UNIVERSITY CASEBOOK SERIES

CASES AND MATERIALS

ADMIRALTY

FOURTH EDITION

by

JO DESHA LUCAS
Arnold I. Shure Professor of Law, Emeritus
University of Chicago

WESTBURY, NEW YORK
THE FOUNDATION PRESS, INC.
1996

Library of Congress Cataloging-in-Publication Data

Lucas, Jo Desha, 1921–
  Cases and materials on admiralty / by Jo Desha Lucas. — 4. ed.
    p. cm. — (University casebook series)
  Includes index.
  ISBN 1–56662–337–5
  1. Admiralty—United States—Cases. I. Title. II. Series.
KF1103.L8 1996
343.7309'6—dc20
[347.30396]   96–371

 TEXT IS PRINTED ON 10% POST CONSUMER RECYCLED PAPER    Printed with Printwise Environmentally Advanced Water Washable Ink

PREFACE

In the preface to the first edition of these materials, which appeared in 1969, the opinion was expressed that a one term course in admiralty cannot create a proctor and if it were designed with that in mind the student market for such a course would be small indeed. Such a course, however, can achieve certain desirable ends in the usual law school curriculum. It can fill a common gap in the student's study of federal jurisdiction. It can serve as a model of a body of law developed around the operation of a single, if variegated, industry. It can serve as a sort of domestic course in comparative law, exposing the student to different solutions to problems they have learned to work out along different lines in their common law courses. It can serve as a model of state-federal relations quite different from those worked out in most other areas of the law, affording a picture of what the world might look like without the Erie doctrine. It can be used to examine the weight of history and tradition in the law, and the relative success of statutory and case-to-case development. This is not to say, of course, that any of these objectives could not be, or is not, pursued in other courses. Since the curriculum is elective, however, educational objectives properly overlap the subject matter.

This fourth edition retains the biases that determined the selection of materials in the first. Part I is devoted to the admiralty jurisdiction in its setting in a federal republic and its administration within our dual system of courts. In Part II an effort has been made to illustrate the process by which the substantive law of the admiralty has grown, and to cover the major areas in which it departs significantly from common law principles. The gaps in coverage in the first edition remain. Detailed consideration of the commercial law aspects of transactions involving ocean transport has been left other opportunities; the law of marine insurance, always an important background consideration in carriage transactions, works its way into the materials only intersticially; and the large number of problems raised by the complex pattern of subsidies and regulation within which the shipping industry operates has been ignored. This is, perhaps, a pity, but casebooks must stop somewhere if students are to carry them around. In an area with as many faces as maritime law, each chapter is an iceberg and a choice must be made between a full set of very small tips and a smaller set sufficiently exposed to reveal, at least, their general contours.

In the twenty-seven years since the publication of the first edition, the Supreme Court had repudiated a number of hoary doctrines of the admiralty, creating out of whole cloth a general maritime action for wrongful death; rejecting the traditional rule that maritime jurisdiction in tort cases depends upon location alone; and abandoning the traditional rule for the assessment of damages in mutual fault collisions by moieties, in favor of a rule of proportional fault. These "revolutionary" changes occurred largely during the first decade after the publication of the first edition, and since that time the Supreme Court has kept busy trying to reconcile the changes with related doctrine. In the case of the new action for wrongful death under the general maritime law, the task was complicated by the sweeping amendments to the LHWCA that occurred on the heals of its creation, largely eliminating the the problem that prompted the Court to take the initiative and leaving in doubt the precise relationship of the new cause of action with the LHWCA, the Jones Act, and the Death on the High Seas Act.

Nor has the Court's shift away from location alone as the litmus for tort jurisdiction in favor of an additional requirement of maritime nexus, been altogether uneventful, and over a decade after the recognition of the general requirement of maritime nexus, a vocal segment of the Court is calling for return to a "bright line" locational rule.

There have also been changes in the jurisdictional statutes of potential importance in admiralty and maritime cases. In 1990 § 1367 was added to provide for "supplemental jurisdiction," providing a statutory basis for "pendent" jurisdiction of claims and parties, with special limitations in the case of diversity cases, creating new problems under the saving to suitors clause and in connection with the jury trial in maritime cases. Similarly, in 1991, the Removal Statute was amended to eliminate the derivative jurisdiction theory.

In the preface to the Third Edition, the author expressed the opinion that the next area for reform might be carriage of goods. This has not developed. The issue continue to simmer, however, and the student should give the matter an attentive eye. The area that has been most reform resistant over the longest period has been limitation of liability. Does the Court's recent development of a broad concept of "maritime nexus" put pressure on the issue of limitation?

JO DESHA LUCAS

CHICAGO, ILLINOIS
MARCH, 1996

SUMMARY OF CONTENTS

PREFACE -- iii

TABLE OF CASES --- xxi

PART I Admiralty and Maritime Jurisdiction and Practice -- 1

CHAPTER 1 Introduction -- 1

CHAPTER 2 Navigable Waters of the United States ------------------- 38
A. Navigability in Fact --- 38
B. Present Navigability in Fact ------------------------------------- 41
C. Regulation of Navigable Waters ---------------------------------- 50

CHAPTER 3 Locality and Subject Matter in Determining Jurisdiction --- 56
A. Jurisdiction in Contract -- 56
B. Jurisdiction in Tort Cases -------------------------------------- 92
   1. Maritime Location --------------------------------------- 92
   2. The Admiralty Extension Act of 1948 --------------------- 97
   3. Maritime Connection ------------------------------------ 104
C. Criminal Jurisdiction -- 126
D. Jurisdiction in Prize Cases ------------------------------------ 128
E. The Outer Continental Shelf Lands Act -------------------------- 129
F. Amount in Controversy in Admiralty Causes --------------------- 131

CHAPTER 4 Vessels and Jurisdiction ------------------------------- 132

CHAPTER 5 Admiralty Jurisdiction and Federalism ----------------- 144
A. The Saving to Suitors Clause ----------------------------------- 144
B. Statutory Proceedings -- 161
   1. The Death on the High Seas Act ------------------------- 161
   2. The Limitation of Liability Act ------------------------ 161
   3. Suits Against the United States ------------------------ 162
   4. The Ship Mortgage Act of 1920 -------------------------- 162
C. Ancillary or Pendent Jurisdiction ------------------------------ 162
   1. Joinder of Nonmaritime Claims -------------------------- 162
   2. Counterclaims -- 163
   3. Third Party Practice ----------------------------------- 165
   4. Joinder of Parties ------------------------------------- 168
D. Removal Jurisdiction --- 174
E. Limitations on Remedies in Admiralty -------------------------- 177

CHAPTER 6 Admiralty Jurisdiction and the Federal Judicial System 204
Introductory Note --- 204
CHAPTER 7 Jurisdiction in Rem; In Personam; Attachments in the Admiralty --- 247
A. Jurisdiction in Rem -- 247
   1. Arrest --- 247
   2. Security; Release -------------------------------------- 264

B. Notice and Hearing; Rules B and C of the Supplemental Rules as Amended in 1985 -- 271
C. Attachment and Garnishment ------------------------------------ 272
D. Personal Jurisdiction -- 281
    1. Service on an Agent -- 281
    2. Long Arm Jurisdiction -------------------------------------- 284

CHAPTER 8 Venue in Suits in Admiralty ------------------------- 295
A. Note on Venue in Admiralty and Maritime Proceedings -------------- 295
B. Forum Non Conveniens -- 298
C. Note on Forum Selection Agreements ----------------------------- 306

CHAPTER 9 Appeals in Suits in Admiralty ------------------------- 308

CHAPTER 10 Suits Against the Government ----------------------- 312
A. Suits Against the United States -------------------------------- 312
B. Note on Suits Against the State -------------------------------- 338
C. Note on Suits Against Municipal Corporations ------------------- 340
D. Note on Suits Against Foreign States --------------------------- 340

PART II Substantive Law of the Admiralty ----------------------- 343

CHAPTER 11 Sources of the Substantive Law ---------------------- 343
A. Sea Law as a Body of International Custom; The Codes and the Text Writers -- 343
B. The Common Law as a Source of Maritime Substantive Law -------- 357
C. Problems of Federalism; State Courts and Federal Rights; Federal Courts and State Rights -------------------------------- 366

CHAPTER 12 The Maritime Lien --------------------------------- 386
A. Origin and Nature of the Maritime Lien ------------------------- 386
    1. Introductory Note -- 386
    2. Nature of Maritime Liens on Vessels -------------------------- 387
    3. Liens on Cargo --- 411
B. Transactions Importing Liens ---------------------------------- 414
    1. The Mariner's Lien for Wages --------------------------------- 414
    2. Liens Arising Out of Contracts of Affreightment -------------- 417
    3. Liens for Repairs, Supplies and Other Necessaries ----------- 430
    4. Preferred Ship Mortgages ------------------------------------ 465
    5. Tort Liens -- 469
    6. Other Transactions Giving Rise to Maritime Liens ------------ 478
    7. Liens Under State Law --------------------------------------- 479
    8. Advances and Liens by Subrogation --------------------------- 480
C. Priority of Liens --- 486
D. Extinguishment of Liens --------------------------------------- 511
    1. Destruction of the Res -------------------------------------- 511
    2. Judicial Sale --- 513
    3. Release of Vessel on Bond ----------------------------------- 516
    4. Reduction of Claim to Judgment in Personam ----------------- 520
    5. Waiver --- 525
    6. Laches --- 531
    7. Foreclosure of Maritime Liens After Initiation of Insolvency Proceedings -- 536

CHAPTER 13 Carriage of Passengers ----------------------------------- 544

CHAPTER 14 Carriage of Goods --- 558

A. Contracts of Affreightment-- 558

   1. Common and Private Carriers---------------------------------- 558

   2. Charter Parties --- 559

   3. Tug and Tow -- 576

   4. Bills of Lading --- 587

B. The Harter Act -- 589

C. Coverage of Harter and Cogsa-------------------------------------- 596

D. Carrier's Responsibilities --- 603

   1. Seaworthiness-- 603

   2. Care and Custody of Cargo ----------------------------------- 607

E. Excepted Perils-- 610

   1. Act of God -- 610

   2. Perils of the Sea -- 617

   3. Fire --- 621

   4. Errors in Management -- 631

   5. Other Causes Without Fault or Neglect --------------------- 633

F. Damages; Limitation --- 639

G. Deviation-- 649

CHAPTER 15 Salvage --- 664

A. Property the Subject of Salvage----------------------------------- 664

B. Who May Be a Salvor? --- 667

C. Salvage Situations; Peril -- 677

D. Acts Constituting Salvage Services ------------------------------- 683

E. Necessity for Request -- 693

F. Conduct Forfeiting a Salvage Award ----------------------------- 694

G. Rival Salvors -- 696

H. Amount of Award; Distribution; Life Salvage --------------------- 701

I. Salvage Contracts -- 713

CHAPTER 16 General Average -- 720

A. General Average Sacrifices --- 721

B. Imminent Peril--- 733

C. Common Adventure -- 737

D. Peril the Result of Negligence-------------------------------------- 741

E. Extraordinary Expense as General Average --------------------- 746

F. Note on Salvage Expenses as General Average ----------------- 757

CHAPTER 17 Collision -- 759

A. Fault-- 759

   1. Inscrutable Fault and the Inevitable Accident ------------- 759

   2. The Rules of Navigation --------------------------------------- 763

   3. The Rule of the Pennsylvania--------------------------------- 765

   4. Supervening Negligence, the Major–minor Fault Rule, and the
       Last Clear Chance -- 774

   5. Errors in Extremis -- 780

B. Damages-- 784

   1. Computation of Damages-------------------------------------- 784

   2. Apportionment of Damages, the Moieties Rule------------- 806

B. Damages—Continued
    3. Abrogation of the Moieties Rule ---------------------------------- 811
CHAPTER   18   Tort Law in General ------------------------------- 820
Introductory   Note --- 820
CHAPTER   19   Maritime Law of Industrial Accidents --------------- 844
A. Seamen --- 844
    1. Who Is a Seaman -- 844
    2. The Traditional Seamen's Remedies ------------------------- 859
    3. Maintenance and Cure -------------------------------------- 866
    4. The Warranty of Seaworthiness --------------------------- 896
    5. Action for Negligence Under the Jones Act --------------- 911
    6. Remedies of Government Employees ----------------------- 954
B. Longshoremen and Harbor Workers ------------------------------ 955
    1. Historical Note -- 955
    2. The Longshore and Harbor Workers' Compensation Act --------- 980
CHAPTER   20   Death Actions -------------------------------------- 1010
CHAPTER   21   Limitation of Liability ---------------------------- 1026
A. Vessels --- 1026
B. Owners --- 1039
C. Limitable Claims --- 1044
    1. Debts and Liabilities ------------------------------------- 1044
    2. Personal Contracts --------------------------------------- 1050
D. Privity or Knowledge -- 1053
    1. Corporations --- 1053
    2. Individuals --- 1065
E. Limitation Proceedings -- 1070
    1. Amount of the Fund -------------------------------------- 1070
    2. Issues Triable in a Limitation Proceeding --------------- 1075
    3. Limitation and the Savings Clause ----------------------- 1081
    4. Limitations in Limitation Proceedings ------------------- 1088
F. Note on Limitation of Liability in Water Pollution Cases ------------- 1097
CHAPTER   22   Postscript on Federal Preemption ------------------- 1099

INDEX --- 1109

TABLE OF CONTENTS

PREFACE -- iii
TABLE OF CASES -- xxi

PART I Admiralty and Maritime Jurisdiction and Practice -- 1

CHAPTER 1 Introduction -- 1

Jackson v. The Steamboat Magnolia -- 4
Note on the Extension of Admiralty and Maritime Jurisdiction ---------- 29

CHAPTER 2 Navigable Waters of the United States ------------- 38

A. **Navigability in Fact** -- 38
B. **Present Navigability in Fact** -- 41
   Finneseth v. Carter --- 41
   Note -- 48
C. **Regulation of Navigable Waters** --- 50
   Land & Lake Tours, Inc. v. Lewis -- 50
   Note -- 54

**CHAPTER 3 Locality and Subject Matter in Determining
      Jurisdiction** --- 56

A. **Jurisdiction in Contract** --- 56
   New England Mutual Marine Ins. Co. v. Dunham --------------------- 56
   Sirius Ins. Co. (UK) Ltd. v. Collins --- 62
   Note -- 66
   North Pacific Steamship Co. v. Hall Brothers Marine Railway &
      Shipbuilding Co. -- 67
   Note -- 72
   Terminal Shipping Co. v. Hamberg --- 73
   Note -- 74
   General Engine & Machine Works, Inc. v. Slay and the F/V
      Danlyn -- 76
   Note -- 79
   Exxon Corp. v. Central Gulf Lines, Inc. ---------------------------------- 79
   Note -- 85
   Flota Maritima Browning De Cuba v. Ciudad De La Habana ------- 86
   Note -- 90
B. **Jurisdiction in Tort Cases** --- 92
   1. Maritime Location --- 92
      The Admiral Peoples --- 92
      Note --- 94
   2. The Admiralty Extension Act of 1948 --------------------------------- 97
      Duluth Superior Excursions, Inc. v. Makela ----------------------- 97
      Note --- 101

B. **Jurisdiction in Tort Cases**—Continued
    3. Maritime Connection ----- 104
       Jerome B. Grubart, Inc. v. Great Lakes Dredge & Dock Co. ----- 104
       Note ----- 121
C. **Criminal Jurisdiction** ----- 126
    Note ----- 127
D. **Jurisdiction in Prize Cases** ----- 128
    Note ----- 129
E. **The Outer Continental Shelf Lands Act** ----- 129
F. **Amount in Controversy in Admiralty Causes** ----- 131

CHAPTER 4 Vessels and Jurisdiction ----- 132

Pavone v. Mississippi Riverboat Amusement Corp. ----- 132
Note ----- 139

CHAPTER 5 Admiralty Jurisdiction and Federalism ----- 144

A. **The Saving to Suitors Clause** ----- 144
    The Hine v. Trevor ----- 144
    Note ----- 146
    C.J. Hendry Co. v. Moore ----- 147
    Note ----- 154
    Rounds v. Cloverport Foundry & Machine Co. ----- 155
    Note ----- 158
    Sellick v. Sun Harbor Marina, Inc. ----- 159
    Note ----- 161
B. **Statutory Proceedings** ----- 161
    1. The Death on the High Seas Act ----- 161
    2. The Limitation of Liability Act ----- 161
    3. Suits Against the United States ----- 162
    4. The Ship Mortgage Act of 1920 ----- 162
C. **Ancillary or Pendent Jurisdiction** ----- 162
    1. Joinder of Nonmaritime Claims ----- 162
    2. Counterclaims ----- 163
    3. Third Party Practice ----- 165
       Galt G/S v. Hapag–Lloyd A.G. ----- 165
       Note ----- 168
    4. Joinder of Parties ----- 168
       Loeber v. Bay Tankers, Inc. ----- 168
       Note ----- 172
D. **Removal Jurisdiction** ----- 174
    Alleman v. Bunge Corp. ----- 174
    Note ----- 175
E. **Limitations on Remedies in Admiralty** ----- 177
    Ward v. Peck ----- 177
    Note ----- 177
    Rice v. Charles Dreifus Co. ----- 178
    The Annie H Smith ----- 180
    Note ----- 183
    Archawski v. Hanioti ----- 183

E. Limitations on Remedies in Admiralty—Continued
Marine Transit Corp. v. Dreyfus 186
Kynoch v. The Propeller S.C. Ives 189
*Swift & Company Packers v. Compania Colombiana Del Caribe,
    S. A.* 192
Note 197
Pino v. Protection Maritime Ins. Co., Ltd. 197
Note 200

**CHAPTER 6   Admiralty Jurisdiction and the Federal Judicial
    System** 204

Introductory   Note 204
Beeler v. United States 205
Note 208
Crookham v. Muick 208
Note 210
Thomas v. Peninsular & Oriental Steam Navigation Co. 210
La Capria v. Compagnie Maritime Belge 212
Note 214
Haskins v. Point Towing Co. 215
Teal v. Eagle Fleet, Inc. v. Penrod Drilling Corp. 221
Powell v. Offshore Navigation, Inc. 227
Duhon v. Koch Exploration Co. 236
Note 244

**CHAPTER   7   Jurisdiction in Rem; In Personam; Attach-
    ments in the Admiralty** 247

A. Jurisdiction in Rem 247
    1. Arrest 247
    There'll Always Be an England 247
    The King v. Joseph Lane 247
    Belcher Co. of Alabama, Inc. v. M/V Maratha Mariner 249
    Note 253
    The Resolute 254
    United States v. Freights, etc., of the Mount Shasta 256
    Note 258
    Thyssen Steel Corp. v. Federal Commerce & Nav. Co. 259
    Note 261
    2. Security; Release 264
    Stevedoring Services of America v. Ancora Transport, N.V. 264
    Note 268
**B. Notice and Hearing; Rules B and C of the Supplemental
    Rules as Amended in 1985** 271
C. Attachment and Garnishment 272
    Royal Swan v. Global Container Lines, Ltd. 272
D. Personal Jurisdiction 281
    1. Service on an Agent 281
    Ontario Paper Co., Ltd. v. Salenrederierna A/B 281
    Note 283
    2. Long Arm Jurisdiction 284

D. **Personal Jurisdiction**—Continued

DeJames v. Magnificence Carriers, Inc. ----- 284

Note ----- 293

CHAPTER 8 Venue in Suits in Admiralty ----- 295

A. **Note on Venue in Admiralty and Maritime Proceedings** ----- 295

B. **Forum Non Conveniens** ----- 298

De Oliveira v. Delta Marine Drilling Co. ----- 298

Abraham v. Universal Glow, Inc. ----- 303

Note ----- 306

C. **Note on Forum Selection Agreements** ----- 306

CHAPTER 9 Appeals in Suits in Admiralty ----- 308

Note on Appeals in Maritime Cases ----- 308

CHAPTER 10 Suits Against the Government ----- 312

A. **Suits Against the United States** ----- 312

United States v. United Continental Tuna Corp. ----- 312

Note ----- 323

Canadian Transport Co. v. United States ----- 325

Note ----- 333

Jones & Laughlin Steel, Inc. v. Mon River Towing, Inc. ----- 333

Note ----- 338

B. **Note on Suits Against the State** ----- 338

C. **Note on Suits Against Municipal Corporations** ----- 340

D. **Note on Suits Against Foreign States** ----- 340

PART II Substantive Law of the Admiralty ----- 343

CHAPTER 11 Sources of the Substantive Law ----- 343

A. **Sea Law as a Body of International Custom; The Codes and the Text Writers** ----- 343

Thompson v. The Catharina ----- 343

1 Molloy, de Jure Maritimo XIX–XXIV ----- 348

Story, Miscellaneous Writings (1835) ----- 350

1 Hay & Marriott XI ----- 352

Swinney v. Tinker ----- 355

Note ----- 356

B. **The Common Law as a Source of Maritime Substantive Law** ----- 357

The Sea Gull ----- 357

Note ----- 358

DeLoach v. Companhia de Navegacao Lloyd Brasileiro ----- 359

Note ----- 365

C. **Problems of Federalism; State Courts and Federal Rights; Rights; Federal Courts and State Rights** ----------------- 366
    Kalleck v. Deering --- 366
    Southern Pacific Co. v. Jensen ------------------------------- 367
    Note -- 373
    Chelentis v. Luckenbach S.S. Co. ---------------------------- 375
    Note -- 377
    Calhoun v. Yamaha Motor Corp., U.S.A. --------------------- 377
    Note -- 384

CHAPTER 12 The Maritime Lien ----------------------------- 386

A. **Origin and Nature of the Maritime Lien** ------------------ 386
  1. Introductory Note --- 386
    The Nestor -- 386
    2 Browne, Admiralty 142–143 ---------------------------------- 386
    Gilmore and Black, The Law of Admiralty --------------------- 387
  2. Nature of Maritime Liens on Vessels ---------------------- 387
    Note on Subjects to Which the Lien Attaches ------------------ 387
    The Bold Buccleugh -- 389
    Cavcar Co. v. M/V Suzdal ------------------------------------- 392
    Note -- 399
    Oil Shipping (Bunkering) B.V. v. Sonmez Denizcilik Ve Ticaret A.S. --- 401
    Note -- 410
  3. Liens on Cargo --- 411
    4,885 Bags of Linseed --- 411
    Note -- 413
B. **Transactions Importing Liens** --------------------------- 414
  1. The Mariner's Lien for Wages ---------------------------- 414
    Harrison v. The Beverly Lynn --------------------------------- 414
    Note -- 416
  2. Liens Arising Out of Contracts of Affreightment ---------- 417
    Osaka Shosen Kaisha v. Pacific Export Lumber Co. ----------- 417
    Note -- 421
    Krauss Bros. Lumber Co. v. Dimon Steamship Corp. ---------- 422
    United States v. Steamship Lucie Schulte --------------------- 426
    Note -- 428
    Shipowners' Lien for Charter Hire ----------------------------- 429
  3. Liens for Repairs, Supplies and Other Necessaries --------- 430
    A. Necessaries -- 430
      J. Ray McDermott & Co. v. The Off–Shore Menhaden Co. --- 430
      Note -- 433
    B. Furnishing to the Ship ------------------------------------- 434
      Redcliffe Americas Limited v. M/V Tyson Lykes ------------ 434
      Note -- 440
    C. The Owner or a Person Authorized by the Owner ----------- 441
      (1) The Owner -- 441
        Diaz v. The Seathunder ------------------------------ 441
        Freedom Line Inc. v. Vessel Glenrock ---------------- 442
      (2) Master --- 446
        Yacht, Mary Jane v. Broward Marine, Inc. ----------- 446

B. Transactions Importing Liens—Continued

Note 447

    (3) Or a Person Authorized by the Owner 447

       Crescent City Marine, Inc. v. M/V Nunki 447

       Note 452

  D. Charter Clauses Prohibiting Liens 453

    Ferromet Resources, Inc. v. Chemoil Corp. 453

    Cardinal Shipping Corp. v. M/S Seisho Maru 456

    Note 461

  E. Reliance on the Credit of the Vessel 462

    Farrell Ocean Services, Inc. v. United States 462

4. Preferred Ship Mortgages 465

  The Favorite 465

5. Tort Liens 469

  The Anaces 469

  Note 473

  The Florence 473

  Oriente Commercial, Inc. v. American Flag Vessel, M/V Floridi-
    an 475

  Note 478

6. Other Transactions Giving Rise to Maritime Liens 478

7. Liens Under State Law 479

8. Advances and Liens by Subrogation 480

  Findley v. Lanasa (The Josephine Lanasa) 480

  Note 485

C. Priority of Liens 486

  The C. J. Saxe 486

  Note 487

  The William Leishear 488

  Note 492

  The John G. Stevens 492

  Note 498

  The Frank G. Fowler 499

  Note 500

  Todd Shipyards Corporation v. The City of Athens 501

  Note 506

  The City of Tawas 506

  Note 508

  The Home 508

  Note 511

D. Extinguishment of Liens 511

1. Destruction of the Res 511

  Walsh v. Tadlock 511

  Note 513

2. Judicial Sale 513

  South Carolina State Ports Authority v. Silver Anchor, S.A.,
    (Panama) 513

  Note 515

3. Release of Vessel on Bond 516

  Hawgood & Avery Transit Co. v. Dingman 516

4. Reduction of Claim to Judgment in Personam 520

  Pratt v. United States 520

D. Extinguishment of Liens—Continued

    5. Waiver 525
      Newport News Shipbuilding & Dry Dock Co. v. S.S. Independence 525
      Note 531
    6. Laches 531
      Usher v. M/V Ocean Wave 531
      Note 535
    7. Foreclosure of Maritime Liens After Initiation of Insolvency Proceedings 536
      United States v. LeBouf Bros. Towing Co., Inc. 536
      Note 542

CHAPTER 13 Carriage of Passengers 544

Introductory Note 544
Kornberg v. Carnival Cruise Lines, Inc. 545
Note 548
Rainey v. Paquet Cruises, Inc. 552
Note 555

CHAPTER 14 Carriage of Goods 558

A. Contracts of Affreightment 558
    1. Common and Private Carriers 558
    2. Charter Parties 559
      Pacific Employers Ins. Co. v. M/V Gloria 559
      Complaint of Admiral Towing and Barge Co. 566
      Note 573
    3. Tug and Tow 576
      Agrico Chemical Co. v. M/V Ben W. Martin 576
      Note 581
      Dillingham Tug & Barge Corp. v. Collier Carbon & Chem. Corp. 582
      Note 587
    4. Bills of Lading 587
B. The Harter Act 589
  The Carib Prince 589
  May v. Hamburg–Amerikanische Packetfahrt Aktiengesellschaft 592
  Note 595
C. Coverage of Harter and Cogsa 596
  Caterpillar Overseas, S.A. v. S.S. Expeditor 596
  Note 601
D. Carrier's Responsibilities 603
    1. Seaworthiness 603
      International Navigation Company v. Farr & Bailey Manufacturing Company 603
      Note 605
    2. Care and Custody of Cargo 607
      Knott v. Botany Worsted Mills 607
      Note 609

E. **Excepted Perils** -- 610
  1. Act of God --- 610
    Mamiye Bros. v. Barber Steamship Lines ----------------- 610
    Note -- 616
  2. Perils of the Sea --- 617
    The Vallescura --- 617
    Note -- 621
  3. Fire -- 621
    Westinghouse Elec. Corp. v. M/V Leslie Lykes ------------ 621
    Note -- 631
  4. Errors in Management -------------------------------------- 631
    Firestone Synthetic Fibers Co. v. M/S Black Heron ---------- 631
    Note -- 632
  5. Other Causes Without Fault or Neglect ------------------- 633
    Tubacex, Inc. v. M/V Risan ------------------------------ 633
    Note -- 638
F. **Damages; Limitation** --- 639
  Minerais U.S. Inc., Exalmet Div. v. M/V Moslavina --------- 639
  Note --- 641
  Hayes–Leger Associates, Inc. v. M/V Oriental Knight ---------- 641
  Note --- 648
G. **Deviation** --- 649
  General Elec. Co. Intern. v. S.S. Nancy Lykes --------------- 649
  Yutana Barge Lines v. Northland Services ------------------- 656
  Note --- 659

CHAPTER 15   Salvage -- 664

A. **Property the Subject of Salvage** ------------------------------ 664
  Provost v. Huber -- 664
  Note --- 666
B. **Who May Be a Salvor?** -- 667
  Mason v. The Blaireau --- 667
  Note --- 672
  Nicholas E. Vernicos Shipping Co. v. United States ----------- 673
  Note --- 677
C. **Salvage Situations; Peril** ------------------------------------ 677
  Faneuil Advisors, Inc. v. O/S Sea Hawk ----------------------- 677
  Note --- 683
D. **Acts Constituting Salvage Services** --------------------------- 683
  Saint Paul Marine Transp. Corp. v. Cerro Sales Corp. -------- 683
  Note --- 692
E. **Necessity for Request** -- 693
  Merritt & Chapman Derrick & Wrecking Co. v. United States --- 693
F. **Conduct Forfeiting a Salvage Award** -------------------------- 694
  M/T Norseman -- 694
G. **Rival Salvors** -- 696
  Schooner Brindicate II --------------------------------------- 696
  (Dominguez v. Schooner Brindicate II) ------------------------ 696
  The Acara --- 699
  (Rickard v. Pringle) --- 699
  Note --- 701

H. **Amount of Award; Distribution; Life Salvage** ------------------ 701
   Trico Marine Operators, Inc. on its own Behalf and on Behalf of
     the M/V Manatee River and M/V Wolf River v. Dow Chemicalco.
     and Security Pacific Leasing, Inc. ----------------------------- 701
   Note -- 706
   Warshauer v. Lloyd Saboudo S.A. ------------------------------ 710
   Note -- 713
I. **Salvage Contracts** -- 713
   The Elfrida --- 713
   Note -- 719

CHAPTER 16 General Average ---------------------------------- 720

A. **General Average Sacrifices** -------------------------------- 721
   Barnard v. Adams -- 721
   Note -- 725
   Ralli v. Troop -- 726
   Note -- 731
B. **Imminent Peril** --- 733
   The West Imboden -- 733
   (Ravenscroft v. United States) ------------------------------ 733
   Note -- 736
C. **Common Adventure** --- 737
   S. C. Loveland Co. v. United States ------------------------- 737
   Note -- 740
D. **Peril the Result of Negligence** --------------------------- 741
   The Jason --- 741
   Note -- 746
E. **Extraordinary Expense as General Average** ----------------- 746
   Eagle Terminal Tankers, Inc. v. Insurance Co. of U.S.S.R. --- 746
   Note -- 755
F. **Note on Salvage Expenses as General Average** -------------- 757

CHAPTER 17 Collision --------------------------------------- 759

A. **Fault** --- 759
  1. Inscrutable Fault and the Inevitable Accident ------------- 759
    The Jumna --- 759
    Note -- 761
  2. The Rules of Navigation ----------------------------------- 763
  3. The Rule of the Pennsylvania ------------------------------ 765
    Hellenic Lines, Ltd. v. Prudential Lines, Inc. ---------- 765
    Note -- 771
  4. Supervening Negligence, the Major–minor Fault Rule, and the
     Last Clear Chance ------------------------------------- 774
    Exxon Company v. Sofec, Inc. ---------------------------- 774
    Note -- 779
  5. Errors in Extremis -- 780
    The Bywell Castle --------------------------------------- 780
    Note -- 782

B. Damages --- 784
   1. Computation of Damages ----------------------------------- 784
     Howard Olson v. Marine Leopard ------------------------- 784
     Compania Pelineon De Navegacion, S.A. v. Texas Petroleum Co. -- 794
     Note --- 799
   2. Apportionment of Damages, the Moieties Rule ------------ 806
     The Woodrop–Sims -------------------------------------- 806
     Vanderplank v. Miller ---------------------------------- 807
     1 Conkling, Admiralty 300 ----------------------------- 807
     Note --- 808
   3. Abrogation of the Moieties Rule ------------------------- 811
     United States v. Reliable Transfer Co., Inc. ----------- 811

CHAPTER 18   Tort Law in General ---------------------------- 820

Introductory Note -- 820
Leathers v. Blessing --- 821
Orient Mid–East Lines v. Bowen --------------------------------- 824
Kermarec v. Compagnie Generale Transatlantique ----------------- 825
Note --- 829
Lewis v. Timco, Inc. --- 830
Note --- 834
Ocean Barge Transp. Co. v. Hess Oil Virgin Islands Corp. ------- 835
Note --- 839
Note on Indemnity and Contribution ------------------------------- 840
M. Muratore v. M/S Scotia Prince ------------------------------- 840
Note --- 843

CHAPTER 19   Maritime Law of Industrial Accidents ---------- 844

A. Seamen -- 844
   1. Who Is a Seaman -------------------------------------- 844
     Chandris, Inc. v. Latsis ------------------------------- 844
   2. The Traditional Seamen's Remedies -------------------- 859
     The Osceola -- 859
     Note --- 866
   3. Maintenance and Cure -------------------------------- 866
     Warren v. United States -------------------------------- 866
     Koistinen v. American Export Lines, Inc. --------------- 871
     Note --- 874
     Farrell v. United States ------------------------------- 877
     Note --- 884
     Vaughan v. Atkinson ------------------------------------ 885
     Note --- 893
     Rejection of Medical Care -------------------------------- 895
   4. The Warranty of Seaworthiness ----------------------- 896
     A. What Constitutes Unseaworthiness ------------------ 896
       Hughes v. ContiCarriers and Terminals, Inc. ------- 896
       Usner v. Luckenbach Overseas Corp. ---------------- 902
       Note --- 908
     B. What Vessels Are Warranted Seaworthy -------------- 910

A. **Seamen**—Continued
    5. Action for Negligence Under the Jones Act ------------------------ 911
        A. "Any Seaman" -- 911
           Nicol v. Gulf Fleet Supply Vessels, Inc. ------------------ 911
        B. In the Course of His Employment------------------------ 920
           McAleer v. Smith-- 920
           Note -- 931
           Colon v. Apex Marine Corp. ---------------------------- 932
           Note -- 940
        C. Standard of Care Under the Jones Act ---------------- 940
           Smith v. Trans–World Drilling Co. ------------------------ 940
           Note -- 946
        D. Damages -- 948
           Horsley v. Mobil Oil Corp. ------------------------------ 948
           Note -- 953
        E. Wrongful Death and Survival Under the Jones Act ---------- 953
    6. Remedies of Government Employees ------------------------------ 954
B. **Longshoremen and Harbor Workers** ------------------------ 955
    1. Historical Note -- 955
    2. The Longshore and Harbor Workers' Compensation Act ---------- 980
        A. Coverage-- 980
           Chesapeake and Ohio Ry. v. Schwalb ------------------ 980
           Note -- 986
        B. Third Person Liability ---------------------------------- 991
           Howlett v. Birkdale Shipping Co., S.A. ---------------- 991
           Burchett v. Cargill, Inc. -------------------------------- 1000
           Note -- 1002

CHAPTER 20 Death Actions ------------------------------ 1010

Miles v. Apex Marine Corp. ---------------------------------- 1010
Note -- 1020

CHAPTER 21 Limitation of Liability ------------------ 1026

A. **Vessels** -- 1026
    The Yacht Julaine -- 1026
    (Petition of H.T. Porter) ---------------------------------- 1026
    Note-- 1029
    Carolina Floral Import, Inc. v. M. v. Eurypylus ------------ 1029
B. **Owners** -- 1039
    In re Marine Recreational Opportunities, Inc. -------------- 1039
    Lady Jane, Inc., Lim. Procs. ------------------------------ 1041
    Note-- 1043
C. **Limitable Claims** -- 1044
    1. Debts and Liabilities -------------------------------------- 1044
        Seven Resorts v. Cantlen -------------------------------- 1044
        Note -- 1048
    2. Personal Contracts -- 1050
        Cullen Fuel Co. Inc. v. W.E. Hedger, Inc. -------------- 1050
        Note -- 1051

D. **Privity or Knowledge** --- 1053
    1. Corporations --- 1053
       Petition of Kinsman Transit Co. --------------------------- 1053
       Note --- 1055
       Farrell Lines, Inc. v. Jones ------------------------------ 1058
       Note --- 1065
    2. Individuals --- 1065
       Coryell Et Al. v. Phipps Et Al. --------------------------- 1065
       (The Seminole) -- 1065
       Note --- 1068
E. **Limitation Proceedings** ----------------------------------- 1070
    1. Amount of the Fund ------------------------------------- 1070
    2. Issues Triable in a Limitation Proceeding ---------------- 1075
       British Transport Commission v. United States ------------ 1075
       (The Haiti Victory) -------------------------------------- 1075
       Note --- 1081
    3. Limitation and the Savings Clause ---------------------- 1081
       Jefferson Barracks Marine Services, Inc. v. Casey -------- 1081
       Note --- 1086
    4. Limitations in Limitation Proceedings ------------------- 1088
       Cincinnati Gas & Elec. Co. v. Abel ---------------------- 1088
       Note --- 1093
F. **Note on Limitation of Liability in Water Pollution Cases** ---- 1097

CHAPTER   22   Postscript on Federal Preemption ---------------- 1099

Yamaha Motor Corp., U.S.A. v. Calhoun ------------------------------- 1099
Note -- 1108

INDEX --- 1109

TABLE OF CASES

Principal cases are in bold type. Non-principal cases are in roman type. References are to Pages.

A A B Elec. Industries, Inc. v. Control Masters,Inc., 72
Abraham v. Universal Glow, Inc., 303
Acker v. The City of Athens, 421, 544
Acwoo Intern. Steel Corp. v. Toko Kaiun Kaish, Ltd., 588
Adams v. Pease, 37
Adams v. Texaco, Inc., 885
Addison v. Gulf Coast Contracting Services, Inc., 176
Admiral Towing and Barge Co., Complaint of, 566
Admiral Towing Co. v. Woolen, 1069
Adventure Bound Sports, Inc., Matter of, 1056
Agfa–Gevaert, Inc. v. S/S TFL ADAMS, 663
Agrico Chemical Co. v. M/V Ben W. Martin, 576
Ahlgren v. Red Star Towing & Transp Co, 809
Ainsworth v. Penrod Drilling Corp., 953
Ajubita v. S/S Peik, 434
A. Kemp Fisheries, Inc. v. Castle & Cooke, Inc., Bumble Bee Seafoods Div., 607
Akron Corp. v. M/T Cantigny, 803
Alaska Steamship Company v. Petterson, 968, 969, 977, 978
Albany Ins. Co. v. M.V. Istrian Exp., 478
Albert E. Reed & Co. v. M/S Thackeray, 589
Alcoa S. S. Co., Inc. v. M/V Nordic Regent, 306
Aldinger v. Howard, 173, 173
Alford v. Appalachian Power Co., 48
Alfred Dunhill of London, Inc. v. Republic of Cuba, 341
Alkmeon Naviera, S.A. v. M/V Marina L, 802
All Alaskan Seafoods, Inc. v. M/V Sea Producer, 478
Alleman v. Bunge Corp., 174
Allen v. Hixson, 556
Allen v. Matson Nav. Co., 556, 830
Allen v. The Contessa, 433, 434, 440
Allied Chemical Intern. Corp. v. Companhia de Navegacao Lloyd Brasileiro, 663
All Pacific Trading, Inc. v. Vessel M/V Hanjin Yosu, 253
Allstate Ins. Co. v. International Shipping Corp., 662, 663

Alpert v. Zim Lines, 556
Aluminios Pozuelo Limited v. S. S. Navigator, 648
Alva S. Co., Petition of, 340
Alva S.S. Co., Ltd., Petition of, 340
Alyeska Pipeline Service Co. v. Bay Ridge, 272
Al–Zawkari v. American S.S. Co., 894
Ameejee Valleejee and Sons v. M/V Victoria U., 485
Amella v. United States, 338
Amerada Hess Corp. (Hess Oil & Chemical Div.) V. S/T Mobil Apex, 758
American Anthracite & Bituminous Coal Corp. v. Leonardo Arrivabene, S. A., 531
American Commercial Lines, Inc. v. United States, 1097
American Dredging Co. v. Miller, 306, 385
American Dredging Co., Complaint of, 1056
American Exp. Co. v. United States Lines, Inc., 662
American Home Assur. Co. v. L & L Marine Service, Inc., 746
American Home Assur. Co. v. M/V Sletter, 575
American Petrofina Pipeline Co. v. M/V Shoko Maru, 763
American President Lines, Ltd. v. Green Transfer and Storage, Inc., 74
American Stevedores v. Porello, 973
American Tel. & Tel. Co. v. M/V Cape Fear, 1050
American Union Transport, Inc. v. United States, 811
Ammon, The Vigilancia, 422, 440
Amoco Cadiz Off Coast of France on March 16, 1978, Matter of, 1044
Amoco Transport Co. v. S/S Mason Lykes, 805
Anderson v. Cunard Line Ltd., 932
Anglo–American Grain Co. v. The Mina D'Amico, 263
Anheuser–Busch, Inc., Complaint of, 1043
Anthony v. International Paper Co., 773
Antilles Ins. Co. v. Transconex, Inc., 649
Appalachian Elec. Power Co., United States v., 40
Aquila, The, 356

Aquino v. Alaska S.S. Co., 365
Archawski v. Hanioti, 183
Armstrong v. United States, 480
Arques Shipyards v. The Charles Van Damme, 141, 513
Askew v. American Waterways Operators, Inc., 385, 1098
Associated Metals and Minerals Corp. v. Alexander's Unity MV, 310, 410, 478
Associated Metals and Minerals Corp. v. Etelae Suomin Laiva, 621
A & S Transp. Co., Inc. v. Tug Fajardo, 802
Atkins v. Fibre Disintegrating Co., 295
Atlanta Shipping Corp., Inc. v. Chemical Bank, 197
Atlantic Coast Line R. Co. v. Erie Lackawanna R. Co., 975
Atlantic & Gulf Stevedores, Inc. v. Ellerman Lines, Limited, 741, 976
Atlantic Mut. Ins. Co., United States v., 811
Atlantic Pipe Line Co. v. Dredge Philadelphia, 809
Atlantic Steamer Supply Co. v. The Tradewind, 433
A.T. & T. v. Steuart Transp. Co., 761
Autin v. Otis Engineering Corp., 894
Avera v. Florida Towing Corp., 1057
Avis v. Cunard S.S. Co., 551
Avondale Marine Ways, v. Henderson, 963
Ayers v. Parker, 962

Bach v. Trident Steamship Co., Inc., 932
Bagrowski v. American Export Isbrandtsen Lines, Inc., 990
Baker v. Raymond Intern., Inc., 574
Baker v. S/S Cristobal, 973
Ballard v. Alcoa S. S. Co., 385
Ballard Shipping Co. v. Beach Shellfish, 385
Baltimore & O.R. Co. v. Baugh, 377
B & A Marine Co., Inc. v. American Foreign Shipping Co., Inc., 333
Banco de Credito Indus., S.A. v. Tesoreria General, 417
Bankers Trust Co., Matter of, 806
Bankers Trust Co., Complaint of, 1058
Banks v. Hanover S. S. Corp., 245
Barbachym v. Costa Line, Inc., 551
Barbe v. Drummond, 1024
Barber Lines A/S v. M/V Donau Maru, 805
Barbetta v. S/S Bermuda Star, 550
Barcelona, The, 1058
Bard v. The Silver Wave, 516
Barge Ivernia, The, 1051
Barge NL–5—Chesapeake Bay Bridge and Tunnel Dist. v. Oil Screw Prince, 1058
Barger v. Petroleum Helicopters, Inc., 142, 143
Barnard v. Adams, 721, 740
Barnes v. Andover Co., L.P., 894
Barnouw v. S. S. Ozark, 417
Barretto Peat, Inc. v. Luis Ayala Colon Sucrs., Inc., 602
Barrios v. Pelham Marine, Inc., 1004, 1008
Barton v. Borit, 799

Bassis v. SS Caribia, 269
Bauer S.S. Corp., In re, 429
Beach Salvage Corp. of Fla. v. The Cap't. Tom, 683
Beacon Theatres, Inc. v. Westover, 164, 165
Beeler v. United States, 205, 208
Belcher Co. of Alabama, Inc. v. M/V Maratha Mariner, 249
Belden v. Chase, 808, 820
Bell, Billy Joe v. Zapata Haynie Corp., 894
Bennett v. Perini Corp., 988
Bergen Shipping Co., Ltd. v. Japan Marine Services, Ltd., 85
Bergeron v. Mire, 894
Bergher v. General Petroleum Co., 719
Berizzi Bros. Co. v. The Pesaro, 340
Berkshire Fashions, Inc. v. M.V. Hakusan II, 660
Bermuda Exp., N.V. v. M/V Litsa (Ex. Laurie U), 441
Bernard v. Binnings Const. Co., Inc., 142
Bertram v. Freeport McMoran, Inc., 876
Bethlehem Steel Corp., Matter of, 804
Beverly Hills Nat. Bank & Trust Co. v. Compania De Navegacione Almirante S. A., Panama, 202, 203, 429
Bhatnagar v. Surrendra Overseas Ltd., 306
Bienvenido Shipping Co. v. Sub–Freights of the S.S. Andora, 429
Billedeaux v. Tidex, 947
Birney R., 764
Bissett–Berman Corp., United States v., 400
Bisso v. Inland Waterways Corp., 587
Bjaranson v. Botelho Shipping Corp., Manila, 1005
Blackler v. F. Jacobus Transportation Co., 1070
Blair v. M/V Blue Spruce, 434
Blakey v. U.S.S. Iowa, 333, 955
Blanchard v. Engine & Gas Compressor Services, Inc., 141
Blanchard Lumber Co. v. S. S. Anthony II, 602
Blanco v. United States, 323
Blevins v. United States, 909
Blouin v. American Export Isbrandtsen Lines, Inc., 876
Bodden v. Osgood, 245
Bogart v. the John Jay, 465
Boh Bros. Const. Co., Inc. v. M/V Tag–Along, 801
Bold Buccleugh, The, 389
Booth S.S. Co. v. Tug Dalzell No. 2, pp. 263, 809
Bosnor, S.A. de C.V. v. Tug L.A. Barrios, 253
Boston, City of v. S.S. Texaco Texas, 773 F.2d 1396, p. 761
Boston, City of v. SS Texaco Texas, 599 F.Supp. 1132, p. 762
Boston Metals Co. v. The Winding Gulf, 587
Boudoin v. Lykes Bros. S. S. Co., 102, 909
Boudreau v. Boat Andrea G. Corp., 161
Bovell v. United States Dept. of Defense, 324
Bowns v. Royal Viking Lines, Ltd., 550
Bowoon Sangsa Co., Ltd., Matter of, 309

Boyden, United States v., 143

Boyer, In re, 38, 40

Boyle v. Pool Offshore Co., a Div. of Enserch Corp., 947

Boyles v. Cunard Line Ltd., 550

Brandon v. S. S. Denton, 417

Brister v. A.W.I., Inc., 1049

British Transport Commission v. United States, 1075

Brock v. S.S. Southampton, 440, 485

Brooklyn Eastern District Terminal v. United States, 802, 803

Brown v. C. D. Mallory & Co., 296

Brown v. United States, 894

Brown & Root Marine Operators, Inc. v. Zapata Off–Shore Co., 1073

Brunet v. Boh Bros. Const. Co., Inc., 141

Brunet v. United Gas Pipeline Co., 1056

B. Turecamo Towing Corp. v. United States, 581

Buchanan v. Stanships, Inc., 829

Bucolo, Inc. v. S/V Jaguar, 783

Bundens v. J.E. Brenneman Co., 141, 989, 1008

Bunge Corp. v. American Commercial Barge Line Co., 806, 1097

Bunge Corp. v. M/V Furness Bridge, 761, 762

Bunge Edible Oil Corp. v. M/Vs' Torm Rask and Fort Steele, 663

Bunting v. Sun Co., Inc., 948

Burchett v. Cargill, Inc., 141, 176, **1000**

Burdine v. Walden, 479

Burks v. American River Transp. Co., 141, 142

Burton S S Co., In re, 434

B. V. Bureau Wijsmuller v. United States, 800

Bynum v. Premier Cruise Lines, Ltd., 876

Byrd v. Byrd, 821

Bywell Castle, The, 780

Cactus Pipe & Supply Co., Inc. v. M/V Montmartre, 263, 574

Cada v. Costa Line, Inc., 551

Caicedo, United States v., 128

Calbeck v. Travelers Ins. Co., 960, 961, 962, 989

Calcagni v. Hudson Waterways Corp., 909

Calhoun v. Daly, 385, 966

Callas' Estate v. United States, 325

Caminiti v. Tomlinson Fleet Corp., 713

Campbell Industries, Inc. v. Offshore Logistics Intern., Inc., 1006

Canadian Transport Co. v. United States, 325

Canal Barge Co., Inc. v. China Ocean Shipping Co., 772

Candiano v. Moore–McCormack Lines, Inc., 972

Capt'n Mark v. Sea Fever Corp., 773

Carbone v. Ursich, 804

Cardinal Shipping Corp. v. M/S Seisho Maru, 456

Carey v. Berkshire Railroad, 1020

Cargill Ferrous Intern. v. M/V ARCTIC CONFIDENCE, 573

Cargill, Inc. v. C & P Towing Co., Inc., 582

Caribbean Sea Transport, Ltd., Complaint of, 1073

Carlisle Packing Co. v. Sandanger, 1022

Carnival Cruise Lines, Inc. v. Shute, 307, 552

Carpenter v. Klosters Rederi A/S, 550

Carpenter v. Universal Star Shipping, S.A., 1004, 1005

Carroll v. Protection Maritime Ins. Co., Ltd., 122

Carson v. Blazer, 37

Cary Marine, Inc. v. Motorvessel Papillon, 183

Castriot v. Nicoll, 31

Caterpillar Financial Services Inc. v. Aleutian Chalice, 479

Caterpillar Overseas, S.A. v. Marine Transport Inc., 660

Caterpillar Overseas, S. A. v. S. S. Expeditor, 596

Catlin v. United States, 308

Catrakis v. Nautilus Petroleum Carriers Corp., 894

Caulfield v. AC & D Marine, Inc., 896

Cavcar Co. v. M/V Suzdal, 392

Cedarville—Topdalsfjord, 1057

Central Hudson Gas and Elec. Corp. v. Empresa Naviera Santa, SA, 401

Cerro Sales Corp. v. Atlantic Marine Enterprises, Inc., 663

CF Industries, Inc., United States v., 1049

Chadade S. S. Co., Petition of, 556

Challenger, Inc. v. Durno, 410

Chan v. Society Expeditions, Inc., 1024

Chance v. Certain Artifacts Found and Salvaged from The Nashville, 707

Chance v. United States, 416

Chandris, Inc. v. Latsis, 844

Chapman v. City of Grosse Pointe Farms, 96, 97, 97

Chapman v. the Engines of Greenpoint, 513

Chapman v. United States, 324

Chelentis v. Luckenbach S.S. Co., 375, 377, 808, 820, 954, 957, 1022

Chervy v. Peninsular & Oriental Steam Nav. Co., 549

Chesapeake and Ohio Ry. Co. v. Schwalb, 980, 986, 987, 988

Chesapeake Shipping, Inc., Complaint of, 1043

China Trade and Development Corp. v. M.V. Choong Yong, 201

China Union Lines, Limited v. A. O. Andersen & Co., 772

Churchill v. F/V Fjord, 5 F.3d 374, p. 1070

Churchill v. F/V FJORD, 892 F.2d 763, pp. 210, 400

Cia. Atlantica Pacifica, S. A. v. Humble Oil & Refining Co., 632

Cincinnati Gas & Elec. Co. v. Abel, 1088, 1093, 1094, 1096

City of (see name of city)

C.J. Hendry Co. v. Moore, 147, 158

Claborn v. Star Fish & Oyster Co., Inc., 909

Claim of Gypsum Carrier, 774

Clem Perrin Marine Towing, Inc. v. Panama Canal Co., 91

Cleveland Tankers, Inc., Petition of, 1024

Clevenger v. Star Fish & Oyster Co., 909

Close v. Anderson, 660

Cobelfret–Cie Belge v. Samick Lines Co., Ltd., 283

Colavito v. Gonzales, 557

Colburn v. Bunge Towing, Inc., 893, 947

Colgate Palmolive Co. v. S/S Dart Canada, 174

Collie v. Fergusson, 488

Colon v. Apex Marine Corp., 932

Colonial Press of Miami, Inc. v. The Allen's Cay, 270, 433

Columbus Co. v. Shore, 609

Columbus–McKinnon, Inc. v. Gearench, Inc., 1004

Colvin v. Kokusai Kisen Kabushiki Kaisha, 965

Commodity Service Corp. v. Hamburg–American Line, 588

Compagnia Maritima La Empresa, S. A. v. Pickard, 485

Compania De Navegacione Almirante S. A. Panama v. Certain Proceeds of Cargo, 429

Compania Pelineon De Navegacion, S. A. v. Texas Petroleum Co., 794

Compania Peruana De Vapores, United States v., 763

Complaint of (see name of party)

Connolly v. Farrell Lines, Inc., 296, 876

Conoco v. Varco International, Inc., 779

Consolidated Aluminum Corp. v. C.F. Bean Corp., 804

Consolidated Grain & Barge Co. v. Marcona Conveyor Corp., 582

Consolidated Rail Corp. v. Gottshall, 953

Construction Exporting Enterprises, Uneca v. Nikki Maritime Ltd., 308

Contact Lumber Co. v. P.T. Moges Shipping Co. Ltd., 306

Containerschiffsreedei T.S. Columbus New Zealand v. Corporation of Lloyd's, 757

Conti–Lines, S.A. v. M/V BARONESS V, 486

Continental Cas. Co. v. Canadian Universal Ins. Co., 244

Continental Grain Co. v. Federal Barge Lines, Inc., 263

Continental Grain Co. v. The FBL–585, 297

Continental Oil Co. v. Bonanza Corp., 1056

Cookmeyer v. Louisiana Dept. of Highways, 140

Cooper v. Loper, 1006

Cooper Stevedoring Co. v. Fritz Kopke, Inc., 975, 975, 1002

Cope v. Vallette Dry–Dock Co, 143

Corat Intern., Inc. v. Saudi Nat. Lines, 663

Cornish Shipping Ltd. v. International Nederlanden Bank N.V., 430

Coryell v. Phipps (The Seminole), 1065

Cosmopolitan Shipping Co. v. McAllister, 931, 932

Couch v. Cro–Marine Transport, Inc., 1002, 1009

Coulter v. Ingram Pipeline, Inc., 896

Cowart, Estate of v. Nicklos Drilling Co., 1003

Craine v. United States, 574

Creole Shipping, Ltd. v. Diamandis Pateras, Ltd., 761

Crescent City Marine, Inc. v. M/V Nunki, 447

Crescent Towing & Salvage Co. v. Dixilyn Drilling Corp., 587

Crescent Towing & Salvage Co., Inc. v. M/V Anax, 516

Crisis Transp. Co. v. M/V Erlangen Exp., 589

Crookham v. Muick, 208, 210

Crown Zellerbach Corp. v. Ingram Industries, Inc., 783 F.2d 1296, p. 1072

Crown Zellerbach Corp. v. Ingram Industries, Inc., 745 F.2d 995, p. 1072

Crumady v. The Joachim Hendrik Fisser, 969, 970, 971, 972

Crustacean Transp. Corp. v. Atalanta Trading Corp., 485

Cullen Fuel Co. v. W. E. Hedger, Inc., 1050

Culver v. Slater Boat Co., 215

Cummiskey v. Chandris, S.A., 550

Cunard S.S. Co. Ltd. v. Salen Reefer Services AB, 543

Cupit v. McClanahan Contractors, Inc., 1056

Curacao Drydock Co., (N.Y. Curacaose Dok Maatschappli) v. M/V Akritas, 310

Curry v. Fluor Drilling Services, Inc., 893

Dabney v. New England Mut. Marine Ins. Co., 731

Dailey, Thomas D. v. Alcoa S. S. Co., 875

Damodar Bulk Carriers, Ltd., Complaint of, 631

Dann v. Dredge Sandpiper, 513

David Crystal, Inc. v. Cunard S. S. Co., 649

Davis v. Bender Shipbuilding and Repair Co., Inc., 1024

Davis v. City of Jacksonville Beach, Fla., 97

Davis v. Department of Labor and Industries of Washington, 960, 962

Davis v. Matson Nav. Co., 176

Davis v. Odeco, Inc., 893

Davis v. United States, 1069

Dean v. United States, 911

De Bardeleben Coal Corp. v. Henderson, 963

De Centeno v. Gulf Fleet Crews, Inc., 946

Deep Sea Tankers, Limited v. The Long Branch, 783, 1073, 1088, 1094

Deffes v. Federal Barge Lines, Inc., 977

Defrier v. The Nicaragua, 548

Deisler v. McCormack Aggregates, Co., 894

DeJames v. Magnificence Carriers, Inc., 654 F.2d 280, p. **284**

DeJames v. Magnificence Carriers, Inc., 491 F.Supp. 1276, pp. 293, 294

Delaney v. Merchants River Transp., 1002

Del Greco v. New York Harbor Independent Pilots, 75

DeLoach by DeLoach v. Companhia de Navegacao Lloyd Brasileiro, 359, 365

DeLovio v. Boit, 2, 29, 32, 94

Delphinus Maritima, S.A., Matter of Complaint of, 660

Delta Country Ventures, Inc. v. Magana, 126, 1049, 1049

Delta S.S. Lines, Inc. v. Avondale Shipyards, Inc., 802

Dempsey v. Mac Towing, Inc., 947

De Oliveira v. Delta Marine Drilling Co., 298, 306

Deutsche Shell Tanker Gesellschaft mbH v. Placid Refining Co., 746

Dianella Shipping Corp. v. Hernandez, 1006

Diaz v. The Seathunder, 433, **441**

Dick v. United States, 1043, 1044

Dickens v. United States, 947

Diesel Tanker Ira S. Bushey, Inc. v. Tug Bruce A. McAllister, 800

DiGiovanni v. Traylor Bros., Inc., 141

Dillingham Tug & Barge Corp. v. Collier Carbon & Chemical Corp., 582, 587

Director, Office of Workers' Compensation Programs, United States Dept. of Labor v. Perini North River Associates, 988

Dixilyn Drilling Corp. v. Crescent Towing & Salvage Co., 587

Dominican Maritime, S.A. v. M/V Inagua Beach, 801

Doran v. Lee, 40

Double D Dredging Co., In re, 50

Dowdle v. Offshore Exp., Inc., 894

Doxsee Sea Clam Co., Inc. v. Brown, 1095

Dragon v. United States (The Lucky Lindy), 40

Drake v. Raymark Industries, Inc., 1005

Dugas v. National Aircraft Corp., 1024

Duhon v. Koch Exploration Co., 236

Duluth Superior Excursions, Inc. v. Makela, 97, 549

Dwyer Oil Transport Co. v. Tug Matton, 772

Eagle–Picher Industries, Inc. v. United States, 955, 991

Eagle Terminal Tankers, Inc. v. Insurance Co. of U.S.S.R. (Ingosstrakh), Ltd., 637 F.2d 890, p. **746**

Eagle Terminal Tankers, Inc. v. Insurance Co. of U.S.S.R. (Ingosstrakh), Ltd., 489 F.Supp. 920, p. 755

Eagle Terminal Tankers, Inc. v. Insurance Co. of United StatesS.R., (Ingosstrakh), Ltd., 755

Easton, Ex parte, 74

East River S.S. Corp. v. Transamerica Delaval, Inc., 95, 123, 161, 839, 843

Economu v. Bates, 91

Economy Light & Power Co. v. United States, 40

Eddie S.S. Co. Ltd. v. P.T. Karana Line, 200

Edmonds v. Compagnie Generale Transatlantique, 1002

Edwards v. Elliott, 49

Edwards v. Hurtel, 724 F.2d 689, p. 50

Edwards v. Hurtel, 717 F.2d 1204, p. 49

Effron v. Sun Line Cruises, Inc., 552

Egan Marine Contracting Co., Inc. v. South Sea Shipping Corp., 283

Eklof Marine Corp. v. United States, 333

Elia Salzman Tobacco Co. v. S. S. Mormacwind, 609

Ellerman Lines Ltd. v. Gibbs, Nathaniel (Canada) Ltd., 741, 755

Elna II–Mission San Francisco (Petition of Oskar Tiedemann and Company), 809

Emerson G.M. Diesel, Inc. v. Alaskan Enterprise, 215, 805

Emery v. Rock Island Boatworks, Inc., 1024

Empresa Lineas Maritimas Argentinas S.A. v. United States, 1058

Encyclopaedia Britannica, Inc. v. S. S. Hong Kong Producer, 662

Enelow v. New York Life Ins. Co., 309

English Whipple Sailyard, Ltd. v. Yawl Ardent, 801

Epstein v. Corporacion Peruana de Vapores, 447

Equilease Corp. v. M/V Sampson, 479

Erie, City of v. S. S. North American, 410

Erie R Co v. Erie & Western Transp Co, 377, 809

Erie Sand S.S. Co. v. Peter Kiewit and Sons Co., Inc., 1096

Esso Brussels v. C.V. Sea Witch, 1097

Esso Intern., Inc. v. Steamship Captain John, 453

Esta Later Charters, Inc. v. Ignacio, 1095

Estate of (see name of party)

Etheridge v. Norfolk & Western Ry. Co., 986, 987, 1007

Ettelson v. Metropolitan Life Ins. Co., 309

Evans v. Buchanan, 830

Evans v. United Arab Shipping Co. S.A.G., 932, 948

Evansville & Bowling Green Packet Co. v. Chero Cola Bottling Co., 139

Evergreen Intern. (USA) Corp. v. Standard Warehouse, 310

Executive Jet Aviation, Inc. v. City of Cleveland, Ohio, 94, 95, 121, 123, 131, 174, 230, 324, 365

Exner Sand and Gravel Corp. v. Maher Stevedoring Corp., 800

Ex parte (see name of party)

Exxon Co. v. Sofec, Inc., 774

Exxon Corp. v. Central Gulf Lines, Inc., 79

Famiano v. Enyeart, 1087

Faneuil Advisors, Inc. v. O/S Sea Hawk, 478, **677**

Farrandoc (Canada Exch. 1967), 606

Farrell v. United States, 877, 884, 885

Farrell Lines Inc., In re, 1065

Farrell Lines Inc. v. Jones, 1058

Farrell Ocean Services, Inc. v. United States, 462

Farr Sugar Corp., United States v., 808

Farwest Steel Corp. v. Barge Sea–Span 241, 828 F.2d 522, p. 452

Farwest Steel Corp. v. Barge Sea–Span 241, 1984 WL 1908, p. 441

Faust v. South Carolina State Highway Dept., 339

Favorite, The, 75

Federal Barge Lines, Inc. v. Granite City Steel Div. of Nat. Steel Corp., 574

Federal Barge Lines, Inc. v. SCNO Barge Lines, Inc., 574

Federal Ins. Co. v. Lake Shore Inc., 294

Federal Marine Terminals, Inc. v. Burnside Shipping Co., 1006

Federazione Italiana Dei, Consorzi Agrari v. Mandask, 606, 1057

F.E.R.C., State ex rel. New York State Dept. of Environmental Conservation v., 55

Feres v. United States, 333, 955

Ferromet Resources, Inc. v. Chemoil Corp., 453

Figueroa v. Campbell Industries, 953, 990

Filippou v. Italia Societa Per Azioni Di Navizione, 245

Findley v. Lanasa, 480

Finley v. United States, 173

Finneseth v. Carter, 41, 48, 49

Finora Co., Inc. v. Amitie Shipping, Ltd., 575

Fireman's Fund Ins. Companies v. M/V Vignes, 606

Firestone Synthetic Fibers Co.–Division of Firestone Tire & Rubber Co. v. M/S Black Heron, 606, **631,** 632

First Bank & Trust v. Knachel, 416

First Nat. Bank & Trust Co. of Escanaba v. Oil Screw Olive L. Moore Barge Wiltranco, 388

Fitzgerald v. United States Lines Co., 162, 163

Flores v. Carnival Cruise Lines, 885

Flores, United States v., 127, 128

Florida Dept. of State v. Treasure Salvors, Inc., 339

Florida, Dept. of State, State of v. Treasure Salvors, Inc., 264

Florida East Coast Ry. Co. v. Revilo Corp., 772

Flota Maritima Browning De Cuba, Sociadad Anonima v. Motor Vessel Ciudad De La Habana, 86

Flota Maritima Browning De Cuba, Sociadad Anonima v. The Ciudad De La Habana, 90

Flowers Transp., Inc. v. M/V Peanut Hollinger, 310

Folkstone Maritime, Ltd. v. CSX Corp., 269

Follett, Petition of, 1069

Fontenot v. AWI, Inc., 988

Fontenot v. Mesa Petroleum Co., 988, 1006

Ford Motor Co. v. Wallenius Lines, 74

Foremost Ins. Co. v. Richardson, 49, 122, 124, 365

Foret v. Co–Mar Offshore Corp., 875

Forkin v. Furness Withy & Co., 977

Forrester v. Ocean Marine Indem. Co., 575

Foss Launch and Tug Co. v. Char Ching Shipping U.S.A., 434

Foster v. United States, 365

Fourco Glass Co. v. Transmirra Products Corp., 296, 297

4,885 Bags of Linseed, In re, 411, 478

Francese v. United States, 208

Francis v. Dietrick, 215

Francosteel Corp. v. M/V Charm, 261

Francosteel Corp. v. N. V. Nederlandsch Amerikaansche, Stoomvart–Maatschappij, 663

Frank L. III, The, 1068

Fraser River Pile & Dredge Ltd. v. Empire Tug Boats Ltd., 582

Fredelos v. Merritt–Chapman & Scott Corp., 487, 492

Freedom Line Inc. v. Vessel Glenrock, 416, **442**

Freeport Sulphur Co. v. S/S Hermosa, 800

Freights, etc., of the Mount Shasta, United States v., 256, 258, 264

Fretz v. Bull, 38

Fuentes v. Shevin, 272

Fuller v. Golden Age Fisheries, 536

F/V Sylvester F. Whalen, United States v., 226 F.Supp. 617, p. 473

F/V Sylvester F. Whalen, United States v., 217 F.Supp. 916, p. 388

Galban Lobo Trading Co. S/A v. The Diponegaro, 388

Galehead, Inc. v. M/V Fratzis M., 535

Galt G/S v. Hapag–Lloyd A.G., 165

Gamma–10 Plastics, Inc. v. American President Lines, Ltd., 601

Garay v. Carnival Cruise Line, Inc., 876

Garcia v. Queen, Ltd., 67

Gardiner v. Sea–Land Service, Inc., 894

Garrett v. United States Lines, Inc., 829

Garvin v. Alumax of South Carolina, Inc., 1004, 1008

Gaspar v. United States, 761

Gaspard v. Taylor Diving & Salvage Co., Inc., 894

Gaudet v. Sea–Land Services, Inc., 1024

Gauthier v. Crosby Marine Service, Inc., 893

Gave v. Grace Line, Inc., 128

Gay v. Barge 266, 1008, 1008

Gaymon v. Quinn Menhaden Fisheries of Tex., Inc., 948

Gayner v. The New Orleans, 416

Gebhard v. S.S. Hawaiian Legislator, 977

Gele v. Wilson, 806

General Accident, Fire & Life Assur Corporation v. Crowell, 991
General Elec. Co. Intern. Sales Div. v. S.S. Nancy Lykes, 649, 663
General Elec. Credit & Leasing Corp. v. Drill Ship Mission Exploration, 410, 416
General Engine & Mach. Works, Inc. v. Slay, 76
Gerald v. United States Lines Co., 909
Getty Refining and Marketing Co. v. MT FADI B, 803
G & G Shipping Co., Ltd. of Anguilla, Complaint of, 783
Gibboney v. Wright, 555, 556
Gilbert Imported Hardwoods, Inc. v. 245 Packages of Guatambu Squares, More or Less, 413
Gillespie v. United States Steel Corp., 308, 954, 955, 1023
Glacier Bay, In re, 1049
Gloria S. S. Co. v. Smith, 310
Glynn v. Roy Al Boat Management Corp., 895, 953
Gonsalves v. Amoco Shipping Co., 176
Gooden v. Sinclair Refining Co., 885
Gore v. Clearwater Shipping Corp., 884
Gough v. Natural Gas Pipeline Co. of America, 953, 953
Goumas v. K. Karras & Son, 85
Grace v. Keystone Shipping Co., 953
Grand Bahama Petroleum Co., Ltd. v. Canadian Transp. Agencies, Ltd., 272
Grant Smith–Porter Ship Co. v. Rohde, 958, 959, 960, 960
Great Lakes Dredge & Dock Co., Complaint of, 1052
Great Lakes Dredge & Dock Co v. Kierejewski, 958
Great Lakes Towing Co v. St Joseph–Chicago S S Co, 1053
Greenburg v. Puerto Rico Maritime Shipping Authority, 588
Greenshields, Cowie & Co. v. Stephens & Sons, 732
Greenway v. Buzzard Point Boatyard Corp., 74
Greer v. United States, 801
Gremillion v. Gulf Coast Catering Co., 141
Griffin v. Oceanic Contractors, Inc., 417
Griffis v. Gulf Coast Pre–Stress Co., Inc., 1004
Grillea v. United States, 910, 970, 971, 973
Grover v. American President Lines, Inc., 947
Grow v. Steel Gas Screw Loraine K, 86, 479
Grubart, Inc. v. Great Lakes Dredge & Dock Co., 104, 141, 1029, 1049
Gryar v. Odeco, Inc., 557
Guenther v. Sedco, Inc., 535
Guevara v. Maritime Overseas Corp., 895
Guey v. Gulf Ins. Co., 1095
Guidry v. South Louisiana Contractors, Inc., 932
Guilles v. Sea–Land Service, Inc., 988, 1007
Gulf and Southern Terminal Corp. v. S.S. President Roxas, 264

Gulf Atlantic Transp. Co. v. The F. L. Hayes, 809
Gulf Oil Trading Co. v. Creole Supply, 511
Gulf Oil Trading Co. v. M/V Freedom, 462
Gulf Oil Trading Co., a Div. of Gulf Oil Co. v. M/V CARIBE MAR, 461
Gutierrez v. Waterman S. S. Corp., 102, 413, 976, 977, 978
Guzman v. Pichirilo, 979

Hagans v. Farrell Lines, Inc., 102
Halcyon Lines v. Haenn Ship Ceiling & Refitting Corp., 973, 974, 975
Hamilton v. Seariver Maritime, Inc., 940
Hanke, In re, 1069
Harmon v. Baltimore & Ohio R.R., 1007
Harper v. Zapata Off–Shore Co., 895
Harrell v. Dixon Bay Transp. Co., 895
Harrell, United States v., 49
Harrison v. Glendel Drilling Co., 245
Harrison Boat House, Inc., Complaint of, 556
Hartford Acc. & Indem. Co. v. Costa Lines Cargo Services, Inc., 1007
Hartford Fire Ins. Co. v. Pacific Far East Line, Inc., 649
Haskins v. Point Towing Co., 163, **215**
Hassinger v. Tideland Elec. Membership Corp., 96
Hastings v. Mann, 96
Hatch v. Durocher Dock and Dredge, Inc., 141
Hatteras, Inc. v. United StatesS. Hatteras, 707
Haughton v. Blackships, Inc., 908
Hawgood & Avery Transit Co. v. Dingman, 516
Hayes v. Wilh Wilhelmsen Enterprises, Ltd., 1005
Hayes–Leger Associates, Inc. v. M/V Oriental Knight, 641
Hayford v. Doussony, 140
Hays v. Carnival Cruise Lines, Inc., 556
Hebert v. Air Logistics, Inc., 143
Hechinger, Matter of, 947
Hecht v. Cunard Line Ltd., 551
Hellenic Lines, Limited v. S. S. Union Metropole, 771, 802
Hellenic Lines, Ltd. v. Prudential Lines, Inc., 765
Hellweg v. Baja Boats, Inc., 1094
Hemba v. Freeport McMoran Energy Partners, Ltd., 142
Henderson v. United States, 338
Henley Drilling Co. v. McGee, 649
Herb's Welding, Inc. v. Gray, 987
Hercules Carriers, Inc. v. Claimant State of Fla., Dept. of Transp., 1058, 1065
Hercules Carriers, Inc., Complaint of, 614 F.Supp. 16, p. 800
Hercules Carriers, Inc., Complaint of, 1982 A.M.C. 2888, p. 762.
Hercules, Inc. v. Stevens Shipping Co., 780
Hernandez v. M/V Rajaan, 1006
Hershey Chocolate Corp. v. The Mars, 633

Hewlett v. Barge Bertie, 800

Hewlett v. Tug Evelyn, 800

H & F Barge Co., Inc. v. Garber Bros., Inc., 295

H. & H. Wheel Service, Petition of, 1069, 1069

Hicks v. Ocean Drilling & Exploration Co., 142

Hill v. United Fruit Co., 176

Hines v. British Steel Corp., 1005

Hiram Walker & Sons, Inc. v. Kirk Line, R.B. Kirkconnell & Bro., Ltd., 601

Hixon v. Sherwin–Williams Co., 173

Hocking, Petition of, 1069, 1075

Hodes v. S.N.C. Achille Lauro ed Altri–Gestione, 551

Hoegh Lines v. Green Truck Sales, Inc., 601

Hokanson v. Maritime Overseas Corp., 875

Holmes v. J. Ray McDermott & Co., Inc., 895

Hoopengarner v. United States, 128

Hopson v. Texaco, Inc., 946

Horsley v. Mobil Oil Corp., 948, 1024

Horton v. Horton, Inc. v. The Robert E. Hopkins, 810

Howard Olson & Co. v. Marine Leopard, 784, 810, 1075

Howlett v. Birkdale Shipping Co., S.A., 991

Hudson Harbor 79th Street Boat Basin, Inc. v. Sea Casa, 74, 142

Huff v. Italian Line, 557

Hughes v. ContiCarriers and Terminals, Inc., 896

Hunt v. Paco Tankers, Inc., 295, 295

Hurston v. Director, Office of Workers Compensation Programs, 987

Hydaburg Co-op. Ass'n v. Alaska S. S. Co., 632

Iligan Integrated Steel Mills, Inc. v. S.S. John Weyerhaeuser, 662

Illinois—Union Star, 801

Imm v. Union R. Co., 131

Impala Trading Corp. v. Hawthorne Lumber Co., 262

Incas and Monterey Printing and Packaging, Ltd. v. M/V Sang Jin, 308

Indussa Corp. v. S. S. Ranborg, 307, 602

Industria Nacional Del Papel, CA. v. M/V Albert F, 574

Ingram v. Threadgill, 36

Ingram River Equipment, Inc. v. Pott Industries, Inc., 843

Inland Credit Corp. v. M/T Bow Egret, 269

In Matter of Complaint of Korea Wonyang Fisheries Co., Ltd., 1049

In re (see name of party)

Interlake S. S. Co. v. Nielsen, 96

International Adjusters, Ltd. v. M.V. MANHATTAN, 757

International Milling Co. v. Brown Steamship Co., 311

International Nav. Co. v. Farr & Bailey Mfg. Co., 603

International Paint Co., Inc. v. M/V Mission Viking, 416

International Seafoods of Alaska, Inc. v. Park Ventures, Inc., 269, 452, 486

International Shoe Co. v. State of Wash., Office of Unemployment Compensation and Placement, 293

International Stevedoring Co. v. Haverty, 958, 966, 967, 990

Irving Trust Co. v. The Golden Sail, 411

Isthmian Steamship Co., United States v., 163

Italia Di Navigazione, S.p.A. v. M.V. Hermes I, 662

Italia Societa per Azioni di Navigazione v. Oregon Stevedoring Co., 974, 979

Jack Neilson, Inc. v. Tug Peggy, 90

Jackson v. Inland Oil & Transport Co., 258

Jackson v. Lykes Bros. S. S. Co., 980

Jackson v. Marine Exploration Co., Inc., 75

Jackson v. The Steamboat Magnolia, 4, 29, 38, 155

James v. River Parishes Co., Inc., 762

Jane B. Corp., United States v., 485

Jefferson Barracks Marine Service, Inc. v. Casey, 1081, 1087

Jernigan v. Lay Barge Delta Five, 416

J. Gerber & Co. v. S.S. Sabine Howaldt, 621

Jig Third Corp. v. Puritan Marine Ins. Underwriters Corp., 123

Johansen v. United States, 955

Johnson v. G.T. Elliott, Inc., 990

Johnson v. Mobile Towing & Wrecking Co., 829

Johnson v. Odeco Oil and Gas Co., 142

Johnson v. Penrod Drilling Co., 215

Johnson v. United States, 979

Jones v. Bender Welding & Mach. Works, Inc., 805

Jones v. Fruchtreederei Harald Schuldt & Co., 978

Jones v. One Fifty Foot Gulfstar Motor Sailing Yacht, Hull No. 01, 91

Jones v. Reagan, 895

Jones v. United States, 876

Jones & Laughlin Steel Corp. v. Pfeifer, 1007

Jones & Laughlin Steel, Inc. v. Mon River Towing, Inc., 333, 338

Jordan v. United States Lines, Inc., 908

J. Ray McDermott & Co. v. The Off-Shore Menhaden Co., 430, 433

Juda, United States v., 128

Justice v. United States, 333

Kaiser Aetna v. United States, 41

Kalleck v. Deering, 359, **366**

Kane v. M/V Leda, 462

Kanematsu–Gosho Ltd. v. M/T Messiniaki Aigli, 641

Kathriner v. Unisea, Inc., 975 F.2d 657, p. 1004

Kathriner v. Unisea, Inc., 740 F.Supp. 768, p. 245

Keen v. Overseas Tankship Corp., 102

Keeping v. Dawson, 875

Keller v. United States, 1005, 1009

Kelly v. Pittsburgh & Conneaut Dock Co., 1007

Kelly v. Smith, 95, 123

Kelly v. S/S "Queen Elizabeth 2", 660

Kennecott Copper Corp. v. State Tax Com'n, 339, 340

Kermarec v. Compagnie Generale Transatlantique, 359, 825, 829, 830

Kerr–McGee Corp. v. Ma–Ju Marine Services, Inc., 1005

Kesselring v. F/T Arctic Hero, 388

Ketchum v. Gulf Oil Corp., 1005

Kettell v. Wiggin, 659

Keys Jet Ski, Inc. v. Kays, 1029

Kiesel v. State of Fla., Dept. of Natural Resources, 340

Kiewit Pacific Co., Matter of Complaint of, 1095

King v. Alaska S.S. Co., 377

King Fisher Marine Service, Inc. v. NP Sunbonnet, 582, 799, 802

Kingston Shipping Co., Inc. v. Roberts, 803

Kingston, The, 417

King, The v. Joseph Lane, 247

Kinsman Transit Co., Petition of, 779, 810, 1053

Kirsch v. United States, 910

Klarman, Howard, Petition of, 1081

Kline v. Maritrans CP, Inc., 948

Knapp, Stout & Co. Company v. McCaffrey, 76

Knickerbocker Ice Co. v. Stewart, 374, 377, 957, 1023

Knott v. Botany Worsted Mills, 607

Koistinen v. American Export Lines, 871, 874, 875

Konica Business Machines v. SEA–LAND CONSUMER, 660

Kornberg v. Carnival Cruise Lines, Inc., 545, 548, 549, 556

Kossick v. United Fruit Co., 895

Kotsopoulos v. Asturia Shipping Co., 806

Kraljic v. Berman Enterprises, Inc., 895

Kratzer v. Capital Marine Supply, Inc., 895

Krauss Bros. Lumber Co. v. Dimon S.S. Corp., 422, 498US19

K/S Ditlev Chartering A/S & Co. v. Egeria S.p.A. di Navigazione, 283

Kynoch v. The Propeller S.C. Ives, 189

La Capria v. Compagnie Maritime Belge, 212

Lackey v. Atlantic Richfield Co., 176

Lady Jane, Inc., Complaint of, 1041, 1043

Lake Tankers Corp. v. Henn, 1086

Lambros Seaplane Base v. the Batory, 666

Land and Lake Tours, Inc. v. Lewis, 50

Langnes v. Green, 1087, 1088, 1094

L'Arina v. Manwaring, 75

Larios v. Victory Carriers, Inc., 536, 972

Larsen v. Northland Transp. Co., 740

La Vengeance, United States v., 33

Lawrence v. Minturn, 736

L.B. Harvey Marine, Inc. v. M/V River Arc, 268

Leathers v. Blessing, 821

Leather's Best, Inc. v. S.S. Mormaclynx, 168, 172, 649

LeBouf Bros. Towing Co., Inc., United States v., 536, 543

Ledet v. United Aircraft Corp., 161

Leith v. Oil Transport Co., 296, 296

Lekas & Drivas, Inc. v. Goulandris, 616, 632, 661

Leslie Salt Co. v. United States, 55

Lewis v. S. S. Baune, 197

Lewis v. Timco, Inc., 830, 834

Lewis v. United States, 245

Liberty Seafood, Inc., Complaint of, 885

Lightfoot v. F/V ARCTIC STORM, 535

Lindgren v. United States, 954, 955, 1023

Linton v. Great Lakes Dredge & Dock Co., 176

Lirette v. N.L. Sperry Sun, Inc., 176

Liverpool, Brazil & River Plate Steam Nav. Co. v. Brooklyn Eastern Dist. Terminal, 1073, 1074

Liverpool & G.W. Steam Co. v. Phenix Ins. Co., 548, 556

Livingston v. United States, 48, 49

Lloyd's Leasing Ltd. v. Conoco, 805

Lockheed Aircraft Corp. v. United States, 955, 991, 1005

Loc–Wood Boat & Motors, Inc. v. Rockwell, 40, 556

Loeber v. Bay Tankers, Inc., 168

Lohman v. Royal Viking Lines, Inc., 550

Long Island Tankers Corp. v. S. S. Kaimana, 417

Louis Dreyfus Corp. v. 27,946 Long Tons of Corn, 606

Louisiana ex rel. Guste, State of v. M/V Testbank, 804

Louisiana Ship Management, Inc., In re, 542, 543

Louisville and N. R. Co. v. M/V Bayou Lacombe, 803

Louisville Underwriters, In re, 295

Lousararian v. Royal Caribbean Corp., 550

Luke, Harry B. v. Hirsch and the Myab III, 783

Luna v. Star of India, 141

L.W. Richardson Const. Co., Matter of, 1094

Lynch v. McFarland, 49

Macedo v. F/V Paul & Michelle, 875, 893, 894

Mackensworth v. S.S. American Merchant, 263

Madole v. Johnson, 40

Madruga v. Superior Court of State of Cal. in and for San Diego County, 158

Magnolia Marine Transport Co., Inc. v. Laplace Towing Corp., 1044

Magnolia Ocean Shipping Corp. v. M/V Mercedes Maria, 91

Magnussen v. Yak, Inc., 947

Mahnich v. Southern S. S. Co., 910, 966, 967, 968, 972, 1022, 1023

Mahramas v. American Export Isbrandtsen Lines, Inc., 931

Mali v. Keeper of the Common Jail of Hudson County, 128

Mamiye Bros. v. Barber S. S. Lines, Inc., 610

Manhattan Oil Transp. Co. v. M/V Salvador, 746

Mapco Petroleum, Inc. v. Memphis Barge Line, Inc., 1094

Marcona Corp. v. Oil Screw Shifty III, 773

Marek v. Marpan Two, Inc., 551

Marine Fuel Supply & Towing, Inc. v. M/V Ken Lucky, 447, 452

Marine Recreational Opportunities, Inc. v. Berman, 1039, 1043

Marine Sports, Inc., Complaint of, 1056

Marine Stevedoring Corp. v. Oosting, 963, 964

Marine Transit Corporation v. Dreyfus, 186

Maritime Underwater Surveys, Inc. v. Unidentified, Wrecked and Abandoned Sailing Vessel, 262, 339

Mark v. South Continental Ins. Agency, Inc., 666

Markakis v. S/S Volendam, 708

Martha Anne–Cearal (Atkins v. Lorentzen), 763

Martin v. John W. Stone Oil Distributor, Inc., 948

Marvirazon Compania Naviera S.A. v. H.J. Baker & Bro., Inc., 283

Marx v. Government of Guam, 308

Maryland Cas. Co. v. Cushing, 1071, 1072

Maryland Ins. Co. v. Le Roy, 661

Mascuilli v. United States, 909, 972

Mason v. The Blaireau, 667, 672

Massman–Drake v. Towboat M/V Hugh C. Blaske, 762

Mathiesen v. M/V Obelix, 602, 805

Matson Nav. Co., United States v., 95, 97

Matter of (see name of party)

Matthews v. Gulf & South Am. S. S. Co., 875

Max Morris, the v. Curry, 820, 835

Maxon Marine, Inc. v. Director, Office of Workers' Compensation Programs, 991

Maxwell v. Hapag–Lloyd Aktiengesellschaft, Hamburg, 762

May v. Hamburg–Amerikanische Packetfahrt Aktiengesellschaft, 592

May v. Transworld Drilling Co., 1003

McAleer v. Smith, 920, 932

McAllister v. United States, 311

McCann v. Falgout Boat Co., 1081

McCarthy v. American Eastern Corp., 141

McCarthy v. The Bark Peking, 141, 1004

McClenahan v. Paradise Cruises, Ltd., 1049

McClendon v. OMI Offshore Marine Service, 940, 947

McCormick v. United States, 680 F.2d 345, p. 324

McCormick v. United States, 645 F.2d 299, p. 324

McCorpen v. Central Gulf S. S. Corp., 876

McDermott, Inc. v. AmClyde, 840

McDermott, Inc. v. Boudreaux, 141

McDermott, Inc. v. M/V ANGELA BRILEY, 543

McDermott Intern., Inc. v. Wilander, 989

Mears v. American Export Lines, Inc., 909

Melancon v. Petrostar Corp., 953

Melwire Trading Co., Inc. v. M/V Cape Antibes, 428

Mendez v. Ishikawajima–Harima Heavy Industries Co., Ltd., 535

Mengel Box Co. v. Joest, 161

Merrill–Stevens Dry Dock Co. v. M/V Laissez Faire, 197

Merritt & Chapman Derrick & Wrecking Co v. United States, 693

Miami River Boat Yard, Inc. v. 60' Houseboat, Serial No. SC–40–2860–3–62, 142

Michalic v. Cleveland Tankers, Inc., 909

Milanovich v. Costa Crociere, S.p.A., 551

Miles v. Apex Marine Corp., 895, **1010,** 1023, 1024, 1025

Miller v. Griffin–Alexander Drilling Co., 96

Miller v. International Freighting Corp, 551, 603

Miller v. United States, 955

Miller Industries v. Caterpillar Tractor Co., 805, 839

Miller Yacht Sales Inc. v. M.V. 'OCEAN FRIEND', 661

Milwaukee, City of v. Cement Div., Nat. Gypsum Co., 806

Minerais United States Inc., Exalmet Div. v. M/V Moslavina, 639, 641

Mink v. Genmar Industries, Inc., 95

Minnehaha Creek Watershed Dist. v. Hoffman, 55

Minnie v. Port Huron Terminal Co., 96

Mitchell v. W. T. Grant Co., 272

Mitsui & Co., Ltd. v. American Export Lines, Inc., 648

Mobile Life Ins Co v. Brame, 358, 1021

Mobil Oil Corp. v. Higginbotham, 1024

Mobil Sales and Supply Corp. v. Panamax Venus, 511

Molett v. Penrod Drilling Co., 1003

Montauk Oil Transp. Corp. v. Sonat Marine, Inc., 197

Moon Engineering Co. v. The Valiant Power, 410

Moor v. Alameda County, 340

Moore v. Phillips Petroleum Co., 1005

Moore–McCormack Lines, Inc. v. Richardson, 1074

Moore–McCormack Lines, Inc. v. Russak, 556

Moragne v. States Marine Lines, Inc., 384, 1023, 1108

Morak v. Costa Armatori S.P.A. Genova, 551

Morales v. Dampskibs A/S Flint, 413

Moran v. Bay State Trawler Corp., 875

Morania Barge No. 190, Inc., Complaint of, 1096

Moran Towing & Transp. Co., United States v., 143

Moran Towing & Transp. Co., Inc. v. Lombas, 896

Morel v. Sabine Towing & Transp. Co., Inc., 893

Morgan Guar. Trust Co. of New York v. Hellenic Lines Ltd., 542

Morton v. De Oliveira, 557

Motor Ship Pacific Carrier, In re, 95, 123

Moyer v. Wrecked and Abandoned Vessel, known as Andrea Doria, 264

M/S Bremen v. Zapata Off–Shore Co., 306, 587, 1095

M/T Alva S. S. Co., In re, 1075

M/T Norseman, 694

Muratore, M. v. M/S Scotia Prince, 550, 840

Murray v. Hildreth, 127

Murray v. New York Central Railroad Company, 1088, 1094

Murray v. Schwartz, 479

M/V Marilena P, United States v., 607

M/V Wuerttemberg, United States v., 783, 783

Nacirema Operating Co. v. Johnson, 96, 964

Nadeau v. Costley, 557

Nadle v. M.V. Tequilla, 488

National Iranian Tanker Co. (Nederland), N. V. v. Tug Dalzell 2, 810

National Steel Corp. v. Great Lakes Towing Co., 802

Navigazione Generale Italiana v. Spencer Kellogg & Sons, Inc. (The S.S. Minicio), 736

Neirbo Co. v. Bethlehem Shipbuilding Corp., 295, 296

Nelsen v. Research Corp. of University of Hawaii, 953

Neptune Maritime Co. of Monrovia v. Vessel Essi Camilla, 762

New England Mut. Marine Ins. Co. v. Dunham, 56

New England Transp. Co., In re, 508

New Jersey Steam–Boat Co v. Brockett, 557

New Orleans for Use and Ben. of Sewerage and Water Bd. of New Orleans, City of v. American Commercial Lines, Inc., 801

Newpark Shipbuilding & Repair, Inc. v. M/V Trinton Brute, 271

Newport News Shipbuilding and Dry Dock Co. v. S.S. Independence, 525

New York, In re, 41 S.Ct. 588, p. 338

New York, In re, 41 S.Ct. 592, p. 338

New York State Dept. of Environmental Conservation, State ex rel. v. F.E.R.C., 55

New York & Virginia S.S. Co. v. Calderwood, 38

N.H. Shipping Corp. v. Freights of S/S Jackie Hause, 429

Nicholas E. Vernicos Shipping Co. v. United States, 673

Nichols v. Petroleum Helicopters, Inc., 1024

Nicol v. Gulf Fleet Supply Vessels, Inc., 911

N.J. Theriot, Inc., Complaint of, 1049

N.M. Paterson & Sons, Limited v. City of Chicago, 324 F.2d 254, p. 809

N.M. Paterson & Sons, Limited v. City of Chicago, 209 F.Supp. 576, p. 808

Nobles, Complaint of, 1043, 1070

Nordasilla Corp. v. Norfolk Shipbuilding & Drydock Corp., 803

North Atlantic & Gulf Steamship Co., In re, 429

Northeast Marine Terminal Co., Inc. v. Caputo, 987, 987, 988

North Georgia Finishing, Inc. v. Di–Chem, Inc., 272

Northland Navigation Co., Ltd v. Patterson Boiler Works Ltd., 740, 741, 758

North Pac. S.S. Co. v. Hall Bros. Marine Ry. & Shipbuilding Co., 67

North River Ins. Co. v. Fed Sea/Fed Pac Line, 663

Norwich, City of, 1070

Notarian v. Trans World Airlines, Inc., 96

Nugent, In re v. Smith, 559

Nunley v. M/V Dauntless Colocotronis, 677, 719, 762

Nygren v. American Boat Cartage, Inc., 808

O'Brien v. City of New York, 990

Ocean Barge Transport Co. v. Hess Oil Virgin Islands Corp., 835

Ocean Recovery Group v. O/S Northern Retriever, 389

Ocean Science & Engineering Inc. v. International Geomarine Corp., 91

O'Connell Machinery Co., Inc. v. M.V. Americana, 662

Odeco Oil and Gas Co., Drilling Div. v. Bonnette, 95

Odishelidze v. Aetna Life & Cas Co., 244

O'Donnell v. Great Lakes Dredge & Dock Co., 311

O'Donnell v. Latham, 310

Offshore Logistics, Inc. v. Tallentire, 176, 210, 1024

O'Hare, Ex parte, 127

Ohio River Co. v. Carrillo, 1096

Oil Shipping (Bunkering) B.V. v. Sonmez Denizcilik Ve Ticaret A.S., 388, 401

Oil Spill by Amoco Cadiz off Coast of France on March 16, 1978, In re, 173

O'Keeffe v. Atlantic Stevedoring Co., 96, 601

Oliver v. Maryland Ins. Co., 661, 662

Olsen v. Shell Oil Co., 141

Olympic Towing Corp. v. Nebel Towing Co., 1072

Oman v. Johns–Manville Corp., 125, 365

Omar v. Sea–Land Service, Inc., 876

Omni Capital Intern. v. Rudolf Wolff & Co., Ltd., 294

Ontario Paper Co. Ltd. v. Salenrederierna A/B, 281, 283

Orduna S.A. v. Zen–Noh Grain Corp., 843

Oregon, State of, United States v., 49

Oriente Commercial, Inc. v. American Flag Vessel, M/V Floridian, 475

Orient Mid–East Lines, Inc. v. Bowen, Inc., 824

Orient Mid–East Lines, Inc. v. Shipment of Rice on Board S.S. Orient Transporter, 746

Orr v. United States, 297

Osaka Shosen Kaisha v. Pacific Export Lumber Co., 417, 544

Oseredzuk v. Warner Co., 50

Owen Equipment & Erection Co. v. Kroger, 168, 172, 173

Pacific Employers Ins. Co. v. M/V Gloria, 559

Pacific Vegetable Oil Corp. v. M/S Norse Commander, 478

Palmer v. Waterman S. S. Corp., 876

Panaconti Shipping Co., S.A. v. M/V Ypapanti, 263

Panama Transport Co., United States v., 783

Parden v. Terminal Ry. of Alabama State Docks Dept., 339, 991

Parker v. Motor Boat Sales, 960, 962

Parker Towing Co. v. Yazoo River Towing, Inc., 802

Patterson Terminals, Inc. v. S. S. Johannes Frans, 801

Pavone v. Mississippi Riverboat Amusement Corp., 132, 141

P.C. Pfeiffer Co. v. The Pacific Star, 417

P & E Boat Rentals, Inc., Matter of, 806

Pelotto v. L & N Towing Co., 895

Peninsular & Oriental Steam Nav. Co. v. Overseas Oil Carriers, Inc., 553 F.2d 830, p. 709

Peninsular & Oriental Steam Nav. Co. v. Overseas Oil Carriers, Inc., 418 F.Supp. 656, p. 713

Pennsylvania R. Co. v. S. S. Marie Leonhardt, 762

Penny v. United Fruit Co., 932

Pennzoil Producing Co. v. Offshore Exp., Inc., 1056

Pentelikon v. Verdi, 783

Peoples Natural Gas Co. v. Ashland Oil, Inc., 761, 772

Peter Paul, Inc v. Rederi A/B Pulp, 606

Petersen v. Chesapeake and Ohio Ry. Co., 125

Petersen v. Interocean Ships, Inc., 417

Petition of (see name of party)

Petro v. Jada Yacht Charters, Ltd., 102

Peyroux v. Howard (The Planter), 36, 147

Peytavin v. Government Emp. Ins. Co., 140

PG&E Resources Offshore Co. v. Zapata Gulf Marine Corp., 1056

Pierside Terminal Operators, Inc. v. M/V Floridian, 462

Pino v. Protection Maritime Ins. Co., Ltd., 197

Pioneer–Wallschiff, 809

Piper Aircraft Co. v. Reyno, 306

Pittman Mechanical Contractors, Inc. v. Director, Office of Workers' Compensation Programs, 986

Pizani v. M/V Cotton Blossom, 800

Platoro Ltd., Inc. v. Unidentified Remains of a Vessel, 263, 264

Platoro Ltd., Inc. v. Unidentified Remains of a Vessel, Her Cargo, Apparel, Tackle, and Furniture, in a Cause of Salvage, Civil and Maritime, 339, 707

Point Landing, Inc. v. Alabama Dry Dock & Shipbuilding Co., 531

Polly v. Carlson, 1070

Pope & Talbot v. Hawn, 808, 835

Port of Portland v. M/V Paralla, 452

Port Ship Service, Inc. v. Norton, Lilly & Co., Inc., 253

Port Welcome Cruises, Inc. v. S. S. Bay Belle, 416

Potash Co. of Canada Ltd. v. M/V Raleigh, 487

Powell v. Offshore Nav., Inc., 227

PPG Industries, Inc. v. Bean Dredging, 804

Pratt v. United States, 520

Prendis v. Central Gulf S. S. Co., 876

Price v. Price, 48

Pride Shipping Corp. v. Tafu Lumber Co., 269

Proceeds of the Gratitude, 508

Provost v. Huber, 644, 666

Prudential Ins. v. United States Lines, Inc., 417

Pure Oil Co. v. Suarez, 210, 297

Purnell v. Norned Shipping B.V., 990, 1006

Puthe v. Exxon Shipping Co., 953

Quaker Oats Co. v. M/V Torvanger, 638

Quick v. Hansen, 49

Rainey v. Paquet Cruises, Inc., 552, 830

Ralli v. Troop, 726

Ralston v. the State Rights, 37

Randall v. Chevron U.S.A., Inc., 575, 988, 1005, 1024

Ray v. Lykes Bros. S.S. Co., Inc., 1007

Rea v. The Eclipse, 201, 202

Redcliffe Americas Ltd. v. M/V Tyson Lykes, 434, 440

Red Cross Line v. Atlantic Fruit Co., 161

Rederi A/B Soya v. S. S. Grand Grace, 783

Red Star Barge Line, Inc. v. Nassau County Bridge Authority, 799

Red Star Towing & Transp. Co. v. Department of Transp. of State of N.J., 339

Reed v. S. S. Yaka, 975, 978, 979, 980, 1008

Reed v. Steamship Yaka, 1007

Reeves v. Offshore Logistics, Inc., 143

Reichert v. Chemical Carriers, Inc., 1008

Reid v. Quebec Paper Sales & Transp. Co., 971

Reliable Transfer Co., Inc., United States v., 779, 780, **811**

Reliance Marine Ins. Co. v. New York & C. Mail S. S. Co., 732

Republic Marine, Inc., United States v., 263

Republic Nat. Bank of Miami v. United States, 268, 270, 271

Republic of Peru, Ex parte, 340

Ressler v. States Marine Lines, Inc., 876

Result Shipping Co., Ltd. v. Ferruzzi Trading USA Inc., 308

Rex v. _____ (see opposing party)

Rice v. Charles Dreifus Co., 178, 202

Richard Bertram & Co. v. Yacht Wanda, 91

Richardson v. Harmon, 1048

Richardson v. St. Charles–St. John the Baptist Bridge and Ferry Authority, 131

Richendollar v. Diamond M Drilling Co., Inc., 819 F.2d 124, p. 1003

Richendollar v. Diamond M Drilling Co., Inc., 784 F.2d 580, p. 122

Riggs v. Scindia Steam Nav. Co., 1004

Ring Power Corp. v. Oil Screw Tug Snipe, 461

River Queen, In re, 49

Riverside Bayview Homes, Inc., United States v., 55

Roach v. M/V Aqua Grace, 1008

Roberts v. Offshore Logistics Services, Inc., 556, 830

Roberts v. United States, 124, 125

Robertson Lim. Procs., 1069

Robins Dry Dock & Repair Co. v. Flint, 385, 803, 804, 805

Robinson v. F/V Shenanegan, 400

Robinson v. Pocahontas, Inc., 895

Rockwell International Corp. v. M/V Incotrans Spirit, 663

Roco Carriers, Ltd. v. M/V Nurnberg Exp., 173

Rodco Marine Services, Inc. v. Migliaccio, 1074, 1074

Rodrigue v. Aetna Cas. & Sur. Co., 130

Rodriguez Alvarez v. Bahama Cruise Line, Inc., 885

Rogers v. Texaco, Inc., 1072

Rogers v. United States Lines, 969, 978

Rogers v. Yachts America, Inc., 75

Romaniuk v. Locke, 962

Romero v. Bethlehem Steel Corp., 246

Romero v. International Terminal Operating Co., 162, 175, 176, 204, 205

Roper v. United States, 910

Rose v. Bloomfield S. S. Co., 875

Rounds v. Cloverport Foundry & Mach. Co., 155, 158

Rowley, Complaint of, 1069

Roy v. M/V Kateri Tek, 410

Royal Indem Co v. Puerto Rico Cement Corp, 958

Royal Ins. Co. of America v. Pier 39 Ltd. Partnership, 66, 67

Royal Swan Navigation Co. Ltd. v. Global Container Lines, Ltd., 272

Russell v. City Ice & Fuel Co. of Point Pleasant, 140

Ryan v. Pacific Coast Shipping Co., Liberia, 509 F.2d 1054, p. 973

Ryan v. Pacific Coast Shipping Co., Liberia, 448 F.2d 525, p. 972

Ryan Stevedoring Co. v. United States, 413, 974, 975, 979

Ryan Walsh Stevedoring Co., Inc. v. James Marine Services, Inc., 802

Ryder v. United States, 829

Sagastume v. Lampsis Nav. Ltd., Drosia, 1097

Saint Paul Marine Transp. Corp. v. Cerro Sales Corp., 683

Salem v. United States Lines Co., 909

Saratoga Fishing Co. v. Marco Seattle Inc., 840

Savas v. Maria Trading Corp., 485

Schade v. National Sur. Corp., 606

Scheel v. Conboy, 557

Schoenamsgruber v. Hamburg American Line, 309

Schooner Brindicate II (Dominguez v. Schooner Brindicate), 692, 696

Schoremoyer v. Barnes, 1069

Schrader v. Royal Caribbean Cruise Line, Inc., 550

Schroeder v. Tug Montauk, 800

Schuede v. Zenith S.S. Co., 956

Scindia Steam Nav. Co., Ltd. v. De Los Santos, 1005, 1008, 1009

S. C. Loveland Co. v. United States, 737, 740, 758

S.C. Loveland Co., Inc. v. Barge Arlington, 673

Scrap Loaders, Inc. v. Pacific Coast Shipping, Co., Liberia, 972

Seaboard Air Line R. Co. v. Marine Industries, Inc., 800

Seacarriers Maritime Co. v. M/T Stolt Jade, 763

Seagrist, United States v., 127

Sea Land Industries, Inc. v. General Ship Repair Corp., 72

Sea–Land Service, Inc. v. Director, Office of Workers' Compensation Programs, United States Dept. of Labor, 987

Seas Shipping Co. v. Sieracki, 966, 967, 968, 969, 973, 976, 977, 978, 979, 1023

Seattle–First National Bank v. Northern Belle 95, 389

Sea Vessel, Inc. v. Reyes, 96

Sedco, Inc. v. S.S. Strathewe, 617, 661

Self v. Great Lakes Dredge & Dock Co., 762, 805, 1006

Sellick v. Sun Harbor Marina, Inc., 159
S & E Shipping Corp. v. Chesapeake & O. Ry. Co., 1052
Seven Resorts, Inc. v. Cantlen, 66, **1044,** 1048, 1049
Shakit v. M/V Forum Trader, 308
Shanferoke C. & S. Corp. v. Westchester Service Corp., 309
Shankles v. Costa Armatori, S.P.A., 550
Sharp v. Johnson Bros. Corp., 989
Shaw, Ex parte, 296
Shaw v. Ohio River Co., 893
Shea v. Rev–Lyn Contracting Co., Inc., 1004
Shell Oil Co. v. M/T GILDA, 261
Shell Oil Co. M/V EB II, In re, 1044
Sheppard v. Taylor, 75
Shogry v. Lewis, 40, 50
Siderius v. M.V. Amilla, 575
Sierra Pacific Power Co. v. F. E. R. C., 55
Signal Oil & Gas Co. v. Barge W–701, 1052
Simpson Timber Co. v. Parks, 413
Singapore Nav. Co., S./A. v. Mego Corp., 660
Sinkler v. Missouri Pacific Railroad Company, 946
Sirius Ins. Co. (UK) Ltd. v. Collins, 62
Sisson v. Ruby, 49, 1029
Skibinski v. Waterman S. S. Corp., 971, 979
Smallwood v. American Trading & Transp. Co., 1024
Smith v. Lauritzen, 909
Smith v. Pan Air Corp., 124
Smith v. Pinell, 245
Smith v. Trans–World Drilling Co., 940
Smith v. United States, 875
Smith, Rex v., 36
Snavely v. Lang, 803
Sniadach v. Family Finance Corp. of Bay View, 272
Snyder v. Four Winds Sailboat Centre, Ltd., 91
Societe Generale v. Federal Ins. Co., 588
Sook v. Great Pac. Shipping Co., 1096
South American S. S. Co. v. Atlantic Towing Co., 692
South Carolina State Highway Dept. v. Jacksonville Shipyards, Inc., 1074
South Carolina State Ports Authority v. Silver Anchor, S.A., (Panama), 513
Southern Oregon Production Credit Assn. v. Oil Screw Sweet Pea, 264, 270
Southern Pac. Co. v. Denton, 296
Southern Pac. Co. v. Jensen, 367, 373, 374, 377, 384, 385, 820, 954, 956, 957, 963, 1021
Southwestern Sugar & Molasses Co. v. River Terminals Corp., 587
Southwest Marine, Inc. v. Gizoni, 989
Soya Atlantic, United States v., 783
Spartus Corp. v. S/S Yafo, 661
Spataro v. Kloster Cruise, Ltd., 551
SPM Corp. v. M/V Ming Moon, 663
Srodes v. the Collier, 513
S. S. Bethflor v. Thomas, 295
S.S. Clarke's Wharf, 802
S.S. Hai Chang, 163

S. S. Lucie Schulte, United States v., 426
S.S. Percy Jordan, The, 536
Staffer v. Bouchard Transp. Co., Inc., 173
Standard Electrica, S. A. v. Hamburg Sudamerikanische Dampfschiffahrts–Gesellschaft, 649
Standard Oil Co. of New Jersey v. Southern Pac. Co., 799
Stanga v. McCormick Shipping Corp., 556, 556
Stanley T. Scott & Co., Inc. v. Makah Development Corp., 86
Starlight Trading, Inc. v. S.S. San Francisco Maru, 732, 732
State Establishment for Agr. Product Trading v. M/V Wesermunde, 602
State ex rel. v. _____ (see opposing party and relator)
State Industrial Commission of State of New York v. Nordenholt Corporation, 97, 957, 963, 976
State of (see name of state)
States Marine Corp. of Del. v. Producers Coop. Packing Co., 609
States S. S. Co. v. United States, 606
Stephen Bros. Line, United States v., 558
Stern, Hays & Lang, Inc. v. M/V Nili, 433
Stevedoring Services of America v. Ancora Transport, N.V., 264, 270
Stevens v. F/V Bonnie Doon, 731 F.2d 1433, pp. 800, 806
Stevens v. F/V Bonnie Doon, 655 F.2d 206, p. 772
Stevens v. the White City, 581
Stevens Institute of Technology v. United States, 801
St. Johns N.F. Shipping Corp. v. S.A. Companhia Geral Commercial do Rio de Janeiro, 603, 662
Stoller v. Evergreen Intern. (United StatesA.) Corp., 932
Stowers v. Consolidated Rail Corp., 986, 987
Strawbridge v. Curtiss, 204
Strika v. Netherlands Ministry of Traffic, 102
Sturgeon Bay Shipbuilding & Dry Dock Co. v. The Nautilus, 262
Sumitomo Corp. v. M/V Cosmos, 841
Sun Harbor Marina, Inc. v. Sellick, 480
Sunkist Growers, Inc. v. Adelaide Shipping Lines, Ltd., 631
Sun Oil Co., Petition of, 673
Sun Ship, Inc. v. Pennsylvania, 989
Sutton v. Earles, 333, 1024
Sutton River Services, Inc. v. Inland Tugs Co., 801
Swift & Co. Packers v. Compania Colombiana Del Caribe, 192, 197, 202, 308
Swinney v. Tinker, 355
Szyka v. United States Secretary of Defense, 95, 123

Tabb Lakes, Ltd. v. United States, 55
Ta Chi Navigation (Panama) Corp. S. A., Complaint of, 1029

Ta Chi Nav. (Panama) Corp. S.A., Complaint of, 492, 709
Taino Lines, Inc. v. M/V Constance Pan Atlantic, 410
Tai Ping Ins. Co., Ltd. v. M/V Warschau, 309
Taisho Marine & Fire Ins. Co., Ltd. v. M/V Sea–Land Endurance, 621
Tamblyn v. River Bend Marine, Inc., 515
Tate v. A/B Svenska Amerika Linein, 908
Taylor v. Alaska Rivers Nav. Co., 829
Taylor v. Bunge Corp., 1008
Taylor v. Carryl, 262
Taylor v. Costa Lines, Inc., 550
Taylor v. Tracor Marine, Inc., 270
Teal v. Eagle Fleet, Inc., 221, 245
Techem Chemical Co., Ltd. v. M/T Choyo Maru, 272
Tenneco Resins, Inc. v. Davy Intern., AG, 588
Terminal Shipping Co. v. Hamberg, 73, 86
Terminal Shipping Co. v. Traynor, 991
Texaco, Inc., Matter of, 762
Texas Eastern Transmission Corp. v. McMoRan Offshore Exploration Co., 804
Texport Oil Co. v. M/V Amolyntos, 478, 641
Teyseer Cement Co. v. Halla Maritime Corp., 268
The Aberfoyle, 544
The Acara (Rickard v. Pringle), 699
The Admiral Peoples, 92, 94, 95, 97
The Alabama, 810
The America, 500, 501
The Anaces, 469, 473
The Andree, 478
The Annie H Smith, 180
The Ansaldo San Giorgio I v. Rheinstrom Bros. Co., 649
The Ardell Marine Corp v. Mars, 433
The Atlas, 809
The Audrey II, United States v., 410
The Augusta, 388
The Baltimore, 800
The Barge Murray Mac (Guillot v. Cenac Towing Co.), 1072, 1073
The Belfast, 38
The Bella, 422
The Bella Dan, 339
the Betsey and Charlotte, United States v., 33
The Boat La Sambra v. Lewis, 79
The Bremen, 708
The Brig Ann, 262
The Carib Prince, 589
The Chattahoochee, 811
The Chester, 416
The Chickasaw (Petition of Waterman Steamship Corp.), 1057
The Chickie, 1088, 1094
The China, 399, 400
The Cimbria, 485
The City of Tawas, 506
The C.J. Saxe, 486
The Clarita, 673
The Commerce, 38
The Conqueror, 803

The Cora P White, 440
The Corsair, 1021
The Daniel Ball, 39, 40, 49
The Del Sud (Mississippi Shipping Co. v. Zander & Co.), 605, 633
The Dodge–Michael, In re Petition of, 1075
The Eagle, 155, 964
The Edith, 508
The Elfrida, 713
The Emilia S. De Perez, 429
The Emma Kate Ross, 802
The Eugene F. Moran v. New York Central & Hudson River R. Co., 809
The Exchange, 75
The Favorite, 465
The Florence, 473
The Fort Gaines, 416
The Frank G Fowler, 499, 500
The Gazelle, 516
The General Smith, 146, 147
The Genesee Chief v. Fitzhugh, 35, 782
The Great Western, 1071
The Hamilton, 1021
The Harrisburg, 358, 1021
The Harrison v. Beverly Lynn, 414
The Herbert L. Rawding, 416
The Hine v. Trevor, 144, 146, 147, 430, 479
The Home, 508
The Hope, 388
The Indrapura, 661, 662
The Interstate No. 1, 501, 508
The Interstate No 2, 508
The Ionnasis P. Goulandris, 1051
The Ira M. Hedges, 809
The Jason, 741
The J.C. Pfluger, 683
The John D. Rockefeller, 764
The John E Berwind, 800
The John G. Stevens, 492, 498, 499, 500, 501
The Joseph Warner, 388
The J.P. Donaldson, 740
The Julia Blake, 757
The Jumna, 759
The Kearney, 394
The Kensington, 551, 603
The Kiersage, 440
The Leviathan, 603
The Lord Derby, 413
The Lottawanna, 88 U.S. 558, p. 2
The Lottawanna, 87 U.S. 201, p. 147
The Main v. Williams, 1073
The Margaret, 809
The Marine Sulphur Queen, 161, 163, 176
The Meridian, 1070
The Meton, 966
The Mona, 434
The Montello, 40
The Mormackile, 1051
The Moses Taylor, 147
The Murphy Tugs, 485
The Muskegon, 434
The Nestor, 386
The North Star, 810
The Oceana, 452

The Oceano, 478
The Odysseus III, 485
The Oregon, 15 S.Ct. 804, p. 761
The Oregon, 133 Fed. 609, p. 556
The Osceola, 103, 859, 866, 955, 968
The Owego, 429
The Pacific, 544
The Palmyra, 308
The Pennsylvania, 771, 772, 773, 774
The Plymouth, 94, 95, 97, 820
The Poznan, 410, 410
The Priscilla, 55 F.2d 32, p. 802
The Priscilla, 114 Fed. 836, p. 422
The Puritan, 485
The Resolute, 254
The Rio Grande, 269
Theriot v. J. Ray McDermott & Co., Inc., 947, 953
The Roanoke, 147
The Robert Hadden, 801
The Rolph, 102
The Samuel Little, 508
The Schooner Exchange v. McFaddon, 340
The Schooner Sally, 33
The Sea Gull, 357
The Showboat, 140, 385
The Slingsby, 967
The Soerstad, 1051
The S.S. Andros Tower (Maroceano Compania Naviera S.A. of Panama v. Los Angeles), 763
The Steamboat Orleans, 34, 147
The Sterling, 434
The Susan (In re Wood's Petition), 1052
The Tashmoo, 672
The Thomas Jefferson, 32, 35
The Trenton, 515
The Trillora II (Petition of Guggerteim), 1069
The Trojan, In re, 1043
The Vallescura, 617
The Washington, 811
The Western Maid, 400
The West Point, 340
The William Leishear, 488, 501
The Winnebago, 516
The Wordsworth, 736
The Worthington and Davis, 761
The Yacht Juliane (Petition of Porter), 1026
The Zarco, United States v., 388
Thomas v. Newton Intern. Enterprises, 1009
Thomas v. Peninsular & Oriental Steam Nav. Co., 210
Thompson v. The Catharina, 343
Thompson v. Trent Maritime Co., 311
Thomson v. Chesapeake Yacht Club, Inc., 96
Thornton v. Steiner Products, Ltd., 946
Thorsteinsson v. M/V Drangur, 515
Three Buoys Houseboat Vacations United StatesA. Ltd. v. Morts, 49
Thyssen, Inc. v. S/S Eurounity, 575, 641
Thyssen, Inc. v. S.S. Fortune Star, 663

Thyssen Steel Corp. v. Federal Commerce & Nav. Co., 259
Tidelands Barge No. 5 (Boudoin v. J. Ray McDermott & Co.), 762
Titan Nav., Inc. v. Timsco, Inc., 308
Tittle v. Aldacosta, 555, 557
T.J. Falgout Boats, Inc. v. United States, 124
T.N.T. Marine Service, Inc. v. Weaver Shipyards & Dry Docks, Inc., 245
Todd Shipyards Corp. v. The City of Athens, 501, 506
Todd Shipyards Corp. v. United States, 746
Tonnesen v. Yonkers Contracting Co., 1004
Topgallant Lines, Inc., Matter of, 485
Toro Shipping Corp. v. Bacon–McMillan Veneer Mfg. Co., 429
Toyomenka, Inc. v. S.S. Tosaharu Maru, 649
Tradeways II, 309
Tramp Oil and Marine, Ltd. v. M/V Mermaid I, 486
Trans–Asiatic Oil Ltd., S.A. v. Apex Oil Co., 269
Transnational Maritime, Inc. (Republic of Bangladesh), Matter of, 341
Traub v. Holland–America Line, 556
Treasure Salvors, Inc. v. Unidentified Wrecked & Abandoned Sailing Vessel, 640 F.2d 560, pp. 200, 701, 707
Treasure Salvors, Inc. v. Unidentified Wrecked and Abandoned Sailing Vessel, 569 F.2d 330, pp. 339, 706
Trico Marine Operators, Inc. v. Champagne, 706, 989
Trico Marine Operators, Inc. v. Dow Chemical Co., 701
Trinidad Corp. v. Cmwlth., 761
Trojan Yacht Co. v. Productos Pesqueros Mexicanos, S.A., 306
T. Smith & Son, Inc. v. Rigby, 86
T. Smith & Son, Inc. v. Wilson, 962
Tubacex, Inc. v. M/V Risan, 633, 638
Tug Ocean Prince, Inc. v. United States, 773, 1057
Tullis v. Fidelity & Cas. Co. of New York, 556
Twery v. Houseboat Jilly's Yen, 762
Twin City Barge & Towing Co. v. Aiple, 91

Ulster Oil Transport Corp. v. the Matton No. 20, 803
Ultramar Canada, Inc. v. Mutual Marine Office, Inc., 741
Uncle Ben's Intern. Div. of Uncle Ben's, Inc. v. Hapag–Lloyd Aktiengesellschaft, 601
Unimac Co., Inc. v. C.F. Ocean Service, Inc., 602, 663
Unimills B.V. v. Statistix Shipping, N.V., 602
Union Oil Co. v. Oppen, 804
United Continental Tuna Corp. v. United States, 323
United Continental Tuna Corp., United States v., 312, 323
United Kingdom Mut. S.S. Assur. Ass'n (Bermuda) Ltd. v. State Establishment For Agr. Product Trading, 602

United Mine Workers of America v. Gibbs, 173

United Overseas Export Lines, Inc. v. Medluck Compania Maviera, S.A., 763

United States v. _____ (see opposing party)

United States, Petition of, 425 F.2d 991, p. 616

United States, Petition of, 229 F.Supp. 241, p. 692

United States Bulk Carriers, Inc. v. Arguelles, 417

United States Steel Corp. v. Fuhrman, 805

United Texas Transmission Co. v. United States Army Corps of Engineers, 54

United Transportation & Lighterage Co. v. New York & Baltimore Transp. Line, 164

University of Texas Medical Branch at Galveston v. United States, 1049

Ure v. Coffman, 38

Urubamba–Tug Coot, 801, 811

Usher v. M/V Ocean Wave, 531

Usner v. Luckenbach Overseas Corp., 902, 910, 972, 973, 978

Valero Refining, Inc. v. M/T Lauberhorn, 574

Valley Line Co. v. Ryan, 1087

Valley Towing Service, Inc. v. S/S American Wheat, Freighters, Inc., 772

Valm v. Hercules Fish Products, Inc., 908

Vance v. American Hawaii Cruises, Inc., 843

Vanderplank v. Miller, 807

Van Der Salm Bulb Farms, Inc. v. Hapag Lloyd, AG, 641

Vanniman v. Tug Diane, 462

Vatican Shrimp Co., Inc. v. Solis, 1093, 1094

Vaughan v. Atkinson, 885

Veazie v. Moor, 39

Vella v. Ford Motor Co., 884

Vickers v. Chiles Drilling Co., 142

Victory Carriers, Inc. v. Law, 97, 122, 978, 1003

Vilanova v. United States, 989, 990

Vimar Seguros y Reaseguros, S.A. v. M/V Sky Reefer, 307, 602

Voris v. Texas Emp. Ins. Ass'n, 991

Wabco Trade Co., Div. of World Standard Export Ltd. v. S.S. Inger Skou, 660

Wactor v. Spartan Transp. Corp., 876

Wahlstrom v. Kawasaki Heavy Industries, Ltd., 1024

Waldron v. Moore–McCormack Lines, Inc., 909

Walker–Skageth Food Stores v. the Bavois, 434

Wallin v. Keegan, 310

Walls Industries, Inc. v. United States, 955

Walsh v. Rogers, 38

Walsh v. Tadlock, 511, 513

Walters v. Moore–McCormack Lines, Inc., 909

Walthew v. Mavrojami, 741

Ward v. Peck, 177

Waring v. Clarke, 34

Warner v. the Bear, 86

Warren v. United States, 866, 874

Warshauer v. Lloyd Saboudo S. A., 710, 713

Washington, State of v. W.C. Dawson & Co., 374, 957

Waterman S.S. Corp. v. Chrysanthi, 802

Waterman S. S. Corp. v. Dugan & McNamara, Inc., 974

Watson v. Joshua Hendy Corporation, 876

Watz v. Zapata Off–Shore Co., 910

Weinstein v. Eastern Airlines, Inc., 97, 163

Wemhoener Pressen v. Ceres Marine Terminals, Inc., 602

Wenzel's Estate by Mirikitani v. Seaward Marine Services, Inc., 142

West v. United States, 910

West Imboden, The (Ravenscroft v. United States), 733

Westinghouse Elec. Corp. v. M/V Leslie Lykes, 621, 631

West Winds, Inc. v. M.V. Resolute, 417

Weyerhaeuser S. S. Co. v. Nacirema Operating Co., 974

Weyher/Livsey Constructors, Inc. v. Prevetire, 986, 987

Wheeler v. Marine Navigation Sulphur Carriers, Inc., 1087

White v. Florio & Co., 991

White v. United States, 95

Whitney S.S. Co. v. United States, 780

Wilburn Boat Co. v. Fireman's Fund Ins. Co., 67, 384, 385, 1108

Willard v. Dorr, 75

William P. Brooks Const. Co., Inc. v. Guthrie, 91

Williams v. McAllister Bros. Inc., 932

Wilmington Trust v. United States Dist. Court for Dist. of Hawaii, 164

Wimmer v. Hoage, 991

Windjammer Cruises, Inc. v. Paradise Cruises, Ltd., 535

Windsor Mount Joy Mut. Ins. Co. v. Giragosian, 385

Wolsiffer v. Atlantis Submarines, Inc., 932

Wong Wing Fai Co., S.A. v. United States, 575

Wood v. Diamond M Drilling Co., 894

Woodrop–Sims, The, 806

Woods v. Sammisa Co., Ltd., 1005

Workman v. Mayor, Aldermen, and Commonality of the City of New York, 340

W. R. Grace & Co. v. Charleston Lighterage & Transfer Co., 388

Wright v. United States, 126

Wyandotte Transp. Co. v. United States, 1049

Yacht Charlotte (Petition of Colonial Trust Co.), 1048

Yacht, Mary Jane v. Broward Marine, Inc., 446

Yamaha Motor Corp., U.S.A. v. Calhoun, 116 S.Ct. 619, p. **1099,** 1108

Yamaha Motor Corp., U.S.A. v. Calhoun, 40 F.3d 622, 310, **377,** 1024

Yang Mach. Tool Co. v. Sea–Land Service, Inc., 649, 663
Young v. Armadores de Cabotaje, S.A., 1009
Yutana Barge Lines, Inc. v. Northland Services, Inc., 656, 663

Zahn v. International Paper Co., 173, 173
Zapata Marine Service v. O/Y Finnlines, Ltd., 306
Zebroid Trawling Corp., Petition of, 1074
Zim Israel Nav. Co. v. T. Chatani & Co., 163

ADMIRALTY

*

PART I

ADMIRALTY AND MARITIME JURISDICTION AND PRACTICE

CHAPTER 1

INTRODUCTION

CONSTITUTION OF THE UNITED STATES

ARTICLE III

Section 1. The judicial Power of the United States shall be vested in one supreme Court, and in such inferior Courts as the Congress may from time to time ordain and establish. * * *

Section 2. The judicial Power shall extend * * * to all Cases of admiralty and maritime Jurisdiction * * *.

" * * * But by what criterion are we to ascertain the precise limits of the law thus adopted? The Constitution does not define it. It does not declare whether it was intended to embrace the entire maritime law as expounded in the treatises, or only the limited and restricted system which was received in England, or lastly such modification of both of these as was accepted and recognized as law in this country. Nor does the Constitution attempt to draw the boundary line between maritime law and local law. It assumes that the meaning of the phrase 'admiralty and maritime jurisdiction' is well understood. It treats this matter as it does the cognate ones of common law and equity, when it speaks of 'cases in law and equity,' or of 'suits at common law,' without defining those terms, assuming them to be known and understood." Mr. Justice Bradley in The Lottawanna, 88 U.S. (21 Wall.) 558, 22 L.Ed. 654 (1874).

" * * * What is the true interpretation of the clause 'all cases of admiralty and maritime jurisdiction'? If we examine the etymology, or received use, of the words 'admiralty' and 'maritime jurisdiction,' we shall find, that they include jurisdiction of all things done upon and relating to the sea, or, in other words, all transactions and proceedings relative to commerce and navigation, and to damages or injuries upon the sea. [footnote omitted] In all the great maritime nations of Europe, the terms 'admiralty jurisdiction' are uniformly applied to the courts exercising jurisdiction over maritime contracts and concerns. We shall find the terms just as familiarly known among the jurists of *Scotland, France, Holland* and *Spain,* as of *England,* and applied to their own courts, possessing substantially the same jurisdiction, as the English Admiralty in the reign of *Edward* the third [footnote omitted]. If we pass from the etymology and use of these terms (i.e. 'admiralty jurisdiction') in foreign countries, the only expositions of them, that seem to present themselves, are, that they refer 1. to the jurisdiction of the admiralty as acknowledged *in England* at the American Revolution; or 2. at the emigration of our ancestors; or 3. as acknowledged and exercised *in the United States* at the American Revolution; or 4. to the ancient and original jurisdiction, inherent in the admiralty of *England* by virtue of its general organization." Mr. Justice Story, in his opinion on circuit in DeLovio v. Boit, 2 Gall. 398, 7 F.Cas. 418 (1815).

13 RICH. II, c. 5

* * * that the admirals and their deputies shall not meddle henceforth of any thing done within the realm, but only of a thing done upon the sea, according as it hath been duly used in the time of the noble King Edward [III], grandfather of our lord the king that now is.

15 RICH. II, c. 3

* * * that of all manner of contracts, pleas and quereles and of all other things done or arising within the bodies of counties, as well by land as by water; and also of wreck of the sea, the admiral's court shall have no manner of cognizance, power nor jurisdiction; but all such manner of contracts, pleas and quereles, and all other things rising within the bodies of counties, as well by land as by water, as afore, and also wreck of the sea, shall be tried, determined, discussed and remedied, by the laws of the land, and not before or by the admiral, nor his lieutenant, in any wise. Nevertheless the death of a man, and of a maihem done in great ships, being hovering in the mainstream of great rivers, only, beneath the bridges of the same rivers nigh to the sea, and in none other places of the same rivers, the admiral shall have cognizance; and also to arrest ships in the great flotes for the great voyages of the king and of the realm; saving always to the king all manner of forfeitures and profits thereof coming; and he shall have jurisdiction upon the said flotes during the said voyages, only saving always to the lords, cities and boroughs, their liberties and franchises.

2. HEN. IV, c. 11

* * * that the statute of 13 Rich. II be firmly holden and kept, and put in
due execution; and that, as touching a pain to be set upon the admiral or
his lieutenant, that the statute and the common law be holden against
them; and that he, that feeleth himself grieved against the form of the said
statute, shall have his action grounded upon the case against him that doth
so pursue in the admiral's court, and recover his double damages against
the pursuant, and the same pursuant shall incur the pain of £10 to the king
for the pursuit so made, if he be attained.

Hale, De Juris Maris Cap III (1787)

There be some streams or rivers, that are private not only in propriety or
ownership, but also in use, as little streams and rivers that are not a
common passage for the king's people. Again, there may be other rivers,
as well fresh as salt, that are of common or publick use for carriage of boats
and lighters. And these, whether they are fresh or salt, whether they flow
and reflow or not, are *prima facie publici juris,* common highways for man
or goods or both from one inland town to another. Thus the rivers of Wey,
of Severn, of Thames, and divers others, as well above the bridges and
ports as below, as well above the flowings of the sea as below, and as well
where they are become to be of private propriety as in what parts they are
of the king's propriety, are publick rivers *juris publici.* And therefore all
nuisances and impediments of passages of boats and vessels, though in the
private soil of any person, may be punished by indictments, and removed;
and this was the reason of the statute of *Magna Charta cap. 23.*

*Omnes kidelli deponantur per Thamisiam et Medwayam, et per totam
Angliam nisi per costeram maris.*

These kinds of nuisances were such, as hindered or obstructed the
passage of boats, as wears, piles, choaking up the passage with filth,
diverting of the river by cutts or trenches, decay of the banks, or the like.

And they were reformed.

Sometimes by indictments or presentments in the leets, sessions of the
peace, oyer and terminer, or before justices of assize.

Oftentimes in the king's bench; as Hil. 50 E. 3. B.R.Rot. 23. for
nuisances in the river of Trent; H. 23 E. 3. B.R.Rot. 61. in the river Ouse;
H. 21. E. 1. in the river Severn; Tr. E. 3. Rot. 29. in the river Leigh; and
generally in all other rivers within the bodies of counties, which had
common passage of boats or barges, whether the water were fresh or salt,
the king's or a subject's, Rot. Parliamenti 14. R. 2. n. 34. Mich. 36. E. 3.
B.R.Rot. 65. Mich. 18, 19. E. 1. B.R. and infinite more.

Sometimes by special commission; as for the river of Leigh, 19 Afs. 6.

And sometimes by the parties, that were prejudiced by such nuisance,
without any process of law.

More of this we shall see when we come to consider of common
nuisances in havens and ports.

But if any person at his own charge makes his own private stream to be passable for boats or barges, either by making of locks or cutts, or drawing together other streams; and hereby that river, which was his own in point of propriety become now capable of carriage of vessels; yet this seems not to make it *juris publici,* and he may pull it down again, or apply it to his own private use. For it is not hereby made to be *juris publici,* unless it were done at common charge, or by a publick authority, or that by long continuance of time it hath been freely devoted to a public use. And so it seems also to be, if he that makes such a new river or passage doth it by way of recompence or compensation for some other public stream that he hath stopped for his own conveniency; as in the case of the Abbot of St. Austin's Canterbury, mentioned in the Register. So likewise if he purchaseth the king's charter to make a reasonable toil for the passage of the king's subjects, and puts it in use, these seem to be devoting and as it were consecrating of it to the common use. As he, that by an *ad quod damnum,* and license thereupon obtained, changeth a way, and sets out another in his own land; this new way is thereupon become *juris publici,* as well as a way by prescription. For no man can take a settled or constant toll even in his own private land for a common passage without the king's licence.

Molloy: De Jure Maritimo (1769) to the Reader, XXIV

* * * In the whole Work I have no where medled with the *Admiralty* or its Jurisdiction (unless by the by, as incidently falling in with other Matters) knowing well, that it would have been impertinent and saucy in me to enter into the Debate of *Imperium merum, Imperium mixtum, Jurisdictio simplex,* and the like, and of the bounding out of Jurisdictions, which in effect tends to question the Government, and trip up the Power that gives Laws and Protection to us; since all that can be said, as well on the one side as the other, hath been so fully and learnedly handled and treated of by several worthy Persons (that have indeed said all that can be said) but more especially in that famous Dispute, not long since before His Sacred Majesty in Council, where the most elaborate and ingenious Reasons that could be drawn by the Skill of a learned Civilian, were asserted in vindicating the Admiralties Jurisdiction, by the Judge of the Same, Sir Leoline Jenkins, and in Answer of whom was produced that *Great Good Man* the Lord Chief Justice *Hale,* who as well by Law positive as other his great Reasons, soon put a Period to that Question, which during his Days slept, and it may modestly be presumed will hardly (if ever) be awakened.

Jackson v. The Steamboat Magnolia

Supreme Court of the United States, 1857.
61 U.S. (20 How.) 296, 15 L.Ed. 909.

■ MR. JUSTICE GRIER delivered the opinion of the court.

The only question presented for our consideration on this appeal is, whether the court below had jurisdiction.

The libel purports to be in a cause of collision, civil and maritime. It alleges that the steamboat Wetumpka, a vessel of three hundred tons burden, was on a voyage from New Orleans to the city of Montgomery, in Alabama; that while ascending the Alabama river, she was run into and sunk by the steamboat Magnolia, which was descending the same.

The answer of the respondents, among other things, alleges "that the collision took place far above tide-water, on the Alabama river, in the county of Wilcox, in the State of Alabama, and therefore not within the jurisdiction of the District Court sitting in admiralty."

This plea was sustained by the court, and the libel dismissed. The record does not disclose the reasons on which this judgment was based. It is presumed, therefore, to be founded on the facts stated in the plea, viz:

1. That the collision was within the body of a county.

2. That it was above tide-water.

1. The Alabama river flows through the State of Alabama. It is a great public river, navigable from the sea for many miles above the ebb and flow of the tide. Vessels licensed for the coasting trade, and those engaged in foreign commerce, pass on its waters to ports of entry within the State. It is not, like the Mississippi, a boundary between coterminous States. Neither is it, like the Penobscot, (see Veazie v. Moor, 14 How., 568,) made subservient to the internal trade of the State by artificial means and dams constructed at its mouth, rendering it inaccessible to sea-going vessels. It differs from the Hudson, which rises in and passes through the State of New York, in the fact that it is navigable for ships and vessels of the largest class far above where its waters are affected by the tide.

Before the adoption of the present Constitution, each State, in the exercise of its sovereign power, had its own court of admiralty, having jurisdiction over the harbors, creeks, inlets, and public navigable waters, connected with the sea. This jurisdiction was exercised not only over rivers, creeks, and inlets, which were boundaries to or passed through other States, but also where they were wholly within the State. Such a distinction was unknown, nor (as it appears from the decision of this court in the case of Waring v. Clarke, 5 How., 441) had these courts been driven from the exercise of jurisdiction over torts committed on navigable water within the body of a county, by the jealousy of the common-law courts.

When, therefore, the exercise, of admiralty and maritime jurisdiction over its public rivers, ports, and havens, was surrendered by each State to the Government of the United States, without an exception as to subjects or places, this court cannot interpolate one into the Constitution, or introduce an arbitrary distinction which has no foundation in reason or precedent.

The objection to jurisdiction stated in the plea, "that the collision was within the county of Wilcox, in the State of Alabama," can therefore have no greater force or effect from the fact alleged in the argument, that the Alabama river, so far as it is navigable, is wholly within the boundary of the State. It amounts only to a renewal of the old contest between courts

decided jurisdiction [illegible] within state already

of common law and courts of admiralty, as to their jurisdiction within the body of a county. This question has been finally adjudicated in this court, and the argument exhausted, in the case of Waring v. Clark. After an experience of ten years, we have not been called on by the bar to review its principles as founded in error, nor have we heard of any complaints by the people of wrongs suffered on account of its supposed infringement of the right of trial by jury. So far, therefore, as the solution of the question now before us is affected by the fact that the tort was committed within the body of a county, it must be considered as finally settled by the decision in that case.

2. The second ground of objection to the jurisdiction of the court is founded on the fact, that though the collision complained of occurred in a great navigable river, it was on a part of that river not affected by the flux and reflux of the tide, but "far above it."

already decided this issue also

This objection, also, is one which has heretofore been considered and decided by this court, after full argument and much deliberation. In the case of the Genesee Chief, (12 How. 443,) we have decided, that though in England the flux and reflux of the tide was a sound and reasonable test of a navigable river, because on that island tidewater and navigable water were synonymous terms, yet that "there is certainly nothing in the ebb and flow of the tide that makes the waters peculiarly suitable for admiralty jurisdiction, nor anything in the absence of a tide that renders it unfit. If it is a public navigable water on which commerce is carried on between different States or nations, the reason for the jurisdiction is precisely the same. And if a distinction is made on that account, it is merely arbitrary, without any foundation in reason—and, indeed, contrary to it." The case of the Thomas Jefferson (10 Wheaton) and others, which had hastily adopted this arbitrary and (in this country) false test of navigable waters, were necessarily overruled.

Since the decision of these cases, the several district courts have taken jurisdiction of cases of collision on the great public navigable rivers. Some of these cases have been brought to this court by appeal, and in no instance has any objection been taken, either by the counsel or the court, to the jurisdiction, because the collision was within the body of a county, or above the tide. (See Fritz v. Bull, 12 How., 466; Walsh v. Rogers, 13 How., 283; The Steamboat New World, 16 How., 469; Ure v. Coffman, 19 How., 56; New York and Virginia S.B. Co. v. Calderwood, 19 How., 245.)

Holding

In our opinion, therefore, neither of the facts alleged in the answer, nor both of them taken together, will constitute a sufficient exception to the jurisdiction of the District Court.

It is due however, to the learned counsel who has presented the argument for respondent in this case, to say, that he has not attempted to impugn the decision of this court in the case of Waring v. Clark, nor to question the sufficiency of the reasons given in the case of the *Genesee Chief* for overruling the case of the *Thomas Jefferson;* but he contends that the case of the *Genesee Chief* decided that the act of Congress of 1845, "extending the jurisdiction of the District Court to certain cases upon the lakes," & c., was not only constitutional, but also that it conferred a new jurisdiction, which the court did not possess before; and consequently, as that act was confined to the lakes, and "to vessels of twenty or more tons burden, licensed and employed in the business of commerce and navigation between ports and places in different States and Territories," it cannot authorize the District Courts in assuming jurisdiction over waters and subjects not included in the act, and more especially where the navigable portion of the river is wholly within the boundary of a single State. It is contended also that the case of Fritz v. Bull, and those which follow it, sustaining the jurisdiction of the court of admiralty over torts on the Mississippi river, cannot be reconciled with the points decided in the former case, as just stated, unless on the hypothesis that the act of 1845 be construed to include the Mississippi and other great rivers of the West; which it manifestly does not.

But it never has been asserted by this court, either in the case of Fritz v. Bull, or in any other case, that the admiralty jurisdiction exercised over the great navigable rivers of the West was claimed under the act of 1845, or by virtue of anything therein contained.

The Constitution, in defining the powers of the courts of the United States, extends them to "all cases of admiralty and maritime jurisdiction." It defines how much of the judicial power shall be exercised by the Supreme Court only; and it was left to Congress to ordain and establish other courts, and to fix the boundary and extent of their respective jurisdictions. Congress might give any of these courts the whole or so much of the admiralty jurisdiction as it saw fit. It might extend their jurisdiction over all navigable waters, and all ships and vessels thereon, or over some navigable waters, and vessels of a certain description only. Consequently, as Congress had never before 1845 conferred admiralty jurisdiction over the Northern fresh-water lakes *not* "navigable from the sea," the District Courts could not assume it by virtue of this clause in the Constitution. An act of Congress was therefore necessary to confer this jurisdiction on those waters, and was completely within the constitutional powers of Congress; unless, by some unbending law of nature, fresh-water lakes and rivers are necessarily within the category of those that are not "navigable," and which, consequently, could not be subjected to "admiralty jurisdiction," any more than canals or railroads.

When these States were colonies, and for a long time after the adoption of the Constitution of the United States, the shores of the great lakes of the North, above and beyond the ocean tides, were as yet almost uninhabited, except by savages. The necessities of commerce and the progress of steam navigation had not as yet called for the exercise of admiralty jurisdiction, except on the ocean border of the Atlantic States.

The judiciary act of 1789, in defining the several powers of the courts established by it, gives to the District Courts of the United States "exclusive original cognizance of all civil cases of admiralty and maritime jurisdiction, including all seizures, & c., when they are made on waters which are *navigable from the sea* by vessels of ten or more tons burden, & c., as well as upon the high seas."

So long as the commerce of the country was centered chiefly on the Eastern Atlantic ports, where the fresh-water rivers were seldom navigable above tide-water, no inconvenience arose from the adoption of the English insular test of "navigable waters." Hence it was followed by the courts without objection or inquiry.

But this act does not confine admiralty jurisdiction to tide-waters; and if the flux and reflux of the tide be abandoned, as an arbitrary and false test of a "navigable river,". it required no further legislation of Congress to extend it to the Mississippi, Alabama, and other great rivers, "navigable from the sea." If the waters over which this jurisdiction is claimed be within this category, the act makes no distinction between them. It is not confined to rivers or waters which bound coterminous States, such as the Mississippi and Ohio, or to rivers passing through more than one State; nor does the act distinguish between them and rivers which rise in and pass through one State only, and are consequently *"infra corpus comitatus."* The admiralty jurisdiction surrendered by the States to the Union had no such bounds as exercised by themselves, and is clogged with no such conditions in its surrender. The interpolation of such conditions by the courts would exclude many of the ports, harbors, creeks, and inlets, most frequented by ships and commerce, but which are wholly included within the boundaries of a State or the body of a county.

It seems to have been assumed, in the argument of this case, that because the District Courts had not exercised their admiralty jurisdiction above tide-water before the decision of this court of the case of the *Genesee Chief,* that such jurisdiction had been exercised by them as conferred by the act of 1845. It is upon this mistaken hypothesis that any difficulty is found in reconciling that case with the case of Fritz v. Bull, which immediately followed it.

The act of 1845 was the occasion and created the necessity for this court to review their former decisions.

It might be considered in fact as a declaratory act reversing the decision in the case of the *Thomas Jefferson.* We could no longer evade the question by a judicial notice of an occult tide without ebb or flow, as in the case of Peyroux v. Howard, (7 Pet., 343). The court were placed in the position, that they must either declare the act of Congress void, and shock the common sense of the people by declaring the lakes not to be "navigable waters," or overrule previous decisions which had established an arbitrary distinction, which, when applied to our continent, had no foundation in reason.

In conclusion, we repeat what we then said, that "courts of admiralty have been found necessary in all commercial countries, not only for the safety and convenience of commerce, and a speedy decision of controversies where delay would be ruin, but also to administer the laws of nations in a season of war, and to determine the validity of captures and questions of prize or no prize in a judicial proceeding. And it would be contrary to the first principles on which this Union was formed, to confine these rights to the States bordering on the Atlantic, and to the tide-water rivers connected with it, and to deny them to the citizens who border on the lakes, and the great navigable streams of the Western States. Certainly, such was not the intent of the framers of the Constitution; and if such be the construction finally given to it by this court, it must necessarily produce great public inconvenience, and at the same time fail to accomplish one of the great objects of the framers of the Constitution; that is, perfect equality in the rights and privileges of the citizens of the different States, not only in the laws of the General Government, but in the mode of administering them."

The decree of the court below, dismissing the libel for want of jurisdiction, is therefore reversed, and it is ordered that the record be remitted, with directions to further proceed in the case as to law and justice may appertain.

■ MR. JUSTICE MCLEAN delivered a separate opinion, and MR. JUSTICE CATRON, MR. JUSTICE DANIEL, and MR. JUSTICE CAMPBELL, dissented, MR. JUSTICE CATRON concurred with MR. JUSTICE CAMPBELL in the opinion delivered by him.

■ MR. JUSTICE MCLEAN:

I agree to the decision in this case; but as I wish to be on one or two points somewhat more explicit than the opinion of the court, I will concisely state my views.

The Constitution declares that the judicial power shall extend "to all cases of admiralty and maritime jurisdiction." The judiciary act of 1789 provides, "that the District Courts shall have exclusive original cognizance of all civil cases of admiralty and maritime jurisdiction."

The act of the 25th February, 1845, is entitled "An act to extend the jurisdiction of the District Courts to certain cases upon the lakes and navigable waters connecting with the same." This act was considered by Congress as extending the jurisdiction of the District Court; and it was so, very properly, treated by the court in the case of the Genesee Chief.

In the opinion, it was said this act was not passed under the commercial power, but under the admiralty and maritime jurisdiction given in the Constitution. No terms could be more complete than those used in the Constitution to confer this jurisdiction. In all cases of admiralty and maritime jurisdiction, such suits may be brought in the District Court.

This jurisdiction was limited in England to the ebb and flow of the tide, as their rivers were navigable only as far as the tide flowed. And as in this country the rivers falling into the Atlantic were not navigable above tide-water, the same rule was applied. And when the question of jurisdiction was first raised in regard to our Western rivers, the same rule was adopted, when there was no reason for its restriction to tide-water, as in the rivers of the Atlantic. And this shows that the most learned and able judges may, from the force of precedent, apply an established rule where the reason or necessity on which it was founded fails.

In England and in the Atlantic States, the ebb and flow of the tide marked the extent of the navigableness of rivers. But the navigability of our Western rivers in no instance depends upon the tide.

By the civil law, the maritime system extends over all navigable waters. The admiralty and maritime jurisdiction, like the commonlaw or chancery jurisdiction, embraces a system of procedure known and established for ages. It may be called a system of regulations embodied and matured by the most enlightened and commercial nations of the world. Its origin may be traced to the regulations of Wisbuy, of the Hanse Towns, the laws of Oleron, the ordinances of France, and the usages of other commercial countries, including the English admiralty.

It is, in fact, a regulation of commerce, as it comprehends the duties and powers of masters of vessels, the maritime liens of seamen, of those who furnish supplies to vessels, make advances, & c., and, in short, the knowledge and conduct required of pilots, seamen, masters, and everything pertaining to the sailing and management of a ship. As the terms import, these regulations apply to the water, and not to the land, and are commensurate with the jurisdiction conferred.

By the Constitution, "Congress have power to regulate commerce with foreign nations, and among the several States, and with the Indian tribes." The provision, "among the several States," limits the power of Congress in the regulation of commerce to two or more States; consequently, a State has power to regulate a commerce exclusively within its own limits; but beyond such limits the regulation belongs to Congress. The admiralty and maritime jurisdiction is essentially a commercial power, and it is necessarily limited to the exercise of that power by Congress.

Every voyage of a vessel between two or more States is subject to the admiralty jurisdiction, and not to any State regulation. A denial of this doctrine is a subversion of the commercial power of Congress, and throws us on the Confederation. It also subverts the admiralty and maritime jurisdiction of the Federal courts, given explicitly in the Constitution and in the judiciary act of 1789.

In this case, the steamboat Wetumpka was engaged in a commerce between New Orleans, in Louisiana, and Montgomery, in Alabama. The Magnolia was running between Mobile and Montgomery, in the State of Alabama. The Wetumpka, within the State of Alabama, was as much under the Federal jurisdiction as it was in the State of Louisiana. No one will contend that one State may regulate the commerce of another; nor can it be maintained that the power to regulate the commerce of the Wetumpka in this case was in either State. It was a commerce between the two States, which comes within the definition of commerce expressly given to Congress. While thus protected and regulated by the power of Congress, the Wetumpka was run into by the Magnolia, and sunk, in the Alabama river; and it is earnestly contended that the admiralty can give no remedy for this aggravated trespass. Since the decision in the case of the Genesee Chief by seven judges, only one dissenting, the admiralty jurisdiction has been constantly applied on all our lakes and rivers of the North; and some of the cases have been reviewed in this court without objection. The navigators of the Alabama river must have been more prudent and skilful than those of the North, or their voyages were less frequent, if the above collision is the first that has occurred on the Alabama river.

It is true, the Magnolia was engaged in a commerce strictly within the State; but this does not exonerate her, as the trespass was on a vessel protected by the admiralty law. Cases have frequently occurred on the Ohio and Mississippi rivers, where steamboats, having run down and sunk flat-boats, were held responsible for the injury in the admiralty. And if a steamer is liable in such cases, a remedy for an injury done to it cannot be withheld in the same court.

In the Genesee Chief case, (12 How., 443), this court held: "The admiralty jurisdiction granted to the District Courts of the United States under the Constitution extends to the navigable rivers and lakes of the United States, without regard to the ebb and flow of the tides of the ocean." It is difficult to perceive how this language could have been mistaken, as alleged by the counsel in argument. All the lakes and all the navigable rivers in the Union are declared to be subject to this jurisdiction without reference to the tide, and it overrules all previous decisions on that subject.

It was said in that case the act of 1845 extended the jurisdiction of the admiralty; and this was so, as by the act of 1789 it was limited to rivers navigable from the sea by vessels of ten tons burden and upwards.

It is alleged that the assumption of this jurisdiction will absorb matters of controversy and the punishment of offences and misdemeanors now cognizable in the courts of the State, without the trial by jury, and before a foreign tribunal, contrary to the wishes and interests of a State.

The admiralty and maritime jurisdiction has been in operation on all the navigable rivers of our Atlantic coast since the organization of the Government, and its exercise has not been found dangerous or inconvenient. Experience is a better rule of judgment than theory. If this jurisdiction has been found salutary in that part of our country which is most commercial, it cannot be injurious or dangerous in those parts which are less commercial.

The Federal courts have no cognizance of common-law offences, on the land or on the water. Jurisdiction has been conferred on them of common law and chancery in specified cases, in every State and Territory of the Union; but I am not aware that this has been considered a foreign jurisdiction, or one that has been dangerous to the people of any State. Occasional conflicts of jurisdiction have arisen between this tribunal and the State courts, to preserve the rights guarantied by the Federal Constitution; but this became necessary in maintenance of the fundamental law of the Union. And if Congress should deem it necessary for the regulation of our internal commerce, amounting to more than ten hundred millions of dollars annually, to enact laws for its protection, they will no doubt be as mindful of the rights of the States as of those who, by their enterprise and wealth, carry on the commerce of the country.

Every one knows how strenuously the admiralty jurisdiction was resisted in England by the common-law lawyers, headed by Coke. The contest lasted for two centuries. The admiralty civilians contended that the statutes of Richard II and 2 H. IV did not curtail the ancient jurisdiction of the admiralty over torts and injuries upon the high seas, and in ports within the ebb and flow of the tide, which was shown by an exposition of the ancient cases, as was opposed by the common-law courts; but they continued the contest until they acquired a concurrent jurisdiction over all maritime causes, except prize. The vice-admiralty courts in this country, under the colonial Government, exercised jurisdiction over all maritime contracts, and over torts and injuries, as well in ports as upon the high seas, and this was the jurisdiction conferred on our courts by the Constitution.

But it was not until a late period that the jurisdiction of the admiralty in England was settled by the statute of 3 and 4 Victoria, c. 67, passed in 1840. This is entitled "An act to improve the practice and extend the jurisdiction of the High Court of Admiralty in England." And it is gratifying to the bar and bench of this country to know, that the above statute has placed the English admiralty substantially on the same footing that it is maintained in this country. To this remark it is believed there are but two or three exceptions. Insurance, ransom, and surveys, are believed to constitute the only exceptions. The flow of the tide, as before remarked, is used to designate the navigableness of their rivers. Whether an insurance is within the admiralty, has not been considered by this court. It is singular, that while the English admiralty, by its extension, has been placed substantially upon the same basis as our own, ours should be denounced as having a dangerous tendency upon our interests and institutions, and a desire expressed to abandon the enlightened rules of the civil law, and follow the misconstrued statutes of Richard II.

Antiquity has its charms, as it is rarely found in the common walks of professional life; but it may be doubted whether wisdom is not more frequently found in experience and the gradual progress of human affairs; and this is especially the case in all systems of jurisprudence which are matured by the progress of human knowledge. Whether it be common, chancery, or admiralty law, we should be more instructed by studying its present adaptations to human concerns, than to trace it back to its beginnings. Every one is more interested and delighted to look upon the majestic and flowing river, than by following its current upwards until it becomes lost in its mountain rivulets.

■ MR. JUSTICE DANIEL dissenting:

Against the opinion of the court in this cause, and the doctrines assumed in its support, I feel constrained solemnly to protest.

* * *

Having, in cases formerly before this court, * * * traced with some care the origin of the admiralty jurisdiction in England, and the modes and limits to which that jurisdiction was there subjected, no farther reference will here be made to the authorities by which that investigation has been guided, than is necessary to illustrate the origin and extent of the like jurisdiction as appertaining to the tribunals of the United States. * * * The only known difference between the administration in admiralty courts in the mother country and in her American colonies, was created *by express statute,* with reference to the *revenue;* was limited to the single regulation prescribed by the statute; and has, by every writer upon the subject, been treated as a *special* direction, applicable solely to the matter of which it treated, and as neither entering into, nor deducible from, any regular and constitutional attribute of the admiralty jurisdiction. It was an exception, an anomaly, and in its nature and operation was unique and solitary. Of the same character, precisely, is the provision of the eleventh section of the judiciary act of 1789, which invests the District Courts with jurisdiction in cases of seizure under the laws of imposts of the United States.

* * *

The conclusion, then, from the eleventh section of the judiciary act, is inevitably this: that the power thereby vested with respect to *seizures,* is not an *admiralty* power—was never conferred by the investment of admiralty power in accordance with the Constitution; but is in its character distinct therefrom, and is peculiar and limited in its extent. Such appears to have been the opinion of two distinguished commentators upon the admiralty jurisdiction of the courts of the United States, Chancellor Kent and Mr. Dane; the former of whom, in the 1st vol. of his Commentaries, p. 376, holds this language: "Congress had a right, in their discretion, to make all seizures and forfeitures cognizable in the District Courts; but it may be a question whether they had any right to declare them to be cases of admiralty jurisdiction, if they were not so by the law of the land when the Constitution was made. The Constitution secures to the citizen trial by jury in all criminal prosecutions, and in all civil suits at common law where the value in controversy exceeds twenty dollars. These prosecutions for forfeitures of large and valuable portions of property, under the revenue laws, are highly penal in their consequences; and the Government and its officers are always parties, and deeply concerned in the conviction and forfeiture. And if, by act of Congress or by judicial decisions, the prosecution can be turned over to the admiralty side of the District Court, as being neither a criminal prosecution nor a suit at common law, the trial of the cause is then transferred from a jury of the country to the breast of a single judge. It is probable, however, that the judiciary act did not intend to do more than to declare the jurisdiction of the District Courts over these cases; and that all the prosecutions for penalties and forfeitures upon seizures under laws of imposts, navigation, and trade, were not to be considered of admiralty jurisdiction when the case admitted of a prosecution at common law; for the act saves to *suitors in all cases* the right to a common-law remedy, where the common law was competent to give it. We have seen that it is competent to give it; because, under the vigorous system of the English law, such prosecutions *in rem* are in the exchequer, according to the course of the common law; and it may be doubted whether the case of La Vengeance, on which all subsequent decisions of the Supreme Court have rested, was sufficiently considered. The vice-admiralty courts in this country when we were colonies, and also in the West Indies, obtained jurisdiction in *revenue causes* to an extent totally unknown to the jurisdiction of the English admiralty, and with powers as enlarged as those claimed at the present day. But this extension, *by statute,* of the jurisdiction of the American vice-admiralty courts beyond their ancient limits to revenue cases and penalties, was much discussed and complained of at the commencement of the Revolution." Judge Conkling also, in his *Treatise on the Admiralty,* vol. 2, p. 391, says: "In England, all revenue seizures are cognizable *exclusively* in the *exchequer;* and such of them as are cognizable on the admiralty side of the District Courts of the United States are made so *only by force of a legislative act."*

* * *

It may here be pertinently asked, how, with this exposition of the law, can be reconciled the assertion that at the time of the American Revolution, and down to the adoption of the Constitution of the United States, there were vested in the colonial courts of England, and were appropriate to them as courts of admiralty, powers which never were vested in their superior, by whom they were created, and by whom they were to be supervised and controlled? With perfect respect, it would seem to imply an incongruity, if not an absurdity, to ascribe to any tribunal an appellate or revisory power with reference to matters beyond its legitimate jurisdiction, and which confessedly belonged to a different authority. Yet is this assertion of jurisdiction in admiralty in the colonial courts beyond that of their creator and superior, constantly renewed *arguendo,* whilst, in reply to repeated challenges of authority by which the assumption may be sustained, not one adjudication in point has been adduced. Again, it may be asked whether, in the history of jurisprudence, another instance can be found in which it is alleged that a *system, a corpus juris,* has grown up and been established, and yet not an ingredient, not a fragment of any such *system* can be discovered? But there have been decisions which were made in this country—decisions contemporaneous with the event of the separation from the mother country; but these decisions, respectable for their learning and ability, so far from sustaining the *obiter* assertion above mentioned, divest it of even plausibility; for they affirm and maintain a complete conformity and subordination of the admiralty jurisdiction in the colonies, to that which had prevailed in England from the time of the statutes of Richard, and from the days of Owen, Brownlow, Hobart, Fortescue, and Coke. I refer to the case of Clinton v. The Brig Hannah, decided by Judge Hopkinson, of Pennsylvania, in 1781, and the case of Shrewsbury v. The Sloop Two Friends, decided by Judge Bee, of South Carolina, in 1786. And, indeed, the phrase "admiralty jurisdiction," except in the acceptation received by us from the English courts, is without intelligible or definite meaning, for under no other system of jurisprudence is the law of the marine known to be administered under the same organization.

Let us now take a view of the claims advanced for the admiralty power, in its constant attempts at encroachment upon the principles and genius of the common law, and of our republican and peculiar institutions, at least from the decision in the case of the Thomas Jefferson, in the 10th of Wheaton, p. 428, to that of the Genesee Chief v. Fitzhugh, in the 12th of Howard, 443, inclusive; this last a case, to my apprehension, more remarkable and more startling as an assumption of judicial power than any which the judicial history of the country has hitherto disclosed, prior to the case now under consideration.

By the statute of 13th Richard II, cap. 15th, it is enacted, that "the Admirals and their deputies shall meddle with nothing done *within the realm,* but only with things done upon the *sea;* "and by the 15th of Richard II, cap. 3d, "that in all contracts, pleas, and quarrels, and other things done within the bodies of counties, *by land or water,* the Admiral shall have no cognizance, but they shall be tried by the law of the land." The language of these provisions is truly remarkable. By that of the first is denounced the exclusion, utterly, of the Admiral's power from the entire realm; by that of the second, is as explicitly denied to him all cognizance of things done *in the bodies of the counties, either by land or by water.* And the statute of Henry IV, cap. 11, by way of insuring a sanction of these exclusions, provides, "that he who finds himself aggrieved against the form of the statutes of Richard, shall have his action grounded upon the case against him who so pursues in the admiralty, and recover double damages." Lord Hale, in his *History of the Common Law,* speaking of the court of admiralty, says, (p. 51:) "This court is not bottomed or founded upon the authority of the civil law, but hath both its powers and jurisdiction by the law and custom of the realm in such matters as are proper for its cognizance." And again, in an enumeration of matters not within the cognizance of the admiralty, he continues: "So also of damages in *navigable rivers within the bodies of counties,* things done upon the shore at low-water mark, wreck of the sea, & c.; these things belong not to the Admiral's jurisdiction." And the cause, the only cause assigned as the foundation of that jurisdiction, is the peculiar locality of each instance, viz: its being neither within the body of any county or vicinage, nor *infra fauces terrae,* so that the *venue or pays* can be summoned for its trial. No one pretends to doubt that thus stood the admiralty law of the realm of England at the period of separation from the American colonies, and perhaps in the particulars above mentioned it may remain the unchanged law of that country to the present moment, as it is a fact recorded in history, that for a departure from that law, one of the most learned and brilliant of her admiralty judges (Sir William Scott, afterwards Lord Stowell) was condemned in a very heavy verdict. Such, I say, was the law of the realm of England, and I think that the fallacy or pretence of any change in the admiralty law proper of that realm, in its application to the colonies, has been clearly demonstrated.

The admiralty law of England, according to every accurate test, was the admiralty law of the United States at the period of the adoption of the Constitution. It is pertinent in this place to remark, that the jurisdiction of the admiralty having been, both by the common law and by the language of the statutes of Richard II and Henry IV, excluded not only from the body of the counties, both on the land and on the water, and even from the *realm,* it followed, *ex consequenti,* that the locality of that jurisdiction was (and necessarily so) within the ebb and flow of the tide. Hence, it is more than probable, arose the adoption and use of the phrase as a portion of the description of the locus of that jurisdiction, viz: that it was *maritime,* i.e., connected with or was upon the sea, and was neither upon the land nor within the *fauces terrae,* nor upon any navigable water within a county, and was within the ebb and flow of the tide.

Under such a state of the admiralty law, conceded to be the law of England, and as I contend, the law of the United States, came before this court for decision the case of the Thomas Jefferson, in the 10th of Wheaton, p. 428. In this case, not a single ingredient required by the English cases to give jurisdiction existed. It could by no possibility or by any propriety of language be styled *maritime,* as every fact it presented occurred at the distance of a thousand miles from the ocean, and it could not be shown that there ever existed a tide in the water-course on which the occurrences that produced the suit originated. Yet, in the absence of these essential ingredients of admiralty jurisdiction, the court, with that greed for power by which courts are so often impelled beyond the line of strict propriety, makes a query, whether, under the show of *regulating commerce,* Congress might not assert a distinctive and original authority, viz: the power of the admiralty. The court, however, felt itself constrained to concede the necessity of a locality within the ebb and flow of the tide, and for the want of that requisite to deny the jurisdiction.

* * *

These several decisions, founded, as they are believed to have been, in error, and upon a misconstruction of the law, of the Constitution, and the history of the country, in so far as they sought to permit invasions of the territorial, municipal, and political rights of the States, are, nevertheless, not entirely without their value. By the limit they prescribed to the admiralty, viz: the ebb and flow of the tide, they at least rejected the ambitious claim to undefined and undefinable judicial discretion over the Constitution and the law, (and the indispensable territorial rights of the States,) and so far fortified the foundations of a Government, based, in theory at any rate, upon restricted and exactly-defined delegations of power only. It was under the stress of the aforegoing decisions, and, as is well known, upon an application of a portion of this court, that the act of Congress of February 26, 1845, cap. 22, was passed, with the sole view of extending the admiralty jurisdiction to cases arising upon the lakes, and upon the rivers connecting the said lakes, on which there were no tides, and which (i.e., *the lakes*) were within no State limits. Here, then, we have the exception, the solitary exception, fortifying the general rule as to the admiralty jurisdiction, which jurisdiction is again described and defined in this provision of the statute above quoted, as existing upon the *high seas* or upon the *tide-waters* of the United States only.

* * * The repeated and explicit decisions of this court already cited, and the act of Congress of 1845, might, it is supposed, have been regarded as some earnest of uniformity and certainty in defining the admiralty jurisprudence of the United States, at least upon the points adjudged, and as to the provisions of the statute; but, in this age of *progress,* such anticipations are held to be amongst the wildest fallacies. It is now discovered that the principles asserted by the admiralty courts in England, or said to have been propounded by the mysterious, unedited, and unproduced proceedings of the colonial vice-admiralty courts, so often avouched here in argument; the decisions of this court and the provisions of the act of 1845, are all to be thrown aside, as wholly erroneous. That the admiralty power is not to be restricted by its effect upon the territorial, political, or municipal rights and institutions upon which it may be brought to bear, nor by any checks from the authority of the common law. That there is but one rule by which its extent is to be computed, and that is the rule which measures it by miles or leagues; that the scale for its admeasurement can be applied only as the discretion of the judiciary may determine, upon its necessity or policy, irrespective of the Constitution, the statute, or the character of the element on which it is to be exerted, or the adjudications of this court on this last point. That the admiralty of the fixed and limited realm of England, and as known to the framers of the Constitution, cannot be the admiralty of this day; and, of course, the admiralty of our time and of our present day must be changed according to the judgment or discretion of the courts, in the event of further acquisitions of territory.

Such are the conclusions regularly deducible from the opinion of this court in the case of the *Genesee Chief*—conclusions, in my deliberate judgment, the most startling and dangerous innovations, anterior to that decision, ever attempted upon the powers and rights of internal government appertaining to the States. * * *

* * * In quest of certainty, under this new doctrine, the inquiry is naturally suggested, what are navigable waters? Will it be proper to adopt, in the interpretation of this phrase, an etymological derivation from *navis,* and to designate, as navigable waters, those only on whose bosoms ships and navies can be floated? Shall it embrace waters on which sloops and shallops, or what are generally termed river craft, can swim; or shall it be extended to any water on which a batteau or a pirogue can be floated? These are all, at any rate, *practicable* waters, navigable in a certain sense. If any point between the extremes just mentioned is to be taken, there is at once opened a prolific source of uncertainty, of contestation and expense. And if the last of these extremes be adopted, then there is scarcely an internal water-course, whether in its natural condition, or as improved under the authority and with the resources of the States, or a canal, or a mill-pond, some of which are known to cover many acres of land, (and, as

this court can convert rivers without tides into *seas,* may be metamorphosed into small lakes,) which would not by this doctrine be brought within the grasp of the admiralty. Some of our canals are navigated by steam, and some of them by sails; some of them are adjuncts to rivers, and form continuous communications with the ocean; all of them are fed by, and therefore are made portions of, rivers. Under this new regime, the hand of Federal power may be thrust into everything, even into a vegetable or fruit basket; and there is no production of a farm, an orchard, or a garden, on the margin of these water-courses, which is not liable to be arrested on its way to the next market town by the *high admiralty power,* with all its parade of appendages; and the simple, plain, homely countryman, who imagined he had some comprehension of his rights, and their remedies under the cognizance of a justice of the peace, or of a county court, is now, through the instrumentality of some apt fomenter of trouble, metamorphosed and magnified from a country attorney into a proctor, to be confounded and put to silence by a learned display from Roccus de Navibus, Emerigon, or Pardessus, from the Mare Clausum, or from the Trinity Masters, or the Apostles.

* * *

In truth, the extravagance of these claims to an all-controlling central power, their utter incongruity with any just proportion or equipoise of the different parts of our system, would exhibit them as positively ludicrous, were it not for the serious mischiefs to which, if tolerated, they must inevitably lead—mischiefs which should characterize those pretensions as fatal to the inherent and necessary powers of self-preservation and internal government in the States; as at war with the interests, the habits and feelings of the people, and therefore to be reprobated and wholly rejected. For myself, I can only say, that to whatsoever point they may, under approbation here or elsewhere, have culminated, they never can offer themselves for my acceptation, but they must encounter my solemn rebuke.

■ MR. JUSTICE CAMPBELL dissenting:

I dissent from the judgment of the court in this cause, and from the opinion delivered by the judges composing a majority of the court.

* * *

It is my opinion that this court claims a power for the District Court not delegated to the Federal Government in the Constitution of the United States, and that Congress, in organizing the judiciary department, have not conferred upon any court of the United States. That this court has assumed a jurisdiction over a case only cognizable at the common law, and triable by a jury; and that its opinion and judgment contravene the authority and doctrine of a large number of decisions pronounced by this court, and by the Circuit Courts, after elaborate arguments and mature deliberation, and which for a long period have formed a rule of decision to the court, and of opinion to the legal profession; and that no other judgment of this court affords a sanction to this.

* * *

The reign of Richard II was an epoch to be remembered with interest, and studied with care, by those concerned in administering the constitutional law of England or the United States. A formal complaint was made by the Commons of defects in the administration, as well about the King's person and his household as in his courts of justice, and redress was demanded. Measures were taken for placing the judicial institutions of England upon a solid constitutional foundation, and to exclude from the realm the odious systems of the continent. The first of the enactments was directed against the usurpations of the great military officers, who administered justice by virtue of their seignoral powers—the Lords' Constable and the Earl Marshal. The acts of 8th and 13th Richard II provide that, "because the Commons do make a grievous complaint that the court of the Constable and Marshal have accroached to them, and do daily accroach, contracts, covenants, trespasses, debts, detinues, and many other actions pleadable at the common law, in great prejudice to the King, and to the great grievance and oppression of the people," therefore they were prohibited, and their jurisdiction confined "to contracts and deeds of arms without the realm," and "things that touch more within the realm which cannot be determined and discussed by the common law."

The Lord High Admiral received a similar rebuke. The preamble of the act of 13 Richard II recites, "that complaints had arisen because Admirals and their deputies hold their sessions within divers places of the realm, accroaching to them greater authority than belonged to their office, to the prejudice of the King, & c." It was declared that the Admiral should not meddle with anything done within the realm, but only with things done upon the sea, as had been used in the time of Edward III. But this did not suffice to restrain the accroaching spirit of that feudal lord and his deputies.

Two years after, the Parliament enacted, "that the court of admiralty hath no manner of cognizance, power, nor jurisdiction of any manner of contract, plea, or quarrel, or of any other thing done or rising within the bodies of counties, either by land or water, and also with wreck of the sea; but all such manner of contracts, pleas, and quarrels, and all other things rising within the bodies of counties, as well by land as by water as aforesaid, and also wreck of the sea, shall be tried, termined, discussed, and remedied by the laws of the land, and not before, nor by the Admiral or his lieutenant, in no manner. Nevertheless, of the death of a man and of a mayhem done in great ships, being and hovering in the main stream of the great rivers, beneath the points of the same rivers, and in no other place of the same rivers, the Admiral shall have cognizance."

In the sixteenth year of the reign of Richard II, the rule of the Roman chancery, like that of the Lords' Constable, Marshal, and Admiral, was banished from England. In that year it was enacted that, "Both those who shall pursue or cause to be pursued, in the court of Rome or *elsewhere,* any processes, or instruments, or other things whatsoever, which touch the King, against his crown and regality, or his realm, shall be outlawed and placed out of the King's protection." In the following reign the accroaching spirit of the courts of admiralty received a further rebuke.

Upon the prayer of the Commons, the statutes of Richard II were confirmed, and a penalty was inflicted upon such as should maintain suits in the admiralty, contrary to their spirit.

This body of statute law served in a great degree to check the usurping tendencies of these anomalous jurisdictions, and to prevent in a measure the removal of suits triable at the common law *ad aliud examen,* and to be discussed *per aliam legem.* It placed upon an eminence the common law of the realm, and enabled the Commons to plead with authority against other encroachments and usurpations upon the general liberty. But, though a foreign law and despotism were not allowed to enter the kingdom through the courts martial, ecclesiastical, or admiral, the preversion of judiciary powers to purposes of oppression was not effectually prevented. The courts of the Star Chamber and of High Commission, originally limited to specific objects, "assumed power to intermeddle in civil causes and matters only of private interest between party and party, and adventured to determine the estates and liberties of the subject, contrary to the law of the land and the rights and privileges of the subject," and "had been by experience found to be an intolerable burden, and the means to introduce an arbitrary power and government." Among the cases of jurisdiction claimed by the Star Chamber were those between merchant strangers and Englishmen, or between strangers, and for the restitution of ships and goods unlawfully taken, or other deceits practiced on merchants.

One of the most practiced proctors of this court has left his testimony: "That since the great Roman Senate, so famous in all ages and nations as that they might be called *jure mirum orbis,* there hath no court come so near them, in state, honor, and adjudication, as this." But, by the 16th of Charles I, it was enacted, both in respect of this and the High Commission Court, "that from henceforth no court, council, or place of judicature, shall be erected, ordained, constituted, or appointed, which shall have, use, or exercise the same or like jurisdiction as is or hath been used, practiced, or exercised," in those courts.

But the statute did not terminate with this. The patriot leaders of that time, reviewing in the preamble to the act the various parliamentary enactments in regard to the legal institutions of England, and reciting those declarations of the public liberties which had extended over a period of four hundred years, proceeded to add another. It was solemnly enacted, "that neither his Majesty, nor his Privy Council, have, or ought to have, any jurisdiction, power, or authority, by English bill, petition, articles, libel, or any other arbitrary whatsoever, to examine or draw in question, determine, or dispose of the lands, tenements, hereditaments, goods, and chattels, of any of the subjects of this realm, but that the same ought to be tried and determined in the ordinary courts of justice, and by the ordinary course of the law."

This selection of a few sections from various English statutes, and the historical facts I have mentioned, is designed to illustrate the intensity and duration of the contest which resulted in placing the judiciary institutions of England on their existing foundation. In the midst of that contest, the settlements were formed in America in which those institutions were successfully planted.

They have been incorporated into the Constitution of the United States, and prevail from the Atlantic Ocean to the Pacific, and from the Lakes to the Gulf of Mexico. These statutes show how the courts martial, ecclesiastical, admiral, and courts proceeding from an arbitrary royal authority, were either limited or suppressed.

The inquiry arises, how would a case like that before this court have been decided in England, either at the period of the Declaration of Independence, or at the adoption of the Constitution of the United States, in the court of admiralty?

In 1832, a question arose in that court, whether a cause of collision, arising between steam vessels navigating the river Humber, a short distance from the sea, within the ebb and flow of the tide, within the port of Hull, below the first bridges, when the tide was three-fourths flood, was cognizable by the court. The judge of the admiralty, an exact and conscientious judge, answered: "Since the statutes of Richard II and of Henry IV, *it has been strictly held* that the court of admiralty cannot exercise jurisdiction in civil causes arising *infra corpus comitatus.*" I cite this opinion not simply as evidence of the law in 1832, but also as affording authentic evidence of the historical fact it enunciates. (The Public Opinion, 2 Hagg., 399.)

I proceed now to inquire of the admiralty jurisdiction as exercised by the courts of vice-admiralty in the colonies and in the United States before the adoption of the Constitution.

The jurisdiction included four subjects, and a separate examination of each title of jurisdiction will shed light upon the discussion. These are— prize; breaches of the acts of navigation, revenue, and trade; crimes and misdemeanors on the high seas; and cases of civil and maritime jurisdiction.

* * *

The admiralty court of Great Britain and the vice-admiralty courts of the colonies were vested with jurisdiction over cases for the violation of a series of statutes for the regulation of trade and revenue in the colonies. The origin and extent of this jurisdiction are explained in the case of the Columbus, decided in the British admiralty in 1789, on an appeal from the vice-admiralty court of Barbados. The learned judge of that court said: "The court of admiralty derives no jurisdiction in causes of revenue from the patent of the judge, or from the ancient customary and inherent jurisdiction of the prerogative of the Crown, in the person of its Lord High Admiral, and exercised by his lieutenant. Not a word is mentioned of the King's revenue, which seems to have been entirely appropriated to the Court of Exchequer, which is both a court of law and equity. If, therefore, there is any inherent prerogative right of judging of seizures upon the sea, for the rights and dues of the Crown, whether of peace or of war, as in the right of prize and reprisal, that prerogative jurisdiction is put in motion by special commission or by act of Parliament. The first statute which places judgment of revenue in the plantations with the courts of admiralty, is the 12th of Charles II, ch. 18, sec. 1, which act has been followed by subsequent statutes." This lucid opinion has not been cited in any previous discussion of the subject in this court, from the fact that it is not published in the regular series of the admiralty reports. (2 Coll.Jur., 82; 2 Dod.Adm.R., 352.)

By an act of the 22d and 23d Charles II, to regulate the trade of the plantations, suits were authorized for breaches of its enactments "in the court of the High Admiral of England, or of any of his vice-admirals," or in any court of record. The acts of 7th and 8th of William III, 6th George II, 4th, 5th, 6th, 7th, and 8th, of George III, confer plenary jurisdiction upon the same courts, in cases of navigation, trade, and revenue, in the colonies, and the later statutes extend their authority to seizures upon the land as well as water. * * *

The first of these acts was passed when the colonial settlements in New England and Virginia were in their infancy, and before those in the remaining colonies had been fairly commenced. The jurisdiction was familiar to the colonists, and these acts explain the origin of the clause of the judiciary act of 1789 on the same subject. The judiciary act confers on the District Courts "cognizance of all civil causes of civil and maritime jurisdiction, including all seizures under laws of impost, navigation, or trade, of the United States, when the seizures are made on waters which are navigable from the sea by vessels of ten or more tons burden, within their respective districts, as well as upon the high seas." It is difficult to comprehend on what principle the court can construe the grant of jurisdiction in this act over cases of seizure under the law of impost and trade upon navigable waters, to an extension of the civil jurisdiction of the admiralty to the same localities. The admiralty jurisdiction, in cases of seizure, is a special jurisdiction, not belonging to the original constitution of the courts of admiralty, and this act treats it as such. And so this court, until the revolution in its doctrines in these latter years, uniformly treated it. The long and painful discussions from Delovio v. Boit to the New Jersey Navigation Case, are without meaning on any other hypothesis. If the jurisdiction in both classes of cases had been supposed to rest on the same foundation, the whole controversy would have been settled by the case of "La Vengeance," reported in 3 Dall., 297.

The civil and maritime jurisdiction of the vice-admiralty courts extended to the same subjects and was exercised under the same limitations in the colonies as in Great Britain. "Upon the establishment of colonial Governments," says a learned judge of one of those courts, "it was deemed proper to invest the Governors with the same civil and maritime jurisdiction; and therefore it became usual for the Lord High Admiral or the Lords Commissioners to grant a commission of vice-admiral to them." The office thus conferred on the Governor was precisely the same with that of the vice-admirals in England, and was confined to that civil and maritime jurisdiction which was the original branch of his authority. (Stewart's V.Ad.R., 394, 405.) These courts were subordinate to the admiralty court of England, and, until the late reign of William IV, it received appeals from them. (1 Dod.Adm.R., 381.) The incompatibility of the criminal jurisdiction of the Admiral on the high seas with the legal constitution of England, was declared and corrected by the 28 H. VIII, ch. 15.

* * *

There can be no room for doubt that the statesmen and jurists who composed the Congress of 1774 regarded the limits of the courts of admiralty as settled by the statutes of Richard II, Henry IV, Henry VIII, and the early acts of navigation and trade, and that the enlargement of this jurisdiction was such a wrong as to justify a resort to arms. Their declarations bear no other interpretation; and the admiralty system of the States before the Constitution was administered upon this opinion. (Bee's Adm.R., 419, 433; 1 Dall., 33.)

* * *

The judicial power of the United States was organized to comprehend all cases that might properly arise under the Constitution, laws, and treaties of the United States, and, in addition, cases of which, from the character of the parties, the decision might involve the peace and harmony of the Union. This principle was accepted without dissent among the framers of the Constitution. The clause "all cases of admiralty and maritime jurisdiction" appears in the draught of the Constitution imputed to Charles Pinckney, and submitted at a very early stage of the session of the Convention. It was reported by the committee of detail in their first report, and was adopted without debate. In one of the sittings, in an incidental discussion, Mr. Wilson, of Pennsylvania, remarked: *"That the admiralty jurisdiction ought to be given wholly to the National Government, as it related to cases not within the jurisdiction of a particular State,* and to a scene *in which controversy with foreigners would be most likely to happen."* (2 Mad.De., 799.) No other observation in the Convention illustrates this clause.

The judiciary clause is expounded in the numbers of the Federalist, by Alexander Hamilton.

He says, the judicial power extends—1st, to all those cases which arise out of the laws of the United States, passed in pursuance of their just and constitutional powers of legislation; 2d, to all those which concern the execution of the provisions expressly contained in the Articles of Union; 3d, to all those in which the United States are a party; 4th, to all those which involve the peace of the Confederacy, whether they relate to the intercourse between the United States and foreign nations, or to that between the States themselves; 5th, to all those which originate on the high seas, and are of admiralty or maritime jurisdiction; and, lastly, to all those in which the State tribunals cannot be supposed to be unbiassed and impartial.

In regard to the 5th class, he says: "The most bigoted idolizers of State authority have not thus far shown a disposition to deny the national judiciary the cognizance of maritime causes. These so generally depend on the laws of nations, and so commonly affect the rights of foreigners, that they fall within the considerations relative to the public peace. The most important of them are, by the present Confederation, submitted to Federal jurisdiction."

Similar remarks are to be found in the debates in various of the Conventions of the States which adopted the Constitution, as incidentally occurring. In none of the Conventions was the judiciary clause of the Constitution considerately examined, except in Virginia; and in the Convention of Virginia no objection was made to this clause. Gov. Randolph said there, that "cases of admiralty and maritime jurisdiction cannot with propriety be vested in particular State courts. As our national tranquillity, reputation, and intercourse with foreign nations, may be affected by admiralty decisions, as they ought therefore to be uniform, and as there can be no uniformity if there be thirteen distinct independent jurisdictions, the jurisdiction ought to be in the Federal judiciary." Mr. Madison, in a luminous exposition of the article, expressed a similar opinion. He said: "The same reasons supported the grant of admiralty jurisdiction as existed in the grant of cognizance of causes affecting ambassadors and foreign ministers." "As our intercourse with foreign nations will be affected by decisions of this kind, they ought to be uniform." In the same speech, this statesman affirmed, *that all controversies directly between citizen and citizen will still remain with the local courts.* And after the Constitution was adopted, we find Chief Justice Jay, in analyzing the judicial power of the United States, and assigning reasons for the grant, says of this portion of it, "because, as the seas are the joint property of nations, whose rights and privileges relative thereto are regulated by the law of nations and treaties, such cases necessarily belong to a national jurisdiction." The instance jurisdiction of the court, now the object of such ambition and interest, and involving questions so threatening, was hardly referred to by the friends of the Constitution, and not an alarm was expressed by any of its vigilant and jealous opponents. The prize jurisdiction of the court— that which concerned the foreign relations of the Union in war or in peace, and which is so intimately related to the honor and dignity of the country— was in the minds of all those statesmen who referred to the subject.

It did not enter the imagination of any opponent of the Constitution to conceive that a jurisdiction which for centuries had been sternly repelled from the body of any county could, by any authority, artifice, or device, assume a jurisdiction through the whole extent of every lake and water-course within the limits of the United States. The collision described in the libel of the appellants occurred at a place which in 1789 formed a part of the State of Georgia. Had a similar cause then arisen, I can affirm with perfect safety that not an individual member of any Convention, whether State or Federal, who was concerned in the making or the ratifying of the Constitution, would have admitted the existence of an admiralty jurisdiction over the case. Such being the facts, I affirm that no change in the opinion of men, nor in the condition of the country, nor any apparent expediency, can render that constitutional which those who made the Constitution did not design to be so.

"If any of the provisions of the Constitution are deemed unjust," said the Chief Justice, in Scott v. Sandford, 19 How., 393, "there is a mode prescribed in the instrument itself by which it may be amended; but, while it remains unaltered, it must be construed as it was understood at the time of its adoption. It is not only the same in words, but the same in meaning, and delegates the same powers to the Government, and secures the same rights and privileges to the citizen; and as long as it continues to exist in its present form, it speaks not only in the same words, but with the same meaning with which it spake when it came from the hands of its framers, and was voted on and adopted by the people of the United States."

That the framers of the Constitution designed to secure to the Federal Government a plenary control over all *maritime* questions arising in their intercourse with foreign nations, whether of peace or war, which assumed a juridical form through courts of its own appointment, is more than probable from the instrument and the contemporary expositions I have quoted. This was the primary and designed object of the authors of the Constitution in granting this jurisdiction. It is likewise probable that the jurisdiction which had been exercised from the infancy of the colonies to the reign of George III, by courts of admiralty, under laws of navigation, trade, and revenue, was considered as forming a legitimate branch of the admiralty jurisdiction. Such was the opinion of the First Congress under the Constitution, and it has been confirmed in this court. (3 Dall., 397; 2 Cr., 405; 4 Cr., 443; 2 H., 210.) If the instance jurisdiction of the court was at all remembered, the reminiscence was not of a nature to create alarm. The cases for its employment were few and defined. Those did not depend upon any purely municipal code, nor affect any question of public or political interest. They related for the most part to transactions at a distance, which did not involve the interests nor attract the observation of any considerable class of persons. No one could imagine that this jurisdiction, by the interpretation of those who were to exercise it, could penetrate wherever a vessel of ten tons might enter within any of the States.

The question arises, what are the power and jurisdiction claimed for the courts of the United States by this reversal of the judgment of the District Court of Alabama?

The Supreme Court requires that court to take cognizance of cases of admiralty and maritime jurisdiction that arise on lakes and on rivers, as if they were high seas. Dunlap, defining the constitutional jurisdiction in 1835, said, that "it comprehends all maritime contracts, torts, and injuries.

The latter branch is necessarily bounded by locality; the former extends over all contracts, whensoever they may be made and executed, or whatever may be the form of the stipulation which relates to the navigation, business, or commerce of the sea." (Dunlap's Pr., 43.)

This was the broad pretension for the admiralty set up by Mr. Justice Story, in Delovio v. Boit, in 1815, under which the legal profession and this court staggered for thirty years before being able to maintain it. The definition to be deduced from the present decision deprives that of any significance. That affords no description of the subject.

The definition under this decree, if carried to its logical extent, will run thus: "That the admiralty and maritime jurisdiction of the courts of the United States extends to all cases of contracts, torts, and injuries, which arise in or concern the navigation, commerce, or business of citizens of the United States, or persons commorant therein, on any of the navigable waters of the world."

I proceed now to examine the jurisprudence of the courts of the United States, to ascertain the various stages in the progress to the goal which has been to-day attained. The tendency of opinion in the first years of the existence of the Union was to limit the admiralty jurisdiction according the constitution of the British court of admiralty. Justice Washington so declared in 1806; United States v. McGill, 4 Dall., 395; and his learned successor maintained the same doctrine. (Bald.R., 544.)

This opinion was assailed by Justice Story in Delovio v. Boit, 2 Gall., 398, in the year 1815.

The question of jurisdiction arose on a libel founded on a policy of insurance, and the jurisdiction of the court was sustained. I believe I express a general, if not universal, opinion of the legal profession, in saying that this judgment was erroneous. I understand Justice Curtis to intimate the existence of such an opinion in the Gloucester Insurance Company v. Younger, 2 Curt.R., 322.

The opinion of Justice Story, in the cause of Delovio v. Boit, is celebrated for its research, and remarkable, in my opinion, for its boldness in asserting novel conclusions, and the facility with which authentic historical evidence that contradicted them is disposed of. The examination of the English authorities resulted in the following conclusions.

In the construction of the statutes of Richard II and Henry IV, "the admiralty has *uniformly* and *without hesitation*," he says, "maintained that they were never intended to abridge or restrain the rightful jurisdiction of the court; that they meant to take away any pretence of entertaining suits upon contracts arising wholly upon land, and referring solely to terrene affairs; and upon torts or injuries which, though arising in ports, were not done within the ebb and flow of the tide; and that the language of these statutes, as well as the manifest object thereof, as stated in the preambles, and in the petitions on which they were founded, is fully satisfied by this exposition. So that, consistently with the statutes, the admiralty may still exercise jurisdiction: 1. Over torts and injuries upon the high seas, and in ports within the ebb and flow of the tide, and in great streams below the first bridges; 2. Over all maritime contracts arising at home or abroad; 3. Over matters of prize and its incidents." In regard to the conclusions of the courts of common law he says:

That the common-law interpretation of these statutes abridges the jurisdiction to things wholly done on the sea. 2. That the common-law interpretation of these statutes is indefensible upon principle, and the decisions founded upon it are inconsistent and unsatisfactory. 3. That the interpretation of the same statutes does not abridge any of its ancient jurisdiction, but leaves to it cognizance of all maritime contracts, torts, injuries, and offences upon the high seas, and in ports as far as the ebb and flow of the tide. 4. That this is the true limit of the admiralty jurisdiction, on principle. In regard to the case of the collision between ships and steamboats, we have the authoritative declaration of the judge of the admiralty. I have cited it to show that this statement of the English law is not accurate. And Sir John Nicholl, in the same court, in 3 Hagg., 257, 283, differs materially from other portions of the same statement. It may be true that the English court of admiralty, with the approbation of the King, took cognizance of causes arising within the limits of England, in despite of the prohibition by Parliament. But the great charter, and other statutes of importance to the liberties of the realm, were also violated by the same authority. It is also true that the twelve judges of England, and the attorney general, in the presence of the King and the Privy Council, after solemn debate, in 1632, signed an agreement to concede to the admiralty a larger jurisdiction. But such an act was illegal, and by the judges extra-judicial. Ten of those judges, four years later, presided in the case against Hampden for ship money; the attorney general was the inventor of the writ for its levy; the Privy Council was that which Strafford and Laud had organized to rule England without a Parliament, and which was made hateful by its arbitrary and violent proceedings. And the contract itself was denounced as unconstitutional by Lord Coke, who, but a few years before, had prepared the Petition of Right in which the legal constitution of England was embodied. For all contracts, pleas, and quarrels, made and done upon a river, haven, or creek, within the realm of England, he said, "the Admiral, without question, hath not jurisdiction, for then he should hold plea of things done within the body of the county, which are triable by verdict of twelve men, and merely determinable by the common law, and not within the admiralty and by the civil law; for that were to change and alter the law in such cases." (4 Co.Inst., 135.) And finally, in 1640, to close the door upon all such attempts of the King and his Privy Council, the fifth section of the act "For the regulating of the Privy Council, and for taking away the court commonly called the Star Chamber," which I have already quoted, was adopted.

The great and controlling question of contest in this long period of contest was as to the supremacy of the Parliament, and a very important form of that question related to its organization of the courts and its regulation of their jurisdiction. When the supremacy of Parliament had been established by the Revolution, its enactments which had defined the constitutional limits of the courts of judicature were no longer opposed or contradicted. The error of the opinion in Delovio v. Boit, on this subject, in my judgment, consists in its adoption of the harsh and acrimonious censures of discarded and discomfited civilians on the conduct of the great patriots of England, whose courage, sagacity, and patriotism, secured the rights of her people, as any evidence of historical facts.

* * *

If the principle of this decree is carried to its logical extent, all cases arising in the transportation of property or persons from the towns and landing-places of the different States, to other towns and landing-places, whether in or out of the State; all cases of tort or damage arising in the navigation of the internal waters, whether involving the security of persons or title to property, in either; all cases of supply to those engaged in the navigation, not to enumerate others, will be cognizable in the District Courts of the United States. If the dogma of judges in regard to the system of laws to be administered prevails, then this whole class of cases may be drawn *ad aliud examen,* and placed under the dominion of a foreign code, *whether they arise among citizens or others.* The States are deprived of the power to mould their own laws in respect of persons and things within their limits, and which are appropriately subject to their sovereignty. The right of the people to self-government is thus abridged—abridged to the precise extent, that a judge appointed by another Government may impose a law, not sanctioned by the representatives or agents of the people, upon the citizens of the State. Thus the contest here assumes the same significance as in Great Britain, and, in its last analysis, involves the question of the right of the people to determine their own laws and legal institutions. And surely this objection to the decree is independent of any consideration whether the river is subject to tides, or is navigable from the sea.

This decree derives no strength from the legislation of Congress, but a strong argument is to be deduced from the act of 1845 in opposition to it. The learned author of the opinion in Delovio v. Boit, and in the case of the *Thomas Jefferson,* (Justice Story,) has the reputation of being the author of the act. He proposed to bring under the judicial administration of the United States, cases that did not belong to the jurisdiction of the admiralty under the authoritative exposition of the Constitution by this court. The first suggestion of the feasibility of such a law is to be found in the opinion given in the case of the *Thomas Jefferson,* in 1825, and is enough to relieve this court from the imputation of having decided that case without a proper appreciation of the magnitude of the question.

The act of 1845 involves the admission, that cases arising on waters within the limits of the United States other than tide-waters were cases at common law, and that a jury, under the seventh amendment of the Constitution, must be preserved. It was framed on the hypothesis that Congress might increase the judicial power of the United States, so as to comprise all cases arising on, or which related to, any subject to which its legislation extended. It is apparent that this court in 1847, and afterwards in 1848, when the suits of Waring v. Clark, and the New Jersey Navigation

Co. v. The Merchants' Bank, were so elaborately discussed, were wholly unconscious of the fact that this act contained a recognition of any jurisdiction in admiralty, additional to what had been previously exercised.

The only inference that can be drawn properly from the act of 1845, in my opinion, is, that Congress recognised the limit that the decisions in the earlier cases in this court had established for the admiralty and maritime jurisdiction, and its own incapacity to confer a more enlarged jurisdiction of that kind.

I have performed my duty, in my opinion, in expressing at large my convictions on the subject of the powers of the courts of the United States under the clause of the Constitution I have considered.

There have been cases, since I came into this court, involving the jurisdiction of the court on the seas and their tide-waters, the lakes, and the Mississippi river. I have applied the law as settled in previous decisions, in deference to the principle of *stare decisis,* without opposing any objection—though in a portion of those decisions the reasons of the court did not satisfy my own judgment. I consider that the present cases carries the jurisdiction to an incalculable extent beyond any other, and all others, that have heretofore been pronounced, and that it must create a revolution in the admiralty administration of the courts of the United States; that the change will produce heart-burning and discontent, and involve collisions with State Legislatures and State jurisdictions. And, finally, it is a violation of the rights reserved in the Constitution of the United States to the States and the people.

NOTE ON THE EXTENSION OF ADMIRALTY AND MARITIME JURISDICTION

Jackson v. The Steamboat Magnolia was the last case in which there was more than token dissent from the proposition that "admiralty and maritime jurisdiction," insofar as the term is defined by locality, extends to all water navigable in interstate and foreign commerce. The antiquaries among admiralty students will wish to explore more thoroughly the dispute that was put to rest in that case. A good place to start is Mr. Justice Story's opinion in De Lovio v. Boit, 2 Gall. 398, 7 Fed.Cas. 418 (1815). Though the matter in controversy in that case was the jurisdiction over a dispute arising under a marine insurance policy, and accordingly did not involve the question of locality, Mr. Justice Story proceeded to a "thorough examination of the whole jurisdiction of the admiralty." The opinion covers over seventy-five pages in the reports and the student will find in its copious footnotes an excellent bibliography of sources available at the time. The student must judge for himself the justice of Mr. Justice Campbell's observation in *Jackson v. The Steamboat Magnolia* that the opinion in *DeLovio* was remarkable for "* * * its boldness in asserting novel conclusions, and the facility with which authentic historical evidence that contradicted them is disposed of." Certainly he will find that a good deal of Story's history today is subject to very serious question, though it is still repeated. One example will suffice. One of the principal arguments mustered to support an interpretation of Art. III, section 2, of the Constitution as unburdened by the restrictions of the statutes of Richard II was the assertion that the jurisdiction of the vice-admiralty courts in the colonies was similarly unburdened. Reference was made to the wording of the commissions of the vice-admiralty judges in several of the colonies, and the statement was made that "In point of fact the vice admiralty court of Massachusetts, before the revolution, exercised a jurisdiction far more extensive, than that of the admiralty in England."

This "history" has become part of the general lore of admiralty jurisdiction. Judge Hough, in his Reports of Cases in the Vice Admiralty of the Province of New York and in the Court of Admiralty of the State of New York, 1715–1788, states that an examination of the New York cases substantiates Mr. Justice Story's "celebrated remark." The student should brouse among those cases, however, before he agrees with Judge Hough. Of particular interest is Archibald Kennedy Qui Tam & C Agt. 32 Barrells & C of Gunpowder, appearing on p. 82 of the collection.

"Aug 30 1754 The Case before the Court is whether the Admiralty hath Jurisdiction in this Cause. It is agreed by both sides that the seizure of the Gunpowder was made within the body of the City and County of New York; and what the Lybellant Insists gives the Admiralty Jurisdiction is the statute of the 7th & 8th of Will. 3d for preventing frauds and Regulating abuses in the Plantation Trade; in the seventh section of which act it is enacted that all the Penalties and forfeitures before mentioned & c. are to be Recovered in any of His Majesties Courts at Westminster or in the Kingdom of Ireland, or in the Court of Admiralty held in his Majesties Plantations Respectively where such offence shall be Committed, at the pleasure of the Officer or Informer.

"The Claimants say the Statutes of the 13th and 15th of Richard 2d take away all jurisdiction from the Admiralty of Matters and Causes arising on the Land within the body of any County, which statutes are now in force, not being Repealed by any subsequent statute.

"Let us consider what the Design and Intention of the Act of Parliament of the 7th and 8th of King William is: By the Title & Preamble it appears to be for the preventing frauds and Regulating abuses in the Plantation Trade; and I conceive these frauds & abuses may be Committed as well within the Admiralty Jurisdiction as within the Body of any County; & that appears by the act, because it is left to the pleasure of the Officer or Informer where he will prosecute the offence. But that pleasure must be Limitted by the Law. That is if the fraud and abuse be Committed within the Body of the County it must be his pleasure to prosecute the offence in the Courts of Common Law. If Committed within the Admiralty Jurisdiction his pleasure must be to prosecute it in the Admiralty Court.

* * *

"Upon the whole I am of the opinion that the plea to the Jurisdiction is a good plea, and that the Admiralty hath no power to try the offence by the Act of the 7 and 8 of King William as this Case is Circumstanced; the seizure of the powder being made within the Body of the City and County of New York. But as to what Powder is already condemned the plea to the Jurisdiction is too late."

See also the short report of Castriot v. Nicoll, set forth on p. 167, a libel by a surgeon on a privateer for prize money allegedly wrongfully withheld. Said the judge:

> "May 8, 1759 In this case I am clearly of opinion that the Admiralty have no Jurisdiction. The Prizes with all their lading taken by the Oliver Cromwell were condemned in this Court as Lawfull prizes & if John Bigs Castriot is entitled to anything taken on these prizes it is by a contract made on land previous to the capture, and whether that contract has been complied with or not must be determined in the Courts of Common Law. Therefore I Dismiss the Lybell."

As to the use of prohibitions in the colonies, see Gilmore and Black, *The Law of Admiralty* 10 (1975) "It has long been part of received lore that [the admiralty] jurisdiction was not sliced away by writs of prohibition, the statutes under which these had issued not applying to the colonies. The truth seems to be much more complicated than this, and is only partly recoverable."

See, also, Charles M. Andrews, in Records of the Vice–Admiralty Court of Rhode Island 1716–1752, edited by Dorothy S. Towle.

> " * * * Prohibitions were available for a great variety of uses, and a thorough analysis of the circumstances under which they were issued and of the ends which they were designed to serve would go far to elucidate one very important aspect of the history of the common law in America.

> "The writ was made use of probably in all the colonies at one time or another, but we have no certain evidence of its exercise in Maryland, Virginia, and Antigua. Of the other colonies illustrations are few from Bermuda and Barbados. But in Massachusetts, Rhode Island, New York, Pennsylvania, and the two Carolinas, prohibitions were frequently employed, with Pennsylvania offering almost no instances after 1727, when occurred the case of the *Sarah* seized at Newcastle for illegal trading and that of the *Phoenix* in the same year. The conflict between the two jurisdictions reaches its highest point of belligerency in Massachusetts, as might have been expected, for there the enmity of the provincials for all royal officials and institutions was of long standing, and had been increased and deepened by the activities of Edward Randolph and the administration of Andros. There too the local common law courts had attained a position of great strength and assurance and, until the advent of the vice-admiralty court and its procedure under the civil law, had completely controlled the exercise of justice in the colony. Massachusetts fought long and hard for juries and the common law, and in no colony was the use of the writs so frequent or the complaints of the judges of vice-admiralty so bitter as in this old Puritan commonwealth."

Having established to his own satisfaction that the English statutes limiting the jurisdiction of the High Court of the Admiralty were no embarrassment to the free exercise of maritime jurisdiction in the colonial vice-admiralty courts, Mr. Justice Story proceeded to describe the true and immemorial jurisdiction of maritime courts as extending to all contracts the subject matter of which was maritime, and to torts and injuries taking place on waters within the ebb and flow of the tide.

In DeLovio v. Boit, another argument marshalled by Mr. Justice Story to demonstrate that torts committed on water *infra corpus comitatus* and *infra fauces terrae* were subject to the jurisdiction of the colonial and early state admiralty courts was the wording of the Judiciary Act of 1789, as follows:

> "Section 9. *And be it further enacted,* That the district courts * * * shall also have exclusive original cognizance of all civil causes of admiralty and maritime jurisdiction, including all seizures under laws of impost, navigation or trade of the United States, where the seizures are made, on waters which are navigable from the sea by vessels of ten or more tons burthen, within their respective districts as well as upon the high seas; saving to suitors, in all cases, the right of a common law remedy, where the common law is competent to give it; and shall also have exclusive original cognizance of all seizures on land, or other waters than as aforesaid, made, and of all suits for penalties incurred, under the laws of the United States. * * * And the trial of issues of fact, in the district courts, in all causes except civil causes of admiralty and maritime jurisdiction, shall be by jury."

Story argued that Congress had no power to extend the admiralty jurisdiction beyond the limit imposed by Article III, section 2, of the Constitution, and therefore the definition of admiralty and maritime jurisdiction to include seizures in navigable streams obviously within the body of some county negated any intention to be bound by the statutes of Richard II.

The Thomas Jefferson and The Steamboat Orleans

The question of locational jurisdiction of the admiralty court did not reach the Supreme Court until 1825, ten years after the decision in De Lovio v. Boit. In The Thomas Jefferson, 23 U.S. (10 Wheat.) 428, 6 L.Ed. 358, the libellant sought wages for services performed on a steamboat that was engaged in a voyage from Shippingport, Kentucky, up the Missouri River and back to that port. Perhaps with an eye to the argument in DeLovio v. Boit, the libellant placed some reliance on the ninth section of the Act of 1789, for the place at which the services were performed was navigable from the sea by vessels of ten tons burthen.

In a unanimous decision the Court held that the service, having been performed several hundred miles above the ebb and flow of the tide, was not maritime service, and therefore the admiralty court had no jurisdiction over a claim for wages. The argument on the Act of 1789 was brushed aside with the remark that this was a "statuteable provision, and limited to the cases there stated." Is this position reconcilable with the discussion of the Act of 1789 in DeLovio v. Boit? Is it possible that the term "cases of admiralty and maritime jurisdiction" could mean different things in the Constitution and in the Judiciary Act of 1789? Is it possible, for example, that Article III, section 2, of the Constitution permits trial of cases involving seizures under the revenue and trade laws in the admiralty court without a jury despite the fact that the seizures take place above the ebb and flow of the tide, while the same language in the Judiciary Act, modified as it is by the "including" clause, is limited to cases occurring within the ebb and flow of the tide except in the cases specified? The early cases on section 9 of the Judiciary Act are not very helpful. In the first of these cases, United States v. La Vengeance, 3 U.S. (3 Dall.) 297, 1 L.Ed. 610 (1796), the United States District Attorney had brought an information seeking the forfeiture of a vessel for illegal export of arms, allegedly from Sandy Hook, New Jersey, to Port de Paix in the West Indies. The district court ordered the vessel forfeit. This decision was reversed by the Circuit Court (Mr. Justice Chase) and the United States sued out a writ of error, assigning the "general errors." The cause was heard and the court declared its opinion affirming the Circuit Court. Then Charles Lee, the Attorney General of the United States, asked to be heard further on the subject of jurisdiction. It was his contention that either (1) the proceeding below was criminal in nature, or (2) civil but outside the admiralty jurisdiction. He did not argue the place of seizure, however, or jurisdiction over torts committed *infra corpus comitatus* on water, or the ebb and flow of the tide. It was his view, rather, that the offence named in the statute ("exporting from the United States") necessarily began on land and that under the old authorities when a thing was done partially on land and partially on water, the admiralty had no jurisdiction. The Court put the case over a day to hear this argument, but adhered to its original decision. Mr. Justice Marshall observed, "We are perfectly satisfied upon the two points that have been agitated in this cause. In the first place, we think, that it is a cause of admiralty and maritime jurisdiction. The exportation of arms and ammunition is, simply, the offence; and exportation is entirely a water transaction. It appears, indeed, on the face of the libel, to have commenced at Sandy Hook; which, certainly, must have been upon the water."

In The Schooner Sally, 6 U.S. (2 Cranch.) 406, 2 L.Ed. 320 (1805) the Court affirmed the forfeiture by the admiralty court of a vessel engaged in the slave trade. There was no argument and no opinion. Three years later, however, in United States v. The Betsey and Charlotte, 8 U.S. (4 Cranch.) 443, 2 L.Ed. 673 (1808) the question arose again. The seizure had taken place in Alexandria, Virginia, and the forfeiture was had for violation of an act of congress suspending commercial intercourse with certain portions of the Island of Santa Domingo. The case was argued for the claimant by Charles Lee. After the Court indicated that it took the case to be governed by *La Vengeance,* Lee stated, "I hope to show that this case is distinguishable from those; and to be permitted to argue at large the point of law, for this is not a case of admiralty jurisdiction. I argued the case of *The Vengeance,* and I know it was not so fully argued as it might have been; and some of the judges may recollect that it was a rather sudden decision." Mr. Justice Chase responded, "I recollect, that the argument was no great thing, but the court took time and considered the case well. The reason of the legislature for putting seizures of this kind on the admiralty side of the court was, the great danger to the revenue, if such cases should be left to the caprice of juries." Mr. Lee was permitted to make his argument, and from the outcome it may be inferred that, like his argument in *La Vengeance,* it was "no great thing." In an opinion of two short paragraphs Mr. Justice Marshall held that the case was governed by *La Vengeance.*

The Thomas Jefferson was the first case, then, to place squarely the question of admiralty jurisdiction above tide waters. It should be noted that the case was a libel for wages, that is to say, a case contractual in nature, illustrating, of course, that the locational aspects of jurisdiction have an effect on contract as well as tort cases. Thus in a contract case the question is not locality of creation, or of performance, but it is locality of the employment of the vessel.

The Thomas Jefferson was followed 12 years later by The Steamboat Orleans, 36 U.S. (11 Pet.) 175, 9 L.Ed. 677 (1837) in which this concept was worked out at greater length. The vessel was one employed in making trips from New Orleans north to inland cities on the Mississippi. Thus one terminus of at least some of her voyages was within tide waters. Mr. Justice Story observed, "But the case is not one of a steamboat engaged in maritime trade or navigation. Though, in her voyages, she may have touched, at one *terminus* of them, in tide-waters, her employment has been, substantially, on other waters * * *. The true test of [admiralty] jurisdiction in all cases of this sort is, whether the vessel be engaged, substantially, in maritime navigation, or in interior navigation and trade not on tide-waters. In the latter case there is no jurisdiction. So that, in this view, the district court had no jurisdiction over the steamboat involved * * * as she was wholly engaged in voyages on such interior waters."

Waring v. Clarke

Waring v. Clarke, 46 U.S. (5 How.) 441, 12 L.Ed. 226 (1847) was a case arising out of a collision between two steamboats on the Mississippi River. The collision took place about 90 miles north of New Orleans. One of the steamboats involved was on a voyage from Bayou Sarah to New Orleans, and the other was on a voyage from New Orleans to Bayou Sarah. Thus each vessel was involved in internal commerce rather than maritime or tide-water commerce, as that distinction was explained in The Steamboat Orleans. Thus jurisdiction could not be predicated upon the nature of the commerce involved. Conceding that the precise issue was before the Court for the first time, Mr. Justice Wayne, for the Court, took the position that *The Thomas Jefferson*, Peyroux v. Howard, and The Steamboat Orleans established the proposition that insofar as determined by locality, admiralty jurisdiction extended to waters affected by the tide. Since a case of tort was a case in which jurisdiction is to be determined by locality, the court found the jurisdiction proper. Mr. Justice Woodbury wrote an elaborate dissent in which he was joined by Mr. Justice Daniel and Mr. Justice Grier. Mr. Justice Catron confined his opinion to holding that jurisdiction was proper when the libel was brought *in rem* against the ship, for otherwise, he reasoned, there would be an hiatus and the right to proceed against the ship would be lost.

The Genesee Chief

The first departure from the ebb and flow of the tide as the locality test for admiralty jurisdiction took place in The Propeller Genesee Chief v. Fitzhugh, 53 U.S. (12 How.) 443, 13 L.Ed. 1058 (1851). In the decision in *The Thomas Jefferson* in 1825, Mr. Justice Story had observed that he saw no need to express an opinion on whether jurisdiction in admiralty could be extended to cover inland waters by statute framed as a regulation of commerce. In 1845, Congress had picked up this suggestion and enacted the following provision (Act of February 26, 1845, Chapter 20, 5 Stat. 726–727):

> "That the district courts of the United States shall have, possess, and exercise, the same jurisdiction in matters of contract and tort, arising in, upon, or concerning, steamboats and other vessels of twenty tons burden and upwards, enrolled and licensed for the coastal trade, and at the time employed in business of commerce and navigation between ports and places in different States and Territories upon the lakes and navigable waters connecting said lakes, as is now possessed and exercised by the said courts in cases of the like steamboats and other vessels employed in navigation and commerce upon the high seas, or tide waters, within the admiralty and maritime jurisdiction of the United States; and in all suits brought in such courts in all such matters of contract or tort, the remedies, and the forms of process, and the modes of proceeding, shall be the same as are or may be used by such courts in cases of admiralty and maritime jurisdiction; and the maritime law of the United States, so far as the same is or may be applicable thereto, shall constitute the rule of decision in such suits, in the same manner, and to the same extent, and with the same equities, as it now does in cases of admiralty and maritime jurisdiction; saving, however, to the parties the right of trial by jury of all facts put in issue in such suits, where either party shall require it; and saving also to the parties the right of a concurrent remedy at the common law, where it is competent to give it, and any concurrent remedy which may be given by the State laws, where such steamer or other vessel is employed in such business of commerce and navigation."

This Act was undoubtedly inspired by Mr. Justice Story's observation in The Thomas Jefferson, and it has been said that Story authored the bill. See discussion of the point in Mr. Justice Campbell's dissent in The Steamboat Magnolia, supra. In *The Genesee Chief* Chief Justice Taney held that the Congress did not intend to exercise its powers to regulate commerce, that in any event that clause of the Constitution could not support a jurisdiction broader than was conferred in Article III, and that the Act must fall unless the subject matter fell within the definition of "cases of admiralty and maritime jurisdiction." This led to a reappraisal of the doctrine that the jurisdiction was bounded by tide water. The following excerpt from the opinion gives the general basis of the Chief Justice's reasoning.

> "Now there is certainly nothing in the ebb and flow of the tide that makes the waters peculiarly suitable for admiralty jurisdiction, nor anything in the absence of a tide that renders it unfit. If it is a public navigable water, on which commerce is carried on between different States

or nations, the reason for the jurisdiction is precisely the same. And if a distinction is made on that account, it is merely arbitrary, without any foundation in reason; and, indeed, would seem to be inconsistent with it.

"In England, undoubtedly the writers upon the subject and the decisions in its courts of admiralty, always speak of the jurisdiction as confined to tide-water. And this definition in England was a sound and reasonable one, because there was no navigable stream in the country beyond the ebb and flow of the tide; nor any place where a port could be established to carry on trade with a foreign nation, and where vessels could enter and depart with cargoes. In England, therefore tide-water and navigable water are synonymous terms, and tide-water, with a few small and unimportant exceptions, meant nothing more than public rivers, as contradistinguished from private ones; and they took the ebb and flow of the tide as the test, because it was a convenient one, and more easily determined the character of the river. Hence the established doctrine in England, that the admiralty jurisdiction is confined to the ebb and flow of the tide. In other words, it is confined to public navigable waters."

Mr. Justice Taney went on to say that quite naturally we took over this definition of public navigable water because on the East coast the rivers were much the same as in England, not navigable above tide-water, and that gradually under the influence of precedents we lost sight of the thing defined (public navigable water) and fell into the error of holding that the admiralty was limited in its jurisdiction to tide-water.

Does this explanation for the evolution of the rule of The Thomas Jefferson put Chief Justice Taney's questionable geography pick-a-back on Mr. Justice Story's questionable history? Unless he had reference to navigability *from the sea,* there is no factual basis for the statement that English rivers were navigable only so far as the tide ebbed and flowed; vide the discussion in Hale's De Juris Maris of the Wey, Severn, Thames, and "divers others" (p. 3, supra).

There is some basis for the statement that in England "navigable" and "tidal" were used as synonymous. This usage did not derive from cases dealing with the jurisdiction of the High Court of the Admiralty, but, rather, from the law of riparian rights. Under the developed law, the soil under rivers "navigable" in this special sense belonged to the crown, and absent special grant or prescription, fishing rights belonged to the crown, and were therefore public. See the discussion in Ingram v. Threadgill, 14 N.C. (3 Dev.) 59 (1831). Does Chief Judge Taney put the proposition backward? Did the English courts use "tidal" to mean "navigable"? Or did they use "navigable" to mean "tidal"? Nor does it appear that this usage was thought to be a reflection of the want of navigability in fact above the tide. In Rex v. Smith [1685] 2 Doug. 441, the court shows that it was fully aware of most of the changes that could be rung on this theme, including the distinction between salt water and fresh water that rises and falls under pressure from the tide. See Peyroux v. Howard (The Planter) 32 U.S. (7 Pet.) 324, 8 L.Ed. 700 (1833).

Nor did the American courts drift into confusion between navigable water and tidal water because the rivers in the eastern United States, like those in England, were not navigable above the tide. The special English usage that equated "navigable" to "tidal" was well known to the American bar at the time of the decision of The Thomas Jefferson. The English rule had been rejected in some states. See, e.g., Carson v. Blazer, 2 Binn. 475 (1810). It was adopted in others. See, e.g., Adams v. Pease, 2 Conn. 481 (1818).

If Chief Justice Taney's attempt to tie the evolution of the American definition of admiralty and maritime jurisdiction to the English law deserves low marks, how important is such a tie? The jurisdictional line between the common law courts and the High Court of the Admiralty divided business between two of the same king's courts (albeit courts following different procedures and often administering different substantive rules). They were both national courts and the rules of decision in both were subject to the same legislative authority. In the United States, by contrast, Art. III, section 2 of the Constitution effected a distribution of the judicial power between central government and its constituent parts. Is it not reasonable to mark the line with an eye to the function of central government in regulating commerce among the several states?

Viewed in this perspective, is the mid-nineteenth century expansion of the American admiralty and maritime jurisdiction best explained by the following "trivia" from an entertaining and informative entry in the Encyclopaedia Britannica, "Mississippi River Steam Boat"? In 1814, there were hardly 20 steamboat arrivals in New Orleans; by 1834, the figure had reached 1,200. From 1810 to 1850 an estimated 4,000 persons had perished in steamboat disasters, and "classic accounts describe the drowning of scores, the hurling of bodies across banks * * * many lingered on, horribly burned, others were never found." A large proportion of the disasters could be traced to races on the river. Safety precautions were flouted, and engines pushed beyond capacity.

Nor was "steamboat fever" limited to the Mississippi. See, e.g., Ralston v. The Steamboat State Rights, 20 Fed.Cas. 201, Crabbe 22 (C.C.D.Pa.1836), in which it appeared that a large steamboat equipped with an icebreaker deliberately rammed a smaller, slower competitor operating on the Delaware River, prompting Judge Hopkinson to observe, "This company, for the very purpose of putting down the competition, if it could be so-called, which the Linnaeus had entered into with their large and superior boats, so excellent in their accommodations, speed, and general management, had an undoubted legal right to run the State Rights, or any other boat, at twelve cents, or at one cent, a passenger. Yet I cannot but believe that it would be more worthy of their high character and overwhelming strength to imitate the generosity of the Eagle who 'suffers little birds to sing,' rather than to pounce upon every unfortunate sparrow that might cross their path * * *"

CHAPTER 2

NAVIGABLE WATERS OF THE UNITED STATES

A. NAVIGABILITY IN FACT

"In quest of certainty, under this new doctrine, the inquiry is naturally suggested, what are navigable waters?" Mr. Justice Daniel dissenting in The Magnolia (p. 17, supra).

In 1851, when the Supreme Court adopted "navigable waters of the United States" as the locational test of admiralty and maritime jurisdiction, this term had appeared in the steamboat registration and inspection Act of 1838, 5 Stat. 130 ("in or upon the bays, lakes, rivers, or other navigable waters of the United States"). Since this Act dealt with the operation of steamboats carrying passengers and merchandise, its application could hardly have raised a question of navigability vel non, although the phrase "of the United States" was calculated to raise the issue of the interstate character of the waterway.

The Genesee Chief involved a collision on Lake Ontario, obviously a waterway navigable in interstate commerce. Fretz v. Bull, 53 U.S. (12 How.) 466, 13 L.Ed. 1068 (1851), arose out of a collision between two steamboats on the Mississippi River. The same was true of Walsh v. Rogers, 54 U.S. (13 How.) 283, 14 L.Ed. 147 (1852). In Ure v. Coffman, 60 U.S. (19 How.) 56, 15 L.Ed. 567 (1856), a steamboat ran down a flatboat (also on the Mississippi). In New York & Virginia S.S. Co. v. Calderwood, 60 U.S. (19 How.) 241, 15 L.Ed. 612 (1856), a steamboat ran down a schooner in the Elizabeth River at a location that would have satisfied the test of tidal waters. The Magnolia, as we have seen, involved a steamboat collision on the Alabama River, spoken of by Mr. Justice Grier as "navigable for ships and vessels of the largest class far above where its waters are affected by the tide."

In The Commerce, 66 U.S. (1 Black) 574, 17 L.Ed. 107 (1861), involving a collision on the Hudson River, it was made plain that the jurisdiction was governed by the use of the waters in interstate commerce, without regard to whether either or both vessels were themselves engaged in interstate commerce. In The Belfast, 74 U.S. (7 Wall.) 624, 19 L.Ed. 266 (1868), it was held that admiralty and maritime jurisdiction of contract claims depends upon the same "test by waters" applied in tort cases. The question of the fact of navigability in interstate commerce as a linchpin to admiralty and maritime jurisdiction did not arise in the Supreme Court until the decision in Ex parte Boyer, 109 U.S. 629, 3 S.Ct. 434, 27 L.Ed.

1056 (1884).   In a closely analogous case, however, it was held that on a river wholly within one state, in which navigation from the sea was made impossible by a series of dams, the state had the power to grant an exclusive license to operate steamboats on improved sections of the river above the dams.   Veazie v. Moor, 55 U.S. (14 How.) 568, 14 L.Ed. 545 (1852).   The decision in *Veazie* appears to be the only majority opinion Mr. Justice Daniel ever wrote on the subject of navigable waters.

In The Daniel Ball, 77 U.S. (10 Wall.) 557, 19 L.Ed. 999 (1870), the Supreme stated, "Those rivers must be regarded as public navigable rivers in law which are navigable in fact when they are used or are susceptible of being used, in their ordinary condition, as highways for commerce, over which trade or travel are or may be conducted in the customary modes of travel and trade on water.   And they constitute navigable waters of the United States within the meaning of the acts of Congress, in counterdistinction from the navigable waters of the States when they form in their ordinary condition by themselves, or by uniting with other waters, a continued highway over which commerce is or may be carried on with other states or foreign countries in the customary modes in which such commerce is conducted by water."

This definition has often been described as a definition of navigable waters for the purposes of admiralty and maritime jurisdiction.   It was so spoken of in Ex parte Boyer.   Yet it is quite clear that in The Daniel Ball no issue of navigability was discussed or decided.   The case was a libel to enforce the provisions of the steamboat inspection Act of 1838, as amended in 1852.   On the issue of the navigability of the water involved (the Grand River in Michigan) the Court had "no doubt."   Indeed, it could hardly be questioned.   From the conceded facts it appeared that the river was "capable of bearing a steamer of one hundred and twenty-three tons burden, laden with merchandise and passengers, as far as Grand Rapids, a distance of forty miles from its mouth in Lake Michigan.   And by its juncture with the lake it forms a continued highway for commerce, both with other States and foreign countries."   The more serious question agitated in The Daniel Ball was whether the transportation of passengers and cargo on an intrastate leg of an interstate trip constituted interstate commerce within the power of congressional regulation.

The Montello, also quoted in *Finneseth*, was, like The Daniel Ball, a libel to enforce the registration and inspection law.   As in the case of The Daniel Ball, there was no question at all about the current navigability of the Fox River, the water on which the subject steamboat operated.   The argument advanced in The Montello was that The Fox River was not navigable in its natural state and therefore it was not navigable water of the United States, and thus it was beyond the commerce power to impose the steamboat regulations on such as did not themselves operate in interstate commerce.   The Court, relying upon the definition given in The Daniel Ball, vide the phrase in that definition "in its ordinary condition," found it necessary to address the question of whether the river was navigable in its natural state.   Based on evidence of its historical use as a highway for interstate commerce, it determined that it had been and therefore still was "navigable water of the United States."

A decade after the decision in The Montello, in Ex parte Boyer, supra, the Supreme Court held that the admiralty jurisdiction extended to a collision occurring on an artificial canal forming a link in the interstate or international waters. Unless it be supposed that the power of Congress under the Commerce Clause is less broad than the admiralty jurisdiction, the decision in Ex parte Boyer rejected the supposition of The Montello that the commerce power extends only over such waters as were navigable in interstate commerce in their natural state.

In Economy Light & Power Co. v. United States, 256 U.S. 113, 41 S.Ct. 409, 65 L.Ed. 847 (1921), an action to enjoin the construction of a dam, brought under § 10 of the Rivers and Harbors Appropriation Act of 1899 (33 U.S.C.A. § 403), the Supreme Court, building in part on the decision in The Montello, held that under the Act of 1899 the power to regulate obstructions on navigable waters of the United States extends to waters navigable in their natural state, even though, because of artificial obstructions, they are no longer navigable. In United States v. Appalachian Electric Power Co., 311 U.S. 377, 61 S.Ct. 291, 85 L.Ed. 243 (1940), it was held that a stream is also navigable water, although not presently navigable in fact, if it can be made navigable through reasonable expenditure. The Court found support for this view in the phrase used in The Daniel Ball definition, "natural and ordinary condition," and further support in the statutory definition in the Federal Power Act, which read, "which either in their natural or improved condition" are used or suitable for use. See 16 U.S.C.A. § 796(8).

A composit definition of "navigable waters" read from statements made the the Court in The Daniel Ball, The Montello, Ex Parte Boyer, Economy Light & Power, and Appalachian Electric Power, would define navigable waters as waters that were navigable, are navigable, or might be made navigable, and was sometimes applied to determine the boundaries of admiralty and maritime jurisdiction under 28 U.S.C.A. § 1333. See, e.g., Loc–Wood Boat & Motors, Inc. v. Rockwell, 245 F.2d 306, 1957 A.M.C. 2085 (8th Cir.1957)(Lake of the Ozarks); Madole v. Johnson, 241 F.Supp. 379, 1965 A.M.C. 2610 (W.D.La.1965)(Lake Hamilton in Arkansas). The court in both these cases reasoned that the river that fed the lake was navigable water of the United States before the dam was constructed, and the dam was an artificial obstruction that, under the decisions in Economy Light & Power Co. did not destroy navigability.

In the case of natural lakes located wholly in one state and fed by streams themselves not navigable in interstate commerce, admiralty jurisdiction was denied, though the lake was traversed by a commercial ferry that carried cars some of which were on an interstate trip in which the lake was a link. Shogry v. Lewis, 225 F.Supp. 741 (W.D.Pa.1964).

The application of the property and regulation cases in the determination of jurisdiction was questioned in Dragon v. United States (The Lucky Lindy) 76 F.2d 561, 1935 A.M.C. 553 (5th Cir.1935); Doran v. Lee, 287

F.Supp. 807 (W.D.Pa.1968), and this was called "completely logical and valid." See Guinn, An Analysis of Navigable Waters of the United States, 18 Baylor L.Rev. 559, 568 (1966). Professor Guinn noted that at that time the Supreme Court had never adopted this view, though he read the cases as *interpreting* the definition more broadly in property and regulation cases than in jurisdiction cases.

In Kaiser Aetna v. United States, 444 U.S. 164, 100 S.Ct. 383, 62 L.Ed.2d 332 (1979), the Supreme Court recognized the contextual character of the term "navigable water" and indicated that the litmus for admiralty jurisdiction is present navigability in interstate commerce. It indicated that federal regulation under the Commerce Clause requires neither historical nor present navigability in interstate commerce, nor for that matter water at all. The immediate question posed in *Kaiser Aetna* involved an Hawaiian fish pond. This pond was adjacent to the ocean, but separated from it by a reef or bar over which water flowed at high tide. These "fishing ponds" were recognized as private property under Hawaiian law and could be bought, sold, or inherited. The subject "pond" was developed for residential purposes. A large marina was built and the reef or bar was cut to permit ingress and egress of boats. The United States Corps of Army Engineers took the position that the development constituted public navigable water of the United States and the proprietors could not exclude the public from entering the area or making a charge therefor. The Supreme Court held that the navigable servitude of the United States for the benefit of the public is limited to waters navigable in their natural state, and appropriation of public rights in waters that are private property and made navigable by expenditure of private funds and must be compensated. The Court indicated, however, that once joined to the ocean the water of the "pond" would be subject to the admiralty jurisdiction.

B.   PRESENT NAVIGABILITY IN FACT

Finneseth v. Carter

United States Court of Appeals, Sixth Circuit, 1983.
712 F.2d 1041, 1983 A.M.C. 2391, 1983 A.M.C. 2391.

■ CORNELIA G. KENNEDY, CIRCUIT JUDGE.

Appellant Finneseth appeals from a final order in this action seeking damages in connection with a boating accident dismissing her complaint insofar as it invoked the admiralty jurisdiction of the District Court under 28 U.S.C. § 1333(1); 46 U.S.C. § 740. The remainder of the complaint, predicated upon negligence and invoking the diversity jurisdiction of the District Court, remains before the District Court.

On April 10, 1979, two pleasure craft collided on Dale Hollow Lake killing appellant Finneseth's husband and son. Dale Hollow Lake lies in both Kentucky and Tennessee and was formed when the Army Corps of

Engineers constructed a dam on the Obey River. The former riverbed of the Obey River laid entirely in Tennessee. When the dam was erected, however, the reservoir created extended upstream beyond the confluence of the Obey and Wolf Rivers. The former riverbed of the Wolf River meandered back and forth across the Kentucky–Tennessee state line. The reservoir thus has boundaries in both states. The boating accident occurred somewhere above the former riverbed of the Wolf River. It is unclear whether the accident occurred in Kentucky or Tennessee. At present Dale Hollow Lake supports seven to eleven commercial marinas. The only maritime traffic which presently operates on the lake is in the form of pleasure craft. The pleasure craft may traverse the lake between Kentucky and Tennessee but cannot go downstream beyond the dam because the dam is without locks. An official report by the Army Corps of Engineers, made pursuant to its regulatory authority under the Rivers and Harbors Appropriation Act of 1899, 33 U.S.C. §§ 401 et seq., indicated that the Obey River was navigable and historically navigated by flatboats, barges, log rafts, loose floating logs and steam and gasoline powered boats carrying minerals, naval stores, agricultural staples and forest products. The report indicated that the Wolf River was also navigable and historically navigated by loose floating logs. The record indicates that in "its present condition the Obey River could support, during all seasons, commercial navigation of the ordinary type * * * on Dale Hollow Lake, which extend[s] from Mile 7.3 to Mile 58.2 on Obey River, Mile 10.0 on East Fork, Mile 6.0 on West Fork, and Mile 16.6 on Wolf River. Navigation on these streams is by recreational craft at present." App. 102, 113, Ex. A, "Determination of Navigability, Obey River and Tributaries."[1] There are presently no restrictions against the use of the lake by individuals exploring for petroleum deposits located near the lake. The possibility of ferry service across the lake between Kentucky and Tennessee was not addressed.

On appellee Carter's motion, the District Court dismissed the complaint to the extent it invoked the court's admiralty jurisdiction on the ground that Dale Hollow Lake was not "navigable" within the meaning of 28 U.S.C. § 1333(1) and 46 U.S.C. § 740. The District Court found the lake to be non-navigable because it is not currently being used as an artery of commerce. Appellant Finneseth appeals this determination.

In Kaiser Aetna v. United States, 444 U.S. 164, 100 S.Ct. 383, 62 L.Ed.2d 332 (1979), the Supreme Court indicated that the term "navigability," as used in past Supreme Court decisions, has been used to define four separate and distinct concepts: to delineate the boundaries of navigational servitudes; to define the scope of Congress' regulatory authority under the Interstate Commerce Clause; to determine the extent of authority of the Army Corps of Engineers under the Rivers and Harbors Appropriation Act

---

1. In order to have jurisdiction over both the Obey and Wolf Rivers, a necessary prerequisite to the Army Corps of Engineers construction of the dam, both rivers had to be determined navigable under the Rivers and Harbors Appropriation Act of 1899. 33 U.S.C. § 403. The requirement of navigability under that Act and navigability for admiralty jurisdiction are not the same. See discussion of Kaiser Aetna v. United States, 444 U.S. 164, 100 S.Ct. 383, 62 L.Ed.2d 332 (1979).

of 1899; and, to establish the limits of the jurisdiction of the federal courts conferred by Article III, § 2 of the United States Constitution over admiralty and maritime cases. Id. 171–72, 100 S.Ct. at 388.

In Executive Jet Aviation, Inc. v. City of Cleveland, 409 U.S. 249, 93 S.Ct. 493, 34 L.Ed.2d 454 (1972), the Supreme Court set forth the test for admiralty jurisdiction. Admiralty jurisdiction under 28 U.S.C. § 1333(1) and 46 U.S.C. § 740 exists if: (1) the alleged wrongful injury occurred upon navigable waters, and (2) the alleged acts or omissions of the defendants significantly relates to traditional maritime activity. Id. 249, 93 S.Ct. at 493. Accord, Foremost Insurance Co. v. Richardson, 457 U.S. 668, 673, 102 S.Ct. 2654, 2658, 73 L.Ed.2d 300 (1982). Both appellant Finneseth and appellee Carter agree that the second requirement in *Executive Jet* is met in this case because the collision on Dale Hollow Lake involved the operation of two pleasure craft which may constitute traditional maritime activity. *Foremost Insurance,* supra (collision of two pleasure craft on navigable waters squarely within admiralty jurisdiction). At issue, then, is whether the first requirement, whether the alleged wrongful acts of appellee Carter occurred upon "navigable waters," is met in this case.

In The Daniel Ball, 77 U.S. (10 Wall.) 557, 19 L.Ed. 999 (1871), the Supreme Court stated a definition of navigability for purposes of establishing admiralty jurisdiction.[2]

> Those rivers must be regarded as public navigable rivers in law which are *navigable in fact.* And they are navigable in fact when they are *used, or are susceptible of being used,* in their ordinary condition, as highways for commerce, over which trade and travel *are or may be conducted* in the *customary* modes of trade and travel on water. And they constitute navigable waters of the United States within the meaning of the acts of Congress, in contradistinction from the navigable waters of the States, when they form in their ordinary condition by themselves, or by uniting with other waters, a *continued highway over which commerce is or may be carried on with other States* or foreign countries in the customary modes in which such commerce is conducted by water (emphasis added).

---

2. *Executive Jet* only added a second requirement to the test for admiralty jurisdiction: it did not alter the test of "navigability" set forth by prior Supreme Court precedent in the admiralty context. In *Executive Jet,* the navigability of Lake Erie was assumed; in *Kaiser Aetna* the issue was a definition of navigability for purposes of imposing a navigational servitude on a Hawaiian fishpond; and in *Foremost Insurance* the navigability of the Amite River in Louisiana was assumed. Subsequent to *Executive Jet,* the Supreme Court has not had the occasion to address the issue of the definition of navigable waters for purposes of admiralty jurisdiction. Although dicta, in *Kaiser Aetna,* the Supreme Court indicated that navigable waters subject to admiralty jurisdiction were defined as including waters that were navigable in fact. *Kaiser Aetna,* supra, 172 n. 7, 100 S.Ct. at 389 n. 7, citing The Propeller Genesee Chief v. Fitzhugh, 53 U.S. (12 How.) 443, 13 L.Ed. 1058 (1852)(admiralty jurisdiction). The recent Supreme Court case of Director, Office of Workers' Compensation Programs, United States Department of Labor v. Perini North River Associates, 459 U.S. 297, 103 S.Ct. 634, 74 L.Ed.2d 465 (1983), addressed the issue of coverage under the Longshoremen's & Harbor Workers' Compensation Act for injuries sustained by workers on navigable waters of the United States. It is not probative of the issue on appeal.

Id. 563.   In The Montello, 87 U.S. (20 Wall.) 430, 22 L.Ed. 391 (1874), the Supreme Court again addressed the definition of navigability in the admiralty context and stated:

> [T]he true test of the navigability of a stream does not depend on the mode by which commerce *is, or may be,* conducted, nor the difficulties attending navigation.   * * * The *capability of use* by the public for purposes of transportation and commerce *affords the true criterion of the navigability of a river, rather than the extent and manner of that use.*   (emphasis added).

Id. 441.   Although The Daniel Ball defined "navigability in fact" as a water body's susceptibility for use as a highway of commerce in its ordinary condition, subsequent Supreme Court cases in the admiralty context have made it clear that an artificial water body is navigable in fact if it is used or susceptible for use as a highway of commerce.   Ex Parte Boyer, 109 U.S. 629, 3 S.Ct. 434, 27 L.Ed. 1056 (1884)(Illinois and Michigan Canal);   The Robert W. Parsons, 191 U.S. 17, 24 S.Ct. 8, 48 L.Ed. 73 (1903)(New York State Barge Canal);   Marine Transit Corp. v. Dreyfus, 284 U.S. 263, 52 S.Ct. 166, 76 L.Ed. 282 (1932)(New York State Barge Canal).   See also United States v. Appalachian Electric Power Co., 311 U.S. 377, 408–09, 61 S.Ct. 291, 299–300, 85 L.Ed. 243 (1940)(applicability of Federal Power Act of 1920 under the Commerce Clause).

The principles to be distilled from the above-mentioned Supreme Court cases are that an artificial water body, such as a man-made reservoir, is navigable in fact for purposes of conferring admiralty jurisdiction if it is used or capable or susceptible of being used as an interstate highway for commerce over which trade or travel is or may be conducted in the customary modes of travel on water.

In this case Dale Hollow Lake clearly meets the requirement that the lake be an *interstate* highway for commerce because it straddles Kentucky and Tennessee.   Because the interstate nexus is satisfied in this manner, it is not probative that maritime traffic on the lake is prevented from traveling downstream by the lockless dam.   Two cases cited by appellee Carter, Chapman v. United States, 575 F.2d 147 (7th Cir.)(en banc), cert. denied, 439 U.S. 893, 99 S.Ct. 251, 58 L.Ed.2d 239 (1978), and Adams v. Montana Power Co., 528 F.2d 437 (9th Cir.1975), are distinguishable from the case on appeal in that the reservoirs created by lockless dams were wholly within the confines of one state.   Thus, the threshold requirement that the water body be available as an interstate highway of commerce was not satisfied.

Dale Hollow Lake also meets the requirement that it be used or capable or susceptible of being used for any trade or travel that is or may be conducted in the customary modes of trade or travel on water.   Because of the liberal definition given to "customary modes of trade and travel on water,"[3] and the fact that Dale Hollow Lake is currently suitable for

---

3.   See, e.g., The Montello, 87 U.S. (20   Wall.) 430, 440–43, 22 L.Ed. 391 (1874)(Dur-   ham boats).

maritime traffic by large pleasure craft, there is no evidence before the Court which indicates that Dale Hollow Lake is not susceptible or capable of being used for transportation and commerce between Kentucky and Tennessee, whatever the modes may be. In fact, the only evidence before the District Court regarding the present capability or susceptibility of Dale Hollow Lake for commercial maritime traffic indicates that Dale Hollow Lake can support commercial navigation of the ordinary type during all seasons. App. 102, 113, Ex. A, "Determination of Navigability, Obey River and Tributaries." Fed.R.Civ.P. 50(a); Coffy v. Multi–County Narcotics Bureau, 600 F.2d 570, 579 (6th Cir.1979).[4] No Supreme Court case imposes the requirement that navigability only exists, for purposes of admiralty jurisdiction, if the lake or river is currently or presently being used as a highway for interstate commerce. This requirement has been imposed, however, by the Eighth Circuit, despite the contrary language of futurity, such as "susceptibility," "capability," and "may be" conducted or carried on, in early Supreme Court cases. Livingston v. United States, 627 F.2d 165 (8th Cir.1980).

In *Livingston,* the Eighth Circuit, relying upon *Chapman* and *Adams,* found a reservoir created by the damming of a river which straddled the states of Arkansas and Missouri to be non-navigable because commercial maritime activity ceased on the river which created the reservoir at the time the dam was constructed. The *Livingston* court held that navigability in admiralty is limited to describing a present capability of the water body to sustain commercial shipping and that admiralty jurisdiction turns on contemporary navigability in fact. *Livingston,* supra, 170. In *Livingston,* the court indicated that because extensions of admiralty jurisdiction have followed the opening of new waters to commercial shipping, it follows that the closing of waters to commercial shipping should likewise have the effect of eliminating admiralty jurisdiction over them. Id. 169.

Livingston appears to be erroneously decided to the extent that it requires contemporary, current or present commercial maritime activity as a prerequisite for navigability under the admiralty laws because the definition of "navigability in fact" as "susceptible of being used" in The Daniel Ball and the criterion of "capability for use" in The Montello specifically contradict this requirement. Accord, Sawczyk v. United States Coast

---

4. The report of the Army Corps of Engineers, made pursuant to its regulatory authority under the Rivers and Harbors Appropriation Act of 1899, 33 U.S.C. § 401 et seq., also provides evidence of the navigability of Dale Hollow Lake at the point of the Wolf River. We are mindful that the *Kaiser Aetna* Court was clear to point out that meeting the definition of navigability under one of the four uses of "navigability" was not dispositive of meeting each of the other definitions. Id. 444 U.S. 172–73, 100 S.Ct. at 388–89. Although determinations by the Army Corps of Engineers, the Coast Guard, or the courts, with respect to navigability under the Rivers and Harbors Appropriation Act of 1899 or the Commerce Clause, are not controlling in a navigability determination for admiralty jurisdiction, they are not without significance and may be taken into account by a court in determining whether a water body is navigable. See United States v. Oregon, 295 U.S. 1, 23–24, 55 S.Ct. 610, 619, 79 L.Ed. 1267 (1935); Sawczyk v. United States Coast Guard, 499 F.Supp. 1034, 1039 (W.D.N.Y.1980).

Guard, 499 F.Supp. 1034 (W.D.N.Y.1980)(lower rapids and whirlpool below Niagara Falls navigable).

The *Livingston* court relied upon the decisions of the Ninth and Seventh Circuits in *Adams* and *Chapman,* supra. This reliance failed to note that in both cases the courts relied not only on the fact that the waterbody was not currently used for commercial navigation but also that it was not susceptible of such use in its present state.

Adams involved a reservoir existing wholly in the state of Montana, created by the damming of a river which continued below the dam into the Mississippi. The Ninth Circuit held that the river above the lockless dam, which was no longer used for commercial maritime activity after the reservoir was established, was not navigable for purposes of admiralty jurisdiction, even though it would have been navigable under the Commerce Clause. The *Adams* court observed that, absent some present or *potential* commercial maritime activity, there was no justifiable federal interest for finding federal admiralty jurisdiction. *Adams,* supra, 439–40. It recognized that the test of navigability is whether the waterway "is used or *susceptible* of being used as an artery of commerce." (emphasis added) Id. 439. The *Adams* court confused, however, the two requirements of *Executive Jet,* merged them together and found that the operation of pleasure craft does not affect commercial maritime activity—a position which was squarely rejected by the Supreme Court in the recent case of *Foremost Insurance.* See *Adams,* supra, 439.

Chapman involved an accident on the Kankakee River in Illinois. Although the river continued into the Mississippi, at the point it was dammed it was wholly in the state of Illinois. No commercial maritime activity took place on the Kankakee River above the lockless dam after its erection in 1931. Since that time, the river has been solely used for recreational purposes. The *Chapman* court determined that it was unusable and held that a recreational boating accident does not give rise to a claim within the admiralty jurisdiction of the federal courts when it occurs on waters which are not in fact currently used for commercial maritime activity and are not susceptible of such use in their present state. *Chapman,* supra, 151. Thus, neither *Chapman* nor *Adams* mandates that there be present usage. Both permit consideration of whether the river or reservoir is susceptible of such use as well. In *Chapman,* there is also the implication that the Kankakee River is unusable for some reason pertaining to the physical characteristics of the water body itself, rather than the practical realities or economics of future commercial activity.

All three courts state that no federal interest is served by asserting admiralty jurisdiction where there is presently or currently no commercial maritime activity ongoing. In *Foremost Insurance,* the Supreme Court found admiralty jurisdiction where a complaint alleged a collision between two pleasure boats on navigable waters. The Court found no requirement that the maritime activity giving rise to admiralty jurisdiction be exclusively commercial. The *Foremost Insurance* Court based its decision on the breadth of the federal interest in protecting maritime commerce, stressing the need for uniform rules to govern conduct and liability, the potential impact on maritime commerce when two vessels collide on navigable waters, and the uncertainty that would necessarily accompany a jurisdictional test tied to the commercial or noncommercial use of a given boat. *Foremost Insurance,* supra, 457 U.S. 668, 674–75, 102 S.Ct. at 2658–59. Because of these same broad federal interests, there can be no requirement that commercial maritime activity be presently or currently engaged in on a particular water body before admiralty jurisdiction may attach where that water body is susceptible to or capable of being used as an interstate highway of commerce over which trade or travel may be conducted in the customary modes of travel upon water. The concern of the *Foremost Insurance* Court with the potential, rather than actual, impact on maritime commerce by pleasure craft suggests that federal interests in protecting maritime commerce extend to creating a climate conducive to commercial maritime activity on water bodies which are not presently or currently being used as interstate highways of commerce but are susceptible to or capable of such use.

Finding admiralty jurisdiction in a case, such as *Livingston* and the case on appeal, where the water bodies are potential interstate highways of commerce because they are susceptible to or capable of such use, serves the purpose of making uniform rules of conduct, including the navigational rules, "Rules of the Road," light requirements, etc., applicable to all interstate maritime traffic, whether commercial or pleasure. Having uniform rules in place is conducive to commercial maritime activity because commercial maritime activity could begin on such a water body, despite its prior absence or a hiatus in activity, without providing notice to the pleasure boating public of a change in rules and conduct. Conversely, pleasure boaters would operate under uniform rules of conduct and liability without regard to commercial caprice or economic whim. Otherwise, reservoirs such as Dale Hollow Lake, which are clearly interstate, would be subject to either federal or state rules of conduct and liability, which may differ radically from one another, depending on the coincidence of whether commercial maritime activity is currently or presently being engaged in at the time of any tortious occurrence. For example, if current or present commercial maritime activity is the test, a ferry could operate on Dale Hollow Lake between Kentucky and Tennessee one day and go out of business the next and tortious occurrences happening on each of the two days would be subject to different rules of conduct and liability. This addition or subtraction of commercial maritime traffic on Dale Hollow Lake would require that all pleasure boat operators suddenly change their rules of conduct and liability from federal to state or vice versa causing great uncertainty and confusion. In addition, interstate maritime activity is by definition not local. A scattering of states applying their own parochial rules of law could lead to inconsistent rules of conduct depending on a pleasure boater's precise location within the territorial jurisdiction of one state or another and inconsistent rules of liability depending on the location of a tortious occurrence. Uniform, stable and in-place rules of maritime conduct and liability would eliminate difficulties in determining which state's law applies in cases such as the one on appeal where the precise location of the accident is unknown.   They would preclude the possibility of inconsistent findings or the denial of jurisdiction or a cause of action in any state forum and eliminate the specter of parallel or conflicting rules attending interstate pleasure boaters who cross state lines.   All of these considerations support a federal interest in protecting interstate commerce by creating a climate conducive to commercial maritime activity where a water body is susceptible or capable of being used as an interstate highway of commerce.

Because Dale Hollow Lake is an interstate water body susceptible or capable of being used as an interstate highway of commerce, even though it is not presently so used, it meets the Supreme Court's requirements for navigability for admiralty jurisdiction under 28 U.S.C. § 1333(1) and 46 U.S.C. § 740.   Accordingly, the decision of the District Court is reversed and the case remanded for further proceedings consistent with this opinion.

NOTE

The geographical setting in which *Finneseth* arose, a lockless dam that creates a lake or reservoir above and leaves no navigable connection between the lake and the stream below, has become familiar.   See McCaughan, Federal Maritime Jurisdiction over Inland Intrastate Lakes, 26 Wash. & Lee L.Rev. 1 (1969).   Typically the lake above the dam has been developed for recreational boating and aquatic sports.   In *Finneseth,* the lake above the dam spanned the state line and the event out of which the litigation arose occurred on the lake.   In these circumstances, when the lake itself is capable of supporting interstate travel, the cases appear to be unanimous in holding that the location requirement for admiralty jurisdiction has been satisfied, despite the failure to show present commercial use. When the lake is located wholly within a single state and and there exists no route by which commerce could proceed between states without going over the dam, it has been held that the waters of the lake are not navigable waters of the United States.   Compare, in this respect Price v. Price, 929 F.2d 131 (4th Cir.1991) sustaining admiralty jurisdiction in a personal injury action arising out of an incident occurring on Buggs Island Lake, created by a dam on the Roanoke River and forming the boundary between Virginia and North Carolina, with Alford v. Appalachian Power Co., 951 F.2d 30 (4th Cir.1991), in which the court upheld dismissal of admiralty claims arising out of an accident occurring on Smith Mountain Lake, formed by a dam upstream on the same river at a point in which the lake lies wholly in Virginia.   The distinction can be very important to the litigants.   In Alford, the dismissal of maritime claims resulted in the application of the Virginia law, under which contributory negligence constituted a bar.

In Livingston v. United States, 627 F.2d 165, 1982 A.M.C. 1065 (8th Cir.1980), sharply criticized in *Finneseth,* the subject accident took place in the river below the dam.   The court found that when the generators of the dam were not running, the river could not be navigated without portages.   When the generators were running, the water was deeper, but actual navigation had been confined to small skiffs used for recreational fishing.   On these findings the court held that the plaintiff had not demonstrated navigability in fact.

The statement in *Finneseth* that the *Livingston* court "found a reservoir created by the damming of a river which straddled the states of Arkansas and

Missouri to be non-navigable because commercial activity ceased on the river which created the reservoir at the time the dam was constructed" is a misstatement, is it not? Does the *Finneseth* court read the Eighth Circuit test correctly when it suggests that it includes a requirement of "current or present commercial maritime activity"? See Edwards v. Hurtel, 717 F.2d 1204 (8th Cir.1983). See also Three Buoys Houseboat Vacations U.S.A. Ltd. v. Morts, 921 F.2d 775 (8th Cir.1990), holding the Lake of the Ozarks nonnavigable, overruling Loc-Wood Boat & Motors, Inc. v. Rockwell, 245 F.2d 306 (8th Cir.1957).

The location of the lake itself in a single state is not a guarantee that there is no admiralty jurisdiction, for while a lockless dam destroys navigability from the lake downstream, it may possibly create navigability upstream, and if the dam were to cause the water in a tributary stream to become navigable to commercial traffic across state lines, it might bring the lake into the admiralty jurisdiction upstream. See Lynch v. McFarland, 808 F.Supp. 559, 1994 A.M.C. 2407 (W.D.Ky.1992), in which it was held that limited canoe and raft traffic on the Big South Fork River from Tennessee into Kentucky did not render Lake Cumberland a highway of commerce. Cf. United States v. Harrell, 926 F.2d 1036 (11th Cir.1991).—Navigability of a tributary stream only during unusual and infrequent temporary flooding done not make a tributary stream subject to a navigational servitude. Would it support admiralty jurisdiction during these short periods?

In *Finneseth,* the court stresses potential use, as distinct from present use, for purposes of interstate commerce. Does it concede that there must be at least a potential use for the commercial transportation of cargo or passengers, as distinct from interstate movement of pleasure craft? How does one measure the potential? Is it to be measured by the depth and navigability alone, or is the commercial potential also to be taken into account? In *Livingston,* for example, is it significant that the court found that the river below the dam was about three miles long, running from the foot of the dam to its confluence with another stream, and that the United States owned the dam, and both banks of the river for its entire length?

In understanding the *Adams, Chapman, Livingston, Finneseth,* and *Edwards* cases, how important is their chronology in relation to the decisions of the Supreme Court in *Executive Jet, Kaiser Aetna,* and *Foremost Insurance?*

In Sisson v. Ruby, discussed in the following chapter, the Supreme Court defined the requirement of maritime nexus in tort cases as limiting the jurisdiction to the type of activity or event with a potential for disruption of maritime commerce. Does this definition support the argument that admiralty jurisdiction does not cover tort claims arising out of recreational boating accidents on waters on which there is in fact no such commerce? Or does the potential disruption of the potential commerce suffice?

Determining navigability

The holding of *The Daniel Ball* that those waters are navigable in law that are navigable in fact raises the fact-law distinction in the determination of jurisdiction. If navigability is a fact rather than a matter of law, it must be proved by competent evidence. See, e.g., United States v. Oregon, 295 U.S. 1, 55 S.Ct. 610, 79 L.Ed. 1267 (1935). There a special master was appointed to take evidence and heard, inter alia, testimony from witnesses in the area as to whether they had operated boats on the water in question or had seen others operating them. See Guinn, An Analysis of Navigable Waters of the United States, 18 Baylor L.Rev. 559. Who has the burden of proof? See Quick v. Hansen, 1975 A.M.C. 791 (9th Cir.1974); In re River Queen, 275 F.Supp. 403, 1968 A.M.C. 1374 (W.D.Ark.1967), aff'd 402 F.2d 977 (8th

Cir.1968), to the effect that the burden lies with the party asserting the existence of jurisdiction.   This is simply a statement of a general proposition that a party asserting jurisdiction has the burden of showing it if it is challenged, is it not? Notice that in Shogry v. Lewis affidavits were considered.   For an inconclusive discussion of the use of judicial notice to establish navigability, see Edwards v. Hurtel, 724 F.2d 689 (8th Cir.1984).   If the issue were to arise in an action in which jurisdiction depended upon the waters test, the question of a jury trial could not arise, since there is no right to a jury trial in an action cognizable only on the basis of the admiralty jurisdiction.   Note, however, that the Jones Act, extending the Federal Employers Liability Act to seamen (see Chapter 16, infra) gives a right to a jury trial.   Its application depends upon the navigability of the waters on which the vessel operates.   See, e.g., Oseredzuk v. Warner Co., 354 F.Supp. 453, 1972 A.M.C. 2007 (E.D.Pa.1972), aff'd 485 F.2d 680, 1974 A.M.C. 254 (3d Cir.1973).   In a Jones Act action would the plaintiff have a right to have the issue of navigability in fact put to a jury?   Notice that it has been held that the issue as to whether the plaintiff is a seaman (a member of the crew of a vessel), and the issue of whether the structure he worked on is a vessel, must go to the jury when this fact is contested.

If the action were one brought under the saving to suitors clause, and the issue were not jurisdiction under § 1333, but whether or not the court should apply state law or maritime law, would navigability be a jurisdictional fact, or an element of the cause of action, or a problem of choice of law?   If a jury were demanded, how would the issue be decided?

It has been held that the navigability of the waters on which a subject accident takes place can be established by estoppel.   In re Double D Dredging Co., 467 F.2d 468, 1972 A.M.C. 2377 (5th Cir.1972).   See Moore's Federal Practice, ¶ .200[3] (1976–77).

C.   REGULATION OF NAVIGABLE WATERS

Land & Lake Tours, Inc. v. Lewis

United States Court of Appeals, Eighth Circuit, 1984.
738 F.2d 961, cert. denied 469 U.S. 1038, 105 S.Ct. 517, 83 L.Ed.2d 406 (1984).

■ McMILLIAN, CIRCUIT JUDGE.

Drew Lewis,[1] Secretary of the Department of Transportation, and the United States Coast Guard appeal from a final order of the District Court for the Western District of Arkansas granting summary judgment in favor of Land & Lake Tours, Inc. (hereinafter L & L).   For reversal appellants argue that the district court erred in determining that the Coast Guard lacked jurisdiction to conduct safety inspections of L & L's amphibious vehicles operating on Lake Hamilton, Arkansas.   For the reasons discussed below, we reverse.

Since 1962 L & L has operated a business conducting sightseeing tours in Garland County, Arkansas.   L & L transports tourists in ten World War

---

1.   Elizabeth Dole became Secretary of   litigation began.
the Department of Transportation after this

II vintage amphibious vehicles called DUKWs, but commonly referred to as "ducks." These vehicles carry up to twenty-two passengers, who are shown a number of attractions in and around Hot Springs, Arkansas, and over the waters of Lake Hamilton. Between 1962 and 1976, the state regulated L & L's business.

In 1976 a representative of the Coast Guard informed L & L that the agency was assuming jurisdiction over the inspection of the "ducks" pursuant to 46 U.S.C. §§ 390(b), 390a (repealed 1983).[2] These statutes required the Coast Guard to conduct triennial safety inspections of the vehicles and set minimum federal specifications for passenger-carrying vessels. Although L & L attempted to comply, allegedly at great expense, the Coast Guard continued to cite L & L for safety violations and required certain modifications of the "ducks" before they could be operated on Lake Hamilton.

In 1982 L & L decided to challenge the Coast Guard's jurisdiction to regulate its business. L & L contended that it had operated for twenty years without incident under state regulation and was not financially able to comply with the Coast Guard's regulations. On cross-motions for summary judgment, the district court ruled in favor of L & L and enjoined appellants from any further regulation or inspection of the "ducks." The district court based its jurisdiction on 28 U.S.C. § 1333 (admiralty and maritime jurisdiction). Relying on Livingston v. United States, 627 F.2d 165 (8th Cir.1980), cert. denied, 450 U.S. 914, 101 S.Ct. 1354, 67 L.Ed.2d 338 (1981), the district court held that the Coast Guard lacked admiralty jurisdiction to regulate any vehicles operating on Lake Hamilton because Lake Hamilton was not "presently navigable in fact." Land & Lake Tours, Inc. v. Lewis, No. 82–6014 (W.D.Ark. Apr. 4, 1983). This appeal followed.

Appellants concede on appeal that no federal admiralty jurisdiction exists with respect to Lake Hamilton. Appellants argue, however, that Lake Hamilton is a navigable water of the United States for commerce clause purposes, and Congress' authority to require inspection of L & L's vehicles is premised on the commerce clause, U.S. Const. art. I, § 8, cl. 3, and does not involve the admiralty jurisdiction clause, U.S. Const. art. III,

---

2. 46 U.S.C. § 390a provided for the triennial inspection of passenger-carrying vessels and set forth the criteria for those inspections. Section 390(b) defined "passenger-carrying vessel" and stated that the term included "any domestic vessel operating on the navigable waters of the United States." These provisions were repealed by the Act of Aug. 26, 1983, Pub.L. 98–89, § 4(b), 97 Stat. 599, 604, 605. Section 4(b) of the Act provides that the repeal is effective "except for * * * proceedings that were begun, before the date of enactment of this Act and except as provided by section 2 of this Act." 46 U.S.C.A.App. § 4(b)(West Supp.1983). Section 2(d) of the Act states that "[a]n action taken or an offense committed under a law replaced by this Act is deemed to have been taken or committed under the corresponding provision of this Act." Id. § 2(d). 46 U.S.C. § 390a corresponds to 46 U.S.C.A. §§ 3301(8)(small passenger vessel), 3305 (West Supp.1983). 46 U.S.C. § 390(b), defining a passenger-carrying vessel, corresponds to 46 U.S.C.A. § 2101(21)(B)(passenger on a small passenger vessel), (35) (small passenger vessel)(West Supp.1983).

§ 2, cl. 1.[3]

In Kaiser Aetna v. United States, 444 U.S. 164, 174, 100 S.Ct. 383, 389–90, 62 L.Ed.2d 332 (1979)(emphasis added), the Supreme Court stated:

> [United States v.] Appalachian Power Co., [311 U.S. 377, 61 S.Ct. 291, 85 L.Ed. 243 (1940),] indicates that *congressional authority over the waters of this Nation does not depend on a stream's "navigability."* And, as demonstrated by this Court's decisions in NLRB v. Jones & Laughlin Steel Corp., 301 U.S. 1 [57 S.Ct. 615, 81 L.Ed. 893] (1937), United States v. Darby, 312 U.S. 100 [61 S.Ct. 451, 85 L.Ed. 609] (1941), and Wickard v. Filburn, 317 U.S. 111 [63 S.Ct. 82, 87 L.Ed. 122] (1942), a wide spectrum of economic activities "affect" interstate commerce and thus are susceptible of congressional regulation under the Commerce Clause *irrespective of whether navigation, or, indeed, water, is involved.* The cases that discuss Congress' paramount authority to regulate waters used in interstate commerce are consequently best understood when viewed in terms of more traditional Commerce Clause analysis than by reference to whether the stream in fact is capable of supporting navigation or may be characterized as "navigable water of the United States."

The Court cautioned that because the concept of navigability has been used for several purposes (for example, to define the scope of Congress' regulatory authority under the commerce clause and to delimit the admiralty and maritime jurisdiction of federal courts under art. III, § 2 of the Constitution), "any reliance upon judicial precedent must be predicated upon careful appraisal of the *purpose* for which the concept of 'navigability' was invoked in a particular case." Id. at 171, 100 S.Ct. at 388 (quoting with approval from the district court opinion, 408 F.Supp. 42, 49 (D.Hawai'i 1976)(emphasis in original)).

In the present case, the district court's reliance on *Livingston* was misplaced. *Livingston* involved a wrongful death action against the government based on the district court's admiralty jurisdiction as set forth in 28 U.S.C. § 1333. We held there that "the district court lacked admiralty jurisdiction because the accident occurred on waters that, though once used for commercial shipping, are no longer navigable in fact." 627 F.2d at 165. The case at bar did not involve the district court's article III admiralty jurisdiction, but instead Congress' article I power to regulate interstate commerce. As noted in Kaiser Aetna v. United States, 444 U.S. at 173–74, 100 S.Ct. at 389–90, Congress' article I power to regulate interstate commerce does not depend upon "navigability." Here, the federal government has an intense interest in the safety of passenger vessels, and the safety of passenger vessels has a substantial effect on interstate commerce.[4]

---

3. Because present navigability in fact is the linchpin of admiralty jurisdiction, the district court's finding that Lake Hamilton was currently non-navigable arguably ousted the court of jurisdiction under 28 U.S.C. § 1333. We find, however, that the issues before the district court raised federal questions involving Congress' power under the commerce clause, and jurisdiction therefore obtained under 28 U.S.C. § 1331.

4. The original laws [governing the inspection and certification of vessels] were directly related to the safety of the relatively new and potentially dangerous steam vessel. The demand for Federal remedial legislation began during the early 1800's after frequent

Undoubtedly Congress may require the inspection of passenger vessels, impose safety requirements, and "exercise its authority for such other reason as may seem to it in the interest of furthering navigation or commerce." Id. at 174, 100 S.Ct. at 390.

Thus, the vessel safety specifications and periodic safety inspection requirements represent an exercise of Congressional power under the commerce clause, which has been delegated to the Coast Guard. Although characterization of Lake Hamilton as "navigable waters of the United States" is not necessary to support Congressional authority to regulate vessel safety under the commerce clause after Kaiser Aetna v. United States, id. at 173–74, 100 S.Ct. at 389–90, we note that the term "passenger-carrying vessel" is in part defined in 46 U.S.C. § 390(b) (now repealed)[5] to include "any vessel operating on the navigable waters of the United States." In Adams v. Montana Power Co., 528 F.2d 437, 440 (9th Cir.1975)(citations omitted), a case decided before *Kaiser Aetna,* the court discussed the meaning of "navigable waters of the United States" in the context of commerce clause regulation:

> The commerce clause vests power in Congress to regulate all waters navigable in interstate or foreign commerce. In determining the scope of navigable waters for purposes of exercising the commerce power, the courts developed the doctrine that if a waterway was navigable in its natural and ordinary condition, it remained so despite subsequent obstruction.

Cf. Livingston v. United States, 627 F.2d 165, 169–70 (8th Cir.1980)(comparison of admiralty jurisdiction, which requires present navigability in fact for commercial shipping, with commerce clause jurisdiction, which requires historical navigability), cert. denied, 450 U.S. 914, 101 S.Ct. 1354, 67 L.Ed.2d 338 (1981). Lake Hamilton is part of the navigable waters of the United States because the part of the Ouachita River which was obstructed by dams to create Lake Hamilton was navigable in its natural and ordinary

---

and disastrous explosions of steam boilers on passenger vessels. This directly led to the first maritime safety laws in 1838 that required periodic inspection and certification of vessels engaged in the transportation of passengers and freight on the waters of the United States. This was followed by a more extensive steamboat inspection law in 1852. * * *

In 1864 the principal inspection and licensing provisions of the 1852 Act were made applicable to ferries, towing vessels, and canal boats. However, steamboat explosions continued with high loss of life and property. One of the greatest of all disasters, the destruction of the passenger vessel *Sultana* by explosion and fire with a loss of life estimated at more than 1,500 lives in April 1865, led to renewed legislation efforts. In 1871 this culminated with legislation that combined a number of new requirements into a coherent

and unified body of maritime safety laws. * * *

In the more than 100 years since then, as the public recognized the need for vessel safety legislation, primarily as the result of maritime disasters, other classes of vessels [than steam vessels] were subjected to Federal inspection or regulatory control. These included * * * all vessels carrying more than six passengers in 1956. * * *

H.R.Rep. No. 338, 98th Cong., 1st Sess. 136–37, reprinted in 1983 U.S.Code Cong. & Ad. News 948–49.

5. The definition of "small passenger vessel" in the 1983 Act does not include a reference to the "navigable waters of the United States." 46 U.S.C.A. § 2101(21)(B), (35)(West Supp.1983).

condition. See Madole v. Johnson, 241 F.Supp. 379, 382 (W.D.La.1965)(specific finding that the Ouachita River in its natural and ordinary state is or was capable of being used as a highway for commerce); see also Cooper v. United States, 489 F.Supp. 200, 203 (W.D.Mo.)(similar lake created by dam on river and located within one state; vessels operating on lake subject to vessel safety inspection and certification by Coast Guard), vacated on other grounds, 500 F.Supp. 191 (1980). Thus, the ducks operated on Lake Hamilton by L & L are vessels operating on the navigable waters of the United States and as such are subject to the Coast Guard's vessel safety specifications and periodic safety inspections.

Accordingly, the order of the district court is reversed.

NOTE

Since the statute enforced in Land & Lake Tours imposed safety standards and inspections on vessels carrying passengers, it was necessarily limited in its effect to waters navigable in the primitive sense. The issue, then, was whether it was applicable to vessels that operated upon interstate waters. Under today's conception of the commerce power, it is necessary only that the activity regulated, wet or dry, affect interstate commerce. Beyond that, the reach of regulations is to be determined by applying ordinary canons of statutory interpretation. In Land & Lake Tours, the statute in force at the time the plaintiff sought a declaration excluding his activity from its requirements, defined "passenger-carrying vessel" as including "any domestic vessel operating on the navigable waters of the United States." By the time the case reached the court of appeals, the statute had been repealed and a new statute enacted. The replacement statute deleted the language referring to "navigable waters of the United States." Does that leave the regulation applicable to waters navigable in interstate commerce neither currently nor historically? E.g., does it apply to the fish pond project in Kaiser–Aetna?

Section 10 of the Rivers and harbors Act of 1899, as amended, 46 U.S.C.A. § 403, interdicts "[t]he creation of any obstruction not affirmatively authorized by Congress , to the navigable capacity of any of the waters of the United States . . ." Generally this provision has been construed to enforce the "navigational servitude" of the United States in waters that are, or were, navigable in their natural state or with reasonable expenditure could be made so. The Act is enforced by the Army Corps of Engineers, and the building of structures in "any port, roadstead, haven, harbor, canal, navigable river, or other water of the United States" is prohibited without prior approval of the Corps. Section 10 has been held to adopt the definition of "navigable waters" derived from The Daniel Ball, The Montello, and Economy Light & Power. What are "reasonable improvements" in this context? Is it limited to improvements of the waterway itself, or does it embrace widening the waterway to include abutting dry land? See United Texas Transmission Co. v. United States Army Corps of Engineers, 7 F.3d 436 (5th Cir.1993), holding that the United States could, having issued a permit for a pipeline crossing navigable water could, under the terms of the permit, require the owner of the pipeline to pay for relocation of so much of the line as crossed the navigable water, when relocation was necessary to accommodate a flood control project, but could not require payment for such portions of the line as were above the high water mark of the water and had been located on easements acquired from the owners of abutting dry land. The Court of Appeals rejected as "bootstrap"the argument that widening the body of water to include such land would bring it within the definition of "navigable waters" for purposes of allocating the cost of relocation.

The Federal Power Act, like the Rivers & Harbors Act, is aimed at protecting interstate commerce by preventing the destruction of navigability of bodies of water which could form avenues of interstate commerce and travel, and has been construed to embody the same definition. See State ex rel. N.Y. State Dept. of Environmental Conservation v. FERC, 954 F.2d 56 (2d Cir.1992), in which the court of appeals held that navigability was established by a showing that logs were floated downstream, even in the absence of a showing that any were ever floated over the falls, and reversed a holding by FERC that a license was not required for construction of power houses. But some potential for interstate travel must be shown. See Sierra Pacific Power Co. v. FERC, 681 F.2d 1134 (9th Cir.1982), holding that the Truckee River, which runs from Lake Tahoe in California to Pyramid Lake in Nevada is not navigable water of the United States, based on the finding that the river is navigable in portions in California, and also in portions in Nevada, but never was and is not now, and could not with reasonable expenditure be made, navigable in the portion that crosses the state line. See also Minnehaha Creek Watershed Dist. v. Hoffman, 597 F.2d 617 (8th Cir.1979).

Particular waters have sometimes been excluded from the definition of "navigable waters." See e.g., 33 U.S.C.A. § 47 ("Eagle Lake, which lies partly within the limits of the State of Mississippi, in Warren County, and partly within the limits of the State of Louisiana, in Madison Parish, is declared to be a nonnavigable stream for the purpose of the Constitution and laws of the United States. The right to alter, amend, or repeal this section is expressly reserved."). Others have been more limited. See 33 U.S.C.A. § 37 ("Nodaway River, in the counties of Andrew, Holt, and Nodaway, in the State of Missouri, is declared to be not a navigable water of the United States within the meaning of the laws for the preservation and protection of such waters. The right to alter, amend, or repeal is expressly reserved."). And see sec. 591 ("The prohibitions and provisions for review and approval concerning wharves and piers in waters of the United States as set forth in sec. 403 and 565 of this title shall not apply to any body of water located entirely within one State which is, or could be, considered to be a navigable body of water of the United States solely on the basis of historical use in interstate commerce.").

The problem that is dealt with in the environmental statutes differs from that at which the Rivers and Harbors Act and the Federal Power Act are aimed, for the effects of pollution do not depend upon "navigability in fact," let alone historical navigability. The distinction is not, however, easy to frame. The Clean Water Act applies to "navigable waters" but defines "navigable waters" as "waters of the United States." This definition has been amplified by regulations to include a variety of wetlands adjacent to navigable and this extension was upheld in United States v. Riverside Bayview Homes, Inc., 474 U.S. 121, 106 S.Ct. 455, 88 L.Ed.2d 419 (1985). When wetlands that are not adjacent to waters navigable in interstate commerce constitute "waters of the United States" is not altogether clear. *Kaiser–Aetna* makes indicates that the power of Congress to regulate the use of wetlands does not turn upon navigability, but upon conventional analysis of the exercise of powers under the Commerce Clause. Therefore if draining or filling wet lands affects interstate commerce, that is sufficient. See Leslie Salt Co. v. United States, 896 F.2d 354 (9th Cir.1990), cert. denied 498 U.S. 1126, 111 S.Ct. 1089, 112 L.Ed.2d 1194 (1991), holding that jurisdiction under the Act could rest on the basis that the waters may provide a habitat for migratory birds. See also Tabb Lakes, Ltd. v. United States, 10 F.3d 796 (Fed.Cir.1993), discussing the question without deciding it.

CHAPTER 3

LOCALITY AND SUBJECT MATTER IN DETERMINING JURISDICTION

A. JURISDICTION IN CONTRACT

New England Mutual Marine Ins. Co. v. Dunham

Supreme Court of the United States, 1870.
78 U.S. (11 Wall.) 1, 20 L.Ed. 90.

■ MR. JUSTICE BRADLEY delivered the opinion of the court.

* * *

The case, as thus brought before us, presents the question, whether the District Court for the District of Massachusetts, sitting in admiralty, has jurisdiction to entertain a libel *in personam* on a policy of marine insurance to recover for a loss.

This precise question has never been decided by this court. But, in our view, several decisions have been made which determine the principle on which the case depends. The general jurisdiction of the District Courts in admiralty and maritime cases has been heretofore so fully discussed that it is only necessary to refer to them very briefly on this occasion.

The Constitution declares that the judicial power of the United States shall extend "to all cases of admiralty and maritime jurisdiction," without defining the limits of that jurisdiction. Congress, by the Judiciary Act passed at its first session, 24th of September, 1789, established the District Courts, and conferred upon them, among other things, "exclusive original cognizance of all civil cases of admiralty and maritime jurisdiction."

As far as regards civil cases, therefore, the jurisdiction of these courts was thus made coextensive with the constitutional gift of judicial power on this subject.

Much controversy has arisen with regard to the extent of this jurisdiction. It is well known that in England great jealousy of the admiralty was long exhibited by the courts of common law.

The admiralty courts were originally established in that and other maritime countries of Europe for the protection of commerce and the administration of that venerable law of the sea which reaches back to sources long anterior even to those of the civil law itself; which Lord Mansfield says is not the law of any particular country, but the general law of nations; and which is founded on the broadest principles of equity and justice, deriving, however, much of its completeness and symmetry, as well as its modes of proceeding, from the civil law, and embracing, altogether, a system of regulations embodied and matured by the combined efforts of the most enlightened commercial nations of the world. Its system of procedure has been established for ages, and is essentially founded, as we have said, on the civil law; and this is probably one reason why so much hostility was exhibited against the admiralty by the courts of common law, and why its jurisdiction was so much more crippled and restricted in England than in any other state. In all other countries bordering on the Mediterranean or the Atlantic the marine courts, whether under the name of admiralty courts or otherwise, are generally invested with jurisdiction of all matters arising in marine commerce, as well as other marine matters of public concern, such as crimes committed on the sea, captures, and even naval affairs. But in England, partly under strained constructions of parliamentary enactments and partly from assumptions of public policy, the common law courts succeeded in establishing the general rule that the jurisdiction of the admiralty was confined to the *high* seas and entirely excluded from transactions arising on waters within the body of a county, such as rivers, inlets, and arms of the sea as far out as the naked eye could discern objects from shore to shore, as well as from transactions arising on the land, though relating to marine affairs.

In England = locality test

With respect to contracts, this criterion of locality was carried so far that, with the exception of the cases of seamen's wages and bottomry bonds, no contract was allowed to be prosecuted in the admiralty unless it was made upon the sea, and was to be executed upon the sea; and even then it must not be under seal.

Of course, under such a construction of the admiralty jurisdiction, a policy of insurance executed on land would be excluded from it.

But this narrow view has not prevailed here. This court has frequently declared and decided that the admiralty and maritime jurisdiction of the United States is not limited either by the restraining statutes or the judicial prohibitions of England, but is to be interpreted by a more enlarged view of its essential nature and objects, and with reference to analogous jurisdictions in other countries constituting the maritime commercial world, as well as to that of England. "Its boundary," says Chief Justice Taney,[1] "is to be ascertained by a reasonable and just construction of the words used in the Constitution, taken in connection with the whole instrument, and the purposes for which admiralty and maritime jurisdiction was granted to the Federal government." "Courts of admiralty," says the same judge in another case,[2] "have been found necessary in all commercial countries, not only for the safety and convenience of commerce, and the speedy decision of controversies where delay would often be ruin, but also to administer the laws of nations in a season of war, and to determine the validity of captures and questions of prize or no prize in a

---

1. The Steamer St. Lawrence, 1 Black, 527.

2. The Genesee Chief, 12 Howard, 454 (1851).

judicial proceeding. And it would be contrary to the first principles on which the Union was formed to confine these rights to the States bordering on the Atlantic, and to the tide-water rivers connected with it, and to deny them to the citizens who border on the lakes and the great navigable streams which flow through the Western States.''

In accordance with this more enlarged view of the subject, several results have been arrived at widely differing from the long-established rules of the English courts.

First, as to the *locus* or territory of maritime jurisdiction; that is, the place or territory *where* the law maritime prevails, where torts must be committed, and where business must be transacted, in order to be maritime in their character; a long train of decisions has settled that it extends not only to the main sea, but to all the navigable waters of the United States, or bordering on the same, whether land-locked or open, salt or fresh, tide or no tide.

* * *

Secondly, as to *contracts,* it has been equally well settled that the English rule which concedes jurisdiction, with a few exceptions, only to contracts made upon the sea and to be executed thereon (making *locality* the test) is entirely inadmissible, and that the true criterion is the nature and subject-matter of the contract, as whether it was a maritime contract, having reference to maritime service or maritime transactions.

* * *

In this court, in the case of The New Jersey Navigation Company v. Merchants' Bank,[3] which was a libel *in personam* against the company on a contract of affreightment to recover for the loss of specie by the burning of the steamer Lexington on Long Island Sound, Justice Nelson, delivering the opinion of the court, says:[4] "If the cause is a maritime cause, subject to admiralty cognizance, jurisdiction is complete over the person as well as over the ship. * * * On looking into the several cases in admiralty which have come before this court, and in which its jurisdiction was involved, it will be found that the inquiry has been, not into the jurisdiction of the court of admiralty in England, but into the nature and subject-matter of the contract, whether it was a maritime contract, and the service a maritime service, to be performed upon the sea or upon waters within the ebb and flow of the tide." [The last distinction based on tide, as we have seen, has since been abrogated.] Jurisdiction in that case was sustained by this court, as it had previously been in cases of suits by ship-carpenters and materialmen on contracts for repairs, materials, and supplies, and by pilots for pilotage: in none of which would it have been allowed to the admiralty courts in England.[5] In the subsequent case of Morewood v. Enequist,[6] decided in 1859, which was a case of charter-party and affreightment,

3. 6 Howard, 344 (1848).

4. Ib. 392.

5. See cases cited by Justice Nelson, 6 Howard, 390, 391 (1848).

6. 23 Howard, 493 (1859).

Justice Grier, who had dissented in the case of The Lexington, but who seems to have changed his views on the whole subject, delivered the opinion of the court, and, amongst other things, said: "Counsel have expended much learning and ingenuity in an attempt to demonstrate that a court of admiralty in this country, like those of England, has no jurisdiction over contracts of charter-party or affreightment. They do not seem to deny that these are maritime contracts, according to any correct definition of the terms, but rather require us to abandon our whole course of decision on this subject and return to the fluctuating decisions of English common law judges, which, it has been truly said, 'are founded on no uniform principle, and exhibit illiberal jealousy and narrow prejudice.'" He adds that the court did not feel disposed to be again drawn into the discussion; that the subject had been thoroughly investigated in the case of The Lexington, and that they had then decided "that charter-parties and contracts of affreightment were 'maritime contracts,' within the true meaning and construction of the Constitution and act of Congress, and cognizable in courts of admiralty by process either *in rem* or *in personam.*" The case of The People's Ferry Co. v. Beers,[7] being pressed upon the court, in which it had been adjudged that a contract for building a vessel was not within the admiralty jurisdiction, being a contract *made* on land and to be *performed* on land, Justice Grier remarked: "The court decided in that case that a contract to build a ship is *not a maritime contract;* " but he intimated that the opinion in that case must be construed in connection with the precise question before the court; in other words, that the effect of that decision was not to be extended by implication to other cases.

In the case of *The Moses Taylor,*[8] it was decided that a contract to carry passengers by sea as well as a contract to carry goods, was a maritime contract and cognizable in admiralty, although a small part of the transportation was by land, the principal portion being by water. In a late case of affreightment, that of The Belfast,[9] it was contended that admiralty jurisdiction did not attach, because the goods were to be transported only from one port to another in the same State, and were not the subject of interstate commerce. But as the transportation was on a navigable river, the court decided in favor of the jurisdiction, because it was a maritime transaction. Justice Clifford, delivering the opinion of the court, says:[10] "Contracts, claims, or service, purely maritime, and touching rights and duties appertaining to commerce and navigation, are cognizable in the admiralty courts. Torts or injuries committed on navigable waters, of a civil nature, are also cognizable in the admiralty courts. Jurisdiction in the former case depends upon the nature of the contract, but in the latter it depends entirely upon the locality."

It thus appears that in each case the decision of the court and the reasoning on which it was founded have been based upon the fundamental inquiry whether the contract was or was not a *maritime contract.* If it was,

7. 20 Ib. 401.

8. 4 Wallace, 411 (1866).

9. 7 Wallace, 624 (1868).

10. 7 Ib. 637.

the jurisdiction was asserted; if it was not, the jurisdiction was denied. And whether maritime or not maritime depended, not on the place where the contract was made, but on the *subject-matter* of the contract. If that was maritime the contract was maritime. This may be regarded as the established doctrine of the court.

* * *

It only remains, then, to inquire whether the contract of marine insurance, as set forth in the present case, is or is not a maritime contract.

It is objected that it is not a maritime contract because it is made on the land and is to be performed (by payment of the loss) on the land, and is, therefore, entirely a common law transaction. This objection would equally apply to bottomry and respondentia loans, which are also usually made on the land and are to be paid on the land. But in both cases payment is made to depend on a maritime risk; in the one case upon the loss of the ship or goods, and in the other upon their safe arrival at their destination. So the contract of affreightment is also made on land, and is to be performed on the land by the delivery of the goods and payment of the freight. It is true that in the latter case a maritime service is to be performed in the transportation of the goods. But if we carefully analyze the contract of insurance we shall find that, in effect, it is a contract, or guaranty, on the part of the insurer, that the ship or goods shall pass safely over the sea, and through its storms and its many casualties, to the port of its destination; and if they do not pass safely, but meet with disaster from any of the misadventures insured against, the insurer will pay the loss sustained. So in the contract of affreightment, the master guarantees that the goods shall be safely transported (dangers of the seas excepted) from the port of shipment to the port of delivery, and there delivered. The contract of the one guarantees against loss from the dangers of the sea, the contract of the other against loss from all other dangers. Of course these contracts do not always run precisely parallel to each other, as now stated; special terms are inserted in each at the option of the parties. But this statement shows the general nature of the two contracts. And how a fair mind can discern any substantial distinction between them on the question whether they are or are not, maritime contracts, is difficult to imagine. The object of the two contracts is, in the one case, maritime service, and in the other maritime casualties.

And then the contract of insurance, and the rights of the parties arising therefrom, are affected by and mixed up with all the questions that can arise in maritime commerce,—jettison, abandonment, average, salvage, capture, prize, bottomry, & c.

Perhaps the best criterion of the maritime character of a contract is the system of law from which it arises and by which it is governed. And it is well known that the contract of insurance sprang from the law maritime, and derives all its material rules and incidents therefrom. It was unknown to the common law; and the common law remedies, when applied to it, were so inadequate and clumsy that disputes arising out of the contract were generally left to arbitration, until the year A.D. 1601, when the statute of 43 Elizabeth was passed creating a special court, or commission, for hearing and determining causes arising on policies of insurance.

* * *

Suffice it to say, that in every maritime code of Europe, unless England is excepted, marine insurance constitutes one of the principal heads. It is treated in nearly every one of those collected by Pardessus, except the more ancient ones, which were compiled before the contract had assumed its place in written law. It is, in fact, a part of the general maritime law of the world; slightly modified, it is true, in each country, according to the circumstances or genius of the people. Can stronger proof be presented that the contract is a maritime contract?

But an additional argument is found in the fact that in all other countries, except England, even in Scotland, suits and controversies arising upon the contract of marine insurance are within the jurisdiction of the admiralty or other marine courts.[11] The French Ordinance of 1681 touching the Marine, in enumerating the cases subject to the jurisdiction of the judges of admiralty, expressly mentions those arising upon policies of assurance, and concludes with this broad language: "And generally all contracts concerning the commerce of the sea."[12] The Italian writer, Roccus, says: "These subjects of insurance and disputes relative to ships are to be decided according to maritime law, and the usages and customs of the sea are to be respected. The proceedings are to be according to the forms of maritime courts and the rules and principles laid down in the book called 'The Consulate of the Sea,' printed at Barcelona in the year 1592."[13]

It is also clear that, originally, the English admiralty had jurisdiction of this as well as of other maritime contracts. It is expressly included in the commissions of the Admiral.[14] Dr. Browne says: "The cognizance of policies of insurance was of old claimed by the Court of Admiralty, in which they had the great advantage attending all their proceedings as to the examination of witnesses beyond the seas or speedily going out of the kingdom."[15] But the intolerance of the common law courts prohibited the exercise of it. In the early case of Crane v. Bell, 38 Hen. VIII, A.D. 1546, a prohibition was granted for this purpose.[16] Mr. Browne says, very pertinently: "What is the *rationale,* and what the true principle which ought to govern this question, viz.: What contracts should be cognizable in admiralty? Is it not this? All contracts which relate purely to maritime affairs, the natural, short, and easy method of enforcing which is found in the admiralty proceedings."[17]

11. See Benedict's Admiralty, § 294, ed. 1870.

12. Sea Laws, 256.

13. Roccus on Insurance, note 80.

14. Benedict, § 48.

15. 2 Browne's Civil and Admiralty Law, 82.

16. See 4 Institutes, 139.

17. 2 Civil and Admiralty Law, 88.

Another consideration bearing directly on this question is the fact that the commissions in admiralty issued to our colonial governors and admiralty judges, prior to the Revolution, which may be fairly supposed to have been in the minds of the Convention which framed the Constitution, contained either express jurisdiction over policies of insurance or such general jurisdiction over maritime contracts as to embrace them.[18]

The discussions that have taken place in the District and Circuit Courts of the United States have not been adverted to. Many of them are characterized by much learning and research. The learned and exhaustive opinion of Justice Story, in the case of De Lovio v. Boit,[19] affirming the admiralty jurisdiction over policies of marine insurance, has never been answered, and will always stand as a monument of his great erudition. That case was decided in 1815. It has been followed in several other cases in the first circuit.[20] In 1842 Justice Story, in reaffirming his first judgment, says that he had reason to believe that Chief Justice Marshall and Justice Washington were prepared to maintain the jurisdiction. What the opinion of the other judges was he did not know.[21] Doubts as to the jurisdiction have occasionally been expressed by other judges. But we are of opinion that the conclusion of Justice Story was correct.

The answer of the court, therefore, to the question propounded by the Circuit Court will be, that the District Court for the District of Massachusetts, sitting in admiralty, has jurisdiction to entertain the libel in this case.

Answer accordingly.

Sirius Ins. Co. (UK) Ltd. v. Collins

United States Court of Appeals, Second Circuit, 1994.
16 F.3d 34, 1994 A.M.C. 1683.

■ LEVAL, CIRCUIT JUDGE:

The insured owner of a stolen pleasure boat appeals from a declaratory judgment entered after bench trial in the United States District Court for the Eastern District of New York (Leonard D. Wexler, Judge) holding that the plaintiff-insurers are not liable on the theft protection clause of a policy of vessel insurance, by reason of the insured's breach of condition of coverage. Appellant contends first, that the action was not within the admiralty jurisdiction of the United States Courts under 28 U.S.C. sec. 1333, and, second, that the ambiguity in the policy required that it be construed in the insured's favor.

Background

Plaintiff-insurers issued a Certificate of Insurance for one year beginning May 18, 1991, under the High Performance Marine Program to defendant

---

18. Benedict, chap. ix.

19. 2 Gallison, 398.

20. Gloucester Insurance Co. v. Younger, 2 Curtis, 332–333.

21. Hale v. Washington Insurance Co., 2 Story 183 (1842).

Collins covering his vessel, a 1988 37' Midnight Express 37 Sport (and trailer). The policy included a "theft warranty" relating to periods of out-of-water storage that conditioned coverage upon certain precautions to be taken by the insured, as well as on the theft occurring in specified fashion. This provision read as follows:

> THEFT WARRANT: It is hereby understood and agreed and warranted that:
>
> While the insured boat is stored on a trailer it shall be:
>
> 1. Kept in locked fences [sic.] enclosure, garage, or building.
>
> 2. Secured with a trailer ball lock while attached to a vehicle.
>
> It is understood and agreed that this certificate does not cover loss or damage caused by theft of the insured boat(s), and/or equipment, while stored on a trailer unless occasioned by persons or persons making:
>
> 1. Entry to the locked fenced enclosure, garage or building, or
>
> 2. Destruction of the ball lock.
>
> Provided the above is accompanied by actual force and violence of which there shall be visible marks made by tools, explosives, electricity, or chemicals.

On or around January 5, 1992, Collins, according to the testimony, loaded the boat onto the insured trailer, removed it from the water for winter storage, and towed it to his parents' home in West Islip, New York. He parked his truck and the trailered boat, attached with a ball lock, on the circular driveway at the front of his parents, home, planning, according to the district court's findings of fact, to leave it there "for an indefinite period of time." He fastened a chain between two posts located at one outlet of the driveway before leaving; the other outlet remained open. The following day the truck, trailer and boat were missing from the driveway. According to Collins, the chain across the driveway had been broken.

The district court held that the theft warranty required the defendant to place the boat, while stored on a trailer, in a locked fenced enclosure, and that the defendant had failed to do so in breach of the warranty. Judgment was accordingly awarded to the insurers.

Discussion

Collins contends that because the theft occurred ashore, litigation under the policy is not within the specialized exclusive maritime jurisdiction conferred on federal courts by 28 U.S.C. sec. 1333. He relies primarily on Atlantic Mut. Ins. v. Balfour Maclaine Int'l, Ltd., 968 F.2d 196 (2d.Cir.1992), and Lewis Charters, Inc. v. Huckins Yacht Corp., 871 F.2d 1046 (11th Cir.1989) which we discuss below. We disagree with Collins' contentions and hold that this is a maritime claim properly lodged in our admiralty jurisdiction.

The Supreme Court explained in 1871 that, in determining whether admiralty jurisdiction applies to a *contract* dispute, "the fundamental inquiry [has been] whether the contract was or was not a *maritime contract.* . . . and whether maritime or not maritime depended on the *subject matter* of the contract.   If that was maritime the contract was maritime."   Insurance Co. v. Dunham, 78 U.S. (11 Wall.) 1, 29, 20, 20 L.Ed. 90 l.Ed. 90 (1871).   It has been long settled that the maritime jurisdiction applies to "all contracts ... which relate to the navigation, business, or commerce of the sea," *Atlantic Mutual*, quoting from De Lovio v. Boit, 7 F.Cas. 418, 444 (C.C.D.Mass 1815)(No. 3,776)(Story, J.).   Although it was once disputed whether marine insurance contracts were maritime, in view of the fact that they were made and performed ashore, see *Dunham*, 78 U.S. (11 Wall.) at 30, it has long been settled that because their subject is maritime, they fall within the admiralty jurisdiction.   See id. at 30–35, citing De Lovio v. Boit, supra,; *Atlantic Mutual*, 968 F.2d, at 199.

Under the old, now outdated rule, the jurisdiction was said to be reserved to "contracts", claims, and services *purely* maritime, Rea v. The Eclipse, 135 U.S. 599, 608, 10 S.Ct. 873, 876, 34 L.Ed. 269 (1890)(emphasis added).   The test has, however, been loostened considerably so that admiralty jurisdiction is held to cover also contracts whose nonmaritime elements are "incidental" to a primarily maritime purpose, as well as the separable maritime portions of mixed contracts that are not primarily maritime, if these can be separately litigated without prejudice.   *Atlantic Mutual*, Simon v. Intercontinental Transport (ICT) B.V. 882 F.2d 1435, 1442 (9th Cir.1989).

In *Atlantic Mutual*, we ruled that, in appraising those questions, the court should consider "whether an issue related to maritime interests has been raised," 968 F.2d at 199, bearing in mind that the " 'fundamental interest giving rise to maritime jurisdiction is the protection of maritime commerce.' "   Id. at 200, quoting Sisson v. Ruby, 497 U.S. 358, 367, 110 S.Ct. 2892, 2898, 111 L.Ed.2d 292 (1990);   Foremost Ins. Co. v. Richardson, 457 U.S. 668, 674, 102 S.Ct. 2654, 2658, 73 L.Ed.2d 300 (1982).

Applying these principles to the claim before us, we are satisfied that the policy of marine insurance, which covered a vessel against a wide variety of perils during its normal use "afloat," as well as during transportation and storage ashore, serves "the protection of maritime commerce," and that a claim based upon the theft of the vessel is "related to maritime interests," not withstanding that the policy included coverage during land storage and that the theft occurred in those circumstances.

There are few objects—perhaps none—more essentially related to maritime commerce than vessels.   They have no utility on land;   they are taken ashore solely to make or keep them fit for use in the water, or to transport them from one body of water to another.[22]   Furthermore, taking smaller boats ashore for these purposes is important or essential to their use on the water.   The risk of theft of boats is an important concern of maritime commerce.   And whether theft of a vessel occurs while it is afloat or ashore, the impact of the theft is on maritime commerce.   Policies

22. *As in Werner Herzog's Film, Fitzcarroldo (1982).*

providing insurance covering such theft relate importantly to the protection of maritime commerce.

Given all these considerations, we might find it difficult to decide whether this policy should be considered "purely" maritime or as having nonmaritime elements that are merely "incidental" to a primarily maritime purpose. But the question is academic. For in either case, the claim is to be litigated within the maritime jurisdiction. Atlantic. Mut. Ins. Co. v. Balfour Maclaine Int'l, Ltd., 968 F.2d F.196, 199 (2d Cir.1992); Simon v. Intercontinental Transport (ICT) B.V., 882 F.2d 1435, 1442 (9th Cir.1989).

Collins relies on our denial of admiralty jurisdiction in *Atlantic Mutual*, where the policy covered the cargo during land transport and warehousing, as well as during ocean carriage, and the losses occurred during warehousing on land. That case presented significantly different facts. The policy there covered not a boat, but coffee, which does not have an inherently maritime character. Secondly, although part of the policy was designed to cover maritime transportation, other portions, with separately calculated premiums, covered the coffee during inland transportation, storage, and milling. The contract was neither purely maritime nor even primarily maritime. Furthermore the thefts occurred while the coffee was in indefinite land storage without ever having entered maritime commerce. It was indeed questionable whether it would ever enter maritime commerce as the eventual transportation from Mexico to the United States might have occurred by truck, rather than ship. Thus, although *Atlantic Mutual* has points in common with the present case—to wit that both policies provided shore coverage and both losses occurred during such shore coverage—we consider the two situations fundamentally different. In *Atlantic Mutual*, "the subject matter of the dispute[was].... so attenuated from the business of maritime commerce that it [did] not implicate the concerns underlying admiralty ... jurisdiction." 968 F.2d at 200. Here the contrary is true.

Nor is Collins helped by Lewis Charters, Inc. v. Huckins Yacht Corp., 871 F.2d 1046 (11th Cir.1989), which held that a negligence action for destruction of a boat by fire in a shoreside painting shed was not properly litigated in admiralty. See also Latin American Property and Casualty Ins. Co. v. Hi-Lift Marina, Inc., 887 F.2d 1477 (11th Cir.1989). For *Lewis* was a tort case—not a contract case. Admiralty tort jurisdiction is determined quite differently from admiralty contract jurisdiction. See Foremost Ins. Co. v. Richardson, 457 U.S. 668, 672–74, 102 S.Ct. 2654, 2657–58, 73 L.Ed.2d 300 (1982)(describing admiralty tort jurisdiction). *Lewis Charters* is therefore not helpful to Colins's argument.

There is no validity in appellant's contention that the admiralty jurisdiction is not applicable to a pleasure boat, as opposed to a commercial vessel. Albeit in the more compelling context of the need for uniform application of the Rules of the Road to commercial vessels and pleasure craft alike, the Supreme Court made clear in *Foremost* that admiralty jurisdiction extends to matters involving pleasure boats. *Foremost*, 457 U.S. at 675–76, 102 S.Ct. at 2658–59. Although they are not *employed* in commercial endeavors, pleasure boats constitute an important part of maritime commerce.

Nor is Collins aided by the holding of Frank B. Hall & Co. v. S.S. Seafreeze Altantic, 423 F.Supp. 1205 (S.D.N.Y.1976). The district court there held that the admiralty jurisdiction was inapplicable to a claim on a ship that had been mothballed, laying idle for several years, without any likely prospect of its returning to navigation. Collins never contended below that his boat was mothballed. He testified that he removed the boat from the water "for winter storage." Although Judge Wexler found that Collins "intended to leave the vessel in the driveway of his parents' residence ... *for an indefinite period of time* (emphasis added), it is clear that the judge meant this in the context of winter storage, not permanent mothballing."

* * *

Conclusion

The judgment of the district court is affirmed.

N O T E

In the *Dunham* case, the Supreme Court rejected a locality test for admiralty contract jurisdiction and stated that the "true criterion" in such cases to be "the nature and subject matter of the contract, as whether it was a maritime contract, having reference to maritime service or maritime transactions." Of course this does not eliminate all consideration of locality. Remember that in *The Thomas Jefferson* (p. 32, supra), the Court held that a libel for wages could not be maintained in the district court if the voyage giving rise to the wage claim took place above the ebb and flow of the tide. Substituting "navigable waters of the United States" for "ebb and flow of the tide," it is still true, is it not, that the contract must relate to some activity with a maritime location. See Seven Resorts v. Cantlen 57 F.3d 771, 1995 A.M.C. 2087 (9th Cir.1995), reproduced below at p. 1044, in which defendant owner, co-defendant in an action arising out of the operation of a rented houseboat on a non-navigable lake, sought unsuccessfully to place admiralty jurisdiction on the rental contract.

In Royal Insurance of America v. Pier 39. Ltd., 738 F.2d 1035, 1986 A.M.C. 2392 (9th Cir.1984), it was held that an insurance policy insuring a floating breakwater and a floating dock, the dock secured to the bottom and the shore and the breakwater to the bottom alone and sheltering the dock, was not a maritime contract. The court first noted that all insurance policies on vessels are maritime, but that neither of the structures was a vessel. Treating the structures as analogous to traditional wharves and docks, it held that excepting contracts with particular vessels, such as contracts for wharfage, contracts with wharves and docks are not maritime. At the policy level, the court observed:

"Not only has Royal failed to show that its policies are like other contracts that have been held within admiralty jurisdiction, it has also failed to show that bringing them within the jurisdiction would serve the interests that lie behind the constitutional grant of admiralty jurisdiction. Because the breakwater and dock, unlike vessels, are immobile, an insurer dealing on the credit of the structures does not need the in rem process of admiralty to prevent their leaving port before he can enforce his claim. The breakwater and dock will not be subject to claims in distant ports, so their owner and insurer need neither admiralty's guarantee of a neutral federal forum to guard against the possible prejudice of local courts, nor its guarantee of a nationwide uniform maritime law. Unlike seamen, neither the owners nor insurers of floating breakwaters and docks are a favored class whose interests admiralty courts seek to protect. The only possible reason to bring Royal's policies within the jurisdiction is to ensure that the standard marine insurance clauses appearing in them receive the same interpretation that they would if they appeared in policies on vessels and cargo so as to avoid contaminating federal marine insurance law with inconsistent state precedents. But future admiralty courts construing insurance on vessels and cargos will easily be able to distinguish any state decisions regarding floating breakwaters and docks. Moreover, even a federal court sitting in admiralty might construe Royal's policies according to state law rather than federally-defined admiralty rule. See Wilburn Boat Co. v. Fireman's Fund Insurance Co., 348 U.S. 310, 75 S.Ct. 368, 99 L.Ed. 337 (1955).''

In *Royal Ins.*, the breakwater broke loose and damaged itself and the dock.

Section 1 of the English Marine Insurance Act of 1906 defines ''marine insurance'' as follows, ''* * * a contract whereby an insurer undertakes to indemnify the assured, in manner and to the extent thereby agreed, against marine losses, that is to say, the losses incident to marine adventure.'' Section 3(2) defines ''marine adventure'' and ''maritime perils.'' A ''marine adventure'' exists where:

''(a) Any ship goods or other movables are exposed to maritime perils. Such property is in this Act referred to as 'insurable property.'

''(b) The earning or acquisition of any freight, passage money, commission, profit, or other pecuniary benefit, or the security for any advances, loan, or disbursements, is endangered by the exposure of insurable property to maritime perils;

''(c) Any liability to a third party may be incurred by the owner of, or other person interested in, or responsible for, insurable property, by reason of maritime perils.''

''Maritime perils'' are defined to mean, ''* * * the perils consequent on, or incidental to, the navigation of the sea, that is to say, perils of the seas, fire, war perils, pirates, rovers, thieves, captures, seizures, restraints and detainments of princes and peoples, jettisons, barratry, and any other perils, either of the like kind or which may be designated by the policy.''

Is a workmen's compensation policy a maritime contract if the employer is engaged in work pursuant to maritime contracts, e.g., a stevedore? Cf. Garcia v. Queen, Ltd. 487 F.2d 625 (5th Cir.1973). There a policy described as a ''workmen's compensation and employer's liability policy'' was construed to cover claims under the Jones Act and the general maritime law. The action was brought as a civil action against the employer and his insurers, and a jury was demanded. Had it been identified as maritime, could it have been maintained against the insurer?

North Pacific Steamship Co. v. Hall Brothers Marine Railway & Shipbuilding Co.

Supreme Court of the United States, 1919.
249 U.S. 119, 39 S.Ct. 221, 63 L.Ed. 510.

■ MR. JUSTICE PITNEY delivered the opinion of the court.

This is a direct appeal under § 238, Judicial Code (Act of March 3, 1911, c. 231, 36 Stat. 1087, 1157), involving only the question whether the cause was within the admiralty jurisdiction of a District Court of the United States.

* * *

The facts were these: In the month of May, 1911, the Steamship Company was the owner of the American steamer *Yucatan,* which then lay moored or tied up at dock upon the waters of Puget Sound at Seattle, in the State of Washington. The vessel, which was of steel construction, was in need of extensive repairs. She had been wrecked, and had remained submerged for a long time; ice floes had torn away the upper decks, and some of her bottom plates also needed to be replaced. She was under charter for an Alaskan voyage, to be commenced as soon as the repairs could be completed. The Shipbuilding Company was the owner of a shipyard, marine railway, machine shops, and other equipment for building and repairing ships, situate upon and adjacent to the navigable waters of Puget Sound at Winslow, in the same State, and had in its employ numerous mechanics and laborers. Under these circumstances it was agreed between the parties that the Shipbuilding Company should tow the vessel from where she lay to the shipyard, haul her out as required upon the marine railway to a position on dry land adjacent to the machine shop—the place being known as the "dry dock," and the hauling out being described as "docking"—and should furnish mechanics, laborers and foremen as needed, who were to work with other men already in the employ of the Steamship Company, and under its superintendence; and the Shipbuilding Company was also to furnish plates and other materials needed in the repairs, and the use of air compressors, steam hammers, riveters, boring machines, lathes, blacksmith forge, and the usual and necessary tools for the use of such machines. At the time the contract was made, another vessel (the *Archer*) was upon the dry dock, and it was uncertain how soon she could be returned to the water. It was understood that the *Yucatan* should be hauled out as soon as the *Archer* came off, should remain upon the dry dock only during such part of the work as required her to be in that position, and at other times should lie in the water alongside the plant. For the services to be performed and the materials and equipment to be furnished the Shipbuilding Company was to receive stated prices, thus: for labor of all classes, the actual rate of wages paid to the men plus 15 per cent.; for use of tug and scow, a stated sum per hour; for hauling out the vessel and the use of the marine railway, a stated sum for the first 24 hours, and a specified rate per day for 6 "lay days" immediately following the hauling out; for each working day thereafter, another rate; for vessel lying alongside the dock for repairs, no charge; for the running of air compressors, a certain charge per hour; for the use and operation of other machines, certain rates specified; and for materials supplied, invoice prices and cost of freight to plant, with 10 per cent. additional.

The vessel was docked and repaired in the manner contemplated by the agreement; she was brought to the shipyard on the 27th of May, and lay in the water alongside of the dock there until the 17th of June, during which time upper decks and beams were put in and other work of a character that could be done as well while she was afloat as in the dry dock. On June 17 she was hauled out and remained in dry dock for about two weeks while her bottom plates were renewed. During the same period the propeller was removed to permit of an examination of the tail shaft, and as the shaft showed deterioration a new one was ordered to be supplied by a concern in San Francisco. Upon completion of the work upon the bottom plates, and on the 5th of July, the vessel was returned to the water and lay there for about two weeks awaiting arrival of the new tail shaft. When this arrived the vessel was again hauled out, the tail shaft and propeller were fitted, and the remaining repairs completed. Libelant's claim was for work and labor performed, services rendered, and materials furnished under the circumstances mentioned, and was based upon the agreed scale of compensation.

The question in dispute is whether a claim thus grounded is the subject of admiralty jurisdiction; appellant's contention being that the contract, or at least an essential part of it, was for the use by appellant of libelant's marine railway, shipyard, equipment, and laborers in such manner as appellant might choose to employ them, and that it called for the performance of no maritime service by libelant.

The Constitution, Art. III, § 2, extends the judicial powers of the United States to "all cases of admiralty and maritime jurisdiction"; and the legislation enacted by Congress for carrying the power into execution has been equally extensive. Act of September 24, 1789, c. 20, § 9, 1 Stat. 73, 77; Rev.Stats., § 563(8); Judicial Code, § 24(3), 36 Stat. 1087, 1091, c. 231. In defining the bounds of the civil jurisdiction, this court from an early day has rejected those trammels that arose from the restrictive statutes and judicial prohibitions of England. Waring v. Clarke, 5 How. 441, 457–459, 12 L.Ed. 226 (1847); Insurance Co. v. Dunham, 11 Wall. 1, 24, 20 L.Ed. 90 (1870); The Lottawanna, 21 Wall. 558, 576, 22 L.Ed. 654 (1874).

It must be taken to be the settled law of this court that while the civil jurisdiction of the admiralty in matters of tort depends upon locality— whether the act was committed upon navigable waters—in matter of contract it depends upon the subject-matter—the nature and character of the contract; and that the English rule, which conceded jurisdiction, with a few exceptions, only to contracts made and to be executed upon the navigable waters, is inadmissible, the true criterion being the nature of the contract, as to whether it have reference to maritime service or maritime transactions. People's Ferry Co. v. Beers, 20 How. 393, 401, 15 L.Ed. 961 (1857); Philadelphia, Wilmington & Baltimore R.R. Co. v. Philadelphia, etc., Steam Towboat Co., 23 How. 209, 215, 16 L.Ed. 433 (1859); Insurance Co. v. Dunham, 11 Wall. 1, 26, 20 L.Ed. 90 (1870); The Eclipse, 135 U.S. 599, 608, 10 S.Ct. 873, 34 L.Ed. 269 (1890).

In some of the earlier cases the influence of the English rule may be discerned, in that the question whether a contract was to be performed upon the navigable waters was referred to as pertinent to the question whether the contract was of a maritime nature (The Thomas Jefferson, 10 Wheat. 428, 429, 6 L.Ed. 358 (1825); The Planter [Peyroux v. Howard], 7 Pet. 324, 341, 8 L.Ed. 700 (1833); Steamboat Orleans v. Phoebus, 11 Pet. 175, 183, 9 L.Ed. 677 (1837); New Jersey Steam Navigation Co. v. Merchants' Bank, 6 How. 344, 392, 12 L.Ed. 465 (1848)); but a careful examination of the opinions shows that the place of performance was dealt with as an evidential circumstance bearing with more or less weight upon the fundamental question of the nature of the contract. If they go beyond this, they must be deemed to be overruled by Insurance Co. v. Dunham, supra.

Neither in jurisdiction nor in the method of procedure are our admiralty courts dependent alone upon the theory of implied hypothecation; it being established that in a civil cause of maritime origin involving a personal responsibility the libelant may proceed *in personam* if the respondent is within reach of process. The General Smith, 4 Wheat. 438, 443, 4 L.Ed. 609 (1819); Manro v. Almeida, 10 Wheat. 473, 486, 6 L.Ed. 369 (1825); New Jersey Steam Navigation Co. v. Merchants' Bank, 6 How. 344, 390, 12 L.Ed. 465 (1848); Morewood v. Enequist, 23 How. 491, 16 L.Ed. 516 (1859); The Belfast, 7 Wall. 624, 644, 19 L.Ed. 266 (1868); The Kalorama, 10 Wall. 204, 210, 19 L.Ed. 941 (1869); The Sabine, 101 U.S. 384, 386, 25 L.Ed. 982 (1879); In re Louisville Underwriters, 134 U.S. 488, 490, 10 S.Ct. 587, 33 L.Ed. 991 (1890); Workman v. New York City, 179 U.S. 552, 573, 21 S.Ct. 212, 45 L.Ed. 314 (1901); Ex parte Indiana Transportation Co., 244 U.S. 456, 37 S.Ct. 717, 61 L.Ed. 1253 (1917).

That a materialman furnishing supplies or repairs may proceed in admiralty either against the ship *in rem* or against the master or owner *in personam* is recognized by the 12th Rule in Admiralty, adopted in its present form in the year 1872 (13 Wall. xiv) after a long controversy that began with The General Smith, 4 Wheat. 438, 4 L.Ed. 609 (1819), and ended with The Lottawanna, 21 Wall. 558, 579, 581, 22 L.Ed. 654 (1874). See The Glide, 167 U.S. 606, 17 S.Ct. 930, 42 L.Ed. 296 (1897).

It is settled that a contract for building a ship or supplying materials for her construction is not a maritime contract. People's Ferry Co. v. Beers, 20 How. 393, 15 L.Ed. 961 (1857); Roach v. Chapman, 22 How. 129, 16 L.Ed. 291 (1859); Edwards v. Elliott, 21 Wall. 532, 553, 557, 22 L.Ed. 487 (1874); The Winnebago, 205 U.S. 354, 363, 27 S.Ct. 509, 51 L.Ed. 836 (1907). In the case in 20 Howard the court said (p. 402): "So far from the contract being purely maritime, and touching rights and duties appertaining to navigation (on the ocean or elsewhere), it was a contract made on land, to be performed on land." But the true basis for the distinction between the construction and the repair of a ship, for purposes of the admiralty jurisdiction, is to be found in the fact that the structure does not become a ship, in the legal sense, until it is completed and launched. "A ship is born when she is launched, and lives so long as her identity is preserved. Prior to her launching she is a mere congeries of wood and iron—an ordinary piece of personal property—as distinctly a land structure as a house, and subject to mechanics' liens created by state law enforcible in the state courts.   In the baptism of launching she receives her name, and from the moment her keel touches the water she is transformed, and becomes a subject of admiralty jurisdiction." Tucker v. Alexandroff, 183 U.S. 424, 438, 22 S.Ct. 195, 46 L.Ed. 264 (1902).

In The Robert W. Parsons, 191 U.S. 17, 33, 34, 24 S.Ct. 8, 13, 48 L.Ed. 73 (1903), it was held that the admiralty jurisdiction extended to an action for repairs put upon a vessel while in dry dock; but the question whether this would apply to a vessel hauled up on land for repairs was reserved, the language of the court, by Mr. Justice Brown, being: "Had the vessel been hauled up by ways upon the land and there repaired, a different question might have been presented, as to which we express no opinion; but as all serious repairs upon the hulls of vessels are made in dry dock, the proposition that such repairs are made on land would practically deprive the admiralty courts of their largest and most important jurisdiction in connection with repairs."

In The Steamship Jefferson, 215 U.S. 130, 30 S.Ct. 54, 54 L.Ed. 125 (1910), it was held that the admiralty jurisdiction extends to a claim for salvage service rendered to a vessel while undergoing repairs in a dry dock.

What we have said sufficiently indicates the decision that should be reached in the case at bar.   The contract as made contemplated the performance of services and the furnishing of the necessary materials for the repairs of the steamship *Yucatan*.   It was an entire contract, intended to take the ship as she was and to discharge her only when completely repaired and fit for the Alaskan voyage.   It did not contemplate, as is contended by appellant, either a lease, or a contract for use in the nature of a lease, of the libelant's marine railway and machine shop.   The use of these was but incidental; the vessel being hauled out, when consistent with the progress of other work of the Shipbuilding Company, for the purpose of exposing the ship's bottom to permit of the removal and replacement of the broken plates and the examination of the propeller and tail shaft.   In The Planter (Peyroux v. Howard), 7 Pet. 324, 327, 341, 8 L.Ed. 700 (1833), the vessel, requiring repairs below the water line as well as above, was to be and in fact was hauled up out of the water; and it was held that the contract for materials furnished and work performed in repairing her under these circumstances was a maritime contract.   We think the same rule must be applied to the case before us; that the doubt intimated in The Robert W. Parsons, 191 U.S. 17, 33, 34, 24 S.Ct. 8, 48 L.Ed. 73 (1903) must be laid aside; and that there is no difference in character as to repairs made upon the hull of a vessel dependent upon whether they are made while she is afloat, while in dry dock, or while hauled up by ways upon land.   The nature of the service is identical in the several cases, and the admiralty jurisdiction extends to all.

This is recognized by the Act of Congress of June 23, 1910, c. 373, 36 Stat. 604, which declares that "Any person furnishing repairs, supplies, or other necessaries, including the use of dry dock or marine railway, to a vessel, whether foreign or domestic,'' upon the order of a proper person, shall have a maritime lien upon the vessel.

The principle was recognized long ago by Mr. Justice Nelson in a case decided at the circuit, Wortman v. Griffith, 3 Blatchf. 528, 30 F.Cas. 648, No. 18,057 (1856), which was a libel *in personam* to recover compensation for services rendered in repairing a steamboat. Libelant was the owner of a shipyard with apparatus consisting of a railway cradle and other fixtures and implements used for the purpose of hauling vessels out of the water and sustaining them while being repaired. Certain rates of compensation were charged for hauling the vessel upon the ways, and a per diem charge for the time occupied while she was under repair, in cases where the owner of the yard and apparatus was not employed to do the work but the repairs were made by other shipmasters, as was done in that case. The owner of the yard and apparatus, together with his employees, superintended and conducted the operation of raising and lowering the vessel and also of fixing her upon the ways preparatory to the repairs, a service requiring skill and experience and essential to the process of repair. Mr. Justice Nelson held there was no substantial distinction between such a case and the case where the shipmaster was employed to make the repairs; and that the admiralty jurisdiction must be sustained.

Nor is the present case to be distinguished upon the ground that the repairs in which libelant was to furnish work and materials and the use of a marine railway and other equipment were to be done under the superintendence of the Steamship Company. This affected the quantum of the services and the extent of the responsibility, but not the essential character of the services or the nature of the contract, which, in our opinion, were maritime.

Decree affirmed.

N O T E

Just as the question of whether or not an insurance policy is a maritime contract becomes cloudy at the edge of the sea, so with the repair contract. See, e.g., Sea Land Industries, Inc. v. General Ship Repair Corp., 530 F.Supp. 550, 1982 A.M.C. 2120 (D.Md.1982), where it was held that a contract to repair a shoreside crane used to load and discharge containerships is not maritime.

In AAB Electrical Industries, Inc. v. Control Masters, Inc., 1980 A.M.C. 1795 (E.D.La.1980), the Gulf agent of a vessel in Houston contracted with a Houston repairman to repair one of the ship's generators. The repairman realized that it did not have the facilities for the repair and contracted with a New Orleans electrical concern to perform the repairs. The generator was shipped to the New Orleans concern. On arrival, the New Orleans concern realized that it was not equipped for the job and took the generator to another New Orleans firm, which actually performed the work. When the generator finally arrived back in Houston, it was discovered that the original trouble had not been corrected. On a finding that the New Orleans electrical concern that had contracted with the Houston repairman did not know at the time that the generator was to be installed in a vessel, the district court held that its contract claim against the repairman was not within the admiralty and maritime jurisdiction.

Terminal Shipping Co. v. Hamberg

District Court of Maryland, 1915.
222 Fed. 1020.

■ ROSE, DISTRICT JUDGE.   This is a libel in personam with a clause of foreign attachment.   It sets up a contract between the respondents and the libelant, by which the latter until December 31, 1915, was to do all stevedoring work required by the respondents' vessels at the port of Baltimore, except when some charter otherwise provided.   It alleges that the Bertha arrived at this port, but that its master declined to permit the libelant to do the stevedoring work, although it tendered its services and had rigged up its gears and was ready and willing to perform.   It is asserted that by such refusal the libelant lost $75, that being the amount of profit which it says it would have made, had it done the work under the contract and been paid the contract price.

To this libel the respondents have excepted, and on two grounds: First, that the cause of action is not within the jurisdiction of a court of admiralty;   and secondly, that the damages sought to be recovered are purely speculative.

There are cases in which recovery made be had for loss of profits. Pennsylvania Steel Co. v. New York City Ry. Co., 117 C.C.A. 503, 198 F. 721 (1912).   Under other circumstances they cannot be.   De Ford v. Maryland Steel Co., 51 C.C.A. 59, 113 F. 72 (1902).   Whether in this case they can be will depend upon the facts as they may be shown in evidence. The question should not be determined on the face of the pleadings alone.

The second exception will therefore be overruled.

The breach of an executory contract does not, ordinarily, at least, give the injured party a maritime lien upon the ship, and therefore a libel filed in rem may not be filed to recover therefor.   Schooner Freeman v. Buckingham, 18 How. 182, 15 L.Ed. 341 (1855), Scott v. Ira Chaffee, 2 F. 401 (D.C.Mich.1880).   It has also been decided that executory contracts to furnish all provisions that certain ships may require at a particular port, or all coal that they will need at that place, are not maritime contracts, and that admiralty has no jurisdiction, even in personam, to award damages for their breach.   Diefenthal v. Hamburg–Amerikanische Packetfahrt Actien– Gesellschaft, 46 F. 397 (D.C.La.1891);   Steamship Overdale Co., Ltd. v. Turner, 206 F. 339 (D.C.Pa.1913).   In the case last cited it was pointed out that a contract to buy coal or provisions is not in its nature maritime, and does not become so until the coal or the stores are furnished to the ship.

The libelant in this case says that a contract to do stevedoring work on a ship calls for a service which can never be otherwise than maritime. Whatever may have been the original difference of opinion on the subject, it is now clearly settled that stevedoring services are maritime.   Atlantic

Transport Co. of West Virginia v. Imbrovek, 234 U.S. 52, 34 S.Ct. 733, 58 L.Ed. 1208, 51 L.R.A.,N.S., 1157 (1914). Respondent replies that the contract is executory, and that for a breach of such a contract there is no remedy in the admiralty.

The reasoning, if not the express language, of Justice Story on circuit in Andrews v. Essex Fire & Marine Ins. Co., 1 Fed.Cas. 889, goes far to justify this contention. In a number of cases in which a right of action in rem has been denied, doubt has been expressed as to whether there was any jurisdiction even in personam. The Seven Sons, 69 F. 271 (D.C.Pa. 1895). On the other hand, the jurisdiction in personam has been expressly sustained in a case on all fours with this. The Allerton, 93 F. 219 (D.C.Or.1899). The Circuit Court of Appeals for the Seventh Circuit has upheld such jurisdiction where the breach complained of was that of an executory contract for towing. Boutin v. Rudd, 27 C.C.A. 526, 82 F. 685 (1897).

The question seems to have been foreclosed in this circuit by the decision of the Circuit Court of Appeals in Baltimore Steam-Packet Co. v. Patterson, 45 C.C.A. 575, 106 F. 736, 66 L.R.A. 193 (1901). It was there distinctly held that for the failure of a shipper to furnish cargo which he had bargained to ship recovery may be had in the admiralty upon a libel in personam.

It follows that the first exception must also be overruled.

NOTE

The advent of container shipping has introduced interesting problems of line drawing between maritime and terrestrial contracts. See, e.g., American President Lines, Ltd. v. Green Transfer and Storage Inc., 568 F.Supp. 58, 1983 A.M.C. 2444 (D.Or.1983), in which an action for breach of a contract between a shipper and a land-based mover and hauler for the loading of shipper's containers in Portland, to be sent by truck to Seattle for shipment to Japan, was held to be within the admiralty and maritime jurisdiction.

Would a contract with a cargo surveyor for inspection of the cargo after discharge be a maritime contract? In Ford Motor Co. v. Wallenius Lines,M/V Atlantic Cinderella, 476 F.Supp. 1362, 1980 A.M.C. 1114 (E.D.Va.1979), the court held that it isn't, but entertained the claim on the theory of pendent jurisdiction.

Stevedoring contracts are, of course, but one example of a great number of contracts for services provided to ships operating on navigable waters, and therefore maritime in nature. As in the case of contracts of insurance, repair contracts, and stevedoring contracts, each presents its problem of fixing the line between land and water.

Wharfage contracts are maritime. Ex parte Easton, 95 U.S. (5 Otto) 68, 24 L.Ed. 373 (1877). See Hudson Harbor 79th Street Boat Basin, Inc. v. Sea Casa, 469 F.Supp. 987, 1979 A.M.C. 2401 (S.D.N.Y.1979), in which it was held that a floating houseboat capable of being towed from one location to another was a vessel within the Lien Act and subject to a lien for wharfage. With The Sea Casa, compare Greenway v. Buzzard Point Boatyard Corp., 217 A.2d 599 (D.C.App.1966), in which boatyard was permitted to proceed under the District of Columbia landlord-tenant law. Is a contract for winter storage of a pleasure boat maritime when the storage is on land? See Rogers v. Yachts America Inc., 1983 A.M.C. 417 (D.Md.1982).

Actions for pilotage lie within the admiralty and maritime jurisdiction. See Jackson v. Marine Exploration Co., Inc., 614 F.2d 65, 1980 A.M.C. 2098 (5th Cir.1980), where such a claim is spoken of as a classic example of admiralty jurisdiction. Would an agreement among pilots, through their organization, for collection of fees by a collection agent and distribution to individual members of the association on the basis of a share system be a maritime contract? See Del Greco v. New York Harbor Independent Pilots, 1983 A.M.C. 2221 (S.D.N.Y.1983), in which the district court found the maritime "flavor" insufficient.

Suits for wages were adjudicated in the English High Court of the Admiralty from very early times. In The Courtney [1810] Edw.Adm. 239, Sir William Scott observes that such a jurisdiction was exercised "from the first establishment of such a court," though he notes the view of the common law courts that this exercise proceeded "more from a kind of toleration founded upon the general convenience of the practice, than by any direct jurisdiction properly belonging to it." In *The Courtney*, Scott declined to exercise the jurisdiction to enforce the American penalty wages provisions in favor of an American, but indicated that had it been made part of the contract the court would entertain the suit. The jurisdiction of the United States district courts of wage claims seems never to have been doubted, and wage cases appear in substantial numbers in the early American admiralty reports. See, e.g., Babbel v. Gardner and The Catherine, Bee's Adm.Rep. 87 (1796).

Officers, with the exception of the master, appear to be treated in this respect no differently from seamen. See Sheppard v. Taylor, 30 U.S. (5 Pet.) 675, 8 L.Ed. 269 (1831). In L'Arina v. Brig Exchange, 14 Fed.Cas. 1148, Bee's Adm.Rep. 198 (1803), a person taken on as captain in name only, but not in fact master of the vessel, was permitted to maintain a libel against the vessel and its owners for monthly wages under an agreement with the true master. It was held there, however, that the vessel and owner were not liable for a sum of $200 which, under the same agreement, was promised to the plaintiff in the event he should be discharged or the voyage was altered. The plaintiff then sued the master for this sum. Judge Bee found this to insufficiently connected with the voyage to bring it within the admiralty jurisdiction. L'Arina v. Manwaring, 14 Fed.Cas. 1149, Bee's Adm.Rep. 199 (1803).

It is stated in L'Arina v. Brig Exchange, supra, that had the plaintiff been a master of the vessel, he could not have sued in the admiralty. This was clearly the rule in England at about the same time. The Favorite, 2 C.Rob. 223 (1799). Sir William Scott found, however, that the plaintiff's contract was to serve as mate and in the event of the death or removal of the actual master, to take on the additional duties of master; therefore he was entitled to his mate's wages, but would have to sue "elsewhere" for the balance. In England the master's action for wages was put on a parity with that of other seamen by the Merchant Shipping Act of 1854 (17 & 18 Vict, ch. 104, § 191). In the United States, the master was not given a statutory lien on the vessel for wages until 1968, a matter discussed in ch. 12, infra. When the issue arose, however, it was held that the master could sue in admiralty in personam. Willard v. Dorr, 3 Mason 91, 29 Fed.Cas. 1275 (C.C.Mass.1822)(Story, J.). This principle does not appear to have been questioned since.

Since seamen have a lien of very high priority, the question often arises whether claims are wage claims (see chap. 12, infra). In such cases, it would usually be conceded that the claims are service claims within the admiralty and maritime jurisdiction, and often that they are lien claims, the disagreement centering around the question of priorities.

Actions on salvage contracts are within the maritime jurisdiction. See Chap. 15(D, infra. Towing contracts are, as well. See Knapp, Stout & Co. Company v. McCaffrey, 177 U.S. 638, 20 S.Ct. 824, 44 L.Ed. 921 (1900). As in the case of wages and services, both salvage and towage contracts import liens, but of a different priority. The line-drawing, therefore, is usually for the purpose of establishing priorities.

General Engine & Machine Works, Inc. v. Slay and the F/V Danlyn

United States District Court, Southern District of Alabama, 1963.
222 F.Supp. 745, 1964 A.M.C. 552.

■ DANIEL H. THOMAS, D.J. This libel was brought by General Engine against Danny Slay and the F/V *Danlyn, in personam* and *in rem* in an effort to establish and enforce a maritime lien arising out of an oral contract having as its subject matter certain work, materials, supplies, and equipment furnished to the respondents by the libellant.

The oral contract was a so-called "gentlemen's agreement" and was replete with uncertainties and ambiguities. In general terms, the respondent Danny Slay sought assistance from General Engine with respect to the installation of a certain type marine engine in the *Danlyn,* as well as General Engine's assistance in "rigging the boat." A "rough" price was agreed upon, as was the trade-in value of an engine already in the possession of the respondent. The total price was to be paid upon completion of the work. The respondent Danny Slay paid a portion of the amount in advance. At the time the initial agreement between the parties was made, the *Danlyn* was under construction on the ways at Sunset Boat Works, located on Fish River, in Baldwin County, Alabama. As stated above, the agreement between the parties was equivocal. The price therefore was subject to change due to the exigencies of time-labor-material contracts. The final completion date was also subject to change for the same reason.

Nevertheless, the libellant undertook to embark on the fulfillment of its portion of the contract while the *Danlyn* was still on the ways. After the pre-launch work was accomplished, the *Danlyn* was launched and remained for a short while at Sunset's place of business. She was later towed by the respondent to another location on Fish River, and soon after September 1, 1961, she was towed, still incomplete, to the Industrial Canal in Mobile County.

The libellant was engaged in working on the various aspects pertaining to the installation and rigging of the *Danlyn* at intervals while the hull of the *Danlyn* was still on the ways, after the *Danlyn* was launched and afloat at Sunset Boat Works, and also while the *Danlyn* was moored in the Industrial Canal.

The libellant contends that the reasonable value of such labor, materials, supplies and equipment furnished to the respondent amounts to $5748.75.

The libellant further contends that after $1000 credit on the trade-in engine is deducted from the above amount, as well as payments previously made by the respondent, there remains $2765.75 still due and owing libellant by respondent.

The value of the work performed is not disputed by the respondent. However, the respondent claims:

(1) That the libellant agreed to perform the aforesaid work for $850 in addition to the $1000 credit allowed on the respondent's marine engine.

(2) That irrespective of the amount and value of the libellant's work, labor, supplies, equipment and material, this court is without admiralty jurisdiction because the contract between the libellant and the respondent was a contract for original construction of a vessel, and would therefore not support a maritime lien.

Since a jurisdictional matter is raised, the court is obligated to consider the respondent's second position first.

The general rule with regard to maritime liens permits a lien to attach to any vessel for any service rendered to such vessel of a nature so as to facilitate its use as an instrument of navigation. 55 C.J.S. Maritime Liens §§ 12–23.

It is possible for a maritime lien to arise out of either a contract or a tort. 55 C.J.S. Maritime Liens § 12.

However, in order for a maritime lien to arise out of a contract, the contract itself must be of a clearly maritime nature. 2 C.J.S. Admiralty § 24.

A maritime contract is an agreement which concerns transportation by sea, relates to navigation or maritime employment, or involves navigation and commerce on navigable waters. 2 C.J.S. Admiralty § 24, note 23.

If a contract is not directly or substantially related to navigation, even though it is to be performed on water, or on board, or for the benefit of a vessel, such contract cannot be enforced in a court of admiralty. W.T. Blunt, D.C.Mich., 291 Fed. 899, 1923 A.M.C. 1109 (1923).

It is well settled that a contract to build a ship is non-maritime and is not within the jurisdiction of admiralty tribunals. Thames Co. v. "Francis McDonald," 254 U.S. 242, 41 S.Ct. 65, 65 L.Ed. 245 (1920). In that case, hull had been completed and launched. The original builder found itself unable to proceed further and after an agreement with the owner, the appellant towed the hull to another location. More work was accomplished on the hull while it was in possession of the appellant. The ship was manifestly incomplete when the appellant received it. The masts were not in, nor were the bolts, beams, and gaff. The forward house was not constructed and she was not in "condition to carry on any service." The appellant worked on the vessel for some six weeks.

The court was faced squarely with the same issue in *"Francis Mc-Donald"* that is presented to this court in the instant case; i.e., whether a contract to furnish materials, work, and labor for the completion of a vessel not sufficiently advanced to discharge the functions for which intended is within the admiralty and maritime jurisdiction of the federal courts.

The court held that there was no federal jurisdiction in the cause and stated, p. 244:

"Notwithstanding possible and once not inappropriate criticism, the doctrine is now firmly established that contracts to construct entirely new ships are non-maritime because not nearly enough related to any rights and duties pertaining to commerce and navigation."

Further, at p. 245:

" * * * we think the same reasons which exclude such contracts from admiralty jurisdiction likewise apply to agreements made after the hull is in the water, for work and material necessary to consummate a partial construction and *bring the vessel into condition to function as intended.*" (Emphasis supplied.)

It is apparent to the court that the decisions are harmonious and the law well settled with respect to the rule that all work accomplished before a vessel is actually launched is regarded as original construction. However, there has been some conflict on the question of whether work done and materials furnished after the vessel had been launched, but before final completion should be classed as construction. The general and more widely accepted view is as set out in *"Francis McDonald,"* supra.

The opposite view holds that a structure becomes a ship as soon as she is launched and rides upon her destined element. Eliza Ladd, 8 Fed.Cas. No. 4364.

In 1907, this problem was decided by the United States Supreme Court in The Winnebago, 205 U.S. 354, 27 S.Ct. 509, 51 L.Ed. 836. This case was decided some thirteen years before *"Francis McDonald,"* and contributed a great deal toward the provisions of a sounder, broader judicial framework upon which to rest future decisions.

The Supreme Court dealt with the aspect of admiralty and maritime jurisdiction as regards the establishment of maritime liens against a *newly* constructed vessel for the value of work, labor, materials, and supplies furnished her by the libellant subsequent to her launching, but prior to her first voyage.

The court concluded that there was no admiralty jurisdiction, and commented at p. 363:

"Thus, * * * admiralty jurisdiction does not extend to a contract for building a vessel, *or to work done or materials furnished in the construction.* * * * " (Emphasis supplied.)

One further subdivision of the rule with regard to the admiralty jurisdiction of cases of this sort is possible: where the hull is completed and launched, but where certain work remains yet to be done to her. Some courts have held that a contract made after the launching with respect to the completion of such work is a maritime contract, and admiralty courts will take jurisdiction of any dispute arising therefrom. The Manhattan, 46

F. 797 (D.C.Wash.1891); Revenue Cutter, No. 2, 20 F.Cas. 568, No. 11,714. The contract between the parties in the instant case was entered into prior to the launching of the *Danlyn,* and work performed thereunder by the libellant was in the nature of original construction, irrespective of the fact that some of the work involved necessarily took place after the launching of the hull.

The libellant cites in support of its contentions the well known cases of: Tucker v. Alexandroff, 183 U.S. 424, 22 S.Ct. 195, 46 L.Ed. 264 (1902); New Bedford Dry Dock Co. v. Purdy, 258 U.S. 96, 42 S.Ct. 243, 66 L.Ed. 482 (1922); The Scorpio, 181 F.2d 356, 1950 A.M.C. 756 (5 Cir.1950); and Pleason v. Gulfport Shipbuilding Corporation, 221 F.2d 621, 1955 A.M.C. 794 (5 Cir.1955).

The case of Tucker v. Alexandroff, supra, is distinguishable from the instant case. That case involves the meaning of the word "ship" as it pertained to a treaty agreement with a foreign nation. *New Bedford Dry Dock case,* supra, as well as *Scorpio,* and the *Pleason* cases, supra, are all concerned with the conversion of already existing hulls or vessels, and none of them pertains to contracts of original construction.

The rule as set out by the Supreme Court in the *"Francis Mc-Donald"* case, supra, applies here. The court, therefore, is of the opinion that this proceeding does not trench upon the exclusive jurisdiction of the federal courts in admiralty cases. The cause must necessarily be dismissed, and it is unnecessary for the court to consider the respondents' first contention regarding the actual amount in controversy.

NOTE

In the *"Francis McDonald,"* adverted to in the instant case, a shipbuilder contracted to build the vessel in question in Groton, Connecticut, and launched the hull. The shipbuilder found itself unable to complete its contract and a second company agreed with the owner to complete the work and for this purpose the hull was towed to New London. In pursuance of the second contract certain work and labor was furnished. The second company was not able to complete the construction, however, and ultimately the vessel was towed to Hoboken and finished by a third company. The action was brought by the second company for supplies and labor. The Supreme Court held that when the vessel was turned over to the libellant, it was obviously unfinished and therefore the work and supplies that were furnished were in the nature of ship construction and therefore fell within the rule that a construction contract is non-maritime. See also The Boat La Sambra v. Lewis, 321 F.2d 29, 1966 A.M.C. 691 (9th Cir.1963).

Exxon Corp. v. Central Gulf Lines, Inc.

Supreme Court of the United States, 1991.
500 U.S. 603, 111 S.Ct. 2071, 114 L.Ed.2d 649, 1991 A.M.C. 1817.

■ JUSTICE MARSHALL delivered the opinion of the Court.

This case raises the question whether admiralty jurisdiction extends to claims arising from agency contracts. In Minturn v. Maynard, 58 U.S. (17 How.) 477 (1855), this Court held that an agent who had advanced funds for repairs and supplies necessary for a vessel could not bring a claim in admiralty against the vessel's owners. *Minturn* has been interpreted by some lower courts as establishing a per se rule excluding agency contracts from admiralty. We now consider whether *Minturn* should be overruled.

I

This case arose over an unpaid bill for fuels acquired for the vessel, *Green Harbour ex William Hooper (Hooper)*. The *Hooper* is owned by respondent Central Gulf Lines, Inc. (Central Gulf) and was chartered by the Waterman Steamship Corporation (Waterman) for use in maritime commerce. Petitioner Exxon Corporation (Exxon) was Waterman's exclusive worldwide supplier of gas and bunker fuel oil for some 40 years.

In 1983, Waterman and Exxon negotiated a marine fuel requirements contract. Under the terms of the contract, upon request, Exxon would supply Waterman's vessels with marine fuels when the vessels called at ports where Exxon could supply the fuels directly. Alternatively, in ports where Exxon had to rely on local suppliers, Exxon would arrange for the local supplier to provide Waterman vessels with fuel. In such cases, Exxon would pay the local supplier for the fuel and then invoice Waterman. Thus, while Exxon's contractual obligation was to provide Waterman's vessels with fuel when Waterman placed an order, it met that obligation sometimes in the capacity of "seller" and other times in the capacity of "agent."

In the transaction at issue here, Exxon acted as Waterman's agent, procuring bunker fuel for the *Hooper* from Arabian Marine Operating Co. (Arabian Marine) of Jeddah, Saudi Arabia. In October 1983, Arabian Marine delivered over 4,000 tons of fuel to the *Hooper* in Jeddah and invoiced Exxon for the cost of the fuel. Exxon paid for the fuel and invoiced Waterman, in turn, for $763,644. Shortly thereafter, Waterman sought reorganization under Chapter 11 of the Bankruptcy Code; Waterman never paid the full amount of the fuel bill. During the reorganization proceedings, Central Gulf agreed to assume personal liability for the unpaid bill if a court were to hold the *Hooper* liable *in rem* for that cost.

Subsequently, Exxon commenced this litigation in federal district court against Central Gulf *in personam* and against the *Hooper in rem*. Exxon claimed to have a maritime lien on the *Hooper* under the Federal Maritime Lien Act, 46 U.S.C. § 971 (1982 ed.).[23] The District Court noted that "[a] prerequisite to the existence of a maritime lien based on a breach of contract is that the subject matter of the contract must fall within the admiralty jurisdiction." 707 F.Supp. 155, 158 (S.D.N.Y.1989). Relying on the Second Circuit's decision in Peralta Shipping Corp. v. Smith & Johnson

---

23. The relevant provision of the Federal Maritime Lien Act has been amended and recodified at 46 U.S.C. § 31342.

(Shipping) Corp., 739 F.2d 798 (2 Cir.1984), cert. denied, 470 U.S. 1031, 105 S.Ct. 1405, 84 L.Ed.2d 791 (1985), the District Court concluded that it did not have admiralty jurisdiction over the claim. See 707 F.Supp., at 159–161. In *Peralta*, the Second Circuit held that it was constrained by this Court's decision in Minturn v. Maynard, supra, and by those Second Circuit cases faithfully adhering to *Minturn*, to follow a *per se* rule excluding agency contracts from admiralty jurisdiction. See *Peralta*, supra, 739 F.2d at 802–804. The District Court also rejected the argument that Exxon should be excepted from the *Minturn* rule because it had provided credit necessary for the *Hooper* to purchase the fuel and thus was more than a mere agent. To create such an exception, the District Court reasoned, " 'would blur, if not obliterate, a rather clear admiralty distinction.' " 707 F.Supp., at 161, quoting *Peralta*, supra, 739 F.2d at 804 [24]

The District Court denied Exxon's motion for reconsideration. The court first rejected Exxon's claim that in procuring fuel for Waterrnan it was acting as a seller rather than an agent. Additionally, the District Court declined Exxon's invitation to limit the *Minturn* rule to either general agency or preliminary service contracts.[25] Finally, the District Court determined that even if it were to limit *Minturn*, Exxon's contract with Waterman was both a general agency contract and a preliminary services contract and thus was excluded from admiralty jurisdiction under either exception. See 1989 AMC 2943, 2951–55, 717 F.Supp. 1029, 1031–1037 (S.D.N.Y.1989).

The Court of Appeals for the Second Circuit summarily affirmed the judgment of the District Court "substantially for the reasons given" in the District Court's two opinions. Reported at 904 F.2d 33 (1990). We granted certiorari to resolve a conflict among the Circuits as to the scope of the *Minturn* decision[26] and to consider whether *Minturn* should be overruled.

24. In the same action, Exxon also claimed a maritime lien on the *Hooper* for a separate unpaid fuel bill for approximately 42 tons of gas oil Exxon had supplied directly to the *Hooper* in New York. The District Court held that because Exxon was the "supplier" rather than an agent with respect to the New York delivery, the claim for $13,242 fell within the court's admiralty jurisdiction. The court granted summary judgment in Exxon's favor on this claim. 707 F.Supp., at 161–162. This ruling is not at issue here.

25. The preliminary contract rule, which excludes "preliminary services" from admiralty, was enunciated in the Second Circuit as early as 1881. See The Thames, 10 Fed. 848 (S.D.N.Y.1881)("The distinction between preliminary services leading to a maritime contract and such contracts themselves have [sic] been affirmed in this country from the first, and not yet departed from"). In the Second Circuit, the agency exception to

admiralty jurisdiction—the *Minturn* rule—has been fused with the preliminary contract rule. See Cory Bros. & Co. v. United States, 51 F.2d 1010, 1012 (2 Cir.1931)(explaining *Minturn* as involving a preliminary services contract). In denying Exxon's motion for reconsideration, the District Court declined to "disentangle" the two rules, asserting that Circuit precedent had established the rule of *Minturn* "as a subset of the preliminary contract rule." 717 F.Supp. 1029, 1036 (S.D.N.Y.1989).

26. Compare E. S. Binnings, Inc. v. M/VSaudi Riyadh, 815 F.2d 660, 662–665, and n.4 (11 Cir.1987)(general agency contracts for performance of preliminary services excluded from admiralty jurisdiction); and Peralta Shipping Corp. v. Smith & Johnson Shipping Corp., 739 F.2d 798 (2 Cir.1984)(all general agency contracts excluded), cert. denied, 470 U.S. 1031, 105 S.Ct. 1405, 84 L.Ed.2d 791(1985) with Hinkins Steamship

Holdings

498 U.S. 1045, 111 S.Ct. 750, 112 L.Ed.2d 770 (1991). Today we are constrained to overrule *Minturn* and hold that there is no *per se* exception of agency contracts from admiralty jurisdiction.

II

Section 1333(1) of Title 28 U.S.C. grants federal district courts jurisdiction over "[a]ny civil case of admiralty or maritime jurisdiction." In determining the boundaries of admiralty jurisdiction, we look to the purpose of the grant. See Insurance Co. v. Dunham, 78 U.S. (11 Wall.) 1, 24, 20 L.Ed. 90 (1871). As we recently reiterated, the "fundamental interest giving rise to maritime jurisdiction is 'the protection of maritime commerce.' " Sisson v. Ruby, 497 U.S. 358, 367, 110 S.Ct. 2892, 2897, 111 L.Ed.2d 292 (1990), quoting Foremost Ins. Co. v. Richardson, 457 U.S. 668, 674, 102 S.Ct. 2654, 2658, 73 L.Ed.2d 300 (1982). This case requires us to determine whether the limits set upon admiralty jurisdiction in *Minturn* are consistent with that interest.

The decision in *Minturn* has confounded many, and we think the character of that three-paragraph opinion is best appreciated when viewed in its entirety:

> "The respondents were sued in admiralty, by process in personam. The libel charges that they are owners of the steamboat Gold Hunter; that they had appointed the libellant their general agent or broker; and exhibits a bill, showing a balance of accounts due libellant for money paid, laid out, and expended for the use of respondents, in paying for supplies, repairs, and advertising of the steamboat, and numerous other charges, together with commissions on the disbursements, & c.

> "The court below very properly dismissed the libel, for want of jurisdiction. There is nothing in the nature of a maritime contract in the case. The libel shows nothing but a demand for a balance of accounts between agent and principal, for which an action of assumpsit, in a common law court, is the proper remedy. That the money advanced and paid for respondents was, in whole or in part, to pay bills due by a steamboat for repairs or supplies, will not make the transaction maritime, or give the libellant a remedy in admiralty. Nor does the local law of California, which authorizes an attachment of vessels for supplies or repairs, extend to the balance of accounts between agent and principal, who have never dealt on the credit, pledge, or security of the vessel.

> "The case is too plain for argument." 58 U.S. (17 How.) 477, 15 L.Ed. 235.

Agency, Inc. v. Freighters, Inc., 498 F.2d 411, 411–412 (9 Cir.1974)(per curiam)(looking to the character of the work performed by a "husbanding agent" and concluding that the contract was maritime because the services performed were "necessary for the continuing voyage"); and id., 498 F.2d at 412 (arguably limiting *Minturn* to general agency as opposed to special agency contracts); and Hadjipateras v. Pacifica, S.A., 290 F.2d 697, 703–704, and n.15 (5 Cir.1961)(holding an agency contract for management and operation of a vessel within admiralty jurisdiction and limiting *Minturn* to actions for "an accounting as such"). See also Ameejee Valleejee & Sons v. M/V Victoria U., 661 F.2d 310, 312 (4 Cir.1981)(espousing a "general proposition of law" that a general agent may not invoke admiralty jurisdiction while a special agent can).

While disagreeing over what sorts of agency contracts fall within *Minturn's* ambit, lower courts have uniformly agreed that *Minturn* states a *per se* rule barring at least some classes of agency contracts from admiralty. See n.4, supra.[27]

Minturn appears to have rested on two rationales: (1) that the agent's claim was nothing more than a "demand for a balance of accounts" which could be remedied at common law through an action of assumpsit; and (2) that the agent had no contractual or legal right to advance monies "on the credit, pledge, or security of the vessel." The first rationale appears to be an application of the then-accepted rule that "the admiralty has no jurisdiction at all in matters of account between part owners," The Steamboat Orleans v. Phoebus, 36 U.S. (11 Pet.) 175, 182, 9 L.Ed. 677 (1837), or in actions in assumpsit for the wrongful withholding of money, see Archawski v. Hanioti, 350 U.S. 532, 534, 76 S.Ct. 617, 620, 100 L.Ed. 676 (1956)("A line of authorities emerged to the effect that admiralty had no jurisdiction to grant relief in such cases"). The second rationale appears to be premised on the then-accepted rule that a contract would not be deemed maritime absent a "hypothecation" or a pledge by the vessel's owner of the vessel as security for debts created pursuant to the contract. In other words, to sue in admiralty on a contract, the claimant had to have some form of a lien interest in the vessel, even if the action was one in personam. See e.g., Gardner v. The New Jersey, 9 Fed.Cas. 1192, 1195 (No. 5233)(D. Pa.1806); see generally, Note, 17 Conn. L. Rev. 595, 597–598 (1985).

Both of these rationales have since been discredited. In *Archawski*, supra, the Court held that an action cognizable as assumpsit would no longer be automatically excluded from admiralty. Rather, "admiralty has jurisdiction, even where the libel reads like indebitatus assumpsit at common law, provided the unjust enrichment arose as a result of the breach of a maritime contract." 350 U.S. at 536, 76 S.Ct. at 621. Only 15 years after *Minturn* was decided, the Court also cast considerable doubt on the "hypothecation requirement." In Insurance Co. v. Dunham, 78 U.S. (11 Wall.) 1, 20 L.Ed. 90 (1871), the Court explained that, in determining whether a contract falls within admiralty, "the true criterion is the nature and subject-matter of the contract, as whether it was a maritime contract, having reference to maritime service or maritime transactions." Id., at 26. Several subsequent cases followed this edict of *Dunham* and rejected the relevance of the hypothecation requirement to establishing admiralty jurisdiction. See North Pacific S.S. Co. v. Hall Bros. Marine Railway & Shipbuilding Co., 249 U.S. 119, 126, 39 S.Ct. 221, 223, 63 L.Ed. 510 (1919); Detroit Trust Co. v. The Thomas Barlum, 293 U.S. 21, 47–48, 55 S.Ct. 31, 40, 79 L.Ed. 176 (1934) [28]

27. As early as 1869, however, this Court narrowed the reach of *Minturn* and cast doubt on its validity. See The Kalorama, 77 U.S. (10 Wall.) 204, 217, 19 L.Ed. 941 (1869)(distinguishing *Minturn* and allowing agents who had advanced funds for repairs and supplies for a vessel to sue in admiralty where it was "expressly agreed that the advances should be furnished on the credit of the steamer").

28. These decisions were part of a larger trend started in the 19th century of eschewing the restrictive prohibitions on admi-

Thus, to the extent that *Minturn's* theoretical underpinnings can be discerned, those foundations are no longer the law of this Court. *Minturn's* approach to determining admiralty jurisdiction, moreover, is inconsistent with the principle that the "nature and subject-matter" of the contract at issue should be the crucial consideration in assessing admiralty jurisdiction. Insurance Co. v. Dunham, supra, at 26. While the *Minturn* Court viewed it as irrelevant "[t]hat the money advanced and paid for respondents was, in whole or in part, to pay bills due by a steamboat for repairs or supplies," the trend in modern admiralty case law, by contrast, is to focus the jurisdictional inquiry upon whether the nature of the transaction was maritime. See e.g., Kossick v. United Fruit Co., 365 U.S. 731, 735–738, 81 S.Ct. 886, 890–892, 6 L.Ed.2d 56 (1961). See also Krauss Bros. Lumber Co. v. Dimon S.S. Corp., 290 U.S. 117, 124, 54 S.Ct. 105, 107, 78 L.Ed. 216 (1933)("Admiralty is not concerned with the form of the action, but with its substance").

Finally, the proposition for which *Minturn* stands—a *per se* bar of agency contracts from admiralty—ill serves the purpose of the grant of admiralty jurisdiction. As noted, the admiralty jurisdiction is designed to protect maritime commerce. See supra, at 608. There is nothing in the nature of an agency relationship that necessarily excludes such relationships from the realm of maritime commerce. Rubrics such as "general agent" and "special agent" reveal nothing about whether the services actually performed pursuant to a contract are maritime in nature. It is inappropriate, therefore, to focus on the status of a claimant to determine whether admiralty jurisdiction exists. Cf. *Sisson*, 497 U.S. at 364, n. 2, 110 S.Ct., at 2896, n. 2 ("the demand for tidy rules can go too far, and when that demand entirely divorces the jurisdictional inquiry from the purposes that support the exercise of jurisdiction, it *has* gone too far").

We conclude that *Minturn* is incompatible with current principles of admiralty jurisdiction over contracts and therefore should be overruled. We emphasize that our ruling is a narrow one. We remove only the precedent of *Minturn* from the body of rules that have developed over what types of contracts are maritime. Rather than apply a rule excluding all or certain agency contracts from the realm of admiralty, lower courts should look to the subject matter of the agency contract and determine whether the services performed under the contract are maritime in nature. See generally *Kossick*, supra, 365 U.S. at 735–738, 81 S.Ct. at 890–892 (analogizing the substance of the contract at issue to established types of

---

ralty jurisdiction that prevailed in England. See e.g.,Waring v. Clarke, 46 U.S. (5 How.) 441, 454–459, 12 L.Ed. 226 (1847)(holding that the constitutional grant of admiralty jurisdiction did not adopt the statutory and judicial rules limiting admiralty jurisdiction in England); The Propeller Genesee Chief v. Fitzhugh, 53 U.S. (12 How.) 443, 456–457, 13 L.Ed. 1058 (1852)(rejecting the English tide-water doctrine that "measure[d]the jurisdiction of the admiralty by the tide"); Insurance Co. v. Dunham, 78 U.S. (11 Wall.) at 26 (rejecting the English locality rule on maritime contracts "which concedes[admiralty] jurisdiction, with a few exceptions, only to contracts made upon the sea and to be executed thereon").

"maritime" obligations and finding the contract within admiralty jurisdiction).

III

There remains the question whether admiralty jurisdiction extends to Exxon's claim regarding the delivery of fuel in Jeddah. We conclude that it does. Like the District Court, we believe it is clear that when Exxon directly supplies marine fuels to Waterman's ships, the arrangement is maritime in nature. See 707 F.Supp. at 161. Cf. The Golden Gate, 52 F.2d 397 (9 Cir.1931)(entertaining an action in admiralty for the value of fuel oil furnished to a vessel), cert. denied sub nom. Knutsen v. Associated Oil Co., 284 U.S. 682, 52 S.Ct. 199, 76 L.Ed. 576 (1932). In this case, the only difference between the New York delivery over which the District Court asserted jurisdiction, see n.2, supra, and the Jeddah delivery was that, in Jeddah, Exxon bought the fuels from a third party and had the third party deliver them to the *Hooper*. The subject matter of the Jeddah claim, like the New York claim, is the value of the fuel received by the ship. Because the nature and subject-matter of the two transactions are the same as they relate to maritime commerce, if admiralty jurisdiction extends to one, it must extend to the other. Cf. *North Pacific*, supra, at 128, 39 S.Ct. at 224 ("[T]here is no difference in character as to repairs made upon . . . a vessel . . . whether they are made while she is afloat, while in dry dock, or while hauled up [on] land. The nature of the service is identical in the several cases, and the admiralty jurisdiction extends to all").[29] We express no view on whether Exxon is entitled to a maritime lien under the Federal Maritime Lien Act. That issue is not before us, and we leave it to be decided on remand.

The judgment of the Court of Appeals is reversed, and the case is remanded for further proceedings consistent with this opinion.

NOTE

A contract to supply a crew for a vessel has been held to be non-maritime. See, e.g., Goumas v. K. Karras & Son, 51 F.Supp. 145, 1943 A.M.C. 818 (S.D.N.Y.1943), aff'd 140 F.2d 157 (2d Cir.1944). But when the contract provided for involvement in the daily operation of the vessel, including paying the crew and using its good offices in labor negotiations involving grievances concerning "daily life on board," a suit arising out of refusal of the crew to perform its duties was held to be maritime. Bergen Shipping Co., Ltd. v. Japan Marine Services, Ltd., 386 F.Supp. 430, 1975 A.M.C. 490 (S.D.N.Y.1974).

29. As noted, the District Court regarded the services performed by Exxon in the Jeddah transaction as "preliminary" and characterized the rule excluding agency contracts from admiralty as "a subset" of the preliminary contract doctrine. See supra, at 1820, and n.3. This Court has never ruled on the validity of the preliminary contract doctrine, nor do we reach that question here. However, we emphasize that Minturn has been overruled and that courts should focus on the nature of the services performed by the agent in determining whether an agency contract is a maritime contract.

A contract to procure maritime insurance has been held non-maritime. See Warner v. The Bear, 126 F.Supp. 529, 1955 A.M.C. 1123 (D.Alaska 1955). But cf. Stanley T. Scott & Co., Inc. v. Makah Development Corp., 496 F.2d 525, 1974 A.M.C. 934 (9th Cir.1974). There it was held that a suit by an insurance agent for reimbursement of amount advanced on an oral binder on a marine policy obtained by the agent for the vessel owner was maritime. The court disposed of the jurisdictional issue in two short paragraphs without a nod to the cases holding contracts to obtain insurance non-maritime, observing that a marine insurance contract is maritime and that the agent's claim "arises out of a maritime contract" and is thus within the admiralty jurisdiction. Judge Wallace dissented. Is the distinction between *Scott* and the contract to procure cases that breach of a contract to procure arises out of the preliminary dealings and no maritime contract was entered into, while in the premium cases the "claim" could not exist until there was an acceptance of the binder? Note that actions for recovery of insurance premiums have long been entertained in admiralty. See Gilmore & Black, Law of the Admiralty, 22 (1975). See also Grow v. Steel Gas Screw Loraine K, 310 F.2d 547, 1963 A.M.C. 2044 (6th Cir.1962), cited by the court in *Scott*.

When does a claim, not otherwise maritime "arise" out of a maritime contract? In the *Terminal Shipping Co.* case, supra at p. 73, suppose the libelant had entered into contracts with a third party for the lease of equipment to be used in the loading and unloading of the vessel. Would a breach of these contracts be within the admiralty jurisdiction? See T. Smith & Son, Inc. v. Henry F. Rigby Dozer Service, 305 F.Supp. 418, 1969 A.M.C. 2092 (E.D.La.1969) holding such an equipment rental contract non-maritime.

Flota Maritima Browning De Cuba v. Ciudad De La Habana

United States Court of Appeal, Fourth Circuit, 1964.
335 F.2d 619, 1966 A.M.C. 1999.

■ CLEMENT F. HAYNSWORTH, JR., CH. J. Banco Para El Comerico Exterior de Cuba and the Republic of Cuba seek, in addition to other incidental relief, to set aside an order of the United States District Court for the District of Maryland directing the sale, pursuant to Admiralty Rule 12, of the motor vessel Ciudad de la Habana. The source of the controversy and the details of related litigation appear more fully in other opinions.[1]

Banco is a Cuban corporation, organized by the Republic of Cuba for the advancement of its foreign trade. Banco's predecessor negotiated with an American citizen, Browning, for an agreement to operate certain vessels then owned by it. To this end Browning, together with other American citizens, formed a Cuban corporation, Flota Maritima Browning de Cuba, Sociedad Anonima, with which Banco entered into two agreements[2] to lease

---

1. Flota Maritima Browning v. Motor Vessel Ciudad de la Habana, 335 F.2d 619 (4 Cir.1964) 1964 A.M.C. 1641, affirming, 218 F.Supp. 938, 1963 A.M.C. 1734; Flota Maritima Browning v. Ciudad de la Habana, 181 F.Supp. 301, 1960 A.M.C. 496 (D.C.Md.1960).

2. One agreement, the "English Lease Purchase Contract," covers six vessels for a term of fifteen years. The other, the "Canadian Lease Purchase Contract," relates to eight vessels purchased by Banco from Canadian National (West Indies) Steamships, Ltd.,

the vessels. Flota Maritima was given an option to purchase the vessels, with previously paid rentals to be applied to the purchase price. Banco retained the right to convert the leases into a contract of sale with a marine mortgage in an amount equal to the unpaid purchase price, computed as if Flota Maritima had exercised its option. Each agreement required Flota Maritima to pay a specified monthly rental which, over the term of the agreement, would equal or exceed the purchase price.

In October, 1958, after the motor vessel, Cuidad de la Habana had been brought to Baltimore for outfitting pursuant to one of the agreements, a dispute arose between the parties over the performance of the contracts, and Flota Maritima delivered the vessels back to Banco which then continued the outfitting of the Habana in Baltimore. On June 9, 1959, allegedly, the vessels were transferred by Banco to the Republic of Cuba. The original libel, filed June 22, 1959, was *in rem* against the Habana and *in personam* with a clause of foreign attachment against Banco. An amended libel was filed October 9, 1959. Since June, 1959, the Habana has been in the custody of a United States Marshal in dead anchorage in Baltimore harbor, unmaintained and unmanned; its condition has deteriorated steadily.

In its libel, Flota Maritima sought to recover as damages sums expended in outfitting the vessels and loss of the profits anticipated in the performance of the lease. Banco has filed a cross libel against Flota Maritima, also for breach of the lease-purchase agreement. Cuba has filed a claim as owner of the vessel.

After our earlier disposition of the claim of sovereign immunity,[3] Flota Maritima moved for an order, pursuant to Admiralty Rule 12, directing sale of the Habana. Banco moved for cross-security on its cross libel under Admiralty Rule 50, and Cuba moved for an order compelling the Marshal to restore the Habana or to procure a bond securing the cost of restoration. Banco and Cuba appeal the adverse determination of these motions.

Appellants interpose again[4] on this appeal the argument that ship lease-purchase agreements are not within the jurisdiction of an admiralty court. Although subjected to recent criticism,[5] the prevailing rule has been that a contract for the sale of a ship is not a maritime contract.[6] The

---

and three other vessels owned by Banco. It extended for a term of seven years and included the Ciudad de la Habana, formerly the Canadian Challenger. The libel pursuant to which the Habana was seized contains a cause of action based upon an alleged breach of each contract.

3. Flota Maritima Browning v. Motor Vessel Ciudad de la Habana, 335 F.2d 619, (4 Cir.1964), 1964 A.M.C. 1641, affirming 218 F.Supp. 938, 1963 A.M.C. 1734.

4. This argument was rejected in Flota Maritima Browning v. Ciudad de la Habana, 181 F.Supp. 301, 1960 A.M.C. 496 (D.C.Md.

1960), and no appeal was taken. It was not advanced when the case was here before. Unquestionably, however, lack of jurisdiction over the subject matter may be raised at any time.

5. Flota Maritima Browning, supra, note 4; Gilmore & Black, Admiralty, 24–25; Note, the Law of Admiralty and Ship Sale Contracts, 6 Stan.L.Rev. 540.

6. The Ada, 250 F. 194 (2 Cir.1918); Grand Banks Fishing Co. v. Styron (Caracara), 114 F.Supp. 1, 1953 A.M.C. 2172 (D.C.Me.1953); Hirsch v. San Pablo, 81 F.Supp. 292, 1948 A.M.C. 1992. Similarly,

[handwritten margin note: Where mixed maritime & non-maritime elements — if one can separate out the maritime elements — jurisdiction]

charter of a vessel, however, is maritime.[7] Banco advances the principle that if a contract is not wholly maritime there is no admiralty jurisdiction. While the principle is one of general validity when the non-maritime elements of the contract are substantial and inseparable from the maritime elements,[8] it has long been recognized that where the maritime elements of a contract are susceptible to separate adjudication, admiralty jurisdiction may be exercised to that extent. Compagnie Francaise de Navigation a Vapeur v. Bonnasse, 19 F.2d 777, 779, 1927 A.M.C. 1325 (2 Cir.1927); Eastern Mass. Street Ry. v. Transmarine Corp., 42 F.2d 58, 1930 A.M.C. 1454 (1 Cir.1930); Berwind White Coal Mining Co. v. City of New York, 135 F.2d 443, 1943 A.M.C. 682 (2 Cir.1943).

We agree with the District Judge, largely for the reasons expressed by him in a thoughtful opinion,[9] that the maritime aspects of this lease-purchase agreement are separable and that the specific claims may be adjudicated in an admiralty court.

In Ada, 250 F. 194 (2 Cir.1918), the court held that claims arising out of the breach of a charter agreement containing an option to purchase were not cognizable in admiralty. From the three separate opinions filed by the court, however, it is apparent that each judge considered the agreement primarily one for the sale of the vessel. The lease agreement there was limited to a period of six months. During that period the charterer had the use of the vessel upon payment of a fixed sum in specified installments. It also had an option to purchase the vessel at any time for the same sum, the owner agreeing to deposit a bill of sale in escrow as soon as possible. At the time of the breach of the contract, the charterer had in fact exercised his option to purchase, thereby converting the agreement into a contract of sale.

an admiralty court does not have jurisdiction to compel specific performance of a contract to purchase a vessel. Rea v. Eclipse, 135 U.S. 599, 10 S.Ct. 873, 34 L.Ed. 269 (1890); Guayaquil, 29 F.Supp. 578, 1939 A.M.C. 1294 (S.D.N.Y.1939).

7. See J.B. Effenson Co. v. Three Bays Corp., 1957 A.M.C. 16, 238 F.2d 611 (5 Cir. 1957); Cory Bros. & Co. v. United States, 51 F.2d 1010, 1931 A.M.C. 1442 (2 Cir.1931); Gronvold v. Suryan, 12 F.Supp. 429, 1936 A.M.C. 105 (W.D.Wash.1935).

8. The Ada, 250 Fed. 194 (2 Cir.1918); Compagnie Francaise de Navigation a Vapeur v. Bonnasse, 19 F.2d 777, 1927 A.M.C. 1325 (2 Cir.1927); D.C. Andrews & Co. v. United States, 124 F.Supp. 362, 1954 A.M.C. 2221 (Ct.Cl.1954). But see, Sword Line, Inc. v. United States, 228 F.2d 344, 1956 A.M.C. 47 (2 Cir.1956), aff'd 351 U.S. 976, 76 S.Ct. 1047, 100 L.Ed. 1493, 1956 A.M.C. 1464 (jurisdiction in admiralty over charterer's suit in

quasi contract to recover excess charges); Luckenbach S.S. Co. v. Coast Mfg. & Sup. Co., 185 F.Supp. 910, 916, 1960 A.M.C. 2076 (S.D.N.Y.1960), (incidental to admiralty elements and non-separable); Gronvold v. Suryan, supra, note 7 (incidental elements and non-separable). Where the non-maritime elements of a contract are considered separable from those maritime, and admiralty court is ousted of jurisdiction over the former. Pillsbury Flour Mills Co. v. Interlake S.S. Co., 40 F.2d 439, 1930 A.M.C. 774 (2 Cir.1930), cert. denied 282 U.S. 845, 51 S.Ct. 24, 75 L.Ed. 750; Armstrong Cork Co. v. Farrell, 81 F.Supp. 848, 1948 A.M.C. 1708 (E.D.Pa. 1948); Ciano, 63 F.Supp. 892, 1945 A.M.C. 1474 (E.D.Pa.1946).

9. Flota Maritima Browning v. Ciudad de la Habana, 181 F.Supp. 301, 1960 A.M.C. 496 (D.C.Md.1960).

Under other lease-purchase agreements, however, claims may arise which are clearly founded upon the lease provisions and which would be within admiralty jurisdiction. The primary opinion in *Ada* clearly recognized this possibility.

In this case the agreements were to extend for periods of seven and fifteen years. The economic compulsion to exercise the purchase option is clearly not so great where the cost of use for a long period approximates purchase price as it is where the cost of use for six months is the same as the purchase price. Nor is there an indication that the rentals here were so unreasonably high as to suggest a disguised sale. Although the contract could have been converted into a sale at the option of either party, up to the time of its termination it had not been. Unlike the contract in *Ada*, at the time the libel was filed, the parties had operated only under the lease provisions and the purchase-sale options were unexercised. The character of the contract was thus fixed, as between the parties, as a charter.

The District Court's opinion rested in part upon an interpretation of the Canadian agreement which gave the lessee a right to terminate at any time without penalty. That interpretation is challenged here, but the absence of such a provision does not mean that the lease provisions must be disregarded and the agreement treated as a contract of sale.

The damages sought are for loss of the profits of operating the vessels and for certain sums expended in outfitting the ship. The maritime character of contracts to operate[10] or repair[11] a vessel is clear. It would be an unduly strict limitation of traditional admiralty jurisdiction to hold that power to deal with these maritime claims was lost merely because they were based upon an agreement which contained dormant, non-maritime as well as maritime provisions.[12] Where such non-maritime provisions are contingent and have never been given effect, it is not difficult to separate them from the contract and permit separate adjudication in admiralty of the maritime claims arising out of the contract.

Objection to the order of sale on the basis of asserted lack of admiralty jurisdiction, with which we have dealt, is supplemented by a reiteration of the claim of sovereign immunity. That claim was first advanced on behalf of the Republic of Cuba long after it had entered a general appearance. It was denied by the District Court.[13] We affirmed on the ground that the claim in both its jurisdictional and execution aspects had been effectively waived.[14] The Supreme Court denied leave to file a petition for a writ of

10. See note 7, supra.

11. New Bedford Drydock Co. v. Purdy, 258 U.S. 96, 42 S.Ct. 243, 66 L.Ed. 482; The Scorpio, 181 F.2d 356, 1950 A.M.C. 756 (5 Cir.1950).

12. See Eastern Mass. Street Ry. v. Transmarine Corp., 42 F.2d 58, 1930 A.M.C. 1454 (1 Cir.1930).

13. 218 F.Supp. 938, 1963 A.M.C. 1734 (D.C.D.Md.1963).

14. 335 F.2d 619, 1964 A.M.C. 1641 (4 Cir.1963).

prohibition or mandamus.[15]

The Czechoslovakian Ambassador, on behalf of the Republic of Cuba, now undertakes a fragmentation of the claim of execution immunity. We have held only, he says, that a claim of the vessel's immunity from arrest and continued detention may not be asserted; immunity from sale, he contends, is another question.

We think not. When Banco and Cuba entered their general appearance, the claim of sovereign immunity from execution was waived; there were no explicit or implicit limitations. We held previously that because seizure was for the purpose of execution as well as jurisdiction, immunity in both aspects was waived when the general appearance was entered without reservation.

In its execution aspect, the arrest of the vessel, and its subsequent detention, were solely for the purpose of securing payment of the claim out of the proceeds of a sale or out of a bond if the owner obtains the vessel's release. For execution purposes, detention of the vessel, or the bond which stands in her stead, is meaningful only in terms of its ultimate conversion into money for the benefit of the libellant. The things are inseparable, and a general waiver of immunity during any stage of the proceedings.

The immunity claim, as an objection to an order of sale, was fully adjudicated when the case was here before.

There are other objections to the order of sale and appeals from denial of Banco's motion for cross security and of Cuba's motion to require the United States Marshal to restore the vessel to her former condition. We affirm the District Court in all of those respects for reasons which sufficiently appear in its opinion of August 16, 1965.[16]

The order of sale is affirmed, and this Court's order staying the sale during the pendency of these appeals is dissolved. A certified copy of the judgment in lieu of a mandate will issue forthwith.

Affirmed.

■ ALBERT V. BRYAN, CT. J., dissenting.

NOTE

The Ciudad De La Habana was followed in the Fifth Circuit in Jack Neilson, Inc. v. Tug Peggy, 428 F.2d 54, 1970 A.M.C. 1490 (5th Cir.1970). See Note, Admiralty Jurisdiction and Ship Sale Contracts, 6 Stan.L.Rev. 540 (1954), referred to by Judge Wisdom as "an important commentary on the origin of the ship-sale rule and its history in the courts". Cf. Clem Perrin Marine Towing, Inc. v. Panama Canal Co.,

15. 380 U.S. 970, 85 S.Ct. 1349, 14 L.Ed.2d 281 (1965).

16. Flota Maritima Browning de Cuba, Sociadad Anonima vs. Motor Vessel Ciudad de la Habana, 245 F.Supp. 205, 1965 A.M.C.

1816 (D.Md.1965). We do not grant the motions to dismiss the appeals because of the substantial effect a sale of the vessel may have upon the ultimate rights of the parties.

730 F.2d 186 (5th Cir.1984), in which the court found it unnecessary to address the lease-purchase issue because there would be jurisdiction in any event.

Contracts of sale simpliciter remain outside the admiralty and maritime jurisdiction. See Twin City Barge & Towing Co. v. Aiple, 709 F.2d 507 (8th Cir.1983). In an unpublished opinion in Magnolia Ocean Shipping v. M/V Mercedes Maria, 644 F.2d 880 (4th Cir.1981)(Table), printed at 1982 A.M.C. 731, the Fourth Circuit noted criticism of the ship-sale rule, mentioning in particular Moore's Federal Practice, adding, "A learned commentator, especially one of the stature of Professor Moore, may more readily indulge himself in the luxury of disclaiming a developed line of authority than a federal judge." Does the failure to publish the opinion and disposition of the appeal in the "table" suggest a reluctance to add to the store of precedents supporting the ship-sale rule?

In addition to the cases dealing with the lease with option to buy, there are other transactions that skirt the edges of the ship-sale rule. What of a sale with free storage for the winter. In Snyder v. 4 Winds Sailboat Centre, 701 F.2d 251 (2d Cir.1983), the plaintiff traded his boat in for a larger model under a contract of sale which entitled him to free storage for the winter. He took possession of the new boat in October, and on November 4, he told them to "lock it up for winter." The boat disappeared and was never heard from again. Should a suit for the loss of the boat be brought in admiralty?

The fact that there has been a sale does not rob the admiralty court of jurisdiction to entertain a petitory or possessory libel. See Jones v. One Fifty Foot Gulfstar Motor Sailing Yacht, Hull No. 01, 625 F.2d 44, 1981 A.M.C. 1005 (5th Cir.1980). In that case the purchaser of a yacht was permitted to maintain a petitory libel in admiralty to test his legal title against the assertion of a secured interest in the seller's inventory.

But see Richard Bertram & Co. v. Yacht Wanda, 447 F.2d 966 (5th Cir.1971), where it was held that an action framed as a possessory or petitory action was of maritime jurisdiction whether viewed as a suit to enforce a security interest or mortgage, a suit to try or quiet title, or for breach of contract for sale, or for breach of contract to construct a vessel.

Suppose a claim under a contract of sale is pleaded as a counterclaim. See William P. Brooks Const. Co. v. Guthrie, 614 F.2d 509, 1981 A.M.C. 303 (5th Cir.1980). There plaintiff, who was title holder of record, brought a possessory action in admiralty to recover possession of the vessel and defendant filed a cross-action asserting an oral contract of sale. The court held that the sale contract defense embodied in the "cross-action" did not deprive the court of jurisdiction.

As with a contract of purchase, a contract between parties to purchase and operate a vessel for their mutual profit is not a maritime contract. Economu v. Bates, 222 F.Supp. 988, 1965 A.M.C. 1289 (S.D.N.Y.1963).

Mixed Contracts

When taken as a whole the contract is maritime, the particular claim of breach needn't be maritime. See, e.g., Ocean Science & Engineering Inc. v. International Geomarine Corp., 312 F.Supp. 825, 1971 A.M.C. 143 (D.Del.1970). There a contract was for the conduct of geophysical surveys, making of geological observations and measurements, and collection of geological samples, for the purpose of mapping in detail and determining the geophysical make-up and mineral composition of the sea bottom sediments and intersticial brines of a designated area of the Red Sea. The contract was held to be maritime when it provided that the work should be carried out from a certain vessel.

B.   JURISDICTION IN TORT CASES

1.   MARITIME LOCATION

The Admiral Peoples

Supreme Court of the United States, 1935.
295 U.S. 649, 55 S.Ct. 885, 79 L.Ed. 1633.

■ MR. CHIEF JUSTICE HUGHES delivered the opinion of the Court.

Petitioner was a passenger on the steamship "Admiral Peoples" on her voyage from Wilmington, California, to Portland, Oregon.   While disembarking at Portland petitioner was injured by falling from a gangplank leading from the vessel to the dock.   This libel *in rem* against the vessel alleged that respondent placed the gangplank so that it sloped from the ship toward the dock at an angle of from ten to fifteen degrees;   that it was approximately two feet in width and eighteen feet in length and was equipped with the usual rope railings which terminated approximately three feet from each end;   that the level of the plank at the shore end was about six inches above the level of the dock, thereby creating a step from the plank to the dock;   that upon instructions from one of respondent's officers, libelant proceeded along the plank and as she reached its lower end, being unaware of the step and having no warning, she fell from the plank and was "violently and forcibly thrown forward upon the dock in such manner as to cause the injuries hereinafter set forth."   Libelant alleged negligence in failing to provide a handrope or railing extending along either side of the gangplank to the shore end, in failing to have the plank flush with the dock or taper off to the level of the dock, and in failing to give warning of the step.

Respondent's exception to the libel, upon the ground that the case was not within the admiralty jurisdiction, was sustained by the District Court, and its judgment dismissing the libel was affirmed by the Circuit Court of Appeals.   In view of an asserted conflict with other decisions of the federal courts,[1] we granted a writ of certiorari.

This is one of the border cases involving the close distinctions which from time to time are necessary in applying the principles governing the admiralty jurisdiction.   That jurisdiction in cases of tort depends upon the locality of the injury.   It does not extend to injuries caused by a vessel to persons or property on the land.   Where the cause of action arises upon the

---

1. Compare The Strabo, 90 F. 110 (D.C.N.Y.1898); Id., 98 F. 998 (2d Cir.1900); The H.S. Pickands, 42 F. 239 (D.C.Mich. 1890); The Aurora, 163 F. 633 (D.C.Or. 1908); Id., 178 F. 587 (D.C.Or.1910); Aurora Shipping Co. v. Boyce, 191 F. 960 (9 Cir. 1912); The Atna, 297 F. 673 (D.C.Wash. 1924); The Brand, 29 F.2d 792 (D.C.Or. 1929).

land, the state law is applicable. The Plymouth, 3 Wall. 20, 33, 18 L.Ed.
125 (1865); Johnson v. Chicago & Pacific Elevator Co., 119 U.S. 388, 397, 7
S.Ct. 254, 30 L.Ed. 447 (1886); Cleveland Terminal & V.R. Co. v. Cleveland
Steamship Co., 208 U.S. 316, 319, 28 S.Ct. 414, 52 L.Ed. 508 (1908);
Atlantic Transport Co. v. Imbrovek, 234 U.S. 52, 59, 34 S.Ct. 733, 58 L.Ed.
1208 (1914); State Industrial Comm'n v. Nordenholt Corp., 259 U.S. 263,
272, 42 S.Ct. 473, 66 L.Ed. 933 (1922); Smith & Son v. Taylor, 276 U.S.
179, 181, 48 S.Ct. 228, 72 L.Ed. 520 (1928); compare Vancouver S.S. Co. v.
Rice, 288 U.S. 445, 448, 53 S.Ct. 420, 77 L.Ed. 885 (1933).

The basic fact in the instant case is that the gangplank was a part of
the vessel. It was a part of the vessel's equipment which was placed in
position to enable its passengers to reach the shore. It was no less a part
of the vessel because in its extension to the dock it projected over the land.
Thus, while the libelant was on the gangplank she had not yet left the
vessel. This was still true as she proceeded to the shore end of the plank.
If while on that part of the vessel she had been hit by a swinging crane and
had been precipitated upon the dock, the admiralty would have had
jurisdiction of her claim. See Minnie v. Port Huron Terminal Co., decided
this day, ante, p. 647. If instead of being struck in this way, the negligent
handling of the vessel, as by a sudden movement, had caused her to fall
from the gangplank, the cause of action would still have arisen on the
vessel. We perceive no basis for a sound distinction because her fall was
due to negligence in the construction or placing of the gangplank. By
reason of that neglect, as the libel alleges, she fell from the plank and was
violently thrown forward upon the dock. Neither the short distance that
she fell nor the fact that she fell on the dock and not in the water, alters
the nature of the cause of action which arose from the breach of duty owing
to her while she was still on the ship and using its facility for disembarking.

This view is supported by the weight of authority in the federal courts.
In The Strabo, 90 F. 110 (D.C.N.Y.1899), aff'd 98 F. 998, 39 C.C.A. 375,
libelant, who was working on a vessel lying at a dock, attempted to leave
the vessel by means of a ladder which, by reason of the master's negligence,
was not secured properly to the ship's rail and in consequence the ladder
fell and the libelant was thrown to the dock and injured. The District
Court, sustaining the admiralty jurisdiction, asked these pertinent questions (90 Fed. p. 113): "If a passenger, standing at the gangway, for the
purpose of alighting, were disturbed by some negligent act of the master,
would the jurisdiction of this court depend upon the fact whether he fell on
the dock, and remained there, or whether he was precipitated upon the
dock in the first instance, or finally landed there after first falling on some
part of the ship? If a seaman, by the master's neglect, should fall
overboard, would this court entertain jurisdiction if the seaman fell in the
water, and decline jurisdiction if he fell on the dock or other land? The
inception of a cause of action is not usually defined by such a rule." The
Circuit Court of Appeals of the Second Circuit, affirming the decision of the
District Court (98 Fed. p. 1000), thought it would be a too literal and an
inadmissible interpretation of the language used in The Plymouth, supra,

to say that "if a passenger on board a steamship should, through the negligence of the owners, stumble on the ship upon a defective gangplank, and be precipitated upon the wharf, the injury would not be a maritime tort." "The language employed in the *Plymouth* decision," said the court, "and which was applicable to the circumstances of that case, does not justify such a conclusion." And, deciding the case before it, the Circuit Court of Appeals said: "The cause of action originated and the injury had commenced on the ship, the consummation somewhere being inevitable. It is not of vital importance to the admiralty jurisdiction whether the injury culminated on the stringpiece of the wharf or in the water." See, also, The Atna, 297 F. 673, 675, 676 (D.C.Wash.1924); The Brand, 29 F.2d 792 (D.C.Or.1929).

In L'Hote v. Crowell, 54 F.2d 212 (5 Cir.1932) a longshoreman, who had been working on a wharf in putting bales in a sling which was raised by the ship's tackle and then lowered into its hold, was riding on the last load when the sling struck against the rail or side of the ship, with the result that he fell to the wharf and was injured. The Circuit Court of Appeals of the Fifth Circuit said that he had "finished his work on the wharf and from the time he was lifted from it by the sling by means of the ship's tackle was under the control of an instrumentality of the ship"; and, in that view, the jurisdiction of admiralty was sustained. The ruling in that case was not disturbed by our decision on certiorari (as the Circuit Court of Appeals in the instant case mistakenly supposed), as our writ was expressly limited to the question raised by the review of the deputy commissioner's finding as to the dependency of a claimant for compensation under the Longshoremen's and Harbor Workers' Compensation Act, 33 U.S.C.A. §§ 901–950. 285 U.S. 533, 52 S.Ct. 406, 76 L.Ed. 928 (1932). We decided simply that the finding of the deputy commissioner, upon evidence, against the dependency of the claimant, was final, and accordingly we directed the affirmance of his order. 286 U.S. 528, 52 S.Ct. 499, 76 L.Ed. 1270 (1932). See Voehl v. Indemnity Insurance Co., 288 U.S. 162, 166, 53 S.Ct. 380, 77 L.Ed. 676 (1933).

We think that the libel presented a case within the jurisdiction of admiralty. The decree of the Circuit Court of Appeals is reversed and the cause is remanded for further proceedings in conformity with this opinion. Reversed.

NOTE

The general doctrine of *The Plymouth*, as developed in *The Admiral Peoples*, that admiralty tort jurisdiction is bounded by locality, had been taken for granted for a long time. In DeLovio v. Boit, 7 Fed.Cas. 418, 2 Gall. 398 (1815), Justice Story, after a detailed analysis to demonstrate that the true criterion of admiralty contract jurisdiction was the maritime character of the subject matter, observed in one short sentence that jurisdiction in tort is "necessarily bounded by locality." And this principle was recognized by the Supreme Court without serious question until the decision in Executive Jet Aviation, Inc. v. City of Cleveland, 409 U.S. 249, 93 S.Ct. 493, 34 L.Ed.2d 454, 1973 A.M.C. 1 (1972), discussed in the following subhead. In

Victory Carriers v. Law, decided the year before, the Court cited over 40 cases to that effect, a fact it noted in *Executive Jet*. 409 U.S. at 254 n. 4, 93 S.Ct. at 497 n. 4.

Apart from the fact that The Plymouth and the Admiral Peoples fortified the doctrine that tort jurisdiction depends on the locality of the tort, they served as exemplars of where torts take place for purposes of the locality doctrine. In cases involving similar facts the rule of *The Admiral Peoples* has generally been followed. See, e.g., White v. United States, 53 F.3d 43, 1995 A.M.C. 1904 (4th Cir.1995), in which a security guard lost her balance and stumbled when she stepped upon a small wooden platform at the end of the gangway of the Government's vessel, and ultimately collided with equipment stored near a building on the pier.

And in Odeco Oil & Gas Co. v. Bonnette, 4 F.3d 401, 1994 A.M.C. 506 (5th Cir.1993), it was held that injury in a fall of a rescue capsule from a fixed drilling platform into the water is "sufficiently salty" to support admiralty jurisdiction.

The Plymouth and *The Admiral Peoples* did not cover all possibilities. In *The Plymouth*, although the breach of duty took place on the the vessel, no injury to the person or property of the plaintiff occurred there. In such circumstances it was held that an action for damages did not lie in the admiralty, and this holding survived until the expansion of the jurisdiction in the Extension Act of 1948. See United States v. Matson Navigation Co., 201 F.2d 610, 614 (9th Cir.1953). The mirror image of the *The Plymouth* would be the case of a fire on the pier that spread to a vessel, or where a bridge or other land structure causes damage to a vessel in navigable water. In such cases it was held that redress could be had in admiralty. Cases are collected in 1 Benedict on Admiralty, 6th Ed.,§ 128b, noted by the court in *Matson, supra*. The effect of the Extension Act is discussed in the following subhead.

This principle that injury on navigable waters through a breach of duty or wrongful act occurring on land constitutes a maritime tort survived so long as locality of the tort was recognized as the sole criterion of admiralty jurisdiction in tort cases, and still governs the location of the tort to the extent that maritime location is required.

Injury to passengers on a small boat from bullets fired from the shore have been held to be maritime torts. Kelly v. Smith, 485 F.2d 520, 1973 A.M.C. 2478 (5th Cir.1973).

Shelling close to plaintiff in his boat by military installation located on land. Szyka v. U.S. Secretary of Defense, 525 F.2d 62, 1975 A.M.C. 2504 (2d Cir.1975).

Emission of smoke by a paper mill located on land, that allegedly caused a collision between a vessel and a bridge by reducing the visibility. Gypsum Carrier, Inc. v. Union Camp Corp., 489 F.2d 152, 1974 A.M.C. 227 (5th Cir.1974).

Negligent design and manufacture of a vessel or its component parts causing injury on navigable waters. Mink v. Genmar Industries, Inc., 29 F.3d 1543, 1995 A.M.C. 36 (11th Cir.1994), applying three year statute for maritime torts to bar action by purchaser of speed boat injured on a demonstration run, allegedly through failure of the manufacturer to provide adequate handholds on the boat.

Turbines installed in a new vessels by a subcontractor, when the failure of the turbines occurred on the high seas. East River Steamship Corp. v. Transamerica Delaval, Inc. , 476 U.S. 858, 106 S.Ct. 2295, 90 L.Ed.2d 865, 1986 A.M.C. 2027 (1986).

The rule of The Admiral Peoples and its mirror image are more difficult to apply. In that case the gravamin was negligence in the provision of a safe method of egress from the vessel, and the accident was that the passenger tripped. Thus the minimum reading of the decision is merely that in a slip and fall accident, the accident takes place where the victim *slips and falls*, not where he *lands*. This does not exhaust the possibilities, however, and the reported cases on tort location include a fascinating collection of marginal situations. There have been cases in which the victim has been standing on the pier and struck by a sling load of cargo suspended from the vessel's equipment. Nacirema Operating Co. v. Johnson, 396 U.S. 212, 90 S.Ct. 347, 24 L.Ed.2d 371, 1969 A.M.C. 1967(1969). There one victim was picked up by the ship's equipment and dropped on the pier while another was crushed against the side of a gondola car. There have been cases in which the injured party was on the vessel and knocked to the pier. Minnie v. Port Huron Terminal Co., 295 U.S. 647, 55 S.Ct. 884, 79 L.Ed. 1631, 1935 A.M.C. 879 (1935). There have been cases in which the victim was picked up by the vessel's equipment and dropped, but it was not possible to tell whether he struck the pier, the vessel, or went directly into the water. O'Keeffe v. Atlantic Stevedoring Co., 354 F.2d 48, 1966 A.M.C. 209 (5th Cir.1965). There have been cases in which the victim fell through a hole in the pier. Thomson v. Chesapeake Yacht Club, 255 F.Supp. 555, 1965 A.M.C. 2442 (D.Md.1965). There have been cases in which the victim was standing in the water. Hastings v. Mann, 340 F.2d 910, 1965 A.M.C. 549 (4th Cir.1965). There have been cases in which the victim was above the water. Notarian v. TWA, 244 F.Supp. 874, 1966 A.M.C. 1384 (W.D.Pa.1965). There have been cases in which the victim dove off the pier into the water. Chapman v. City of Grosse Pointe Farms, 385 F.2d 962, 1968 A.M.C. 386 (6 Cir.1967). And there have been cases in which he drove off the pier in an automobile. Interlake Steamship Co. v. Nielsen, 338 F.2d 879, 1965 A.M.C. 1542 (6 Cir.1964), cert. denied 381 U.S. 934, 85 S.Ct. 1765, 14 L.Ed.2d 699 (1965).

Cliff-hangers continue to turn up. See, e.g., Parker by and Through Parker v. Gulf City Fisheries, Inc. There jurisdiction was upheld in an action against a physician who, while on dry land, allegedly failed to give adequate medical advice when consulted by a seaman's wife while the seaman was on board a vessel, and the seaman suffered a stroke after returning from the voyage. With Miller v. Griffin–Alexander Drilling Co., 873 F.2d 809 (5th Cir.1989). There it was held that treatment by a doctor on shore of a mud man who had been injured on a drilling barge did not give rise to a maritime tort. The court found the facts of the *Parker* case were unique. The district court also declined as a matter of discretion to exercise pendent party jurisdiction. For discussion of the present state of the doctrine of pendent party jurisdiction, see Ch. 5, subhead 4 infra.

A tort occurring on a vessel while it is in drydock on navigable waters occurs on navigable waters for purposes of admiralty jurisdiction, although the vessel has been lifted out of the water. Sea Vessel, Inc. v. Reyes, 23 F.3d 345, 1994 A.M.C. 2736 (11th Cir.1994), in which the court declined to draw a distinction in this respect between kinds of drydocks.

And it has been held that a navigable waterway is bounded by the median highwater mark, so that a vessel may be on dry land and yet satisfy the maritime location requirement. See Hassinger v. Tideland Electric Membership Corp., 781 F.2d 1022 (4th Cir.1986), cert. denied 478 U.S. 1004, 106 S.Ct 3294, 92 L.Ed.2d 709 (1986), in which a sailor beaching a boat in a storm was electricuted when the mast came in contact with overhead electric wires.

The assumption indulged in in The Admiral Peoples that the admiralty tort jurisdiction embraced *all* torts that occurred on navigable waters of the United

States, was subject to some doubt over the years. Most of the decided cases, however, adhered to the locality rule. Thus it was held that a surfboard accident was maritime, since it occurred on the ocean. Davis v. City of Jacksonville Beach, Florida, 251 F.Supp. 327, 1966 A.M.C. 1231 (M.D.Fla.1965). The crash of a domestic airplane in domestic waters was likewise held to give rise to a maritime cause of action for negligence in the construction of the aircraft, though the building of an airplane could not be said to be maritime since even the building of a ship is not maritime. Weinstein v. Eastern Airlines, Inc., 316 F.2d 758, 1963 A.M.C. 1450 (3d Cir.1963). The first court of appeals case to reject the locality rule as a sole test was Chapman v. City of Grosse Pointe Farms, 385 F.2d 962, 1968 A.M.C. 386 (6th Cir.1967), dismissing for want of jurisdiction an action by a plaintiff who dove from a pier into 18 inches of water and sued for the resultant injuries.

Location of personal injuries has been an issue most often in connection with injuries to harbor workers, who often work on and off the vessel. They are engaged, very largely, in work under a maritime contract between their employer and the vessel owner but the location of a given accident is purely fortuitous. At the time of the decision in *The Plymouth* the jurisdictional issue was dependent upon general concepts. By the time of the decision in *The Admiral Peoples,* however, the Longshoremen's and Harbor Workers Compensation Act had been enacted and the coverage of that Act was stated in terms as limited to occurrences "on navigable waters of the United States." The history of the LHWCA is discussed at length in the HISTORICAL NOTE at p. 955 infra. Suffice it to say here that generally accidents occurring on the pier were not compensated under its provisions. See, e.g. State Industrial Commission of New York v. Nordenholt Corp., 259 U.S. 263, 42 S.Ct. 473, 66 L.Ed. 933 (1922). See also Victory Carriers, Inc. v. Law, 404 U.S. 202, 92 S.Ct. 418, 30 L.Ed.2d 383 (1971).

In those relatively rare situations in which tort jurisdiction was invoked outside the industrial tort area, it was generally stated that the jurisdiction also depended upon locality, that is that the tort must occur on navigable waters, despite the obvious maritime connection between event and injury. Thus until the enactment of the Admiralty Extension Act of 1948, collisions between a vessel and a land structure did not afford a maritime cause of action for damage to a land structure. See United States v. Matson Navigation Co., 201 F.2d 610 (9th Cir.1953). The Extension Act is discussed in the following subhead.

In *Grosse Pointe Farms*, supra, why was it necessary to consider whether the incident had a nexus with maritime affairs? Weren't the circumstances a mirror image of The Admiral Peoples? Was the breach of duty to prevent people from diving off the pier, or was it to provide deeper water? Or is the difference the fact that the plaintiff in The Admiral Peoples tripped, while the plaintiff in *Grosse Pointe Farms* dived voluntarily?

It is interesting to note that the Federal Tort Claims Act applies the law of the State in which the act or omission complained of takes place. 28 U.S.C.A. § 1346.

2.   THE ADMIRALTY EXTENSION ACT OF 1948

Duluth Superior Excursions, Inc. v. Makela

United States Court of Appeals, Eighth Circuit, 1980.
623 F.2d 1251, 1980 A.M.C. 2518.

■ BRIGHT, CIRCUIT JUDGE.

Duluth Superior Excursions, Inc. and Flamingo Excursions, Inc. (collectively, Excursions) brought this action in federal court seeking to limit their potential liability to Joseph Makela under the Shipowner's Limitation of Liability Act, 46 U.S.C. §§ 181–189 (1976). The district court dismissed the action, holding that Excursions had failed to establish federal admiralty jurisdiction under 28 U.S.C. § 1333(1)(1976). For the reasons set forth below, we conclude that this determination was erroneous. Accordingly, we reverse.

I. *Background*

On the night of August 12, 1977, Joseph Makela was struck and seriously injured by a car while crossing Harbor Drive in Duluth, Minnesota. The driver of the car was allegedly intoxicated. Both Makela and the car's driver had just disembarked from the S.S. Flamingo after a three-hour privately chartered cruise around the Duluth–Superior harbor. The organizers of the charter cruise, having advertised it as a "booze cruise," had brought several kegs of beer on board. The Flamingo was owned by appellant Flamingo Excursions, Inc., and operated by appellant Duluth Superior Excursions, Inc.

In September 1977, Makela's attorney notified Excursions that a tort claim would be filed against them. Excursions responded by filing the present action in federal court on February 10, 1978, seeking to limit their potential liability to the value of the S.S. Flamingo, her equipment, and any pending freight as of August 12, 1977. See 46 U.S.C. § 183(a) (1976).[1] Excursions offered an ad interim stipulation for value in the sum of $51,000, alleging that this sum exceeded the aggregate value of their interest in the vessel.

In October 1978, Makela filed a tort action in Minnesota state court, naming as defendants the driver of the car that struck him, the driver's father, the cruise organizers, and Excursions.[2] Makela's claim against Excursions was that Excursions inadequately supervised the passengers aboard the Flamingo, who consequently became illegally intoxicated, and that Excursions failed to provide a safe means of exit for these passengers. The federal action brought by Excursions against Makela was dismissed for want of jurisdiction on November 8, 1979.

II. *Analysis*

In Executive Jet Aviation v. City of Cleveland, 409 U.S. 249, 93 S.Ct. 493, 34 L.Ed.2d 454 (1972), the Supreme Court recounted the history of

---

1. 46 U.S.C. § 183(a) provides in pertinent part as follows:

(a) The liability of the owner of any vessel, whether American or foreign, for any * * * act, matter, or thing, loss, damage, or forfeiture, done, occasioned, or incurred, without the privity or knowledge of such owner or owners, shall not, except in the cases provided for in subsection (b) of this section, exceed the amount or value of the interest of such owner in such vessel, and her freight then pending.

The district court did not reach the issue of whether this statute applies here; neither do we.

2. The parties have informed us that this lawsuit has not yet gone to trial.

maritime tort jurisdiction. Traditionally, the test of jurisdiction was whether the tort was "located" on navigable waters. E.g., The Plymouth, 70 U.S. (3 Wall.) 20, 18 L.Ed. 125 (1866). Because this test has proven unsatisfactory in many cases, the Court in *Executive Jet* placed its imprimatur on the more modern test of whether the alleged wrong is related to traditional maritime activity. See id. at 261, 93 S.Ct. at 501.[3]

In the case at hand, there is little question that the wrongs allegedly committed by Excursions took place on navigable waters.[4] The district court held, however, that Excursions failed to show the requisite relationship between these wrongs and traditional maritime activities. The district court based this holding upon its conclusion that inadequate supervision, illegal intoxication, and failure to provide a safe exit are not traditional maritime acts.

The district court may well have been correct in this surmise. The question before the court, however, was whether these alleged acts were related to (i.e., occurred in connection with) traditional maritime activities. Carrying passengers for hire is undoubtedly a traditional maritime activity, and suits in tort for personal injuries to passengers are clearly included in admiralty jurisdiction. E.g., St. Hilaire Moye v. Henderson, 496 F.2d 973 (8th Cir.), cert. denied, 419 U.S. 884, 95 S.Ct. 151, 42 L.Ed.2d 125 (1974). See G. Gilmore and C. Black, *The Law of Admiralty* 23 & 23 n. 77 (2d ed. 1975). The nature of the allegedly negligent acts underlying Makela's claims against appellants is largely irrelevant. It is sufficient for purposes of admiralty jurisdiction in this case that a passenger is suing for personal injuries allegedly due to the negligence of the vessel's owners and crew on navigable waters. See Kermarec v. Compagnie Generale, 358 U.S. 625, 79 S.Ct. 406, 3 L.Ed.2d 550 (1959); Gibboney v. Wright, 517 F.2d 1054, 1059 (5th Cir.1975).

To be sure, the accident that injured Makela occurred on dry land. Under the terms of the Admiralty Extension Act, 46 U.S.C. § 740 (1976), however, this circumstance does not destroy admiralty jurisdiction over Makela's claims against the appellants. The Admiralty Extension Act provides in pertinent part:

> The admiralty and maritime jurisdiction of the United States shall extend to and include all cases of damage or injury, to person or property, caused by a vessel on navigable water, notwithstanding that such damage or injury be done or consummated on land.

In Gutierrez v. Waterman S.S. Corp., 373 U.S. 206, 210, 83 S.Ct. 1185, 1188, 10 L.Ed.2d 297 (1963), the Supreme Court held that the Admiralty

3. At issue in *Executive Jet* was a claim for property damage to an airplane that crashed and sank in Lake Erie. The Court in that case held specifically that, absent either a showing of a significant relationship between the wrong and traditional maritime activity or legislation to the contrary, claims arising from airplane accidents over naviga-ble waters are not cognizable in admiralty. Id. at 268, 93 S.Ct. at 504.

4. It is true, as Makela notes, that the injury he suffered was consummated on dry land. That fact, however, does not change the locale of appellants' alleged wrongs, nor does it destroy admiralty jurisdiction in this case. See text at note 5 infra.

Extension Act applies not only to injuries caused by the impact of a vessel itself, but also to those due to alleged acts of negligence by a vessel's crew. In that case, a longshoreman was injured when he slipped on loose beans that had been spilled on the dock from defective bags in the course of unloading. The defendant argued that the federal courts lacked jurisdiction to hear the longshoreman's claims. The Court held, however, that admiralty jurisdiction is established when

> it is alleged that the shipowner commits a tort while or before the ship is being unloaded, and the impact of which is felt ashore at a time and place not remote from the wrongful act. [Id. at 210, 83 S.Ct. at 1188 (footnote omitted).]

These conditions for admiralty jurisdiction are fully satisfied in the present case.[5] Cf. Tullis v. Fidelity and Casualty Co. of New York, 397 F.2d 22, 23–24 (5th Cir.1968)(admiralty jurisdiction established by a crew boat passenger's allegation that defendant boat owner failed to provide a reasonably safe means of debarking).[6]

Makela cites a number of cases in support of the district court's holding that it lacked jurisdiction. In our view, all of these cases are

---

5. Although it might be argued that Makela's injury is remote from the wrongful act, the accident occurred some six minutes after the S.S. Flamingo docked, on a street that adjoins the dock. In our view, this is not sufficiently remote in time and space to destroy admiralty jurisdiction. We intimate no view as to whether Makela's injury was remote in the sense of not having been proximately caused by the appellants' alleged acts of negligence. That issue remains for the trier of fact to decide. But cf. Pryor v. American President Lines, 520 F.2d 974 (4th Cir. 1975), cert. denied, 423 U.S. 1055, 96 S.Ct. 787, 46 L.Ed.2d 644 (1976), and cases there cited (requiring proximate cause to invoke the Admiralty Extension Act where the only permissible inference is that the vessel did not proximately cause the injury).

6. In Gutierrez v. Waterman S.S. Corp., supra, the Supreme Court not only found admiralty jurisdiction, but also held that the defendant shipowner was negligent towards the plaintiff longshoreman and strictly liable for breach of its warranty of seaworthiness. The Court restricted the scope of this latter holding in Victory Carriers, Inc. v. Law, 404 U.S. 202, 92 S.Ct. 418, 30 L.Ed.2d 383 (1971), another longshoreman suit for dockside injuries, this time caused by equipment owned and operated by the stevedore. After observing that "in Gutierrez, supra, federal admiralty jurisdiction was clearly present since the Admiralty Extension Act on its face reached the injury there involved[,]" the Court stated:

> The decision in Gutierrez turned, not on the "function" the stevedore was performing at the time of his injury, but, rather, upon the fact that his injury was caused by an appurtenance of a ship, the defective cargo containers, which the Court held to be an "injury, to person * * * caused by a vessel on navigable water" which was consummated ashore under 46 U.S.C. § 740. The Court has never approved an unseaworthiness recovery for an injury sustained on land merely because the injured longshoreman was engaged in the process of "loading" or "unloading." [Id. at 210–11, 92 S.Ct. at 424. (footnote omitted).]

Since Victory Carriers, courts faced with on-shore seaworthiness claims have typically attempted to ascertain whether the allegedly defective piece of equipment causing the injury was, at the time of the accident, an appurtenance of a vessel. See, e.g., Kinsella v. Zim Israel Navigation Co., Ltd., 513 F.2d 701 (1st Cir.1975). In the case at hand, however, this issue does not arise, as there is no claim of unseaworthiness. Makela simply alleges that the appellants were negligent in operating the S.S. Flamingo on navigable waters and in providing a safe means of exit for its passengers. See generally 7A Moore's Federal Practice ¶ .325[4] (2d ed. 1979).

dissimilar in crucial respects from the case at hand. For example, in Peytavin v. Government Employees Ins. Co., 453 F.2d 1121 (5th Cir.1972), the plaintiff sued for whiplash injuries sustained when he was struck from behind by another automobile while parked on a floating pontoon at a ferry landing. The court held that the plaintiff's claim did not come within federal admiralty jurisdiction, observing that neither the conduct of the parties (apart from their use of the pontoon), nor the nature or apparent cause of the accident, nor the injury sustained demonstrated a connection with maritime activities or interests. Id. at 1126–27.

Notwithstanding this language, the very factors that led the court in *Peytavin* to distinguish its earlier decision in Byrd v. Napolean Ave. Ferry Co., Inc., 227 F.2d 958 (5th Cir.1955), aff'g per curiam 125 F.Supp. 573 (E.D.La.1954), cert. denied, 351 U.S. 925, 76 S.Ct. 783, 100 L.Ed. 1455 (1956)(upholding admiralty jurisdiction), support our determination that jurisdiction exists here. See Peytavin v. Government Employees Ins. Co., supra, 453 F.2d at 1127. Here, Mr. Makela, like the plaintiff in *Byrd,* was a passenger aboard a commercial vessel and the defendants are its owners and operators. Their alleged negligence, unlike that of the defendant driver in *Peytavin,* involves their performance of maritime duties in caring for their passengers. Cf. St. Hilaire Moye v. Henderson, supra (admiralty defendants found negligent in their operation of a pleasure boat).[7] Finally, we note that the sequence of causal events alleged in this case started on board the vessel and ended on land, calling into play the Admiralty Extension Act. None of the cases cited by Makela shares this last critical feature. Nor do they address the duties of vessel owners or operators to their passengers, a traditional maritime concern.

We conclude, then, that Makela's claim against Excursions comes within the admiralty jurisdiction of the federal courts.[8] We reverse the decision of the district court dismissing the appellants' action, and remand the case for further proceedings consistent with this opinion.

N O T E

Notice that Makela brought his action in the state court against the driver of the automobile, his father, the organizer of the cruise, and the vessel owner, and the issue of admiralty jurisdiction arose because the vessel owner filed a petition for limitation of liability. Had Makela brought his action in the federal court, would the claims against the driver, his father, and the cruise organizer have been

7. Makela points out that his injuries, like those of the whiplash victim in *Peytavin,* show no particular maritime character. The same thing is true, however, of the fall on spilled beans suffered by the plaintiff long-shoreman in *Gutierrez,* supra. Cf. The Admiral Peoples, 295 U.S. 649, 55 S.Ct. 885, 79 L.Ed. 1633 (1935)(admiralty plaintiff who fell off a step at the end of a gangplank onto the dock recovered damages). We do not consider the nature of the plaintiff's injury to be critical in determining the scope of admiralty jurisdiction.

8. The issue of whether the district court has jurisdiction to entertain Makela's claims against the other parties named in his state court action is not before us. See generally Maryland Port Administration v. S.S. American Legend, 453 F.Supp. 584, 587–89 (D.Md.1978), and cases there cited.

cognizeable as admiralty claims? Cf. Petro v. Jada Yacht, 854 F.Supp. 698, 1994 AMC 1146 (D.Hawai'i 1994), another "booze cruise" case, in which after disembarcation one of the passengers was assaulted in the parking lot by an enebriated fellow passenger and sued his attacker and the vessel owner. The court held that the claim against the vessel owner was maritime, but the claim against the attacker was not. For discussion of supplemental jurisdiction under 28 U.S.C.A. sec.1367, see Ch.11, infra.

In Gutierrez v. Waterman Steamship Corp., 373 U.S. 206, 83 S.Ct. 1185, 10 L.Ed.2d 297 (1963), discussed infra at p. 1016, libelant, a longshoreman working on the pier unloading a cargo of beans, was injured when he slipped on some loose beans that spilled from defective bags. The Court brushed off a challenge to the jurisdiction based upon the non-maritime location of the accident, observing:

"* * * Whatever validity this proposition may have had until 1948, the passage of the Extension of Admiralty Jurisdiction Act, 62 Stat. 496, 46 U.S.C.A. § 740, swept it away when it made vessels on navigable water liable for damage or injury 'notwithstanding that such damage or injury be done or consummated on land.' Respondent and the carrier amici curiae would have the statute limited to injuries actually caused by the physical agency of the vessel or a particular part of it—such as when the ship rams a bridge or when its defective winch drops some cargo onto a longshoreman. Cf. Strika v. Netherlands Ministry of Traffic, 185 F.2d 555 (2 Cir.1951); Hagans v. Farrell Lines, Inc., 237 F.2d 477 (3 Cir.1956). Nothing in the legislative history supports so restrictive an interpretation of the statutory language. There is no distinction in admiralty between torts committed by the ship itself and by the ship's personnel while operating it, any more than there is between torts 'committed' by a corporation and by its employees. And ships are libeled as readily on an unduly bellicose mate's assault on a crewman, see Boudoin v. Lykes Bros. S.S. Co., 348 U.S. 336, 339, 340, 75 S.Ct. 382, 99 L.Ed. 354, 358, 359 (1955) amended 350 U.S. 811, 76 S.Ct. 38, 100 L.Ed. 727 (1955); The Rolph, 299 F. 52 (9 Cir.1962), or for having an incompetent crew or master, see Keen v. Overseas Tankship Corp., 194 F.2d 515, 517 (2 Cir.1952), as for a collision. Various far-fetched hypotheticals are raised, such as a suit in admiralty for an ordinary automobile accident involving a ship's officer on ship business in port, or for someone's slipping on beans that continue to leak from these bags in a warehouse in Denver. We think it sufficient for the needs of this occasion to hold that the case is within the maritime jurisdiction under 46 U.S.C.A. §§ 740 when, as here, it is alleged that the shipowner commits a tort while or before the ship is being unloaded, and the impact of which is felt ashore at a time and place not remote from the wrongful act." (Footnotes omitted)

"Nothing in the legislative history supports so restrictive an interpretation of the statutory language" is perhaps an overstatement. See U.S.Code Cong.Serv., 1948, v. 2, p. 1898, where the report of the Senate Judiciary Committee and letters from a number of government officials are reproduced. It seems quite clear from these materials that the statute was aimed at the inequities that resulted from the extension of the doctrine of The Plymouth to ship-to-shore collisions. The report reads, in part:

"As a result of the denial of admiralty jurisdiction where injury is done on land, when a vessel collides with a bridge through mutual fault and both are damaged, under existing law the owner of the bridge, being denied a remedy in admiralty, is barred by contributory negligence from any recovery in an action at law. But the owner of the vessel may by a suit in admiralty recover half damages from the bridge, contributory negligence operating merely to reduce the recovery. Further, where a collision between a vessel and a land structure is caused by the fault of a compulsory pilot, the owner of the land structure is without remedy for his injuries since at law a compulsory pilot is not deemed the servant of the vessel's master or owner. Homer Ramsdell Transportation Co. v. Compagnie Generale Transatlantique (182 U.S. 406, 416). But if the vessel sheers off the land structure to collide with another vessel in the vicinity, the owner of the second vessel, by an in rem proceeding in admiralty, may recover full damages, for the wrong is viewed as that of the vessel itself and compulsory pilotage is no defense. The China (74 U.S. 53, 68). The bill under consideration would correct these inequities as a result of providing that the admiralty courts shall take cognizance of all of them.

"The bill will bring United States practice respecting maritime torts into accord with that followed by the British, who by a series of statutes, beginning in 1840, have restored admiralty jurisdiction in situations of this character and brought the British law into harmony with that of most European countries. For a number of years the American Bar Association and the Maritime Law Association of the United States have pressed for legislation of this character. Bills similar to H.R. 238 have been introduced in each Congress since the Seventy-fifth. Such bills have heretofore been approved in principle by the Maritime Commission, War Shipping Administration, and the Navy Department but not by this Department.

"Congress has failed on several occasions to pass legislation of this kind. For example, it was thought undesirable, while the United States was at war and operating many vessels, both through the War Shipping Administration and in the military and naval service, to impose additional liabilities on the United States for injuries caused by its vessels. Courts have held jurisdiction under the Public Vessels Act, 1925, to be confined to cases where a private admiralty proceeding could be maintained. State of Maine v. United States (45 F.Supp. 35, affirmed 134 F.2d 574, cert. denied 319 U.S. 772). Since the act (46 U.S.C.A. § 781) covers, without exception, all 'damages caused by a public vessel' a contrary result appears justified by its plain language as well as its purpose (see 66 Congressional Record, 3560) and the construction given the similar language of the British statutes. See especially The Uhla (19 L.T.R. (n.s.) 89, 90). But the Department formerly thought it wise to oppose alteration of the rule."

The report goes on to say that since the passage of the Federal Tort Claims Act in 1946, extension of the admiralty jurisdiction to such cases will not cost the United States much if anything. As to the construction of the British statute, see Mr. Justice Brown's opinion in The Osceola, 189 U.S. 158, 23 S.Ct. 483, 47 L.Ed. 760 (1903). There the contention was made that a Wisconsin statute patterned after the British statute had the effect of creating a lien on behalf of a seaman injured through the negligence of the officers and crew of a vessel. In rejecting this contention the Court observed:

"It is insisted, however, that a lien is given upon the vessel by a local statute of Wisconsin, Rev.Stat. of 1898, sec. 3348, repeating a previous statute upon the same subject, which provides that every ship, boat or vessel used in navigating the waters of that State shall be liable 'for all damages arising from injuries done to persons or property by such ship, boat or vessel,' and that the claim for such damages shall constitute a lien upon such ship, boat or vessel, which shall take precedence of all other claims or liens thereon. As the accident happened within three miles of the port of Milwaukee, and as the constitution of Wisconsin fixes the center of Lake Michigan as the eastern boundary of the State, there is no doubt that the vessel was navigating the waters of that State at the time of the accident. But the vital question in the case is whether the damages arose from an injury done to persons or property *by such ship,* boat or vessel. The statute was doubtless primarily intended to cover cases of collision with other vessels or with structures affixed to the land, and to other cases where the damage is done by the ship herself, as the offending thing, to persons or property outside of the ship, through the negligence or mismanagement of the ship by the officers or seamen in charge. To hold that it applies to injuries suffered by a member of the crew on board the ship is to give the act an effect beyond the ordinary meaning of the words used. Would it apply, for instance, to injuries received in falling through an open hatchway? Or to a block blown against a seaman by the force of the wind, though the accident in either case might have resulted from the negligence of the master? We think not.

"The act in this particular uses the same language as the seventh section of the English Admiralty Court Act of 1861, which declares that 'the High Court of Admiralty shall have jurisdiction over any claim for damage done by any ship.' Construing that act, it has been held by the Court of Admiralty that it applies to damages occasioned by a vessel coming in collision with a pier, The Uhla, L.R. 2 Ad. & Ec. 29, note, and also to cases of personal injury, The Sylph, L.R. 2 Ad. & Ec. 24, where a diver, while engaged in diving in the river Mersey, was caught by the paddle wheel of a steamer and suffered considerable injury; but not to a case where personal injuries were sustained by a seaman falling down into the hold of a vessel, owing to the hatchway being insufficiently protected, The Theta, 1894, P.D. 280, or to loss of life, The Vera Cruz, 9 P.D. 96. As we have indicated above the statute was confined to cases of damage done by those in charge of a ship with the ship as the 'noxious instrument,' and that cases of damages done *on board* the ship were not within the meaning of the act of damages done *by the ship.*

"In the case under consideration the damage was not done by the ship in the ordinary sense of the word, but by a gangway which may be assumed to be an ordinary appliance of the ship, being blown against the libellant by the force of the wind."

3. MARITIME CONNECTION

Jerome B. Grubart, Inc. v. Great Lakes Dredge & Dock Co.

Supreme Court of the United States, 1995.
513 U.S. ___, 115 S.Ct. 1043, 130 L.Ed.2d 1024, 1995 A.M.C. 913.

■ JUSTICE SOUTER delivered the opinion of the Court.

On April 13, 1992, water from the Chicago River poured into a freight tunnel running under the river and thence into the basements of buildings in the downtown Chicago Loop. Allegedly, the flooding resulted from events several months earlier, when the respondent Great Lakes Dredge and Dock Company had used a crane, sitting on a barge in the river next to a bridge, to drive piles into the river bed above the tunnel. The issue before us is whether a court of the United States has admiralty jurisdiction to determine and limit the extent of Great Lakes's tort liability. We hold the case to be within federal admiralty jurisdiction.

I

The complaint, together with affidavits subject to no objection, alleges the following facts. In 1990, Great Lakes bid on a contract with the petitioner city of Chicago to replace wooden pilings clustered around the piers of several bridges spanning the Chicago River, a navigable waterway within the meaning of The Daniel Ball, 77 U.S. 557, 19 L.Ed. 999, 10 Wall. 557, 563 (1871). See Escanaba Co. v. Chicago, 107 U.S. 678, 683, 2 S.Ct. 185, 188–189, 27 L.Ed. 442 (1883). The pilings (called dolphins) keep ships from bumping into the piers and so protect both. After winning the contract, Great Lakes carried out the work with two barges towed by a tug. One barge carried pilings; the other carried a crane that pulled out old pilings and helped drive in new ones.

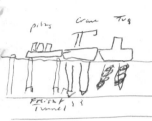

In August and September 1991, Great Lakes replaced the pilings around the piers projecting into the river and supporting the Kinzie Street Bridge. After towing the crane-carrying barge into position near one of the piers, Great Lakes's employees secured the barge to the river bed with spuds, or long metal legs that project down from the barge and anchor it. The workers then used the crane on the barge to pull up old pilings, stow them on the other barge, and drive new pilings into the river bed around the piers. About seven months later, an eddy formed in the river near the bridge as the collapsing walls or ceiling of a freight tunnel running under the river opened the tunnel to river water, which flowed through to flood buildings in the Loop.

After the flood, many of the victims brought actions in state court against Great Lakes and the city of Chicago, claiming that in the course of replacing the pilings Great Lakes had negligently weakened the tunnel structure, which Chicago (its owner) had not properly maintained. Great Lakes then brought this lawsuit in the United States District Court, invoking federal admiralty jurisdiction. Count I of the complaint seeks the protection of the Limitation of Vessel Owner's Liability Act (Limitation Act), 46 U.S.C.App. § 181 *et seq.*, a statute that would, in effect, permit the admiralty court to decide whether Great Lakes committed a tort and, if so, to limit Great Lakes's liability to the value of the vessels (the tug and two barges) involved if the tort was committed "without the privity or knowledge" of the vessels' owner, 46 U.S.C.App. § 183(a). Counts II and III of Great Lakes's complaint ask for indemnity and contribution from the city for any resulting loss to Great Lakes.

The city, joined by petitioner Jerome B. Grubart, Inc., one of the state-court plaintiffs, filed a motion to dismiss this suit for lack of admiralty jurisdiction. Fed.Rule Civ. Proc. 12(b)(1). The District Court granted the motion, the Seventh Circuit reversed, Great Lakes Dredge & Dock Co. v. Chicago, 3 F.3d 225 (7th Cir.1993), and we granted certiorari, 510 U.S. ___, 114 S.Ct. 1047, 127 L.Ed.2d 370 (1994). We now affirm.

II

The parties do not dispute the Seventh Circuit's conclusion that jurisdiction as to Counts II and III (indemnity and contribution) hinges on jurisdiction over the Count I claim. See 3 F.3d, at 231, n. 9; see also 28 U.S.C. § 1367 (1988 ed., Supp. V)(supplemental jurisdiction); Fed.Rules Civ.Proc. 14(a) and (c)(impleader of third parties). Thus, the issue is simply whether or not a federal admiralty court has jurisdiction over claims that Great Lakes's faulty replacement work caused the flood damage.

A

A federal court's authority to hear cases in admiralty flows initially from the Constitution, which "extend[s]" federal judicial power "to all Cases of admiralty and maritime Jurisdiction." U.S. Const., Art. III, § 2. Congress has embodied that power in a statute giving federal district courts "original jurisdiction ... of ... [a]ny civil case of admiralty or maritime jurisdiction...." 28 U.S.C. § 1333(1).

The traditional test for admiralty tort jurisdiction asked only whether the tort occurred on navigable waters. If it did, admiralty jurisdiction followed; if it did not, admiralty jurisdiction did not exist. See, e.g., Thomas v. Lane, 23 F.Cas. 957, 960 (No. 13902) (C.C.Me.1813)(Story, J., on Circuit). This ostensibly simple locality test was complicated by the rule that the injury had to be "wholly" sustained on navigable waters for the tort to be within admiralty. The Plymouth, 70 U.S. 20, 18 L.Ed. 125, 3 Wall. 20, 34 (1866)(no jurisdiction over tort action brought by the owner of warehouse destroyed in a fire that started on board a ship docked nearby). Thus, admiralty courts lacked jurisdiction over, say, a claim following a ship's collision with a pier insofar as it injured the pier, for admiralty law treated the pier as an extension of the land. Martin v. West, 222 U.S. 191, 197, 32 S.Ct. 42, 43, 56 L.Ed. 159 (1911); Cleveland T. & V.R. Co. v. Cleveland S.S. Co., 208 U.S. 316, 319, 28 S.Ct. 414, 415, 52 L.Ed. 508 (1908).

This latter rule was changed in 1948, however, when Congress enacted the Extension of Admiralty Jurisdiction Act, 62 Stat. 496. The Act provided that

> "[t]he admiralty and maritime jurisdiction of the United States shall extend to and include all cases of damage or injury, to person or property, caused by a vessel on navigable water, notwithstanding that such damage or injury be done or consummated on land." 46 U.S.C.App. § 740.

The purpose of the Act was to end concern over the sometimes confusing line between land and water, by investing admiralty with jurisdiction over "all cases" where the injury was caused by a ship or other vessel on navigable water, even if such injury occurred on land. See, e.g., Gutierrez v. Waterman S.S. Corp., 373 U.S. 206, 209–210, 83 S.Ct. 1185, 1187–1188, 10 L.Ed.2d 297 (1963); Executive Jet Aviation, Inc. v. City of Cleveland, 409 U.S. 249, 260, 93 S.Ct. 493, 500–501, 34 L.Ed.2d 454 (1972). After this congressional modification to gather the odd case into admiralty, the jurisdictional rule was qualified again in three decisions of this Court aimed at keeping a different class of odd cases out. In the first case, *Executive Jet, supra,* tort claims arose out of the wreck of an airplane that collided with a flock of birds just after take-off on a domestic flight and fell into the navigable waters of Lake Erie. We held that admiralty lacked jurisdiction to consider the claims. We wrote that "a purely mechanical application of the locality test" was not always "sensible" or "consonant with the purposes of maritime law," id., at 261, 93 S.Ct., at 501, as when (for example) the literal and universal application of the locality rule would require admiralty courts to adjudicate tort disputes between colliding swimmers, id., at 255, 93 S.Ct., at 498. We held that "claims arising from airplane accidents are not cognizable in admiralty" despite the location of the harm, unless "the wrong bear[s] a significant relationship to traditional maritime activity." Id., at 268, 93 S.Ct., at 504.

The second decision, Foremost Ins. Co. v. Richardson, 457 U.S. 668, 102 S.Ct. 2654, 73 L.Ed.2d 300 (1982), dealt with tort claims arising out of the collision of two pleasure boats in a navigable river estuary. We held that admiralty courts had jurisdiction, id., at 677, 102 S.Ct., at 2659, even though jurisdiction existed only if "the wrong" had a significant connection with traditional "maritime activity," id., at 674, 102 S.Ct., at 2658. We conceded that pleasure boats themselves had little to do with the maritime commerce lying at the heart of the admiralty court's basic work, id., at 674–675, 102 S.Ct., at 2658–2659, but we nonetheless found the necessary relationship in

> "[t]he potential disruptive impact [upon maritime commerce] of a collision between boats on navigable waters, when coupled with the traditional concern that admiralty law holds for navigation...." Id., at 675, 102 S.Ct. at 2658.

In the most recent of the trilogy, Sisson v. Ruby, 497 U.S. 358, 110 S.Ct. 2892, 111 L.Ed.2d 292 (1990), we held that a federal admiralty court had jurisdiction over tort claims arising when a fire, caused by a defective washer/dryer aboard a pleasure boat docked at a marina, burned the boat, other boats docked nearby, and the marina itself. Id., at 367, 110 S.Ct., at 2898. We elaborated on the enquiry exemplified in *Executive Jet* and *Foremost* by focusing on two points to determine the relationship of a claim to the objectives of admiralty jurisdiction. We noted, first, that the incident causing the harm, the burning of docked boats at a marina on navigable waters, was of a sort "likely to disrupt [maritime] commercial activity." Id., 497 U.S., at 363, 110 S.Ct., at 2896. Second, we found a "substantial relationship" with "traditional maritime activity" in the kind of activity from which the incident arose, "the storage and maintenance of a vessel ... on navigable waters." Id., at 365–367, 110 S.Ct., at 2897–2898.

After *Sisson*, then, a party seeking to invoke federal admiralty jurisdiction pursuant to 28 U.S.C. § 1333(1) over a tort claim must satisfy conditions both of location and of connection with maritime activity. A court applying the location test must determine whether the tort occurred on navigable water or whether injury suffered on land was caused by a vessel on navigable water. 46 U.S.C.App. § 740. The connection test raises two issues. A court, first, must "assess the general features of the type of incident involved," 497 U.S., at 363, 110 S.Ct., at 2896, to determine whether the incident has "a potentially disruptive impact on maritime commerce," id., at 364, n. 2, 110 S.Ct., at 2896, n. 2. Second, a court must determine whether "the general character" of the "activity giving rise to the incident" shows a "substantial relationship to traditional maritime activity." Id., at 365, 364, and n. 2, 110 S.Ct., at 2897, 2896, and n. 2. We now apply the tests to the facts of this case.

B

The location test is, of course, readily satisfied. If Great Lakes caused the flood, it must have done so by weakening the structure of the tunnel while it drove in new pilings or removed old ones around the bridge piers. The weakening presumably took place as Great Lakes's workers lifted and replaced the pilings with a crane that sat on a barge stationed in the Chicago River. The place in the river where the barge sat, and from which workers directed the crane, is in the "navigable waters of the United States." *Escanaba Co.*, 107 U.S., at 683, 2 S.Ct., at 188–189. Thus, if Great Lakes committed a tort, it must have done it while on navigable waters.

It must also have done it "by a vessel." Even though the barge was fastened to the river bottom and was in use as a work platform at the times in question, at other times it was used for transportation. See 3 F.3d, at 229. Petitioners do not here seriously dispute the conclusion of each court below that the Great Lakes barge is, for admiralty tort purposes, a "vessel." The fact that the pile-driving was done with a crane makes no difference under the location test, given the maritime law that ordinarily treats an "appurtenance" attached to a vessel in navigable waters as part of the vessel itself. See, e.g., Victory Carriers, Inc. v. Law, 404 U.S. 202, 210–211, 92 S.Ct. 418, 424–425, 30 L.Ed.2d 383 (1971); *Gutierrez*, 373 U.S., at 209–210, 83 S.Ct., at 1187–1188.[1]

Because the injuries suffered by Grubart and the other flood victims were caused by a vessel on navigable water, the location enquiry would seem to be at an end, "notwithstanding that such damage or injury have been done or consummated on land." 46 U.S.C.App. § 740. Both Grubart

---

1. Grubart argues, based on Margin v. Sea–Land Services, Inc., 812 F.2d 973, 975 (C.A.5 1987), that an appurtenance is considered part of the vessel only when it is defective. See Brief for Petitioner in No. 93–762, pp. 34–35 (Grubart Brief). *Margin*, however, does not so hold. It dealt with a land-based crane that lowered a ship's hatch cover dangerously close to a welder working on a dock, and its result turned not on the condition of the hatch cover, the putative appurtenance, but on the fact that the plaintiff did not allege that "vessel negligence proximately caused his injury." 812 F.2d at 977. Indeed the argument that Congress intended admiralty jurisdiction to injuries caused by defective appurtenances, but not to appurtenances in good condition when operated negligently, makes no sense. See *Gutierrez*, 373 U.S., at 210, 83 S.St., at 1188 ("There is no distinction in admiralty between torts committed by the ship itself and by the ship's personnel while operating it . . .").

and Chicago nonetheless ask us to subject the Extension Act to limitations not apparent from its text. While they concede that the Act refers to "all cases of damage or injury," they argue that "all" must not mean literally every such case, no matter how great the distance between the vessel's tortious activity and the resulting harm. They contend that, to be within the Act, the damage must be close in time and space to the activity that caused it: that it must occur "reasonably contemporaneously" with the negligent conduct and no "farther from navigable waters than the reach of the vessel, its appurtenances and cargo." For authority, they point to this Court's statement in *Gutierrez*, supra; that jurisdiction is present when the "impact" of the tortious activity "is felt ashore at a time and place not remote from the wrongful act." Id. at 210, 83 S.Ct., at 1188.[2]

The demerits of this argument lie not only in its want of textual support for its nonremoteness rule, but in its disregard of a less stringent but familiar proximity condition tied to the language of the statute. The Act uses the phrase "caused by," which more than one Court of Appeals has read as requiring what tort law has traditionally called "proximate causation." See, e.g., Pryor v. American President Lines, 520 F.2d 974, 979 (C.A.4 1975), cert. denied, 423 U.S. 1055, 96 S.Ct. 787, 46 L.Ed.2d 644 (1976); Adams v. Harris County, 452 F.2d 994, 996–997 (C.A.5 1971), cert. denied, 406 U.S. 968, 92 S.Ct. 2414, 32 L.Ed.2d 667 (1972). This classic tort notion normally eliminates the bizarre, cf. Palsgraf v. Long Island R. Co., 248 N.Y. 339, 162 N.E. 99 (1928), and its use should obviate not only the complication but even the need for further temporal or spatial limitations. Nor is reliance on familiar proximate causation inconsistent with *Gutierrez*, which used its its nonremote language, not to announce a special test, but simply to distinguish its own facts (the victim having slipped on beans spilling from cargo containers being unloaded from a ship) from what the Court called "[v]arious far-fetched hypotheticals," such as injury to someone slipping on beans that continue to leak from the containers after they had been shipped from Puerto Rico to a warehouse in Denver. 373 U.S., at 210, 83 S.Ct., at 1188. See also *Victory Carriers*, supra, 404 U.S at 210–211, 92 S.Ct., at 424–425.

The city responds by saying that, as a practical matter, the use of proximate cause as a limiting jurisdictional principle would undesirably force an admiralty court to investigate the merits of the dispute at the outset of a case when it determined jurisdiction.[3] The argument, of course,

---

2. At oral argument, counsel for the city undercut this argument by conceding that admiralty jurisdiction would govern claims arising from an incident in which a ship on navigable waters slipped its moorings, drafted into a dam, and caused a breach in the dam that resulted in flooding of surrounding territory. Tr. of Oral Arg. 17.

3. The city in part bases its assertion about the practical effects of a proximate cause rule on a reading of Crowell v. Benson,

285 U.S. 22, 54–56, 52 S.Ct. 285, 293–295, 76 L.Ed. 598 (1932), which, according to the city, held that the Longshoremen's and harbor Worker's Compensation Act could not constitutionally apply to an employee absent a finding that he was actually injured on navigable waters. Thus, the city argues, a construction of the Extension Act that would permit the assertion of federal jurisdiction over land-based injuries absent a finding, on the merits, of actual causation "would raise

assumes that the truth of jurisdictional allegations must always be determined with finality at the threshold of litigation, but that assumption is erroneous. Normal practice permits a party to establish jurisdiction at the outset of a case by means of a nonfrivolous assertion of jurisdictional elements, see, e.g., Bray v. Alexandria Women's Health Clinic, 506 U.S. 263, ___, 113 S.Ct. 753, 768, 122 L.Ed.2d 34 (1993)(slip op., at 21); Bell v. Hood, 327 U.S. 678, 682–683, 66 S.Ct. 773, 776, 90 L.Ed. 939 (1946), and any litigation of a contested subject-matter jurisdictional fact issue occurs in comparatively summary procedure before a judge alone (as distinct from litigation of the same fact issue as an element of the cause of action, if the claim survives the jurisdictional objection). See 2A J. Moore & J. Lucas, Moore's Federal Practice 11 12.07[2.—1] (2d ed. 1994); 5A C. Wright & A. Miller, Federal Practice and Procedure § 1350 (2d ed. 1990). There is no reason why this should not be just as true for proximate causation as it is for the maritime nature of the tortfeasor's activity giving rise to the incident. See *Sisson*, 497 U.S., at 365, 110 S.Ct., at 2897. There is no need or justification, then, for imposing an additional nonremoteness hurdle in the name of jurisdiction.

We now turn to the maritime connection enquiries, the first being whether the incident involved was of a sort with the potential to disrupt maritime commerce. In *Sisson*, we described the features of the incident in general terms as "a fire on a vessel docked at a marina on navigable waters," id., at 363, 110 S.Ct., at 2896, and determined that such an incident "plainly satisf[ied]" the first maritime connection requirement, ibid., because the fire could have "spread to nearby commercial vessels or ma[d]e the marina inaccessible to such vessels" and therefore "[c]ertainly" had a "potentially disruptive impact on maritime commerce." Id., at 362, 110 S.Ct., at 2896. We noted that this first prong went to potential effects, not to the "particular facts of the incident," noting that in both *Executive Jet* and *Foremost* we had focused not on the specific facts at hand but on whether the "general features" of the incident were "likely to disrupt commercial activity." 497 U.S. at 363, 110 S.Ct., at 2896.

The first *Sisson* test turns, then, on a description of the incident at an intermediate level of possible generality. To speak of the incident as "fire" would have been too general to differentiate cases; at the other extreme, to describe the fire as damaging nothing but pleasure boats would have

serious constitutional questions." See Brief for Petitioner in No. 93–1094, pp. 18–19 (City Brief).

Even if the city's interpretation of *Crowell* is correct, it is not dispositive here. Constitutional difficulties need not arise when a court defers final determination of facts upon which jurisdiction depends until after the first jurisdictional skirmish. In the standing context, for example, we have held that "the Constitution does not require that the plaintiff offer … proof [of the fact that plaintiff sustained actual injury] as a thresh-old matter in order to invoke the district court's jurisdiction." Gwaltney of Smithfield, Ltd. v. Chesapeake Bay Foundation, Inc., 484 U.S. 49, 66, 108 S.Ct. 376, 386, 98 L.Ed.2d 306 (1987). We see no reason why a different rule should apply here, and find ourselves in the company of the city's own *amici*. See Brief for National Conference of State Legislatures, et al. as *as amici curiae* 18–19, n. 9 (suggesting that "a court need not decide the merits of causation issues to resolve a jurisdictional challenge").

ignored, among other things, the capacity of pleasure boats to endanger commercial shipping that happened to be nearby. We rejected both extremes and instead asked whether the incident could be seen within a class of incidents that posed more than a fanciful risk to commercial shipping.

Following *Sisson*, the "general features" of the incident at issue here may be described as damage by a vessel in navigable waters to an underwater structure. So characterized, there is little question that this is the kind of incident that has a "potentially disruptive impact on maritime commerce." As it actually turned out in this case, damaging a structure beneath the river bed could lead to a disruption in the water course itself, App. 33 (eddy formed above the leak); and, again as it actually happened, damaging a structure so situated could lead to restrictions on the navigational use of the waterway during required repairs. See Pet. for Cert. in No. 93–1094, p.22a (District Court found that after the flood "[t]he river remained closed for over a month," "[r]iver traffic ceased, several commuter ferries were stranded, and many barges could not enter the river system ... because the river was lowered to aid repair efforts"). Cf. Pennzoil Producing Co. v. Offshore Express, Inc., 943 F.2d 1465 (C.A.5 1991)(admiralty suit when vessel struck and ruptured gas pipeline and gas exploded); Marathon Pipe Line Co. v. Drilling Rig Rowan/Odessa, 761 F.2d 229, 233 (C.A.5 1985)(admiralty jurisdiction when vessel struck pipeline, "a fixed structure on the seabed"); Orange Beach Water, Sewer, and Fire Protection Authority v. M/V Alva, 680 F.2d 1374 (C.A.11 1982)(admiralty jurisdiction when vessel struck underwater pipeline).

In the second *Sisson* enquiry, we look to whether the general character of the activity giving rise to the incident shows a substantial relationship to traditional maritime activity. We ask whether a tortfeasor's activity, commercial or noncommercial, on navigable waters is so closely related to activity traditionally subject to admiralty law that the reasons for applying special admiralty rules would apply in the case at hand. Navigation of boats in navigable waters clearly falls within the substantial relationship, *Foremost*, 457 U.S., at 675, 102 S.Ct., at 2658–2659; storing them at a marina on navigable waters is close enough, *Sisson*, supra, 497 U.S., at 367, 110 S.Ct., at 2898; whereas in flying an airplane over the water, *Executive Jet*, 409 U.S., at 270–271, 93 S.Ct., at 505–506, as in swimming, id, at 255–256, 93 S.Ct., at 498–499, the relationship is too attenuated.

On like reasoning, the "activity giving rise to the incident"in this case, *Sisson*, supra, 497 U.S., at 364, 110 S.Ct., at 2897, should be characterized as repair or maintenance work on a navigable waterway performed from a vessel. Described in this way, there is is no question that the activity is substantially related to traditional maritime activity, for barges and similar vessels have traditionally been engaged in repair work similar to what Great Lakes contracted to perform here. See, e.g., Shea v. Rev–Lyn Contracting Co., 868 F.2d 515, 518 (C.A.1 1989)(bridge repair by crane-carrying barge); Nelson v. United States, 639 F.2d 469, 472 (C.A.9 1980)(Kennedy, J.)(repair of wave suppressor from a barge); In re New York Dock Co., 61 F.2d 777 (C.A.2 1932)(pile-driving from crane-carrying barge in connection with the building of a dock); In re P. Sanford Ross, Inc., 196 F.921, 923–924 (E.D.N.Y.1912)(pile driving from crane-carrying barge close to water's edge), rev'd on other grounds, 204 F. 248 (C.A.2 1913); cf. In re The V–14813, 65 F.2d 789, 790 (C.A.5 1933)("[t]here are many cases holding that a dredge, or a barge with a pile driver, employed on navigable waters, is subject to maritime jurisdiction"); Lawrence v. Flatboat, 84 F. 200 (S.D.Ala.1897)(pile driving from crane-carrying barge in connection with the creation of bulkheads), aff'd *sub nom* Southern Log Cart & Supply Co. v. Lawrence, 86 F. 907 (C.A.5 1898).

The city argues, to the contrary, that a proper application of the activity prong of *Sisson* would consider the city's own alleged failure at properly maintaining and operating the tunnel system that runs under the river. City Brief 48–49. If this asserted proximate cause of the flood victims' injuries were considered, the city submits, its failure to resemble any traditional maritime activity would take this case out of admiralty.

The city misreads *Sisson*, however, which did not consider the activities of the washer/dryer manufacturer, who was possibly an additional tortfeasor, and whose activities were hardly maritime; the activities of *Sisson*, the boat owner, supplied the necessary substantial relationship to traditional maritime activity. Likewise, in *Foremost*, we said that "[b]ecause the 'wrong' here involves the negligent operation of a vessel on navigable waters, we believe that it has a sufficient nexus to traditional maritime activity to sustain admiralty jurisdiction...." 457 U.S;, at 674, 102 S.Ct. at 2658. By using the word "involves," we made it clear that we need to look only to whether one of the arguably proximate causes of the incident originated in the maritime activity of a tortfeasor: as long as one of the putative tortfeasors was engaged in traditional maritime activity the allegedly wrongful activity will "involve" such traditional maritime activity and will meet the second nexus prong. Thus, even if we were to identify the "activity giving rise to the incident" as including the acts of the city as well as Great Lakes, admiralty jurisdiction would nevertheless attach. That result would be true to *Sisson's* requirement of a "substantial relationship" between the "activity giving rise to the incident" and traditional maritime activity. *Sisson* did not require, as the city in effect asserts, that there be a complete identity between the two. The substantial relationship test is satisfied when at least one alleged tortfeasor was engaging in activity substantially related to traditional maritime activity and such activity is claimed to have been a proximate cause of the incident.

Petitioners also argue that we might get a different result simply by characterizing the "activity" in question at a different level of generality, perhaps as "repair and maintenance," or, as "pile driving near a bridge." The city is, of course, correct that a tortfeasor's activity can be described at a sufficiently high level of generality to eliminate any hint of maritime connection, and if that were properly done *Sisson* would bar assertion of admiralty jurisdiction. But to suggest that such hyper-generalization ought to be the rule would convert *Sisson* into a vehicle for eliminating admiralty jurisdiction. Although there is inevitably some play in the joints in selecting the right level of generality when applying the *Sisson* test, the inevitable imprecision is not an excuse for whimsy. The test turns on the comparison of traditional maritime activity to the arguably maritime character of the tortfeasor's activity in a given case; the comparison would merely be frustrated by eliminating the maritime aspect of the tortfeasor's activity from consideration.[4]

Grubart makes an additional claim that *Sisson* is being given too expansive a reading. If the activity at issue here is considered maritime-related, it argues, then virtually "every activity involving a vessel on navigable waters" would be "a traditional maritime activity sufficient to invoke maritime jurisdiction." Grubart Brief 6. But this is not fatal criticism. This Court has not proposed any radical alteration of the traditional criteria for invoking admiralty jurisdiction in tort cases, but has simply followed the lead of the lower federal courts in rejecting a location rule so rigid as to extend admiralty to a case involving an airplane, not a vessel, engaged in an activity far removed from anything traditionally maritime. See *Executive Jet*, 409 U.S., at 268–274. 93 S.Ct., at 504 506; see also Peytavin v. Government Employees Ins. Co., 453 F.2d 1121, 1127 (C.A.5 1972)(no jurisdiction over claim for personal injury by motorist who was rearended while waiting for a ferry on a floating pontoon serving as the ferry's landing); Chapman v. Grosse Pointe Farms, 385 F.2d 962 (C.A.6 1967)(no admiralty jurisdiction over claim of swimmer who injured himself when diving off pier into shallow but navigable water). In the cases after *Executive Jet*, the Court stressed the need for a maritime connection, but found one in the navigation or berthing of pleasure boats, despite the facts that the pleasure boat activity took place near shore, where States have a strong interest in applying their own tort law, or was not on all fours with the maritime shipping and commerce that has traditionally made up the business of most maritime courts. *Sisson*, 497 U.S., at 367, 110 S.Ct., at 2898; *Foremost*, 457 U.S., at 675, 102 S.Ct., at 2658–2659. Although we agree with petitioners that these cases do not say that every tort involving a vessel on navigable waters falls within the scope of admiralty jurisdiction no matter what, they do show that ordinarily that will be so.[5]

III

Perhaps recognizing the difficulty of escaping the case law, petitioners ask us to change it. In cases "involving land based parties and injuries," the city would have us adopt a condition of jurisdiction that

---

4. The city also proposes that we define the activity as "the operation of an underground tunnel connected to Loop buildings." City Brief 49–50. But doing this would eliminate the maritime tortfeasor's activity from consideration entirely. This (like the choice of a supreme level of generality, described in the text) would turn Sisson v. Ruby, 497 U.S. 358, 110 S.Ct. 2892, 111 L.Ed.2d 292 (1990), on its head, from a test to weed out torts without a maritime connection into an arbitrary exercise for eliminating jurisdiction over even vessel-related torts connected to traditional maritime commerce.

5. Because we conclude that the tort alleged in Count I of Great Lakes's complaint satisfies both the location and connection tests necessary for admiralty jurisdiction under 28 U.S.C. § 1333(1), we need not consider respondent's alternative argument that the Extension of Admiralty Jurisdiction Act, 46 U.S.C. § 740 provides an independent basis of federal jurisdiction over the complaint.

"the totality of the circumstances reflects a federal interest in protecting maritime commerce sufficiently weighty to justify shifting what would otherwise be state court litigation into federal court under the federal law of admiralty."   City Brief 32.

Grubart and the city say that the Fifth Circuit has applied a somewhat similar "four-factor test" looking to "the functions and roles of the parties; the types of vehicles and instrumentalities involved; the causation and the type of injury; and traditional concepts of the role of admiralty law." Kelly v. Smith, 485 F.2d 520, 525 (C.A.5 1973); see also Molett v. Penrod Drilling Co., 826 F.2d 1419, 1426 (C.A.5 1987)(adding three more factors: the "impact of the event on maritime shipping and commerce"; "the desirability of a uniform national rule to apply to such matters"; and "the need for admiralty 'expertise' in the trial and decision of the case"), cert. denied sub nom.   Columbus-McKinnon, Inc. v. Gearench, Inc., 493 U.S. 1003, 110 S.Ct. 563, 107 L.Ed.2d 558 (1989). Although they point out that *Sisson* disapproved the use of four-factor or seven-factor tests "where all the relevant entities are engaged in similar types of activity," this rule implicitly left the matter open for cases like this one, where most of the victims, and one of the tortfeasors, are based on land.   See 497 U.S., at 365, n. 3, 110 S.Ct. at 2897 ("Different issues may be raised by a case in which one of the instrumentalities is engaged in a traditional maritime activity, but the other is not").   The city argues that there is a good reason why cases like this one should get different treatment.   Since the basic rationale for federal admiralty jurisdiction is "protection of maritime commerce through uniform rules of decision," the proposed jurisdictional test would improve on *Sisson* in limiting the scope of admiralty jurisdiction more exactly to its rationale.   A multiple factor test would minimize, if not eliminate, the awkward possibility that federal admiralty rules or proce- dures will govern a case, to the disadvantage of state law, when admiralty's purpose does not require it.   Cf. *Foremost*, supra, at 677–686, 102 S.Ct., at 2659–2659–2664 (Powell, J., dissenting).

Although the arguments are not frivolous, they do not persuade.   It is worth recalling that the *Sisson* tests are aimed at the same objectives invoked to support a new multifactor test, the elimination of admiralty jurisdiction where the rationale for the jurisdiction does not support it.   If the tort produces no potential threat to maritime commerce or occurs during activity lacking a substantial relationship to traditional maritime activity, *Sisson* assumes that the objectives of admiralty jurisdiction proba- bly do not require its exercise, even if the location test is satisfied.   If, however, the *Sisson* tests are also satisfied, it is not apparent why the need for admiralty jurisdiction in aid of maritime commerce somehow becomes less acute merely because land-based parties happen to be involved.   Cer- tainly Congress did not think a land-based party necessarily diluted the need for admiralty jurisdiction or it would have kept its hands off the primitive location test.

Of course one could claim it to be odd that under *Sisson* a land-based party (or more than one) may be subject to admiralty jurisdiction, but it would appear no less odd under the city's test that a maritime tortfeasor in the most traditional mould might be subject to state common-law jurisdiction. Other things being equal, it is not evident why the first supposed anomaly is worse than the second. But other things are not even equal. As noted just above, Congress has already made the judgment, in the Extension Act, that a land-based victim may properly be subject to admiralty jurisdiction. Surely a land-based joint tortfeasor has no claim to supposedly more favorable treatment.

Nor are these the only objections to the city's position. Contrary to what the city suggests, City Brief 10, 14–15, 25–26, 30, exercise of federal admiralty jurisdiction does not result in automatic displacement of state law. It is true that, "[w]ith admiralty jurisdiction comes the application of substantive admiralty law." East River S.S. Corp. v. Transamerica Delaval Inc., 476 U.S. 858, 864, 106 S.Ct. 2295, 2298–2299, 90 L.Ed.2d 865 (1986). But, to characterize that law, as the city apparently does, as "federal rules of decision," City Brief 15, is

"a destructive oversimplification of the highly intricate interplay of the States and the National Government in their regulation of maritime commerce. It is true that state law must yield to the needs of a uniform federal maritime law when this Court finds inroads on a harmonious system. But this limitation still leaves the States a wide scope." Romero v. International Terminal Operating Co., 358 U.S. 354, 373, 79 S.Ct. 468, 480–481. 3 L.Ed.2d 368 (1959)(footnote omitted).

See *East River*, supra, at 864–865, 106 S.Ct., at 2298–2299 ("Drawn from state and federal sources, the general maritime law is an amalgam of traditional common-law rules, modifications of those rules, and newly created rules" (footnote omitted)). Thus, the city's proposal to synchronize the jurisdictional enquiry with the test for determining the applicable substantive law would discard a fundamental feature of admiralty law, that federal admiralty courts sometimes do apply state law. See, e.g., American Dredging Co. v. Miller, 510 U.S. __, __, 114 S.Ct. 981, 987, 127 L.Ed.2d 285 (1994); see also 1 S. Friedell, Benedict on Admiralty § 112 p. 749 (7th ed. 1994).[6]

---

6. We will content ourselves simply with raising a question about another of the city's assumptions, which does not go to anything dispositive for us. It is true that this Court has said that "the primary focus of admiralty jurisdiction is unquestionably the protection of maritime commerce," Foremost Ins. Co. v. Richardson., 457 U.S. 668, 674, 102 S.Ct. 2654, 2658, 73 L.Ed.2d 300 (1982); see *Sisson*, 497 U.S., at 367, 110 S.Ct., at 2898; see id., at 364, n. 2, 110 S.Ct., at 2896–2897, n. 2, a premise that has recently been questioned, see Casto, The Origins of Federal Admiralty Jurisdiction in an age of Privateers, Smugglers, and Pirates, 37 Am.J.Legal Hist., 117 (1993). However that may be, this Court has never limited the interest in question to the "protection of maritime commerce through uniform rules of decision," as the city would have it. City Brief 19. Granted, whatever its precise purpose, it is likely that Congress thought of uniformity of substantive law as a subsidiary goal conducive to furthering that purpose. See Currie, Federalism and the Admiralty: "The Devil's Own Mess," 1960 S.Ct.Rev. 158, 163 ("[A] uniform law was apparently one reason for the establishment of the admiralty law in 1789" (footnote omitted). But we are unwilling to rule out that the first Congress saw a value in federal admiralty courts beyond fostering uniformity of substantive law, stemming, say, from a concern with local bias similar to the presupposition for diversity jurisdiction. See The Federalist No. 80, p. 538 (J.Cooke ed.

Finally, on top of these objections going to the city's premises there is added a most powerful one based on the practical consequences of adopting a multifactor test. Although the existing case law tempers the locality test with the added requirements looking to potential harm and traditional activity, it reflects customary practice in seeing jurisdiction as the norm when the tort originates with a vessel in navigable waters, and in treating departure from the locality principle as the exception. For better or worse, the case law has thus carved out the approximate shape of admiralty jurisdiction in a way that admiralty lawyers understand reasonably well. As against this approach, so familiar and relatively easy, the proposed four or seven-factor test would be hard to apply, jettisoning relative predictability for the open-ended rough-and-tumble of factors, inviting complex argument in a trial court and a virtually inevitable appeal.

Consider, for example, just one of the factors under the city's test, requiring a district court at the beginning of every purported admiralty case to determine the source (state or federal) of the applicable substantive law. The difficulty of doing that was an important reason why this Court in *Romero*, supra, was unable to hold that maritime claims fell within the scope of the federal-question jurisdiction statute, 28 U.S.C. § 1331. 358 U.S., at 375–376, 79 S.Ct., at 481–482 ("sound judicial policy does not encourage a situation which necessitates constant adjudication of the boundaries of state and federal competence"). That concern applies just as strongly to cases invoking a district court's admiralty jurisdiction under 28 U.S.C. § 1333, under which the jurisdictional enquiry for maritime torts has traditionally been quite uncomplicated.

Reasons of practice, then, are as weighty as reasons of theory for rejecting the city's call to adopt a multifactor test for admiralty jurisdiction for the benefit of land-based parties to a tort action.

Accordingly, we conclude that the Court of Appeals correctly held that the District Court had admiralty jurisdiction over the respondent's Limitation Act suit. The judgment of the Court of Appeals is

Affirmed.

■ JUSTICE STEVENS and JUSTICE BREYER took no part in the decision of this case.

■ JUSTICE O'CONNOR, concurring.

I concur in the Court's judgment and opinion. The Court properly holds that, when a court is faced with a case involving multiple tortfeasors, some of whom may not be maritime actors, if one of the putative tortfeasors was engaged in traditional maritime activity alleged to have proximately caused

1961)(A. Hamilton)("maritime causes ... so commonly affect the rights of foreigners"); 1 M. Farrand, Records of the Federal Convention of 1787, p. 124 (1911); 2 id, at 46; see generally D. Robertson, Admiralty and Federalism 95–103 (1970). After all, if uniformity of substantive law had been Congress's only concern, it would have left admiralty jurisdiction in the state courts subject to an appeal to a national tribunal (as it did with federal question jurisdiction until 1875, and as the Articles of Federation had done with cases of prize and capture).

the incident, then the supposedly wrongful activity "involves" traditional maritime activity. The possible involvement of other, nonmaritime parties does not affect the jurisdictional inquiry as to the maritime party. Ante, 1051–1052. I do not, however, understand the Court's opinion to suggest that, having found admiralty jurisdiction over a particular claim against a particular party, a court *must* then exercise admiralty jurisdiction over *all* the claims and parties involved in the case. Rather, the court should engage in the usual supplemental jurisdiction and impleader inquiries. See 28 U.S.C. § 1367 (1988 ed., Supp. V); Fed.Rule Civ.Proc. 14; see also ante, at 1047. I find nothing in the Court's opinion to the contrary.

■ JUSTICE THOMAS, with whom JUSTICE SCALIA joins, concurring in the judgment.

I agree with the majority's conclusion that 28 U.S.C. § 1333(1) grants the District Court jurisdiction over the great Chicago flood of 1992. But I write separately because I cannot agree with the test the Court applies to determine the boundaries of admiralty and maritime jurisdiction. Instead of continuing our unquestioning allegiance to the multifactor approach of Sisson v. Ruby, 497 U.S. 358, 110 S.Ct. 2892, 111 L.Ed.2d 292 (1990), I would restore the jurisdictional inquiry to the simple question whether the tort occurred on a vessel on the navigable waters of the United States. If so, then admiralty jurisdiction exists. This clear, bright-line rule, which the Court applied until recently, ensures that judges and litigants will not waste their resources in determining the extent of federal subject-matter jurisdiction.

I

This case requires the Court to redefine once again the line between federal admiralty jurisdiction and state power due to an ambiguous balancing test. The fact that we have had to revisit this question for the third time in a little over 10 years indicates the defects of the Court's current approach. The faults of balancing tests are clearest, and perhaps most destructive, in the area of jurisdiction. Vague and obscure rules may permit judicial power to reach beyond its constitutional and statutory limits, or they may discourage judges from hearing disputes properly before them. Such rules waste judges' and litigants' resources better spent on the merits, as this case itself demonstrates. It is especially unfortunate that this has occurred in admiralty, an area that once provided a jurisdictional rule almost as clear as the 9th and 10th verses of Genesis: "And God said, Let the waters under the heaven be gathered together unto one place, and let the dry land appear: and it was so. And God called the dry land Earth and the gathering together of the waters called he Seas: and God saw that it was good." The Holy Bible, Genesis 1:9–10 (King James Version).

As recently as 1972, courts and parties experienced little difficulty in determining whether a case triggered admiralty jurisdiction, thanks to the simple "situs rule." In The Plymouth, 70 U.S. 20, 18 L.Ed. 125, 3 Wall. 20, 36 (1866), this Court articulated the situs rule thus: "[e]very species of tort, however occurring, and whether on board a vessel or not, if upon the high seas or navigable waters, is of admiralty cognizance." This simple, clear test, which Justice Story pronounced while riding circuit, see Thomas v. Lane, 23 F.Cas. 957, 960 (C.C.Me.1813), did not require alteration until 1948, when Congress included within the admiralty jurisdiction torts caused on water, but whose effects were felt on land. See Extension of Admiralty Jurisdiction Act, 62 Stat. 496, 46 U.S.C.App. § 740.

The simplicity of this test was marred by modern cases that tested the boundaries of admiralty jurisdiction with ever more unusual facts. In Executive Jet Aviation, Inc. v. City of Cleveland, 409 U.S. 249, 93 S.Ct. 493, 34 L.Ed.2d 454 (1972), we held that a plane crash in Lake Erie was not an admiralty case within the meaning of § 1333(1) because the tort did not "bear a significant relationship to traditional maritime activity." Id, at 268, 93 S.Ct., at 504. What subsequent cases have failed to respect, however, is *Executive Jet 's* clear limitation to torts involving aircraft. As we said:

> "One area in which locality as the exclusive test of admiralty tort jurisdiction has given rise to serious problems in application is that of aviation. . . . [W]e have concluded that maritime locality alone is not a sufficient predicate for admiralty jurisdiction in aviation tort cases." Id., at 261, 93 S.Ct., at 501 (emphasis added).

Our identification of the "significant relationship" factor occurred wholly in the context of a discussion of the difficulties that aircraft posed for maritime law. In fact, while we recognized the extensive criticism of the strict locality rule, we noted that "for the traditional types of maritime torts, the traditional test has worked quite satisfactorily." Id, at 254, 93 S.Ct., at 497. Thus, *Executive Jet,* properly read, holds that if a tort occurred on board a vessel on the navigable waters, the situs test applies, but if the tort involved an airplane, then the "significant relationship" requirement is added.

Although it modified the strict locality test, *Executive Jet* still retained a clear rule that I could apply comfortably to the main business of the admiralty court. Nonetheless, the simplicity and clarity of this approach met its demise in Foremost Ins. Co. v. Richardson, 457 U.S. 668, 102 S.Ct. 2654, 73 L.Ed.2d 300 (1982). That case involved the collision of two pleasure boats on the navigable waters, a tort that some commentators had argued did not fall within the admiralty jurisdiction because it did not implicate maritime commerce. See, e.g., Stolz, Pleasure Boating and Admiralty: Erie at Sea, 51 Calif.L.Rev. 661 (1963). The Court could have resolved the case and found jurisdiction simply by applying the situs test. Instead, responding to the arguments that admiralty jurisdiction was limited to commercial maritime activity, the Court found that the tort's significant connection with "traditional maritime activity" and the accident's "potential disruptive impact" on maritime commerce prompted an exercise of federal jurisdiction. 457 U.S., at 674–675, 102 S.Ct., at 2658–2659.

It is clear that *Foremost* overextended *Executive Jet*, which had reserved the significant relationship inquiry for aviation torts. As Justice

Scalia noted in *Sisson*, *Executive Jet* is better "understood as resting on the quite simple ground that the tort did not involve a vessel, which had traditionally been thought required by the leading scholars in the field." 497 U.S., at 369–370, 110 S.Ct., at 2899 (opinion concurring in judgment). *Executive Jet* did not in the least seek to alter the strict locality test for torts involving waterborne vessels. *Foremost,* however, converted *Executive Jet's* exception into the rule. In addition to examining situs, *Foremost* required federal courts to ask whether the tort bore a significant relationship to maritime commerce, and whether the accident had a potential disruptive impact on maritime commerce. 457 U.S., at 673475 102 S.Ct., at 2657–2659. The lower courts adopted different approaches as they sought to apply *Foremost 's* alteration of the *Executive Jet* test. See *Sisson,* supra, 497 U.S., at 365, n. 4, 110 S.Ct., at 2897, n. 4 (citing cases).

Sisson then affirmed the inherent vagueness of the *Foremost* test. *Sisson* involved a marina fire that was caused by a faulty washer-dryer unit on a pleasure yacht. The fire destroyed the yacht and damaged several vessels in addition to the marina. In finding admiralty jurisdiction, the Court held that the federal judicial power would extend to such cases only if: (1) in addition to situs, (2) the "incident" poses a potential hazard to maritime commerce, and (3) the "activity" giving rise to the incident bears a substantial relationship to traditional maritime activity. 497 U.S., at 362–364, 110 S.Ct., at 2895–2897. The traditional situs test also would have sustained a finding of jurisdiction because the fire started on board a vessel on the waterways. Thus, what was once a simple question——did the tort occur on the navigable waters—had become a complicated, multifactor analysis.

The disruption and confusion created by the *Foremost-Sisson* approach is evident from the post-*Sisson* decisions of the lower courts and from the majority opinion itself. Faced with the task of determining what is an "incident" or "activity" for *Sisson* purposes, the Fourth, Fifth, and Ninth Circuits simply reverted to the multi-factor test they had employed before *Sisson.* See Price v. Price, 929 F.2d 131, 135–136 (C.A.4 1991); Coats v. Penrod Drilling Corp., 5 F.3d 877, 885–886 (C.A.5 1993); Delta Country Ventures, Inc. v. Magana, 986 F.2d 1260, 1263 (C.A.9 1993). The District Court's opinion in this case is typical: while nodding to *Sisson,* the court focused its entire attention on a totality-of-the-circumstances-test, which includes factors such as "the functions and roles of the parties" and "[t]he traditional concepts of the role of admiralty law." Pet. for Cert. of Chicago 32a. Such considerations have no place in the *Sisson* test and should have no role in any jurisdictional inquiry. The dangers of a totality-of-the-circumstances approach to jurisdiction should be obvious. An undefined test requires courts and litigants to devote substantial resources to determine whether a federal court may hear a specific case. Such a test also introduces undesirable uncertainty into the affairs of private actors—even those involved in common maritime activities—who cannot predict whether or not their conduct may justify the exercise of admiralty jurisdiction.

Although the majority makes an admirable attempt to clarify what *Sisson* obscures, I am afraid that its analysis cannot mitigate the confusion of the *Sisson* test. Thus, faced with the "potential to disrupt maritime commerce" prong ante, at 1050, the majority must resort to "an intermediate level of possible generality" to determine the "'general features'"of the incident here, id., at 1051. The majority does not explain the origins of "levels of generality," nor, to my knowledge, do we employ such a concept in other areas of jurisdiction. We do not use "levels of generality" to characterize residency or amount in controversy for diversity purposes, or to determine the presence of a federal question. Nor does the majority explain why an "intermediate" level of generality is appropriate. It is even unclear what an intermediate level of generality is, and we cannot expect that district courts will apply such a concept uniformly in similar cases. It is far from obvious how the undefined intermediate level of generality indicates that the "incident" for *Sisson* purposes is that of a vessel damaging an underwater structure.

The majority also applies levels of generality to the next prong of *Sisson*—whether the tortfeasor is engaged in "activity" that shows a "substantial relationship to traditional maritime activity." The majority decides that the activity is repair work by a vessel on a navigable waterway. But, as the petitioners rightly argue, the "activity" very well could be bridge repair or pile driving. One simply cannot tell due to the ambiguities intrinsic to *Sisson* and to the uncertainty as to the meaning of levels of generality. The majority's response implicitly acknowledges the vagueness inherent in *Sisson*: "Although there is inevitably some play in the joints in selecting the right level of generality when applying the *Sisson* test, the inevitable imprecision is not an excuse for whimsy." Ante, at 1052. The Court cannot provide much guidance to district courts as to the correct level of generality; instead, it can only say that any level is probably sufficient so long as it does not lead to "whimsy." When it comes to these issues, I prefer a clearer rule, which this Court has demanded with respect to federal question or diversity jurisdiction. Indeed, the "play in the joints" and "imprecision" that the Court finds "inevitable" easily could be avoided by returning to the test that prevailed before *Foremost*. In its effort to create an elegant, general test that could include all maritime torts, *Sisson* has only disrupted what was once a simple inquiry.

II

It should be apparent that this Court does not owe *Sisson* the benefit of stare decisis. As shown above, *Sisson* and *Foremost* themselves overextended *Executive Jet* and deviated from a long tradition of admiralty jurisprudence. More importantly, the new test of *Sisson* and *Foremost* did not produce greater clarity or simplicity in exchange for departing from a century of undisturbed practice. Instead, as discussed earlier, the two cases have produced only confusion and disarray in the lower courts and in this Court as well. It would seem that in the area of federal subject-matter jurisdiction, vagueness and ambiguity are grounds enough to revisit an unworkable prior decision.

In place of *Sisson* I would follow the test described at the outset. When determining whether maritime jurisdiction exists under § 1333(1), a federal district court should ask if the tort occurred on a vessel on the navigable waters. This approach won the approval of two Justices in *Sisson*, see 497 U.S., at 373, 110 S.Ct., at 2901 (Scalia, J., joined by White, J., concurring in judgment). Although Justice Scalia's *Sisson* concurrence retained a "normal maritime activities" component, it recognized that anything a vessel does in the navigable waters would meet that requirement; and that "[i]t would be more straightforward to jettison the 'traditional maritime activity' analysis entirely." Id., at 374, 110 S.Ct., at 2902. I wholly agree and have chosen the straightforward approach, which, for all of its simplicity, would have produced the same results the Court arrived at in *Executive Jet, Foremost, Sisson*, and this case. Although this approach might leave within admiralty jurisdiction a few "unusual actions," ibid., such freakish cases will occur rarely. In any event, the resources needed to resolve them "will be saved many times over by a clear jurisdictional rule that makes it unnecessary to decide" what is a traditional maritime activity and what poses a threat to maritime commerce. Id., at 374–375, 110 S.Ct., at 2901–2902.

In this case, a straightforward application of the proposed test easily produces a finding of admiralty jurisdiction. As the majority quite ably demonstrates, the situs requirement is satisfied because the tort was caused by a "spud barge" on the Chicago River. Ante, at 1048–1049. Although the accident's effects were felt on land, the Extension of Admiralty Jurisdiction Act brings the event within § 1333(1). While I agree with the majority's analysis of this question, I disagree with its decision to continue on to other issues. A simple application of the situs test would yield the same result the Court reaches at the end of its analysis.

This Court pursues clarity and efficiency in other areas of federal subject-matter jurisdiction, and it should demand no less in admiralty and maritime law. The test I have proposed would produce much the same results as the *Sisson* analysis without the need for wasteful litigation over threshold jurisdictional questions. Because *Sisson* departed from a century of precedent, is unworkable, and is easily replaced with a bright-line rule, I concur only in the judgment.

N O T E

As the Court notes, the maritime nexus requirement can be traced to Executive Jet Aviation Co. v. City of Cleveland. The facts of *Executive Jet,* as stated by the Court, were as follows:

"When the crash occurred, the plane was manned by a pilot, a co-pilot, and a stewardess, and was departing Cleveland on a charter flight to Portland, Maine, where it was to pick up passengers and then continue to White Plains, New York. After being cleared for takeoff by the respondent Dicken, who was the federal air traffic controller at the airport, the plane took off, becoming airborne at about half the distance down the runway. The takeoff flushed the seagulls on the runway, and they rose into the airspace directly ahead of the ascending plane. Ingestion of the birds into the plane's jet engines caused an almost total loss of power. Descending back toward the runway in a semi-stalled condition, the plane veered slightly to the left, struck a portion of the airport perimeter fence and the top of a nearby pickup truck, and then settled in Lake Erie just off the end of the runway and less that one fifth of a statute mile off shore. There were no injuries to the crew, but the aircraft soon sank and became a total loss." 409 U.S. at 249, 93 S.Ct. 495.

If we applied The Admiral Peoples, where would you say the tort occurred? The court of appeals thought that it occurred on land. The want of maritime connection was an alternative theory.

In Foremost Ins. Co. v. Richardson, the action arose out of a collision between two pleasure craft on the Amite River in Louisiana. There was no question that the river at that point was navigable, but Judge Thornberry expressed the view that admiralty jurisdiction required that in addition to being navigable, the waterway must also function as an integral or major "artery of commerce." See Ch. 2, supra.

In Carroll v. Protection Maritime Ins. Co., 512 F.2d 4, 1975 A.M.C. 1633 (1st Cir.1975), the First Circuit held that an action against an insurance carrier charging that the defendant "blacklisted" seamen by refusing coverage to employers if they hired seamen who had brought actions for injuries, was within the maritime jurisdiction because the natural consequences of the actions of the defendant was to prevent maritime employment. The court purported to follow the *Executive Jet* test, calling particular attention to the Supreme Court's mention of frequent exceptions that had been made to the requirement of maritime location, and reading the case as adopting a maritime connection test. Looking at those exceptions, do they go beyond situations in which the plaintiff and the defendant are directly linked in a maritime relationship and the duties alleged to have been breached are those arising out of their relationship? If it is a maritime tort to act in a way that will prevent the defendant from providing a maritime service, would an automobile accident in which a mariner broke his leg give rise to an action for a maritime tort? If a sailor on leave is hit on the head with a whiskey bottle or contracts venereal disease, does he have a cause of action within § 1333? In *Carroll,* the court was also prompted to its decision by what it considered the anomoly in holding that in the blacklist situation the seaman's action against the employer would be cognizable as an action for breach of a maritime contract and the joinder of the tortfeasor would be precluded by want of jurisdiction. Is this possible anomaly precluded by the doctrine of pendent jurisdiction? See Chapter 6C, infra. It must be remembered, however, that if the problem is resolved within the pendent jurisdiction doctrine, the pendent claim is governed by state law. By contrast, if the act is recognized as a maritime tort, the federal court is free to design the remedy.

Most of the decisions read *Executive Jet* and *Foremost Insurance* to require in most cases maritime location as well as maritime nexus. See, e.g., Richendollar v. Diamond M. Drilling Co., Inc., 784 F.2d 580 (5th Cir.1986). The *Richendollar* court points out that the requirement of maritime location was plainly stated in Victory Carriers, Inc. v. Law, 404 U.S. 202, 92 S.Ct. 418, 30 L.Ed.2d 383 (1971).

The other face of *Executive Jet* is, of course, the question of how "salty" a tort must be to be maritime. Experience with maritime nexus as a touchstone to contract jurisdiction suggests that any line will be a wavering one. *Foremost Insurance* makes it clear that the nexus that is required does not relate alone to commercial transportation. The Court goes as far as to say that the operation of a recreational vessel on the navigable waters of the United States is a maritime activity, making negligent operation of such a vessel a maritime tort. Since *Foremost* involved a collision between two vessels on water conceded to be navigable, it leaves many changes to be rung. Is it the maritime activity of the tortfeasor that controls? Does so much flow from the literal language of the Admiralty Extension Act? ("extend to and include all cases of damage or injury, to person or property, caused by a vessel on navigable water, notwithstanding that such damage or injury be done or consummated on land."). As Mr. Justice Marshall notes in *Foremost,* the term "vessel" as used in the Extension Act is not limited to commercial vessels. Since the purpose of the Extension Act might be characterized as dealing with extension and not restatement, perhaps reliance cannot be put on the Act itself. Nevertheless it would be anomalous indeed to hold that damage caused by a recreational vessel on navigable water gives rise to an action within the maritime jurisdiction and is governed by federal law if the damage is done or consummated on land, but is not within the maritime jurisdiction and is governed by state law if the damage is done or consummated on navigable waters.

Damage to a vessel on navigable waters flowing from an act or omission on land was thought to give rise to an action for maritime tort under the pre-*Executive Jet* locality theory. It was this lack of equivalence that led to the 1948 Extension Act. Generally the cases since *Executive Jet* have sustained the jurisdiction in such cases. See, e.g., Kelly v. Smith, 485 F.2d 520, 1973 A.M.C. 2478 (5th Cir.1973). There plaintiffs were deer poachers on a private hunting preserve ashore and were escaping in a small boat on the Mississippi River when they were injured by bullets fired at them from the shore.

Similarly in Szyka v. United States Secretary of Defense, 525 F.2d 62, 1975 A.M.C. 2504 (2d Cir.1975), the court of appeals held that a complaint alleging shelling close to the plaintiff and his family in their boat by a land-based military installation arose under the Suits in Admiralty Act and not the Tort Claims Act.

And in Gypsum Carrier, Inc. v. Union Camp Corp., 489 F.2d 152, 1974 A.M.C. 227 (5th Cir.1974), jurisdiction was upheld in a suit by the owners of a vessel that collided with a bridge, against a land based paper mill that allegedly caused the accident by the emission of smoke that reduced visibility.

In Jig the Third Corp. v. Puritan Marine Ins. Underwriters Corp., 519 F.2d 171, 1976 A.M.C. 118 (5th Cir.1975), the action was brought under the diversity jurisdiction and thus the issue of maritime jurisdiction vel non did not arise. The court held, however, that negligent design of a vessel causing it to sink in the navigable waters constituted a maritime tort and therefore was governed by the federal maritime law.

In East River S.S. Corp. v. Transamerica Delaval, Inc., 476 U.S. 858, 106 S.Ct. 2295, 90 L.Ed.2d 865 (1986), the Supreme Court upheld the jurisdiction in an action against manufacturers of turbines used on oil tankers for losses occasioned by the malfunction of the turbines. Maritime location was found because the damage to the turbines occurred on the high seas while the turbines were in use, and maritime nexus because the vessels were engaged in maritime commerce, a primary concern of admiralty law. The substantive aspects of *East River S.S.* are discussed at page 839, infra.

Cases like *Jig the Third Corp.* and *Delaval Turbine* are not brought about by the *Executive Jet* doctrine, inasmuch as maritime location was found to exist in each, and prior to *Executive Jet* location alone would have sufficed. They do reject the argument, however, that the "nexus" requirement announced in *Executive Jet* leaves negligent breach of a terrestrial contract, like a contract to build a ship, or a contract to supply parts or equipment to a shipbuilder outside the admiralty jurisdiction.

While the decision in *Foremost Insurance* holds that the operation of recreational vessels on navigable water meets the maritime nexus test, it left open the issue, already discussed in Chapter 2 above, whether bodies of water not used or suitable for commercial use, but navigable interstate by small recreational vessels are navigable waters of the United States for the purpose of applying the locational arm of the *Executive Jet* test.

In the case of aircraft accidents, the Court in *Executive Jet* left open the question of whether an accident in the course of a flight over the ocean would come within the maritime jurisdiction. Some cases in the lower courts have held that they do. See, e.g., Roberts v. United States, 498 F.2d 520 (9th Cir.1974), cert. denied 419 U.S. 1070, 95 S.Ct. 656, 42 L.Ed.2d 665 (1974). There the claims grew out of the crash of a private cargo plane into navigable waters as it was approaching an air base on Okinawa. It was transporting cargo between the United States and Viet Nam, and Okinawa was "merely" one of the intermediate stopping points. The court noted that transoceanic transportation of cargo is recognized as a traditional maritime activity, and that prior to the advent of aviation such shipping could be performed only by waterborne vessels.

Similarly it has been held that the crash in navigable waters of a helicopter used to transport workers to offshore oil facilities has sufficient maritime nexus to support the exercise of the admiralty and maritime jurisdiction. Smith v. Pan Air Corp., 684 F.2d 1102, 1983 A.M.C. 2836 (5th Cir.1982). See also Barger v. Petroleum Helicopters, Inc., discussed in the NOTE ON VESSELS in Chapter 4, infra.

And in T.J. Falgout Boats, Inc. v. United States, 508 F.2d 855, 1975 A.M.C. 343 (9th Cir.1974) the plaintiff sued the United States under the Federal Tort Claims Act for damages when a Sidewinder missile released from a naval aircraft at the time over navigable waters struck a privately owned vessel being operated on navigable waters. The United States defended on the ground that the action was cognizable only under the Suits in Admiralty Act and was barred by the prescription provision in that statute. In affirming the dismissal of the action the court of appeals observed:

> "Unlike the aircraft in *Executive Jet,* the subject craft is by its very nature maritime. Without question, the release of the Sidewinder from the naval aircraft over navigable waters created a potential hazard to navigation, and the activities of the aircraft at the time were maritime in nature. The United States Navy exists, in major part, for the purpose of operating vessels and aircraft in, on, and over navigable waters. Its aviation branch is fully integrated with the naval service and, whether land-based or sea based, functions essentially to serve in sea operations. * * * Surely, it cannot be said that the naval plane's activity over water in the instant case was entirely 'fortuitous' as was the plane involved in *Executive Jet*. We seriously doubt if appellants should question the applicability of the Suits in Admiralty Act if the aircraft had been stationed on an aircraft carrier. The record is silent on this point. It is our studied conclusion that *Executive Jet* is clearly distinguishable and does not control the facts before us."

The court found the *Roberts* case closely in point and observed that "before the birth of aviation, the firing at sea of explosive projectiles was performed only by waterborne vessels."

In *Roberts* how pertinent is it that before aviation freight went from Los Angeles to Viet Nam by surface vessel? Or that before aviation "projectiles" were fired on water from ships? Before the completion of the trans-Siberian railway, freight went from St. Petersburg to Vladivostoc by water. Would that make a railroad accident in Usbeck maritime?

In *T.J. Falgout Boats* is the stress laid upon the "naval" character of the navy warranted? Notice the number of changes that can be rung on the facts:

1. The missile was discharged by a navy plane over water and struck a vessel.

2. The missile was discharged by a navy plane over water and struck a land structure.

3. The missile was discharged by a navy plane over land and struck a vessel in the water.

4. The missile was discharged by a navy plane over land and struck a land structure.

5 to 8. The missile was discharged by an army plane.

9 to 12. The missile was discharged by a marine corps plane.

Perhaps the best example of the difficulties in applying the maritime nexus theory in the tort area lies in the cases in which shipyard workers have sought to invoke the admiralty jurisdiction in actions for damages from exposure to asbestos particles in their work. The decisions are unanimous in holding that these asbestosis claims lack the requisite maritime nexus and accordingly are not within the admiralty and maritime jurisdiction. See Oman v. Johns–Manville Corp., 764 F.2d 224 (4th Cir.1985), in which the Fourth Circuit overruled the only court of appeals indication that there was jurisdiction of such actions. In Petersen v. Chesapeake & Ohio Ry. Co., 784 F.2d 732 (6th Cir.1986), the Sixth Circuit joined the view expressed in the other circuits that the asbestosis claims lacked maritime nexus, but went on to hold that a seaman could bring an action under the Jones Act for negligence, there being no requirement of admiralty jurisdiction in such an action. It then proceeded to hold that the Jones Act plaintiff, who alleged that the plaintiff's decedent had acquired asbestosis while working on defendant-employer's car floats, could maintain an action for unseaworthiness under the general maritime law pendent to the claim under the Jones Act. If the asbestosis claim has insufficient maritime nexus to be cognizable under the admiralty and maritime jurisdiction, on what basis does he have a substantive claim for unseaworthiness?

In appraising the importance of the *Sisson-Grubart* analysis one must remember the fact, adverted to by Justice Souter, that in cases like this "[t]his Court has not proposed any radical alteration of the traditional criteria for invoking admiralty jurisdiction, but has simply followed the lead of the lower federal courts in rejecting a location rule so rigid as to extend admiralty to a case involving an airplane, not a vessel, engaged in an activity far removed from anything traditionally maritime." Even Justices Scalia and Thomas concede the exclusion of cases involving the airplane on a domestic flight that happens to fall in the water.

But the reason does not appear to be that the incident is not a threat to maritime commerce. An airplane could fall on a steamer, and the wreckage of an airplane would disturb maritime commerce on the Chicago River as surely as the hole in top of the tunnel.

Does the *Sisson-Grubart* analysis help outside the area of physical damage? It is easy to conceive of a collision (*Richardson*), or a fire (*Sisson*), or a hole in the bottom of the Chicago River (*Grubart*) as interfering with commerce. Even lesser physical intrusions fit the theory. See Wright v. United States, 883 F.Supp. 60, 1995 A.M.C. 899 (D.S.C.1994), holding that negligence in allowing a passenger to jump off a rented pontoon boat in a no-swimming area passed the *Grubart* because an unauthorized swimmer presented a potential of injury to other pontoon boats.

Where there is no potential of physical interference with commerce, what is the test? In a post-*Sisson*, pre-*Grubart* case, it was held that there was no admiralty jurisdiction of an action for injuries to a fifteen year old boy, injured while diving for recreation off a pleasure craft anchored in navigable waters. Delta Country Ventures, Inc. v. Magana, 986 F.2d 1260, 1993 A.M.C. 855 (9th Cir.1993). Judge Kozinski dissented. Does the opinion in *Grubart* illuminate the issue?

When the injury is in the course of commercial maritime activity, is there any requirement that the accident be such as to interrupt or interfere with commerce?

C.   Criminal Jurisdiction

18 U.S.C.A. § 1111

Murder.—(a) * * *

(b) Within the special maritime and territorial jurisdiction of the United States,

Whoever is guilty of murder in the first degree, shall suffer death unless the jury qualifies its verdict * * *

Whoever is guilty of murder in the second degree * * *

Section 1111 is illustrative of a number of sections of the Criminal Code dealing with crimes against the person.

18 U.S.C.A. § 7

Special maritime and territorial jurisdiction of the United States defined. —The term "special maritime and territorial jurisdiction of the United States," as used in this title, includes:

(1) The high seas, any other waters within the admiralty and maritime jurisdiction of the United States and out of the jurisdiction of any particular State, and any vessel belonging in whole or in part to the United States or any citizen thereof, or to any corporation created by or under the laws of the United States, or of any State, Territory, District, or possession thereof, when such vessel is within the admiralty and maritime jurisdiction of the United States and out of the jurisdiction of any particular State.

(2) Any vessel registered, licensed, or enrolled under the laws of the United States, and being on a voyage upon the waters of any of the Great Lakes, or any of the waters connecting them, or upon the Saint Lawrence River where the same constitutes the International Boundary Line.

(3) * * *

(4) * * *

CONSTITUTION OF THE UNITED STATES

Art. III, Sec. 2

* * *

The Trial of all Crimes, except in Cases of Impeachment, shall be by Jury; and such Trial shall be held in the State where the said Crimes shall have been committed; but when not committed within any State, the Trial shall be at such Place or Places as the Congress may by law have directed.

Note

In England the jurisdiction of the High Court of Admiralty over crimes, like its jurisdiction over civil proceedings, was subject to some controversy. Quite clearly the court tried crimes committed on the high seas outside the body of any county. By the Statute of 15 Rich. II, c. 3, set forth supra at p. 2, it also tried cases of homicide and mayhem done aboard ship in the great rivers below the first bridges. The early admiralty judges also claimed criminal jurisdiction in cases occurring in "rivers, creeks, and havens" within the flux and reflux of the tide. In addition, the statutes gave the court jurisdiction over a variety of crimes directly related to maritime commerce. Prior to the Statute of 28 Hen. VIII, c. 15, in 1537, admiralty crimes were tried according to the civil law. No jury was used and conviction required a confession or testimony of two witnesses (the same rule written into the United States Constitution for the trial of treason). Under this statute, however, it was provided that admiralty crimes would be handled through grand jury indictment and petit jury trial. See 2 Browne, Admiralty ch. XI.

The criminal jurisdiction of the admiralty is of no importance, then, in defining an area of peculiar procedure or separate practice. It remains of some importance in defining the line between state and federal prosecution. The provisions of 18 U.S.C.A. § 1111 are typical of the sections of Title 18 providing for punishment of personal crimes.

It will be noted that these sections limit the application of their provisions to (a) the high seas, (b) the Great Lakes and connecting waters in some cases, and (c) other waters within the admiralty jurisdiction of the United States but not within the jurisdiction of any state. It is clear that "high seas" includes waters within the three mile limit, though they may be subject to state jurisdiction. Murray v. Hildreth, 61 F.2d 483 (5th Cir.1932). What of a ship fastened to the land by cables and communicating with the shore by use of its boats? See United States v. Seagrist, 27 Fed.Cas. 1002 (No. 16,245) (S.D.N.Y.1860). What of water enclosed by a breakwater to provide protected anchorage? See Ex parte O'Hare, 179 Fed. 662, 103 C.C.A. 220 (2d Cir.1910). Is the territorial water of a foreign country within the maritime jurisdiction of the United States so that crimes aboard American ships in foreign ports are punishable under the statutes that are limited to the "special maritime and territorial jurisdiction?" See United States v. Flores, 289 U.S. 137, 53 S.Ct. 580, 77 L.Ed. 1086, 1933 A.M.C. 649 (1933).

high seas
Great Lakes
other waters

Other sections of the criminal code define crimes without reference to the "special maritime and territorial jurisdiction." See, e.g., 18 U.S.C.A. § 1151 dealing with misconduct, negligence, or neglect of duty of employees on a vessel resulting in loss of life. Prior to the adoption of the Judicial Code of 1948, this provision had been located in chapter 11 of the Criminal Code of 1909 and limited to the high seas and other waters within the admiralty jurisdiction and outside the jurisdiction of any particular state. The 1948 revision removed it from this limitation. What, then, is the present scope of the application of § 1151? Is it limited to navigable waters of the United States as defined for the purposes of the civil jurisdiction?

Since an occurrence on the high seas or in the Great Lakes and connecting waters might take place within the jurisdiction of a particular state, is there anything that negatives the state jurisdiction? See Hoopengarner v. United States, 270 F.2d 465 (6th Cir.1959). Notice that the federal law does not apply to crimes occurring aboard a foreign vessel, when the foreign vessel is in the territorial waters of one of the United States. May the crime then be prosecuted under the state law? See Mali v. Keeper of the Common Jail of Hudson County, 120 U.S. 1, 7 S.Ct. 385, 30 L.Ed. 565, and see discussion of the point by the Court in *Flores,* supra, at p. 127. See also Gave v. Grace Line, Inc., 237 F.Supp. 557, 1965 A.M.C. 71 (E.D.Pa. 1964). There a seaman on an American vessel located in Valparaiso, Chile, was arrested aboard the vessel on the charge of selling 10,000 rounds of 22–caliber rifle cartridges while he was ashore on his lunch break. He was convicted and sentenced by the Chilean courts but released on appeal and upon his return sued the ship owner and officers for the alleged illegal detainment and refusal to repatriate him. While the allegation that the crime was perpetrated ashore might have been enough to distinguish the case from *Mali* (where a murder had been committed on board), the fact of arrest on board led the court to hold that where the crime is of a nature calculated "to disturb the peace and tranquility of the country to which the vessel has been brought, the offenders have never by comity or usage been entitled to any exemption from the operation of the local laws for their punishment, if the local tribunals see fit to assert their authority * * *".

Where the vessel is stateless it has been held by the American courts that the crew of a stateless vessel has no legitimate expectation of the protection of any particular state and can be subjected to the laws of any nation. See United States v. Juda, 46 F.3d 961, 1995 A.M.C. 1096 (9th Cir.1995), in which the Coast Guard stopped and searched a vessel apparently on its way to the United States, notwithstanding a false claim of British registry, and upon discovery of illegal drugs seized the vessel and arrested the crew. They were charged with illegal possession with intent to distribute. The court of appeals held that no nexus with the United States need be charged or proved. See also, to the same effect, United States v. Caicedo, 47 F.3d 370, 1995 A.M.C. 1085 (9th Cir.1995).

D.   JURISDICTION IN PRIZE CASES

28 U.S.C.A. § 1333(2)

1333.   Admiralty, maritime and prize cases. —The district courts shall have original jurisdiction, exclusive of the courts of the States, of:

* * *

(2) Any prize brought into the United States and all proceedings for the condemnation of property taken as prize.

N O T E

As a practical matter the prize jurisdiction has not been of much importance in American courts since the Spanish American War. In World War I there was considerable prize litigation in England. The cases have been extracted from Lloyd's Lists and published in a ten volume series called Lloyd's Prize Cases. See also Garner, Prize Law During the World War (1927), and Colombos, Law of Prize (1949). After the entry of the United States in World War II, the American prize law was refurbished in the statute of 1942 (Public Law 704, 77th Congress) and in several reciprocal agreements entered into by the United States and its co-belligerents (See 6 Benedict on *Admiralty* 536–541). Though there was some prize litigation during the war, none developed under the American statute. The statute of 1942 was rewritten in 1956 and appears in the present Code as 10 U.S.C.A. §§ 7651–81. For a contemporary application of the principles of prize law, see Brown, World War Prize Law Applied in a Limited War Situation: Egyptian Restrictions on Neutral Shipping with Israel, 50 U.Minn.L.Rev. 849 (1966), where it is argued that cases during World War I and World War II expanding the permissible belligerent control of neutral shipping are not properly applied in the context of limited warfare.

The student who is interested in the prize jurisdiction will find an entertaining introduction to the subject in D. Martens, Essay on Privateers, Captures, and Particularly on Recaptures (Horne Translation, 1801). Another entertaining background volume is Statham, Privateers and Privateering (1910). The first American textual treatment of the subject is to be found in two notes, the first at 1 Wheat. 494 and the second at 2 Wheat., p. 1 of the Appendix. These notes were later acknowledged to be the work of Justice Story and were published after Story's death in a small volume entitled Story, Principles and Practice of Prize Courts (1854). It includes also a response from Sir William Scott and Sir John Nicholl, sometime judges of the English High Court of the Admiralty, to a letter directed to them by John Jay inquiring about the English practice in prize courts, and a variety of specimen papers and documents.

E. THE OUTER CONTINENTAL SHELF LANDS ACT

As part of the Outer Continental Shelf Lands Act, Act of Aug. 7, 1953, Ch. 345, 67 Stat. 462, it was declared that the Constitution and laws of the United States were extended to "the subsoil and seabed of the outer Continental Shelf and to all artificial islands and fixed structures which may be erected thereon for the purposes of transporting such resources therefrom" to the same extent as if the Continental Shelf were a federal enclave. 43 U.S.C.A. § 1333(a)(1).

Having extended the law of the United States to the Shelf, it was provided that to the extent that they were not inconsistent with "this subchapter or with other federal laws," or with regulations of the Secretary, the civil and criminal laws of each adjacent State[s] as of August 7, 1953 should be the law of the United States for "that portion of the seabed of the outer Continental Shelf, and artificial islands and fixed structures thereon, which would be within the area of the State if its boundaries were extended seaward to the margin of the Continental Shelf." Section 1333 was amended in 1975 to eliminate the static conformity provision and provide, instead, that the laws of each adjacent state "now in effect or hereafter adopted" shall be the law of the United States on artificial islands and fixed structures. Act of January 3, 1975, Pub.L. 93–627, § 19(f), 88 Stat. 2146 (43 U.S.C.A. § 1333(a)(2)).

As in other cases in which the federal law has adopted the state law, the interpretation of the Outer Continental Shelf Lands Act was not entirely free from difficulty. Arguably, the general maritime law could be looked upon as within the language "other federal laws" and there was some authority for this interpretation. See Rodrigue v. Aetna Cas. & Sur. Co., 395 F.2d 216, 1970 A.M.C. 413 (5th Cir.1968). The Supreme Court reversed. Rodrigue v. Aetna Cas. & Sur. Co., 395 U.S. 352, 89 S.Ct. 1835, 23 L.Ed.2d 360 (1969), holding that the state law of personal injuries and wrongful death applies, and not the general maritime law and the Death on the High Seas Act. This reading was reiterated in Chevron Oil Co. v. Huson, 404 U.S. 97, 92 S.Ct. 349, 30 L.Ed.2d 296 (1971). In that case, however, the Court recognized the difficulties imposed by reliance on the Fifth Circuit cases, and held that the *Rodrigue* decision would not be applied retroactively to bar a claim under the state statute of limitations.

Notice that both § 1331(a)(1) and (a)(2) to this point applied only to "artificial islands and fixed structures." What of moveable structures? Not only did (a)(2) not adopt the state law as the law of the United States, but (a)(1) did not in terms extend the law of the United States to movable structures resting on the seabed on the Continental Shelf. Was this an oversight, or was the understanding that on movable structures the admiralty law would apply, the locale being the high seas, and therefore an extension of the law of the United States would be unnecessary? In 1978, subsection (a)(1) was amended to extend the law of the United States to "all artificial islands, and all installations and other devices permanently or temporarily attached to the seabed, which may be erected thereon for the purpose of exploring for, developing, or producing resources thereon, or any such installation or other device (other than a ship or vessel) for the purpose of transporting such resources." Act of September 18, 1978, Pub.L. 95–372, Tit. II, § 203, 92 Stat. 635. The 1978 revision of § 1333(a)(2) renumbered subsection (a)(2) as (a)(2)(A), but made no change in the text. Thus, while under present subsection (a)(1) extends the law of the United States to installations and devices temporarily attached to the seabed, "to the same extent as if the outer Continental Shelf were an area of exclusive federal jurisdiction," in such cases the "civil and criminal laws of each adjacent state" are not extended as the law of the United States under subsection (a)(2)(A).

How much difference does the 1978 amendment make? Does this depend upon the extent to which state law is borrowed in cases dealing with events in areas of exclusive jurisdiction located within a state? Most of the cases in which the issue of controlling law is put are cases of personal injury and death. In the case of death, it is clear, is it not, that if the occurrence falls within the provisions of subsection (a)(1), but not within the provisions of (a)(2)(A), it is governed by the Death on the High Seas

Act. In the case of injury, if, had it occurred in a federal enclave, it would be within the admiralty and maritime jurisdiction, then it would be governed by the maritime law if it occurred on the outer Continental Shelf. These distinctions are of much less importance because under 43 U.S.C.A. § 1333(b), added in 1978, injuries or death of an employee "resulting from any injury occurring as the result of operations conducted on the outer Continental Shelf for the purposes of exploring for, developing, removing or transporting by pipeline the natural resources * * * " are brought within the Longshore and Harbor Workers' Compensation Act, excepting officers and members of the crew of vessels and government employees. It is to be noted that coverage under the LHWCA depends upon the nature of the "operations" and not on the temporary or permanent nature of a structure.

Section 1333 is not applicable to waters within the three mile limit. On these territorial waters, the line to be drawn is one between the state law and the admiralty law, which since the decision of *Executive Jet* will depend upon the maritime location and maritime nexus. In general, employees engaged in off-shore development of natural resources are not thought to be engaged in maritime employment. See Herb's Welding, Inc. v. Gray, discussed in connection with the coverage of the LHWCA under its own provisions, p. 980, infra.

F. AMOUNT IN CONTROVERSY IN ADMIRALTY CAUSES

When a plaintiff elects to bring a maritime claim under the "saving to suitors" clause, he may bring it in the federal court only on a showing of some head of federal jurisdiction other than 28 U.S.C.A. § 1333. If the only such basis is diversity of citizenship, he must meet the requirement of § 1332 that there be in excess of $10,000 in controversy. Prior to 1980, the same requirement appeared in § 1331, and as a consequence the plaintiff in a statutory action within the admiralty and maritime jurisdiction, and involving $10,000 or less, had the option of proceeding in the federal court under § 1333, without a jury, or in the state court with a jury, but could not bring the action in the federal court and demand a jury unless the particular statute under which the claim arose created a claim cognizable under some jurisdictional section other than § 1331, e.g., a civil rights claim, or a claim arising under a statute enacted under the commerce power, cognizable under § 1337. In Imm v. Union Railroad Co., 289 F.2d 858 (3d Cir.1961), cert. denied 368 U.S. 833, 82 S.Ct. 55, 7 L.Ed.2d 35 (1961), it was held that an action under the F.E.L.A. was cognizable under § 1337, and the *Imm* decision was extended to Jones Act cases in Richardson v. St. Charles–St. John the Baptist Bridge and Ferry Authority, 274 F.Supp. 764, 1968 A.M.C. 538 (E.D.La.1967). See also Brown v. Sinclair Refining Co., 227 F.Supp. 714, 1968 A.M.C. 428 (S.D.N.Y.1964), in which the court applied the *Imm* decision to an event that took place during an actual interstate voyage. Since the 1980 amendment, of course, the issue cannot arise.

CHAPTER 4

Vessels and Jurisdiction

Pavone v. Mississippi Riverboat Amusement Corp.

United States Court of Appeals, Fifth Circuit, 1995.
52 F.3d 560, 1995 A.M.C. 2038.

■ JACQUES L. WIENER, JR., CT.J.:

The appeals we hear in consolidation today are brought by two plaintiffs-appellants who claim that they were injured while working on a Jones Act vessel, but whose claims were dismissed on summary judgments rendered by different district courts. Both claims arose in the context of the dockside casino facet of the burgeoning gaming industries in two of the states of this circuit. In our plenary review of the district courts' summary judgments, we exercise our authority to affirm for reasons differing somewhat from those of the trial courts.

I. Facts and Proceedings

A. *Pavone.*

In the first of the cases we review today, Plaintiff–Appellant Christopher Pavone filed suit in Louisiana state court against Defendants–Appellants, Mississippi Riverboat Amusement Corporation, et al. (Riverboat Companies), alleging a work-related accident and seeking recovery under the Jones Act[1] for disablement, lost wages, impairment of future earning capacity, mental and physical pain and suffering, and loss of enjoyment of life. In addition to compensatory damages, Pavone seeks punitive damages and attorneys' fees. Pavone maintains that he was employed as a bartender on the Biloxi Belle, a floating dockside casino moored in Biloxi, Mississippi, and claims that he injured his foot during the course and scope of his employment while working at a related restaurant located dockside of the *Biloxi Belle.* In particular, Pavone alleges that he stepped on a screw, which penetrated his shoe and punctured his foot, at a time when the Biloxi Belle was being prepared for its grand opening, scheduled for the following day.

The Riverboat Companies were served with process on or about September 16,1993, after which they timely removed the case to federal court for the Eastern District of Louisiana on October 12, 1993. More than thirty days later, on November 15, 1993, Pavone filed a motion to remand, contending that his Jones Act case was not removable. Fifteen days thereafter the Riverboat Companies filed a motion for summary judgment,

---

1. 46 U.S.C. App. § 688 (1988).

insisting that the *Biloxi Belle* was neither a Jones Act vessel nor "in navigation" at the time of Pavone's alleged accident.

On December 20, 1993, the district court denied Pavone's motion to remand, apparently concluding, *inter alia*, that the motion was untimely, and on February 16, 1994, the court denied Pavone's motion for reconsideration. Twice the court granted Pavone continuances, but eventually granted the Riverboat Companies' motion for summary judgment, holding, as a matter of law, that the *Biloxi Belle* was not a Jones Act vessel.

Pavone's timely filing of a notice of appeal led to this review, in which he assigns the following as points of reversible error: (1) his motion to remand was not untimely when filed within thirty-three days following the filing by the Riverboat Companies of their notice of removal; (2) his suit comprised a nonremovable Jones Act claim; (3) the "saving to suitors" clause prohibits removal of state court maritime actions; (4) his last motion to continue the Riverboat Companies' motion for summary judgment should have been granted; and (5) the *Biloxi Belle* and similar floating casinos are either conventional vessels or special purpose craft, in either case satisfying requirements for vessel status under the Jones Act.

B. *Ketzel*

Plaintiff–Appellant Kathleen L. Ketzel alleges that she was injured while working as a cocktail waitress on the *Biloxi Belle* and filed suit in federal court for the Southern District of Mississippi against her employer, one of the Riverboat Companies, Defendant–Appellee, Mississippi Riverboat Amusement, Ltd. (Mississippi Riverboat Amusement). Ketzel seeks recovery under the Jones Act and the general maritime law for severe injuries to her knee, which she claims occurred when she tripped over a garbage can lid and fell during the course and scope of her employment aboard the *Biluxi Belle*.

In April 1994, Mississippi Riverboat Amusement filed a motion for summary judgment, contending that Ketzel was not a seaman when she was injured on the *Biloxi Belle* because it was not a vessel in navigation under the Jones Act or the general maritime law. Ketzel filed her own summary judgment motion, which Mississippi Riverboat Amusement answered by filing a motion seeking an extension of time within which to respond, which the district court granted. Several months later, the district court also granted Mississippi Riverboat Amusement's summary judgment motion, concluding that, as a matter of law, the *Biloxi Belle* "is nothing but a 'floating casino' ... not a 'vessel' under the Jones Act."[2] Ketzel timely filed her notice of appeal.

2. In Preston O. King v. The President Riverboat Casino-Mississippi, Inc., No. 1:94CV233GR (Mar. 10, 1995), the same district court that decided *Ketzel*, held that it lacked admiralty subject matter jurisdiction over a claim by a plaintiff who alleged that he was injured aboard a floating casino that is essentially identical to the *Biloxi Belle*. The plaintiff argued that he was entitled to "passenger" status under the Jones Act, but the district court disagreed, holding that a floating casino is not a Jones Act vessel and that the activity associated with the alleged injury (i.e., dockside gaming) lacked a sufficient nex-

C.   *The Biloxi Belle*

1.   *History*

The structure now known as the *Biloxi Belle* is situated on a barge that was constructed at Morgan City, Louisiana, for the express purpose of supporting a floating restaurant and bar that was to be located at Corpus Christi, Texas. In preparation therefor, the completed barge was towed from Morgan City to a shipyard in Rockport, Texas, where the restaurant structure was added and the name *Wayward Lady* was affixed. The *Wayward Lady* was towed from Rockport to Corpus Christi, where it was operated as a restaurant and bar, as originally contemplated. After a while, the *Wayward Lady* was moved from Corpus Christi to Aransas Pass, Texas, where it remained moored for approximately two and a half more years before being re-outfitted as a casino, towed to Biloxi, and renamed the *Biloxi Belle*.

In preparation for its use as a dockside floating casino, the *Biloxi Belle* was moored to shore by lines tied to sunken steel pylons that were filled with concrete. The first level of the *Biloxi Belle* was connected to the pier by steel ramps, and the second level was joined to a shoreside building. In addition, numerous shore-side utility lines—telephone, electric, gas, sewer, domestic fire and water, cable TV, and computer—were connected permanently (or at least indefinitely) to the *Biloxi Belle*. Only by removing steel pins from the ramps and letting loose all lines and cables could the *Biloxi Belle* be disconnected from the shore.

2.   *Vessel Features*

The barge upon which the casino structure of the *Biloxi Belle* rests has a steel hull, a raked bow to facilitate its being towed, bilge pumps, functional ballast tanks, an auxiliary generator to supply emergency electrical power, and below-deck features including storage facilities and a galley for employee meals and work breaks. It is 217 feet long, 44 feet wide, has a 10–foot draft, and a gross and net tonnage of 2587 tons. The barge is documented by the United States Coast Guard, is assigned an official registration number, is authorized to engage in the coastwise trade, is approved to undertake voyages between ports of the United States with no restrictions, and is home-ported in New Orleans. In addition, an engineer from the American Bureau of Shipping Marine Services, Inc. reviewed the stability of the *Biloxi Belle* and rendered an evaluation of the "vessel's intact stability." The *Biloxi Belle* Casino is licensed for gaming by the Mississippi Gaming Commission pursuant to the Mississippi Gaming Control Act, which allows such licenses to be issued only to operators of "vessels" or "cruise vessels." A continual stand-by towing contract with Alario Brothers Towing commits that company to supply the equipment, facilities, and expertise required to tow the Biloxi Belle to sheltered waters in the event potentially damaging weather is forecast. (The *Biloxi Belle* was towed to sheltered waters on August 23, 1992, when Hurricane Andrew threatened.)

us to traditional maritime activity to confer
admiralty jurisdiction on the court.

3. *Nonvessel Features*

The *Biloxi Belle* has no engine, no captain, no navigational aids, no crewquarters and no lifesaving equipment. For visual effect only, the *Biloxi Belle* is outfitted with a decorative pilot house containing no operating parts other than a single light switch. This faux pilot house contains no steering mechanism, but is decorated with an antique wheel for purely aesthetic purposes. Decorative ring buoys are located on the *Biloxi Belle*, but they too are purely visual effects and are not intended for life-saving use.

Likewise, a motorized but nonfunctional paddle wheel is affixed to the *Biloxi Belle*. The paddle wheel is turned by a small engine, and water outlets around the wheel produce spray to give the appearance of function, but the wheel rests permanently above the water level and serves no propulsion function.

Despite having been towed from its place of manufacture in Louisiana to two restaurant and bar locations in Texas and eventually to its dockside casino location in Biloxi, the subject barge has never been used as a seagoing vessel to transport passengers, cargo, or equipment across navigable waters. Neither was it originally constructed to do so. Even though the barge floats on navigable waters, its quite substantial dockside attachment to land is indefinite, if not permanent, save only for its ability to be unmoored and towed to sheltered waters in advance of approaching hurricanes or other violent weather. The *Biloxi Belle* employs no navigational or nautical crew; all workers thereon are employed solely in connection with the casino operation.

II. Analysis

A. *Standard of Review*

Both cases consolidated here on appeal were terminated in the district courts by summary judgments in favor of the Defendants–Appellees. We review de novo a district court's grant of summary judgment.[3] In so doing, we determine whether "all of the pleadings, depositions, answers to interrogatories, admissions on file, together with affidavits, if any, show that there is no genuine issue as to any material fact and that the moving party is entitled to judgment as a matter of law."[4] The moving party need not support its motion with affidavits or other evidence, but to defeat a motion for summary judgment the nonmovant must present evidence sufficient to establish the existence of each element of his claim as to which he will have the burden of proof at trial.[5] We view this evidence, and the inferences to be drawn from it, in the light most favorable to the nonmovant.[6]

---

3. Simpson v. Lykes Bros. Inc., 22 F.3d 601, 602 (5th Cir.1994).

4. Fed.R.Civ.P. 56(c).

5. Celotex Corp. v. Catrett, 477 U.S. 317, 322, 106 S.Ct. 2548, 2552, 91 L.Ed.2d 265 (1986).

6. Unida v. Levi Strauss & Co., 986 F.2d 970, 975 (5 Cir.1993).

B. *Seaman Status*

To recover under either the Jones Act or the general maritime law, a plaintiff must be a "seaman."[7] The determination of "seaman" status is generally one of fact.[8] "However, seaman status may be decided on summary judgment where the evidence does not support a finding, as a matter of law, that the claimant is permanently assigned to a Jones Act vessel."[9] The substantive issue at the core of both cases that we review today is whether the *Biloxi Belle* is a Jones Act vessel or was one at the times when the subject accidents are alleged to have occurred. Albeit for reasons different from those expressed by the district courts, we agree with their conclusions that the *Biloxi Belle* was not a vessel in navigation for purposes of the Jones Act at the pertinent times. Consequently, neither Pavone nor Ketzel was a seaman, and summary judgment against them both was proper.

C. *Preliminary Matters*

* * * [Discussion of removability, untimely motion to remand and denial of continuance, and footnotes 10–21 omitted—Eds.]

D. *Jones Act Vessels: Yea or Nay?*

Again, as both Pavone and Ketzel depend for recovery on the ability to sustain their claims to having been Jones Act "seamen" when they were injured, and as the *Biloxie Belle* was concededly situated on navigable waters at the times when the subject accidents are alleged to have occurred, thereby meeting the "situs" test for Jones Act purposes, the core question is whether the "status" of the *Biloxi Belle* was that of Jones Act vessel at the times in question. And in the context of indefinitely moored floating casinos, that question is *res nova* in this circuit.[22] With the assistance of able counsel, our esteemed colleagues of the Southern District of Mississippi and the Eastern District of Louisiana, respectively, have rendered opinions in the instant cases crafted in classical maritime methodology for determining, on the basis of a watercraft's unique physical and functional attributes, whether such a craft—here the Biloxi Belle—is a "vessel," conventional or nonconventional, for purposes of the Jones Act or the general maritime law. We are not prepared to say that either opinion is flawed; that the analysis in either is erroneous; or that the result reached on the narrow question whether the *Biloxi Belle* was a Jones Act vessel vis-à-vis Pavone and Ketzel at the times their accidents occurred is wrong. We have nagging concerns nevertheless that vessel analyses of the kinds

7. Hebert v. Air Logistics, Inc., 720 F.2d 853, 856 (5 Cir.1983).

8. Gremillion v. Gulf Coast Catering Co., 904 F.2d 290, 292 (5 Cir.1990).

9. Id.

22. With the recent and presumably continuing proliferation of such "gaming" establishments in Louisiana and Mississippi, and the question of legalized casino gaming still being openly discussed and debated in Texas, we speculate that the cases we consider today are merely the vanguard of a host of future legal efforts to advance as maritime causes of action all sorts of personal injury and property damage claims arising from occurrences on or near moored floating casinos and similar establishments.

performed by the district courts in the instant cases could be overbroad, albeit through inadvertence, and thereby return to haunt us in slightly differing contexts in the future.[23] We conclude that the correct result reached by the district courts in these cases can be achieved in a narrower—and thus a jurisprudentially more principled—way, thereby avoiding the potentiality of undesirable future side effects. The approach to which we refer comprehends the analysis of putative "vessels" that were either withdrawn from navigation at the time in question or never placed in navigation. In particular, we examine the status of the *Biloxi Belle* as of the times pertinent to the alleged injuries in these cases to determine if it was a Jones Act vessel—assuming arguendo that the subject craft was built and used for nonvessel purposes, was moored other than temporarily to the bank, and either had been "withdrawn from navigation" or was being used as a "work platform," or both.[24]

The concepts of "withdrawn from navigation" and "work platform," both usually eschewing vessel status, are not infrequently intertwined. The withdrawn-from-navigation idea has been recognized for decades, distinguishing craft or structures that meet the general dictionary definition of "vessel" from those that meet Jones Act or the general maritime law vessel status at a given time, such as when the craft or structure has been " 'laid up for the winter' ". [25] Both that concept and the work platform concept are certainly alive and well in this circuit, as perhaps best illustrated by a triumvirate of relatively recent decisions.

In the 1984 Jones Act case of Bernard v. Binnings Construction Co.,[26] the "vessel" in question was a small raft or "work punt" stationed alongside a piling that was being driven near the shore of a canal. We noted first the teachings of our earlier cases establishing that dry docks and analogous structures of which the primary purpose is to provide a work platform—even if the structures are afloat—are not Jones Act vessels, as a matter of law.[27] In *Bernard*, we recognized that:

> In a line of cases beginning with Cook v. Belden Concrete Products,[[28]] we
> have extended [the rationale that a floating dry dock is not a "vessel"

23. For example, whether floating casinos, bars, restaurants, etc. would be Jones Act vessels for purposes of accidents occurring while they were being towed to a new location or to a shipyard or dry dock for work or repairs or to sheltered waters in avoidance of a hurricane. The approach we adopt infra also avoids the conflict in "vessel" status among the Jones Act, the general maritime law, state casino licensing classification, Coast Guard documentation, and "dictionary" definitions.

24. In limiting our consideration to vessels withdrawn from navigation or being used as work platforms, we also avoid the always problematic issue of special purpose vessels. See, e.g., Gremillion v. Gulf Coast Catering

Co., 904 F.2d 290, 293 (5 Cir.1990)("Nevertheless, exotic craft may qualify as vessels, especially if frequently navigated, or if exposed to the perils associated with maritime service, or if injury occurs during ocean transport")

25. Desper v. Starved Rock Ferry Co., 342 U.S. 187, 191, 72 S.Ct. 216, 218, 96 L.Ed. 205 (1952)(quoting Hawn v. American S.S. Co., 107 F.2d 999, 1000 (2 Cir.1939)).

26. 741 F.2d 824 (5 Cir.1984).

27. 741 F.2d at 830 & n. 21.

28. 472 F.2d 999 (5 Cir.)(finding that floating construction platform moored alongside employer's concrete yard is legally indis-

while moored at the bank and operated as a dry dock], by analogy, to structures that lack the permanency of fixation to shore or the bottom that is common to dry docks, but nonetheless are used primarily as work platforms.[29]

The *Bernard* court then laid out what has become the starting point in this circuit for analyzing such work-platform cases:

> Since *Cook* we have, despite our reluctance to take Jones Act claims from the trier of fact, affirmed findings that, as a matter of law, other floating work platforms are not vessels. A review of these decisions indicates three factors common to them: (1) The structures involved were constructed and used primarily as work platforms; (2) they were moored or otherwise secured at the time of the accident; and (3) although they were capable of movement and were sometimes moved across navigable waters in the course of normal operations, any transportation function they performed was merely incidental to their primary purpose of serving as work platforms.[30]

The next case in our trilogy is Ducrepont v. Baton Rouge Enterprises, Inc.,[31] in which we were called on to classify a structure as a vessel or nonvessel under the Longshoremen's and Harbor Workers' Compensation Act (LHWCA)[32] as well as under the Jones Act and the general maritime law. In *Ducrepont*, we slightly expanded one element of the *Bernard* test by recognizing that a structure could meet the work-platform definition under the *Bernard* factors even if it had not originally been constructed for that purpose, as long as it was used primarily as a work platform at the time in question and met the other *Bernard* factors.[33] Then came Gremillion v. Gulf Coast Catering Co.[34] in which we heeded the lesson of our earlier decision in Blanchard v. Engine & Gas Compressor Servs., Inc.,[35] stating that, "[a]s a general principle, where the vessel status of an unconventional craft is unsettled, it is necessary to focus upon the 'purpose for which the craft is constructed and the business in which it is engaged.'"[36] We then proceeded in Gremillion to reinforce the *Bernard* analysis as follows:

> Our decisions in this area instruct, however, that as a matter of law certain dry docks and floating work platforms will not qualify as Jones Act vessels. [citing in a footnote, examples from our prior jurisprudence: floating platform used for cleaning and stripping; repair barge; oil production platform that had not moved for twenty-four years; gulf rig moved only twice in twenty years; small raft-like work platform used to drill pilings; floating work platform used in unloading grain barges.] A survey of the case law demonstrates three common attributes for nonvessels:

tinguishable from floating dry docks and holding it not to be a Jones Act vessel, as matter of law), cert. denied, 414 U.S. 868, 94 S.Ct. 175, 38 L.Ed.2d 116 (1973).

29. *Bernard*, 1985 AMC at 794, 741 F.2d at 830.

30. .741 F.2d at 831.

31. 877 F.2d 393 (5 Cir.1989).

32. 33 U.S.C. § 905(b)(1988).

33. *Ducrepont*, 877 F.2d at 395.

34. 904 F.2d 290 (5 Cir.1990).

35. 575 F.2d 1140 (5 Cir.1978).

36. *Gremillion*, 904 F.2d at 293 (quoting *Blanchard*, 575 F.2d at 1142).

(1) The structure was constructed to be used primarily as a work platform;

(2) the structure is moored or otherwise secured at the time of the accident; and

(3) although the platform is capable of movement, and is sometimes moved across navigable waters in the course of normal operations, any transportation function is merely incidental to the platform's primary purpose.[37]

When the undisputed facts of the instant cases are plugged into (1) the *Desper/Hawn* withdrawn-from-navigation factors, or (2) the *Bernard/Gremillion* work-platform attributes, or both, and are compared to the functional and nautical characteristics and mooring statuses of the various craft that in earlier cases were held as a matter of law to be nonvessels for Jones Act purposes, there can be little doubt that indefinitely moored, shore-side, floating casinos, such as the *Biloxi Belle*, must be added to that list. Here, the semi-permanently or indefinitely moored barge supporting the *Biloxi Belle* casino was constructed *ab initio* to be the floating site of a restaurant and bar (not a key factor given *Ducrepont's* recognition that original construction as a work platform is not a prerequisite).[38] From its inception the instant barge was used first as a floating restaurant and bar until its conversion to a casino and its renaming as the *Biloxi Belle*, after which it has been used only for casino purposes. Upon its arrival in Mississippi from Texas, the *Biloxi Belle* was moored to the shore in a semi-permanent or indefinite manner, and continued to be thus moored before, during, and after the accidents in question. The *Biloxi Belle* is susceptible of being moved, and in fact was moved across navigable waters one time in the course of "normal operations" (assuming that movement to avoid the threat of a hurricane on a single occasion can be deemed "normal operations"), which one–time movement was purely incidental to the barge's primary purpose of physically supporting a dockside casino structure. We hold, therefore, that at the times of the Pavone and Ketzel accidents, the *Biloxi Belle* (1) was removed from navigation, and (2) was a work platform. Under either circumstance, it was not then a vessel for purposes of the Jones Act or the general maritime law. For the foregoing reasons, the summary judgments in the cases consolidated for review herein are, in all respects, affirmed.

NOTE

There is a substantial number of cases in which floating structures that are more or less permanently moored to the land or to a pier or other service structure have been held not to be a vessel. See Evansville & Bowling Green Packet Co. v. Chero Cola Bottling Co., 271 U.S. 19, 46 S.Ct. 379, 70 L.Ed. 805, 1926 A.M.C. 684 (1926), holding that a wharfboat was not a vessel for the purposes of the limitation

---

37. 904 F.2d at 293–94 (citing Daniel v. Ergon, Inc., 892 F.2d 403, 407 (5 Cir.1990)(citing Bernard v. Binnings Constr. Co., 741 F.2d 824, 831 (5 Cir.1984))).

38. Ducrepont v. Baton Rouge Enters., Inc., 877 F.2d 393, 395 (5 Cir.1989).

of liability Act. The Supreme Court described the wharfboat and its employment as follows:

"The wharfboat in question was built in 1884 and was used at Hopefield, Arkansas, on the Mississippi River. In 1901 it was towed to Madison, Indiana, where it was overhauled, and then to Louisville, Kentucky, where it was used. In 1910, after more repairs at Madison, it was taken to Evansville. Appellant acquired it in 1915. Each winter it was towed to Green River Harbor to protect it from ice. While in use in Evansville it was secured to the shore by four or five cables and remained at the same point except when moved to conform to the stage of the river. The lower part of the structure was rectangular, 243 feet long, 48 feet wide and six feet deep. It was built of wood and, to strengthen it and keep the water out, was lined around the sides and ends, extending 18 or 20 inches from the bottom, with concrete eight inches thick. It had no machinery or power for propulsion and was not subject to government inspection as are vessels operated on navigable waters. There was plumbing in the structure, and it was connected with the city water system; it obtained current for electric from the city plant, and had telephone connections. Appellant's office and quarters for the men in charge were located in one end of the structure. There were floats and an apron making a driveway between the land and a door at each end. The wharfboat was used to transfer freight between steamboats and land and from one steamboat to another. Charges made for services performed by its use were for storage and handling and not for transportation."

In Cookmeyer v. Louisiana Dep't of Highways, 309 F.Supp. 881, 1970 A.M.C. 584 (E.D.La.1970), aff'd on the opinion of the district court 433 F.2d 386 (5th Cir.1970), it was held that two steel barges attached to a permanent pivot piling structure as part of a bridge assembly that would swing open to permit passage of water traffic fell within the holding in the *Chero Cola* case. See also Russell v. City Ice and Fuel Co. of Point Pleasant, 539 F.2d 1318 (4th Cir.1976)(floating fuel flat "more or less permanently moored to the shore" was part of the dock and not a vessel for purposes of the Jones Act). Is there a difference between a holding that a thing is not a vessel and a holding that it is part of the dock. See Peytavin v. Government Employees Ins. Co., 341 F.Supp. 1286 (D.La.1971), aff'd 453 F.2d 1121 (5th Cir.1972). There plaintiff was a victim of a rear end collision on a pontoon ferry ramp while waiting to buy a ticket for the ferry. The parties were not diverse in citizenship and jurisdiction hinged on whether the subject accident was within the maritime tort jurisdiction. The district court held that the ramp was an extension of the land and therefore the accident lacked maritime location. The court of appeals affirmed the dismissal for want of jurisdiction but declined to accept the determination that the ramp was an extension of the land, putting its decision, instead, on the ground that there was insufficient maritime connection to give rise to a maritime cause of action.

In *Pavone* it could be found that the structure was never intended to be used as a vessel, and that the vessel-like accoutrements were faux. Does this matter? See Hayford v. Doussony, 32 F.2d 605 (5 Cir.1929), holding that a platform, formerly a ship in navigation, but secured to the dock with cables and clamps around clusters of pilings and used as a dance platform is not a vessel for the purpose of the Lien Act. Cf. The Showboat, 47 F.2d 286 (D.Mass.1930), in which it was held that a moored vessel used as a restaurant and dance hall, but which kept aboard a master or mate and two or three seamen, and which could easily be disconnected from the moorings and leave, was a vessel for purposes of the Lien Act. It was held, however, that merchandise purchased on conditional sale for use in the restaurant and dance hall was not subject to the maritime liens. The present use would not in any case destroy maritime liens that might have attached while the vessel was in service. See Arques Shipyards v. S.S. Charles Van Damme, 175 F.Supp. 871, 1959 A.M.C. 1570 (N.D.Cal.1959). If you were attending the melodrama on the Golden-rod Showboat at the pier in St. Louis and were hit by a ill-aimed turnip, could you proceed in rem against the boat?

In McCarthy v. The Bark Peking, 716 F.2d 130, 1984 A.M.C. 1 (2d Cir.1983), cert. denied 465 U.S. 1078, 104 S.Ct. 1439, 79 L.Ed.2d 760 (1984) it was held that for the purposes of § 905(b), a museum vessel on exhibit as an artifact was a vessel and therefore a museum worker injured while painting the upper mainmast and spars could maintain an action against the vessel for negligence. The Bark Peking was floating in the water, but the rudder was welded in one position and she had not been to sea under her own power for half a century. In similar circumstances it has been held that an injured visitor may sue the vessel in admiralty. Luna v. Star of India, 356 F.Supp. 59, 1973 A.M.C. 1597 (S.D.Cal.1973). Can *McCarthy* be reconciled with *Pavone*? Is display of boats of the past a more venerable maritime use than riverboat gambling?

A "quarterboat" which served as a floating hotel for 40 to 60 personnel and was designed to service oil companies working on inland waterways and shallow offshore areas was not a vessel for the purposes of the Jones Act. It lacked self-propulsion and was usually towed to a desired location where it was "spudded down" on one side to the sea floor, with the other side fixed, directly or indirectly, to a bank. Gremillion v. Gulf Coast Catering Co., 904 F.2d 290 (5th Cir.1990).

A platform moored in a river and used for transfer of cargo from barges on one side to vessels on the other, and having no more than an incidental transportation function, and movable only by winching in or paying out lines, is not a vessel for the purposes of the Jones Act. Burchett v. Cargill, 48 F.3d 173, 1995 A.M.C. 1576 (5th Cir.1995).

It is generally held that permanent structures resting on the land beneath the water are not vessels. Thus for the purposes of 46 U.S.C.A. § 905(b), exempting from the exclusive remedy provisions of the LHWCA an action by a covered worker against the owner of a vessel for negligence, a fixed drilling platform has been held not to be a vessel. Olsen v. Shell Oil Co., 708 F.2d 976, 1984 A.M.C. 580 (5th Cir.1983), cert. denied 464 U.S. 1045, 104 S.Ct. 715, 79 L.Ed.2d 178 (1984). And similarly, it has been held that a compressor building constructed on a submerged barge is not a Jones Act vessel. Blanchard v. Engine and Gas Compressor Services, Inc., 575 F.2d 1140 (5th Cir.1978).

Barges or floating platforms that not only support special equipment but are regularly used to transport it from one job to another have regularly been held to be vessels. Jerome B. Grubart, Inc. v. Great Lakes Dredge & Dock Co., 513 U.S. ___, 115 S.Ct. 1043, 130 L.Ed.2d 1024 (1995). See also: Bundens v. J.E. Brenneman Co., 46 F.3d 292, 1995 A.M.C. 1330 (3d Cir.1995); Brunet v. Boh Bros. Construction Co., 715 F.2d 196, 1984 A.M.C. 1264 (5th Cir.1983)(a pile driving barge); McDermott, Inc. v. Boudreaux, 679 F.2d 452 (5th Cir.1982)(a pipe laying barge). Both of these cases involved the Jones Act. And see Burks v. American River Transp. Co., 679 F.2d 69, 1983 A.M.C. 2208 (5th Cir.1982)(a barge which was towed to a vessel and made fast to its side and used in the process of loading it). *Burks* was decided under § 905(b). Cf. Hatch v. Durocher D. & D., Inc., 33 F.3d 545, 1994 A.M.C. 2188 (6th Cir.1994) and DiGiovanni v. Traylor Bros., Inc., 959 F.2d 1119, 1992 A.M.C. 1521 (1st Cir.1992)(en banc), cert. denied 506 U.S. 827, 113 S.Ct. 87, 121 L.Ed.2d 50, 1993 A.M.C. 2998 (1992). In *Hatch*, it was held that a flat deck barge built as a derrick and work platform and used in construction work was not a vessel for purposes of the Jones Act, except when actually in navigation.   How much do such cases differ from *Grubart*?

To the effect that a jack-up barge can be a vessel, see Vickers v. Chiles Drilling Co., 822 F.2d 535 (5th Cir.1987), citing Hicks v. Ocean Drilling and Exploration Co., 512 F.2d 817 (5th Cir.1975), cert. denied 423 U.S. 1050, 96 S.Ct. 777, 46 L.Ed.2d 639 (1976).   But a drilling rig attached to the bottom by pilings and not intended to be moved often , and had been moved only twice in the preceding 20 years, was held not to be a vessel for purposes of the Jones Act in Hemba v. Freeport McMoran Energy Partners, Ltd., 811 F.2d 276 (5th Cir.1987).   The court of appeals mentioned, also, that the rig had no navigation lights or lifesaving gear, was not registered with the Coast Guard as a vessel, and had no galley or crew quarters.   In Johnson v. Odeco Oil and Gas Co., 864 F.2d 40 (5th Cir.1989), the court indicated that more recent cases, including *Hemba* had narrowed the holding in *Hicks*.   See, in particular, Bernard v. Binnings Construction Co., 741 F.2d 824 (5th Cir.1984), in which the court attempted to state factors to be considered in determining whether an off-shore platform qualifies as a vessel.   These include: (1) navigational aids; (2) raked bow; (3) lifeboats and other lifesaving equipment; (4)bilge pumps; (5) crew quarters; (6) registration as a vessel with the Coast Guard.

Houseboats that are capable of being towed from place to place are usually regarded as vessels for purposes of the Lien Act.   See Hudson Harbor 79th Street Boat Basin, Inc. v. Sea Casa, 469 F.Supp. 987 (S.D.N.Y.1979).   See also Miami Riverboat Yard v. 60′ Houseboat, 390 F.2d 596, 1968 A.M.C. 336 (5th Cir.1968).

There is a general definition of the word "vessel" in 1 U.S.C.A. § 3, "every description of watercraft or other artificial contrivance used, or capable of being used, as a means of transportation on water."   In *Burks*, supra, Judge Brown observed that "[n]o doubt the three men in a tub would also fit within our definition and one probably could make a convincing case for Jonah inside the whale."   Under this definition some fairly strange structures have been held to be vessels.

For a "strange creature" case that rivals any of Judge Brown's examples, see Estate of Wenzel v. Seaward Marine Services, Inc., 709 F.2d 1326 (9th Cir.1983).   There the court of appeals held that it was error for the district court to determine as a matter of law that a "submerged cleaning and maintenance platform" [SCAMP] was not a vessel for purposes of the Jones Act.   The SCAMP is a device for the cleaning of the hulls of vessels.   The court described it as follows: "It is a saucer shaped unit which is six feet in diameter and twenty inches deep, which is equipped with an impeller.   The SCAMP travels on a horizontal patch at a pre-set speed of fifty-four feet a minute.   The saucer shape of the SCAMP and the impeller cause it to adhere to the underwater surfaces of a ship's hull.   The SCAMP can be operated by remote control or steered manually by divers.   It can advance, reverse, or stop.   It is equipped with lights."

In Barger v. Petroleum Helicopters, Inc., 692 F.2d 337, 1983 A.M.C. 2854 (5th Cir.1982), cert denied 461 U.S. 958, 103 S.Ct. 2430, 77 L.Ed.2d 1316 (1983), a helicopter used to carry passengers to work on the outer Continantal Shelf crashed into the Gulf of Mexico, forty miles offshore, killing all aboard.   The survivors of the pilot brought an action against his employer under the Jones Act and under the general maritime law, urging that the helicopter was a vessel and he was a member of its crue.   A divided court of appeals held that the helicopter was not a vessel and therefore, under the Outer Continental Shelf Lands Act (OCSLA) the survivors' remedy was limited to death benefits under the LHWCA.   Judge Brown dissented, being of the opinion that the intention to take a broad view of "vessel" was manifested in the adoption in 1977 of the International Regulations for Preventing Collisions at Sea, which defines "vessel" as including "nondisplacement craft and seaplanes."   33 U.S.C.A. § 1601(1).

Is it easier to hold that a strange structure is a vessel than it is to hold a helicopter is a vessel?   After all, we have another name for a helicopter.   The decision in *Barger* has been criticized.   See Moore's Federal Practice, ¶ .215[4] (1984–1985 Supp. by Pelaez) Professor Pelaez refers to the district court decision reversed in *Barger* as "enlightened," and Judge Brown's dissent as "strong."   But the *Barger* holding has since been reiterated by the Fifth Circuit.   See Hebert v. Air Logistics, Inc., 720 F.2d 853, 1984 A.M.C. 1512 (5 Cir.1983);   Reeves v. Offshore Logistics, Inc., 720 F.2d 835 1984 A.M.C. 2552 (5 Cir.1983) Co.   On the general subject of aircraft as vessels, see Symposium: Aircraft as vessels under the Jones Act and General Maritime Law, 22 S.Tex.L.J. 595 et seq. (1982).   See also Moore's Federal Practice, ¶ .200 Moore & Pelaez (1983).

Despite the statutory definition of "vessel," the cases make it clear that the same structure may be treated as a vessel for some purposes and not for others. Thus a houseboat, while it has been treated as a vessel for the purposes of the Lien Act, has been held to be a structure requiring a permit under § 10 of the Rivers and Harbors Appropriation Act of 1899.   See United States v. Boyden, 696 F.2d 685 (9th Cir.1983).   In like fashion, a floating drydock, though held not to be a vessel for purposes of marine salvage (Cope v. Vallette Dry–Dock Co., 119 U.S. 625, 7 S.Ct. 336, 30 L.Ed. 501 (1887)), has been held to be a vessel, raft, or other craft within the provisions of the Wreck Act.   United States v. Moran Towing & Transp. Co., 374 F.2d 656, 1967 A.M.C. 1733 (4th Cir.1967), vac'd 389 U.S. 575, 88 S.Ct. 689, 19 L.Ed.2d 775 (1968), on remand 409 F.2d 961 (4th Cir.1969).   A large number of "vessels" cases classified and discussed under headings related to the purpose of the designation as a "vessel," is to be found in Moore's Federal Practice, ¶ .215 (2d Ed.1983, by Moore and Pelaez).

CHAPTER 5

ADMIRALTY JURISDICTION AND FEDERALISM

A. THE SAVING TO SUITORS CLAUSE

The Hine v. Trevor

Supreme Court of the United States, 1867.
71 U.S. (4 Wall.) 555, 18 L.Ed. 451.*

Error to the Supreme Court of the State of Iowa; the case, as disclosed by the record, having been in substance this:

A collision occurred between the steamboats Hine and Sunshine, on the Mississippi River, at or near St. Louis, in which the latter vessel was injured. Some months afterwards, the owners of the Sunshine caused the Hine to be seized while she was lying at Davenport, Iowa, in a proceeding under the laws of that State, to subject her to sale in satisfaction of the damages sustained by their vessel. The code of Iowa, under which this seizure was made, gives a lien against any boat found in the waters of that State, for injury to person or property by said boat, officers or crew, & c.; gives precedence in liens; authorizes the seizure and sale of the boat, without any process against the wrongdoer, whether owner or master, and saves the plaintiff all his common-law rights, but makes no provision to protect the owner of the vessel.

The owners of the Hine interposed a plea to the jurisdiction of the State court. The point being ruled against them, it was carried to the Supreme Court of the State, where the judgment of the lower court was affirmed; and by the present writ of error this court was called upon to reverse that decision. * * *

■ MR. JUSTICE MILLER delivered the opinion of the court.

The record distinctly raises the question, how far the jurisdiction of the District Courts of the United States in admiralty causes, arising on the navigable inlands waters of this country, is exclusive, and to what extent the State courts can exercise a concurrent jurisdiction? * * *

[In an omitted portion of the opinion the court held that the admiralty jurisdiction extended to the Mississippi River.]

* The Court's footnotes have been omitted.

144

At the same time, the State courts have been in the habit of adjudicating causes, which, in the nature of their subject-matter, are identical in every sense with causes which are acknowledged to be of admiralty and maritime cognizance; and they have in these causes administered remedies which differ in no essential respect from the remedies which have heretofore been considered as peculiar to admiralty courts. This authority has been exercised under State statutes, and not under any claim of a general common-law power in these courts to such a jurisdiction.

It is a little singular that, at this term of the court, we should, for the first time, have the question of the right of the State courts to exercise this jurisdiction, raised by two writs of error to State courts, remote from each other, the one relating to a contract to be performed on the Pacific Ocean, and the other to a collision on the Mississippi River. The first of these cases, The Moses Taylor, had been decided before the present case was submitted to our consideration.

The main point ruled in that case is, that the jurisdiction conferred by the act of 1789, on the District Courts, in civil causes of admiralty and maritime jurisdiction, is exclusive by its express terms, and that this exclusion extends to the State courts. The language of the ninth section of the act admits of no other interpretation. It says, after describing the criminal jurisdiction conferred on the District Courts, that they "shall also have *exclusive* original cognizance of all civil causes of admiralty and maritime jurisdiction, including all seizures under laws of impost, navigation, or trade of the United States, when the seizures are made on waters which are navigable from the sea by vessels of ten or more tons burden." If the Congress of the United States has the right, in providing for the exercise of the admiralty powers, to which the Constitution declares the authority of the Federal judiciary shall extend, to make that jurisdiction exclusive, then, undoubtedly, it has done so by this act. This branch of the subject has been so fully discussed in the opinion of the court, in the case just referred to, that it is unnecessary to consider it further in this place.

It must be taken, therefore, as the settled law of this court, that wherever the District Courts of the United States have original cognizance of admiralty causes, by virtue of the act of 1789, that cognizance is exclusive, and no other court, state or national, can exercise it, with the exception always of such concurrent remedy as is given by the common law. * * *

If the facts of the case before us in this record constitute a cause of admiralty cognizance, then the remedy, by a direct proceeding against the vessel, belonged to the Federal courts alone, and was excluded from the State tribunals. * * *

It is said that the statute of Iowa may be fairly construed as coming within the clause of the ninth section of the act of 1789, which "saves to suitors, in all cases, the right of a common-law remedy where the common law is competent to give it."

But the remedy pursued in the Iowa courts, in the case before us, is in no sense a common-law remedy. It is a remedy partaking of all the essential features of an admiralty proceeding in rem. The statute provides that the vessel may be sued and made defendant without any proceeding against the owners, or even mentioning their names. That a writ may be issued and the vessel seized, on filing a petition similar in substance to a libel. That after a notice in the nature of a monition, the vessel may be condemned and an order made for her sale, if the liability is established for which she was sued. Such is the general character of the steamboat laws of the Western States.

While the proceeding differs thus from a common-law remedy, it is also essentially different from what are in the West called suits by attachment, and in some of the older States foreign attachments. In these cases there is a suit against a personal defendant by name, and because of inability to serve process on him on account of nonresidence, or for some other reason mentioned in the various statutes allowing attachments to issue, the suit is commenced by a writ directing the proper officer to attach sufficient property of the defendant to answer any judgment which may be rendered against him. This proceeding may be had against an owner or part owner of a vessel, and his interest thus subjected to sale in a common-law court of the State.

Such actions may, also, be maintained in personam against a defendant in the common-law courts, as the common law gives; all in consistence with the grant of admiralty powers in the ninth section of the Judiciary Act.

But it could not have been the intention of Congress, by the exception in that section, to give the suitor all such remedies as might afterwards be enacted by State statutes, for this would have enabled the States to make the jurisdiction of their courts concurrent in all cases, by simply providing a statutory remedy for all cases. Thus the exclusive jurisdiction of the Federal courts would be defeated.   * * *

The Judgment is reversed, and the case is remanded to the Supreme Court of Iowa, with directions that it be dismissed for want of jurisdiction.

NOTE

Is the Court in *The Hine* simply reacting to the ambiguity in the Judiciary Act? The district court is given "exclusive" jurisdiction of admiralty and maritime causes, but the right of "a common law remedy" is saved to suitors in all cases. If *something* is to be exclusive, and if it is a "common law remedy" that is saved to suitors, then the intention must have been to preserve the traditional admiralty remedy, the libel in rem to foreclose a maritime lien, as an exclusively federal province. There is some historical justification for this view of the matter for the existence of a maritime lien was often taken as the measure of admiralty jurisdiction. See the discussion of the home port lien doctrine in the chapter on maritime liens, infra. It could be, however, that in *The Hine* the Court was at least partially motivated by its views on the propriety of home port supply liens in general. In The General Smith, 17 U.S. (4 Wheat.) 438, 4 L.Ed. 609 (1819), the Court had held that no lien for home port necessaries existed under the general maritime law, but suggested that such a lien could be created by state statute, a proposition later established in Peyroux v. Howard, 32 U.S. (7 Pet.) 324, 8 L.Ed. 700 (1833), and The Orleans, 36 U.S. (11 Pet.) 175, 9 L.Ed. 677 (1837).   This view was later incorporated into the Admiralty Rules of 1844.   In 1858, however, the rules were changed to provide that the state created liens for "supplies, repairs, or other necessaries" might be enforced in personam in the admiralty but not in rem, thus recognizing the maritime nature of the contract but the absence of a lien.   *The Hine* and The Moses Taylor, 71 U.S. (4 Wall.) 411, 18 L.Ed. 397 (1866), had the practical effect of abolishing the home port lien for necessaries.   Under the traditional maritime law, there was none.   Under Rule 12 of the Admiralty Rules the federal court would not enforce a state created lien; under *The Hine* and *The Moses Taylor*, the state court could not.   The possibility was always open, however, that the rule might be changed and such liens again enforced in the federal courts.   This happened in 1872.   In the following year, in *The Lottawanna*, 87 U.S. (20 Wall.) 201, 22 L.Ed. 259 (1873), the Court reaffirmed the doctrine of The *General Smith*.   It was not until 1903, in *The Roanoke*, 189 U.S. 185, 23 S.Ct. 491, 47 L.Ed. 770 (1903), that a state lien statute was struck down as unconstitutional, and not until 1910 that the Congress turned its attention to the home port lien problem.   The present status of state created liens is discussed in the chapter on maritime liens, infra.

What is the importance of preserving the exclusive jurisdiction of the federal court over lien foreclosures?

C.J. Hendry Co. v. Moore

Supreme Court of the United States, 1943.
318 U.S. 133, 63 S.Ct. 499, 87 L.Ed. 663, 1943 A.M.C. 156.

■ MR. CHIEF JUSTICE STONE delivered the opinion of the Court.

The Fish and Game Commission of California, having seized a purse net while it was being used for fishing in the navigable waters of the state in violation of the State Fish and Game Code, brought the present proceeding under Sec. 845 of the Code for forfeiture of the net.   The question for decision is whether the state court's judgment, directing that the net be forfeited and ordering the commission to sell or destroy it, is a "common law remedy" which the "common law is competent to give" within the statutory exception to the exclusive jurisdiction in admiralty conferred on district courts of the United States by Sec. 9 of the Judiciary Act of 1789, 1 Stat. 76–77, 28 U.S.C.A. §§ 41(3) and 371 (Third).

Section 845 of the California Fish and Game Code declares that a net used in violation of the provisions of the Code is a public nuisance and makes it the duty of any arresting officer to seize the net and report its seizure to the commission.   The statute requires the commission to institute proceedings in the state superior court for the forfeiture of the seized net and authorizes the court, after a hearing and determination that the net was used unlawfully, to make an order forfeiting it and directing that it be sold or destroyed by the commission.

In this case the commission seized the net while it was being used by the fishing vessel Reliance in navigable coastal waters of the state in violation of Sections 89 and 842, which prohibit fishing by net in the area in question, and respondents, the members of the commission, brought this proceeding in the state superior court for the forfeiture of the net. Petitioners appeared as claimants and after a trial the court gave judgment that the net be forfeited, ordering respondents to sell or destroy it. The Supreme Court of California at first set the judgment aside, but after rehearing affirmed, 18 Cal.2d 835, 118 P.2d 1, 3 (1941), holding that the remedy given by the judgment is a "common law remedy" which "the common law is competent to give," and that the case is not within the exclusive jurisdiction in admiralty conferred on the federal courts by the Judiciary Act and hence was properly tried in the state court. Cf. Knapp, Stout & Co. v. McCaffrey, 177 U.S. 638, 20 S.Ct. 824, 44 L.Ed. 921 (1900); The Hamilton, 207 U.S. 398, 404, 28 S.Ct. 133, 134, 52 L.Ed. 264 (1908); Red Cross Line v. Atlantic Fruit Co., 264 U.S. 109, 123, 44 S.Ct. 274, 276, 68 L.Ed. 582 (1924). We granted certiorari, 316 U.S. 643, 62 S.Ct. 1036, 86 L.Ed. 1728 (1942), the question being of importance in defining the jurisdiction of state courts in relation to the admiralty jurisdiction.

Only a single issue is presented by the record and briefs—whether the state is precluded by the Constitution and laws of the United States from entertaining the present suit. It is not questioned that the state has authority to regulate fishing in its navigable waters, Manchester v. Massachusetts, 139 U.S. 240, 11 S.Ct. 559, 35 L.Ed. 159 (1891); Lawton v. Steele, 152 U.S. 133, 139, 14 S.Ct. 499, 501, 38 L.Ed. 385 (1894); Lee v. New Jersey, 207 U.S. 67, 28 S.Ct. 22, 52 L.Ed. 106 (1907); Skiriotes v. Florida, 313 U.S. 69, 75, 61 S.Ct. 924, 928, 85 L.Ed. 1193 (1941); and it is not denied that seizure there of a net appurtenant to a fishing vessel is cognizable in admiralty. But petitioners insist that the present proceeding is not one which can be entertained by a state court since the judgment in rem for forfeiture of the net is not a common law remedy which the common law is competent to give, and that the case is therefore not within the statutory exception to the exclusive admiralty jurisdiction of the federal courts. In this posture of the case, and in the view we take, we find it necessary to consider only this contention.

Section 371 (Third) of 28 U.S.C.A., derived from Sec. 9 of the Judiciary Act of 1789, confers exclusive jurisdiction on the federal courts "of all civil causes of admiralty and maritime jurisdiction, saving to suitors in all cases the right of a common-law remedy where the common law is competent to give it. * * *" A characteristic feature of the maritime law is its use of the procedure in rem derived from the civil law, by which a libellant may proceed against the vessel, naming her as a defendant and seeking a judgment subjecting the vessel, and hence the interests of all persons in her, to the satisfaction of the asserted claim. Suits in rem against a vessel in cases of maritime tort and for the enforcement of maritime liens are familiar examples of a procedure by which a judgment in rem is sought, "good against all the world."

The question whether a maritime cause of action can be prosecuted in the state courts by such a procedure was first discussed by this Court

seventy-seven years after the adoption of the Constitution and the Judiciary Act, in The Moses Taylor, 4 Wall. 411 (1866), which held that a lien
upon a vessel, created by State Statute, could not be enforced by a
proceeding in rem in the state courts. Decision was rested on the ground
that exclusive jurisdiction of the suit was vested in the federal courts by the
Judiciary Act, since a judgment in rem to enforce a lien is not a remedy
which the common law is competent to give, a ruling which has since been
consistently followed. The Hine v. Trevor, 4 Wall. 555, 18 L.Ed. 451
(1866); The Belfast, 7 Wall. 624, 19 L.Ed. 266 (1868); The Glide, 167 U.S.
606, 17 S.Ct. 930, 42 L.Ed. 296 (1896); The Robert W. Parsons, 191 U.S.
17, 36–38, 24 S.Ct. 8, 14, 15, 48 L.Ed. 73 (1903); Rounds v. Cloverport
Foundry Co., 237 U.S. 303, 307, 308, 35 S.Ct. 596, 597, 598, 59 L.Ed. 966
(1915). Eleven years earlier this Court in Smith v. Maryland, 18 How. 71,
15 L.Ed. 269 (1855), without discussion of the point now at issue, had
sustained the seizure and forfeiture of a vessel in a state court proceeding
in rem, all pursuant to state statutes, for violation of a Maryland fishing
law within the navigable waters of the state. The Court declared that the
statute, which prescribed the procedure in rem in the state court, conflicted
"neither with the admiralty jurisdiction of any court of the United States
conferred by Congress, nor with any law of Congress whatever" (p. 76).
The authority of that decision has never been questioned by this Court.

The common law as it was received in the United States at the time of
the adoption of the Constitution did not afford a remedy in rem in suits
between private persons. Hence the adoption of the saving clause in the
Judiciary Act, as this Court has held in the cases already cited, did not
withdraw from the exclusive jurisdiction of admiralty that class of cases in
which private suitors sought to enforce their claims by the seizure of a
vessel in proceedings in rem. But to the generalization that a judgment in
rem was not a common remedy there is an important exception. Forfeiture
to the Crown of the offending object, because it had been used in violation
of law, by a procedure in rem was a practice familiar not only to the
English admiralty courts but to the court of Exchequer. The Exchequer
gave such a remedy for the forfeiture of articles seized on land for the
violation of law. And, concurrently with the admiralty, it entertained true
proceedings in rem for the forfeiture of vessels for violations on navigable
waters. Such suits in the Exchequer were begun on information and were
against the vessel or article to be condemned. Under the provisions of
many statutes the suit might be brought by an informer qui tam, who was
permitted to share in the proceeds of the forfeited article; the judgment
was of forfeiture and the forfeited article was ordered to be sold. This was
the established procedure certainly as early as the latter part of the
seventeenth century. Proceedings in rem, closely paralleling those in the
Exchequer, were also entertained by justices of the peace in many forfeiture cases arising under the customs laws (see Hoon, The Organization of
the English Customs System, 1696–1786, pp. 277, 280–83), and the Act of 8
Geo. I, c. 18, Sec. 16, placed within that jurisdiction the condemnation of
vessels up to fifteen tons charged with smuggling.

While the English Acts of Navigation and Trade and numerous other forfeiture statutes conferred jurisdiction on all the English common law courts of record to entertain suits for forfeiture, nevertheless suitors having ready access to the convenient procedure of exchequer or admiralty in qui tam actions seem to have had little occasion to resort to the King's Bench or Common Pleas. In the occasional reported forfeiture cases brought in King's Bench, the English reports give us little light on the procedure followed or the precise form of judgment entered. In one case, Roberts v. Withered, 5 Mod. 193, 12 Mod. 92, the court seems to have adapted the common law action of detinue to forfeiture cases by resort to the fiction that bringing the action was the equivalent of a seizure which vested the property in the Crown so that a suit in detinue or replevin in personam to gain possession would lie. See Stephen, Pleading (3rd Am. ed.) pp. 47, 52, 69, 74; Ames, Lectures on Legal History, pp. 64, 71. Cf. Wilkins v. Despard, 5 Term Rep. 112.

Separate courts exercising the jurisdiction of the Court of Exchequer were never established in the American Colonies. Instead, that jurisdiction was absorbed by the common law courts which entertained suits for the forfeiture of property under English or local statutes authorizing its condemnation. Long before the adoption of the Constitution the common law courts in the Colonies—and later in the states during the period of Confederation—were exercising jurisdiction in rem in the enforcement of forfeiture statutes. Like the Exchequer, in cases of seizure on navigable waters they exercised a jurisdiction concurrently with the courts of admiralty. But the vice-admiralty courts in the Colonies did not begin to function with any real continuity until about 1700 or shortly afterward. See Andrews, Vice–Admiralty Courts in the Colonies, in Records of the Vice–Admiralty Court of Rhode Island, 1617–1752 (ed. Towle, 1936), p. 1; Andrews, The Colonial Period of American History, vol. 4, ch. 8; Harper, The English Navigation Laws, ch. 15; Osgood, The American Colonies in the 18th Century, vol. 1, pp. 185–222, 299–303. By that time, the jurisdiction of common law courts to condemn ships and cargoes for violation of the Navigation Acts had been firmly established, apparently without question, and was regularly exercised throughout the colonies. In general the suits were brought against the vessel or article to be condemned, were tried by jury, closely followed the procedure in Exchequer, and if successful resulted in judgments of forfeiture or condemnation with a provision for sale.

The rise of the vice-admiralty courts—prompted in part by the Crown's desire to have access to a forum not controlled by the obstinate resistance of American juries—did not divest the colonial common law courts of their jurisdiction to proceed in rem in cases of forfeiture and condemnation. The trial records have not yet been made available for all the Colonies, and in some instances perhaps can never be. But there is no reason to suppose that in this respect the judicial history of forfeiture proceedings in New York, manuscript records of which we have examined, is not typical of the others, and there is ample support for the conclusion that in the seaboard states forfeiture proceedings in rem, extending to seizures on navigable waters of the state, were an established procedure of the common law courts before the Revolution. It was the admiralty courts, not the common law courts, which had difficulty in establishing their jurisdiction, although in 1759 the Board of Trade was able to write that "With regard to breaches of the Law of Trade they are cognizable either in the courts of common law in the plantations, or in the courts of Admiralty, which have in such cases, if not in all, a concurrent jurisdiction with the courts of common law" (quoted in Andrews, Vice–Admiralty Courts in the Colonies, supra, at p. 7); and Stokes reported that the same situation prevailed at the outbreak of the Revolution. See Stokes, A View of the Constitution of the British Colonies (1783), pp. 270, 357 et seq.

In New York, admiralty jurisdiction was vested in the Mayor's Court in 1678, and that court continued to exercise jurisdiction in all maritime cases, including those arising under the Navigation Acts, throughout the colonial period even after the establishment of a court of vice-admiralty. See Select Cases of the Mayor's Court of New York City, 1674–1784 (ed. Morris, 1935) pp. 39–40, 566 et seq. But cases of forfeiture were also regularly prosecuted before the common law courts of the colony—in the General Quarter Sessions of the Peace in New York City during the 1680's, and, after the reorganization of the judiciary in 1691, in the Supreme Court of Judicature, which was given jurisdiction "of all pleas, Civill Criminall, and Mixt, as fully & amply to all Intents & purposes whatsoever, as the Courts of Kings Bench, Common Pleas, & Exchequer within their Majestyes Kingdom of England, have or ought to have," 1 Colonial Laws of New York (1894) p. 229. * * *

The records of the New York Supreme Court of Judicature contain numerous instances of forfeiture proceedings during the eighteenth century. One is Hammond qui tam v. Sloop Carolina, a prosecution in 1735 for a false customs certificate, which resulted in the discharge of the ship and her cargo for failure of proof. Later cases show more in detail how closely that court's procedure in forfeiture cases followed the essentials of the procedure in rem which had been developed in the English Exchequer. Nor did the creation of a state Court of Admiralty after the Revolution effect a withdrawal of such jurisdiction from the common law courts. Statutes enacted in New York during the period of the Confederation, like the English and local legislation which preceded them, continued to employ forfeiture as a sanction, and forfeiture proceedings continued to be brought in the Supreme Court and other common law tribunals. * * *

In Pennsylvania we have a record of a similar exercise of jurisdiction in 1787 by the Philadelphia Court of Common Pleas in Phile qui tam v. The Ship Anna, 1 Dall. 197, 1 L.Ed. 98 (1787), where the jury condemned the ship.

Examination of the legislative history of the Judiciary Act of 1789 does not disclose precisely what its framers had in mind when in Sec. 9 they used the phrase "common law remedy." But it is unlikely that, in selecting this phrase as the means of marking the boundary of the jurisdiction of state courts over matters which might otherwise be within the exclusive jurisdiction of admiralty, the draftsmen of Sec. 9 intended to withdraw from the state courts a jurisdiction and remedy in forfeiture cases which had been so generally applied by nonadmiralty courts both in England and America, and which had become a recognized part of the common law system as developed in England and received in this country long before the American Revolution. Nor can we accept the suggestion that Congress, in this use of the phrase "common law remedy," was harking back some hundreds of years to a period before the Exchequer had taken its place as one of the three great courts administering the common law, and was likewise disregarding the experience of the common law courts in America with which it was familiar—all without any indication of such a purpose. Considerations of practical convenience in the conduct of forfeiture proceedings for violations of local statutes occurring on state waters, as well as the contemporary and later history of the exercise of the admiralty jurisdiction, indicate that there was no purpose to limit such proceedings to the exclusive jurisdiction of the admiralty.

Shortly after the adoption of the Constitution, state legislation was enacted regulating state tidal waters and authorizing forfeiture in the state courts of fish nets and vessels illegally used in fishing there. Such a statute was considered in 1823 in Corfield v. Coryell, 4 Wash.C.C. 371, Fed.Cas. No. 3230, (cited in Smith v. Maryland, supra, 18 How. at 75), where a New Jersey state court forfeiture of a vessel under a statute regulating the Delaware Bay was upheld as constitutional by Justice Washington, without question of the state court's jurisdiction because of the in rem nature of the proceeding. No suggestion is to be found in that case or elsewhere that the Judiciary Act struck down the large body of state legislation, enacted shortly after 1789, which provided for the forfeiture in state courts of vessels or nets seized in navigable waters of a state for violating state fishing laws. And such legislation has become rooted in the law enforcement programs of about half the states, without intimation from this or any other court that the Judiciary Act prohibited it. See Boggs v. Commonwealth, 76 Va. 989, 993–96 (1882); Dize v. Lloyd, 36 F. 651, 652–53 (1888); Johnson v. Loper, 46 N.J.L. 321 (1884); Bradford v. DeLuca, 90 N.J.L. 434, 103 A. 692 (1917); Doolan v. The Greyhound, 79 Conn. 697, 66 A. 511 (1907); Ely v. Bugbee, 90 Conn. 584, 98 A. 121 (1916); State v. Umaki, 103 Wash. 232, 174 P. 447 (1918); State v. Mavrikas, 148 Wash. 651, 269 P. 805 (1928); Osborn v. Charlevoix, 114 Mich. 655, 663–66, 72 N.W. 982 (1897).

It is noteworthy that Blackstone's Commentaries, more read in America before the Revolution than any other law book, referred to the information in rem in the Court of Exchequer as the procedure by which forfeitures were inflicted for violation of Acts of Parliament. Bk. III, p. 262. And Kent, in his Commentaries, pointed out that "seizures, in England, for violation of the laws of revenue, trade or navigation, were tried by a jury in the Court of Exchequer, according to the course of the common law; and though a proceeding be in rem, it is not necessarily a proceeding or cause in the admiralty" (12th ed., Vol. 1, p. 374). He declared that, within the meaning of Sec. 9 of the Judiciary Act, the common law was competent to give such a remedy "because, under the vigorous system of the English law, such prosecutions in rem are in the Exchequer, according to the course of the common law" (p. 376).

Upon the adoption of the Constitution the national government took over the regulation of trade, navigation and customs duties which had been prolific sources of forfeiture proceedings in the state courts. This Court in suits brought in admiralty sustained the admiralty jurisdiction over forfeitures prescribed by Congress for the violation of federal revenue and other laws where the seizure had occurred on navigable waters. United States v. La Vengeance, 3 Dall. 297, 1 L.Ed. 610 (1796); United States v. Schooner Sally, 2 Cranch 406, 2 L.Ed. 320 (1805); United States v. Schooner Betsey and Charlotte, 4 Cranch 443, 2 L.Ed. 673 (1808); Whelan v. United States, 7 Cranch 112, 3 L.Ed. 286 (1812); The Samuel, 1 Wheat. 9, 4 L.Ed. 23 (1816). Those decisions held that when the seizure occurred on navigable waters the cause was maritime and hence triable without a jury in the federal courts. But they obviously did not determine, and there was no occasion to determine, whether forfeiture proceedings belonged in the category of maritime causes that might also be tried in state courts because, within the meaning of the saving clause, the common law was competent to give the remedy.

The Court has never held or said that the admiralty jurisdiction in a forfeiture case is exclusive, and it has repeatedly declared that, in cases of forfeiture of articles seized on land for violation of federal statutes, the district courts proceed as courts of common law according to the course of the Exchequer on informations in rem with trial by jury. The Sarah, 8 Wheat. 391, 396, n. (a), 5 L.Ed. 644 (1823); 443 Cans of Frozen Egg Product v. United States, 226 U.S. 172, 33 S.Ct. 50, 57 L.Ed. 174 (1913), and cases cited. In United States v. 422 Casks of Wine, 1 Pet. 547, 7 L.Ed. 257 (1828), Justice Story defined such an action as a libel or information in rem on the Exchequer side of the court. And see Chief Justice Marshall's reference, in Schooner Hoppet v. United States, 7 Cranch 389, 393, 3 L.Ed. 380 (1813), to "proceedings in Courts of common law, either against the person or the thing, for penalties or forfeitures." In all this we perceive a common understanding of judges, lawyers and text writers, both before and after the adoption of the Constitution, of the common law nature of the procedure and judgment in rem in forfeiture cases and of its use in such proceedings in the Exchequer and in the American common law courts.

We conclude that the common law as received in this country at the time of the adoption of the Constitution gave a remedy in rem in cases of forfeiture, and that it is a "common law remedy" and one which "the common law is competent to give" within the meaning of Sec. 9 of the Judiciary Act of 1789. By that Act the states were left free to provide such a remedy in forfeiture cases where the articles are seized upon navigable waters of the state for violation of state law. It follows that Smith v. Maryland, supra, was rightly decided and is not in conflict with The Moses Taylor, supra, and cases following it, and that the judgment of the Supreme Court of California should be

Affirmed.

■ Mr. Justice Black, dissenting:

If this case involved only a fishnet, I should be inclined to acquiesce in the holding of the Court.   Indeed, we have held that a state may seize and condemn a fishnet of trifling value without following the formal procedure of court action at all.   Lawton v. Steele, 152 U.S. 133, 14 S.Ct. 499, 38 L.Ed. 385 (1894).   But the principle laid down here involves far more than a fishnet, for under it state courts are authorized through in rem proceedings to seize and condemn, for violation of local law, any equipment or vessel employed in maritime activity.   Today's in rem action is against a fishnet used in patently illegal fashion;   tomorrow's may be an action against a tramp-steamer or ocean liner which violates a harbor regulation or otherwise offends against the police regulations of a state or municipality.   Persons guilty of violating state laws affecting maritime activity may be prosecuted by in personam actions in state courts, and the admiralty courts themselves can helpfully enforce state laws through in rem proceedings.   I do not believe, however, that the Judiciary Act permits states, through state common law courts which cannot reasonably be expected to have knowledge of admiralty law and practice, to give permanent halt to any portion of the maritime trade and commerce of the nation by bring in rem proceedings against ships.

The Judiciary Act of 1789 places in the federal admiralty courts exclusive jurisdiction over admiralty cases except where the common law provides an equivalent remedy.   It is conceded that as a general proposition the common law courts have no in rem remedy in maritime cases.   However, the Court holds squarely, for the first time in its history, that there is an exception to this rule which permits states to bring in rem forfeiture proceedings in common law courts.   The Court brushes aside as mere generalizations the many cases hereafter considered which declare that no equivalent of an admiralty in rem proceeding may be brought at common law.   Today's holding is rested principally on the English and colonial practice prior to 1789 and on one case in this Court.   I disagree, believing that the English practice is irrelevant, that the colonial law was not in accord with the English practice, and that a long series of cases since 1789 have clearly considered the proposition put by the Court, and have given the Judiciary Act a meaning squarely opposite to that now announced.
* * *

NOTE

In connection with the argument of the majority based upon the history of enforcement of seizures under the revenue law in the admiralty courts and the Court of Exchequer, consider the language of Sec. 9 of the Judiciary Act of 1789, vesting in the district court jurisdiction over "all seizures under laws of impost, navigation or trade of the United States, where the seizures are made, on waters which are navigable from the sea by vessels of ten or more tons burthen * * * and also * * * all seizures on land, or other waters than aforesaid, made, and of all suits for penalties and forfeitures incurred, under the laws of the United States * * *."

Since the district court is given no jurisdiction to entertain qui tam proceedings to enforce forfeitures under state laws, an interpretation of the "saving to suitors" clause to exclude state court qui tam proceedings would have had the result of abolishing such proceedings altogether.   In view of the long history of such practice, is this likely?   Of course this argument ignores the perhaps more tenable argument of Mr. Justice Daniel in *Jackson v. The Steamboat Magnolia* and earlier cases extending the locational jurisdiction inward that the provision referred to bespoke an understanding of a much more restricted constitutional admiralty jurisdiction. Sec. 9 of the Act of 1789 has had a rather peculiar forensic history.   It was referred to by Mr. Justice Story as demonstrating that the jurisdiction was not limited to the area outside the county, and Mr. Justice Daniel's argument brushed off in the process of extending the jurisdiction to all navigable waters.   Note that if one posits an admiralty jurisdiction broader than the seizure jurisdiction, the only purpose of the section would be to specifically limit admiralty seizure.   This interpretation was rejected in The Eagle, 75 U.S. (8 Wall.) 15, 19 L.Ed. 365 (1868), where the validity of Mr. Justice Daniel's interpretation was given a backhanded recognition.   The Court took the position that the statute was intended as an enlargement but since the Congress had enacted the statute unaware of the breadth of the admiralty jurisdiction, a statute designed to enlarge would not be read to restrict.   This made the language meaningless and ultimately the language was dropped from the section.   Under the present statutory pattern there is a specific grant of jurisdiction over seizures under the laws of the United States that do not occur on waters within the maritime jurisdiction to depend upon the general grant of admiralty and maritime jurisdiction.   See 28 U.S.C.A. §§ 41(3), 371(4)(1940); 28 U.S.C.A. § 1356 (1948).   This leaves the state jurisdiction to depend upon the "saving to suitors" provision, for clearly the jurisdiction to try seizure cases involving navigable waters no longer depends upon the early admiralty jurisdiction over revenue cases.   Yet can it be supposed that in the revision of the code it was intended to saddle the federal courts with this sort of case?

Rounds v. Cloverport Foundry & Machine Co.

Supreme Court of the United States, 1915.
237 U.S. 303, 35 S.Ct. 596, 59 L.Ed. 966.

■ MR. JUSTICE HUGHES delivered the opinion of the court:

The Cloverport Foundry & Machine Company, the defendant in error, brought this suit against F.T. Rounds and S.A. Jesse, of Owensboro, Kentucky, in the Breckinridge circuit court of that state, to recover the sum of $5,668.65 for work and materials furnished under a contract to repair and rebuild a steamboat formerly known as the "R.D. Kendall," and renamed the "Golden Girl."   The defendants were the owners of the vessel.   A specific attachment was issued under §§ 2480 to 2486 of the Kentucky Statutes, which provided for a lien upon watercraft for work and supplies, etc., and the defendants procured a release of the boat by executing a forthcoming bond.   By special demurrer, the defendants challenged the jurisdiction of the court to entertain the action upon the ground that the subject-matter was exclusively cognizable in the admiralty.   The demurrer was overruled, and the defendants, reasserting the absence of authority in the court, answered, denying the allegations of the petition, and setting up a counterclaim for damages alleged to have been caused by

defective work and by delay in completion.   Upon the trial, the counterclaim was dismissed and the company had judgment against the defendants
for the amount demanded in its petition; it was further adjudged that, by
virtue of the attachment and the applicable law, the plaintiff had a lien
upon the vessel for the payment of the judgment, and the vessel was
ordered to be sold and the proceeds applied to the debt.   The court of
appeals of the state affirmed the judgment.   159 Ky. 414, 167 S.W. 384.

The question presented on this writ of error relates solely to the
jurisdiction of the state court.   It is contended by the plaintiffs in error
that the contract in suit was for repairs on the vessel, and therefore was
maritime in character; that the proceeding was *in rem* and beyond the
competency of the local tribunal.   See The Moses Taylor, 4 Wall. 411, 18
L.Ed. 397 (1866);   The Hine v. Trevor, 4 Wall. 555, 18 L.Ed. 451 (1866);
The Belfast, 7 Wall. 624, 19 L.Ed. 266 (1868);   The J.E. Rumbell, 148 U.S.
1, 13 S.Ct. 498, 37 L.Ed. 345 (1893);   The Glide, 167 U.S. 606, 17 S.Ct. 930,
42 L.Ed. 296 (1897);   The Robert W. Parsons (Perry v. Haines) 191 U.S. 17,
24 S.Ct. 8, 48 L.Ed. 73;   act of June 23, 1910, chap. 373, 36 Stat. at L. 604,
Comp.Stat.1913, § 7783.   On the other hand, the defendant in error denies
that the contract was maritime, contending that the old boat was dismantled, its identity destroyed, and a new boat built, and that the case in this
aspect falls within the decisions relating to contracts for the original
construction of a vessel.   People's Ferry Co. v. Beers, 20 How. 393, 15
L.Ed. 961 (1857);   Roach v. Chapman, 22 How. 129, 16 L.Ed. 291 (1859);
Edwards v. Elliott, 21 Wall. 532, 22 L.Ed. 487 (1874);   The Winnebago
(Iroquois Transp. Co. v. Delaney Forge & Iron Co.) 205 U.S. 354, 27 S.Ct.
509, 51 L.Ed. 836 (1907).   Further, it is urged in support of the judgment
that the proceeding was *in personam,* and not *in rem*;   that the attachment
and direction for sale were incidental to the suit against the owners and for
the purpose of securing satisfaction of the personal judgment.   Accordingly,
it is said, the proceeding was within the scope of the "common-law
remedy" saved to suitors by the judiciary act.   1 Stat. at L. 77, chap. 20;
Rev.Stat. § 563, Judicial Code, § 24 [36 Stat. at L. 1091, chap. 231,
Comp.Stat.1913, § 991].

As the last point is plainly well taken, it is unnecessary to go further.
It is well settled that in an action *in personam* the state court has
jurisdiction to issue an auxiliary attachment against the vessel;   and,
whether or not the contract in suit be deemed to be of a maritime nature, it
cannot be said that the state court transcended its authority.   The proceeding *in rem* which is within the exclusive jurisdiction of admiralty is one
essentially against the vessel itself as the debtor or offending thing,—in
which the vessel is itself "seized and impleaded as the defendant, and is
judged and sentenced accordingly."   By virtue of dominion over the thing
all persons interested in it are deemed to be parties to the suit;   the decree
binds all the world, and under it the property itself passes, and not merely
the title or interest of a personal defendant.   The Mary, 9 Cranch 126, 144,
3 L.Ed. 678, 684 (1815);   The Moses Taylor, 4 Wall. 411, 18 L.Ed. 397
(1866);   The Hine v. Trevor, 4 Wall. 555, 18 L.Ed. 451 (1866);   The Belfast,
7 Wall. 624, 19 L.Ed. 266 (1868);   The Glide, 167 U.S. 606, 17 S.Ct. 930, 42

L.Ed. 296 (1897); The Robert W. Parsons (Perry v. Haines) 191 U.S. 17, 24 S.Ct. 8, 48 L.Ed. 73 (1903); Bird v. The Josephine, 39 N.Y. 19, 27 (1868). Actions *in personam* with a concurrent attachment to afford security for the payment of a personal judgment are in a different category. The Belfast, 7 Wall. 624, 19 L.Ed. 266 (1868); Taylor v. Carryl, 20 How. 583, 598, 599, 15 L.Ed. 1028, 1033, 1034 (1857); The Robert W. Parsons (Perry v. Haines) 191 U.S. 17, 24 S.Ct. 8, 48 L.Ed. 73 (1903). And this is so not only in the case of an attachment against the property of the defendant generally, but also where it runs specifically against the vessel under a state statute providing for a lien, if it be found that the attachment was auxiliary to the remedy *in personam*. Leon v. Galceran, 11 Wall. 185, 20 L.Ed. 74 (1870); see also Johnson v. Chicago & P. Elevator Co., 119 U.S. 388, 398, 399, 7 S.Ct. 254, 30 L.Ed. 447, 450, 451 (1886); Knapp, S. & Co. v. McCaffrey, 177 U.S. 638, 646, 648, 20 S.Ct. 824, 44 L.Ed. 921, 925, 926 (1901).

In the case of Leon v. Galceran, supra, the suit was *in personam,* in a court of the state of Louisiana, to recover mariner's wages. Under a statute of the state the vessel was subject to a lien or privilege in favor of the mariner; and accordingly at the beginning of the suit, on the application of the plaintiff, who asserted his lien, a writ of sequestration was issued and levied upon the vessel, which was afterwards released upon the execution by the owner, the defendant in the suit, of a forthcoming bond, with surety. Judgment was recovered by the plaintiff for the amount claimed, and the vessel not being returned, suit was brought in the state court against the surety. Upon writ of error from this court to review the judgment in the latter action, it was contended, with respect to the issue and levy of the writ of sequestration, that the vessel had been seized under admiralty process in a proceeding *in rem* over which the state court had no jurisdiction *ratione materiae,* and hence that the bond was void. The contention was overruled and the jurisdiction of the state court maintained. As this court said in Johnson v. Chicago & P. Elevator Co., 119 U.S. 388, 398, 399, 7 S.Ct. 254, 30 L.Ed. 447, 450, 451 (1886), in reviewing Leon v. Galceran, supra, it was held that "the action *in personam* in the state court was a proper one, because it was a common-law remedy, which the common law was competent to give, although the state law gave a lien on the vessel in the case, similar to a lien under the maritime law, and it was made enforceable by a writ of sequestration in advance, to hold the vessel as a security to respond to a judgment, if recovered against her owner, as a defendant; that the suit was not a proceeding *in rem,* nor was the writ of sequestration; that the bond given on the release of the vessel became the substitute for her; that the common law is as competent as the admiralty to give a remedy in all cases where the suit is *in personam* against the owner of the property; and that these views were not inconsistent with any expressed in The Moses Taylor, in the Hine v. Trevor, or in the Belfast."

The result of the decisions is thus stated in Knapp, S. & Co. v. McCaffrey, 177 U.S. 638, 646, 648, 20 S.Ct. 824, 44 L.Ed. 921, 925, 926 (1900). "The true distinction between such proceedings as are and such as are not invasions of the exclusive admiralty jurisdiction is this: If the cause of action be one cognizable in admiralty, *and* the suit be *in rem* against the thing itself, though a monition be also issued to the owner, the proceeding is essentially one in admiralty. If, upon the other hand, the cause of action be not one of which a court of admiralty has jurisdiction, *or* if the suit be *in personam* against an individual defendant, with an auxiliary attachment against a particular thing, or against the property of the defendant in general, it is essentially a proceeding according to the course of the common law, and within the saving clause of the statute (Rev.Stat. § 563) of a common-law remedy."

In the present case, as we have said, the suit was *in personam* and the attachment was in that suit. It had no other effect than to provide security for the payment of the personal judgment which was recovered, and it was for the purpose of satisfying this judgment that, in the same proceeding and by the terms of the judgment, the vessel was directed to be sold. It was within the scope of the common-law remedy to sell the property of the judgment debtors to pay their debt. We are not able to find any encroachment upon the exclusive jurisdiction vested in the Federal court in admiralty.

Judgment affirmed.

N O T E

In the *Hendry* case, Mr. Justice Black observes, "I do not believe, however, that the Judiciary Act permits states, through common law courts * * * to give permanent halt to any portion of the maritime trade and commerce of the nation by bringing in rem proceedings against ships." What does he mean by "permanent halt"? Is the halt in *Hendry* any more permanent than the halt in *Cloverport*? Note that in *Cloverport,* the Court attachment was characterized as purely "auxiliary" to secure payment of a personal judgment. In many state cases, however, attachment and garnishment are employed partially to obtain security for the payment of an in personam judgment, but partially to obtain jurisdiction over an absent defendant to the extent of the property attached or garnished in the event that personal service cannot be made. Foreign attachments are, of course, not unknown in admiralty practice. They were provided for in former Admiralty Rule 2 and presently are provided for in Supplemental Rule B of the F.R.C.P. Until 1963, since there was no provision of such attachments in the F.R.C.P., jurisdiction over an absent party could not be obtained in a common law suit in the federal court. Since then, however, Rule 4(e) has provided for utilization of the state procedure in such cases. Supplemental Rule B also permits use of the state procedure as an alternative to the federal procedure for process in personam with a clause of foreign attachment.

Eleven years after *Cloverport,* in Madruga v. Superior Court, 346 U.S. 556, 74 S.Ct. 298, 98 L.Ed. 290 (1954), the Court held that the state court had jurisdiction in a partition suit seeking a sale of a ship. Mr. Justice Black wrote the majority opinion. He observed:

"The scarcity of reported cases involving such partition since the Constitution was adopted indicates that establishment of a national partition rule is not of major importance to the shipping world. We can foresee at this time no possible injury to commerce or navigation if states continue to be free to follow their own customary partition procedures. Easily accessible local courts are well equipped to handle these essentially local disputes. Ordering the sale of property for partition is part of their everyday work. Long experience has enabled states to develop simple legislative and judicial partition procedures with which local judges and counsel are familiar. Federal courts have rarely been called upon to try such disputes and have established no settled rules for partition. In some parts of the country the inaccessibility of federal courts as compared with state courts would cause needless expense and inconvenience to parties."

Given the rather extreme view of the geographical jurisdiction of the admiralty, cannot much of what Mr. Justice Black says be applied to in rem proceedings in general? Mr. Justice Frankfurter dissented, joined by Mr. Justice Jackson. They could see in the partition suit nothing but an in rem proceeding. It was not for the Court, they observed, to provide the state courts with a concurrent jurisdiction in admiralty when the Judiciary Act vested such jurisdiction exclusively in the federal district courts, just because "establishment of a national partition rule is not of major importance to the shipping world."

Sellick v. Sun Harbor Marina, Inc.

United States Court of Appeals, Ninth Circuit, 1967.
384 F.2d 870, 1967 A.M.C. 2309.

■ WALTER L. POPE, CT. J. On October 21, 1962, the appellant sold the vessel here in controversy under a conditional sales contract to some persons named Potter. The Potters berthed the vessel at the appellee's wharf thereby incurring wharfage fees which were paid until April, 1963. Thereafter they were unable to pay the wharfage due. The appellee claimed a possessory lien upon the vessel for unpaid storage charges after appropriate demands upon the Potters and upon the appellant for payment of these charges and after notice of sale in the manner prescribed by the California Civil Code, appellee sold the vessel at public auction to satisfy its lien and purchased the vessel at the sale.

Thereafter the appellee brought in a California Superior Court an action against the appellant and the Potters to quiet title to the vessel. The appellant appeared by answer in that action and filed a cross-complaint against the appellee alleging substantially the matters complained of in the appellant's complaint filed in the court below in the cause now before us. Following trial of that action the Superior Court made findings of fact and conclusions of law in favor of the plaintiff in that suit (the appellee here), and entered its decree quieting title to the vessel in the appellee against the appellant and the Potters. The appellant then proceeded to take an appeal from the Superior Court judgment to the District Court of Appeal which affirmed the Superior Court decree. Hearing was denied by the Supreme Court. The decision of the District Court of Appeal is reported at 58 Cal.Rptr. 459.

Claiming that the California state courts were without jurisdiction to entertain that action and that their judgments were void, the appellant filed his libel *in personam* in the court below seeking damages for the alleged conversion of the ship. His libel was dismissed by the district court and he brings this appeal.

It is plain that if the state court had jurisdiction to enter its quiet title decree, that decree ended all the appellant's rights or claims as to the vessel. Therefore, the fundamental question before us is whether the State court had jurisdiction.

Appellant made the same claim of want of jurisdiction in his appeal in Sun Harbor Marina, Inc. v. Sellick, supra, in the District Court of Appeal. That court upheld the state court's jurisdiction upon the ground that jurisdiction was granted under the saving to suitor's clause * * *.

In his argument here the appellant, noting that the saving to suitors clause does not confer upon state courts the right to entertain proceedings *in rem* against vessels, The Moses Taylor, 71 U.S. 411, 18 L.Ed. 397 (1866), The Hine v. Trevor, 71 U.S. 555, 18 L.Ed. 451 (1866) asserts that the "state court conducted an *in rem* action as the action of giving appellees quiet title is an *in rem* action."

The fallacy in appellant's argument is apparent from what was said by the Supreme Court in Madruga v. Superior Court, 346 U.S. 556, 74 S.Ct. 298, 98 L.Ed. 290, 1954 A.M.C. 405 (1954). The Court there noted, 346 U.S. at page 560, 1954 A.M.C. at 409, that : "Admiralty jurisdiction is 'exclusive' only as to those maritime causes of action begun and carried on as proceedings *in rem,* that is, where a vessel or thing is itself treated as the offender and made the defendant by name or description in order to enforce a lien." That was a case in which action was brought in a California court for sale of a vessel and partition of the proceeds pursuant to a California statute. The Supreme Court, upholding the state court's jurisdiction, said * * * "The proceedings in this California partition case were not *in rem* in the admiralty sense. The plaintiffs' quarrel was with their co-owner, not with the ship. Manuel Madruga, not the ship, was made defendant. Thus the state court in this proceeding acts only upon the interests of the parties over whom it has jurisdiction *in personam,* and it does not affect the interests of others in the world at large, as it would if this were a proceeding *in rem* to enforce a lien. The California court is 'competent' to give this partition remedy and therefore has jurisdiction of the cause of action."

In like manner it must be said here that the state court action to quiet title, an action in aid of the lien foreclosure sale, was not brought against the ship but solely against the individuals Sellick and the Potters and hence the District Court of Appeal was correct in holding that the saving to suitors clause was applicable and that the state courts had jurisdiction to enter the quiet title decree.[1]

The judgment is affirmed.

---

1. In this holding we should not be understood to be approving the suggestion made in the opinion of the District Court of Appeal that the changes made in the saving to suitors clause in the 1948 revision of the statute had a "broadening effect." See the discussion of this matter in Gilmore & Black, *The Law of Admiralty,* p. 35.

NOTE

See Red Cross Line v. Atlantic Fruit Co., 264 U.S. 109, 44 S.Ct. 274, 68 L.Ed. 582 (1924), upholding the jurisdiction of a state court in an action for specific performance of an arbitration clause; Mengel Box Co. v. Joest, 127 Miss. 461, 90 So. 161 (1921), permitting replevin suit in the state court.

B.   STATUTORY PROCEEDINGS

1.   THE DEATH ON THE HIGH SEAS ACT

The Death on the High Seas Act, 46 U.S.C.A. § 761, provides that in cases under its coverage, "* * * the personal representative of the decedent may maintain a suit for damages in the district courts of the United States, in admiralty * * *". Until recent years most of the cases read this language to confer on the federal district courts an exclusive jurisdiction of actions under the DOHSA. The cases are collected in Boudreau v. Boat Andrea G. Corp., 350 Mass. 473, 215 N.E.2d 907, 1963 A.M.C. 1270 (1966). There was authority to the contrary. See, e.g., Ledet v. United Aircraft Corp., 10 N.Y.2d 258, 219 N.Y.S.2d 245, 176 N.E.2d 820, 1963 A.M.C. 1334 (1961). It is now established, over half a century after its passage, that the Act does not preclude the exercise of concurrent jurisdiction by the state courts. East River S.S. Corp. v. Transamerica Delaval Inc., 476 U.S. 858, 106 S.Ct. 2295, 90 L.Ed.2d 865 (1986). For discussion of the effect of the *East River S.S.* decision on removal of actions, see subdivision D, infra. The application of the substantive provisions of the DOHSA in actions in the federal and state courts is discussed in Chapter 20, infra.

From the standpoint of practical administration the supposed exclusiveness of the district court's jurisdiction has caused some trouble. It is not always apparent whether the death occurred more than a marine league from shore and therefore it is sometimes advantageous to join the Death on the High Seas count with a count under the possibly applicable state wrongful death statute. This could be done in the federal district court in admiralty, but in this event there would be a waiver of the right to jury trial on the state law count. The problems attending the joinder of admiralty proceedings and actions at law in the federal district court are treated in Subdivision C, infra. Whatever their solution, the counts cannot be joined in the state court. See The Marine Sulphur Queen, 231 F.Supp. 934, 1965 A.M.C. 340 (S.D.N.Y.1964).

2.   THE LIMITATION OF LIABILITY ACT

The Limitation of Liability Act provides in part, "The vessel owner, within six months after a claimant shall have given to or filed with such owner written notice of claim, may petition a district court of the United States of competent jurisdiction for limitation of liability * * *" 46 U.S.C.A. § 185. The previous section provides, however, that whenever the loss is suffered by several freighters or owners of goods on the same voyage, they are to receive compensation in proportion to their losses and "* * * for that purpose the freighters and owners of property, and the owner of the vessel, or any of them, may take the appropriate proceedings in any court, for the purpose of apportioning the sum for which the owner of the vessel may be liable among the parties entitled thereto."

These sections, read together, have been taken to mean that the federal district court has exclusive jurisdiction of proceedings to determine the right to limit liability under the act, but that the state courts have concurrent jurisdiction of proceedings to determine liability on the underlying claims and to apportion the fund, so long as the right to a litigation of the limitation issue in the federal court is not denied. These matters are discussed in greater detail in the chapter on Limitation of Liability, infra.

3.   SUITS AGAINST THE UNITED STATES

Both the Suits in Admiralty Act, 46 U.S.C.A. §§ 741–752, and The Public Vessels Act, 46 U.S.C.A. §§ 781–790, provide in terms for libels in personam in admiralty in the district court. Since both these sections deal with suits against the United States, the question of state court jurisdiction is not involved. The sections have caused some problems in the federal courts because of the doubt at times as to whether a cause falls under their provisions, or under the Tort Claims Act. This matter is treated in Chapter 10, infra.

4.   THE SHIP MORTGAGE ACT OF 1920

Under the Ship Mortgage Act of 1920, now codified as 46 U.S.C.A. §§ 31322–31330, proceedings in rem to foreclose a preferred ship mortgage on a documented vessel, or a vessel to be documented under chapter 121, or a foreign vessel, must be brought in the United States district court in admiralty. 46 U.S.C.A. § 31325(c). Under § 31325 (b)(2), however, a mortgagee may enforce a claim for outstanding indebtedness in an in personam action in admiralty or civil action in personam for the outstanding indebtedness or any deficiency in full payment of the indebtedness. Would a state court have jurisdiction under § 954(a)? As to whether a bankruptcy court could foreclose a preferred ship mortgage, see Gilmore & Black, The Law of Admiralty, § 9–94 (1975).

C.   ANCILLARY OR PENDENT JURISDICTION

1.   JOINDER OF NONMARITIME CLAIMS

In Romero v. International Terminal Operating Co., 358 U.S. 354, 79 S.Ct. 468, 3 L.Ed.2d 368 (1959), the Supreme Court held that claims under the general maritime law could be treated as pendent to claims under the Jones Act in an action brought at law in the federal district court. The Court declined to decide whether the "pendent" claims could be submitted to a jury. The Court was very cautious in its statement about the application of Hurn v. Oursler in the admiralty. In Fitzgerald v. United States Lines,

374 U.S. 16, 83 S.Ct. 1646, 10 L.Ed.2d 720 (1963), the Supreme Court held that when a count under the Jones Act was brought on the law side of the court, counts for breach of the warranty of seaworthiness of the vessel and for maintenance and cure must be treated as pendent to the Jones Act claim and submitted to the same jury. It has been held that the basis of the *Fitzgerald* decision does not lie in the pendent jurisdiction of the law court over the admiralty claim, but in a more general principle that the related claims should be tried together to the jury as a matter of proper judicial administration. See Haskins v. Point Towing Co., 395 F.2d 737, 1968 A.M.C. 1193 (3d Cir.1968), reproduced in Chapter 6, infra, at p. 239. Neither the *Fitzgerald* nor the *Haskins* case, however, answers the question of whether a claim under the state law can be brought in the federal court on the theory that it is pendent to a claim brought in admiralty. There is some authority on the subject that suggests that it may not. See, e.g., Weinstein v. Eastern Airlines, Inc., 316 F.2d 758 (3d Cir.1963). While there was no discussion of the pendent jurisdiction question, the court held that counts for negligence could be heard by the admiralty court, but counts for breach of warranty could not. Compare the *Weinstein* decision with the decision in The Marine Sulphur Queen, 231 F.Supp. 934, 1965 A.M.C. 341 (S.D.N.Y.1964). There the court hints that affording a jury trial on the pendent claim would overcome the difficulty. And see The S.S. Mormaclynx, p. 172, infra.

2.   COUNTERCLAIMS

Under former Admiralty Rule 50, a cross-libel could be brought only if it arose out of the same contract or transaction out of which the original libel arose. Zim Israel Navigation Co. v. T. Chatani & Co., 249 F.Supp. 535, 1966 A.M.C. 1575 (S.D.N.Y.1966). In the *Zim Israel* case, Judge Herlands makes it plain that he was in favor of extending Rule 13 to admiralty cases. See also United States v. Isthmian Steamship Co., 359 U.S. 314, 79 S.Ct. 857, 3 L.Ed.2d 845 (1959), in which Chief Justice Warren indicated that any liberalization of the admiralty practice along the lines of Rule 13 of the F.R.C.P. would have to await rule changes. In the amendments made in 1966 to effect the merger of the civil and admiralty rules, no limitation was placed on the application of Rule 13 to admiralty cases, and absent any such limitation, the rule is fully applicable. "Clearly, the clause in Rule 1, subjecting admiralty proceedings to the Federal Rules, must mean that all admiralty proceedings are bound by all the Rules and not just the amended ones." Judge Tenney in The S.S. Hai Chang, 259 F.Supp. 75, 1966 A.M.C. 2239 (S.D.N.Y.1966). It follows that under Rule 13(b), a permissive counterclaim can be brought in an admiralty proceeding. Since Rule 9(h) speaks of "[a] pleading or count setting forth a claim for relief," and this language, as defined in Rule 8, plainly covers an answer setting up a counterclaim as well as a complaint, Rule 9(h) applies to counterclaims. If the claim is both within the court's admiralty jurisdiction and also cognizable under some other jurisdictional head, e.g., if the parties are diverse, the party asserting the claim may at his election identify it as maritime, or may bring it at law under the "saving to suitors" clause. Of course, if the claim is cognizable only under the admiralty jurisdiction, it will be treated as an admiralty claim under Rule 9(h) whether it is so identified or not. A permissive counterclaim under Rule 13(b) must be supported by independent grounds of jurisdiction. See Moore's Federal Practice ¶ 13.19 (1972). If a counterclaim is non-maritime, therefore, and as a consequence not supportable under 28 U.S.C.A. § 1333, it would have to be maintainable under some other head of federal jurisdiction.

The application of Rule 13(a), dealing with compulsory counterclaims, is somewhat more complex. Clearly it applies to admiralty proceedings, so at least in the case in which admiralty jurisdiction supports the claim, or it is otherwise within the jurisdiction of the district court, it must be brought or lost. What of the application of Rule 9(h) to such a claim? May the defendant pleading a counterclaim insist upon a jury trial by failing to identify his claim as maritime? Under the former admiralty practice, since he was not obligated to file a cross-libel, he could have had a jury trial by bringing his claim as an independent action under the "saving to suitors" clause. Since under Rule 13(a) he is forced to bring it in the form of a counterclaim, is there any reason for depriving him of this option? On the other hand, under the former practice, the original cause would go forward and the libelant would have had the benefit of his election to litigate in admiralty before the court. Is the experience with the merger of law and equity pertinent? See Beacon Theatres, Inc. v. Westover, 359 U.S. 500, 79 S.Ct. 948, 3 L.Ed.2d 988 (1959).

See Wilmington Trust v. United States District Court for Dist. of Hawaii, 934 F.2d 1026 (9th Cir.1991), in which the holder of a second preferred mortgage intervened in an in rem mortgage foreclosure proceeding brought by the holder of a first preferred mortgage, answered the complaint and filed a number of claims designated as counterclaims, together with a demand for jury trial. Applying *Beacon Theatres*, the court of appeals entered a mandamus requiring the district court to honor the jury demand, observing, "We note that our holding may result in the entire case being tried to a jury. This result is likely to occur if the claims are closely related factually ..."

What of a counterclaim within Rule 13(a) that is non-maritime in character? Under the former admiralty practice such a counterclaim could not be brought. United Transportation & Lighterage Co. v. New York & Baltimore Transportation Line, 180 Fed. 902 (S.D.N.Y.1910); The Kearney, 14 F.2d 949, 1926 A.M.C. 1640 (3d Cir.1926). The latter case was read by Benedict to permit such a cross-libel to be maintained so long as the original libel remained pending but required its dismissal if for any reason the original libel was dismissed. See 1 Benedict, *Admiralty* 454 (6th ed. (Knauth) 1940). If the Benedict view of The Kearney is sound, could the defendant be forced to litigate his counterclaim in admiralty? Would this be in effect to elevate the "saving to suitors" clause above the Seventh Amendment? In any event would it not be strange to permit the defendant whose claim *could* be litigated in admiralty a choice under Rule 9(h) and *require* the defendant whose claim could *not* be litigated in admiralty independently to bring it there?   On the other hand, if the *Beacon Theatres* case requires that the jury trial take place first, and the counterclaim is such as to call into operation the doctrine of collateral estoppel, has the plaintiff who exercised his option under Rule 9(h) been deprived of the major benefit of such an election?

3.   THIRD PARTY PRACTICE

Galt G/S v. Hapag–Lloyd A.G.

United States Court of Appeals, Ninth Circuit, 1995.
60 F.3d 1370.

■ BRUNETTI, CIRCUIT JUDGE:

The district court awarded judgment to third-party plaintiff Hapag–Lloyd A.G. and against third-party defendant Safeway Stores after a nonjury trial of California law indemnification and subrogation claims.   The third-party claims were ancillary to an admiralty cargo damage suit instituted by Galt G/S against Hapag–Lloyd.   We reverse the judgment of the district court for lack of subject matter jurisdiction and remand for the district court to dismiss Galt's third-party subrogation claim against Safeway and determine whether diversity jurisdiction exists for Hapag–Lloyd's third-party indemnification claim against Safeway.

I

The admiralty action alleged that Hapag–Lloyd or one of three other carriers of a shipment of hams damaged the hams during the shipment. The International Trading Company (ITC) arranged in 1987 for the importation of 2160 tins of canned ham from a supplier in Aarhus, Denmark, and consigned them for delivery to Safeway Stores (Safeway).   Safeway more than a week after delivery, discovering that the ham was covered with ice, frozen, and thereby spoiled, notified ITC.   ITC agreed to rescind the sale, notified Galt G/S (Galt), its insurer, and requested coverage in the amount of $53,243.21, the net loss.

Galt sued the four carriers that delivered the ham to Safeway, seeking recovery by way of subrogation: Hapag–Lloyd A.G. (Hapag–Lloyd), which had shipped the ham by sea from Denmark to Oakland, California; Can Transport, Inc., which delivered the unloaded ham by truck to Sacramento; Crystal Ice & Cold Storage, which stored it in Sacramento until; D & D Services delivered it by truck and unloaded it at Safeway's meat plant in Stockton.   The ham sat in this plant in storage for eleven days before Safeway employees opened it and discovered that it was frozen.

Hapag–Lloyd assumed the tenders of the ground carriers' defenses. Hapag–Lloyd denied that any of the carriers had frozen the ham; it argued that Safeway employees froze the ham in the eleven days after receiving and before opening it.   During discovery, Hapag–Lloyd found evidence indicating that the ham's temperature had never dropped below 28°F, its freezing temperature, during its ocean voyage and ground delivery. Hapag–Lloyd also discovered that Safeway's Stockton plant had both a cooler and a freezer, and that, in the four years between the freezing and the litigation discovery, Safeway employees had destroyed the record indicating in which room the ham had been stored.

The district court granted a motion by Hapag–Lloyd to implead Safeway as a defendant. Under Federal Rule of Civil Procedure 14(c)(Rule 14(c)), the district court tendered to Safeway the defenses of separate California law claims by Hapag–Lloyd and Galt. Galt's pendent claim was for recovery from Safeway, by way of subrogation, of ITC's loss from rescinding the consignment to Safeway. Hapag–Lloyd's ancillary claim was for indemnification from Safeway of the amount of any judgment against Hapag–Lloyd on the cargo damage claim in the principal action. The day before trial, Hapag–Lloyd paid Galt $13,500 to settle the principal cargo damage action and acquire the assignment of Galt's subrogation claim against Safeway. Hapag–Lloyd's indemnification claim and Galt's subrogation claim (the latter now in Hapag–Lloyd's hands) went to a bench trial.

The district court ruled for Hapag–Lloyd on Galt's claim but not on its own. The court concluded that Safeway was liable for the entire $53,-243.21 net loss to Hapag–Lloyd on the claim assigned by Galt. The court declined to consider Hapag–Lloyd's claim for indemnification for the costs of settling with Galt because Hapag–Lloyd had won on Galt's claim.

Safeway filed a timely notice of appeal; Hapag–Lloyd cross-appeals. Safeway appeals from the grant of the motion to implead it and from two trial issues. Hapag–Lloyd appeals from the district court's refusal to consider its claim for indemnification for its settlement costs.

II

We first inquire whether the district court correctly exercised subject matter jurisdiction over Safeway. We review de novo whether subject matter jurisdiction exists. United States v. City of Twin Falls, Idaho, 806 F.2d 862, 866–67 (9th Cir.1986). We may review issues regarding subject matter jurisdiction sua sponte. Rath Packing Co. v. Becker, 530 F.2d 1295, 1303 (9th Cir.1975), aff'd, 430 U.S. 519, 97 S.Ct. 1305, 51 L.Ed.2d 604 (1977).

Safeway argues that ancillary jurisdiction did not exist over the third party claims against it. However, before we address ancillary jurisdiction, we inquire sua sponte whether admiralty or diversity jurisdiction provided the district court with an independent basis for federal subject matter jurisdiction over Safeway. Cf. Joiner v. Diamond M. Drilling Co., 677 F.2d 1035, 1038–39 (5th Cir.1982).

* * * [The court's discussion of admiralty and diversity jurisdiction is omitted. It found that admiralty jurisdiction did not exist and that failure to identify the corporate parties' principal place of business made it impossible to tell whether or not diversity existed—Ed.]

C

We now focus on ancillary jurisdiction, the basis for jurisdiction on which the district court actually relied. The district court concluded that the claims from Safeway arose from the same transaction or occurrence as the cargo damage claim and exercised ancillary jurisdiction accordingly. Having exercised jurisdiction, it then granted Hapag–Lloyd's motion to implead Safeway under Rule 14(e).

Safeway was a pendent party because it was not already a party to the lawsuit when Hapag–Lloyd moved to implead it and because the district court had no independent basis for federal jurisdiction over it. Before the district court could implead Safeway under Rule 14(e), it needed to establish that ancillary jurisdiction existed. Rule 14(e) could not provide the basis for jurisdiction. Fed.R.Civ.P. 82. Instead, the exercise of jurisdiction over the pendent and ancillary actions had to establish a constitutionally required minimal nexus to the principal action and find explicit authorization in a jurisdiction-conferring statute. See Finley v. United States, 490 U.S. 545, 109 S.Ct. 2003, 104 L.Ed.2d 593 (1989)(determining whether ancillary jurisdiction existed by analyzing the constitutional minimum for jurisdiction and the jurisdictional statute at issue, 28 U.S.C. § 1346(b), but not the procedure for impleader, Rule 14(a)).

Galt and Hapag–Lloyd's claims must have been part of the same constitutional "case" as Galt's cargo damage claim. At a minimum, the indemnification claims must have arisen from the same transaction or occurrence as the cargo damage claim. See Finley, 490 U.S. at 549, 109 S.Ct. at 2006–07. If the claims all had been part of the same constitutional case, ancillary jurisdiction would have existed if the language or the legislative history of the statute conferring jurisdiction over the cargo damage claim, in this case 28 U.S.C. § 1333, could have overcome the presumption that the statute does not confer jurisdiction over a pendent party like Safeway. See Finley, 490 U.S. at 549, 552, 554, 109 S.Ct. at 2006–07, 2008, 2009–10.[2]

We conclude that the cargo damage claim and the ancillary claims arise from different occurrences. The alleged occurrence in the cargo damage claim is whether Hapag–Lloyd or one of the carriers mishandled the ham during shipment; the alleged occurrence in the indemnification claim is whether Safeway stored the ham improperly. The two occurrences are separated by the carriers' relinquishing control over the hams. They are also separated in time. Accordingly, the district court erred in exercising ancillary jurisdiction over the California indemnification claims against Safeway.

We recognize that this result means that Hapag–Lloyd may have to press its claims against Safeway in a second suit in state court. However, this outcome is sometimes unavoidable in a federal system. The limited

---

2. 28 U.S.C. § 1367 supersedes this second *Finley* requirement for all suits arising from complaints filed after December 1, 1990. Pub.L. No. 101650, § 310(c), 104 Stat. 5089, 5114 (1990). However, Galt filed its complaint in 1989.

nature of federal courts' jurisdiction "means that the efficiency and convenience of a consolidated action will sometimes have to be forgone in favor of separate actions in state and federal courts." Id. at 555, 109 S.Ct. at 2010.

Conclusion

We reverse the district court's exercise of ancillary jurisdiction over the state law claims against Safeway. The district court may have diversity jurisdiction over Hapag–Lloyd and the other transportation defendants' indemnity claim against Safeway. We remand the case to the district court to consider in its discretion whether to grant Hapag–Lloyd leave to amend its third party complaint to establish such jurisdiction and pursue its third party claim under Rule 14(a). See Nugget Hydroelectric, L.P. v. Pacific Gas & Elec. Co., 981 F.2d 429, 438 (9th Cir.1992). However, even if diversity jurisdiction exists between Galt and Safeway, Rule 14(a) would not allow Hapag–Lloyd to tender Safeway with the defense of Galt's subrogation claim against it. The district court should thus dismiss this claim on remand.

REVERSED and REMANDED.

NOTE

It has long been assumed that a third party claim brought under Rule 14(a)(b), does not require an independent source of jurisdiction. See Moore's Federal Practice, ¶ 14.26 (2d ed.1994). Thus in a diversity case, a defendant may implead an indemnitor though there is no diversity between the third party defendant and either the plaintiff or the defendant. The reason is not easy to explain but is thought to rest upon the fact that the claim for indemnity or contribution is created by the main claim, and therefore in a sense can be viewed as ancillary or dependent. In Owen Equipment & Erection Co. v. Kroger, 437 U.S. 365, 98 S.Ct. 2396, 57 L.Ed.2d 274 (1978), the Supreme Court, assuming this to be the case, held that in a diversity action the plaintiff could not amend its complaint to state a claim directly against the third party defendant absent an independent basis for jurisdiction.

The practice under Rule 14(c) supports a strong analogy to *Owen Equipment*, since in both the action is converted into one in which the plaintiff is arraigned against two defendants, against one of whom it could not bring an independent action. As a consequence, the jurisdiction of non-maritime claims brought as third-party claims under Rule 14(c) and the question of pendent party jurisdiction generally coalesced. Thus in Leather's Best, Inc. v. The Mormaclynx, discussed in the NOTE on p. 172 below, which the court held that a non-maritime co-defendant could be joined without an independent basis for jurisdiction, Judge Friendly observed that it would be with great reluctance that he would hold differently in a case of impleader.

4. JOINDER OF PARTIES

Loeber v. Bay Tankers, Inc.

United States Court of Appeals, Fifth Circuit, 1991.
924 F.2d 1340, 1992 A.M.C. 1500.

■ PER CURIAM:

The Plaintiffs–Appellants, Charlene and Glen Loeber, individually and on behalf of their daughter Gretchen Loeber, appeal the district court's order

(1) sustaining the motion by the United States that summary judgment be granted, dismissing their suit against the United States for want of jurisdiction; and (2) denying the Loebers' motion to file a third amended and supplemental complaint in which they sought to have the court exercise pendent-party jurisdiction over Violet Dock Port, Inc. We affirm the grant of summary judgment and reverse the denial of the motion to file an amended complaint.

I. Operable Facts

Plaintiff Glen Loeber was the first assistant engineer aboard the USNS *Pollux*, a vessel owned by the United States. On June 13, 1988, the *Pollux* was moored outboard of, and alongside, the USNS *Regulus*, another vessel owned by the United States, which was moored at the Violet Dock Port in Violet, Louisiana. On that day while Glen's wife, Charlene, and his two daughters, Gretchen and Glennis, were visiting Glen and standing on the dock adjacent to the *Regulus*, a wake from a passing merchant vessel, the M/V *Meteora*, allegedly caused the *Regulus* to surge. That surge in turn caused the *Regulus's* accommodation ladder to roll across the dock. The ladder struck Gretchen, knocked her down, and rolled along her legs, breaking her right femur bone. Both parents claim that they too sustained personal injuries while they were attempting to extricate Gretchen from beneath the ladder.

* * *

IV. Pendent–Party Jurisdiction

In denying the Loebers' motion for leave to file an amended and supplemental complaint to add Violet Dock Port, Inc. (Violet) as a party defendant, the district court declined to exercise pendent-party jurisdiction over a party against whom, as the Loebers concede, no independent basis for federal jurisdiction exists. As no federal question is involved, jurisdiction does not lie under 28 U.S.C. § 1331; as the citizenship of the parties is not diverse, jurisdiction does not lie under 28 U.S.C. § 1332; as the claim against Violet is grounded on state law, the district court has jurisdiction over the claim against Violet only if pendent-party jurisdiction is available in admiralty cases. The district court has jurisdiction over Metropolitan under Article III, § 2 of the constitution and under 28 U.S.C. § 1333(1).

We have previously held that "a federal court entertaining a maritime claim has the discretion to adjudicate non-federal claims derived from a common nucleus of operative fact, including claims against a party not before the court in the federal action." Feigler v. Tidex, Inc., 826 F.2d 1435, 1439 (5 Cir.1987). However, because the Supreme Court's decision in Finley v. United States, 490 U.S. 545, 109 S.Ct 2003, 104 L.Ed.2d 593 (1989), places in question the doctrine of pendent party jurisdiction in any context, we must examine anew whether the doctrine survives in admiralty cases.[3] Fortunately, we have the guiding wisdom of the Second Circuit on this very question to enlighten our analysis. See Roco Carriers, Ltd. v. M/V Nurnberg Express, 899 F.2d 1292 (2 Cir.1990).

In *Finley* the Supreme Court held that pendent-party jurisdiction is unavailable when the primary claim is brought under the Federal Tort Claims Act (FTCA), 28 U.S.C. § 1346(b). 490 U.S. at 550–51. More generally, it declared that the inquiry into whether pendent jurisdiction exists over a different nondiverse defendant on a non-federal claim does not end with an inquiry into whether the federal and state claims derive from a common nucleus of operative fact. *Finley*, 490 U.S. at 550–51 (citing United Mine Workers v. Gibbs, 383 U.S. 715 (1966)). Federal courts must additionally examine "the posture in which the nonfederal claim is asserted and the specific statute that confers jurisdiction over the federal claim." Id. (quoting Owen Equipment & Erection Co. v. Kroger, 437 U.S. 365, 373, 98 S.Ct. 2396, 57 L.Ed.2d 274 (1978)).

In terms of the relevant statutory grants of jurisdiction, the Second Circuit has distinguished an action brought into federal court pursuant to the court's admiralty jurisdiction and one, such as in *Finley*, sought to be brought pursuant to FTCA. *Roco*, 899 F.2d at 1295. In the latter action jurisdiction is predicated upon a waiver of sovereign immunity permitting tort claims against the United States, and such jurisdictional grants are ordinarily interpreted narrowly. Id. (citing *Sherwood*, 312 U.S. 584, 590 (1941)). In contrast, waiver of sovereign immunity is not an issue in the Loebers' action, their claims against the United States having been dismissed. Consequently, the "posture" or the context in which the Loebers assert their nonfederal claim against Violet is entirely different from the posture described in *Finley*. See 490 U.S. at 551–52.

The Court in *Finley* declared that " 'neither the convenience of the litigants nor considerations of judicial economy can suffice to justify' " jurisdiction over state-law claims involving additional parties without an independent basis for jurisdiction. Id. 490 U.S. at 552 (quoting *Kroger*, 437 U.S. 365, 376–77 (1978)). But the policy of permitting claims arising in admiralty to be resolved in a single setting entails, as the court in Roco noted, more than the mere convenience of the parties. See *Roco*, 1990 AMC at 918–19, 899 F.2d at 1296. The policy arises, instead, from the historical recognition that maritime claims in particular should be subjected to efficient and uniform procedures and treatment. Id. (citing In re Oil Spill by Amoco Cadiz Off Coast of France, 1983 AMC 1633, 1635–37, 699 F.2d 909, 913–14 (7 Cir.), cert. denied sub nom. Astilleros Espanoles, S.A. v. Standard Oil Co., 464 U.S. 864, 104 S.Ct. 196, 78 L.Ed.2d 172 (1983)).

3. We must examine the doctrine of pendent-party jurisdiction even though Congress has effectively overruled *Finley*. The Judicial Improvements Act of 1990, Pub.L. No.101–650, § 310, 104 Stat. 5089, 5113–14 (1990)(codified at 28 U.S.C. § 1367), provides the explicit authorization of pendent-party jurisdiction that in *Finley* the Supreme Court found to be absent. Because the instant action commenced before the enactment of the Judicial Improvements Act on December 1, 1990, that Act does not apply to the instant case. See Pub.L. No. 101–650, § 310.

Resolution of pendent-party jurisdiction, the Court in *Finley* emphasized, demands " 'careful attention to the relevant statutory language.' " *Finley*, 490 U.S. at 550 (quoting Aldinger v. Howard, 427 U.S. 1, 17 (1976)). The language of the relevant statutory grants of jurisdiction in *Finley* and in the Loebers' case differs substantially. See *Roco*, 1990 AMC at 918–19, 899 F.2d at 1296. The Supreme Court emphasized that the grant in the FTCA of jurisdiction over "claims against the United States," 28 U.S.C. § 1346(b), was limited to claims against a specific party, the United States. The Court held, therefore, that the statute defines jurisdiction "in a manner that does not reach defendants other than the United States." *Finley*, 490 U.S. at 553. But the statute supplying admiralty jurisdiction is "strikingly broad." *Roco*, 899 F.2d at 1296. It confers admiralty jurisdiction over "[a]ny civil case of admiralty or maritime jurisdiction...." 28 U.S.C. § 1333(1).

The admiralty statute does not limit jurisdiction to a particular party, as do the FTCA and the Federal Employers' Liability Act (FELA), 45 U.S.C. § 51 et seq., 56. See Lockard v. Missouri Pac. R.R. Co., 894 F.2d 299 (8 Cir.1990)(45 U.S.C. § 51 imposes liability on "[e]very common carrier by railroad"); see also Iron Workers Mid–South Pension Fund v. Terotechnology Corp., 891 F.2d 548, 551 (5 Cir.1990)(no pendent-party jurisdiction under Employee Retirement Income Security Act,29 U.S.C. § 1132(e), over state-law claim to enforce lien). Neither does the Act limit jurisdiction to a certain category of claims. Instead, it provides jurisdiction over an admiralty "case." 28 U.S.C. § 1333(1).

Therefore, unlike the FTCA which "confers jurisdiction over 'claims against the United States and no one else,' *Finley*, 490 U.S. at 552, admiralty jurisdiction extends to an entire case, including non-admiralty claims against a second defendant." *Roco*, 899 F.2d at 1296. Cf. Nolan v. Boeing Co., 919 F.2d 1058, 1064 (5 Cir.1990)(in contrast to *Finley* which confers jurisdiction only over "claims," Foreign Sovereign Immunities Act (FSIA) provides jurisdiction over "*action* against a foreign state" (emphasis added) and, therefore, includes claims against parties other than foreign state); Teledyne, Inc. v. Kone Corp., 892 F.2d 1404, 1409 (9 Cir.1989)(FSIA provides pendent-party jurisdiction). That the admiralty statute uses "case" and not "action" as in the FSIA is a distinction without a difference. This court has recently reiterated that "[i]n federal practice the terms refer to the same thing, i.e., the entirety of a civil proceeding." *Nolan*, 919 F.2d at 1066.

In conclusion, we agree with the Second Circuit, *Roco*, 899 F.2d at 1297, that "[i]n light of the broadly worded jurisdiction over admiralty cases and 'the strong policy in favor of providing efficient procedures for resolving maritime disputes,' *In re Oil Spill*, 1983 AMC 1637, 699 F.2d at 914, we see no reason at this juncture to depart from the established rule of this Circuit that pendent party jurisdiction is available in the unique area of admiralty." Accordingly, we hold that the district court erred in not allowing the Loebers to amend their complaint to add Violet.

V. Conclusion

Because the Loebers failed to comply with the requirement in the AEA, 46 U.S.C. App. § 740, that they file a claim with the appropriate federal agency and then wait six months before filing suit, the district court correctly granted summary judgment in favor of the United States. The Loebers' action is also time barred. A plaintiff who files an action within the two-year period prescribed by 46 U.S.C. App. § 745 (Suits in Admiralty Act), but who fails to comply with the six-month requirement of the AEA loses his action after the two-year limitation period has expired.

Because the admiralty jurisdiction statute broadly bestows jurisdiction over "[a]ny civil case of admiralty or maritime jurisdiction" and because courts have historically acknowledged the pressing need to subject all claims in admiralty to efficient and uniform procedures, the district court properly has pendent-party jurisdiction over Violet Dock Port, Inc. Accordingly, the order of the district court granting summary judgment in favor of the United States is affirmed, and its order denying the Loebers leave to file an amended complaint in which they add Violet Dock Port, Inc. is reversed and the case remanded for further proceedings consistent with this opinion.

NOTE

Joinder of common law or equitable claims with maritime claims is permitted in terms by Rule 18(a), and the extent to which joinder of parties is permitted by Rule 20 does not depend upon the law-equity-admiralty distinction. The Rules do not affect jurisdiction, however, and so the problem of the scope of a case or controversy remains.

By the time of the decision in *Owen Equipment*, discussed in the NOTE on p. 169, above, the *Gibbs* theory of pendent jurisdiction had been extended by some of the lower court decisions to embrace the joinder of parties as well as claims, and some six years before *Owen*, had been applied to joinder of parties in an admiralty action. See Leather's Best, Inc. v. S.S. Mormaclynx, 451 F.2d 800, 1971 A.M.C. 2383 (2d Cir.1971). In The Mormaclynx, a large container of leather goods was unloaded by stevedores and placed in a large terminal area to await pick up by the shipper. The area was accessible through four gates. Two were open 24 hours a day and supposedly under the continuous supervision of watchmen. The other two were open only from 9:00 A.M. to 4:00 P.M. on weekdays and similarly guarded at those times. One roving watchman was on duty to see that there were no unauthorized persons on the pier and that no one opened any container. When the shipper's trucker arrived to pick up the container it could not be found. Next day it was found by the police 25 miles away and empty. The shipper brought suit against the carrier and the operator of the pier, in admiralty, being of the opinion that the claims were all under the contract of carriage. The court of appeals found that the claim against the pier operator lacked a basis for admiralty jurisdiction and the parties were not diverse. The court's solution was to treat the state law claim against the pier operator as "pendent" to the admiralty claim. There was no jury demand so the question of pendent claims and the right to a jury trial. Judge Friendly observed that he saw no reason why the same rule should not obtain in the case of compulsory counterclaims and in third party claims.

Since the decision in The Mormaclynx, the pendent parties doctrine has come full cycle. The Supreme Court was slow to recognize the basis for such jurisdiction. See Zahn v. International Paper Co., 414 U.S. 291, 94 S.Ct. 505, 38 L.Ed.2d 511 (1973)(each member of a class suing in the federal courts on the basis of diversity must demonstrate the minimum amount in controversy); Aldinger v. Howard, 427 U.S. 1, 96 S.Ct. 2413, 49 L.Ed.2d 276 (1976)(an action against a municipality under State law cannot be brought pendent to an action against individuals under the civil rights statutes); Owen Equipment Co. v. Kroger, supra. Despite these straws in the wind, the maritime cases generally followed The Mormaclynx, being of the opinion that § 1333 could be distinguished from § 1332 (*Zahn* and *Owen Equipment*)and § 1343 (*Aldinger*).

Finally, in Finley v. United States, 490 U.S. 545, 109 S.Ct. 2003, 104 L.Ed.2d 593 (1989), the Supreme Court held that an action against an alleged joint tortfeasor cannot be brought as pendent to a claim against the United States under the Federal Tort Claims Act (28 U.S.C. § 1346(b)), and stated in general terms that a basis for pendent party jurisdiction must appear in the jurisdictional statute and could not be derived from the *Gibbs* doctrine. Although there was initial doubt about the survival of The Mormaclynx after *Finley*, the Second Circuit again found a basis for distinction and sustained the exercise of pendent party jurisdiction in maritime cases. Roco Carriers, Ltd. v. M/V Nurnberg Express, 899 F.2d 1292 (2d Cir.1990), despite an earlier dictum to the contrary. Staffer v. Bouchard Transp. Co., 878 F.2d 638, 643 n. 5 (2d Cir.1989).

In December 1990, as part of the Judicial Reform Act of 1990, Congress added § 1367 to title 28, covering explicitly the exercise of "supplemental" jurisdiction, and making it clear that a district court with original jurisdiction of a claim may exercise "supplemental" jurisdiction over all claims that are part of the constitutional case or controversy out of which arose the claim over which the court has original jurisdiction, whether or not these claims require the addition of other parties. The statute exempts cases in which the jurisdiction of the court is founded solely on § 1332. In such cases the court may not exercise "supplemental" jurisdiction of claims by the plaintiffs against persons made parties under Rules 14, 19, 20, or 24, or over claims by persons proposed to be joined under Rule 19, or seeking to intervene under Rule 24. Insofar as admiralty and maritime cases are concerned, § 1367 vindicates the decision in The Mormaclynx. In the case of motions to add parties under Rule 19, or motions to intervene under Rule 24, if the original action is identified as maritime under Rule 9(h) the statute clearly confers supplemental jurisdiction of claims within the *Gibbs* doctrine. If the claim is pleaded without identification and jurisdiction is pitched on diversity, and the parties needed for just adjudication, or those of a petitioner for intervention are maritime will "supplemental" jurisdiction support their joinder, or should the plaintiff be required to elect between dismissal of the action under Rule 19, and amending his complaint to identify his claim as maritime? In the case of a proposed intervenor, is it significant that the petitioner could file an independent action and move for consolidation?

Aside from the jury problem the issue of "pendent party jurisdiction" must be viewed, the Supreme Court has instructed, as a matter of statutory construction. See Aldinger v. Howard, 427 U.S. 1, 96 S.Ct. 2413, 49 L.Ed.2d 276 (1976). In cases such as The Mormaclynx, for example, the question reduces itself to a construction of 28 U.S.C.A. § 1333. Where does this lead us? Cf. In re Oil Spill by Amoco Cadiz Off Coast of France, 699 F.2d 909, 1983 A.M.C. 1633 (7th Cir.1983)("Although many recent decisions, including our circuit's decision in Hixon v. Sherwin–Williams Co., 671 F.2d 1005, 1008–09 (7th Cir.1982), reject 'pendent parties,' jurisdiction as a basis for allowing a diversity plaintiff to bring in an additional defendant against whom the plaintiff has a state law claim that does not satisfy the minimum amount in controversy requirement of the diversity statute, 28 U.S.C. § 1332, the admiralty setting is distinguishable. The tradition of liberal joinder, reflected in Rule 14(c), illustrates the strong admiralty policy in favor of providing efficient procedures for resolving maritime disputes").

The doctrine of pendent jurisdiction presupposes, of course, that there is no independent basis for jurisdiction of the claim referred to as pendent, and it results in the application of the land law (often the state law) in treating the merits of the claim. See, e.g., Colgate Palmolive Co. v. S/S Dart Canada, 724 F.2d 313, 1984 A.M.C. 305 (2d Cir.1983), in which it was held that an action for lost cargo against a terminal owner brought as pendent to an action against the carrier (as in The Mormaclynx), state law governs the validity of a contract term extending to the terminal owner the $500 package limitation of liability under COGSA. See Chapter 14 F, infra.

Where the court can find admiralty jurisdiction of all claims, it can eliminate both the jury trial problem and the choice of law problem. If the view expressed in Carroll v. Protection Maritime Ins. Co. (discussed in the note on p. 122 above) to the effect that *Executive Jet* extended to the tort jurisdiction the contract rule that jurisdiction is predicated upon maritime nexus and not location, would it pare down sharply the area in which recourse to the pendent jurisdiction would have to be made?

D. REMOVAL JURISDICTION

Alleman v. Bunge Corp.

United States Court of Appeals, Fifth Circuit, 1984.
756 F.2d 344.

■ REAVLEY, CIRCUIT JUDGE:

Bunge Corp. and Insurance Co. of North America (hereinafter referred to collectively as Bunge) appeal a summary judgment in favor of eight insurance companies.[1] Bunge attempts to base this appeal on 28 U.S.C. § 1292(a)(3)(1982), which permits appeal of interlocutory decrees in admiralty cases. Because this appeal is not from a maritime action and no other jurisdiction exists, we dismiss the appeal.

James and Shirley Allerman brought suit in Louisiana state court to recover for personal injuries that resulted from James' falling in an open hole on a grain barge while employed by Bunge as a longshoreman. The Allemans brought claims under the Longshoremen's and Harbor Workers' Compensation Act, 33 U.S.C. §§ 901, 950 (1982), general maritime law, and Louisiana state law, La.Civ.Code,Ann.art. 2315 (West Supp.1984), against, among others, Bunge and eight other insurance companies with which

---

1. The insurance companies are: Continental Insurance Co., Belafonte Insurance Co., Midland Insurance Co., Northeastern Insurance Co., Penn Lumberman Insurance Co., Ranger Insurance Co., and Republic Insurance Co.

Bunge had an insurance policy. Bunge removed the action to federal court on the basis of diversity jurisdiction. 28 U.S.C. § 1332(a)(1982). The federal court then granted the eight insurance companies summary judgment on grounds that their policy with Bunge excluded coverage of claims by employees.

The admiralty jurisdiction of the federal courts, 28 U.S.C. § 1333 (1982), could have been invoked in this case. The Allemans could have filed their complaint with a statement identifying it as a maritime claim., Fed.R.Civ.P. 9(h),[2] in admiralty court. Bynum v. Patterson Truck Lines, Inc., 655 F.2d 643, 644 (5th Cir.1981)(Longshormen's and Harbor Workers' Compensation Act is a maritime cause of action). Instead, the Allemans exercised their "historic option," Romero v. International Terminal Operating Co., 358 U.S. 354, 371, 79 S.Ct. 468, 480, 3 L.Ed.2d 368 (1959), under the saving-to-suitors clause of 28 U.S.C. § 1333(1)(1982). Numerous and important consequences flow from the Alleman's decision to bring their action in state court. See T.N.T. Marine Service, Inc. v. Weaver Shipyards & Dry Docks, Inc., 702 F.2d 585, 586–87 (5th Cir.), cert. denied, 464 U.S. 847, 104 S.Ct. 151, 78 L.Ed.2d 141 (1983)(jurisdiction invoked governs venue, interlocutory appeals, remedies available, right to jury trial, and the law that applies). By removing this action, Bunge could not alter the Allemans' substantive rights or destroy their right to presecute their action in a common law court. Bunge could have remove this action only to a federal diversity court. Cf. Gaitor v. Peninsular and Occidental Steamship Co., 287 F.2d 252, 255, (5th Cir.1961)(maritime action brought in state court could be removed only if diversity existed). Therefore the Allemans' action is not in the federal court's admiralty jurisdiction.

Because 28 U.S.C. 1292(a)(3)(1982), may be used only if the federal court's admiralty jurisdiction has been invoked, Fed.R.Civ.P. 9(h), Bunge cannot base jurisdiction for this appeal on that statute. Because no other basis for this appeals exists,[3] it is DISMISSED.

N O T E

Prior to the decision of the Supreme Court in Romero v. International Terminal Operating Co., 358 U.S. 354, 79 S.Ct. 468, 3 L.Ed.2d 368 (1959), there was some difference of opinion in the lower courts as to whether a maritime cause brought in the state court under the "saving to suitors" clause was removable by the defendant to the federal court absent some non-maritime basis of jurisdiction. Until the 1948 revision of 28 U.S.C.A. § 1441 the problem was simply whether or not an action brought in the state court was one arising under the laws of the United States, which was decided in the negative in *Romero*. In that year, however, the removal statute was broadened to provide for removal in cases in which the district

2. Setting forth Rule 9(h).

3. The district court did not certify this summary judgment under Fed.R.Civ.P. 54(b). See Boudeloche v. Tnemec Co., 693 F.2d 546, 547 (5th Cir.1982)(order adjudicating fewer than all claims as to fewer to all parties not appealable as final judgment unless certified pursuant to Rule 54(b)).

court would have had original jurisdiction, except "as otherwise expressly provided by Act of Congress."

In 1956, in Davis v. Matson Nav. Co., 143 F.Supp. 537 (N.D.Cal.1956), Judge Carter of the Northern District of California held that a case could be removed to the admiralty side of the federal court. He reasoned that certainly the cause was within the original jurisdiction of the district court, and that the "saving to suitors" provision in 28 U.S.C.A. § 1333(1) could not qualify as an express provision exempting maritime causes from the language of § 1441(a).

The holding in the *Davis* case was rejected the following year by Judge Mathes in the Southern District of California in Hill v. United Fruit Co., 149 F.Supp. 470 (S.D.Cal.1957). Judge Mathes read the "saving to suitors" clause as an option that would be nullified by removal of the case.

Since the decision in *Romero*, it has been held in a number of cases that a civil action brought in the state court under the "saving" clause may not be removed under § 1441(b) on the ground that it is within the admiralty jurisdiction. E.g., *Alleman* above. See also Linton v. Great Lakes Dredge & Dock Co., 964 F.2d 1480, 1992 A.M.C. 2789 (5th Cir.1992). In *Linton*, the court of appeals held that the fact that plaintiff had waived a jury trial did not make the action removable.

Suppose that the action is one within the exclusive jurisdiction of the federal district court. Prior to the decision in Offshore Logistics , Inc. v. Tallentire, 477 U.S. 207, 106 S.Ct. 2485, 91 L.Ed.2d 174 (1986), holding that the state courts have concurrent jurisdiction of actions under the Death on the High Seas Act, and the enactment, during the same year, of 28 U.S.C.A. § 1441(e), which eliminated the doctrine that removal jurisdiction being derivative, the DOHSA actions posed a problem, because it was not always possible to state with certitude where the death occurred. See The Marine Sulfur Queen (Cunningham v. Bethleham Steel Co.), 231 F.Supp. 934, 1965 A.M.C. 340 (S.D.N.Y.1964).

Actions under the FELA that are brought in the state court cannot be removed by the defendant. 28 U.S.C.A. § 1445(a), and this section is applied in Jones Act cases. The question arises whether a suit stating a Jones Act claim and joining it with a separate and distinct claim itself removable can be removed in its entirety under § 1441(c). See Addison v. Gulf Coast Contracting Services, Inc., 744 F.2d 494, 1985 A.M.C. 1254 (5th Cir.1984); Gonsalves v. Amoco Shipping Co., 733 F.2d 1020, 1984 A.M.C.2665 (2d Cir.1984). In neither case was the court of appeals willing to state that there might not be claims sufficiently separate to permit removal of a Jones Act claim under § 1441(c), but both courts were of the opinion that the claims under the general maritime law usually coupled with an action under the Jones Act—a claim for breach of warranty of seaworthiness and a claim for maintenance and cure—are too closely related to the Jones Act claim to justify whole case removal.

It has been held that the statutory bar to removal is waived by the litigant's failure to object to removal in the district court. Lirette v. N.L. Sperry Sun, Inc., 820 F.2d 116 (5th Cir. 1987).

And fraudulent joinder of a Jones Act claim to prevent removal. See Burchett v. Cargill, Inc., 48 F.3d 173, 1995 A.M.C. 1576 (5th Cir.1995), affirming a refusal to remand on the ground that the structure on which the plaintiff was injured was, as a matter of law, not a vessel. Compare with Lackey v. Atlantic Richfield Co., 990 F.2d 202 (5th Cir.1993) applying the same principle but finding remand proper since the defendant failed to prove that plaintiff's claim of the seaman status as a borrowed servant was fraudulent.

* * *

E. LIMITATIONS ON REMEDIES IN ADMIRALTY

Ward v. Peck

Supreme Court of the United States, 1855.
59 U.S. (18 How.) 267, 15 L.Ed. 383.

■ MR. JUSTICE GRIER delivered the opinion of the court.

The pleadings in this case present but the single question of the title or ownership of the Bark Mopang.

Originally, the court of admiralty in England entertained jurisdiction of petitory as well as mere possessory actions. Since the Restoration, that court, through the jealous interference of courts of law, had ceased to pronounce directly on questions of ownership or property. Petitory suits were silently abandoned, and, if in a possessory action a question of mere property arose, especially of a more complicated nature, it declined to interfere.

This "submission to authority rather than reason" has continued till the statute of 3 and 4 Vict. c. 65, § 4, restored to the admiralty plenary jurisdiction of such questions. See case of The Aurora, 3 Rob. 133, 136, and the Warrior, 2 Dodson, 288, 2 Brown Civ. & Ad. 430.

In this country, where the courts of admiralty have not been subjected to such jealous restraints, the ancient jurisdiction over petitory suits or causes of property has been retained. In the case of The Tilton, (5 Mason 465)(1830), Mr. Justice Story has examined this question with his usual learning and ability. The authority of that case has never been questioned in our courts. See Taylor v. Royal Saxon, 1 Wall. 322 (1863). In the case of the New England Ins. Co. v. Brig Sarah Anne, 13 Pet. 387 (1839), in this court, the only question was the title or ownership of the brig, yet the cause was entertained without any expression of doubt as to jurisdiction.

The judgment of the circuit court is affirmed.

N O T E

Mr. Justice Daniel, who we know did not share Mr. Justice Grier's admiration for Mr. Justice Story's "usual learning and ability," dissented in an opinion the flavor of which is preserved in a short quotation:

"Too true does it seem to me the case, that the ambitious and undefined pretensions of this branch of jurisprudence have found greater favor here than, in my view, is compatible with civil liberty, with public policy, or private benefit; and hence I have been the more inclined to watch and prevent its dangerous encroachments, and in all sincerity can, in contemplating the favor extended to those encroachments exclaim, *'hinc illae lachrymae.'* "

He went on to make the doleful prediction that if the theories of that civil law professor, Mr. Arthur Brown, be recognized as authority,

> "there is no excess of extravagance to be found in the exploded notions of Sir Leoline Jenkins, or anywhere else, which will not find an apology, nay, a full justification, in the book of this civil-law doctor. If the theories of this professor are to be regarded as binding, his disciples may look forward at no distant day to an announcement from this bench, as there has been formerly from that of one of the circuits, of the doctrine, that a policy of insurance (a mere wager laid upon the safety of a vessel) is strictly and essentially a maritime contract, because, forsooth, the vessel had to navigate the ocean."

As a predictor Mr. Justice Daniel was obviously better than he was as a forestaller. He died in 1860, so missed by a decade the agony of seeing his prediction materialize in Insurance Co. v. Dunham.

Rice v. Charles Dreifus Co.

United States Court of Appeals, Second Circuit, 1938.
96 F.2d 80.

■ L. HAND, CIRCUIT J. The Williamsburg–Flushing Scrap Iron Corporation appeals from a decree in the admiralty holding it primarily liable for injury to libelant's scow Elizabeth R, while being loaded with fabricated iron and steel at a pier at the foot of Gansevoort, north river. In July, 1936, the Dreifus Company had agreed in writing to buy some fabricated iron and steel of the Williamsburg–Flushing Corporation, which that company was to deliver alongside scows at a wharf at the foot of Gansevoort street. A number of barges chartered by the Dreifus Company were laded between August and October, among which was the Elizabeth R, owned by the libelant, Rice, which he had chartered to the Dreifus Company. In September, while this scow was being laden with the iron and steel, her decks were crushed because of insufficient dunnage; all agree that the Dreifus Company is liable for this damage as charterer, and the only question is whether Mitchell Lachow was in charge and the Williamsburg Corporation was his employer. Rice sued the Dreifus Company upon his charter, and the Dreifus Company impleaded the Williamsburg Corporation under the Fifty–Sixth Admiralty Rule, 28 U.S.C.A. following section 723. The judge entered a decree primarily against the Williamsburg Corporation; while its appeal was pending, a judge of this court allowed it to amend its answer by alleging a release of the Dreifus Company, and allowed that company to reply by alleging that, if the release was broad enough to cover the claim, it was executed and delivered by mutual mistake and should be reformed.

The Dreifus Company and the Williamsburg Corporation fell into differences regarding the execution of the contract we have mentioned, and the Williamsburg Corporation sued in the municipal court for goods sold and delivered. The Dreifus Company counterclaimed for delay in delivery; and while the action was pending, the parties came to a composition on February 19, 1937, by which the Dreifus Company executed and received a release and made a payment.   The general terms of this release concededly cover any claim which the Dreifus Company might have arising out of the negligence of Mitchell and Lachow and it is curious that the Williamsburg Corporation made no effort to plead it in this suit until after appeal.   The Dreifus Company asserts that in spite of its language the release was not intended to cover anything but the controversy in the municipal court; and the evidence leaves no doubt in our minds that this is true.   * * * Therefore beyond peradventure the parties did not understand that the release was to cover the cause of suit at bar, and the only question is whether these facts are available by way of reply to an answer in a suit in the admiralty.

It is true, no doubt, that the admiralty has no jurisdiction over a libel to reform a written instrument.   Justice Story so decided in Andrews v. Essex Fire & M. Ins. Co., 3 Mason 6, Fed.Cas.No. 374 (1822), and his holding has been again and again approved.   The Eclipse, 135 U.S. 599, 10 S.Ct. 873, 34 L.Ed. 269 (1890), is the chief authority in the Supreme Court upon the incapacity of an admiralty court to entertain equitable causes of suit;   there, a petition of cestuis que trustent who tried to intervene and assert their equitable rights, was refused.   In United Transportation & L. Co. v. New York & Baltimore T. Line, 185 F. 386 (2 Cir.1911), we refused to consider on the merits a cross-libel depending upon the reformation of a contract before any relief could be granted.   With the exception, however, of Meyer v. Pacific Mail S.S. Co., 58 F. 923 (D.C.Cal.1893), and Koninklijke Nederlandsche Stoomboot Maatschappij v. Yglesias & Co., 37 F.2d 103 (D.C.N.Y.1930), we have found no decision that when a release, accord and satisfaction, account stated, or other transaction of discharge is pleaded to a claim justiciable in the admiralty, the court will not pass upon any facts in avoidance which would be good in equity;   but that the libelant must file a bill in equity to enjoin the defense.   Certain it is that in libels for seamen's wages courts of admiralty have again and again felt themselves not so limited, though it must be owned that the point was always assumed sub silentio.   Whiteman v. Neptune, 1 Pet.Adm. 180, Fed.Cas.No.17,569 (1806);   Thompson v. Faussat, 1 Pet.C.C. 182, Fed.Cas.No.13,954 (1815); The David Pratt, 1 Ware 509, Fed.Cas.No.3,597 (1839);   The Topsy, 44 F. 631 (D.C.S.C.1890);   The Adonis, 38 F.2d 743 (3 Cir.1930);   Harmon v. United States, 59 F.2d 372 (5 Cir.1932).   Luckenbach S.S. Co. v. Berwind–White Coal Co., 7 F.2d 793 (2 Cir.1925), arose upon a libel for demurrage to which the respondent pleaded what was in effect an accord and satisfaction, which the libelant met by an allegation of mutual mistake, incorporated into its libel by amendment.   We held that since the cause of suit was itself maritime, we might dispose of it altogether and at once, and we considered the matter in avoidance upon its merits.   Southern Cotton Oil Co. v. United States, 84 F.2d 509 (5 Cir.1836), involved the same question, and, while the court did not apparently observe the point of jurisdiction, it too considered the merits.

The supposed embarrassment appears to us to result from failing to consider why it was ever necessary to resort to a court of chancery to avoid a transaction of discharge.   A court of law was entirely indifferent to how a release or other discharge was obtained, provided indeed that the obligee meant to execute it. Fraud, mistake, duress, and other circumstances to which equity was sensitive, were wholly irrelevant to it. The discharge was a good bar, if it was once proved; hence it was crucial for the plaintiff in some way to prevent the defendant from pleading it, else his action was lost. He could only do that by getting an injunction from a court of equity, and indeed if the defendant had the hardihood to defy the chancellor, even the injunction was fruitless. When, however, a defendant in equity pleaded a release or the like, it would have been absurd for that court to require the plaintiff to file a separate bill to enjoin its use, because any facts which would justify an injunction, would be good avoidance. Such matter therefore was always pleadable in the main suit, and if special replications had not been abolished (Street, Federal Equity Practice, § 790), it would not have appeared until the plaintiff replied. However, after general replications alone were permissible, the plaintiff's only course was either to avoid the plea in his bill in anticipation, or to amend after the defendant had pleaded it. Op.cit. §§ 791, 1093. Courts of admiralty have always professed to proceed upon equitable principles, unlike courts of law; therefore if they were not to recognize equitable avoidances of transactions of discharge, it could not be because in substance the facts were irrelevant, but for some procedural reason. However, procedure in the admiralty is proverbially plastic and no such reason exists; it must therefore be possible to reply to a release by showing grounds for reformation. We think it is. The question is of much importance, because if we are wrong, the defect would be beyond the power of Congress, being a limitation upon the constitutional powers of the admiralty court. That jurisdiction depends in our judgment altogether upon the cause of suit which the libelant brings before the court; if that be once maritime, the court may dispose of it completely without the need of any other suit in the same, or any other court; it is omnicompetent within its sphere. We do not of course mean that this extends to the entertainment of causes of action, or causes of suit, by way of cross-libel, counterclaim, or set-off, which are not themselves maritime; that is another question, and we need not concern ourselves with it now.

Decree affirmed.

The Annie H Smith

United States District Court, Southern District of New York, 1878.
10 Ben. 110, 1 F.Cas. 968.

■ CHOATE, J. This is a suit of licitation and partition brought by the owners of a moiety of the ship Annie H. Smith, against the ship and the owners of the other moiety. The libel prays a sale of the ship under the decree of the Court and the distribution of the proceeds among the owners. That the Courts of Admiralty have jurisdiction of such a suit, seems to be settled by authority, so far as this country is concerned. There are three reported cases in which the Court has entertained such a suit, and granted the relief here prayed for. They are the case of the sloop Hope in the District Court of South Carolina in 1793 (Bee's Rep. 2), the case of The Seneca in the Circuit Court for the Eastern District of Pennsylvania in 1829 (18 Amer.Jur. 486), and the case of The Vincennes in the District Court of Maine, in 1851 (cited 2 Parsons on Shipping and Adm., 343). These decisions have received the emphatic approval of eminent text writers as being in accordance with the principles of the maritime law. (Story on Partnership, § 438; Benedict's Admiralty 2d Ed., § 274; 2 Parsons A. & S. 343; Dunlap's Adm.Pr., p. 67; 2 Kent Com., 370.)

In the case of The Seneca, Judge Hopkinson, of the District Court, denied the relief on the ground that the Court had not jurisdiction, and the English Court of Admiralty has also declined to exercise this power, but the great weight of authority is in favor of the jurisdiction; and in cases where the relief is shown to be necessary, the sale by decree of the Court seems to be the only practicable means of restoring the ship to its proper use as a vehicle of commerce, and therefore highly beneficial to those public interests which are peculiarly the care of the Admiralty. The fact that the power is not exercised in England may be accounted for, perhaps, by the well known restrictions to which the jurisdiction of the English Admiralty Courts was subjected in early times through the jealousy and the greater power of the other Courts. This power of sale, so far as the cases have gone, has only been exercised where the owners are equally divided in respect to the employment of the ship or appointment of the master. Where they are unequally divided, the rights of the majority and minority owners respectively are for the most part well settled. The majority in interest have the right to employ the ship in navigation, notwithstanding the objection and protest of the minority and their refusal to join in the adventure, but in such a case the minority may require security for the safe return of the vessel. If the majority in interest unreasonably refuse to employ the ship, it has been suggested that a sale may be enforced. (Willings v. Blight, 2 Pet.Adm. 290, Fed.Cas.No.17,765 (D.C.Pa.1800).)

Of the cases where a sale has been decreed upon a disagreement between equal moiety part owners, the case of The Seneca is the only one reported with sufficient fullness to show the particular circumstances under which the power was exercised, and the views of the Court as to the reasons and grounds for the exercise of the power to decree a sale as between the equal part owners, which reasons and grounds must, of course, limit and control the action of the court, in ordering or refusing a sale in each case presented to it. In the case of The Seneca, the respondent was owner of one-half of the vessel, was in possession of her, and had made several voyages in her as master, to the dissatisfaction of the owners of the other half, whose interest the libellants had purchased; and he had projected another voyage, and insisted on fitting her out at great expense, and upon going in her as master. The libellants on the other hand had refused to incur any expense for the outfit of the vessel for a voyage to be conducted by the respondent. They had appointed or attempted to appoint another master, and were ready and willing to employ the ship. It is obvious that the disagreement between the part owners in that case was such in its nature and effect, under the circumstances in which the vessel was placed, that it operated effectually to prevent the present use or employment of the vessel at all in navigation. The parties being equal in their right to control the employment of the ship and the appointment of the master, the effect of the disagreement was, as Mr. Justice Washington distinctly points out (p. 492), that "the vessel must remain unemployed, since neither owner can otherwise than tortiously send her to sea against the will of the other."

I think, also, that it is clear from the report of the case, that it was the opinion of that learned judge, that the power of the court to interfere and order a sale depends upon this as an essential and controlling element; that in the situation of the parties and the ship, as existing when the suit is brought, the ship cannot rightfully be sent to sea by either party. And it also appears from the authorities upon which he relies as supporting his opinion, that such is the ground or one of the chief grounds upon which the power to sell rests, as the same has been declared or recognized in the foreign maritime codes to which he refers. Thus he cites with approval, the following statement of the provisions of the Roman Marine Code: "(1.) That the opinion and decision of the majority in interest of the owners concerning the employment of the vessel is to govern, and, therefore, they may on any probable design, freight out or send the ship to sea, though against the will of the minority. (2.) But if the majority refuse to employ the vessel, though they cannot be compelled to it by the minority, neither can their refusal keep the vessel idle, to the injury of the minority, or to the public detriment; and since, in such a case, the minority can neither employ her themselves, nor force the majority to do so, the vessel may be valued and sold. (3.) If the interest of the owners be equal, and they differ about the employment of the vessel, one-half being in favor of employing her, and the other opposed to it, in that case the willing owner may send her out." He also cites the 6th Article of the Marine Code of France, said to have been published as early as 1681, as follows: "No person can constrain his partner to proceed to the public sale of a ship held in common, except the opinions of the owners be equally divided about the undertaking of some voyage." And he also cites and accepts as just and reasonable, Valin's commentary on this rule, as follows: "The case excepted in this article is where the opinions of the parties are equally divided on the undertaking of some voyage, upon which we may remark, that the question is not of two equal opinions, of which one is to leave the vessel without any kind of voyage, and the other to undertake such or such a voyage, there being no doubt in that case, that the opinion favorable to a voyage ought to prevail, saving the right to discuss the projected voyage; but solely of the case of two opinions equally divided upon the particular enterprise projected by one moiety of the persons interested, and rejected by the other moiety; whether that moiety proposes, on its part, another voyage, or confines itself to a disapproval of it, provided, nevertheless, that it gives plausible reasons for its conduct; otherwise this would have the air of an absolute refusal to permit the vessel to be navigated, which justice could not tolerate, being contrary to the object of the vessel, to the original intention of the parties, and the interests of commerce." The particular point of disagreement in the case of The Seneca, was, as to who should go as master; and Mr. Justice Washington held that although not expressly mentioned in these foreign codes, the case was within their reason, because a disagreement as to the master operated as effectually as a disagreement as to the voyage to be undertaken, to prevent the ship from being sent to sea; and he held further, that if the moiety objecting to a master, honestly entertained an objection to him, on the ground of their want of confidence in his skill or integrity, they did assign a plausible reason for their conduct. From this case, therefore, and the authorities on which it rests, may be deduced these rules, as governing and limiting the exercise of this power of sale on the application of a moiety of the owners; first, that the disagreement must be such as prevents the present employment of the ship in navigation; and, secondly, that the objecting moiety asking for a sale, must either propose a different employment of the ship, or, if they merely object to the voyage or the master proposed by the other moiety, their objection must be based on reasonable grounds. And this result is entirely in accordance with the principles applied by Courts of Admiralty in dealing with the rights, duties and powers of part owners of ships, whether equally or unequally divided in opinion, and which are well expressed by Judge Peters, in the case of Willings v. Blight, 2 Peter's Adm.Dec. p. 292: "It is a principle discernible in all Maritime Codes, that every encouragement and assistance should be afforded to those who are ready to give to their ships constant employment, and this not only for the particular profit of owners, but for the general interests and prosperity of commerce. * * * "

Turning now to the facts of this particular case, it will be seen that the libellants' case does not come in either particular within the rule thus established by the case of The Seneca; the disagreement between these part owners does not operate to prevent the present employment of the ship, nor do the libellants, the party objecting to the employment of the ship proposed by the other moiety, either propose any other employment, or allege or show any plausible grounds for objection to that proposed by the other party. * * *

[The facts are set forth in detail in an omitted portion of the opinion.]

Libel dismissed with costs.

NOTE

Although Supplemental Rule D provides for in rem proceedings in possessory, petitory, and partition actions, the procedures there provided are available only when there is admiralty jurisdiction. Thus when the action for possession of a vessel rested on the breach of a contract of sale, which was not a maritime contract, in rem process could not be had under Rule D. Cary Marine, Inc. v. Motorvessel Papillon, 872 F.2d 751 (6th Cir.1989).

Archawski v. Hanioti

Supreme Court of the United States, 1956.
350 U.S. 532, 76 S.Ct. 617, 100 L.Ed. 676.

■ MR. JUSTICE DOUGLAS delivered the opinion of the Court.

Dist Ct - adjvs.
Ct. Appeals: CL

The sole question in the case is whether the cause of action alleged comes within the admiralty jurisdiction of the District Court. The District Court held that this was an action on a maritime contract, within the admiralty jurisdiction, 129 F.Supp. 410. The Court of Appeals reversed, holding that the suit was in the nature of the old common law *indebitatus assumpsit* for money had and received, based upon the wrongful withholding of money. 223 F.2d 406. The case is here on a petition for certiorari which we granted, 350 U.S. 872, because of the seeming conflict of that ruling with Krauss Bros. Lumber Co. v. Dimon S.S. Corp., 290 U.S. 117, 124, 54 S.Ct. 105, 107, 78 L.Ed. 216 (1933).[1]

The libel alleges that respondent, doing business in his own and in various trade names, owned and controlled a passenger vessel, known as the City of Athens, and held out that vessel as a common carrier of passengers for hire, and that petitioners paid moneys for passage upon the vessel, scheduled for July 15, 1947, to Europe. A contract for the transportation of passengers is a maritime contract within admiralty jurisdiction.[2] The Moses Taylor, 4 Wall. 411, 18 L.Ed. 397 (1866). The allegations so far mentioned are plainly sufficient to establish such a contract. The libel goes on to allege a breach of that contract through an abandonment of the voyage. If this were all, it would be plain that petitioners stated a claim for breach of a maritime contract. But the libel further alleges that the sums paid by petitioners as passage money were "wrongfully and deliberately" applied by respondent to his own use and benefit "in reckless disregard of his obligations to refund the same" and that respondent "has secreted himself away and manipulated his assets * * * for the purpose of defrauding" petitioners. Then follow allegations of certain fraudulent acts and transactions.

The allegations of wrongfulness and fraud do not alter the essential character of the libel. For the ancient admiralty teaching is that, "The rules of pleading in the admiralty are exceedingly simple and free from technical requirements." Dupont de Nemours & Co. v. Vance, 19 How. 162, 171–172, 15 L.Ed. 584 (1856). And see 2 Benedict, American Admiralty (6th ed. 1940), §§ 223, 237. Though these particular allegations of the libel sound in fraud or in the wrongful withholding of moneys, it is plain in the context that the obligation to pay the moneys arose because of a breach of the contract to transport passengers. Lawyers speak of the obligation in terms of *indebitatus assumpsit,* a concept whose tortuous development gave

---

1. There is also an apparent conflict with Sword Line v. United States, 228 F.2d 344, 346 (1955), decided, after we granted certiorari, by a different panel of the Second Circuit from the one which sat in the instant case.

2. The Court in New Jersey Steam Navigation Company v. Merchant's Bank, 6 How. 344, 392, 12 L.Ed. 465 (1848), stated that in determining admiralty jurisdiction the inquiry is "into the nature and subject-matter of the contract,—whether it was a maritime contract, and the service a maritime service, to be performed upon the sea, or upon waters within the ebb and flow of the tide. And, again, whether the service was to be substantially performed upon the sea, or tide-waters, although it had commenced and had terminated beyond the reach of the tide; if it was, then jurisdiction has always been maintained."

expression to "the ethical character of the law." See Ames, The History of Assumpsit, 2 Harv.L.Rev. 1, 53, 58 (1888). As Mr. Justice Holmes once put it, "An obligation to pay money generally is enforced by an action of assumpsit and to that extent is referred to a contract even though it be one existing only by fiction of law." Thomas v. Matthiessen, 232 U.S. 221, 235, 34 S.Ct. 312, 314, 58 L.Ed. 577 (1914).

The fiction sometimes distorted the law. A line of authorities emerged to the effect that admiralty had no jurisdiction to grant relief in such cases "because the implied promise to repay the moneys which cannot in good conscience be retained—necessary to support the action for money had and received—is not a maritime contract."[3] United Transp. & L. Co. v. New York & B.T. Line, 185 F. 386, 391 (1911). Yet that duty to pay is often referable, as here, to the breach of a maritime contract. As Mr. Justice Stone said in Krauss Bros. Co. v. Dimon S.S. Corp., supra, at 124:

> "* * * Even under the common law form of action for money had and received there could be no recovery without proof of the breach of the contract involved in demanding the payment, and the basis of recovery there, as in admiralty, is the violation of some term of the contract of affreightment, whether by failure to carry or by exaction of freight which the contract did not authorize."

The truth is that in a case such as the present one there is neither an actual promise to repay the passage moneys nor a second contract. The problem is to prevent unjust enrichment from a maritime contract. See Morrison, The Remedial Powers of the Admiralty, 43 Yale L.J. 1, 27 (1933). A court that prevents a maritime contract from being exploited in that way does not reach beyond the domain of maritime affairs. We conclude that, so long as the claim asserted arises out of a maritime contract, the admiralty court has jurisdiction over it.

The philosophy of *indebitatus assumpsit* is, indeed, not wholly foreign to admiralty. Analogous conceptions of rights based on quasi-contract are found in admiralty. One who saves property at sea has the right to an award of salvage, regardless of any agreement between him and the owner. See Mason v. Ship Blaireau, 2 Cranch 240, 266, 2 L.Ed. 266 (1804); The Sabine, 101 U.S. 384, 390, 25 L.Ed. 982 (1879); 1 Benedict, supra § 117 et seq. Likewise, where cargo is jettisoned, the owner becomes entitled to a contribution in general average from the owners of other cargo which was saved without the aid of any agreement. See Barnard v. Adams, 10 How. 270, 303–304, 13 L.Ed. 417 (1850); Star of Hope, 9 Wall. 203, 228–230, 19 L.Ed. 638 (1869); 1 Benedict, supra, § 98. Other examples could be given. See Chandler, Quasi Contractual Relief in Admiralty, 27 Mich.L.Rev. 23 (1928). Rights which admiralty recognizes as serving the ends of justice are often indistinguishable from ordinary quasi-contractual rights created to prevent unjust enrichment. How far the concept of quasi-contracts may be applied in admiralty it is unnecessary to decide. It is sufficient this day

---

3. And see Israel v. Moore & McCormack Co., 295 F. 919 (D.C.N.Y.1920); Home Ins. Co. v. Merchant's Transp. Co., 16 F.2d 372 (9 Cir.1927); Silva v. Bankers Commercial Corp., 163 F.2d 602 (2 Cir.1947).

to hold that admiralty has jurisdiction, even where the libel reads like *indebitatus assumpsit* at common law, provided that the unjust enrichment arose as a result of the breach of a maritime contract. Such is the case here.

The judgment is reversed and the case is remanded to the Court of Appeals for proceedings in conformity with this opinion.

Reversed and remanded.

Marine Transit Corp. v. Dreyfus

Supreme Court of the United States, 1932.
284 U.S. 263, 52 S.Ct. 166, 76 L.Ed. 282.

■ MR. CHIEF JUSTICE HUGHES delivered the opinion of the Court.

The petitioner, Marine Transit Corporation, entered into a written booking agreement with the respondents, Louis Dreyfus & Company, to furnish insurable canal tonnage for about 200,000 bushels of wheat, to be carried from Buffalo to New York. The contract provided that it should be "subject to New York Produce Exchange Canal Grain Charter Party No. 1 as amended." That charter party contained the following provision as to disputes:

"All disputes arising under this contract to be arbitrated before the Committee on Grain of the New York Produce Exchange whose decision shall be final and binding."

Under this contract, the Marine Transit Corporation, in September, 1928, provided the barge Edward A. Ryan to carry 19,200 bushels of the above-stated amount. This was a shipment, as the bill of lading of the Marine Transit Corporation shows, to the order of the Bank of Nova Scotia and was from Fort William, Ontario, "in bond, for export," to be delivered "on surrender of original Lake bill of lading properly endorsed." While in tow of the petitioner's tug Gerald A. Fagan on the New York Barge Canal, and approaching the federal lock at Troy, the Edward A. Ryan struck the guide wall and sank with its cargo. The respondents, Louis Dreyfus & Company, filed a libel in admiralty against the Marine Transit Corporation in personam, and against the tug Gerald A. Fagan, in rem, to recover damages for the loss of the wheat. The libel was also against a barge John E. Enright, one of the boats in the tow, but the action as to that boat was subsequently discontinued. A claim for the tug Gerald A. Fagan was made by the Marine Transit Corporation and a stipulation for value was filed by it, as claimant, in the sum of $26,000, with the usual provision that the stipulation should be void if the claimant and the stipulator (the Continental Casualty Company) should abide by all orders of the court and pay the amount awarded by its final decree, and that otherwise the stipulation should remain in full force.

After answer to the libel had been filed by the Marine Transit Corporation, as respondent and as claimant of the tug Gerald A. Fagan, the libellants moved for a reference of the dispute to arbitration in accordance with the provision of the booking contract. This motion was granted "only as to the issues raised by the contract between the libellants and the Marine Transit Corporation," and the latter was ordered to submit to arbitration as to these issues before the Committee on Grain of the New York Produce Exchange. The arbitration proceeded and resulted in an award against the Marine Transit Corporation for the sum of $23,016, with interest and the costs and expenses of the arbitration. The award was confirmed by the District Court and an order—in substance, a final decree—was entered for the recovery by the libellants against the Marine Transit Corporation of the amount of the award, with the further provision that, if payment was not made within ten days, execution should issue against the Marine Transit Corporation and the stipulator. A motion to restrain the libellants from recovering from the claimant or its stipulator on behalf of the tug Gerald A. Fagan was denied. The decree entered upon the award was affirmed by the Circuit Court of Appeals, 49 F.2d 215, and the case comes here on writ of certiorari.

There is no question that the controversy between the petitioner and the respondents was within the arbitration clause of the booking contract. That provision was valid, Red Cross Line v. Atlantic Fruit Co., 264 U.S. 109, 122, 44 S.Ct. 274, 68 L.Ed. 582 (1924), and, as it related to all disputes arising under the contract, it applied to the controversy with the Marine Transit Corporation as operating owner of the tug Gerald A. Fagan, which was used for the agreed transportation. The questions presented are (1) whether the action of the District Court was authorized by the United States Arbitration Act,[1] and (2) whether that Act, as thus applied, is constitutional.

First. In construing the statute, we deal only with the questions raised by the present record. The loss occurred upon a waterway which was part of the navigable waters of the United States, The Robert W. Parsons, 191 U.S. 17, 24 S.Ct. 8, 48 L.Ed. 73 (1903), and while the cargo was being transported by the petitioner under a maritime contract. The subject matter of the controversy thus lay within the jurisdiction of admiralty. The ambiguities of the statute have been stressed in argument, but we think that its provisions embrace a case such as the one before us[2] and it is not necessary to discuss others. Section 4 authorizes a court, which would otherwise have jurisdiction in admiralty "of the subject matter of a suit arising out of the controversy between the parties" to a written agreement for arbitration, to "make an order directing the parties to proceed to arbitration in accordance with the terms of the agreement."

1. Act of February 12, 1925, c. 213, 43 Stat. 883; [U.S.C.A., Tit. 9, §§ 1–15] * * *

2. The Committee on the Judiciary of the House of Representatives, in its report upon the bill, which with the Senate amendment became the Act in question, said:

"The purpose of this bill is to make valid and enforcible agreements for arbitration contained in contracts involving interstate commerce or within the jurisdiction of admiralty, or which may be the subject of litigation in the federal courts * * *. The remedy is founded also upon the federal control over interstate commerce and over admiralty." House Rep. No. 96, 68th Cong., 1st Sess. See, also, Cong.Rec., vol. 66, pt. 3, 68th Cong., 2d Sess., pp. 3003, 3004.

Section 8 explicitly provides that where a cause of action is "otherwise justiciable in admiralty, then, notwithstanding anything herein to the contrary, the party claiming to be aggrieved may begin his proceeding hereunder by libel and seizure of the vessel or other property of the other party according to the usual course of admiralty proceedings," and the court may then "direct the parties to proceed with the arbitration and shall retain jurisdiction to enter its decree upon the award."

In this instance, the libel against the vessel came directly within the provision of § 8. * * * We conclude that the order directing the arbitration of the issues arising under the contract between the libellants and the Marine Transit Corporation was authorized by the statute. * * *

Second. The constitutional question raised by this application of the statute, is whether it is compatible with the maintenance of the judicial power of the United States as extended to cases of admiralty and maritime jurisdiction (Const. Art. III).

In Red Cross Line v. Atlantic Fruit Co., supra (at pp. 122, 123), this Court pointed out that in admiralty "agreements to submit controversies to arbitration are valid," and that "reference of maritime controversies to arbitration has long been common practice." "An executory agreement," said the court, "may be made a rule of court" and the "substantive right created by an agreement to submit disputes to arbitration is recognized as a perfect obligation." The question, then, is one merely as to the power of the Congress to afford a remedy in admiralty to enforce such an obligation. It was because the question was one of remedy only, that this Court decided that a State, by virtue of the clause saving to suitors "the right of a common law remedy,"[3] had the power "to confer upon its courts the authority to compel parties within its jurisdiction to specifically perform an agreement for arbitration, which is valid by the general maritime law, as well as by the law of the State," and is contained in a maritime contract made within the State and there to be performed. Red Cross Line v. Atlantic Fruit Co., supra, at p. 124. The general power of the Congress to provide remedies in matters falling within the admiralty jurisdiction of the federal courts, and to regulate their procedure, is indisputable. The petitioner contends that the Congress could not confer upon courts of admiralty the authority to grant specific performance. But it is well settled that the Congress, in providing appropriate means to enforce obligations cognizable in admiralty, may draw upon other systems. Thus the Congress may authorize a trial by jury in admiralty, as it has done in relation to certain cases arising on the Great Lakes.[4] Courts of Admiralty may be empowered to grant injunctions, as in proceedings for limitation of liability.[5] Similarly, there can be no question of the power of Congress to

3. Judicial Code, § 24(3); U.S.C.A., Tit. 28, § 41(3).

4. Act of February 26, 1845, c. 20, 5 Stat. 726; R.S. 566; U.S.C.A., Tit. 28, § 770; The Genesee Chief, 12 How. 443, 459, 460, 13 L.Ed. 1058 (1851); The Eagle, 8 Wall. 15, 25, 19 L.Ed. 365 (1868).

5. Hartford Accident & Indemnity Co. v. Southern Pacific Co., 273 U.S. 207, 218, 47 S.Ct. 357, 360, 71 L.Ed. 612 (1927).

authorize specific performance when that is an appropriate remedy in a matter within the admiralty jurisdiction. As Chief Justice Taney said in The Genesee Chief, 12 How. 443, 460, 13 L.Ed. 1058 (1851): "The Constitution declares that the judicial power of the United States shall extend to 'all cases of admiralty and maritime jurisdiction.' But it does not direct that the court shall proceed according to ancient and established forms, or shall adopt any other form or mode of practice. * * * In admiralty and maritime cases there is no such limitation as to the mode of proceeding, and Congress may therefore in cases of that description give either party right of trial by jury, or modify the practice of the court in any other respect that it deems more conducive to the administration of justice."

In this instance a remedy is provided to fit the agreement. The Congress has authorized the court to direct the parties to proceed to arbitration in accordance with a valid stipulation of a maritime contract, and to enter a decree upon the award found to be regular and within the terms of the agreement. We think that the objection on constitutional grounds is without merit.

Decree affirmed.

Kynoch v. The Propeller S.C. Ives

United States District Court, Northern District of Ohio, 1856.
1 Newb. 205, 14 F.Cas. 888.

The libel was filed August 6th, 1856, and sets forth that on the 9th day of May, 1856, the claimant, Wm. C. Neilson, being the owner of the propeller S.C. Ives (then called the Dick Tinto), entered into a contract for the sale to the libelant, of one-half of said propeller, her steam pump, submarine armors, & c., * * *.

The libel further alleged that as a part of the consideration of said contract, it was agreed that Kynoch should have the sole charge and management of the propeller, and that she should be employed in the business of wrecking: that the propeller had been fitted out according to the contract, payment tendered by the libelant, and possession and a conveyance of a moiety demanded, but that said Neilson refused to make any conveyance or give possession, declaring it to be his intention to send the propeller on a voyage to the St. Clair river, beyond the reach of libelant.

The libel, therefore, prayed process against the propeller, and a decree for the possession, offering to give bonds pendente lite for her safe return to abide the decree, and also for a monition to Neilson to show cause why he should not be required to perform, all and singular, the undertakings to his agreement.

To this libel, exceptions to the jurisdiction of the court were filed by Willey & Cary, proctors for claimants, on a preliminary hearing of which the court refused to grant possession to the libelant, but ordered possession to be redelivered to the claimant Neilson, on his entering into the usual stipulation, with sureties, & c. * * *

■ WILLSON, J. The libel in this case, partakes much of the character of a bill in chancery, which seeks to enforce the specific performance of a contract, for the purchase of property. It also seeks the further object of obtaining, for the libelant, the possession and control of the propeller S.C. Ives.

The only question in the case, is, has this court jurisdiction of the subject matter of the suit?

As a preliminary inquiry, it is proper to examine and determine the effect of the contract referred to in the libel, upon the title to the moiety of the vessel claimed to be purchased; or in other words, to determine the question whether Kynoch obtained by the contract, a legal, or only an equitable title to the property. * * *

I am clear that Kynoch obtained by the agreement only an equitable interest in the vessel.

If the libelant, then, has only an equitable title to the property, how stands this suit? We have in the record the case presented: First, an equitable owner, not in possession, seeking by a proceeding in rem, the interposition of a court of admiralty to give control of the vessel; and second, a demand upon a court of admiralty to decree the specific performance of a contract for the purchase of vessel property.

It has long been settled that a court of admiralty will not hold an equitable title sufficient to justify its interposition against a legal title to obtain possession, although it may sometimes deem such an equitable interest sufficient to restrain it from interference with an existing possession under it. The province of the admiralty is to carry into effect the declarations of the maritime law. Titles to ships and vessels depend chiefly upon the maritime law, as recognized and enforced in the common law. It is laid down by Godolphin, and also by Brown and in Clerk's Praxes, that suits in admiralty touching property in ships, are of two kinds; one called petitory suits, in which the mere title to the property is litigated and sought to be enforced, independently of any possession which has accompanied or sanctioned that title; the other, called possessory suits, which seek to restore to the owner the possession, of which he has been unjustly deprived, when that possession has followed a legal title, or as it is sometimes phrased, when there has been a possession under a claim of title with a constat of property.

I am aware, that so far as the question of jurisdiction is concerned, this distinction between petitory and possessory suits has never obtained recognition by the courts in this country. The early decision of Judge Story in the case of De Lovio v. Boit, 2 Gal. 398, Fed.Cas.No.3,776 (1815), furnished an authority which has been acted upon with confidence by the courts ever since. And this distinction has lately been substantially abolished even in England by the 3 and 4 Victoria, entitled "An act to improve the practice and extend the jurisdiction of the high Court of Admiralty" in England.

But with all this growing liberality and modern favor towards the jurisdiction of the courts, it has never been held or claimed anywhere, that in contests between part owners of a ship for possession or disputes about title, the admiralty would entertain jurisdiction to support an equitable title for either purpose. Possession must follow the legal title, and that title lies at the foundation of the jurisdiction. It belongs to other tribunals to establish the legal title, and when that is done, such title brings with it all its incidents in controversies between part owners in courts of admiralty.

Upon the first proposition, therefore, I hold that the libelant not having had possession of the propeller, cannot, upon a mere equitable title, come into this court and ask possession and control of the vessel.

In the second place, can the demand made in this libel for the specific performance of the contract in question, be enforced in the admiralty?

Courts of admiralty have no general jurisdiction to administer relief as courts of equity. If a maritime contract is broken, the admiralty, concurrent with courts of law, can only give damages for the breach of it; whereas the chancery may compel the party, in some cases, to a specific performance. A court of admiralty has no more power to decree such specific performance, than it has to set aside the contract for fraud, or correct a mistake, or decree the execution of a trust. These are matters properly subject to the cognizance of courts of equity and not of the admiralty. Both courts have their origin in the polity of the civil law. From the time the Rhodian Code was incorporated into the Pandects, the maritime law has ever been declared in written ordinances and codes of maritime regulations. The admiralty courts had no power to modify or change them. On the contrary the Praetors of Rome exercised jurisdiction in cases where there was no written law to govern them, and granted relief where, by the enforcement of the written law, equity and good conscience would be perverted.   * * *

Such departure from written ordinances and codes of maritime regulations was never known in courts of admiralty, although, as to form, their course of proceeding has always been in accordance with the Roman law.

But the decisions of our own courts are decisive of the question. In the case of Andrews & Shepherd v. Essex Fire and Marine Ins. Co., 3 Mason R. 16 (1822), Mr. Justice Story broadly declares that courts of admiralty cannot entertain a libel for specific performance, or to correct a mistake, or to grant relief against fraud. Courts of admiralty, he says, "have jurisdiction over maritime contracts when executed, but not over those leading to the execution of maritime contracts. If there were a contract to build a ship, or to sign a shipping paper, or to execute a bottomry bond, and the party refused to perform it, the admiralty cannot take jurisdiction and enforce its performance. But if the contract be maritime and executed, the jurisdiction attaches; and the admiralty may then administer relief upon it according to equity and good conscience. The law looks to the proximate, and not to the remote cause, as the source of jurisdiction, and deals with it only when it has assumed its final shape as a maritime contract."

Such being the rules of law governing the admiralty jurisdiction of this court, it follows that we have not cognizance of the subject matter of this suit in a proceeding in rem.

But it was claimed by the counsel for the libelant, in the argument, that the contract of purchase being maritime, the case should be retained and proceeded with in personam upon the question of damages for a breach of the contract.

It is, perhaps, unnecessary to determine whether this contract is, in its nature, maritime or not. * * *

The obstacle in the way here is not necessarily in the character of the contract, but in the mode of procedure claimed by counsel. The twenty-second rule in admiralty prescribed by the Supreme Court of the United States, directs the mode of procedure in all petitory or possessory suits between part owners or adverse proprietors of a ship. It declares the process shall be by an arrest of the vessel and by a monition to the adverse party to appear and make answer to the suit. The rule requires a joint proceeding in rem and in personam. The libel is the foundation for the action of the court, and it determines the character of the decree. It cannot be amended to change the form of the action any more than a proceeding in the common law action of ejectment could be changed into an action of trespass.

Such, however, would be the case if the suit should now be allowed to proceed in personam. An amended libel seeking damages for a breach of the contract would be the virtual institution of a new suit, and a novelty in admiralty practice.

The exceptions to the jurisdiction of the court are sustained, and the libel dismissed without prejudice.

Swift & Company Packers v. Compania Colombiana Del Caribe, S. A.

Supreme Court of the United States, 1950.
339 U.S. 684, 70 S.Ct. 861, 94 L.Ed. 1206.

■ MR. JUSTICE FRANKFURTER delivered the opinion of the Court.

The question before us is the propriety of an order of the District Court for the Canal Zone vacating a foreign attachment of a vessel made in a libel in personam. We granted certiorari because important questions relating to the scope of admiralty jurisdiction and its exercise are in issue. 338 U.S. 813, 70 S.Ct. 76, 94 L.Ed. 492.

On March 7, 1948, the libel was filed against Compania Transmaritima Colombiana, S. A., a Colombian corporation, by Swift & Company Packers, a Nevada corporation, certain Cuban corporations and individuals, and a Colombian citizen. They brought the libel as owners of rice shipped from

Ecuador to Cuba. It was alleged that the cargo had been delivered in good order to the M/V Cali, owned and operated by Transmaritima, and that the vessel had sunk, or partially sunk, off the island of Grand Cayman with resulting nondelivery of the cargo. This was supplemented by allegations of negligence. Process was prayed with the further request that if the respondent could not be found its goods and chattels be attached, particularly a vessel known as the Alacran, or Caribe. This vessel was thereupon attached by the marshal.

On March 8, libellants filed a supplemental and amended libel, and on the basis of the following allegations joined the Compania Colombiana Del Caribe, S. A., as respondent. On or shortly prior to March 4, the Compania Del Caribe had been organized under the laws of Colombia and the Alacran had been transferred by Transmaritima to Del Caribe in fraud of the rights of libellants. The latter company had been organized by directors, officers and stockholders of Transmaritima, but no funds had been paid into its treasury for the issue of its stock, and the transfer of the Alacran was without real consideration. Del Caribe was "merely the creature or alter ego" of Transmaritima and "they should be held to be, as they are, one and the same." Del Caribe, on or about March 4, had had the vessel's name changed from Alacran to Caribe, and a new register had been issued accordingly. In the alternative, the claim was that Del Caribe was indebted to Transmaritima for at least a substantial part if not all of the purchase price of the Caribe.

Attachment of the vessel was again prayed on what appears to have been either of two grounds: since Transmaritima and Del Caribe were really one and the same, it mattered not which was deemed to be the owner of the Caribe; since the transfer of the Caribe to Del Caribe was a fraudulent transfer to be set aside, the vessel was in reality Transmaritima's property and Del Caribe should be garnished. On the basis of the amended libel another attachment of the Caribe was made. * * *

On August 16, Del Caribe gave notice of a motion to dismiss the libel as to it and vacate the attachment. Various grounds were urged calling into question the jurisdiction of the court, the propriety of its exercise, and the adequacy of the allegations to state a claim in the libel. An accompanying affidavit set forth matters relating to the transfer.

On September 20, the District Court found that the nondelivery of the cargo was due to the beaching of the Cali in January, 1948; that Del Caribe had been organized in the latter part of February, 1948; and that Transmaritima had sold and transferred the Caribe to Del Caribe on February 25. From these facts the district judge concluded that there was no jurisdiction in admiralty to inquire into the relations between the two respondent companies or the sale of the Caribe. In any event, the court declined to exercise jurisdiction to look into the transfer since it had taken place between two foreign corporations and in a foreign country. Accordingly, the attachment was ordered to be vacated. While libellants submitted additional evidence upon a rehearing, the court adhered to its original views. 83 F.Supp. 273.

The Court of Appeals affirmed. It held that jurisdiction to set aside a fraudulent transfer before judgment on the main claim was at best "doubtful," that there was discretion to decline jurisdiction on principles of forum non conveniens, and that, in any event, libellants had not sustained their burden of producing proof that the transfer was fraudulent. 175 F.2d 513.

This we believe to be a fair résumé of an uncommonly confused and opaque record. It is especially hampering that the record is not clearer than it is when legal issues of real complexity are in controversy. * * *

On finding that the Caribe had been sold by Transmaritima to Del Caribe prior to the filing of the libel, the District Court deemed itself without jurisdiction to determine whether the transfer was fraudulent. In consequence it felt compelled to treat Del Caribe as the owner of the vessel, and since only the property of Transmaritima could be validly attached the attachment had to be vacated.

The reasoning of the District Court was based on the view that a claim of fraud in the transfer of a vessel was a matter for determination by a court of equity and therefore outside the bounds of admiralty jurisdiction. There is a good deal of loose talk to this effect in the reports, concurrent with talk that courts of admiralty exercise their jurisdiction upon equitable principles. Even as to admiralty jurisdiction we must be wary of verbal generalizations unrelated to their applications. Not the least creative achievement of judicial law-making is the body of doctrines that has been derived from the brief words of the Constitution extending the judicial power "to all Cases of admiralty and maritime Jurisdiction." U.S.Const. Art. III, para. 2. But it would be beyond human achievement even of a long line of judges especially equipped for dealing with admiralty matters to have produced a wholly harmonious body of admiralty law, or to have written opinions that should not have lent themselves through largeness or looseness of statement beyond the scope of their adjudications.

Unquestionably a court of admiralty will not enforce an independent equitable claim merely because it pertains to maritime property. E.g., The Eclipse, 135 U.S. 599, 608, 10 S.Ct. 873, 875, 34 L.Ed. 269 (1890), and cases cited. The reasoning of the District Court would be pertinent if the libellants, as creditors of Transmaritima, had gone into admiralty by way of a creditor's bill to set aside a pretended sale of the Caribe as a fraudulent transfer. But that is not the case before us. Libellants went into admiralty on a claim arising upon a contract of affreightment supplemented by charges of negligence in the nondelivery of a sea cargo—matters obviously within admiralty jurisdiction. As an incident to that claim, in order to secure respondents' appearance and to insure the fruits of a decree in libellants' favor, they made an attachment under General Admiralty Rule 2. The issue of fraud arises in connection with the attachment as a means of effectuating a claim incontestably in admiralty. To deny an admiralty court jurisdiction over this subsidiary or derivative issue in a litigation clearly maritime would require an absolute rule that admiralty is rigorously excluded from all contact with nonmaritime transactions and from all equitable relief, even though such nonmaritime transactions come into play, and such equitable relief is sought, in the course of admiralty's exercise of its jurisdiction over a matter exclusively maritime. It would be strange indeed thus to hobble a legal system that has been so responsive to the practicalities of maritime commerce and so inventive in adapting its jurisdiction to the needs of that commerce. Controversies between admiralty and common law are familiar legal history. See Mr. Justice Story's classic opinion in De Lovio v. Boit, 7 Fed.Cas. 418, No. 3,776, 2 Gall. 398 (1815); 4 Benedict on Admiralty cc. 61–63 (Knauth ed. 1940). We find no restriction upon admiralty by chancery so unrelenting as to bar the grant of any equitable relief even when that relief is subsidiary to issues wholly within admiralty jurisdiction. Certainly there is no ground for believing that this restriction was accepted as a matter of course by the framers of the Constitution so that such sterilization of admiralty jurisdiction can be said to have been presupposed by Article III of the Constitution.

A few illustrative cases will take us out of the fog of generalities, for the decisions dealing with concrete situations afford a working approach even if not a rigid rule.

Nonmaritime contracts may be examined to determine whether they constitute a valid defense, although the same contracts will not support a libel or cross-libel for affirmative relief. Armour & Co. v. Fort Morgan S. S. Co., 270 U.S. 253, 258–60, 46 S.Ct. 212, 213, 70 L.Ed. 571 (1926). An equitable claim which does not support a possessory suit may be availed of as a valid defense against a similar suit by the holder of legal title. Chirurg v. Knickerbocker Steam Towage Co., 174 F. 188 (1910); cf. The Daisy, 29 F. 300 (1887); see Morrison, Remedial Powers of the Admiralty, 43 Yale L.J. 1, 21 (1933). Admiralty cannot entertain a suit to reform a release from liability executed under a mutual mistake merely because it pertains to a maritime claim; but when such a release is pleaded in defense against assertion of that claim, admiralty is not barred from determining whether it was executed by the parties under mutual mistake. Rice v. Charles Dreifus Co., 96 F.2d 80. And so as to accounting, "It is true that a court of admiralty will not entertain a suit for an accounting as such: as, for example, an accounting between co-owners of a vessel, or between maritime adventurers, or between principal and agent * * * [citing cases]. Nevertheless, it has never been true, when an accounting is necessary to the complete adjustment of rights over which admiralty has independent jurisdiction, that it will suspend its remedies midway and require the parties to resort to another court." W. E. Hedger Transp. Corp. v. Ira S. Bushey & Sons, Inc., 155 F.2d 321, 323 (2 Cir.1946), per Learned Hand, J.

In each of these cases a holding that admiralty must stay its hands as to a matter intrinsically nonmaritime but "necessary to the complete adjustment of rights over which admiralty has independent jurisdiction" would have seriously impaired the discharge by admiralty of the task which belongs to it. To recognize these subsidiary powers of admiralty to deal justly with the claims that are within its jurisdiction is not to enlarge the admiralty jurisdiction but to avoid its mutilating restriction. To generalize beyond this is to invite misleading or empty abstractions.

We can now see the immediate problem in its proper perspective. The process of foreign attachment is known of old in admiralty. It has two purposes: to secure a respondent's appearance and to assure satisfaction in case the suit is successful. Manro v. Almeida, 10 Wheat. 473, 489, 6 L.Ed. 369 (1825). While the process may be utilized only when a respondent is not found within the jurisdiction, an attachment is not dissolved by the subsequent appearance of respondent. See Birdsall v. Germain Co., 227 F. 953, 955 (1915); 2 Benedict on Admiralty § 290 (Knauth ed. 1940). Disputes over ownership of attached vessels are of course inevitable since only the respondent's property may be attached. E.g., Cushing v. Laird, 107 U.S. 69, 2 S.Ct. 196, 27 L.Ed. 391 (1883); cf. McGahern v. Koppers Coal Co., 108 F.2d 652 (3 Cir.1940); Kingston Dry Dock Co. v. Lake Champlain Transp. Co., 31 F.2d 265 (2 Cir.1929). Inevitably such disputes may involve transactions not themselves the subject matter of an independent libel. If jurisdiction be wanting in a court of admiralty when such a controversy arises in the context of an attachment made in a libel over which the court indubitably has jurisdiction, a congenital defect would have to be attributed to the ancient process of foreign attachment. If colorable transfers of property were immune to challenge in a court of admiralty when a libel in personam has been brought in a District where the respondent cannot be personally served, admiralty jurisdiction would be sacrificed to a sterile theory of judicial separatism. No support for such a conclusion is to be found in any decision of this Court or in those of the lower courts which have had so large a share in the development of admiralty law. The relevant rulings look the other way.

In Lee v. Thompson, 15 Fed.Cas. 233, No. 8,202, 3 Woods 167 (1878), Mr. Justice Bradley held that an admiralty court had power to look into an allegedly fraudulent transfer where the question was relevant to execution upon a decree in admiralty. He fully recognized that a libel based solely on the transfer could not be maintained, but where that issue was "incidental to its general jurisdiction, and for maintaining the same, it [the admiralty court] has plenary power to decide, and frequently does decide, conflicting claims to property. Without such power its jurisdiction would often be defeated." 15 Fed.Cas. at 235; 3 Woods at 173. The force of Mr. Justice Bradley's decision is sought to be cut down in that it dealt with execution on a judgment and not with an attachment. The fact is, however, that Mr. Justice Bradley relied in his reasoning on the process of foreign attachment, and reason rejects any significant distinction between the jurisdiction of admiralty to inquire into a fraudulent transfer in the two situations. In both admiralty is not seized of jurisdiction to correct a fraud simply because it is a fraud; that's the business of equity. The basis of admiralty's power is to protect its jurisdiction from being thwarted by a fraudulent transfer, and that applies equally whether it is concerned with executing its judgment or authorizing an attachment to secure an independent maritime claim. Cf. The New York, 113 F. 810; The Columbia, 100 F. 890 (judgment in admiralty vacated because obtained by fraud).

We must conclude that the District Court was not without power to look into the transfer of the Caribe under the circumstances of this suit. * * *

The case must be reversed and remanded for proceedings not inconsistent with this opinion.

Reversed and remanded.

NOTE

Independent of the applicability of the pendent jurisdiction doctrine in admiralty proceedings, there is the question of the extent to which the court may issue injunctions in matters ancillary to the proceeding. See Lewis v. S.S. Baune, 534 F.2d 1115, 1976 A.M.C. 1275 (5th Cir.1976). There the court of appeals held that in an admiralty action the district court had jurisdiction to issue an injunction prohibiting the defendants from harassing the plaintiffs. The court did not draw a clear distinction between ancillary and pendent jurisdiction. Even if there would be no jurisdiction of a claim for an injunction in the complaint, would the holding in S.S. Baune—Key Trader be proper?

See Merrill-Stevens Dry Dock Co. v. The Laissez Faire, 421 F.2d 430, 1970 A.M.C. 38 (5th Cir.1970), where it was held that the district court may set aside a marshall's sale for fraud.

The general statement in *Swift and Company* that admiralty courts will apply equitable principles to matters within their jurisdiction was applied in Montauk Oil Transp. Corp. v. Sonat Marine, Inc., 871 F.2d 1169 (2d Cir.1989), in which the court of appeals held that a misstatement of an employee of the vessel owner to the charterer about the possibility of terminating the charter made it inequitable to charge the charterer with a full hire for 20 days during which the subject barge and tug sat idle during a strike delay.

Swift and Company was distinguished in Atlanta Shipping Corp. v. Chemical Bank, 818 F.2d 240 (2d Cir.1987), when the plaintiff sought to void a transfer in an action in which there was no admiralty jurisdiction of any primary claim.

Pino v. Protection Maritime Ins. Co., Ltd.

United States Court of Appeals, First Circuit, 1979.
599 F.2d 10, 1979 A.M.C. 2459, cert. denied 444 U.S. 900, 100 S.Ct. 210, 62 L.Ed.2d 136 (1979).

■ LEVIN H. CAMPBELL, CIRCUIT JUDGE.

This admiralty case involves allegations that the defendant maritime insurance companies,[1] owned and operated by Ernest Enos, were "blacklisting" plaintiff-appellees (a group of seamen working, at one time or another, out of Gloucester, Massachusetts) by demanding higher insurance premiums from the owners of vessels on which they worked. The plaintiffs claimed, *inter alia,* that the higher premiums were unjustified and that the defen-

---

1. The named defendants also included the vessel owners, but they were not the real   parties in interest and no judgment against them was entered.

dants had tortiously interfered with their employment rights.[2]   Their suit was alleged to be within the admiralty jurisdiction of the federal courts, and both injunctive relief and damages were sought.

* * *

The court awarded interim injunctive relief pending a hearing on the issue of damages.   That injunction enjoined defendants from:

> "1.   charging any additional premium to the owner of any commercial fishing vessel because he has signed on as a crewmember any one or more of [the eight prevailing plaintiffs]; and
>
> 2.   demanding as a condition for the issuance, maintenance, or continuation of any insurance policy that the owner of the fishing vessels make available to any of the three defendants * * * a settlement sheet which contains the names of any crewmember."

It is from this judgment and temporary injunction that defendants appeal. See 28 U.S.C. § 1292(a)(1).

Defendants challenge the admiralty jurisdiction of the court and argue that, even if the court did have jurisdiction, it was not empowered to grant injunctive relief.   * * *

AUTHORITY TO GRANT INJUNCTIVE RELIEF

The major question raised on appeal is whether a court sitting in admiralty has the authority to award injunctive relief.   Defendants argue that it cannot, pointing out, correctly, that admiralty courts historically have been thought not to have that power.   See G. Gilmore and C. Black, Law of Admiralty 40–43 (2d ed. 1975) [hereinafter Law of Admiralty]; H. Zobel, "Admiralty Jurisdiction, Unification, and the American Law Institute," 6 San Diego L.Rev. 375 (1969).   This doctrine was anchored in the traditional common law distinction between law, admiralty and equity, and was voiced by the Supreme Court in Schoenamsgruber v. Hamburg American Line, 294 U.S. 454, 457–58, 55 S.Ct. 475, 79 L.Ed. 989 (1935)(dicta).   But the Court, while it has assumed, has in few, if any, cases held that injunctive relief is not available, see *Law of Admiralty* 43, and its later decisions have taken a somewhat different tack.   In Swift & Co. Packers v. Compania Colombiana Del Caribe, S. A., 339 U.S. 684, 70 S.Ct. 861, 94 L.Ed. 1206 (1950), the Court held that an admiralty court disposing of a claim against a shipper for lost goods had jurisdiction to determine whether the shipper had fraudulently conveyed a ship to a dummy corporation to avoid its attachment by the court.   Justice Frankfurter, writing for the Court, observed that to deny an admiralty court jurisdiction over such a subsidiary equitable issue would strangely "hobble" the legal system, and said, "We find no restriction upon admiralty by chancery so unrelenting as to bar the grant of any equitable relief even when that relief is subsidiary to issues wholly within admiralty jurisdiction."   Id. at 691–92, 70 S.Ct. at 866.   And eleven years later, in Vaughan v. Atkinson, 369 U.S. 527, 530, 82

---

2.   The plaintiffs made other statutory claims (e.g., allegations of antitrust violations) that were without merit and are not pressed on appeal.

S.Ct. 997, 999, 8 L.Ed.2d 88 (1962), the Court said, in discussing an award of counsel's fees, that, "Equity is no stranger in admiralty; admiralty courts are, indeed, authorized to grant equitable relief."

Four years after *Vaughan,* in 1966, Congress extended the Federal Rules of Civil Procedure to admiralty cases. See Fed.R.Civ.P. 1. Some commentators took this as a further sign that admiralty could award whatever relief was appropriate in a given case. The idea that admiralty could not grant injunctive relief was, they said, archaic jetsam; anchored in no more solid ground than history, it was best not left to be a "derelict on the waters of the law," Lambert v. California, 355 U.S. 225, 232, 78 S.Ct. 240, 245, 2 L.Ed.2d 228 (1957)(Frankfurter, J., dissenting). See *Law of Admiralty* 43; cf. *Zobel,* supra, at 382–85.

The question whether injunctive relief could be awarded was first addressed directly after 1966 by the Fifth Circuit. In Lewis v. S.S. Baune, 534 F.2d 1115 (5th Cir.1976), it adopted the words of its Chief Judge in an earlier case and held that district courts sitting in admiralty may grant injunctive relief under Fed.R.Civ.P. 65:

> "The Chancellor is no longer fixed to the woolsack. He may stride the quarterdeck of maritime jurisprudence and, in the role of admiralty judge, dispense, as would his landlocked brother, that which equity and good conscience impels."

534 F.2d at 1121, quoting Compania Anonima Venezolana De Navegacion v. A. J. Perez Export Co., 303 F.2d 692, 699 (5th Cir.), cert. denied, 371 U.S. 942, 83 S.Ct. 321, 9 L.Ed.2d 276 (1962). Accord, McKie Lighter Co. v. City of Boston, 335 F.Supp. 663, 666–67 (D.Mass.1971); see Guillot v. Cenac Towing Co., 366 F.2d 898, 904 (5th Cir.1966).

Defendants distinguish *Lewis* as a case in which injunctive relief was awarded on a claim ancillary to the maritime claim that formed the basis of jurisdiction. This is an accurate characterization of the case on its facts,[7] but the Fifth Circuit's discussion of the issue did not distinguish between injunctive relief for admiralty claims and such relief for claims heard in admiralty by virtue of the court's ancillary jurisdiction. Rather it suggested a rule of general applicability, noting the 1966 unification of procedure and the doctrinal development we have outlined above.

This circuit has discussed injunctive relief in admiralty in the past, but has not, until now, been faced directly with the question. In *Carroll,* supra, 512 F.2d at 9, we assumed that equitable relief was not available from admiralty courts. In 1976, however, in A & R Marine Salvage v. McAllister Lighterage Line, 544 F.2d 551, 553, we questioned whether this

---

7. *Lewis* was an appeal from a permanent injunction and a conviction of contempt for violating a district court's temporary restraining order. The t.r.o. had been directed at preventing a shipping company's attorneys from contacting the plaintiffs directly, rather than through their attorneys (who were on contingency), in an effort to settle litigation arising out of a fatal ship collision. Although the court held that admiralty courts could award injunctive relief, it found that the district court's orders were improper. 534 F.2d at 1121–24.

was "the present law," noting that the rule had been subject to great criticism and that the Supreme Court had suggested its demise.

[We hold, with the question now before us, that courts sitting in admiralty may award injunctive relief in accordance with Fed.R.Civ.P. 65 in situations where such relief would be appropriate on land.] This is a departure from the traditional rule, but we find no constitutional, statutory or policy reasons of substance for recognizing a continued limitation upon the power of federal courts sitting in admiralty, nor does it seem likely that the Supreme Court would today adhere to the traditional rule. See *Swift & Co.,* supra, 339 U.S. at 692, 70 S.Ct. 861. District courts sitting in admiralty, which now operate under virtually the same procedures as they do otherwise, should be able to provide the kind or degree of remedy that will properly and fully redress an injury within their jurisdiction, in keeping with the same principles they would apply in other comparable cases. See *Swift & Co.,* supra, 339 U.S. at 691, 70 S.Ct. 861; Law of Admiralty 43. This is not to say, of course, that the rules and constraints affecting equitable jurisdiction on land will be ignored in admiralty—but merely that where equitable relief is otherwise proper under usual principles, it will not be denied on the ground that the court is sitting in admiralty.

* * *

The judgment of liability is affirmed, as is the order temporarily enjoining defendants from assessing higher premiums as to the prevailing plaintiffs. The order enjoining the use of settlement sheets is remanded for reconsideration in light of this opinion.

So ordered.

NOTE

The First Circuit reading of The S.S. Beaune in the Fifth Circuit as relating to admiralty claims as well as ancillary claims was vindicated in Treasure Salvors v. Unidentified Wrecked, etc., 640 F.2d 560, 1981 A.M.C. 1857 (5th Cir.1981). There the court upheld the power of the district court to entertain a claim by a would-be salvor of a long abandoned vessel for injunctive relief against operations by a rival in the area it had marked off as the site of the sunken vessel.

The Second Circuit has approached the injunction issue with more caution. See Eddie S.S. Co. Ltd. v. P.T. Karana Line, 739 F.2d 37, 1984 A.M.C. 2543 (2d Cir.1984), cert. denied 469 U.S. 1073, 105 S.Ct. 568, 83 L.Ed.2d 508 (1984). There the court of appeals vacated a district court order requiring a South African company to obtain vacation of an attachment of a vessel belonging to a Chinese business entity which it had obtained from a South African court as security on a claim against the Chinese entity for losses in connection with a fire aboard another vessel which the Chinese entity had chartered from the company. The court observed:

"This court has concluded that although the proscription against equitable relief stated in *The Eclipse* has been eroded by subsequent cases, 'the power of an admiralty court to grant injunctive relief remains severely circumscribed.

See Moran Towing & Transportation v. United States, 290 F.2d 660, 662 (2d Cir.1961).' New York State Waterways Association, Inc. v. Diamond, 469 F.2d 419, 421 n. 2 (2d Cir.1972). The view that the equity powers of an admiralty court remain severely circumscribed was followed most recently in Tradax Limited v. M.V. Holendrecht, 550 F.2d 1337 (2d Cir.1977).

"Much of the reason for the original rule has vanished, see, e.g., G. Gilmore & C. Black, The Law of Admiralty § 1–14 (2d ed.1975); Note, Admiralty Practice After Unification: Barnacles on the Procedural Hull, 81 Yale L.J. 1154, 1157–63 (1972), and some of our sister Circuits have held that in proper cases admiralty courts may issue injunctions, see Pino v. Protection Maritime Insurance Co., 599 F.2d 10 (1st Cir.), cert. denied 444 U.S. 900, 100 S.Ct. 210, 62 L.Ed.2d 136 (1979); Lewis v. S.S. Baune, 534 F.2d 1115 (5th Cir.1976). Indeed, we may well join those circuits when we are confronted with an appropriate case. Given the record in the present case, however, we see no persuasive reason here to depart from the traditional principle."

See also China Trade & Development Corp. v. M.V. Choong Yong, 837 F.2d 33, (2d. Cir.1987). The court called attention to the fact that it has not as yet found occasion to consider the abandonment of the doctrine that admiralty courts do not issue injunctions, but for the purposes of the case at hand only, assumed the power and held that international comity would make an injunction inappropriate.

Judge Swygert, from the Seventh Circuit, sitting by designation, dissented and would have affirmed the grant of the injunction.

The same principle advanced in support of the supposed want of authority of an admiralty court to grant an injunction, is applicable, theoretically, to other remedies equitable in nature. The doctrine is usually traced to Rea v. The Eclipse Braithwaite, 135 U.S. 599, 10 S.Ct. 873, 34 L.Ed. 269 (1890). In The Eclipse, two individuals and three business entities entered into an agreement to purchase a vessel. The agreement was to the effect that the vessel, when purchased, should be held in trust by the two individuals and operated by one of them. From the earnings the amount advanced by the three entities should be first paid and when fully paid the title of the vessel should revert to the two individuals. In February, 1881, while the vessel was ice bound in the river where she had wintered, all parties entered into an agreement under which a committee was formed with authority to accept any offer for the purchase of the vessel not less than $11,500 cash. The committee entered into a tentative agreement with the agent of one, Leighton, to sell the vessel for $11,500 on condition that the vessel be not damaged beyond $500. On or about April 1, after the vessel had been freed from the ice and brought to port, the committee executed a bill of sale to Leighton, but the operating part owner refused to sign and indicated that his interest was not for sale. The other three interests libeled the vessel and the operating part owner intervened as claimant. Leighton also intervened. The court held that the legal title to the vessel was in the two individual part owners as trustees, and that although they were equal owners, the operating part owner was entitled to possession under the terms of the agreement between them. It declined to address the claims of the non-operating part owner, creditors and putative purchaser. The Supreme Court affirmed. Chief Justice Fuller observed:

"So far as the creditors and intervenors were concerned, if the former desired to wind up the trust, or the latter to enforce an alleged contract of sale, which is indeed what is asked by this intervention, they should have resorted to a different tribunal. While the court of admiralty exercises its jurisdiction upon equitable principles, it has not the characteristic powers of a court of equity. It cannot entertain a bill or libel for specific performance, or to correct a mistake, (Andrews v. Insurance Co., 3 Mason 6, 16) or declare or enforce a trust or an equitable title, (Ward v. Thompson22 How. 330; The Amelia, 6 Ben. 475; Kellum v. Emerson, 2 Curt., 79) or exercise jurisdiction in matters of account merely, (Grant v. Poillon, 20 How. 162; Minturn v. Maynard, 17 How. 477; The Ocean Belle, 6 Ben. 253) or decree the sale of a ship for an unpaid mortgage, or declare her to be the property of the mortgagees and direct possession of her to be given to them. (Bogart v. The John Jay, 17 How. 399.) The jurisdiction embraces all maritime contracts, torts, injuries or offences, and it depends, in cases of contract, upon the nature of the contract, and is limited to contracts claims and services purely maritime, and touching rights and duties appertaining to commerce and navigation. People's Ferry Co. v. Beers, 20 How. 393, 401. There was nothing maritime about the claims of the intervenors, and the intervention was properly dismissed for want of jurisdiction over the subject matter.''

To what extent is the matter of equitable remedies one of subject matter jurisdiction? In Rice v. Charles Dreifus Co., 96 F.2d 80 (2d Cir.1938), in which it was held that in an action on a maritime contract the admiralty court could consider on its merits matter in avoidance that would be good in equity despite the historical practice of requiring that the matter be presented to the chancellor in a separate suit to enjoin recourse to law, Judge Hand observed, "The question is of much importance, because if we are wrong, the defect would be beyond the power of Congress, being a limitation upon the constitutional powers of the admiralty court.''

Note that among the equitable remedies that are stated to be outside the authority of the admiralty court in *The Eclipse* was a decree for the sale of a vessel for an unpaid mortgage, citing Bogart v. The John Jay. As we shall see, Congress has provided for preferred ship mortgages and made provision for foreclosing them. Is this consistent with Judge Hand's observation? Or does the substantive statute bring the remedy within Article III as a controversy arising under the laws of the United States?

To what extent is the matter cured by the development of the doctrine of pendent jurisdiction? Or ancillary jurisdiction? See, e.g., Beverly Hills Nat'l Bank & Trust Co. v. Compania De Navegacione Almirante S.A., 437 F.2d 301, cert. denied 402 U.S. 996, 91 S.Ct. 2173, 29 L.Ed.2d 161 (1971). There an exporter was indebted to a bank and the debt was secured to some extent by a lien on scrap. Pursuant to an agreement between the exporter and the bank, the exporter sold the scrap in Japan, and chartered plaintiff's vessel to deliver it. While the scrap was en route, the vessel owner sued for its charter hire. The cargo was delivered to the purchaser without condition and the bank collected purchaser's drafts, which included prepaid freight.

The district court held that the vessel owner lost its lien on the cargo when it was unconditionally delivered, but found that the bank held the collected funds as constructive trustee for the vessel owner to the extent that they included prepaid freight. On appeal the court of appeals held that the constructive trust claim was an independent claim over which the court would have no independent admiralty jurisdiction under *The Eclipse* and *Swift*. It found, however, two bases for the exercise of jurisdiction of both the lien and the constructive trust claims. First, the two "claims" were simply two theories of recovery and cognizable under the *Gibbs* doctrine. It noted that since the claim for the imposition of a constructive trust was equitable in nature there would be no right to a jury trial and therefore the question of whether a legal claim can be appended to an admiralty claim without affording the parties a right to trial by jury could not arise.

Note that there is some difference between the proposition that the court may award equitable remedies in an admiralty case and the solution of the problem through the doctrine of pendent jurisdiction, vide the S/S Dart Canada, discussed at p. 174 supra. In *Beverly Hills,* this problem was avoided, since all parties conceded that either state law would apply or the matter would be decided upon general equitable principles.

CHAPTER 6

ADMIRALTY JURISDICTION AND THE FEDERAL JUDICIAL SYSTEM

Introductory Note

The pre-merger practice—Sides of the court and analogies to pendent jurisdiction.

In Romero v. International Terminal Operating Co., 358 U.S. 354, 79 S.Ct. 468, 3 L.Ed.2d 368, a Spanish sailor on a vessel of Spanish registry sailing under the Spanish flag and and owned by a Spanish corporation, was injured aboard ship in Hoboken. The sailor brought suit in the Southern District of New York, against four corporations, Transatlantica, his employer and the owner of the vessel, Garcia & Dias, a New York Corporation serving as husbanding agent in New York for Transatlantica, both under the Jones Act and under the general maritime law for breach of the warranty of seaworthiness and maintenance and cure, and two corporations working on board of the vessel at the time of the accident, International Terminal Operating Co., a Delaware stevedoring corporation engaged in loading cargo, and Quinn Lumber, a New York corporation doing carpentry work on board at the time of the accident, for maritime tort. Alienage jurisdiction was thus present in the case of Garcia & Dias, Terminal Operating, and Quinn Lumber, but jurisdiction of the claim against Transatlantica was pleaded under 28 U.S.C.A. § 1331 and the Jones Act. The district court dismissed the action, holding that the Jones Act is inapplicable to an injury to a Spanish seaman injured on a Spanish vessel. The claims against the other three corporations were dismissed for want of complete diversity under the rule in Strawbridge v. Curtiss.

The Supreme Court agreed that the Jones Act was inapplicable, but vacated the judgment on the ground that (1) the claim under the Jones Act was more than merely colorable and therefore not subject to dismissal for want of jurisdiction, and by analogy to pendent jurisdiction, the court could retain the case and adjudicate the claims against Transatlantica under the general maritime law, and (2) since the viable claim under the Jones Act provided an independent basis for jurisdiction of the claim of the only nondiverse party, diversity jurisdiction of the claims against the remaining defendants was not destroyed.

Justice Brennan concurred, but was of the opinion that under the jurisdictional Act of 1975, a maritime claim arises under the laws of the United States and is cognizable under § 1331. He felt the analogy to the doctrine of pendent jurisdiction strained.

It was the *Romero* case that led to Professor Brainerd Currie's article, The Silver Oar and All That: A Study of the Romero Case, 27 U.Chi.L.Rev. 1 (1959). Professor Currie was later to serve as Reporter to the Advisory Committee on the Admiralty Rules during the period during which that Committee and the Advisory Committee on the Rules of Civil Procedure worked out the amendments adopted by the Supreme Court that effected the merger of the admiralty and civil rules.

Beeler v. United States

United States Court of Appeals, Third Circuit, 1964.
338 F.2d 687, 1965 A.M.C. 1904.

■ WILLIAM H. KIRKPATRICK, D.J. In this case the cause of action pleaded derives from an injury to the plaintiff, incurred when a boat in which she was a passenger was swept over a dam in the Allegheny River. The complaint charged that the accident was due to the negligent failure of the Corps of Engineers to post properly located signs warning water craft of the dam. These facts, concisely set out in the complaint, stated a cause of action of maritime tort, cognizable under the Suits in Admiralty Act (46 U.S.C.A. § 741 et seq.). However, instead of pleading that Act, the complaint contained an averment that "This Court has jurisdiction of this cause under the * * * Federal Torts Claim (*sic*) Act,"[1] was captioned as under the Federal Tort Claims Act, and ended with a demand for a jury trial. The clerk docketed the suit as "Civil Action No. 63–345."

The defendant moved for summary judgment, and, pending disposition of that motion, the plaintiffs moved to amend the complaint by deleting the demand for a jury trial and by substituting the Suits in Admiralty Act for the Tort Claims Act in the jurisdictional averment and the caption. Without having acted upon the motion to amend, the judge entered summary judgment of dismissal. Subsequently, he entered an order refusing the amendment. These orders are now before this court on appeal. The two-year limitation of the Suits in Admiralty Act has expired and no new suit under that Act can be begun.

It is not questioned that the Federal Tort Claims Act conferred no right of action upon the plaintiffs nor that the Suits in Admiralty Act provided their sole remedy. Had the plaintiffs' proposed amendment been allowed, the action could have proceeded on the admiralty side of the court, but the court, concluding that it was without jurisdiction, dismissed it.[2] Thus the sole question upon this appeal is whether it was error to refuse the amendment.

---

1. 28 U.S.C.A. § 1346.

2. It is not necessary to decide whether the court could, without any amendment, have simply treated the complaint as a libel under the Suits in Admiralty Act, transferred the case to the admiralty docket and proceed-ed with the suit—a course not entirely un-supported by authority. The case has been presented by both parties upon the postulate that, in the absence of an amendment, the court had no course open but to dismiss.

The defendant's position is, in effect, that the plaintiffs' failure to invoke the Suits in Admiralty Act by a reference to it in their complaint deprived the District Court of jurisdiction to entertain an otherwise well pleaded cause of maritime tort and of power to amend the complaint or transfer the cause to the admiralty docket and, further, that such transfer would have been beyond the power of the court even if the court had obtained jurisdiction of the case. These views we believe to have been also the substance of the court's reasons for its rulings. With them we cannot agree.

It is well settled that the recitation of a statute can neither deprive a court of jurisdiction nor confer jurisdiction upon it. It is the operative facts pleaded which alone can do that. "A plaintiff is not required to state under what law he brings his action, but is only required to plead facts which under the law—that is, any law applicable to the case—entitle him to recover." Newberry v. Central of Georgia Ry. Co., 276 F. 337, 341 (5 Cir.1922). See also Adams v. State Fair, 11 F.2d 295 (W.D.La., 1926).

Here was a complaint which accurately and succinctly stated a cause of action created by the Suits in Admiralty Act. To hold that, having set forth facts which if proved would entitle him to recover, a plaintiff in a case like the present one loses, beyond hope of redemption, the right to pursue his action because he has cited the wrong statute as the basis for it would be indeed a sterile technicality. Fortunately, however, there is a wealth of authority, including the decision of this court in Wounick v. Pittsburgh, etc., Coal Co., 283 F.2d 325 (1960), 1961 A.M.C. 1160, recognizing such a plaintiff's right to have the error corrected by amendment and the suit transferred.

The facts in the *Wounick case* were that an injured seaman brought a suit at law under the Jones Act, basing the action on negligence and unseaworthiness. The District Court, holding that the statute of limitations barred the action on the law side, directed a verdict for the defendant, and later refused to open the judgment or allow a new trial. In reversing, this court said (283 F.2d p. 327, 1961 A.M.C. p. 1162): "Plaintiff's only available remedy for his cause of action, which was in part grounded on a right based on the ancient maritime law, was in admiralty. * * * We think that, in these circumstances, the cause should have been transferred to the admiralty side of the court, and the doctrine of laches applied."

Cases where the complaint was erroneously brought under the Tort Claims Act, in which transfer to the admiralty side of the court was ordered, are Liberty Mutual Insurance Co. v. United States, 183 F.Supp. 944, 1960 A.M.C. 1835 (E.D.N.Y.1960); Mings v. United States, 222 F.Supp. 996, 1964 A.M.C. 707 (S.D.Cal., 1963); Weiss v. United States, 168 F.Supp. 300, 1965 A.M.C. 1912 (D.N.J.1958). A case allowing transfer from the law side to the admiralty side is Modin v. Matson Nav. Co., 128 F.2d 194, 1942 A.M.C. 961 (9 Cir.1942).

The appellee, in support of its position, cites Higa v. Transocean Airlines, 230 F.2d 780, 1956 A.M.C. 122, 1956 U.S.Av.R. 30 (9 Cir.1956), but the decision in that case does not touch the point here involved, because the plaintiff, who had sued on the law side of the court in a diversity suit in which recovery could have been only in admiralty under the Death on the High Seas Act (46 U.S.Code, sec. 761), never moved to amend or transfer the case to the admiralty docket until the Court of Appeals had affirmed the lower court's dismissal of the action. He raised the question for the first time in his petition for rehearing, and the Court of Appeals denied it on the ground that allowance of the transfer, after affirmance of the judgment of dismissal, would have been enlarging the scope of the appeal. Prior to this the plaintiff had persisted in his position that he had the right to try the case at law. The court at no point intimated that power was lacking to transfer the cause to admiralty had a transfer been timely moved.

Dixie, 30 F.Supp. 215, 1940 A.M.C. 70 (S.D.Tex.1939), also relied on by the appellee, is authority only for the proposition that, in a case where the plaintiff's admiralty remedy had not been barred by the statute, the judge in his discretion could refuse the amendment and dismiss the case without prejudice to begin a new suit in admiralty—a discretion which may have been properly exercised under the circumstances of that case. "Of course, the grant or denial of an opportunity to amend is within the discretion of the District Court, but outright refusal to grant the leave without any justifying reason appearing for the denial is not an exercise of discretion; it is merely abuse of that discretion and inconsistent with the spirit of the Federal Rules." Foman v. Davis, 371 U.S. 178, 182, 83 S.Ct. 227, 230, 9 L.Ed.2d 222 (1962). This is particularly true in a case like the present in which the allowance of the amendment cannot adversely affect the defendant while refusal to allow it might put an end to the plaintiffs' right to pursue their cause of action.[3]

The appellee's argument, based upon the legislative history of the 1960 amendment to the Suits in Admiralty Act, is entirely without merit. That amendment was the third section of an act, the first two sections of which authorized transfers from the Court of Claims to a District Court. The appellee argues, in effect, that the fact that transfer from law to admiralty and vice versa was not specifically provided for in the third section indicates that Congress did not intend to permit such transfers. We think the contrary conclusion is to be drawn. Prior to the adoption of the amendment, transfers from the Court of Claims to a District Court had not been permitted but transfers from the law side of the District Court to the admiralty side and vice versa had been long recognized as within the powers of the District Court.[4] It is hardly conceivable that Congress in enacting the amendment to the Suits in Admiralty Act meant to deprive plaintiffs who had misfiled their suits of an already existing right to correct

3. Walker v. Dravo Corp., 210 F.Supp. 386, 1965 A.M.C. 1909 (W.D.Pa., 1962), also relied upon by the appellee, was clearly based upon a misinterpretation of Wounick v. Pittsburgh, etc., Coal Co., supra.

4. See opinion of Judge Clark in Civil v. Waterman S.S. Corp., 217 F.2d 94, 97, 1955 A.M.C. 21 (2 Cir.1955), citing United States ex rel. Pressprich & Son Co. v. James W. Elwell & Co., 250 F. 939 (2 Cir.1918) and several other cases.

the mistake. Likewise, to hold that Congress intended that the Government's consent to be sued should be conditioned upon the Act's being pleaded *eo nomine* and the pleading being designated "libel" instead of "complaint" would be to attribute to Congress an intent to give overriding effect to mere technicalities—an intent which would be directly contrary to the whole purpose and spirit of the legislation. This this court is unwilling to do.

The judgment will be reversed and the cause remanded for further proceedings not inconsistent with this opinion.

NOTE

In Francese v. United States, 229 F.Supp. 10, 1965 A.M.C. 974 (E.D.N.Y.1964), involving, like *Beeler*, a motion to dismiss for want of subject matter jurisdiction an action brought under the FTCA which, it was contended, could be maintained only under the SIAA, the court noted the established authority to transfer cases from one "side" of the court to another when filed on the wrong side, but added that in a case such as the one at bar in which the proper head of jurisdiction remained doubtful, transfer was not necessary to avoid dismissal and the court could continue with the case an let the decision of whether the jurisdiction was civil or maritime abide the event.

Crookham v. Muick

United States District Court, Western District of Pennsylvania, 1965.
246 F.Supp. 288, 1966 A.M.C. 1522.

■ EDWARD DUMBAULD, D.J. On May 12, 1965, libellant filed in Admiralty (No. 65–30) a complaint *in rem* against the M/V Diesel and *in personam* against two individuals (who apparently have not been served with process) and two corporations seeking damages for personal injury alleging negligence and unseaworthiness (jury trial demanded) and also seeking maintenance and cure. An amended libel filed June 2, 1965, repeats the same claims, adding in paragraph 5:

"That this action is brought under the general maritime law and the doctrine of seaworthiness, with pendent rights under the provisions of the Jones Act. That there is diversity of citizenship between libellant and the corporate respondents as his employer and operators of said vessel. Both Seneca Oil & Transport Co. and Seneca Towing Co. are Ohio companies, with principal offices at Cleveland, Ohio."

In the original libel there was included in the maintenance and cure count but not in the negligence and unseaworthiness counts an allegation that libellant is a citizen and resident of Pennsylvania. This allegation disappeared in the amended libel. In each count it is alleged that over $10,000 is involved. In the Exceptions of the corporate respondents and their answer to the amended libel, it is stated that they are Delaware corporations with their principal offices in Cleveland, Ohio. Insofar as the Jones Act is involved, they raise the issue of venue.

In a Jones Act case on the law side, venue is properly laid only in the district of the residence or principal office of the seaman's employer. In this case, that would be Delaware or Ohio. Leith v. Oil Transport Co., 321 F.2d 591, 593, 1964 A.M.C. 2152 (3 Cir.1963); Panama R.R. Co. v. Johnson, 264 U.S. 375, 385, 44 S.Ct. 391, 68 L.Ed. 748, 1924 A.M.C. 551 (1924).

The instant action is clearly one in admiralty, however, and not on the law side. In admiralty the court applies the law of the sea, maritime law. Originally such law did not permit recovery for negligence. Osceola, 189 U.S. 158, 175, 23 S.Ct. 483, 47 L.Ed. 760 (1903). But Congress may modify and modernize such law. Detroit Trust Co. v. Thomas Barlum, 293 U.S. 21, 43–44, 55 S.Ct. 31, 79 L.Ed. 176, 1934 A.M.C. 1417 (1934); see also Panama R.R., supra, 264 U.S. at 386, 388, 1924 A.M.C. at 557. It has done so in the Jones Act of June 5, 1920, 41 Stat. 1007, 46 U.S.C.A. § 688. Though not clearly stated in the terms of the act, the effect of the legislation is to recognize negligence as a ground for recovery. See Id., 264 U.S. at 389, 1924 A.M.C. at 557. The cause of action thus recognized by the modified maritime law may be brought on the admiralty side, as well as on the law side. On the admiralty side, however, the procedural right to jury trial which the Jones Act makes available if the seaman elects to sue on the law side is not available. Id., 264 U.S. at 391, 1924 A.M.C. at 558. Nor does the venue provision of the Jones Act apply in admiralty (Leith, supra, 321 F.2d at 593, 1964 A.M.C. at 2157; Brown v. C.D. Mallory & Co., 122 F.2d 98, 103–104, 1941 A.M.C. 1043 (3 Cir.1941)).

Hence it is clear that libellant is entitled to trial of his entire case in this Court without a jury, if he so desires.

However, he seems to wish to eat his cake and have it too. He has demanded jury trial. He contends that the Jones Act action is "pendent" to the claims cognizable under the historic law of the sea, and that thus all three claims are transubstantiated into matters triable by jury.

This contention would permit the tail to wag the dog. Since negligence and unseaworthiness are merely separate grounds for a single recovery. (Id., 321 F.2d at 592, 1964 A.M.C. at 2154), the law permits the admiralty law claims to be treated as pendent to a civil action on the law side under the Jones Act, with the right of jury trial. Romero v. Int. Terminal Co., 358 U.S. 354, 381, 79 S.Ct. 468, 3 L.Ed.2d 368, 1959 A.M.C. 832 (1959); Fitzgerald v. United States Lines, 374 U.S. 16, 21, 83 S.Ct. 1646, 10 L.Ed.2d 720, 1963 A.M.C. 1093 (1963); *Leith,* supra, 1964 A.M.C. at 2156, 321 F.2d at 594.

We know of, and libellant has referred us, however, to no case where the Jones Act negligence claim has been treated as *pendent to the admiralty claims.* On the contrary, as Judge Hastie says (Id., 321 F.2d at 593, 1964 A.M.C. at 2154) the civil claim is regarded as the "principal" claim, to which the admiralty claim is pendent or ancillary.

Presumably libellant should be given the option of seeking transfer to a jurisdiction where venue is proper over the Jones Act claim, if he wishes to insist on the right to jury trial. Id., 1964 A.M.C. at 2154, 321 F.2d at 593.

Accordingly we grant libellant until October 15, 1965, to elect whether to file an application for transfer, to withdraw the libel, or to proceed to trial non-jury in due course. In the event no election of the first two alternatives is filed by that date, the case will be treated as one for disposition by the Court as a non-jury case, since, as previously stated, the entire cause of action pleaded falls within our traditional admiralty jurisdiction.

N O T E

The choice of venue in Jones Act cases was greatly expanded by the Supreme Court's decision in Pure Oil Co. v. Suarez, 384 U.S. 202, 86 S.Ct. 1394, 16 L.Ed.2d 474 (1966), holding that the venue provision of the Act did not preclude bringing the action in a district in which the venue would be proper under the general venue provision. See Ch. 9, infra.

In *Crookham*, both claims could have been pleaded as maritime and the attempt was to avoid the venue requirement by pleading the Jones Act claims as pendant to the maritime claims and at the same time and at the same time preserve the right to a jury trial. In a somewhat similar situation, in which the plaintiff, lacking diversity, pleaded an action in rem in the district court, with a pendent claim under the Owner Responsibility Statute, and demanded a jury trial on the pendent claim, the court of appeals held that a claim that can be brought only as pendent to an admiralty claim is, for jury purposes, maritime, and will be tried to the bench. Churchill v. F/V FJORD, 892 F.2d 763 (9th Cir.1988) cert. denied 497 U.S. 1025, 110 S.Ct. 3273, 111 L.Ed.2d 783 (1990). To the same effect, in the Fifth Circuit, see Offshore Logistics, Inc. v. Tallentire, 477 U.S. 207, 106 S.Ct. 2485, 91 L.Ed.2d 174 (1986), on remand 800 F.2d 1390 (5th Cir.1986).

Thomas v. Peninsular & Oriental Steam Navigation Co.

United States District Court, Eastern District of Pennsylvania, 1965.
246 F.Supp. 592, 1966 A.M.C. 115.

■ RALPH C. BODY, D.J. The plaintiff, a longshoreman who sustained injuries on July 18, 1961 while helping to unload cargo from the Steamship Cambridge, brought this civil action on October 27, 1961 against the defendant, Peninsular & Oriental Steam Navigation Company. In its answer, defendant admitted ownership of the vessel but averred that it was an owner out of possession at the time of the alleged accident and consequently could not be held liable for plaintiff's injuries. Defendant further averred in its answer that the Federal Steam Navigation Company, Ltd. managed, operated and controlled the Cambridge at all times pertinent to this action.

At a pre-trial conference before The Honorable A. Leon Higginbotham, Jr. defendant again asserted its defense of an owner out of possession. Since counsel for plaintiff was unable to disprove said defense, Judge Higginbotham entered a pre-trial order on February 8, 1965 in which plaintiff was given twenty-one (21) days in which to file a petition to withdraw the civil action or, in the alternative, to file a petition requesting that the civil action be transferred to the admiralty side of the court for consolidation with another action subsequently to be commenced in admiralty.

On February 23, 1965 plaintiff instituted a libel *in personam* against both Peninsular & Oriental Steam Navigation Company and Federal Steamship Navigation Company, Ltd. He also filed a libel *in rem* against the Steamship Cambridge. The respondents answered the above libels and setting forth the defense of laches, and Peninsular again asserted its defense of owner out of possession.

The matter is now before this Court on plaintiff's motion to transfer this pending Civil Action No. 30459 to the admiralty side of the Court for consolidation with the above-mentioned libel actions.

Plaintiff argues that such a transfer from the civil to the admiralty side of the Court, which is a well established practice [Francese v. United States, 229 F.Supp. 10, 1965 A.M.C. 974 (E.D.N.Y.1964); Beeler v. United States, 338 F.2d 687, 1965 A.M.C. 1904 (3 Cir.1964)] should be allowed especially in a situation such as this where the transfer and later consolidation in admiralty would expedite the litigation and make available to the Court all pertinent documents and papers. [Ellerman Lines, Ltd. v. Atlantic & Gulf Stevedores, Inc., 339 F.2d 673, 1965 A.M.C. 283 (3 Cir.1964)].

Defendant, on the other hand, attempts to distinguish the *Francese* and *Beeler cases,* supra, on the ground that there the plaintiffs were longshoremen who had brought civil actions against the United States Government under the Federal Tort Claims Act. Since the court held in both cases that the Tort Claims Act was not applicable, the transfers were allowed because the respective plaintiff's sole remedy lay with the Suits in Admiralty Act. However, defendant argues that in the case at bar plaintiff already has another *in personam* and *in rem* action pending against the defendant in admiralty and would therefore not be deprived of his right to sue if his motion to transfer is denied. We agree with defendant's distinction.

Another compelling reason for denying plaintiff's motion to transfer is found in the policy of preserving the right of trial by jury. Rule 38(d) of the Federal Rules of Civil Procedure, 28 U.S.Code, provides that:

> "A demand for trial by jury * * * may not be withdrawn without the consent of the parties."

Plaintiff demanded a jury trial when he instituted this civil action and defendant is entitled to rely on that demand with the effect that plaintiff cannot dispense with a jury trial without the consent of the defendant. [Cf. Barron & Holtzoff, Federal Practice and Procedure, sec. 877, Vol. 2B, p. 49, Wright Ed.1961]. Professor Moore has stated in this respect:

> " * * * Thus if the plaintiff makes a timely general demand for jury the defendant may rely thereon and the plaintiff cannot dispense with a

jury trial as to some or all of the issues between them without the consent of the defendant."

[5 Moore's Federal Practice, p. 344, sec. 38.45] Therefore, since plaintiff here has not obtained defendant's consent to the transfer, which would be, in effect, a withdrawal of the demand for a jury, the transfer should not be made to the admiralty side where, of course, the case is tried by the court without a jury. [Yates v. Dann, 223 F.2d 64, 1955 A.M.C. 1214 (3 Cir.1955)].

The defendant, in addition to opposing plaintiff's motion to transfer, has urged the Court to dismiss the instant civil action. As previously mentioned, the plaintiff in this case has conceded that he cannot disprove defendant Peninsular's assertion that it is an owner out of possession and therefore not liable for plaintiff's injuries. Where possession and control of a vessel is transferred from one shipping company to another (referred to as "owner *pro hac vice* "), the original owner is relieved of all liability for unseaworthiness. [Vitozi v. Balboa Shipping Co., Inc., 163 F.2d 286, 1948 A.M.C. 695 (1 Cir.1947)].

Even if plaintiff hopes to hold the Steamship Cambridge liable *in rem,* regardless of the fact that the vessel was in the possession of Federal Steam Navigation Company, Ltd., the owner *pro hac vice,* such theory can be tested in the *in rem* admiralty action. And although plaintiff faces the defense of laches in that *in rem* action, a transfer of the present civil action would not affect plaintiff's theory since a mere transfer would not convert the present civil action into an *in rem* action in admiralty. Therefore, the transfer would not affect any possible advantage plaintiff might hope to gain regarding the defense of laches.

Accordingly, it appearing from the review of the record and briefs that no useful purpose would be served by a transfer of this civil action to the admiralty side of the court; and it further appearing that there is no legal merit to this action in that plaintiff cannot disprove defendant Peninsular's defense of owner out of possession, the motion of plaintiff to transfer is denied and the action is dismissed without prejudice.

La Capria v. Compagnie Maritime Belge

United States Court of Appeals, Second Circuit, 1967.
373 F.2d 579, 1967 A.M.C. 726.

■ FRIENDLY, CIRCUIT JUDGE. Santo La Capria, a longshoreman employed by Transoceanic Stevedoring Corp., brought this action to recover for personal injuries in the District Court for the Southern District of New York in 1962 against Compagnie Maritime Belge and Wm. Spencer & Son Corporation. Federal jurisdiction was grounded on diverse citizenship, 28 U.S.C.A. § 1332, plaintiff being allegedly a citizen of New Jersey and the defendants Belgian and New York corporations, respectively, and a jury trial was demanded. In their respective answers Wm. Spencer also demanded a jury trial but Compagnie Maritime Belge did not. Wm. Spencer later impleaded Transoceanic, plaintiff's employer; the latter also demanded a jury trial.

Santo La Capria died in 1964, a resident of New York; an alien who was appointed his administrator by the New York courts was substituted as plaintiff, and the complaint was amended to assert a claim for Santo's wrongful death.

After 265 pages of pleadings, motions and memoranda had accumulated in the files of the District Court and discovery had been had, a pre-trial conference was held in June, 1965; here, apparently for the first time, Wm. Spencer challenged the court's jurisdiction on the basis that Santo La Capria had been a resident of New York when the suit was brought. Some fifteen months later the administrator moved for leave to amend the complaint to identify it as in admiralty under F.R.Civ.Proc. rule 9(h) and to transfer the action to a non-jury calendar. A rather muddy moving affidavit claimed that although Santo was a resident of New York at the date of the accident and also of his death, he had resided in New Jersey for a short period when the action was brought but expressed apprehension whether there was jurisdiction over the death claim under 28 U.S.C.A. § 1332. Wm. Spencer's attorney responded with the argument, rather inconsistent with its previous position of lack of jurisdiction under the diversity statute, that all this was a pretense on the part of plaintiff to avoid a jury trial; it relied on the principle that once diversity jurisdiction has attached, a subsequent change in citizenship does not destroy it. See Wright, Federal Courts § 28 (1963). Compagnie Maritime Belge supported plaintiff's motion, stating its belief that plaintiff had some real cause for worry both about Santo's citizenship in 1962 and over the death claim, which it thought would be regarded as a separate claim not cognizable under § 1332(a)(2) because of the presence of aliens on both sides.[1] Finding that "as presented by either side the diversity issue is not factually convincing," Judge Cooper denied the motion "without prejudice to renewal at the proper time." When plaintiff immediately renewed the motion on somewhat fuller papers, which the judge regarded as containing "persuasive evidence that this Court lacks diversity jurisdiction," he granted the motion. Amended pleadings were served, bringing the file to the impressive total of 369 pages; Wm. Spencer appealed; and plaintiff, with the continued assent of Compagnie Maritime Belge, moved to dismiss for want of appellate jurisdiction.

No discussion is required to show that the order appealed from is neither a final decision under 28 U.S.C.A. § 1291 nor an interlocutory decree "determining the rights and liabilities of the parties to admiralty cases in which appeals from final decrees are allowed," 28 U.S.C.A. § 1292(a)(3), see In re Wills Lines, Inc., 227 F.2d 509 (2 Cir.1955), cert. denied Tankport Terminals Inc., v. Wills Lines, 351 U.S. 917, 76 S.Ct. 709, 100 L.Ed. 1450 (1956). Hence the only possible basis for jurisdiction in this court is that the district judge enjoined proceedings on the "law side" and directed them on the "admiralty side," thereby making an interlocutory injunctive order within 28 U.S.C.A. § 1292(a)(1). So, appellant argues, Modin v. Matson Navigation Co., 128 F.2d 194 (9 Cir.1942), held, on

---

1. We intimate no position as to any of these questions.

the authority of Enelow v. New York Life Ins. Co., 293 U.S. 379, 55 S.Ct. 310, 79 L.Ed. 440 (1935). But *Enelow,* its companion, Shanferoke Coal & Supply Corp. v. Westchester Service Corp., 293 U.S. 449, 55 S.Ct. 313, 79 L.Ed. 583 (1935), decided the same day, and their progeny, notably Ettelson v. Metropolitan Life Ins. Co., 317 U.S. 188, 63 S.Ct. 163, 87 L.Ed. 176 (1942), were cases where a judge was thought to have acted as a chancellor and to have enjoined proceedings at law because of an equitable defense or a claim for arbitration—the kind of action that an equity court might have taken when law and equity were separate, see 293 U.S. at 381–382, 55 S.Ct. 310. These well-known and much debated decisions did not present a situation where the judge merely held he might be without jurisdiction "at law" because of lack of diversity and could proceed only by availing himself of his jurisdiction in admiralty, the only practical effect being to eliminate jury trial.

As against this we have held that the striking of a plaintiff's jury demand on defendant's motion in what the plaintiff insisted to be an action at law and the defendant claimed to be a suit in equity amounted to an injunction against plaintiff's proceeding with his "law" claim and was therefore appealable under *Enelow* and *Ettelson.* Ring v. Spina, 166 F.2d 546, 548–549 (2 Cir.1948), cert. denied 335 U.S. 813, 69 S.Ct. 30, 93 L.Ed. 368 (1948). But the continued authority of Ring v. Spina on this point has been placed in some doubt by the recent decision in Schine v. Schine, 367 F.2d 685, 688 fn. 1 (2 Cir.1966). Moreover, the principle of Ring v. Spina and also the precise holding in Modin v. Matson Navigation Company, supra,[2] are scarcely applicable when, as here, it is the plaintiff who no longer wishes to proceed at law; to envision the chancellor contemplating an injunction to require a plaintiff to keep on proceeding at law despite the plaintiff's desire to shift to admiralty in order to avoid jurisdictional doubts would carry the "element of fiction" recognized as inhering in *Enelow,* see Baltimore Contractors, Inc. v. Bodinger, 348 U.S. 176, 184, 75 S.Ct. 249, 99 L.Ed. 233 (1955), beyond permissible bounds. Prior criticism of the conceptualism on insistence on the two-sidedness of a single court, see B. Currie, The Silver Oar and All That: A Study of the Romero Case, 27 U.Chi.L.Rev. 1, 6–7, 23–40 (1959), gains added force from the recent amendment of the Federal Rules of Civil Procedure to include admiralty cases.

We think it high time that this long-pending case be tried.

The motion to dismiss the appeal is granted.

N O T E

The issue of whether a plaintiff, having asserted diversity jurisdiction or federal question jurisdiction and demanded a jury trial may subsequently change his mind

---

2. Professor Moore regards the *Modin* decision as "questionable," 6 Federal Practice ¶ 54.06[5] at 43 (1964 ed.); because of the distinction above noted, we are not required to decide whether we would follow it on its own facts. See also 5 Moore, Federal Practice ¶ 39.13[2].

and identify his claim as maritime under Rule 9(h), or after a demand for a jury has been made by another party, may avoid the demand by amending the complaint to identify the claim as maritime, has produced some difference of opinion. Compare Emerson G.M. Diesel, Inc. v. Alaskan Enterprise, 732 F.2d 1468, 1985 A.M.C. 2069 (9th Cir.1984) with Johnson v. Penrod Drilling Co., 469 F.2d 897, 903, 1973 A.M.C. 1862, 1868–70 (5th Cir.1972), reh'g 510 F.2d 234, 1975 A.M.C. 2161 (5th Cir.1975), cert. denied 423 U.S. 839, 96 S.Ct. 68, 69, 46 L.Ed.2d 58 (1975), overruled on other grounds in Culver v. Slater Boat Co., 688 F.2d 280, 283, 1983 A.M.C. 2251 (en banc) (5th Cir.1982), cert. denied 469 U.S. 819, 105 S.Ct. 90, 83 L.Ed.2d 37 (1984).

Is the issue of whether a jury demand once made cannot be withdrawn without consent of the opposing party the same issue as that presented by a request to amend to identify a claim as maritime under Rule 9(h)? The redefinition of the claim to preclude a jury trial after timely demand rarely arises outside the context of Rule 9(h), but it can. See, e.g., Francis v. Dietrick, 682 F.2d 485 (4th Cir.1982), in which the plaintiff amended his complaint to delete his claim for damages, leaving only equitable issues to be tried. The court of appeals found this different from the amendment found offensive in *Penrod Drilling*.

In an action at law in which a party makes a timely jury demand and later withdraws it, is the procedure objectionable because the opposing party was entitled to a jury trial on seasonable demand, but may have failed to make a jury demand in reliance upon his opponent's demand? If so, then the admiralty case is different, for the defendant did not have a right to a jury trial.

Haskins v. Point Towing Co.

United States Court of Appeals, Third Circuit, 1968.
395 F.2d 737, 1968 A.M.C. 1193.

■ ABRAHAM L. FREEDMAN, CT. J. A confused pleading presents us with the problem whether plaintiff[1] was entitled to a trial by jury of his Jones Act[2] claim for negligence and his maritime claims for unseaworthiness and maintenance and cure. He was compelled to have all these claims tried by a judge without a jury and he brings this appeal from the decision of the district judge dismissing his action on the merits.

Plaintiff brought the action by filing what he designated as a "Libel in Admiralty, *in rem* and *in personam* * * * against Point Towing Co. and the M/V H.E. Bowles, a motor vessel, her boilers, engines, tackle, apparel and furniture, and Bulk Towing, Inc., in a cause of contract and damage, civil and maritime * * *." He demanded trial by jury. In his "First Cause of Action" he alleged that he was an assistant engineer and member of the crew of the motor vessel H.E. Bowles and sought recovery for personal injuries "as a seaman * * * pursuant to the general maritime law and the doctrine of seaworthiness * * *." In the same cause of action he claimed "pendent rights" under the Jones Act for negligence. In the "Second Cause of Action" he sought recovery for maintenance and cure. He alleged

---

1. Although the parties are referred to in the pleadings as libellant and respondent, in view of the uniform designation provided under the 1966 amendments to the Federal Rules of Civil Procedure (see Rules 1, 4(b)), we shall refer to the parties as plaintiff and defendant.

2. 46 U.S.C.A. § 688.

damages in excess of $10,000, exclusive of interest and costs in each cause of action. The pleading concluded with a prayer that process issue against the vessel in accordance with the practice in admiralty and maritime jurisdiction and in the alternative that attachment of property of the defendants be made "as on foreign attachment, *in personam.*"

The Clerk of the Court docketed the action in admiralty but placed it on the civil jury list. Process issued but was returned unexecuted and shortly thereafter counsel entered an appearance for Point Towing Co. and subsequently filed an answer to the libel. No appearance was entered for Bulk Towing, Inc., which therefore dropped out of the case.

After discovery proceedings Point Towing Co., which will be referred to as the defendant, filed a motion to remove the case from the jury list and to assign it to a nonjury list on the ground that there was no right to trial by jury because the action was in admiralty. The district court agreed and granted the motion.[3] It was also of the opinion that plaintiff had not shown venue at law under the Jones Act[4] because the defendant did not reside or have its principal office within the jurisdiction. It therefore gave plaintiff an election to seek a transfer to a jurisdiction where venue existed, to withdraw the action, or to proceed to trial by a judge without a jury. The court specified that the case would be treated as a nonjury case if plaintiff did not choose either of the first two alternatives within fifteen days. All this was prior to the effective date of the new merged civil and admiralty rules. Plaintiff made no such choice and the case proceeded to trial as a nonjury action.

Ultimately the district court dismissed the action because defendant was not liable for any negligence or unseaworthiness which may have occasioned plaintiff's injury. It found that the vessel was being operated by Bulk Towing, Inc., the unserved defendant, under a "bare boat charter" from defendant, that the landing where the vessel was tied was operated by another corporation and that defendant was not the plaintiff's employer.[5]

Analysis of the problem of the right to jury trial must begin in the light of the guidance established by the Supreme Court in Fitzgerald v. United States Lines Co., 374 U.S. 16, 83 S.Ct. 1646, 10 L.Ed.2d 720, 1963 A.M.C. 1093 (1963). There it was held error to refuse plaintiff a jury trial of his

---

3. See Crookham v. Muick, 246 F.Supp. 288, 1966 A.M.C. 1522 (W.D.Pa.1965), on which the district court relied.

4. The Jones Act provides:

"Any seaman who shall suffer personal injury in the course of his employment may, at his election, maintain an action for damages at law, with the right of trial by jury, and in such an action all statutes of the United States modifying or extending the common-law right or remedy in cases of personal injury to railway employees shall apply.   * * * Jurisdiction in such actions shall be un-

der the court of the district in which the defendant employer resides or in which his principal office is located." (46 U.S.C.A. § 688).

The term "jurisdiction" in the Jones Act has been interpreted to mean venue. See Panama R. R. Co. v. Johnson, 264 U.S. 375, 383–85, 44 S.Ct. 391, 68 L.Ed. 748, 1924 A.M.C. 551, 553 (1924).

5. The court also found that the vessel was not unseaworthy "with respect to its equipment, including means of ingress and egress."

claim for maintenance and cure coincident with the jury trial of his claims under the Jones Act for negligence and under maritime law for unseaworthiness.[6] The Court made no attempt to define precisely how plaintiff had labeled his claims, whether in admiralty or at law, although the opinion of the Court of Appeals[7] indicates that jurisdiction at law was asserted for the claim under the Jones Act with the unseaworthiness and maintenance and cure claims joined as pendent to it on the law side, under the doctrine of Romero v. International Terminal Operating Co., 358 U.S. 354, 380, 79 S.Ct. 468, 3 L.Ed.2d 368, 1959 A.M.C. 832, 853 (1959).[8] The Court based its decision on the fundamental factors of simplicity, utility to litigants and the interest of justice in having one tribunal decide the three claims which in general arise from a unitary set of circumstances. Mr. Justice Black said "Although remedies for negligence, unseaworthiness, and maintenance and cure have different origins and may on occasion call for application of slightly different principles and procedures, they nevertheless, when based on one unitary set of circumstances, serve the same purpose of indemnifying a seaman for damages caused by injury, depend in large part upon the same evidence, and involve some identical elements of recovery. Requiring a seaman to split up his lawsuit, submitting part of it to a jury and part to a judge, unduly complicates and confuses a trial, creates difficulties in applying doctrines of *res judicata* and collateral estoppel, and can easily result in too much or too little recovery."[9] Because of these considerations Mr. Justice Black concluded: "Only one trier of fact should be used for the trial of what is essentially one lawsuit to settle one claim split conceptually into separate parts because of historical developments. And since Congress in the Jones Act has declared that the negligence part of the claim shall be tried by a jury, we would not be free, even if we wished, to require submission of all the claims to the judge alone. Therefore, the jury, a time-honored institution in our jurisprudence, is the only tribunal competent under the present congressional enactments to try all the claims. Accordingly, we hold that a maintenance and cure claim joined with a Jones Act claim must be submitted to the jury when both arise out of one set of facts."[10]

6. The district court had followed the Second Circuit practice in permitting the claim of unseaworthiness to be tried before the jury together with the negligence claim under the Jones Act. Balado v. Lykes Bros. S. S. Co., 179 F.2d 943, 945, 1950 A.M.C. 609 (2 Cir.1950). Similarly, see McCarthy v. American Eastern Corp., 175 F.2d 724, 1953 A.M.C. 1864 (3 Cir.1949), cert. denied 338 U.S. 868, 70 S.Ct. 144, 94 L.Ed. 532 (1949), relying on the fact that each of these claims is res adjudicata of the other.

7. See Fitzgerald v. United States Lines Co., 306 F.2d 461, 463, 1962 A.M.C. 2251 (2 Cir.1962), reversed 374 U.S. 16, 83 S.Ct.

1646, 10 L.Ed.2d 720, 1963 A.M.C. 1093 (1963).

8. Romero held that a federal court which has jurisdiction over a Jones Act claim on the law side of the court, also has pendent jurisdiction to hear unseaworthiness and maintenance and cure claims joined on the law side, even though there is no independent jurisdiction at law over the maritime claims.

9. Fitzgerald v. United States Lines Co., 374 U.S. at 18–19, 83 S.Ct. at 1649, 1963 A.M.C. at 1095 (1963).

10. Id., 374 U.S. at 21, 83 S.Ct. 1650,- 1963 A.M.C. 1097.

It therefore is beyond question that a plaintiff who files a complaint at law under the Jones Act and demands a jury trial, has the right to join with it and have tried before a jury as pendent to it his claims under maritime law for unseaworthiness and for maintenance and cure. The Jones Act, however, provides the right to trial by jury only in an action at law,[11] and for such an action establishes a venue requirement.[12] The district court concluded that plaintiff's action did not satisfy the venue requirement of an action at law under the Jones Act because Pennsylvania was not the place of residence or principal place of business of the defendant. It held that all the claims could proceed in admiralty, whose venue requirement is that the action be brought wherever the defendant may be served with process or wherever defendant's property may be attached.[13] It was proper to proceed with all the claims in admiralty since the claims for unseaworthiness and maintenance and cure are creatures of admiralty and the Jones Act has been construed to permit a Jones Act claim for negligence to be maintained as an independent admiralty action.[14]

The district court's conclusion on venue, however, was based on a misapprehension of the factual situation. It was undisputed that defendant was incorporated within the judicial district in which the action was brought. This was the place of defendant's residence for venue under the Jones Act,[15] and since the Jones Act's requirement for venue in an action at law therefore was satisfied, plaintiff could have obtained trial by jury of his Jones Act negligence claim and with it, under *Fitzgerald*, trial before the same jury of his unseaworthiness and maintenance and cure claims if they had been made pendent to it on the law side of the court.

Plaintiff did not, however, seek the trial of all his claims on the law side of the court, but brought the unseaworthiness and maintenance and cure claims in admiralty. Nevertheless, we must interpret his demand for a jury trial of his claims and his designation of the Jones Act claim as a civil rather than a maritime claim, and as a pendent rather than an independent claim in admiralty, as indicating a choice that the Jones Act claim be designated as an action at law. In these circumstances we think that plaintiff was entitled to have his Jones Act claim tried before a jury as an action at law and to have his claims for unseaworthiness and maintenance and cure which were brought in admiralty submitted to the same jury. We see no reason why a plaintiff who sues at law under the Jones Act for negligence must make his claims for unseaworthiness and maintenance and cure pendent to it on the law side in order to maintain his right to trial by

11. Panama R. R. Co. v. Johnson, supra, 264 U.S. at 391, 1924 A.M.C. at 560; Yates v. Dann, 223 F.2d 64, 66, 1955 A.M.C. 1214 (3 Cir.1955); Texas Menhaden Co. v. Palermo, 329 F.2d 579, 1964 A.M.C. 2136 (5 Cir.1964); O'Brien v. U.S. Tank Ship Corp., 16 F.Supp. 478, 1936 A.M.C. 1552 (S.D.N.Y. 1936).

12. Leith v. Oil Transport Co., 321 F.2d 591, 1964 A.M.C. 2152 (3 Cir.1963).

13. Brown v. C. D. Mallory & Co., 122 F.2d 98, 104, 1941 A.M.C. 1043 (3 Cir.1941).

14. Panama R. R. Co. v. Johnson, supra, n. 4, 264 U.S. at 391, 44 S.Ct. 391, 1924 A.M.C. at 560 (1924).

15. See Pure Oil Co. v. Suarez, 384 U.S. 202, 203–4, 86 S.Ct. 1394, 16 L.Ed.2d 474, 1966 A.M.C. 1117 (1966).

jury on all three claims. To require this would compel him to lose the advantages which inhere in the characteristic admiralty claims, such as *in rem* process,[16] interlocutory appeals,[17] admiralty attachment[18] and the right to obtain depositions within twenty days of commencement of the action without permission of the court.[19] There is no reason to make relinquishment of the procedural advantages of these inherent admiralty claims for unseaworthiness and maintenance and cure the price for a jury trial. *Fitzgerald* has made it clear that the reason for trial by jury in claims for unseaworthiness and maintenance and cure is not that they are actions at law, but rather that there should be one fact finder and that when they are joined with the Jones Act claim under which a right of trial by jury is guaranteed, they, too, may be tried by the same jury. The Court in *Fitzgerald* did not justify its decision by characterizing the claims for unseaworthiness and maintenance and cure as having been brought on the law side, but instead specifically declared that it was creating a right to trial by jury in admiralty cases in the interest of judicial administration by virtue of the power left to it by Congress to fashion the controlling rules of admiralty law.[20]

There is no novelty in permitting a joint trial of claims in admiralty and claims at law.[21] For some years before *Romero* we required that claims for maintenance and cure be brought on the admiralty side of the court, subject to admiralty procedures and without trial by jury, rather than as pendent to an action at law under the Jones Act. Jordine v. Walling, 185 F.2d 662, 1951 A.M.C. 43 (3 Cir.1950). Yet in maintaining this distinction between the nature of the claims we nevertheless approved the practice in this circuit permitting a joint trial of the claim for maintenance and cure with the claim at law under the Jones Act for negligence and the claim for unseaworthiness, although the maintenance and cure claim was decided by the judge and the others by a jury. Jordine v. Walling, supra, 185 F.2d at 671, 1951 A.M.C. at 55.[22]

---

16. Rule C, Supplemental Rules for Certain Admiralty and Maritime Claims, Federal Rules of Civil Procedure.

17. Rule 73(h), Federal Rules of Civil Procedure; 28 U.S.C.A. § 1292(a)(3).

18. Rule B, Supplemental Rules for Certain Admiralty and Maritime Claims, Federal Rules of Civil Procedure.

19. Rule 26(a), Federal Rules of Civil Procedure; Rev.Stat. secs. 863–65.

20. Fitzgerald v. United States Lines, supra, 374 U.S. at 20–21, 83 S.Ct. 1646, 1963 A.M.C. at 1097 (1963).

21. See Continental Grain Co. v. Barge FBL–585, 364 U.S. 19, 80 S.Ct. 1470, 4 L.Ed.2d 1540, 1961 A.M.C. 1 (1960); McAfoss v. Canadian Pacific Steamships, Ltd., 243 F.2d 270, 1957 A.M.C. 982, (2 Cir.1957), cert.

denied 355 U.S. 823, 78 S.Ct. 32, 2 L.Ed.2d 39, 1957 A.M.C. 2493 (1957).

22. A dictum in Leith v. Oil Transport Co., supra, 321 F.2d at 592, 1964 A.M.C. at 2156, that a Jones Act claim and an unseaworthiness claim must be brought on the same side of the court does not preclude our permitting an unseaworthiness claim to be brought on the admiralty side, joined with a Jones Act claim at law where both are tried to a jury. The statement in *Leith* was made in the context of deciding that the definition in 28 U.S.C.A. § 1391(c) of a corporation's residence for venue did not apply to venue under the Jones Act, which was overruled in Pure Oil Co. v. Suarez, supra, n. 15. The dictum had reference to the fact that the claims must be brought together to avoid *res adjudicata*. This need is met if the claims

The unification of the civil and admiralty rules of procedure, which became effective July 1, 1966,[23] specifically authorizes a hybrid proceeding in which claims in admiralty and claims at law are tried together, yet distinctive maritime remedies and procedures are preserved on claims identified as being brought within the admiralty jurisdiction[24] under Rule 9(h).[25] The problems which such hybrid proceedings present are not fundamentally different from those created when law and equity were merged but not obliterated in the original rules, and will exist in the future under the present merger of the civil and admiralty rules. Prior to the unification the same problems required similar treatment in the circumstances of this case and therefore permitted unseaworthiness and maintenance and cure claims to be maintained in admiralty although joined with a Jones Act claim at law with a right to trial by jury on all three claims.

The provisions of the new merged rules do not, as defendant argues, prevent us from allowing a jury trial on the admiralty claims. It is true that the draftsmen took care to provide that the rules did not create a right of trial by jury in an admiralty or maritime claim,[26] and one of the reasons for the requirement in Rule 9(h) of a statement identifying a claim as an admiralty or maritime claim is to determine whether the action is one in which there is a right to trial by jury. However, the right to jury trial on admiralty claims joined with a Jones Act claim stems not from the merger of the civil and admiralty rules, but from a court-created right to trial by jury in such cases in the interest of the administration of justice. There is nothing in Rule 9(h) which prevents a jury trial on an admiralty claim when the right to trial by jury does not depend on the distinction whether it is in law or in admiralty. Although the unified rules were adopted and became effective after *Fitzgerald* was decided, they make no attempt to deal with the *Fitzgerald* decision and we must not construe them as indicating that the Supreme Court in approving and transmitting them to Congress

---

are brought on different "sides of the court" but are tried by the same fact finder.

23. 383 U.S. 1029, 1031.

24. Rules 1, 8(e), 18. The Advisory Committee on Maritime Rules which drafted the amendments to the Rules of Civil Procedure in which the merger of civil and admiralty rules was accomplished said in its letter of transmittal to the Committee on Rules of Practice and Procedure: "Unification does not mean complete uniformity. There are certain distinctively maritime remedies that must be preserved, as distinctively equitable remedies were preserved in the merger of equity and law. In addition, history or the exigencies of maritime litigation occasionally require procedures different from those now provided by the Civil Rules." 34 F.R.D. 331, 335.

25. Rule 9(h) provides:

"A pleading or count setting forth a claim for relief within the admiralty and maritime jurisdiction that is also within the jurisdiction of the district court on some other ground may contain a statement identifying the claim as an admiralty or maritime claim for the purposes of Rules 14(c), 26(a), 38(e), 73(h), 82, and the Supplemental Rules for Certain Admiralty and Maritime Claims. If the claim is cognizable only in admiralty it is an admiralty or maritime claim for those purposes whether so identified or not. The amendment of a pleading to add or withdraw an identifying statement is governed by the principles of Rule 15."

26. Rule 38(e) provides:

"These rules shall not be construed to create a right to trial by jury of the issues in an admiralty or maritime claim within the meaning of Rule 9(h)."

on February 28, 1966[27] meant to uproot the right to trial by jury in an admiralty action when it is joined with a claim under the Jones Act.

Since we conclude that the district court erred in holding that there was a lack of venue at law, that the claims therefore were required to be heard in admiralty, and hence that there was no right to trial by jury, the judgment of the district court must be vacated and the cause remanded for further proceedings. On remand plaintiff will be required to comply with Rule 9(h) which now will be applicable and to supplement his complaint by identifying those counts which he seeks to pursue as claims in admiralty. If he does not designate the Jones Act claim for negligence as being in admiralty for the purpose of Rule 9(h), he will be entitled to have all three claims decided by a jury as he has demanded.[28]

It has been suggested to us that defendant may be entitled by uncontroverted evidence to a dismissal of the action as a matter of law. Defendant had moved for a directed verdict at the close of all the evidence, but since the case was heard by a judge without a jury the motion was not formally ruled on as such. The findings of fact and conclusions of law of the trial judge afford no clear foundation for a determination whether plaintiff's claims were dismissed as a matter of law or on factual grounds. On remand the district court should therefore afford defendant an opportunity by appropriate motion to raise the question of the sufficiency of the evidence as a matter of law to make out a case for consideration by a jury. If the court finds the evidence inadequate for that purpose a judgment for the defendant as a matter of law will be appropriate; otherwise, if plaintiff does not file a statement designating the Jones Act claim as being in admiralty, he will be entitled to have his three claims submitted to a jury.

The judgment of the district court will be vacated and the cause remanded for further proceedings consistent with this opinion.

Teal v. Eagle Fleet, Inc. v. Penrod Drilling Corp.

United States Court of Appeals, Fifth Circuit, 1991.
933 F.2d 341.

■ PER CURIAM. Edwin Teal and his wife seek to appeal the district court's denial of motions seeking to set aside a settlement agreement the Teals entered into with Penrod Drilling Corporation ("Penrod"). The district court denied these various motions on procedural grounds. The Teals also contest the district court's decision to grant Penrod's motion to dismiss for failure to state a claim, arguing that the district court erred in dismissing Penrod without first addressing the merits of the settlement agreement.

---

27. 383 U.S. 1029, 1030.

28. In view of the basis of our decision, we do not pass upon the effect of the belated effort of plaintiff to show that diversity existed in the citizenship of the parties. See Atlantic & Gulf Stevedores, Inc. v. Ellerman Lines, Ltd., 369 U.S. 355, 359–60, 82 S.Ct. 780, 7 L.Ed.2d 798, 1962 A.M.C. 565 (1962); Philadelphia & R. R. Co. v. Berg, 274 F. 534, 539 (3 Cir.1921), cert. denied 257 U.S. 638, 42 S.Ct. 50, 66 L.Ed. 410 (1921); Advisory Committee Note to Rule 9(h), 39 F.R.D. 69, 75.

Because we find that the issue of the validity of the settlement agreement was never properly before the district court, we affirm.

I.   Facts and Proceedings Below

This action arises out of an accident in which Edwin Teal, a roustabout employed by Penrod, was injured when a crane operator on a Penrod jackup rig lowered him from a personnel basket onto the M/V AMERICAN EAGLE, a vessel owned and operated by Eagle Fleet, Inc. ("Eagle"). On August 20, 1986, Teal and his wife entered into a settlement agreement with Penrod. Under the terms of the settlement agreement, the Teals retained their rights to sue Eagle.

Subsequent to entering into their settlement agreement with Penrod, the Teals brought this action against Eagle and the M/V AMERICAN EAGLE. On August 1, 1989, Eagle filed a third party complaint against Penrod, tendering Penrod to the Teals pursuant to Federal Rule of Civil Procedure 14(c). Eagle also filed a motion to set aside the settlement between the Teals and Penrod, arguing that the district court should declare this agreement invalid because Penrod procured it through over-reaching and without obtaining the Teals' full understanding of its content and consequences.

Penrod timely filed an answer to Eagle's third party complaint and also filed a motion to dismiss, asserting lack of jurisdiction and, alternatively, failure to state a claim upon which relief could be granted. Subsequently, the district court denied Eagle's motion to set aside the settlement, finding that Eagle lacked standing to attack the settlement agreement because it was not prejudiced by the settlement. On October 27, 1989, Eagle filed a motion for reconsideration, arguing that it had standing to challenge the settlement agreement because it would suffer legal prejudice if the court failed to reduce its liability to the Teals by the amount of Penrod's liability. Eagle's motion for reconsideration was set for hearing on December 12, 1989. Two months after this scheduled hearing date, the Teals filed a memorandum in support of Eagle's motion for reconsideration.

On February 26, 1990, the Teals filed their first motion to set aside the settlement. When the Teals filed this motion, the trial was set for March 19, 1990. The court's standard pretrial order specifically stated that all dispositive motions must be filed sixty days prior to the pre-trial date. On March 13, 1990, the court entered an order denying both Eagle's motion for reconsideration and the Teals' motion to set aside the settlement. The court held that Eagle would not be prejudiced by the settlement with Penrod because the court would apportion damages pro rata in accordance with Leger v. Drilling Well Control, Inc., 592 F.2dr 1246 (5th Cir.1979). In addition, the district court denied the Teals' motion to set aside the settlement as "obviously" untimely.

In an order dated March 16, 1990, the district court addressed Penrod's motion to dismiss. The court held that it did have subject matter jurisdiction over Penrod because the Teals properly invoked admiralty jurisdiction, and therefore Eagle properly tendered Penrod to the plaintiffs pursuant to Rule 14(c). Nevertheless, the court granted Penrod's motion to dismiss for failure to state a claim, finding that Penrod had already settled with the Teals and Eagle was not prejudiced by that settlement.

On March 29, 1990, the Teals filed a motion for reconsideration of the court's order refusing to set aside the settlement agreement, arguing once again that the Teals did not understand the nature of the settlement agreement, and also arguing that Penrod had breached the agreement. The Teals attached to this motion for reconsideration certain exhibits and an affidavit from Teal which had not previously been submitted to the court. The district court denied the Teals' motion for reconsideration, noting that they could have presented the additional evidence in their first motion and, therefore, relief was not available, under a motion to reconsider.

Prior to the district court's denial of their motion for reconsideration, the Teals settled their claim with Eagle for an undisclosed sum and, upon the district court's denial of the Teals' motion for reconsideration, the matter was dismissed. The Teals subsequently filed this appeal, arguing that the district court erred when it dismissed the Teals' claims against Penrod without addressing the validity of the settlement agreement.

II. Discussion

A. Jurisdiction

Penrod argued in the district court, and argues now on appeal, that the district court never properly acquired jurisdiction over it. According to Penrod, the Teals' failure to specifically plead their cause as one arising under Rule 9(h), Fed.R.Civ.P. precluded Eagle from filing a Rule 14(c)[1] demand against Penrod. Rule 9(h) provides in pertinent part:

> A pleading or count setting forth a claim for relief within the admiralty and mantime jurisdiction that is also within the jurisdiction of the district court on some other ground may contain a statement identifying the claim as an admiralty or maritime claim for the purposes of Rule 14(c).

Fed.R.Civ.P. 9(h). The Teals titled their complaint as follows: "COMPLAINT WITHIN THE ADMIRALTY AND MARITIME JURISDICTION PURSUANT TO THE GENERAL MARITIME LAW OF THE UNITED STATES OF AMERICA...." Their complaint goes on to state that: "This case is cognizable under the admiralty and maritime jurisdiction pursuant to the General Maritime Law of the United States of America, 28 U.S.C. [§]1333 and diversity of citizenship...." In addition, the Teals pled an in rem action against the M/V AMERICAN EAGLE.

---

1. Third party claims under Rule 14(c) are only available in admiralty or maritime claims. Fed.R.Civ.P. 14(c). Rule 14(c) allows a defendant to implead a third party who he claims is wholly or partly liable, either to the plaintiff or to [himself] ... on account of the same transaction, occurrence, or series of transactions or occurrences.— Id. Where such a demand is made, Rule 14(c) provides that "the third-party defendant shall make his defenses to the claims of the plaintiff ... and the action shall proceed as if the plaintiff had commenced it against the third-party defendant as well as the third-party plaintiff." Id.

Although the Teals' complaint did not specifically invoke Rule 9(h), this court has held that a case cognizable under both admiralty and diversity jurisdiction will be treated as an admiralty action if the plaintiff asserts "a simple statement asserting admiralty or maritime claims." T.N.T. Marine Serv., Inc. v. Weaver Shipyards & Dry Docks, Inc., 702 F.2d 585, 588 [36 Fed Rules Serv.2d 293] (5th Cir.), cert. denied, 464 U.S. 847, 104 S.Ct. 151, 78 L.Ed.2d 141 (1983); cf. 5 Wright & Miller, Federal Practice and Procedure: Civil 2d § 1313 at 719 (1990)(preferred technique is to expressly invoke Rule 9(h)). Therefore, under our jurisprudence, a party need not make a specific reference to Rule 9(h) in order to fall under our admiralty jurisdiction. See Durden v. Exxon Corp., 803 F.2d 845, 848–50 [6 Fed Rules Serv.3d 806] (5th Cir.1986); T.N.T. Marine, 702 F.2d at 586–88.

In T.N.T. Marine and Durden, the plaintiffs asserted both admiralty and diversity jurisdiction. In addition, in both cases in rem actions were pled against the vessel involved. Although neither plaintiff's complaint specifically mentioned Rule 9(h), both complaints contained simple statements asserting admiralty or maritime claims or jurisdiction. Consequently, in both cases this court held that the plaintiff had properly invoked admiralty jurisdiction. See T.N.T. Marine, 702 F.2d at 587; Durden, 803 F.2d at 850; cf. Bodden v. Osgood, 879 F.2d 184, 186 [14 Fed Rules Serv.3d 1083] (5th Cir.1989)(where complaint alleged suit brought under admiralty and general maritime laws, but where suit was filed in state court which lacked jurisdiction and plaintiff failed to object to defendant's removal to federal court solely on diversity grounds, no admiralty jurisdiction). Because this court finds that the Teals properly invoked admiralty rules and procedures in their original complaint, we hold that Eagle properly tendered Penrod to the plaintiffs pursuant to Rule 14(c).

B. The Settlement Agreement

[16e.2, 60b.27, 60b.311] In the district court, Eagle moved to set aside the Teals' settlement with Penrod, arguing that the court should declare this agreement invalid because it was procured through: overreaching and without the Teals' full understanding of its content and consequences. We hold that the district court correctly denied this motion because Eagle did not have standing to attack the validity of the settlement when it was not prejudiced by that agreement.

The general rule in this court is that "a non-settling defendant ... [who] is not prejudiced by the settlement ... has no standing to complain about the settlement." In re Beef Indus. Antitrust Litig., 607 F.2d 167, 172 [28 Fed Rules Serv.2d 940] (5th Cir.1979), cert. denied, 452 U.S. 905, 101 S.Ct. 3029, 69 L.Ed.2d 405 (1981); see also Bass v. Phoenix Seadrill/78 Ltd., 749 F.2d 1154, 1160 n. 10 (5th Cir.1985). The district court correctly held that any damages awarded to the Teals would be allocated among the parties proportionate with their degree of fault. See Leger v. Drilling Well Control, Inc., 592 F.2d 1246, 1248 (5th Cir.1979).[2] Therefore Eagle was

---

2. Eagle argued that the application of the credit doctrine enunciated in Hernandez v. M/V RAJAAN, 841 F.2d 582 (5th Cir.1988), would prejudice Eagle. Hernandez provides

not prejudiced by the settlement because the court would have reduced any judgment in favor of the Teals by the proportion of negligence attributable to Penrod and Eagle would only have had to pay their proportionate share. Consequently Eagle lacked any claim against Penrod. For similar reasons, the court correctly denied Eagle's motion for reconsideration.

Moreover, the Teals did not timely contest the settlement agreement. It is well established that seamen, like Teal, are wards of admiralty whose rights federal courts are duty-bound to jealously protect. Bass v. Phoenix Seadrill/78, Ltd., 749 F.2d 1154, 1160–61 (5th Cir.1985); see also Garrett v. Moore–McCormack Co., 317 U.S. 239, 63 S.Ct. 246, 87 L.Ed. 239 (1942). In addition, this court has long recognized that courts must be particularly vigilant to guard against overreaching when a seaman purports to release his right to compensation for personal injuries. See, e.g., Wink v. Rowan Drilling Co., 611 F.2d 98, 100 (5th Cir.)("releases or settlements involving seaman's rights are subject to careful scrutiny"), cert. denied, 449 U.S. 823, 101 S.Ct. 84, 66 L.Ed.2d 26 (1980).

It does not follow, however, that a district court must independently reject a settlement agreement which has not been attacked by a party to the agreement with standing to object. Bass, 749 F.2d at 1160 n. 10, 1161 n. 12. Although a district court may have inherent authority to sua sponte raise the validity of a seaman's release, a court is certainly not required to do so. Id. Therefore, the district court was not required to independently inquire into the merits of the Teals' settlement with Penrod unless the issue was raised in a timely manner by a party to the agreement, i.e. the Teals.

The Teals' first formal challenge to the settlement was not filed until February 28, 1990, even though more than four months earlier the district court specifically pointed out in its ruling denying Eagle's motion to set aside the settlement that Eagle lacked standing to attack the validity of the settlement and that the Teals had not filed any pleadings attacking the settlement. In their memorandum in support of Eagle's motion for reconsideration, filed February 12, 1990, the Teals merely sought application of the Hernandez dollar for dollar allocation doctrine, and alternatively suggested that the court examine the settlement. On February 28, 1990, the Teals filed their first independent motion to set aside the settlement agreement.

When both of these pleadings were filed, the trial of this matter was scheduled for March 19, 1990. According to the district court's standard pretrial order concerning deadlines, all dispositive motions had to be fled no later than sixty days prior to the pre-trial date. The district court enjoys broad discretion in controlling its own docket. Edwards v. Cass County, Tex., 919 F.2d 273, 275 (5th Cir.1990). Since the Teals made no showing that their delay in challenging the settlement was warranted, the district

---

a dollar for dollar reduction to the nonsettling party, as opposed to the pro rata reduction espoused in Leger. The district court correctly held that Leger was applicable to this case.

court's denial of the motion as untimely was well within the court's discretion. The district court should not be obliged to interrupt the orderly proceedings of its docket to rule on this issue when the Teals could have easily presented these matters earlier. Id. at 275–76.

The district court subsequently addressed Penrod's motion to dismiss. After correctly finding that admiralty jurisdiction was properly invoked, the court ruled that since Penrod settled with the Teals before Eagle instituted the third party action against Penrod, the Teals no longer had a cause of action against Penrod. This was correct because even though the Teals were not barred from contesting the validity of the settlement, they had not exercised this right in a timely fashion. Furthermore, in the absence of a direct attack on the settlement agreement, when the "plaintiff settles with and grants a release as to one or more [defendants], reserving his rights against the remaining [defendants], the settling defendants are relieved of any further liability to the plaintiff." Leger, 592 F.2d at 1248. Therefore, since neither Eagle nor the Teals had an asserted, valid claim against Penrod, the district court correctly granted Penrod's motion to dismiss. See Fed.R.Civ.p, 12(b)(6).

The trial scheduled for March 19, 1990, never occurred because after the court dismissed Penrod, the Teals settled their claim with Eagle. After the district court dismissed Penrod, the Teals filed a motion to reconsider and set aside the settlement, arguing that they did not have a full understanding of the effect of the agreement when they signed it, and arguing that Penrod had breached the settlement agreement. The Teals attached to this motion for reconsideration certain exhibits and an affidavit from Teal which had not previously been submitted to the court. The district court also denied this motion on procedural grounds.

As the district court correctly noted, the Federal Rules of Civil Procedure do not specifically provide for a "motion for reconsideration." Lavespere v. Niagara Mach. & Tool Works, Inc., 910 F.2d 167, 173 [17 Fed Rules Serv.3d 654] (5th Cir.1990). This court has held, however, that such a motion which challenges the prior judgment on its merit will be treated as either a motion "to alter or amend under Rule 59(e) or a motion for relief from judgment under Rule 60(b)."[3] Since the district court had already dismissed Penrod from the action when the Teals filed their motion for reconsideration, we find that this motion essentially challenged the court's judgment in dismissing Penrod. Since this motion was filed more than ten days after the rendition of the judgment dismissing Penrod, it falls under Rule 60(b). Lavespere, 910 F.2d at 173.[4]

---

3. Id.; see also Forsythe v. Saudi Arabian Airlines Corp., 885 F.2d 285, 288 (5th Cir.1989); Harcon Barge Co. v. D & G Boat Rentals, Inc., 784 F.2d 665, 669–70, 14 Fed Rules Serv.3d 1 (5th Cir.)(en banc), cert. denied, 479 U.S. 930. 107 S.Ct. 398, 93 L.Ed.2d 351 (1986).

4. Whether this court treats the motion under Rule 59(e) or Rule 60(b) depends on the time at which the motion is served. If the motion is served within ten days of the. rendition of judgment, the motion falls under Rule 59(e); if it is served after that time, it falls under Rule 60(b). Lavespere, 910 F.2d at 173; Harcon Barge, 784 F.2d at 667.

Under Rule 60(b), in order to prevail the Teals must have demonstrated that the evidence in support of their motion to reconsider was not presented in their original motion to upset the settlement due to: "(1) mistake, inadvertence, surprise, or excusable neglect; (2) newly discovered evidence . . .; (3) fraud . . .; (4) the judgment is void; (5) the judgment has been satisfied, released or discharged . . .; or (6) any other reason justifying relief from the operation of the judgment." Fed.R.Civ.P. 60(b). The district court enjoys considerable discretion when determining whether the movant has satisfied any of these Rule 60(b) standards. Lavespere, 910 F.2d at 173; see also Smith v. Alumax Extrusions, Inc., 868 F.2d 1469, 1471 [13 Fed Rules Serv.3d 667] (5th Cir.1989).

In their motion for reconsideration, the Teals did not even attempt to explain why their new evidence could not have been brought as part of their initial motion to set aside the settlement. Indeed, the district court's careful review of the new evidence revealed that all of the evidence was available at the time the Teals filed their first motion. Therefore, the district court did not abuse its discretion when it denied the Teals' motion for reconsideration.

III. Conclusion

For the above-stated reasons, we affirm the decision of the district court.

Powell v. Offshore Navigation, Inc.

United States Court of Appeals, Fifth Circuit, 1981.
644 F.2d 1063.

■ RANDALL, CIRCUIT JUDGE:

This appeal arises from a judgment in favor of defendants in a maritime action based on negligence and unseaworthiness. The primary issue is the district court's denial of the plaintiff's request for trial by jury, which request was based on plaintiff's assertion of diversity jurisdiction as an alternative to federal admiralty jurisdiction. We hold that diversity jurisdiction did not lie because of the absence of complete diversity between the plaintiff and all of the defendants, and that this defect was not remedied by the plaintiff's assertion of admiralty jurisdiction over the non-diverse defendant. We affirm the judgment of the district court in favor of the defendants.

I

Tyrone Powell, an employee of the Department of the Interior, file suit in August, 1976 in the United States District Court for the Eastern District of Louisiana seeking compensation for personal injuries allegedly sustained as a result of his consumption of contaminated drinking water aboard a private vessel hired by the Department of the Interior to perform geological survey work in the Gulf of Mexico. Powell's suit was based solely on the unseaworthiness of the vessel and on the negligence of certain *in personam* defendants. In his original complaint, Powell named as defendants the

M/V DRAKO, the vessel on which the injury occurred; Atlas Offshore Boat Service, Inc. (Atlas), the owner of the vessel; and Offshore Navigation, Inc. (Offshore), the charterer of the vessel.   Powell sought jurisdiction pursuant to 28 U.S.C. § 1391(b) and (c)(1976) and "the General Maritime Laws,"[1] and asserted the applicability of Federal Rule of Civil Procedure 9(h),[2] thereby identifying his action as an admiralty claim for purposes of the federal rules.   Powell also requested a trial by jury.

The defendants responded by moving, *inter alia*, to strike Powell's request for a jury trial.   They argued that no right to trial by jury exists with respect to claims brought under federal admiralty jurisdiction, and that Powell had by his Rule 9(h) request specifically invoked such jurisdiction.   These contentions of the defendants were clearly correct.   See Harrison v. Flota Mercante Grancolombiana S.A., 577 F.2d 968, 985–88 (5th Cir.1978).   Moreover, we note that jurisdiction could not have been established on any basis other than admiralty on the facts stated in the original complaint.   Diversity jurisdiction could not lie because Powell was a citizen of Louisiana and both Atlas and Offshore were asserted to be Louisiana corporations; and since Powell's complaint stated only maritime claims, his case could not be heard under the general federal question jurisdiction of 28 U.S.C. § 1331.   Romero v. International Terminal Operating Co., 358 U.S. 354, 79 S.Ct. 468, 3 L.Ed.2d 368 (1959).   Accordingly the district court granted the defendants' motion to strike Powell's request for a jury trial, but granted a motion by Powell to amend his complaint so as to assert a basis for diversity jurisdiction.

Powell thereupon filed an amended complaint in which he named three diverse defendants in addition to the nondiverse defendants named in the original complaint: Texaco, Inc., the manufacturer of a coating used on the inside of the vessel's water tanks; Old Reliable Fire Insurance Co. (Old Reliable), Altas's insurer; and American Home Assurance Co. (American Home), Offshore's insurer.   Powell asserted that these three defendants were all foreign corporations, and also amended his complaint to assert that Offshore was a foreign corporation.   An assertion in the original complaint that Atlas was a Louisiana Corporation was not changed.   Powell then invoked the diversity jurisdiction of the court, 28 U.S.C. § 1332 with respect to his claims against the diverse defendants (Offshore, Texaco, Old Reliable, and American Home), and the admiralty jurisdiction of the court, 28 U.S.C. § 1333, with respect to the nondiverse defendants (Atlas and the M/V/ DRACO).[3]   Powell again requested a jury trial, but this time only

---

1.   28 U.S.C. § 1391 is of course the federal venue statute and does not grant any form of federal jurisdiction. We assume on the basis of Powell's reference to "the General Maritime Laws" and his assertion of Fed. R.Civ.P 9(h), that Powell intended in his original complaint to invoke the federal admiralty jurisdiction, 28 U.S.C. § 1333.

2.   [Setting forth the text of the rule].

3.   Since the action against the M/V DRACO is *in rem*, it falls within the exclusive admiralty jurisdiction of the federal courts and thus could not in any event be sued upon under federal diversity jurisdiction. While we therefore classify the vessel as "non-diverse," this does not mean that its is non-diverse in all senses in which a person may be so classified. For purposes of the complete diversity requirement, discussed in greater detail be-with respect to the diversity defendants. He argued, in brief, that his claim against these defendants arose at common law and was therefor excepted from exclusive federal jurisdiction over maritime claims by the "saving-to-suitors" clause of section 1333;[4] Powell contended that his suit against the diverse defendants could therefore be brought in federal court by virtue of diversity jurisdiction, in which case the usual rule denying the right to jury trial in admiralty cases would not apply.

No party has disputed Powell's contention that a party asserting a maritime claim arising under the common law and brought in federal court by virtue of its diversity jurisdiction may indeed be tried by a jury. Although the substance of such a claim is generally no different from the merits of a maritime claim brought at admiralty in a federal court,[5] a common law claim heard under the court's diversity jurisdiction is nevertheless beyond the reach of the admiralty rule restricting the right of trial by jury. This confusing distinction arises from the existence of alternative admiralty and non-admiralty remedies in *in personam* actions which fall within the scope of section 1333. As Professors Gilmore and Black succinctly explain:

> The Judiciary Act of 1789, it will be recalled, while bestowing exclusive "admiralty" jurisdiction on the District Courts, saved "to suitors, in all cases, the right of a common law remedy where the common law is competent to give it." [now codified at 28 U.S.C.A. § 1333; see, supra note 4 for revised version now in force] . . .

> Summarily, the result of the cases is that a suitor who holds an *in personam* claim, which might be enforced by suit *in personam* in admiralty, may also bring suit, at his election, in the "common law" court—that is, by

---

low, we treat the vessel as neither diverse nor non-diverse, for its presence in the suit in no way implicates the rationale behind diversity jurisdiction, that is, the protection of out-of-state litigants against bias in state courts.

4. A maritime claim brought in the common law state courts or, by diversity jurisdiction, on the law side of the federal courts, is governed by the same principles as govern actions brought at admiralty, i.e. by *federal maritime law*. E.g., Pope & Talbot, Inc. v. Hawn, 346 U.S. 406, 409–11, 74 S.Ct. 202, 204–05, 98 L.Ed. 143 (1953); Garrett v. Moore–McCormack Co., 317 U.S. 239, 243–46, 63 S.Ct. 246, 249–50, 87 L.Ed. 239 (1942). State law may of course supplement federal maritime law, as in the exercise of its police powers or in the provision of an additional tort remedy; state law may not, however, conflict with federal maritime law, as it would by redefining the requirements or limits of a remedy available in admiralty. E.g., Askew v. American Waterways Operators, Inc.

5. A maritime claim brought in the common law state courts or, by diversity jurisdiction, on the law side of the federal courts, is governed by the same principles as govern actions brought at admiralty, i.e., by *federal maritime law*. E.g., Pope & Talbot, Inc. v. Hawn, 346 U.S. 406, 409–11, 74 S.Ct. 202, 204–05, 98 L.Ed. 143 (1953); Garrett v. Moore–McCormack Co., 317 U.S. 239, 243–46, 63 S.Ct. 246, 249–50, 87 L.Ed. 239 (1942). State law may of course supplement federal maritime law, as in the exercise of its police powers or in the provision of an additional maritime tort remedy; state law may not, however, conflict with federal maritime law, as it would be redefining the requirements or limits of a remedy available at admiralty. E.g., Askew v. American Waterways Operators, Inc., 411 U.S. 325, 93 S.Ct. 1590, 36 L.Ed.2d 280 (1973); Romero v. International Terminal Operating Co., supra 358 U.S. 373– 74, 79 S.Ct. 480–81; Just v. Chambers, 312 U.S. 383, 387–92, 61 S.Ct. 687, 690–93, 85 L.Ed. 903 (1941).

ordinary civil action in state court, or in federal court without reference to "admiralty," given diversity of citizenship and the requisite jurisdictional amount.

G. Gilmore & C. Black, Jr., The Law of Admiralty § 1–13 at 37 (1975). See 7A J.Moore & A. Pelaez, Moore's Federal Practice ¶ .210 (1979). Since a federal court exercising diversity jurisdiction to hear an *in personam* maritime claim is sitting as a common law court, the parties in a diversity action may assert their right to trial by jury despite the limitations associated with actions in admiralty. A. & G. Stevedores v. Ellerman Lines, Ltd., 369 U.S. 355, 360, 82 S.Ct. 780, 784, 7 L.Ed.2d 798 (1962). Powell's *in personam* claims, which are based on defendants' alleged negligence and on the vessel's alleged lack of seaworthiness, may of course be brought in state common law courts as well as in federal admiralty courts. Seas Shipping Co. v. Sieracki, 328 U.S. 85, 88–89, 66 S.Ct. 872, 874, 90 L.Ed. 1099 (1946). Therefore Powell was entitled to a jury trial if he could invoke the diversity jurisdiction of the district court to hear his maritime claims at law.

The difficulty with Powell's assertion of diversity jurisdiction is the apparent absence of complete diversity in this case, for Powell has named at least one defendant (Atlas) which is a citizen of the same state as is Powell. The rule of Strawbridge v. Curtiss, 3 Cranch (7 U.S.) 267, 2 L.Ed. 435 (1806), bars diversity actions where *any* defendant is a citizen of the same state as is the plaintiff. The ancient rules rests on the purpose of the original grant of diversity jurisdiction, which seems to have provided a national forum for the protection of out-of-state litigants against bias in favor of state residents. Since the chance of such bias decreases where citizens of one state are on opposing sides of the same lawsuit, the justification for diversity jurisdiction is diminished absent diversity between each plaintiff and each defendant. See Wright, A. Miller & E. Cooper, Federal Practice & Procedure § 3605 (1975). The complete diversity requirement is accorded particular deference because of its continued application over such a long period of our history. As the Supreme Court explained in Owen Equipment and Erection Co. v. Kroger, 437 U.S. 365, 98 S.Ct. 2396, 57 L.Ed.2d 274 (1978):

> Over the years Congress has repeatedly re-enacted or amended the statute conferring diversity jurisdiction, leaving in tact this rule of complete diversity. Whatever may have been the original purposes of diversity-of-citizenship jurisdiction, this subsequent history clearly demonstrates a Congressional mandate that diversity jurisdiction is not to be available when any plaintiff is a citizen of the same State as any defendant.

437 U.S. at 373–74 (footnotes omitted). This court too has emphasized the importance of the complete diversity requirement. See, e.g., Fawvor v. Texaco, Inc., 546 F.2d 636, 638–39 (5th Cir.1977).

Powell recognizes that the rule of *Strawbridge v. Curtiss* would bar a diversity action against all the named defendants in a single suit. However, Powell argues that his complaint asserts an "independent federal cause of action" (under federal admiralty jurisdiction, 28 U.S.C.A. § 1333) against the non-diverse defendant (Atlas) and that the non-diverse defendant therefore should not be counted for purposes of the complete diversity requirement. For this proposition Powell relies on Romero v. International Terminal Operating Co., 358 U.S. 354, 79 S.Ct. 468, 3 L.Ed.2d 368 (1959), in which the Supreme Court held, *inter alia*, that the naming of a non-diverse in a maritime case would not violate the complete diversity requirement where the plaintiff had stated a Jones Act claim against that defendant. The Court explained its holding as follows:

> Respondents [New York and Delaware corporations] are of diverse citizenship from the petitioner, a Spanish subject. Since the Jones Act provides an independent basis of federal jurisdiction over the non-diverse respondent [a Spanish corporation], the rule of Strawbridge v. Curtiss, 3 Cranch 267, [2 L.Ed. 435] does not require dismissal of the claims against the diverse respondents. Accordingly the dismissal of these claims for lack of jurisdiction was erroneous.

358 U.S. at 381, 79 S.Ct. at 485. In terms of *Romero*, then, Powell's argument is that his claim against Atlas should not bar diversity jurisdiction over the other defendants because that claim rests on an "independent basis of federal jurisdiction"—i.e., the admiralty jurisdiction of section 1333.

In response, the defendants note that the non-diverse defendant in *Romero* was brought into the action by virtue of a *Jones Act* claim, which rests on a non-admiralty grant of jurisdiction. Since the Jones Act establishes a federal statutory basis for recovery, see 46 U.S.C. § 688, jurisdiction of a Jones Act claim is founded on general federal question jurisdiction, 28 U.S.C. § 1331, and not on federal admiralty jurisdiction, 28 U.S.C § 1333. See G. Gilmore & C. Black, Jr., at § 6–62. The non-diverse defendant in this case, however, is named solely on the basis of federal admiralty jurisdiction, 28 U.S.C. § 1333. On this basis the defendants argue that section 1333 is not an "independent basis of federal jurisdiction" in the context of the *Romero* holding at issue here. The district court agreed with this analysis and refused Powell's request for a jury trial with respect to the diverse defendants. The court explained its decision on rehearing of the issue as follows:

> Disregarding our admiralty jurisdiction, as we must in questioning whether or not this general maritime tort action is attended by a right to jury trial by virtue of the saving-to-suitors clause of 28 U.S.C. § 1333, we denied the plaintiff's motion for a jury trial as to defendant's purportedly diverse from him, for lack of complete diversity under Strawbridge v. Curtiss, 3 Cranch 267, 2 L.Ed. 435.

All parties agree, and the district court seems to have assumed, that *Romero* excepts the *Strawbridge* requirement with respect to common law maritime claims only where the non-diverse defendant is the subject of an "independent" basis of federal "jurisdiction." The question before us is therefore a narrow one: is federal admiralty jurisdiction an "independent basis of federal jurisdiction" which will allow suit against a non-diverse defendant in a maritime case without violating the rule of *Strawbridge v. Curtiss* and thereby destroying diversity jurisdiction over diverse defendants sued in the same action under the saving-to suitors clause of section 1333?

II

This question, which does not appear to have previously addressed,[6] arises because of the ambiguity in the Supreme Court's use of the phrase "independent basis of federal jurisdiction." Two possibilities arise from a cursory reading of the *Romero* language. First the court might have used "independent" to denote any jurisdictional basis other than diversity. This interpretation is urged by Powell, who relies on federal admiralty jurisdiction for his claim against the non-diverse defendant. Second, the Court might have used "independent" to denote any *non-admiralty* basis of jurisdiction. This interpretation, urged by the defendants, rests heavily on the fact that *Romero* involved a Jones Act claim, which of course arises under general federal question jurisdiction.

There is a marked difference between these two possibilities. Federal admiralty jurisdictions is "independent" of maritime claims allowed by the saving-to-suitors clause and brought in federal court by virtue of diversity jurisdiction only in a very limited conceptual sense. Every maritime claim that is brought in diversity may also be brought under federal admiralty jurisdiction for the saving-to-suitors clause of section 1333 merely allows concurrent, not exclusive, jurisdiction to the state common law courts. Moreover, as a general rule the same substantive law governs the case whether it is brought under the admiralty jurisdiction of the federal courts or instead by the saving-to-suitors clause under either the common law jurisdiction of the states or the diversity jurisdiction of the federal courts. See See supra at note 5. The choice between the two different routes through which a maritime claim my reach the federal courts (admiralty and diversity) is therefore determinative only of whether the suit is "at admiralty" or "at law;" the choice affects various procedural matters (most importantly the right to trial by jury) but does not affect the substantive rights of the parties. On the other hand, a Jones Act claim is "independent" of maritime claims brought in diversity in a more important substantive sense. The Jones Act creates a cause of action for the seaman who is injured in the course of his employment by his employer's negligence, thereby allowing a maritime tort recovery by seamen against their employers. The general maritime law—whether applied by federal courts sitting in admiralty or by state common law courts—does not provide for such claims. See generally G. Gilmore & C. Black, Jr., supra, at §§ 6–20 to 6–28. A Jones Act claim is therefore a different cause of action altogether from claims that can be brought in federal court under admiralty jurisdiction; the parameters of this cause of action are defined by the statute and not by the general maritime law. The Jones Act, for example, incorporates

---

6. But see Serrano v. Empresa Lineas Maritimas Argentinas, 257 F.Supp. 870, 875 (D.Md.1966)(apparently concluding that admiralty jurisdiction is an "independent basis of federal jurisdiction" within the meaning of the *Romero* exception to *Strawbridge v. Curtiss*).

the terms of the Federal Employers Liability Act, 45 U.S.C. §§ 51–60, which provisions do not affect maritime claims under section 1333. See id.

With the two possible interpretations of the phrase "independent basis of federal jurisdiction" thus understood, we think it clear that the *Romero* exception to to the rule of *Strawbridge v. Curtiss*, applies only in the narrower circumstances stated by the district court—*i.e.,* where a *non-admiralty* basis of jurisdiction exists over the non-diverse defendant. The broader interpretation urged by Powel—*i.e.,* that the *Romero* exception applies whenever *any* basis of jurisdiction other than diversity can be asserted against the non-diverse defendant—leads to a result much broader than anything possibly contemplated in *Romero*. As noted above, *any* action which may be brought at common law under the saving-to-suitors clause (and therefore into the federal court via diversity) may also be brought under federal admiralty jurisdiction. Conversely, *any* claim brought under admiralty jurisdiction but falling under the saving-to-suitors clause (i.e. any *in personam* maritime claim) may also be brought in federal court as a diversity action, provided of course that the plaintiff establishes diversity and the requisite jurisdictional amount. Thus a maritime claim against several defendants but not involving Jones Act or other statutory claims states a series of claims which may alternatively be brought either at admiralty or at law. Although the plaintiff might prefer to try his suit at law, he has the alternative with respect to each claim of bringing his suit at admiralty. If the plaintiff is allowed to assert diversity jurisdiction against diverse defendants while he asserts admiralty jurisdiction against the non-diverse, the result is the abolition of the complete diversity requirement in maritime cases, for in such cases the plaintiff will *always* have the option of suing each non-diverse defendant at admiralty. We think it clear that *Romero* did not, however, abolish the *Strawbridge v. Curtiss* requirement in the context of admiralty suits: the opinion rests on the proposition that "the Jones Act provides an independent basis of jurisdiction," a statement which on its face presumes that maritime cases do indeed exist where no such "independent basis" exists.

There is of course a certain artificiality in this analysis, for whether or not the rule of *Strawbridge v. Curtiss* bars diversity jurisdiction in this case, it is clear that jurisdiction over each claim is at least within the bounds of federal admiralty jurisdiction. The real issue was whether Powell was entitled to trial by jury, and that is a question which only by historical accident hinges upon the nature of of the jurisdictional basis. Still, however, the district court's narrow interpretation of *Romero* is most consistent with the legal framework now in place for determining whether a right to trial by jury exists in a maritime case tried in the federal courts. If the broader interpretation of *Romero* were accepted, i.e., if admiralty were such an "independent basis" of jurisdiction as would exempt the non-diverse defendant from the *Strawbridge* requirement, then the existence of alternative admiralty and common law claims would in effect allow a plaintiff to circumvent the complete diversity requirement altogether, for each non-diverse defendant could be sued under the admiralty alternative. This would leave the district court with two choices with respect to the granting of a trial by jury in all maritime cases in which minimal diversity is present; each of these choices, however, is inconsistent with the jurisdictional framework established by Congress and developed by the Supreme Court.

First, the court could hold a jury trial with respect to the diverse defendants, whose claims are "at law," and a bench trial with respect to the non-diverse defendants whose claims are "at admiralty." A similar splitting of the case between fact-finders was, however, condemned by the Supreme Court in Fitzgerald v. United States Lines, 374 U.S. 16, 83 S.Ct. 1646, 10 L.Ed.2d 720 (1963)(a maintenance and cure claim joined by pendent jurisdiction with a Jones Act claim must be submitted to the jury when both arise from one set of facts). As the Court explained:

> Requiring a seaman to split up his law suit, submitting part of it to a jury and part to a judge, unduly complicates and confuses a trial, creates difficulties in applying doctrines of *res judicata* and collateral estoppel, and can easily result in too much or too little recovery.

374 U.S. at 18–19. Of course the splitting in *Fitzgerald* was particularly striking because it had the effect of dividing interrelated causes of action between the two fact-finders; recovery under the admiralty claims (tried by the judge) depended in part on factual findings made with respect to the Jones Act claim (tried by the jury, whose particular findings and reasoning could only be guessed by the judge). In this case each defendant would have its claims decided by a single fact-finder and there would be no need to split causes of action against any one defendant. It should be obvious, however, that the facts necessary to establish claims against the various defendants are nevertheless interrelated in a manner analogous to the confusion between the causes of action at issue in *Fitzgerald*, for the claims against all defendants arise out of the same maritime accident. We think the interest at stake in *Fitzgerald* is therefore no less relevant here, and that consequently one trier of fact should be used with respect to all defendants.

The second alternative is for the district court to grant a jury trial with respect to all defendants, both diverse and non-diverse. While this approach is arguably consistent with that taken in *Fitzgerald*,[7] it would cause a far greater change in the number and type of claims cognizable only at admiralty but nevertheless tried to a jury. In *Fitzgerald* the Supreme Court allowed a seaman to submit a maritime claim against a single defendant to the jury along with the seaman's Jones Act claim against the same defendant. However, the joinder of claims for trial by jury would allow a plaintiff to assert a right to trial by jury against *all* named

---

7. We note however that the question here is quite distinct from that raised in *Fitzgerald*. The *Fitzgerald* opinion rests on the proper assumption that the plaintiff was entitled to a trial by jury at least with respect to his cause of action under the Jones Act. Here by contrast we are faced with the threshold question of whether the right to a trial by jury exists at all with respect to any of the defendants named in the case. The choice in *Fitzgerald* was between splitting the case and trying the whole matter to a jury; here we have the additional option of trying the whole matter to the court.

defendants in *all* maritime cases in which even a single diverse defendant could be named. As this case illustrates, that task is not a difficult one ; having lost his initial bid for a jury trial, Powell merely amended his complaint to add the two out-of-state insurers and an out-of-state manufacturer of a product involved in the accident.

The consequent expansion in the use of juries in federal admiralty cases admiralty cases may or may not be desirable as a matter of public policy, but it is certainly contrary to the still extant division between actions at admiralty and actions at law.[8] In this respect we find instructive the Supreme Court's guidance on the distinction between admiralty and general federal question jurisdiction. In *Romero v. International Terminal Operating Co.*, supra, the Court rejected an assertion by the plaintiff that cases based on general maritime law arose under general federal question jurisdiction, 28 U.S.C. § 1331. Although maritime claims seem literally to fall within this provision,[9] the Court emphasized the absence of any intent behind the act establishing general federal question jurisdiction to so include within it what was already cognizable under federal admiralty jurisdiction. As the Court explained:

> There is not the slightest indication of any intention, or of any professional or lay demands for a change in the time-sanctioned mode of trying suits in admiralty without a jury, from which it can be inferred that the new grant of cases "arising under the Constitution or laws" a drastic innovation was impliedly introduced into admiralty procedure, whereby Congress changed the method by which federal courts had administered admiralty for almost a century. To draw such an inference is to find that a revolutionary procedural change had undesignedly come to pass.

358 U.S. at 354. The question now before us is analogous to the section 1331 issue decided by the Supreme Court in *Romero*. Here the plaintiff seeks an action at law and therefore a jury trial by virtue of diversity jurisdiction rather than by virtue of general federal question jurisdiction. Here the issue is more complex than in *Romero,* for the saving-to suitors clause undeniably allows maritime claims to be brought at common law and, when diversity jurisdiction is present, on the law side of the federal courts. So long as diversity and the requisite jurisdictional amount is established, therefore, the jurisdictional system does indeed allow a plaintiff to do through diversity jurisdiction what he could not do through general federal question jurisdiction. What the plaintiff asks here, however, is a definition of diversity which is different from that applied in any other context. As we have explained, the rule urged by Powell would in effect require only minimal diversity in maritime cases, since any non-diverse defendant could be sued under federal admiralty jurisdiction and thereby

---

8. The Federal Rules of Civil Procedure were amended in 1966 so as to rescind the Rules of Practice in Admiralty and Maritime Cases and thereby unify civil and admiralty practice. A number of distinctive admiralty rules of procedure were nevertheless retained, both in the Federal Rules of Civil Procedure and in the Supplemental Rules for Certain Admiralty and Maritime Claims. See generally 7A. J. Moore & A. Pelaez, Moore's Federal Practice ¶¶ .01–.03, .53, .90 (1979).

9. [Text of § 1331].

be exempted from the effects of *Strawbridge v. Curtiss*. Even assuming that Congress somehow intended, by virtue of the saving-to-suitors clause of section b 1333, to allow some maritime claims to be tried on the law side of the federal courts through diversity jurisdiction, we think it unreasonable to assume that Congress intended a lesser standard of diversity to apply in such cases. No party to this action has suggested such an intent on the part of Congress, and our research has failed to uncover any evidence of one.[10] An expansion of such magnitude in diversity jurisdiction over maritime cases would render diversity a very different concept in the maritime context than in other areas and as a practical matter would allow an unintended alternative to admiralty jurisdiction in most maritime cases. We think that such an extension would conflict with the thrust of *Romero*, for the Supreme Court's opinion in that case makes it clear that if the age-old absence of jury trials in admiralty cases is to be remedied, that remedy is in the province of Congress. To extend the right of trial by jury to admiralty cases by requiring only minimal diversity is no more in harmony with the statutory scheme as it now exists than is the attempted extension by virtue of general federal question jurisdiction. We hold, therefore, that while a non-diverse defendant may be sued under the Jones Act or some other non-admiralty basis of federal jurisdiction without destroying diversity as to diverse defendants sued on maritime claims in the same suit, the presence of a non-diverse defendant solely on the basis of federal admiralty jurisdiction will indeed implicate the rule of *Strawbridge v. Curtiss* and thereby destroy diversity jurisdiction of the case. Accordingly, we conclude that the district court properly denied Powell's request for trial by jury.

III

Powell also argues that the district court's findings of fact with regard to the proximate cause of his injuries were clearly erroneous. We have reviewed the record and we conclude that the court's findings are adequately supported by the evidence. We therefore affirm the judgment of the district court.

AFFIRMED

Duhon v. Koch Exploration Co.

United States District Court, District of Louisiana, 1986.
628 F.Supp. 925.

■ VERON, DISTRICT JUDGE.

This matter comes before the court upon the motion of defendants, Koch Exploration Company and Koch Industries, Inc., to strike the jury demand

---

10. The question of legislative intent is somewhat more elusive than in *Romero*. Unlike the provision of general federal question jurisdiction, which was enacted as part of the Judiciary Act of 1875, the rule of complete diversity was originally developed by the Supreme Court and has never explicitly been added to the statute by Congress. Thus it is only by virtue of the long-standing survival of the rule in the face of numerous reenactments of the diversity jurisdiction statute that the Supreme Court attributed to the rule the force of a "Congressional mandate" in *Owen Equipment & Erection Co. v Kroger*, supra. Nevertheless we find pursuasive in this case the Congressional silence which in *Owen Equipment & Erection Co.* led the Court to accept the rule of complete diversity. Congress also could have, but did not, exempt maritime cases from the reach of that rule.

of plaintiffs, Curtis J. Price and Timothy Fruge in this consolidated action. The motion gives rise to several considerations due to the hybrid nature of this consolidated action under the Federal Rules of Civil Procedure, which embody the 1966 merger of the civil and admiralty rules. See generally, G. Gilmore & C. Black, The Law of Admiralty 2, 19 (2d ed. 1975). While there is no novelty in conducting a joint trial of claims in admiralty and claims at law, such a consolidation presents procedural issues which profoundly affect the rights and remedies available to the parties. As the determination of these issues depends upon whether the causes of action alleged are characterized as arising under this court's jurisdiction "in admiralty" or "at law," it is necessary to examine the manner in which each plaintiff has framed his action.

Each of these actions arise [sic] from the alleged allision between the M/V/CAPTAIN JUDE, a shrimpboat owned by Plaintiff Wayne Duhon, and some sort of submerged structure owned by defendants in the Gulf of Mexico on or about July 14, 1983. On or about September 22, 1983, plaintiffs Wayne Duhon and George Duhon commenced suit against defendants in the Thirty-eighth Judicial District Court for the Parish of Cameron, State of Louisana, alleging damages in the loss of the M/V CAPTAIN JUDE, which sank as a result of the allision. After the Duhons amended their state court petition to demand a trial by jury, defendants Koch Exploration and Koch Industries, Inc. [hereafter collectively referred to as "Koch"] removed the action to this Court on the basis of diversity of citizenship, 28 U.S.C.§ 1332.

On December 30, 1983, plaintiff Curtis J. Price, Captain of the M/V CAPTAIN JUDE, commenced suit before this Court alleging damages as a result of the personal injuries he sustained as a result of the aforesaid allision. Paragraph 3 of Price's complaint states, "This is a case of admiralty in maritime jurisdiction, as hereinafter more fully appears." In the closing paragraph, however, Price "prays that this cause be tried to a jury."

On July 11, 1984, this Court ordered that the Duhon's cause of action be consolidated with that of Price pursuant to Rule 42. Subsequent to that consolidation, Koch filed a third-party complaint for indemnity and/or contribution against Wayne Duhon, George Duhon and Curtis Price on October 15, 1984. The Court takes note that despite the consolidation of the two actions, they are still treated as being separate and distinct so it is not improper to name the plaintiff in one action as a third-party defendant in the other action with which it has been consolidated.[1] In paragraph 8 of

---

1. Case consolidation does not "merge" the cases, or make a party to one action a party to the action with which it is consolidated. Oelze v. C.I.R., 723 F.2d 1162, reh. denied, 726 F.2d 165 (5th Cir.1983). Thus a party to one action "may cause a third-party complaint to be served upon a person not a party to the action" but who *is* a party to the action with which has been consolidated. See Rule 14(a).

the third-party complaint, Koch invokes the application of Rule 14(c),[2] (thereby tendering third-party defendant Price as a direct defendant to the Duhons in CV No. 83–3279.),[3] In paragraph 13 of the third-party complaint, Koch similarly invokes Rule 14(c) to pose the third-party defendants George Duhon and Wayne Duhon as direct defendants to Curtis J. Price in CV No. 83–3275.

On April 18, 1985, Price was allowed to amend his complaint, adding his spouse as a plaintiff, adding Weaver Exploration Co. as a defendant, alleging diversity jurisdiction and demanding a trial by jury. Koch opposed such an amendment principally on the ground that its invocation of Rule 14(c) made it impossible for this Court to obtain diversity jurisdiction because non-diverse parties, i.e., George Duhon and Wayne Duhon, were posed as direct defendants to the plaintiff Price.[4]

On July 15, 1985, plaintiff Timothy J. Fruge filed a complaint against Koch Exploration Co. Koch Industries, Inc. and Wayne Duhon, alleging jurisdiction pursuant to the Jones Act and the General Maritime Law and seeking a trial by jury. As alleged, Fruge was employed by Wayne Duhon as a seaman aboard the M/V CAPTAIN JUDE at the time of the vessel's allision with the submerged structure of Koch. On September 27, 1985, Fruge's cause of action, CV No. 83–3275 was consolidated with those of Wayne Duhon, George Duhon, and Curtis J. Price. Koch amended its third-party complaint to include Fruge as a third-party defendant and tender Fruge as a direct defendant to Price pursuant to Rule 14(c). Additionally Koch filed a third-party complaint against Curtis J. Price and Weaver Exploration Co., tendering said third-party defendants as direct defendants to Fruge, in CV No.85–2070, under Rule 14(c). Koch has now moved to strike the jury demands of Price and Fruge, contending that their complaints state admiralty and maritime claims within the meaning of Rule 9(h), Fed.R.Civ.Pro., and that a jury trial of such claims is inappropriate under the present circumstances. The Court finds Koch's contentions to be without merit, and will address the issues relative to each plaintiff.[5]

Curtis J. Price (CV No. 83–3275)

Koch urges Price's demand for a jury trial should be stricken because there is no complete diversity of citizenship between the parties and the only jurisdictional basis of this suit (CV No. 83–3275) lies in admiralty, 28 U.S.C. § 1333. Koch further contends that it will be unduly prejudiced if

---

2. [Rule]

3. As discussed infra, this is a wholly improper use of Rule 14(c) because the cause of action filed by the Duhons was removed to this Court *solely* on the basis of diversity jurisdiction and the Duhon's complaint does not assert an admiralty or maritime claim within the meaning of Rule 9(h).

4. This same argument is urged in support of the motion presently under consideration.

5. Koch does not dispute the propriety of a jury trial on the claims of Wayne Duhon and George Duhon, as their cause of action (CV No. 83–2379) was removed to this Court by Koch on the basis of diversity of citizenship. Because the Duhon's cause of action is on the law side of this Court, however, Koch improperly attempts to invoke the application of Rule 14(c) by tendering Curtis J. Price and Timothy J. Fruga as direct defendants to the Duhons.

If Price is permitted to shift from the "admiralty side" of the court to the "law side" because it will lose the valuable benefits of Rule 14(c) and because the filing of the amended complaint came sixteen months after the institution of this proceeding.

In his second amended complaint, Price again prays for a jury trial but also states: "This is a maritime tort case with diversity jurisdiction with the minimum jurisdictional amount being met." Koch argues, however, that there is not complete diversity because its Rule 14(c) third-party complaint against George Duhon and Wayne Duhon poses two Louisiana residents as direct defendants to Price, also a Louisiana resident.[6] Thus, Koch argues that its Rule 14(c) third-party complaint precludes Price's subsequent invocation of diversity jurisdiction. The Court finds this line of reasoning without merit. In essence Koch desires to characterize the amended complaint as a new proceeding, which it is not. Koch's position furthermore fails to recognize the inherent power of the plaintiff, as pleader, to determine procedural consequences under Federal Rule of Civil Procedure 9(h).

The amendment to the complaint, just as the amendment of a pleading to add or withdraw a statement identifying an admiralty and maritime claim under Rule 9(h), is governed by the principles of Rule 15. Under Rule 15(c),[7] Price's assertion of diversity jurisdiction relates back to the date of the filing of his original complaint. Because Koch's third-party complaint was, necessarily, filed subsequent to that date, it cannot serve to create the "jurisdictional defect" alleged by Koch and will not preclude plaintiff from asserting the diversity jurisdiction which he may have originally asserted.

While Koch may desire to retain the procedural benefits of Rule 14(c) by having the suit proceed in admiralty, the plaintiff's original choice of the admiralty side was not an irrevocable election. Fisher v. Danos, 671 F.2d 904, 905 (5th Cir.1982); Doucet v. Wheless Drilling Co., 467 F.2d 336 339 (5th Cir.1972); see also Notes of Advisory Committee on Rule 9(h), 1966 Amendment. Clearly it is the plaintiff who has the power of determining procedural consequences under the Federal Rules of Civil Procedure by the manner in which he chooses to frame his pleadings. See *Doucet*, supra; see also Rachal v. Ingram Corp., 600 F.Supp. 406, 407 (W.D.La.1984); Wright & Miller, Federal Practice & Procedure § 1314 (1969). Because Price has now amended his complaint to assert diversity jurisdiction and

---

6. Rule 14(c) provides that, as a result of being filed, "... the action shall proceed as if the plaintiff had commenced it against the third-party defendant as well as the third-party plaintiff." * * * In the Notes of Advisory Committee on Rules, the Committee remarks that such a result was also originally incorporated in Rule 14, applying to all civil actions. One reason why it was eliminated by the 1946 amendment to the rule "... was that where jurisdiction depended on diversity of citizenship the impleader of an adversary having the same citizenship as the plaintiff was not considered possible."

7. Rule 15(c) provides: "Relation back of Amendments. Whenever the claim or defense asserted in the amended pleading arose out of the conduct, transaction or occurrence set forth or attempted to be set forth in the original pleading, the amendment relates back to the date of the original pleading."

has *not* requested that this action be identified as "an admiralty or maritime claim for the purposes of rules 14(c), 38(e), 82, and the Supplemental Rules for Certain Admiralty and Maritime Claims" in accordance with Rule 9(h), the action has been shifted from the admiralty side to the law side of this Court.[8]   Price therefore is entitled to a jury trial "in accordance with the principles governing civil actions generally."   Romero v. Bethlehem Steel Corp., 515 F.2d 1249, 1252 (5th Cir.1975).   As such, Koch's third-party complaint is now governed by the provisions of Rule 14(a) and is no longer entitled to the benefits of Rule 14(c).   See Lirette v. Popich Bros., Water Transport, Inc., 699 F.2d 725, 727 n. 6 (5th Cir.1983).

The Court is unpursuaded by Koch's contention that it will be unfairly prejudiced by this result.   While the plaintiff's "shift" from the admiralty side to the law side came sixteen months after the commencement of the action, it nevertheless occurred a year before the presently scheduled trial date.   Moreover, Price's cause of action has been consolidated with the diversity action of George Duhon and Wayne Duhon since less than six months after the filing of Price's complaint, and Koch therefore knew that the presentation of the consolidated case was going to be made to a jury even though the Court would act as the ultimate fact-finder as to the Price action.   Cf. *Doucet*, supra at 341 n. 5 ("For defense counsel to shift on short notice from preparing defense of a non-jury trial to preparing defense of a jury trial may pose difficulties.")   In finding an utter lack of prejudice to Koch as a result of the date of filing of Price's amended complaint, the Court also observes that Price's original pleading set forth facts showing that the parties were of diverse citizenship and included a jury demand, despite the fact that Price did not assert diversity jurisdiction.[9]   As such Koch is presumed to have known that Price could have chosen to proceed on the law side of the court and that Price's initial choice to proceed in

---

8.   Under Rule 9(h), no specific "identifying statement" is needed "[i]f th claim is cognizable only in admiralty," and the parties will not be entitled to a jury trial.   When the pleading show that both admiralty and some other basis of federal jurisdiction exist, however, the plaintiff must employ an "identifying statement" in accordance with Rule 9(h) in order to be entitled to the admiralty procedures and remedies, including a nonjury trial.   Romero v. Bethlehem Steel Corp., 515 F.2d 1249, 1252 (5th Cir.1975).   Because a Rule 9(h) declaration has not been made by Price, and because a non-maritime ground for subject matter jurisdiction exists, Price, "therefore is entitled to a jury trial" in accordance with the principles governing civil actions generally.   Id., citing Moore, Federal Practice, ¶ 38.–35[1], at 271.   See also Oroco Marine, Inc. v. National Marine Service, Inc., 71 F.R.D. 220, 221 (S.D.Tex.1976);   Compare

T.N.T. Marine Service v. Weaver Shipyards & Dry Docks, Inc., 702 F.2d 585, 587 (5th Cir. 1983)(no right to a jury trial where the complaint did contain a Rule 9(h) declaration even though diversity jurisdiction existed as well) with Lirette v. Popich Bros., Water Transport, Inc., 699 F.2d 725, 727 n. 6 (5th Cir.1983)(defendant not entitled to benefits of Rule 14(c) where plaintiff's complaint— based on the Jones Act and General maritime Law, "did not expressly contain" a Rule 9(h) declaration).

9.   The civil coversheet, however, indicates that jurisdiction is based "on the maritime laws of the United States; on the basis of diversity; and on the laws of the State of Louisiana."   If Price originally intended to bring his case on law side of the Court under diversity jurisdiction, however, his original complaint was far from making it clear.

admiralty was not an irrevocable election under the established law discussed above.

Timothy J. Fruge (CV No. 85–2070)

As in the action of Curtis J. Price, Koch similarly moves that Fruge's jury demand be stricken because Fruge's complaint provides that it is brought "under the Admiralty and Maritime Jurisdiction pursuant to . . . the Jones Act (46 USCA 688) and pursuant to the General Maritime Law of the United States of America . . . Alternatively, jurisdiction is based on 28 USCA 1331 as this action arises under the Constitution, laws, or treaties of the United States. . . ." At first blush, Koch's position seems meritorious in light of the fact that Fruge's complaint reads that the suit is in admiralty pursuant to the Jones Act. Certainly the Jones Act has been recognized to afford an injured seaman the choice of proceeding either in admiralty without a jury or at law with a jury. Panama R.R. Co. v. Johnson, 264 U.S. 375, 390–91, 44 S.Ct. 391, 395, 68 L.Ed. 748 (1923); Texas Menhaden Co. v. Palermo, 329 F.2d 579, 580, (5th Cir.1964). But because Fruge's complaint requests a trial by jury, and also references federal question jurisdiction under 28 U.S.C. § 1331, this Court views Fruge's Jones Act claim against Wayne Duhon as sitting on the law side. Clearly no right to a jury trial would exist if Fruge brought his Jones Act claim in admiralty, unless the Great Lakes Act, 28 U.S.C. § 1873, applied.[10a] The Court therefore must presume that where the Jones Act claim is coupled with a jury demand, it is its civil jurisdiction which is invoked, and Fruge will receive a jury trial.[10b]

10a. 28 U.S. § 1873 provides:

In any case of admiralty and maritime jurisdiction relating to any matter of contract or tort arising upon or concerning any vessel of twenty tons or upward, enrolled and licensed for the coasting trade, and employed in the business of commerce and navigation between places in different states upon the lakes and navigable waters connecting said lakes, the trial of all issues of fact shall be by jury if either party demands it.

10b. While the Court is also persuaded by the fact that Fruge pleaded federal question jurisdiction in the alternative, there might be some question as to whether Fruge included that reference only because "there is a federal question involving the interpretation of 33 USC § 490 [sic]." Fruge's Memorandum in Opposition to Defendant's Motion to Strike the Jury Demand, p.2. If Fruge intended his claims against Koch under the Wreck Act, 33 U.S.C § 409, to arise under 28 U.S.C. § 1331, he is mistaken. The Wreck Statute is a federal *criminal* statute, which nevertheless "reflects a legislative judgment of the standard of care to which owners of sunken vessels should be held in civil ac-

tions." Morania Barge No. 140, Inc. v. M. & J. Tracy, Inc., 312 F.2d 78, 80 (2d Cir.1962). While violation of the statutory duties is evidence of negligence and may give rise to the liability of the owner of the sunken or submerged vessel, this Court is only aware of such liability being imposed in suits *in admiralty* (apart from where an action is maintained under the Suits in Admiralty Act against the United States). Humble Oil & Refining Co. v. Tug Crochet, 422 F.2d 602 (5th Cir.1970); Ingram Corp. v. Ohio River Co., 505 F.2d 1364 (6th Cir.1974); Chesapeake Bay Bridge & Tunnel District v. Lauritzen, 404 F.2d 1001 (4th Cir.1968); *Morania Barge No. 140, Inc.*, supra. As has been noted the Wreck Act is simply declaratory of the obligation to use due care which exists under the General Maritime Law. THE YFNX–6, 156 F.Supp. 325, 333 (D.Md.1957), aff'd sub nom. 262 F.2d 559 (4th Cir.1959). The statute itself *does not* establish a substantive maritime right under which Fruge's cause of action "arises" for purposes of 28 U.S.C. § 1331. As such, the only basis for federal question jurisdiction in the case at bar is pursuant to the Jones Act, 46 U.S.C.

Fruge's other claims, however, remain on the other side of the Court. In opposing Koch's motion to strike his jury demand, Fruge strenuously contends that he never designated *any* of his claims as being Rule 9(h) admiralty actions. As previously discussed,[11] however, no such designation is required "[i]f the claim is cognizeable only in admiralty." Fed.R.Civ. Pro. 9(h). Unlike the admiralty and maritime claims of plaintiffs george Duhon, Wayne Duhon, and Curtis J. Price, over which the Court has jurisdiction *at law* by virtue of diversity of citizenship,[12] the admiralty and maritime claims asserted by Fruge are cognizeable *only* in admiralty because there is not complete diversity in Fruge's suit. Fruge therefore has no choice but to proceed in admiralty with regard to his claims arising under the General Maritime Law.[13]

While the Court's jurisdiction over Fruge's claims is thus based both on the law side and the admiralty side, Fruge is yet entitled to a jury trial on his maritime as well as his Jones Act claims. In Fitzgerald v. United States Lines Co., 374 U.S. 16, 83 S.Ct. 1646, 10 L.Ed.2d 720, 1963 A.M.C. 1093 (1963), the Supreme Court held that a plaintiff who asserts a Jones Act claim at law, demanding a trial by jury, has the right to have his maritime claims for unseaworthiness and maintenance and cure determined by the jury as sole fact-finder.[14] In accordance with the well-

§ 688, and any civil civil breach of the duties imposed by the Wreck Statute is jurisdictionally grounded in admiralty.

11. Note 8, supra.

12. The Duhons and Price may maintain their maritime causes of action on the law side of this Court by virtue of the "saving-to-suitors" clause set forth in 28 U.S.C. § 1333. This clause serves to "save" plaintiffs the right to enforce their maritime causes of action in a law court; i.e., a state court or a federal court that has jurisdiction at law due to diversity or federal question jurisdiction. Because the Duhons and Price have more than one basis of jurisdiction to bring their maritime claims , their election not to make a Rule 9(h) declaration means that their action shall proceed at law. Romero v. Bethlehem Steel Corp., 515 F.2d 1249, 1252 (5th Cir.1975).

13. The claims of Fruge which are cognizeable only in the admiralty jurisdiction of the Court are for maintenance and cure, unseaworthiness, and for violation of the Wreck Statute, 33 F.S.C § 409. As discussed previously, supra note 10b, the Wreck Statute does not establish any substantive maritime rights which causes of action might "arise under" for purposes of federal jurisdiction, but it simply reflects various obligations of due care existing under the General Maritime Law.

14. Delivering the opinion of the Court, Mr. Justice Black stated:

"Although remedies for negligence, unseaworthiness, and maintenance and cure have different origins and may on occasion call for application of slightly different principles and procedures, they nevertheless, when based on one unitary set of circumstances, serve the same purpose of indemnifying a seaman for damages caused by injury, depend in large part on the same evidence, and involve some identical elements of recovery. Requiring a seaman to split up his law suit, submitting part of it to a jury and part to a judge, unduly complicates and confuses a trial, creates difficulties in applying the doctrines of *res judicata* and collateral estoppel and can easily result in too much or too little recovery."

In light of these considerations, Mr. Justice Black concluded:

"Only one trier of fact should be used for the trial of what is essentially one law suit to settle one claim split conceptually into separate parts because of historical developments. And since Congress in the Jones Act has declared that the negligence part of the claim shall be tried by a jury, we would not be free, even if we wished, to require sub-

established case precedent, Fruge is certainly entitled to a jury trial in the interest of fairless and effective judicial administration. Id.

This does not mean, however, that Fruge's entire action is to be characterized as one at law. Fruge's entitlement to a jury trial on admiralty claims joined with a Jones Act claim does not result in the admiralty claims becoming pendent to the Jones Act claim on the law side of the court. Haskins v. Point Towing Co., 395 F.2d 737, 741–43, 1968 A.M.C. 1193 (3d Cir.1968), subseq. app. 421 F.2d 532, cert. denied 400 U.S. 834, 91 S.Ct. 68, 27 L.Ed.2d 66[15] Fawcett v. Pacific Far East Lines, Inc., 76 F.R.D. 519, 520–21 (N.D.Cal.1977); Saus v. Delta Concrete Co., 368 F.Supp. 297, 297–98 (W.D.Pa.1973). Fruge's claims for maintenance and cure, unseaworthiness, and for violation of the Wreck Statute, 33 U.S.C. § 409, are yet within the cognizance of this Court *solely* in admiralty.[16] Because Koch is posed as a defendant only on the admiralty side of the court, its Rule 14(c) joinder of Weaver Exploration Co. and Price is entirely proper. Fruges's maritime claims are to be governed according to the traditional rules of practice in admiralty, even though he is entitled to a jury trial under *Fitzgerald*.

Conclusion

The joint trial of these claims at law and in admiralty, as well as the consolidation of the four plaintiffs' actions, has been allowed in accordance with the best interests of fairness and of the efficient administration of justice. The joinder of claims "in admiralty" with claims "at law" serves these interests, even though the characterization of those claims may "wake[ ] echoes in the deepest metaphysics of admiralty."[17] Inartful

mission of all the claims to the judge alone. Therefore the jury, a time-honored institution in our jurisprudence, is the only tribunal competent under the present congressional enactments to try all the claims. Accordingly we hold that a maintenance and cure claim joined with a Jones Act claim must be submitted to the jury when both arise out of one set of facts. 374 U.S. at 18–21, 83 S.Ct. at 1649–50. See also Moncada v. Lemuria Shipping Corp., 491 F.2d 470, 473 (2d Cir.1974)."

15. *Fitzgerald* made it clear that the reason for trial by jury in claims for unseaworthiness and maintenance and cure is not that they are actions at law, but rather that there should be one fact finder and that when they are joined with the Jones Act claim under which a right of trial by jury is guaranteed, they, too, may be tried by the same jury. The Court in *Fitzgerald* did not justify its decision by characterizing the claims for unseaworthiness and maintenance and cure as having been brought on the law side, but

instead specifically declared that it was creating a right to trial by jury in admiralty cases in the interest of judicial administration by virtue of the power left to it by Congress to fashion the controlling "rules of admiralty law." 395 F.2d at 741–42, citing Fitzgerald v. United States Lines, supra, 374 U.S. at 20–21, 83 S.Ct. at 1650.

16. See note 10b, supra, regarding Fruge's claims against Koch under the Wreck Statute, 33 U.S.C.§ 409, as being grounded in admiralty.

17. G. Gilmore & C. Black, The Law of Admiralty 33 n. 118 (1957). Subsequent to the time when these renowned publicists first made this remark, however, the 1966 joinder of the civil and admiralty rules served to simplify the task of characterizing claims by virtue of Rule 9(h). Although Rule 9(h) serves as an effective tool, inartful pleading by plaintiffs yet complicates the characterization. Wright and Miller suggest that when a plaintiff who has alternative bases of jurisdiction wishes to avail himself of the special

pleading by the parties, as in the case at bar, does not serve to facilitate the characterization. Nevertheless, the explicit provisions of Rule 9(h) effectively define "admiralty and maritime claims" and the determinations herein set forth have been made in accordance with that rule. Pursuant to the foregoing analysis, Koch's motion to strike plaintiffs' jury demands is DENIED, and all parties will receive a jury trial. The Court furthermore ORDERS that Koch's third-party demands are to proceed under Rule 14(c) *only* in the matter of Fruge v. Koch Exploration Co., CV No. 85–2070.

N O T E

Pleading jurisdiction generally

The federal courts are courts of limited jurisdiction. The court must inquire into its own jurisdiction; jurisdiction cannot be established by stipulation or waiver. It is necessary, then, that the complaint allege a state of facts that falls within the court's competence. In diversity cases, the plaintiff must allege the citizenship of the parties, and on challenge must establish, in most cases, complete diversity between plaintiffs and defendants. In the case of claims under federal statutes, it must appear that the claim that is pleaded "arises under" the statute. In admiralty cases, it must appear that the claim derives from a maritime contract, or a maritime tort, or arises under a statute creating a maritime claim.

Rule 8(a)(1) requires that a pleading which sets forth a claim for relief "shall contain (1) a short and plain statement of the grounds upon which the court's jurisdiction depends, unless the court already has jurisdiction and the claim needs no new grounds of jurisdiction to support it ..." While failure to include such a jurisdictional statement is an infraction of the rules, it is not itself a jurisdictional requirement. See, e.g., Continental Cas. Co. v. Canadian Universal Ins. Co., 605 F.2d 1340 (5th Cir.1979), in which the plaintiff neglected to include the Rule 8(a)(1) statement, but alleged the citizenship of the parties, and the claim was based upon three maritime contracts, so that jurisdiction appeared from the face of the complaint. And in cases in which the jurisdictional statement is incorrect, it may be amended to show jurisdiction where this is possible, and amendment may be made even on appeal. See 28 U.S.C. § 1653, applied in Odishelidze v. Aetna Life & Cas. Co., 853 F.2d 21 (1st Cir.1988), in which a Puerto Rican plaintiff both neglected to state the defendant's state of incorporation and stated that the defendant corporation maintained its principle place of business in Puerto Rico, which, if correct, would have destroyed diversity, when in fact the defendant's principal place of business was in Connecticut.

Pleading Admiralty Jurisdiction

Official Form 2(d) indicates that in the case of admiralty and maritime claims, the requirements of Rule 8(a)(1) of a "short plain statement" are satisfied by the statement "This is a case of admiralty and maritime jurisdiction, as hereinafter more fully appears [If the pleader wishes to invoke the distinctively maritime

admiralty rules, he should follow his jurisdictional allegation with the statement that: "This is an admiralty or maritime claim within the meaning of Rule 9(h)." Wright & Miller, Federal Practice & Procedure § 1313, at p. 454 (1969).

procedures referred to in Rule 9(h), add the following, or its substantial equivalent: This is an admiralty or maritime claim within the meaning of Rule 9(h).].''

When a claim is cognizeable only as an admiralty or maritime claim, e.g., an action against a vessel in rem, or an action under the general maritime law when the parties are not diverse, it is not necessary to identify the claim as maritime under Rule 9(h), but in such cases Rule 8(a)(1) should be complied with. The quoted sentence from the Official Forms, without the bracketed material, suffices. If there is diversity jurisdiction and the plaintiff wishes to proceed under the saving clause, he may plead diversity and the minimum amount in controversy, and need not assert maritime jurisdiction at all. Nevertheless, in determining the substantive law it may be necessary to advert to the maritime nature of the claim. Therefore, identification of the claim as maritime may be intended to invoke the maritime jurisdiction and proceed according to the special maritime rules, or merely to assert a right under the maritime substantive law in a case brought under the civil jurisdiction. This has sometimes been a source of confusion. There are cases, for example, in which the pleader has included in his Rule 8(a)(1) statement diversity or federal claim jurisdiction and also admiralty jurisdiction, and demanded a jury trial. See, e.g., Kathriner v. Unisea, Inc., 740 F.Supp. 768 (D.Alaska 1990), in which the plaintiff stated a claim for negligence under the Jones Act, and claims for unseaworthiness and maintenance and cure, pleaded admiralty jurisdiction, but did not identify the claim as maritime under Rule 9(h), and demanded a jury trial. The court denied a jury trial, indicating that before a jury trial will be granted, the Jones Act claim must be invoked pursuant to § 1331. Cf. Smith v. Pinell, 597 F.2d 994 (5th Cir.1979). There the plaintiff's Rule 8(a)(1) statement was ''This is a case of admiralty and maritime jurisdiction.'' He pleaded a claim under the Jones Act and for unseaworthiness and demanded a jury on both. He did not specifically identify either claim as maritime under Rule 9(h). See also Harrison v. Glendel Drilling Co., 679 F.Supp. 1413 (W.D.La.1988), holding that a complaint based on the Jones Act and the general maritime law that did not contain an express designation under Rule 9(h), but requested a jury trial, would be treated as a federal question case and not an admiralty case.

In view of the possibility of ambiguity, it has been suggested that the proper procedure is to mention Rule 9(h) by name. See Wright and Miller (1990) § 1333, at 719. See also Banks v. Hanover S.S. Corp., 43 F.R.D. 374, 376–377 (D.Md.1967), and see Lewis v. United States, 812 F.Supp. 620, 626–629 (E.D.Va.1992); Filippou v. Italia Societa Per Azioni Di Navizione, 254 F.Supp. 162, 1967 A.M.C. 1076 (D.Mass.1966). How helpful would such a rule be? Most of the authorities now hold that specific mention of Rule 9(h) is unnecessary. See, e.g., Teal v. Eagle Fleet Inc., 933 F.2d 341, 344–345 (5th Cir.1991). Suppose the plaintiff does mention Rule 9(h) and also demands a jury trial. See T.N.T. Marine Service Inc. v. Weaver Shipyards & Dry Docks Inc., 702 F.2d 585 (5th Cir.1983), cert. denied 464 U.S. 847, 104 S.Ct. 151, 78 L.Ed.2d 141 (1983), in which the plaintiff brought his action for damages incurred from the sinking of its vessel while it awaited drydocking, naming as defendants the dry dock corporation in personam, and its tug in rem. The jurisdictional statement alleged diversity and added ''This is a suit for breach of a maritime contract and for maritime tort,'' and demanded a jury trial. The court of appeals affirmed the denial of the jury demand, but indicated that the plaintiff could have amended its complaint. Of what should such an amendment consist? See also Bodden v. Osgood, 879 F.2d 184 (5th Cir.1989), in which the court of appeals observed that where an action is pleaded as a maritime claim a request for jury trial should merely be struck. In the particular case, however, the action had been filed in the state court and removed on grounds of diversity and the court of appeals held that it therefore would proceed as a civil case unless the plaintiff amended to make a designation under Rule 9(h).

If the pleader brings his action in rem under Rule C of the Supplemental Rules, it is unnecessary to invoke Rule 9(h) because the jurisdiction of actions in rem is maritime only, and therefore no election is necessary. Suppose he identifies the claim as maritime but without specific mention of Rule 9(h) and does not demand a jury trial, or includes in the complaint a prayer for process to attach the defendant's goods and chattels, as provided for in Rule B of the Supplemental Rules. Does inclusion of a Rule B prayer for attachment make an action in personam maritime within Rule 9(h) as exclusively maritime?

Rule 18(a) provides that "[a] party asserting a claim for relief as an original claim, counterclaim, cross-claim, or third-party claim, may join, either as independent or as alternate claims, as many claims, legal, equitable, or maritime, as he has against an opposing party." Rule 9(h) permits the inclusion of an identifying statement in "a pleading or count setting for a claim for relief." Does this permit a plaintiff to state a civil claim for negligence in one count and a maritime claim for unseaworthiness in another, pursuing the first as a jury action under the saving to suitors clause and the second in rem as maritime? Does it permit the further splitting of the cause by pleading the claim for unseaworthiness as civil under the diversity jurisdiction and the action in rem as maritime?

Is there a difference in this respect between an action cognizable either under the maritime or under the diversity jurisdiction and one cognizeable either under the maritime or federal question jurisdiction? If the plaintiff does not plead the facts that bring the action under § 1332, that is, does not state the citizenship of each party, diversity jurisdiction does not appear from the complaint, whereas if the plaintiff states a claim under a federal statute, the jurisdiction does appear from the complaint, although the plaintiff may have failed to comply with Rule 8(a)(1). This is not always fatal.

When plaintiff, a repairman who was injured while working on a vessel, stated in paragraph (1) of his complaint, "Complainant alleges a cause of action based upon negligence in accord with general maritime law and a second cause of action on grounds of unseaworthiness in accord with Rule 9(h) of the Federal Rules of Civil Procedure," in paragraph (2) alleged the citizenship of the parties, and in a third paragraph alleged over $10,000 in damages, and the pretrial order was amended to state "Jurisdiction is based also on Diversity of Citizenship and jurisdictional amount," but the complaint was not amended to delete the reference to Rule 9(h), the court of appeals questioned whether such closely related claims could be split, but decided that in any event it was proper to deny the plaintiff's request for a jury trial absent amendment of the complaint. Romero v. Bethlehem Steel Corp., 368 F.Supp. 890 (E.D.Tex.1974), aff'd 515 F.2d 1249 (5th Cir.1975).

CHAPTER 7

JURISDICTION IN REM; IN PERSONAM; ATTACHMENTS IN THE ADMIRALTY

A. JURISDICTION IN REM

1. ARREST

There'll Always Be an England

[*From the London Daily Telegraph*]

Service of an Admiralty writ by handing it to the master of a Dutch vessel, the Prins Bernhard, 388 tons, instead of nailing it to the vessel's mast, was declared invalid in the Admiralty Court yesterday. The writ itself was declared valid and capable of being reserved.

Mr. Justice Hewson said that fixing a writ to a ship's mast might not be a perfect way of informing all interested parties that there was a claim against the ship, but no other method had been suggested or devised.

From the New Yorker

The King v. Joseph Lane

Marsden 80 (1768).

Dr. Harris.—This is a sute brought by the King in his Office of Admiralty against Joseph Lane, pilot of the New Elizabeth, for contempt.

28th September, 1763, Charles Bowden, Marshal of this Court, arrested the ship New Elizabeth in a cause of subtraction of wages at Rotherithe. After that he told the mate of the ship and the pilot, the master not being on board, that the ship must not be moved till bail was given. But on the representation of the pilot, that the ship was inconveniently situated, he gave leave to move her to a more convenient place. This was Saturday, on the afternoon of which Bowden went to Gravesend; and on his return the next day (Sunday the 29th) he met the New Elizabeth at Barking Shelves in full sail towards Gravesende. Bowden was in a boat rowed by two men, with whom he went on board the Elizabeth and asked the pilot, Lane, how he dared to move her, she being under an arrest. He answered he had orders for so doing, and would carry her to Gravesend in spite of him, and without the consent of Bowden or those who employed him, though Bowden had shewn his mace and warrant, the insignia of his office; in regard to which Lane observed he did not regard his piece of paper or mace, which was only a piece of lead. Bowden replied he would complain to the Trinity Masters and the Lords of the Admiralty. Lane replied he valued them no more than he did him. Bowden afterwards presented a Petition to the Lords of the Admiralty, with an affidavit of the facts annexed. The Lords ordered Lane to be prosecuted. Lane was accordingly arrested, and after laying a week in the Marshalsea Prison, bailed. Articles were given in and admitted, you thinking them all relevant. A negative issue being given, we examined three witnesses, viz., Bowden himself, West and Jordan, who rowed him. Jordan says, on the 24th of September Bowden pulled out the silver mace and piece of parchment, and asked Lane how he durst move the ship. Lane, in reply, damned Bowden and his mace, i.e., the officer and his staff of officer and his staff of office. West says Lane went so far as to challenge Bowden to fight him [with] sword and pistol. Bowden, in his affidavit and interrogatory, says Lane said he would carry the ship where he pleased, in spite of the piece of paper and piece of pewter, and that he regarded the Trinity Masters and Lords of the Admiralty no more than him.

An allegation has been offered by Lane containing defensive matter, which was not opposed, because I would not, in a criminal charge, preclude a man from making his defence. Another reason for not opposing it was that it shewd Bowden behaved very civilly. It states that Bowden did not shew his mace, and that without provocation he threatened to complain and have Lane broke; who answered he had done nothing and was not affraid. On this plea four witnesses are examined, Francis Young, Stephan Smith, Peter Robb, and Patric Kampwell; two of whom deny their seeing the warrant or mace. The two other witnesses say Lane damned Bowden. Kampwell, to the 4th Interrogatory, says Bowden shewd Lane his warrant and mace, who said he knew who he was, and bid him kiss his posteriors. If you think on reading the depositions that they come up to the charge, I hope for example sake you will punish him as severely as you can; otherwise it will be impossible to have your warrants executed and property secured.

Dr. Wynne.—I am council for Joseph Lane, who stands charged with breaking the arrest of this court and treating your officer with contempt. I did not know it began by Petition of Complaint from Bowden, on whose affidavit the Articles are framed. Our four witnesses say, when the ship was arrested, Kampwell and Lane sent Stephen Smith to acquaint his brother John Smith, the master. He returned and told them he had seen the master, who had been at Doctors' Commons and settled the affair, and desired the ship might sail as fast as possible to Gravesende. They did so without stopping at Deptford for fear of being delayed. Smith says, when Bowden met them, he called Lane the pilot rascal, scoundrel, and several other abusive names, and put himself in a great passion. When he came on board they told him Smith's message, upon which he was satisfied, and ordered one of the watermen to rub out the arrest mark (which is an anchor) and said they might proceed on their voyage. That the Marshal afterwards returned, and put an assistant on board. Kampwell, the second mate, swears to Bowden's ill-usage of Lane, by calling him old rascal and scoundrel before he came on board, and asking how they durst move; Lane replyed the ship was discharged. Bowden ordered the anchor to be let go. Lane asked if he knew what he was about; that if the anchor was let go, the ship would never come up again, which was worth £ 30,000. Bowden said he was acquainted with the river. Lane asked if Bowden took charge of the ship? He answered, Yes. Lane said, You are a clever fellow to take charge of a ship who knows nothing of the matter; on which words arose; Bowden called Lane old rogue and rascal; and Lane called Bowden young rogue and rascal. He did not hear any abuse offered to the warrant or badge of office. In answer to the fourth Interrogatory, heard Lane say, Bowden might kiss a * * * but not that his masters or the Lords of the Admiralty might.

[After further interchange of counsel the matter was put to the court and Lane was fined 13s. 4d., and condemned in the amount of £ 5, *nomine expensaarum.*].

Belcher Co. of Alabama, Inc. v. M/V Maratha Mariner

United States Court of Appeals, Fifth Circuit, 1984.
724 F.2d 1161, 1984 A.M.C. 1679.

■ ALVIN B. RUBIN, CIRCUIT JUDGE:

This *in rem* libel against a vessel to recover for fuel bunkers supplied to it was dismissed on the ground that a pending action in the Netherlands, in which jurisdiction had been obtained by attachment of the vessel, was the equivalent of an *in rem* action and hence was *lis alibis pendens*. Because the Netherlands permits no *in rem* actions, and, therefore, the suit pending there is *in personam*, and because the ultimate issues in the two suits are different, we reverse the judgment of dismissal.

Belcher Company of Alabama, Inc. (Belcher), filed an *in rem* libel against the vessel M/V Maratha Mariner of Bombay, India, and against all persons having or claiming any interest in the vessel, alleging that Belcher had supplied fuel bunkers to the vessel and had not been paid the amount due it, $99,344. The vessel had been chartered from its owner, Chowgule Steamship Company, Ltd. (Chowgule), by Armada Bulk Carriers of Denmark (Armada). Armada's broker had ordered fuel from Baymar, a California broker, and Baymar had, in turn, contracted with Belcher, which supplied the fuel to the vessel in Mobile, Alabama. Chowgule asserts that Armada paid Baymar for the fuel and that Baymar, in turn, made partial payment to Belcher and subsequently went out of business before paying the balance.

In 1979, Belcher had the vessel attached in the Netherlands to satisfy the alleged outstanding debt. Chowgule secured the release of the vessel by posting 275,000 Dutch guilders ($138,000 in U.S. dollars) in the form of a letter of undertaking, as security for its claim. That litigation is still pending in Rotterdam, the Netherlands. The vessel was later arrested in Houston, Texas, three years later, and this libel was initiated in the Southern District of Texas.

The Federal Maritime Lien Act provides, "[a]ny person furnishing * * * necessaries, to any vessel, whether foreign or domestic, upon the order of the owner of such vessel, or of a person authorized by the owner, shall have a maritime lien on the vessel, which may be enforced by suit *in rem.* * * *" 46 U.S.C. § 971. This lien attaches when necessaries are ordered by and supplied to a charterer,[1] unless the supplier has notice that the person who orders the necessaries lacked authority to do so.[2] Thus, when Belcher supplied fuel to the M/V Maratha Mariner, a maritime lien may have arisen by operation of law, and, if such a lien did arise, its enforceability may be subject to any defenses that may be available to the vessel owner, such as laches. The owner of the vessel is not itself liable for payment, however, unless it has entered into the contract for the supply of necessaries. It has no personal obligation even though a lien attaches to its vessel.[3]

Under the admiralty law of the United States, *in personam* and *in rem* actions may arise from the same claim, and may be brought separately or in the same suit. Supplemental Admiralty Rule C(1)(b). As its name implies, the *in personam* action is filed against the owner personally. An *in rem* action, on the other hand, is filed against the *res,* the vessel; and a maritime lien on the vessel is a prerequisite to an action *in rem.*[4] There is a third category of claims sometimes known as actions *quasi in rem.* Supplemental Admiralty Rule E. These are actions based on a claim for money begun by attachment or other seizure of property when the court has no jurisdiction over the person of the defendant, but has jurisdiction over a thing belonging to him or over a person who is indebted to, or owes a duty to the defendant.[5] A state has jurisdiction by an action *quasi in rem* to enforce a personal claim against a defendant to the extent of applying the property seized to the satisfaction of the claim.[6]

If American law had been applicable when the vessel was attached in the Netherlands, the supplier of fuel would have had a lien on the vessel and an action *in rem* could have been brought to enforce the maritime lien.

1. 46 U.S.C. § 973, as amended by Pub.L. No. 92–79, 85 Stat. 285 (1971); Dampskibsselskabet Dannebrog v. Signal Oil and Gas Company, 310 U.S. 268, 60 S.Ct. 937, 84 L.Ed. 1197 (1939); G. Gilmore & C. Black, *The Law of Admiralty* 685 (2d ed. 1975) and cases cited therein.

2. 46 U.S.C. §§ 972 & 973; G. Gilmore & C. Black, supra 685 et seq.

3. See generally G. Gilmore & C. Black, supra, § 9–19; but see infra note 8.

4. G. Gilmore & C. Black, § 1–12 at 35; see, e.g., The Rock Island Bridge, 73 U.S. (6 Wall.) 213, 215, 18 L.Ed. 753, 754 (1867)(cited in G. Gilmore & C. Black at id.); The Resolute, 168 U.S. 437, 440, 18 S.Ct. 112, 113, 42 L.Ed. 533, 535 (1897); Rainbow Line, Inc. v. M/V Tequila, 480 F.2d 1024, 1028 (2d Cir.1973).

5. Restatement (Second) of Judgments (1982) § 8; James, Civil Procedure 613 (1965).

6. Restatement (Second) of Judgments (1982) § 9.

The Netherlands action was, however, based on contract principles because Dutch law does not recognize the concept of maritime lien and, therefore, provides no mechanism by which such a lien can be enforced. The fact that an *in rem* action could not be brought in the Netherlands does not convert the attachment there filed into an *in rem* proceeding.

Chowgule contends that Belcher has admitted the foreign action to be in effect *in rem* because Belcher has asserted in the course of that action that, despite the difference in the two legal systems, "the position of the owner of the vessel is not essentially enhanced or changed [under Dutch law]. In the present [Netherlands] case the vessel was attached, whereupon by the law of the U.S.A. a lien could have been served. In order to withdraw this attachment, a guarantee was obtained. Possible judgment against Chowgule and possible noncompliance therewith will lead to compensation under guarantee and therewith indirectly on that item of property which by the law of the U.S.A. would be the debtor."

This is not, however, an admission that the foreign attachment is a libel *in rem*. As Belcher's pleading in the Netherlands case further states:

> By Dutch law of procedure which in effect does not provide for the action in rem, an action in personam must be brought therefore, whereby, be it so, the owner of the vessel becomes debtor of the claim under section 321 paragraph 1 Wvk, whereas by the law of the U.S.A. the case itself, in the present instance the vessel, is the debtor.

Therein the true difference lies. In the *in rem* action, the issues are whether: (1) Belcher delivered the claimed quantity of fuel to the M/V Maratha Mariner; (2) the fuel delivered to the bunkers was a necessary within the meaning of the Maritime Lien Act, 46 U.S.C. § 971; (3) the charges claimed are reasonable in amount; and (4) the person who placed the order had authority to do so, either real, apparent, or statutorily presumed. In the attachment action, the sole question is whether Chowgule became liable to Belcher contractually. While it is necessary to resolve a number of questions to determine that issue, the reasonableness of the charges and the status of the fuel as necessaries are irrelevant, and the methods of proving the authority of the person who placed the order differ.

The distinction between these types of proceedings is made clear by the Supplemental Rules. Attachment issues "with respect to any admiralty or maritime claim in personam" and its purpose is to "attach the defendant's goods and chattels" or other assets if the defendant shall not be found in the jurisdiction. Rule B. Attachment may be used for any debt. An action *in rem* on the other hand, is available only to enforce a maritime lien or when authorized by statute. Rule C. The arrest warrant extends only to the vessel "or other property that is the subject of the action." Rule C(3).

The Fourth Circuit has held that the judicial sale of a vessel in a Mexican bankruptcy action was sufficiently similar in substance to an American *in rem* action to remove an *in rem* lien on the vessel. Gulf and Southern Terminal Corp. v. The SS President Roxas, 701 F.2d 1110 (4th

Cir.), cert. denied, 462 U.S. 1133, 103 S.Ct. 3115, 77 L.Ed.2d 1369 (1983). In that case, the Mexican bankruptcy court had possession of the vessel, and sold it "free of encumbrances." The sale erased the lien despite the fact that Mexican law does not provide explicitly for an *in rem* proceeding both because the procedures employed were "virtually identical to those which are denominated as an *in rem* proceeding under American law" and because "the vessel was an asset of the bankrupt, under the control and proper jurisdiction of the Mexican court." Id. 701 F.2d at 1112. A bankruptcy court that has possession of any property has the power to sell the property free and clear of liens.[7]

Attachment does in many respects resemble arrest. In each proceeding the vessel is seized and it may later be sold to satisfy a judgment. In each, the vessel itself may be released and other security substituted. Nevertheless, not only do the issues in the two actions differ; the basic theory on which each is brought is different. In the *in rem* proceeding the owner bears no personal liability. The vessel is sold solely to satisfy the lien. If the proceeds of the sale are inadequate, there is no liability on the owner's part for the residue. Indeed the admiralty court will not render a personal judgment against the owner in excess of the amount of the release bond.[8] Only a personal action against the owner can establish such liability. In the attachment action, the object of the action is a personal judgment for the full sum due. The vessel is seized only to compel the owner's appearance by subjecting to the court's control property within its territorial jurisdiction. If the proceeds of sale of the vessel do not satisfy the judgment, the owner remains liable for the balance of the debt.

Chowgule asserts that, when it provided security to release the vessel from attachment, this discharged the lien. With respect to the lien sought to be enforced, the release does transfer the lien from the vessel to the fund represented by the bond or letter of undertaking.[9] This does not imply that release from an attachment likewise clears the lien. An execution sale in an *in rem* proceeding clears the vessel of all liens.[10] An execution sale pursuant to a writ of attachment is not, however, the equivalent of a judicial sale in admiralty. The ship is not sold free of all liens; instead

---

7. Matter of Buchman, 600 F.2d 160, 165 (8th Cir.1979).

8. The Susana, 2 F.2d 410, 412–13 (4th Cir.1924); The Morning Star (Red Star Towing & Transp. Co.), 5 F.Supp. 502 (E.D.N.Y. 1933); G. Gilmore & C. Black, supra, at 802.

In a few cases, however, owners appearing in an *in rem* action to contest the libelants' claims have been "treated as if they had been brought into court by personal process" and held personally liable for judgment in excess of the security. The Fairisle, 76 F.Supp. 27, 34 (D.Md.1947), aff'd sub nom. Waterman S.S. Corp. v. Dean, 171 F.2d 408

(4th Cir.1948)(quoted in Treasure Salvors v. The Unidentified Wrecked and Abandoned Sailing Vessel, 569 F.2d 330, 335 (5th Cir. 1978)); see also Mosher v. Tate, 182 F.2d 475, 479–80 (9th Cir.1950); G. Gilmore & C. Black, supra, at 802–04.

9. Gray v. Hopkins–Carter Hardware Co. (The Lois), 32 F.2d 876, 878 (5th Cir. 1929); G. Gilmore & C. Black, supra, at 799.

10. The Trenton, 4 F. 657 (E.D.Mich. 1880); Zimmern Coal Co. v. Coal Trading Association of Rotterdam (The Totila x Harold), 30 F.2d 933 (5th Cir.1929); G. Gilmore & C. Black, supra, at 787, et seq.

only the owner's interest, whatever it may be, is adjudicated.[11] Indeed, it could not do so, for the attachment bond does not substitute for a lien but only for the owner's personal liability.

In its analysis of the *lis alibis pendens* argument, the district court correctly stated the applicable rule: a court having jurisdiction should exercise it unless a compelling reason not to do so is demonstrated.[12] It found compelling reason, however, in the supposed hardship on Chowgule of defending two actions and in the possibility of double recovery. Both of these can readily be averted without the damage to Belcher that dismissal occasions. The Netherlands action has been tried and is awaiting decision. Staying proceedings in this action would avoid repetitive litigation of the issues there involved. If Belcher prevails, its judgment will be satisfied out of the security posted in that court. Thus both the expense of the second litigation and the possibility of double liability will be averted. If Chowgule prevails in the Netherlands action, its undertaking will be released and only those issues unique to the *in rem* action need be determined in the United States court. If, on the other hand, this action is dismissed and Belcher fails to prevail in the Netherlands action, it will be deprived of an opportunity to prove its claim *in rem*. No hardship is imposed on Chowgule by continuing the action, for the same undertaking posted in the Netherlands stands as security for the *in rem* action.

For these reasons the judgment is reversed and the case is remanded for further proceedings consistent with this opinion.

NOTE

The fact that a supplier has a lien on a vessel to secure his claim does not preclude suit against anyone who may be liable in personam. See Port Ship Service, Inc. v. International Ship Management & Agencies Service, Inc., 800 F.2d 1418 (5th Cir.1986). There it was held that a supplier of water taxi services ordered by a maritime agent for various vessels owned by its clients could sue the agent if the principal was not sufficiently revealed, independent of whether the supplier could proceed against the vessels in rem. See also Port Ship Service, Inc. v. Norton, Lilly & Co., 883 F.2d 23 (5th Cir.1989).

When the liability is both in personam and in rem the judgment should be entered jointly against the vessel and the owner. Bosnor, S.A. de C.V. v. Tug L.A. Barrios, 796 F.2d 776 (5th Cir.1986). The legal personality of the vessel is sufficiently separate, however, to require that a notice of appeal must name the vessel as an appellant to bring the in rem judgment up for appeal. All Pacific

---

11. G. Gilmore & C. Black, supra, at 802.

12. See Gulf Oil Corp. v. Gilbert, 330 U.S. 501, 67 S.Ct. 839, 91 L.Ed. 1055 (1947); The Belgenland, 114 U.S. 355, 5 S.Ct. 860, 29 L.Ed. 152 (1885); Chiazor v. Transworld Drilling Co. Ltd., 648 F.2d 1015, 1019 (5th Cir.1981); Poseidon Schiffahrt, G.M.B.H. v. The M/S Netuno, 474 F.2d 203, 204 (5th Cir.1973); Perusahaan Umum Listrik Negara Pusat v. M/V Tel Aviv, 711 F.2d 1231 (5th Cir.1983)(upholding conditional dismissal on forum non conveniens grounds because only connection with U.S. forum was in rem action and adequate alternative forum was substantially more convenient conditional dismissal preserved plaintiffs rights and remedies).

Trading, Inc. v. Hanjin Container Line, Inc., 7 F.3d 1427, 1994 A.M.C. 365 (9th Cir.1993).

The Resolute

Supreme Court of the United States, 1897.
168 U.S. 437, 18 S.Ct. 112, 42 L.Ed. 533.

■ Mr. Justice Brown, after stating the case, delivered the opinion of the court.

The sole question presented by the record in this case is whether the court was correct in assuming jurisdiction of a libel for seamen's wages, which accrued while the vessel was in the custody of a receiver, appointed by a state court, upon the foreclosure of a mortgage upon the property of the Oregon and Pacific Railroad Company, owner of the tug.

Jurisdiction is the power to adjudicate a case upon the merits, and dispose of it as justice may require. As applied to a suit *in rem* for the breach of a maritime contract, it presupposes, first, that the contract sued upon is a maritime contract; and, second, that the property proceeded against is within the lawful custody of the court. These are the only requirements necessary to give jurisdiction. Proper cognizance of the parties and subject-matter being conceded, all other matters belong to the merits.

The contention of libellant is that, as a maritime lien is the sole foundation of a proceeding *in rem,* such facts must be averred as to show that a lien arose in the particular case; or, at least, that if the libel shows that a lien could not have existed, it should be dismissed for want of jurisdiction. The averment relied upon in this libel is that the vessel was at the time the services were rendered in the hands of a receiver appointed by a state court. This fact, however, is not absolutely inconsistent with a lien *in rem* for seamen's wages. Paxson v. Cunningham, 63 Fed.Rep. 132. It may have been expressly bargained for by the receiver, it may be implied from the peculiar circumstances under which the services were rendered, or it might be held to have arisen from the peremptory language of the statute, Rev.Stat. § 4535, that "no seaman shall, by any agreement other than is provided by this title, forfeit his lien upon the ship, or be deprived of any remedy for the recovery of his wages to which he would otherwise have been entitled, and every stipulation in any agreement inconsistent with any provision of this title * * * shall be wholly inoperative." *Prima facie,* the rendition of mariner's services imports a lien, and the mere fact that the vessel is navigated by a receiver does not necessarily negative such lien, although there may be facts in the particular case to show that the above statute does not apply, or that credit was expressly given to the owner, to the charterer or to some third person. In fact, the question of lien or no lien is not one of jurisdiction, but of merits.

It is true that there can be no decree *in rem* against the vessel except for the enforcement of a lien given by the maritime law, or by a state law; but if the existence of such a lien were a question of jurisdiction, then nearly every question arising upon the merits could be made one of jurisdiction. Thus, supplies furnished to a vessel import a lien only when they are sold upon her credit; and the defence ordinarily made to such claims is that they were sold upon the personal credit of the owner or charterer; but certainly it could not be claimed that this was a question of jurisdiction. The existence of a lien for collision depends upon the question of fault or no fault, but it never was heard of that it thereby became a question of jurisdiction. Salvage services, too, ordinarily import a lien of the very highest rank; but it has sometimes been held that, if such services are rendered by seamen in the employ of a wrecking tug, or by a municipal fire department, no lien arises, for the reason that the men are originally employed for the very purpose of rescuing property from perils of the sea, or loss by fire. In the case under consideration a portion of the libellant's claim arises by assignment from Tellefson, and the authorities are almost equally divided upon the question whether such assignment carries the lien of the assignor to his assignee. Obviously these are not jurisdictional questions.

In determining the question of a lien in the case under consideration much may depend upon the manner in which the vessels were sold by the receiver. Were they sold in bulk, and merely as a part of the entire property of the insolvent corporation, upon the foreclosure of the mortgage, or was each vessel sold separately, and subject to the liens for mariner's wages which accrued before and while they were in the possession of the receiver? Did the order direct these vessels to be sold free of maritime liens, or subject to them, or was it silent in this particular? Were the lienholders upon these vessels paid from the purchase money, according to their relative rank, as they would have been had the sale been conducted by a court of admiralty? If they were, that would amount to very strong, if not conclusive, evidence against the subsequent endeavor to enforce the liens in a court of admiralty. We cannot assume that the court would authorize its receiver to run these vessels without making some provision for a preferential payment of their current expenses. Meyer v. Western Car Co., 102 U.S. 1, 26 L.Ed. 59; Kneeland v. American Loan & Trust Co., 136 U.S. 89, 10 S.Ct. 950, 34 L.Ed. 379. None of these were questions which went to the jurisdiction of the court to entertain the libels, but were such as would properly arise, either upon the exception to the libels, or upon an answer putting the facts in issue.

Had the vessel, at the time the warrant of arrest was served, been in the actual custody of the receiver, a different question would have been presented; but the facts of this case show that she had been sold, and had passed into the hands of her purchaser, and that the receiver had been discharged.

The case of Ex parte Gordon, 104 U.S. 515, 26 L.Ed. 814, goes even farther than is necessary to support the action of the District Court in assuming jurisdiction of this case. In that case a writ of prohibition was sought to restrain the District Court for the District of Maryland from proceeding against a vessel to recover damages for loss of life in a collision.

It was held that, as the case was one of a maritime tort, of which the District Court unquestionably had jurisdiction, it was for that court to decide whether the vessel was liable for pecuniary damages resulting from the loss of life. "Having jurisdiction," said the Chief Justice, "in respect to the collision, it would seem necessarily to follow that the court had jurisdiction to hear and decide what liability the vessel had incurred thereby." The question was held not to be jurisdictional, but one properly arising upon the merits. See also The Charkieh, 8 Q.B. 197; Schunk v. Moline, Milburn & Stoddard Co., 147 U.S. 500, 13 S.Ct. 416, 37 L.Ed. 255; Smith v. McKay, 161 U.S. 355, 16 S.Ct. 490, 40 L.Ed. 731.

So, too, in In re Fassett, 142 U.S. 479, 12 S.Ct. 295, 35 L.Ed. 1087, the owner of the yacht Conqueror filed a libel for possession, against her and the collector for the port of New York, claiming delivery of the vessel to him and damages against the collector, who had seized her as a dutiable import. The collector applied to this court for a writ of prohibition, alleging that the District Court had no jurisdiction of the suit. We held that the subject-matter of the libel was a marine tort; that the question whether the vessel was liable to duty was properly justiciable in the District Court, and that that court had jurisdiction. Said Mr. Justice Blatchford, in delivering the opinion of the court, p. 484: "The District Court has jurisdiction to determine the question, because it has jurisdiction of the vessel by attachment, and of Fassett by monition; and for this court to decide in the first instance, and in this proceeding, the question whether the yacht is an article imported from a foreign country, and subject to duty under the customs-revenue laws, would be to decide that question as a matter of original jurisdiction, and not of appellate jurisdiction, while as a question of original jurisdiction, it is duly pending before the District Court of the United States on pleadings which put that very question in issue." See also In re Cooper, 143 U.S. 472, 12 S.Ct. 453, 36 L.Ed. 232.

No. 136 is also a libel for wages, and involves precisely the same questions as are involved in the case of Dowsett, and will be disposed of in the same way. Claimants have mistaken their remedy in these cases, and should have appealed to the Circuit Court of Appeals.

The decrees of the District Court, in so far as they assume jurisdiction of these cases, are therefore

Affirmed.

United States v. Freights, etc., of the Mount Shasta

Supreme Court of the United States, 1927.
274 U.S. 466, 47 S.Ct. 666, 71 L.Ed. 1156.

■ MR. JUSTICE HOLMES delivered the opinion of the Court.

* * *

The United States, owner of the Steamship Mount Shasta, in May, 1920, made a bare boat charter of the vessel to the Mount Shasta Steamship

Company through Victor S. Fox and Company, Inc., an agent of that company, stipulating for a lien upon all cargoes and all sub-freights for any amounts due under the charter party. Victor S. Fox and Company in July, 1920, made a subcharter to Palmer & Parker Company for a voyage to bring a cargo of mahogany logs from the Gold Coast, Africa, to Boston. The vessel arrived in Boston with its cargo on February 19, 1921. There is due to the libellant $289,680 for the hire of the steamship, and the libel alleges that there is due and unpaid freight on the cargo of logs, $100,000, more or less, in the hands of Palmer & Parker Company, on which this libel seeks to establish a lien. It prays a monition against Palmer & Parker Company and all persons interested, commanding payment of the freight money into Court, etc. Palmer & Parker Company was served. That company filed exceptions to the libel, denied the jurisdiction of the Court and answered alleging ignorance of the original charter party and of the relations of the United States and the Mount Shasta S.S. Company to the vessel and setting up counterclaims more than sufficient to exhaust the freight. The cargo had been delivered. The District Court assumed that a libel in rem could be maintained against freight money admitted to be due and payable, but was opinion that the fund must exist when the suit is begun, or that the jurisdiction fails. The Court held that where, as here, the liability was denied in good faith, it did not appear that there was any res to be proceeded against and that the suit must be dismissed. The counsel for Palmer & Parker Company pressed the same considerations here in a somewhat more extreme form.

By the general logic of the law a debt may be treated as a res as easily as a ship. It is true that it is not tangible, but it is a right of the creditor's, capable of being attached and appropriated by the law to the creditor's duties. The ship is a res not because it is tangible but because it is a focus of rights that in like manner may be dealt with by the law. It is no more a res than a copyright. How far in fact the admiralty has carried its proceeding in rem is a question of tradition. We are not disposed to disturb what we take to have been the understanding of the Circuit Courts for a good many years, and what the District Court assumed. American Steel Barge Co. v. Chesapeake & Ohio Coal Agency Co., 53 C.C.A. 301, 115 F. 669 (1902); Bank of British North America v. Freights, Etc., of the Hutton, 70 C.C.A. 118, 137 F. 534, 538 (1905); Larsen v. 150 Bales of Sisal Grass, 147 F. 783, 785 (D.C.Ala.1906); Freights of the Kate, 63 F. 707 (D.C.N.Y.1894).

But if it be conceded that the Admiralty Court has jurisdiction to enforce a lien on sub-freights by a proceeding in rem, and a libel is filed alleging such sub-freights to be outstanding, we do not perceive how the Court can be deprived of jurisdiction merely by an answer denying that such freights are due. The jurisdiction is determined by the allegations of the libel. Louisville & Nashville R. Co. v. Rice, 247 U.S. 201, 203, 38 S.Ct. 429, 62 L.Ed. 1071 (1918). It may be defeated upon the trial by proof that the res does not exist. But the allegation of facts that if true make out a case entitles the party making them to have the acts tried. It is said that the Court derives its jurisdiction from its power, and no doubt its jurisdiction ultimately depends on that. But the jurisdiction begins before actual seizure, and authorizes a warrant to arrest, which may or may not be successful. Here the debtor is within the power of the Court and therefore the debt, if there is one, is also within it. The Court has the same jurisdiction to try the existence of the debt that it has to try the claim of the libellant for the hire of the Mount Shasta. If the proof that there is freight due shall fail it does not matter very much whether it be called proof that the Court had no jurisdiction or proof that the plaintiff had no case. Either way the libel will be dismissed. See Lehigh Valley R. Co. v. Cornell Steamboat Co., 218 U.S. 264, 270, 31 S.Ct. 17, 54 L.Ed. 1039, 20 Am.Ann.Cas. 1235 (1911); Lamar v. United States, 240 U.S. 60, 36 S.Ct. 255, 60 L.Ed. 526 (1916).

Decree Reversed.

■ The separate opinion of MR. JUSTICE MCREYNOLDS.

I am unable to accept the view that an admiralty court may entertain an action in rem when there is nothing which the marshal can take into custody. The technical term "in rem" is used to designate a proceeding against something. This court and textwriters again and again have pointed out the essential nature of such thing. The jurisdiction is founded upon physical power over a res within the district upon the theory that it is "a contracting or offending entity," a "debtor" or "offending thing," something that can be arrested or taken into custody, or which can be fairly designated as tangible property. The Sabine, 101 U.S. (11 Otto) 384, 388, 25 L.Ed. 982 (1879); The Robert W. Parsons, 191 U.S. 17, 37, 24 S.Ct. 8, 48 L.Ed. 73 (1903); Benedict on Admiralty (5th Ed.) §§ 11, 297; Hughes on Admiralty (2d Ed.) 400, 401; admiralty rules 10, 22.

* * *

The decree below should be affirmed.

NOTE

In *The Freights, etc., of the Mount Shasta,* the court had personal jurisdiction over the shipper who allegedly owed the charterer the sum for freight. Why does it make a difference whether we call the proceeding a libel in rem rather than a libel in personam with a clause of foreign attachment? Note that the latter proceeding would be possible only if the Mount Shasta S.S. Co. were not servable in the district. If it were, then the procedure in personam would have to embrace first a suit against Mt. Shasta followed by a supplemental proceeding to capture the debt in the hands of the shipper. The obvious disadvantage of this procedure lies in the possibility that by the time the foundation for the supplemental proceeding has been laid the shipper may have no assets. If the proceeding had been by attachment, would the charterer's preference have been preserved? Cf. The Three Jacks (Jackson v. Inland Oil & Transport Co.), 318 F.2d 802, 1963 A.M.C. 1355 (5th Cir.1963).

Does the principle of *The Freights, etc., of the Mt. Shasta* apply to a vessel or other tangible property?

Thyssen Steel Corp. v. Federal Commerce & Nav. Co.

United States District Court, Southern District of New York, 1967.
274 F.Supp. 18, 1968 A.M.C. 1582.

■ WALTER R. MANSFIELD, D.J.   Plaintiff, Thyssen Steel Corporation ("Thyssen" herein) seeks, among other relief, an injunction compelling the defendant Federal Commerce & Navigation Co., Ltd. ("Commerce" herein), "Carbogas" Societa Di Navigazione S.P.A. ("Carbogas" herein), Penelope Shipping Company ("Penelope" herein), and Stavros Niarchos, to bring the S.S. *World Mermaid* into the port of Halifax, Nova Scotia, so that plaintiff may attain a security interest in the vessel.[1]   The *World Mermaid,* which is owned and operated by defendants Penelope and Niarchos, collided on July 23, 1967 in international waters with the S.S. *Giacinto Motta,* which was carrying plaintiff's cargo and which is owned and operated by Commerce and Carbogas.   As a result of the collision, the S.S. *Giacinto Motta* sank. The S.S. *Mermaid,* although damaged, presently is in international waters off Nova Scotia, or en route to Europe.

The original contention of defendant Penelope[2] is that this Court has never acquired personal jurisdiction over it.   On July 28, 1967, a summons, complaint and order to show cause were served on Transoceanic Marine, Inc., which has admittedly served in the past as "husbanding agent" for Penelope.   This agency entailed Transoceanic's arranging for berths, supplies and incidentals on the five occasions the S.S. *Mermaid* entered United States ports.   While, on occasion, service on a "husbanding agent" has been held to be effective, Murphy v. Arrow S.S. Co., 124 F.Supp. 199, 1954 A.M.C. 1423 (E.D.Pa.1954); Jenkins v. Lykes Bros. S.S. Co., 48 F.Supp. 848, 1943 A.M.C. 534 (E.D.Pa.1943); see Murphy v. International Freighting Corp., 182 F.Supp. 636, 1961 A.M.C. 442 (D.Mass.1960), no court has ever so held on a record as bare as this.   Granite Chemical Corp. v. Northeast Coal & Dock Corp., 249 F.Supp. 597, 1966 A.M.C. 1572 (D.Me. 1966); see George H. McFadden & Bros. v. The Sunoak, 167 F.Supp. 132, 1959 A.M.C. 233 (E.D.Va.1958).   Plaintiff cannot show that the S.S. *Mermaid* made regular stops in the United States; or that the ship ever stopped in this District; or that Transoceanic was performing any service for Penelope at the time of service of process.   See Granite Chemical Corp. v. Northeast Coal & Dock Corp., supra.   Plaintiff contends, however, that, if given the opportunity to indulge in discovery, he would be able to establish such facts.   Possibly he could.   See River Plate Corp. v. Forestal Land, Timber & Ry. Co., Ltd., 185 F.Supp. 832 (S.D.N.Y.1960); 4 Moore's Federal Practice, ¶ 26.16[1]. For the purposes of this motion, however, the Court must on the record presently before it find that it lacks jurisdiction over Penelope.   If plaintiff desires to pursue discovery for the purpose of establishing the existence of personal jurisdiction, it should do so by regular

---

1. Plaintiff has not advised the Court how it would obtain this security interest once the ship proceeded to Halifax.

2. There is no question that defendant Carbogas and Commerce have not been served.   There is an issue as to whether Stavros Niarchos has been served but he has not yet appeared to contest jurisdiction.

notice rather than by emergency order, in the absence of facts indicating the likelihood of success, which so far do not appear.

Even if there were jurisdiction over the person of Penelope, the motion must be denied on its merits for lack of jurisdiction over the subject matter, which is the S.S. *World Mermaid,* and it would be both unrealistic and unreasonable for a court to assume the existence of the power to grant such drastic preliminary relief before the plaintiff has even established its claim. On the contrary, existing authority is to the effect that the court cannot order a shipowner to harbor his ship, which is in international waters, in order that it might provide security for a plaintiff's unproven claim.[3] In Impala Trading Corp. v. Hawthorne Lumber Co., 200 F.Supp. 261, 1962 A.M.C. 2021 (S.D.N.Y.1961), JUDGE FEINBERG, in holding that he could not compel the sale of cargo aboard a ship in Puerto Cortez, Honduras, which plaintiff claimed to be subject to its maritime lien and sought in order to "conserve the assets involved" as security to satisfy its claim, stated (1962 A.M.C. at p. 2023):

"The basic issue on consideration of the petition for sale is the Court's jurisdiction to grant the relief sought. On this point, it appears that Hawthorne's contention that this Court has no jurisdiction over the cargo is correct. The cargo has never been seized and brought into the custody of the Court in accordance with Admiralty Rule 10.

"In the present case, since neither the vessel nor the cargo are within the district, I conclude that the Court is without jurisdiction to enter an order authorizing the sale of the lumber."

Processes *in rem* and of maritime attachment represent an exception to the general rule that in the absence of statutory authorization a plaintiff may not have security for his claim until it is established and reduced to judgment. But these exceptions are predicated on the basis that the *res,* i.e., the ship, is within the court's territorial jurisdiction at the time of seizure.[4] Here the ship is outside of this Court's jurisdiction. To suggest that a defendant may be compelled to bring property into this or any other jurisdiction as a means of preserving it as security to satisfy a plaintiff's claim, is to put the cart before the horse or, perhaps more appropriately in this case, to put the barge before the tug. The plaintiff must first establish his claim before seeking such extraordinary relief.

Furthermore, plaintiff would be required to allege in its complaint that the S.S. *World Mermaid* is in the jurisdiction of the Court or will be during

---

3. Defendant also contends that this Court may not grant plaintiff the relief it seeks since an admiralty court has no jurisdiction to issue such an equitable decree. See 4 Benedict, *Admiralty,* sec. 613. The Advisory Committee's Note to Rule 1, Fed. Rules of Civ.Proc., however, rendered the continuing effect of this long established doctrine of admiralty unclear: "Just as the 1938 rules abolished the distinction between actions at law and suits in equity, this change would abolish the distinction between civil actions and suits in admiralty."

4. See, e.g., Rule E, Supplemental Rules for Admiralty, and Maritime Claims and particularly subdivision (3)(a): *"Territorial Limits of Effective Service.* Process *in rem* and of maritime attachment and garnishment shall be served only within the district," and the Advisory Committee's Note with respect to it.

the pendency of the suit. Supplemental Rules for Admiralty and Maritime Claims, Rule C(2). This Rule clearly does not contemplate the ship's being brought within the jurisdiction of the Court by the process of the Court for the reason that such a holding would render the allegation mere surplusage. Any other decision would inevitably lead to a holding that a defendant in a civil suit would have to bring all his possessions into the district so that they could be attached. Such a complete emasculation of the limitations on the drastic remedy of attachment would be intolerable.

Plaintiff contends that this is an exceptional case in that the S.S. *World Mermaid* is about to sink—a fact which will deprive plaintiff of all security. Penelope, however, which is just as concerned over the S.S. *World Mermaid* as is plaintiff, apparently feels otherwise, stating by affidavit dated July 31, 1967, that the damage is minor and that the ship is seaworthy and well on her way to Europe. Plaintiff's apprehension may be unfounded, and in any event it must wait until the S.S. *World Mermaid* comes within the jurisdiction of the Court. This is the normal procedure in such cases. See Witham v. James E. McAlpine, 96 F.Supp. 723, 1951 A.M.C. 870 (E.D.Mich.1951).

In view of the Court's lack of jurisdiction over the subject matter, the plaintiff's application for a default order against Stavros Niarchos, who did not appear to contest the jurisdiction, must be denied, without prejudice to the plaintiff's right to seek a default judgment on the complaint if Niarchos should choose not to answer, move, or otherwise plead with respect to the complaint within the time fixed by the Federal Rules.

Plaintiff seeks to amend his order to show cause to seek voluminous additional relief. There was no notice of this to Penelope until the day before the show cause order was returnable. It is difficult enough to meet the demands of a show cause order without having also to answer various other prayers for relief which were added as a mere afterthought the day before the motion was returnable. Furthermore, in the light of the Court's ruling, such relief, if it is to be requested, should be sought by motion on proper notice rather than by order to show cause.

Accordingly, the motion is denied.

So ordered.

NOTE

It is axiomatic that before a court can render a valid judgment in rem it must acquire jurisdiction of the res. In the first place, there must be a res. Thus in a cargo case, in which the owner was not amenable to service in personam, but the vessel might have been proceeded against in rem, the fact that the vessel had sunk without possibility of salvage made in rem jurisdiction impossible. Francosteel Corp. v. M/V Charm, 825 F.Supp. 1074, 1994 A.M.C. 136 (S.D.Ga.1993). And assuming a res, it must brought before the court. See, e.g., Shell Oil Co. v. M/T GILDA, 790 F.2d 1209 (5th Cir.1986)(Where the ship was never served, in rem jurisdiction was lacking).

In the *Impala Trading Corp.,* cited by the court in The World Mermaid above, Hawthorne Lumber Co. agreed to ship 225,000 board feet of lumber from Puerto Cortez to other ports in the Caribbean. The lumber was loaded aboard the vessel Tropic Sea at Puerto Cortez. Upon loading, $5,008 became due to Impala. The vessel began to list as the lumber was loaded and some of it had to be jettisoned. Hawthorne refused to pay the freight and Impala refused to give up possession of the lumber until the freight was paid. Impala brought a libel in rem and in personam in the Southern District of New York, seeking an order to enable it to sell the lumber and deposit the fund in the court. The court held that since neither the ship nor the cargo was, or ever had been, in the district, it could not order the sale.

The principle that a court must have jurisdiction of the res is less complex than the question of what it takes to acquire it. The classic mode is, of course, arrest. This is accomplished by the service of the warrant of arrest. Older cases state that there can be no jurisdiction in rem without actual seizure and control by the marshal. See, e.g., Taylor v. Carryl, 61 U.S. (20 How.) 583, 15 L.Ed. 1028 (1857); The Brig Ann, 13 U.S. (9 Cranch) 289, 291, 3 L.Ed. 734 (1815). Accordingly, though the warrant of arrest has been issued, if the vessel departs before it is served, there is no jurisdiction in rem. See, e.g., Sturgeon Bay Shipbuilding & Dry Dock Co. v. The Nautilus, 166 F.Supp. 187, 1958 A.M.C. 1050 (E.D.Wis.1958). *The Bold Buckleugh,* reproduced infra at p. 391.

The mechanics of service of process in rem in admiralty and such other in rem procedures governed by the Supplemental Rules are set out in Supplemental Rule E(4). As to a vessel, which is tangible property, Rule E(4)(b) provides that the marshal shall "take it into his possession for safe custody." or if this is impracticable, "shall execute the process by affixing a copy thereof to the property in a conspicuous place and by leaving a copy of the complaint and process with the person having possession or his agent." If the res is at the bottom of the ocean, must the resolution of issues of ownership or the right to salvage abide its raising except to the extent that they can be resolved in proceedings in personam? See Maritime Underwater Surveys, Inc. v. Unidentified Wrecked and Abandoned Sailing Vessel, Etc., 717 F.2d 6, 1984 A.M.C. 249 (1st Cir.1983), where the court "arrested" the res by floating a buoy over its resting place.

Notice that Supplemental Rule C(5) provides that "[i]n any action in rem in which process has been served as provided by this rule, if any part of the property that is the subject of the action has not been brought within the control of the court because it has been removed or sold or because it is intangible property in the hands of a person who has not been served with process, the court may, on motion, order any person having possession or control of such property or its proceeds to show cause why it should not be delivered into the custody of the marshal or paid into court to abide the judgment; and, after hearing, the court may enter such judgment as law and justice may require." Is it troublesome that "this rule" does not provide for service of process? Rule C(3) provides for the issuance of process for service; Rule E(4) provides for the service. In the case of tangible property, such as a vessel, does this mean that there must be an arrest of the vessel under E(4)(b) before there can be ancillary process? What would ancillary process reach? The text of the rule refers to "property that is the subject of the action." Does this include, in the case of a vessel, parts of the vessel or its gear removed or sold before the process was served, and therefore never seized? See Chapter 13A(2), infra, where the subjects to which a maritime lien attaches is discussed. There it is noted that a lien on a vessel extends to its parts and appurtenances. Suppose that the vessel is within the district and is seized, but by the time it is seized parts of it (lash barges, equipment, parts in need of repair, or what-have-you) have been taken outside the district. Unless property does not become a "subject of the action" until it is arrested, persons having possession of the parts could be required to deliver them up. If after the issuance of process and before service the engines of a vessel have been removed and taken outside the jurisdiction, after seizure of the hull can the person possessing the engines be ordered to turn them over to the court? Suppose that the engines remained within the district but the hull has been towed away. Can the plaintiff seize the engines and obtain ancillary process to require return of the hull?

Despite the theoretical necessity that tangible property be arrested and brought under the control of the court, and the provisions of Rule E(4), in rem proceedings often proceed without any arrest at all. In Continental Grain Co. v. Federal Barge Lines, Inc., 268 F.2d 240, 1959 A.M.C. 2158 (5th Cir.1959), the court of appeals repudiated the suggestion of the district court that the case was not truly in rem because there had been no arrest of the vessel, the parties having proceeded under a "letter of undertaking" that stipulated that the proceeding should go forward as a proceeding in rem and agreed to pay any judgment rendered. And the undertaking survives transfer to another district. See Chap. 8A, infra, at p. 297. Does the letter have to be sent along to preserve the jurisdiction? It was sent along in Mackensworth v. S.S. American Merchant, 28 F.3d 246 (2d Cir.1994).

See Anglo–American Grain Co. v. S/T Mina D'Amico, 169 F.Supp. 908, 1959 A.M.C. 511 (E.D.Va.1959), in which it was held that acceptance of the process by proctors for the claimant "with the same force and effect as if said vessel was physically attached" suffices. And so with a stipulation between the seller of a vessel and the buyer who claimed a mortgage that the seller should receive a partial payment of the contested mortgage and the buyer, as claimant in a foreclosure proceeding, would litigate the dispute in the Eastern District of Louisiana. Pana-conti Shipping Co. , S.A. v. M/V Ypapanti, 865 F.2d 705 (5th Cir.1989). In United States v. Republic Marine, Inc., 829 F.2d 1399 (7th Cir.1987), it was held that the vessel had made an unrestricted appearance and thus had waived the necessity of arrest.

Conceding that physical seizure is not required, is the presence of the property in the district a necessity for jurisdiction? See Booth S.S. Co. v. Tug Dalzell No. 2, 1966 A.M.C. 2615 (S.D.N.Y.1966), in which it was held that filing a claim to the vessel and making a general appearance admitted the vessel's presence in the district and was enough to support an in rem decree. The Dalzell No. 2 shakes the concept of jurisdiction in rem as stemming from control of the res in more ways than one. At the time the action was commenced the vessel, wherever located, was in the constructive possession of the owner's trustee in bankruptcy.

In Cactus Pipe & Supply v. M/V Montmartre, 756 F.2d 1103, 1985 A.M.C. 2150 (5th Cir.1985), the court of appeals, in a split opinion, upheld jurisdiction in rem in a case in which no process had even been issued, much less served, on the vessel, when the owner had filed a claim as owner without reserving the issue of jurisdiction. The court did not discuss the location of the vessel. Treating jurisdiction of the res as analogous to jurisdiction of the person, it was of the opinion that the owner's claim constituted an appearance for the vessel; the vessel, having appeared, was subject to the judgment. How far can this analogy be taken? If the vessel is an "offending thing" which can be served by serving her owner, could she be served under the long arm statutes?

See Platoro, Ltd., Inc. v. Unidentified Remains of a Vessel, 508 F.2d 1113, 1975 A.M.C. 1216 (5th Cir.1975), in which plaintiff had recovered valuable artifacts from the remains of a Spanish vessel sunk in 1555 near Padre Island. He transported them to Gary, Indiana, but later, under pressure sent them to Austin, Texas, where they were given into the custody of the Texas General Land Office. He then brought an action in rem in the Southern District of Texas, seeking a declaration of title or a salvage award. The court of appeals held that there was no jurisdiction since at the time the action was brought the res was not within the district.

With *Platoro,* compare State of Florida v. Treasure Salvors, Inc., 621 F.2d 1340, 1981 A.M.C. 1529 (5th Cir.1980), modified 458 U.S. 670, 102 S.Ct. 3304, 73 L.Ed.2d 1057 (1982), another sunken treasure case, in which the res was partly before the court but partly on the bottom of the ocean beyond the boundaries of the district. See Moyer v. Wrecked and Abandoned Vessel, known as Andrea Doria, 836 F.Supp. 1099, 1994 A.M.C. 1021 (D.N.J.1993), in which the court speaks of this jurisdiction as "quasi in rem."

Actual seizure of the vessel and retention of custody by the court is, of course, to make the vessel hostage to the plaintiff's claim, and affords the owner with a powerful incentive to pay up or give security. And the presence of a vessel or other property in the district may be thought to afford a basis for jurisdiction, as to which, see subchapter C, infra. Does the ritual of seizure (the mace and painted anchor in the King v. Joseph Lane) serve any other purpose? In The M/V Montmartre, above, for example, had the vessel been seized and held to answer the claim, the plaintiff could obtain satisfaction of any judgment by sale of the vessel unless the defendant chose to pay it and obtain restoration of the vessel. Now, however, he may have a judgment in rem against a vessel that may not be in the district, and indeed perhaps not in the country. Could the district court nevertheless sell the Montmartre to satisfy the judgment? Cf. Gulf & S. Terminal Corp. v. S.S. President Roxas, 701 F.2d 1110, 1983 A.M.C. 1521 (4TH Cir.1983), cert. denied 462 U.S. 1133, 103 S.Ct. 3115, 77 L.Ed.2d 1369 (1983). Or would he be required to chase the Montmartre from district to district, or country to country. Cf. Southern Oregon Production Credit Ass'n v. Oil Screw Sweet Pea, 435 F.Supp. 454, 1977 A.M.C. 638 (D.Or.1977).

Is there some reason why the libel of tangible personal property should depend upon arrest while the jurisdiction over the person in possession is all that is required when the res is intangible? In *The Freights, etc., of the Mount Shasta*, supra, p. 256, Mr. Justice Holmes states that a ship is a res not because it is tangible but because it is "a focus of rights that in like manner may be dealt with by the law." What are the shore side parallels? When a lien is foreclosed on a tangible res, is it necessary for the court to physically seize it? Given jurisdiction of the party, can the court order the party to deliver the res into the custody of the court?

2.   SECURITY; RELEASE

Stevedoring Services of America v. Ancora Transport, N.V.

United States Court of Appeals, Ninth Circuit, 1995.
59 F.3d 879.

■ BRUNETTI, CIRCUIT JUDGE:

Stevedoring Services of America (SSA) appealed from an order vacating a writ garnishing funds allegedly held by one of its debtors. We dismissed SSA's appeal in the belief that we lost jurisdiction of the appeal when the district court relinquished control over the funds, the basis for jurisdiction of SSA's admiralty action. 941 F.2d 1378 (9th Cir.1991). The Supreme Court vacated our opinion and remanded the case for further consideration in light of Republic National Bank of Miami v. United States, 506 U.S. 80, 113 S.Ct. 554, 121 L.Ed.2d 474 (1992). 506 U.S. 80, 113 S.Ct. 955, 122 L.Ed.2d 112 (1993). Having considered the case in light of *Republic National Bank*, we conclude we have jurisdiction and affirm the district court's order releasing the funds.

I. *Facts and Proceedings*

The writ of garnishment in question arose out of a maritime contract dispute between Stevedoring Services ("SSA") and Ancora Transport, N.V., a Netherlands Antilles corporation which chartered the M/V RISAN ("Ancora"), Armilla (Rotterdam), Ancora's agent, Armilla (London), the owner of the garnished funds, and Armilla (Houston), the company which SSA alleges to have been Ancora's U.S. agent. SSA had a stevedoring contract to unload cargo from the vessel M/V RISAN in San Diego from October 30 to November 4, 1986. An outstanding balance of $59,502.99 remains in dispute on this contract.

SSA sued Ancora and all three Armilla corporations for the balance of the money due on the contract in the United States District Court for the District of Oregon. SSA asserted that the district court had jurisdiction vis-a-vis a res in Oregon, funds deposited by Armilla (London) with the Sunrise Shipping Agency ("Sunrise") in Portland. The funds were deposited by Armilla (Rotterdam) on behalf of Armilla (London) to pay for the loading of cargo onto the M/V CONTENDER ARGENT. SSA also alleged that Armilla (London), as an alter ego of Armilla (Rotterdam) and Armilla (Houston), is liable for the balance due on SSA's stevedoring contract with Ancora.

On August 7, 1987, the district court ordered the issuance of a writ garnishing the funds deposited with Sunrise and a temporary restraining order pursuant to Rule B(1) of the Federal Rules of Civil Procedure Supplemental Rules for Certain Admiralty and Maritime Claims. Armilla (London) entered a limited appearance pursuant to Rule E(8) of the Federal Rules of Civil Procedure Supplemental Rules for Certain Admiralty and Maritime Claims in order to contest the garnishment and to deny SSA's alter ego claim. Armilla (London) contends that Ancora, not Armilla (London), is liable for the balance due on the stevedoring contract. According to Armilla (London), Ancora chartered the M/V RISAN and Armilla (Rotterdam) acted as Ancora's agent. Armilla (London) and Armilla (Houston) claim that they have no connection to SSA.

After a hearing, the district court vacated the writ of garnishment and granted Armilla (London)'s motion for the summary release of the funds. SSA moved for the district court to reconsider its decision pending additional discovery or in the alternative moved to stay the execution of the order vacating the writ. SSA posted a stay bond. The district court denied the motion for reconsideration and lifted the stay of the order vacating the writ. SSA then petitioned this court for a stay of the release of funds and for a writ of mandamus; we denied this petition on September 15, 1987. There is no evidence in the record that SSA posted or offered to post a supersedeas bond after its petition to this court for a stay was rejected.

After the funds were released, the defendants filed a motion in this court to dismiss the case as moot; we denied this motion, giving them leave to argue this issue in this appeal. We issued an opinion dismissing the appeal in 1989. Stevedoring Servs. v. Ancora Transport, 884 F.2d 1250 (9th Cir.1989), withdrawn, 941 F.2d 1378 (1991). In light of the issues raised by SSA upon petition for rehearing, we withdrew our opinion and issued a new opinion. Stevedoring Servs., 941 F.2d at 1378. In 1993, the Supreme Court vacated our 1991 opinion and remanded the case for further consideration in light of the recent Supreme Court decision in Republic National Bank, ___ U.S. at ___, 113 S.Ct. at 555. We now consider the appeal as remanded.

II.   *Our jurisdiction to consider SSA's appeal*

A.   Appealability

We have jurisdiction of this appeal because the district court's order vacating the garnishment is an appealable collateral order. See Polar Shipping Ltd. v. Oriental Shipping Corp., 680 F.2d 627, 630 (9th Cir.1982).

B.   Quasi in Rem Jurisdiction

The district court had subject matter jurisdiction under 28 U.S.C. § 1333. However, Ancora and the Armilla companies argue that the district court has never exercised personal jurisdiction over them and does not now have control over the res, the funds held by Sunrise. If the appellees are correct, we have no jurisdiction of SSA's appeal because the district court could not enforce any judgment we might enter. We consider this issue in light of the Supreme Court's decision in *Republic National Bank* and its effect on our law.

In *Republic National Bank*, the United States government instituted drug forfeiture proceedings against a house in which the Republic National Bank of Miami asserted an 80% mortgagor's lien interest. The district court conducted a bench trial and entered a judgment denying the bank's claim of interest. After the district court entered judgment, the government transferred the $1.05 million in proceeds from the sale of the house to the United States Treasury Assets Forfeiture Fund. The government then moved for the Eleventh Circuit to dismiss the appeal for want of jurisdiction, on the ground that the district court no longer had jurisdiction over the Treasury-deposited sale proceeds. *Republic Nat'l Bank*, ___ U.S. at ___, 113 S.Ct. at 557.

After the Eleventh Circuit dismissed the case, United States v. One Single Family Residence Located at 6960 Miraflores Avenue, 932 F.2d 1433, 1435–36 (11th Cir.1991), the Supreme Court granted certiorari. Applying admiralty principles to this in rem proceeding as required by 28 U.S.C. § 2461(b), the Court reversed the Eleventh Circuit's judgment of dismissal and announced the following jurisdictional principle: While a district court needs jurisdiction over a res to initiate an in rem action, it does not need to maintain continuous control of the res to maintain jurisdiction of the action. *Republic Nat'l Bank*, 506 U.S. at ___, 113 S.Ct. at 557.

We also note that in *Republic National Bank* the bank neither obtained a stay of execution of the forfeiture judgment nor posted a supersedeas bond in order to preserve jurisdiction over the sale proceeds during the pendency of its appeal. *Republic Nat'l Bank*, ___ U.S. at ___, 113 S.Ct. at 557. We read this fact and the Court's holding to eliminate any requirement on a party seeking to institute a maritime attachment to obtain a stay or post a *supersedeas* bond to preserve the district court's jurisdiction over the garnished funds while it appealed the release of the garnished funds.

The only reason we might hesitate to apply the rule in *Republic National Bank* to this case is that SSA's garnishment instituted an action for *quasi in rem* judgment, while the arrest of the house in *Republic National Bank* instituted an *in rem* action. We conclude that this difference suggests no reason why we should distinguish the Supreme Court's decision in that case. The Supreme Court justified its decision as a way to end exploitation of the fiction of in rem jurisdiction to defeat the right of a losing party to appeal. In jurisdictions in which release of the res extinguished the district court's jurisdiction, the prevailing party could frustrate the losing party's appeal by transferring the res out of the district court's jurisdiction. The Supreme Court objected in no uncertain terms to this practice: "[T]he fictions of *in rem* forfeiture were developed primarily to expand the reach of the courts and to furnish remedies for aggrieved parties, not to provide a prevailing party with a means of defeating its adversary's claim for redress." *Republic Nat'l Bank*, ___ U.S. at ___, 113 S.Ct. at 559 (citations omitted).

This objection applies with equal persuasiveness to *quasi in rem* proceedings instituted under Rule B. The attachment procedure provides aggrieved parties an opportunity to gain satisfaction against defendants they might not be able to reach through ordinary in personam proceedings. *Polar Shipping Ltd.*, 680 F.2d at 637; see 2 Thomas J. Sehoenbaum, Admiralty & Maritime Law § 21–2, at 471. In this respect, maritime attachment's purpose resembles the purpose of the in rem fiction articulated by the Supreme Court. Maintaining a continuous-control requirement in *quasi in rem* proceedings would preserve an advantage for prevailing parties eliminated and criticized in the in rem context, the opportunity to shield a district court victory from review.

We acknowledge that, in admiralty practice, attachment procedures have come under greater criticism than arrest procedures for the opportunity they offer plaintiffs to gain leverage over foreign defendants. Both maritime procedures have come under criticism for allowing maritime plaintiffs to reach res owners with license far broader than civil procedure allows. 7A James Wm. Moore, Moore's Federal Practice 11 E.05, at E–205 to E–206 (1993). See generally George Rutherglen, The Contemporary Justification for Maritime Arrest and Attachment, 30 Wm. & Mary L.Rev.

541 (1989). However, Rule B attachments have drawn even stronger criticism than Rule C arrests because the res in an attachment proceeding need not have any relation to the lawsuit—it is merely a means to extract relief in the lawsuit. See Rule B(1); Joseph Kalo, The Meaning of Contact and Minimum National Contacts, 59 Tul.L.Rev. 24, 30 (1984); Rutherglen, 30 Wm. & Mary L.Rev. at 561.

However, this criticism of Rule B does not affect our conclusion. The criticism focuses on the opportunity Rule B creates for a plaintiff to harass a garnishee by instituting the attachment. The problem before us focuses on the opportunity the continuous-control requirement creates for the prevailing party, after the merits of the attachment proceeding have been decided, to deprive the losing party of the chance to appeal. We are concerned here with abuse of the release, not of the initial attachment.

We conclude that the district court's release of the garnished funds in SSA's action for *quasi in rem* judgment did not divest the court of jurisdiction over the res. Accord 2 Schoenbaum § 21–2, at 470 & n. 11 (citing *Republic Nat'l Bank*). Because the district court retains jurisdiction, we may review SSA's appeal without concern that we are reviewing an action with defendants now out of the district court's control.

III.   *SSA's appeal from the district court's order*

Having determined that we have jurisdiction to review the district court's order vacating the writ of garnishment, we consider whether the court erred in concluding that the garnished funds did not belong to a debtor of SSA. We review the court's legal conclusions de novo and its findings of fact for clear error. Nike, Inc. v. Comercial Iberica De Exclusivas Deportivas, S.A., 20 F.3d 987, 990 (9th Cir.1994).

Armilla (London) introduced evidence that Ancora was the only party to the stevedoring contract with SSA and that Armilla (London), not Ancora, owned the funds in question. SSA offered little more than bare assertions that Armilla (London) was an alter ego of Ancora. The district court correctly concluded that the only proper defendant against SSA's action was Ancora and that Armilla (London) was liable neither on the face of SSA's contract nor as Ancora's alter ego. There was no error in the court's determination that it did not have jurisdiction over the funds under Rule B because Ancora, the actual defendant, did not own them. We thus affirm the district court's release of the garnished funds.

AFFIRMED.

NOTE

For cases decided before *Republic National Bank* holding that release of security in an an action in rem under Rule C, or the fund attached an action by attachment under Rule D, had the effect of mooting an appeal, see Teyseer Cement Co. v. Halla Maritime Corp., 794 F.2d 472 (9th Cir.1986); L.B.Harvey Marine, Inc. v. M/V ''River Arc,'' 712 F.2d 458 (11th Cir.1983).

But cf. Inland Credit Corp. v. M/T Bow Egret, 552 F.2d 1148, 1977 A.M.C. 2359 (5th Cir.1977), in which a holder of a preferred ship mortgage sued to foreclose his mortgage, and a number of creditors intervened, and the mortgagor took assignments of all the creditor claims except one supply claim and the claims of two persons who claimed for advances to pay off existing maritime liens. The vessel was sold and the proceeds were distributed to the supply claimant and to the mortgagor in respect of its assigned claims and the mortgage. The court held that the two who claimed for advances could not take from the sale fund, but ordered that they be paid from an operating fund held by the mortgagor, with one of them to be paid in full and the remainder to go to the second. The operating fund proved insufficient to pay the first claim for advances, so the second received nothing. The disappointed claimants for advances appealed, and the mortgagor cross appealed, contending that the money in the operating fund should have gone to it. Judge Tuttle conceded authority to the effect that the removal of the res ends jurisdiction in rem, but indicated that in view of the fact that the action had been brought in personam and the mortgagor was before the court of appeals partly in the capacity of an appellant, the court had jurisdiction of the person of the mortgagor and should exercise its in personam jurisdiction to supply any want of jurisdiction in rem.

And when a claimant made an appearance initially limited to the issue of constitutionality of a Rule B(1) attachment and having lost on this issue made no objection to a pretrial order that stated "there is no dispute between the parties that the court has jurisdiction over the parties and the subject matter of this action", and proceeded to litigate fully the merits of the dispute, dissolution of the attachment did not moot the plaintiff's appeal. Trans–Asiatic Oil Ltd., S.A. v. Apex Oil Co., 804 F.2d 773 (1st Cir.1986). Even if there was a general appearance, release would moot an appeal from the order of release. Pride Shipping Corp. v. Tafu Lumber Co., 898 F.2d 1404 (9th Cir.1990). See also Folkstone Maritime, Ltd. v. CSX Corp., 866 F.2d 955 (7th Cir.1989), cert. denied 493 U.S. 813, 110 S.Ct. 60, 107 L.Ed.2d 27 (1989), (holding that release moots an appeal from an order fixing the amount of security).

And it has been held that the posting of a bond for release of a vessel is not consent to in personam jurisdiction. The action remains in rem. International Seafoods of Alaska, Inc. v. Park Ventures, Inc., 829 F.2d 751 (9th Cir.1987).

The spectre of losing jurisdiction has sometimes made courts very careful to keep its hands on the vessel. See, e.g., Bassis v. SS Caribia, 309 F.Supp. 989, 1969 A.M.C. 1591 (E.D.N.Y.1969), in which Judge Judd indicated that a vessel in the custody of the court under in rem process and in need of repairs should be repaired in Brooklyn, Manhattan, Queens, or Richmond, and not moved to a pier in New Jersey since substantial doubt exists as to whether or not the court would lose jurisdiction if the vessel were moved outside the state.

While theoretically it would not matter how the res was removed from the court's jurisdiction, it was held that accidental, fraudulent, or improper removal did not deprive the court of jurisdiction. This exception to the general rule is traced to The Rio Grande, 90 U.S. (23 Wall.) 458, 23 L.Ed. 158 (1874), given as the authority for the accidental, fraudulent, or improper removal exception, the vessel was libelled in the District of Alabama on a claim for repairs. The district court dismissed the libel, and within a few minutes of the order of dismissal libellant moved for allowance of an appeal to the circuit court. The court allowed the appeal and fixed the amount of the bonds. The following day, based upon a clerical irregularity, the court released the vessel to the respondent, who immediately sent it to sea. The appeal was heard by the circuit court, which reversed the decree of the district court and entered a decree for the libellant. The vessel having departed, the decree could not be enforced by sale. Subsequently, however, the libellant had the vessel arrested in the District of Louisiana, and appended to his complaint a copy of the record of the decree of the circuit court. The Supreme Court held that the circuit court decree was conclusive in the second proceeding. On the subject of the jurisdiction of the circuit court to hear the appeal, Mr. Justice Hunt observed: "We hold the rule to be that a valid seizure and actual control of the res by the marshal gives jurisdiction of the subject matter, and that an accidental or fraudulent or improper removal of it from his custody, or a delivery of it to the party upon security, does not destroy jurisdiction." 90 U.S. at 465. The court found that under the statutes governing appeals the allowance of an appeal had the effect of an automatic stay, and therefore the return of the vessel "was in direct violation of the statute on appeals, and did not operate to destroy the jurisdiction of the Circuit Court." The result of the decision in The Rio Grande is that the vessel is sold in the district in which it is found to satisfy the judgment in rem.

For a more recent case, see Colonial Press of Miami, Inc. v. The Allen's Cay, 277 F.2d 540, 1960 A.M.C. 1598 (5th Cir.1960), in which a vessel of foreign registry arrested in Florida simply steamed away, no security having been posted, and no undertaking having been entered into. Since no sworn claim was made to the vessel, the district court had entered a default decree, but at a hearing on the amount heard the arguments of the ship's master respecting the existence of a lien and dismissed the libel. The court of appeals reversed and remanded for a hearing solely on the issue of amount.

See Southern Oregon Production Credit Ass'n v. The Oil Screw Sweet Pea, 435 F.Supp. 454, 1977 A.M.C. 638 (D.Or.1977). There the plaintiff had The Sweet Pea arrested in California on a claim of maritime lien in respect of repairs performed on the vessel. The vessel was released to the owner on a stipulation by the owner that he would give security in the amount of $5,000, would make over insurance policies to the benefit of the plaintiff, and would deposit with the court the ship's title documents. In fact the title documents were not deposited with the court. The judgment totalled $29,000, of which $4,000 was realized from the security. Subsequently the plaintiff intervened in an action in the district in Oregon brought for the purpose of foreclosing a preferred ship mortgage, asserting his judgment in the district court in California. The district court in Oregon held that the release of the vessel in the first case on stipulation had the effect of transferring the lien on the ship into a lien on the security, and extinguishing the original lien.

And in Taylor v. Tracor Marine, Inc., 683 F.2d 1361, 1983 A.M.C. 2968 (11th Cir.1982), cert. denied 460 U.S. 1012, 103 S.Ct. 1252, 75 L.Ed.2d 481 (1983), the vessel was arrested on claims for wages and penalty wages, and sold, with the proceeds deposited in the registry of the court. The court decreed various sums to various plaintiffs and some of the plaintiffs filed notices of appeal. A motion was made to disburse the funds pending appeal. Appellants strenuously opposed the motion, but the district court granted it and paid out all the money in the fund. The court of appeals dismissed the appeal for want of jurisdiction, indicating that the appellants should have sought mandamus to prevent the disbursement of the fund.

Does the rule of *Republic Nat'l Bank* avert the practical problem that arises when there is no in personam jurisdiction and the res has disappeared and no security has been given? *Ancora Transport* created no problem of relief. Is that because the garnishee won? In *Taylor*, supra, what chance would there be of getting the ship back from the purchaser? Or the wages back from the seamen?

In Newpark Shipbuilding & Repair, Inc. v. M/V Trinton Brute, 2 F.3d 572, 1994 A.M.C. 133 (5th Cir.1993), a lienor took a judgment against the vessel, bought the vessel at the marshal's sale, using the judgment as the purchase price, and then sold it to the claimant (its former owner). Meanwhile the claimant had appealed. Is there any way in which a reversal of the judgment could be enforced. The court of appeals found that the case came within the "useless judgment" exception to *Republic Nat'l Bank*.

Release of Vessel

The release of vessels on the giving of security is governed by Supplemental Rule E(5). The claimant may obtain release of the vessel by filing a special bond (a bond to secure a particular claim) which absent stipulation is to be fixed "at an amount sufficient to cover the plaintiff's claim fairly stated with accrued interest and costs," but not more than twice the amount of the claim or "the value of the property on due appraisal." Or he may file a general bond (a bond to secure the plaintiff's claim and all or any actions that may be brought thereafter in such court) in an amount "at least double the aggregate amount claimed by plaintiffs in all actions begun and pending." Section 2464 of Title 28 provides that a special bond shall be double the amount of the claim. See Gilmore & Black, op. cit., p. 797. There it is observed that "[p]resumably the Committee's rewriting of § 2464 is in no more danger of challenge than the original admiralty rules." Is there any reason to suppose that the subject of the amount of a release bond is outside the Rules Enabling Act? Cf. Former Rule 73(d) of the F.R.C.P., which dealt with the amount of a supersedeas bond. See also Rule 7 of the F.R.A.P. If the subject is procedural, is there any question about the fact that the rules supersede "[a]ll laws in conflict with them"? See 28 U.S.C.A. § 2072.

B.   NOTICE AND HEARING; RULES B AND C OF THE SUPPLEMENTAL RULES AS AMENDED IN 1985

Seizure of vessels under in rem process without benefit of prior notice or hearing had a very long history in admiralty proceedings. Rule IX of the Admiralty Rules of 1844 provided:

> In all cases of seizure and in other suits and proceedings in rem, the process, unless otherwise provided for by statute, shall be by a warrant of arrest of the ship, goods, or other thing to be arrested, and the marshall shall thereupon arrest and take the ship, goods or other thing into his possession for safe custody; and shall cause public notice thereof and for the time assigned for the return of such process and the hearing of the cause to be given in such newspaper within the district as the District Court shall order, and if there is no newspaper published therein then in such other public places in the district as the court shall direct.

Rule IX (1844) was carried forward without substantial alteration as Rule 10 of the Rules of 1920. The same principles were followed in drafting Supplemental Rule C(3) in 1966. As originally promulgated, Supplemental Rule C(3) read:

> (3) PROCESS. Upon the filing of the complaint the clerk shall forthwith issue a warrant for the arrest of the vessel or other property that is the subject of the action and deliver it to the marshal for service. If the property that is the subject of the action consists in whole or in part of

freight, or the proceeds of property sold, or other intangible property, the clerk shall issue a summons directing any person having control of the funds to show cause why they should not be paid into court to abide the judgment.

Three years after the promulgation of the Supplemental Rules, in Sniadach v. Family Finance Corp., 395 U.S. 337, 89 S.Ct. 1820, 23 L.Ed.2d 349 (1969), the Supreme Court began a series of decisions examining for procedural due process state statutes providing for seizure of property prior to notice and an opportunity to be heard.

As the Court worked out the due process requirements for prejudgment seizure of property on land in Fuentes v. Shevin, 407 U.S. 67, 92 S.Ct. 1983, 32 L.Ed.2d 556 (1972), Mitchell v. W.T. Grant Co., 416 U.S. 600, 94 S.Ct. 1895, 40 L.Ed.2d 406 (1974), and North Georgia Finishing, Inc. v. Di-Chem, Inc., 419 U.S. 601, 95 S.Ct. 719, 42 L.Ed.2d 751 (1975), doubt was expressed in a number of quarters about the constitutionality of Supplemental Rules B and C. See, Techem Chemical Co., Ltd. v. M/T Choyo Maru, 416 F.Supp. 960, 1976 A.M.C. 1954 (D.Md.1976). In two district court cases these doubts were converted into holding. See Alyeska Pipeline Service Co. v. Bay Ridge, 509 F.Supp. 1115, 1981 A.M.C. 1086 (D.Alaska 1981), appeal dism'd 703 F.2d 381 (9th Cir.1983), cert. denied 467 U.S. 1247, 104 S.Ct. 3526, 82 L.Ed.2d 852 (1984)(Rule C); Grand Bahama Petroleum Co. v. Canadian Transportation Agencies, Ltd., 450 F.Supp. 447, 1978 A.M.C. 789 (W.D.Wash.1978). In some districts local rules were adopted to supplement the Supplemental Rules to save the practice from attack under the *Sniadach* line of cases. To the extent that the issue of constitutionality reached the courts of appeals, however, both Supplemental Rule B and Supplemental Rule C were held to be valid.

It is not necessary that rules shave procedural due process as close as constitutionally possible, however, and effective August 1, 1985, Supplemental Rules B, C, and E were amended in substance to require some judicial scrutiny prior to seizure and the guarantee of a prompt post-seizure hearing. The background of the proposal of August, 1983, which, mutatis mutandis, became the present text, and its evolution during the intervening two years is discussed in Culp, Charting a New Course: Proposed Amendments to the Supplemental Rules for Admiralty Arrest and Attachment, 103 F.R.D. 319 (1985).

* * *

C.   ATTACHMENT AND GARNISHMENT

Royal Swan v. Global Container Lines, Ltd.

United States District Court, Southern District of New York, 1994.
868 F.Supp. 599, 1995 A.M.C. 1265.

■ HAROLD BAER, D.J.:

This case involves a motion to vacate an *ex parte* attachment of defendant's bank account ordered pursuant to Rule B of the Supplemental Rules for

Certain Admiralty and Maritime Claims of the Federal Rules of Civil Procedure. Three days following the order the court provided for a post-attachment hearing. At that time, the defendant made the instant motion and moved as well for damages, attorneys' fees, expenses and costs incurred in connection with the attachment.

I. Background

Plaintiff Royal Swan Navigation Company Limited ("Royal Swan") is a foreign navigation company and hires out its ships to shipping companies. Defendant Global Container Lines Ltd. ("Global")[1] is a foreign corporation that ships goods overseas. On December 1, 1993, the parties entered into an agreement, or "charter party," in which the defendant would charter the plaintiff's vessel, *Master Panos*. Shortly after the vessel set sail in January of 1994, she encountered rough weather off the coast of Canada. As a result, some of the defendant's deck cargo came loose forcing the *Master Panos* to take refuge in Newfoundland, Canada. The *Master Panos* remained in Newfoundland while defendant restored her cargo and made her fit to sail.

In March of 1994, defendant deducted from the amount it owed plaintiff the time period and expenses spent in Newfoundland restowing the cargo. Plaintiff claims that clause 64 of their charter party, which states that "[a]ll deck cargo [is] to be carried at Charterer's risk," entitles it to the deducted portion. Defendant, meanwhile, contends that the shifting of the cargo and subsequent necessity of taking refuge were the fault of plaintiff's captain. On April 29, 1994, the plaintiff demanded arbitration in accordance with clause 17 of the charter party, which provides that the parties will arbitrate disputes in New York City. On May 23, 1994, the defendant appointed its arbitrator. On June 21, the panel was ready to proceed with the arbitration. The arbitration proceedings, which will take place in the Southern District of New York ("Southern District"), have not yet commenced. On September 30, 1994, plaintiff filed for the Rule B attachment in order to obtain security for the unpaid amount. The attachment was granted on October 31, and on that day, the warrant of attachment was served on defendant's account at Mashreq Bank in the Southern District.

Global asserts several grounds in support of its position that the attachment should be vacated. First, it asserts that the attachment violated Rule B because Global could be "found within" the Southern District. Second, it argues that even if it could not be "found within" the Southern District, the attachment should be set aside because it is abusive in that Royal Swan has exploited the artificial boundary between the Southern and Eastern Districts of New York by pursuing a Rule B

---

1. In its papers, Global identifies itself without a comma between "Lines" and "Ltd.", but Royal Swan had made no motion to amend the caption.

attachment in the Southern District when it could easily pursue the more common route of an in personam action in the Eastern District.

I find that Global could not be "found within" the Southern District for the purposes of Rule B, because there were no individuals authorized to accept service of process on behalf of Global who were present in the Southern District on a regular basis. Nonetheless, I find the attachment must be vacated as "unfair." Royal Swan has not shown it requires security for any arbitral award it may eventually obtain against Global.

II. Discussion

A. *"Found Within" A Given District Under Supplementary Rule B*

Rule B authorizes, in admiralty and maritime cases, attachment of a defendant's assets as a means of obtaining jurisdiction over a defendant provided the defendant cannot be "found within" the federal district in which the assets are sought to be attached. Supp.R.Fed.R.Civ.P. B(1). The purpose of Rule B is to enable the plaintiff both to acquire jurisdiction over the defendant and obtain security for any resulting judgment. Swift & Co. Packers v. Compania Colombiana Del Caribe, SA., 339 U.S. 684, 70 S.Ct. 861, 94 L.Ed. 1206, 1950 AMC 1089 (1950). Cases have held that being "found within" a given district consists of "a two-pronged inquiry: first, whether [the defendant] can be found within the district in terms of jurisdiction [("prong one")], and second, if so, whether it can be found for service of process [("prong two")]." Seawind Compania, S.A. v. Crescent Line, Inc., 320 F.2d 580, 582, 1964 AMC 617, 620 (2 Cir.1963) (citing United States v. CIA Naviera Continental S.A., 178 F.Supp. 561, 563, 1961 AMC 750, 752 (S.D.N.Y.1959)). Because I find, as detailed below, that Global could not be "found within" the Southern District of New York for the purposes of service of process, it is not necessary to consider whether Global's activities in connection with the Southern District rendered it subject to in personam jurisdiction here. Service upon a corporation can be made, in accordance with Rules 4(e)(1) and 4(h)(1) of the Federal Rules of Civil Procedure and § 311 of the New York Civil Practice Law and Rules (McKinney 1990), by, among other methods, delivering a copy of the summons and complaint to a director, officer, managing agent, general agent, cashier, or assistant cashier of the corporation, or any other agent authorized by appointment to receive service.

Global argues that Royal Swan could have served process on it within the Southern District in several different ways. Global first states that Royal Swan "commenced the [underlying] arbitration with Global by serving [Global's lawyers] with its formal demand for arbitration thereby using [Global's lawyers, whose office is in the Southern District] as agents for service of process," and then argues that Royal Swan "could have commenced [an in personam action] by again serving [Global's attorneys] who would have again accepted service on behalf of Global." While status as a party's attorney, without more, does not render the attorney an agent of the party for purposes of service of process, Integrated Container Serv., Inc. v. Starlines Container Shipping Ltd., 1980 AMC 736, 742, 476 F.Supp.

119, 125 (S.D.N.Y.1979), a party can of course appoint virtually anyone, including an attorney, as agent for that purpose. Here, however, Global stops short of asserting that its lawyers were its agents for service of process. Instead Global merely asserts that Royal Swan "us[ed]" its lawyers as such agents, and that its lawyers would have "again accepted service." Physically accepting process for another party does not mean the acceptor was appointed to do so. (In such a case, however, the party might choose to waive the deficiency in service.) And even if Global's attorneys had been appointed to accept arbitration demands, that does not necessarily mean they were also appointed to accept process. Thus, there is insufficient evidence to conclude that Global had appointed its attorneys as its agents for the purposes of accepting service of process.

Next, Global states that one of its directors travels to the Southern District "almost once a week to appear at the United Nations Headquarters, Purchase and Transportation Service Division at the U.N. Plaza." In addition, Global continues, given that the parties' pending arbitration is set to proceed in the Southern District, a "Global director or authorized personnel" would "most surely . . . have attended the [arbitration] hearings. . . ." Consequently, Global argues, it "could have easily been found and served" in the Southern District. Moreover, Global contends, although the arbitration panel was ready to proceed by June 21, 1994, Royal Swan "has done nothing since to commence hearings in the arbitration." In this manner, Global asserts, Royal Swan's actions are analogous to those in Shewan v. Hallenbeck, 150 Fed. 231 (S.D.N.Y.1906), where the Southern District vacated an attachment obtained pursuant to a predecessor rule to Rule B because the party seeking the attachment strategically delayed pursuing an action against its adversary solely in order that an attachment could be obtained when the adversary, as expected, left the Southern District a year later. Royal Swan refutes this, claiming that it has not delayed the commencement of hearings for the purpose of obtaining a Rule B attachment, but instead needed time to obtain and instruct an expert who will "determine the cause of the shifting deck cargo" and testify at the hearings.

While a party seeking a Rule B attachment must make a bona fide effort to find its adversary in the given district, e.g., Seawind Compania, S.A. v. Crescent Line, Inc., 320 F.2d 580, 1964 AMC 617 (2 Cir.1963), it is not necessary that an exhaustive search be conducted. Indeed, in contrast to the instant case, where Global asserts that the transient presence of certain individuals in the Southern District satisfies prong two of the Rule B test, most cases concern whether a party has searched enough to locate an existing permanent office where individuals capable of being served can regularly be found—something much easier to discover than the presence of a transient individual. E.g., Federazione Italiana Dei Consorzi Agrari v. Mandask Compania De Vapores, S.A., 158 F.Supp. 107 (S.D.N.Y.1957). The presence of a Global director "almost once a week" at a certain office at the United Nations Headquarters is insufficient to satisfy prong two of the test. It exceeds a bona fide effort to effect service under such circumstances, because Royal Swan would first have had to ascertain that a director even went to that office on a somewhat regular basis. Then, Royal Swan would have had to discover a specific week, day, and time at which a Global director would appear at the given office. Furthermore, Royal Swan would had to have gained familiarity with the appearance of the several Global directors in order that they be recognized by the process server. Not only would obtaining such information be difficult, but it would also potentially alert Global to the imminent attachment.

The likely presence of a director or individual authorized to receive process at the arbitration hearings, however, poses a more difficult question, as Royal Swan would, in that situation, at least know all potential dates upon which such an individual might appear, and, indeed, based on the progress of the hearings, could anticipate his or her attendance. For example, if the testimony of a Global director was not finished on a given day, Royal Swan could bring a process server to serve process the following day when the director returned to complete his or her testimony. In certain circumstances, I find that the presence of individuals authorized to accept process at arbitration hearings taking place in the district at issue can satisfy prong two of the Rule B test. This would include the situation where arbitration hearings are underway and the authorized individuals consistently attend. Here, however, there is no certainty as to when an authorized individual will attend, or that one will attend at all. In addition, the hearings have not even commenced. The prong is therefore not satisfied, because a party should not be precluded from obtaining a Rule B attachment merely because its adversary will at some future time enter the district. A party should not have to wait before initiating an action nor is there anything improper per se in moving quickly to obtain an attachment.[2] Global's assertion that Royal Swan delayed the commencement of the arbitration hearings for over three months in order to obtain the attachment stretches credibility, given that obtaining an attachment requires relatively little time.

Global might argue that, although it could not be served while physically within the Southern District, it still satisfied prong two of the Rule B test due to Rule 4 of the Federal Rules of Civil Procedure, which enables Royal Swan to serve Global beyond the Southern District boundaries, namely within the Eastern District of New York where it maintains an office and where several of its directors reside and work. The Second Circuit ruled that the attachment should not be available under such circumstances in Chilean Line Inc. v. United States, 344 F.2d 757, 1965 AMC 1387 (2 Cir.1965). See also D/S A/S Flint v. Sabre Shipping Corp., 228 F.Supp. 384, 1965 AMC 238 (E.D.N.Y.1964), aff'd on other grounds sub nom. Det Bergenske Dampskibsselskab v. Sabre Shipping Corp., 341 F.2d 50, 1965 AMC 235 (2 Cir.1965). Subsequent to *Chilean Line*, however, the Advisory Committee Notes to Rule B indicated that the Advisory Commit-

---

2. Depending on the nature of the defendant's ultimate presence in the district, however, the attachment might be deemed "unfair," as discussed below. This might exist where a defendant moved its headquarters into the district, as that would likely mean that the plaintiff no longer needed the security of the attachment.

tee had rejected the idea of restricting the availability of Rule B attachments in this manner.

B.   *"Abusive" Attachments Under Supplementary Rule B*

Global further argues that, even if it could not be "found within" the Southern District, Royal Swan's attachment should be set aside because it is "abusive." Explains Global, "Instead of easily pursuing Global [by way of an in personam action] in the Eastern District [of New York] ... Plaintiff has chosen to cross the artificial boundary into the Southern District in order to attach Global's bank account...." Indeed, Global might point out that Royal Swan simply could have remained in the Southern District and pursued an in personam action instead of utilizing the Rule B attachment (assuming that Global's activities in connection with the Southern District rendered it subject to in personam jurisdiction here). In making its argument, Global relies heavily on the Southern District case of Integrated Container Service, Inc. v. Starlines Container Shipping, Ltd., 1980 AMC 736, 476 F.Supp. 119 (S.D.N.Y.1979). Over a decade after the Advisory Committee had issued the Notes discussed above, the Integrated court, while following the Notes as I do here, held that "where an attachment is obtained unfairly in one district where a proper lawsuit could be commenced in another district without unfairness or inconvenience, the courts may easily remedy the situation by exercising discretion to set aside an unfair attachment."[3] *Integrated*, 476 F.Supp. at 124 (citing D/S A/S Flint v. Sabre Shipping Corp., 228 F.Supp. 384 (E.D.N.Y.1964), aff 'd on other grounds sub nom. Det Bergenske Dampskibsselskab v. Sabre Shipping Corp., 341 F.2d 50 (2 Cir.1965)). Integrated found that the attachment at issue was not "unfair," because "[t]here can be no doubt that plaintiffs' need for security is real, that their quest for attachment is not a tactic of harassment." Id. See also Central Hudson Gas and Elec. Corp. v. Empresa Naviera Santa, SA, 845 F.Supp. 150, 153 (S.D.N.Y.1994)("The Rule was not abused, inasmuch as there was a substantial risk that [plaintiff] would not be able to locate sufficient assets to satisfy its claims, which in turn were not frivolous." (citations omitted)); Western Bulk Carriers (Australia), Pty. v. P.S. Int'l, Ltd., 762 F.Supp. 1302, 1309 (S.D.Ohio 1991)("[T]he Court does have discretion to set aside an unfair attachment where the use of the maritime remedy is abusive, such as where an attachment is obtained unfairly in one district while a proper lawsuit could be commenced in another district without unfairness or convenience.") (cited *Integrated*).

---

3. Because the charter party that Royal Swan and Global had entered into required arbitration of disputes arising thereunder, filing an in personam action against Global would have of course accomplished nothing whether it be in the Southern or Eastern District. It is therefore true in such a situation that an *in personam* action cannot be viewed as an alternative to a Rule B attachment. Nevertheless, the fact that Royal Swan was able to file a valid *in personam* action against Global does reflect that Global engages in significant business activity within the district at issue, and therefore, in accordance with my opinion, necessitates an inquiry as to whether the security of a Rule B attachment is needed.

The *Integrated* holding appears consistent with Rule B's purpose, which, as noted above, was explained by the Supreme Court in Swift & Co Packers v. Compania Colombiana Del Caribe, S.A., 339 U.S. 684, 70 S.Ct. 861, 94 L.Ed. 1206 (1950), as enabling the plaintiff to acquire jurisdiction over a defendant and obtain security for any resulting judgment against the defendant. Under circumstances where the plaintiff can obtain jurisdiction over the defendant in the same or a nearby[4] district independently of a Rule B attachment, and where the plaintiff does not need the security of the attachment to satisfy any judgment it may obtain—a situation that the Advisory Committee may not have considered[5]—the need for either of Rule B's recognized functions does not exist.[6] Employing a Rule B attachment in those situations is consequently "unfair," given, at the least, the inconvenience, and at the worst, the significant financial injury, that the defendant experiences, and should not be permitted.[7]

4. As noted by Professor Moore, a Rule B attachment would not appear as objectionable where, for example, the adjacent districts of the Eastern and Western districts of Pennsylvania are concerned, because in that situation a plaintiff could "eliminat[e] the 300–mile, cross state trip for execution that may otherwise be necessitated." 7A *Moore's Federal Practice* ¶ B.06 (2d ed.1993). In that context, a Rule B attachment would also benefit, for example, a plaintiff who resided in the district where the assets are located, because it could then potentially avoid having to litigate the claim 300 miles away (assuming that the defendant was not otherwise subject to *in personam* jurisdiction in the district where the assets are located).

5. The Fifth Circuit in LaBanca v. Ostermunchner, 664 F.2d 65, 68 n. 4, 1982 AMC 205, 208 (5 Cir.1981), while relying on the Advisory Committee's Notes in refusing to vacate an attachment on the Florida bank account of two individuals from Venezuela where an in personam action could have been initiated in the same district, noted the fact that, without the attachment, the plaintiff "would have little hope of securing the appearance of, or satisfying a judgment against, [the] Venezuela citizens." In so doing, the Fifth Circuit at least left open the possibility that it might rule differently where the need for such security did not exist.

6. By providing jurisdiction simply by virtue of the attachment of assets, Rule B can also enable plaintiffs to litigate their claims in districts that are far more convenient for them than districts where an *in personam* suit could be brought. See supra note 4. Whether that possibility by itself is sufficient to warrant the use of a Rule B attachment is a question I need not address here, where the parties' agreement to arbitrate precludes litigation of the underlying dispute, see supra note 3, and, even if the dispute could be litigated. Royal Swan could file an *in personam* action against Global in the Southern District if, as Global contends, its activities in connection with the Southern District cause it to be subject to in personam jurisdiction here.

Whether the Rule B attachment would have enabled Royal Swan to eliminate a "300–mile, cross-state trip" to satisfy its arbitral award, see supra note 4, is not at issue here, as Global does of course have assets in the Southern District where the dispute will be arbitrated, and even if Global moved those assets, the proximity of its offices to the Southern District likely means the magnitude of the distance contemplated by Professor Moore does not exist in the instant case, Id. Besides, Royal Swan did not contend that Eastern District is a less convenient forum for it than the Southern District in terms of enforcing a judgment.

Moreover, it is not necessary to consider whether the added step required to enforce judgments across the more substantive boundaries of state lines by itself justifies a Rule B attachment, because here the federal districts at issue are within the same state.

7. Professor Moore appears to suggest that an otherwise permissible Rule B attachment should be denied only where both "the plaintiff and defendant carry on substantial and continuing business activities in another district where an in personam proceeding

C. *Royal Swan's Need for Security*

In Integrated, three months before the attachments were granted, the defendants, foreign corporations, had closed their common New York office, disconnected their common telephone line in New York, and in fact, ceased doing business anywhere. *Integrated*, 476 F.Supp. at 123. Those facts left little doubt as to the plaintiff's need for security. Accordingly, at the post-attachment hearing in the instant case, the court indicated that one of its primary concerns in adjudicating the motion to vacate revolved around whether or not Royal Swan needed the security of the attachment in light of Global's oral assertions, reflected in its papers, that Global "has continuously maintained ... offices in Garden City, New York since 1985," has maintained the account that was attached with the same bank since 1985, which account is Global's "primary bank account," and "regularly conducts business in the City of New York[8] with ship owners, ship brokers, insur-

---

could have been commenced." 7A Moore's Federal Practice 11B.06 (2d ed. 1993)(footnote omitted). I do not make such a holding, and explain by way of example, which, I will emphasize, consists of facts that do not exist in the instant case. A profitable defendant corporation may have its only offices and production facilities in the Eastern District of New York, engage in substantial business in the Southern District of New York, have a bank account in the Southern District of New York, and be available for service of process only in the Eastern District, where all potential recipients of service work and reside. A plaintiff corporation that only has offices in California would naturally prefer to obtain a Rule B attachment in the Southern District rather than pursue an in personam suit in that same district or the Eastern District due to the added pressure and inconvenience experienced by the defendant when its assets are attached. In that situation, because the defendant is subject to jurisdiction in the Southern District and can receive process at its offices in the Eastern District issued from the Southern District, and because the defendant's operations are profitable and all of its offices and production facilities are located in New York State, the attachment should not be granted. In accordance with my holding above, the plaintiff can independently obtain jurisdiction over the defendant and does not need the security of an attachment for any subsequent judgment. This analysis does not change simply because there exists no jurisdiction where both "the plaintiff and defendant carry on substantial and continuing business activities ... where an in personam proceeding could have been commenced."

Cf. Western Bulk Carriers (Australia), Pty. v. P.S. Int'l, Ltd., 762 F.Supp. 1302, 1309, 1991 AMC 2828, 2837 (S.D.Ohio 1991)(following Professor Moore's position in permitting a Rule B attachment even though an in personam action could have been instituted in an adjacent federal district, located in an adjoining state, primarily because the plaintiff was an Australia corporation that did not engage in any business in that adjacent district).

8. By merely stating "New York City," without more, Global leaves in doubt whether all, some, or none of the noted activities occurred in New York City's Bronx and New York counties, which are within the confines of the Southern District of New York, as opposed to New York City's three remaining counties—Kings, Queens, and Richmond—which fall within the Eastern District of New York's jurisdiction. 28 U.S.C. § 112(b)-(c) (1993). Although Global's Supplemental Affidavit refers to the "other business activities in Manhattan as mentioned in [the] [initial] affidavit," it likewise fails to specify which of those "other business activities" occurred in New York City's Borough of Manhattan, which consists of the identical geographical area as New York State's New York County.

Because I find, as explained above, that Global could not be "found within" the Southern District of New York for the purposes of service of process it is not relevant to this case what portion, if any, of the stated activities occurred in the Southern District, as opposed to the Eastern District, of New York. This was not clear at the time of the hearing, however, and Royal Swan's failure to raise the matter, either at the hearing, or

ance companies, lawyers, accountants, suppliers, and other professionals engaged in the shipping business."

Pursuant to Rule 12 of the Admiralty Rules of the Southern District of New York, the party seeking to maintain the attachment bears the burden of showing "why the . . . attachment should not be vacated" after the adversary has "show[n] . . . any improper practice or a manifest want of equity on the part of the" other party. Indeed, this burden was detailed in the order that granted the attachment, which order Royal Swan had itself drafted for my signature. In the memorandum that it prepared at my direction after the post-attachment hearing, however, Royal Swan made no claim that it would have difficulty satisfying any ultimate arbitral award against Global. It did not allege, for example, that Global was financially troubled or that it would encounter difficulty in locating Global's assets. Nor did it request discovery on the matter.

During the ex parte correspondence that the court engaged in with Royal Swan in the court's efforts to ascertain if "the conditions set forth in [Rule B] appear to exist," as it is required to do by that rule, Royal Swan indicated that it was ignorant of the nature and size of Global's presence in Garden City[9] and could not state one way or the other whether Global engaged in business activity in the Southern District. After Global made its assertions at the hearing and in its initial papers, and after the court informed the parties of what it identified as the relevant issues, Royal Swan's failure to address them in the memorandum it subsequently submitted can be taken to mean only that Royal Swan is now sufficiently informed. Global has maintained offices in Garden City continuously since 1985 and there are no allegations that Global is financially troubled. Global has not resisted arbitration nor given any other indication that it is attempting to avoid adjudication of the dispute, a factor that might lead a plaintiff to suspect the need for security. It therefore appears that Royal Swan does not need security for its claim any more than the typical plaintiff might, and, in the absence of even an assertion by Royal Swan to the contrary, I cannot find that it needs the security of the Rule B attachment. I therefore vacate the attachment.

D.   *Global's Motion for Expenses*

My decision indicates that although an attachment is available in accordance with the letter of Rule B, it should not be granted if it does not accord with the spirit of the rule. As indicated above, the ex parte correspondence this court engaged in with Royal Swan sought to ascertain

in the memorandum that it subsequently filed, therefore serves as another example of its failure to address the dispositive, or potentially dispositive, issues of the case. This appears especially egregious by noting that the specific confines of the Southern District had only recently been impressed upon Royal Swan when the court informed Royal Swan that the affidavit it submitted *ex parte* when it requested the attachment indicated searches of only those telephone listings for the Southern District counties within New York City, and none of those for the remaining Southern District counties of Dutchess, Orange, Putnam, Rockland, Sullivan, and Westchester.

9. Royal Swan referred to it as an "agent or office."

whether the desired attachment satisfied both the letter and spirit of the rule, by examining whether Royal Swan had a need for security. In that regard, Royal Swan informed the court that it was unaware of the extent of Global's presence in the Eastern and Southern Districts. Because the court understood the difficulty of obtaining that information without alerting Global to the possible attachment, it granted the attachment with the intention that the adversarial process, including discovery, would quickly reveal whether a need for security exists. Notwithstanding that I have vacated the attachment, the awarding of expenses is inappropriate where, as here, obtaining the information needed to conclude whether an attachment is permissible may very well render the issue moot by alerting the other party of the plaintiff's plans. See supra pp.1269–70 (discussing how Royal Swan had no duty to discover the presence of certain Global directors at the United Nations Headquarters particularly because it would "potentially alert Global to the imminent attachment"). If, however, Global has reason to believe that Royal Swan was cognizant of the extent of Global's presence, whether as a result of its interaction with Global in connection with the charter party at issue, Global's stature in the industry, or other circumstances, it may bring a motion for reconsideration of this motion for expenses, where the court will also consider the imposition of sanctions for the misrepresentations that might have been made to the court.

III. Conclusion

The Rule B attachment is vacated. The motion for expenses is denied.

D. PERSONAL JURISDICTION

1. SERVICE ON AN AGENT

Ontario Paper Co., Ltd. v. Salenrederierna A/B

United States District Court, Southern District of New York, 1978.
1979 A.M.C. 1037.

■ LAWRENCE W. PIERCE, D.J.:

This is an action to recover for alleged damage to cargo shipped by the defendants. It is undisputed that plaintiffs are Canadian corporations and that defendants are Swedish corporations. On June 16, 1972, plaintiffs through a charterer delivered a shipment of newsprint aboard the M/S *Husaro*. The voyage charterer, Quebec and Ontario Transportation Co., chartered the vessel M/S *Husaro* from defendants Salenrederierna A/B and Rederi A/B Rex. The cargo was shipped from Quebec to Port Everglades, Florida, where the plaintiffs claim, 300 rolls of paper were found to be damaged by water.

Plaintiffs commenced this action by the filing of a complaint on September 24, 1976. Process was served on the defendants by serving

Skaarup Chartering Corp. Skaarup was the charter broker for the voyage and signed the charter party on behalf of the defendants.

Defendants now move to dismiss the complaint pursuant to Fed. R.Civ.P. 12(b)(5) for failure to obtain *in personam* or *in rem* jurisdiction. Although Rule 12(b)(5) technically addresses the issue of insufficiency of service of process, the Court construes defendants' motion to also assert lack of personal jurisdiction pursuant to Fed.R.Civ.P. 12(b)(2) and notes that plaintiffs have also responded to the motion on this basis. See 5 Wright & Miller, Federal Practice and Procedure, sec. 1353, at 580 (1969).

Plaintiffs have the burden of substantiating allegations of agency which would sustain the validity of service of process under Fed.R.Civ.P. 4(d)(3). See Insurance Co. of North America v. S/S Jotina, 1974 AMC 1190 (S.D.N.Y. 1974); Klishewich v. Mediterranean Agencies, Inc., 1967 AMC 841, 42 F.R.D. 624 (E.D.N.Y. 1966). In the present case, plaintiffs have failed to sustain the burden of showing that Skaarup acted in any capacity other than that of charter broker. Ordinarily, a charter broker is not an agent authorized to receive process on behalf of the party for whom it acted. "The business of ship brokerage is well recognized and carries with it no implication of agency * * *." Klishewich v. Mediterranean Agencies, Inc., supra, 1967 AMC at 845, 42 F.R.D. at 627. The mere fact that Skaarup also signed for the defendants four addenda to the original charter party does not constitute additional functions indicating an agency relationship as in Arpad Szabo v. Smedvig Tankrederi A.S., 1951 AMC 481, 95 F.Supp. 519 (S.D.N.Y.1951). Furthermore, even if Skaarup were a proper agent for service of process, plaintiffs have not presented the Court with any evidence indicating that Skaarup is doing business in New York. Even in the complaint, Skaarup is identified as being located in Greenwich, Connecticut.

In ruling on Rule 12(b)(5) motion, the court has "broad discretion to dismiss the action or to retain the case but quash the service that has been made on the defendant." 5 Wright & Miller, Federal Practice and Procedure sec. 1354, at 585 (1969)(footnotes omitted). In exercising this discretion, courts will generally quash service and retain jurisdiction where "there is a reasonable prospect that plaintiff asserts that an alternative means of service may be effective if the court should find service to be invalid, a quashing of service rather than dismissal of the complaint is warranted." Aquascutum of London, Inc. v. S.S. American Champion, 1970 AMC 679, 684, 426 F.2d 205, 210 (2 Cir., 1970).

Plaintiffs claim that there is personal jurisdiction in New York over the defendants through the activities of A. Willard Ivers, Inc. which acted as port agent for the defendants. It is undisputed that Ivers does business in New York for jurisdictional purposes. However, defendants contend that Ivers was not invested by defendants with the type of discretion that would make Ivers subject to service of process for the defendants. See Fed. R.Civ.P. 4(d)(3) and Grammenos v. Lemos, 1972 AMC 608, 457 F.2d 1067 (2 Cir.1972); Green v. Compania de Navigacion Isabella Ltd., 1960 AMC 2131, 26 F.R.D. 616 (S.D.N.Y.1960). The affidavit of John Cregan, Vice-president of Ivers, states that Ivers performed husbanding functions for defendants including arranging tugs, pilots, line handlers, and visitation of customs and immigration.   In addition, Ivers rendered a disbursement account and collected freights from charterers and remitted these funds to the defendants.   The Court concludes that these activities represent more than "incidental contact" on the part of defendants with New York and that defendants, therefore, could be subject to the Court's *in personam* jurisdiction.   See Koupetoris v. Konkar Intrepid Corp., 1976 AMC 1451, 1456, 535 F.2d 1392, 1395 (2 Cir.1976).

Accordingly, there appearing to be a reasonable prospect that proper service will be made, the Court declines to dismiss this action and denies defendants' motion.   However, service of process on Skaarup is hereby quashed.   In rendering this opinion, the Court makes no determination regarding the propriety of serving Ivers as agent for defendants since it is noted that plaintiffs have not refuted defendant's showing that Ivers ceased acting as port agent for defendants six months prior to the filing of this action.

Plaintiffs are hereby given twenty days from entry of this order within which to effect valid service of process.

NOTE

The question of the propriety of the service of process on Skarrup in *Ontario Paper* relates, of course, to the provisions of Rule 4(d)(3), which in the case of service on a corporation or entity capable of being sued in its common name, requires that the summons and complaint be delivered to an "officer," a "managing or general agent," or "any other agent authorized by appointment or by law to receive service of process."

The court declined to decide whether service on Ivers, the "port agent," who performed "husbanding" functions for the defendant was sufficient.   See Cobelfret–Cie Belge v. Samick Lines Co., Ltd., 542 F.Supp. 29, 1983 A.M.C. 547 (W.D.Wash. 1982):

"Although some courts have found that service upon a local port agent providing ordinary husbanding services on a ship to ship basis is valid service on a foreign shipowner, see e.g., Murphy v. Arrow Steamship Co., 124 F.Supp. 199, 1954 A.M.C. 1423 (E.D.Pa.1954), the majority of courts have held that subagents or husbanding agents are not authorized to accept service of process which will bind the vessel's owner.   See Serpe v. Eagle Ocean Transport Agency Co., 53 F.R.D. 21, 1971 A.M.C. 748 (E.D.Wis.1971); Amicale Industries, Inc. v. The S.S. Rantum, 259 F.Supp. 534, 1967 A.M.C. 96 (D.S.C.1966)."

See also Marvirazon v. H.J. Baker, 1979 A.M.C. 625 (S.D.N.Y.1978), indicating that if service is to be made on a husbanding agent, the latter's activities must be substantial and continuous, not just on a ship to ship basis.   And see K/S Ditlev Chartering A/S & Co. v. Egeria S.p.A., 20 B.R. 625, 1982 A.M.C. 1817 (E.D.Va. 1982), to the effect that a mere husbanding agent can receive service of process only while the vessel is still in the district and he is still acting on behalf of the principal.

Notice that Rule 4(d)(3) also permits service upon an agent authorized by law to receive service of process.   See, e.g., Egan Marine Contracting Co., Inc. v. South

Sea Shipping Corp., 612 F.Supp. 1, 1985 A.M.C. 1489 (D.Md.1983), holding that a foreign corporation the chartered vessels of which had made six calls in Baltimore and incurred indebtedness of $220,000 within a six months period was doing business in the state and since it had not designated an agent for service of process, service could be made upon the Maryland Department of Assessments and Taxation pursuant to statute.

2.   Long Arm Jurisdiction

DeJames v. Magnificence Carriers, Inc.

United States Court of Appeals, Third Circuit, 1981.
654 F.2d 280, 1981 A.M.C. 2105, cert. denied 454 U.S. 1085, 102 S.Ct. 642, 70 L.Ed.2d 620 (1981).

■ Seitz, Chief Judge.

Joseph DeJames appeals from an order of the district court dismissing his admiralty claim against Hitachi Shipbuilding and Engineering Co., Ltd. (Hitachi) for lack of personal jurisdiction and insufficient service of process. Although the complaint was not dismissed as to all defendants, the district court determined that there was no just reason for delay and entered final judgment for Hitachi pursuant to rule 54(b) of the Federal Rules of Civil Procedure.   The district court had admiralty jurisdiction pursuant to 28 U.S.C. § 1333 (1976).   This court has jurisdiction under 28 U.S.C. § 1291 (1976).

I

DeJames, a New Jersey longshoreman, was injured while working on the M.V. Magnificence Venture (the vessel) when it was moored to a pier in Camden, New Jersey.   DeJames filed a complaint in the United States District Court for the District of New Jersey, alleging negligence and strict liability in tort against, *inter alia,* the charterers of the vessel and Hitachi, a Japanese corporation with its principal place of business in Japan. Hitachi had converted the vessel in Japan from a bulk carrier to an automobile carrier.   DeJames alleged that Hitachi's conversion work was defective.

After the complaint was filed, process was served on Hitachi at its place of business in Japan by the Japanese Minister of Foreign Affairs apparently in accordance with the requirements of an international treaty. See Convention on the Service Abroad of Judicial and Extrajudicial Documents in Civil or Commercial Matters, 20 U.S.T. 361–367 (1969).   Hitachi filed a motion to dismiss for lack of personal jurisdiction pursuant to rule 12(b)(2) of the Federal Rules of Civil Procedure.   In support of this motion, Hitachi submitted an affidavit from Kiyoshi Ohno, the manager of its ship repair business department in Tokyo, Japan.   According to this affidavit, Hitachi completed all work on the vessel at its Japanese shipyard and had no further contact with the vessel after it left Osaka, Japan.   The affidavit also states that Hitachi does not maintain an office, have an agent of any type, or transact any business in New Jersey.

After completion of discovery, briefing, and oral argument on the question of jurisdiction, the district court dismissed the complaint against Hitachi. The district court held that there were insufficient contacts with the state of New Jersey to support in personam jurisdiction. See DeJames v. Magnificence Carriers, Inc., 491 F.Supp. 1276, 1279–81 (D.N.J.1980). The court then considered whether it would be appropriate to aggregate all of Hitachi's contacts with the United States for the purpose of establishing personal jurisdiction. The district court believed that a defendant's national contacts might be a viable basis for jurisdiction where service could be effected through wholly federal means. See id. at 1284. However, because Congress has not authorized nationwide service of process for admiralty actions, and because it was necessary for DeJames to utilize New Jersey's long-arm rule, the court concluded that the jurisdictional inquiry was limited to the question whether Hitachi's contacts with New Jersey were sufficient to confer personal jurisdiction. See id.

On appeal, DeJames makes two arguments for reversing the district court. First, he argues that Hitachi's contacts with the state of New Jersey are sufficient to support personal jurisdiction. Alternatively, he argues for the first time on appeal that service was made by wholly federal means, and thus that the district court erred in not considering Hitachi's national contacts.

II

Because this suit arises under the district court's admiralty jurisdiction, the due process clause of the fifth amendment determines whether the district court has personal jurisdiction over Hitachi. See Fraley v. Chesapeake & Ohio Railway, 397 F.2d 1, 4 (3d Cir.1968). However, the principle announced in diversity cases such as International Shoe Co. v. Washington, 326 U.S. 310, 66 S.Ct. 154, 90 L.Ed. 95 (1945), and its progeny is also applicable to nondiversity cases. See *Fraley*, 397 F.2d at 3. This standard provides that a defendant is subject to a forum's jurisdiction only if its contacts with the forum are such that maintenance of the suit will not offend traditional notions of fair play and substantial justice. It is unclear whether the *Fraley* court meant that the fifth amendment requires a defendant to have minimum contacts with the forum state, or whether the court intended only that the *International Shoe* test be applied by analogy, so that a defendant need only have minimum contacts with the United States as a whole. In any event, even in nondiversity cases, if service of process must be made pursuant to a state long-arm statute or rule of court, the defendant's amenability to suit in federal district court is limited by that statute or rule. See Hartley v. Sioux City & New Orleans Barge Lines, Inc., 379 F.2d 354, 357 (3d Cir.1967).

With these principles in mind, we will examine DeJames' arguments that the district court erred in dismissing his claim against Hitachi for lack of personal jurisdiction. In the district court, DeJames claimed that service had been made pursuant to New Jersey Court Rule 4:4–4. Although he now claims alternatively that service was made by wholly federal means, we address first his argument that Hitachi's contacts with the state of New Jersey alone are sufficient to support personal jurisdiction under that state's long-arm rule.

A

The New Jersey long-arm rule is intended to extend as far as is constitutionally permissible. In enacting its long-arm rule, the state of New Jersey is limited by the due process constraints of the fourteenth amendment. Therefore, we believe that Hitachi's amenability to suit in the District of New Jersey must be judged by fourteenth amendment standards. We recognize that this creates an anomalous situation because it results in a federal court in a nondiversity case being limited by the due process restrictions imposed on the states by the fourteenth amendment as opposed to those imposed on the federal government by the fifth amendment. However, it would be equally anomalous to utilize a state long-arm rule to authorize service of process on a defendant in a manner that the state body enacting the rule could not constitutionally authorize. The anomaly of a federal court being limited by the requirements of the fourteenth amendment in a nondiversity case where service must be made pursuant to a state long-arm rule could be easily rectified by congressional authorization of nationwide service of process for admiralty cases. It is not within our province to create such authorization.

DeJames directs our attention to only one contact that Hitachi has had with the state of New Jersey: the vessel on which Hitachi had done conversion work was docked in Camden, New Jersey when DeJames was injured.[1] DeJames argues that this contact is sufficient to support the exercise of in personam jurisdiction over Hitachi.

The evolution of the due process standards that guide courts in determining whether a defendant is amenable to suit in a particular forum has been detailed on numerous occasions and need not be repeated at length here. The primary consideration in the jurisdictional inquiry is that of fundamental fairness to the defendant. The Supreme Court held in *International Shoe:*

> [D]ue process requires only that in order to subject a defendant to a judgment *in personam,* if he be not present within the territory of the forum, he have certain minimum contacts with it such that the maintenance of the suit does not offend "traditional notions of fair play and substantial justice."

326 U.S. at 316, 66 S.Ct. at 158 (quoting Milliken v. Meyer, 311 U.S. 457, 463, 61 S.Ct. 339, 342, 85 L.Ed. 278 (1940)). In Hanson v. Denckla, 357 U.S. 235, 253, 78 S.Ct. 1228, 1239, 2 L.Ed.2d 1283 (1958), the Supreme

---

1. In his appellate brief, DeJames refers to contacts that a subsidiary of Hitachi has with the state of New Jersey. However, counsel for DeJames expressly abandoned reliance on the subsidiary's contacts at oral argument before the district court, and we will not consider them on appeal.

Court further refined its due process analysis by stating that "it is essential in each case that there be some act by which the defendant purposefully avails itself of the privilege of conducting activities within the forum State, thus invoking the benefits and protections of its laws." Recently, in Shaffer v. Heitner, 433 U.S. 186, 97 S.Ct. 2569, 53 L.Ed.2d 683 (1977), Kulko v. Superior Court, 436 U.S. 84, 98 S.Ct. 1690, 56 L.Ed.2d 132 (1978), and World–Wide Volkswagen Corp. v. Woodson, 444 U.S. 286, 100 S.Ct. 559, 62 L.Ed.2d 490 (1980), the Supreme Court indicated that due process requires that the defendant have a reasonable expectation that the nature of its conduct is such that it may be "haled before a court" in the forum state. Standing alone, the fact that the defendant could foresee that its conduct might affect the forum state, or that its product might find its way to the forum state, is too attenuated to constitute such a "reasonable expectation." See World–Wide Volkswagen, 444 U.S. at 297, 100 S.Ct. at 567.

DeJames argues that the conversion work done by Hitachi on the vessel in effect makes Hitachi the "manufacturer" of the vessel, and thus distinguishes Hitachi from the local retailer and the regional distributor in *World-Wide Volkswagen.* Because Hitachi "manufactured" a ship capable of transporting automobiles, DeJames asserts that Hitachi should be amenable to process in any port where the ship docks and injury occurs as a result of Hitachi's allegedly defective work.

In making this argument, DeJames places substantial reliance on the numerous cases adopting the "stream-of-commerce" theory as a basis for jurisdiction over a foreign manufacturer. See, e.g., Stabilisierungsfonds Fur Wein v. Kaiser Stuhl Wine Distributors Pty. Ltd., 647 F.2d 200 (D.C.Cir.1981); Duple Motor Bodies, Ltd. v. Hollingsworth, 417 F.2d 231 (9th Cir.1969).[2] We believe this reliance is misplaced.

The stream-of-commerce theory developed as a means of sustaining jurisdiction in products liability cases in which the product had traveled through an extensive chain of distribution before reaching the ultimate consumer. Under this theory, a manufacturer may be held amenable to process in a forum in which its products are sold, even if the products were sold indirectly through importers or distributors with independent sales and marketing schemes. Courts have found the assumption of jurisdiction in these cases to be consistent with the due process requirements identified above: by increasing the distribution of its products through indirect sales within the forum, a manufacturer benefits legally from the protection provided by the laws of the forum state for its products, as well as economically from indirect sales to forum residents. Underlying the assumption of jurisdiction in these cases is the belief that the fairness requirements of due process do not extend so far as to permit a manufacturer to insulate itself from the reach of the forum state's long-arm rule by

---

2. For a more detailed discussion of the stream-of-commerce theory, and a more extensive compilation of cases using this theory, see Currie, The Growth of the Long Arm: Eight Years of Extended Jurisdiction in Illinois, 1963 Ill.L.F. 533; Note, The Long–Arm Reach of the Courts After Kulko v. Superior Court, 65 Va.L.Rev. 175 (1979).

using an intermediary or by professing ignorance of the ultimate destination of its products. See Note, supra note 2, at 179, 189.

In contrast to the manufacturers in the stream-of-commerce cases, Hitachi did not utilize the owners of the vessel it "manufactured" as distributors of its product and thus did not take advantage of an indirect marketing scheme. Moreover, Hitachi received no economic benefit, either direct or indirect, from residents of New Jersey. Although it could be argued that Hitachi receives some derivative benefit from the international market for Japanese cars and from the fact that the charterers of the vessel were permitted to unload cars in New Jersey, we believe that this attenuated benefit is insufficient to support the assertion of personal jurisdiction. The only benefit that Hitachi derives from the ability of the vessel to dock in New Jersey and the international market for Japanese cars transported on the vessel is that Hitachi may do more conversion of large vessels into automobile carriers, as opposed to work on smaller ships or other kinds of ship repair. This derivative benefit is similar to the benefit that the local retailer and the regional distributor in *World-Wide Volkswagen* derived from the fact that the cars they sold could freely travel across state lines and stop within the forum state. The ability of the consumer to drive the car sold by the *World-Wide Volkswagen* defendants into the forum state, like the ability of the charterers of the vessel to sail the ship "manufactured" by Hitachi into the forum state, arguably increases the demand for the services performed by the defendants. However, this derivative benefit was found insufficient to support personal jurisdiction over the defendants in *World-Wide Volkswagen,* and we likewise find it insufficient to support personal jurisdiction over Hitachi in New Jersey.

We recognize that a single contact between the defendant and the forum state may be sufficient to support the assertion of personal jurisdiction over the defendant in a suit arising from this contact. See McGee v. International Life Insurance Co., 355 U.S. 220, 78 S.Ct. 199, 2 L.Ed.2d 223 (1957). However, we believe that initially we must focus on the defendant's conduct to determine whether the nature of this conduct can be said to have put the defendant on notice that it may be called to defend its actions in the forum state. We do not believe that the conversion work performed by Hitachi in Japan constitutes this kind of conduct. It is true that Hitachi could have foreseen that a ship of this size was capable of transporting cars to any port in the world. However, the Supreme Court put to rest the notion in *World-Wide Volkswagen* that this kind of foreseeability alone is a sufficient basis for personal jurisdiction under the due process clause. See World–Wide Volkswagen, 444 U.S. at 295–97, 100 S.Ct. at 566–67. If it were sufficient, the Supreme Court noted, "[e]very seller of chattels would in effect appoint the chattel his agent for service of process. His amenability would travel with the chattel." Id. at 296, 100 S.Ct. at 566. The Supreme Court found this result unacceptable. Were we to accept DeJames' foreseeability argument in this case, Hitachi would be amenable to suit in every forum where a ship on which it had done conversion work, and over which it exercised no control, could be found.

The conversion work done by Hitachi was performed exclusively in Japan and had no connection with the state of New Jersey. Even accepting DeJames' characterization of Hitachi as the "manufacturer" of the vessel, Hitachi sold its product to the ultimate "consumer" when it returned the converted vessel to its owners in Japan. The fortuitous circumstance that the owners chose to dock in New Jersey is insufficient to support the assertion of jurisdiction over Hitachi under the New Jersey long-arm rule.

B

Having affirmed the conclusion of the district court that Hitachi's contact with the state of New Jersey was insufficient to support the assertion of personal jurisdiction over Hitachi, we now address DeJames' argument that the district court erred in refusing to aggregate Hitachi's contacts with the United States as a whole. On appeal, DeJames does not quarrel with the conclusion of the district court that when Congress has not authorized nationwide service of process, a federal district court's power to require a defendant to submit to its jurisdiction is limited by the Federal Rules of Civil Procedure, and through them by the long-arm rule of the state in which it sits. As we noted above, we believe the district court was correct in reaching this conclusion. * * *

III

The order of the district court dismissing the complaint against Hitachi will be affirmed.

■ GIBBONS, CIRCUIT JUDGE, dissenting:

I agree with the majority that the Convention on the Service Abroad of Judicial and Extrajudicial Documents in Civil or Commercial Matters, 20 U.S.T. 361–367 (1969), does not afford a "wholly federal" means of service of process on a foreign national corporation. Like the majority, I believe the Convention, rather than creating an independent source of adjudicatory competence, facilitates and provides a uniform method of service of process pursuant to some already extant state or federal statute or rule. Unlike the majority, however, I believe Hitachi's relation to New Jersey satisfies the fourteenth amendment due process concerns the Supreme Court enunciated in World–Wide Volkswagen Corp. v. Woodson, 444 U.S. 286, 100 S.Ct. 559, 62 L.Ed.2d 490 (1980). The majority relies on *World-Wide Volkswagen* to hold that Hitachi had no "reasonable expectation" of being haled before a court in New Jersey. The majority analogizes Hitachi to the local dealers involved in *World-Wide Volkswagen*. This analogy is off the mark.

In *World-Wide Volkswagen* the Supreme Court held that a local dealer may not be called to account in a distant place for a product not of its manufacture sold in a restricted market. The Court made clear that Judge Soboloff's famous hypothetical of the California gas station owner who sells a tire that blows out following a cross country trip to Pennsylvania, Erlanger Mills, Inc. v. Cohoes Fibre Mills, Inc., 239 F.2d 502, 507 (4th Cir.1956), cited in *World-Wide Volkswagen,* supra, at 296, would remain confined to Civil Procedure texts. See Comment, Federalism, Due Process and Minimum Contacts: World–Wide Volkswagen v. Woodson, 80 Colum.L.Rev. 1341, 1358–61 (1980). At the same time, the court reaffirmed the principle that a manufacturer who injects a product into the stream of interstate commerce may be subject to personal jurisdiction in the state where the product causes harm. 444 U.S. at 297, 100 S.Ct. at 567. That manufacturer may be subject to a foreign state's jurisdiction even if his defective product arrived in the forum through the activities of a manufacturer or distributor further down the chain of production or sale. The Court's approving reference to the Illinois Supreme Court's celebrated decision in Gray v. American Radiator and Standard Sanitary Corp., 22 Ill.2d 432, 176 N.E.2d 761 (1961), 444 U.S. at 298, 100 S.Ct. at 568; is particularly pertinent here. In *Gray,* a defective valve made in Ohio was incorporated into a water heater manufactured in Pennsylvania. The water heater exploded in Illinois. Although Titan Valve Manufacturing Co. maintained it had no contacts with Illinois, the Illinois court held that Titan's indirect contacts through the manufacture and sale of valves to be incorporated in water heaters destined for interstate markets, including Illinois, satisfied the *International Shoe* minimum contacts and fairness tests.

Thus, *World-Wide Volkswagen* permits assertion of jurisdiction over one who manufactures a finished product and sells it to another manufacturer or distributor who will send the product into interstate commerce, even though the first manufacturer's only direct contact with the forum state is the harm its product caused. One who forms an integral link in the chain of interstate manufacture or distribution is not a "local dealer." A local dealer is at the end of the chain of production or distribution. A local dealer has no interest in the ultimate destination of the goods once they have been purchased by the consumer. It did not matter to the New York car distributors in *World-Wide Volkswagen* or to Judge Sobeloff's California gas station owner whether, once purchased, their products traveled out of state or around the corner. These sellers derived no benefit from their customers' choice of where to take the product. In contrast, Titan Valve, while not directly responsible for the appearance of its product in Illinois, benefitted by selling its goods to American Radiator for inclusion in products intended for interstate sale. Titan could not reasonably claim not to expect, nor disavow the desire that its product would end up in foreign fora.

Applying these principles to Hitachi, it is readily apparent that Hitachi is not a local dealer. It is true that Hitachi converts bulk carriers to automobile carriers in Japan, to the order of Japanese vessel owners. It is also true that Hitachi does not control the ultimate destination of its products. But these facts do not reveal the whole story. Hitachi's ships are an integral part of the chain of international commerce in Japanese automobiles. Hitachi's ships carry Japanese automobiles to American and New Jersey ports. The Port of New York–New Jersey is this nation's largest, receiving over 185,292,125 tons of cargo per year. The New Jersey ports of Paulsboro, Camden–Glouster, and Trenton Harbor together account for another 28,533,725 tons per year. 1981 World Almanac and Book of Facts at 204. It is not "merely foreseeable," but virtually inevitable that ships Hitachi converts will dock in New Jersey.

Nor can it be said that Hitachi has no substantial interest in the destination of the ships it converts. Just as Titan Valve benefitted by sale of its products to another manufacturer who would send the valves into interstate commerce, so Hitachi benefits by selling its vessels to shipowners who will take them to New Jersey ports. Hitachi's ship conversion business is a vital component of the process of distribution of Japanese automobiles in the United States. The American market for Japanese cars enhances Hitachi's ship conversion business. The majority suggests this derivative benefit is too attenuated, for were there no American market for Japanese cars, Hitachi would convert vessels to something other than automobile carriers. At 285. That argument misses the point. The relevant question is whether Hitachi's status as an intermediate link in the chain of Japanese car distribution benefits the business in which Hitachi is in fact engaged.

The majority also suggests that there is a dispositive distinction between Hitachi's relation to the vesselowners and a manufacturer who through a subsequent manufacturer or distributor "takes advantage of an indirect marketing scheme." At 285–286. It is true that the vesselowners do not market Hitachi's ships. But both the vesselowners and Hitachi aid in the American marketing of Japanese cars. The majority looks at the wrong market. The relevant market is not the Japanese market for Japanese automobile carriers, but the market for which Japanese automobile carriers are essential—the American market for Japanese cars. I perceive no valid distinction between a manufacturer whose product serves as a link in the chain of production of another product, and one whose product forms an essential link in the chain of distribution of another product, at least when sale of the second product directly promotes production and sale of the first product. Thus I would hold that assertion of personal jurisdiction in New Jersey over Hitachi is consistent with *World-Wide Volkswagen.*

Finally, while it is not crucial to the disposition of this case, I believe the misconception underlying the majority's statement that the fourteenth amendment governs amenability to suit on a federal claim, at 284–285, should be exposed and criticized. The fourteenth amendment due process clause does not properly apply in all its aspects to federal question claims. In International Shoe Co. v. Washington, 326 U.S. 310, 66 S.Ct. 154, 90 L.Ed. 95 (1945), the Supreme Court established a two-pronged test to determine the constitutionality of a state's assertion of personal jurisdiction over an out-of-state defendant. A state's exercise of jurisdiction must comport with traditional notions of fundamental fairness, and it must be consistent with the values of federalism embodied in the fourteenth amendment. See Jonnet v. Dollar Savings Bank, 530 F.2d 1123, 1132, 1140 (3d Cir.1976)(Gibbons, J., concurring). Cf. World–Wide Volkswagen Corp. v. Woodson, 444 U.S. 286, 292, 100 S.Ct. 559, 564, 62 L.Ed.2d 490 (1980).

When a court asserts personal jurisdiction over a foreign defendant on the basis of a state law claim, it must ensure that the forum state does not unduly encroach on a sister state's interests. When a court, state or federal, adjudicates a federal claim, the federalism issue is of no relevance, for the court determines the parties' rights and liabilities under uniform, national law. No state intrudes on another's interests. The only relevant interest is the national one. Thus the applicable constitutional due process provision should not be the fourteenth amendment, but the fifth amendment.

The fifth amendment requires only that the forum be a fair and reasonable place at which to compel defendant's appearance, and that he have had notice and a reasonable opportunity to be heard. See Stabilisierungsfonds Fur Wein et al. v. Kaiser Stuhl Wine Distributors Pty. Ltd., et al., 647 F.2d 200 (D.C.Cir.1981), at 203 & n. 4. A defendant's *national* contacts enter into the fifth amendment fairness analysis, for it would be unreasonable to subject to suit in the United States a foreign national defendant who had but one fleeting connection with this country. But it is not necessary, under the fifth amendment due process clause, that that defendant's contacts relate primarily to the particular United States location in which the claim arose. Thus, for example, it would not be unfair under the fifth amendment to subject a foreign national shipper to suit in New Jersey on the basis of an admiralty claim that arose in that state, even if the offending ship was the only one ever to dock in New Jersey, and all of defendant's other ships land in Texas. The hypothetical defendant has sufficient contacts with the United States, and the availability of witnesses points to the District of New Jersey as the most convenient forum for the litigation. Cf. Shaffer v. Heitner, 433 U.S. 186, 204, 97 S.Ct. 2569, 2579, 53 L.Ed.2d 683 (1977)(central concern of jurisdictional inquiry is relationship among the defendant, the forum, and the litigation).

Similarly, were a state court adjudicating a federal claim, the relevant due process standard should remain the fifth amendment. The nature of the claim, not the identity of the court, should determine the appropriate due process test. New Jersey has enacted a "constitutional" long arm: its courts may assert personal jurisdiction to the limits of the relevant due process clause. A federal court in a federal question case referred under Federal Rule of Civil Procedure 4(e) to the New Jersey long arm thus must ask two questions: Would assertion of personal jurisdiction violate the fifth amendment? and, Has New Jersey placed any restriction on the constitutionally exercisable scope of jurisdiction? The answer to the second question is no, and therefore when addressing a federal claim, the federal court, or for that matter, a New Jersey court, need consider only the issue of fifth amendment fairness in determining whether to assert personal jurisdiction over the foreign defendant.

On the other hand, one might ask whence derives a state legislature's authority to enact a competence statute of national application. The majority implies that a state legislature may permit assertion of adjudicatory competence to the limits of judicial jurisdiction under the fourteenth amendment, but it may not implement the fifth amendment by conferring competence to the limits of the federal due process clause. But a state long arm implements neither the fourteenth nor the fifth amendment. A state's authority to promulgate rules of competence derives from a state's sovereign power to adjudicate state law and federal question cases, and indeed to rule on controversies arising under a foreign nation's law. This power is preserved to the states through the tenth amendment, although it may be limited by congressional provision for exclusive federal court subject matter jurisdiction.[1] The fifth amendment simply defines the boundaries within which a state may adopt a rule of competence to assert personal jurisdiction in federal question cases.

Thus, while Rule 4(e) has the effect of converting a federal court into a state court for purposes of determining personal jurisdiction, the rule does not automatically make the fourteenth amendment the guiding due process provision. The rule's real "anomaly" arises in instances where a federal court is referred to the long arm of a state whose legislature, unlike New Jersey's, has determined not to permit assertion of personal jurisdiction to the full extent constitutionally permissible. In those instances, Congress' failure to enact a general federal question competence statute has the result of bringing to bear on federal claims, to which federalism concerns have no relevance, individual state legislatures' decisions in effect to protect out-of-state defendants from suit on state law claims. Cf. von Mehren & Trautman, Jurisdiction to Adjudicate: A Suggested Analysis, 79 Harv.L.Rev. 1121, 1123–25 n. 6 (referencing cases in which general federal policies qualify statutory incorporation of state law, and suggesting courts disregard state law provisions that are irrelevant in the federal context).

Since both as a matter of fourteenth amendment due process and as a matter of fifth amendment due process, the majority's analysis of jurisdiction to adjudicate in this case is flawed, I dissent. I would reverse the judgment dismissing the complaint for lack of personal jurisdiction.

NOTE

In portions of the opinion in *DeJames* here omitted, the majority held that the Convention on the Service Abroad of Judicial and Extrajudicial Documents in Civil and Commercial Matters, 20 U.S.T. 361–367 (1969) did not form the basis for personal jurisdiction, and having held that the exercise of long arm jurisdiction under Rule 4(e) was to be measured by *International Shoe—Worldwide Volkswagen* criteria, went on to hold that under these criteria the State of New Jersey could not exercise personal jurisdiction of Hitachi. Judge Gibbons agreed with the court's interpretation of the "service abroad" treaty, but would have held that the tie of Hitachi's business to the Japanese automobile business worldwide and the predict-

---

1. In the case of admiralty claims, federal court jurisdiction is exclusive over the subject matter, but state laws concerning competence to assert personal jurisdiction still obtain, since rather than preempting them with an applicable federal competence statute, Congress through rule 4(e) has referred back to state rules of adjudicatory competence. Compare 15 U.S.C. § 77v (Securities Act of 1933); 15 U.S.C. § 78aa (Securities Exchange Act of 1934).

ability of the risk of injury in New Jersey made the case analogous to a manufacturer who places his product in the stream of commerce.

The majority decision in *De James* is applied in Federal Ins. Co. v. Lake Shore Inc., 886 F.2d 654 (4th Cir.1989) In Omni Capital Intern. v. Rudolf Wolff & Co., Ltd. 484 U.S. 97, 108 S.Ct. 404, 98 L.Ed.2d 415 (1987), it was held that absent a statute providing for nationwide service, long-arm service under Rule 4(e) may be made only in circumstances in which service could be had in the state courts.   The Court declined to comment on the constitutional analysis in the *De James* dissent.

CHAPTER 8

VENUE IN SUITS IN ADMIRALTY

A. NOTE ON VENUE IN ADMIRALTY AND MARITIME PROCEEDINGS

The limitations on proper venue imposed upon civil actions by the general venue statute have not been applied to admiralty proceedings. Thus it was held that despite the fact that suits in personam commenced by attaching property or credits of the defendant in a district other than that of his residence could not be brought in the federal district court, a libel in admiralty could be so commenced. Atkins v. Fibre Disintegrating Co., 85 U.S. (18 Wall.) 272, 21 L.Ed. 841 (1873). Similarly, without the necessity of resorting to the waiver reasoning relied upon in Neirbo Co. v. Bethlehem Shipbuilding Corp., 308 U.S. 165, 60 S.Ct. 153, 84 L.Ed. 167 (1939), it was held that a libel in personam could be maintained outside the district of the respondent's residence by serving respondent's agent appointed under the state laws regulating insurance. In re Louisville Underwriters, 134 U.S. 488, 10 S.Ct. 587, 33 L.Ed. 991 (1890). There, Mr. Justice Gray, writing for an unanimous court, observed:

> "By the ancient and settled practice of courts of admiralty, a libel *in personam* may be maintained for any cause within their jurisdiction, whenever a monition can be served upon the libelee, or an attachment made of any personal property or credits of his; and this practice has been recognized and upheld by the rules and decisions of this court * * *".

In Hunt v. Paco Tankers, Inc., 226 F.Supp. 279, 1966 A.M.C. 1107 (S.D.Tex.1964), it was held that while the jurisdiction of the district court is coextensive with the boundaries of the state in which it sits, the admiralty rule to the effect that the action could be brought wherever the monition could be served limited the venue in admiralty proceedings to the district or division in which the monition was served. Accordingly a libel in personam brought in the Galveston Division of the Southern District of Texas by service in the Houston Division would be transferred to the latter. In S.S. Bethflor v. Thomas, 364 F.2d 634, 1966 A.M.C. 1897 (5 Cir.1966), however, the Fifth Circuit questioned the correctness of the holding in *Paco Tankers,* and held that the district judge did not abuse his discretion in dismissing without prejudice an action which, like that in *Paco Tankers,* had been brought in the Galveston Division by service in the Houston Division, and under the authority of *Paco Tankers* had been transferred. Judge Brown, after an extensive review of the cases, held that the plaintiff in an admiralty case may forum shop all he wants to so far as any venue requirements are concerned, matters of convenience being left to the operation of 28 U.S.C.A. § 1404(a). See H & F Barge Co., Inc. v. Garber Bros., Inc., 65 F.R.D. 399, 1975 A.M.C. 1241 (E.D.La.1974).

While the general venue provision with respect to actions in admiralty is thus coextensive with personal jurisdiction, the Jones Act, importing the FELA into the maritime law, contains the provision, "Jurisdiction in such actions shall be under the court of the district in which the defendant employer resides or in which his principal office is located." 46 U.S.C.A. § 688. This provision has been construed to relate to venue rather than jurisdiction. The Jones Act was adopted in 1920. At that time the general venue provision applicable to federal claim cases limited proper venue to the district "of which he was an inhabitant." In the case of corporations this language was interpreted to limit venue in suits against a corporation to the state of its incorporation. Ex parte Shaw, 145 U.S. 444, 12 S.Ct. 935, 36 L.Ed. 768 (1892); Southern Pacific Co. v. Denton, 146 U.S. 202, 13 S.Ct. 44, 36 L.Ed. 942 (1892). See also Roberts, J., dissenting in Neirbo Co. v. Bethlehem Shipbuilding Corp., 308 U.S. 165, 60 S.Ct. 153, 84 L.Ed. 167 (1939). Thus at the time of its passage the Jones Act provided a venue rule to some extent broader than the general venue provision, but somewhat more restrictive than the traditional venue rule in admiralty proceedings. In 1948, the general venue provision was amended to provide, in part,

"A corporation may be sued in any judicial district in which it is incorporated or licensed to do business, and such judicial district shall be regarded as the residence of such corporation for venue purposes." 28 U.S.C.A. § 1331(c).

Two sorts of problems have arisen in fitting together these three venue patterns. First, since the Supreme Court has held that a Jones Act claim may be brought on the admiralty side of the district court, may the libellant in such a proceeding avail himself of the board traditional admiralty venue rule? See Brown v. C.D. Mallory & Co., 122 F.2d 98 (3d Cir.1941), holding that the special venue rule of the Jones Act applies only when the injured seaman elects to bring his action at law. If he is willing to waive the jury trial and proceed by libel in admiralty, he may proceed wherever he can obtain service or attach property or credits. When the suit was initially brought at law and a jury was demanded, however, the same court of appeals held that when the subject matter of the dispute had no connection with the district in which it was brought it was not an abuse of the district judge's discretion to refuse to permit amendment of the pleadings to convert the action into an admiralty proceeding and remanded with instructions to permit the plaintiff 30 days to apply for transfer of the cause under 28 U.S.C.A. § 1406(a) to a district in which the venue would be proper. Leith v. Oil Transp. Co., 321 F.2d 591 (3d Cir.1963).

Second, the question arises as to the effect of the addition of § 1331(c) upon the venue provision in the Jones Act. In Fourco Glass Co. v. Transmirra Prod. Corp., 353 U.S. 222, 77 S.Ct. 787, 1 L.Ed.2d 786 (1957), the Supreme Court held that the 1948 revision had no applicability in patent cases governed by special venue provisions, and the court in the *Leith* case took the holding in *Fourco* to apply to the Jones Act. In Connolly v. Farrell Lines, Inc., 268 F.2d 653, 1960 A.M.C. 1068 (1st Cir.1959), the First Circuit had stated in a footnote that the section was applicable, without mentioning the *Fourco* case. The matter was ultimately settled by the decision of the Supreme Court in Pure Oil Co. v. Suarez, 384 U.S. 202, 86 S.Ct. 1394, 16 L.Ed.2d 474 (1966), in which it was held that in view of the general remedial purpose of the Jones Act it could not be assumed that the Congress intended to exclude seamen's actions from the benefits of the amendments broadening venue generally.

A similar problem faced the Court in determining whether or not the provisions of 28 U.S.C.A. §§ 1404 and 1406 applied to libels in admiralty. It is to be noted that these sections appear in the general venue statute. Section 1331(b), stating the limits of civil actions other than those based wholly on diversity, has no application, we have seen, to the libel in admiralty. A possible distinction might be made between the two sections. Section 1406 refers to "cases," while § 1404 refers to "civil actions." Does this indicate a broader coverage under § 1406? In this connection it should be noted that § 1404 is essentially a limitation upon venue. Did Congress intend to limit the traditionally broad admiralty venue rule? Transfer under § 1406, on the other hand, is intended to eliminate dismissal for want of proper venue with the attendant dangers of intervening limitations. Does this danger apply equally to admiralty cases? Note that libels in admiralty are governed by the doctrine of laches rather than by a statute of limitations, but that the period before the libel will be barred for laches is often measured by borrowing local statutes of limitations. In 1949, the Second Circuit held that § 1406 applied in an admiralty proceeding. Orr v. United States, 174 F.2d 577 (2d Cir.1949). Despite the holding in the *Orr* case, the district court in Oregon held that § 1404 did not apply in admiralty. Judge McCulloch, in a very worried opinion, admitted the difficulty of holding that one section was applicable and the other not, but was convinced that § 1404 could not be applied without conceding the applicability of § 1391(b) and could not read the Congressional intent to extend so far. Is Judge McCulloch's view bolstered by the fact that the term "civil action" is the term applied to describe actions in law and equity in the Federal Rules of Civil Procedure? Rule 2 has since been amended, of course, to include within that definition the libel in admiralty. The great majority of lower court decisions were to the effect that both sections applied, and the matter was put to rest without comment in Continental Grain Co. v. The FBL–585 and Federal Barge Lines, Inc., 364 U.S. 19, 80 S.Ct. 1470, 4 L.Ed.2d 1540, 1961 A.M.C. 1 (1960).

The *Continental Grain* case involved another and perhaps more difficult problem of admiralty procedure. The case arose out of the sinking of a barge at Memphis, Tennessee. The barge was raised and moved to New Orleans. Subsequently the barge owner brought an action against the cargo owner in the state court in Tennessee, alleging that the sinking was the product of negligence of the cargo owner in loading it. This case was removed to the federal district court in Memphis. The cargo owner commenced a libel in personam against the barge owner and joined with it a libel in rem against the barge. These proceedings were commenced in New Orleans, as process in rem against the barge could be had only where the barge was located. Before the barge was arrested the owner wrote a letter to the libellant indicating that in consideration of the fact that the barge had not actually been arrested and that it had not been required to post bond for its release, it agreed to file claim and answer and to pay any judgment entered, the proceeding to proceed in the ordinary course as a proceeding in rem. It then moved to transfer the cause to Memphis for joinder with its suit against the cargo owner. The district court observed that a proceeding in rem normally cannot be brought except in the district in which the res is located and a transfer under § 1404 cannot be made except to a district where the action "might have been brought," but decided that since no arrest had actually been made he could make the transfer. An appeal was permitted under 28 U.S.C.A. § 1292(b) and the court of appeals affirmed but discounted the fact that the barge had not been seized, treating the case as one in which seizure had been made and the vessel released under bond. It pointed out that in such a case there was no actual transfer of the res, observing:

> " * * * Before the transfer can be made, a claim must have been filed and the vessel released under bond (stipulation). Once that is done, the lien on the vessel is discharged for all purposes, ceases to exist, and the release of libel bond is sole security. Traditional notions are not affected if that security floats with the cause wherever the law navigates it." Continental Grain Co. v. Federal Barge Lines, 268 F.2d 240, 1959 A.M.C. 2664 (5th Cir.1959).

The Supreme Court did not mention this portion of the court of appeal opinion but instead took occasion to observe:

> "The idea behind sec. 1404(a) is that where a 'civil action' to vindicate a wrong—however brought in a court—presents issues and requires witnesses that make one District Court more convenient than another, the trial judge can, after findings, transfer the whole action to a more convenient court. That situation exists here. Although the action in New Orleans was technically brought against the barge itself as well as its owner, the obvious fact is that, whatever other advantages may result, this is an alternative way of bringing the owner into court. * * * Treating both methods for sec. 1404(a) purposes for what they are in a case like this—inseparable parts of one single 'civil action'—merely permits or requires parties to try their issues in a single 'civil action' in a court where it 'might have been brought.' To construe sec. 1404(a) this way merely carries out its design to protect litigants, witnesses and the public against unnecessary inconvenience and expense, not to provide a shelter for *in rem* admiralty proceedings in costly and inconvenient forums."

B.   FORUM NON CONVENIENS

De Oliveira v. Delta Marine Drilling Co.

United States Court of Appeals, Fifth Circuit, 1983.
707 F.2d 843, 1985 A.M.C. 753.

■ PER CURIAM:

Acting in response to the application for rehearing, we withdraw the prior opinion in this case, 684 F.2d 337 (5th Cir.1982) and substitute the following:

Delta Marine Drilling Co. (Delta) brings an interlocutory appeal from the District Court's denial of its motion to dismiss 527 F.Supp. 332 on grounds of *forum non conveniens*. Finding that the district court erroneously based its ruling on the single ground that the vessel aboard which the plaintiff was injured had substantial contacts with the United States, we reverse and remand for entry of an order of dismissal conditioned, however, on Delta's consent to appear in the forum it contends to be convenient.

I

Aristeu Fontes de Oliveira, a Brazilian national and a lifetime resident of Brazil, was employed by Schlumberger, Ltda., a Brazilian corporation operating only in Brazil. Schlumberger contracted with Petrobas, the Brazilian national oil company, to provide well logging services for a well that was being drilled under a separate contract by Delta's Brazilian subsidiary, Perbas, from a drilling platform. De Oliveira and the members of the well-logging crew were transported by crew boat from Aracaju, Brazil, on May 26, 1976, to the vessel, DELTA NINE.

All of the drilling equipment utilized in the operation was provided by Delta and transported on the DELTA NINE. The DELTA NINE is an oceangoing vessel and was on its maiden assignment as a tender vessel. It had been moved adjacent to the platform. When the logging crew arrived, its members were transferred from the crew boat to the vessel by a personnel basket lifted by a crane.

De Oliveira and his coworkers then proceeded to the Petrobas platform via a catwalk gruesomely but accurately known in the trade as a widowmaker. See Law v. Sea Drilling, 510 F.2d 242 (5th Cir.1975). This linked the platform to the DELTA NINE. Many of the tools and the equipment which de Oliveira used were placed on the widowmaker. A Schlumberger engineer was in charge of the well logging crew. The drilling operations were supervised by an American, Dale Clements, who was employed by Delta. Clements was in charge of safety on both the platform and the DELTA NINE.

While de Oliveira was gathering tools on the widowmaker early in the pre-dawn morning of May 27, 1976, a submerged portion of the port anchor chain holding the tender vessel parted. The bow of DELTA NINE drifted downwind from the platform, the widowmaker came unhooked, and de Oliveira tumbled into the sea. As he fell, the widowmaker and his tool box struck him. Although, fortunately, no widow was made, de Oliveira sustained severe injuries, aggravated by his remaining in the water for over half an hour before being brought up to the deck.[1]

---

1. De Oliveira receives compensation for his injuries under the Brazilian worker's compensation plan.

In a suit brought in the U.S. District Court for the Southern District of Texas, de Oliveira contended that he was injured by its negligence, the unseaworthiness of the DELTA NINE and the concurrent negligence of his employer, Schlumberger. He joined as codefendants Schlumberger and two Texas corporations, Schlumberger Limited and Schlumberger Well Services, contending that Schlumberger (Brazil) is their alter ego. These claims have now been dismissed, so the only remaining claim is against Delta. Contending that this claim is governed by Brazilian law, Delta moved to dismiss the suit on the basis of *forum non conveniens*.

In such cases we must decide what body of law applies, United States or foreign. We have held that, if United States law applies, a federal court should entertain the suit. Fisher v. Agios Nicolaos V, 628 F.2d 308, 315 (5th Cir.1980), cert. denied sub nom., Valmas Bros. Shipping, S.A. v. Fisher, 454 U.S. 816, 102 S.Ct. 92, 70 L.Ed.2d 84 (1981); Volyrakis v. M/V Isabelle, 668 F.2d 863 (5th Cir.1982). But see Piper Aircraft v. Reyno, 454 U.S. 235, 257, 102 S.Ct. 252, 266, 70 L.Ed.2d 419, 437 (1981). If, however, foreign law applies, the court may dismiss the suit if there is another more convenient forum. Fisher v. Agios Nicolaos V, supra, 628 F.2d at 314. If the district court decides that foreign law applies, "its discretion in granting a *forum non conveniens* dismissal will not ordinarily be disturbed." Id., 628 F.2d at 318. But whether American or foreign law applies, the choice of the applicable law is itself a question of law, and we fully review the district court's choice of law as we would any other legal decision. Bailey v. Dolphin International, Inc., 697 F.2d 1268, 1274 (5th Cir.1983).

II

To determine what set of legal precepts controls, the district court properly referred to the seven choice of law factors of Lauritzen v. Larsen, 345 U.S. 571, 73 S.Ct. 921, 97 L.Ed. 1254 (1953), as well as the eighth factor added by Hellenic Lines Ltd. v. Rhoditis, 398 U.S. 306, 90 S.Ct. 1731, 26 L.Ed.2d 252 (1970)("the shipowner's base of operations"), and held that "substantial and significant contacts exist" between the accident and the forum. 527 F.Supp. 332 (S.D.Tex.1981). It reached this conclusion because the complete operation and ultimate control of the work was in the hands of Americans employed by Delta; the vessel could not operate without receiving replacement parts from the United States and without American personnel; the vessel's base of operations was in the United States; de Oliveira's work supported the vessel's mission; and substantial and daily operational control of the DELTA NINE was exercised by Delta from its headquarters in Tyler, Texas. The district court also relied on Delta's failure to show that any remedy available to de Oliveira in Brazil is adequate and certain. We note, however, that no act of negligence at Delta's headquarters is alleged but only the negligence of Clements on the Brazilian job site.

Lauritzen-Rhoditis tell us that we must decide what body of law is applicable by looking at eight factors. We do not merely add up the scores for and against, for the test is neither arithmetic nor mechanistic. Hellenic

Lines Ltd. v. Rhoditis, 412 F.2d 919 (5th Cir.1969), aff'd, 398 U.S. 306, 90 S.Ct. 1731, 26 L.Ed.2d 252 (1970), reh. den. 400 U.S. 856, 91 S.Ct. 23, 27 L.Ed.2d 94 (1970). The Supreme Court said, in *Rhoditis,* "If, as stated in Bartholomew v. Universe Tankships Inc., 263 F.2d 437, the liberal purposes of the Jones Act are to be effectuated, the facade of the operation must be considered as minor, compared with the real nature of the operation and a cold objective look at the actual operational contacts which this ship and this owner have with the United States." In *Rhoditis,* a Greek citizen was injured in the Port of New Orleans. The Court refused to permit the vessel's "alien owner, engaged in an extensive business operation in this country, * * * an advantage over citizens engaged in the same business. * * *" 358 U.S. at 310, 90 S.Ct. at 1734, 26 L.Ed.2d at 256. The "base of operations" test was, under *Rhoditis'* circumstances, another, albeit an important, factor to add to place of injury and residence of the seaman. It is not a paramount criterion, overriding the seven *Lauritzen* factors. Thus, in *Fisher,* we found that United States law "may" apply when the injury occurred in a United States port, the vessel had a substantial base of operations in the United States and its owners derived substantial revenues from United States trade. 628 F.2d at 317.

In Chiazor v. Transworld Drilling Co., Ltd., 648 F.2d 1015 (5th Cir.1981), cert. denied, 455 U.S. 1019, 102 S.Ct. 1714, 72 L.Ed.2d 136 (1982), published after the district court entered its findings, we considered the choice of law problem in the context of a foreign accident. The estate of Chiazor, a Nigerian citizen employed by a Nigerian corporation who suffered fatal injuries on a platform off the coast of Nigeria, brought suit, after unraveling the chain of relationship, against the American parent corporation. The district court dismissed on the basis of *forum non conveniens,* finding too tenuous a connection with the United States. Stating that he should first have determined which nation's law is applicable, we held that Nigerian law was because of "the substantiality of the contacts herein with Nigeria warrants the non-application of American law. We are unable to state, and *Rhoditis* in fact does not command us to hold, that the shipowner's base of operations is the sole controlling factor in a choice-of-law situation." Id. 648 F.2d at 1018.

There are, of course, factual distinctions that push the present case closer to United States jurisdiction. *Chiazor* involved a vessel (a submersible drilling rig) that had been anchored off the Nigerian coast for a number of years. Day-to-day operational activities aboard the vessel were in fact conducted in Nigeria. Whether there were American supervisors aboard the vessel does not appear, but we noted that "most witnesses would be located in Nigeria." 648 F.2d at 1019, n. 6. Here the vessel had only recently come to Brazil. But Brazil was the place of the alleged wrongful act, the place of allegiance of de Oliveira, and the place of his employment contract with his direct employer, Schlumberger, itself a Brazilian corporation. The negligent acts and most of the events causing the vessel to be allegedly unseaworthy occurred in Brazil. While de Oliveira alleges he was a Jones Act seaman, he was not directly employed as a crew member, and would acquire that status only if he were a borrowed servant by virtue of the relationship of the duties performed for his direct employer to the vessel and its mission.

For these reasons we hold that Brazilian law is applicable.

III

This alone does not resolve the matter. The convenience or inconvenience of a United States forum for resolution of a dispute involving Brazilian law is a separate question. *Chiazor,* supra, 648 F.2d at 1018. In deciding whether a case should be dismissed because filed in a *forum non conveniens,* we consider such factors as the (1) private interests of the litigants, (2) relative ease of access to sources of proof, (3) availability of compulsory process, (4) cost of obtaining attendance of willing witnesses, and (5) the possibility of view of the premises. Gulf Oil Corporation v. Gilbert, 330 U.S. 501, 67 S.Ct. 839, 91 L.Ed. 1055 (1947); *Chiazor,* supra, 648 F.2d at 1019. "Unless the balance is strongly in favor of the defendant, the plaintiff's choice of a forum should rarely be disturbed." Gulf Oil Corporation v. Gilbert, supra, 330 U.S. at 508, 67 S.Ct. at 843, 91 L.Ed. at 1062. We consider these factors:

1. Private interests of the litigants: de Oliveira is a Brazilian national and is a permanent resident of Brazil. He obtained employment with a Brazilian corporation. His duties to that corporation brought him aboard the vessel.

2. Relative ease of service of process: The other members of the Schlumberger crew were apparently Brazilians. De Oliveira was treated in Brazil. Thus the attending medical personnel are located in Brazil.

3. Compulsory process: The vessel itself is apparently still in Brazilian waters and, by our order, we will insure the availability of compulsory process against the defendant.

4. Cost of obtaining attendance of willing witnesses. These all apparently reside in Brazil, save Clements who is apparently still assigned there.

5. The possibility of a view of the vessel. This can be obtained only in Brazil.

We find the balance strongly in favor of the defendant. Retention of jurisdiction by the United States court would work an injustice particularly since Brazilian law would apply.

If, on the motion of Delta, this suit is dismissed de Oliveira should not be required to face another forum challenge. Therefore, in accordance with our action in a number of recent cases, the district court shall condition its order of dismissal substantially as follows: that, if the plaintiff should file suit in an appropriate Brazilian court within ninety days of the dismissal order, Delta shall submit to service of process and to the jurisdiction of the court; Delta will there formally waive any statute of limitations that has matured since the commencement of this action in the Southern District of Texas; Delta will formally agree in the Brazilian court to make available in Brazil all relevant witnesses and documents within its control;

depositions, answers to interrogatories and the like filed herein may be used in the Brazilian proceeding to the same extent as if they had originated therein; as to witnesses not in its control, Delta will use its best efforts to locate those witnesses and make them available for depositions; Delta will formally agree in the Brazilian proceeding to satisfy any final judgment rendered by that court; and, should Delta fail to promptly meet any of these conditions, the district court will resume jurisdiction over the case. The conditional order may also provide that it can be made final by Delta (1) if de Oliveira does not file suit in the appropriate Brazilian court within 90 days after the order becomes effective or, (2) if the case is timely filed, Delta has complied with all of the conditions of the order, and the appropriate Brazilian court has not finally declined jurisdiction. However, should the appropriate Brazilian court subsequently finally decline jurisdiction over the case, it may be reopened by de Oliveira in the district court if it was timely filed in Brazil in accordance with this order and limitations will not run during the period from the initial filing herein until 90 days after the Brazilian court's declining of jurisdiction. Notice of a motion to make the conditional order final, of course, must be given to de Oliveira and de Oliveira must be given the opportunity to resist the motion on grounds of noncompliance only. Vaz Borralho v. Keydril Co., 696 F.2d 379 (5th Cir.1983).

Reversed and Remanded.

Abraham v. Universal Glow, Inc.

United States Court of Appeals, Fifth Circuit, 1982.
681 F.2d 451.

■ ALVIN B. RUBIN, CIRCUIT JUDGE:

United States courts are seductive to injured foreign seamen for, under the Jones Act, liability can be established by showing slight negligence, trial by jury is available, the remedy is in tort instead of being limited by worker's compensation strictures, and verdicts are generous. Yet the federal courts are not an appropriate forum for the litigation of all of the claims of all of the world's seamen. Although the Jones Act extends a remedy to foreign as well as to United States seamen, the screen by which claims that should be litigated in domestic courts are separated from those that should, in the interests of justice, be decided in foreign courts is the inconvenient forum doctrine: the rule that, if the United States courts are more inconvenient than a foreign forum, the claim should be litigated in that other and less inconvenient court. Here, a foreign seaman attracted to an American court as the forum for his personal injury claim contends that he is not barred by the inconvenience of the forum because he also has a good faith claim for back wages, over which federal jurisdiction is mandatory. Because we are unable from the record to determine whether the seaman is indeed presenting a good faith claim for unpaid wages, we remand the case for further proceedings.

Abraham, a citizen of Sri Lanka, alleges that he was injured while working as a seaman aboard the M/V APPOLLON when the vessel was en route from Reserve, Louisiana, to Port Arthur, Texas. His original complaint alleged Jones Act and general maritime law jurisdiction. He subsequently amended his complaint to allege a cause of action for unpaid wages pursuant to 46 U.S.C. § 596 (1976).[1]

Finding that foreign law is applicable under the principles set forth in the *Lauritzen-Romero–Rhoditis* trilogy,[2] and a United States forum inconvenient under the additional considerations expressed in Gulf Oil Corp. v. Gilbert, 330 U.S. 501, 506–07, 67 S.Ct. 839, 842, 91 L.Ed. 1055, 1061 (1947), the district court dismissed the suit. The court found that the incident occurred in international waters, the ship was sailing under a foreign flag, the plaintiff and the defendant are foreign domiciliaries, the seaman's contract was executed on foreign soil, a foreign forum is available, and the defendant ship owner neither has a "base of operations" in the United States nor derives substantial revenue from the United States. The court's dismissal was appropriately conditioned on the defendant's submission to jurisdiction in an appropriate forum and its waiver of any defense relating to a statute of limitations. The memorandum order does not discuss the wage claim, and hence states no opinion concerning whether it was brought in good faith.

Abraham filed a motion to reconsider, arguing that, in the absence of bad faith, the district court was required to exercise its jurisdiction over his wage claim. The court denied the motion without written reasons.

"[J]urisdiction over a wage claim made in good faith under 46 U.S.C. § 596 is mandatory." Dutta v. Clan Grahan, 528 F.2d 1258, 1260 (4th Cir.1975); accord, Grevas v. M/V Olympic Pegasus, 557 F.2d 65, 67 (4th Cir.), cert. denied, 434 U.S. 969, 98 S.Ct. 515, 54 L.Ed.2d 456 (1977). The court in *Dutta* stated that, generally, if there is jurisdiction over the wage

---

1. That statute provides:

The master or owner of any vessel making coasting voyages shall pay to every seaman his wages within two days after the termination of the agreement under which he was shipped, or at the time such seaman is discharged, whichever first happens; and in case of vessels making foreign voyages, or from a port on the Atlantic to a port on the Pacific, or vice versa, within twenty-four hours after the cargo has been discharged, or within four days after the seaman has been discharged, whichever first happens; and in all cases the seaman shall be entitled to be paid at the time of his discharge on account of wages a sum equal to one-third part of the balance due him. Every master or owner who refuses or neglects to make payment in the manner hereinbefore mentioned without sufficient cause shall pay to the seaman a sum equal to two days' pay for each and every day during which payment is delayed beyond the respective periods, which sum shall be recoverable as wages in any claim made before the court; but this section shall not apply to masters or owners of any vessel the seaman of which are entitled to share in the profits of the cruise or voyage. This section shall not apply to fishing or whaling vessels or yachts.

2. Hellenic Lines, Ltd. v. Rhoditis, 398 U.S. 306, 90 S.Ct. 1731, 26 L.Ed.2d 252 (1970); Romero v. International Terminal Operating Co., 358 U.S. 354, 79 S.Ct. 468, 3 L.Ed.2d 368 (1959); Lauritzen v. Larsen, 345 U.S. 571, 73 S.Ct. 921, 97 L.Ed. 1254 (1953).

claim, the court should also entertain personal injury claims made in the same suit and dispose of the entire case on the merits. *Dutta,* 528 F.2d at 1260; accord, *Grevas,* 557 F.2d at 67; see G. Gilmore & C. Black, *The Law of Admiralty* 479 (2d ed. 1975).

The district court enjoys wide latitude in determining whether a wage claim is asserted in good faith. "Good faith" is, of course, as elusive here as it is in other contexts. Id. at 479; accord, Morewitz v. Andros Compania Maritima, S.A., 614 F.2d 379, 381 (4th Cir.1980). "A good faith issue presents a factual question and the district court's decision will not be disturbed unless it is clearly erroneous." Id. at 381–82.

In Dorizos v. Lemos and Pateras, Ltd., 437 F.Supp. 120, 123–124 (S.D.Ala.1977), the district court, relying on Mihalinos v. Liberian S.S. Trikala, 342 F.Supp. 1237 (S.D.Cal.1972), declined jurisdiction over a wage claim, finding that the good faith requirement had not been met. Noting the potential for abuse in a rule requiring a court to assume jurisdiction over a seaman's suit whenever a wage claim is asserted, regardless of other considerations, the court stated that, when contacts with the country are minimal and the defendant denies liability for a wage claim, a plaintiff must come forward with evidence to establish that the claim was made in good faith. *Dorizos,* 437 F.Supp. at 123 (quoting *Mihalinos,* 342 F.Supp. at 1242).

The defendant asserts that its counsel, in argument before the district judge, asserted that the wage claim was not made in good faith and was filed in an effort to avoid dismissal as a result of a pending motion to dismiss; that its counsel advised the court that he had received a telex "from the vessel's interests" stating that all wages had been paid; and that Abraham never submitted any evidence of his wage claim or even made any specific allegations of fact to support his lone conclusory charge that wages were due and unpaid. The defendant further contends that Abraham's counsel was informed that the court would act on the motion to dismiss unless Abraham offered some proof of his claim and that five weeks passed without action by Abraham or his counsel. After the action was dismissed, the subsequent motion to reconsider was devoid of proof of good faith.

All of this may be correct, but the record contains nothing but the defendant's motion for dismissal, the judgment granting dismissal, Abraham's motion for reconsideration of the § 596 claim, and the district judge's denial of that motion without explanation. There is nothing in the record to show that the district judge even considered the wage claim, or if he did, his reasons for dismissing it.

Acting on so bare a record, we must remand the case. This does not preclude the defendant from raising the issue of good faith and proving the facts it asserts in its brief. If Abraham cannot controvert these facts or otherwise demonstrate his bona fides, dismissal would be proper. In the absence of some evidentiary basis in the record to contradict the allegations of the complaint, they must, however general, be accepted.

For these reasons, the judgment of dismissal is REVERSED and the case is REMANDED for further proceedings consistent with this opinion.

Reversed and Remanded.

NOTE

While the doctrine of forum non conveniens is not a special doctrine of admiralty law, the adoption of 28 U.S.C.A. § 1404(a), providing for transfer on ground of inconvenience having largely eliminated dismissal for inconvenient forum within the United States courts, admiralty cases, in which it is frequently argued that no American forum is convenient, make up a large proportion of the cases in which the doctrine is urged.

To the proposition that the court should not relegate to a foreign forum a case to which the law of the United States is to be applied, the court in *De Oliveira* cites as "cf." Piper Aircraft Co. v. Reyno, 454 U.S. 235, 102 S.Ct. 252, 70 L.Ed.2d 419 (1981). There, in a case arising out of an aircraft accident, the Supreme Court held that the fact that a court has held the American law applicable and that the foreign law might be less advantageous to the plaintiff, does not automatically preclude dismissal on the ground of forum non conveniens. Is there any reason to suppose that the rule should be different in admiralty cases?

It has also sometimes been argued that a case brought by an American citizen in an American court in which jurisdiction has been obtained over the person of the defendant or over the res should not be dismissed and the plaintiff left to sue abroad. This rule of thumb was rejected by the Second Circuit in Alcoa S.S. Co., Inc. v. M/V Nordic Regent, 654 F.2d 147, 1980 A.M.C. 309 (2d Cir.1980)(en banc). In The Nordic Regent a split panel affirmed the dismissal of an action by an American corporation brought in the Southern District of New York against a Liberian Corporation with a general agent in New York and against the Nordic Regent in rem, for damages sustained when the Nordic Regent collided with its pier in Trinidad. On rehearing the panel split the other way and reversed, and on rehearing en banc the court returned to the view of the first panel decision.

In Bhatnagar v. Surrendra Overseas Ltd., 52 F.3d 1220, 1995 A.M.C. 1716 (3d Cir.1995), the court of appeals affirmed the denial of a motion to dismiss for forum non convenience in an action by an Indian national, injured on an Indian vessel on the high seas, and though the cause would be governed by Indian law, on the ground that extreme delay could be expected in the Indian court system.

Cf. Contact Lumber Co. v. P.T. Moges Shipping Co., Ltd. 918 F.2d 1446, 1991 A.M.C. 678 (9th Cir.1990). The court observed that the court should consider both private and public factors. Among the public factors are (1) court congestion, (2) local interest in resolving the controversy, and (3) the desirability of litigating in a forum acquainted with the law that should be applied.

The federal doctrine of forum non convenience is not obligatory on the states. American Dredging Co. v. Miller, 510 U.S. ——, 114 S.Ct. 981, 127 L.Ed.2d 285 (1994), in which the Court viewed forum non convenience as essentially procedural and related to venue.

C. NOTE ON FORUM SELECTION AGREEMENTS

In M/S Bremen and Unterweser Reederei v. Zapata Off–Shore Co., 407 U.S. 1, 92 S.Ct. 1907, 32 L.Ed.2d 513 (1972), the Supreme Court upheld the validity of a clause in an international ocean towing contract providing that all disputes should be litigated in London, England, despite the fact that the effect would be the application of English law which would reduce the liability of the tower to its tow, a matter discussed in chapter 14, below.

Like the doctrine of forum non conveniens, the enforceability of a forum selection agreement is not uniquely a maritime matter, and the same principles have been applied by land and by sea. See Zapata Marine Service v. O/Y Finnlines, Ltd., 571 F.2d 208, 1978 A.M.C. 1740 (5th Cir.1978), enforcing an agreement providing for litigation in London in respect of a collision when the agreement was entered into after the collision had taken place. And see Trojan Yacht Co. v. Productos Pesqueros Mexicanos, S.A. de C.V., 1978 A.M.C. 1539 (E.D.Va.1978), an action on a shipbuilding contract brought as a diversity case, in which the district court stated that the Supreme Court in The M/S Bremen had indicated that selection clauses in international transactions are to be encouraged. The Fourth Circuit affirmed the decision per curiam, but took occasion in an unpublished opinion to repudiate this statement, 1978 A.M.C. 2680 (4th Cir.1978).

Following the lead of the Second Circuit case of Indussa Corp. v. S.S. Ranborg, 377 F.2d 200, 1967 A.M.C. 589 (2d Cir.1967)(en banc), it had been held in many cases that were governed by the COGSA, clauses requiring an American shipper to litigate in a foreign country placed an extra burden upon him in violation of section 3(8) of the Act. This view has now been repudiated by the Supreme Court. See Vimar Seguros y Reaseguros v. M/V Sky Reefer, 515 U.S. ___, 115 S.Ct. 2322, 132 L.Ed.2d 462, 1995 A.M.C. 1817 (1995), upholding the validity of a clause requiring arbitration in Japan. Is there a difference, in this respect, between arbitration and litigation?

Domestic forum selections have also been upheld. Carnival Cruise Lines v. Shute, 499 U.S. 585, 111 S.Ct. 1522, 113 L.Ed.2d 622, 1991 A.M.C. 1697 (1991), holding enforceable a clause in a cruise ticket requiring litigation in Florida.

CHAPTER 9

APPEALS IN SUITS IN ADMIRALTY

NOTE ON APPEALS IN MARITIME CASES

What constitutes a final order for purposes of appeal under 28 U.S.C.A. § 1291 is governed by the same principles applicable in other cases. One classical description of a final judgment appears in Catlin v. United States, 324 U.S. 229, 233, 65 S.Ct. 631, 89 L.Ed. 911 (1945)—"one which ends the litigation ... and leaves nothing for the court to do but to execute the judgment." The *Catlin* concept of finality was applied in maritime cases as well as civil, from an early time. See The Palmyra, 23 U.S. (10 Wheat.) 502, 6 L.Ed. 375 (1825), holding that an admiral decree of restitution was not a final order for purposes of appeal until the damages report of the commissioners was acted upon.

The considerable number of statutes and judicially created doctrines that have liberalized the finality principle are all applicable in admiralty and maritime cases. The collateral order doctrine has been applied. Swift & Co. Packers c. Compania Transmaritima Columbiana del Caribe, 339 U.S. 684, 70 S.Ct. 861, 94 L.Ed. 1206 (1950), holding that an order dissolving an attachment is appealable. And its application in admiralty cases does not differ on that basis. See Marx v. Government of Guam, 866 F.2d 294 (9th Cir.1989)(denial of a claim of sovereign immunity appealable); Titan Nav., Inc. v. Timsco, Inc., 808 F.2d 400 5th Cir.1987)(order to give counter security on pain of losing its security on the main claim appealable); Result Shipping Co., Ltd. v. Ferruzzi Trading USA Inc., 56 F.3d 394 (2d Cir.1995)(denial of countersecurity; Cf. Shakit v. M/V Forum Trader, 14 F.3d 5, 1994 A.M.C. 68 (5th Cir.1993)(order allegedly fixing security too low not appealable).

Cf. Incas and Monterey Printing and Packaging, Ltd. v. M/V Sang Jin, 747 F.2d 958, 1985 A.M.C. 968 (5th Cir.1984), holding that an order releasing defendant's security for plaintiff's claims is appealable, with Construction Export Enterprises, UNECA v. Nikki Maritime, Ltd., et al, 718 F.2d 1085, 1984 A.M.C. 342 (2d Cir.1983), holding that an order denying a motion to vacate an attachment is not appealable (statement accompanying dismissal of the appeal which cannot be cited).

The rather hazy doctrine of "practical finality" sometimes applied in cases in which remand would be inefficient and not serve the purposes of justice was derived from a maritime case. Gillespie v. United States Steel Corp., 379 U.S. 148, 85 S.Ct. 308, 13 L.Ed.2d 199 (1964).

Since 1966, Rule 54(b), permitting the district court to enter as a final judgment an order in a multi-claim or multi-party case disposing of one or more but fewer than all the claims or the claims of one or more but fewer than all the parties, has been applicable to admiralty cases.

The statutes that govern interlocutory appeals are also generally applicable to admiralty cases.

Section 1292(a)(1) of Title 28 provides for an appeal from "[i]nterlocutory orders * * * granting, continuing, modifying, refusing or dissolving injunctions, or refusing to dissolve or modify injunctions, except where a direct review may be had in the Supreme Court." As we have seen in Chapter 6E above, there has been continued doubt about the extent of the power of the court to grant injunctions in admiralty cases. To the extent that injunctions are granted, however, § 1292(a)(1) has been applied. See, e.g., Tai Ping Insurance Co., Ltd. v. M/V Warschau, 731 F.2d 1141, 1985 A.M.C. 575 (5th Cir.1984), in which an order staying arbitration was held appealable as an injunction, and Matter of Bowoon Sangsa Co., Ltd., 720 F.2d 595, 1984 A.M.C. 97 (9th Cir.1983), sustaining jurisdiction under § 1292(a)(1) of an appeal from an order entered in a limitation proceeding dissolving a restraining order staying other proceedings. But an order granting an extension of time within which claims may be filed in a limitation proceedings is not an order modifying an injunction for purposes of the statute. Tradeways II, 373 F.2d 860, 1968 A.M.C. 200 (2d Cir.1967).

The historical distinction between admiralty courts and law courts did have an impact, however, on the appealability of orders assimilated to injunctions for the purposes of § 1292(a)(1). In Enelow v. New York Life Ins. Co., 293 U.S. 379, 55 S.Ct. 310, 79 L.Ed. 440 (1935), the plaintiff filed an action to recover on an insurance policy. The defendant raised the affirmative defense of fraud and petitioned to have the fraud defense tried in equity in advance of the action at law. The Supreme Court held that an order providing for the trial of the equitable defense and staying the action at law was the equivalent of an injunction and appealable under the predecessor section of § 1292(a)(1). In Shanferoke Coal & Supply Corp. v. Westchester Service Corp., 293 U.S. 449, 55 S.Ct. 313, 79 L.Ed. 583 (1935), decided the same day, the principle of the *Enelow* case was applied to permit interlocutory appeal of an order staying an action at law to await arbitration. In Schoenamsgruber v. Hamburg American Line, 294 U.S. 454, 55 S.Ct. 475, 79 L.Ed. 989 (1935), decided the same year, it was held that an order of a court of admiralty staying its proceedings pending arbitration and report did not constitute an injunction for purposes of the statute. In Ettelson v. Metropolitan Life Ins. Co., 317 U.S. 188, 63 S.Ct. 163, 87 L.Ed. 176 (1942) it was held that the *Enelow* decision survived the adoption of the F.R.C.P.

The *Schoenamsgruber* decision survived the argument that merger of the admiralty and civil rules in 1966 had the result of making the *Enelow-Ettleson* rule applicable to maritime cases. The problem disappeared in 1988 when the Supreme Court repudiated the *Enelow-Ettelson* formulation, part and parcel, and the 1988 revision of Title 9 of the Code, which now governs explicitly appeals from orders ordering or refusing to order arbitration. See 9 U.S.C.A. §§ 1–15.

Section 1292(b), permitting the district court to certify controlling questions of law as to which there is reasonable doubt and the early settlement of which "may materially advance the ultimate termination of the litigation," and the court of appeals, in its discretion, to grant leave to appeal, is also applicable in maritime cases. See, e.g., Yamaha Motor Corp. v. Calhoun, ___ U.S. ___, 116 S.Ct. 619, 133 L.Ed.2d 578 (1996), presently before the Supreme Court. See Flowers Transp., Inc. v. M/V Peanut Hollinger, 664 F.2d 112, 1983 A.M.C. 302 [DRO] (5th Cir.1981). And the Federal Rules of Appellate Procedure are applied in the same fashion in admiralty cases as elsewhere. See, e.g., Curacao Drydock Co. v. M/V Akritas, 710 F.2d 204, 1984 A.M.C. 596 (5th Cir.1983), to the effect that the notice of appeal must be filed within the 30 day limit imposed by F.R.A.P. 4(a), which superseded the provision for 90 days in admiralty cases found in 28 U.S.C.A. § 2107.

The only special provisions that are made for admiralty cases are in 28 U.S.C.A. § 1292(a)(3), the courts of appeals are given jurisdiction of "[i]nterlocutory decrees of such district courts or the judges thereof determining the rights and liabilities of the parties to admiralty cases in which appeals from final decrees are allowed." This provision reflected a practice, common in admiralty at the time of its enactment, of trying liability and entering an interlocutory decree, with damages left to determination by commissioners. See Moore's Federal Practice, ¶ 110.19[3] (1970). It has been extended to other sorts of orders, however. See, e.g., Associated Metals and Minerals Corp. v. M/V Alexander's Unity, 41 F.3d 1007, 1995 A.M.C. 1006 (5th Cir.1995), holding that an order determining priority of claims exceeding the amount in the registry of the court was appealable under § 1292(a)(3). See also Gloria S.S. Co. v. Smith, 376 F.2d 46, 1968 A.M.C. 723 (5th Cir.1967), where it was held that § 1292(a)(3) applies to an order dismissing a motion to implead a third-party.

With these cases compare Evergreen International (USA) Corp. v. Standard Warehouse, 33 F.3d 420, 1995 A.M.C. 635 (4th Cir.1994), holding that the grant of summary judgment for one co-defendant is not appealable while all the claims of the plaintiff remain live against another defendant. And see Wallin v. Keegan, 426 F.2d 1313, 1970 A.M.C. 2390 (5th Cir.1970), in which it was held that an order dismissing a counterclaim without prejudice to its maintenance in a separate suit does not determine the rights of the parties.

Note the overlap between § 1292(a)(3) and Rule 54(b) of the F.R.C.P., which became applicable to maritime cases in 1966. Under Rule 54(b) the district court, upon express determination that there is no just reason for delay, and express direction for entry of judgment, may convert into a final judgment an order disposing of all the claims of one party in a multiparty suit, or disposing of a claim in a multiclaim suit. Absent such an express determination and direction such an order remains interlocutory. Some orders fall under both the statute and the rule, do they not? In such a case, if the action is an admiralty case, the order may be appealed despite the failure of the district court to make the express determination and direction. See O'Donnell v. Latham, 525 F.2d 650, 1976 A.M.C. 61 (5th

Cir.1976). There the plaintiff sued the owner of a fishing boat and his insurer in respect of injuries received on board while the boat was being operated by plaintiff and friends under a rental agreement. The district court dismissed the action against the insurer on the ground of noncoverage, and plaintiff appealed. The court of appeals found compliance with Rule 54(b) unnecessary in view of the statute.

There are also cases in which an order will fit within § 1292(a)(3) that could not be made final even with the express determination and direction under Rule 54(b). Since Rule 54(b) applies only when there are multiple parties or multiple claims, an order determining liability but not damages would be interlocutory in any case, but in an admiralty case appealable under the statute. Are there orders that could be made final under Rule 54(b) but could not be appealed under § 1292(a)(3)? What of the order in Wallin v. Keegan, supra? See Moore's Federal Practice, loc. cit.

Does § 1292(a)(3) also overlap with the collateral order doctrine? In *Alex's Unity*, for example, the court indicated that the order determining priority was also an appealable collateral order.

What is an admiralty case for purposes of § 1292(a)(3)? In the *O'Donnell* case, Judge Clark observed, "Finally, without deciding that it would be a *sine qua non* in a case like this, we note that the maritime character of the principle claim was clearly set forth in the complaint."

Prior to the 1966 merger of the rules it was held that § 1292(a)(3) had no application to an action at law under the saving clause and Rule 54(b) governed. See, e.g., Thompson v. Trent Maritime Co., 343 F.2d 200, 1966 A.M.C. 1601 (3d Cir.1965). In connection with the merger amendments, former Rule 73 was amended to add subdivision (h), which read, "These rules do not affect the appealability of interlocutory judgments in admiralty cases pursuant to Title 28, U.S.C.A. § 1292(a)(3). The reference in that statute to admiralty cases shall be construed to mean admiralty and maritime claims within the meaning of Rule 9(h)." What effect did Rule 73(h) have? In 1967, effective in 1968, Rule 73 was abrogated in connection with the promulgation of the Federal Rules of Appellate Procedure. Rule 73(h) was not picked up in the F.R.A.P. What effect did the abrogation of this provision have?

Final judgments in admiralty cases are reviewed in the same fashion as judgments in other cases. 28 U.S.C.A. § 1291. Formerly appeals in admiralty were considered appeals de novo. See 3 Benedict, *Admiralty* § 571 (6th Ed.1940). For the history of the ups and downs of the de novo theory, see International Milling Co. v. Brown S.S. Co., 264 F.2d 803, 1959 A.M.C. 907 (2d Cir.1959). In 1954, the Supreme Court held that the clearly erroneous principle applied in admiralty. McAllister v. United States, 348 U.S. 19, 75 S.Ct. 6, 99 L.Ed. 20 (1954), in which the Supreme Court stated, "No greater scope of review is exercised by the appellate tribunals in admiralty cases than they exercise under Rule 52(a) of the Federal Rules of Civil Procedure." With the merger of the rules in 1966 of course Rule 52(a) is directly applicable.

CHAPTER 10

SUITS AGAINST THE GOVERNMENT

A. SUITS AGAINST THE UNITED STATES

United States v. United Continental Tuna Corp.

Supreme Court of the United States, 1976.
425 U.S. 164, 96 S.Ct. 1319, 47 L.Ed.2d 653, 1976 A.M.C. 258.

■ MR. JUSTICE MARSHALL delivered the opinion of the Court.

Respondent, a Philippine corporation owned largely by Americans, brought this suit against the United States in the United States District Court for the Central District of California alleging jurisdiction under the Suits in Admiralty Act, 41 Stat. 525, as amended, 46 U.S.C. § 741 et seq., and the Public Vessels Act, 43 Stat. 1112, as amended, 46 U.S.C. § 781 et seq. It sought recovery for damages resulting from the sinking of its fishing vessel, the *Orient,* after a collision with the *U.S.S. Parsons,* a naval destroyer of the United States.

Upon the United States' motion for summary judgment, the District Court held that since the naval destroyer was a "public vessel of the United States," the suit was governed by the provisions of the Public Vessels Act. See 46 U.S.C. § 781. In particular, the court held that respondent was subject to the Act's reciprocity provision, which bars any suit by a foreign national under the Act unless it appears that his government, "under similar circumstances, allows nationals of the United States to sue in its courts." 46 U.S.C. § 785. Finding no such reciprocity, the District Court dismissed the complaint.

The Court of Appeals for the Ninth Circuit reversed on the ground that respondent's action, although involving a public vessel, is maintainable under the Suits in Admiralty Act without reference to the reciprocity provision of the Public Vessels Act. 499 F.2d 774 (1974). We granted certiorari, 420 U.S. 971, 95 S.Ct. 1390, 43 L.Ed.2d 651 (1975), and we now reverse.

I

It is undisputed that before 1960 suits involving public vessels could not be maintained under the Suits in Admiralty Act. The Act then authorized suits involving vessels owned by, possessed by, or operated by or for the United States as follows:

"In cases where if such vessel were privately owned or operated, or if such cargo were privately owned and possessed, a proceeding in admiralty could be maintained at the time of commencement of the action herein provided for, a libel in personam may be brought against the United States * * * *provided that such vessel is employed as a merchant vessel * * *.*" 46 U.S.C. § 742 (1958)(emphasis added).[1]

In 1960, however, Congress amended this provision of the Suits in Admiralty Act by deleting the proviso, italicized above, that the vessel must be "employed as a merchant vessel." 74 Stat. 912. Reading the amended provision literally, the Court of Appeals held that suits involving public vessels could not be brought under the Suits in Admiralty Act, free from the restrictions imposed by the Public Vessels Act. The court reached this result in spite of its acknowledgment that "such a conclusion permits the [Public Vessels Act's] reciprocity provision to be circumvented in a manner neither explicitly authorized nor perhaps contemplated by Congress." 499 F.2d, at 778.

The Court of Appeals' result would permit circumvention of not only the reciprocity requirement, but also several other significant limitations imposed upon suits brought under the Public Vessels Act. Under 46 U.S.C. § 784, for example, officers and members of the crew of a public vessel may not be subpoenaed in connection with any suit authorized by the Public Vessels Act without the consent of the Secretary of the Department, the commanding officer, or certain other persons. In time of war, the Secretary of the Navy can obtain a stay of any suit brought under the Public Vessels Act when it appears that prosecution of the suit would tend to interfere with naval operations. 10 U.S.C. §§ 7721–7730. And under the Public Vessels Act, unlike under the Suits in Admiralty Act, interest on judgments does not accrue prior to the time of judgment. Compare 46 U.S.C. § 782 with 46 U.S.C. § 745.

Under the Court of Appeals' interpretation of the 1960 amendment to the Suits in Admiralty Act, circumvention of these restrictive provisions of the Public Vessels Act would not be limited to a handful of cases. Since there is virtually no reason for a litigant to prefer to have his suit governed by the provisions of the Public Vessels Act,[2] the import of the Court of Appeals' interpretation is to render the restrictive provisions of the Public Vessels Act ineffectual in practically every case to which they would otherwise have application. If Congress had intended that result, it might just as well have repealed the Public Vessels Act altogether.

The Public Vessels Act was not amended in 1960, and, as the Court of Appeals recognized, the 1960 amendment to the Suits in Admiralty Act

---

1. We need not concern ourselves in this case with the definitions of the terms "merchant vessel" and "public vessel." It suffices to say that the terms are mutually exclusive, and that the naval destroyer in this case is beyond question a "public vessel."

2. The only apparent advantage to bringing suit under the Public Vessels Act lies in its broader venue provision. Both the Suits in Admiralty Act and the Public Vessels Act provide venue in the district in which the vessel or cargo is found, and in the district in which any plaintiff resides or has a place of business (under the Suits in Admiralty Act it must be the principal place of business in the United States). 46 U.S.C. §§ 742, 782. But the Public Vessels Act provides further that if there is no such district, suit may be brought in any district in the United States. 46 U.S.C. § 782.

contains no language expressly permitting claims previously governed by the Public Vessels Act to be brought under the Suits in Admiralty Act, free from the restrictive provisions of the Public Vessels Act. What amounts to the effective repeal of those provisions is urged as a matter of implication. It is, of course, a cardinal principle of statutory construction that repeals by implication are not favored. See, e.g., Regional Rail Reorganization Act Cases, 419 U.S. 102, 133, 95 S.Ct. 335, 353, 42 L.Ed.2d 320, 347 (1974); Amell v. United States, 384 U.S. 158, 165–166, 86 S.Ct. 1384, 1388, 16 L.Ed.2d 445, 449–450 (1966); Silver v. New York Stock Exchange, 373 U.S. 341, 357, 83 S.Ct. 1246, 1257, 10 L.Ed.2d 389, 400 (1963); United States v. Borden Co., 308 U.S. 188, 198–199, 60 S.Ct. 182, 188, 84 L.Ed. 181, 190–191 (1939). The principle carries special weight when we are urged to find that a specific statute has been repealed by a more general one. See, e.g. Morton v. Mancari, 417 U.S. 535, 550–551, 94 S.Ct. 2474, 2482–2483, 41 L.Ed.2d 290, 300–301 (1974); Bulova Watch Co. v. United States, 365 U.S. 753, 758, 81 S.Ct. 864, 867, 6 L.Ed.2d 72, 75 (1961); Rodgers v. United States, 185 U.S. 83, 87–89, 22 S.Ct. 582, 583–584, 46 L.Ed. 816, 818–819 (1902).

To be sure, the principle of these cases is not precisely applicable in this case—for here the argument is not that the Public Vessels Act can no longer have application to a particular set of facts, but simply that its terms can be evaded at will by asserting jurisdiction under another statute. We should, however, be as hesitant to infer that Congress intended to authorize evasion of a statute at will as we are to infer that Congress intended to narrow the scope of a statute. Both types of "repeal"—effective and actual—involve the compromise or abandonment of previously articulated policies, and we would normally expect some expression by Congress that such results are intended. Indeed, the expectation that there would be some expression of an intent to "repeal" is particularly strong in a case like this one, in which the "repeal" would extend to virtually every case to which the statute had application.

The ultimate question in this case is whether Congress intended, by the deletion of the "employed as a merchant vessel" proviso from the Suits in Admiralty Act, to authorize the wholesale evasion of the restrictions specifically imposed by the Public Vessels Act on suits for damages caused by public vessels. An examination of the history of the Suits in Admiralty Act, the Public Vessels Act and, in particular, the 1960 amendment to the Suits in Admiralty Act, indicates quite clearly that Congress had no such intent.

II

A

The history of the Suits in Admiralty Act and the Public Vessels Act has been the subject of the Court's attention on several prior occasions. See Canadian Aviator v. United States, 324 U.S. 215, 218–225, 65 S.Ct. 639, 641–644, 89 L.Ed. 901, 905–909 (1945); American Stevedores, Inc. v. Porello, 330 U.S. 446, 450–454, 67 S.Ct. 847, 849–850, 91 L.Ed. 1011, 1016–

1018 (1947); Johansen v. United States, 343 U.S. 427, 432–434, 72 S.Ct. 849, 853, 96 L.Ed. 1051 (1952); Amell v. United States, 384 U.S. at 164–166, 86 S.Ct. at 1387–1388, 16 L.Ed.2d at 449–450. The history is quite clear and, for our purposes, can be stated briefly.

Prior to 1916, the doctrine of sovereign immunity barred any suit by a private owner whose vessel was damaged by a vessel owned or operated by the United States. Recognizing the inequities of denying recovery to private owners and the difficulties inherent in attempting to grant relief to deserving private owners through private acts of Congress, Congress provided in the Shipping Act of 1916 that Shipping Board vessels employed as merchant vessels were subject to "all laws, regulations, and liabilities governing merchant vessels." 46 U.S.C. § 808. In The Lake Monroe, 250 U.S. 246, 39 S.Ct. 460, 63 L.Ed. 962 (1919), this Court held that the Shipping Act had subjected all Shipping Board merchant vessels to proceedings *in rem* in admiralty, including arrest and seizure. Congress, concerned that the arrest and seizure of Shipping Board merchant vessels would occasion unnecessary delay and expense, promptly responded to *The Lake Monroe* decision by enacting the Suits in Admiralty Act.[3] The Act prohibited the arrest or seizure of any vessel owned by, possessed by, or operated by or for the United States. 46 U.S.C. § 741. In the place of an *in rem* proceeding, the Act authorized a libel *in personam* in cases involving such vessels, if such a proceeding could have been maintained had the vessel been a private vessel, and "provided that such vessel is employed as a merchant vessel." 46 U.S.C. § 742 (1958). Significantly, Congress was urged to include in the Suits in Admiralty Act authorization for suits against the United States for damages caused by public vessels, but the suggestion was rejected in Committee as a "radical change" in policy that might "materially delay passage" of the Act.[4]

Until 1925 the only recourse for the owner of a vessel or cargo damaged by a public vessel was to apply to Congress for a private bill. In that year, Congress enacted the Public Vessels Act, which authorized a libel *in personam* against the United States "for damages caused by a public vessel of the United States." 46 U.S.C. § 781. The Act provided that suits involving public vessels "shall be subject to and proceed in accordance with the provisions of [the Suits in Admiralty Act] or any amendment thereof, insofar as the same are not inconsistent herewith * * *." 46 U.S.C. § 782. Some of the inconsistencies lay in the Public Vessels Act's provisions, referred to above, restricting subpoenas to officers and crew members of a public vessel, barring recovery of prejudgment interest, and imposing a requirement of reciprocity. Each of these provisions must be assumed to have reflected deliberate policy choices by Congress. In particular, the notion of reciprocity was central to the scheme enacted by Congress. One of the spurs to enactment of the Public Vessels Act was Congress' recognition that the principal maritime nations, notably England, France, and

---

3. See S.Rep.No.223, 66th Cong., 1st Sess. (1919); H.R.Rep.No.497, 66th Cong., 2d Sess. (1919).

4. H.R.Rep.No.497, 66th Cong., 1st Sess. 4 (1919).

Germany, already permitted their nations and foreigners to bring suit for damages caused by public vessels.[5] And while the debates on the Public Vessels Act were sparse, the Act's requirement of reciprocity was specifically mentioned on the House floor in response to a question whether the Act gave foreign nationals the same rights as citizens to bring suit.[6]

B

The 1960 amendment to the Suits in Admiralty Act, which formed the basis of the Court of Appeals' decision, was an outgrowth of severe jurisdictional problems facing the plaintiff with a maritime claim against the United States. Both the Suits in Admiralty Act and the Public Vessels Act authorized suits on the admiralty side of the district courts, and were viewed as providing the exclusive remedy for claims within their coverage. See 46 U.S.C. § 745; Johnson v. United States Shipping Board Emergency Fleet Corp., 280 U.S. 320, 50 S.Ct. 118, 74 L.Ed. 451 (1930); Aliotti v. United States, 221 F.2d 598 (C.A.9 1955). But these Acts were not generally interpreted to encompass all actionable maritime claims against the United States. Maritime tort claims deemed beyond the reach of both Acts could be brought only on the law side of the district courts under the Federal Tort Claims Act. 28 U.S.C. §§ 1346(b), 2671 et seq. More importantly for our purposes, contract claims not encompassed by either Act fell within the Tucker Act, which lodged exclusive jurisdiction in the Court of Claims for claims exceeding $10,000. 28 U.S.C. §§ 1346(a)(2), 1491.

A plaintiff with a contract claim against the United States for more than $10,000 often found himself in a difficult position. He had to choose between proceeding in the district court under one of the admiralty acts, and proceeding in the Court of Claims under the Tucker Act. And he had to choose his forum wisely, for cases were not transferable between the district courts and the Court of Claims, and an incorrect choice could result in the applicable statute of limitations having run by the time the error was discovered.[7] The solution of filing claims in both the district court and the Court of Claims was unavailable, because under 28 U.S.C. § 1500 the Court of Claims has no jurisdiction over any claim that is the subject of a pending suit in any other court. See Wessel, Duval & Co. v. United States, 124 F.Supp. 636, 129 Ct.Cl. 464 (1954).

Because of serious uncertainties about the reach of the Suits in Admiralty and Public Vessels Acts on the one hand, and the Tucker Act on

---

5. H.R.Rep.No.913, 68th Cong., 1st Sess., 5–6, 15–16 (1924); S.Rep.No. 941, 68th Cong., 2d Sess., 5–6, 15–16 (1925); 66 Cong. Rec. 2088 (1925) (remarks of Rep. Underhill).

6. 66 Cong.Rec. 2088 (1925)(remarks of Reps. Denison, Underhill, and Bulwinkle).

7. H.R.Rep.No.523, 86th Cong., 1st Sess., 2 (1959)(hereinafter cited as House Report); S.Rep.No.1894, 86th Cong., 2d Sess., 3

(1960)(hereinafter cited as Senate Report), U.S.Code Cong. & Admin.News 1960, p. 3583. The problem was most severe when suit was incorrectly brought in the Court of Claims under the Tucker Act, which has a six-year statute of limitations, 28 U.S.C. § 2401(a); the Suits in Admiralty and Public Vessels Acts have two-year limitation periods, 46 U.S.C. §§ 745, 782.

the other, the crucial determination of the appropriate forum for a claim was often a difficult one.[8]   The jurisdictional uncertainties under these acts were illustrated in Calmar S. S. Corp. v. United States, 345 U.S. 446, 73 S.Ct. 733, 97 L.Ed. 1140 (1953).   In that case the private owner of a steamship under charter to the United States brought suit for additional charter hire for the loss of its vessel, which was bombed by enemy airplanes while carrying military supplies and equipment.   The vessel was clearly not a "public vessel" under the Public Vessels Act, because it was privately owned and operated.   The question was whether the vessel, "undoubtedly 'operated * * * for the United States', was 'employed as a merchant vessel' within the meaning of the [Suits in Admiralty] Act while carrying military supplies and equipment for hire."   Id., at 447, 73 S.Ct. at 734, 97 L.Ed. at 1142.   The District Court held that it was a merchant vessel, and assumed jurisdiction under the Suits in Admiralty Act.   The Court of Appeals reversed on the ground that while the vessel could have been employed as a merchant vessel under its charter, it was not so employed while transporting war materiel.   Having thus successfully argued to the Court of Appeals that the suit was not cognizable under either the Suits in Admiralty Act or the Public Vessels Act, the Government reversed its position in this Court. It argued, and the Court held, that the nature of the cargo was irrelevant and that the vessel was employed as a merchant vessel within the meaning of the Suits in Admiralty Act.   The Court was clearly sensitive to the fact that a contrary ruling would have relegated the plaintiff to the Court of Claims, id., at 455, 73 S.Ct. at 737, 97 L.Ed. at 1146, but even after *Calmar* there remained the possibility that a particular vessel would be held to be neither a "public vessel" nor "employed as a merchant vessel."

The sharp reversals of position by the Government and the courts in the *Calmar* case were but illustrative of the jurisdictional uncertainties faced by potential litigants.   In several instances, courts reached conflicting results as to whether certain types of claims should be brought in the district court under the Suits in Admiralty Act or Public Vessels Act on the one hand, or in the Court of Claims under the Tucker Act on the other.[9]

---

8.   The respective House and Senate Committee Reports explained the problem as follows:

> "Since the applicability of [the Suits in Admiralty, Public Vessels and Tucker Acts] to a given factual situation is frequently exceedingly difficult to determine and a question on which reasonable men may differ, lawyers in maritime practice occasionally and unavoidably bring suit in the wrong forum."   House Report, at 2; Senate Report, at 3, U.S.Code Cong. & Admin.News 1960, p. 3584.

9.   See House Report, at 3; Senate Report, at 4.   Compare Aliotti v. United States, 221 F.2d 598 (C.A.9 1955), with Eastern S. S. Lines v. United States, 187 F.2d 956 (C.A.1 1951); Lykes Bros. S. S. Co. v. United States, 124 F.Supp. 622, 129 Ct.Cl. 455 (1954), with States Marine Corp. v. United States, 120 F.Supp. 585 (S.D.N.Y.1954), rev'd, 220 F.2d 655 (C.A.2 1955); Smith–Johnson S. S. Corp. v. United States, 139 F.Supp. 298, 135 Ct.Cl. 869, cert. denied, 351 U.S. 988, 76 S.Ct. 1047, 100 L.Ed. 1501 (1956), with Sword Line v. United States, 228 F.2d 344 (C.A.2 1955), 230 F.2d 75 (C.A.2), aff'd 351 U.S. 976, 76 S.Ct. 1047, 100 L.Ed. 1493 (1956)(after *Sword Line* was affirmed, the Court of Claims reversed itself in Smith–Johnson v. United States, 135 Ct.Cl. 866, 142 F.Supp. 367 (1956)).

It was the difficulty in determining the appropriate forum for a maritime claim against the United States that moved Congress to amend the Suits in Admiralty Act in 1960. The amendment first passed by the House in 1959 was designed to ameliorate the harsh consequences of misfilings by authorizing the transfer of cases between the district courts and the Court of Claims.[10] The transfer provision would "prevent dismissal of suits which would become time-barred when the appropriate forum had finally been determined."[11] But the Senate Committee on the Judiciary found the House bill inadequate:

"The transfer bill would operate to prevent ultimate loss of rights of litigants, but it did nothing to eliminate or correct the cause of original erroneous choices of forum while it could increase the existing delays."[12]

Accordingly, the Committee, while accepting the House amendment, proposed several additional amendments, whose purpose was stated succinctly as follows:

"The purpose of the amendments is to make as certain as possible that suits brought against the United States for damages caused by vessels and employees of the United States through breach of contract or tort can be originally filed in the correct court so as to proceed to trial promptly on their merits."[13]

Two amendments were designed to clarify the jurisdictional language of the Suits in Admiralty Act. First, the Committee added language authorizing suits against the United States where a suit would be maintainable "if a private person or property were involved." The prior version of the Act had authorized suits against the United States only when suits would be maintainable if the "vessel" or "cargo" were privately owned, operated or possessed, and that language had generated considerable confusion.[14]

10. The House had passed an identical bill in 1958, H.R. 3046, 85th Cong., 2d Sess., but it did not emerge from the Senate Committee on the Judiciary before the expiration of the 85th Congress.

11. House Report, at 3; Senate Report, at 4, U.S.Code Cong. & Admin. News 1960, p. 3587.

12. Senate Report, at 6, U.S.Code. Cong. & Admin.News 1960, p. 3587.

13. Id., at 2, U.S.Code Cong. & Admin.News, 1960, p. 3583.

14. Senate Report, at 5, citing Ryan Stevedoring Co. v. United States, 175 F.2d 490 (C.A.2), cert. denied, 338 U.S. 899, 70 S.Ct. 249, 94 L.Ed. 553 (1949). Compare Lykes Bros. S. S. Co. v. United States, 124 F.Supp. 622, 129 Ct.Cl. 455 (1954), with States Marine Corp. v. United States, 120 F.Supp. 585 (S.D.N.Y.1954), rev'd, 220 F.2d 655 (C.A.2 1955).

This amendment, which has no bearing on this case, has generally been held to require that those maritime tort claims that were previously cognizable only on the law side of the district courts under the Federal Tort Claims Act now be brought on the admiralty side of the district courts under the Suits in Admiralty Act. See T. J. Falgout Boats, Inc. v. United States, 361 F.Supp. 838 (C.D.Cal.1972), aff'd, 508 F.2d 855 (C.A.9 1974), petition for certiorari filed March 22, 1975 (No. 74–1215); Roberts v. United States, 498 F.2d 520 (C.A.9), cert. denied, 419 U.S. 1070, 95 S.Ct. 656, 42 L.Ed.2d 665 (1974); De Bardeleben Marine Corp. v. United States, 451 F.2d 140 (C.A.5 1971); Utzinger v. United States, 246 F.Supp. 1022 (S.D.Ohio 1965); Tankrederiet Gefion A/S v. United States, 241 F.Supp. 83 (E.D.Mich. 1964); Tebbs v. Baker–Whitely Towing Co., 227 F.Supp. 656 (D.Md.1964); Beeler v. Unit-

Second, the Committee made the change that concerns us in this case: it deleted the language in the jurisdictional section of the Suits in Admiralty Act requiring that a vessel be "employed as a merchant vessel." We have already noted the confusion evidenced by the Government and the courts in the *Calmar* case over whether the vessel in question was "employed as a merchant vessel." In addition, the Senate Report referred to other cases in which the "employed as a merchant vessel" language had caused jurisdictional difficulties. For example, in Continental Casualty Co. v. United States, 156 F.Supp. 942, 140 Ct.Cl. 500 (1957), the Court of Claims had held that a suit on a contract for the repair of a vessel that had been out of service for several years was not authorized by the Suits in Admiralty Act, because at the time the repairs were made "the vessel was not employed at all," and could not therefore be said to have been "employed as a merchant vessel." Similarly, in Eastern S. S. Lines v. United States, 187 F.2d 956 (C.A.1 1951), the Court of Appeals affirmed the dismissal of a vessel owner's contract claim against the United States for the amount necessary to recondition its vessel as a cargo and passenger ship after the Army had used it for troop transport and hospital services. The Court of Appeals held that the Suits in Admiralty Act had no application because the Army had not employed the vessel as a merchant vessel. The results in *Continental Casualty* and *Eastern S. S. Lines* were, the Senate Report noted, contrary to results reached in other cases "on essentially identical facts."[15] It was to make clear that such cases could be brought on the admiralty side of the district courts that the Committee recommended the deletion of the confusing "employed as a merchant vessel" proviso.

C

Respondent contends that the deletion of the "employed as a merchant vessel" proviso was intended to abolish the distinction between a merchant vessel and a public vessel, and thereby enable suits previously cognizable under the Public Vessels Act to be brought under the Suits in Admiralty Act, free from the restrictive provisions of the Public Vessels Act. There is no indication that Congress had any such broad purpose.[16] The legislative history contains no explicit suggestion that Congress intended to render nugatory the provisions of the Public Vessels Act. Nor does it express any broad intent to put an end to all litigation over whether a vessel is a public vessel.

ed States, 224 F.Supp. 973 (W.D.Pa.), rev'd on other grounds, 338 F.2d 687 (C.A.3 1964).

15. Senate Report, at 5, citing James Shewan & Sons v. United States, 266 U.S. 108, 45 S.Ct. 45, 69 L.Ed. 192 (1924); Aliotti v. United States, 221 F.2d 598 (C.A.9 1955); Sinclair Refining Co. v. United States, 129 Ct.Cl. 474, 124 F.Supp. 628 (Ct.Cl.1954). Of course, this Court's decision in the *Calmar* case cast doubts on at least some decisions narrowly defining the scope of admiralty jurisdiction under the Suits in Admiralty and Public Vessels Acts. Congress was understandably of the view that confusion remained after *Calmar*.

16. We do not view the dictum in Amell v. United States, 384 U.S. 158, 164, 86 S.Ct. 1384, 1387, 16 L.Ed.2d 445, 449 (1966), as requiring a result different from the one we reach today.

The definitions of "merchant vessel" and "public vessel" were of interest to Congress only insofar as they related to Congress' basic purpose: to remove uncertainty over the proper forum for a claim against the United States. In this regard, it is quite clear that Congress' concern was not with uncertainty whether a suit should be brought under the Suits in Admiralty Act or under the Public Vessels Act, since in either event the proper forum was the admiralty side of the district court. See *Calmar S. S. Corp.*, supra, 345 U.S., at 454–455, 73 S.Ct. at 737, 97 L.Ed. at 1145–1146. The Senate Report stated the concern precisely:

> "The serious problem, and the one to which this bill is directed, arises in claims exceeding $10,000 where there is uncertainty as to whether a suit is properly brought under the Tucker Act [in the Court of Claims] on the one hand or the Suits in Admiralty or Public Vessels Act [on the admiralty side of the district court] on the other."[17]

In short, Congress saw confusion between the category of suits cognizable under the Suits in Admiralty Act or Public Vessels Act on the one hand, and the category of suits cognizable under the Tucker Act on the other. It attempted to eliminate the confusion between these two categories by expanding the scope of the Suits in Admiralty Act at the expense of the Tucker Act—thereby virtually eliminating the quasi-admiralty jurisdiction of the Court of Claims under the Tucker Act.[18] But Congress did nothing to alter the distinction between the Suits in Admiralty Act and the Public Vessels Act, or expand the one at the expense of the other.

That the House and Senate Reports contain a reference to "confusion in establishing whether a vessel is a 'merchant vessel' or a 'public vessel,' "does not suggest otherwise. That reference appears in the course of a discussion of the difficulty in choosing the proper forum for a claim. To a limited extent, doubt whether a vessel was a merchant vessel or a public vessel created uncertainty over the proper forum. The Reports explained:

> "If [a vessel is] a 'merchant vessel', under the Suits in Admiralty Act exclusive jurisdiction is in the district court in admiralty. If a 'public vessel' jurisdiction may be either in admiralty under the Public Vessels Act or under the Tucker Act, depending on the nature of the claim. It will be recalled that a claim under the Tucker Act exceeding $10,000 must be brought in the Court of Claims."[19]

Congress' concern was that because of differences in the authorizational language of the Suits in Admiralty Act and the Public Vessels Act, some claims that would clearly have been within the jurisdiction of the district court if merchant vessels were involved had been held to be beyond the

---

17. Senate Report, at 3, U.S.Code Cong. & Admin.News 1960, p. 3584.

18. The Court of Claims has not been completely deprived of jurisdiction over claims arising in a maritime context. In Amell v. United States, 384 U.S. 158, 86 S.Ct. 1384, 16 L.Ed.2d 445 (1966), we held that wage claims exceeding $10,000 by government employees working aboard government vessels are still cognizable exclusively in the Court of Claims, where wage claims by government employees have traditionally been cognizable.

19. House Report, at 2; Senate Report, at 3, U.S.Code Cong. & Admin.News 1960, p. 3584.

district court's jurisdiction when public vessels were involved. Thus, some courts had held that contract claims other than those expressly authorized by the Public Vessels Act were generally not cognizable under the Act.[20] Litigants with certain types of contract claims therefore faced the possibility that the appropriate forum would depend on the type of vessel involved. Congress' deletion of the "employed as a merchant vessel" proviso was clearly intended to recover such uncertainty as to the proper forum by bringing within the Suits in Admiralty Act whatever category of claims involving public vessels was beyond the scope of the Public Vessels Act.[21] But claims like the instant one that fell within the Public Vessels Act, presented none of the problems with which Congress was concerned in 1960, and there is therefore no reason to infer that Congress intended to affect them.

III

In sum, the interpretation of the 1960 amendment advanced by the respondent and adopted by the Court of Appeals would effectively nullify specific policy judgments made by Congress when it enacted the Public Vessels Act, by enabling litigants to bring suits previously subject to the terms of the Public Vessels Act under the Suits in Admiralty Act. The language of the amendment does not explicitly authorize such a result, and the legislative history reflects a narrow congressional purpose that would not be advanced by that result. We therefore hold that claims within the scope of the Public Vessels Act remain subject to its terms after the 1960 amendment to the Suits in Admiralty Act. Since there is no dispute that respondent's claim falls within the embrace of the Public Vessels Act, the Court of Appeals erred in concluding that the reciprocity provision of the Public Vessels Act is inapplicable.

Respondent urges two additional grounds for affirmance. First, it contends that the reciprocity provision, even if applicable, does not bar its claim, because the owners of 99% of its stock are Americans and it is in substance an American owner. The District Court rejected this contention, and the Court of Appeals did not address it since it found the reciprocity provision inapplicable. Second, respondent argues that if it is considered a national of the Philippines, whose suit would fall within the prohibition of the reciprocity provision, that provision denies it due process in violation of the Fifth Amendment. This argument was not even presented to the District Court, and was not addressed by the Court of Appeals. We leave

20. See, e.g., Eastern S.S. Lines v. United States, 187 F.2d 956, 959 (C.A.1 1951); Continental Casualty Co. v. United States, 156 F.Supp. 942, 140 Ct.Cl. 500 (1957). Other than claims for "damages caused by a public vessel of the United States," the only claims expressly authorized by the Public Vessels Act are claims "for compensation for towage and salvage services, including contract salvage, rendered to a public vessel of the United States." 46 U.S.C. § 781.

21. It is not to be assumed that contract claims other than those expressly authorized by the Public Vessels Act were necessarily beyond the scope of the Act. As in Calmar S. S. Corp. v. United States, 345 U.S., at 456 n. 8, 73 S.Ct. at 738, 97 L.Ed. at 1147, we intimate no view on the subject.

the consideration of these two additional contentions, to the extent they were adequately raised, to the Court of Appeals on remand.

The judgment of the Court of Appeals is reversed, and the case remanded for further proceedings consistent with this opinion.

It is so ordered.

Reversed and remanded.

■ MR. JUSTICE STEVENS took no part in the consideration or decision of this case.

■ MR. JUSTICE STEWART, dissenting.

Congress amended the Suits in Admiralty Act in 1960 to eliminate the distinction the Act formerly drew between public vessels and merchant vessels owned or operated by the United States. Act of Sept. 13, 1960, Pub.L. No. 86–770, § 3, 74 Stat. 912. See S.Rep. No. 1894, 86th Cong., 2d Sess., 3. See also S.Rep. No. 92–1079, 92d Cong., 2d Sess., 5–6. Six years later the then Solicitor General explained the effect of that amendment in a brief filed on behalf of the Government in this Court:

> "As originally enacted, the Suits in Admiralty Act was limited to government merchant vessels and tugboats, and excluded public vessels. The latter were separately covered in the Public Vessels Act. * * * Because of the uncertainty engendered by the public-merchant vessel distinction, * * * Congress in 1960 amended Section 2 of the Suits in Admiralty Act to delete the reference to merchant vessels. * * * Thus, the Suits in Admiralty Act now extends to government public as well as merchant vessels." Brief for the United States at 9 n. 1, Amell v. United States, 384 U.S. 158, 86 S.Ct. 1384, 16 L.Ed.2d 445.[1]

In the present case the Government has steered an entirely different course, arguing that Congress did not intend to expand the scope of the Suits in Admiralty Act to include public vessels, and that the plain language of the Act should be ignored. I cannot accept this boxing of the compass. At best, the United States has demonstrated only that the legislative history indicates that Congress was concerned with more than one problem in amending the law. But ambiguous legislative history surely cannot suffice to undermine the plain words of the statute, when no persuasive policy considerations[2] and no repeal by implication[3] are involved.

---

1. This Court agreed: "In 1960, * * * Congress abolished the distinction between public and merchant vessels, a matter which had sorely confused attorneys. * * *" Amell v. United States, 384 U.S. 158, 164, 86 S.Ct. 1384, 1388, 16 L.Ed.2d 445, 449.

2. Since the United States could have sued the owners of the fishing boat in the Philippines had the fishing boat rammed the destroyer, it would do no violence to the concept of reciprocity to allow the owners of the boat to sue the United States in a federal court. And while the United States would no longer be able *sua sponte* to prevent the enforcement of subpoenas or stay proceedings against naval vessels and their crews, it is not realistic to think that a federal court would refuse such relief if national security were in any way at stake. Finally, prejudgment interest is awardable under the Suits in Admiralty Act, and not under the Public Vessels Act, but the amount of money involved in such awards is not large and the award of interest is discretionary in any event. The

---

3. See note 3 on page 323.

The plain language of the Suits in Admiralty authorizes anyone to sue the United States for damages caused by any U.S. vessel. There is no need to inquire further: "When there is no ambiguity in the words, there is no room for construction. The case must be a strong one indeed, which would justify a Court in departing from the plain meaning of words * * * in search of an intention which the words themselves did not suggest." United States v. Wiltberger, 5 Wheat. 76, 95–96, 5 L.Ed. 37, 92 (Marshall, C.J.). As the Court said 10 years ago in construing the Suits in Admiralty Act, "If we are here misconstruing the intent of Congress, it can easily set the matter to rest by explicit language." Amell v. United States, supra, 384 U.S. at 166, 86 S.Ct. at 1389, 16 L.Ed.2d at 450. So long as the law reads as it now does, I think the Court of Appeals correctly understood it, and I would, therefore, affirm the judgment before us.[4]

NOTE

In a sequel to the *United Continental Tuna* decision, the plaintiffs urged on remand that the vessel should be treated as an American vessel in view of the 99% American ownership, an issue noted by the Supreme Court, but not decided. The court of appeals declined to permit them to thus pierce their own corporate veil, and rejected the application of a contacts test such as that employed under the Jones Act. United Continental Tuna Corp. v. United States, 550 F.2d 569, 1977 A.M.C. 660 (9th Cir.1977).

In Blanco v. United States, 775 F.2d 53 (2d Cir.1985) the Public Vessels Act was held applicable to an action under the Jones Act for wrongful death of a crewman on a vessel under bareboat charter to the United States, and the action dismissed under the reciprocity provision when it appeared that it was brought on behalf of a wife and thirteen children, all Honduran nationals, despite the fact that the decedent and the representative plaintiff, the decedent's eldest son, were both citizens of the United States. The court of appeals indicated that an action for pain and suffering, or an action for the son's own pecuniary loss would not have been barred by the statute, but the record was bare of any indication that death was not instantaneous or any proof of loss by the representative plaintiff.

In *United Continental Tuna*, the issue was whether the restrictions of the Public Vessels Act could be avoided by pleading under the Suits in Admiralty Act, as amended in 1960. In making the point that the 1960 amendments were not intended to repudiate the policy decisions reflected in the restrictions written into the PVA the Court emphasized the purpose of the 1960 amendments to eliminate confusion over the application of the Tucker Act and the admiralty statutes. It did

---

Scotland, 118 U.S. 507, 519, 6 S.Ct. 1174, 1175, 30 L.Ed. 153, 155. None of these governmental interests supposedly served by the Public Vessels Act, but not by the Suit in Admiralty Act, is therefore significant.

3. The judgment of the Court of Appeals does not amount to a repeal of the Public Vessels Act, since there will still be cases cognizable only under that Act by reason of its broader venue provisions. Compare 46 U.S.C. § 742 with 46 U.S.C. § 782.

4. While no other Court of Appeals has ruled on the precise issue presented here, two have indicated that they would reach the same result as did the Ninth Circuit. United Philippine Lines, Inc. v. Submarine USS Daniel Boone, 475 F.2d 478, 480 n. 5 (C.A.4); Ira S. Bushey & Sons, Inc. v. United States, 398 F.2d 167, 169 (C.A.2). See also DeBardeleben Marine Corp. v. United States, 451 F.2d 140, 145–146 (C.A.5).

not reach the question of the relationship between the Suits in Admiralty Act and the Federal Tort Claims Act, but noted in n. 14 to the opinion that the lower courts had construed the statute to embrace all maritime claims against the United States, to the exclusion of claims under the FTCA. At the time of the 1960 amendments would this interpretation be calculated to eliminate confusion? Remember that then the maritime jurisdiction in tort was bounded by location alone. Since the decision in *Executive Jet* has placed the boundary on both location and maritime nexus, is the identification of the admiralty claim so easy? Note that under the Tort Claims Act the action must be filed within two years from the occurrence or within six months from the denial of an administrative claim, whichever is later. See 28 U.S.C.A. § 2401(b). Under the Suits in Admiralty Act it must be filed within two years of the occurrence. Is there any justification for the possible trap that these discrepancies produce? In McCormick v. United States, the plaintiff filed an administrative claim under the F.T.C.A. for damages incurred when their pleasure boat collided with an obstruction allegedly negligently placed in navigable water by the Government. The incident occurred on August 22, 1976. The administrative claims were submitted to the Department of the Army on January 25, 1978, and July 21, 1978. The claims were denied on September 22, 1978. The action was filed on November 6, 1978. The district court dismissed on the ground that the Suits in Admiralty Act afforded the exclusive remedy and the two year statute of limitations had run when the action was commenced. In the first appeal the court of appeals reversed, reading the S.A.A. to leave under the F.T.C.A. actions nonoperational maritime torts, such as the placing of obstructions in water. McCormick v. United States, 645 F.2d 299, 1982 A.M.C. 61 (5th Cir.1981). On rehearing, the court indicated that it had reconsidered and was convinced that its interpretation of the relevant statutes had been incorrect, but held that the S.A.A. is subject to tolling and reversed and remanded for fact finding on the tolling issue. McCormick v. United States, 680 F.2d 345, 1984 A.M.C. 1799 (5th Cir.1982).

In Bovell v. United States Dept. of Defense, 735 F.2d 755 (3d Cir.1984), the injuries alleged occurred in December, 1979, when plaintiff (apparently an employee of government contractor) fell from a ladder on a vessel owned by the United States. Two years after the occurrence, short two days, he filed a claim under the F.T.C.A. The claim was denied in three weeks, and something over four months later, plaintiff filed his action. The district court dismissed on the ground that an action under the Public Vessels Act was the plaintiff's exclusive remedy and was time barred. The court of appeals affirmed, holding that the two year statute of limitations under the S.A.A., applicable to actions under the P.V.A. is not subject to tolling, and added that even if it were to agree with the Fifth Circuit in *McCormick* that it might be tolled in "appropriate circumstances," it did not consider the circumstances appropriate.

Is it possible to avoid the situation in which the plaintiffs in *McCormick* and *Bovell* found themselves by pleading the F.T.C.A. and the S.A.A. as alternatives? This was done in Chapman v. United States, 575 F.2d 147, 1978 A.M.C. 2202 (7th Cir.1978)(en banc), cert. denied 439 U.S. 893, 99 S.Ct. 251, 58 L.Ed.2d 239 (1978). The action was brought in respect of a recreational boating accident allegedly caused by the United States in failing to mark a dam privately constructed in 1948 on a stream not used for commercial navigation since 1931. The action was pleaded under both the F.T.C.A. and the S.A.A. The count under the F.T.C.A. was dismissed by the district court on a finding that the plaintiff had been negligent and therefore could not recover under the F.T.C.A. The court tried the claim under the S.A.A. to the bench and awarded damages. This award was sustained on appeal, but reheard en banc and dismissed for want of jurisdiction. The dismissal of the count under the F.T.C.A. was not appealed.

It was also done in Estate of Callas v. United States, 682 F.2d 613 (7th Cir.1982), with more satisfactory results. The plaintiff in an action charging negligence in the operation of a lock and dam, pleaded under both the S.A.A. and F.T.C.A. The district dismissed the count under the F.T.C.A. and found the United States negligent, but asserted in its final judgment that it was rendered under the F.T.C.A. The court of appeals found the dismissal of the F.T.C.A. claim correct and the misstatement in the judgment harmless error.

Canadian Transport Co. v. United States

United States Court of Appeals, District of Columbia Circuit, 1980.
663 F.2d 1081, 1980 A.M.C. 2103.

ROBB, CIRCUIT JUDGE:

Appellants Canadian Transport Company and Bocimar, N.V. sued the United States in the District Court, seeking damages for the refusal of the Coast Guard to permit M/V TROPWAVE to enter the port of Norfolk, Virginia on or about April 20, 1974. The ground of the refusal was that the master and officers of TROPWAVE were Polish nationals whose presence posed a risk to national security. Appellants asserted three causes of action in their complaint. The first alleged the tort of intentional interference with contract rights and was based upon the Suits in Admiralty Act, 46 U.S.C. § 741 et seq. (1976). The second, based on 28 U.S.C. § 1350 (1976), alleged that the Coast Guard's action violated the treaty obligations of the United States. Finally, appellants asserted that they had been deprived of their property without due process of law in violation of the Fifth Amendment.[1] On the parties' cross motions for summary judgment, the District Court granted the motion of the United States and dismissed all three counts for failure to state a claim upon which relief may be granted.[2] Plaintiffs appeal.

I

* * *

The Coast Guard's decision to bar TROPWAVE from Norfolk harbor was made pursuant to the Special Interest Vessel (SIV) Program. This program is administered by the Coast Guard under regulations issued by the Secretary of the Treasury. The Secretary's authority to prescribe these regulations derives from the Magnuson Act, which authorizes him to "make rules and regulations governing the anchorage and movement of any vessels, foreign or domestic, in the territorial waters of the United States" when the President "declares a national emergency to exist by reason of actual or threatened war, insurrection, or invasion, or disturbance or threatened disturbance of the international relations of the United

---

1. The parties stipulated that venue was appropriate in the District of Columbia.

2. Canadian Transport Co. v. United States, 430 F.Supp. 1168 (D.D.C.1977).

States." 50 U.S.C. § 191 (1976). In addition, the Act gives the President authority to issue regulations governing the anchorage and movement of "foreign flag vessels" whenever he finds that "the security of the United States is endangered by reason of actual or threatened war, or invasion, or insurrection or subversive activity * * *." Id. In 1950, President Truman issued Executive Order 10173, reprinted in 3 C.F.R. 356 (1949–53 Comp.), in which he stated that "the security of the United States is endangered by reason of subversive activity", and prescribed various regulations pursuant to section 191. The Secretary of the Treasury, relying upon this proclamation, adopted additional regulations, including the SIV program.[6] The SIV regulations are classified in the interest of national security. No publication of the ports to which it applies or its criteria for denying a vessel access to a port has been made.

II

Appellants first allege that the Coast Guard's actions amount to an intentional interference with their contract rights under the charter and subcharter agreements. They characterize this cause of action as a tort suit[7] brought under the Suits in Admiralty Act. * * *

A. *The Discretionary Function Exemption*

The government contends that the Coast Guard was engaged in the performance of a "discretionary function" and that the United States is therefore completely immune from suit in this case. Appellants note that the Suits in Admiralty Act contains no express exception for discretionary functions. By contrast, the Federal Tort Claims Act explicitly provides such an exemption:

> The provisions of this chapter and section 1346(b) of this title shall not apply to—
>
> (a) Any claim based upon an act or omission of an employee of the Government, exercising due care, in the execution of a statute or regulation, whether or not such statute or regulation be valid, or based upon the exercise or performance or the failure to exercise or perform a discretionary function or duty on the part of a federal agency or an employee of the Government, whether or not the discretion involved be abused.

28 U.S.C. § 2680 (1976).

Appellants argue that the failure of Congress to include such language in the Suits in Admiralty Act indicates its intent that no similar exception apply in admiralty cases brought against the United States. This view has been explicitly adopted by the Court of Appeals for the Fourth Circuit[9] and

---

6. Appellants do not dispute the authority of the Secretary to adopt these regulations.

7. Appellants state that the tort of intentional interference with contract rights is recognized in admiralty, citing Aljassim v. S. S. South Star, 323 F.Supp. 918 (S.D.N.Y. 1971).

9. Lane v. United States, 529 F.2d 175 (4th Cir.1975).

endorsed in dictum by the Court of Appeals for the Fifth Circuit,[10] but rejected by the Court of Appeals for the First Circuit.[11]

We believe that respect for the doctrine of separation of powers requires that in cases arising under the Suits in Admiralty Act, courts should refrain from passing judgment on the appropriateness of actions of the executive branch which meet the requirements of the discretionary function exception of the FTCA. Accordingly, we align ourselves with the views expressed in the *Gercey* case and hold that a discretionary function exemption is implicit in the Suits in Admiralty Act.

* * *

The legislative history of the "private person" language focuses exclusively upon the difficulties that had been created by the necessity of choosing between the court of claims and the district courts. The history did not focus on the extent of the liability in tort to which the United States was consenting.

Although the legislative history of the Suits in Admiralty Act is inconclusive on this point, the legislative history of the FTCA suggests that the exemption for discretionary functions in that Act was derived from the doctrine of separation of powers, a doctrine to which the courts must adhere even in the absence of an explicit statutory command. In Dalehite v. United States, 346 U.S. 15, 73 S.Ct. 956, 97 L.Ed. 1427 (1953), the Supreme Court reviewed this legislative history at length. Id. at 24–30, 73 S.Ct. at 962–65. The Court noted that the exception "was drafted as a clarifying amendment", id. at 26, 73 S.Ct. at 963, and referred to testimony of the Assistant Attorney General, who advised the House Judiciary Committee that "'the cases embraced within [the new] subsection *would have been exempted from [the prior bill] by judicial construction. It is not probable that the courts would extend a Tort Claims Act into the realm of the validity of legislation or discretionary administrative action, but H.R. 6463 makes this specific'*". Id. at 27, 73 S.Ct. at 963.[14] [Emphasis added].

Our recognition of a discretionary function exception in the Suits in Admiralty Act, therefore, is not an attempt to rewrite the statute, but merely an acknowledgement of the limits of judicial power. See 3 K. Davis, Administrative Law Treatise § 25.13 (1958) & (1970 Supp.); L. Jaffee, Judicial Control of Administrative Action, 244, 256–60 (1965).

Our conclusion that the discretionary function exception of the FTCA must be read into the Suits in Admiralty Act requires us to delineate the proper scope of that exception. The government appears to argue that if an action involves the exercise of judgment by a government employee, the action is discretionary and the United States is immune from suit. (Appel-

---

10. De Bardeleben Marine Corp. v. United States, 451 F.2d 140, 143–44 & note 15 (5th Cir.1971).

11. Gercey v. United States, 540 F.2d 536 (1st Cir.), cert. denied, 430 U.S. 954, 97 S.Ct. 1599, 51 L.Ed.2d 804 (1977).

14. (Quoting Hearings on H.R. 5373 and H.R. 6463 Before the Committee on the Judiciary, House of Representatives, 77th Cong., 2d Sess. at 29 (testimony of Asst. Attorney General Shea)).

lees' Br. at 35–36) Courts have recognized, however, that giving such a broad reading to the term "discretionary" would effectively immunize almost all government activity from suit under the FTCA.

In the *Dalehite* decision the Supreme Court attempted to narrow the meaning of "discretionary" somewhat by distinguishing between decisions made at the "planning" level, which are within *the exception,* and those made at the "operational" level, which are not subject to it. 346 U.S. at 42, 73 S.Ct. at 971. We think however that the result in this case should not turn upon whether the Coast Guard's actions can be labelled as "planning" or "operational". Although that distinction provides a useful guideline, a proper decision can be reached only by keeping the purposes of the discretionary function exemption in mind. The exercise of judgment which the exemption protects must be one which would otherwise involve courts in making a decision entrusted to other branches of the government. Decisions which require a government official to weigh competing policy alternatives are entitled to immunity for such decisions are the ordinary responsibility of the legislative and executive branches. In the *Dalehite* opinion itself, the Court stated that "[w]here there is room for *policy judgment* and decision, there is discretion." 346 U.S. at 36, 73 S.Ct. at 968. (Emphasis added) In Mr. Justice Jackson's words, "it is not a tort for government to govern. * * *" Id. at 57, 73 S.Ct. at 978 (dissenting opinion). Conversely, if the decision involves only the implementation of policy choices already made, there is usually no reason for a court to refrain from passing judgment on the question of whether the statutory or regulatory mandate has been complied with.

The distinction between decisions which require judgment in the formulation of policy and those which involve only the implementation of policy choices already made has been recognized and approved by many courts, e.g., Downs v. United States, 522 F.2d 990 (6th Cir.1975); Griffin v. United States, 500 F.2d 1059 (3d Cir.1974); Eastern Air Lines v. Union Trust Co., 95 U.S.App.D.C. 189, 221 F.2d 62, aff'd per curiam sub nom. United States v. Union Trust Co., 350 U.S. 907, 76 S.Ct. 192, 100 L.Ed. 796 (1955); Johnson v. State, 69 Cal.2d 782, 73 Cal.Rptr. 240, 447 P.2d 352 (1968); K. Davis, supra, § 25.08 (Supp.1970). See also Rieser v. District of Columbia, 183 U.S.App.D.C. 375, 388, 563 F.2d 462, 475 (1977), modified on other grounds 188 U.S.App.D.C. 384, 580 F.2d 647 (1978)(*en banc*)(applying the distinction to determine liability of the District of Columbia). Although the line dividing decisions which involve a choice between competing policy considerations and those which involve the implementation of choices already made may not always be well-defined, we believe that recognition of the purposes of the discretionary function exception requires a court to attempt to draw such a line.

B.   *The Coast Guard's Failure to Give Notice*

* * *

We think the decision to keep the details, and even the existence, of the SIV program classified is immunized by the discretionary function exemption which we find in the Suits in Admiralty Act. The officials responsible for the promulgation of the regulations were required to weigh the benefits to the maritime industry that might result from providing some notice of the existence of the program against the danger to national security that might result from publishing the details of the program.[17] We think the decision to protect the national security at the expense of whatever inconvenience might befall vessels such as TROPWAVE was a decision to favor one competing policy over another. It is not the province of the courts to second-guess such a decision in a damage action against the United States brought under either the Federal Tort Claims Act or the Suits in Admiralty Act.[18] Consequently, the District Court correctly dismissed the claim based upon the Coast Guard's failure to give any notice of the program.

C. *Arbitrary Administration of the SIV Program*

Appellants have advanced an alternative argument. They maintain that there is a basis in the record for concluding that the Coast Guard officers who made the actual decision to bar TROPWAVE did so arbitrarily, and that the United States is not immune from suit for such actions.   * * *

The government contends that the decision to bar TROPWAVE called for "considerable evaluation and discussion" and an "exercise of judgment" (Appellee's Br. at 35) that the Coast Guard was therefore engaged in a discretionary function and no damage action may be maintained under the Suits in Admiralty Act.

Although we have recognized that the Suits in Admiralty Act contains a discretionary function exception, we have limited the exception's scope to the exercise of discretion in formulating government policy making authority to the officers responsible for administering the program. At this stage of the proceedings, therefore, we cannot say that the Coast Guard was performing a discretionary function when it admitted TROPWIND and Polish fishing vessels but excluded TROPWAVE. By failing to show that the Coast Guard officers were making policy judgments when these actions were taken, the government has failed to meet its burden of establishing that it is entitled to summary judgment as a matter of law.[24] Accordingly, we cannot affirm the grant of summary judgment to the government on this ground.

The District Court did not rely on the discretionary function exception, but held that there has been no waiver of sovereign immunity for any claim

---

17. It appears from the manner in which appellants learned of the restrictions that there was public knowledge that the Port of Norfolk was a restricted area. TAN 4.

18. We do not hold that courts must uncritically accept every decision to withhold information which the executive branch seeks to justify in the interest of national security. It is clear that when information is sought because of its relevance to a judicial proceed-

ing, "[t]he court itself must determine whether the circumstances are appropriate for the claim of privilege." United States v. Reynolds, 345 U.S. 1, 8, 73 S.Ct. 528, 532, 97 L.Ed. 727 (1953). See also Committee for Nuclear Responsibility, Inc. v. Seaborg, 149 U.S.App.D.C. 385, 391, 463 F.2d 788, 794 (1971).

24. Semaan v. Mumford, supra, note 21.

of wrongful administration of the SIV regulations because the Coast Guard's activity was "uniquely governmental".[25]   The court cited the language in the Suits in Admiralty Act which waives sovereign immunity only in cases where a proceeding could be maintained "if a private person or property were involved".   46 U.S.C. § 742 (1976).   The court noted that the legislative history was not helpful in interpreting this provision, and that there has been relatively little case law construing it.   It looked to the similar language in the FTCA,[26] however, and concluded that it should rely upon FTCA case law, believing that the two provisions should be construed *in pari materia*.

We believe the District Court was correct in looking to the FTCA cases in construing the Suits in Admiralty Act's "private person" language.   We think that the court erred, however, in concluding that those cases establish an exception for "uniquely governmental" action.

The District Court relied upon Feres v. United States, 340 U.S. 135, 71 S.Ct. 153, 95 L.Ed. 152 (1950).   In that case the Court held that a soldier on active duty could not recover against the United States for injuries which "arise out of or are in the course of activity incident to service."   Id. at 146, 71 S.Ct. at 159.   The Court cited five factors influencing its holding: (1) the absence of a parallel private liability, since no private person has the power to organize a military force; id. at 141–42, 71 S.Ct. at 156–57; (2) the presence of a comprehensive compensation system for military personnel, id. at 144–45, 71 S.Ct. at 158; (3) the small number of private bills which had sought compensation for members of the military, id. at 140, 71 S.Ct. at 156; (4) the exclusively federal nature of the relationship between a soldier and the United States, id. at 143–44, 71 S.Ct. at 157–58; (5) the variations of state law to which members of the military would be subjected involuntarily, since they have no choice in where they are sent, id. at 142–43, 71 S.Ct. at 157.

The government argues that the first factor identified in Feres v. United States is present here, that the protection of national security and conduct of foreign affairs are activities that only the United States conducts.   Therefore, says the government, no liability can be imposed upon the United States because no private person would ever undertake such actions, let alone be held liable for performing them wrongfully.

We conclude however that subsequent Supreme Court decisions have so narrowed the *Feres* holding that the case will no longer support the government's position.   In Indian Towing Co. v. United States, 350 U.S. 61, 76 S.Ct. 122, 100 L.Ed. 48 (1955), the Court noted that "all Government activity is inescapably 'uniquely governmental' in that it is performed by the Government.   * * * 'Government is not partly public or partly

---

25.   430 F.Supp. at 1171.

26.   "The United States shall be liable * * * in the same manner and to the same extent as a private individual under like circumstances.   * * * "28 U.S.C. § 2674 (1976). See also id. § 1346(b)(United States liable

"under circumstances where the United States, if a private person, would be liable to the claimant in accordance with the law of the place where the act or omission occurred.")

private, depending upon the governmental pedigree of the type of a particular activity or the manner in which the Government conducts it.' " Id. at 67–68, 76 S.Ct. at 125–26, quoting Federal Crop Ins. Corp. v. Merrill, 332 U.S. 380, 383–84, 68 S.Ct. 1, 2–3, 92 L.Ed. 10. In deciding that a suit could be brought against the United States for the Coast Guard's negligent operation of a lighthouse, an activity which the government had contended was "uniquely governmental", the Court stated, "we would be attributing bizarre motives to Congress were we to hold that it was predicating liability on such a completely fortuitous circumstance—the presence or absence of identical private activity." 350 U.S. at 67, 76 S.Ct. at 125. (footnote omitted)

In Rayonier Inc. v. United States, 352 U.S. 315, 77 S.Ct. 374, 1 L.Ed.2d 354 (1957), the Court held that the FTCA would permit recovery against the United States for the negligence of the Forest Service in fighting a fire. It cited Indian Towing v. United States for the proposition that "an injured party cannot be deprived of his rights under the Act by resort to an alleged distinction, imported from the law of municipal corporations, between the Government's negligence when it acts in a 'proprietary' capacity and its negligence when it acts in a 'uniquely governmental' capacity." Id. at 319, 77 S.Ct. at 376. (footnote omitted) And in United States v. Muniz, 374 U.S. 150, 83 S.Ct. 1850, 10 L.Ed.2d 805 (1963), a unanimous Court appeared to limit the *Feres* decision to its particular facts:

> In the last analysis, *Feres* seems best explained by the "peculiar and special relationship of the soldier to his superiors, the effects of the maintenance of such suits on discipline and the extreme results that might obtain if suits under the Tort Claims Act were allowed for negligent orders given or negligent acts committed in the course of military duty. * * *"

Id. at 162, 83 S.Ct. at 1857, quoting United States v. Brown, 348 U.S. 110, 112, 75 S.Ct. 141, 143, 99 L.Ed. 139 (1954).[27]

* * *

We do not construe the "private person" language of the Suits in Admiralty Act as totally without force, however. The statute requires that the United States can be sued only if an action in admiralty can be maintained "if a private person or property were involved". This language means that a cause of action in admiralty would exist for the injury complained of by the plaintiff if that injury had been caused by a private person. Appellants maintain that a cause of action does exist in admiralty for intentional

---

27. The extent of the limitations placed upon Feres v. United States may also be observed by comparing the Court's declaration in that case that the effect of the FTCA was to waive immunity "from recognized causes of action and was not to visit the Government with novel and unprecedented liabilities", 340 U.S. at 142, 71 S.Ct. at 157, with the subsequent statement in Rayonier v. United States that the very purpose of the Tort Claims Act was to waive the Government's traditional all-encompassing immunity "from tort actions and to establish novel and unprecedented governmental liability." 352 U.S. at 319, 77 S.Ct. at 376. See also United States v. Muniz, supra, at 159, 83 S.Ct. at 1856; "The Act extends to novel and unprecedented forms of liability as well."

interference with contractual rights by a private person,[28] and the government does not dispute this.[29]   The government argues, however, that in order to determine whether the Coast Guard *wrongfully* interfered with the appellants' contractual rights, the District Court must judge whether the SIV regulations were properly applied, a standard that by its very nature does not apply to private persons.   Courts have not hesitated, however, to evaluate the conduct of government employees in light of federal regulations in order to determine whether there has been a breach of duty actionable in tort.   In Downs v. United States, 522 F.2d 990 (6th Cir.1975) supra, the court held that because the FBI's policy for dealing with hijackers had been embodied in regulations, an FBI agent would be required to implement those regulations with the degree of skill expected of an FBI agent with comparable training in handling such matters.   Id. at 1002.   Similarly, liability has been imposed for the failure of air traffic controllers to follow federal regulations governing the handling of aircraft. Yates v. United States, supra; Ingham v. Eastern Air Lines, supra.   Not every violation by the government of its regulations will give rise to an action under the Tort Claims Act or the Suits in Admiralty Act.   If, however, a cause of action would normally require proof that a private person acted wrongfully or without authority, the presence of that element may be proven in an action against the United States by reference to standards applicable to federal employees.[30]

We therefore hold that if the Coast Guard officers acted arbitrarily and in violation of regulations in diverting TROPWAVE, the United States is not immune from a damage action brought under the Suits in Admiralty Act.   * * *

* * *

CONCLUSION

The order denying appellants' motion for summary judgment is affirmed. The order granting summary judgment to the United States on appellants' second and third causes of action is also affirmed.   The order granting summary judgment to the United States on appellants' first cause of action is affirmed with regard to the claim of failure to give notice of the regulations.   With regard to the claim of arbitrary administration of the program, the judgment of the District Court is reversed, and the case is remanded for further proceedings in accordance with this opinion.

So ordered.

28.   See note 7 supra.

29.   Appellee's Br. at 28.

30.   The government argues that for the District Court to decide whether the SIV regulations were applied improperly, it must "become involved in making substantive decisions under the SIV program", such as whether TROPWAVE's diversion was warranted by national security considerations, or whether alternatives less drastic than diversion would have been appropriate.   It also argues that the court would be involved in political questions related to the conduct of foreign affairs which are beyond its competence.   (Appellee's Br. at 29) Because we do not know the contents of the regulations, these assertions are speculative at this time.

N O T E

Cf. Eklof Marine Corp. v. United States, 762 F.2d 200, 1985 A.M.C. 2141 (2d Cir.1985), in which the court held that inasmuch as the placing of buoys to mark a Hudson River reef was not a "discretionary" act within the discretionary function doctrine, it was not necessary to reach the question of whether the discretionary function doctrine applied under the Suits in Admiralty Act.

In Sutton v. Earles, 26 F.3d 903, 1994 A.M.C. 2007 (9th Cir.1994), a case involving a collision with a buoy in its weapon station open to use by boaters, claims of negligence in not monitoring safety, not briefing boaters, not maintaining a system of permits to police competence, and not taking steps to protect users from the hazards of intoxication were barred by the discretionary function exception, but failure to post signs and to place lights on the buoys were not.

It has been stated that the only possible action for defamation by an agent of the United States is an action against the United States, and this is precluded by the defamation exception in the FTCA. B & A Marine Co., Inc. v. American Foreign Shipping Co., Inc., 23 F.3d 709 (2d Cir.1994). If a defamation suit is brought against the United States is it always under the FTCA, or can it have a "maritime nexus?" If so, is the defamation exception imported into the SIAA?

The core holding in *Feres* that an active member of the armed services may not sue the United States in tort for injuries incurred in active duty remains. See Blakey v. U.S.S. Iowa. 991 F.2d 148 (4th Cir.1993), affirming dismissal of an action under the S.I.A,A, for the wrongful death of a seaman killed by an explosion on the U.S.S. Iowa, on the authority of *Feres* and the action of his family under the FTCA for emotional distress caused by negligence in carrying out the investigation of the death, on the ground of the discretionary function exception.

It is to be noted that the statute of limitation under the SIAA and the PVA and the FTCA are all two years, compared with the tort statute of three years. For discussion of equitable tolling of these statutes, see Justice v. United States, 6 F.3d 1474, 1994 A.M.C. 317 (11th Cir.1993).

Jones & Laughlin Steel, Inc. v. Mon River Towing, Inc.

United States Court of Appeals, Third Circuit, 1985.
772 F.2d 62, 1986 A.M.C. 609.

■ GIBBONS, CIRCUIT JUDGE:

This appeal presents an issue of first impression for the Third Circuit: Whether in an admiralty suit against the United States under the Suits in Admiralty Act, service of process, timely within Rule 4 of the Federal Rules of Civil Procedure, is nevertheless untimely—and thus time-barred—because such service was not made on the local United States Attorney and the Attorney General "forthwith," as required by the Act. The district court concluded that service was untimely and dismissed the action for lack of subject matter jurisdiction. We reverse.

The Maxwell Lock and Dam, which is owned and operated by the Army Corps of Engineers, is situated on the Monongahela River in Fayette County, Pennsylvania. Jones and Laughlin Steel, Inc. (J & L), the appellant here, operates a preparation plant on the river that depends upon water transportation. On January 31, 1982, an empty barge owned by the

Mon River Towing Company (Mon River) broke free, floated down the river, and lodged in an open gate at the dam. To facilitate release of the barge, the Corps of Engineers lowered the river's water level, an action that J & L alleges interrupted its steel production and thereby caused it damage.

J & L notified the Corps of Engineers of its losses, and the Corps acknowledged the claim by mailing to J & L Standard Recovery Form 95. J & L completed and filed the form in a timely fashion. When the Corps did not agree to make payment, J & L, in order to comply with the applicable statute of limitations, filed a complaint against Mon River and the United States in the Federal District Court for the Western District of Pennsylvania on January 18, 1984. Jurisdiction was predicated on the general admiralty jurisdiction statute, 28 U.S.C. § 1333 (1982), on the Suits in Admiralty Act, 46 U.S.C. §§ 741–752 (1982), and on the Federal Tort Claims Act, 28 U.S.C. §§ 1346(b), 2671–2680 (1982).

A copy of the summons and complaint was served on Mon River on January 24, 1984, and by certified mail on the Corps of Engineers in Pittsburgh, Pennsylvania on January 19, 1984. The summons and complaint thus were served upon the United States agency having primary responsibility for investigating the claim one day after J & L filed its complaint.

On March 15, 1984, J & L's counsel received from an Assistant United States Attorney a letter contending that the January 19 service was defective because J & L had failed to comply with Rule 4(d)(4), which, when read in conjunction with Rule 4(j), requires service of process upon the Attorney General and the appropriate United States Attorney within 120 days of the filing of a complaint in an action against the United States. The letter advised that if such service was not made within ten days the United States would move to dismiss the action against it. The letter evidenced a belief that Rule 4(d)(4) specified the proper mode of service.

Well within the ten days specified in the March 15, 1984 letter, and well within the 120 days specified in Rule 4(j), J & L effected service upon the Attorney General of the United States and upon the United States Attorney. These officers obviously had notice of the filing and of the substance of the complaint by March 15, 1984. Both were personally served with additional process no later than March 20, 1984.

The United States subsequently changed its position with respect to the applicability of Rule 4. Contending that the sole basis of subject matter jurisdiction in the suit against the United States was the Suits in Admiralty Act, the government moved for the district court to dismiss the suit against it. It argued that, because service of process had not been accomplished in the manner and within the time provided by the Act, the court lacked subject matter jurisdiction over the case. The government did not contend that it was in any way prejudiced by the fact that the Corps of Engineers, rather than the United States Attorney, was served on January 19, 1984.

The district court, relying on authorities in the Court of Appeals for the Second and Ninth Circuits, dismissed the complaint against the United States, as well as Mon River's cross-claim against the United States, for lack of subject matter jurisdiction. This appeal followed.[1]

II

Congress waived the federal government's sovereign immunity to certain admiralty suits when it enacted the Suits in Admiralty Act in 1920. See Suits in Admiralty Act, Pub.L. No. 156, 41 Stat. 525 (1920)(codified at 46 U.S.C. §§ 741–752 (1982)). Section 1 of the Act prohibited in rem actions against merchant vessels or cargoes of the United States. See id. § 1, 41 Stat. at 525 (codified at 46 U.S.C. § 741 (1982)). Section 2 provided that

> in cases where if such vessel were privately owned or operated, or if such cargo were privately owned and possessed, a proceeding in admiralty could be maintained * * *, a libel in personam may be brought against the United States * * *, provided such vessel is employed as a merchant vessel or is a tug boat.

Id. § 2, 41 Stat. at 525–26 (codified at 46 U.S.C. § 742 (1982)).[2]

Plainly, Congress intended to put the United States, when operating merchant vessels, in the same position as were private owners. That is confirmed by section 3 of the Act, which provides that "[s]uch suits shall proceed and shall be heard and determined according to the principles of law and to the rules of practice obtaining in like cases between private parties." Id. § 3, 41 Stat. at 526 (codified at 46 U.S.C. § 743 (1982)).

Congress addressed service of process in the third and fourth sentences of section 2 of the Act. According to this portion of the Act,

> The libelant shall forthwith serve a copy of his libel on the United States Attorney for such district and mail a copy thereof by registered mail to the Attorney General of the United States, and shall file a sworn return of such service and mailing. Such service and mailing shall constitute valid service on the United States.

Id. § 2, 41 Stat. at 526 (codified at 42 U.S.C. § 742 (1982)).[3]

Before addressing the significance of this language to this case a preliminary observation is in order. The district court asserted, and rather puzzlingly the parties to this appeal appear to agree, that the exclusive

---

1. Both J & L and the United States contend that the order is appealable pursuant to 28 U.S.C. § 1291 (1982). However, since J & L's complaint against Mon River has not been disposed of, there is no final judgment as defined in Rule 54(b). But we have appellate jurisdiction under 28 U.S.C. § 1292(a)(3)(1982). See Bankers Trust Co. v. Bethlehem Steel Corp., 761 F.2d 943, 945 n. 1 (3d Cir.1985).

2. In 1960 Congress broadened the scope of this waiver by removing the restriction as to merchant vessels. See Act of Sept.

13, 1960, Pub.L. No. 86–770, § 3, 74 Stat. 912, 912 (codified at 46 U.S.C. § 742 (1982)).

3. When in 1926 Congress enacted the Public Vessels Act, which waived sovereign immunity even with respect to public as well as merchant vessels, it simply provided that "[s]uch suits shall be subject to and proceed in accordance with the provisions of [the Suits in Admiralty Act]." Public Vessels Act, Pub.L. No. 546, § 2, 43 Stat. 1112, 1112 (1925)(codified at 42 U.S.C. § 782 (1982)).

basis for tort claims sounding in admiralty is the Suits in Admiralty Act. Plainly that is not the case. When Congress enacted the Federal Tort Claims Act (FTCA), 28 U.S.C. §§ 1346(b), 2671–2680 (1982), in 1946, it included jurisdiction over maritime torts committed by the government, except for those torts for which a remedy was provided by either the Suits in Admiralty Act or the Public Vessels Act, 46 U.S.C. §§ 781–790 (1982). See Federal Tort Claims Act, Pub.L. No. 773, §§ 2674, 2680, 62 Stat. 869, 983, 984 (1948)(codified at 28 U.S.C. §§ 2674, 2680 (1982)). Because those acts waived the federal government's sovereign immunity to damages attributable only to its vessels, the FTCA, by waiving sovereign immunity for all other maritime torts, provided a cause for admiralty claims that did not involve vessels. The Supreme Court recognized this in Indian Towing Co. v. United States, 350 U.S. 61, 76 S.Ct. 122, 100 L.Ed. 48 (1955), in which it held that an admiralty action was maintainable under the FTCA for damages caused by the government's negligence in permitting a light-house to go dark. See id. at 69, 76 S.Ct. at 126; see also H. Baer, Admiralty Law of the Supreme Court 727 (3d ed. 1979).

J & L does not allege that a vessel of the United States caused it damage. A dam is not a vessel. Thus, since neither the Suits in Admiralty Act nor the Public Vessels Act may provide a cause of action in this case, J & L may be able to recover under the FTCA. In its complaint J & L invoked the FTCA, and, unquestionably, service of process was timely under that act. This alone would seem to require reversal of the district court's dismissal of the complaint. Yet, because the parties, for reasons known only to them, have not addressed the applicability of the FTCA, prudence suggests that we address the merits of the district court's interpretation of the Suits in Admiralty Act.

In ruling that it lacked subject matter jurisdiction over J & L's action, the district court relied on a series of cases in the Second and Ninth Circuits, all of which woodenly followed City of New York v. McAllister Brothers, Inc., 278 F.2d 708 (2d Cir.1960), a Second Circuit decision. In that case the court concluded that the service of process on the United States Attorney more than two months after the filing of a bill of libel, although such service was within the statute of limitations, was not service "forthwith" within the meaning of the Suits in Admiralty Act. It then held that the Act's requirement of forthwith service was jurisdictional and that the plaintiff's failure to comply with the requirement therefore de-prived the district court of subject matter jurisdiction over the suit. See id. at 710.

The Second Circuit subsequently affirmed *McAllister* in Battaglia v. United States, 303 F.2d 683 (2d Cir.), cert. denied, 371 U.S. 907, 83 S.Ct. 210, 9 L.Ed.2d 168 (1962). In *Battaglia* Judge Friendly wrote a concurring opinion demonstrating that *McAllister's* conclusion that the Act's forthwith requirement was jurisdictional could not reflect the intent of Congress. He nonetheless concurred because he felt bound by circuit precedent, which had consistently accepted that conclusion. See id. at 686–87 (Friendly, J., concurring).

When the Ninth Circuit first discussed this issue, it noted Judge Friendly's criticism. See Owens v. United States, 541 F.2d 1386, 1388 (9th Cir.1976), cert. denied, 430 U.S. 945, 97 S.Ct. 1580, 51 L.Ed.2d 792 (1977). But, in Kenyon v. United States, 676 F.2d 1229 (9th Cir.1981)(per curiam), the court adopted the *McAllister* interpretation of the Act, see id. at 1231 (describing compliance with the Act's forthwith requirement as "a condition precedent to the congressional waiver of the Government's sovereign immunity") and affirmed a district court's dismissal of a complaint in a case in which the plaintiff had served the Attorney General after the statute of limitation had run. Judge Boochever, like Judge Friendly, vigorously disputed the *McAllister* interpretation of the statute. However, he also felt bound by circuit precedent. See id. at 1231–32 (Boochever, J., concurring). Despite this criticism, the Ninth Circuit still follows *McAllister,* even in cases such as this, in which service on both the Attorney General and the United States Attorney is made within the statute of limitations but not "forthwith." See, e.g., Amella v. United States, 732 F.2d 711, 713 (9th Cir.1984).

Unlike Judge Friendly and Judge Boochever, we are not bound by precedent on this issue. We conclude that the Act's requirement of forthwith service of process is not jurisdictional but rather is procedural.

In light of this conclusion, recent developments concerning the Federal Rules of Civil Procedure are relevant to disposition of this case. On February 28, 1966, the Supreme Court adopted rules that unified, generally speaking, admiralty procedure with the Federal Rules of Civil Procedure. See Amendments to Rules of Civil Procedure for the United States District Courts, *reported in* 383 U.S. 1029 (1966). Thus Rule 4(d)(4) now governs the method of service of process in admiralty actions, as well as service of process on the United States in all civil cases to which it is a party. Rule 4(j), a recent addition to the rule, see Act of Jan. 12, 1983, Pub.L. No. 97– 462, § 2, 1982 U.S.Code Cong. & Ad.News (96 Stat.) 2527, 2528, requires that service of the summons and complaint be made "upon a defendant within 120 days after the filing of the complaint."

This congressional enactment of a uniform 120–day period for accomplishing service of process must be read in light of 28 U.S.C. § 2072 (1982), which states that "[a]ll laws in conflict with such rules shall be of no further force or effect after such rules have taken effect." Rule 4(j) therefore supersedes the Suits in Admiralty Act's requirement of forthwith service. Cf. C. Wright & A. Miller, Federal Practice and Procedure § 1106, at 412 (1969)("Rule 4(d)(4) supersedes prior statutes providing for service in suits against the United States to the extent they are inconsistent with it."). As noted above, J & L effected service upon the appropriate United States Attorney and the Attorney General well within 120 days of the date on which it filed its complaint.

III

The order dismissing J & L's complaint must be reversed. Rule 4 governs the service of process in this case. This is so for two independent reasons.

First, J & L's complaint relies on the FTCA and states a claim for a maritime tort falling under that act. Rule 4 governs service on the United States in FTCA cases. Second, even if J & L has a cause of action under the Suits in Admiralty Act, the 1966 amendments to the Admiralty Rules and the recently adopted Rule 4(j) supersede the method of service of process specified in the Act. See 28 U.S.C. § 2072 (1982). In either case, J & L satisfied the requirements of Rule 4.

The judgment of the district court will be reversed.

NOTE

In Amella v. United States, which in *Jones & Laughlin Steel* the Third Circuit declined to follow, the plaintiff's fishing vessel sank while in tow of the United States Coast Guard. Plaintiff filed an action on October 15, 1981, asserting negligence on the part of the Coast Guard. He mailed the process to the United States Attorney and to the Attorney General. The process reached the United States Attorney on October 19, and reached the Attorney General on October 21. The process sent to the United States Attorney contained a request for acknowledgement of receipt of process. Instead of acknowledging receipt of process the United States Attorney's Office wrote to the plaintiff early in December to inform him that proper service had not been made, as the statute and Rule 4(d)(4) of the Federal Rules of Civil Procedure require personal service upon the United States Attorney, and advised appellant's counsel to voluntarily dismiss and to refile the action, serving the Attorney General by registered mail and the United States Attorney by personal service. Instead of doing this counsel chose to make personal service of the original complaint upon the United States Attorney. This was accomplished on December 17, 63 days after the action was filed. The United States informed the plaintiff that it did not consider the 63 days to be forthwith and repeatedly urged counsel to dismiss, refile, and forthwith reserve the process on the Attorney General and the United States Attorney before the statute of limitations ran. The court of appeals affirmed a dismissal of the action, though Judge Kennedy observed, "It is a sad case."

Subsequent cases have generally followed *Amella*. Most recently, see Henderson v. United States, 51 F.3d 574, 1995 A.M.C. 1918 (5th Cir.1995), cert. granted ___ U.S. ___, 116 S.Ct. 493, 133 L.Ed.2d 419 (1995).

B.   NOTE ON SUITS AGAINST THE STATE

Suits against the state must take account of the Eleventh Amendment. Under the Eleventh Amendment, as construed, suits against a state eo nomine cannot be brought in a federal court without the consent of the state to be sued, except insofar as they are authorized by Act of Congress enacted under the Fourteenth Amendment enforcement clauses.

The Eleventh Amendment applies to suits in admiralty, and may not be avoided by proceeding in rem against the property of the state. See Ex parte New York, 256 U.S. 490, 41 S.Ct. 588, 65 L.Ed. 1057 (1921)(Ex parte New York No. 1); 256 U.S. 503, 41 S.Ct. 592, 65 L.Ed. 1063 (1921). (Ex Parte New York No. 2).

Nevertheless it has been held that by analogy to suits against state officers to test the legality of their conduct (the Ex Parte Young suit), an action in rem in admiralty can be brought, against the property, with ancillary process under Supplemental Rule C(5) directed to state officers in possession of the property, directing them to deliver it to the court. Florida Department of State v. Treasure Salvors, Inc., 458 U.S. 670, 102 S.Ct. 3304, 73 L.Ed.2d 1057 (1982). The Court indicated, however, that the district court erred in determining the ownership of the property as between the plaintiff and the state. On remand this was read by the court of appeals to sanction the delivery of the property to the plaintiff, and the entry of a judgment in rem confirming plaintiff's title against the world except for the State of Florida.

The First Circuit has read *Treasure Salvors* to proceed on the view that the State of Florida had no colorable claim to the artifacts recovered from the Atocha and lying on the ocean floor beyond the territorial limits of the state. See Maritime Underwater Surveys, Inc. v. Unidentified Wrecked and Abandoned Sailing Vessel, 717 F.2d 6, 1984 A.M.C. 249 (1st Cir.1983), affirming the dismissal of an action in rem to confirm the plaintiff's title to the remains of a vessel located half a mile from the coast of Massachusetts, when the process summoned in all states making a claim and was obviously pointed at adjudicating the claim of the state of Massachusetts.

In the sunken treasure cases it has been assumed that the state could waive its immunity and submit its rights to the federal courts. In some cases it has been held that waiver can be derived from conduct. See Parden v. Terminal Railway, 377 U.S. 184, 84 S.Ct. 1207, 12 L.Ed.2d 233 (1964), in which it was held that operating a railroad gave the state's consent to be sued under the F.E.L.A. Is there any doubt that the *Parden* principle covers suits under the Jones Act? But the courts have been reluctant to expand this exception. In Red Star Towing & Transp. Co. v. Department of Transp. of State of N.J., 423 F.2d 104, 1970 A.M.C. 11 (3d Cir.1970), refusing to apply the *Parden* case to the operation of an interstate bridge. A contrary view was expressed by the Fourth Circuit in The Bella Dan, 404 F.2d 1001, 1968 A.M.C. 900 (4th Cir.1968). But the decision in The Bella Dan was later repudiated. Faust v. South Carolina State Highway Dept., 721 F.2d 934, 1984 A.M.C. 851 (4th Cir.1983), cert. denied 467 U.S. 1226, 104 S.Ct. 2678, 81 L.Ed.2d 874 (1984). Note that the employees of states are specifically excluded from the coverage of the LHWCA. See Chapter 17 below.

Assuming that *Parden* carries with it the Jones Act, does a State by operating a vessel consent to be sued for breach of the warranty of seaworthiness? A state provide for suit against itself in its own courts without subjecting itself to suits in admiralty in the federal courts. See, e.g., Kennecott Copper Corp. v. State Tax Commission, 327 U.S. 573, 66 S.Ct. 745, 90 L.Ed. 862 (1946). Unless a waiver of immunity is explicitly applicable only to suits in the state courts, however, the federal courts have been reluctant to assume this intention. See, e.g., Platoro Ltd., Inc. v. Unidentified Remains, Etc., 695 F.2d 893, 1984 A.M.C. 2288 (5th Cir.1983), cert. denied 464 U.S. 818, 104 S.Ct. 77, 78 L.Ed.2d 89 (1983); Kiesel v. Florida Dept. of Nat. Resources, 479 F.2d 1261, 1973 A.M.C. 2133 (5th Cir.1973).

Note that in general the State can permit suits in its own courts without subjecting itself to suit in the federal courts. See, e.g., Kennecott Copper Corp. v. State Tax Commission, 327 U.S. 573, 66 S.Ct. 745, 90 L.Ed. 862 (1946).

C. NOTE ON SUITS AGAINST MUNICIPAL CORPORATIONS

The Eleventh Amendment does not protect municipal corporations and subdivisions of the State such as counties that may be sue and be sued against suit in the federal courts. Moor v. Alameda County, 411 U.S. 693, 93 S.Ct. 1785, 36 L.Ed.2d 596 (1973). Under state law they may not be liable for torts of their servants acting in a governmental capacity. In Workman v. Mayor of New York, 179 U.S. 552, 21 S.Ct. 212, 45 L.Ed. 314 (1900), a closely divided Court held that the City of New York could be sued in admiralty in personam in respect of a collision between a privately owned vessel and a city fire boat engaged at the time in fighting a fire. The Court conceded that since the fire boat was held by the city for use in performing its governmental functions it was not subject to an action in rem. In The West Point, 71 F.Supp. 206, 1946 A.M.C. 1532 (E.D.Va.1947) a ferry boat owned jointly by a city and a county was the subject of a suit in rem. How does one draw the line between property held for governmental use and that held for proprietary use?

Assuming that in an action against a municipality the maritime law is applicable, what is the maritime law of municipal liability in tort? See Petition of Alva S.S. Co., Ltd., 405 F.2d 962, 1969 A.M.C. 805 (2d Cir.1969), in which the Second Circuit indicated that there remains a midground in which the admiralty court might apply the law of the state. See also the same case at 616 F.2d 605, 1980 A.M.C. 857 (2d Cir.1980).

D. NOTE ON SUITS AGAINST FOREIGN STATES

Suits against foreign states are governed by chapter 97 of Title 28, added, effective January 1, 1977, by the Foreign Sovereign Immunities Act of 1976. Prior to the enactment of chapter 97, a foreign sovereign was almost completely immune to suit in the courts of the United States, absent its consent. Indeed no provision existed in either the statutes or the Rules for service of process. From a fairly early time, however, attempts were made, largely unsuccessful, to proceed in rem in the admiralty against vessels belonging to foreign sovereigns. See The Schooner Exchange v. McFaddon, 11 U.S. (7 Cranch) 116, 3 L.Ed. 287 (1812). As late as 1926 it was held that even a purely commercial vessel owned by a foreign sovereign was immune. Berizzi Bros. Co. v. The Pesaro, 271 U.S. 562, 46 S.Ct. 611, 70 L.Ed. 1088 (1926). In Ex Parte Republic of Peru, 318 U.S. 578, 63 S.Ct.

793, 87 L.Ed. 1014 (1943), however, the Court made it clear that the district court had jurisdiction of actions in rem against vessels belonging to a foreign sovereign and in each case, absent a recognition of the immunity by the Department of State, should proceed to determine whether the sovereign actually owned the vessel at the time of its seizure and whether it was of a character entitling it to immunity. In the particular case the Department of State had recognized the immunity and the Court held that the Department's determination was conclusive. In 1952, in the so-called "Tate Letter," the Department of State announced its intention to depart from the classic doctrine of sovereign immunity and follow the "restricted" doctrine followed by that time in many countries, under which "the immunity of the sovereign is recognized with regard to sovereign or public acts (*jure imperii*)of a state, but not with respect to private acts (*jure gestionis*)." In Alfred Dunhill of London v. Republic of Cuba, 425 U.S. 682, 96 S.Ct. 1854, 48 L.Ed.2d 301 (1976), while the case did not directly involve sovereign immunity, Mr. Justice White, speaking for three members of a five man majority, stated that "* * * it is fair to say that the 'restrictive theory' of sovereign immunity appears to be generally accepted as the prevailing law in this country," but no other justice joined in this part of the opinion. Thus the matter of immunity stood at the time of the enactment of the 1976 Act. The want of specific provision for service of process remained troublesome in initiating actions in personam even in cases in which there was contractual consent to be sued, e.g., actions to enforce an arbitration clause. There is an extended discussion of this matter by Judge Tenney in Transnational Maritime—Ta Peng S.S. Co. (Arb.), 1975 A.M.C. 1411 (S.D.N.Y.1975). The 1976 Act contains rather elaborate provisions for service of process. See 28 U.S.C.A. § 1608.

The Act is wholly preclusive of suits against foreign states, defined to include their political subdivisions, agencies, and instrumentalities, except such as are citizens of a State of the United States under 28 U.S.C.A. § 1332(c) or (d), or created under the laws of a third country, except as provided in 28 U.S.C.A. §§ 1605–1607. See 28 U.S.C.A. § 1604. Similarly § 1609 provides that the property of the sovereign is immune from attachment, arrest, and execution except as provided by the Act. The exceptions to such immunity are set forth in §§ 1610–1611.

Aside from expropriation cases, which of course might involve a vessel or cargo, the Act destroys the immunity of the foreign sovereign in two classes of cases that previously would have been, in given circumstances, within the jurisdiction of the district courts under § 1333. First, it withdraws the immunity "* * * in any case * * * in which the action is based upon the commercial activity carried on in the United States by the foreign state; or upon an act performed in the United States in connection with a commercial activity of the foreign state elsewhere; or upon an act outside the territory of the United States in connection with a commercial activity of a foreign state elsewhere and that act causes a direct effect in the United States." 28 U.S.C.A. § 1605(2). Second, it withdraws the immunity in cases "* * * not otherwise encompassed in paragraph (2) above, in which money damages are sought against a foreign state for personal injury or death, or damage to or loss of property, occurring in the United States and caused by the tortious act of any official or employee of that foreign state while acting within the scope of his office or employment * * *" "The United States" is defined to include "all territory and waters, continental or insular, subject to the jurisdiction of the United States." 28 U.S.C.A. § 1603(c). A commercial activity carried on in the United States by a foreign state is defined to include commercial activity having "substantial contact" with the United States. See 28 U.S.C.A. § 1603(d).

Given these definitions the Act appears to cover most admiralty claims arising out of shipping to and from the United States, does it not?

Of particular interest in the admiralty area is the fact that the Act absolutely precludes the knowing procurement of in rem process against a vessel or cargo of a foreign sovereign. Under 28 U.S.C.A. § 1605(b), if a claim is such that it would import a maritime lien, the plaintiff may initiate proceedings in the district in which the vessel or cargo is found by serving notice upon the person in whose possession the vessel or cargo is at the time, but thereupon must begin process in personam within days. If he knowingly has the vessel or cargo arrested, he loses the right to proceed in personam. If unwittingly he has the vessel or cargo arrested, he must begin process in personam within 10 days after he becomes aware of the interest of the foreign sovereign, or he will lose his right to proceed with the action. See 28 U.S.C.A. § 1605(b). Thus under the Act as under the Suits in Admiralty Act and the Public Vessels Act a suit to foreclose a maritime lien is converted into an action in personam against the sovereign.

Part II

Substantive Law of the Admiralty

CHAPTER 11

Sources of the Substantive Law

A. Sea Law as a Body of International Custom; The Codes and the Text Writers

Thompson v. The Catharina

United States District Court, District of Pennsylvania, 1795.
1 Pet.Adm. 104.

This was the case of a foreign ship, which came before the court on a claim for wages by her seamen, who by their contracts had engaged to return to the port from which they shipped. During the progress of the cause, the following opinion was given by the district judge.

"An objection is made, though not very seriously pressed, to my decision on a point, on which our own municipal laws are silent. This objection, however, obliges me to give my sentiments on the question '*What laws or rules shall direct or govern the decisions of maritime courts here, in points on which we have no regulations established by our own national legislature?*'"

There are, in most nations concerned in commerce, municipal and local laws relative to contracts with mariners, and other maritime covenants and agreements; though the great leading principles, or outlines, are in all nearly the same. On this account among others, I have avoided taking cognizance, as much as possible, of disputes in which foreign ships and seamen, are concerned. I have in general, left them to settle their differences before their own tribunals. On several occasions, I have seen it part of the contract, that the mariners should not sue in any other than their own courts;—and I consider such a contract lawful. It would be against law, and void, if it were, that the mariner should *not sue in any case;* or, that he should *not sue in the proper court, or courts of his country.* But where the voyage of a foreign ship ended here, or was broken up, and no treaty or compact designated the mode of proceeding, I have permitted suits to be prosecuted. In such cases, I have determined according to the laws of the country to which the ship belonged, if there existed any peculiar variance or difference from those generally prevailing. I have seldom found any very material difference in principle. The laws and customs of Spain,[1] relating to mariners, are more rigid than those of other nations, on similar points. Among other points of variance from other laws, those of Spain grant the master, a lien on the ship, for his wages. In the present case, the contract was in part, with mariners of the United States; and these seamen were to be discharged in an *American port.* I apply the authority of this court to the case of our own citizens. If by our own municipal laws, there are rules established, our courts are bound exclusively to follow them. But in cases where no such rules are instituted, we must resort to the regulations of other maritime countries, which have stood the test of time and experience, to direct our judgments, as rules of decision. We ought not to betray so much vanity, as to take it for granted, that we could establish more salutary and useful regulations than those which have, for ages, governed the most commercial and powerful nations, and led them to wealth and greatness.

The laws of the *Rhodians* were followed and adopted by the Romans, in their most prosperous state of commerce and power. Those in the celebrated *Consolato del mare,*[2] prevailing in the *Mediterranean,* and estab-

---

1. *Spain* cannot be said to have a general national code. She possesses a number of local collections and ordinances, operating in different maritime districts of that extensive kingdom.

1. Their civil law consists of a great number of particular laws compiled in the form of *codes.*

2. Each has particular titles. See Azuni, M.L. vol. i, pp. 404, 405.

3. The *Consolato del Mare,* is an adopted code, and governs in the Spanish courts of the *Mediterranean.*

4. The laws and ordinances of the *Consulate of Bilboa,* prevail on the *Spanish* coasts of the *Atlantic.*

5. The commerce of the *Indies* is regulated by a particular *code,* distinct from others. It is governed by, and subject to, the usages of the *Contractacion,* or *Consulate* of *Seville.* See Azuni, of whom, in addition to many more antient writers, I have made much use on those subjects.

2. *Il Consolato del Mare.* These are the most ancient, celebrated and authentic *sea laws,* after those of the *Rhodians, Greeks,* and *Romans.* Yet *Hubner,* because he found (as *Emerigon* alleges), a passage in them contradictory to a favorite dogma, vituperates and depreciates them, to his own disgrace, and not to their disparagement. As a respectable part of the laws of nations, they have always been received in the *English* courts of admiralty, and those of this country. Their origin is enveloped in obscurity, though attributed to several nations, as well as to the *Pisans,* to whom a modern author labours to ascribe them. Their influence, value and authority, have been appreciated by claims to their origin, set up by various

lished, in concert with other trading states and countries, by the *Venetians* and *Genoese,* in the periods of their naval power and commercial prosperity, are collections of, and improvements on, more ancient customs and laws. Of these, the *Amalfitan code* (the first and most respected of what are called, as they relate in point of time to those of the *Rhodians* and *Romans,* *"modern sea laws,"*)furnished the predominant and most generally received principles.[3] The laws of *Oleron,* occupy now a portion of the famous *Black book of the British admiralty,* which is consulted by all their courts on subjects of maritime and commercial controversy. These laws of Oleron were not entirely of British growth. They were compiled at first, as French authors assert, and from the face of them it would seem probable, by Queen Eleonora, Dutchess of Guienne, for her continental dominions, and afterwards improved and enlarged by her son Richard the First, of England, in no small degree from the maritime laws and customs, not only of his own country, but also from the laws and customs prevailing among the continental trading nations. Of these, the Saxons were, at an early period, the most conspicuous and practically intelligent in nautical affairs. They introduced into England their maritime knowledge, as they did some valuable principles of the common law. What was entitled, the Saxon shore, extended from the western parts of Denmark, to the western parts of France. The excellence and importance of these laws of Oleron, are evinced by a contest for their origin between two great nations, who have wisdom and liberality enough to follow them, be the fact of origin how it may. The maritime ordinances of *France* (where also the laws of Oleron, or Roll d'Oleron, are in force, and claimed, as of French origin) are very much grounded on the sea laws of other nations, mixed with their own. Those of *Louis the Fourteenth,* were compiled under the direction of the people of maritime countries. Those laws have prevailed in the countries occupying the coasts of the *Mediterranean,* and the neighbouring parts of southern *Europe,* for centuries. Although some special and local laws exist, in several national districts of that region, yet the *Consolato del Mare* is, to this day, the leading directrix, in their maritime jurisprudence, and naval affairs.

This body of maritime law is a *compilation* "of the best maritime laws then existing, comprising judicial proceedings, principles and decisions, settled by men of great experience and consummate prudence; who, having reason and custom for their guides, established these excellent regulations, concerning navigation and maritime contracts." It may, indeed, be called the *common law of maritime Europe,* where it is universally adopted and respected.

3. The city of *Amalfi* was situate in, what is now called, the province of *Salerno,* in the kingdom of *Naples.* Nothing great remains of it, but its celebrity for the most extensive commerce of its time, its immense wealth and magnificence, and its great weight in all questions of maritime concern. Like the *Rhodians,* the *Amalfitans* furnished principles for the codes of other maritime countries of southern *Europe.* These remain engrafted into the laws of other nations; though the *Amalfitan* code, or, as it is sometimes called, *"Table,"* is not preserved. To the *Amalfitans,* the invention of the mariner's compass, is ascribed. Dr. *Robertson* gives the discovery to a native of *Amalphi.* But no opinion about ancient transactions, seems to be at rest. *Azuni* says, the *French* invented—the *Amalfitans* improved—and the *Portuguese* perfected, this *compass,* in their discoveries of the New World. The *Chinese,* forestal the whole, in the antiquity of their claims, to this most eminent of all useful inventions. The *Pisans* and the *Amalfitans* share the credit of the discovery and preservation of the *Pandects* of Justinian, after their having been long buried in obscurity, during the barbarous ages.

great minister *Colbert,* from such materials, with local additions, suited to that country.   The laws of the *Hanse Towns,*[4] are nearly in substance the same with those called the laws of *Wisbuy,* and both are principally founded on those of Oleron.   The sea laws of *Spain* are, in no small degree, collections from those of other nations.   There is a striking similarity in the leading principles of all these laws.   So far from sound principles becoming obsolete, or injured by time, that it will be found, on careful investigation, that the oldest sea laws we know, those of the Rhodians[5], have furnished the outline and leading character of the whole.   With such examples before us, we need not hesitate to be guided by the rules and principles, established in the maritime laws of other countries.   As the ocean is common, it is proper and essentially convenient, that its laws should be also common to all who travel this *"high road of nations."*

I shall not contend with those who say, we ought to have a maritime code of our own, about the binding force of all these laws on us.   By the general laws of nations we certainly are bound.   These apply, most frequently, in the prize court; but there are many cases of *salvage, wreck,* & c. on the *Instance* or civil side of the court, which, necessarily must be determined under the general law.   The wisdom and experience, evidenced in the particular maritime institutions of other commercial countries, ought at least to be greatly respected.   If they serve only as faithful guides, and tried and long established rules of decision, in similar cases, they are of

4.   The laws of the *Hanse Towns* were published first in 1591, and reviewed in 1614, and posterior to those of *Wisbuy* or *Oleron.* The history of this commercial confederacy is well known.   Although in itself and its dependencies, it consisted of 62 cities, originally, it is now reduced to six, consisting of *Lubeck, Hamburgh, Dantzig, Bremen, Rostock,* and *Cologne.*   Its existence to this day, in any state of respectable combination, is a singular instance of survivorship over the ravages of time, the jealousies of powerful nations, and the exposure to interior danger and dissension; to which all multitudinous associations, whether national or individual, are constantly, often fatally, liable.

5.   In a note to the case of *Walton and others, vs. the Neptune,* it will appear, that *Azuni,* in his book on Maritime Law collects all the authorities for and against the authenticity of the fragments of *Rhodian Laws,* published by *Simon Scardius* and others, and continued to our time, in collections of *Sea Laws* as genuine.   *Azuni* declares them spurious.   But although, according to him, these may not be genuine, as to the text and *very words* (which other respectable writers either impliedly or positively assert they are) they contain many of the principles we see in other codes and works.   *Azuni* allows, agree-

ably to a cloud of authorities he could not controvert, that "the *Rhodian laws,* whatever may be the period of their publication, are the *fountain of maritime jurisprudence"* Azuni, M.L. vol. i, 277.   N. York edition 1806.

The *Rhodians* applied themselves exclusively to commerce, and avoided every idea of extension of territory.   Their fleet was so powerful, and their naval regulations so excellent, that they were courted by the most mighty nations of their time.   They held the empire of the sea, and by confining their strength and resources to maritime objects, they not only protected and extended their own commerce, but scoured the ocean of pirates who annoyed the trade of all countries. *Alexander the Great* treated them with marked distinction.   The *Romans* were their admirers, allies and friends.   These powerful Islanders entitled themselves to the friendship and esteem of other commercial nations, by aiding and protecting, and not by restraining similar pursuits.   Their superiority, in mercantile and naval talent and enterprise, gained them the admiration and respect of their contemporaries; when a spirit of monopoly, jealousy and plunder, would have handed them down to us, not to be imitated, but detested.

high and exemplary importance. It must be granted, that it is safer to follow them, than to trust entirely to the varying and *crooked line* of discretion.[6]

Where a reciprocity of decision, in certain cases, is necessary, the court of one country is often guided by the customs, laws, and decisions of the tribunals of another, in similar cases.

But the change in the form of our government has not abrogated all the laws, customs and principles of jurisprudence, we inherited from our ancestors; and possessed at the period of our becoming an independent nation. The people of these states, both individually and collectively, have the *Common law,*[7] in all cases, consistent with the change of our government, and the principles on which it is founded. They possess, in like manner, the *Maritime law,* which is part of the *Common law,* existing at the same period; and this is peculiarly within the cognizance of courts, invested with *maritime* jurisdiction; although it is referred to, *in all our courts on maritime* questions. It is, then, not to be disputed, on sound principles, that this court must be governed in its decisions, by the *maritime code* we possessed at the period before stated; as well as by the particular laws since established by our own government, or which may hereafter be enacted. These laws and the decisions under them, must be received as authorities, in this, and other courts of our country *"in all cases*

6. The foregoing enumeration of some of the *maritime codes,* is not intended to comprehend the *whole,* which would swell the account too extensively. It is given merely to shew, that the most renowned maritime nations always adopted the principles, when long tried and tested, of their predecessors, or contemporaries. *England* has not collected into a body, or code, the maritime laws by which she deems herself bound peculiarly, though she has enacted some laws, in addition to the laws or judgments of *Oleron;* such as the statute *De Mercatoribus,* the articles of *Quinsborough,* the acts relative to the powers of the admiralty, her navigation act, prize acts, & c. Her *law merchant,* and that part of it relating to *assurances* particularly, as well as *maritime law,* are chiefly collected in the decisions of her courts. These are founded on usages and established customs, as well of her own, as of all countries possessing respectable codes or principles of maritime law. When they are duly canvassed, and have stood the test of time and sound discussion, they become part of their common law, and settled as precedents of indisputable authority. In their courts, respectable foreign jurists and publicists are cited, and their reasonings, opinions and statements regarded, in the decision of maritime questions. Such has also been the practice in the courts, particularly of maritime jurisdiction, of our country.

Holland, though its existence depended on commerce, has never had any peculiar national code of maritime laws.—Possibly owing to the division of her territory into separate provinces.

7. The *feudal parts* of this law, and such as are inconsistent with the principles of our government are not, nor can they be, in force. Those who are best acquainted with its wise and just principles, as they relate to contracts, and the property, as well as the personal rights of individuals, admire the *Common law* as the venerable and solid bulwark of both liberty and property, *Statute laws* innovating upon it, have seldom been found, on experience, to be real improvements. Those who do not know the Common law suppose it to be every thing, *that it is not.* Its rules and principles are not arbitrary, but *fixed* and *settled* by the wisdom and decisions of the most respectable and intelligent sages, of both ancient and modern times. Many of the objections raised against it shew a want of acquaintance with its system and principles. Some of these objections are founded in innovation *made by statutes* altering or obscuring, the Common law. Others have nothing in either common or statute law to support them.

of admiralty and maritime jurisdiction," to which, by the constitution, it is declared *"the judicial power of the United States shall extend."* Nor shall I think myself warranted to exclude more modern expositions, or adjudged cases from being produced here. Whatever may, in strictness, be thought of their *binding* authority, I shall always be ready to hear the opinions of the learned and wise jurisprudents or judicial characters of any country. On subjects agitated in this court, often deeply affecting the property and reputation of the suitors, I am not so confident in my own judgment, as not to wish for all the lights and information, it may be in my power to obtain, from any respectable sources.

If, in any instance, the laws or the decisions under them, shall be found or deemed severe, or not suited to a particular exigency or course of trade, parties may mould their contracts at their will, according to circumstances, by mutual agreement and consent. Let the law be what it may, *Modus et conventio vincunt legem,* in all contracts, not radically against common justice, moral and political obligation, and those principles which the law will not suffer to be destroyed or perverted for private purposes.[8] If under a contract, by a casualty, a particular inconvenience arises from the general principles of the maritime law, the party must submit. He must consider what he loses or pays as a contribution to the great and general interests of commerce, or the predominant policy and advantage of his country.[9]

1 Molloy, de Jure Maritimo XIX–XXIV

(9th Ed. 1769).

* * *

The consideration of all which gives some Sparks of Encouragement to the writing [of] the ensuing Tract, especially when reflecting, that among all

8. The conditions of bonds, or considerations of promises, or agreements in contracts accounted illegal and void, are numerous and well known to lawyers. A contract cannot be legally binding which defeats its own object—such as that no suit shall be brought at all for a *bona fide* debt, agreed to be paid—a condition in a deed to do an act *malum in se,* as to beat, or kill a man, or commit any crime—Insurance on an illegal voyage—Bonds for general restraint of trade are void, though good where the condition is not to carry it on in any particular place—A bond to a third person that the obligor, a witness, shall not prosecute one confined for felony, perjury, & c. and many other instances which might be given.

A bond with impossible conditions is absolute, and the condition a nullity. An agreement or contract not to bring a suit to en-

force performance is, if made at the time, well. But if made posterior to the bond, contract or agreement, it amounts to a general release.

9. The cause, in which the foregoing opinion was delivered, was of a mixed character. Part of the complainants were foreigners; and bound to return home with the ship. Although with a view to sail out of our port, at our high wages, they endeavoured on pretext of deviation, to obtain their discharge; the cause was dismissed as to them—they were referred to their own courts for decision. Wages were decreed to two *American* seamen, who were by contract to be discharged here.

In the case of *Willendson vs.* the *Försöket, post,* the principles adopted by the court, relative to foreign seamen are further elucidated and explained.

Nations, there is a Common Law which governs the mighty Thing of
Navigation and Commerce; I had some Impulses more than ordinary to
induce me to the same, especially at a time when Navigation and Commerce were never (from the Erection by Divine Instinct of that mighty
Prototype, the Ark to the present Age) in greater Esteem than now, and by
which we have found vast and great Easements and Discharges from those
royal and just Rights and Dues, which now and of old were justly due to
those that governed this Empire; therefore ought by all Ways and Means
to be fortified and encouraged, be it by whatsoever Art, Science or Thing
that does in the least point out towards the same. Nor was it the wanting
in Thoughts to promote and incite the Professors of the Law, raising and
stirring up their Genius to the Advancement of the Law in this Point; and
though I believe many have wished that such a thing might be, yet none
that I can find have ever yet attempted the same: Nor is it possible, unless
those things which are by Law *constituted and known,* be rightly separated
from those that are natural; for natural Law is immutably and always the
same, therefore may easily be collected into Art: But things that come from
Constitution, because they often vary and change, and are divers in divers
Places, are put without Art, as other precepts of Laws positive or municipal; hence it was that the Constitutions and Laws of *Rhodes,* for their
Justice and Equity, got footing amongst the Romans, as well as amongst
other bordering People on the *Mediterranean,* * * *; yet when they, as
well as the *Romans,* became subject to Fate, they then remained only as
Examples of Justice and Reason for others to imitate and follow: An
obsequious Adorer of which was the great *Justinian,* who caused them to
be inserted into the Civil Law; and though they obtained a Place amongst
others of the Ancient *Romans* as well as the Modern, yet have they not all
received by Custom such a force as may make them Laws, but remain only
as they have the authority in Shew of Reason, which binds not always
alike, but varies according to Circumstances of Time, Place, State, Age, and
what other Conveniences or Inconveniences meet with it; nor have those
Laws, instituted at *Oleron,* obtained any other or greater Force than those
of *Rhodes* or Imperial, considered only from the Reason the which are not
become by any particular Custom or Constitution, but only esteemed and
valued by the Reasons found in them, and applied to the Case emergent.

'Tis true, that in *Rome,* and some other Parts of *Italy* and *Germany,*
and the Kingdom of *Portugal,* in all those Cases wherein the municipal
Ordinances of those Countries have failed in providing, the Imperial Laws
(if the Case be such as that it *non Tragua peccado,* or be not spiritual) is
there made of Force; but there is no other Nation, State or Republic can be
named, where any Part of the Body of those Imperial Laws hath obtained
the just Force of a Law, otherwise than as Custom hath particularly
induced it; and where no such settled Custom hath made it a Law, there it
hath Force only according to the Strength of Reason and Circumstance
joined with it, or as it shews the Opinion and Judgment of those that made
it, but not at all as if it had any commanding Power of Obedience * * *.
And since this Kingdom, as well as most others, being free from all
Subjection to the Empire, having a constituted and known Law of its own,

excludes all Imperial Power and Laws, otherwise than as Custom hath variously made some Admission, I applied myself to the Collection of such Matters, according to my inconsiderable Judgment, as are either constituted by the supreme Authority of the Three Estates, or that which hath in some measure obtained by continued Custom the Force of Law in reference to Matters Maritime, and of Commerce, as well in Cases publick as private.

By the first Part of which I thought it necessary, since Nature by Traffick hath made us all Kinsmen, to consider and examine upon what Grounds, and in what manner, Commerce was first procured and established, which is by the Laws of Leagues, Embassies, and the like, which is a thing fit to be known; so likewise of what may interrupt the same, and likewise of those that have any reference to Seafaring Causes in Matters Civil.

In the Prosecution of this Work, I have taken care to refer those things, which pertain to the Laws of Nature, unto Notions so certain, that no Man, without offering of Violence to himself, may deny them; and to ascertain the Truth of such, I have used the Testimonies of such Authority, as in my weak Judgment are of Credit to evince the same; and as to that Law, which we call the Law of Will, or Common Consent, or the Law of Nations, for that which cannot by sure Consequence be deduced out of sure Principles, and yet appears every where observed, must needs have its Rise from free Will and Consent, which is that which is called the *Law of Nations;* both which (as much as possible) hath been endeavoured to be kept asunder where the Matter hath required it. And for the Civil Law, I have ascertained the several Authorities which I have made use of, that is of the *Romans* into three sorts, the *Pandects,* the *Codes of Theodosius* and *Justinian, the Novel Constitutions,* and these most excellent *Jurisconsults,* that have by their Profoundness of Judgment illustrated the obscure Paths of the same Law; the third those most excellent Persons who joined Policy to Law, as *Grotius, Ralegh, Bacon, Selden,* and the like. Of other Pieces, that of Shardius, intituled, Leges Navales Rhodiorum, & Selectae Rhodiorum, Petrus Pekius the Zealander, Locinius, Vinius, that of Oleron collected by Garasias alias Ferrand and Cleriack. * * *

Story, Miscellaneous Writings (1835)

[Excerpts from a review by Joseph Story of a translation of a work entitled "Of the Laws of the Sea, etc." by Frederick J. Jacobsen and published in 1815. The review appeared in North American Review in 1818.]

As to the manuscript, found in the library of Francis Pithou, a celebrated jurist of the sixteenth century, which was published first at Basle in 1561 by Simon Scardius, and afterwards at Frankfort in 1596 by Marquardus Freer and Leunclavius, as genuine fragments of the Rhodian Laws, it may be observed, that, if their genuineness were completely established, they would not increase our veneration for the wisdom, or the commercial polity of the nation, whose name they bear. But the critical sagacity of modern civilians has not hesitated to reject these fragments, as more than apocryphal, as the fictions of some jurist, as late, at least, as the middle ages. It is true, that they have been silently quoted or directly asserted as genuine, by Cujas, by Selden, Godefroi, Vinnius, and other eminent jurists. Bynker-shoek first boldly denied their authenticity; the cautious and accomplished Heineccius followed in the same path; and their opinion has been generally adopted by the learned of the eighteenth century. Rejecting, therefore, as we do, the Fragments of the Rhodian Laws, as a modern fraud, there is nothing, which has reached us, except the codes and the compilations of the Roman emporers, which even wears the habiliments of ancient maritime jurisprudence, as embraced in the titles of the Corpus Juris Civilis. The circumstances under which the Roman codes were compiled, do, as we think, fully justify these remarks. * * * If this be a just view of the case, and we have no doubt it is, the Roman law, as collected by Justinian, contains in itself the substance of all the maritime law of all antiquity, improved by the philosophy and the learning of Roman jurisconsults. Yet, how narrow is the compass, within which the whole maritime law of Rome is compressed! It scarcely fills a half dozen short titles in the Pandects, and about as many in the Justinian Code, mixed up with matter properly appertaining to other subjects. * * * But the very circumstance, that so little is here to be found, after Rome had been for so many ages the mistress of the world in commerce and in arms, seems a decisive proof, that neither she, nor any more ancient nation, on the shores of the Mediterrane-an, had ever digested at any period a general system of maritime law.

The glory of having reduced the principles of maritime law to a science belongs to later times; * * *

Let it not, therefore, be imagined, that the maritime law, as acknowl-edged and practiced upon by the most enlightened nations of the present day, was produced *per saltum,* by the sudden start of a single mind or nation, generalizing and analyzing the principles at a single effort. Far different is the case. It arrived at its present comparative perfection by slow and cautious steps; by the gradual accumulations of distant times, and the contributions of various nations. Industry and patience first collected the scattered rays, emitting from a thousand points through the dim vista of past ages; and philosophy reflected them back with tenfold brilliancy and symmetry. If, indeed, a professional mind might indulge in a momentary enthusiasm, it would perceive, that in this process had been realized the enchantment and wonders of the Kaleidoscope, where broken and disjointed materials, however rude, are shaped into inexhaustible varieties of figures, all perfect in their order and harmonies, by the adjustment of reflected light under the guidance of philosophy.

* * *

The title of this curious collection, Consolato del Mare (Consulate of the Sea) is derived from the name consolato (consulate or consular court) which was, by almost all of the commercial nations of the Mediterranean, given to their maritime courts. The value of this collection has been differently estimated in modern times by learned men. Hubner, with his usual petulence has treated it as an ill chosen mass of maritime usages and positive ordinances of the middle ages, or of times very little enlightened, which are now obsolete and of no authority. Bynkershoek, in his usual bold and determined manner, treats it with as little ceremony. After approving of its decision in a particular case, he adds, "Vellem omnia, quae in illa farragini legum nauticarum reperiuntur, aeque proba et recta essent, sed non omnia ibi sunt tam bonae frugis." To these opinions we justly oppose the discreet yet liberal praise of Casaregis, Emérigon, Valin, Vinnius, and Lubeck. But in our judgment it is not necessary to resort to *testimonia eruditorum*. The fact, that the substance of its regulations was eagerly embraced, and immediately incorporated into the usages and ordinances of all the maritime nations of the continent, pronounces an eulogy on its merits, which no formal vindication can surpass. Emérigon very justly states, that its decisions have united the suffrages of all nations; and it has furnished ample materials for the maritime ordinances of France of 1681, an ordinance which has immortalized the ministry of Louis XIV., and which, perhaps, more than the maritime code of any other nation, deserves the praise of philosophic jurists. Nay, more, the Consolato del Mare contains the rudiments of the law of prize, as it is presently administered; and its authority has, perhaps, weighed more than any other, in settling the great controversy of our times, relative to the question, whether free ships make free goods. England, in asserting the negative, (as we think with vast force of reasoning,) has reposed on this venerable monument, as affording the surest proof of the antiquity and the general recognition of the rule, which she has so justly sought to establish, and which has stood approved to the good sense of the three greatest civilians of modern times, Grotius, Bynkershoek, and Heineccius.

* * *

1 Hay & Marriott XI
(1801).

* * * The British cruizers covered the ocean: the instructions of the British Government were peremptory, and scarcely a neutral ship left a neutral or enemy's port without having the property of French subjects on board openly, or covered. The activity of cruizers made them bold in a praedatory war: merchants of all nations interested directly or indirectly, were loud in their clamours to the ministers of their respective countries; all were animated with the desire of making themselves of consequence, or gaining some profit. The doctrine of "free ship, free goods," and treaties, were ill understood or overlooked. "Free ship, free goods," is a short pithy sentence; but the application is from misapplication of the sense, or from taking for granted that the proposition is true universally; for all neutral ships are not free by the law and usage of nations, but only those that are privileged specifically by treaties; and nations although pretending to be non-belligerents, must make themselves actual parties in war when they assist one of the belligerents. It can never be so much for their interest as to be simple carriers: what would be the fate of neutral waggons attempting to go through the lines and posts of a belligerent power? The British government was alarmed with a fear that all the northern maritime powers would form a confederacy, and enforce a free commerce, which would render a naval war and ascendancy of the fleets and armaments of Great Britain not only of no avail, but even give a preponderancy to those of France. Our own merchants, particularly the insurers, felt with the enemies of England. The question was acutely debated in the committee of the States General of Holland, whether they should not declare war against England. The forwardest of the foreign courts upon this occasion was that of Prussia, scarcely with a ship or a port, its flag was to be held up to protect the world.

The elector of Brandenburg had a personal dislike to the elector of Hanover and King of England. A low man, with a low establishment, was sent hither in a diplomatic character, to shew contempt, to affront, and complain. The common lawyers of England, who are the great counsellors of its government, but who knew little of the Admiralty Court and the law of nations, arrogated all power and knowledge to themselves, but were, when called upon, unable to answer the memorial of the Prussian minister, Monr Michel. To Sir George Lee, the archbishop's Judge of the Prerogative Court, and Dr. Paul, the Advocate General of the king, two eminent civilians; were added two great common lawyers, the Attorney General, Sir Dudley Ryder, and the Solicitor General, Mr. Murray: who all of them drew up an answer and signed it. The latter, from the place of his birth, had a predilection for the imperial or civil law, which he quoted on many occasions, and piqued himself on a superior knowledge: he took to himself the principal merit of this performance, which was ushered into the world with great eclat, and by high authority.

Notwithstanding all this, there is reason to believe, that the king of Prussia having threatened to invade Hanover, the whole matter was put to sleep by our Government privately restoring the value of the ships and cargoes, protected, as it was insisted, by the Prussian flag, although the property of the enemies of England.

The pertinacity of the king of Prussia was unfortunately increased by Lord Grenville, favorite of King George II, and the great advisor of his councils, having used a lively expression, "that he never heard of the flag of Berlin before, and should as soon have expected to have heard of the flag of Frankfort."

The same notions of "free ship, free goods," were again revived in the last war by the late Empress of Russia, not understanding them, and putting herself at the head of what was called the armed neutrality. One Carlo Beerens, a Livonian, merchant, lawyer, and politician, in a furious memorial informed the Empress, that he and others of her subjects were greatly obstructed in their commerce by the English cruizers; that England could not command a ball of packthread without her, and that she had nothing to do but speak the word. The immense profit of the ballance of trade between Great Britain and Russia, was never stated or considered. To her resentment expressed too hastily on this occasion, the British government thought proper to submit, and a quantity of sail-cloth, sufficient to have fitted out the whole Spanish fleet from Ferrol and Cadiz, was restored upon reversal of the decree of condemnation in consequence of an appeal, and the captor absolutely condemned in costs and damages. But the effect of the sentence in the first instance was the stopping the Spanish fleet. The idea of government was, that this great lady must not be put out of humour, and that in granting so much to the Russian flag for the moment, there was nothing very material granted in fact, because it was notorious that the Russians have but few merchant or carrier ships of their own, perhaps not half a dozen; and that the true doctrine of the law of nations is, *that the ship confers the privilege on the flag, and not the flag upon the ship;* and lastly with respect to the armed neutrality, Denmark, Sweden, & c. must be judged in cases of capture by their own separate and several treaties, as well as they would be guided by their own particular interests.

* * *

It is by the principle, and not by the precedent of the decree matters should be adjudged * * * One should suppose that justice was one of the simplest ideas in nature, but how complicated must it appear when we travel from the *tractus tractatuum* down to the latest publications on all sorts of law? Little ought to be our surprise, when we find that German and Dutch *"magnificent"* professors as they call themselves, and who in general are only schoolmasters, are the numerous and principal writers on the laws ecclesiastical, civil, and of nature, and of nations. A Bynkershoek, a Huberus, a Vattel, a Hubner, a Schlegel, a Busch, a Heineccius, a Grotius, or Pufendorf are men who have written to serve a particular private personal, or otherwise some public political purpose. Had the wife of Grotius published her opinion upon some certain subjects, said a reader of lectures upon the Roman and civil law in one of our own universities, she would have been of a different opinion. It is well known that in the foreign universities that whosoever takes a degree (and degrees are mostly taken in Law) print and publish Theses which they make or are made for them. Nothing can be more ridiculous, when it is as notorious that a thesis may be bought, as well as burghers briefs and false passes, for one or a few rix-dollars, than to see such things dressed up with all the professional pendantry of learning, and the authors as theatrically antiquated as if they appeared in trunk hose, jackboots, slashed doublets, great slouched hats and feathers, ruffs or bands. Well might a late fighting and writing monarch exclaim, "O droit de gens, comment ten etude est inutil," to which at the same time all sovereign princes appeal, and most violate it, as if they wished to be judged and approved by the rational and humane part of mankind at the very moment they are guilty of sophistry, cruelty, and deceit, and shew how much they despise all other human beings over whom a providential birth and generation have placed them.

From this reflection, must be excepted the Sovereign of this country, as the most equitable on earth, and who may well say, what was once said by a monarch of France, "That if truth and justice fled from all the rest of the world, they ought to find a refuge in the breast of princes."

Swinney v. Tinker

Marsden 139 (1774).

Court (1).—In this case a suit is brought for four guineas as the wages due for the run from Gainsborough to London and back. It is admitted a dispute arose at London respecting the duty to be done on the delivery of the cargo. A deputy fruit meter was on board to weigh the potatoes, on whom that duty lies. The carriage of the fruit from the ship to the craft and thence on shore is admitted to be the business of the owners. The dispute arises on the question, who is bound to shovel, fill, and hoist the potatoes out of the hold? The men insist that they are not obliged to do it without additional pay of 6d. per ton or 2s. per day. This ship had eighty tons of potatoes; 40s. is a heavy load on the freight, if due. It is in evidence the owners sometimes send men to shovel the fruit, to prevent it being carelessly cut. It is highly probable this duty lies on the master of the ship. If so, it lies on the seamen, whom he desires to do the duty of the ship. In the common course of the trade the owners of the cargo release the crew and send other men. But if the master is obliged under the general contract, the mariners are bound equally. The witnesses all speak to it as a duty on the mariners, and so understood on the general hiring at Gainsborough. Nothing is said as to the lading, what the mariners are obliged to do. The cause is not fully instructed. The evidence of the mariners in respect to the custom of paying a specific sum is not to be relied on, as the witnesses who depose thereto, though competent, are interested. It is not like the evidence as to navigating the ship, because there no other witnesses can be had; in this case there may. It appears to me the mariners are not entitled to wages, unless they perform the voyage for which they are hired, and the services attending it. The men do not return to Gainsborough on board the vessel. The master refusing them victuals, the men go on shore. They ask the master whether he will or has discharged them. He answers in the negative. In the coal and corn trade the custom is established, that the mariners have nothing further to do when they arrive in the river at the ship's moorings. The coalheavers then supply their place in unloading the cargo. In this trade I am far from being satisfied that the Captain must hire other men or pay the mariners this exorbitant demand. They have usually been satisfied with a gratuity, and have not made a demand from the master. The consignees of the cargo often employ other persons in the business to prevent the fruit being cut by the shovels and negligence of the crew. I cannot say the mariners shall obtain judgment on the evidence of their interested parties. Nor am I sufficiently instructed to say the non-compliance of the mariners with the Captain's request shall operate as forfeiture of wages. There is a sort of admission that something more should be given than the common wages for doing the duty. I will not say the mariner is obliged to do it. I would much less establish a demand on the master. The sailors shall be entitled to their wages for the duty done. No tender has been made. The master should have discharged the men for refusing to do their duty. As I am averse to establishing the custom, so I should be unwilling to deny them any consideration. I pronounce therefore for two guineas being due to the plaintiff. It must be very easy in the future to set the matter right by a special agreement. I shall consider about costs, but must give some, as no tender was made, and I have pronounced for two guineas being due. [I] therefore desire the costs may be moderately taxed.

NOTE

Obviously Story and Marriott have been selected as representative of extremes in pendantry on the one hand and anti-intellectualism on the other. Perhaps Judge Peters' solicitation of "all the lights and information, it may be in my power to obtain, from any respectable sources" represents a fair average. There were no printed opinions of cases adjudicated in the High Court of the Admiralty until 1801, so the ancient codes, the Black Book of the Admiralty, the text writers, and the exigencies of the case at hand were mixed in the early decisions. This was equally true of the early printed decisions in England. See, e.g., The Aquila, 1 C.Rob. 37 (1798). This case deals with the salvage of a derelict. It was argued to the court that the salvors were entitled to a moiety of the property. Sir William Scott observed:

"But another question is started: whether, although the crown is allowed to have exclusive right of property, in cases where no owner appears, there is not an universal rule that gives to the finder, in all cases alike, without regard to the degrees of merit or service, one moiety of the thing preserved? We should certainly not be very desirous to find such a rule; nor could we wish to reduce to one dead level the various degrees of merit that perpetually occur, according to the particular circumstances of each separate case.—If there was such a rule, however, it would be my duty to obey it; but I can find no such rule in the general maritime law: I have looked into the books on this subject; in the *Consolato del Mare,* and in other books, I find no such rule: I find no such rule established by the practice of other *European* nations.

"By the citations which have been made from the Black Book of the Admiralty, it does indeed appear that anciently the division which usually took place between the Lord High Admiral and the finder of derelict, was by moieties; and the papers to which my attention has been called by Dr. Swabey, do show something of a continuance of such rule down to the time of *Charles* II.—It appears from those papers, that the whole was condemned as of right to the king, and half was afterwards given to the finder. There still remains some ambiguity, however, in what manner this share was given; whether in conformity to a general rule then conceived to be binding, may be doubted: though I am inclined to think it was.

"In later cases, however, I find no observance of any such rule. In 1777, there was a case of considerable merit, in which Sir *G. Hay* gave only a third. In 1779, there was another case of a bag of money found in the sea, of which three eighths were given. A case has been cited by the Advocate of the Admiralty, in which Sir *W. Wynne,* then King's Advocate, and the then Advocate of the Admiralty, recommended it to the crown to allow a moiety; but I do not understand that opinion to have been given in conformity to any positive or prevailing rule, but from the particular circumstances of the case, and imply therefore a denial of the existence of any express rule at that time.— The notes of Sir *E. Simpson,* which I have before cited, prove that he knew of no such rule; for after saying, 'In such a case it becomes a perquisite of Admiralty;' had there been such a rule, he would naturally have added: not, as the words now stand, *'The salvor must be satisfied for their expense and trouble;'* but the salvors shall 'take a moiety:' he therefore had no knowledge of such a rule.

"On a view of the whole argument, and looking at the latest practice of these courts, I am of the opinion that there is no such rule: it may have existed, and become obsolete.   Many alterations in practice we know have taken place since the compilation of the Black Book of the Admiralty; and perhaps there may have been a change on this point.   If such a rule ever existed, it is become obsolete; and as there is nothing reasonable in the principle, that should induce us to wish for its revival, I shall pronounce the salvors not to be *de jure* entitled to a moiety: but applying the discretion of the Court to the circumstances of this case, I shall decree to them two-fifths of the cargo saved."

Note that in Swinney v. Tinker, the matter of extra compensation for loading and unloading is covered by one of the ancient codes.   Art V. of the Laws of Wisbuy provides, "The mariners shall have three deniers a last for loading, and three for unloading, which is to be reckoned only as their wages for guindage or hoisting." There is no reference to this fact in the report of the case.   The custom that becomes important is the custom in the potato trade in England, and the analogy drawn is not to the universal and immemorial custom of nations, but to the coal trade in England.

B.   THE COMMON LAW AS A SOURCE OF MARITIME SUBSTANTIVE LAW

The Sea Gull

United States Circuit Court, Maryland, 1865.
Chase C.C.Rep. 145, 21 F.Cas. 909.

■ CHASE, C.J.—The libel in this case seeks redress for injuries to the wife of the libellant, terminating in her death.   It alleges that the wrongs complained of were occasioned by the collision of the steamer Sea Gull with the steamer Leary, and that the collision occurred through the fault of the Sea Gull.

The owners of the Sea Gull responded to the libel by a plea, that the matters alleged were not within the cognizance of the court; that the libellant had no right to sue for the alleged wrong, and the court had no jurisdiction in the premises; and that if it had jurisdiction, the proceedings should be *in personam,* and not *in rem.*

Upon the hearing the libel was dismissed by the District Court, and the cause comes here by appeal.

* * *

The *objection to jurisdiction,* made by the plea, rests upon the propositions that a husband can not recover for injuries to his wife, after her death. It was urged in support [of] this objection that *personal actions die with the person.* But this maxim does not seem to apply to the case before us. The suit is not prosecuted by an administrator, but by the husband of the deceased, and redress is sought for damages to him through injuries to her.

There are cases, indeed, in which it has been held that in a suit at law, no redress can be had by the surviving representative for injuries occasioned by the death of one through the wrong of another; but these are all common-law cases, and the common law has its peculiar rules in relation to this subject, traceable to the feudal system and its forfeitures.

The case of Baker v. Boardman [sic] (1 Campbell, 493) is the leading English decision, followed in Massachusetts by the case of Carey v. Berkshire R.R. Co. (1 Cushing, 475). The English Parliament has corrected the English law, and supplied a remedy. The Massachusetts legislature has done the same thing for the Massachusetts law. In other states the English precedent has not been followed. In Ford v. Monroe (20 Wendell, 210), a father recovered damages for the death of his son, killed by the negligence of the defendant's servants; and in James v. Christy (18 Missouri, 162), an action was maintained against the owner of a boat, brought by a father to recover damages for the death of his son, occasioned by a defect in the machinery. These latter authorities were approved by Judge Sprague, in the case of Cutting v. Seabury. He observes that "the weight of authority in common-law courts seems to be against the action, but natural equity and the general principles of law are in favor of it." He adds: "It is not controverted that if a father be willfully and wrongfully deprived of the services, society, and control of his minor son, he may maintain an action against the wrong-doer if the son survive. Why, then, if the same wrong be done and aggravated by the death of the child, should his right of action be lost?" It is difficult to answer this question, and certainly it better becomes the humane and liberal character of proceedings in admiralty to give than to withhold the remedy, when not required to withhold it by established and inflexible rules.

These considerations require that the plea be overruled.

* * *

A decree will be entered in favor of the libellant for twenty-one hundred dollars.

Decree entered accordingly.

NOTE

The Sea Gull was repudiated by the Supreme Court in The Harrisburg, 119 U.S. 199, 7 S.Ct. 140, 30 L.Ed. 358 (1886). It is to be noted that during the intervening years one of the New York cases on which Mr. Justice Chase rested his decision in The Sea Gull had been substantially overruled and the doctrine of Baker v. Bolton generally accepted in the state courts in common law litigation. Further, in Mobile

Life Insurance Co. v. Brame, 95 U.S. (5 Otto) 754, 24 L.Ed. 580 (1877), the Supreme Court had accepted it as a part of the federal common law. The Court in The Harrisburg read The Sea Gull as based primarily on Mr. Justice Chase's reading of the then current state of the law, rather than a pronouncement of a difference between the land law and the sea law. See Lucas, Flood Tide, Some Irrelevant History of the Admiralty, 1964 Sup.Ct.Rev. 249, 270. It must be noted that these decisions were made prior to the decision in Erie v. Tomkins, *vide* the statement in Kalleck v. Deering, reproduced at p. 368, infra, "But it is hardly to be expected that different views of the substantive law should be enforced by the same judges sitting in different courts." In the post-*Erie* period, of course, the problem is a different one. Since the common law to be applied is the law of the states, there is no reason to suppose that the Supreme Court will agree with the resolution of the substantive rule evolving in the state courts, and since the parallel development of the law in admiralty and maritime cases remains a pocket of federal "common law," it may or may not follow the common law development. See, e.g., Kermarec v. Compagnie Generale Transatlantique, reproduced at p. 873, infra, in which it was held that the common law status distinctions in determining the duty of care imposed upon the owner of premises upon which injury occurs are not applicable in the maritime law. The question to be asked is whether, but for *Erie,* these distinctions would be followed by the Supreme Court in diversity cases. Is there anything particular about admiralty cases that commends the *Kermarec* rule as proper in wet torts that would not be equally convincing in the case of dry torts?

DeLoach v. Companhia de Navegacao Lloyd Brasileiro

United States Court of Appeals, Third Circuit, 1986.
782 F.2d 438.

■ WEIS, CIRCUIT JUDGE.

In these cases the minor plaintiff seeks damages for the loss of companionship and guidance of his father who was injured in the course of his employment as a longshoreman. The district court denied the claims, finding them unsupported by authoritative precedent in either maritime or common law. We will affirm.

The two separate suits filed by the minor plaintiff were dismissed under Fed.R.Civ.P. 12(b)(6) for failure to state a claim. These appeals followed.

The plaintiff's father, Glen M. DeLoach, sustained severe injury to his shoulder when he was struck by a crate that fell while being lifted by a crane owned and leased by the defendant Markim Crane Rental. The accident occurred on January 6, 1984 in the port of Philadelphia aboard a ship owned and operated by the defendant, Companhia de Navegacao Lloyd Brasileiro.

Glen DeLoach and his wife filed suits against both defendants seeking damages for his personal injuries and his spouse's loss of consortium. The minor plaintiff, age 5, filed separate suits against each defendant. He asserted claims for loss of parental consortium, care, love, companionship, playtime, guidance, educational help, financial and nonfinancial support, services, aid and comfort of his father, and mental distress occasioned by his father's disability.

In passing on the minor plaintiff's claim against the shipowner, the court found that the Longshoremen's and Harbor Workers' Compensation Act, 33 U.S.C. §§ 901, et seq., provided no cause of action for loss of parental consortium. The district judge then examined the general maritime law. Finding no authoritative precedent in that area, he looked to the common law where the overwhelming majority of states have rejected similar claims by children of injured parents. Persuaded by the state courts' reasoning, the district court concluded that the plaintiff's claim against the ship owner was not cognizable in maritime law.

The child's claim for mental distress was denied as well. The minor plaintiff had not witnessed the accident, nor was he near the scene; therefore, even under state court decisions allowing recovery for emotional shock by a bystander, the plaintiff's claim was not viable. The district court made similar rulings on both counts of the suit against the crane owner.

I

On appeal, plaintiff does not dispute the district court's conclusion that he cannot recover against the ship owner under the Longshoremen's and Harbor Workers' Act; therefore, the focus of our inquiry is on general maritime law. We are urged to construe maritime law in a humanitarian fashion and follow the growing minority of state courts which allow claims for deprivation of parental consortium.

Plaintiff relies heavily on Sea–Land Services, Inc. v. Gaudet, 414 U.S. 573, 94 S.Ct. 806, 39 L.Ed.2d 9 (1974). In that case, the Court permitted the widow of a longshoreman who had died from his injuries to maintain a maritime wrongful death action and recover for loss of consortium, despite the fact that during his lifetime the decedent had settled his own claim for personal injuries.

The Court further extended general maritime law in American Export Lines, Inc. v. Alvez, 446 U.S. 274, 100 S.Ct. 1673, 64 L.Ed.2d 284 (1980) by allowing the wife of an injured longshoreman to recover damages for the loss of his society. The Court concluded that the deprivation suffered by a longshoreman's spouse is compensable under general maritime law whether his injuries are fatal or nonfatal, notwithstanding that such damages are precluded by the Death on the High Seas Act and the Jones Act. In coming to that decision, the Court relied on the holdings of the vast majority of states that a spouse could recover for loss of society.

The Supreme Court has not addressed the rights asserted by the minor plaintiff here, but in Madore v. Ingram Tank Ships, Inc., 732 F.2d 475, 479 (5th Cir.1984), a court of appeals rejected recovery for loss of parental consortium in a Jones Act case. Finding no authorization in the statute, the court relied on the "overwhelming majority of the courts" that had denied such claims under state tort law. However, a district court, influenced by a state statute authorizing such recovery, did entertain children's suits for loss of parental services under general maritime law in Kelly v. T.L. James Co., Inc., 603 F.Supp. 390 (W.D.La.1985).

In this case the district court recognized that where the statutory or general maritime law does not provide clear precedent, courts may look to the prevailing common law. American Export Lines, Inc. v. Alvez, 446 U.S. 274, 100 S.Ct. 1673, 64 L.Ed.2d 284 (1980). Until 1980 the state courts were unanimous in denying societal claims by children, but in that year Massachusetts abandoned its earlier position and allowed recovery in Ferriter v. Daniel O'Connell's Sons, Inc., 381 Mass. 507, 413 N.E.2d 690 (1980). In the next few years five other states followed that lead: Michigan, Iowa, Wisconsin, Washington, and Vermont.[1]

The reasoning of those cases, however, has not convinced other courts that have confronted the issue since 1980. Florida, New York, Oregon, Georgia, North Dakota, Minnesota, Texas, and Illinois, among others,[2] continue to deny recovery, adhering to the rule previously announced by the courts in some twenty states. The Restatement (Second) of Torts § 707(a) as revised in 1969, also did not recognize liability for the loss suffered by children of negligently injured parents. See Annot. 11 A.L.R.4th 549 (1982).[3]

Although common law and statutory differences among the states have played a role in the results reached in various cases, major reasons cited both for and against recognition of the cause of action fall into frequently repeated patterns.

Courts favoring the new claim stress the similarity to spousal consortium, the inconsistency of recognizing loss of services of a deceased parent

1. See Berger v. Weber, 411 Mich. 1, 303 N.W.2d 424 (Mich.1981); Weitl v. Moes, 311 N.W.2d 259 (Iowa 1981), overruled in part, Audubon–Exira Ready Mix, Inc. v. Illinois Central Gulf R.R. Co., 335 N.W.2d 148 (Iowa 1983)(claim permitted statutorily, not under Weitl's common law theory); Theama v. City of Kenosha, 117 Wis.2d 508, 344 N.W.2d 513 (Wis.1984); Ueland v. Reynolds Metals Co., 103 Wash.2d 131, 691 P.2d 190 (Wash.1984); Hay v. Medical Center Hospital of Vermont, 145 Vt. 533, 496 A.2d 939 (1985).

2. See Zorzos v. Rosen, 467 So.2d 305 (Fla.1985); DeAngelis v. Lutheran Medical Center, 84 A.D.2d 17, 445 N.Y.S.2d 188 (1981), aff'd 58 N.Y.2d 1053, 462 N.Y.S.2d 626, 449 N.E.2d 406 (1983); Norwest v. Presbyterian Intercommunity Hospital, 293 Or. 543, 652 P.2d 318 (1982); W.J. Bremer Co., Inc. v. Graham, 169 Ga.App. 115, 312 S.E.2d 806 (1983); Morgel v. Winger, 290 N.W.2d 266 (N.D.1980); Salin v. Kloempken, 322 N.W.2d 736 (Minn.1982); Bennight v. West-

ern Auto Supply Co., 670 S.W.2d 373 (Tex. App.1984); Mueller v. Hellrung Constr. Co., 107 Ill.App.3d 337, 63 Ill.Dec. 140, 437 N.E.2d 789 (1982).

3. Scholarly comment, both before and after 1980, generally favored the extension of liability in such circumstances. See, e.g., Love, Tortious Interference with the Parent–Child Relationship: Loss of an Injured Person's Society and Companionship, 51 Ind.L.J. 590 (1976); Note, The Child's Right to Sue for Loss of a Parent's Love, Care, and Companionship Caused by Tortious Injury to the Parent, 56 B.U.L.Rev. 722 (1976); Note, The Child's Claim for Loss of Consortium Damages: A Logical and Sympathetic Appeal, 13 San.Diego L.Rev. 231 (1975); Cooney & Conway, The Child's Right to Parental Consortium, 14 J.Mar.L.Rev. 341 (1981). The foregoing is but a partial listing of the extensive bibliography on the issue. See also W. Prosser & W. Page Keeton, The Law Of Torts § 125 at 935 (5th ed. 1984).

under wrongful death statutes but not permitting recovery when an injured parent survives, and an assumed need to compensate for an acknowledged loss to the children.

Those courts brush aside such countervailing considerations as increased litigation and insurance costs, finding them speculative and insufficient to prevent creation of a new cause of action. They also point out that courts presently award monetary damages for such intangibles as emotional distress as well as pain and suffering. Declining to await legislative action, the courts that have adopted the new theory of recovery have relied on their duty, as they perceive it, to mold the common law to meet society's needs.

The courts refusing to recognize the children's claims question the advisability of equating parental society with a monetary value. In addition, they point to the difficulties inherent in defining the limits of the new right (e.g., whether it would apply only to minor children, whether it would extend to those standing *in loco parentis*), and note the probable increased insurance costs and added burden on the courts. A number of the courts also believe that this issue, essentially one of policy, should be resolved by the legislature.

There is room to question the desirability of a court's decision to create a new cause of action without adequate demonstration of both need and cost. Curiously, with respect to increased costs of administering the claims, both the courts which dismiss that factor as insubstantial, as well as those which use it as an argument against recognition of a new cause of action, do so without any empirical data or statistical projections. In a concurring opinion, one judge has acknowledged that legislatures possess superior resources with which to weigh all potentially affected interests, Norwest v. Presbyterian Intercommunity Hospital, 293 Or. 543, 652 P.2d 318, 333 (Tanzer, J. concurring).

The majority in *Norwest* emphasized that in tort law, negligence generally imposes an obligation to compensate only the person immediately injured, not all those who predictably suffer loss as a consequence of the injury. Analogies to the existing exceptions to that principle—spousal consortium, parents' actions for their children's injuries, and statutory wrongful death damages—were considered inadequate justification for further expansion to include a child's consortium claim.

Other courts have also questioned the use of spousal consortium as support for a child's right of action, pointing out the differing nature of the relationship. Those judges also doubt the wisdom of earlier decisions attempting to promote equality of treatment by extending the right of consortium to the wife from its common law origins with the husband. Because the husband's right is a "historical curiosity", it has been suggested that the better way to achieve equality would be the abolition of consortium for both spouses. See Berger v. Weber, 303 N.W.2d at 431 (Levin, J. dissenting).

The arguments on both sides of the issue have merit, but unquestionably as the common law now stands, the overwhelming majority of the states have declined to allow recovery by children for the loss of companionship caused by negligent injury to their parents. Plaintiff therefore derives no significant support from that source of contribution to maritime law.

Our inquiry is not at an end, however. If the common law denies recovery, we must decide whether adequate reason exists for an admiralty court to allow the claim nevertheless. Igneri v. Cie. de Transports Oceaniques, 323 F.2d 257, 260 (2d Cir.1963), overruled on other grounds, American Export Lines, Inc. v. Alvez, 446 U.S. 274, 100 S.Ct. 1673, 64 L.Ed.2d 284 (1980). After careful consideration, we conclude that there is not sufficient justification for the suggested expansion of maritime law.

Unlike the extension of consortium from husband to wife, which was accomplished within fairly well established bounds, the creation of an analogous right in children raises a host of easily foreseeable problems, and no doubt many unexpected ones as well. For example, should an award be confined to minor children, should it be made to children as a class or individually, and is it appropriate only where the parent is severely injured. It may well be that a longshoreman kept at home by injuries of a less serious nature may be able to devote more time to the rearing of his children than if he suffered no disability and was required to spend most of his day on the job.

Furthermore, if one accepts the premise that money may compensate for the loss of the love and companionship of a parent—a most questionable concept even in today's materialistic society[4]—it is not readily apparent why the line should be drawn at the parent-child relationship. In many instances the child may have received his rearing from grandparents, uncles and aunts, siblings, or friends. The loss a child sustains through injury to any of those persons would be no less severe than if they had been his natural parents. Denial of a cause of action in those circumstances would be arbitrary. Once the nature of the limitation is recognized as being arbitrary, it would appear that the better policy is to draw the line at the spousal relationship, an area which is more readily defined and confined.

To the extent that any recovery of the child is based on economic loss resulting from his parent's inability to earn money, the award would duplicate damages the injured parent himself is entitled to recover from the tortfeasor.

---

4. In denying recovery the California Supreme Court said "social policy must at some point intervene to delimit liability." Borer v. American Airlines, Inc., 19 Cal.3d 441, 446, 138 Cal.Rptr. 302, 305, 563 P.2d 858, 861 (1977). "[M]onetary compensation will not enable plaintiffs to regain the companionship and guidance of a mother. * * * To say that plaintiffs have been 'compensated' for their loss is superficial; in reality they have suffered a loss for which they can never be compensated; they have obtained, instead, a future benefit essentially unrelated to that loss." Id. at 447, 138 Cal.Rptr. at 306, 563 P.2d at 862.

We are also concerned with maintaining logical limits on recovery by one who suffers only indirect injury. The historical support that exists for spousal consortium does not extend to other forms of indirect injury. Courts have traditionally recognized that liability for negligence must have limits—arbitrarily selected but necessary, nevertheless. For example, an employee deprived of his livelihood because of injury to his employer has no right to recover from a tortfeasor for this tangible and calculable loss.[5]

Nor should we overlook the economic effects of the creation of this new cause of action. Unlike those state courts which had no hesitancy in declining to await legislative determination of the basic policy questions, we feel constrained by Congress's demonstrated interest in regulating the liability of stevedores and shipowners for injuries to longshoremen. The legislative history of the 1972 amendments to the Act addressing that concern indicates that they were the result of compromise and concession between the competing interests.

Although the Supreme Court in *Gaudet* and *Alvez* apparently did not believe that recognizing a right of action for spousal consortium would disturb the balance that Congress had struck, we see a substantial distinction in the vague and logically expansive right asserted here. In this context, too, the special solicitude of the maritime law for "those men who under[take] to venture upon hazardous unpredictable sea voyages," Moragne v. States Marine Lines, Inc., 398 U.S. 375, 387, 90 S.Ct. 1772, 1780, 26 L.Ed.2d 339 (1970), should be tempered by the congressional provision of remedies for injured longshoremen who do not venture on such voyages.

Consequently, we conclude that maritime law does not grant children a right to recover for the loss of society and companionship of their parent longshoreman who has been injured by the negligence of a shipowner.

II

Plaintiff also seeks damages for mental distress caused by "the constant exposure to the crippling and deforming injury of his father." The plaintiff did not witness the accident, nor was he in the area at the time it occurred.

Again, no federal statutory or decisional law provides for such a cause of action.[6] Some states allow recovery where the plaintiff either witnesses the accident from outside the "zone of danger" or comes on the scene soon after it and while the injured person is still present. Sinn v. Burd, 486 Pa. 146, 404 A.2d 672 (1979); Dziokonski v. Babineau, 375 Mass. 555, 380

---

5. This is hardly a fanciful concern. Members of a judge's staff, for example, would lose their positions if the judge were severely injured and thereby forced to retire. Similarly, employees of a small business might find themselves without a job if an injury incapacitated the sole proprietor whose skill or specialized knowledge was essential to the operation of the enterprise. It is highly questionable that the employees' calculable loss would be any less than that of the child whose parent may be unable to work or play, but may have more time to offer guidance and companionship.

6. In Sea–Land Services v. Gaudet, 414 U.S. at 585–86 n. 17, 94 S.Ct. at 815 n. 17, the Supreme Court refused to permit recovery for mental anguish of the surviving spouse in a wrongful death action.

N.E.2d 1295 (1978); Dillon v. Legg, 68 Cal.2d 728, 69 Cal.Rptr. 72, 441 P.2d 912 (1968). This, however, is as far as state courts have gone. See also Prosser and Keaton, § 54 at 359.

The plaintiff's claim for emotional injury does not come within even the most expansive holdings of a few state courts. The common law provides no support for the plaintiff's maritime claim, nor do we perceive any reason why the maritime law should venture into these unchartered waters that state courts have expressly declined to enter. Thus, we conclude that the trial court did not err in dismissing the plaintiff's emotional distress count for failure to state a claim.

As noted earlier, in addition to the suit alleging negligence against the owner of the ship, plaintiff also filed a companion suit, consolidated on appeal, against the owner of the crane involved in the accident. Although that claim does not implicate the same congressional concern for the interests of stevedores and ship owners, the complaint otherwise presents essentially the same issues as the case against the defendant ship owner. Because we find no countervailing considerations which would justify a different conclusion, we reach the same result as to the plaintiff's claims against defendant Markim.

Accordingly, the judgment of the district court will be affirmed in each of the consolidated cases.

NOTE

In an action such as *DeLoach,* in which a longshoreman was injured on board a vessel while working at his occupation, there is no serious question about admiralty jurisdiction. Assuming jurisdiction, what is the admiralty law of tort? If slander is a tort at sea, does the picturesque parlance of the sailor make language innocuous that would be defamatory on shore? If one says of an able bodied seaman that he is a landlubber, is it slanderous per se? In Foster v. United States, 156 F.Supp. 421 (S.D.N.Y.1957), in which the court declined to dismiss an action for libel and slander what will be the maritime rule on truth as a defense? In Aquino v. Alaska S.S. Co., 199 Wash. 490, 91 P.2d 1014 (1939), a passenger was bitten by a dog owned by another passenger. What is the maritime doctrine of scienter? Is a sea dog entitled to one bite?

Under *Executive Jet* and *Foremost Insurance,* we now demand maritime nexus as a precondition to admiralty jurisdiction. Does the determination of maritime nexus involve considerations very similar to those involved in *DeLoach?* Notice, however, that when jurisdiction is rejected, the result is the application of the state law. Thus the decision on nexus relates to considerations of uniformity without regard to the substance of the rule to be applied. Are *Foster* and *Aquino* cases in which there should be a uniform rule in the admiralty?

With *DeLoach,* compare Oman v. Johns–Manville Corp., 764 F.2d 224, 1985 A.M.C. 2317 (4th Cir.1985)(en banc), cert. denied 474 U.S. 970, 106 S.Ct. 351, 88 L.Ed.2d 319 (1985), in which it was found that actions against shipowners for damages incurred through exposure to asbestos in the course of employment in the shipbuilding and ship repair business lacked the required maritime nexus. Why is uniformity of rule more necessary on the subject of children's loss of companionship than on the subject of vessel owner liability for industrial disease?

Is there a third alternative? Could the court find sufficient nexus to justify the exercise of the jurisdiction but insufficient to justify the fashioning of a maritime rule, and in effect borrow the state law? See Wilburn Boat Co. v. Fireman's Fund Ins. Co., at p. 380, infra. The question is touched upon again in Chapter 20, infra, dealing with actions for wrongful death.

C. Problems of Federalism; State Courts and Federal Rights; Federal Courts and State Rights

Kalleck v. Deering

Supreme Court of Massachusetts, 1894.
161 Mass. 469, 37 N.E. 450.

■ Holmes, J. This is an action of tort for personal injuries suffered on board a coasting vessel while in harbor, through the breaking of a triangle on which the plaintiff was sitting and scraping a mast. As the case comes before us, we must take it that the defendants did their duty in furnishing materials for the construction of the triangle, that the mate was in control of the vessel at the time, and that the cause of the plaintiff's injury was some negligence on the mate's part in constructing the triangle and in ordering the plaintiff to use it. The question is whether the defendants are answerable for this conduct of the mate.

By the common law as understood in this State, the work of construction was not one of the matters which the defendants were bound at their peril to see done with reasonable care, and therefore, if those engaged upon it were fellow servants in their general standing and occupation, the plaintiff took the risk of their negligence. They were not removed from the class of fellow servants for the time being by the nature of their occupation, to adopt the mode of expression which has been used. * * *

But it is argued that a different doctrine obtains in the admiralty, and that we ought to follow the law which would be administered by the courts especially constituted for the affairs of seamen. For this argument it does not matter precisely where the vessel was. If the accident happened within the body of the county the admiralty jurisdiction would not be excluded; Waring v. Clarke, 5 How. 441; The Commerce, 1 Black, 574; and if upon the high seas, that of the common law is not to be denied. Percival v. Hickey, 8 Johns. 257. Wilson v. Mackenzie, 7 Hill, (N.Y.) 95, 97.

The case most relied on is The A. Heaton, 43 F. 592 (C.C.Mass.1890) followed by The Frank & Willie, 45 F. 494 (D.C.N.Y.1891), and The Julia Fowler, 49 F. 277 (D.C.N.Y.1892). Compare Morse v. Slue, 1 Vent. 238; S.C. 3 Keb. 135, 1 Molloy de Jure Marit. book 2, c. 2, § 2. If the American cases meant that the admiralty courts had worked out the liability for the acts of the captain from their own peculiar principles, it might be necessary to inquire whether the personal liability of the owner necessarily followed from the same premises, and if it did, why the common law should yield to the admiralty rather than the admiralty to the common law. But it is hardly to be expected that different views of the substantive law should be enforced by the same judges sitting in different courts. * * * Under these circumstances the Circuit Court cases do not seem to us a sufficient reason for departing from the common law because the accident happened on board ship. Moreover, it is very plain that we cannot adopt the admiralty law as a whole. We cannot divide the damages when the plaintiff has been guilty of contributory negligence, as was done in *The Julia Fowler.* See The Max Morris v. Curry, 137 U.S. 1, 11 S.Ct. 29, 34 L.Ed. 586 (1890). See Dowell v. Steam Navigation Co., 5 El. & Bl. 195, 206.

Verdict set aside.

Southern Pacific Co. v. Jensen

Supreme Court of the United States, 1917.
244 U.S. 205, 37 S.Ct. 524, 61 L.Ed. 1086.

■ MR. JUSTICE MCREYNOLDS delivered the opinion of the court.

Upon a claim regularly presented, the Workmen's Compensation Commission of New York made the following findings of fact, rulings and award, October 9, 1914:

* * *

"3. On said date Christen Jensen was operating a small electric freight truck. His work consisted in driving the truck into the steamship El Oriente where it was loaded with cargo, then driving the truck out of the vessel upon a gangway connecting the vessel with Pier 49, North River, and thence upon the pier, where the lumber was unloaded from the truck. The ship was about 10 feet distant from the pier. At about 10:15 A.M., after Jensen had been doing such work for about three hours that morning, he started out of the ship with his truck loaded with lumber, a part of the cargo of the steamship El Oriente, which was being transported from Galveston, Texas, to New York City. Jensen stood on the rear of the truck, the lumber coming about to his shoulder. In driving out of the port in the side of the vessel and upon the gangway, the truck became jammed against the guide pieces on the gangway. Jensen then reversed the direction of the truck and proceeded at third or full speed backward into the hatchway. He failed to lower his head and his head struck the ship at the top line, throwing his head forward and causing his chin to hit the lumber in front of him. His neck was broken and in this manner he met his death."

* * *

Article III, § 2, of the Constitution, extends the judicial power of the United States "To all cases of admiralty and maritime jurisdiction;" and Article I, § 8, confers upon the Congress power "To make all laws which may be necessary and proper for carrying into execution the foregoing powers and all other powers vested by this Constitution in the government of the United States or in any department or officer thereof." Considering our former opinions, it must now be accepted as settled doctrine that in consequence of these provisions Congress has paramount power to fix and determine the maritime law which shall prevail throughout the country. Butler v. Boston & Savannah Steamship Co., 130 U.S. 527, 9 S.Ct. 612, 32 L.Ed. 1017 (1889); In re Garnett, 141 U.S. 1, 14, 11 S.Ct. 840, 35 L.Ed. 631 (1891). And further, that in the absence of some controlling statute the general maritime law as accepted by the federal courts constitutes part of our national law applicable to matters within the admiralty and maritime jurisdiction. The Lottawanna, 21 Wall. 558, 22 L.Ed. 654 (1874); Butler v. Boston & Savannah Steamship Co., 130 U.S. 527, 557, 9 S.Ct. 612, 32 L.Ed. 1017 (1889); Workman v. Mayor of New York City, 179 U.S. 552, 21 S.Ct. 212, 45 L.Ed. 314 (1901).

In *The Lottawanna*, Mr. Justice Bradley speaking for the court said: "That we have a maritime law of our own, operative throughout the United States, cannot be doubted. The general system of maritime law which was familiar to the lawyers and statesmen of the country when the Constitution was adopted, was most certainly intended and referred to when it was declared in that instrument that the judicial power of the United States shall extend 'to all cases of admiralty and maritime jurisdiction.' * * * One thing, however, is unquestionable; the Constitution must have referred to a system of law coextensive with, and operating uniformly in, the whole country. It certainly could not have been intended to place the rules and limits of maritime law under the disposal and regulation of the several States, as that would have defeated the uniformity and consistency at which the Constitution aimed on all subjects of a commercial character affecting the intercourse of the States with each other or with foreign states."

By § 9, Judiciary Act of 1789, 1 Stat. 76, 77, the District Courts of the United States were given "exclusive original cognizance of all civil causes of admiralty and maritime jurisdiction; * * * saving to suitors, in all cases, the right of a common law remedy, where the common law is competent to give it." And this grant has been continued. Judicial Code, §§ 24 and 256.

In view of these constitutional provisions and the federal act it would be difficult, if not impossible, to define with exactness just how far the general maritime law may be changed, modified, or affected by state legislation. That this may be done to some extent cannot be denied. A lien upon a vessel for repairs in her own port may be given by state statute, The Lottawanna, 21 Wall. 558, 579, 580, 22 L.Ed. 654, 663, 664 (1874); The J.E. Rumbell, 148 U.S. 1, 13 S.Ct. 498, 37 L.Ed. 345 (1893); pilotage fees fixed, Cooley v. Board of Wardens, 12 How. 299, 13 L.Ed. 996 (1851); Ex parte McNiel, 13 Wall. 236, 242, 20 L.Ed. 624, 626 (1871); and the right given to recover in death cases, The Hamilton, 207 U.S. 398, 28 S.Ct. 133, 52 L.Ed. 264 (1908); La Bourgogne, 210 U.S. 95, 138, 28 S.Ct. 664, 52 L.Ed. 973, 993 (1908). See The City of Norwalk, 55 Fed.Rep. 98, 106. Equally well established is the rule that state statutes may not contravene an applicable act of Congress or affect the general maritime law beyond certain limits. They cannot authorize proceedings *in rem* according to the course in admiralty, The Moses Taylor, 4 Wall. 411, 18 L.Ed. 397 (1866); American Steamboat Co. v. Chase, 16 Wall. 522, 534, 21 L.Ed. 369, 372 (1872); The Glide, 167 U.S. 606, 17 S.Ct. 930, 42 L.Ed. 296 (1897); nor create liens for materials used in repairing a foreign ship, The Roanoke, 189 U.S. 185, 23 S.Ct. 491, 47 L.Ed. 770 (1903). See Workman v. Mayor of New York City, 179 U.S. 552, 21 S.Ct. 212, 45 L.Ed. 314 (1901). And plainly, we think, no such legislation is valid if it contravenes the essential purpose expressed by an act of Congress or works material prejudice to the characteristic features of the general maritime law or interferes with the proper harmony and uniformity of that law in its international and interstate relations. This limitation, at the least, is essential to the effective operation of the fundamental purposes for which such law was incorporated into our national laws by the Constitution itself. These purposes are forcefully indicated in the foregoing quotations from The Lottawanna.

A similar rule in respect to interstate commerce deduced from the grant to Congress of power to regulate it is now firmly established. "Where the subject is national in its character, and admits and requires uniformity of regulation, affecting alike all the States, such as transportation between the States, including the importation of goods from one State into another, Congress can alone act upon it and provide the needed regulations. The absence of any law of Congress on the subject is equivalent to its declaration that commerce in that matter shall be free." Bowman v. Chicago & Northwestern Ry. Co., 125 U.S. 465, 507, 508, 8 S.Ct. 1062, 1066, 1067, 31 L.Ed. 700 (1888); Vance v. W.A. Vandercook Co., 170 U.S. 438, 444, 18 S.Ct. 674, 676, 42 L.Ed. 1100, 1103 (1898); James Clark Distilling Co. v. Western Maryland Ry. Co., 242 U.S. 311, 37 S.Ct. 180, 61 L.Ed. 326 (1917). And the same character of reasoning which supports this rule, we think, makes imperative the stated limitation upon the power of the States to interpose where maritime matters are involved.

The work of a stevedore in which the deceased was engaging is maritime in its nature; his employment was a maritime contract; the injuries which he received were likewise maritime; and the rights and liabilities of the parties in connection therewith were matters clearly within the admiralty jurisdiction. Atlantic Transport Co. v. Imbrovek, 234 U.S. 52, 59, 60, 34 S.Ct. 733, 58 L.Ed. 1208, 1211, 1213 (1914).

If New York can subject foreign ships coming into her ports to such obligations as those imposed by her Compensation Statutes, other States may do likewise. The necessary consequence would be destruction of the very uniformity in respect to maritime matters which the Constitution was designed to establish; and freedom of navigation between the States and with foreign countries would be seriously hampered and impeded. A far more serious injury would result to commerce then could have been inflicted by the Washington statute authorizing a materialman's lien condemned in *The Roanoke*. The legislature exceeded its authority in attempting to extend the statute under consideration to conditions like those here disclosed.   So applied, it conflicts with the Constitution and to that extent is invalid.

Exclusive jurisdiction of all civil cases of admiralty and maritime jurisdiction is vested in the Federal District Courts, "saving to suitors, in all cases, the right of a common law remedy, where the common law is competent to give it."   The remedy which the Compensation Statute attempts to give is of a character wholly unknown to the common law, incapable of enforcement by the ordinary processes of any court and is not saved to suitors from the grant of exclusive jurisdiction.   The Hine v. Trevor, 4 Wall. 555, 571, 572, 18 L.Ed. 451 (1866); The Belfast, 7 Wall. 624, 644, 19 L.Ed. 266, 272 (1868); American Steamboat Co. v. Chase, 16 Wall. 522, 531, 533, 21 L.Ed. 369, 371, 372 (1872); The Glide, 167 U.S. 606, 623, 17 S.Ct. 930, 42 L.Ed. 296, 302 (1897).   And finally this remedy is not consistent with the policy of Congress to encourage investments in ships manifested in the Acts of 1851 and 1884 (Rev.Stats., §§ 4283–4285; § 18, Act of June 26, 1884, c. 121, 23 Stat. 57) which declare a limitation upon the liability of their owners.   Richardson v. Harmon, 222 U.S. 96, 104, 32 S.Ct. 27, 56 L.Ed. 110 (1912).

The judgment of the court below must be reversed and the cause remanded for further proceedings not inconsistent with this opinion.

Reversed.

■ MR. JUSTICE HOLMES, dissenting.

The Southern Pacific Company has been held liable under the statutes of New York for an accidental injury happening upon a gang-plank between a pier and the company's vessel and causing the death of one of its employees.   The company not having insured as permitted, the statute may be taken as if it simply imposed a limited but absolute liability in such a case. The short question is whether the power of the State to regulate the liability in that place and to enforce it in the State's own courts is taken away by the conferring of exclusive jurisdiction of all civil causes of admiralty and maritime jurisdiction upon the courts of the United States.

There is no doubt that the saving to suitors of the right of a common-law remedy leaves open the common-law jurisdiction of the state courts, and leaves some power of legislation at least, to the States.   For the latter I need do no more than refer to state pilotage statutes, and to liens created by state laws in aid of maritime contracts.   Nearer to the point, it is decided that a statutory remedy for causing death may be enforced by the state courts, although the death was due to a collision upon the high seas. American Steamboat Co. v. Chase, 16 Wall. 522, 21 L.Ed. 369 (1872). Sherlock v. Alling, 93 U.S. 99, 104, 23 L.Ed. 819, 820 (1876).   Knapp, Stout & Co. v. McCaffrey, 177 U.S. 638, 646, 20 S.Ct. 824, 44 L.Ed. 921 (1900). Minnesota Rate Cases, 230 U.S. 352, 409, 33 S.Ct. 729, 57 L.Ed. 1511 (1913).   The misgivings of Mr. Justice Bradley were adverted to in The Hamilton, 207 U.S. 398, 28 S.Ct. 133, 52 L.Ed. 264, and held at least insufficient to prevent the admiralty from recognizing such a state-created right in a proper case, if indeed they went to any such extent. LaBourgogne, 210 U.S. 95, 138, 28 S.Ct. 664, 52 L.Ed. 973 (1908).

The statute having been upheld in other respects, New York Central R.R. Co. v. White, 243 U.S. 188, 37 S.Ct. 247, 61 L.Ed. 667 (1917), I should have thought these authorities conclusive. The liability created by the New York act ends in a money judgment, and the mode in which the amount is ascertained, or is to be paid, being one that the State constitutionally might adopt, cannot matter to the question before us if any liability can be imposed that was not known to the maritime law. And as such a liability can be imposed where it was unknown not only to the maritime but to the common law, I can see no difference between one otherwise constitutionally created for death caused by accident and one for death due to fault. Neither can the statutes limiting the liability of owners affect the case. Those statutes extend to non-maritime torts, which of course are the creation of state law. Richardson v. Harmon, 222 U.S. 96, 104, 32 S.Ct. 27, 56 L.Ed. 110, 113 (1912). They are paramount to but not inconsistent with the new cause of action. However, as my opinion stands on grounds that equally would support a judgment for a maritime tort not ending in death, with which admiralty courts have begun to deal, I will state the reasons that satisfy my mind.

No doubt there sometimes has been an air of benevolent gratuity in the admiralty's attitude about enforcing state laws. But of course there is no gratuity about it. Courts cannot give or withhold at pleasure. If the claim is enforced or recognized it is because the claim is a right, and if a claim depending upon a state statute is enforced it is because the State had constitutional power to pass the law. Taking it as established that a State has constitutional power to pass laws giving rights and imposing liabilities for acts done upon the high seas when there were no such rights or liabilities before, what is there to hinder its doing so in the case of a maritime tort? Not the existence of an inconsistent law emanating from a superior source, that is, from the United States. There is no such law. The maritime law is not a *corpus juris*—it is a very limited body of customs and ordinances of the sea. The nearest to anything of the sort in question was the rule that a seaman was entitled to recover the expenses necessary for his cure when the master's negligence caused his hurt. The maritime law gave him no more. The Osceola, 189 U.S. 158, 175, 23 S.Ct. 483, 47 L.Ed. 760, 764 (1903). One may affirm with the sanction of that case that it is an innovation to allow suits in the admiralty by seamen to recover damages for personal injuries caused by the negligence of the master and to apply the common-law principles of tort.

Now, however, common-law principles have been applied to sustain a libel by a stevedore *in personam* against the master for personal injuries suffered while loading a ship, Atlantic Transport Co. v. Imbrovek, 234 U.S. 52, 34 S.Ct. 733, 58 L.Ed. 1208 (1914); and The Osceola recognizes that in some cases at least seamen may have similar relief. From what source do these new rights come? The earliest case relies upon "the analogies of the municipal law," The Edith Godden, 23 F. 43, 46 (D.C.N.Y.1885),—sufficient evidence of the obvious pattern, but inadequate for the specific origin. I recognize without hesitation that judges do and must legislate, but they can do so only interstitially; they are confined from molar to molecular motions. A common-law judge could not say I think the doctrine of consideration a bit of historical nonsense and shall not enforce it in my court. No more could a judge exercising the limited jurisdiction of admiralty say I think well of the common-law rules of master and servant and propose to introduce them here *en bloc*. Certainly he could not in that way enlarge the exclusive jurisdiction of the District Courts and cut down the power of the States. If admiralty adopts common-law rules without an act of Congress it cannot extend the maritime law as understood by the Constitution. It must take the rights of the parties from a different authority, just as it does when it enforces a lien created by a State. The only authority available is the common law or statutes of a State. For from the often repeated statement that there is no common law of the United States, Wheaton v. Peters, 8 Pet. 591, 658, 8 L.Ed. 1055, 1079 (1834); Western Union Telegraph Co. v. Call Publishing Co., 181 U.S. 92, 101, 21 S.Ct. 561, 45 L.Ed. 765, 770 (1901) and from the principles recognized in Atlantic Transport Co. v. Imbrovek having been unknown to the maritime law, the natural inference is that in the silence of Congress this court has believed the very limited law of the sea to be supplemented here as in England by the common law, and that here that means, by the common law of the State. Sherlock v. Alling, 93 U.S. 99, 104, 23 L.Ed. 819, 820 (1876). Taylor v. Carryl, 20 How. 583, 598, 15 L.Ed. 1028, 1033 (1857). So far as I know, the state courts have made this assumption without criticism or attempt at revision from the beginning to this day; e.g. Wilson v. MacKenzie, 7 Hill (N.Y.), 95. Gabrielson v. Waydell, 135 N.Y. 1, 11, 31 N.E. 969 (1892). Kalleck v. Deering, 161 Mass. 469, 37 N.E. 450 (1894). See Ogle v. Barnes, 8 T.R. 188. Nicholson v. Mounsey, 15 East, 384. Even where the admiralty has unquestioned jurisdiction the common law may have concurrent authority and the state courts concurrent power. Schoonmaker v. Gilmore, 102 U.S. 118, 26 L.Ed. 95 (1880). The invalidity of state attempts to create a remedy for maritime contracts or torts, parallel to that in the admiralty, that was established in such cases as The Moses Taylor, 4 Wall. 411, 18 L.Ed. 397 (1866), and The Hine v. Trevor, 4 Wall. 555, 18 L.Ed. 451 (1866), is immaterial to the present point.

The common law is not a brooding omnipresence in the sky but the articulate voice of some sovereign or quasi-sovereign that can be identified; although some decisions with which I have disagreed seem to me to have forgotten the fact. It always is the law of some State, and if the District Courts adopt the common law of torts, as they have shown a tendency to do, they thereby assume that a law not of maritime origin and deriving its authority in that territory only from some particular State of this Union also governs maritime torts in that territory—and if the common law, the statute law has at least equal force, as the discussion in The Osceola assumes.⟩ On the other hand the refusal of the District Courts to give remedies coextensive with the common law would prove no more than that they regarded their jurisdiction as limited by the ancient lines—not that they doubted that the common law might and would be enforced in the courts of the States as it always has been. This court has recognized that in some cases different principles of liability would be applied as the suit should happen to be brought in a common-law or admiralty court. Compare The Max Morris v. Curry, 137 U.S. 1, 11 S.Ct. 29, 34 L.Ed. 586 (1890), with Belden v. Chase, 150 U.S. 674, 691, 14 S.Ct. 264, 269, 37 L.Ed. 1218, 1224 (1893). But hitherto it has not been doubted authoritatively, so far as I know, that even when the admiralty had a rule of its own to which it adhered, as in Workman v. Mayor of New York City, 179 U.S. 552, 21 S.Ct. 212, 45 L.Ed. 314 (1901), the state law, common or statute, would prevail in the courts of the State. Happily such conflicts are few.

It might be asked why, if the grant of jurisdiction to the courts of the United States imports a power in Congress to legislate, the saving of a common-law remedy, i.e., in the state courts, did not import a like if subordinate power in the States. But leaving that question on one side, such cases as American Steamboat Co. v. Chase, 16 Wall. 522, 21 L.Ed. 369 (1872); The Hamilton, 207 U.S. 398, 28 S.Ct. 133, 52 L.Ed. 264 (1908), and Atlantic Transport Co. v. Imbrovek, 234 U.S. 52, 34 S.Ct. 733, 58 L.Ed. 1208 (1914), show that it is too late to say that the mere silence of Congress excludes the statute or common law of a State from supplementing the wholly inadequate maritime law of the time of the Constitution, in the regulation of personal rights, and I venture to say that it never has been supposed to do so, or had any such effect.

As to the spectre of a lack of uniformity I content myself with referring to The Hamilton, 207 U.S. 398, 406, 28 S.Ct. 133, 52 L.Ed. 264, 270 (1908). The difficulty really is not so great as in the case of interstate carriers by land, which "in the absence of Federal statute providing a different rule are answerable according to the law of the State for nonfeasance or misfeasance within its limits." The Minnesota Rate Cases, 230 U.S. 352, 408, 33 S.Ct. 729, 57 L.Ed. 1511, 1545 (1913), and cases cited. The conclusion that I reach accords with the considered cases of Lindstrom v. Mutual Steamship Co., 132 Minn. 328, 156 N.W. 669 (1916); Kennerson v. Thames Towboat Co., 89 Conn. 367, 94 A. 372 (1915); and North Pacific S.S. Co. v. Industrial Accident Commission of California, 163 P. 199 (1917), as well as with the New York decision in this case. 215 N.Y. 514, 109 N.E. 600 (1915).

■ MR. JUSTICE PITNEY, dissenting.

* * *

NOTE

The *Jensen* case has been characterized as one of the two most ill-advised admiralty decisions ever handed down by the Supreme Court, the other being The General Smith. See Gilmore and Black, *Law of Admiralty* 642 (1975). There was almost immediate congressional reaction to the *Jensen* case. The saving to suitors clause was amended that year to preserve "the rights and remedies under the workmen's compensation law of any state." 40 Stat. 395 (1917). This provision came before the Court in 1920, in Knickerbocker Ice Co. v. Stewart, 253 U.S. 149, 40 S.Ct. 438, 64 L.Ed. 834 (1920). In an opinion by Mr. Justice McReynolds, it held the Act of 1917 unconstitutional, observing:

" * * * we conclude that Congress undertook to permit application of Workmen's Compensation Laws of the several States to injuries within the admiralty and maritime jurisdiction; and to save such statutes from the objections pointed out by Southern Pacific Co. v. Jensen. It sought to authorize and sanction action by the States in prescribing and enforcing, as to all parties concerned, rights, obligations, liabilities and remedies designed to provide compensation for injuries suffered by employees engaged in maritime work.

"And so construed, we think the enactment is beyond the power of Congress. Its power to legislate concerning rights and liabilities within the maritime jurisdiction and remedies for their enforcement, arises from the Constitution, as above indicated. The definite object of the grant was to commit direct control to the Federal Government; to relieve maritime commerce from unnecessary burdens and disadvantages incident to discordant legislation; and to establish, so far as practicable, harmonious and uniform rules applicable throughout every part of the Union.

Considering the fundamental purpose in view and the definite end for which such rules were accepted, we must conclude that in their characteristic features and essential international and interstate relations, the latter may not be repealed, amended, or changed except by legislation which embodies both the will and deliberate judgment of Congress. The subject was intrusted to it to be dealt with according to its discretion—not for delegation to others. To say that because Congress could have enacted a compensation act applicable to maritime injuries, it could authorize the States to do so as they might desire, is false reasoning. Moreover, such an authorization would inevitably destroy the harmony and uniformity which the Constitution not only contemplated but actually established—it would defeat the very purpose of the grant. See Sudden & Christenson v. Industrial Accident Commission, 182 Cal. 437, 188 P. 803."

Mr. Justice Holmes dissented, joined by Justices Pitney, Brandeis, and Clarke. In 1922, Congress enacted another amendment to the saving to suitors clause, providing substantially the same thing it had attempted in the Act of 1917, but this time exempting from its provisions the master and members of the crews of vessels. 42 Stat. 634. This provision was struck down in State of Washington v. W.C. Dawson & Co., 264 U.S. 219, 44 S.Ct. 302, 68 L.Ed. 646 (1924).

Note that the application of state workmen's compensation to members of the crew of vessels would raise problems of the necessity for an owner of a foreign vessel to qualify under the statute of every state in which it did business, the spectre raised by Mr. Justice McReynolds in *Jensen*. Is the same thing true of the application of such statutes to shore-side personnel? The longshoreman is usually the employee of the master stevedore. If he is injured outside the maritime jurisdiction, he is covered by the state act. He works wholly within the state. Is there any reason for denying Congress the authority to draw this line in so hazy an area? Is there any reason for uniformity of treatment of personal injury cases arising in the New York harbor and, say, the San Francisco harbor? Compare the treatment of the line drawing problem by Congress in the act of 1922 with the treatment of the same problem by the Court. See Chapter 19(B), infra.

Chelentis v. Luckenbach S.S. Co.

Supreme Court of the United States, 1918.
247 U.S. 372, 38 S.Ct. 501, 62 L.Ed. 1171.

■ MR. JUSTICE MCREYNOLDS delivered the opinion of the court.

In December, 1915, petitioner was employed by respondent, a Delaware corporation, as fireman on board the steamship "J.L. Luckenbach" which it then operated and controlled. While at sea, twenty-four hours out from New York, the port of destination, petitioner undertook to perform certain duties on deck during a heavy wind; a wave came aboard, knocked him down and broke his leg. He received due care immediately; when the vessel arrived at destination he was taken to the marine hospital where he remained for three months; during that time it became necessary to amputate his leg. After discharge from the hospital, claiming that his injuries resulted from the negligence and an improvident order of a superior officer, he instituted a common law action in Supreme Court, New York County, demanding full indemnity for damage sustained. The cause was removed to the United States District Court because of diverse citizenship. Counsel did not question seaworthiness of ship or her appliances and announced that no claim was made for maintenance, cure, or wages. At conclusion of plaintiff's evidence the court directed verdict for respondent, and judgment thereon was affirmed by the Circuit Court of Appeals. 243 F. 536, 156 C.C.A. 234 (1917).   * * *

The work about which petitioner was engaged is maritime in its nature; his employment was a maritime contract; the injuries received were likewise maritime and the parties' rights and liabilities were matters clearly within the admiralty jurisdiction. Atlantic Transport Co. v. Imbrovek, 234 U.S. 52, 59, 60, 34 S.Ct. 733, 734, 735, 58 L.Ed. 1208 (1914). And unless in some way there was imposed upon the owners a liability different from that prescribed by maritime law, petitioner could properly demand only wages, maintenance and cure. Under the doctrine approved in Southern Pacific Co. v. Jensen, no State has power to abolish the well recognized maritime rule concerning measure of recovery and substitute therefor the full indemnity rule of the common law. Such a substitution would distinctly and definitely change or add to the settled maritime law; and it would be destructive of the "uniformity and consistency at which the Constitution aimed on all subjects of a commercial character affecting the intercourse of the States with each other or with foreign states."

Two acts of Congress are relied upon, and it is said that under each petitioner has the right to recover full indemnity according to the common law. They are: (1) Section 9, Judiciary Act of 1789, 1 Stat. 76, 77, whereby District Courts of the United States were given exclusive original cognizance of all civil causes of admiralty and maritime jurisdiction, "saving to suitors, in all cases, the right of a common law remedy, where the common law is competent to give it" (Judicial Code, §§ 24, 256); and (2) section 20 of Act to Promote the Welfare of American Seamen, approved March 4, 1915, c. 153, 38 Stat. 1164, 1185, which provides—"That in any suit to recover damages for any injury sustained on board vessel or in its service seamen having command shall not be held to be fellow-servants with those under their authority.''

The precise effect of the quoted clause of the original Judiciary Act has not been delimited by this court and different views have been entertained concerning it. In Southern Pacific Co. v. Jensen we definitely ruled that it gave no authority to the several States to enact legislation which would work ''material prejudice to the characteristic features of the general maritime law or interfere with the proper harmony and uniformity of that law in its international and interstate relations.'' In The Moses Taylor, 4 Wall. 411, 431, 18 L.Ed. 397 (1866), we said: ''That clause only saves to suitors 'the right of a common-law remedy, where the common law is competent to give it.' It is not a remedy in the common-law courts which is saved, but a common-law remedy. A proceeding *in rem*, as used in the admiralty courts, is not a remedy afforded by the common law; it is a proceeding under the civil law.'' And in Knapp, Stout & Co. v. McCaffrey, 177 U.S. 638, 644, 648, 20 S.Ct. 824, 827, 44 L.Ed. 921 (1900): ''Some of the cases already cited recognize the distinction between a common law action and a common law remedy. Thus in *The Moses Taylor,* * * * it is said of the saving clause of the Judiciary Act: 'It is not a remedy in the common law courts which is saved, but a common law remedy.' '' ''If the suit be *in personam* against an individual defendant, with an auxiliary attachment against a particular thing, or against the property of the defendant in general, it is essentially a proceeding according to the course of the common law, and within the saving clause of the statute * * * of a common law remedy. The suit in this case being one in equity to enforce a common law remedy, the state courts were correct in assuming jurisdiction.''

The distinction between rights and remedies is fundamental. A right is a well founded or acknowledged claim; a remedy is the means employed to enforce a right or redress an injury. Bouvier's Law Dictionary. Plainly, we think, under the saving clause a right sanctioned by the maritime law may be enforced through any appropriate remedy recognized at common law; but we find nothing therein which reveals an intention to give the complaining party an election to determine whether the defendant's liability shall be measured by common-law standards rather than those of the maritime law. Under the circumstances here presented, without regard to the court where he might ask relief, petitioner's rights were those recognized by the law of the sea.

Section 20 of the Seamen's Act declares ''seamen having command shall not be held to be fellow-servants with those under their authority,'' and full effect must be given this whenever the relationship between such parties becomes important. But the maritime law imposes upon a shipowner liability to a member of the crew injured at sea by reason of another member's negligence without regard to their relationship; it was of no consequence therefore to petitioner whether or not the alleged negligent order came from a fellow servant; the statute is irrelevant. The language of the section discloses no intention to impose upon shipowners the same measure of liability for injuries suffered by the crew while at sea as the common law prescribes for employers in respect of their employees on shore.

The judgment of the court below is

Affirmed.

■ MR. JUSTICE HOLMES concurs in the result.

■ MR. JUSTICE PITNEY, MR. JUSTICE BRANDEIS and MR. JUSTICE CLARKE dissent.

N O T E

In *Jensen,* it was held that it was a common law *remedy* that was saved to suitors by the savings clause. The workmen's compensation scheme being "wholly unknown to the common law [and] incapable of enforcement by the ordinary processes of any court," was not saved to suitors. In *Chelentis,* on the other hand, the action was begun at common law in the state court and removed to the federal district court. It was not the uncommon character of the remedy, then, that was at issue, but the question of whether the maritime or common law rule was to be applied. Note that while the Court states that "no state has power to abolish the well recognized maritime rule concerning measure of recovery and substitute therefor the full indemnity rule of the common law," that question is not directly at issue, for the case was decided before the decision in the *Erie* case and were the common law to be applied in the federal court under the diversity jurisdiction, under the rule in Baltimore & O.R. Co. v. Baugh, 149 U.S. 368, 13 S.Ct. 914, 37 L.Ed. 772 (1893), the federal court would take its own reading of the common law rather than follow the state law. Under the *Baugh* case, the fellow servant doctrine would be applied independent of the maritime rule.

Compare the statement in *Jensen* that in addition to the fact that the workmen's compensation remedy was unheard of at common law, it was "not consistent with the policy of Congress to encourage investments in ships" manifested in the limitation acts with the act of 1915 nullified in *Chelentis,* as well as the acts of 1917 and 1922 declared unconstitutional in *Knickerbocker Ice* and *W.C. Dawson.*

Absent a federal statute, when an action maritime in character is brought at law under the diversity jurisdiction and the saving clause, the maritime doctrine of laches governs. King v. Alaska S.S. Co., 431 F.2d 994, 1970 A.M.C. 2119 (9th Cir.1970).

Calhoun v. Yamaha Motor Corp., U.S.A.

United States Court of Appeals, Third Circuit, 1994.
40 F.3d 622, 1995 A.M.C. 1.

■ BECKER, CIRCUIT JUDGE.

These consolidated interlocutory cross appeals before us pursuant to 28 U.S.C. § 1292(b)(1993) present an interesting and important question of maritime law: whether state wrongful death and survival statutes are displaced by a federal maritime rule of decision concerning the remedies available for the death of a recreational boater occurring within state territorial waters,[1] which are explicitly excluded from the reach of the

---

1. "State territorial waters" refers to waters within the territorial limits of a state, as well as "the coastal waters less than three nautical miles from the shore of a state."

Death on the High Seas Act, 46 U.S.C.A. § 761 (1975). The remedies at issue are loss of society, loss of support and services, loss of future earnings, and punitive damages.

This case arose when Natalie Calhoun, the twelve year old daughter of plaintiffs Lucien and Robin Calhoun, was killed in a boating accident in the waters off Puerto Rico. Natalie had been riding a "Wavejammer," a type of jet ski manufactured by Yamaha Motor Corporation, U.S.A., and its parent company, Yamaha Motor Company, Ltd. (collectively referred to as "Yamaha"). Plaintiffs sued Yamaha seeking recovery under the Pennsylvania wrongful death and survival statutes, 42 Pa.Cons.Stat.Ann. §§ 8301–8302 (1982 & Supp.1994). In granting partial summary judgment for Yamaha on the issue of available damages, the district court held that federal maritime law displaced both state remedies, and fashioned a federal common law rule applicable to cases involving the death of a non-seaman in territorial waters under which future earnings and punitive damages are not recoverable but damages for loss of society or support are. Each party sought certification to appeal the portion of the court's ruling that was unfavorable.

We do not reach the question whether the district court fashioned the proper federal common law remedy, however, because we conclude that the federal maritime law does not displace state wrongful death or survival statutes in this context. Rather, applying traditional admiralty choice of law principles, we hold that the appropriate rule of decision in this area should be supplied by state law. Our analysis of the Supreme Court's maritime wrongful death jurisprudence reveals that there is no federal substantive policy with which state wrongful death or survival statutes conflict here. In the absence of a clear conflict, state law rules of decision should apply. We will therefore affirm the district court's order denying Yamaha partial summary judgment, reverse the order granting Yamaha partial summary judgment, and remand the case for further proceedings consistent with this opinion. On remand, the district court will have to determine whether the plaintiffs' claims are governed by the laws of Pennsylvania or of Puerto Rico, and how the wrongful death and survival laws of those Commonwealths bear upon plaintiffs' damages.

I. FACTS, PROCEDURAL HISTORY, AND SCOPE OF THE INTERLOCUTORY APPEAL

On July 6, 1989, while vacationing at Palmas Del Mar Resort, Humacao, Puerto Rico, Natalie Calhoun rented a Yamaha "Wavejammer." While she was riding the "Wavejammer," Natalie slammed into a vessel anchored in the waters off the hotel frontage and was killed. At the time of her death, Natalie was twelve years old. Her parents, Lucien and Robin Calhoun, individually and in their capacities as administrators for the estate of their daughter, sued Yamaha in the District Court for the Eastern District of

William C. Brown, III, Problems Arising from the Intersection of Traditional Maritime Law and Aviation Death and Personal Injury Liability, 68 Tul.L.Rev. 577, 581 (1994).

Pennsylvania seeking recovery under the Pennsylvania wrongful death statute, 42 Pa.Cons.Stat.Ann. § 8301 (1982 & Supp.1994), and the Pennsylvania survival statute, Pa.Const.Stat.Ann. § 8302 (1982). Their complaint invoked federal jurisdiction both on the basis of diversity of citizenship, 28 U.S.C.A. § 1332 (West 193),[2] and admiralty, 28 U.S.C.A. § 1333 (West 1993). The theories of recovery alleged in the complaint included negligence, strict liability, and breach of the implied warranties of merchantability and fitness for purpose. The complaint sought damages for lost future earnings, loss of society, loss of support and services, and funeral expenses. It also requested punitive damages. * * *

II.   ADMIRALTY LAW AND DISPLACEMENT OF STATE LAW: GENERAL PRINCIPLES

As we have noted, the plaintiffs' complaint alleged federal jurisdiction on the basis of both diversity of citizenship, 28 U.S.C.A. § 1332 (West 1993), and admiralty, 28 U.S.C.A. § 1333 (West 1993).[5] The Supreme Court has instructed us that "[w]ith admiralty jurisdiction comes the application of substantive admiralty law." East River S.S. Corp. v. Transamerica Delaval, 476 U.S. 858, 864, 106 S.Ct. 2295, 2298–99, 90 L.Ed.2d 865 (1986). But knowing that substantive admiralty law applies does not really resolve the question whether federal or state law provides the relevant rule of decision. "Although the corpus of admiralty law is federal in the sense that it derives from the implications of Article III evolved by the courts, to claim that all enforced rights pertaining to matters maritime are rooted in federal law is a destructive oversimplification of the highly intricate interplay of the States and the National Government." Romero v. International Terminal Operating Co., 358 U.S. 354, 373–75, 79 S.Ct. 468, 480, 3 L.Ed.2d 368 (1959); see also American Dredging Co. v. Miller, ___ U.S. ___, ___, 114

---

2. The Calhouns are citizens of Pennsylvania; Yamaha Motor Corporation, U.S.A. is a California corporation, and Yamaha Motor Company, Ltd. is a Japanese corporation.

5. Since the accident involved the allision of a pleasure craft (the "Wavejammer") with another vessel on navigable waters, admiralty jurisdiction appears to have been appropriate. See Sisson v. Ruby, 497 U.S. 358, 366–68, 110 S.Ct. 2892, 2898, 111 L.Ed.2d 292 (1990); Foremost Ins. Co. v. Richardson 457 U.S. 668, 677, 102 S.Ct. 2654, 2659, 73 L.Ed.2d 300 (1982)(collision of two boats , neither of which had ever been engaged in commercial maritime activity, and when site of accident was on waters seldom, if ever, used for commercial activity, was within admiralty jurisdiction). The Calhouns now argue that admiralty jurisdiction is inappropriate. Although they are entitled to so argue and have reserved their right to appeal that question from a final order, we doubt that

the existence or non-existence of admiralty jurisdiction matters to the question of remedies. Even if this were solely a diversity case (in which event we would still have subject matter jurisdiction over these cross-appeals) or the parties were in state court, a federal maritime rule of decision applicable to the controversy would still displace a state rule that was in conflict. Although Erie R.R. Co. v. Tompkins, 304 U.S. 64, 58 S.Ct. 817, 82 L.Ed. 1188 (1938), states that there is no *general* federal common law, it is well settled that there are areas in which *specific* bodies of federal common law operate, particularly admiralty. And where a federal rule (either statutory or common law) supplies a rule of decision in a particular case, it applies regardless of the basis of jurisdiction. This is in part what the reverse-*Erie* doctrine tells us. See Offshore Logistics, Inc. v. Tallentire, 477 U.S. 207, 223, 106 S.Ct. 2485, 2494, 91 L.Ed.2d 174 (1986).

S.Ct. 981, 987, 127 L.Ed.2d 285 (1994)(reorganizing the continued vitality of this principles from *Romero*).

State and federal authorities jointly exercise regulatory authority over maritime matters. *Romero*, 358 U.S. at 375, 79 S.Ct. at 481. As a result, state law can, and often does, provide the relevant rule of decision in admiralty cases. See, e.g., Wilburn Boat Co. v. Fireman's Fund Ins. Co., 348 U.S. 310, 321, 75 S.Ct. 368, 374, 99 L.Ed. 337 (1955)(state law determines the effect of breach of warranty in a marine insurance policy). Indeed, "[i]n the field of . . . maritime torts, the National Government has left much regulatory power in the States." Id. at 313, 75 S.Ct at 370.

Whether a state law may provide a rule of decision in an admiralty case depends on whether the state rule "conflicts" with the substantive principles of federal admiralty law. As Judge Aldisert explained in Floyd v. Lykes Bros. Steamship Co., 844 F.2d 1044, 1047 (3d Cir.1988), "state law may supplement maritime law when maritime law is silent or where a local matter is at issue, but state law may not be applied where it would conflict with [federal] maritime law." See also Askew v. American Waterways Operators, Inc., 411 U.S. 325, 341, 93 S.Ct. 1590, 1600, 36 L.Ed.2d 280 (1973)(courts in admiralty cases may reach beyond maritime precedents and apply state law "absent a clear conflict with the federal law"); Pope & Talbot, Inc. v. Hawn, 346 U.S. 406, 409–10, 74 S.Ct. 202, 205, 98 L.Ed. 143 (1953)("[S]tates may sometimes supplement federal maritime policies. . . ."); Sosebee v. Rath, 893 F.2d 54, 56–57 (3d Cir.1990)(maritime law preempts territorial attorney fees provision that directly conflicts with federal law). Thus, in the context of this case, the Pennsylvania wrongful death and survival statutes (or the Puerto Rico death and survival actions) may apply unless they conflict with a substantive rule of federal admiralty law.

We view this question as being quite similar, if not identical, to the preemption analysis articulated in Clearfield Trust Co. v. United States, 318 U.S. 363, 63 S.Ct. 573, 87 L.Ed. 838 (1943), and its progeny, see, e.g., United States v. Little Lake Misere Land Co., 412 U.S. 580, 594, 93 S.Ct. 2389, 2398, 37 L.Ed.2d 187 (1973); United States v. Kimbell Foods, Inc., 440 U.S. 715, 728–29, 99 S.Ct. 1448, 1458–59, 59 L.Ed.2d 711 (1979); Boyle v. United Technologies Corp., 487 U.S. 500, 507 n. 3, 108 S.Ct. 2510, 2516 n. 3, 101 L.Ed.2d 442 (1988); O'Melveny & Myers v. F.D.I.C., ___ U.S. ___, 114 S.Ct. 2048, 2053, 129 L.Ed.2d 67 (1994). These cases recognize that there are areas of unique federal interest which are entirely governed by federal law, but where federal law nevertheless "borrows," see *Little Lake Misere*, 412 U.S. at 594, 93 S.Ct. at 2398, or "incorporates" or "adopts," see *Kimbell Foods*, 440 U.S. at 728–30, 99 S.Ct. at 1458–59, state law except where a significant conflict with federal policy exists.

While it is clear that under certain circumstances the general maritime law—including the wrongful death rule of *Moragne*—may incorporate state law as its rule of decision, the Supreme Court has begun to view the distinction between federal law incorporating state law as a rule of decision and state law operating of its own force as of theoretical importance only.

See *O'Melveny & Myers,* ___ U.S. at ___, 114 S.Ct. at 2048 ("In any event, knowing whether 'federal law governs' in the *Kimbell Foods* sense—a sense which includes federal adoption of state-law rules—does not much advance the ball. The issue in the present case is whether the [state] rule of decision is to be applied . . . or displaced, and if it is applied it is of only theoretical interest whether the basis for that application is [the state's] sovereign power or federal adoption of the state's disposition.")(citation omitted). More precisely, although drawing such a distinction identifies the sovereign "power" being exercised, it does not have any real bearing on the practical question whether the state law rule of decision will apply or be displaced. See id.[6] Thus, because it makes little practical difference as to whether the general maritime law has incorporated state law or whether state law provides a rule of decision of its own force, we simply refer to the problem as "displacement of state law." [7]

In admiralty law, determining whether federal maritime law conflicts with and thus displaces state law has proven to be extremely tricky. Although we are told time and again under maritime preemption doctrine that a conflict exists where state law prejudices the "characteristic features" of federal maritime law, or interferes with the "proper harmony and uniformity of that law," Southern Pac. Co. v. Jensen, 244 U.S. 205, 216, 37 S.Ct. 524, 529, 61 L.Ed. 1086 (1917), the *Jensen* language is little more than a convenient slogan, providing little guidance on the question whether there is a conflict. See American Dredging, ___ U.S. at ___, 114 S.Ct. at 991 (Stevens, J., concurring)("The unhelpful abstractness of [the *Jensen* language] leaves us without a reliable compass for navigating maritime preemption problems."). Indeed, the lack of a clearly delineated conflicts inquiry in this area has been problematic. The Supreme Court has consistently struggled with setting the boundary between conflicting and non-conflicting state regulation in the area of maritime affairs, and has recently admitted,

[i]t would be idle to pretend that the line separating permissible from impermissible state regulation is readily discernible in our admiralty juris-

---

6. See also Boyle, 487 U.S. at 507 n. 3, 108 S.Ct. at 2516 n. 3 ("We refer here to the displacement of state law, although it is possible to analyze it as the displacement of federal-law reference to state law for the rule of decision. [Citing *Little Lake Misere* and *Kimbell* Foods]. We see nothing to be gained by expanding the theoretical scope of the federal pre-emption beyond its practical effect, and so adopt the more modest terminology. If the distinction between displacement of state law and displacement of federal law's incorporation of state law ever makes a practical difference, it at least does not do so in the present case."); Martha Field, Sources of Law: The Scope of Federal Common Law. 99 Harv.L.Rev. 881, 977 & n. 408 (1986)("[The] distinction between state law applying directly and state law applying through federal reference is of dubious relevance.")

7. The correct analytic conclusion, we believe, is that admiralty law simply has not spoken to the factual situation of this case, see infra at 637–39, 63943, and that state laws accordingly apply of their own force. Were we to find federal admiralty law governing wrongful death and survival actions applicable to the death of a recreational boater occurring within state territorial waters, however, our analysis would likely lead us to hold that admiralty law either does not displace or adopts (or incorporates) state (or territorial) tort law. See infra at n. 33.

> prudence, or indeed is even entirely consistent within our admiralty jurisprudence. Compare [Kossick v. United Fruit Co., 365 U.S. 731, 81 S.Ct. 886, 6 L.Ed.2d 56 (1961)] (state law cannot require provision of maritime contract to be in writing), with Wilburn Boat Co. v. Fireman's Fund Ins. Co., 348 U.S. 310, 75 S.Ct. 368, 99 L.Ed. 337 [(1955)] (state law can determine effect of breach of warranty in marine insurance policy).

American Dredging, ___ U.S. at ___, 114 S.Ct. at 987–88 (parallel citation omitted). See also Grant Gilmore & Charles L. Black, The Law of Admiralty § 1–17, at 49 (2d ed.1975)("The concepts that have been fashioned for drawing [the line between state and federal law] are too vague, as we have seen, to ensure either predictability or wisdom in the line's actual drawing.").

In our view, however, the maritime preemption doctrine is not significantly different from the preemption doctrine applicable to non-maritime contexts. See American Dredging, ___ U.S. at ___, 114 S.Ct. at 992 (Stevens, J., concurring); *Wilburn Boat Co.*, 348 U.S. at 324, 75 S.Ct. at 376 (Frankfurter, J., concurring)(maritime preemption analysis factors "are not unlike those involved when the question is whether a State, in the absence of congressional action, may regulate some matters even though aspects of interstate commerce are affected"); id. at 333, 75 S.Ct. at 381 (Reed, J., dissenting)("Since Congress has power to make federal jurisdiction and legislation exclusive, the [preemption] situation in admiralty is somewhat analogous to that governing state action interfering with interstate commerce."). Therefore, resort to non-maritime preemption doctrine by way of analogy may help sharpen the focus of the inquiry.[8]

Stated succinctly, in the absence of an express statement by Congress (express preemption), (implied) preemption could occur either where Congress intended that federal law occupy the field (field preemption) or where there is an actual conflict between state and federal law such that: (1) compliance with both federal and state law is impossible; or (2) state law stands as an obstacle to the accomplishment and execution of the full

---

8. The analogy is not perfect. In Knickerbocker Ice Co. v. Stewart, 253 U.S. 149, 40 S.Ct. 438, 64 L.Ed. 834 (1920), and Washington v. W.C. Dawson & Co., 264 U.S. 219, 44 S.Ct. 302, 68 L.Ed. 646 (1924), the Supreme Court held that some state regulation of maritime matters, even where authorized by Congress, was precluded directly by the Constitution and the uniformity implications of its grant of federal maritime jurisdiction. See *Knickerbocker*, 253 U.S. at 163–64, 40 S.Ct. at 441; *W.C. Dawson & Co.*, 264 U.S. at 227–28, 44 S.Ct. at 305. In *Knickerbocker*, however, a congressional enactment authorizing state workers' compensation laws to govern maritime workers was held unconstitutional "because their provisions were held to modify or displace essential features of the substantive maritime law." Red Cross Line v. Atlantic Fruit Co., 264 U.S. 109, 124, 44 S.Ct. 274, 277, 68 L.Ed. 582 (1924). And in *W.C. Dawson & Co.*, a similar congressional act was invalidated because it "permit[ted] any state to alter the maritime law and thereby introduce conflicting requirements." W.C. Dawson & Co., 264 U.S. at 228, 44 S.Ct. at 305. Although these cases have not been explicitly overruled by the Court, they rest on a strong nondelegation doctrine the likes of which has not been seen since the 1930s. At all events, by contrast to the situations in *Knickerbocker* and *W.C. Dawson*, as we detail below, here we discern no maritime law governing the plaintiffs' wrongful death and survival actions and no federal interest whose uniformity would be unconstitutionally impaired by application of state law.

purposes and objectives of Congress.   See California v. ARC America Corp., 490 U.S. 93, 100–01, 109 S.Ct. 1661, 1665, 104 L.Ed.2d 86 (1989)(antitrust).[9]

In non-maritime cases, the determination whether there is a conflict between state and federal law in large part turns on interpretation of federal statutes.   See Wallis v. Pan American Petroleum Corp., 384 U.S. 63, 68, 86 S.Ct. 1301, 1304, 16 L.Ed.2d 369 (1966)("Whether latent federal power should be exercised to displace state law is primarily a decision for Congress.").[10]   In addition, non-maritime cases employ a presumption against preemption.   That is, a court should construe a federal substantive rule in such a way that it does not conflict with a state rule in an area traditionally regulated by the states.   See *ARC America*, 490 U.S. at 102, 109 S.Ct. at 1665.   In admiralty law a similar presumption is incorporated in the case law by the requirement that there be a "clear conflict" before state laws are preempted.   See *Askew,* 411 U.S. at 341, 93 S.Ct. at 1600; cf. Ballard Shipping v. Beach Shellfish, 32 F.3d 623, 630 (1st Cir.1994)(stating that where a state remedy is aimed at a "great and legitimate state concern," a federal court must act with caution before finding displacement of state law).   In light of these general principles, the question in this case—whether state statutory remedies can provide the rule of decision when a recreational boater is killed in territorial waters—largely reduces to an inquiry into whether the different substantive admiralty rules articulat-

---

9.   The full *Jensen* preemption analysis is contained in the now famous passage stating that state legislation affecting maritime commerce is invalid "if it contravenes the essential purpose expressed by an act of Congress, or works material prejudice to the characteristic features of the general maritime law, or interferes with the proper harmony and uniformity of that law in its international and interstate relations." *Jensen*, 244 U.S. at 216, 37 S.Ct. at 529.   This language seems to include the express preemption and implied preemption concepts of the non-maritime preemption doctrines.   The language also seems to leave room for field preemption, although it does not appear to reference it as clearly.   But as the First Circuit has recently recognized in Ballard Shipping Co. v. Beach Shellfish, 32 F.3d 623, 626–27 (1st Cir.1994), in *American Dredging*, ___ U.S. at ___, 114 S.Ct. at 987, the Supreme Court gave the *Jensen* "characteristic features" language a limited meaning.   "[I]t rea[d] the phrase to apply—and apparently only to apply—to a federal rule that either 'originated in admiralty' or has 'exclusive application there.'" *Ballard Shipping*, 32 F.3d at 627.   Under this restrictive reading, wrongful death and survival statutes would materially prejudice no "characteristic feature" of admiralty because the wrongful death and survival remedies did not originate in or have exclusive application in admiralty.   Because applying these state remedies would not conflict with any congressional legislation, see infra at 637–39, 639–43, the focus of the inquiry in this case, therefore, is whether the application of state rules of decision will unduly interfere with the uniformity of federal maritime principles.

10.   Maritime law is not simply a creature of statute but is more an amalgam of common law and statutory principles.   But as we discuss in the next section, the development of the federal law of maritime deaths has become increasingly defined by statute, and the federal statutory schemes have taken a preeminent role in shaping the federal maritime death remedies, including those provided by federal common law.   This development, in our view, brings the federal admiralty preemption doctrine more into line with the run-of-the-mill preemption case law, where the focus of the inquiry is in large part on statutory interpretation.   Cf. *Ballard Shipping*, 32 F.3d at 630–31 (looking to a recently enacted statute to determine whether a federal common law rule displaced a state statute).

ed in federal statutes and at common law would be frustrated by the application of state law. *Pope & Talbot, Inc.*, 346 U.S. at 410, 74 S.Ct. at 205 ("[A] state may not deprive a person of any substantial admiralty right as defined in controlling acts of Congress or by interpretative decisions of this Court."); *Wilburn Boat Co.*, 348 U.S. at 332, 75 S.Ct. at 381 (Reed, J., dissenting)("State power may be exercised where it is complementary to the general law.   It may not be exercised where it would have the effect of harming any necessary or desirable uniformity."); Offshore Logistics, Inc. v. Tallentire, 477 U.S. 207, 228, 106 S.Ct. 2485, 2497, 91 L.Ed.2d 174 (1986)("[W]here Congress had spoken, or where general federal maritime law controlled, the States exercising concurrent jurisdiction over maritime matters could not apply conflicting state substantive law.").

But before determining whether the substantive federal policies concerning maritime deaths would be frustrated, it is important to know what policies have, and have not, been articulated.   This requires some understanding of the history behind the development of federal remedies for maritime deaths.   Although the "tortuous development"[11] of the federal remedies for maritime deaths is familiar to many, and has been amply described elsewhere in the case law,[12] it is essential background, and so we will describe at least the major developments.

* * *

N O T E

The Supreme Court affirmed in Yamaha Motor Corp., U.S.A. v. Calhoun, ___ U.S. ___, 116 S.Ct. 619, 133 L.Ed.2d 578 (1996). On the issue of the application of state law in wrongful death cases.   This aspect of the case is treated in Chap. 20 below. Are the wrongful death cases special?   Remember that the state statutes were regularly applied in maritime cases not governed by federal statute from the decision in The Harrisburg in 1886 until the creation of the cause of action under the general maritime law in *Moragne* in 1970, and that in *Jensen* in 1917 the Court recognized them as an exception to the principle of necessary uniformity in the admiralty.   For the text of the Supreme Court opinion and discussion of the future of preemption in admiralty cases, see chap. 22 infra.

There have been other chinks in the *Jensen* armor.   In Wilburn Boat Co. v. Fireman's Fund Ins. Co., 348 U.S. 310, 75 S.Ct. 368, 99 L.Ed. 337, 1955 A.M.C. 467 (1955), the Supreme Courtheld that the Texas law governing the effect of warranties in insurance contracts governed a fire insurance policy on a vessel which burned on Lake Texoma, which spans the boundary between Texas and Oklahoma. Justice Black found no federal law identifiable as admiralty law which governed the particular issue, and declined to find that pre-Erie decisions, some of them dealing with marine policies, as preemptive.   Justice Frankfurter, concurring, believed the

---

11. *Tallentire*, 477 U.S. at 212, 106 S.Ct. at 2488 ("The tortuous development of the law of wrongful death in the maritime context illustrates the truth of Justice Cardozo's observation that '[death] is a composer of strife by the general law of the sea as it was for many centuries by the common law

of the land.' ")(quoting Cortes v. Baltimore Insular Line, Inc., 287 U.S. 367, 371, 53 S.Ct. 173, 174, 77 L.Ed. 368 (1932)).

12. See Miles v. Apex Marine Corp., 498 U.S. 19, 23–27, 111 S.Ct. 317, 320–23, 112 L.Ed.2d 275 (1990); *Tallentire*, 477 U.S. at 212–17, 106 S.Ct. at 2488–91.

result was justified by the local nature of the occurrence, Justices Reed and Burton dissented.

Gilmore & Black, Law of the Admiralty 2–8 (1975) commented as follows: "Even eighteen years after the decision, it still seems wise to cast this chapter in the form of a series of guesses, based on the set of possibilities as to the effect of Wilburn. The reader is sufficiently warned, however, of the incertitudes that case has introduced." See MacChesney, Marine Insurance and the Substantive Maritime Law: A Comment on the Wilburn Boat Co. Case, 57 Mich.L.Rev. 555 (1959).

In insurance cases *Wilburn Boat* has been read to require the application of a settled federal admiralty rule when there is one, but in cases in which there is none, to prefer application of the state law over the creation of a new rule. See Windsor Mount Joy Mutual Insurance Company v. Giragosian, 57 F.3d 50, (1st Cir.1995).

In Askew v. American Waterways Operators, Inc., 411 U.S. 325, 93 S.Ct. 1590, 36 L.Ed.2d 280, 1973 A.M.C. 811, a Florida anti-pollution statute that imposed strict liability for oil spills in navigable waters from any waterfront facility used for drilling or handling the transfer or storage of oil (terminal facility) or any ship destined for or leaving such facility. Justice Douglas characterized the statute as dealing with sea-to-shore injuries, a subject traditionally regulated by the states.

Most recently, in American Dredging Co. v. Miller, 510 U.S. ___, 114 S.Ct. 981, 127 L.Ed.2d 285 (1994), the Court held that state courts are not bound to follow federal standards for dismissal of actions under the doctrine forum non conveniens. The majority of the Court characterized forum non conveniens as a procedural doctrine and although recognizing the holes in the *Jensen* doctrine, thought the issue of substantive uniformity in admiralty was not involved.

In addition to *Calhoun*, see Ballard Shipping Co. v. Beach Shellfish, 32 F.3d 623, 1994 A.M.C. 2705 (1st Cir.1994), holding that Robins Dry Dock & Repair Co. v. Flint, 275 U.S. 303, 48 S.Ct. 134, 72 L.Ed. 290 (1927), denying recovery for purely economic damage in maritime property damage cases, was not an essentially maritime case and does not preempt the Maine water pollution statute creating liability for purely economic damage—in the particular case losses of seafood dealers occasioned by a two week hiatus in fishing activities following an oil spill.

Is there a distinction to be made between a state statute and a common law rule? In *Ballard*, for example, suppose that in a sister state there is no statute but *Robins Dry Dock* has been rejected by the courts. In *Calhoun*, while the availability of various modes of relief in wrongful death and survival actions depends upon statute, damages for loss of society and punitive damages in personal injury cases normally does not. To the extent that the admiralty law might not provide for such awards, what law would govern? Put another way, do *Jensen* and *Chelentis* stand for different doctrines, each with its limitations? Do *Wilburn Boat* and *Askew* represent special areas (insurance and water pollution) in which shared federal-state regulation is thought particularly desirable? Is recreational boating one such? See Stolz, Pleasure Boating and the Admiralty: Erie at Sea, 51 Cal.L.Rev. 661 (1963). Or is the Court moving back toward a more geographical concept of jurisdiction and ameliorating the move by softening the practice regarding rules of decision? Cf. Currie, Federalism and the Admiralty: "The Devil's Own Mess," 160 Sup.Ct.Rev. (Kurland, Ed.) 358.

CHAPTER 12

THE MARITIME LIEN

A. ORIGIN AND NATURE OF THE MARITIME LIEN

1. INTRODUCTORY NOTE

Gilmore and Black observe that "[m]uch wit and learning have been expended in analyzing the 'true nature' of the maritime lien." *The Law of the Admiralty* 589 (1975). It is well to begin with a small sample, reserving judgment as to the category into which it fits.

The Nestor

United States Circuit Court, District of Maine, 1831.
1 Sumn. 73, 18 F.Cas. 9.

■ STORY, J.

* * *

Now a lien by the maritime law is not strictly a Roman hypothecation, though it resembles it, and is often called a tacit hypothecation. It also somewhat resembles what is called a *privilege* in that law, that is, a right of priority of satisfaction out of the proceeds of the thing in a concurrence of creditors. Emerigon says, that this privilege was strictly personal, and gave only a preference against simple contract creditors, and had no effect upon those, who were secured by express hypothecation; and that this personal privilege given by the Roman law is unknown in the French jurisprudence; for by the law of France every privilege carries with it a tacit and privileged hypothecation, at least as to the thing which is the subject of it.

* * *

"Lord Tenterden has remarked, that a contract of hypothecation made by the master does not transfer the property of the ship; but only gives the creditor a privilege or claim upon it, to be carried into effect by legal process. And this is equally true, whether the hypothecation be express or tacit."

2 Browne, Admiralty 142–143

(1st Am.Ed. from 2d Eng.Ed., 1840).

"It is said by the court, in a case reported by a celebrated judge [Justin v. Ballam (1701) 2 Ld. Raymond 805], that by the maritime law every contract with the master of a ship implies an hypothecation, though by the law of England it is otherwise. I know not where this maritime law is to be found. There is no such rule in the civil law. That law doth expressly and *nominatim* enumerate all the tacit pledges which it acknowledges, yet mentions no such one as this. It is said, indeed, that as the repairs of houses at Rome included a tacit pledge, so by analogy we must suppose did those of ships. But Vinnius has refuted this analogy, and agrees with me in opinion, that though the person furnishing money for such repairs was preferred to any other creditor, he had not, without express agreement, any qualified or hypothecatory property in the ship, and his remedy was not the *actio hypothecaria,* but the *actio in factum,* not a mortgage suit, but an action on the case. And Roccus, speaking of the modern maritime law, so far from extending this right of tacit pledge by implication to all contracts of the master, appears to confine it to mariners wages—to money borrowed to purchase a cargo—to furnish provisions for the sailors—or to pay the rent of a store-house for goods landed—mentioning the lender for ships repairs, or payment of customs duties, as merely having a preference to other creditors.

"Where a tacit pledge existed, it did not by the Roman law affect a *bona fide* purchaser. Things tacitly pledged might be freely alienated before they were arrested; as with a bond, without a judgment, doth not follow the land in the hands of a *bona fide* purchaser, though it's said to be an incumbrance on the land.

"The torts of the master cannot be supposed to *hypothecate* the ship; nor, in my humble judgment, in strictness of speech, to produce any lien on it. How then is a ship forfeited, and lost to the owner, by his captain's misconduct? In my apprehension, only in this collateral way, that it is (agreeably to the practice of the Roman law as to its own citizens, extended by the modern maritime law to foreigners) arrested until he gives bail or *fides jussores,* and sold for defaults and contempts if he will not appear."

Gilmore and Black, the Law of Admiralty
590 (1975).

"* * * Anglo–American lien law is a 19th century creation * * * The evocations of the Rhodian law, the Digest of Justinian, the Code of Oleron, the Consulate of the Sea—and all that—which are frequent in the nineteenth century opinions merely illustrate that century's addition to the agreeable pastime of antiquarianism. A gardner may amuse himself by composing an old-fashioned garden, but he puts living plants in freshly spaded soil."

2.   NATURE OF MARITIME LIENS ON VESSELS

NOTE ON SUBJECTS TO WHICH THE LIEN ATTACHES

The question of what is a vessel for purposes of the existence of maritime liens has already been discussed. When the lien attaches to a vessel, it attaches to its hull, engine, tackle, apparel, and furniture. See Galban Lobo Trading Co. v. The Diponegaro, 103 F.Supp. 452, 1952 A.M.C. 181 (S.D.N.Y.1951); The Joseph Warner, 32 F.Supp. 532, 1940 A.M.C. 217 (D.Mass.1939). In the latter case, repairs and supplies for the provision of which the lien was claimed were provided after installation of a deck winch and a pair of gallowses which were removed before the vessel was arrested. The court held that the winch and gallowses must be returned to the vessel. See also United States v. The Zarco, 187 F.Supp. 371, 1961 A.M.C. 78 (S.D.Cal.1960). There, at the time of the seizure of the vessel an armature had been removed from the ship and taken to a repair yard which asserted a possessory lien on it for the price of the repairs. It was stipulated that it should be treated as constructively within the court's custody and jurisdiction. Suppose that the equipment involved was acquired after the creation of the lien. Compare United States v. F/V Sylvester F. Whalen, 217 F.Supp. 916, 1963 A.M.C. 2389 (D.Me.1963), and *The Joseph Warner,* supra, with W.R. Grace & Co. v. Charleston L. & T. Co., 193 F.2d 539, 1952 A.M.C. 689 (4th Cir.1952). Will the reservation by the seller of title under a conditional sales contract prevent a lien from attaching to the vessel's equipment? See The Hope, 191 Fed. 243 (D.Mass. 1911). Cf: The Showboat, 47 F.2d 286 (D.Mass.1930). There it was held that portable fire extinguishers sold for use on the vessel were subject to a maritime lien on the vessel but that furnishings used in the vessel's restaurant and dance hall were not such a part of the vessel's equipment as would subject the conditional vendor's title to maritime liens. Suppose instead of retaining title under a conditional sales agreement the provider of equipment leases it to the shipowner and the vessel is later seized with the equipment aboard. See *Sylvester F. Whalen,* supra, in which the equipment, a fathometer and radar equipment, were under a five year lease. See also The Augusta, 15 F.2d 727 (E.D.La.1920)(wireless equipment). Compare with these cases, The Linda Lee, 1949 A.M.C. 324 (S.D.Cal.1947) in which it was held that radio equipment leased for use aboard a fishing vessel was not subject to a lien on the vessel and her equipment. The test applied in the case of leased equipment has been whether the equipment is "essential to the operation of the vessel." Kesselring v. F/T Arctic Hero, 30 F.3d 1123, 1995 A.M.C. 539 (9th Cir. 1994).

Supplies as well as equipment are considered as part of the vessel. See Oil Shipping (Bunkering) B.V. v. Sonmez Denizcilik Ve Ticaret A.S., 10 F.3d 176, 1994 A.M.C. 879 (3d Cir.1993).

First Nat. Bank & Trust Co. of Escanaba v. Oil Screw Olive L. Moore, 379 F.Supp. 1382 (W.D.Mich.1973), aff'd 521 F.2d 1401 (6th Cir.1975) (Leased compressor put aboard vessel as a stopgap means of operating the winches after boiler breakdown did not become an integral part of the vessel and thus the subject of traditional maritime liens—the court conceded that the case presented a "borderline situation").

In Smith, Ship Mortgages, 47 Tulane L.Rev. 608, 618 (1973), the rule is summarized as follows:

"* * * If title or ownership rests with the owner-mortgagor of the vessel, the lien will reach the property. If title has been retained by a third party, the courts generally but not uniformly make a distinction between title retention based on actual ownership (i.e., where the property is supplied by a lessor or charterer), and the retention of mere security title (i.e., conditional sale). In the latter case, the courts have held that the owner-mortgagor is the owner and titleholder. When title retention is merely a security device, the courts feel that they are dealing merely with a question of priorities upon which the Act is clear. When title is retained on the basis of actual ownership and not simply a disguised conditional sale, however, the courts generally hold that the lien does not reach the property in question [footnotes omitted]."

This summary is quoted with approval in Ocean Recovery Group v. O/S Northern Retriever, 1983 A.M.C. 262 (D.Alaska 1982), a case in which the court released a generator and ordered hoists sold with the ship, applying Section 1–201(37) of the Uniform Commercial Code to characterize the former as leased and the latter bought on conditional sale. What about a lease with option to purchase? See Seattle–First National Bank v. Northern Belle, 1995 A.M.C. 1535 (W.D.Wash.1995).

The Bold Buccleugh

Judicial Committee of the Privy Council of Great Britain (1851).
7 Moo.P.C.C. 267.

This appeal originated in a cause of damage, civil and maritime, promoted by the Respondents, the owners of the barque "William," against the steam-ship, the "Bold Buccleugh," by reason of a collision between these vessels.

The "Bold Buccleugh" belonged to the Edinburgh and Dundee Steam Packet Company, trading between Leith and Kingston-upon-Hull, in Yorkshire, the partners of which Company were all resident in Scotland. The collision took place in the river Humber, on the 14th of December, 1848, when the barque "William" was run down by the "Bold Buccleugh," and totally lost.

On the 19th of the same month, an action for damage was entered in the High Court of Admiralty in England, on behalf of the Respondents (who were domiciled and resided in England), the owners of the barque "William," against the "Bold Buccleugh" and the partners of the Edinburgh and Dundee Steam Company, and a warrant of arrest was extracted and forwarded to Hull to be executed; but the "Bold Buccleugh" had left that port for Leith, before the arrival of the warrant, and consequently could not be arrested. The owners of the "William" then applied to the owners of the "Bold Buccleugh" to give bail to the action, which they declined to do, and the "Bold Buccleugh," still continuing out of the jurisdiction of the Admiralty Court, and within the jurisdiction of the Scotch Courts, the owners of the "William," on the 30th of January, 1849, commenced a suit against the owners of the "Bold Buccleugh," in the Court of Session in Scotland, and the steamer was forthwith arrested in

Leith harbour; but on bail being given to answer the action in that Court, she was released. By a bill of sale, dated the 26th of June, 1849, the owners of the "Bold Buccleugh" sold her absolutely to the Appellant for £4,800, without notice to him of any unsatisfied claim arising out of the damage done to the "William," or any suit pending in regard thereto, in the Court of Session in Scotland; but in August following, the vessel having returned to Hull, was again arrested by virtue of a warrant, under seal of the High Court of Admiralty, and a fresh action commenced in that Court, instructions being sent to Scotland for the immediate abandonment of the suit in the Court of Session. An appearance under protest was entered by the Appellant, and an Act on Petition, brought in on his behalf, disclaiming the jurisdiction of the Court of Admiralty to entertain the second suit.

Judgment was reserved, and now delivered by

■ Sir John Jervis. There were two questions in this case: First, the effect of the pendency of another proceeding in Scotland for the same cause of action. Secondly, the liability of the vessel by a proceeding *in rem* after a *bona fide* sale, without notice.

It is manifest that these two defences are of a totally different nature; the first being a declinatory plea properly the subject of a protest; and the second, an absolute bar. Generally, it is inconvenient to depart from the settled rules of procedure, and to raise such questions differing in degree by the same defence; but as the Court below did not object to this course, we merely notice it to observe, that we do not approve of such a proceeding, and pass on to deliver our opinion upon the two points raised.

Upon the first point we have not, from the commencement of the discussion, entertained any doubt; but we desired the second question to be re-argued, because it was of great general importance, and because we were unable to find any authorities bearing directly upon it; and some of the cases to which we were referred, were apparently conflicting with each other.

The course which was taken upon the second argument, makes it convenient to dispose of the second question in the first instance.

It is admitted that the Court of Admiralty has jurisdiction in a case of collision by a proceeding *in rem* against the ship itself; but it is said that the arrest of the vessel is only a means of compelling the appearance of the owners; that the damage confers no lien upon the ship, and that the owners having appeared, the question is to be determined according to the interests of the party litigant, without reference to the original liability of the vessel causing the wrong. For these propositions, *dicta* have been referred to, which are entitled to great respect, but which, upon consideration, will be found not to support the propositions for which they were cited. In The Johann Friederich (1 W.Rob. 37), Dr. Lushington is reported to have said that proceedings *in rem* in the Court of Admiralty were analogous to those by foreign attachment in the Courts of the City of London. For the purpose for which that allusion was made, viz., the liability of the property of foreigners to be arrested by process out of the Court of Admiralty and the Courts of the City of London, the two proceedings may be analogous; but in other respects they are altogether different. The foreign attachment is founded upon a plaint against the principal debtor, and must be returned *nihil* before any step can be taken against the garnishee; the proceeding *in rem,* whether for wages, salvage, collision, or on bottomry, goes against the ship in the first instance. In the former case, the proceedings are *in personam,* in the latter, they are *in rem.* The attachment, like a Common Law distringas, is merely for the purpose of compelling an appearance; and if the Defendant appears within a year and a day, even after judgment and execution against the garnishee, and puts in bail, the attachment is at an end. If the owners do not appear to the warrant arresting the ship, the proceedings go on without reference to their default, and the decree is confined exclusively to the vessel. Many other distinctions will be found upon reference to the notes to Turbill's case (1 Wms. Saund. 67, n. 1). It is not correct, therefore, to say, that the proceeding *in rem* is in all respects analogous to the proceeding by foreign attachment, and that the former is merely to compel an appearance, because the latter is undoubtedly for that purpose only.

In all proceedings *in rem,* whatever be the foundation of the jurisdiction, the warrant is the same, and the proceedings are conducted in the same form, and there is no reason for saying that a different rule is to prevail, where the foundation of the jurisdiction is a collision, from that which is admitted to be the practice, when the suit is instituted for salvage, or the recovery of wages against the ship.

But it is further said, that the damage confers no lien upon the ship, and a *dictum* of Dr. Lushington, in the case of The Volant (1 W.Rob. 387), is cited as an authority for this proposition. By reference to a contemporaneous report of the same case (1 Notes of Cases, 508), it seems doubtful whether the learned Judge did use the expression attributed to him by Dr. W. Robinson. If he did, the expression is certainly inaccurate, and being a *dictum* merely, not necessary for the decision of that case, cannot be taken as a binding authority.

A maritime lien does not include or require possession. The word is used in Maritime Law not in the strict legal sense in which we understand it in Courts of Common Law, in which case there could be no lien where there was no possession, actual or constructive; but to express, as if by analogy, the nature of claims which neither presuppose nor originate in possession. This was well understood in the Civil Law, by which there might be a pledge with possession, and a hypothecation without possession, and by which in either case the right travelled with the thing into whosesoever possession it came. Having its origin in this rule of the Civil Law, a maritime lien is well defined by Lord Tenterden, to mean a claim or privilege upon a thing to be carried into effect by legal process; and Mr. Justice Story (1 Sumner, 78) explains that process to be a proceeding *in rem,* and adds, that wherever a lien or claim is given upon the thing, then the Admiralty enforces it by a proceeding *in rem,* and indeed is the only Court competent to enforce it. A maritime lien is the foundation of the proceeding *in rem,* a process to make perfect a right inchoate from the moment the lien attaches; and whilst it must be admitted that where such a lien exists, a proceeding *in rem* may be had, it will be found to be equally true, that in all cases where a proceeding *in rem* is the proper course, there a maritime lien exists, which gives a privilege or claim upon the thing, to be carried into effect by legal process. This claim or privilege travels with the thing, into whosesoever possession it may come. It is inchoate from the moment the claim or privilege attaches, and when carried into effect by legal process, by a proceeding *in rem,* relates back to the period when it first attached. This simple rule, which, in our opinion, must govern this case, and which is deduced from the Civil Law, cannot be better illustrated than by reference to the circumstances of *The Aline,* referred to in the argument, and decided in conformity with this rule, though apparently upon other grounds. In that case, there was a bottomry bond before and after the collision, and the Court held, that the claim for damage in a proceeding *in rem,* must be preferred to the first bond-holder, but was not entitled against the second bond-holder to the increased value of the vessel by reason of repairs effected at his cost. The interest of the first bond-holder taking effect from the period when his lien attached, he was, so to speak, a part owner in interest at the date of the collision, and the ship in which he and others were interested was liable to its value at that date for the injury done, without reference to his claim. So by the collision the interest of the claimant attached, and dating from that event, the ship in which he was interested having been repaired, was put in bottomry by the master acting for all parties, and he would be bound by that transaction.

This rule, which is simple and intelligible, is, in our opinion applicable to all cases. It is not necessary to say that the lien is indelible, and may not be lost by negligence or delay where the rights of third parties may be compromised; but where reasonable diligence is used, and the proceedings are had in good faith, the lien may be enforced, into whosesoever possession the thing may come.

The remaining point may be disposed of in a few words. The pleadings show that the proceedings in Scotland were commenced by process against the persons of the Defendants, and that the seizure of the vessel was collateral to that proceeding, for the mere purpose of securing the debt. We have already explained that, in our judgment, a proceeding *in rem* differs from one *in personam,* and it follows, that the two suits being in their nature different, the pendency of the one cannot be pleaded in suspension of the other.

For these reasons, we are of opinion, that the judgment of the Court below must be affirmed, with costs.

* * *

Cavcar Co. v. M/V Suzdal

United States Court of Appeals, Third Circuit, 1983.
723 F.2d 1096, 1984 A.M.C. 609.

■ LOUIS H. POLLAK, DISTRICT JUDGE.

This appeal raises the question whether a vessel may be liable *in rem* for breach of the contract of carriage by the operator of the vessel when the vessel's owner is not liable *in personam* for the breach.   The district court held that there can be no *in rem* liability in such circumstances.   For the reasons stated below, we reverse.

I

This case has a long and complex factual and procedural history which must be reviewed, at least in summary form, in order to understand the legal issues presented on appeal.   In 1975, appellant, Sherkate Sahami Khass Auto Pars ("Auto Pars") ordered 200 Ford Bronco trucks from Ford Export Corporation.   This purchase was financed by two letters of credit issued by Iranian banks.   At the port of Philadelphia, forty-nine of these vehicles were loaded on the M/V FINN AMER ("Finn Amer"), the appellee.

The Finn Amer is registered in Finland and is owned by Amer Sea O/Y ("Amer Sea") a Finnish company.   When this controversy arose, the Finn Amer was time-chartered to Gloucester Shipping Corporation which is not a party to these proceedings.   Although the master of the Finn Amer was employed by Amer Sea, the vessel was operated by Marine Transport Services (MTS), a New Jersey corporation.   The district court found that "MTS provided the operational infrastructure, arranged the stevedoring, solicited cargo, processed all documents and established an agency network in overseas points with respect to the Finn–Amer.   It did not charter that vessel."   App. 347a.

When the forty-nine Broncos were loaded on the vessel, MTS issued a negotiable bill of lading.   The bill of lading specified Bandar Shahpour, a port of Iran, as the destination.   It listed as consignee "Order of: Bank of Teheran Takhte Djamshid Branch, Teheran, Iran" and as "notify party" the appellant, Auto Pars.   Amer Sea was not a party to the bill of lading and the master of the Finn Amer never saw the bill of lading.

The Finn Amer arrived at Bandar Shahpour on January 23, 1976. Auto Pars was notified of the vessel's arrival and was requested by MTS to "preclear" the Broncos.   Preclearance is a procedure by which the customs duty on the cargo is paid in advance of discharge and the consignee takes direct delivery from the side of the vessel.   The district court found that there was no legal requirement of preclearance and that consignees generally resisted the preclearance system.[1]

The Finn Amer was granted berth on February 19, 1976.   It discharged all of its cargo other than the forty-nine Broncos.   The Broncos were the only cargo which was not precleared.   While the vessel was at Bandar Shahpour no bill of lading was presented for these vehicles.   In

---

1. The district court noted that the reason for this reluctance to preclear cargo was the fact that it was difficult to obtain repayment of the duty from the Iranian authorities once the duty had been paid.   In addition, if the cargo was not precleared, the recipient of the cargo could keep it in the customs warehouse for up to four months before being required to provide its own storage facilities.

fact, the original bill of lading remains at the Bank of Teheran, Takhte Djamshid Branch.

On February 23, without giving notice to Auto Pars, MTS ordered the Finn Amer to depart from Bandar Shahpour with the Broncos. It did so and returned the vehicles to Philadelphia as directed by MTS. The Broncos were impounded and eventually sold by United States Customs.

This suit is one of two which arose from the shipping of the forty-nine Broncos. In 1976, MTS filed suit in the federal district court in New Jersey against Auto Pars to recover for losses sustained due to MTS' inability to deliver the vehicles. Auto Pars counterclaimed against MTS for failure to deliver the cargo. That action was later consolidated with the action presently before us—a suit for damages for nondelivery of the Broncos which was filed in 1977 by Auto Pars against the Finn Amer and Amer Sea.[2] After a bench trial, the district court filed detailed findings of fact and conclusions of law. The court determined that MTS was a "carrier" under the Carriage of Goods by Sea Act (COGSA), 46 U.S.C. §§ 1300–15 and was liable to Auto Pars for failure to deliver the cargo. In addition, the court held that Auto Pars was not liable to MTS for any costs related to the return of the vehicles to Philadelphia. Moreover, the court found that neither Amer Sea nor the Finn Amer were parties to the bill of lading and the master of the ship had taken all relevant actions solely under the direction of MTS. The court concluded that Amer Sea, the owner of the Finn Amer, was not liable for the nondelivery of the cargo and that Auto Pars had failed to establish any basis for the imposition of *in rem* liability.

Auto Pars has appealed the district court's decision solely with respect to the finding on *in rem* liability. It does not dispute the lower court's finding that Amer Sea is not personally liable for the nondelivery. The primary issue before us is whether *in rem* liability exists when the charterer or operator of the vessel has breached the contract of carriage but the shipowner is not personally liable for the breach.[3]

---

2. These actions were also consolidated with suits stemming from a shipment of seventy-nine Mack Trucks to Iran by MTS on another vessel, M/V SUZDAL. Marine Transport Services, Inc. v. Cavcar Co., No. 76–0683; Cavcar Company v. M/V SUZDAL, No. 77–0274.

3. The secondary issues are insubstantial:

Appellee Finn Amer contends that Auto Pars is not entitled to present to this court its claim that the Finn Amer was liable *in rem* because the question was not properly presented to the district court. The contention is without merit. The district court's conclusion of law number 55 expressly recites: "Defen-

dants have failed to establish any basis for the imposition of *in rem* liability upon the vessels Suzdal and Finn–Amer." Having been considered and determined below, the question is ripe for review here.

Appellee also contends that, because the Bank of Teheran is the named consignee on the bill of lading, Auto Pars is not "the real party in interest" within the meaning of Federal Rule of Civil Procedure 17(a). We disagree. Auto Pars, having ordered and undertaken to import the trucks covered by the bill of lading, was the "notify party" on the bill of lading, reflecting its beneficial interest in the trucks. That beneficial interest was recognized by the district court in its

II

In arguing to the district court that the Finn Amer was liable *in rem,* Auto Pars relied on the Supreme Court's venerable decision in The Barnstable, 181 U.S. 464, 21 S.Ct. 684, 45 L.Ed. 954 (1901).   In that case the libeled vessel was the British steamship Barnstable which had collided off Cape Cod with the schooner Fortuna—"a collision resulting from the negligence of the officers and crew, who are appointed and paid by the charterers." 181 U.S. at 466, 21 S.Ct. at 685.   The question before the Court was whether, under the terms of the charter party governing the negligently operated Barnstable, ultimate liability lay with the charterers or the owners.   En route to resolving this issue, Justice Brown, speaking for a unanimous Court, observed that, "[w]hatever may be the English rule with respect to the liability of a vessel for damages occasioned by the neglect of the charterer, as to which there appears to be some doubt * * * the law in this country is entirely well-settled that the ship itself is to be treated in some sense as a principal, and as personally liable for the negligence of anyone who is lawfully in possession of her, whether as owner or charterer."   181 U.S. at 467, 21 S.Ct. at 685.

Not surprisingly, the district court in the instant case concluded that *The Barnstable* was of little avail to Auto Pars since Auto Pars' "claim sounded in contract and not negligence * * * *The Barnstable* did not, even remotely, support imposition of liability under the facts of this case."   App. 405a.

Auto Pars may not be able to derive any comfort from the Court's decision in *The Barnstable,* or from what the Court held or said in Reed v. S.S Yaka, 373 U.S. 410, 83 S.Ct. 1349, 10 L.Ed.2d 448 (1963), an *in rem* proceeding of more recent vintage.   Neither of those suits involved the type of claim presented here—an action by a shipper of goods against a vessel *in rem* for breach of the contract of carriage.   On the other hand, nothing in those Supreme Court holdings or opinions forecloses the transposition of that *in rem* analysis to a situation involving a breach of the contract of carriage.

Within the Second Circuit, at both the trial and appellate levels, there has developed over the past six decades a corpus of authority which strongly supports the imposition on the Finn Amer of *in rem* liability for failure to fulfill the various obligations contained in the bill of lading.   The first of these cases was The Esrom, 272 F. 266, 267 (2d Cir.1921), in which a divided panel of the Court of Appeals—each of whose members filed an opinion—found that the vessel was not liable *in rem* for damage to a shipment of prunes.   The damage to the prunes had resulted from delay in the vessel's departure from New York but the delay was held to impose no

findings of fact and conclusions of law. App. 363a, 367a, and 371a.   Assuming *arguendo* that the Bank of Teheran, as named consignee, might have had sufficient interest to sue had it elected to do so, there is no ground for concluding that Auto Pars could not sue, the Bank of Teheran not having done so.   Cf. The Thames, 81 U.S. (14 Wall.) 98, 108, 20 L.Ed. 804 (1871).

See also note 14 infra.

liability on the vessel since the charter bound the vessel not to sail until full and the master had no knowledge of the perishable nature of the goods. Although Judge Manton, writing the principal opinion, found no liability *in rem* under those facts, he observed that as a general proposition "[t]he ship may be held liable *in rem* for damages to the cargo even though no bill of lading or contract of affreightment was signed by the master." 272 F. at 269. This was so because "[i]f the voyage is begun, the vessel must carry the goods to the destination on the terms agreed by the shipper with the charterer; for when the vessel starts upon the voyage, by implication, there is a ratification and adoption by the ship of the charterer's contract with shipper." 272 F. at 271.[4]

In 1921, Judge Learned Hand, then a District Judge, considered a claim which was in important respects closely analogous to the present action. The Poznan, 276 F. 418 (S.D.N.Y.). That suit involved claims by numerous shippers against the ship *in rem* and the shipowner and charterer *in personam* for failure to deliver their goods in Havana, the ship having returned to New York with its cargo after waiting for a berth in Havana for almost two months. The ship was held liable *in rem* although the master had signed only a few of the bills of lading in question. The charter party did not provide for the master to sign the bills of lading but instead contemplated that all of them would be in the charterer's name. Thus, the shipowner was not a party to the contract of carriage. Judge Hand nonetheless held that "[b]eing once laden she was bound for right delivery though the charterers sign. * * * Indeed, the cargo would have a 'privilege' against the ship for right delivery even without any bill of lading." 276 F. at 432. Liability *in rem* was thus found notwithstanding that the shipowner was not liable *in personam* for breach of contract.[5]

Soon thereafter, Judge Hand considered a similar *in rem* claim arising from a ship's deviation from the course established by the bill of lading and again found liability *in rem* although the shipowner had no personal liability under the bill of lading. The Blandon, 287 F. 722 (S.D.N.Y.1922). The charterer had signed the bill of lading and the master had not, but the court found "that the master must be held to ratify all bills of lading once he set sail." 287 F. at 723. Judge Hand noted that this case could be distinguished from *The Esrom* because the charter in *The Esrom* was a voyage charter which would state a destination and, thus, could be viewed as directly establishing the ship's duty. "But this is not possible in a time

---

4. Judge Hough, while "substantially agreeing" with Judge Manton, concluded that whereas the ship could be held liable for "proper stowage, seamanlike management, and right delivery," 272 F. at 273, in the absence of a contract binding the shipowners to the bill of lading, only the charterer could be liable for delay in sailing. Judge Ward, dissenting, found that whether or not the master of the vessel had signed the bill of lading was irrelevant. He would have held the ship liable *in rem* because "[h]aving accepted a shipment of prunes, she was bound to sail within a reasonable time for prunes." 272 F. at 275.

5. Judge Hand did find the owner liable *in personam* for directing the ship's tortious return from Havana to New York; but the ship's *in rem* liability for breach of the contract of carriage was independent of the shipowner's tort liability.

charter, where the destination is not described." 287 F. at 723. However, he declined to relieve the vessel of liability on such a basis. "Whatever, therefore, may be the rule before the ship breaks ground, it seems to me clear that thereafter the bill of lading, though signed by the charterer only, is the measure of the ship's duty and the cargo's 'privilege.'" 287 F. at 724.

Judge Manton's *Esrom* analysis was also followed by Judge Hazel in The G.A. Tomlinson, 293 F. 51 (W.D.N.Y.1923), in which the vessel was held liable *in rem* for misdelivery of cargo when the grain was off-loaded at a grain elevator other than that specified in the bill of lading: "The fact that the bills of lading were issued by the charterer, instead of by the steamship, does not, in my opinion, relieve the personified ship from liability for failure to make right delivery of the cargo. * * * It makes no difference that the master did not sign or issue the bills of lading, for on the Great Lakes they are customarily signed by vessel agencies only, and, being laden, she was required to make right delivery, though bills of lading were signed by the charterer." 293 F. at 52.[6]

Canvassing the same issues forty years later in United Nations Children's Fund v. S/S Nordstern, 251 F.Supp. 833 (S.D.N.Y.1965), Judge Levet concluded that the edifice Judge Hand and his district court colleagues had reared upon *The Esrom* was secure. In *Nordstern,* the shipper proceeded against the shipowner and time charterer *in personam* for damages stemming from the vessel's deviation and resulting failure to deliver at the designated port. The vessel was held liable *in rem* despite the fact that, as in the present action, the master had not signed the bill of lading and the charterer was solely responsible for the decision to bypass the designated port. Judge Levet reviewed the cases discussed above and found that "in this court's opinion, those decisions make good sense. Once the voyage has begun, the goods are beyond the shipper's control. It seems eminently reasonable to hold that the ship has a duty to deliver them to the destination provided in the bill of lading being carried by the ship. * * * Indeed, the maritime lien and the proceeding against the ship itself do seem 'the best and surest pledge for the compensation and indemnity to the injured party.'" 251 F.Supp. at 837–38.[7]

In 1972, the Court of Appeals for the Second Circuit gave its full imprimatur to the ratification principle. Demsey & Associates, Inc. v. S.S.

---

6. Judge Goddard, of the Southern District of New York, addressed the same issue in 1924 in the case of *The Muskegon,* 10 F.2d 817. In that case, the libel was brought *in rem* for failure of delivery and refusal by the vessel to deliver the cargo in accordance with the bills of lading. After discussing the prior cases within the Second Circuit, Judge Goddard found on the facts before him an adoption and ratification of the bills of lading upon sailing since "not a thing was done to indicate any other intention." 10 F.2d at 820.

7. Judge Levet found *in rem* liability particularly reasonable in light of the master's awareness that under the bill of lading he was to proceed to Karachi, the designated port. Similarly, in the present case the district court found that "[t]he master of the Finn–Amer believed that all of his cargo would be discharged in Bandar Shahpour." App. 366a.

Sea Star, 461 F.2d 1009 (2d Cir.1972).[8] Judge Medina, speaking for the court, found that "[a]lthough the Master did not sign the bills of lading, the sailing of the Sea Star with the coils aboard constituted a ratification of the bills of lading. The Muskegon, 10 F.2d 817 (S.D.N.Y.1924); United Nations Children's Fund v. S/S Nordstern, 251 F.Supp. 833 (S.D.N.Y.1965)." 461 F.2d at 1015. Thus, the ship was held liable despite the absence of *in personam* liability of the shipowner.

The consistent trial and appellate court holdings in the Second Circuit that *in rem* liability is justified for breaches of the contract of carriage, whether these breaches take the form of misdelivery, nondelivery, or damage to cargo,[9] find impressive support in the authoritative treatise by Professor Charles L. Black, Jr. and the late Professor Grant Gilmore. The treatise cites with approval the district court opinion affirmed in part in *Demsey*, noting that the shipowner "cannot prevent, of course, the arising of the usual liens against his vessel, where these accrue because of cargo damage or nondelivery, even when he cannot be held personally liable." G. Gilmore & C. Black, Jr., *The Law of Admiralty* § 4–17 (2d ed. 1975).[10] The treatise also points out that such a result is proper as a matter of public policy in that it provides security to those who suffer a wrong through the instrumentality of the ship by creating limited shipowner liability for the actions of third parties to whom they have entrusted control. Id. at § 9–18a.[11]

We find the foregoing analysis doctrinally persuasive and dispositive of the present appeal. Although the master of the Finn Amer did not sign the bill of lading for the forty-nine Broncos, the departure of the ship from Philadelphia with the cargo on board effected an implied ratification of the bill of lading, binding the ship to the obligations therein, including the duty to deliver the goods at the designated port.[12] Therefore, the vessel is liable

8. Forty-six years earlier in The Capitaine Faure, 10 F.2d 950, 967 (2d Cir.1926), the Second Circuit had specifically reserved the question whether the ship's breaking ground resulted in an implied ratification of the charterer's bill of lading, noting that the statements to that effect in *The Esrom* were only dicta.

9. See British West Indies Produce, Inc. v. S/S Atlantic Clipper, 353 F.Supp. 548 (S.D.N.Y.1973)(Weinfeld, J.)(vessel liable *in rem* for damage to cargo of yams, ginger, and pumpkins caused by time charterer's decision to discharge the cargo onto a pier in cold weather upon arrival at the designated destination).

10. As additional support for this conclusion, the treatise refers to the language of the Carriage of Goods by Sea Act, 46 U.S.C. § 1303. This portion of the statute, establishing the grounds for holding a carrier liable, describes the "responsibilities and liabilities of the carrier and *ship*" (emphasis supplied). Subsection 8 specifically declares null and void a contractual provision "relieving the carrier *or the ship* from liability." (emphasis supplied).

11. The Gilmore and Black treatise also advances the view that "the rule of The *Barnstable* might well be expanded to one of unlimited (i.e., *in personam*) liability for the third party's *torts and breaches*, subject to the shipowner's right to recover indemnification from the party subjectively at fault." G. Gilmore & C. Black Jr., *The Law of Admiralty* § 9–18a at 621 (2d ed. 1975)(emphasis supplied). Whether such a breach should give rise to *in personam* shipowner liability is an issue not posed by the present appeal.

12. The district court found that MTS was not a "charterer" of the Finn Amer although it was the "operator" of the vessel

in rem even though Amer Sea is not personally liable in contract for the breach. Our decision does not address the Finn Amer's possible right to indemnification from the party primarily responsible for the injury.[13]   See e.g., Crumady v. The Joachim Hendrik Fisser, 358 U.S. 423, 428, 79 S.Ct. 445, 448, 3 L.Ed.2d 413 (1959); British West Indies Produce, Inc. v. S/S Atlantic Clipper, 353 F.Supp. 548, 555 (S.D.N.Y.1973).

Accordingly, the judgment below will be reversed and the case remanded for proceedings consistent with this opinion.[14]

NOTE

In The China, 74 U.S. (7 Wall.) 53, 19 L.Ed. 67 (1868), it was held that an innocent party in a collision within the pilot waters in the port of New York, could proceed in rem against the vessel at fault, despite the fact that the cause of the collision was negligent navigation by a pilot taken on pursuant to New York statute.   Justice Swayne determined that under the statute the taking on of the pilot was compulsory, but rejecting English decisions to the contrary, held that the vessel was liable. The issue of whether the owner was liable in personam was not before the court, but liability was put on the theory that the collision created a maritime lien on the vessel at fault, which could be perfected by a libel in rem.   Justice Clifford and Justice Field, while they joined in the decision on liability in rem, dissented from any implication that the owner was not liable in personam.   This matter is discussed in Chap. 17 infra.

Justice Swain believed this established principle of the American maritime law was salutary because otherwise the innocent party would have to seek redress from the pilot, who, especially when the damage was very extensive, would not have sufficient resources to respond in damages.   Are there other ways to handle the compulsory pilot problem?   Insurance?   The matter was handled differently in ages past.   Note Article XXIII of The Rules of Oleron, under which the pilot in such

and responsible for the direction and management of the vessel with respect to the pickup and delivery of cargo. It therefore found MTS liable as a "carrier" under the Carriage of Goods by Sea Act. Although the cases in the Second Circuit all involved breaches of the contract of carriage by charterers, we do not believe that MTS' status as "operator" rather than "charterer" involves a distinction of any consequence: The liability-producing activities of MTS stem from functions equivalent to those of the charterers in the Second Circuit cases. Although MTS was not a direct party to the time charter, it was a beneficiary of that agreement and the functional equivalent of the charterer for the purposes of the issues before this court.

13. The district court's conclusion of law number 34 found that "MTS agreed to indemnify the owner against all consequences arising out of the master's compliance with the charterer's orders." In addition, conclusion of law number 36 states "Amer Sea is entitled to enforcement of the indemnification clause." App. 373a.

14. The appellee's "statement of the case" on appeal asserts that the question of *in rem* jurisdiction of the district court was "rendered moot" by that court's resolution of the question of *in rem* liability. This suggests some question as to the existence of *in rem* jurisdiction in the district court. This jurisdictional issue was not raised as an issue in this appeal. A likely explanation is that the question of personal jurisdiction seems not to have been raised in the district court by timely motion or responsive pleading and hence, pursuant to Rule 12(h) of the *Federal Rules of Civil Procedure*, would appear to have been waived. Fish v. Bamby Bakers, Inc., 76 F.R.D. 511 (N.D.N.Y.1977); 5 C. Wright & A. Miller, Federal Practice and Procedure § 1351 at 563 (1969 & Supp.1983).

circumstances was "obliged to make full satisfaction for the same, if he hath wherewithall; and if not, lose his head"—certainly a powerful inducement to insurance. Are there more recent schemes for solving analogous problems? The sheriff's bond?

In The Barnstable, referred to in The M/V Suzdal above, it was held that a vessel at fault may be libelled in rem in respect of collision damage taking place while the vessel is being operated by a bare boat charterer. This result seems a fortiori under The China, does it not, for if one may lose his ship for the negligence of a compulsory pilot in whose selection he has no role, why not for the negligence of a charterer he has chosen?

Cases like The China and The Barnstable have often been referred to as based on the theory that independent of the human source of error, the vessel as a res is liable. Does this concept of the "personality" of the vessel aid analysis? See Gilmore & Black, The Law of Admiralty, § 9–18 (1975), where the authors describe it as largely a useless fiction.

Whatever the utility of the concept, it has never been carried wherever logic might lead. In The Western Maid, 257 U.S. 419, 42 S.Ct. 159, 66 L.Ed. 299 (1922), prior to the adoption of the Public Vessels Act, it was held that collisions involving vessels either owned by or chartered by the United States did not give rise to liens which could be perfected after return of the vessels to commercial use or to their owners. Rejecting the argument that the lien was created and was merely unenforceable while the vessel was in the possession of the United States, and used as a public vessel, Justice Holmes observed, "The personality of a public vessel is merged in that of the sovereign." In The Barnstable, Justice Brown limited his holding to damage done by the vessel through the negligence of one "in lawful possession." See Churchill v. F/V FJORD, 892 F.2d 763 (9th Cir.1988), cert. denied 497 U.S. 1025, 110 S.Ct. 3273, 111 L.Ed.2d 783 (1990).

The whole concept of liability in rem without liability of the owner is sometimes questioned. See, e.g., Robinson v. F/V Shenanegan 1994 A.M.C. 2581, 1994 WL 387867 (N.D.Cal.1994). In The Shenanegan, involving a collision between two fishing boats, the owner of the innocent vessel brought suit in the state court against four partners as owners of the offending vessel. This action was settled. The plaintiffs gave defendants a covenant not to sue, but reserved the right to sue the subsequent purchaser of the boat and "any other entity." They then brought suit against, inter alia, the vessel in rem. In dismissing the suit as barred, the court stated:

"The common law by which an *in rem* action against a ship could be maintained, even though an action against its owner or operator could not, was at one point adopted by the Supreme Court. See, e.g., The China, 74 U.S. (7 Wall.) 53 (1868). Such authority, however, 'has been weakened if not destroyed by subsequent cases.' United States v. Bissett–Berman Corp., 481 F.2d 764 (9th Cir.1973)(following settlement of action as to negligent operator, summary judgment was properly granted to defendant in action against ship *in rem*). Perceived by Judge Hand, that earlier doctrine 'is hard to explain ... on any other theory than as a vestigial devolution out of the notion that anthing that moves and kills a man should be deodand to the king.' *Burns Bros*, 202 F.2d at 912 (footnote omitted).

"There is no contention in the present matter that the alleged negligent party has an ownership interest in the boat [the negligent party was not sued, and the court indicated no opinion on the viability of such a suit— d.]. More important, since those parties which did have such an ownership interest—the partnerships— have already paid their penance, see supra, the *in rem* action is duplicative and properly dismissed. As the Ninth Circuit has generally held, 'In personam liability is a sine qua non for in rem liability against the ship.' *Bissett-Berman Corp.*, 481 F.2d at 771. In a decision which retains its force despite its age, the Supreme Court, too, has spoken to the point:

> To say an owner is not liable, but that his vessel is liable, seems to us like talking in riddles. A man's liability for a demand against him is measured by the amount of the property that may be taken from him to satisfy that demand. In the matter of liability, a man and his property cannot be separated ... The liability of the thing is so exactly the owner's liability, that a discharge or pardon extended to him will operate as a release of his property.

City of Norwich, 6 S.Ct. 1150 (1886)."

Does the court mean to suggest that the plaintiffs in The Shenanegan could not have sued in rem in the first place, despite the absence of a property interest in the negligent person?

Does it make any practical difference whether we say that putting to one side statutory limitation of liability and contract, a vessel owner is fully liable for its own negligence and for the negligence of its servants and agents, and liable for the negligence of anyone lawfully in possession of the vessel only to the extent of the value of the vessel, or we say that it is liable for its own negligence and that of its servants and agents, and the vessel is liable for the negligence of others in legal possession?

As we have seen, it does make a procedural difference. Does it make a difference in a case like The Shenanegan in the application of the rules of res judicata and collateral estoppel? Suppose that the plaintiffs had not been able to collect the state court judgment against the partner-owners. Cf. Central Hudson Gas and Electric Corp. v. Empresa Naviera Santa, S.A., 845 F.Supp. 150, 1994 A.M.C. 2003 (S.D.N.Y.1994), holding that when a bare boat charterer appeared as a claimant and defended a claim in rem, it was bound by the judgment in a later action against it in personam for deficiency.

Oil Shipping (Bunkering) B.V. v. Sonmez Denizcilik Ve Ticaret A.S.

United States Court of Appeals , Third Circuit, 1993.
10 F.3d 176, 1994 A.M.C. 879.

■ HUTCHINSON, CIRCUIT JUDGE.

Appellant, International Marine Fuels of San Francisco, Inc. ("IMF"), appeals an order of the United States District Court for the Eastern District of Pennsylvania disposing of lien claims on a fund created by the judicial sale of the vessel M./V ZIYA S ("ZIYA S") and its bunkers.[1] See Oil Shipping (Bunkering) B.V. v. Royal Bank of Scot. plc, 817 F.Supp. 1254 (E.D.Pa.1993). In that order the district court held IMF, which had supplied fuel bunkers after the ZIYA S had been arrested, did not have a

---

1. A separate appeal, filed at our Docket No. 93–1341, also involves the same arrest of the ZIYA S but presents distinct legal issues. We will resolve that appeal by way of another opinion.

preferred claim or lien superior to that of appellee. The Royal Bank of Scotland plc ("Bank"), for the value of the bunkers. Id. at 1260–61.

* * *

IMF contends that the arrest of the ZIYA S was merely "nominal" and therefore the vessel could continue to incur obligations. IMF also argues it had no duty to inquire as to the status or custody of the ship under the Federal Maritime Lien Act. In the alternative, IMF argues that the fuel it provided to the ship was an *in custodia legis* expense because it was for the common benefit of the vessel's creditors and that the district court therefore abused its discretion when it refused IMF's claim to priority in the proceeds from a separate sale of the fuel. Finally, IMF argues that the district court erred in awarding the proceeds of the sale of the bunkers to the Bank because the Bank's lien did not extend to the bunkers.

We reject these arguments. We hold that the district court and the United States Marshals Service did not nominally arrest the ZIYA S, but rather effectively put her *in custodia legis*. Because no private party can bind a vessel *in custodia legis*, we also conclude the Federal Maritime Lien Act's presumption that a party ordering supplies for a vessel has authority to bind her does not apply once the vessel is in court custody. In addition, we hold that the district court did not abuse its discretion in denying IMF's claim priority as an administrative expense incurred while the vessel was *in custodia legis*. Finally, in accord with long standing principles of maritime law, we hold that the Bank's lien reached the fuel IMF supplied. We will therefore affirm the order of the district court.

I

On March 27, 1992, IMF confirmed in writing its assent to an order from the operator of the vessel the ZIYA S, Sonmez Denizcilik Ve Ticaret AS. ("Sonmez"), Istanbul, Turkey, to provide fuel bunkers to the vessel when she was moored in the Port of Philadelphia. Under the terms of this agreement, the delivery was to take place at 8:00 a.m., March 30 at Pier 122. On March 27, IMF bought the fuel needed to meet the agreement from Texaco International Trade Inc. and Texaco arranged for a towing barge to deliver the fuel on the morning of Monday, March 30, as agreed. The contract price of the bunkers as ultimately delivered was $200,781.31.

In the meantime, on March 27, 1992, Oil Shipping (Bunkering) B.V., a previous supplier of the ZIYA S, had filed an in rem and in personam claim against the ZIYA S, her owners, and managers, in the United States District Court for the Eastern District of Pennsylvania, seeking funds due for bunkering supplied overseas. On March 29, pursuant to a warrant issued by the district court, the United States Marshal ("Marshal") arrested the ZIYA S while she was berthed at Pier 122 in the Port of Philadelphia. The Marshal served the master of the ship with a complaint and posted a copy of the arrest notice on the ship's wheel house. The Marshal then appointed the master of the ship substitute custodian. By order of the district court, the ZIYA S was permitted to continue off-loading cargo, but the district court ordered her to remain within the jurisdiction of the court. A later court order permitted the vessel to move to Pier 82 South.

The next morning, March 30, 1992, the barge arrived carrying the IMF bunkers. The master accepted the fuel on board. The barge captain met with the chief engineer of the ZIYA S who signed a declaration of inspection. The barge transferred the bunkers from approximately 10:00 a.m. to 5:25 p.m. Although the master was well aware of the arrest of the vessel, he never informed the barge captain or crew. The barge delivered 2,185.23 metric tons of bunker fuel and 122.18 metric tons of marine diesel oil to the vessel. At the time of delivery, the ZIYA S already had at least 433.1 metric tons of fuel and 86.9 metric tons of diesel aboard. Following the completion of the delivery, the barge left the ZIYA S. IMF had no actual knowledge of the arrest and did not become aware of it until April 29, 1992, one month later.

On April 2, 1992, the Bank, the holder of a first preferred ship mortgage on the ZIYA S, seeking to foreclose on its mortgage, intervened in the action. Shortly thereafter, the Bank received its own arrest warrant and executed it upon the vessel. The mortgage had been granted and properly recorded following the advance of $11,000,000.00 from the Bank to the vessel owners and operators.

On May 12, 1992, the Marshal sold the ZIYA S at public auction for $1,820,000.00. The sale included the fuel on board at the time of initial arrest but not that supplied by IMF. A few days later, the IMF bunkers were sold at private sale to the successful bidder of the ship for $130,-000.00. The district court ordered the proceeds from both sales held in a single fund.

All claims to the fund except those of IMF, the Bank, and one other party were settled by stipulation after all had made cross-motions for summary judgment with respect to the priorities of their respective liens. In its April 6, 1993, order, the district court granted the Bank's motion and awarded it the remaining funds in the court registry. IMF filed a timely appeal.

II

We will separately address all three of IMF's contentions.

A

It is well settled that once a vessel is under arrest and in judicial custody, her owners and master of the ship no longer have any power to bind her and create a lien.[2] 2 Kingstate Oil v. M/V Green Star, 815 F.2d 918, 922–24 (3d Cir.1987).

> When a vessel is in the custody of the law, having been seized by the marshal, and being either in his actual or constructive possession, no new

2. Absent arrest, a supplier who provides "necessaries" which were ordered or authorized by the owner of the vessel, relying on the vessel's credit, obtains a maritime lien against the ship. See generally 46 U.S.C.A. §§ 31341–31342 (West. Supp.1993).

liens against her may accure [sic], and neither the marshal, the master, nor the owner has the power to impose a lien of any sort beyond such as are necessary for the ship's due care and preservation. Since the seizure revokes all authority to incur liabilities on behalf of the ship, one who renders services without first requiring the Court's permission, does so at his risk.

2 Benedict on Admiralty § 48 at 3–92 to 3–93 (footnotes omitted)(7th ed. 1990). Courts considering this rule have, however, noted that it is not without exception. If the arrest of the vessel is "nominal" and she continues to conduct normal business operations, parties that innocently supply materials to her will not have their liens defeated by virtue of the arrest. See id. at 3–96 ("In order for the vessel to avoid liens while in custodia legis, the possession by the marshal must be actual or constructive and not merely nominal or colorable." Citing Taylor v. Carryl, 61 U.S. (20 How.) 583, 15 L.Ed. 1028 (1858)(other citations omitted)). The case most often relied upon for the nominal arrest theory is THE YOUNG AMERICA, 30 F. 789 (S.D.N.Y.1887). In that case, it stated:

> the vessel was allowed by the marshal to pursue her ordinary business as before; and that she did so, without interruption, for about five months after her first nominal arrest ... [and] that during this time there was no keeper on board, and no notice of attachment posted upon her masts; nor was there any publication of process until the latter part of May. In effect, the vessel was not in the custody of the court at all.

Id. at 791. The court concluded:

> [w]here a plaintiff, as in this case, obtains only a nominal arrest of a vessel, and virtually directs that she be left to pursue her ordinary business, with its attendant liabilities to other persons, in contract or in tort, he must be held to have waived the benefit of the custody of the court as a protection against other liens, and to be estopped from claiming, as against third persons, the exemptions that belong only to a vessel in actual custody. Otherwise, not only would third persons be misled and deceived, but ready means would be offered of running vessels without liability to any further liens at all. Such a practice would be a plain abuse of the process of the court.

Id. at 791–92; see also THE NISSEQOGUE, 280 F. 174, 186 (E.D.N.C. 1922)(where arrested vessel is not monitored by representative on board or notice of the arrest is not posted on board or elsewhere publicly, postarrest repairer may obtain lien).

Innocent supply alone is insufficient to give a supplier lien status. In THE COMMACK, 8 F.2d 151 (S.D.Fla.1925), the supplier provided materials to an arrested vessel that had a keeper on board. The supplier contended that a lien should attach because the master did not reveal the arrest, but the court rejected the supplier's lien claim, stating it knew of "no principle of law which makes it the duty of the custodian to notify parties dealing with the master that he is custodian...." Id. at 153.

We hold the arrest of the ZIYA S was more than nominal. The Marshal had posted notice of arrest in the wheel house of the ZIYA S. The Supreme Court has noted the paramount importance of notice.

The whole world, it is said, are parties in an admiralty cause; and, therefore, the whole world is bound by the decision. The reason on which this dictum is based will determine its extent. Every person may make himself a party, and appeal from the sentence; but notice of the controversy is necessary in order to become a party, and it is a principle of natural justice, of universal obligation, that before the rights of an individual be bound by a judicial sentence, he shall have notice, either actual or implied, of the proceedings against him. Where these proceedings are against the person, notice is served personally, or by publication; where they are *in rem*, notice is served upon the thing itself. This is necessarily notice to all those who have any interest in the thing, and is reasonable because it is necessary, and because it is a part of common prudence for all those who have any interest in it, to guard that interest by person who are in a situation to protect it. Every person, therefore, who could assert any title to THE MARY, has constructive notice of her seizure, and may fairly be considered as a party to the libel.

THE MARY, 13 U.S. 126, 144, 3 L.Ed. 678 (1815). It has long been a maritime tradition to post notice of arrest on the ship. In former times, it was tacked to the mast. See, e.g., THE YOUNG AMERICA, 30 F. at 791. Today it is posted on the wheel house. See U.S. Dep't of Justice, Manual for United States Marshals, § 6.3–12 (1986), reprinted in 1987 A.M.C. 1051, 1053. When the Marshal posted his handbill on the ZIYA S's wheel house, he gave constructive notice of the arrest to the whole world. The district court took other significant steps to secure the res: it appointed a caretaker, posted notice of attachment, ordered the ship not to move about the port without notice to the plaintiff, and otherwise limited the vessel's actions. The Marshal's arrest of the ZIYA S was actual, not "nominal" or merely colorable. Accordingly, when IMF delivered its fuel to the vessel, no maritime lien attached in its favor. GREEN STAR, 815 F.2d at 922. THE YOUNG AMERICA and THE NISSEQOGUE are distinguishable.

The equitable considerations underlying the court's decision in The YOUNG AMERICA are not present here. There, the court expressed concern about the risk of plaintiffs' manipulating the system by having a ship arrested, allowing her to incur liabilities as if the arrest had never happened, and then avoid paying them. This risk is not present here. The YOUNG AMERICA court's concerns are implicated only if it is the arresting party (or some other party seeking payment from the court's fund) who has allowed the liability to be incurred. See The COMMACK, 8 F.2d at 152 (finding nominal arrest exception inapplicable to case where "there was no act of libelant which induced the [suppliers] to expend the labor or furnish the supplies to the vessel...."). As the court in The COMMACK stated, "the acts of the master cannot raise an equity in favor of the [suppliers], entitling them to postpone the payment of intervenors who under the admiralty law are entitled to maritime liens. *The acts of the intervenors might have this effect, but not those of the Master, owner or officers of the Court."* Id. at 153 (emphasis added).

IMF Contends, however, that the 1971 amendments to the Federal Maritime Lien ACt ("the lien act") indicate it no longer has any duty to ascertain the status of the ship receiving supplies and therefore could provide services with impunity, absent actual notice of the arrest. We disagree for the following reasons.

Before 1971, the lien act imposed a duty on a supplier who asserted a maritime lien to use "reasonable diligence" to determine whether the individual requesting the supplies had authority to bind the ship. 46 U.S.C.A. § 973 (amended 1971). Congress amended this part of the lien act to deal with a problem significantly different from that now before us, one which commonly arose when an operator of a ship was acting under charters that had a lien preclusion clause. The legislative history of the lien act amendments specifically states that they were designed to protect materialman from the harsh effect of lien preclusion clauses. It states, in relevant part:

> The purpose of the [lien act amendments] is to protect terminal operators, . . . ship repairers, . . . and other suppliers who in good faith furnish necessaries to a vessel. At the present time, a "prohibition of lien" clause . . . and the [lien act] preclude a supplier from acquiring a lien on a vessel for necessaries furnished to the vessel. The bill would amend the [lien act] to permit a supplier to acquire such a lien despite a "prohibition of lien" clause. . . .

H.R.Rep. No. 92–340, 92d Cong., 1st Sess., reprinted in 1971 U.S.C.C.A.N. 1363, 1363. The House Report concludes: "the bill . . . is necessary in order to protect American materialmen from the operation of a 'no lien provision. . . .'" Id., reprinted in 1971 U.S.C.C.A.N. at 1365.

Gulf Oil Trading Co. v. M/V CARIBE MAR, 757 F.2d 743 (5th Cir. 1985) provides a good overview of the legislative history behind the 1971 amendments. In that case, the charter agreement specifically denied the operator of the vessel the authority to incur a lien binding the vessel. The charterer, however, entered into a bunker agreement which contained a clause permitting the Gulf Oil Trading Company ("Gulf Oil"), the bunker provider, to retain a lien against the vessel for the purchase price of the bunkers. Id. at 745. Two bunker deliveries were made. At the time of the first, the master of the ship notified the barge master of the lien preclusion clause, but did not directly notify Gulf Oil. Before the second delivery, however, Gulf Oil did receive notice of the lien preclusion clause. Despite this, Gulf Oil delivered the bunkers. Id. at 746.

Later, Gulf Oil instituted an in rem proceeding, seeking to secure payment for the bunkers. Id. The district court held that while a valid maritime lien existed for the first bunker delivery, no maritime lien existed for the second delivery because Gulf Oil, at that time, had notice of the lien preclusion clause. Id. On appeal, the United States Court of Appeals for the Fifth Circuit affirmed. It rejected Gulf Oil's argument that the lien act amendments made a lien preclusion clause wholly ineffective to deprive a materialman from obtaining a lien. Id. In so doing the court of appeals reviewed the history of the 1971 amendments. It indicated that the 1971 amendments removed the duty of suppliers or materialmen to assure themselves that the operator ordering supplies for the vessel had authority to bind her. Id. It concluded, however, that the amendments did not create a conclusive presumption that an operator always had power to bind the vessel. Instead, the court concluded that no lien for necessaries could attach if the materialman had actual notice of a lien preclusion clause. Id. at 748–49.

Both legislative history and case law interpreting the 1971 amendments to the lien act indicate that they do no more than relieve a materialman of any duty to ascertain whether a lien preclusion clause is in place.

In a case involving a vessel free to go about its business, some party always exists with authority to bind the vessel even if the owner may have withheld it from the operator. Even a non-consenting owner of a vessel arguably receives a benefit from the supply of necessaries to her because it facilitates the charter. But in the case of a properly arrested vessel, no party has authority to bind the ship without permission of the court. See GREEN STAR, 815 F.2d at 922; 2 Benedict on Admiralty § 48, 13–92. A supplier dealing with an arrested vessel is in a different position than a supplier dealing with a vessel under charter. Suppliers do not have to inquire about authority under the lien act because someone, somewhere, owner or operator, can encumber the vessel without obtaining court permission. In the 1971 amendments, Congress reallocated the burden of inquiry by allowing a lien in favor of a supplier who does not inquire about the operator's authority. Once a ship is under arrest, no lien can be created without court permission. We conclude that in the 1971 amendments to the lien act, Congress did not intend to give a supplier a right to rely on the authority of the master of the ship to create a lien once arrest of the vessel terminated the authority of owner, operator, charter party or anyone else to impose a lien on the vessel absent court approval.

IMF's suggested approach would grant masters and shipowners power to create liens in favor of suppliers even though all private parties have been deprived of that power. Such a power would prevent the arrest from achieving its purpose of freezing the lien positions pending court determination of their existence and priority. IMF cites no authority that would support its expansive interpretation of the 1971 amendment. Given the circumstances under which Congress amended the lien act, we think the extension IMF suggests is inappropriate. Once the vessel is properly in custody, only the court that has issued the process arresting the vessel can bind her and give a claim for supplies lien status. Suppliers who do not get court permission to supply goods to an arrested vessel act at their own peril. IMF would extend the 1971 amendments to relieve a materialman of the duty to inquire as to whether a vessel has been arrested. We do not think Congress intended that result.

B

Secondly, IMF contends that the district court abused its discretion[3] when it refused to give IMF's claim for the value of the bunkers it delivered the

---

3. We disturb district court decisions deciding what claims are accorded the status

of administrative expenses incurred in custodia legis only if the " 'judicial action is arbi-

priority status of an *in custodia legis* expense. Priority for goods supplied *in custodia legis* does not technically flow from any maritime lien, see Benedict on Admiralty § 48, at 3–93, but instead is based upon the equitable powers of a court administering a *res*.

> The most elementary notion of justice would seem to require that services or property furnished upon the authority of the court or its officer, acting within his authority, for the common benefit of those interested in a fund administered by the court, should be paid from the fund as an "expense of justice." This is the familiar rule of courts of equity.... Such preferential payments ... result rather from the self-imposed duty of the court, in the exercise of its accustomed jurisdiction, to require that expenses which have contributed either to the preservation or creation of the fund in its custody shall be paid before a general distribution among those entitled to receive it.

New York Dock Co. v. Steamship POZNAN ("THE POZNAN"), 274 U.S. 117, 121, 47 S.Ct. 482, 484, 71 L.Ed. 955 (1927)(citations omitted). In order to qualify for preferential treatment as an expense *in custodia legis*, an expense must be incurred "upon the authority of the court or its officer," and be "for the common benefit of those interested in [the] fund." GREEN STAR, 815 F.2d at 923 (quoting THE POZNAN, 274 U.S. at 121, 47 S.Ct. at 484). Even if it were possible to infer from the master's authorization, as court appointed custodian, that the court approved the tug's delivery to off-load IMF's bunkers,[4] IMF's argument that it is entitled to administrative priority because the fuel was delivered *in custodia legis* would fail. It has not demonstrated that the bunkers were supplied in order for the common benefit of all the parties interested in the *res* or its proceeds. Expenses furnished *in custodia legis* are allowed administrative priority because they are necessary to preserve the *res*, and it is in the best interest of all creditors that the *res* be preserved. Without a guarantee of priority, suppliers would be hesitant to supply goods and services necessary to preserve a *res* that is the subject of pending judicial proceedings. See *THE POZNAN*, 274 U.S. at 121, 47 S.Ct. at 484 (acknowledging the tradition of courts to elevate administrative expenses); cf 11 U.S.C.A. § 507(a)(1)(West 1993)(granting priority to administrative expenses in bankruptcy proceeding); 11 U.S.C.A. § 506(e)(West 1993)(allowing trustee in bankruptcy to recover from property securing an allowed secured claim the expenses incurred in preserving the property). Here, the district court found that the fuel IMF supplied was not necessary to the preservation of the ZIYA S. We see no basis for overturning that finding. When IMF delivered its fuel and diesel oil to the ZIYA S, she already had more than enough fuel to maneuver around the Port of Philadelphia in the limited fashion the court had allowed. The bunkers supplied did nothing

---

trary, fanciful, or unreasonable, or when improper standards, criteria or procedures are used.' " GREEN STAR, 815 F.2d at 922 (quoting Evans v. Buchanan, 555 F.2d 373, 378 (3d Cir.), cert. denied, 434 U.S. 880. 98 S.Ct. 235, 54 L.Ed.2d 160 (1977)).

4. While we do not decide this issue, we note the lack of any evidence beyond the marshal's instructions to the master to support the inference.

to preserve the res or make possible continued operation to enhance the funds available to creditors. Cf. Roy v. M/V KATERI TEK 238 F.Supp. 813, 815 (E.D.La.1965)(administrative expense for fuel and ice allowed when vessel was under court permission to continue operation in order to supplement fund for creditors); The NEBRASKA, 61 F. 514, 516 (D.Ill. 1894)(claim of fuel supplier allowed only in proportion to extent fuel permitted ship to engage in activity that would enhance the resulting fund), aff'd, 69 F. 1009 (7th Cir.1895).

The fact that the fuel IMF supplied did ultimately increase the fund available to lien creditors after the bunkers were separately sold is not enough to give IMF priority. The class of administrative expenses for goods supplied *in custodia legis* is not broad enough to include every post-arrest expense that might add to the value of the *res* when it is sold. Where the district court has not specifically ordered goods or services, only those expenses that are necessary to preserve the value of the *res* are in the category of *in custodia legis* expenses.[5] Inclusion of every valuable post-arrest supply in the category of administrative expenses would prefer the interests of suppliers whose provisions may not be immediately consumed, such as fuel or equipment suppliers, over those who provide an essential service, such as stevedores, or the suppliers of necessary consumable provisions, such as caterers. The suppliers of durable, or unconsumed, goods could then claim the proceeds of the sale of any tangibles they had supplied which were still on board unconsumed at the time of sale, while the priority of those supplying services or consumables would gradually disappear as their services or supplies were consumed. Classification of an item supplied after arrest as an *in custodia legis* expense depends not only on whether it inured to the benefit of the claimants but also on whether it preserved the *res*. Each is necessary, but each alone is not necessary and sufficient. Here, the bunkers IMF provided did not preserve the *res* nor enable the vessel to continue about its court directed activity as in KATERI TEK While fuel and oil may, in certain circumstances, be necessities for which priority is appropriate, a court does not abuse its discretion when it refuses administrative priority to an expense for fuel that is neither necessary to preserve the *res* nor ordered by the court. The district court did not abuse its discretion in denying IMF's claim, for the value of the oil it supplied, the administrative priority of an *in custodia legis* expense.

---

5. We do not reach or decide whether goods that are not necessary to preserve the res are entitled to the priority of an administrative expense if the district court directly requests a supplier to furnish them. In that case, principles of equity need to be applied to the issue of priority. Here the district court did not request or specifically approve IMF's delivery of the fuel. The temporary custodian, lacking authority, permitted IMF to deliver the fuel and IMF failed to inquire into his authority. Acquiescence in delivery does not create a priority claim. See Vlavianos v. The CYPRESS, 171 F.2d 435, 438 (4th Cir.1948)(no priority expense for post-arrest crew wages; although "crew remained on board with the acquiescence of the marshal ... it is clear that the marshal did not ask them to maintain the vessel...."), cert. denied, 337 U.S. 924, 69 S.Ct. 1168, 93 L.Ed. 1732 (1949).

C

Finally, IMF contends that the lien of the Bank does not extend to the bunkers, and that therefore it is entitled to the proceeds from the separate sale of the bunkers. The crux of IMF's argument is that the Bank's mortgage only extends to bunkers purchased or ordered by Northwest Shipping Corporation ("Northwest"), the owner of the ZIYA S, and that the lien created by the mortgage cannot be considered to extend to IMF's bunkers because they were ordered by Sonmez, the operator of the vessel. We also reject this argument.

* * * For all these reasons, we will affirm the district court's order granting the Bank's priority in the fund resulting from the sale of the ZIYA S. and denying the priority claimed by IMF.

N O T E

It has been held that the doctrine of the *Poznan* does not deprive a lienor of his lien status when the services were rendered a vessel while it was in custody pursuant to an attachment under state law.   City of Erie v. S.S. North American, 267 F.Supp. 875, 1968 A.M.C. 500 (W.D.Pa.1967).

In *The Poznan* the vessel was in the hands of the United States Marshal. Ofttimes after the vessel is seized by the marshal the court appoints a ship keeper. When this is done and services are requested by the person thus appointed, they may be allowed as expenses in custodia legis. See, e.g., General Electric Credit and Leasing Corp. v. Drill Ship Mission Exploration, 668 F.2d 811, 1983 A.M.C. 958 (5th Cir.1982).   There, on joint petition of the owner and the seizing creditor, the captain and relief captain were appointed as keeper and relief keeper. Food and cleaning services performed by a caterer at the request of the keeper were allowed as expenses, ahead of the mortgage.

Suppose that while the vessel is under arrest, the consent keeper is permitted to operate it. Would the suppliers have liens? In Roy v. M/V Kateri Tek, 238 F.Supp. 813, 1966 A.M.C. 1830 (E.D.La.1965), the court held this situation comes within the *Poznan* rule, no lien, but priority of payment granted as an "expense of justice." Note that 46 U.S.C.A. § 953(b)(2) provides that a preferred ship mortgage shall be subordinated to "expenses and fees allowed and costs taxed." See The Challenger v. Durno, 245 F.2d 815, 1958 A.M.C. 125 (5th Cir.1958). See also United States v. The Audrey II, 185 F.Supp. 777, 1960 A.M.C. 1977 (N.D.Cal.1960), in which the court issued an order to the effect that monies advanced by the libellant for operation, maintenance, and insurance be given lien status. In the Moon Engineering Co. v. The Valiant Power, 193 F.Supp. 460, 1961 A.M.C. 226 (E.D.Va.1960), charges for towing vessel under arrest, and for wharfage were allowed priority under the *Poznan* rule, but port insurance charges incurred by the preferred mortgagee without the knowledge or approval of the marshal were not.

In some circumstances the court has named the plaintiff as substitute custodian. Taino Lines, Inc. v. M/V Constance Pan Atlantic, 982 F.2d 20, 1994 A.M.C. 486 (1st Cir.1992), in which the owner gave no security and obtained an injunction against interlocutory sale of the vessel.

And in some cases services or expenditures rendered or incurred in the protection of the res have been allowed though not approved in advance by the marshal or substitute custodian. See Associated Metals and Minerals Corp. v. M/V

Alexander's Unity, 41 F.3d 1007, 1995 A.M.C. 1006 (5th Cir.1995). Suppose the crew stayed on the vessel voluntarily after the arrest, there being no request for their services and no benefit to the marshal. Irving Trust Co. v. The Golden Sail, 197 F.Supp. 777, 1962 A.M.C. 2676 (D.Or.1961).

3. LIENS ON CARGO

4,885 Bags of Linseed

Supreme Court of the United States, 1861.
66 U.S. (1 Black.) 108, 17 L.Ed. 35.

■ MR. CHIEF JUSTICE TANEY. The rights of the parties in this case depend altogether on the contract created by the bill of lading. That instrument does not refer to the charter party, nor can the charter party influence in any degree the decision of the question before us. Augustine Wills was not a party to it, and it is not material to inquire whether he did or did not know of its existence and contents; for there is nothing in it to prevent Wills & Co., the sub-charterers, or Augustine Wills, the consignee, from entering into the separate and distinct contract stated in the bill of lading, and the assignees took the rights of Wills & Co. in this contract, and nothing more. The circumstance that it came to hands of the ship-owners by assignment from the sub-charterers, who knew and were bound by all the stipulations of the charter party, cannot alter the construction of the bill of lading, nor affect the rights or obligations of Augustine Wills.

Undoubtedly the ship-owner has a right to retain the goods until the freight is paid, and has, therefore, a lien upon them for the amount; and, as contracts of affreightment are regarded by the courts of the United States as maritime contracts, over which the courts of admiralty have jurisdiction, the ship-owner may enforce his lien by a proceeding *in rem* in the proper court. But this lien is not in the nature of a hypothecation, which will remain a charge upon the goods after the ship-owner has parted from the possession, but is analogous to the lien given by the common law to the carrier on land, who is not bound to deliver them to the party until his fare is paid; and if he delivers them, the incumbrances of the lien does not follow them in the hands of the owner or consignee. It is nothing more than the right to withhold the goods, and is inseparably associated with his possession, and dependent upon it.

The lien of the carrier by water for his freight, under the ordinary bill of lading, although it is maritime, yet it stands upon the same ground with the carrier by land, and arises from his right to retain the possession until the freight is paid, and is lost by an unconditional delivery to the consignee. It is suggested in the argument for the appellant, that, as a general rule, maritime liens do not depend on possession of the thing upon which the lien exists; but this proposition cannot be maintained in the courts of admiralty of the United States. And, whatever may be the doctrine in the courts on the continent of Europe, where the civil law is established, it has been decided in this court that the maritime lien for a general average in a case of jettison, and the lien for freight, depend upon the possession of the goods, and arise from the right to retain them until the amount of the lien is paid. Cutler v. Rae, (7 How. 729 (1849);) Dupont De Nemours & Co. v. Vance and others, (19 How. 162 (1856)).

In the last mentioned case, the court, speaking of the lien for general average, and referring to the decision of Cutler v. Rae on that point, said: "This admits the existence of a lien arising out of the admiralty law, but puts it on the same footing as a maritime lien on cargo for the price of its transportation, which, as is well known, is waived by an authorized delivery without insisting on payment."

After these two decisions, both of which were made upon much deliberation, the law upon this subject must be regarded as settled in the courts of the United States, and it is unnecessary to examine the various authorities which have been cited in the argument. But it may be proper to say, that while this court has never regarded its admiralty authority as restricted to the subjects over which the English courts of admiralty exercised jurisdiction at the time our Constitution was adopted, yet it has never claimed the full extent of admiralty power which belongs to the courts organized under, and governed altogether by, the principles of the civil law.

But courts of admiralty, when carrying into execution maritime contracts and liens, are not governed by the strict and technical rules of the common law, and deal with them upon equitable principles, and with reference to the usages and necessities of trade. And it often happens that the necessities and usages of trade require that the cargo should pass into the hands of the consignee before he pays the freight. It is the interest of the ship-owner that his vessel should discharge her cargo as speedily as possible after her arrival at the port of delivery. And it would be a serious sacrifice of his interests if the ship was compelled, in order to preserve the lien, to remain day after day with her cargo on board, waiting until the consignee found it convenient to pay the freight, or until the lien could be enforced in a court of admiralty. The consignee, too, in many instances, might desire to see the cargo unladen before he paid the freight, in order to ascertain whether all of the goods mentioned in the bill of lading were on board, and not damaged by the fault of the ship. It is his duty, and not that of the ship-owner, to provide a suitable and safe place on shore in which they may be stored; and several days are often consumed in unloading and storing the cargo of a large merchant vessel. And if the cargo cannot be unladen and placed in the warehouse of the consignee, without waiving the lien, it would seriously embarrass the ordinary operations and convenience of commerce, both as to the ship-owner and the merchant.

It is true, that such a delivery, without any condition or qualification annexed, would be a waiver of the lien; because, as we have already said, the lien is but an incident to the possession, with the right to retain. But in cases of the kind above mentioned it is frequently, perhaps more usually, understood between the parties, that transferring the goods from the ship to the warehouse shall not be regarded as a waiver of the lien, and that the ship-owner reserves the right to proceed *in rem* to enforce it, if the freight is not paid. And if it appears by the evidence that such an understanding did exist between the parties, before or at the time the cargo was placed in the hands of the consignee, or if such an understanding is plainly to be inferred from the established local usage of the port, a court of admiralty will regard the transaction as a deposit of the goods, for the time, in the warehouse, and not as an absolute delivery; and, on that ground, will consider the ship-owner as still constructively in possession, so far as to preserve his lien and his remedy *in rem*.

But in the case before us, there is nothing from which such an inference can be drawn. The goods were delivered, it is admitted, generally, and without any condition or qualification. Upon such a delivery there could be neither actual nor constructive possession remaining in the ship-owner; and, consequently, there could be no right of retainer to support his lien.

The decree of the Circuit Court, dismissing the libel, must therefore be affirmed.

Decree affirmed.

NOTE

Part of the cargo may be withheld from the consignee when the consignee refuses to pay the full freight. Gilbert Imported Hardwoods, Inc. v. 245 Pkgs. Guatambu Squares, 508 F.2d 1116, 1975 A.M.C. 912 (5th Cir.1975).

Quoting Cleirac, *Us et Coutemes de la* Mer 597 (1647), Gilmore and Black suggest that there appears no reason why there might not be a lien on cargo for personal injuries occasioned by the cargo itself rather than the vessel and its owners. They give as an example of such a situation The Lord Derby, 17 Fed. 265 (C.C.La.1883), in which the libelant was bitten by a dog, observing that the court refrained from discussing the question of whether there was a lien on the dog as well as the vessel. Gilmore and Black, *The Law of Admiralty* 631 (1975). There are, of course, more probable examples. In Gutierrez v. Waterman Steamship Corp., 373 U.S. 206, 83 S.Ct. 1185, 10 L.Ed.2d 297 (1963), discussed at p. 976, infra, could the longshoreman who slipped on the beans at large because of improper packaging have libeled the cargo of beans? See also Ryan Stevedoring Co. v. United States, 175 F.2d 490, 1949 A.M.C. 1363 (2d Cir.1949), cert. denied 338 U.S. 899, 70 S.Ct. 249, 94 L.Ed. 553 (1949); Simpson Timber Co. v. Parks, 369 F.2d 324, 1966 A.M.C. 2704 (9th Cir.1966); Morales v. Dampskibs A/S Flint, 264 F.Supp.829 (S.D.N.Y.1966), aff'd 370 F.2d 569, 1967 A.M.C. 744 (2d Cir.1967). Perhaps the reason no such cases appear lies in the fact that the injured party would almost always prefer to sue the shipowner, for in this way he could take advantage of the warranty of seaworthiness and thus avoid the necessity for proving negligence. See Judge Browning's dissenting opinion in the *Simpson Timber Co.* case, supra. In that case the shipper had shipped a cargo of doors. They had openings in them for glass and were packaged in cardboard. Instead of staggering the doors so that the openings would not be aligned, the shipper packaged them with all the openings at the same end. While they were being loaded, a longshoreman carrying a 100 pound bag of flour stepped on the topmost package and fell through the cardboard. The case was a common law action for negligence. If an action against the cargo *in rem* were permitted, what level of duty would be imposed upon the shipper (negligence? seaworthiness?). Even if the standard of care were not changed, problems remain. Could one expect that the court that refused to enforce a lien for charter hire against the American purchaser who had paid in advance would be willing to tell a door purchaser similarly situated that his purchase had been converted into a fund for the payment of an injury to a longshoreman, leaving him to sue perhaps a foreign shipper to get his money back? On the other hand, given liability on the part of the shipowner, isn't the insurance against such happenings an element in the cost of shipment in any event? Who is the best insurer?

B.   TRANSACTIONS IMPORTING LIENS

1.   THE MARINER'S LIEN FOR WAGES

Harrison v. The Beverly Lynn

United States District Court, Puerto Rico, 1959.
172 F.Supp. 719, 1960 A.M.C. 921.

■ CLEMENTE RUIZ–NAZARIO, D.J.   This action is now before the Court on respondent's exceptions to the libel.

As grounds for the exceptions it is alleged:

"First: That the facts averred in the libel do not give rise to any maritime lien upon the M/V Beverly Lynn.

"Second: That the facts averred in the libel do not constitute a cause of action within the admiralty and maritime jurisdiction of this court."

In its memorandum as well as in its oral argument in support of said exceptions, the respondent has contended by quoting paragraphs Twelfth, Thirteenth and Seventeenth of the libel, that inasmuch as libelant seeks support for his claim in 46 U.S.C.A. §§ 531 and 533,

(1) the facts averred in the libel do not give rise to a lien, or

(2) constitute a cause of action, within the admiralty jurisdiction of the Court.

Respondent's reasoning is that 46 U.S.C.A. § 531, Chap. 17 only mentions cod fisheries, or the mackerel fisheries, and since the libel herein concerns a contract dealing with tuna catch or fishery, therefore, neither said section, nor Section 533 of the same 46 U.S.C.A., nor any provision of Chap. 17, thereof, apply to this action, and that on this account the facts averred in the libel do not give rise to a lien on the respondent vessel and in favor of libellant, for his agreed share in the catch or proceeds thereof, in lieu of wages, nor do such facts constitute a cause of action, within the admiralty jurisdiction of the court.

In the first place, the only purpose of 46 U.S.C.A. § 531 is to *compel* the vessels therein mentioned, when engaged in carrying on the bank and other cod fisheries, or the mackerel fishery, bound for a port of the United

States, to make an agreement in writing with every fisherman who may be employed therein, pursuant to the terms provided in said section. It does not *preclude* other fishing vessels, engaged in other fisheries, from making similar agreements with their fishermen, on the basis of a share of the catch of whatever other fish they may be engaged in fishing.

And all that 46 U.S.C.A. § 533, does is to establish, in favor of the cod or mackerel fisherman with whom such a contract for a share of the catch or its proceeds may have been entered into under § 531, a lien on the vessel, which may be proceeded against "in the same form and to the same effect as any other vessel is by law liable, and may be proceeded against for the wages of seamen or mariners in the merchant service."

The court entertains no doubt that fishermen on shares other than cod and mackerel fishermen, have a lien on the vessels on which they are hired and are entitled to bring libels *in rem* against said vessels to recover their shares of the catch or the proceeds thereof, in lieu of wages. See Minna, 11 F. 759 (E.D.Mich.1882); Carrier Dove, 97 F. 111 (1 Cir.1899); Georgiana, 245 F. 321 (1 Cir.1917); I.S.E., (9 Cir.1926), The I.S.E., 15 F.2d 749, 1927 A.M.C. 23; United States v. Laflin (9 Cir.1928), 24 F.2d 683, 1928 A.M.C. 700.

Also see Putnam v. Lower, 236 F.2d 561, at 569, 570, 1956 A.M.C. 2059, at 2070 (9th Cir.1956), where it was said:

"That the initial exercise of power therein was maritime is clear, since the cause originated as a libel for wages and damages resulting from wrongful action relating to a fishing lay. Ever since the opinion of Justice Story in Harden v. Gordon, 2 Mason 541, 11 F.Cas. 480 (1823), it has been settled in the maritime law of the United States that seamen are the wards of Admiralty, and as such the courts of admiralty vigilantly guard against any encroachment upon their rights. The jurisdiction of courts of admiralty over the wage claims of seamen is anciently established. From the dawn of maritime commerce, the necessity for skilled and courageous mariners has been recognized and the law has jealously protected them as to certain and prompt payment of wages or compensation by other methods. Originally, seamen were compensated by a stake or share in the profits of the voyage. More recently, it has become customary to pay fixed wages, but the old form survives in the lay plan employed in the more speculative pursuits of sealing, whaling, and fishing. Fishermen, although possessing wages and customs peculiar to their business, are nonetheless seamen, and in general receive the same protection. Therefore, despite compensational differences, lay fishermen or sharesmen possess a right similar to that enjoyed by regular seamen, to lien the vessel and catch on board to secure their compensation, and this right is maritime in nature."

Moreover, libellant, in his libel, does not limit his request for relief on 46 U.S.C.A. §§ 531, 533, but also "on the general admiralty and maritime law" (See Par. Fourteenth of the libel).

It follows, therefore, that the facts alleged in the libel give rise to a maritime lien upon The M/V Beverly Lynn, and constitute a cause of action within the admiralty and maritime jurisdiction of this court, and that respondent's exceptions to the libel must be denied.

It is so ordered.

NOTE

The lien exists for seaman's wages. It is necessary to determine, therefore, whether the person asserting the lien is a seaman, i.e., a member of the crew of a vessel. What constitutes a vessel is discussed above in Chapter 4. Whether the person asserting the lien is a member of the crew is a matter that produces some litigation. To qualify as a member of the crew of a vessel, it is necessary to show that the vessel is in navigation. See First Bank & Trust v. Knachel, 999 F.2d 107, 1994 A.M.C. 864 (5th Cir.1993), holding that seamen engaged in getting engines of a fishing vessel running, and sailing her from Sabine Pass to two successive yards in Texas for repairs in preparation for a voyage to Haiti, when the hull was intact and no equipment had been removed, were entitled to a lien for wages. What of a fish spotter who flies a seaplane and spots fish for a fishing fleet and is compensated party in cash and partly on a lay arrangement such as that involved in The Beverly Lynn? See Chance v. United States, 266 F.2d 874, 1959 A.M.C. 2045 (5th Cir.1959), holding no. What of maintenance personnel aboard a ship docked in navigable waters. See Port Welcome Cruises, Inc. v. S.S. Bay Belle, 215 F.Supp. 72, 1964 A.M.C. 2674 (D.Md.1963), holding yes. What if the services were provided by a business entity who used its own personnel. Could it claim a wage lien on the theory that its employees had a lien which it had acquired by subrogation. The Fifth Circuit has twice so held. See General Electric Credit & Leasing Corp. v. Drill Ship Mission Exploration, 668 F.2d 811, 1983 A.M.C. 958 (5th Cir.1982); International Paint Co. v. M/V Mission Viking, 637 F.2d 382, 1981 A.M.C. 1487 (5th Cir.1981). Both of these cases involved in part food service provided by a shore based caterer aboard a moored vessel.

What about a diver employed by an independent contractor working from a vessel? See Jernigan v. Lay Barge Delta Five, 296 F.Supp. 127, 1970 A.M.C. 2166 (S.D.Tex.1969), aff'd per curiam 423 F.2d 1327, 1970 A.M.C. 2169 (5th Cir.1970), holding no.

From very early times it was held that the master did not have a lien for his wages. See Freedom Line Inc. v. Vessel Glenrock, 268 F.Supp. 7, 1968 A.M.C. 507 (S.D.Fla.1967). What of the first mate? Cf. The Arie H., 1963 A.M.C. 1595 (S.D.Cal.1963), decided under Liberian law. In 1968 the Shipping Act was amended to provide a lien for master's wages. 46 U.S.C.A. § 606 (1979). In connection with the partial revision of Title 46 in 1983, § 606 was repealed without placement. Where does this leave the master's wage claim?

Assuming that the party asserting the lien is a seaman, the question sometimes arises as to whether the claims are for "wages" within the preference afforded such by the maritime law. Additional wages paid for extra-hazardous service have been held to be wages for the purposes of the lien law. The Herbert L. Rawding, 55 F.Supp. 156, 1944 A.M.C. 156, 1944 A.M.C. 222 (E.D.S.C.1944). So have statutory penalties for delayed payment of wages. The Chester, 25 F.2d 908, 1928 A.M.C. 638 (D.Md.1928). So, too, with statutory extra pay for improper discharge. The Fort Gaines, 18 F.2d 413, 1927 A.M.C. 655 (D.Md.1927). And with contractual dismissal benefits. Gayner v. The New Orleans, 54 F.Supp. 25, 1944 A.M.C. 462 (N.D.Cal.1944). Statutory penalty wages can amount to quite considerable sums. Under 46 U.S.C.A. §§ 10313(g) and 10504(c), failure to pay wages when due "without sufficient cause" may result in a penalty of two days wages for each day of delay. See Griffin v. Oceanic Contractors, Inc., 458 U.S. 564, 102 S.Ct. 3245, 73 L.Ed.2d 973 (1982), in which the seaman recovered $300,000 in penalties for late payment of $412.50 in wages.

"Comp time," which is pay in addition to the base pay, given for each day at sea or within a foreign port, is not "wages" under the Wage Statutes. Petersen v. Interocean Ships, Inc., 823 F.2d 334 (9th Cir.1987).

Would seamen have a lien for unpaid withholding taxes and F.I.C.A. payments? See P.C. Pfeiffer Co. v. The Pacific Star, 183 F.Supp. 932, 1960 A.M.C. 1666 (E.D.Va.1960), holding that where the employer has not deducted these payments the lien is for gross wages. In the particular case the withholding taxes and F.D.I.C. payments were deducted and paid over to the I.R.S. What about payments to retirement, welfare, and vacation funds? See Prudential Insurance v. United States Lines, Inc., 915 F.2d 411 (9th Cir. 1990); West Winds, Inc. v. M/V Resolute, 720 F.2d 1097, 1984 A.M.C. 319 (9th Cir.1983) (cert. denied 467 U.S. 1242, 104 S.Ct. 3513, 82 L.Ed.2d 822 (1984)); Barnouw v. S.S. Ozark, 304 F.2d 717, 1962 A.M.C. 1675 (5th Cir.1962); Brandon v. S.S. Denton, 302 F.2d 404, 1962 A.M.C. 1730 (5th Cir.1962); The Kingston, 1961 A.M.C. 1321 (S.D.Tex.1961). All hold no lien. Does it matter whether the lien is asserted by the fund trustees or the individual seaman? See Long Island Tankers Corp. v. S.S. Kaimana, 265 F.Supp. 723, 1967 A.M.C. 2467 (N.D.Cal.1967), aff'd 401 F.2d 182, 1968 A.M.C. 2778 (9th Cir.1968), cert denied 393 U.S. 1095, 89 S.Ct. 879, 21 L.Ed.2d 785, 1070 A.M.C. 255 (1969). Cf. Banco de Credito Industrial, S.A. v. Tesoreria General de la Seguridad Social de España, 990 F.2d 827, 1993 A.M.C. 2029 (5th Cir.1993), (holding that the Spanish Social Security Administration had no lien on a Spanish vessel securing the payment of social security obligations of seamen).

But if the seaman is personally liable for contributions or suffers a net loss through failure to pay, a wage lien may lie. See discussion in *Banco de Credito*, supra.

In United States Bulk Carriers, Inc. v. Arguelles, 400 U.S. 351, 91 S.Ct. 409, 27 L.Ed.2d 456 (1971), it was held that where seamen's wages are governed by a collective bargaining agreement the seaman need not proceed under § 301 of the Taft Hartley Act for enforcement of the agreement but may sue under 46 U.S.C.A. § 596, which in the 1983 partial revision of Title 46 has been placed in §§ 10313 and 10504.

2.   LIENS ARISING OUT OF CONTRACTS OF AFFREIGHTMENT

Osaka Shosen Kaisha v. Pacific Export Lumber Co.

Supreme Court of the United States, 1923.
260 U.S. 490, 43 S.Ct. 172, 67 L.Ed. 364.

■ MR. JUSTICE McREYNOLDS delivered the opinion of the Court.

March 19, 1917, through its agent at Tacoma, Wash., Osaka Shosen Kaisha, incorporated under the laws of Japan and owner of the Japanese steamer "Saigon Maru," then at Singapore, chartered the whole of that vessel, including her deck, to respondent Lumber Company to carry a full cargo of lumber from the Columbia or Willamette River to Bombay. In May, 1917, the vessel began to load at Portland, Ore. Having taken on a full underdeck cargo and 241,559 feet upon the deck, the captain refused to accept more. After insisting that that the vessel was not loaded to capacity and ineffectively demanding that she receive an additional 508,441 feet, respondent libeled her, setting up the charter party and the captain's refusal, and claimed substantial damages. The owner gave bond; the vessel departed and safely delivered her cargo.

The Lumber Company maintains that it suffered material loss by the ship's refusal to accept a full load; that she is liable therefor under the general admiralty law and also under the Oregon statute (Olson's Laws of Oregon, § 10,281), which declares every vessel navigating the waters of the State shall be subject to a lien for the damages resulting from nonperformance of affreightment contracts.

Petitioner excepted to the libel upon the ground that the facts alleged showed no lien or right to proceed *in rem*. The trial court ruled otherwise and awarded damages upon the evidence. 267 F. 881. The Circuit Court of Appeals approved this action. 272 F. 799 (1921).

Little need be written of the claim under the state statute. The rights and liabilities of the parties depend upon general rules of maritime law not subject to material alterations by state enactments. The Roanoke, 189 U.S. 185, 23 S.Ct. 491, 47 L.Ed. 770 (1902); Southern Pacific Co. v. Jensen, 244 U.S. 205, 37 S.Ct. 524, 61 L.Ed. 1086 (1916); Union Fish Co. v. Erickson, 248 U.S. 308, 39 S.Ct. 112, 63 L.Ed. 261 (1919).

Both courts below acted upon the view that while the ship is not liable *in rem* for breaches of an affreightment contract so long as it remains wholly executory, she becomes liable therefor whenever she partly executes it, as by taking on board some part of the cargo. In support of this view, it is said: Early decisions of our circuit and district courts held that under maritime law the ship is liable *in rem* for any breach of a contract of affreightment with owner or master. That The Freeman, 18 How. 182, 188, 15 L.Ed. 341 (1856), and The Yankee Blade, 19 How. 82, 89, 90, 91, 15 L.Ed. 554 (1857), modified this doctrine by denying such liability where the contract remains purely executory, but left it in full force where the vessel has partly performed the agreement, as by accepting part of the indicated cargo. The Hermitage, 12 F.Cas. 27; The Williams, 29 F.Cas. 1342; The Ira Chaffee, 2 F. 401 (1880); The Director, 26 F. 708 (1886); The Starlight, 42 F. 167 (1890); The Oscoda, 66 F. 347 (1895); The Helios, 108 F. 279 (1901); The Oceano, 148 F. 131 (1906); Wilson v. Peninsula Bark & Lumber Co., 110 C.C.A. 190, 188 F. 52 (1911), were cited.

We think the argument is unsound.

Prior to *The Freeman* and *The Yankee Blade,* this Court had expressed no opinion on the subject; but, so far as the reports show, the lower courts had generally asserted liability of the ship for breaches of affreightment contracts. "It is grounded upon the authority of the master to contract for the employment of the vessel, and upon the general doctrine of the maritime law, that the vessel is bodily answerable for such contracts of the master made for her benefit." The Flash, 1 Abb.Adm. 67, 70; The

Rebecca, 1 Ware, 188; *The Ira Chaffee,* supra.   Since 1857, some of the lower courts have said that the ship becomes liable for breaches of affreightment contracts with her owner or master whenever partly executed by her; but it is forcibly maintained that in none of the cases was the point directly involved.   *The Hermitage, The Williams, The Ira Chaffee, The Director, The Starlight, The Oscoda, The Helios, The Oceano, Wilson v. Peninsula Bark & Lumber Co.,* supra.

The Freeman and *The Yankee Blade* distinctly rejected the theory of the earlier opinions.   They are inconsistent with the doctrine that partial performance may create a privilege or lien upon the vessel.   And in so far as the lower courts express approval of this doctrine in their more recent opinions, they fail properly to interpret what has been said here.

While, perhaps, not essential to the decision, this Court, through Mr. Justice Curtis, said in *The Freeman*: "Under the maritime law of the United States the vessel is bound to the cargo, and the cargo to the vessel, for the performance of a contract of affreightment; but the law creates no lien on a vessel as a security for the performance of a contract to transport cargo, until some lawful contract of affreightment is made, and a cargo shipped under it."

In *The Yankee Blade,* Mr. Justice Grier, speaking for the Court, declared:

"The maritime 'privilege' or lien is adopted from the civil law, and imports a tacit hypothecation of the subject of it.   It is a '*jus in re,*' without actual possession or any right of possession.   It accompanies the property into the hands of a bona fide purchaser.   It can be executed and divested only by a proceeding *in rem*.   This sort of proceeding against personal property is unknown to the common law, and is peculiar to the process of courts of admiralty.   The foreign and other attachments of property in the State courts, though by analogy loosely termed proceedings *in rem,* are evidently not within the category.   But this privilege or lien, though adhering to the vessel, is a secret one; it may operate to the prejudice of general creditors and purchasers without notice; it is therefore '*stricti juris,*' and cannot be extended by construction, analogy, or inference.   'Analogy,' says Pardessus, (Droit Civ., vol. 3, 597,) 'cannot afford a decisive argument, because privileges are of *strict right*.   They are an exception to the rule by which all creditors have equal rights in the property of their debtor, and an exception should be declared and described in express words; we cannot arrive at it by reasoning from one case to another.'

"Now, it is a doctrine not to be found in any treatise on maritime law, that every contract by the owner or master of a vessel, for the future employment of it, hypothecates the vessel for its performance.   This lien or privilege is founded on the rule of maritime law as stated by Cleirac, (597:) 'Le batel est obligée à la marchandise et la marchandise au batel.'   The obligation is mutual and reciprocal.   The merchandise is bound or hypothecated to the vessel for freight and charges, (unless released by the covenants of the charter-party,) and the vessel to the cargo.   The bill of lading usually sets forth the terms of the contract, and shows the duty assumed by the vessel. Where there is a charter-party, its covenants will define the duties imposed on the ship. Hence it is said, (1 Valin, Ordon. de Mar., b. 3, tit. 1, art. 11,) that 'the ship, with her tackle, the freight, and the cargo, are respectively bound (affectée) by the covenants of the charter-party.' But this duty of the vessel, to the performance of which the law binds her by hypothecation, is to deliver the cargo at the time and place stipulated in the bill of lading or charter-party, without injury or deterioration. If the cargo be not placed on board, it is not bound to the vessel, and the vessel cannot be in default for the non-delivery, in good order, of goods never received on board. Consequently, if the master or owner refuses to perform his contract, or for any other reason the ship does not receive cargo and depart on her voyage according to contract, the charterer has no privilege or maritime lien on the ship for such breach of the contract by the owners, but must resort to his personal action for damages, as in other cases. * * *

"And this court has decided, in the case of The Freeman v. Buckingham, 18 How. 188, 15 L.Ed. 341 (1855), 'that the law creates no lien on a vessel as a security for the performance of a contract to transport cargo, until some lawful contract of affreightment is made, and a cargo shipped under it.' "

In Bulkley, Claimant of the Barque Edwin, v. Naumkeag Steam Cotton Co., 24 How. 386, 393, 16 L.Ed. 599 (1860), the barque was libeled to recover damages for not delivering part of the cotton—707 bales—which the master had agreed to carry from Mobile to Boston. With most of the cargo on board the vessel was towed below the bar, there to receive the remainder from lighters. A lighter carrying 100 bales sank, and the cotton was lost or damaged. The barque delivered 607 bales at Boston in good condition. The owner of the vessel claimed exemption for her upon the ground that she never received the 100 bales. This Court said: "In the present case the cargo was delivered in pursuance of the contract, the goods in the custody of the master, and subject to his lien for freight, as effectually as if they had been upon the deck of the ship, the contract confessedly binding both the owner and the shipper; and, unless it be held that the latter is entitled to his lien upon the vessel also, he is deprived of one of the privileges of the contract, when, at the same time, the owner is in the full enjoyment of all those belonging to his side of it."

Later opinions approve the same general rule.

"The doctrine that the obligation between ship and cargo is mutual and reciprocal, and does not attach until the cargo is on board, or in the custody of the master, has been so often discussed and so long settled, that it would be useless labor to restate it, or the principles which lie at its foundation. The case of The Freeman v. Buckingham, decided by this court, is decisive of this case." The Lady Franklin, 8 Wall. 325, 329, 19 L.Ed. 455 (1868).

"It is a principle of maritime law that the owner of the cargo has a lien on the vessel for any injury he may sustain by the fault of the vessel or the master; but the law creates no lien on a vessel as a security for the performance of a contract to transport a cargo until some lawful contract of affreightment is made, and the cargo to which it relates has been delivered to the custody of the master or some one authorized to receive it." The Keokuk, 9 Wall. 517, 519, 19 L.Ed. 744 (1869).

The maritime privilege or lien, though adhering to the vessel, is a secret one which may operate to the prejudice of general creditors and purchasers without notice and is therefore *stricti juris* and cannot be extended by construction, analogy or inference. *The Yankee Blade,* supra. The contract of affreightment itself creates no lien, and this Court has consistently declared that the obligation between ship and cargo is mutual and reciprocal and does not attach until the cargo is on board or in the master's custody. We think the lien created by the law must be mutual and reciprocal; the lien of the cargo owner upon the ship is limited by the corresponding and reciprocal rights of the ship owner upon the cargo. See The Thomas P. Sheldon, 113 F. 779, 782, 783 (D.C.R.I.1902).

The theory that partial acceptance of the designated cargo under a contract of affreightment creates a privilege or lien upon the ship for damages resulting from failure to take all, is inconsistent with the opinions of this Court and, we think, without support of adequate authority. In The S.L. Watson, 55 C.C.A. 439, 118 F. 945, 952 (1902), the court well said:

"The rule of admiralty, as always stated, is that the cargo is bound to the ship and the ship to the cargo. Whatever cases may have been decided otherwise disregarded the universal fact that no lien arises in admiralty except in connection with some visible occurrence relating to the vessel or cargo or to a person injured. This is necessary in order that innocent parties dealing with vessels may not be the losers by secret liens, the existence of which they have no possibility of detecting by any relation to any visible fact. It is in harmony with this rule that no lien lies in behalf of a vessel against her cargo for dead freight, or against a vessel for supplies contracted for, but not actually put aboard. The Kiersage, 2 Curt.C.C. 421, 14 F.Cas. 466 (1855); Pars. Ship. & Adm. (1869), 142, 143. It follows out the same principle that Mr. Justice Curtis states in The Kiersage, 2 Curt.C.C. 421, 14 F.Cas. 466 (1855), that admiralty liens are *stricti juris,* and that they cannot be extended argumentatively, or by analogy or inference. He says, 'They must be given by the law itself, and the case must be found described in the law.' "

Reversed.

NOTE

When the carrier contracted to carry three parcels of cargo, with an option to use two or three vessels, and elected to use three, and loaded the first two onto two vessels, but failed to tender the third vessel for the loading of the third, the shipper could not enforce an arbitration award as a lien. Sumitomo Corp. v. M/V Cosmos, 1983 A.M.C. 595 (S.D.Tex.1982).

The same principle has been applied to executory contracts for transportation of passengers and their baggage. See Acker v. The City of Athens, 177 F.2d 961,

1950 A.M.C. 282 (4th Cir.1949); The Priscilla, 114 F. 836 (2d Cir.1902); The Bella, 91 Fed. 540 (D.Wash.1899). As to what sort of delivery constitutes delivery of the cargo for the purpose of making the contract executed, see The Vigilancia, 58 Fed. 698 (S.D.N.Y.1893). See Gilmore and Black, *Law of Admiralty,* § 9–22 (1975). In *The Vigilancia* it was stated that the goods must be "either actually put on board * * * or * * * brought within the immediate presence or control of the officers of the ship." It should be noted that the court indicated that this rule applied to supplies as well as cargo. The question of delivery of supplies is treated at p. 434, infra.

Krauss Bros. Lumber Co. v. Dimon Steamship Corp.

Supreme Court of the United States, 1933.
290 U.S. 117, 54 S.Ct. 105, 78 L.Ed. 216.

■ MR. JUSTICE STONE delivered the opinion of the Court.

This suit in admiralty was brought by petitioner in the District Court for Western Washington against respondent, the steamship "Pacific Cedar," and its owner, the respondent Dimon Steamship Corporation, to recover an alleged overpayment of freight and to establish a lien on the vessel for the amount of the overpayment. The libel alleges a contract by petitioner with the owner, by which the latter agreed to receive for loading on the "Pacific Cedar," on or about January 18, 1930, at named Pacific Coast ports, a quantity of lumber, and to transport it to Philadelphia and New York at the rate of $10.00 per thousand feet, but with a provision that in the event "a regular intercoastal carrier moves similar cargo at a lower rate," such lower rate should be applied. The libel makes no reference to any bill of lading but sets up that the lumber was shipped and transported, and between March 1st and 20th was delivered, all under the provisions of the contract, and that at the conclusion of the voyage and while the vessel was discharging her cargo, respondents, at destination, demanded and received payment of freight at the $10.00 rate, although in January, 1930, a regular intercoastal carrier had carried a similar cargo from Seattle to Baltimore at $8.50 per thousand feet.

The lien asserted is for the difference between the freight paid and the freight earned at the agreed lower rate. Upon exceptions the District Court dismissed the libel for want of admiralty jurisdiction. 53 F.2d 492 (1932). The Court of Appeals for the Ninth Circuit reversed the decree dismissing the libel *in personam,* but affirmed so much of it as dismissed the libel *in rem.* 61 F.2d 187 (1932). This Court granted certiorari on petition of the libellant alone, 289 U.S. 716, 53 S.Ct. 594, 77 L.Ed. 1469 (1933), to resolve an alleged conflict between the decision below and that of the Court of Appeals for the Sixth Circuit in The Oregon, 55 F. 666, 676 (1893). The only question presented here is whether the petitioner is entitled to a lien on the vessel for the overpaid freight.

While there has been a lack of unanimity in the decisions as to the precise limits of the lien in favor of the cargo, see Osaka Shosen Kaisha v. Pacific Export Lumber Co., 260 U.S. 490, 43 S.Ct. 172, 67 L.Ed. 364 (1922), the cases are agreed that the right to the lien has its source in the contract of affreightment and that the lien itself is justified as a means by which the vessel, treated as a personality or as impliedly hypothecated to secure the performance of the contract is made answerable for nonperformance. See The Freeman, 18 How. 182, 188, 15 L.Ed. 341 (1855); Vandewater v. Mills, 19 How. 82, 90, 15 L.Ed. 554 (1856); Osaka Shosen Kaisha v. Pacific Export Lumber Co., supra; The Flash, 1 Abb.Adm. 67, 9 F.Cas. 252 (1847); The Rebecca, 1 Ware 188, 20 F.Cas. 373 (1830); Scott v. The Ira Chaffee, 2 F. 401 (D.C.Mich.1880). This engagement of the vessel, or its hypothecation, as distinguished from the personal obligation of the owner, does not ensue upon the mere execution of the contract for transportation. Only upon the lading of the vessel, or at least when she is ready to receive the cargo—where there is "union of ship and cargo"—does the contract become the contract of the vessel and the right to the lien attach. No lien for breach of the contract to carry results from failure of the vessel to receive and load the cargo or a part of it. See Osaka Shosen Kaisha v. Pacific Export Lumber Co., supra.

It is not questioned here that the union of ship and cargo, once established, gives rise to the right of the vessel to a lien on the cargo for the freight money and of the cargo on the vessel for failure to carry safely and deliver rightly. The breach now alleged is only that the freight demanded on discharge of the cargo was in excess of that stipulated by the contract, and respondent insists that the liens in favor of cargo growing out of the contract of affreightment are restricted to those claims founded on breach of the obligation to carry and deliver. But the undertaking to charge the agreed freight and no more is an inseparable incident to every contract of affreightment, as essential to it and as properly a subject of admiralty jurisdiction as is the obligation of the cargo to pay freight when earned, or of the vessel to carry safely. See Matson Navigation Co. v. United States, 284 U.S. 352, 358, 52 S.Ct. 162, 76 L.Ed. 336 (1932). It is unlike an agreement to pay a commission to the broker procuring the charter party, Brown v. West Hartlepool Steam Navigation Co., 50 C.C.A. 664, 112 F. 1018 (1902), or a provision for storing cargo in the vessel at the end of the voyage, Pillsbury Flour Mills Co. v. Interlake Steamship Co., 40 F.2d 439 (2 Cir.1945), which, though embodied in the contract of carriage for hire, are no necessary part of it.

It is not denied, and the cases hold, that there is a lien for excessive freight knowingly exacted as a condition of delivery of the cargo, The John Francis, 184 F. 746 (D.C.Ala.1911); The Ada, 233 F. 325 (D.C.Md.1916); The Muskegon, 10 F.2d 817 (D.C.N.Y.1924); Tatsuuma Kisen Kabushiki Kaisha v. Robert Dollar Co., 31 F.2d 401 (9 Cir.1929); cf. The Oregon, 5 C.C.A. 229, 55 F. 666, 677 (1893); but it is argued that in that case the generating source of the right is the failure to perform the transportation contract by refusal to deliver the cargo. The fact that the breach of one term of the contract, the agreement to charge only the stipulated freight, coincides with the breach of another, to make delivery, does not obscure the fact that both terms are broken, and that the substance of the right to recover is for the freight collected in excess of that agreed upon, not damages for failure to make delivery. Nor does the fact that there is breach of both afford any basis for saying that the breach of either term alone could not give rise to the lien. This becomes more apparent upon examination of the numerous cases in which a lien has been imposed for some breach of the freight term.[1]

In *The Oregon*, supra, the time charterer sold the tonnage of the vessel for a single voyage at a rate in advance of that stipulated in the charter party. Her captain collected the freight at the agreed higher rate and retained it. The Court of Appeals for the Sixth Circuit, Judge Taft writing the opinion, sustained the jurisdiction *in rem* to recover the excess on the ground that its collection was incidental to the execution of the maritime contract, and to be treated as an overpayment of freight. This conclusion is obviously inconsistent with the view that the affreightment lien in favor of the cargo is dependent on the failure of the vessel to carry and deliver. The right to a lien for the mistaken overpayment of freight was involved in The Oceano, 148 F. 131 (D.C.N.Y.1906), where the charterer advanced charter freight to provide a fund for the vessel's disbursements, under stipulation that the advance should be deducted from the freight earned under the charter party. Upon settlement at the port of destination the libellant's agent, by mistake, deducted less than the advances made. The court, Judge Hough writing the opinion, held, treating the settlement as an overpayment of the charter freight, that the cause was one of affreightment and that a lien attached to the vessel for the amount of the overpayment.

It was argued to us, as it has been in other cases, that, as the payment for excess freight was made under mistake, the demand is upon a cause of action for money had and received, which lies only at common law and not in admiralty. The objection applies with equal force to the liens allowed for excess freight, payment of which was procured by fraud or duress, or for freight paid in advance where the voyage was abandoned after the ship was loaded.[2] Admiralty is not concerned with the form of the action, but with

---

1. Lien for freight paid in advance but not earned under the terms of the contract of affreightment: The Harriman, 9 Wall. 161, 19 L.Ed. 629 (1869); The Panama, 18 F.Cas. 1073; cf. The A.M. Bliss, 1 F.Cas. 593; Church v. Shelton, 5 F.Cas. 674. (See also Allanwilde Transport Corp. v. Vacuum Oil Co., 248 U.S. 377, 39 S.Ct. 147, 63 L.Ed. 312 (1918) and International Paper Co. v. The Gracie D. Chambers, 248 U.S. 387, 39 S.Ct. 149, 63 L.Ed. 318 (1918), 39 S.Ct. 147, 63 L.Ed. 312, where the lien was denied because the freight was held to have been earned.) Lien for charges or purchase price of the cargo, collected by the master from the consignee for account of the shipper as provided in the contract of affreightment: The Hardy, 11 F.Cas. 503; The St. Joseph, 21 F.Cas. 176; Zollinger v. The Emma, 30 F.Cas. 939; cf. The New Hampshire, 21 F. 924 (D.C.Mich., 1880); Krohn v. The Julia, 37 F. 369,

(C.C.La., 1889). Lien in favor of the charterer for freight earned in violation of the charter party by the ship manned and officered by the owner; The Port Adelaide, 59 F. 174 (D.C.N.Y., 1893). Lien for freight overpaid, as dead freight for shortage of cargo, wrongfully exacted by threat of attachment of the cargo actually shipped and delivered according to the contract: The Lake Eckhart, 31 F.2d 804 (S.D.N.Y.1924). Lien for salvage, payment of which by the cargo was fraudulently procured by the master, who had wilfully stranded the vessel: Church v. Shelton, supra. Lien for the excess of a deposit by the cargo owner in a general average fund, the right of recovery being founded on the master's duty, and hence the ship's, to make the general average adjustment: The Emilia S. De Perez, 22 F.2d 585, (D.C.Md.1928).

2. See note 1, supra.

its substance.   Even under the common law form of action for money had and received there could be no recovery without proof of the breach of the contract involved in demanding the payment, and the basis of recovery there, as in admiralty, is the violation of some term of the contract of affreightment, whether by failure to carry or by exaction of freight which the contract did not authorize.   See The Oceano, supra, 132; but cf. Israel v. Moore & McCormack Co., 295 F. 919 (D.C.N.Y.1920).

It seems equally obvious that lack of knowledge by the parties at the time of the payment that the freight demanded was excessive should have no bearing on the existence of the lien.   There is no hint in the books that the security given by way of lien for the performance of the contract of affreightment depends upon such knowledge.   The liability of the vessel for damage to cargo affords a not infrequent example of a lien which may attach, although at the time of unloading cargo there was no knowledge of the particular events which effected the breach.   See Rich v. Lambert, 12 How. 347, 13 L.Ed. 1017 (1851).

We see no distinction, either in principle or with respect to the practical operation or convenience of maritime commerce, between the lien asserted here for overpayment of freight by mistake and those for overpayments similarly made but induced by other means.   Here, as there, the overpayment, made as the cargo was unloaded, occurred while the union of ship and cargo continued, and the liability asserted was determined by events contemporaneous with that union.   The circumstances which called the lien into being do not differ in point of notoriety from those giving rise to other affreightment liens upon the vessel.   While it is true that the maritime lien is secret, hence is *stricti juris* and not to be extended by implication, this does not mean that the right to the lien is not to be recognized and upheld, when within accepted supporting principles, merely because the circumstances which call for its recognition are unusual or infrequent.

The suggestion made on the argument that the lien asserted here, after the cargo is discharged, is affected by application of the often stated rule that the liens on ship and cargo are mutual and reciprocal, is without basis. It is only the obligations of ship and cargo under the contract of affreightment which are to be characterized as mutual and reciprocal, not the liens which result from the breach of those obligations.   The one lien may come into existence without the other and the lien on the ship in favor of cargo, not being possessory, see Dupont De Nemours & Co. v. Vance, 19 How. 162, 15 L.Ed. 584 (1856); Tatsuuma Kisen Kabushiki Kaisha v. Robert Dollar Co., supra, may survive the lien of ship on cargo which is terminated by unconditional delivery.[3]   In re 4,885 Bags of Linseed, 1 Black 108, 17 L.Ed. 35 (1861).

---

3.   The statement that liens of affreightment on ship and cargo are mutual and reciprocal is based on the frequently quoted phrase of Cleirac (597): "Le batel est obligé à la marchandise et la marchandise au batel."

Judge Hough indicated in The Saturnus, 250 F. 407, 412 (C.C.A.N.Y.1918) that Cleirac's "clever phrase" referred to the mutual obligations flowing from the union of the personified ship and personified cargo.

We note, but do not discuss, the objection that the libel may be taken to allege only a voluntary overpayment of the freight without mistake. We think it may be construed to mean that the payment was made without knowledge at the time that a lower rate controlled. The court below took that to be its meaning. Certiorari was granted to review the question decided below and not the sufficiency of the pleadings to raise it.

Reversed.

■ Mr. Justice McReynolds, Mr. Justice Sutherland, Mr. Justice Butler and Mr. Justice Roberts are of opinion that the challenged judgment should be affirmed.

Secret liens are not favored, they should not be extended by construction, analogy or inference, or to circumstances where there is ground for serious doubt. Osaka Shosen Kaisha v. Pacific Export Lumber Co., 260 U.S. 490, 43 S.Ct. 172, 67 L.Ed. 364 (1922).

United States v. Steamship Lucie Schulte

United States Court of Appeals, Second Circuit, 1965.
343 F.2d 897, 1965 A.M.C. 1516.

■ Henry J. Friendly, Ct. J. This libel, tried on a stipulation of facts and exhibits before the late Judge Dawson, 227 F.Supp. 583, 1965 A.M.C. 1522 (D.C.N.Y.1964), raises questions, seemingly not yet settled by authority, on the old subject of maritime liens.

On two occasions in 1957, Schulte & Bruns, a German partnership owning the Lucie Schulte, time-chartered her to Three Bays Corporation, Ltd., of Nassau, Bahamas. The charters on a standard form (designated "Government Form, approved by the New York Produce Exchange") contained a provision that

"Charterers will not suffer, nor permit to be continued, any lien or encumbrance incurred by them or their agents, which might have priority over the title and interest of the owners in the vessel."

On three occasions during the charter periods the United States, acting through the Navy's Military Sea Transportation Service and the Transportation Office, Patrick Air Force Base, made shipments on the Lucie Schulte from Port Canaveral, Florida, to installations in the British West Indies. The bills of lading, standard Government forms, designated the "transportation company" as "Three Bays Line (MS M/V Lucie Schulte)," and were signed by an officer or agent of Three Bays Lines, Inc., apparently a branch

---

It has often been pointed out that the lien on cargo is not strictly a privilege (see Pothier, Maritime Contract, Translation by Caleb Cushing, Boston, 1821, 94–50; Hennebicq, Principes de droit Maritime, Brussels, 1904, 316) as is the lien on the ship, but is more like the possessory lien of the land carrier and, like it, does not survive the un-conditional delivery of the cargo. See Cutler v. Rae, 7 How. 729, 12 L.Ed. 890 (1849); 4,885 Bags of Linseed, 1 Black 108, 113, 17 L.Ed. 35 (1861); The Bird of Paradise, 5 Wall. 545, 18 L.Ed. 662 (1866); The Eddy, 5 Wall. 481, 494, 18 L.Ed. 486 (1866) and the full discussion in Wellman v. Morse, 22 C.C.A. 318, 76 F. 573 (1896).

of the charterer organized as a Florida corporation. Under a "conference tariff concurrence" filed with the Federal Maritime Board by Three Bays pursuant to 46 U.S.C.A. § 817, the charges on the Government's shipments were limited to those specified in the Leeward & Windward Island & Guianas Conference Southbound Freight Tariff No. 6. Freight was demanded by Three Bays Lines, Inc., and paid by the Government at dates ranging from three weeks to four months after the respective deliveries. Although the vouchers certified "that the rates charged are not in excess of the lowest net rates available for the Government, based on tariffs effective at the date of service," the amounts paid exceeded such rates by $4,288.86. Some three and a half years later the Government brought this libel to recover that amount from the ship *in rem* and Three Bays Lines, Inc., *in personam;* the latter was not served and apparently is insolvent.

The alternative defenses relied on by the claimant-owner were that the overcharges had been made after cessation of the "union of ship and cargo," see Krauss Bros. Lumber Co. v. Dimon S. S. Corp., 290 U.S. 117, 121, 125, 54 S.Ct. 105, 78 L.Ed. 216, 1933 A.M.C. 1578, 1580 (1933), and that under the circumstances the "prohibition of lien" clause of the charter barred the government's assertion of a lien for overpayments exacted by a time-charterer. Agreeing with Judge Dawson's rejection of the first defense, we think he was mistaken in overruling the second.

(1) Supporting its first defense, the owner relies on policy arguments against maritime liens, summed up in the oft-quoted statement that the lien "is a secret one, which may operate to the prejudice of general creditors and purchasers without notice, and is therefore *stricti juris,* and cannot be extended by construction, analogy, or inference." Osaka Shosen Kaisha v. Pacific Export Lumber Co., 260 U.S. 490, 499, 43 S.Ct. 172, 67 L.Ed. 364, 1923 A.M.C. 55, 59 (1923), paraphrasing The Yankee Blade, 60 U.S. 82, 89, 15 L.Ed. 554 (1857). But neither such general considerations nor the decision in Pacific Export, applying to a portion of cargo not yet loaded the settled rule that a lien does not arise from an unjustified refusal to accept the goods for shipment, The Saturnus, 162 C.C.A. 477, 250 F. 407 (1918), cert. denied 247 U.S. 521, 38 S.Ct. 583, 62 L.Ed. 1247 (1918), see Gilmore & Black on *Admiralty,* sec. 9–22 (1957), would support a distinction impossible to justify on any ground of logic or of policy. The *Krauss Bros.* case overrode an attempted distinction far more tenable than that asserted here—namely, between a refusal to deliver unless the excessive charges were paid, amounting to a threat of conversion, and a demand for such charges *simpliciter,* giving rise to liability in contract or quasi contract. Once that barrier has been crossed, it would be altogether irrational to have the existence of a lien turn on whether the demand was made, or the payment received, while the goods were on the ship, on a pier in the ship's control, or later. That the high financial responsibility—or the complicated accounting procedures—of a particular shipper may induce or require the carrier to defer demand and payment is irrelevant to the recognition of a lien in favor of the shipper, the "vice" of which is as great when payment is made earlier as when made later.

The loss of the carrier's possessory lien on the goods on the latters' delivery is similarly irrelevant. "Mutuality", is no more appealing in this branch of the law than elsewhere, see Cardozo, *The Growth of the Law* 14–16 (1924); Zdanok v. Glidden Co., 327 F.2d 944, 954–55 (2 Cir.1964), cert. denied 377 U.S. 934, 84 S.Ct. 1338, 12 L.Ed.2d 298 (1964), and it would be unreasonable to spell out from the mere fact of delivery and receipt an agreement by the shipper to forego any lien to which it would be entitled in the absence of such a release. Indeed, *Krauss Bros.* itself sufficiently settles this point. Although that case was decided on the pleadings, which do not disclose whether payments were simultaneous with the various deliveries or a short time thereafter, 290 U.S. at 120, 1933 A.M.C. at 1583, no one seemed to think anything turned on this, the important point pressed by the ship and rejected by the Supreme Court being that excessive payment was not demanded as a condition of delivery. See Judge L. Hand's analysis of the decision in Sword Line, Inc. v. United States, 228 F.2d 344, 346, 1056 A.M.C. 47 (2 Cir.1955), aff'd on rehearing 230 F.2d 75, 1956 A.M.C. 1277, aff'd 351 U.S. 976, 76 S.Ct. 1047, 100 L.Ed. 1493, 1056 A.M.C. 1464 (1956). Moreover, the Supreme Court's opinion approved 290 U.S. at 124, 1933 A.M.C. at 1582, Judge Hough's decision in The Oceano, 148 F. 131 (S.D.N.Y.1906), recognizing a lien for an overpayment by a charterer's agent, apparently made some days after the "union" of charter-party and vessel had ended. We thus cannot give the statement of Mr. Justice Stone, 290 U.S. at 125, 1933 A.M.C. at 1582,—"the over-payment made as the cargo was unloaded, occurred while the union of ship and cargo continued, and the liability asserted was determined by events contemporaneous with that union"—enough weight to tilt the scales in the owner's favor; context suggests that the opinion was stressing factual similarity with prior cases and not fixing the outer limits of the lien. Only a paragraph later Mr. Justice Stone declared that "it is only the obligations of ship and cargo under the contract which are to be characterized as mutual and reciprocal, not the liens which result from the breach of those obligations." 290 U.S. at 125–26, 1933 A.M.C. 1583.

* * *

Reversed, with instructions to dismiss the libel in rem.

NOTE

See Melwire Trading Co., Inc. v. M/V Cape Antibes, 811 F.2d 1271 (9th Cir.1987). There it was held that a consignee of cargo could not proceed against the vessel in rem for damages allegedly occasioned by the late delivery of cargo when the cargo was delivered undamaged and was worth more than it was on the date on which it should have been delivered. The action could proceed, however, against the carrier in personam. See modified opinion at 830 F.2d 1083 (9th Cir.1987). There the court of appeals expressed the opinion that the decision in *Kraus Bros.* is properly limited to overpayment of freight and otherwise a lien does not arise in favor of cargo except where there is a visible damage to the cargo.

Cargo is not considered an appurtenance of the vessel and therefore is not covered by a maritime lien against the vessel. See 1 Benedict, *Admiralty* § 59 (6th

Ed. (Knauth) 1940).   Under certain circumstances, however, there is a lien on the cargo.   The vessel owner has a lien against cargo for the payment of freight.   The nature of such a lien is discussed in subdivision A.3, supra.   Such a lien is also imposed in the case of demurrage (See The Hyperion's Cargo, 2 Low. 93, 12 Fed.Cas. 1138 (No. 6987) (D.Mass.1871)), lighterage (See The Owego, 292 Fed. 403 (E.D.La.1923)), and general average (See The Emilia S. De Perez, 22 F.2d 585 (D.Md.1927)).   When a vessel is on charter the owner may preserve a lien on cargo to secure payment of amounts due under the charter.   See Gilmore and Black, *Law of Admiralty* §§ 4–9, 4–11 (1975).

SHIPOWNERS' LIEN FOR CHARTER HIRE

When cargo is shipped under a bill of lading or under a time or voyage charter under which freights are collected by the owner or his agents, payment of the freight is enforcible by the carrier through his possessory lien on the cargo, i.e., the carrier can retain the cargo until the freight is paid or through some warehousing or other arrangement avoid an unconditional discharge, thereby preserving his security.   If the vessel is under a bareboat charter or a time charter under which the charterer operates the vessel and collects the freights, the owner, in an effort to secure the payment of sums due under the charter, usually includes a clause giving him a lien on freights or sub-freights, and in effect subrogating the owner to the carrier's lien on cargo.   For an example of the utility of such a provision, see Matter of Bauer S.S. Corp., 167 F.Supp. 909, 1958 A.M.C. 2190 (S.D.N.Y.1957), where the time charterer went bankrupt two days after the cargo was loaded on the vessel. The court held that the lien on sub-freights attached at the moment of loading. The owner's lien on the cargo depends upon notice to the shipper and payment in good faith to the charterer will defeat such a lien.   See, e.g., Toro Shipping Corp. v. Bacon–McMillan Veneer Mfg. Co. (The Nadine), 364 F.2d 928, 1966 A.M.C. 2290 (5th Cir.1966).   There the shipper paid the freight in advance without notice of the reserved lien on cargo.   In the meanwhile the owner had become concerned over failure to pay charter hire and had sent one of its officials to South America to consult with the master of the vessel.   As a result of this consultation the master declined to sail unless the lien notice was put in the bill of lading.   The vessel remained in port an extra day while the parties engaged in a dispute over the matter and then the charterer agreed to the incorporation of the notice.   The shipper (purchaser of the cargo) was totally unaware of any of these goings on.   An earlier shipment of the same sort of cargo had been made to him under bills of lading that did not give notice of the charter provision preserving the lien.   See also In re North Atlantic & Gulf S.S. Co., 252 F.Supp. 724, 1963 A.M.C. 871 (S.D.N.Y. 1966).   When the consignee is on notice of the lien, he may deposit the amount of the freight in escrow and obtain discharge of the cargo.   This was done in N.H. Shipping Corp. v. Freights of S/S Jackie Hause, 181 F.Supp. 165, 1961 A.M.C. 83 (S.D.N.Y.1960).   Cf. Bienvenido Shipping Co. v. Sub–Freights of the S.S. Andora, 168 F.Supp. 127, 1958 A.M.C. 2161 (E.D.N.Y.1957), where an attachment of sub-freights was vacated on a showing that the full amount of the owner's claim had been deposited in court in London pending arbitration.   When the cargo is thus discharged, the owner's lien on the freights is substituted for a possessory lien on cargo.   See Compania De Navegacione Almirante S. A. Panama, v. Certain Proceeds of Cargo, etc. (The Searaven), 288 F.Supp. 77, 1968 A.M.C. 704 (C.D.Cal.1967) rev'd on a finding that as to charter hire the cargo had been unconditionally released 437 F.2d 301 (9th Cir.1971); The Freights of the Jackie Hause, supra.   As we have seen, when the lien exists it may be enforced in a proceeding *in rem* in the admiralty. Freights of the Mount Shasta, supra, at p. 263. It has been held, however, that in an action like The Mount Shasta, the res attached is the obligation of the consignee to pay freight, and not a specific fund in the hands of the consignee, and that therefore after the freight has been paid to the charterer, even after notice, the owner has no lien on the funds in the hands of the charterer or his agent. Cornish Shipping Ltd. v. International Nederlanden Bank N.V., 53 F.3d 499 (2d Cir.1995).

3. Liens for Repairs, Supplies and Other Necessaries

BACKGROUND OF THE LIEN ACT

The early history of the home port supply lien has been discussed in connection with the saving to suitors clause. See note following The Hine v. Trevor, supra at p. 144. After the amendment of the Admiralty Rules in 1872 to permit foreclosure in admiralty of home port liens created by state law, and the refusal of the Supreme Court to create a national lien law in The Lottawanna, there was a period of thirty-eight years during which the Court patched together American lien law from the general law of the admiralty and the state statutes. This process was not without its uncertainties. See Smith, The Confusion in the Law Relating to Materialmen's Liens on Vessels, 21 Harv.L.Rev. 332 (1908). See also Gilmore and Black, *Law of Admiralty,* § 9–29 (1975). The latter sums up the policy of the court on the enforcement of statutory provisions covering filing, duration, and discharge thus: "Sometimes [they] will be enforced and sometimes they will not."

In 1910 Congress enacted the Lien Act. While the draftsmanship of the act has been criticized (See Gilmore and Black, *Law of Admiralty,* § 9–30 (1957)), it has resulted in substantial uniformity in the treatment of materialmen's liens insofar as uniformity is achieved in an area in which Supreme Court review is rare. The provisions of the Lien Act of 1910 were amended and incorporated into the Ship Mortgage Act of 1920, 41 Stat. 1005, 46 U.S.C.A. §§ 971–975. They now appear, mutatis mutandis, as 46 U.S.C §§ 31341–31343.

A. NECESSARIES

J. Ray McDermott & Co. v. The Off–Shore Menhaden Co.

United States Court of Appeals, Fifth Circuit, 1959.
262 F.2d 523, 1959 A.M.C. 527.

■ John R. Brown, Ct. J. In the bankruptcy proceeding of appellant, The Off–Shore Menhaden Company, J. Ray McDermott & Co., Inc. unsuccessfully sought a maritime lien against two vessels of the Bankrupt for the cost of dredging out a special slip on Rattlesnake Bayou, Louisiana, for use as a permanent berth. I affirm.

What we know, and all we know, comes from a stipulation of the parties. It may be briefly summarized. In 1955 the Bankrupt commenced its operations in the processing of menhaden fish into scraps, oils, and solubles. It owned only three vessels. Two were the dumb-barges, Fish Factory No. 1 and Abl 123, the other, the fishing utility towing vessel Bebeco. The barges were equipped with machinery and facilities for the complete processing of menhaden.

In the first season of 1955, the factory barges were anchored in the Gulf of Mexico nearby the supporting fishing vessels. This proved unprofitable because of irretrievable loss of equipment overboard, high wages for the labor force held at sea for long periods of time, and continual interruption of operations by heavy seas, gales and Gulf of Mexico weather disturbances requiring removal of the flotilla to and from ports of haven.

In the second season of 1956 the vessels were anchored in Rattlesnake Bayou. This location was reasonably close both to the fishing grounds in the Gulf, as well as the land market for the finished products. But this, too, proved unsuitable because of loss of equipment overboard, the continued, though less frequent, withdrawals to safe refuge during weather disturbances, and undoubtedly most important, the continual necessity of shifting anchorage to accommodate the substantial movement of nondescript oil field vessels moving up and down the Bayou. These deficiencies for both 1955 and 1956 were the primary cause of the financial[ly] unprofitable operations of the Bankrupt.

To avoid this, Bankrupt in 1957, after securing necessary approval from Federal and State regulatory agencies as well as permission of the owners of the land adjacent to the Bayou, arranged with McDermott to dredge out a berth on Rattlesnake Bayou. The slip was dredged out of the bank to a uniform depth of ten feet. It cut far enough into the shore to accommodate the beam of the two factory barges, to afford protection from weather disturbances, and, at the same time, provide a mooring on the offshore side of the barges for loading and unloading fishing vessels without interfering with the movement of other craft within the established navigational lines of the Bayou.

The slip was dredged in length sufficient to accommodate the factory barges end to end.

The dispute here is whether this was the "furnishing [of] repairs, supplies, towage, use of drydock or marine railway, or other necessaries * * * to [a] vessel" as the Maritime Lien Act prescribes. 46 U.S.C.A. § 971. We approach the problem as we have before with no niggardly begrudging interpretation of "other necessaries." For "we the statutory words 'other necessaries' should not be narrowly interpreted as was done in cases like J. Doherty, The Hatteras, supra (sic), Muskegon, 275 F. 348 (2 Cir.1921), Suelco, 286 F. 286 (E.D.N.Y.1922), but that they should be given a broad meaning, as they were in Rupert City, 213 F. 263 (W.D.Wash.1914), and Henry S. Grove, 285 F. 60 (W.D.Wash.1922), and held to include maritime services generally, at least insofar as port charges are concerned, whether such services consist of the furnishing of labor or material." Western Wave, 77 F.2d 695, 698, 1935 A.M.C. 985 (5 Cir.1935), cert. denied 296 U.S. 633, 56 S.Ct. 156, 80 L.Ed. 450, 1935 A.M.C. 1444. See also

Griffin, The Federal Maritime Lien Act, 37 Harv.L.Rev. * * * (1923), reprinted 1924 A.M.C. 206, and Gilmore & Black, *Admiralty* 542–43 (1957).

But neither this approach which must frequently lead to the allowance of maritime liens to new and infrequent situations, Krauss Bros. Lumber Co. v. Dimon Steamship Corp., 290 U.S. 117, 54 S.Ct. 105, 78 L.Ed. 216, 1933 A.M.C. 1578 (1933), nor the assumption that the act of dredging was a maritime activity of the dredge, Butler v. Ellis, 45 F.2d 951, 1931 A.M.C. 77 (4 Cir.1930); cf. McKie v. Diamond Marine Co., 204 F.2d 132, 1953 A.M.C. 1409 (5 Cir.1953) makes this out to be a lien.

The lien is not here asserted to cover the charge of a *service* rendered to the vessels. This would be the case were it for wharfage, or in the Bayou wilderness, vicarious wharfage for the *use* of the slip by the factory barges. *Western Wave,* supra. What is sought here is not the cost for the service, but rather the cost of constructing the capital facility by which that service is furnished or becomes available. This distinction is emphasized by the repeated use of the word "services" in the closing refrains of McDermott's brief as it urges a favorable contrast of this case with others cited by it. "Surely, appellant's services were no less necessary to enable the subject vessels to earn their revenues, or 'freight,' than were the cooperage services, stevedoring services,[1] canal services,[2] wharfage services,[3] fumigation services,[4] storage services,[5] travel services,[6] and kindred other services involved in the cases cited * * *."

The statutory concept of a maritime lien is phrased in broad generalities. The idea of "other necessaries" unavoidably calls for judicial application in equally broad terms. For example, this has been stated to be "what is reasonably needed in the ship's business," The Penn, 273 F. 990, 991 (3 Cir.1921). And to determine this, "regard must be had to the character of the voyage or the employment in which the vessel is being used." Walker–Skageth Food Stores, Inc. v. Bavois, 43 F.Supp. 109, 110, 1942 A.M.C. 211 (S.D.N.Y.1942) quoting from The Satellite, 188 F. 717, 720 (D.Mass.1910). This means that the decision in individual cases cannot be a mere mechanical one of semantics. It must frequently be a matter of degree. In this light, while this berth was perhaps of operational indispensability to profitable activities of this unique flotilla, this is an effort to obtain a maritime lien for the cost of capital structures and facilities apart from the vessels. If it may be done for a slip, there is no reason why it may not be done for a wharf, if for a wharf, then the adjacent dock and warehouse shed, if for them, the essential railway switching tracks, the overhead cranes, the marine legs for grain and ore handling, banana elevators, railroad car derricks for seatrain vessels, or one hundred and one other such possibilities.

1. Henry S. Grove, 285 F. 60, (W.D.Wash.1922).

2. In re Burton S.S. Co., 3 F.2d 1015, 1925 A.M.C. 335 (D.Mass., 1925).

3. *Western Wave,* supra.

4. The Susquehanna, 3 F.2d 1014, 1923 A.M.C. 643 (D.Mass., 1923).

5. The Artemis, 53 F.2d 672, 1932 A.M.C. 195 (S.D.N.Y., 1931).

6. The Egeria, 294 F. 791, 1924 A.M.C. 126 (9 Cir.1923).

The effort to liken this to the cases of Gulfport, 162 C.C.A. 593, 250 F. 577 (5 Cir.1918), and William Leishear, 21 F.2d 862, 864, 1927 A.M.C. 1770, 1773 (D.Md.1927), is unrealistic. Each of these involved liens for dredging out channels to free vessels then stranded high and dry after severe storms. As both opinions so plainly reflect, these were essentially services in the nature of salvage. We characterized it thus in *Gulfport*: "A service rendered in restoring a vessel so placed to the element in which alone it is of use, from which it was forced by the violence of a storm, is of a nature to facilitate or render possible the continuance of its use as an instrument of navigation. * * *." 250 F. at 580. Unless the services there involved were performed, the vessels would have ended their lives in an ignominious land-locked grave. Here the new slip facilitated the menhaden operation to be sure. But the continued life of the Fishing Factory No. 1 and Abl 123 as floating navigating vessels did not depend on it, as witnesses the departure of the vessels from the slip when they were towed to Appalachicola, Florida, after the collapse of Bankrupt's Louisiana operations.

Affirmed.

N O T E

The more recent cases are in line with those set out in the footnotes in the *McDermott* case. See, e.g., Colonial Press of Miami, Inc. v. The Allen's Cay, 277 F.2d 540, 1960 A.M.C. 1598 (5th Cir.1960). There it was assumed that printing material supplied to an advertising firm on the order of the master of the vessel comes within the term "other necessaries," though the question was not directly before the court since the decision turned on the unchallenged default decree. In the Atlantic Steamer Supply Co. v. The Tradewind, 153 F.Supp. 354, 1957 A.M.C. 2196 (D.Md.1957), it was held that the lien existed for provision of advertising materials such as book matches, pictures of the ship, and advertising pamphlets and stickers when they were provided for use of the passengers. The court declined to hold that there was a lien for furnishing newspaper advertising. In Allen v. The Contessa, 196 F.Supp. 649, 1961 A.M.C. 2190 (S.D.Tex.1961), it was held cigarettes furnished by a grocer were "necessaries." Pilotage comes within the term. Diaz v. The Seathunder, 191 F.Supp. 807, 1961 A.M.C. 561 (D.Md.1961).

Advertising charges have been held to be necessaries independent of delivery of tangible items. Stern, Hays & Lang v. M/V Nili, 407 F.2d 549, 1969 A.M.C. 13 (5th Cir.1969).

Is the emphasis put upon "services" by Judge Brown in the *McDermott* case an accurate guide to the definition of the term "necessaries" ? Note that in the enumeration that under the rule *ejusdem generis* defines the catch-all phrase, are "supplies" and "repairs". Are supplies "services" ? Of course, repairs may be in the nature of services, but is there no lien for the provider of equipment put aboard the vessel in the course of its refurbishing? In The Ardell Marine Corp. v. Mars, 163 F.Supp. 691, 1958 A.M.C. 2193 (E.D.N.Y.1958), for example, it was held that when a vessel was converted from steam to diesel and received a new propeller and a new engine room floor, it was being repaired and not reconstructed and the lien for repairs was good. Were the printing materials provided in *The Allen's Cay* a service? Was the advertising a service and the materials an ingredient, like the new propeller in the repair case?

The first section of the Lien Act of 1910 (36 Stat. 604) read:

"Any person furnishing repairs, supplies, or other necessaries, including the use of dry dock or marine railway, to a vessel, whether foreign or domestic, upon the order of the owner or owners of such vessel, or of a person by him or them authorized, shall have a maritime lien on the vessel which may be enforced by a proceeding in rem, and it shall not be necessary to allege or prove that credit was given to the vessel."

There was a tendency toward strict construction of the provision as to "other necessaries." In The Muskegon, 275 Fed. 348 (2d Cir.1921), for example, it was held that the term was limited to things like repairs and supplies (applying the rule *ejusdem generis*)and that the master stevedore had no lien for his services. Similarly in The Mona, 282 Fed. 468 (4th Cir.1922), it was held that towage did not come within "other necessaries" (applying the act of 1910 in an appeal decided after the enactment of the act of 1920). The amendments of 1920 added towage to the list, but also changed the position of the phrase "use of dry dock or marine railway" to place it within the enumeration that precedes the catch-all phrase. This was taken as a deliberate effort to broaden the construction given to "other necessaries." See In re Burton S.S. Co., 3 F.2d 1015, 1925 A.M.C. 335 (D.Mass.1925).

From the standpoint of grammar, the section appears to indicate that there is a lien for the furnishing of "repairs, supplies, towage, [and] use of dry dock or marine railway", these being illustrations of "necessaries," and then *other* "necessaries." If this phrasing is correct, then it follows that there would be no necessity to demonstrate that "repairs, supplies, towage, [or] use of dry dock or marine railway" was "necessary." In the case of supplies, however, this has not been altogether true. There has been a tendency to require that the supplies furnished were "necessary," that is, supplies reasonably needed in the ship's business. In *The Contessa*, supra, for example, the conclusion of law to the effect that cigarettes were necessary was supported by a finding of fact "That cigarettes are usually included in the supplies that are put on board shrimping vessels such as *The Contessa*." Suppose that there had been included in the order a supply of Romeo y Julietta Churchills instead of the cigarettes? In The Sterling, 230 Fed. 543 (W.D.Wash. 1916), it was held that liquor was not a "necessary" supply on a fishing vessel, despite a showing that the sailors would not sail without it. In Walker–Skageth Food Stores v. The Bovois, 43 F.Supp. 109, 1942 A.M.C. 211 (S.D.N.Y.1942), liquor was determined to constitute a "necessary" supply when furnished to a pleasure yacht at a resort.

Pilotage has been held to be a necessary. See Ajubita v. S.S. Peik, 428 F.2d 1345, 1970 A.M.C. 1463 (5th Cir.1970); Blair v. M/V Blue Spruce, 315 F.Supp. 555, 1970 A.M.C. 1298 (D.Mass.1970).

When the lessor can prove that cargo containers were actually provided to a particular vessel, it has a lien for the rental. Foss Launch and Tug Co. v. Char Ching Shipping USA, 808 F.2d 697, 1987 A.M.C. 913 (9th Cir.1987). See *Redcliffe* below.

* * *

B. FURNISHING TO THE SHIP

Redcliffe Americas Limited v. M/V Tyson Lykes

United States Court of Appeals, Fourth Circuit, 1993.
996 F.2d 47, 1993 A.M.C. 2294.

■ J. MICHAEL LUTTIG, CT.J.:

Defendants in rem, the container vessels M/V *Tyson Lykes* and M/V *Tillie*

Lykes, and their claimant, First American Bulk Carrier Corporation, appeal from an order of the district court granting partial summary judgment to appellee Redcliffe Americas and sustaining Redcliffe's claims for maritime liens against the vessels. We hold that because Redcliffe provided containers to the vessels' charterer rather than to the vessels themselves, maritime liens did not arise in favor of appellee. We therefore reverse.

I

This case arises out of two contracts entered into by Topgallant Group, Inc., an intermodal carrier that transported containerized goods by truck, rail and ship between depots in the United States and in Europe.[1] On April 21, 1987, Topgallant Group chartered the container vessels M/V *Delaware Bay* (since renamed *Tyson Lykes*) and M/V *Chesapeake Bay* (since renamed *Tillie Lykes*)(hereinafter collectively referred to as the "Vessels") from their owner, appellant First American Bulk Carrier Corporation (FABC). A year later, Topgallant Group leased in bulk, pursuant to a three-year equipment rental agreement (the "Agreement"), 245 refrigerated containers from appellee Redcliffe for the purpose of hauling shipments of hard frozen foods from Virginia to American military bases in Europe. The Agreement provided that these containers were "for use in particular on [Topgallant Group's] vessels 'Chesapeake [Bay]' and 'Delaware [Bay]' or such other vessels as agreed between the parties in writing." J.A. at 33.

Consistent with industry practice, Redcliffe provided the containers in bulk to Topgallant Group; it did not deliver the containers directly to the Vessels or earmark specific containers for use on a particular vessel. Topgallant Group in turn distributed the containers to shippers, who loaded them, and then transported the containers to various ports in the United States and Europe. From these ports, the containers were assigned for carriage to either Vessel as Topgallant Group found commercially convenient. After the cargoes reached their final destination, the process repeated itself. The containers thus were apportioned and reapportioned between the two Vessels at the discretion of Topgallant Group.

In April 1989, Topgallant Group transferred its business to an affiliated concern, Topgallant Lines, Inc., and, with FABC's consent, assigned the sub-bareboat charters covering the Vessels to Topgallant Lines. The latter firm began operating the Vessels in July of that year, frequently using the containers leased from Redcliffe. On December 13, 1989, the Topgallant companies filed for bankruptcy. FABC thereafter terminated the charters and retook possession of the Vessels.

Redcliffe brought this *in rem* action against the Vessels in district court for $432,196 in unpaid container rental charges that had accrued between September 1 and December 31, 1989. Redcliffe asserted that,

---

1. The cargoes delivered by intermodal carriers are loaded into special shipping containers that can be transferred easily from one mode of transportation to the next until they reach their final destination. The ocean leg of each voyage is completed through the use of container vessels, which are custom-made to hold such containers.

pursuant to the Federal Maritime Lien Act (FMLA), it was entitled to claim the unpaid charges as maritime liens against the *Tyson Lykes* and the *Tillie Lykes*. FABC appeared in the action as the Vessels' claimant and denied that Redcliffe was entitled to liens.

The district court ultimately granted Redcliffe's motion for partial summary judgment on the issue of liability. Redcliffe Americas Ltd. v. M/V Tyson Lykes, 806 F.Supp. 69 (D.S.C.1992). Rejecting the reasoning of the Ninth Circuit in Foss Launch & Tug Co. v. Char Ching Shipping U.S.A., Ltd., 808 F.2d 697 (9 Cir.), cert. denied, 484 U.S. 828, 108 S.Ct. 96, 98 L.Ed.2d 57(1987), and adopting instead the contrary view expressed in Itel Containers Int'l Corp. v. Atlanttrafik Express Serv. Ltd. (Itel II), 781 F.Supp. 975 (S.D.N.Y.1991),[2] the district court concluded that FMLA's requirement that necessaries be provided "to a vessel" in order for a maritime lien to arise had been satisfied, even though Redcliffe provided containers to Topgallant Group, "not based on the needs of a specific vessel, but indiscriminately in bulk." 806 F.Supp. at 72–73. The court accordingly held that Redcliffe was entitled to maritime liens against the Vessels, leaving for a later date a determination of the proper amount of damages. Id., 806 F.Supp. at 74.

FABC and the defendant Vessels thereafter brought this interlocutory appeal pursuant to 28 U.S.C. § 1292(a)(3), advancing numerous grounds for reversal, only the first of which we need address.

II

A

The maritime lien "had its origin in desire to protect the ship," Piedmont & Georges Creek Coal Co. v. Seaboard Fisheries Co., 254 U.S. 1, 9, 41 S.Ct. 1, 3, 65 L.Ed. 97 (1920). The primary impetus for recognition of the lien was concern for the ship and her needs, not the needs of suppliers or even the ship's owners:

> Since [a ship] is usually absent from the home port, remote from the residence of her owners and without any large amount of money, it is essential that she should be self-reliant-that she should be able to obtain upon her own account needed repairs and supplies.... Because the ship's need was the source of the maritime lien it could arise only if the repairs or supplies were necessary; if the pledge of her credit was necessary to the obtaining of them; if they were actually obtained; and if they were furnished upon her credit.

Id. These general principles of the law of maritime liens were undisturbed by passage of the FMLA in 1910. In particular, as is clear from the Court's decision in *Piedmont*, that Act did not expand the traditionally limited availability of the maritime lien.

---

2. One month after the district court issued its order, the Second Circuit reversed *Itel II*. Itel Containers Int'l Corp. v. Atlant- trafik Express Serv. Ltd. (Itel III), 982 F.2d 765 (2 Cir.1992).

In *Piedmont*, a coal dealer had contracted with a fish oil company to deliver coal for use on the oil company's fleet of steamers and in its factories. The coal was sold to the oil company, placed in its bins, and distributed by the oil company as needed to its ships and factories. When the oil company went into receivership, the coal dealer libeled twelve of the steamers, seeking maritime liens under FMLA for the unpaid price of five loads of coal.

The Supreme Court affirmed the dismissal of the libels, refusing "[t]o hold that a [maritime] lien for the unpaid purchase price of supplies arises in favor of the seller merely because the purchaser, who is the owner of a vessel, subsequently appropriates the supplies to [the vessel's] use." Id. at 8. Because part of the coal was supplied for nonmaritime use in the factories and, more importantly, because the coal had been furnished to the respective steamers not by the coal dealer, but by the oil company "in its discretion as owner of the coal and of the business," the Court held that no liens had arisen in favor of the coal dealer. Id. at 7–8, 13. Even though this result contravened the express understanding of the contracting parties, the Court refused to give a broad reading to FMLA. Under the Act, as before, stated the Court, the maritime lien is a secret one, arising by operation of law. "It may operate to the prejudice of prior mortgagees or of purchasers without notice. It is therefore stricti juris and will not be extended by construction, analogy or inference." Id. at 12; see also *Itel III*, 982 F.2d at 768 ("As a general rule, maritime liens are disfavored by the law.").

Following *Piedmont*, courts consistently have held that a supplier claiming a maritime lien against a vessel must, inter alia, have delivered needed supplies directly to the vessel or somehow earmarked the supplies for use on that particular vessel. See Dampskibsselskabet Dannebrog v. Signal Oil & Gas Co., 310 U.S. 268, 277, 60 S.Ct. 937, 942, 84 L.Ed. 1197 (1940)(distinguishing *Piedmont* and sustaining maritime liens on grounds that "oil was supplied exclusively for the vessels in question [and] was delivered directly to the vessels and was so invoiced"); Bankers Trust Co. v. Hudson River Day Line, 93 F.2d 457, 458 (2 Cir.1937)("the requirements for a maritime lien are met, 'if the supplies, though delivered in mass to the owner of the fleet under a single contract, are expressly ordered by the owner and delivered to him by the supplyman for the use of named vessels in specified portions' " (emphasis supplied by Second Circuit)(*quoting The American Eagle*, 30 F.2d 293, 295 (D.Del.1929))). With the aforementioned principles and these authorities in mind, we turn to the specific issue under consideration.

B

FMLA provides in relevant part that "a person providing necessaries to a vessel on the order of the owner or a person authorized by the owner ... has a maritime lien on the vessel." 746 U.S.C. § 31342.[3] We assume for

---

3. 46 U.S.C. § 31342 superseded 46 U.S.C. § 971 in 1989 without significant change. Section 971 had used the verb "furnishing" rather than "providing". Most of

purposes of this appeal that Topgallant Group, as the Vessels' charterer, was authorized to order the lease of Redcliffe's containers, and that the containers constituted "necessaries" for the Vessels for purposes of the statute.   The sole question before us is whether Redcliffe provided the necessaries to the Vessels within the meaning of the Act.   Two courts of appeals, in cases virtually identical to this one, have addressed this question.   Both the Ninth Circuit in *Foss Launch* and the Second Circuit in *Itel III* came to the same conclusion, with which we agree, that FMLA as construed by the Supreme Court in *Piedmont* simply "does not support a claim of maritime lien by a supplier who furnishes goods in bulk to a fleet owner or charterer, with apportionment among the ships being made at the discretion of the recipient."   *Itel III*, 982 F.2d at 767.[4]

In *Foss Launch* and *Itel III*, as here, an intermodal carrier leased shipping containers from container lessors.   The containers were delivered in bulk to the carriers and individual units were not designated for use on any particular ship.   When the carriers failed to pay charges due under the leases, the container lessors asserted in rem claims for maritime liens against container ships operated by the carriers.

After discussing applicable precedent, the Ninth Circuit noted the parallels between its case and *Piedmont*:

> In each case a materialman provided bulk supplies-coal in Piedmont, containers here-in circumstances where the final allocation of supplies, to any vessel of the group intended to be supplied, was left to the discretion of the procuring authority.   Although, in both cases, it was understood that the supplies provided would predominantly be put to maritime use, in neither case was there any evident attempt to designate any individual vessel to receive any identifiable component of the supplies.

Foss Launch, 808 F.2d at 702.   Because the intermodal carrier, and not the lessors, had unrestricted authority to designate which containers would be used aboard particular vessels in its fleet, the court reversed the district court's judgment sustaining the lien claims, and held that "cargo containers leased in bulk to a time-charterer of a group of vessels for unrestricted use on board the vessels in that group, are not furnished to any particular

---

the cases in this field arose prior to 1989 and therefore discuss the "furnishing" requirement of FMLA.

4.   The court below acknowledged that its decision, like several of those relied upon, embraced a broader interpretation of FMLA's requirements than had generally obtained in the caselaw, but believed that the departure "was appropriate to accommodate and favor the 'modern' practices of the container leasing industry. '806 F.Supp. at 73'; see also Equalease Corp. v. M/V Sampson, 793 F.2d 598, 603 (5 Cir. en banc)(espousing broad reading of FMLA furnishing requirement), cert. denied, 479 U.S. 984, 107 S.Ct. 570, 93 L.Ed.2d 575 (1986); Triton Container Int'l Ltd. v. M/S Itapage, 774 F.Supp. 1349, 1350 (M.D.Fla.1990).   We simply have no authority to abandon the strict precepts in *Piedmont* on the basis of a change in industry custom.   Congress alone is empowered to effect such a change.   See *Foss Launch*, 808 F.2d at 703 ([W]e are not persuaded that 'modern business conditions' in the shipping industry are sufficient justification to expand the 'furnishing to any vessel' requirement of [FMLA].")

vessel of the group, on which they subsequently happen to be employed, within the meaning of [FMLA]." Id. 808 F.2d at 703.

The Second Circuit, citing *Piedmont, Bankers Trust*, and *Foss Launch*, similarly reversed a judgment in favor of the maritime lien claims of several container lessors, *Itel III*, 982 F.2d at 769. Noting that "[t]he concept of an in rem hypothecation will not work in the manner intended ... if there is no identifiable ship to which the lien may attach when the obligation is created," the court observed that, in the case before it, "no one knew to which ship a container would be assigned at any given time." Id., 982 F.2d at 768. Agreeing with the arguments made by the defendants in rem and their owners, the Second Circuit held that "under [FMLA,] maritime liens cannot be claimed for supplies furnished simply to fleet owners," and that "supplies are furnished to vessels within the meaning of [FMLA] only when they are either provided directly to or are earmarked for specific vessels." Id., 982 F.2d at 767.

Redcliffe attempts to distinguish *Foss Launch* and *Itel III* on the ground that the Agreement in this case provided that appellee's containers were to be used only aboard two vessels, both of which were named, and such other vessels that Redcliffe and Topgallant Group agreed to in writing. Appellee's Br. at 12–14. Two ships still constitute a fleet, however, and the containers were neither delivered directly to the Vessels by Redcliffe nor specifically earmarked for use on one of the Vessels or the other. Topgallant Group (and later Topgallant Lines), the Vessels' charterer, had the discretion to allocate and reallocate the leased containers between the two Vessels as, in its sole discretion, it deemed desirable. For example, it could have chosen to carry Redcliffe's containers only aboard one of the Vessels or, for that matter, not to use the containers on either of the Vessels. It is precisely because the charterers retained such discretion that the Second and Ninth Circuits rejected the lien claims in Foss Launch and Itel III.[5]

Accordingly, because Redcliffe did not provide containers to the *Tyson Lykes* and the *Tillie Lykes*, we hold that maritime liens for the amounts

---

5. Redcliffe's reliance upon Carr v. George E. Warran Corp., 2 F.2d 333 (4 Cir. 1924), and Jeffrey v. Henderson Bros., 193 F.2d 589 (4 Cir.1951), in support of a contrary conclusion is misplaced. In both cases, there was no question that the supplies had been specifically provided to the vessels against which the maritime liens were enforced. In *Carr* a coal dealer had sold 835 tons of coal to a fish oil and guano company, fifteen per cent of which was to be used in the company's factory, with the remainder earmarked for use on the company's four steamers. We held that the coal allocated to and used by each steamer had been sufficiently identified to sustain the coal dealer's maritime lien claims against two of the ships because "85 per cent of the coal was sold directly for use of the steamers named, and so billed to the vessels and received and used by them," because this eighty-five per cent portion was used and "billed in equal parts to the four steamers," and because "the coal was placed upon the piers at which the steamers coaled, and was all taken and used by them." 2 F.2d at 334. We upheld the maritime lien in *Jeffrey* because the supplies were provided to the only vessel operated by the owner, and "in most instances the deliveries were made at such places as to indicate that the goods were intended for the vessel." 193 F.2d at 594.

due under the Agreement did not arise in Redcliffe's favor under the FMLA.

III

For the reasons stated herein, the judgment below is reversed. On remand the district court shall dismiss Redcliffe's complaint and release the security posted by FABC.

Reversed and remanded with instructions.

NOTE

"The Piedmont case is all things to all men and is regularly cited on both sides of every case in which it is relevant: since some of Justice Brandeis' facts are always present, it is an authority for shipowner's counsel for denial of the lien; since all of them are never present, it is equally an authority for supplier's counsel in favor of the lien." Gilmore and Black, *Law of Admiralty* 661 (1975). Does *Tyson Lykes* take out some of the mystery?

Some pre-lien act cases indicated that supplies and necessaries must be delivered to the vessel, that is, brought along side. See, e.g., Ammon v. The Vigilancia, 58 Fed. 698 (S.D.N.Y.1893). This did not mean that the supplier could not enter into a contract for an entire fleet (See, e.g., The Kiersage, 2 Curt.C.C. 421, 14 F.Cas. 466 (C.C.Me.1855) so long as the supplies were actually furnished to particular vessels. The matter is discussed in The Cora P. White, 243 Fed. 246 (D.N.J.1917). More recently, see Brock v. S.S. Southampton, 231 F.Supp. 283, 1964 A.M.C. 800–A (D.Or.1964), in which a lien was given a bank that had issued an irrevocable letter of credit to a union to guarantee payment of seamen furnished vessels by the union. The letter was issued to cover the fleet generally, but Judge Solomon held that since it was limited to the payment of wages after they were earned, the payments to the crew of a particular vessel imported a lien against that vessel, noting that he had also ordered payment of claims of an architect who had provided services to the fleet, despite the fact that he had billed the fleet without specifying the amounts due by any particular vessel and had received a part payment. He was permitted to itemize the services to the particular vessel in question and deduct a percentage of the partial payment. Judge Solomon noted that no one objected to this method of computation. See also Brock v. S.S. Southampton, 231 F.Supp. 283, 1964 A.M.C. 1905 (D.Or.1964).

Certainly more recent cases do not require that the supplies be delivered to the vessel or put on board. See, e.g., Allen v. The Contessa, 196 F.Supp. 649, 1961 A.M.C. 2190 (S.D.Tex.1961). There the court found as a fact "[t]hat the groceries, etc., made the basis of libellant's claim were furnished either to the owner * * * in person or to members of the crew of The *M/V Contessa* on his oral orders, and were delivered either to the owner * * * or to persons authorized by him, at the place of business of libellant." In its conclusions of law it was stated "[t]hat under the practice followed in the shrimping industry in and around Aransas Pass, Texas, as found in the Findings of Fact, libellant has discharged his burden of proving that the supplies made the basis of his claim were supplied to the vessel and put on the vessel; and there being no direct proof offered by the claimants defending this action, showing that said supplies were not on board said vessel, no other conclusion is tenable. And when a supplier, like the libellant, turns over supplies such as groceries, etc., to the owner or those authorized by him, as was done in this case, said supplier should not be required, to follow said supplies to the vessel."

When a supplier of steel delivers steel to a repair yard and requests that the steel be segregated for use on a particular barge, the steel was "furnished to the vessel" within the meaning of the Act. Farwest Steel Corp. v. Barge Sea–Span 241, 769 F.2d 620 (9th Cir.1985).

Suppose it is services rather than supplies for which the lien is sought. Do the services have to be performed on board or at shipside? See Bermuda Exp., N.V. v. M/V Litsa (Ex Laurie U), 872 F.2d 554 (3d Cir.1989), cert. denied 493 U.S. 819, 110 S.Ct. 73, 107 L.Ed.2d 40 (1989), holding that a stevedore's lien covers paying the longshoremen under the Union contract, but not the cost of moving a large chassis around when moving it was not directly related to loading or unloading the vessel.

C.   THE OWNER OR A PERSON AUTHORIZED BY THE OWNER

(1) The Owner

Diaz v. The Seathunder

United States District Court, District of Maryland, 1961.
191 F.Supp. 807, 1961 A.M.C. 561.

■ R. Dorsey Watkins, D.J.   * * *

[The case involved an alleged lien for repairs. The defense was to the effect that the vessel was under charter and the charter contained a prohibition of liens clause. In answer to this defense the libellant alleged that the libel sounded in tort for fraudulent concealment, and failing that, that the charterer in question was actually the "economic owner" of the vessel.] It is next suggested that the effect of the Carver decision should be limited to bareboat charters (1) of short duration, (2) where the bareboat charterer is not the "economic owner" of the vessel, and (3) where the general owner has not recovered more than its economic investment with interest. Economic ownership of the Seathunder by Ocean in the instant case arises because the Delhi–Taylor Oil Corporation (Preston's parent) purchased The Seathunder on April 4, 1952, from Colonial Steamship Corporation (Colonial) for $3,150,000. The vessel was then chartered back under bareboat charter to Colonial from that date until October 5, 1953, for which Delhi–Taylor received $1,800,000. Thereafter, on October 6, 1953 until April 4, 1956, she was on a bareboat charter to Colonial from which Preston received $1,593,000 making a total of $3,393,000 received from Colonial in charter hire. The charter from Preston to Ocean, executed on April 6, 1956, was for a period of ten years during which time it was contemplated that Preston would receive from Ocean sums totaling $3,012,-840 in charter hire. The argument is advanced, that since the charter hire received from Colonial plus that contemplated as eventually to be received from Ocean would total $6,405,840, Ocean thereby became the "economic" owner of the Seathunder. Factually, and as a matter of law, this argument is without support. There is no logic in adding the charter hire received from Colonial to that contemplated to be received from Ocean to establish

Ocean's economic ownership of the vessel. The sums Preston was to receive from Ocean over a ten year period are irrelevant when, as a matter of fact, the charter party did not run for ten years but instead was cancelled by mutual agreement on November 19, 1958, approximately only two and one-half years after its execution. No authorities have been cited to the court in support of Maryland's position nor has the court found any through its own research. No standards have been suggested for determining at what point a charter of short duration merges into one of long duration; when and how precisely "economic" ownership arises or how much of a profit is sufficient to strip an owner of his power to prohibit a charterer from creating valid liens against the vessel. Thus Maryland's position, if sound, would again involve the courts in that Serbonian Bog[1] to which Robinson on Admiralty, page 373, refers and from which he states that the courts were partially rescued by the passage of the Federal Maritime Lien Act. In the view that this court takes,[2] the provisions of the Act and the decisions construing the Act prevent the recurrence of such an involvement. "The Act says nothing about types of charters" (The Signal Oil Case, supra, 310 U.S. at page 279, 60 S.Ct. at page 943). It does not differentiate between them on grounds of short or long duration. It makes no mention of "economic ownership" nor does it, having carved out an exception in favor of the recorded holder of title, specify that the exception in favor of the recorded holder of title, specify that the exception no longer applies if the title holder has recovered its initial investment with interest. None of these alleged distinguishing factors can be read into the Federal Maritime Lien Act.

* * *

That Congress never intended the word "owner" as used in the Maritime Lien Act, reenacted in 1920 as part of the Ship Mortgage Act, to extend to an equitable owner or an alleged "economic" owner is evidenced by the history of the Ship Mortgage Act of 1920. The Act was passed to encourage investment in domestic vessels by affording better mortgage security. The purpose can best, if not only, be effectuated by construing "owner" as being limited solely to the holder of recorded title.

* * *

Freedom Line Inc. v. Vessel Glenrock

United States District Court, Southern District of Florida, 1967.
268 F.Supp. 7, 1968 A.M.C. 507.

■ C. CLYDE ATKINS, D.J. This cause came on for trial before me and at the conclusion thereof all parties submitted proposed findings of fact and conclusions of law. These proposals and all memoranda in support of the

---

1. "A gulf profound as that Serbonian Bog Betwixt Damiata and Mount Cassius old, Where armies whole have sunk."

Milton, Paradise Lost II.

2. [footnote omitted].

positions of the respective parties have been carefully considered. Thereupon, the Court makes the following Findings of Fact and Conclusions of Law.

Findings of Fact

1. At the time of filing this libel, Freedom Line Incorporated, a Panamanian corporation, was the holder of a note, secured by a mortgage on the vessel S.S. Glenrock, executed by Hudson Shipping Corporation as owner thereof (hereinafter "Hudson"), dated December 3, 1963, recorded under the laws of the Republic of Panama. The balance as of December 2, 1966, was in the amount of $10,900 plus interest, insurance, costs, expenses and attorneys' fees. The mortgage, at such time was and is now in default and it was necessary for libellant to engage the attorneys who filed the libel in this cause to foreclose such mortgage.

2. Intervenor Brewer Dry Dock Company (hereinafter "Brewer"), is a New York corporation maintaining its principal place of business in Staten Island, New York. It is a company which owns and operates a dry dock and is engaged in the repair, renovation and furnishing of supplies to vessels.

3. Intervenor Bahamas Line, S.A. (hereinafter "Bahamas") is a Panamanian corporation engaged in the shipping business in Miami, Florida.

4. Intervenor Manual Diaz Losada (hereinafter "Diaz") is engaged in the business of ship repairs, primarily on a contract basis. He frequently subcontracts portions of his work to others.

5. Though the mortgage specifically required it, a certified copy of the mortgage was not placed among the vessel's papers or a "Notice of Mortgage" posted in the chart room of the ship.

6. In May, 1964, at the request of R.A. Nichol and Co. (hereinafter "Nichol"), as agents of the owner of the Glenrock who were authorized to act in her behalf, Brewer furnished necessary supplies, materials, services and repairs to and aboard the vessel for a total value of $23,754 on the credit of the vessel. The sum of $23,754 represents a reasonable charge for such services, materials, supplies and repairs. The balance due on said account was $15,754 as of March 15, 1966, and such remains outstanding and unpaid. Such necessaries were furnished at Staten Island, New York.

7. Shortly after March 12, 1966, Brewer engaged counsel in New York to collect the account owed it for work on the Glenrock. Previous efforts to collect the account had been unsuccessful. The whereabouts of the vessel was not determined until June 8, 1966, when Brewer received information from Nichol that the Glenrock was to be sold by the United States Marshal for the Southern District of Florida. After a necessary substitution of counsel, Brewer filed a Petition to Intervene in these proceedings on June 30, 1966.

8. Any delay by Brewer in asserting its claim against the Glenrock has not subjected any of the parties in this cause to a disadvantage in

asserting or establishing any claim against the Glenrock or any defense to the claim of Brewer.

9.   Tropic Carib, S.A. (hereinafter "Tropic") is a Panamanian corporation of which the libellant Diaz was one of the four stockholders and its secretary on January 5, 1966.   On that date, Tropic authorized Bahamas to act as its agent in the purchase of the Glenrock from Hudson Shipping Corporation, likewise a Panamanian corporation.   Bahamas also agreed to lend Tropic funds to purchase and repair the vessel.   As additional security for the loan the stockholders were to pledge their stock as collateral.   After acquiring the Glenrock, Bahamas was to act as operator and manager of the Glenrock.

10.   Bahamas agreed to purchase the Glenrock "as is" from Hudson by a Memorandum of Agreement dated February 10, 1966.   Prior to executing that agreement, two of the four stockholders of Tropic went to San Juan, Puerto Rico to inspect the vessel where it had remained in port for some time.   The vessel was in need of repairs and was then "out of class."   Jhonar Shipping Corporation (hereinafter Jhonar), acting through Rogelio Jhonar, was engaged by Nichol to act for the owner of the Glenrock in the sale and delivery of it to Bahamas at Miami.   The authority of Jhonar to act as an agent for the owner was limited by a letter dated February 17, 1966, from the owner to Jhonar.   Such letter provided, *inter alia*, as follows:

"We refer to our telephone conversation of February 16, at which time we requested that you act as Agents on our behalf in connection with the sale and delivery of the M.V. Glenrock to Bahamas Line, Ltd.   This delivery is to become effective, by agreement, on vessel's arrival at the Pilot Station, Miami and the Terms of the sale are, by agreement, Cash, on delivery $45,000.—less any advances, vessel to be accepted 'as is—where is.' All other terms and conditions are included in a Memorandum of Agreement dated February 10, 1966, a copy of which is in the possession of Messrs. Bahamas Line, Ltd."

The scope of Jhonar's authority to act on behalf of owners was disclosed to Bahamas.

11.   Prior to the arrival of the vessel in Miami for delivery to Bahamas, certain expenditures were made by Bahamas in San Juan, Puerto Rico in order to discharge alleged claims against the vessel so that she might sail.   Such expenditures were made at the request of Jhonar without the knowledge or consent of the owner.   Such advances were made in contemplation of the sale and not on the vessel's credit.

12.   The Glenrock arrived in Miami from Puerto Rico at the Pilot Station on February 18, 1966.   At that time there were wages owing to the crew of the vessel.   Payment thereof was made by Bahamas as authorized by the owners in their letters of authority to Jhonar dated February 17.   A total of $8309.10 was disbursed for this purpose by Bahamas but at least $2,334.30 of this sum was paid to the master of the vessel.   Such disbursement was made in contemplation of the sale but Bahamas also received an

assignment of the above wage claims in the amount of $3,549.16. The original crew of the said vessel was signed off the vessel and a successor crew obtained by Bahamas acting as owner of said vessel.

13.   Bahamas, in anticipation of the arrival of the Glenrock and in contemplation of the sale, arranged a charter party with Inter–American Shipping Co. The charter party agreement was executed on February 11, 1966, by Bahamas Line, S.A., "Owner's Agents," but the vessel did not sail from Miami pursuant to that agreement until February 22, 1966.

14.   During the interim between her arrival in Miami and her departure pursuant to said Charter Party Agreement, certain work, materials and services were furnished to the Glenrock by Diaz. His interest in and relationship to Tropic, for whom Bahamas was to purchase the Glenrock, is set forth above.

15.   To the extent that Diaz incurred expenditures in furnishing supplies, materials and services to the Glenrock prior to her departure in performance of the Charter Party Agreement, Diaz acted as a prospective owner of the vessel and was acting without the authority or approval of the owner, Hudson. Rogelio Jhonar, in purportedly authorizing repairs, services or supplies to said vessel, acted beyond the scope of the limited authority delineated in the letter of February 17, 1966. This limited authority was disclosed to or should have been known by Diaz.

16.   At the outset of the voyage from Miami, pursuant to the Charter Party Agreement negotiated by Bahamas with Interamerican Shipping Co., the vessel broke down. Charges and expenses were incurred in towing the vessel back to port and in making incidental repairs to damages manifested in said voyage. However, the Court is unable to separate those expenses, charges or materials furnished for the repair of the damage to the vessel on that voyage from various other repair, maintenance or conversion items furnished to said vessel by Bahamas and Diaz.

17.   The Court finds it difficult to believe, and therefore it rejects the testimony of Bahamas and Diaz to the effect that substantial sums of money were furnished to the Glenrock by way of services, repairs and supplies on the credit of the vessel or the credit of her owner, Hudson. The Court's finding is made in view of the knowledge both Bahamas and Diaz had of the financial inability of Hudson to satisfy the vessel's obligations in San Juan, Puerto Rico. They also were aware of the owner's inability to satisfy other claims outstanding against the vessel including the mortgage held by libellant. The Court, therefore, finds that Bahamas and Diaz were either acting as prospective owners in incurring the aforesaid expenses or as volunteers having no obligation or valid authorization to so incur expenses. If these expenses were incurred with the approval of Jhonar, they were not within the scope of authority of Jhonar to approve. They were therefore furnished voluntarily, or without authorization by the owner and are not chargeable to the vessel.

Conclusions of Law

Having made the foregoing Findings of Fact, the Court makes and enters the following Conclusions of Law:

1. The court has jurisdiction over the parties to, and the subject matter of, this litigation.

2. Bahamas has a valid maritime lien to the extent of $3,549.16, as the first priority holder of security, representing payment of that amount to the crew of the Glenrock for wages which accrued prior to the acceptance of the vessel at Miami by Bahamas on February 19, 1966, and of which assignments were obtained. Payment made to the master of the vessel for his services does not constitute a maritime lien. Walker v. Woolsey, 186 F.2d 920, 1951 A.M.C. 471 (5 Cir.1951); Burdine v. Walden, 91 F.2d 321, 1937 A.M.C. 1149 (5 Cir.1937). Bahamas is also entitled to interest on the sums paid from the date of each payment. The remainder of the claim asserted by Bahamas does not constitute a maritime lien under Title 46, U.S.Code, sec. 971, Rubin Iron Works, Inc. v. Johnson; Ruesga, et al. v. Johnson, 100 F.2d 871, 1939 A.M.C. 27 (5 Cir.1939).

3. Brewer has a valid maritime lien for the services and supplies furnished to the Glenrock within the confines of the United States in the sum of $15,754 and it is entitled to recover said amount with interest from November 16, 1965, after payment of the above maritime lien.

4. Freedom line has a valid Panamanian Preferred Ship's mortgage, and is entitled to satisfaction of the unpaid balance thereof, including all sums and expenses secured by that instrument, after the above maritime liens have been satisfied, to the extent funds are available.

5. Diaz is not entitled to a maritime lien under Title 46, sec. 971, U.S.Code.

6. Libellant is directed to prepare and submit Final Judgment in conformity with these Findings of Fact and Conclusions of Law within ten days.

(2) Master

Yacht, Mary Jane v. Broward Marine, Inc.

United States Court of Appeals, Fifth Circuit, 1963.
313 F.2d 516, 1963 A.M.C. 868.

■ PER CURIAM: This appeal is from a final decree allowing recovery for maritime liens against the Yacht Mary Jane. Although the decree is for the sum of $5,514.41, the difference between the parties has finally—we say finally with some emphasis—boiled down to approximately $1,100. There appears to be no real question about the work or the price charged by the shipyard, or the fact that it was done. The whole defense rests on the fact that unlike the usual situation in which a master is placed aboard a vessel to command her and incur such obligations as may be necessary to the vessel's operation, what the owner here had under the name master was something quite different.   The nominal captain really could not order anything unless another captain—a marine surveyor—approved it.   This amphibious hydraheaded arrangement perhaps accounted for the fact that the whole case was tried, disposed of, and appealed without so much as even a deferential nod in the direction of the Maritime Liens Act.   46 U.S.C.A. §§ 971, 972, 973.   Cf. Point Landing, Inc. v. Alabama Dry Dock & Shipbuilding Co., 261 F.2d 861, 1959 A.M.C. 148 (5 Cir.1958);   Colonial Press of Miami, Inc. v. Allen's Cay, 277 F.2d 540, 1960 A.M.C. 1598 (5 Cir.1960);   Roberts v. Echternach, 302 F.2d 370, 1963 A.M.C. 137 (5 Cir.1962).

The items in dispute were in the category ordered by the nominal captain, but subsequently disapproved by the other captain.   A review of the record shows that the case presented facts from which the Judge could find that the actual agreement with the shipyard was something less—or more— than what the parties originally spelled out.   From this the Judge concluded that as to each of these items, there was in effect an implied authorization resulting—if from no other thing—from the failure of the owners "real" captain to object while the disputed work was, to his obvious knowledge, going on.

Consequently we think this case—a swearing match between live swearers whose credibility had to be, and was, resolved by the Judge—must end with the trial Court since these findings were not clearly erroneous.

Affirmed and Remanded.

NOTE

When supplies were accepted by the master, who was hired by the owner, the vessel was liable, a no lien clause to the contrary notwithstanding.   Marine Fuel Supply & Towing, Inc. v. The M/V Ken Lucky, 869 F.2d 473 (9th Cir.1988).

The master has no implied authority to purchase necessaries for a whole fleet of ships.   See Epstein v. Corporacion Peruana de Vapores, 325 F.Supp. 535, 1971 A.M.C. 1259 (S.D.N.Y.1971), in which it was held that the supplier had no lien for supplying, inter alia 2,270,000 cigarettes and large quantities of potables including two cases of Drambuie and one of B. & B.

(3) Or a Person Authorized by the Owner

Crescent City Marine, Inc. v. M/V Nunki

United States Court of Appeals, Fifth Circuit, 1994.
20 F.3d 665, 1994 A.M.C. 2195.

■ REYNALDO G. GARZA, CIRCUIT JUDGE:

Crescent City Marine, Inc. and Central Boat Rentals, Inc. appeal the district court's finding that they were not entitled to a maritime lien. Finding no errors we AFFIRM.

I.   FACTS

The M/V NUNKI ("NUNKI") was owned by Impressa Transporti Maritimi SRL, and under the time charter of Scanports Shipping, Ltd. ("Scanports"). Scanports entered into a voyage charter with Energy Transport, LTD., a subsidiary of Cabot Corporation. Scanports, as the "disponet owner" of the NUNKI, appointed Global Steamship Agencies, Inc. ("Global"), to act as local, husbanding agent for the charterers after Global had been nominated by the voyage charterer. Acting on instructions from the voyage charterers, Global arranged to have the "slops"[1] removed from the NUNKI, and disposed ashore by Emerald Refining, Inc. ("Emerald"), an independent Louisiana service company. The voyage charterers agreed to pay Emerald $1 per barrel both to remove and dispose of the slops, plus the opportunity to sell any salvageable crude oil removed from the vessel. After the slops had been removed from the NUNKI, Emerald sent an invoice to the voyage charterers totalling $27,644.64, which was paid in full. Although Emerald agreed with the voyage charterers to remove and dispose of the "slops" for a flat per-barrel charge, Emerald hired appellants Crescent City Marine and Central Boat Rentals' tugs and barges on a per-day basis. After the "slops" had been removed from the ship, Emerald encountered difficulties in disposing of the material. This resulted in Crescent City Marine and Central Boat Rentals' equipment being tied up much longer than had been anticipated by Emerald. Work that was supposed to be completed in two to three days actually required approximately twelve days to finish. The appellants incurred additional transportation costs of $80,768.66. The appellants were never paid for their services and instituted this action by seizing the vessel claiming a maritime lien. The district court found that the appellants were not entitled to a maritime lien and vacated their seizure of the vessel. The appellants timely appealed to this court.

II. DISCUSSION

The appellants claim the district court erred in: (1) finding that the appellants did not perform the work at the request of a person authorized to act for the vessel; (2) finding that the contract price to remove the slops was $1 per barrel; (3) finding that the charges of the appellants were incurred solely because of delays Emerald encountered in disposing of the slops; and (4) failing to hold that a maritime lien attaches when necessaries are ordered by or supplied to a charterer unless the supplier has notice that the person who ordered the necessaries lacked authority to do so. We find that the district court did not err in any of its findings. Therefore, the judgment of the district court is affirmed.

A. *Did the appellants perform the work at the request of a person authorized to act for the vessel?*

The appellants claim that they have met all of the requirements for a maritime lien, and that the trial court erred in holding that they were not

---

1. "Slops" is an industry term used to define the oily water residue in the bottom of the ship's tanks after it has been washed with hot water. This procedure is usually required when there is a change in cargo assignment.

entitled to a maritime lien. The appellants also claim that the district court erred in holding that Emerald was the only contractor hired by the vessel to perform the work, and only it could have acquired a maritime lien. The Federal Maritime Commercial Instruments and Lien Acts provides that:

> [A] person providing necessaries to a vessel on the order of the owner or a person authorized by the owner
>
> (1) has a maritime lien on the vessel;
>
> (2) may bring a civil action in rem to enforce the lien; and
>
> (3) is not required to allege or prove in the action that credit was given to the vessel.

46 U.S.C. § 31342(a).

Appellants assert that the district court erred in holding that they were subcontractors and that by definition, they did not perform the work at the request of a person authorized to act for the vessel. They claim that the "restrictive repair contractor" line of cases relied on by the district court does not apply to this case. See, Bonanni Ship Supply, Inc. v. United States, 959 F.2d 1558 (llth Cir.1992); Farwest Steel Corp. v. Barge SEA–SPAN 241, 828 F.2d 522 (9th Cir.1987), cert. denied, 485 U.S. 1034, 108 S.Ct. 1594, 99 L.Ed.2d 909 (1988). Rather, they claim that the "agent/broker" or "middle-man" line of cases is more consistent with the facts presented in this case. See, Marine Fuel Supply and Towing v. M/V KEN LUCKY, 869 F.2d 473, 475 (9th Cir.1988); Belcher Co. of Alabama, Inc. v. M/V MARATHA MARINER, 724 F.2d 1161 (5th Cir.1984). In the "agent/broker" or "middle-man" cases there were as many as five layers between the owner of the vessel and the service provider, yet the service provider was still permitted a lien against the vessel.

Appellants contend that the Federal Maritime Commercial Instruments and Liens Act broadly defines persons authorized by the owner to procure necessaries for a vessel. Although 46 U.S.C. §§ 31341, et seq. lists those persons presumed to have authority, that presumption is not conclusive. Gulf Oil Trading Co., a Div. of Gulf Oil Co. v. M/V CARIBE MAR, 757 F.2d 743, 748–49 (5th Cir.1985). Appellants assert that persons falling outside the class presumed to have authority might still have authority to procure necessaries; there is merely no presumption of authority. Appellants further assert that it is axiomatic in this court that authorization, either actual, implied or fairly presumed, given prior to, during performance of the services, or ratified subsequent to the performance will suffice. Atlantic & Gulf Stevedores, Inc. v. M/V GRAND LOYALTY, 608 F.2d 197, 202 (5th Cir.1979).

Appellants assert that Steven Long, the President of Emerald, testified that Nick Kandiliotis, President of Global, was informed during their negotiations that:

> (1) Emerald did not own the necessary tug boats and tank barges absolutely required to properly remove, transport and dispose of the NUNKI's slops; and

(2) Emerald was going to arrange with the appellants to provide the tug boats and the tank barges incident to the removal, transportation, and disposal of the NUNKI's slops.

Finally, appellants claim that Cabot and Global gave Emerald implied, fairly presumed and/or apparent authority to bind the vessel for all necessary and incidental equipment required to properly remove, transport and dispose of the vessel's slops. Cabot and Global gave this authority by contracting with Emerald, failing to inquire as to Emerald's abilities to complete the contracted task without the involvement of other parties, with the knowledge that it is the common practice in the industry for jobs of this sort to be farmed out to other parties, and the failure to object or instruct Emerald otherwise.

Appellees, in contrast, assert that the pertinent provision of the Federal Maritime Commercial Instruments and Liens Act states as follows: (a) The following persons are presumed to have authority to procure necessaries for a vessel:

(1) the owner;

(2) the master;

(3) a person entrusted with the management of the vessel at the port of supply; or

(4) an officer or agent appointed by—

(A) the owner;

(B) a charterer;

(C) an owner pro hac vice; or

(D) an agreed buyer in possession of the vessel.

46 U.S.C. § 31341(a).

Appellees contend that the only section applicable is (a)(4), and since the appellants dealt only with Emerald, the specific question before the district court was whether Emerald was an agent appointed by a charterer. Appellees assert that since the district court found as a matter of fact that Emerald was not an agent, and was therefore, without presumptive authority, the appellants' case must fail because they offered no proof that Emerald had actual authority to bind the vessel.

Appellees assert that the district court specifically rejected Steven Long's testimony that Nick Kandiliotis, the President of Global knew that Emerald was going to subcontract the work. The district court in its findings and conclusions stated:

> The voyage charterer and Global dealt only with Emerald Refining. Neither the charterers nor Global were aware that Emerald in fact subcontracted the work to the plaintiffs, and they did not ever learn of plaintiffs' involvement in the job until approximately one month later when Global was contacted by plaintiffs complaining that Emerald had not paid plaintiffs' invoices.

Appellees further assert that under Louisiana law, an agency relationship can be created either by an express appointment or by an implied appointment arising from apparent authority. Richard A. Cheramie Enterprises, Inc. v. Mt. Airy Ref. Co., 708 F.2d 156, 158 (5th Cir.1983). Since there was no evidence that Emerald was expressly appointed as an agent, the only issue is whether there was an implied appointment. In order to establish implied agency, Cheramie, makes clear that the appellants had to prove that (1) the charterer, as principal, made some representation or manifestation directly to the appellants, and (2) the appellants reasonably relied on Emerald's purported authority as a direct consequence of those direct representations. Id. Appellees assert that there is no evidence whatsoever of any communication between the voyage charterer, purported principal, and the appellants. Consequently, there is no evidence that anything the alleged principal (Cabot) did, led the appellants reasonably to believe that Emerald was the charterers' agent. Furthermore, the district court specifically concluded that no one associated with the vessel knew that Emerald would subcontract the work to the appellants. Therefore, there is no evidence to suggest that the vessel either consented to or authorized Emerald's delegation of the work. Appellees finally assert that Harriet Harrison, the President of Crescent City Marine, testified that she knew that Emerald was an independent contractor rather than an agent of the vessel.

We are bound to uphold the district court's findings of fact unless they are clearly erroneous. Chance v. Rice University, 984 F.2d 151, 153 (5th Cir.1993); FED.R.CIV.P. 52(a).

The district court specifically found that the appellants did not perform the work aboard the NUNKI at the request of a person authorized to act for the vessel. The district court further found that the slops were removed from the NUNKI in three days and that Emerald was fully paid for the removal. Finally, the district court found that the additional charges the appellants incurred were due solely to delays Emerald encountered in disposing of the slops.

As the appellees point out, Emerald does not fall within the category of those presumed to have authority to bind the vessel. Furthermore, based on general agency law, the appellants have not provided any evidence that Global did anything that would lead the appellants to reasonably believe that Emerald had implied authority to bind the vessel.

Therefore, the district court did not clearly err in finding that the appellants did not perform the work aboard the NUNKI at the request of a person authorized to act for the vessel.

B. *Did the district court err in finding that the contract price to remove the slops was $1 per barrel?*

* * *

C. *Did the district court err in holding that the appellants' additional charges were incurred solely because of delays Emerald encountered in disposing of the slops?*

* * *

D. *Did the district court err in failing to hold that a maritime lien attaches when necessaries are ordered by or supplied to a charterer unless the supplier has notice that the person who ordered the necessaries lacked authority to do so?*

Appellants assert that Belcher Co. of Alabama, Inc. v. M/V MARATHA MARINER, 724 F.2d 1161, 1163 (5th Cir.1984), states that a maritime lien "attaches when necessaries are ordered by and supplied to a charterer, unless the supplier has notice that the person who orders the necessaries lacked authority do so." The facts of *Belcher* are similar to the case at bar. In *Belcher*, Armada Bulk Carriers of Denmark chartered the vessel. Id. Armada's broker ordered fuel from Baymar, a California broker, and Baymar contracted with Belcher, who actually supplied the fuel. Id. Armada paid Baymar and Baymar made partial payment to Belcher. Id. Belcher then brought an in rem action against the vessel. Id. The issue in *Belcher*, however, was whether Belcher could bring an *in rem* action against the vessel when the there was a pending legal action in Denmark. Therefore, the language appellants cite is *dicta*.

However, this *dicta* is of no help to the appellants. As the appellees point out, the President of Crescent City Marine testified that she knew that Emerald was an independent contractor and not an agent of the vessel. Moreover, the district court specifically found that the appellants knew when they were hired by Emerald, that Emerald was an independent service company with no special relationship to the NUNKI. Therefore, the district court did not err in finding that the appellants were not entitled to a maritime lien in this instance.

III. CONCLUSION

For the foregoing reasons, the district court's judgment is AFFIRMED.

NOTE

A subcharterer in possession and control qualifies as an "authorized person" unless under section q of the Lien Act as amended. Marine Fuel Supply & Towing, Inc. v. M/V Ken Lucky, 869 F.2d 473 (9th Cir.1988).

Where a person is presumed to have authority, secret agreement between the owner and agent does not protect the owner from liens. Port of Portland v. M/V PARALLA, 892 F.2d 825 (9th Cir.1989).

As demonstrated in The N/V NUNKI above, a general contractor hired by the owner to repair a vessel does nor qualify as a person "to whom the management of the vessel at the port of supply is entrusted." As a consequence, the general contractors subcontractors and suppliers do not acquire a lien. See also Farwest Steel Corp. v. Barge Sea–Span 241, 828 F.2d 522 (9th Cir.1987)(Farwest II), cert. denied 485 U.S. 1034, 108 S.Ct. 1594, 99 L.Ed.2d 909 (1988). See also Port of Portland v. M/V Paralla, supra.

The term "agreed purchaser in possession" refers to a purchaser with physical possession of the vessel. International Seafoods of Alaska v. Park Ventures, Inc., 829 F.2d 751 (9th Cir.1987), rejecting the broader definition given in The Oceana, 233 Fed. 139 (E.D.N.Y.1916), modified on other grounds, 244 Fed. 80 (2d Cir.1916), cert. denied, 245 U.S. 656, 38 S.Ct. 13, 62 L.Ed. 533 (1917), as "entirely unsupported dictum."

Ordinary principles of ratification and estoppel apply to dealings with agents of the shipowner. See, e.g., Esso International, Inc. v. S.S. Captain John, 322 F.Supp. 314, 1970 A.M.C. 2086 (S.D.Tex.1970), aff'd 443 F.2d 1144 (5th Cir.1971).

D. CHARTER CLAUSES PROHIBITING LIENS

Ferromet Resources, Inc. v. Chemoil Corp.

United States Court of Appeals, Fifth Circuit, 1993.

5 F.3d 902, 1995 A.M.C. 157.

■ W. EUGENE DAVIS, CH.J.:

Chemoil Corporation (Chemoil) and Hollywood Marine, Inc. (Hollywood) appeal the judgment of the district court granting Ferromet's motion for summary judgment in an action to recover damages for detention of a vessel. We vacate and remand.

I

Ferromet was the time charterer of the M/V *Pantazis L (Pantazis)*. The time charter specifically prohibited Ferromet from incurring any liens on the ship. Ferromet, through its chartering agent, Jansen Chartering, contracted with Associated Bunkering Contractors (ABC) to furnish bunkers for the vessel. This contract was subject to ABC's standard clauses, including a provision that the sale of bunkers is "made on the credit of the receiving vessel" and is subject to all security rights.

Chemoil was contacted to provide bunkers to the *Pantazis* for the account of ABC. Chemoil agreed to bunker the vessel subject to its standard sales agreement which also contains a provision securing the sale of bunkers on the credit of the vessel and subjecting the vessel to a maritime lien for bunkering charges.

Chemoil directed Hollywood, its barge contractor, to deliver the bunkers to the *Pantazis*. On the evening of November 2 and morning of November 3, the *Barge Hollywood 212*, in tow of a tug, moored alongside the *Pantazis* and transferred the bunkers to the ship. According to Ferromet's summary judgment evidence, the *Pantazis* crew notified the *Hollywood* crew of its status as a time charterer and its inability to bind the vessel *in rem* before fuel delivery began. Chemoil denied that Ferromet gave such notice to *Hollywood* until after fuel delivery was complete at around 4:30 a.m. on Sunday, November 3, 1992. It is undisputed that when *Hollywood* completed delivery of the fuel, the captain of the *Pantazis* returned the fuel receipt to the *Hollywood* crew with a stamp that read:

> These services and/or supplies were ordered by time charters for their sole purpose and expense vessel/owners [sic] do not guarantee payment.

Hollywood immediately notified Chemoil of the receipt. Chemoil was concerned that the exceptence of the stamped receipt might destroy its right to a maritime lien. Chemoil's representative instructed *Hollywood* to remain attached to the ship until either 1) the above mentioned clause was deleted from the bunker receipt, 20 other arrangements for prompt payment were made, or 3) the fuel was returned to the barge.

Negotiations continued between Ferromet, Chemoil, and Hollywood representatives for two and a half days until Ferromet agreed to pay the entire purchase price of the bunkers and provide security for Chemoil's claim for bunker barge demurrage during the negotiations. The barge then released the ship, two and a half days after fueling was complete.

Ferromet filed suit against both Chemoil and Hollywood alleging that defendants had committed a maritime tort as well as intentionally interfered with Ferromet's contractual rights. Ferromet sought to recover the charterhire it paid during the two and a half days the ship was detained as well as other expenses incurred as a result of the delay. Both sides filed motions for summary judgment.

The district court granted summary judgment in favor of Ferromet, holding that no set of facts could justify Chemoil and Hollywood's self help actions in detaining the *Pentazis*. Chemoil and Hollywood filed a timely appeal and Ferromet filed a cross appeal seeking an increase in damages.

II

We review a summary judgment *de novo*, applying the same criteria as would a district court. Hanks v. Transcontinental Gas Pipe Line Corp., 953 F.2d 996, 997 (5 Cir.1992). Summary judgment is proper "if the pleadings, depositions, answers to interrogatories, and admissions on file, together with the affidavits, if any, show that there is no genuine issue as to any material fact and that the moving party is entitled to a judgment as a matter of law." Fed.R.Civ.P. 56(c).

Under the Federal Maritime Lien Act, 46 U.S.C.app. § 971 *et seq.*, any person furnishing necessaries such as fuel to a vessel shall have a maritime lien on the vessel. The ship's master or other person, such as a charter, to whom the vessel is entrusted is presumed to have authority to purchase necessaries to the credit of the vessel. The materialman who furnishes necessaries in response to a request from a master, charterer or other person in custody of the vessel has no duty to inquire about that person's authority to bind the vessel. (§ 973). But a supplier's lien is defeated if he has actual knowledge that the person ordering the necessaries has no authority to bind the vessel. Gulf Oil Trading Co. v. M/V Caribe Mar, 1985 AMC 2726, 757 F.2d 743 (5 Cir.1985).

Thus, when Chemoil learned from Hollywood that the vessel's master had stamped a message on the fuel receipt indicating that the custodian of the vessel was without authority to purchase supplies on the vessel's credit, Chemoil was concerned that its fuel sale would not be secured by a maritime lien on this vessel. This concern was justifiable on two fronts.

First the receipt could support an argument that the master told the supplier of his lack of authority to incur liens before the sale was completed. If this argument were accepted, the lien would not arise. Alternatively the ship could argue that acceptance of the receipt even after the fuel was delivered acted as a waiver of the lien by the supplier. See Marine Fuel Supply & Towing, Inc. v. M/V Ken Lucky, 1989 AMC 390, 859 F.2d 1405 (9 Cir.1988).

In sum, under Chemoil's version of the facts, Chemoil and Hollywood were justified in concluding that Ferromet had tricked them into delivering bunkers to the vessel with the promise of a lien only to have the lien destroyed by Ferromet's breach of its promise.

Ferromet argues that even if it tricked Chemoil into delivering the fuel by promising a lien and then reneging on that promise, Chemoil was not justified in resorting to self help and forcibly detaining the ship. The law ordinarily does not favor self help. But this is not universally so. The *Restatement of Torts* recognizes that a party may use reasonable force against another to recapture assets wrongfully taken in very limited circumstances.

> 1) The use of reasonable force against another for the purpose of recaption is privileged if the other
>
> > a) has tortiously taken the chattel from the actor's possession without claim of right, or under claim of right but by force or other duress or fraud, ...

Restatement (Second) of Torts, § 101 (1965). The force used must be reasonable under the circumstances. Id. Certainly force calculated to cause serious bodily harm would never be justified to recapture property. Further, the privilege only exists if the possession is taken wrongfully, such as by theft or fraud. Id. See also Prosser & Keaton on the *Law of Torts* § 22 (5th Ed.1984). Courts in applying this rule, have held that a merchant or his agent has a right to use nondeadly force to retrieve stolen goods or detain a suspect for a reasonable length of time to investigate. Montgomery Ward & Co. v. Freeman, 199 F.2d 720, 723–24 (4 Cir.1952). See also Edwards v. Gross, 633 F.Supp. 267, 271 (D.D.C.1986)(employer privileged to use reasonable force to take back documents from an employee who wrongfully refused to surrender them).

If Ferromet did not give notice of its lack of authority to incur liens before the fuel was delivered and tried to get Hollywood to accept a bunker receipt that threatened the maritime lien, the Ferromet wrongfully interfered with Chemoil's right to security which Ferromet had contractually agreed to provide. Under these circumstances where procured Chemoil's fuel by promising that the sale would be to the credit of the vessel, Ferromet wrongfully obtained possession of Chemoil's property. Under *Restatement (Second) of Torts* § 101, Chemoil was entitled to use reasonable force to get back its property. Chemoil acted reasonably in ordering Hollywood to wait alongside the ship until the ship pumped the fuel back to the barge, furnished a receipt without the offending language, or other arrangements for payment were made.

A material issue of fact is presented on when Ferromet advised Hollywood that Ferromet was without authority to incur liens. If the district court finds that Ferromet did not give notice to Hollywood before the fuel was delivered of its lack of authority to bind the vessel *in rem*, Ferromet cannot recover for damages caused solely by its own wrongful acts in obtaining Chemoil's property. If, on the other hand, the district court finds that Ferromet notified Hollywood before the fuel was delivered of its lack of authority to incur liens, then the district court may find that Chemoil had no justification for detaining the ship and Ferromet is entitled to recover damages for the delay.[1]

For the reasons stated above, we vacate the district court's summary judgment in favor of Ferromet and remand this case to the district court for further proceedings consistent with this opinion.

Cardinal Shipping Corp. v. M/S Seisho Maru

United States Court of Appeals, Fifth Circuit, 1984.
744 F.2d 461, 1985 A.M.C. 2630.

■ GOLDBERG, CIRCUIT JUDGE:

The two cases consolidated for this appeal both involve maritime liens and the effectiveness of "Prohibition-of-Lien" clauses contained in charterparties. We will treat the two cases separately, however, because they raise different peripheral issues and their factual settings differ.

I.   Cardinal Shipping v. M/S Seisho Maru

Aizawa Kaiun K.K. ("Aizawa") owns the M/S Seisho Maru. Aizawa time-chartered the vessel to Nakamura Steamship Co., Ltd., ("Nakamura") under a charterparty dated August 17, 1979. Aizawa and Nakamura are both Japanese Corporations, and the Seisho Maru sails under a Japanese flag. The charterparty gave Nakamura the right to use or sublet the vessel for a set period. The actual operation of the vessel, however, would be the responsibility of a Master and crew provided by Aizawa. On November 17, 1980, Nakamura time-chartered the Seisho Maru to Clover Trading Corporation ("Clover"), a Liberian Corporation. The period of this charter was two years, plus or minus one month at the charterer's option. The charterparty provided for payment of hire to be made in London, semi-monthly in advance.

The time charter from Nakamura to Clover, as well as the head charter from Aizawa to Nakamura, were drawn on the standard New York Produce Exchange form. Both charters contained the following lien clause:

---

1. If the district court awards damages to Ferromet, it should reconsider its damage award. Because of a typographical error, the district court apparently omitted awarding $260 for launch fees incurred in transporting the pilot to and from the vessel. We also see no reason for the court's failure to award Ferromet a pro rata share of the ballast bonus for the two and a half day delay.

18. That the Owners shall have a lien upon all cargoes, and all sub-freights for any amounts due under this Charter, including General Average contributions, and the Charterers to have a lien on the Ship for all monies paid in advance and not earned, and any overpaid hire or excess deposit to be returned at once. *Charterers will not suffer, nor permit to be continued, any lien or encumbrance incurred by them or their agents, which might have priority over the title and interest of the owners in the vessel.*

(emphasis added).

On October 5, 1981, in Charlotte, N.C., Clover entered into a voyage charterparty with Cardinal Shipping Corporation ("Cardinal"), a United States Corporation. The charter contemplated the carriage of six thousand metric tons of steel coils from Oxeloesund, Sweden, to the ports of Detroit and Chicago. Cardinal executed the charter in order to meet its contractual commitment with a shipper of the cargo.[1]

In accordance with the charterparty, Clover delivered the Seisho Maru to Cardinal in Oxeloesund.[2] On November 3, 1981, Cardinal began loading the cargo of coils on board. In the meantime, a dispute had developed between Nakamura and Clover. Payment of hire under their time charter became due on October 28, 1981. The day before, Clover had advised Nakamura that it had instructed its bankers to transfer the amount due to Nakamura's bank. Nakamura's representatives, relying on this communication, waited several days for the transfer of funds. When the transfer had not occurred by November 3, Nakamura's representatives contacted Clover seeking clarification as to the non-payment of hire.

On the following day, November 4, 1981, Nakamura instructed the vessel that loading should cease immediately. Approximately 1800 of the 6000 metric tons had already been loaded; but neither Nakamura nor the Master of the Seisho Maru had signed bills of lading for the cargo. Since payment was not forthcoming, Nakamura gave formal notice on November 5 of the default in payment of hire, expressly reserving Nakamura's right under the charterparty to withdraw the vessel and affording Clover three banking days to cure the default.

When Clover failed to remit payment within that time, Nakamura announced that it would withdraw the vessel from the time charter. Some discussions ensued between Nakamura and Cardinal concerning the carriage of the cargo of steel coils, but no agreement could be reached. Thus, in mid-November, Nakamura discharged the cargo already on board and withdrew the Seisho Maru.

---

1. The shipper is Intercontinental Metals Corporation, a United States company. Its contract with Cardinal is evidenced by a Liner Booking Note executed in Charlotte, North Carolina, on October 13, 1981. We, like the trial court, consider it irrelevant that this note is dated eight days after the voyage charter between Cardinal and Clover.

2. The charter originally designated the Dimitris P. Lemos as the carrying vessel but provided for substitution at the carrier's option. The Seisho Maru was substituted before the date of performance.

Cardinal made alternate arrangements to ship the cargo, allegedly suffering losses as a result. It filed suit in district court to recover damages for breach of the voyage charter. Cardinal brought this action *in rem*, asserting a lien against the Seisho Maru. Aizawa appeared as claimant of the vessel and filed a Motion to Dismiss Cardinal's *in rem* complaint. Cardinal, in turn, filed an Opposition to that motion as well as its own Cross–Motion for Summary Judgment. The trial court granted Aizawa's Motion to Dismiss, holding that the Prohibition-of-Lien Clause in Aizawa's charterparty precluded Cardinal's assertion of a lien. This appeal follows.

A. Issues

A major squall has brewed in this case because Cardinal is suing for breach of a charter to which Aizawa was not a party. Cardinal nevertheless asserts that the Seisho Maru itself is bound to that contract. Cardinal argues that ancient maritime doctrine creates reciprocal liens between the vessel and her cargo once the cargo is loaded on board. Aizawa responds that such a lien does not arise in this case and, in any event, is precluded by the Prohibition-of-Lien clause in the Nakamura–Clover charter. The shipowner argues that Cardinal had a duty of reasonable diligence to discover that clause. Finally, Aizawa argues that Swedish law should apply to this dispute under choice-of-law principles.

Approaching this storm line from the opposite heading, we hold that Swedish law does not apply but that American law precludes Cardinal's lien.

1. Choice of Law

* * *

(b) Prohibition-of-Lien Clause

The Prohibition-of-Lien clause in the two time charters provides an additional ground for rejecting a lien in this case. In *The Schooner Freeman*, the Supreme Court noted that it is "a just and reasonable implication of law that the general owner assents to the creation of liens" by the "special owner." 59 U.S. (18 How.) at 190, 15 L.Ed. 341. The general owner, however, can effectively negate that implication of assent by the inclusion of a clause prohibiting contract liens. See The Valencia v. Ziegler, 165 U.S. 264, 17 S.Ct. 323, 41 L.Ed. 710 (1897); The Kate, 164 U.S. 458, 17 S.Ct. 135, 41 L.Ed. 512 (1896); United States v. S.S. Lucie Schulte, 343 F.2d at 900–901; *Gilmore & Black,* supra, § 9–39, at 668–69, § 9–46a, at 687–88.

Clause 18 of the Aizawa–Nakamura and Nakamura–Clover charters is the standard New York Produce Exchange provision, which has been enforced in a myriad of decisions. See, e.g., Walsh Stevedoring v. M/S Slagen, 361 F.2d 478, 479 (5th Cir.1966); Schilling v. A/S D/S Dannebrog, 320 F.2d 628, 632 (2d Cir.1963). Most of the cases involved materialmen who had furnished repairs and supplies to a ship under charter. Those cases are not particularly enlightening here because they turn on a construction of the Maritime Lien Act, 46 U.S.C. § 971 et seq., which specifically addresses materialmen's liens. See infra at 470; TTT Stevedores of Texas v. M/V Jagat Vijeta, 696 F.2d 1135, 1139 and n. 2 (5th Cir.1983); Walsh Stevedoring, 361 F.2d at 479.

However, in *S.S. Lucie Schulte*, the Second Circuit held that the Prohibition-of-Lien clause also limits a charterer's authority to subject the vessel to liens arising out of contracts of affreightment. 343 F.2d at 900–901. The shipowner (Schulte & Bruns) had time-chartered the S.S. Lucie Schulte to Three Bays Corporation. The charter contained exactly the same anti-lien provision as appears in our case.[11] Three Bays subsequently contracted with the United States Government to ship cargo on the Lucie Schulte. However, Three Bays overcharged its shipper. Eventually, the government discovered the error and brought an action *in rem* to recover the excess tariffs. The court held that the anti-lien clause in the head charter precluded a maritime lien against the vessel:

> Although the prime purpose of the clause may have been to trigger the pertinent provision of the Lien Act, we perceive no tenable ground for narrowing the broad language to materialmen's liens. Neither do we see any basis, either in policy or in authority, why an owner should be forbidden to protect himself against the creation of liens by a charterer under contracts of affreightment if he sufficiently brings the charterer's lack of authority home to the shipper.

343 F.2d at 901.

We agree that an owner should be able to shield himself against liens if he gives sufficient notice to shippers and subcharterers.[12] The question becomes whether the notice was sufficient—or, more precisely, whether the charterer, at the time it chartered the vessel, "knew, or by reasonable diligence could have ascertained," that the ship was already under charter and that the charter contained a Prohibition-of-Lien clause. The Kate, 164 U.S. at 470, 17 S.Ct. at 140; The Lucie Schulte, 343 F.2d at 901. The party entering a contract has a duty of inquiry. See *Gilmore & Black,* at 672, 687–88. If he later seeks a lien for breach of that contract, he must meet the burden of showing that diligent inquiry would not have informed him of the higher charter or the anti-lien clause. See The Lucie Schulte, 343 F.2d at 901. The trial court found nothing in the record before it to indicate that Cardinal did not know and could not by reasonable diligence have discovered the Nakamura–Clover charter or Clause 18. Thus, Cardinal failed to bear its burden of proof on this matter.

Cardinal responds, however, that the rule of *S.S. Lucie Schulte* should no longer apply. It points out that Congress amended the Maritime Lien

---

11. The charter provided:

Charterers will not suffer, nor permit to be continued, any lien or encumbrance incurred by them or their agents, which might have priority over the title and interest of the owners in the vessel.

343 F.2d at 898.

12. We speak only of contract liens. The owner cannot use an anti-lien clause to prevent tort claimants from asserting a lien against the vessel. See *Gilmore & Black*, supra, at 668.

Act in 1971, repealing a provision that required materialmen to exercise due diligence in ascertaining the terms of the ship's charterparty. See Pub.L. No. 92–79 (1971), amending 46 U.S.C. § 973. Cardinal argues that that amendment undermines the reasoning of *S.S. Lucie Schulte*.

We disagree. The amendment certainly affected the power of the *materialman* to acquire a maritime lien, see Atlantic and Gulf Stevedores v. M/V Grand Loyalty, 608 F.2d 197, 201–202 n. 7 (5th Cir.1979); but it had no effect on other contractors. The Maritime Lien Act delineated the rights only of materialmen. When enacted in 1910, it may have subsumed (and perhaps modified[13]) more ancient principles respecting maritime liens. However, it has never purported to govern the shipper's or subcharterer's lien. See *Gilmore & Black*, supra, at 687. Thus, the amendment in 1971 had no direct bearing on the effectiveness of a Prohibition-of-Lien clause vis-a-vis the claim of a subcharterer.

Moreover, the legislative policy supporting the amendment has much less force in the case of non-materialmen. The House Report on the 1971 bill pointed out that the materialman needs protection from anti-lien clauses because he works under great time pressure and usually does not have time to investigate the authority of a charterer.

> Testimony at the hearings on the bill would indicate that this problem is primarily encountered with foreign-flag vessels chartered to foreign operators. In order to protect themselves, the American materialman must ascertain whether a vessel requesting necessaries is under charter and if so, whether the charter contains a "no lien provision." Alternatively, he can make a credit check on the financial responsibility of the vessel operator. Generally, a vessel requiring necessaries is unable to give sufficient notice so that the American materialman can do either, and he usually ends up assuming the risk that his bill will be paid.

> * * *

> After careful consideration of the entire record, your Committee has concluded that, as a matter of equity, the owner should bear the loss in such a situation.

> As a practical matter, the owner can more easily protect himself contractually by bonds or otherwise at the time he charters the vessel, than the American materialman who furnishes necessaries to a vessel under great economic pressure to put back to sea.

H.R.Report No. 92–340, reprinted in 1971 U.S.Code Cong. & Ad.News, 92nd Cong., 1st Sess., 1363, 1364, 1365. A would-be charterer, by contrast, is under much less time pressure and has earlier notice of his need to obtain a vessel. Consequently, he has greater freedom to conduct an adequate inquiry. Furthermore, the corporations that typically charter vessels are more sophisticated and have greater resources to devote to an investigation than has the local materialman. Cf. The Lucie Schulte, 343

---

13. See *Gilmore & Black*, supra, § 9– 44, at 677 (specific form of anti-lien clause required).

F.2d at 901. As between a shipowner, charterer and subcharterer, it is not so obvious that the owner should bear all risks. Permitting a contractual allocation of risks between these parties is much more equitable than in the case of shipowner and materialman.

The Prohibition-of-Lien clause still serves a valid purpose. It encourages freer trade in the chartering and subchartering of vessels. Owners will be more likely to permit their charterers to enter freely into contracts of affreightment if the owners know that no "secret liens" will arise from obscure provisions in sub-agreements.

More important, the duty of inquiry that has been placed on shippers and charterers still serves a valid goal. It prevents them from "shutting their eyes" to facts that they could easily discover. See *Gilmore & Black,* supra, at 672. Because there are no strong counterreasons for shielding these parties from such an obligation, we hold that the rule of *S.S. Lucie Schulte* is still binding.

Thus, Cardinal had the burden of showing that a reasonable inquiry would not have brought the anti-lien clause to surface. It failed to meet that burden, so its lien must likewise fail. The judgment of the trial court is

Affirmed.

NOTE

Despite a no-lien clause in the charter, the owner could authorize the expenditures. In Ring Power Corp. v. Oil Screw Tug Snipe, 1974 A.M.C. 107 (M.D.Fla.1972), aff'd 479 F.2d 1322, 1974 A.M.C. 109 (5th Cir.1973) it was held that on the evidence the owner's officer had authorized the repairs in question by consent in a telephone conversation and by later visiting the site of the work to check on it.

There is a good discussion of the effect of the 1971 amendment in Gulf Oil Trading Co. v. M/V Caribe Mar, 757 F.2d 743, 1985 A.M.C. 2726 (5th Cir.1985). The facts of the case were as follows. Gulf supplied fuel oil to ships owned or chartered by Uiterwyk, a shipping corporation, over a period of about eight years. Toward the end of that period, Gulf and Uiterwyk made an agreement under which Gulf agreed to deliver fuel oil (called "bunkers") to the Caribe Mar in Houston. The Caribe Mar was chartered by Uiterwyk under a charter party containing a prohibition of liens clause. The written confirmation sent by Gulf to Uiterwyk upon receipt of the order contained a provision indicating that the delivery of the bunkers was subject to Gulf's "International Marine Fuel Oil and/or Marine Lubricants Contract and Price Schedule." Both the marine Contract and the Price Schedule contained a clause stating in essence that Gulf would retain a lien against a vessel for the purchase price of any fuel used by the vessel. Gulf hired National, an independent barging service to deliver the bunkers to the Caribe Mar. When the barge was brought alongside the master of the Caribe Mar hand delivered to the barge captain on the fuel delivery receipt, notice that the vessel was chartered and that the charter contained a prohibitions of lien clause. Some dispute then developed over the technical specifications of the bunkers, which was eventually resolved after extended consultations among the master and chief engineer of the Caribe Mar, representatives of Uiterwyk, and Gulf representatives. The prohibition of liens clause was not brought to the attention of Gulf at this time, but two days after the delivery receipt was handed to the barge captain, a letter containing the same notice of the charter and prohibition of liens clause was delivered to Gulf. Later the same month Uiterwyk contracted with Gulf for bunkers for the Caribe Mar, to be delivered at Ceuta, Spanish Morocco, and the bunkers were loaded on board the ship in Ceuta the following month.   Uiterwyk went bankrupt without having paid for either the Houston delivery or the Ceuta delivery and Gulf asserted liens for the purchase price.   The court rejected the argument that notice to the barge captain in Houston was notice to Gulf and upheld the lien.   In the case of the bunkers delivered in Ceuta, however, Gulf had received the documents and therefore had actual notice of the charter and prohibition of liens clause, and therefore it held that it did not acquire a lien.   Would the notice on the receipt delivered to the barge captain have been sufficient without the letter?   See Gulf Oil Trading Co. v. M/V Freedom, 1985 A.M.C. 2738, 1985 WL 4787 (D.Or.1985), holding that notice of a charter and no-lien clause stamped on a prior receipt for bunkers was not sufficient notice to preclude a lien for subsequent bunkers.

In Pierside Terminal Operators, Inc. v. M/V Floridian, 389 F.Supp. 25, 1974 A.M.C. 1954 (E.D.Va.1974), it was held that the 1971 repeal of the "but" clause in § 973, whatever its effect on the enforceability of a no-lien clause, did not have the effect of making the owner liable in personam for repairs made on the order of a bare boat charterer.   In that case the action was brought in rem against the vessel and in personam against the former owner, but in rem process was never obtained.

See also Vanniman v. The Tug Diane, 1975 A.M.C. 71 (E.D.N.C.1974), in which an action for wages, wharfage, and damages for the acts or omissions of a bare boat charterer was brought against the charterer, the vessel in rem, and the owner.   As in *The M/V Floridian,* proper steps were not taken to bring the vessel within the court's jurisdiction and the in rem claim was treated as abandoned.   The plaintiffs feared that the charterer would not be able to respond to a judgment.   The action against the owner was dismissed, with permission to proceed against the charterer in personam if the plaintiff wished to do so.

But if the Act imposes no liability in personam, it does not affect whatever liability the vessel owner may have.   Thus it has been held that despite the fact that a lien has been precluded by want of authority of a charterer to bind the vessel, the owner may be liable in personam on a theory of unjust enrichment.   See Kane v. M/V Leda, 491 F.2d 899, 1974 A.M.C. 425 (5th Cir.1974), aff'g 355 F.Supp. 796, 1973 A.M.C. 2296 (E.D.La.1972).   There new engines had been installed on order of a charterer.   Prior to the commencement of the action the vessel had been sold. The charterer was insolvent and the original owner "substantially insolvent."   The repairman argued his lien and in the alternative unjust enrichment of the new owner.   It was held that there was no lien and that the new owner was not shown to be unjustly enriched.   "For whatever academic interest it may have," however, the court entered a judgment against the original owner on the unjust enrichment theory.

E.   RELIANCE ON THE CREDIT OF THE VESSEL

Farrell Ocean Services, Inc. v. United States

United States Court of Appeals, First Circuit, 1982.
681 F.2d 91, 1983 A.M.C. 1077.

■ COFFIN, CHIEF JUDGE.

The two questions posed by this appeal are whether appellant had a maritime lien on certain Navy vessels and, if such a right existed, whether appellant had waived that right.

In 1976 appellee, the United States, contracted with Bromfield Corporation for the repair of four Navy vessels. Bromfield in turn subcontracted with appellant, Farrell Ocean Services, Inc., to transport the vessels from Norfolk, Virginia, to Boston where they were to be repaired. The vessels were loaded on a barge and towed to Boston, and appellant submitted to Bromfield its invoice for $29,340 for the services provided. After receiving only $5,000 of the amount due from Bromfield, appellant brought an action in rem against appellee on the theory that it had a maritime lien on the vessels it had transported. The district court, 524 F.Supp. 211, found that although appellant had provided a service that ordinarily gave rise to a maritime lien, appellant had waived the lien.

This case is governed by the federal Maritime Lien Act, 46 U.S.C. § 971 et seq., which states in relevant part that "Any person furnishing repairs, supplies, *towage*, use of dry dock or marine railway, or *other necessaries,* to any vessel * * * shall have a maritime lien on the vessel, which may be enforced by suit in rem." Id. § 971 (emphasis added). The Act also provides that a person entitled to a lien may waive it "at any time by agreement or otherwise." Id. § 974. Although the agreement between Bromfield and appellant made no mention of the obligation of the United States to pay should Bromfield not fulfill its contractual responsibility to cover the transportation costs, a lien will be enforceable if it meets the qualifying requirements of § 971 and is found not to have been waived under § 974.

We affirm the district court's finding that the transportation services provided by appellant fall within the category of "other necessaries" recognized by § 971 to be services for which a lien can attach. We have stated previously that the term "other necessaries" should be interpreted broadly in order to encourage the provision of services that will keep ships active and consequently have found it to apply whenever the goods or services that were provided to the vessel were necessary for its continued operation. Payne v. S.S. Tropic Breeze, 423 F.2d 236, 241 (1st Cir.), cert. denied, 400 U.S. 964, 91 S.Ct. 363, 27 L.Ed.2d 383 (1970); see Ajubita v. S.S. Peik, 428 F.2d 1345, 1346 (5th Cir.1970)(term includes expenditures that are not absolutely indispensable but are convenient or useful to vessel).

Under this standard, we find ample reason to believe that the transportation of the vessels to the site where they were to be repaired was a necessary service. Were they not transported, they could not be repaired as required by Bromfield's contract with the government, and without the repair, their operation would have been impaired. Our conclusion is further justified by the fact that the statute explicitly allows liens to be asserted for "towage". 46 U.S.C. § 971. The service rendered in this instance performed the same function as towing the vessels to the point of repair, and there is no reason to distinguish the susceptibility to a lien of vessels that are towed in for repair and those that are carried in on a barge.

Appellee argues that, because the vessels were being carried at the time in question, they should be viewed as cargo and should be subject only to a cargo lien—a lien that appellant lost when it surrendered possession of the vessels. Although the vessels were being treated as cargo, they maintained their identity as "vessels" susceptible to maritime liens: a qualifying "vessel" is one that is capable of use as a vessel even if not functioning as such at the moment in question. See M/V Marifax v. McCrory, 391 F.2d 909, 910 (5th Cir.1968)(per curiam); 1 U.S.C. § 3. These four vessels certainly were fully capable of operating as vessels. As the Fifth Circuit noted in an analogous situation, a kangaroo is no less a kangaroo because it is carried for part of its existence in another kangaroo's pouch. Wirth Ltd. v. S/S Acadia Forest, 537 F.2d 1272, 1278 (5th Cir.1976)(cargo-carrying barge transported by vessel is "ship" as defined by COGSA). Whether or not the vessels may also have been subject to a cargo lien as cargo, we find no reason to conclude that their alternative status as cargo should exempt them from a maritime lien to which they would otherwise be subject.

Proceeding to the issue of waiver, we recognize that the district court's finding that appellant had waived its lien is grounded largely in an analysis of the facts of the particular case and therefore is reversible only if clearly erroneous. Even given this deferential standard of review, however, we do not find sufficient evidence to support the district court's conclusion.

A party can waive a lien by "agreement or otherwise", 46 U.S.C. § 974, but a presumption exists that the service was supplied on the credit of the vessel. The party attacking the lien has the burden of overcoming that presumption by showing that the party rendering the service relied solely on personal credit. Point Landing, Inc. v. Alabama Dry Dock & Shipbuilding Co., 261 F.2d 861, 867 (5th Cir.1958); see W.A. Marshall & Co. v. S.S. "President Arthur", 279 U.S. 564, 568, 49 S.Ct. 420, 421, 73 L.Ed. 846 (1929)(Maritime Lien Act relieved libellant from necessity of proving that credit was given to vessel); Harmon, Discharge and Waiver of Maritime Liens, 47 Tul.L.Rev. 786, 804 (1973).

Appellee points to certain facts to prove waiver: appellant's knowledge that Bromfield was operating on a cash-on-delivery basis when it signed the contract coupled with its failure to expressly retain the right to a lien to protect itself; appellant's failure to negotiate with the government as well as Bromfield about the terms of payment; appellant's submission of an invoice for the amount due solely to Bromfield; and its acceptance of partial payment from Bromfield. Appellee argues that all of these circumstances show that appellant was relying only on the credit of Bromfield and had waived its right to assert a lien against the government property to which it was furnishing the necessary services.

It is not enough, however, to show that the supplier relied in part on the credit of the owner's agent or the owner. See The Everosa, 93 F.2d 732, 735 (1st Cir.1937). The party entitled to the lien must have taken *affirmative* actions that manifest a clear intention to forego the lien. See The Bronx, 246 F. 809, 810 (2d Cir.1917); Nacirema Operating Co. v. S.S.

Al Kulsum, 407 F.Supp. 1222, 1226 (S.D.N.Y.1975).   For example, in Marshall & Co. v. S.S. "President Arthur", supra, the leading case in which waiver was found, the seller of coal to be used on the vessel doubted the financial reliability of the company to which he was selling.   It insisted that payment be in the form of "trade acceptances"—promises of payment— personally endorsed by three individuals, and the resulting contract stated that there was "no outside condition, warranty, agreement, or understanding."   279 U.S. at 566–67, 49 S.Ct. at 420–421.   The intent to rely on personal credit was clear.

The facts of this case do not evidence any such intent.   The fact that the supplier of services may be aware of the receiver's precarious financial state is insufficient when not accompanied by an affirmative, protective action.   See The A.S. Sherman, 51 F.2d 782, 788 (N.D.N.Y.1930).   Nor does the submission of a bill to the owner's agent with whom the supplier has been dealing rather than to the owner and the vessel constitute waiver. The Commack, 299 F. 229, 231 (1st Cir.1924); Lower Coast Transp. Co. v. Gulf Refining Co. of La., 211 F. 336, 337 (5th Cir.1914)(per curiam).   Nor, lastly, does the acceptance of part payment lead to the conclusion that the lien has been waived.   Nacirema Operating Co. v. S.S. Al Kulsum, supra, 407 F.Supp. at 1226.   Even considered cumulatively, these facts show only that appellant expected—as it had a right to expect—that the government would pay Bromfield and Bromfield would pay appellant.   Were we to uphold a finding that appellee could overcome the presumption against waiver on so little evidence, we would undercut the reason for allowing services to be secured by the vessel: the promotion of the provision of services to keep vessels in operation to the maximum extent possible. Payne v. S.S. Tropic Breeze, supra 423 F.2d at 241; The Everosa, supra, 93 F.2d at 735.

The judgment below is affirmed in part and reversed in part.

4.   PREFERRED SHIP MORTGAGES

In Bogart v. The John Jay, 58 U.S. (17 How.) 399, 15 L.Ed. 95 (1854), it was held that a proceeding to foreclose a mortgage was not within the admiralty and maritime jurisdiction of the United States.   Mortgages were possible under state law, and it was held that in the event a vessel were libelled in the admiralty court the mortgagee would be entitled to remnants in the registry of the court after the discharge of the maritime liens, but the claim under the mortgage thus coming last, was often worthless.   In 1920, Congress enacted the Ship Mortgage Act, now Ch. 25 of Tit. 46 of the Code, §§ 911–961.   Recodified in 1988, mutatis mutandis, in 46 U.S.C.A. §§ 31321–31330.

The Favorite

United States Circuit Court of Appeals, Second Circuit, 1941.
120 F.2d 899, 1941 A.M.C. 1073.

■ AUGUSTUS N. HAND, CIRCUIT JUDGE.   This is an appeal from a final decree in admiralty holding a mortgage covering three steamships, made on

December 24, 1929, to secure an indebtedness to the Corn Exchange Bank Trust Company, which was due on April 1, 1930, superior in priority to the maritime lien of Tietjen & Lang Dry Dock Company for repairs to one of the vessels, the Bear Mountain. The repairs were made eight years after the expiration of the date of maturity of the mortgage, which was endorsed on the vessel's documents. The mortgage was recorded in the New York Custom House and thereafter endorsed upon the documents as a preferred ship's mortgage under the Act of 1920, 46 U.S.C.A. Sec. 911 et seq. No extension of the date of the maturity of the mortgage was ever made, recorded or endorsed. The mortgage provided that failure to pay it punctually on April 1, 1930, would result in a default and render it immediately enforceable. The mortgage was not paid off at maturity but the principal of $100,000 had been reduced to $79,000 which, with interest due at the date of the decree, amounted to $83,732.46. No certificate of partial discharge was ever made, recorded or endorsed, and no steps to foreclose were taken until March, 1939, when the present libel of foreclosure was filed in the District Court by the Corn Exchange Bank Trust Company. The cause came on for trial before Judge Conger, who held that the mortgagee was entitled to priority over the maritime lien of Tietjen & Lang Dry Dock Company and dismissed the intervening petition of the latter and granted the libellant judgment against McAllister Navigation Company, Inc., which had executed the bond secured by the mortgage, for the difference between the indebtedness due and the amounts realized through the foreclosure sale.

Tietjen & Lang Dry Dock Company has appealed from the decree on the ground that its maritime lien for repairs is superior to the lien of libellant's mortgage. In our opinion the decree of the District Court granting priority to the mortgage was right and should be affirmed.

The appellant contends that its lien is superior because: (a) the priority given the mortgage by the Act of 1920 expired on the date of maturity upon the analogy of the rule applicable to bottomry bonds; (b) the priority of the mortgage was lost by laches, due to delay in foreclosure.

The claim that the priority of the lien of a preferred mortgage conforming to the provisions of the Merchant Marine Act, 46 U.S.C.A. § 597 et seq., and recorded as required therein is to be determined by analogies derived from the rules of law applicable to bottomry bonds seems quite out of accord with the purpose of the Act.

In Detroit Trust Co. v. Barlum S.S. Co., 293 U.S. 21, 38 et seq., 55 S.Ct. 31, 36, 79 L.Ed. 176 (1934), the Supreme Court remarked that the declared purpose of the Act was "to provide for the promotion and maintenance of the American merchant marine", that: "The report of the Senate Committee on Commerce pointed out that 'mortgage security on ships' was 'practically worthless'; that it was proposed to 'make it good except as to certain demands that should be superior to everything else, such as wages'; and that it was desired to have 'our people and capital interested in shipping and shipping securities.'" The court went on to say: "The bill, with this purpose, was developed in conference. The managers on the part of the House of Representatives, in their statement accompanying the report of the Committee of Conference, observed that by the enlarged provisions of the bill 'the mortgagee under a mortgage upon a vessel of the United States is made more secure in his interest in the vessel than he is under existing admiralty law,' and, referring to the plan of 'creating a preferred mortgage,' added that 'the preferred status arises upon the recording of the mortgage as a preferred mortgage and its indorsement upon vessel's documents.' " * * *

In view of the foregoing and of the broad purposes of the Merchant Marine Act it is entirely clear that the analogy of bottomry bonds cannot control its provisions if they in terms give the libellant's mortgage priority over the maritime lien for repairs. We think the language of the Act renders the priority of the mortgage clear.

46 U.S.C.A. § 922, provides that a preferred mortgage, after recording and endorsement, shall have "the preferred status given by the provisions of section 953". * * *

46 U.S.C.A. § 951, provides that: "A preferred mortgage shall constitute a lien upon the mortgaged vessel in the amount of the outstanding mortgage indebtedness secured by such vessel. Upon the default of any term or condition of the mortgage, such lien may be enforced by the mortgagee by suit in rem in admiralty. * * *"

In the case at bar there was default on the part of the mortgagor through failure to pay the mortgage indebtedness when due. Section 951 contains no requirement that, in order to preserve the preferred status of such a mortgage, the mortgagee must foreclose at maturity or within a reasonable time thereafter, or indeed at any particular time. Accordingly the lien became enforceable, the libel was properly filed and the decree of the District Court in favor of Corn Exchange Bank Trust Company is unassailable.

There can be no reason for supposing that ships' mortgages recorded in conformity with the Act of 1920, which was designed to make such securities desirable investments, should be subjected to limitations that would render their enforcement far more difficult and hazardous than that of similar mortgages covering land or chattels. It was plainly the purpose of the Act to make ships' mortgages as available for investment as other securities with which the public is accustomed to deal and thus to render that class of securities attractive which had been unmarketable before.

The intricate reasoning whereby the appellant has attacked the priority of the libellant's mortgage, like the past attacks upon the constitutionality and scope of the Ship Mortgage Act, appears to be an aftermath of the long struggles of the courts of common law and equity to limit the admiralty jurisdiction. Many of the details of this struggle, which lasted for at least 200 years, are related by Professor Andrews in Volume 4, Chapter VIII of his great work on "The Colonial Period of American History" (Yale University Press 1938), where he gives a sketch of the Vice–Admiralty Courts. This fight that went on in England and its Colonies between the common law and chancery courts and the admiralty judges, and continued in the courts of the states prior to the adoption of the federal constitution, stood in the way of each attempted extension of the jurisdiction of the unpopular maritime courts.   As a result there still remains a hesitancy to assert powers under the maritime jurisdiction, as fully as would be natural, and an inclination to await congressional legislation before taking any new steps.   This self-limiting tendency has manifested itself in the case of ships' mortgages, contracts to build ships, torts on navigable waters which are not a part of the sea itself, and other similar matters, and has encouraged attempts to retain restrictions of the jurisdiction of the courts of admiralty which, if they should prevail, would impair the value of ships' mortgages and thwart the broad purposes of the Ship Mortgage Act.   Doubtless such attempts would hardly have been made in a field where opposition to extensions of jurisdiction was less traditional than that of maritime law.   Cf. Penhallow v. Doane's Adm'rs, 3 Dall. 54 (1795).

The appellant argues that the requirement that the date of maturity of the mortgage be entered in the Custom House record and endorsed on the ship's documents limits the time when the security may be enforced and the lien may have priority.   This contention seems quite unfounded.   The requirement was to enable persons making advances of furnishing repairs to vessels to know when the mortgage matured in order that they might determine whether it was safe for them to risk taking a junior security.   When the intervenor in the case at bar contracted to make the repairs the mortgage was already long overdue and the record indicated that its lien was for a larger amount than was in fact owing after the reduction of the principal by payments of about $21,000.   In the face of this record we can imagine no prejudice to the intervenor because of the omission of the mortgagee to begin foreclosure sooner than it did.   * * *

The analogy of the mortgage to a bottomry bond is illusory.   A bottomry bond ordinarily creates a secret lien.   Here the ship's mortgage was recorded in the Custom House and any subsequent lienor could discover it by examining the record.   The rule for bottomry bonds that enforcement must be contemporaneous with maturity or shortly thereafter originated because such liens were secret.   They should not be allowed to stand in the way of subsequent lienors, having no notice of their existence, any longer than absolutely necessary.   What effect R.S. § 4192, 46 U.S.C.A. § 921 note, permitting bottomry bonds to be recorded had upon their enforcement, and whether special diligence in enforcing such bonds was requisite even though subsequent lienors had notice to their existence before giving credit to the vessel, has not been shown.   But in any event the rule as to enforcement of bottomry bonds has no effect upon the rights of a preferred ship's mortgage made and filed in conformity with the provisions of the Ship Mortgage Act.

Appellant's final contention that the mortgagee is barred from foreclosure by laches has no merit.   The mortgagor not only reduced the principal but kept up the payment of interest until shortly before the libel was filed.   There surely was no showing of laches affecting libellant's cause of action or claim of priority.

Decree affirmed with costs to appellee.

5.   TORT LIENS

The Anaces

United States Circuit Court of Appeals, Fourth Circuit, 1899.
93 Fed. 240.

This is a libel in rem in admiralty instituted by McCollum, the appellant, against the British steamship Anaces to recover damages for injuries received by the libelant while working, as a stevedore, stowing cotton in the hold of the steamship.   The case stated by the libelant is that, while he was at work in the hold, several bales of cotton were suddenly dropped upon him; that he was one of a number of stevedores employed by a master stevedore who had a contract to load the ship; that it was the custom of the port, and one of the terms of the contract for the stevedoring, that the steamship should furnish and operate the winch for hoisting and lowering the cotton, and should provide a man of skill and experience to operate it, so as not to endanger the stevedores working in the hold; that the injury to the libelant was caused by the negligence and incompetency of the man employed by the ship's officers to operate the winch; that the man employed by the master of the ship to operate the winch was an ordinary laborer, entirely inexperienced and unskilled, who was intrusted with a duty requiring experienced judgment in order to avoid injuring the steve-dores working in the hold, and that the master in employing an incompe-tent man, without experience, to operate the winch, was guilty of negli-gence, and failed in a duty which the owners of the ship owed the libelant; that the injury was caused by the incompetency of the winchman, and through no fault of the libelant.   The steamship was arrested, and released upon stipulation.   The master appeared as claimant, and filed an answer controverting the allegations of the libel; denying that the winchman was incompetent; alleging that he was a highly-skilled man, selected by the head stevedore, and that the libelant was injured through his own reckless-ness in not heeding warnings given him.   When the case was called for trial it appears that the respondent made a motion orally to dismiss the libel because improperly brought as a libel in rem.   This defense was not made in the answer, and should properly have been made before answer, by exception (Ben.Adm. Secs. 466, 468); but the court heard the motion, and dismissed the libel, as stated in the decree, "for the reason that a libel in rem for the causes set forth in the libel will not lie in this court."   87 F. 565.   From this decree the libelant has appealed.

■ MORRIS, DISTRICT JUDGE (after stating the facts as above).   The district judge held that the only remedy in admiralty for a personal injury to one lawfully upon the ship, resulting from the negligent failure of the officers of the ship to perform a duty necessary for his safety, is by libel in personam, and that a libel in rem cannot be maintained. * * *

The only action for tort which by express rule is forbidden to be brought in rem is that mentioned in rule 16, which declares that all suits for assaults and beating on the high seas, or elsewhere within the admiralty and maritime jurisdiction, shall be in personam only. It is admitted that the libel charges a maritime tort, and that the admiralty has jurisdiction (Leathers v. Blessing, 105 U.S. 626, 26 L.Ed. 1192 (1881)), and that many maritime torts give a maritime lien, with a right to proceed in rem to recover the damage sustained; but endeavor has been made to show that maritime torts of the particular kind alleged in this libel do not have that privilege. It is admitted that negligence in navigation, resulting in a collision causing injuries to persons, gives a lien, and that suits for injuries to passengers caused by negligence of the ship's officers can be enforced in rem. And it is hardly denied that personal injuries resulting from defective appliances, or want of proper construction of the ship, give a lien; but it is argued that personal injuries which are caused by negligent misuse of a proper appliance do not give a lien, although they do give an action in admiralty against the owners of the ship. This is an attempt to make a distinction which does not find countenance in the reported decisions of admiralty courts of the United States. In The A. Heaton, 43 F. 592 (1 Cir.1899), Mr. Justice Gray, sitting in the circuit court, hearing an appeal from the district court of Massachusetts, in a very careful and learned opinion, said:

"In England, indeed, it appears unsettled, whether a libel in rem can be maintained in admiralty for a personal injury. But on principle, as observed by a recent English writer, it would seem difficult to deny the justice of the view that personal injuries inflicted by a ship might confer a maritime lien, or formulate a satisfactory reason why damages occasioned to a man's property should give rise to rights of a higher nature, or be the subject of a more effective remedy, than an injury occasioned under the same circumstances to his person. 4 Law Quar.Rev. 388. In this country it has been established by a series of judgments of the supreme court of the United States that a libel in admiralty may be maintained against the ship for any personal injury for which the owners are liable under the general law, independently of any local statute. Accordingly, passengers have often maintained libels, as well against the ship carrying them as against other ships, for personal injuries caused by negligence for which the owners were responsible. The New World, 57 U.S. (16 How.) 469, 14 L.Ed. 1019 (1853); The Washington, 76 U.S. (9 Wall.) 513, 19 L.Ed. 787 (1869); The Juniata, 93 U.S. 337, 23 L.Ed. 930 (1876); The City of Panama, 101 U.S. 453, 462, 25 L.Ed. 1061 (1879). The sixteenth admiralty rule, which directs that 'in all suits for an assault or beating upon the high seas, or elsewhere within the admiralty and maritime jurisdiction, the suit shall be in personam only,' does not affect libels for negligence."

In The John G. Stevens, 170 U.S. 113, 120, 18 S.Ct. 544, 547 (1898), Mr. Justice Gray, speaking for the supreme court, said:

"The foundation of the rule that collision gives to the party injured a jus in re in the offending ship is the principle of the maritime law that the ship, by whomsoever owned or navigated, is considered as herself the wrongdoer, liable for the tort, and subject to a maritime lien for the damages. The principle, as has been observed by careful text writers on both sides of the Atlantic, has been more clearly established and more fully carried out in this country than in England. Henry, Adm.Jur. & Proc. Sec. 75; Mars.Mar.Coll. (3d Ed.) 93."

And he cites the following passage from The Malek Adhel, 2 How. 210, 234:

"The ship is also by the general maritime law, held responsible for the torts and misconduct of the master and crew thereof, whether arising from negligence or a willful disregard of duty; as, for example, in cases of collision and other wrongs done upon the high seas, or elsewhere within the admiralty and maritime jurisdiction, upon the general policy of that law, which looks to the instrument itself used as the means of the mischief, as the best and surest pledge for the compensation to the injured party."
* * *

The case of The John G. Stevens is also an authority against the suggestion, made in argument, that the fact that there was no contract in the present case between the libelant and the vessel was a reason for holding that he had no maritime lien for his injuries. * * *

It would appear, therefore, to be the settled rule in the United States that there is a maritime lien for the injury inflicted by maritime torts, with but few exceptions,—for instance, that made by rule 16, that suits for assault and beating shall be in personam only. In our Reports are many such actions in rem in the district and appellate courts in which the maritime lien has not been questioned, and many of them are suits by stevedores and others not having direct contractual relations with the ship. The Rheola, 19 F. 926. This was a libel in rem by a stevedore, one of a number employed by a master stevedore to discharge the ship, who was injured by the breaking of a defective chain furnished by the ship. On appeal to the circuit court, Judge Wallace said:

"As the libelant was not directly employed by the master, and could only look to the master stevedore for his pay, there was no privity of contract between him and the shipowners. Nor did the relation of master and servant, in its technical sense, exist between the libelant and the shipowner. But it is conceived that this does not in the least affect the obligation of the master not to be negligent towards the libelant, or the degree of care which it was incumbent upon him to exercise. The libelant was performing a service in which the shipowners had an interest, and which they contemplated would be performed by the use of the appliances which they agreed to provide. They were under the same obligation to him not to expose him to unnecessary danger that they were to the master stevedore, his employer. This was no express obligation on their part, to either, to provide safe and suitable appliances; but they were under an implied duty to each, and the measure of duty towards each was the same."

Steel v. McNeil, 8 C.C.A. 512, 60 F. 105 (1894), in the circuit court of appeals for the Fifth Circuit, was a libel in rem by one of a number of stevedores, not in the immediate pay of the ship, who was injured by a block which had been negligently rigged with an insufficient shackle bolt by the ship's crew. The libel was maintained.

The City of Panama, 101 U.S. 453–462, 25 L.Ed. 1061 (1879), was an action in rem by a passenger who fell into a hatchway negligently left open by some of the crew of the ship. * * *

Every consideration of justice and of convenience urges that the maritime lien, if it exists, should be maintained in cases like the present one. The owners of the vessel almost invariably are unknown and inaccessible. To require the libelant to serve process on them is practically to deny him any remedy. Under the statutes of the United States, the owners of all the vessel property, foreign and domestic, are given, to the fullest extent, the privilege of limiting their liability to the value of their interest in the vessel. The injured party cannot touch their property, outside of their interest in the ship, if they claim to limit their liability; and there are strong reasons of justice and convenience why he should have a maritime lien upon that specific property, and why distinctions, not founded in reason, between claims of the same general merit, should not gain a place in a system of jurisprudence which is intended to approach natural justice.

It is urged for the appellee that the case of Currie v. McKnight [1897] App.Cas. 97, in the house of lords, is a persuasive decision, of high authority, to establish the contention that there is no maritime lien in the present case. In Currie v. McKnight the master of the vessel against which the maritime lien was asserted had, in order to release her from a position of peril, wrongfully cut the moorings of another ship, and caused her to drift ashore and receive damage. By the judgment of the house of lords it was declared to be the admiralty law, as established in England since the case of The Bold Buccleugh, 7 Moore, P.C. 267, that when a ship is carelessly navigated, so as to occasion injury to another vessel, the injured vessel has a remedy against the corpus of the offending ship, and that this right arises from the fact that the offending ship is the instrument which causes the damage, and it was stated that in the case in hand it appeared from the findings of fact that the damage was not caused by any movement of the vessel proceeded against, in the course of her navigation, but was occasioned by the act of her crew in removing an obstacle to her starting on her voyage. As the result of the judgments delivered in the case, the ruling was that, under the English law, to render a ship liable to a maritime lien the ship itself must be the instrument which causes the damage. Whether the reasoning of the judgments delivered in Currie v. McKnight would be held satisfactory in our courts, which have made, not solely the fact that the ship is the direct instrument which causes the damage the test of a maritime lien, but also the fact that the maritime tort has resulted from the negligent failure of those in charge of the ship to observe some duty in the management of the ship which the law imposes upon them in respect to persons lawfully on the ship, it is not now necessary to discuss; for the case alleged in the libel in the present case charges that it was the negligent misuse of the ship's steam winch which caused the libelant's injury. It is, in effect, the same as if the charge was that a part of the ship itself, as a spar or a block, had, by fault of the ship's officers, fallen upon the libelant. It is therefore the ship itself which, through the negligent management of the officers, caused the damage, and this is within the test attempted to be set up in Currie v. McKnight. We think, therefore, that it is plain that the case stated in the libel in the present case entitled the libelant to proceed in rem under the maritime law as administered in our courts. * * *

The decree appealed from is reversed.

N O T E

Admiralty Rule 16, referred to by the court in *The Anaces*, was carried forward as Rule 15 in the revised admiralty rules of 1920. When the admiralty and civil rules were merged in 1966, however, Rule 15 was eliminated, with the following comment by the Advisory Committee:

> The draft eliminates the provision of Admiralty Rule 15 that actions for assault and beating may be brought only in personam. A preliminary study fails to disclose any reason for the rule. It is subject to so many exceptions that it is calculated to deceive rather than to inform. A seaman may sue in rem when he has been beaten by a fellow member of the crew so vicious as to render the vessel unseaworthy, The Rolph, 293 F. 269, aff'd 299 F. 52 (9 Cir.1923), or where the theory of the action is that a beating by the master is a breach of the obligation under the shipping articles to treat the seaman with proper kindness, The David Evans, 187 F. 775 (C.C.A. 9th.1911); and a passenger may sue in rem on the theory that the assault is a breach of the contract of passage, The Western States, 159 F. 354 (2 Cir.1908). To say that an action for money damages may be brought only in personam seems equivalent to saying that a maritime lien shall not exist; and that, in turn, seems equivalent to announcing a rule of substantive law rather than a rule of procedure. Dropping the rule will leave it to the courts to determine whether a lien exists as a matter of substantive law.

There is no lien created by a cause of action under the Jones Act, and none is created by reducing such a claim to judgment. See United States v. F/V Sylvester F. Whalen, 226 F.Supp. 617, 1964 A.M.C. 1552 (D.Me.1964).

The Florence

United States District Court, Eastern District of Michigan, 1877.
2 Flipp. 56, 9 F.Cas. 294.

Libelant, being the owner of a lighter, averred that the master of the scow had, without authority, seized and used his lighter and neglected to return her, though requested so to do. He claimed $60 damage, and also the rental value of the lighter from the time of seizure, April 15, 1875, to the filing of his libel. Exceptions were taken to the jurisdiction on the ground that the facts did not constitute a lien upon the scow by the admiralty law. The principal allegations in the libel were denied in the answer, and it was claimed that the lighter had been detained by a ship carpenter, who had been directed by the libelant to put certain repairs upon her. The facts were that while the vessel was in a sunken condition the claimant applied to a brother of libelant for permission to use the lighter in carrying off wood to the scow. This the brother, Wallace Lemaire, granted without authority. The claimant used her two or three days only; left her lying near the lake shore where she pounded and became leaky. It was agreed, on demand made by libelant for the lighter, that she should be left at a ship carpenter's to be repaired. After this was finished the carpenter refused to deliver her to libelant, who filed this libel to recover her value. * * *

■ Brown, J.—The principal question discussed upon the argument related to the jurisdiction of the court. The libel sounds in tort, and it was strenuously insisted by claimant's advocate that no lien attached to the scow for the conversion of the lighter, both parties conceding that claimant took possession of her without authority from the owner. Cases of spoliation and damage are of admiralty and maritime jurisdiction. These include illegal seizure or depredations upon vessels or goods afloat. Every violent dispossession of property on the ocean is, prima facie, a maritime tort, and as such belongs to the admiralty jurisdiction. Benedict 310, 311. And the owners of a vessel are liable for torts committed by the master in the course of his employment.

There can be no doubt that if this were a case of contract—that is, if the agent of whom the claimant hired the scow, and whom claimant in good faith believed to have authority to loan it, had in fact possessed that authority, a libel in rem could have been sustained for the use of the lighter. A person furnishing a small boat or a lighter for the use of a vessel has as valid a lien upon her as though he had furnished an anchor, a compass, a chronometer, or any other of the articles usually denominated materials. In the case of The Dick Keys, 1 Bissell, 408, Mr. Justice McLean held that, where the master of a steamboat, on her behalf, agreed to pay $20 per day for the use of a barge, a libel might be maintained against the steamboat for the amount. Mr. Parsons says (2 Parsons on Shipping, 148): "If a barge is necessary to a steamboat, its hire to it will be regarded as material furnished for its equipment;" citing Amis v. Steamboat Louisa, 9 Mo. 629 (1845); Gleim v. The Belmont, 11 Mo. 112 (1847); Steamboat Kentucky v. Brooks, 1 Greene, (Ia.) 398 (1848)—cases which fully sustain the text of the learned commentator.

Now, upon principle, it is difficult to say why, if an action in rem will lie for the use or value of property *lawfully* obtained, a similar action will not lie for the use or value of property *unlawfully* obtained; in other words, where the wrong is greater, the remedy should not be less. The general rule with regard to torts seems to be, that the owners and the vessel are liable for all the acts of the master done in the execution of the business in which he may be employed, by which third persons are injured, whether the injury was occasioned by the unlawful acts or by the negligence or want of skill of the master. Dias v. The Revenge, 3 Wash. 262 (1891); Dean v. Angus, Bee's Admiralty, 369; The Martha Ann, Olcott, 18. The principle underlying these decisions is that, for torts committed in the business of the master as such, or in which the ship is the active, the injuring or the benefited party, the injured party has his remedy as well against the vessel as against her owner and master.   The mere fact that the person committing a tort is master of a vessel, or course, does not make her liable; but, if it be an act done in pursuance of his business as master or is beneficial to the vessel, she becomes liable in rem.   The English cases hold that the vessel is not liable for a willful collision.   This doctrine, however, is denied in the case of Ralston v. The State Rights, Crabbe, 22, where a libel was sustained for running down the libelant's vessel, done by the express direction of the master of the colliding vessel.

* * *

No willful misconduct or wrongful purpose on the part of the claimant need be shown; for the gist of the action is the use of the lighter by the vessel, and I hold that it makes no difference whether the claimant became possessed of her by a contract, or by an act which was technically a conversion.   The exception to the jurisdiction must therefore be overruled.

Ouillette, the owner of the scow, took possession of the lighter without authority from the libelant.   After he had her for some time, and she had been injured either by Ouillette's negligence in allowing her to pound upon the bottom, or by becoming leaky, libelant went to Ouillette and demanded that the lighter should be returned to him in good order.   Ouillette then put her into the hands of a carpenter, who repaired the damages done to her, and also made some alterations and repairs on her at the request of the libelant.   When libelant went to the carpenter to demand her, he refused to give her up, either until the repairs put upon her by Ouillette's directions were paid, as libelant says, or until libelant would release Ouillette from all liability, or would clear Ouillette of the law, as the carpenter says.   As it is clear that libelant offered to pay for the repairs which he had ordered, and the carpenter did not detain her upon that ground, his further detention of her must be attributed to Ouillette, notwithstanding his statement that the carpenter detained her without authority from him.   It was the duty of Ouillette to see that the lighter was returned, and no excuse for the non-performance of that duty, not attributable to the libelant, can be accepted.

There is considerable conflict with regard to the value of the lighter; but, upon all the testimony, I think that $45 is as much as she is worth. There must be a decree for the libelant for this amount, with interest.

Oriente Commercial, Inc. v. American Flag Vessel, M/V Floridian

United States Court of Appeals, Fourth Circuit, 1975.
529 F.2d 221, 1975 A.M.C. 2484.

■ HAYNSWORTH, CHIEF JUDGE: The question presented by this case in admiralty is whether claims against a ship as a common carrier for damage to or loss of cargo are "preferred maritime liens" "for damages arising out of tort," 46 U.S.C. § 953(a), and thus superior to a valid preferred mortgage lien. 46 U.S.C. § 953(b), we hold that they are.

Oriente Commercial, Inc., Black and Decker, Inc., and the United States were among many *in rem* claimants against the M/V Floridian, which was arrested and sold by order of the court in May 1973. The United States held two valid preferred ship mortgages on the vessel. Oriente took a default judgment on its claim that a shipment of meat was negligently damaged in transit. Black and Decker holds a default judgment on its claim that the vessel negligently failed to deliver part of a shipment of machinery. The several claims far exceed the proceeds of the sale, so the question of priority of the liens must be met.

Title 46 U.S.C.A. § 953 provides that the preferred mortgage liens shall have priority over all claims against a vessel sold by judicial order except preferred maritime liens and expenses, fees, and costs allowed by the court. Subsection 953(a)(2) defines "preferred maritime liens" to include "a lien for damages arising out of tort * * *." The district court acknowledged that the asserted liens were maritime and that the cargo claimants had alleged loss and damage due to negligence in operation of the ship as a common carrier, but held that the claims did not give rise to preferred maritime liens. It was reasoned that such claims ought to be brought in contract, but, because of the broad duties of the vessel as a common carrier, almost always may be brought as tort actions. Since such claims are thus "hybrids" and since the Ship Mortgage Act was intended to promote ship financing, the court believed that cargo claims must be subordinate to preferred mortgages. This conclusion was bolstered by the court's observation that if the cargo liens were superior to the preferred mortgage lien, they would also outrank supply and repair liens, which are most in need of priority.

While the district court was led to its conclusion by policy considerations, we believe it gave insufficient weight to earlier cases that strongly support a contrary result. Thus, in The John G. Stevens, 170 U.S. 113, 18 S.Ct. 544, 42 L.Ed. 969 (1898), the Supreme Court held that a lien for damage to a tow due to negligence of its tug sounded in tort, independent of any contract made for towage, and was superior to liens for supplies, which sound solely in contract. See also, Stevens v. The White City, 285 U.S. 195, 201, 52 S.Ct. 347, 76 L.Ed. 699 (1932). The opinion does much to dispel the notion that simply because a lien is a "hybrid" of tort and contract, it does not arise out of tort. The supply lienor had argued that the tug's liability was analogous to that of a common carrier for the loss of goods carried and, being thus contractual in origin, had no priority over the supply lien. In dictum decisive of the instant case, the Court rejected the contention:

> But even an action by a passenger, or by an owner of goods, against a carrier, for neglect to carry and deliver in safety, is an action for the breach of a duty imposed by the law, independently of contract or of consideration, and is therefore founded in tort.

170 U.S. at 124–25, 18 S.Ct. at 549.

The question was more precisely presented to Judge Soper, then a district judge, in The Henry W. Breyer, D.C., Md., 17 F.2d 423 (1927). Among the several creditors in that case were cargo shippers who claimed loss of goods and damages for prepaid freight against the ship as a common carrier. Judge Soper held that the shippers' liens arose in tort and thus had priority over the preferred mortgage lien, stating:

> The intervening libels of the shippers sound in tort, on the theory that they are entitled to recover damages for breach of the carrier's common-law duty, notwithstanding that the carrier's default was also a breach of the contract expressed in the bill of lading. The responsibilities of a common carrier may be restricted by contract, but the nature of its occupation makes it a common carrier still. * * * It is well established that ordinarily the owner of goods damaged by the dereliction of a common carrier has the option to bring action either in contract or tort. "Where, from a given state of facts, the law raises a legal obligation to do a particular act, and there is a breach of that obligation, and a consequential damage, there, although assumpsit may be maintainable upon a promise implied by law to do the act, still an action on the case founded in tort is the more proper form of action." * * * In other words, when the relationship of shipper and carrier is established, there is a duty imposed by law which arises out of the relations which the carrier sustains to the public, and no special contract is necessary.

17 F.2d at 429 (citations omitted).

More recently it has been held that cargo claims such as those in the present case arise out of tort if the loss results from a lack of due diligence on the part of the carrier. Thus, in Morrisey v. S.S. A. & J. Faith, D.C., N.D.Ohio, 252 F.Supp. 54 (1965), the court concluded that the Carriage of Goods by Sea Act, 46 U.S.C. §§ 1300–1315, places a legal obligation, independent of contract, upon the carrier. While the court believed the duty of due diligence to be less burdensome to the carrier than that imposed in the *Breyer* case, either standard is met by the facts of this case. The cargo claimants having taken judgment on their allegations of negligence, have established a violation of the duty of due diligence and, *a fortiori,* of the much stricter obligations of common carriers. Accordingly, whichever standard is applied, it has been broken in this case, and the breach sounds in tort. See also Port Welcome Cruises, Inc. v. S.S. Bay Belle, D.C., Md., 215 F.Supp. 72, 86 (1963), aff'd, 324 F.2d 954 (4th Cir.1963)(failure to return rented property sounds in tort on conversion theory); Potash Co. of Canada Ltd. v. M/V Raleigh, D.C., C.Z., 361 F.Supp. 120 (1973); The Pacific Spruce, D.C., W.D.Wash., 1 F.Supp. 593 (1932).

The St. Paul, D.C., S.D., N.Y., 277 F. 99 (1921), relied upon by the district court, is not necessarily to the contrary. In that case all but two of the cargo claims complaints sounded solely in contract. The two were apparently claims for loss of cargo sustained during a fire which occurred while the vessel was in the custody of the court, as a result of which no lien arose. Id. at 109. So viewed, the case stands for the proposition that a cargo claimant who brings his action solely in contract or who is unable to prove his tort will be subordinate to supply and repair liens. Oriente and

Black and Decker are not such plaintiffs, having brought their actions in tort and taken judgments that are not contested by the United States.

Finally we note that the legislation draws no distinction between cargo claims that sound in tort, the so-called hybrid liens, and any other type of claim for damages arising out of tort. While Congress might have been well advised to subordinate cargo claims, it flatly granted priority to all claims arising out of tort. The result reached by the district court and pressed by the United States would carve out an exception to the statute, unwarranted by its language. Whatever Congress meant, it stated that all tort liens are prior to preferred mortgage liens. In light of cases decided both before and after enactment of the Ship Mortgage Act, holding that cargo claims such as those in the instant case sound in tort, we cannot say that Congress intended something else. Accordingly, we hold that the claims arose out of tort and are preferred maritime liens having priority over the preferred mortgage lien.

Reversed.

NOTE

Accord, Associated Metals and Minerals Corp. v. Alexander's Unity MV, 41 F.3d 1007, 1995 A.M.C. 1006 (5th Cir.1995); Texport Oil Co. v. M/V Amolyntos, 11 F.3d 361, 1994 A.M.C.815 (2d Cir.1993); All Alaskan Seafoods, Inc. v. M/V Sea Producer, 882 F.2d 425, 1989 A.M.C. 2935 (9th Cir.1989). See, in particular the M/V Alexander's Unity, which contains a thorough discussion of the issue.

And it has been held that there needn't be any contract between the shipper and carrier to justify a lien for cargo damage. Albany Ins. Co. v. M/V Istrian Exp., 61 F.3d 709 (9th Cir.1995).

6. OTHER TRANSACTIONS GIVING RISE TO MARITIME LIENS

Salvage. See, e.g., Faneuil Advisors, Inc. v. O/S Sea Hawk, 50 F.3d 88, 1995 A.M.C. 1504 (1st Cir.1995).

General Average Expenses.—A maritime lien exists on the vessel in favor of a freighter who is entitled to general average contribution. The Andree, 47 F.2d 874 (2d Cir.1931), appeal dismissed 296 U.S. 668, 57 S.Ct. 756 (1932). When it is the vessel that is entitled to contribution, the lien exists on the cargo, but like cargo liens in general, it will be lost by unconditional delivery. See *4,885 Bags of Linseed*, supra, p. 411.

Breach of Charter Party.—A lien exists in favor of the charterer for breach of the terms of the charter party. The Oceano, 148 Fed. 131 (S.D.N.Y.1906). See Gilmore and Black, *Law of Admiralty* 631 (1975). See Pacific Vegetable Oil Corp. v. M/S Norse Commander, 264 F.Supp. 625, 1967 A.M.C. 1895 (S.D.Tex.1966). There a subcharterer was held to have a lien for cargo loss.

Bottomry and Respondentia Bonds.—These devices, at one time of importance in the financing of voyages, are no longer in use. Gilmore and Black state that probably no living lawyer has seen an example of either.

Law of Admiralty 632 (1975). The bottomry bond was secured by the vessel and the respondentia bond by the cargo. They were both conditioned upon the successful completion of the voyage, and for that reason likened to a form of insurance contract. See Park, *Marine Insurances,* 869 (1842). No doubt because of this high risk element the interest rate was considerably higher than that obtaining on other forms of loan. See Park, supra. For a literary reference, see Smollett's Adventures of Peregrine Pickle in which Mr. Pickle is tempted into putting his money in bottomry by the "excessive premium." He received £1,000 back on his £800.

7. LIENS UNDER STATE LAW

The Federal Lien Act provides that the act supersedes the state statutes insofar as such statutes purport to create rights of action to be enforced *in rem* in admiralty against vessels for "repairs, supplies, towage, use of drydock or marine railway, and other necessaries." In short, the act is preemptive only within its own coverage. It leaves the states free to create liens to be enforced in admiralty by the federal court, so long as they are not liens for necessaries. While there is a relatively restricted area in which maritime obligations import no lien and do not fall within the description of necessaries, there have been occasional examples of enforcement of state-created liens since the passage of the Lien Act. In Burdine v. Walden, 91 F.2d 321, 1937 A.M.C. 1149 (5th Cir.1937), the court applied a state statute giving a master a lien for his wages, and in Grow v. Steel Screw Loraine K, 310 F.2d 547, 1963 A.M.C. 2044 (6th Cir.1962), a state statute giving a lien for unpaid insurance premiums. Cf. Equilease Corp. v. M/V Sampson, 793 F.2d 598, 1986 A.M.C. 1826 (5th Cir.1986)(en banc), in which the court of appeals, having first upheld the application of a state law privilege for the amount of insurance premiums advanced by an insurance agent, then on rehearing determined that the state law privilege had expired, hear the case en banc and held that the advance imported a maritime lien. See also Caterpiller Fin. Services Inc. v. Aleutian Chalice, 1994 A.M.C. 1767, 1994 WL 468187, holding insurance premiums fall within the Lien Act as "necessaries." In Murray v. Schwartz, 175 F.2d 72, 1949 A.M.C. 1081 (2d Cir.1949), the Second Circuit held that the maritime court would not enforce a lien for wharfage of a dead ship, the contract being nonmaritime. Proceeding from the *Burdine* and *Murray* cases, Gilmore and Black observe that while in theory the state service lien statutes are still in force "as to whatever service liens are not covered by the Lien Act or the general maritime law," in fact the state statutes are "either moribund or dead." Law of Admiralty 659 (1975). The *Grow* case represents the only flicker of life since that time. In the tort area, which, of course, does not come within the Lien Act provisions, the courts have upheld state created liens for wrongful death on territorial waters. The cases are collected in Gilmore and Black, supra.

So long as the state lien is not enforced in a true *in rem* proceeding in the state court in violation of the rule set out in *The Hine,* or does not require enforcement in an admiralty proceeding, the state may create and enforce liens as it sees fit, subject to the possibility that they might be held to be antithetical to the general maritime law. State created liens for provision of labor and materials for a shipbuilder enforced by attachment within four days following the launching were recognized as valid by the Supreme Court in Armstrong v. United States, 364 U.S. 40, 80 S.Ct. 1563, 4 L.Ed.2d 1554 (1960). See also Sun Harbor Marina v. Sellick, 250 Cal.App.2d 281, 58 Cal.Rptr. 459, 1967 A.M.C. 2783 (1967).

8.   ADVANCES AND LIENS BY SUBROGATION

Findley v. Lanasa (The Josephine Lanasa)

United States Court of Appeal, Fifth Circuit, 1960.
276 F.2d 907, 1960 A.M.C. 1444.

■ JOHN R. BROWN, CT. J.   This case deals with the problem of a maritime lien for cash advances made to a master for use in payment of crew's wages. Specifically, the narrow issue is the extent and nature of the proof required to show actual application of the funds to payments of wages. The District Court on rehearing held that a lien existed. The unsuccessful claimant to the vessel, stating himself to be the owner but found by the district court to be a mere non-maritime mortgagee, appeals.

There is a lot of family on both sides of this transaction involving the good ship S.S. Josephine Lanasa. The successful maritime lienor (libellant below appellee here) is Henry P. Lanasa. The money advanced was delivered on the three occasions by his son, Henry M. Lanasa. On the other side of the controversy was the brother of Henry P., Vincent F. Lanasa. Vincent and George Dennis were the owners[1] of the S.S. Josephine Lanasa.

When the case was tried, the Judge had before him the libel of Henry to impress a lien on a vessel *owned* by H.W. Findley. In that trial, Vincent Lanasa and George Dennis, either individually or through their corporation, West Indies Importing Corp., were described as and considered to be charterers. The advance being made by one brother to the master in the employ of the other for the purpose of defraying expenses for charterer's account gave the Court considerable pause. This general circumstance of suspicion was enhanced by other factors. The money was delivered for Henry by his son, Henry M. On each of these three occasions, Vincent was aboard and saw the master receive the cash from Henry M. and in turn give a signed, written receipt[2] stating that it was for crew's wages. Vincent

1. This was through the instrumentality of their wholly owned Panamanian corporation, West Indies Importing Corp. George Dennis was the son-in-law of H.W. Findley, the Claimant, who claimed the Steamship Josephine Lanasa as owner.

2. The three written receipts were typewritten with the master's name typed "Capt.

Peter Penic, Master Steamship Josephine Lanasa" with his original signature signed "P. Penic." The receipts were for $2,300, $2,464, and $3,000 respectively, and each recited at the top "on board the Steamship Josephine Lanasa." In each one payment was acknowledged by Peter Penic, Master, received from "H.P. Lanasa, U.S.A.," and

knew, of course, that the charter party prohibited the master incurring any liens. Consistent with the general maritime law,[3] the supposed charter, of course, contained the traditional exception for crew's wages and salvage. But Vincent knew that crew's wages were, as between owner and charterer, a proper charge for the account of the charterer (Vincent and George Dennis).

Viewing the matter, as he was entitled to in that state of revealed truth, the Judge looked upon the case as one based on "the theory of subrogation" in which "the captain was not the agent of the owner and * * * had no right to pledge the credit of the vessel." The Court sustained the first ground of claimant's motion to dismiss that "the burden of proof is upon libellant to establish that he is entitled to a maritime lien by subrogation to the claims of the seaman whose wages he contends he advanced and [as to which] there is no proof that he did anything but make loans to the captain." Reflecting the significance of ownership by Findley in evaluating the sufficiency of the evidence on the purpose for the advances, the Court had this to say. "In this case the very fact that Vincent F. Lanasa, brother of the libellant and president of the charterer, was present at the delivery of the money to the captain, fully conversant with the charter's provision against pledging the credit of the vessel makes the entire transaction subject to the sharpest scrutiny."

In this atmosphere, the District Court was apparently of the opinion that since there was no direct evidence of payment of any of these sums by the master to crew members, the decisions in The Englewood, 57 F.2d 319, 1932 A.M.C. 343 (E.D.N.Y.1932), Reconstruction Finance Corp. v. William D. Mangold, 99 F.Supp. 651; and The Florine (Fairbanks Morse & Co. v. Freight Boat Florine), 1951 A.M.C. 1589, 1927 A.M.C. 1717 (E.D.La.1927), urged by claimant, required a dismissal for insufficiency of proof.

---

stated "on account crew wages for months October & November, 1954."

3. This general approach finds frequent illustration. See, e.g., 46 U.S.C.A. § 953 under the Preferred Ship Mortgage Act which defines a "preferred maritime lien" to include "* * * (2) a lien * * * for wages of the crew of the vessel * * *." Between execution of the mortgage and its recordation, sec. 924 forbids incurring "any contractual obligation creating a lien * * * other than a lien for wages of the crew * * *." Section 973 of the Federal Maritime Lien Act provides that "[N]othing in this chapter shall be construed to confer a lien when the furnisher knew, or by the exercise of reasonable diligence could have ascertained, that because of the terms of the charter party, agreement for sale of the vessel, or for any other reason, the person ordering the repairs, supplies, or other

necessaries was without authority to bind the vessel therefor." 46 U.S.C.A. § 973. But such a prohibition is ineffective against a claim for crew's wages. Kongo, 155 F.2d 492, 1946 A.M.C. 1200 (6 Cir.1946), cert. denied 329 U.S. 735, 67 S.Ct. 99, 91 L.Ed. 635, 1946 A.M.C. 1496; The S.W. Somers, 22 F.2d 448, 1927 A.M.C. 1753 (D.Md.1927); The Chester, 25 F.2d 908, 128 A.M.C. 638 (D.Md.1928); President Arthur, 25 F.2d 999, 1928 A.M.C. 1377 (S.D.N.Y.1927). The idea has never been more effectively stated than in the nautical figure of Justice Gray recorded in John G. Stevens, 170 U.S. 113, 119, 18 S.Ct. 544, 42 L.Ed. 969 (1898), that "seamen's wages * * * are sacred liens, and, as long as a plank of the ship remains, the sailor is entitled, against all other persons, to the proceeds as a security for his wages."

But before the trial court entered a decree of dismissal upon his memorandum findings, the libellant moved for a rehearing on the basis of newly discovered evidence. The Court granted a rehearing and on the further hearing received in the record what libellant had described as the newly discovered evidence. Since the case was still under active consideration by the Court, the claimant's effort here to convince us that, on principles testing the propriety of a refusal[4] to reopen a record, the granting of a rehearing was an abuse of discretion is completely unavailing.

Whether it was really newly discovered, it was certainly new to the Court. There was no abuse of discretion in granting the rehearing to receive it. Whether, after its receipt, it proved anything is quite a different matter.

At this point, the family dealings over the S.S. Josephine Lanasa became more complicated. For the newly discovered and offered evidence was the record filed in this Court in another one of her numerous legal travails from Baltimore to Texas to Florida to the Canal Zone as empty-handed suppliers sought satisfaction. Findley v. Robert C. Herd & Co., 250 F.2d 77, 1958 A.M.C. 317 (5 Cir.1957). That record comprising testimony concerning the dealings between Findley and his son-in-law, Dennis, as well as Vincent Lanasa, the execution and exchange of various bills of sales and mortgages, was not objected to by claimant on the ground that it was hearsay. The sole ground was that it had no bearing on the issues in the instant case.

The District Court thought otherwise, as do we. For the Court below, as had Judge Connally in the *Texas* case affirmed by us, now found that what he thought was the situation was something altogether different. Findley was no longer the owner whose vessel was exposed to liens incurred by a charterer through possible connivance between an easy going master and two brothers, one supplying money, the other operating the vessel as a charterer. Now the truth revealed that Findley was a mere mortgagee. A bill of sale ostensibly showed him to be the owner and he had, as such "owner" in turn chartered it back to Dennis and Vincent (or their corporation). The charter "hire," however, was stated to be the repayment of the loans previously made by Findley. The whole purpose was to put Findley in a position where he could protect himself against liens of others by virtue of the operation of the clause in the so-called charter forbidding Dennis and Vincent to incur liens. This would, so long as the fiction were preserved, give him protection which an ordinary mortgage, as such, would not.

The evidence was certainly relevant on the question of the master's actual authority. For as an employee of the owner, not the charterer, he had the full authority expressed in the statute[5] to incur liens. And the

---

4. Claimant urges 39 Am.Jur., New Trials, sec. 159, "Time of Discovery; Facts known at Trial" and sec. 160, "Freedom from Negligence; Exercise of Diligence."

5. 46 U.S.C.A. § 972 provides: "The following persons shall be presumed to have authority from the owner to procure repairs, supplies, towage, use of dry dock or marine

attempt to put a restriction on this authority of the master as a direct employee of the owner through the lien prohibition clause in the pretended charter was ineffectual.[6]

It was likewise relevant on the circumstances under which the lien asserted against the vessel came into being. No longer was it the action of an agent having limited authority with some clearly defined exclusions. Now it was the act of the master as a direct agent of the owner. Moreover, the act was performed by the agent in the immediate presence, and with the unreserved consent, of the principal-owner.[7] It was then a case of funds being advanced on the owner's direct order and therefore presumptively on the credit of the vessel until the contrary was proved as the statute prescribes. Point Landing, Inc. v. Alabama Dry Dock & Shipbuilding Co., 261 F.2d 861, at 867, 1959 A.M.C. 148, 156–157 (5 Cir.1958).

Obviously, these new facts had an immediate bearing on the sufficiency of the proof as to the intended use of the funds. With the owner having direct knowledge of the advance for the stated purpose under circumstances which made the receipt by the master the admitted acts of the owner—and for his account and benefit as well—the means of knowledge concerning subsequent application of the funds was likewise in the owner's hands. Until evidence was brought forward by the owner to refute it, the proof offered by the lienor in this setting made out a *prima facie* showing.

The cases mentioned above, so strongly urged by claimant, do not compel a contrary result. Reconstruction Finance Corp. v. William D. Mangold, supra, was a frank appraisal of the evidence as a credibility matter. The Judge, "after observing the witnesses and considering the evidence presented," 99 F.Supp. 651, 653 (1951), 1951 A.M.C. at 1591, simply declined to believe the testimony that $50 was really advanced for payment of crew's wages. Essentially, the same is true as to the *Englewood,* supra. That case does not, nor could it, undertake to declare as the legal rule what sort of evidence is required to establish use of the funds for payment of crew's wages. In the absence of the "so-called advance sheets," that Court merely declined to accept as sufficient "a general statement that a certain sum was paid * * *." 57 F.2d 319, 320, 1932 A.M.C. 343 (1932). Here, as we have shown, there was much more than a general statement. Here was the act of the master in the owner's presence committing the vessel to an agreement that the funds were for crew's wages. In testing this proof, we may even assume that had the master, without the knowledge or acquiescence of the owner, subsequently misappropriated the funds, no lien would have arisen. But until that showing was made, the joint acts

---

railway, and other necessaries for the vessel: The managing owner, ship's husband, master, or any person to whom the management of the vessel at the port of supply is intrusted. * * *"

6. See 46 U.S.C.A. § 973 and note 3, supra.

7. This, of course, makes it a case within the express terms of the Maritime Lien Act as the furnishing of necessaries to a vessel "upon the order of the owner of such vessel" rather than the alternative basis of furnishing them upon the order "of a person authorized by the owner." 46 U.S.C.A. § 971.

of master and owner were adequate to establish *prima facie* that the funds were used for a purpose giving rise to a maritime lien.

Findley, neither as the supposed owner nor as the mortgagee he really was, ever undertook to make any such proof. What was sufficient as *prima facie* proof then became uncontradicted proof and on it, the District Court was entitled to declare the existence of the lien as he did.

Affirmed.

■ Joseph C. Hutcheson, Jr., Ct., J., Dissenting. Stripped of all the rhetorical involvements of the opinion, by which a pretty theory is made to answer for a legal solution, this case is a completely simple one. It presents the single question whether the claimant of a lien for moneys loaned has made sufficient proof, that they were used for crew's wages, to entitle him to a lien priming a mortgage lien. This court's espousal, however, of the district judge's conclusion on rehearing (Rec. 73) that "The discovery by the court that Vincent Lanasa was actually an owner and not a charterer, puts an entirely different complexion on the transaction" supplies *the entire absence of testimony of any person,* that the sums loaned were actually paid to the crew as wages, accepts the false logic that this discovery destroys Findley's admitted priority, as mortgagee of the vessel, over a wholly unproved claim of a lien for moneys loaned, and gives the case an entirely different complexion.

Such a decision, abstractly considered, is neither breath-taking nor earth shaking.

Unfortunately for the law, the use of this sort of chop logic or pseudo reasoning, the substitution of feeling for thinking, the ignoring of a fact for a theory, has appeared in many cases, and there is no guarantee, except the mental activity and the personality of the particular judge or judges, that it will not continue to appear.

Viewed abstractly, therefore, it might well be thought that I should not unpack my heart with words but should content myself with general reflection upon the usual futility of dissents and the particular reflection that my dissent in this case will certainly be read by few and perhaps agreed to by none but the aggrieved appellant. Of the opinion, however, that the conclusion on which the district judge and the majority have made this case turn, that on a second hearing it was shown that Findley was not owner but the owner of a mortgage, is completely without bearing on the decision of this case, I must register my disagreement with and disapproval of the kind of reasoning which led the district judge to his opinion below and persuaded the majority to follow him.

In doing this, I wish to register particular disagreement with the statement on the last page of the majority opinion, *that the fact that the owner was present when the purported loan was made and did not protest it,* is evidence of the fact that the master *used* the funds to pay crew's wages. In the first place, there is no evidence that the owner assented at all. In the second place, the record shows only that he did not protest the loan for the stated purpose, that, indeed, *he said nothing whatever.* This fact can have no bearing on the crucial fact whether the master used the funds for crew's wages. *On this point no evidence was offered by anybody, and until such evidence was offered there was no duty upon Findley, either as the supposed owner or as the mortgagee, to make any proof on the issue.*

The final conclusion of the opinion: "What was sufficient as *prima facie* proof then became uncontradicted proof and on it, the District Court was entitled to declare the existence of the lien as he did." is therefore a complete *non sequitur,* unsupported in fact or in law.

N O T E

See, also, Brock v. S.S. Southampton, 231 F.Supp. 283, 1964 A.M.C. 1905 (D.Or. 1964), in which a bank that had issued a letter of credit to the Administrator of the Marine Engineers Benevolent Association to guarantee wages earned by engineering personnel serving on a fleet of vessels was held to have a wage lien for amounts paid from the fund to engineering personnel aboard the vessel libeled. The lien discharged by advances of money need not be in existence at the time of the advances. Thus a person advancing money to obtain repairs, supplies, or other necessaries obtains a supply lien just as if he had himself provided the repairs, etc. M/V Crustacea, 369 F.2d 656, 1966 A.M.C. 362 (5th Cir.1966). Of course, an owner cannot pay off his own obligation and acquire a lien on his own vessel. See In re Topgallant Lines, 154 B.R. 368, 1993 A.M.C. 2775 (S.D.Ga.1993). This principle has been extended to part owners. When the vessel is owned by a corporation, the question is somewhat more complex. When the stockholder advances money on the credit of the ship and so notifies the master at the time, and there is no unfairness to other stockholders, there is authority for the proposition that a lien exists. The Puritan, 258 Fed. 271 (D.Mass.1919). On the other hand it has been said that a presumption exists that such advances are made on general credit. The Cimbria, 214 Fed. 131 (D.N.J.1914). Cf. The Odysseus III, 77 F.Supp. 297 (S.D.Fla.1948). When other creditors are involved, liens in favor of part owners may be postponed until such creditors are paid. See The Murphy Tugs, 28 Fed. 429 (E.D.Mich.1886). It has been held, however, that a purchaser of a vessel who paid off maritime liens prior to purchase so that the vessel would pass clear, succeeded to the liens, and was preferred over a lien for unpaid federal taxes recorded after the transaction, distinguishing the cases like The *Cimbria* where the owner was discharging a lien on his own vessel. United States v. The Jane B. Corp., 167 F.Supp. 352, 1966 A.M.C. 427 (D.Mass.1958). And see Ameejee Valleejee & Sons v. M/V Victoria U, 661 F.2d 310, 1982 A.M.C. 1557 (4th Cir.1981), where the principle is recognized but it is held that the agent plaintiff in the particular case was not a general agent.

A person classified as a "general agent" is treated as a part owner for these purposes. There is a presumption to the effect that he relies on the credit of the owner, to whom he is no stranger. Savas v. Maria Trading Corp., 285 F.2d 336, 1961 A.M.C. 260 (4th Cir.1960). It has been held, however, that this presumption may be overcome by express agreement for a lien. The cases are collected in Compagnia Maritima La Empresa, S.A. v. Pickard (The M/Eda), 320 F.2d 829, 1964 A.M.C. 109 (5th Cir.1963). In that case it was held that in any event the agent involved, one who was to buy, outfit, maintain, repair, refurbish and undertake to resell a vessel so that he and the financiers would make a profit, was not a general agent.

In Tramp Oil and Marine, Ltd. v. M/V Mermaid I, 805 F.2d 42, 1987 A.M.C. 866 (1st Cir.1986) the court declined to recognize a lien claim of an English broker engaged by an intermediary who was requested by the charterer to make arrangements for the supplying of fuel. The court held that since the Act of 1920 was enacted to protect American materialmen, it would be unfair to recognize a lien of a broker unknown to the vessel owner without benefit to the American materialman. But suppose the foreign party advances money to discharge a lien of an American supplier. See Conti–Lines, S.A. v. M/V BARONESS, 1992 A.M.C. 681, 1991 WL 340173 (M.D.Fla.1991). And see International Seafoods of Alaska v. Park Ventures, Inc., 829 F.2d 751 (9th Cir.1987), in which a lien was recognized on behalf of an "innocent conduit" employed to create a debt relationship running between a purchaser of a fishing vessel and a prospective purchaser of fish, on behalf of the vessel.

Gilmore and Black suggest that the law of advances grew up as a stop-gap during the period during which it was supposed that a maritime lien could not be assigned. *Law of Admiralty* 633 (1975), and that most, if not all, problems that inhere in this branch of the maritime law can be avoided by simple assignment of the lien.

C. PRIORITY OF LIENS

The C. J. Saxe

United States District Court, Southern District of New York, 1906.
145 Fed. 749.

■ ADAMS, DISTRICT JUDGE. A collision took place on the 24th of October, 1905, between the American Linseed Company's barge Andy, in tow of the steamtug C.J. Saxe, on a hawser, and the steamer Staatendam. An action was brought by the Linseed Company against both vessels. The owner of the Staatendam appeared in the action and filed a claim, with a stipulation for value. The Saxe did not appear and upon the default, a decree was entered against her, upon which she was sold and the proceeds, some $615, paid into court. In November, 1905, an action was brought by Etheridge and others against the Saxe to recover the wages due them. The expenses of the sale having been deducted, there remains in court the sum of $429.63 to meet the claims, so far as the Saxe was concerned, and the question now presented is as to the proper method of distributing the fund.

There are $1,535.08 due for collision and $310.69 for wages. The $310.69 include a claim of Walter Thompson for $67.50 and a dispute has arisen whether he was pilot or master. It appears that he was charged with the responsibility of engaging the crew, controlling the tug's movements, making agreements for towage, etc., which ordinarily constitute a part of the master's duties. This case does not fall within the line of authorities cited in The Pauline, 138 F. 271 (D.C.N.Y.1905), determining that under certain circumstances, the pilot, though in control of the navigation of the vessel, is not excluded from asserting a lien. Here, it seems that Thompson was actually the master and is not entitled to a lien.

The principal question is one of priority between seamen's wages and collision damages. It is contended for the latter that under The John G. Stevens, 170 U.S. 113, 18 S.Ct. 544, 42 L.Ed. 969 (1898), and The F.H. Stanwood, 1 C.C.A. 379, 49 F. 577 (1892), the collision claim, which, if allowed, will absorb the entire fund, is entitled to priority. The Stevens Case is an authority for the proposition that a collision claim is entitled to priority over a statutory lien for supplies previously furnished in a vessel's home port. There is nothing in the opinion of the court, however, manifesting an intention to extend to wages claims the principle that liens arising out of tort are to be preferred to those arising out of seamen's contracts. In that connection the court says (170 U.S. 113, 119, 18 S.Ct. 554, 547, 42 L.Ed. 969 (1898)):

"The case at bar, however, presents no question of the comparative rank of seamen's wages, which may depend upon peculiar considerations, and which, according to the favorite saying of Lord Stowell and of Mr. Justice Story, are sacred liens, and, as long as a plank of the ship remains, the sailor is entitled, against all other persons, to the proceeds as a security for his wages."

The whole question was fully considered by Judge Choate in The Orient, 10 Ben. 620, 18 F.Cas. 801, and I do not find anything in the more recent decisions to authoritatively overcome the conclusion that the claims of seamen for their wages should be given priority over collision damages. The later decisions, outside of this district, are in conflict, some of them, The Daisy Day, 40 F. 538 (D.C.Mich.1889), for example, sustain the decisions here, while others, The F.H. Stanwood, supra, for example, take the contrary view. It is urged in connection with the case last cited, that the seamen here being implicated in the Saxe's collision, and, also, having a claim against a solvent owner, are barred from recovery, but I am not convinced that these circumstances are sufficient to defeat the seamen's claims, and I do not find anything to implicate them in the fault. That contention applies with much force to the master's claim. He was conducting the faulty navigation of the vessel and for such reason, as well as that arising from his position as master, he should not be permitted to recover, but the seamen were doubtless free from responsible participation in the negligence, and should not be deprived of their ordinary rights.

A distribution of the fund will be made in conformity herewith.

NOTE

A claim for maintenance and cure has been held to have the same priority as a wage claim. Fredelos v. Merritt–Chapman & Scott (The Padre Island), 447 F.2d 435, 1971 A.M.C. 1347 (5th Cir.1971).

Repatriation expenses have been treated as wages for priority purposes. See Potash Co. of Canada Ltd. v. M/V Raleigh, 361 F.Supp. 120, 1973 A.M.C. 2658 (D.C.Canal Zone 1973).

As a practical matter, penalty wages under 46 U.S.C.A. § 596 (penalties for not paying wages promptly) rank at the bottom in any case in which priority has any importance. They have been accorded lien status (see NOTE, at p. 443, supra), and this appears to be correct since 46 U.S.C.A. § 596, after providing for such penalties, continues, "which sum shall be recoverable as wages in any claim made before the court." When the vessel owner is insolvent, however, and the vessel has been libeled for claims in excess of its value, it has been held that penalty wages under the statute will not be assessed. Collie v. Fergusson, 281 U.S. 52, 50 S.Ct. 189, 74 L.Ed. 696, 1930 A.M.C. 408 (1930). The Supreme Court read the statute as intended to force an owner who could pay the wages due to pay them promptly. It stated that "it can afford no such protection and exert no coercive force where delay in payment, as here, is due to the insolvency of the owner and the arrest of the vessel, subject to accrued claims beyond its value * * *. Otherwise, it would not be imposed on the owner directly or through his interest in the ship, but only upon the lienors, who are neither within the letter nor the spirit of the statute." This language in the *Collie* case has been read to subordinate the claims for penalty wages to those of a mortgagee when the amounts available for payment of the mortgage claim were less than its amount. Nadle v. M.V. Tequila, 1973 A.M.C. 909 (S.D.N.Y.1973). The court held the penalty wage claim in abeyance until it could be determined whether the mortgagee could collect his in personam judgment from other assets, it not having been shown that the owner was insolvent.

The William Leishear

United States District Court, District of Maryland, 1927.
21 F.2d 862, 1927 A.M.C. 1770.

■ COLEMAN, DISTRICT JUDGE. The schooner William Leishear was sold under admiralty process as a result of various libels, and this proceeding is to determine the rights, if any, of the libelants to share according to their respective priorities in the net proceeds of the sale amounting to $1,011.17. The claims are as follows:

(1) For salvage under a written contract dated July 22, 1926, $850.

(2) For labor and materials furnished between September 1 and November 20, 1926, $4,132.90.

(3) For transporting the sails of the vessel on or about October 1, 1926, $45.

(4) For wages of crew during October and November, 1926, $640.

(5) For wharfage from November 20, 1926, to March 26, 1927, $126.

(6) For watchman from January 19, 1927, to March 26, 1927, $198.

It is obvious that the proceeds will be grossly insufficient to pay all demands. Therefore the fund must go to those entitled to priority as far as possible, and the unsatisfied claimants must seek elsewhere for payment. See language of Ware, J., in The Paragon, 18 Fed.Cas. 10708.

The question of priority of maritime liens is filled with confusion. The rules conflict. Tort liens generally rank contract liens. The John G. Stevens, 170 U.S. 113, 18 S.Ct. 544, 42 L.Ed. 969 (1898). Seamen's wage liens are especially favored under the ancient doctrine, that has come down to us, that seamen are in effect wards of the admiralty. The Idlehour, 63 F. 1018 (D.C.N.Y.1894). So also of salvage, since the law wishes to encourage persons in saving maritime property from destruction. Provost v. The Selkirk, 20 Fed.Cas. 11455. All maritime claims rank all nonmaritime. The J.E. Rumbell, 148 U.S. 1, 13 S.Ct. 498, 37 L.Ed. 345 (1892).

There is the general rule that maritime liens rank in an order inverse to the order of their creation (The St. Jago de Cuba, 9 Wheat. 409, 6 L.Ed. 122 (1824)), a principle contrary to what is common in other branches of the law. Without going at any length into the ancient historical reasons for this anomaly suffice it to say that in this country two theories exist as the basis of this admiralty doctrine. They are, first, that each person acquires a jus in re, and becomes a sort of coproprietor in the res, and therefore subjects his claim to the next similar lien which attaches; and, second, that the last beneficial service is the one that continues the activity of the ship as long as possible, and therefore should be preferred, provided that what is produced or contributed to by the service is a voyage. The Glen Island, 194 F. 744 (D.C.N.Y.1912). Under the second theory, there is the consideration that beneficial additions subsequent to earlier liens add to the value of the ship, and that, therefore, to prefer such additions will not deprive the earlier lienors of any interest which they would have had, if no such services had been rendered.

Generally speaking, the law of maritime liens may be said to be made up of exceptions to the above doctrine, which gives priority to the lien latest in point of time, so that today it is possible to deduce, from the decisions, the following order of priority, existing irrespective of time, which represents the weight of authority: (1) Seamen's wages; (2) salvage; (3) tort and collision liens; (4) repairs, supplies, towage, wharfage, pilotage, and other necessaries; (5) bottomry bonds in inverse order of application; (6) nonmaritime claims. This, however, is no more than a very general statement, since any summary is subject to further exceptions of more or less narrow application. With this general background, we may now take up the various claims involved in the present case.

1. The wage claims amounting to $640, are made by five sailors, claiming to have had contracts to ship as crew on board the schooner for the oyster dredging season at a fixed rate per month, and that, whereas, because the schooner was laid up, undergoing repairs, they never actually shipped aboard her, they nevertheless, during part of the period, did various kinds of work aboard her, from carpentering to cooking, and that they are thus entitled to be paid their stipulated wages, just as if the vessel had been in commission. It appears that they did make some effort to obtain other employment after they learned the schooner would not be in commission, but were unsuccessful.

In view of the special consideration universally accorded wage claims by the admiralty courts, it seems not unreasonable to hold upon these facts that the seamen are entitled to a lien for their wages, where, through no fault of their own, they are prevented from earning them aboard the vessel while in navigation. Levering v. Bank of Columbia, 15 F.Cas. 412; The Alanson Sumner, 28 F. 670 (D.C.N.Y.1886). It is also argued that these wages should not be allowed because the libelants were engaged in a profit-sharing arrangement respecting the impending voyage. But the evidence does not sustain this contention.

A lien is therefore allowed to each of these libelants for the respective amounts claimed, aggregating $640. Such are entitled to first priority. The weight of authority seems clear to this effect, especially in view of the fact that the services were performed subsequent to the salvage. See The Lillie Laurie, 50 F. 219 (C.C.Tex.1880); Dahlstrom v. E.M. Davidson, 1 F. 259 (D.C.Wis.1880). It has even been held that claims due seamen, which are not strictly wage claims, such as for penalties and repatriation expenses, are to be classed as wages and entitled to the priority generally accorded to them. The Lancastrian, 290 F. 397, 1923 A.M.C. 840 (D.C.N.Y. 1923); Gerber v. Spencer, 278 F. 886 (C.C.A.Cal.1922).

That wage claims precede repair and supply liens is well established. The Grapeshot, 22 F. 123 (D.C.N.Y.1884); The G.F. Brown, 24 F. 399 (D.C.Conn.1885); The Philomena, 200 F. 873 (D.C.Mass.1913). Wage claims also precede wharfage. The Selkirk, 20 F.Cas. 23.

2. As to the claim in the nature of salvage for floating and delivering the schooner at the shipyard, the evidence is that the vessel, being hard aground in one of the small tributaries of Chesapeake Bay as the result of a storm, and there not being sufficient rise of the tide to float her, the intervening libelant, pursuant to a contract to salvage her, dug a ditch some 300 or 400 feet long, 5 feet deep and 20 feet wide, thereby floating her. While this work was done in the month of July, no claim appears to have been made until the intervening libel was filed, some seven months later. The salvor was the son of the managing owner of the vessel, with whom he contracted, and the only written evidence of the claim is a certificate, signed by the managing owner. In spite of some doubt in the mind of the court as to the entire good faith of this claim as actually made, by reason of its size and the rather peculiar surrounding circumstances, the court believes that a salvage service was performed. The Gulfport, 162 C.C.A. 593, 250 F. 577 (5th Cir.1918). See, also, Simmons v. Steamship Jefferson, 215 U.S. 130, 30 S.Ct. 54, 54 L.Ed. 125, 17 Ann.Cas. 907 (1909).

Salvage is a service voluntarily rendered to a vessel needing assistance, and is designed to relieve her from distress or danger, either present or reasonably apprehended. The Blackwall, 10 Wall. 1, 19 L.Ed. 870 (1869); The Pleasure Bay, 226 F. 55 (D.C.Ala.1915); The Neshaminy, 142 C.C.A. 577, 228 F. 285 (3d Cir.1916). It is true that every salvage contract is not to be set aside because it seems excessive. It is within the discretion of the court to cut down the award, as required by the peculiar circumstances of the case. The Elfrida, 172 U.S. 186, 19 S.Ct. 146, 43 L.Ed. 413 (1898). Therefore a quantum meruit claim in this case would appear to be justified, and the court feels that $350 is reasonable and proper. This lien is entitled to second priority, because it ranks supply and repair liens, The Thomas Morgan, 123 F. 781 (D.C.S.C.1903); The Dredge No. 1, 137 F. 110 (D.C.N.Y.1905); Great Lakes Towing Co. v. St. Joseph–Chicago S.S. Co., 165 C.C.A. 261, 253 F. 635 (1918)(torts and supplies); The Virgo, 46 F. 294 (D.C.N.Y.1891); and also wharfage, Provost v. The Selkirk, supra.

3. As to the claim for labor and materials, which amounts to $4,132.90, there is no evidence that any of the items comprising this bill are unreasonable. It appears that the shipbuilding company, which did the work, received instructions to put her in first-class condition for the approaching oyster season, and that it was found necessary to make very extensive repairs. Hence the large bill. The labor and materials so used created a maritime lien under the Merchant Marine Act of 1920. * * * This lien is third in order of priority. It ranks evenly with all like liens of even date. Saylor v. Taylor, 23 C.C.A. 343, 77 F. 476 (1897); The Estrada Palma, 8 F.2d 103, 1923 A.M.C. 1040 (D.C.La.1923); The Jack–O–Lantern, 282 F. 899 (D.C.Mass.1922).

4. Next is the claim for wharfage. There seems no doubt but that a lien exists for this service even as to a domestic vessel, since this is a necessary maritime service during the course of repairs. The Kate Tremaine, 14 F.Cas. 144 (D.C.N.Y.1871); The Scow No. 15, 35 C.C.A. 149, 92 F. 1008 (1899). But after the filing of the libel the vessel was withdrawn from navigation, and no further lien for wharfage accrues. The Poznan, 9 F.2d 838, 846 (2 Cir.1926). The claim is therefore allowed from and including November 20, 1926, to and including January 19, 1927 or 61 days, which, at $1 per day, amounts to $61. Since the wharfage service was performed about the same time that the materials and supplies were furnished, this claim ranks equally with the claim for the latter. *The Estrada Palma,* supra; Saylor v. Taylor, supra.

5. The claim for services of the watchman covers the period from January 19, 1927, the date of the filing of the libel, to March 26, 1927, the date when the vessel was sold. The vessel being under custody of the marshal during this period, the watchman's services cannot be regarded as maritime. The Fortuna, 206 F. 573 (D.C.Wash.1913). This claim is therefore not allowed.

6. Likewise the claim for transporting sails is not allowed. No part of the service seems to have been rendered upon the vessel. From the libel it appears that nothing was done, other than to haul the sails overland from Crisfield, Md., to the shipyard at White Haven, Md., where the vessel was being rebuilt. This cannot be regarded as a maritime service, and falls in the class of contracts only incidentally maritime. Gilbert v. Roach, 2 F. 393 (C.C.Ill.1880); The New Rochelle, 8 F.2d 59, 1923 A.M.C. 362 (D.C.Ohio 1923). See Benedict, 5th Ed. § 66.

Summarizing the situation with respect to the allowed claims, it is as follows: First, wage claims, $640; second, salvage claim, $350; third, materials, supplies, and wharfage, aggregating $4,193.90. Since the first two allowances will consume all but $21.17 of the total fund in the registry of the court, there is nothing left for the claims of the third group, which rank equally, except a pro rata share of this small residue.

A decree will be signed in accordance with these allowances.

NOTE

In Fredelos v. Merritt–Chapman & Scott Corp. (The Padre Island), 447 F.2d 435, 1971 A.M.C. 1347 (5th Cir.1971), it was held that wage liens and liens for maintenance and cure are superior to salvage liens. But salvage liens come next. See Complaint of Ta Chi Nav. (Panama) Corp. S.A., 583 F.Supp. 1322, 1985 A.M.C. 1367 (S.D.N.Y.1984).

The John G. Stevens

Supreme Court of the United States, 1898.
170 U.S. 113, 18 S.Ct. 544, 42 L.Ed. 969.

■ MR. JUSTICE GRAY, after stating the case, delivered the opinion of the court.

The question presented by this record is whether a lien upon a tug, for damages to her tow by negligent towage bringing the tow into collision with a third vessel, is to be preferred, in admiralty, to a statutory lien for supplies furnished to the tug in her home port before the collision.

This question may be conveniently divided in its consideration by the court, as it was in the arguments at the bar, into two parts: First. Is a claim in tort for damages by a collision entitled to priority over a claim in contract for previous supplies? Second. Is a claim by a tow against her tug, for damages from coming into collision with a third vessel by reason of negligent towage, a claim in tort?

* * *

By our law, then, a claim for damages by collision, and a claim for supplies, are both maritime liens. The question of their comparative rank is now for the first time presented to this court for adjudication; and it has been the subject of conflicting decisions in other courts of the United States, and especially in those held within the State of New York.

In *The America*, (1853) Judge Hall, in the Northern District of New York, appears to have held liens for collisions and those for supplies to be of equal rank, without regard to the date when they attached to the ship. 16 Law Reporter, 264. A claim for damages by collision has been postponed to an earlier claim for supplies, by Judge Brown, in the Southern District of New York, in The Amos D. Carver, 35 F. 665 (D.C.N.Y.1888); but has been preferred to such a claim, by Judge Benedict, in the Eastern District of New York, and by Mr. Justice Blatchford on appeal, in The R.S. Carter & The John G. Stevens, 38 F. 515 (D.C.N.Y.1889) and 40 F. 331 (C.C.N.Y. 1889). And, in an earlier case, a claim for collision had been allowed by Judge Benedict a like preference over a previous bottomry bond. Force v. The Pride of the Ocean, 3 F. 162 (D.C.N.Y.1880).

The preference due to the lien for damages from collision, over earlier claims founded on contract, has been carried so far as to allow the lien for damages to prevail over the claim of seamen for wages earned before the collision, by Judge Lowell, in the District of Massachusetts, in The Enterprise, 1 Low. 455, 8 F.Cas. 731 (1870); by Judge Nixon, in the District of New Jersey, in The Maria & Elizabeth, 12 F. 627 (D.C.N.J.1882) by Judges Gresham and Jenkins, in the Circuit Court of Appeals for the Seventh Circuit, in The F.H. Stanwood, 1 C.C.A. 379, 49 F. 577 (7th Cir.1892); and by Judge Swan, in the Eastern District of Michigan, in The Nettie Woodward, 50 F. 224 (D.C.Mich., 1892).   The opposite view has been maintained, in the Southern District of New York, by Judge Choate, in The Orient, 10 Ben. 620, 18 F.Cas. 801 (1879), as well as by Judge Brown, in The Amos D. Carver, 35 F. 665 (1888) above cited; and in the Eastern District of New York, by Judge Benedict, in The Samuel J. Christian, 16 F. 796 (D.C.N.Y.1883); and in the Western District of Michigan, by Judge Severens, in The Daisy Day, 40 F. 538 (D.C.Mich.1889).

The case at bar, however, presents no question of the comparative rank of seamen's wages, which may depend upon peculiar considerations, and which, according to the favorite saying of Lord Stowell and of Mr. Justice Story, are sacred liens, and, as long as a plank of the ship remains, the sailor is entitled, against all other persons, to the proceeds as a security for his wages.   The Madonna D'Idra, 1 Dodson, 37, 40; The Sydney Cove, 2 Dodson, 11, 13; The Neptune, 1 Hagg.Adm. 227, 239; Sheppard v. Taylor, 30 U.S. (5 Pet.) 675, 710, 8 L.Ed. 269 (1831); Brown v. Lull, 2 Sumner, 443, 452, Fed.Cas. No. 11,185, (1836); Pitman v. Hooper, 3 Sumner, 50, 58, Fed.Cas. No. 11,185 (1837); Abbott on Shipping, pt. 4, c. 4, § 8; 3 Kent Com. 197.   Yet see Norwich & N.Y. Transport Co. v. Wright, 80 U.S. (13 Wall.) 104, 122, 20 L.Ed. 585 (1871).

Nor does this case present any question between successive liens for repairs or supplies, the general rule as to which is that they are to be paid in inverse order, because it is for the benefit of all the interests in the ship that she should be kept in condition to be navigated.   Abbott on Shipping, pt. 2, c. 3, § 32; The St. Jago de Cuba, 22 U.S. (9 Wheat.) 409, 416, 6 L.Ed. 122 (1824); The J.E. Rumbell, 148 U.S. 1, 9, 13 S.Ct. 498 (1893); The Fanny, 2 Low. 508, 8 F.Cas. 993 (1876).

Nor does it present a question of precedence between two claims for distinct and successive collisions, as to which there has been a difference of opinion in the Southern District of New York; Judge Choate, in the District Court, giving the preference to the later claim, upon the ground that the interest created in the vessel by the first collision was subject, like all other proprietary interests in her, to the ordinary marine perils, including the second collision; and Mr. Justice Blatchford, in the Circuit Court, reversing the decree, because the vessel libelled had not been benefited, but had been injured, by the second collision.   The Frank G. Fowler, 8 F. 331, and 17 F. 653 (C.C.N.Y.1883).

Nor yet does it present the question whether a lien for repairs made after the collision, so far as they increase the value of the vessel, may be preferred to the lien for the damages by the collision, in accordance with the English cases of *The Aline* and *The Bold Buccleugh,* cited at the beginning of this opinion.

But the question we have to deal with is whether the lien for damages by the collision is to be preferred to the lien for supplies furnished before the collision.

The foundation of the rule that collision gives to the party injured a *jus in re* in the offending ship is the principle of the maritime law that the ship, by whomsoever owned or navigated, is considered as herself the wrongdoer, liable for the tort, and subject to a maritime lien for the damages. This principle, as has been observed by careful text writers on both sides of the Atlantic, has been more clearly established, and more fully carried out, in this country than in England. Henry on *Admiralty,* § 75, note; Marsden on *Collisions,* (3d ed.) 93.

The act of Congress of December 22, 1807, c. 5, laid an embargo on all ships and vessels, within the limits and jurisdiction of the United States, bound to any foreign port or place; and the supplemental act of January 9, 1808, § 3, provided that any ship or vessel proceeding, contrary to the provisions of the act, to a foreign port or place, should be forfeited. 2 Stat. 451, 453. Upon the trial of a libel in the Circuit Court of the United States to enforce the forfeiture of a vessel under those acts, Chief Justice Marshall said: "This is not a proceeding against the owner; it is a proceeding against the vessel, for an offence committed by the vessel, which is not less an offence, and does not the less subject her to forfeiture, because it was committed without the authority and against the will of the owner." The Little Charles, 1 Brock 347, 354, 26 F.Cas. 979 (1818).

Upon a libel of information for the condemnation of a piratical vessel, under the act of Congress of March 3, 1819, c. 77, continued in force by the act of May 15, 1820, c. 113, (3 Stat. 510, 600,) Mr. Justice Story, delivering the opinion of this court, and referring to seizures in revenue causes, said: "The thing is here primarily considered as the offender, or rather the offence is attached primarily to the thing; and this, whether the offence be *malum prohibitum* or *malum in se.* The same principle applies to proceedings *in rem,* on seizures in the admiralty." The Palmyra, 25 U.S. (12 Wheat.) 1, 14, 6 L.Ed. 531 (1827).

In The Malek Adhel, 43 U.S. (2 How.) 210, 233, 234, 11 L.Ed. 239 (1844), Mr. Justice Story, in delivering judgment, stated the principle more fully, saying: "It is not an uncommon course in the admiralty, acting under the law of nations, to treat the vessel in which or by which, or by the master or crew thereof, a wrong or offence has been done, as the offender, without any regard whatsoever to the personal misconduct or responsibility of the owner thereof. And this is done from the necessity of the case, as the only adequate means of suppressing the offence or wrong, or insuring an indemnity to the injured party." And, after quoting the passages above cited from the opinions in *The Little Charles* and in *The Palmyra,* he added: "The ship is also, by the general maritime law, held responsible for the torts and misconduct of the master and crew thereof, whether arising from negligence or a wilful disregard of duty; as, for example, in cases of collision and other wrongs done upon the high seas, or elsewhere within the admiralty and maritime jurisdiction, upon the general policy of that

law, which looks to the instrument itself, used as the means of the
mischief, as the best and surest pledge for the compensation and indemnity
to the injured party."

In The China, 74 U.S. (7 Wall.) 53, 68, 19 L.Ed. 67 (1868), by the
application of the same principle, a ship was held liable for damages by
collision through the negligence of a pilot whom she had been compelled by
law to take on board; and Mr. Justice Swayne, in delivering judgment,
said: "The maritime law as to the position and powers of the master, and
the responsibility of the vessel, is not derived from the civil law of master
and servant, nor from the common law. It had its source in the commercial usages and jurisprudence of the middle ages. Originally, the primary
liability was upon the vessel, and that of the owner was not personal, but
merely incidental to his ownership, from which he was discharged either by
the loss of the vessel or by abandoning it to the creditors. But while the
law limited the creditor to this part of the owner's property, it gave him a
lien or privilege against it in preference to other creditors." "According to
the admiralty law, the collision impresses upon the wrongdoing vessel a
maritime lien. This the vessel carries with it into whosesoever hands it
may come. It is inchoate at the moment of the wrong, and must be
perfected by subsequent proceedings."

The same principle has been recognized in other cases. Cushing v.
The John Fraser, 62 U.S. (21 How.) 184, 194, 16 L.Ed. 106 (1858); The
Merrimac, 81 U.S. (14 Wall.) 199, 20 L.Ed. 873 (1871); The Clarita & The
Clara, 90 U.S. (23 Wall.) 1, 23 L.Ed. 146 (1874); Ralli v. Troop, 157 U.S.
386, 402, 403, 15 S.Ct. 657 (1894).

That the maritime lien upon a vessel, for damages caused by her fault
to another vessel, takes precedence of a maritime lien for supplies previously furnished to the offending vessel, is a reasonable inference, if not a
necessary conclusion, from the decisions of this court, above referred to, the
effect of which may be summed up as follows:

The collision, as soon as it takes place, creates, as security for the
damages, a maritime lien or privilege, *jus in re,* a proprietary interest in
the offending ship, and which, when enforced by admiralty process *in rem,*
relates back to the time of the collision. The offending ship is considered
as herself the wrongdoer, and as herself bound to make compensation for
the wrong done. The owner of the injured vessel is entitled to proceed *in
rem* against the offender, without regard to the question who may be her
owners, or to the division, the nature or the extent of their interests in her.
With the relations of the owners of those interests, as among themselves,
the owner of the injured vessel has no concern. All the interests, existing
at the time of the collision, in the offending vessel, whether by way of part-
ownership, of mortgage, of bottomry bond or of other maritime lien for
repairs or supplies, arising out of contract with the owners or agents of the
vessel, are parts of the vessel herself, and as such are bound by and
responsible for her wrongful acts. Any one who had furnished necessary
supplies to the vessel before the collision, and had thereby acquired, under
our law, a maritime lien or privilege in the vessel herself, was, as was said

in *The Bold Buccleugh,* before cited, of the holder of an earlier bottomry bond, under the law of England, "so to speak, a part owner in interest at the date of the collision, and the ship in which he and others were interested was liable to its value at that date for the injury done, without reference to his claim." 7 Moore P.C. 285.

We are then brought to the question, whether a claim by a tow against her tug, for damages from coming into collision with a third vessel because of negligent towage, is a claim in tort, standing upon the same ground as a claim of the third vessel for damages against the tug.

Upon this question, again, there have been conflicting opinions in the District Courts of the United States.

On the one hand, it has been held by Judge Benedict, in the Eastern District of New York, in several cases, including the case at bar, that a claim by a tow against her tug for damages caused by the negligence of the latter is founded on a voluntary contract between the owner of the tow and the owner of the tug, and should be postponed to a claim against the tug for necessary supplies or repairs furnished before the contract of towage was made. The Samuel J. Christian, 16 F. 796 (D.C.N.Y.1883); The John G. Stevens, 58 F. 792 (D.C.N.Y.1893); The Glen Iris, 78 F. 511 (D.C.N.Y. 1897). The same conclusion has been reached by Judge Brown, in the Southern District of New York, proceeding upon the hypothesis that the security for the maritime obligation created by the contract of towage is subject to all liens already existing upon the vessel, and upon the theory that, by the general maritime law, liens *ex delicto,* including all liens for damage by collision, are inferior in the rank of privilege to liens *ex contractu.* The Grapeshot, 22 F. 123 (D.C.N.Y.1884); The Young America, 30 F. 789 (D.C.N.Y.1887); The Gratitude, 42 F. 299 (D.C.N.Y.1890).

On the other hand, the claim by a tow against her tug for damages caused by negligent towage has been held to be founded in tort, arising out of the duty imposed by law, and independent of any contract made, or consideration paid or to be paid, for the towage, by Mr. Justice Blatchford, when District Judge, in The Brooklyn, 2 Ben. 547, 4 F.Cas. 238 (1868) and in The Deer, 4 Ben. 352, 7 F.Cas. 351 (1870); by Judge Lowell, in The Arturo, 6 F. 308 (C.C.Mass.1881); and by Judge Swing, in the Southern District of Ohio, in The Liberty, 7 F. 226, 230 (D.C.Ohio 1881). In *The Arturo,* Judge Lowell said: "These cases of tow against tug are, in form and fact, very like collision cases. The contract gives rise to duties very closely resembling those which one vessel owes to others which it may meet. There is, therefore, an analogy between the two classes of cases so close that the tow may sue, in one proceeding for damage, her own tug and a strange vessel with which there has been a collision." 6 F. at 312. And it has accordingly been held, by Judge Nixon, and by Judge Severens, that such a claim by a tow against her tug is entitled to priority of payment over liens on the tug for previous repairs or supplies. The M. Vandercook, 24 F. 472, 478 (D.C.N.J.1885); The Daisy Day, 40 F. 538 (D.C.Mich.1889).

The decisions of this court are in accordance with the latter view, and are inconsistent with any other.

It was argued that the liability of a tug for the loss of her tow was analogous to the liability of a common carrier for the loss of the goods carried. But even an action by a passenger, or by an owner of goods, against a carrier, for neglect to carry and deliver in safety, is an action for the breach of a duty imposed by the law, independently of contract or of consideration, and is therefore founded in tort. Philadelphia & Reading Railroad v. Derby, 55 U.S. (14 How.) 468, 485, 14 L.Ed. 502 (1852); Atlantic & Pacific Railroad v. Laird, 164 U.S. 393, 17 S.Ct. 120 (1896).

In Norwich & N.Y. Transport Co. v. Wright, 80 U.S. (13 Wall.) 104, 122, 20 L.Ed. 585 (1871), Mr. Justice Bradley, referring to Maclachlan on Shipping, (1st ed.) 598, laid down these general propositions: "Liens for reparation for wrong done are superior to any prior liens for money borrowed, wages, pilotage, etc. But they stand on an equality with regard to each other if they arise from the same cause." Although these propositions went beyond what was required for the decision of that case, which was one of a collision between two vessels, owing to the fault of one of them, causing the loss of her cargo, as well as of the other vessel and her cargo, yet the very point adjudged was that the lien on the offending vessel for the loss of her own cargo was a lien for reparation of damage, and therefore was upon an equality with the lien upon her for the loss of the other vessel and her cargo.

This court, more than once, has directly affirmed that a suit by the owner of a tow against her tug, to recover for an injury to the tow by negligence on the part of the tug, is a suit *ex delicto* and not *ex contractu*.

In The Quickstep, 76 U.S. (9 Wall.) 665, 670, 19 L.Ed. 767 (1869) a libel by the owner of a tow against her tug set forth a contract with the tug, for a stipulated price, to tow directly, and a deviation and unreasonable delay in its performance, and that the tug negligently backed into the tow and injured her. An objection that the libel could not be maintained, because the contract alleged was not proved, was overruled by this court. Mr. Justice Davis, in delivering judgment, said: "The libel was not filed to recover damages for the breach of a contract, as is contended, but to obtain compensation for the commission of a tort. It is true it asserts a contract of towage, but this is done by way of inducement to the real grievance complained of, which is the wrong suffered by the libellant in the destruction of his boat by the carelessness and mismanagement of the captain of the Quickstep."

Again, in The Syracuse, 79 U.S. (12 Wall.) 167, 171, 20 L.Ed. 382 (1870), which was a libel by a tug against her tow for negligently bringing her into collision with a vessel at anchor, the court, speaking by the same justice, said: "It is unnecessary to consider the evidence relating to the alleged contract of towage, because if it be true, as the appellant says, that by special agreement the canal boat was being towed at her own risk, nevertheless the steamer is liable, if, through the negligence of those in charge of her, the canal boat suffered loss. Although the policy of the law has not imposed on the towing boat the obligation resting on a common carrier, it does require, on the part of the persons engaged in her management, the exercise of reasonable care, caution and maritime skill, and if these are neglected, and disaster occurs, the towing boat must be visited with the consequences." And see The J.P. Donaldson, 167 U.S. 599, 603, 17 S.Ct. 951 (1897).

The essential likeness between the ordinary case of a collision between two ships, and the liability of a tug to her tow for damages caused to the latter by a collision with a third vessel, is exemplified by the familiar practice in admiralty, (followed in the very proceeding in which the question now before us arose,) which allows the owner of a tow, injured by a collision caused by the conduct of her tug and of another vessel, to sue both in one libel, and to recover against either or both, according to the proof at the hearing. The Alabama & The Game–Cock, 92 U.S. 695, 23 L.Ed. 763 (1875); The Atlas, 93 U.S. 302, 23 L.Ed. 863 (1876); The L.P. Dayton, 120 U.S. 337, 7 S.Ct. 568 (1887); The R.S. Carter & The John G. Stevens, 38 F. 515 (E.D.N.Y., 1889), and 40 F. 331 (E.D.N.Y.1889).

The result of applying to the case at bar the principles of the maritime law of the United States, as heretofore declared by this court, is that the lien for the damages occasioned by negligent towage must be preferred to the previous lien for supplies.

In the argument of this case, copious references were made to foreign codes and commentaries, which we have not thought it important to consider, because they differ among themselves as to the comparative rank of various maritime liens, and because the general maritime law is in force in this country, or in any other, so far only as administered in its courts, or adopted by its own laws and usages. The Lottawanna, 88 U.S. (21 Wall.) 558, 572, 22 L.Ed. 654 (1874); The Belgenland, 114 U.S. 355, 369, 5 S.Ct. 860, 29 L.Ed. 152 (1885); Liverpool & G.W. Steam Co. v. Phenix Ins. Co., 129 U.S. 397, 444, 9 S.Ct. 469, 32 L.Ed. 788 (1888); Ralli v. Troop, 157 U.S. 386, 407, 15 S.Ct. 657, 39 L.Ed. 742 (1895).

Question certified answered in the affirmative.

NOTE

The John G. Stevens is the last word the Supreme Court has had to say on the subject of lien priorities. See Gilmore and Black, *Law of Admiralty,* § 9–59 (1975). In The John G. Stevens, the question presented directly was whether a subsequent collision lien is to be preferred over a previous lien for supplies. The Court held that it was. It arrived at this holding by reference to the theory that the injured party obtains a claim on the ship regardless of the ownership. A supplier of services to the ship at an earlier date is treated, then, as a part owner. Its interests are subjected to the claim in the same fashion as other interests. If this is the basis for the preference, does it suggest that there is no rank priority at all? If each lien holder becomes a part owner, then as to subsequent contract claims the provision of the services or supplies would be conferring a benefit on *his* vessel, and as to tort liens, it would be *his* vessel that committed the offence. The doctrine seems to apply to wage liens as well. Yet the Court is careful to note that the question of wage lien priority may be different because of the "sacred" nature of that lien, and careful to note that it is not called upon to decide as to successive collisions, successive liens for services, or later service liens as against earlier liens for collision damage, with regard to all of which it recognizes that there is difference of opinion in the lower courts.

The John G. Stevens also takes up the problem of what constitutes a tort lien as against a lien on a contract claim. Given the basis on which the determination is made that the later collision claim is preferred to the earlier service claim, why is it necessary to determine that the later claim is a claim in tort rather than in contract? Could the Court have decided just as easily that the "interest" of the supplier was affected by the negligent discharge of the ship's contract? Does the Court's failure to subsume this case under the rule of inverse priority by time of accrual that it states for supply liens among themselves indicate that it is unwilling to state a rule that will equate liens for breach of affreightment contracts to liens for supplies and necessaries? It will be noted, of course, that this view of the matter is required by the Ship Mortgage Act, for under that act the mortgage lien is made superior to subsequent service liens but inferior to liens for earlier necessaries, and liens for tort damage, wages, general average, and salvage. If the lien for negligent towage were classified as a contract lien, then, it would by the terms of the act be subordinate to the mortgage, at least if it were anterior to the recordation of the mortgage. The Ship Mortgage Act does not apply, of course, to cases in which there is no mortgage, and by its terms it does not affect the priority of preferred liens among themselves. On the other hand is it evidence that the liens that are made "preferred liens" were considered superior in rank to the service lien, and that contract liens not made superior are inferior? This accentuates, of course, the importance of the classification of a lien as tort rather than contract. See the discussion of the tort character of breach of the affreightment contract in Section B. 6, supra.

The Frank G. Fowler

United States Circuit Court, Southern District of New York, 1883.
17 Fed. 653.

■ BLATCHFORD, JUSTICE. The district court awarded priority of claim and lien to the Phenix Insurance Company, and directed that the $4,500 and all accumulations of interest thereon be paid to it. The Conways appeal from such award and direction. The view of the district court was that the interest or lien of the Conways in the tug, growing out of the damage suffered by the canalboat and cargo at the earlier date, was liable to respond for the damage to the barge at the later date. I cannot concur in this view. This is a case where there was no priority of attachment or seizure of the vessel, although the libel for the second damage was first filed, and it is not a case where either claim can be considered as other than one sounding in damages for a tort. The contention on the part of the Phenix Insurance Company is that the claims arising out of the two torts are to be paid in the inverse order of their creation, on the view that though they are claims of the same class they are not claims of the same rank of privilege. It may very well be that among creditors he is to be preferred "who has contributed most immediately to the preservation of the thing;" that "the last bottomry bond is preferred to those of older date;" and "that repairs and supplies furnished a vessel in her last voyage take precedence of those furnished in a prior voyage." But the principle governing such cases is that "the services performed at the latest hour are most efficacious in bringing the vessel and her freightage to their final destination;" and that "each foregoing incumbrance, therefore, is actually benefited by reason of the succeeding incumbrance." This principle can have no place except where services are rendered, such as loaning money, furnishing supplies, making repairs, salvage, and claims arising out of contract generally. Such services benefit the vessel, make her better, preserve her, contribute to save her or improve her or keep her in running or going order for the benefit of all who have prior liens or claims on her. But a second tort or collision can have no such effect in reference to a party injured by a prior tort or collision. The second tort or collision does not benefit the vessel or add to her value or preserve her. It only tends to injure her, and the sufferer by the first tort or collision, in having recourse against the vessel after the second tort or collision, must take her as he finds her, damaged, perhaps, by a second collision. He ought not to lose the benefit of his lien arising out of the first tort or collision, unless the circumstances are such that in judgment of law he may fairly be held to have waived his lien, or postponed it, as regards the lien arising out of the second tort or collision. In the present case there was no waiver or postponement. No case cited declares any doctrine which sanctions the giving of priority in the present case to the Phenix Insurance Company, except what is found in the case of The America, 6 Monthly Law Rep. (N.S.) 264. That case is not sustained by authority, nor is it sustainable on principle. There was nothing in the mere fact of the second tort to extinguish the lien arising out of the first tort, and, when both torts were of the same character, each arising out of negligence towards a tow in fulfilling a contract of towage, and each claimant arrests the vessel at the same time, to respond, there is no principle of the maritime law, and no interest of commerce or navigation, which requires that the elder lienor, not guilty of laches, and not having committed any waiver or abandonment, should have his claim postponed to that of the younger lienor.

The decree of the district court must be reversed, as to the matters appealed from, with costs of the appeal, and priority of lien and of payment out of the fund be awarded to the Conways, and both cases be remanded to the district court, with directions to that court to proceed with the reference in the suit brought by the Conways, and to take such further proceedings thereafter as may not be inconsistent with the findings and opinion of this court.

NOTE

In The America, 168 Fed. 424 (D.N.J.1909), the decision in the *Frank G. Fowler* was repudiated on authority of *The John G. Stevens*. Judge Cross, after reviewing the conflict of authority that existed on the subject before *The John G. Stevens*, observed.

"* * * Judge Blatchford's reasoning was in effect that, since the second collision did not benefit the vessel, it was not entitled to priority over the lien created by the first collision, thereby seemingly adopting the rule that a subsequent lien is entitled to priority only when it has benefited or increased the value of the vessel out of which all liens are to be satisfied. It is manifest, however, that priorities between collision liens cannot be determined on the theory of benefit to the offending vessel. No collision, be it the first, the second, or the third, can or does benefit the vessel. *The John G. Stevens,* supra, moreover, expressly held that a tort lien, although it did not benefit the vessel, nevertheless had priority over an earlier lien for supplies, which presumably did. There is no apparent reason why the rule in cases of collision should be different than it is in the matter of successive liens for repairs or supplies, which are ordinarily paid in their inverse order. The proprietary interest created in the vessel in favor of the party injured by the first collision is subject, like all other proprietary interests in her, to subsequent marine perils, including collisions. That a maritime lien created by collision gives a proprietary interest in the res to the injured party is laid down in many cases, among them *The John G. Stevens,* supra * * *''

The rule of *The America* seems to be taken as the law today. See, e.g., Gilmore and Black, *Law of Admiralty,* § 9–62 (1975). The authority cited is the *John G. Stevens* and *The America.* Is the rationale of *The America* a sound one? If it is, would one expect that a later lien for repairs and supplies would outrank an earlier collision lien? If a later collision is a maritime peril, why is not the need for repairs? In The Interstate No. 1, 290 Fed. 926 (2d Cir.1923), liens for negligent towage were subordinated to those for supplies on the same voyage. The court observed, "That part of the decree in the case now before the court which postpones the claim for negligent towage to the liens for repairs and supplies is not challenged on this appeal. The law on that subject seems now so well established as to be beyond controversy." Gilmore and Black, supra, state that all tort claims rank all contract claims, citing *The Interstate No. 1* for the proposition that despite the holding in *The John G. Stevens* negligent towage has not remained "firmly anchored" on the tort side. Note that in *The William Leishear,* the court states that tort liens generally rank contract liens, and cites for this proposition *The John G. Stevens.* Note that this rule is not to be deduced from the theory of the lien as a *jus in re.*

Todd Shipyards Corporation v. The City of Athens

United States District Court, District of Maryland, 1949.
83 F.Supp. 67, 1949 A.M.C. 572.

■ CHESTNUT, DISTRICT JUDGE. The SS "City of Athens", a trans-Atlantic passenger-cargo ship, was libelled in the Port of Baltimore on July 12, 1947 by the Todd Shipyards Corporation of New York, for the balance due for repairs and reconstruction of the ship in the total amount of $491,077. Many intervening libels and other claims against the ship were filed; and in due course the ship was sold by the Marshal of the court on August 13, 1947 to the Panamanian Lines, Inc., for $400,000, which sum (together with the sum of $1837.71 representing earned freight) less certain expenses of administration, represents the total sum available for lien claims in the amount of $775,457.82. On August 14, 1947 the case was referred to Mr. L. Vernon Miller, * * *, as Commissioner, "to take evidence therein and to report to the Court his findings of law and fact therein with all convenient speed", and the clerk was directed to give notice by publication that all claims against the proceeds of the ship should be filed within a specified time. The Commissioner's report was filed October 7, 1948. * * *

Schedule X (the last page of the report) lists in summary all claims allowed as liens. They embrace basic wages of the crew in the amount of $24,-733.74; additional wages for the crew at $15,141.54; one extra month's pay for certain members of the crew $2,033; repatriation claims $945; additional wages to skeleton crew July 12 to July 22, 1947, $1,375.66; maintenance and cure $236.25; personal injury claims $4,000, and unclassified crew claims in the amount of $8,422.25; head tax claims of $1,624, and cargo claims $1,074.57. The total of such claims was $59,586.01. Other claims for supplies or "necessaries" to the ship on various voyages allowed as liens aggregated $715,871.81. Of this latter amount those accruing in the calendar year 1947 amounting to $291,921.68 were determined to be paid in full as having priority, and the remainder $423,950.13, a large amount of which was allowed to the Todd Shipyards Corporation arising in 1946, was to be deferred to the prior payment claims. The estimated net fund available for distribution after deducting certain expenses of administration including the Commissioner's fee, will be about $380,000. The total claims allowed priority in payment and thus to be paid in full, aggregate $351,507.69. As the deferred claims aggregate $423,950.13, and the remainder of the fund available for distribution is only about $30,000, it appears that the claims deferred in payment by the Commissioner's report will receive a dividend of less than 10%.

* * *

The second question of general importance arising on the exceptions relates to the *marshalling of maritime liens*. The applicable law is to be found in judicial decisions, and is not controlled by any federal statute. With respect to the ranking of liens of different classes, the judicial decisions, while not entirely uniform, are substantially in accord. The law was conveniently summarized in this court by Judge Coleman twenty years ago in the case of The William Leishear, 21 F.2d 862, 863 (D.C.Md.1927). * * * In the instant case there are several classes of liens including seamen's wages, a tort claim, and liens for repairs, supplies and other necessaries; but as the case presents no controversy with respect to the preferred payment of seamen's wages and the tort claim, the only question of priority of payment arising with respect to the claims for repairs, supplies and other necessaries, all of which are claims of the same class and rank. But as the fund for distribution is insufficient to pay all of them in full, there is necessarily involved here the question where the line is to be drawn between those claims of this latter class.

On this point it has sometimes been said that the judicial decisions are in confusion; but an examination of very many cases leads to the conclusion that this statement is correct only insofar as it is applicable to other than ocean voyages of ships. The rule originally developed in admiralty law and still the basic rule is that the maritime liens of the same class are entitled to priority of payment in the inverse order of the time of accrual and that therefore liens arising in connection with the last voyage of the ship have priority of payment over liens accruing on a prior voyage. The rule was thus expressed by Judge Brown in the well-known case of The Proceeds of the Gratitude, 42 F. 299, at page 300 (D.C.N.Y.1890)—

"The general maritime law adjusts all liens by the voyage. * * * By the general rule * * * the priority of liens continues only till the next voyage. The liens connected with every new voyage start with a priority over all former ones after the ship has sailed, if there has previously been opportunity to enforce them."

See also generally Robinson on Admiralty, p. 425; Benedict on Admiralty, Vol. 3, s. 465; The St. Jago de Cuba, 22 U.S. 409, 9 Wheat. 409, 6 L.Ed. 122 (1824); The John G. Stevens, 170 U.S. 113, 18 S.Ct. 544, 42 L.Ed. 969 (1898); 33 Yale Law Journal, 841 (1924); The Interstate No. 1, 290 F. 926, 934 (2 Cir.1923), certiorari denied 262 U.S. 753, 43 S.Ct. 701, 67 L.Ed. 1216; The Steam Dredge A, 204 F. 262, 264 (4 Cir.1913).

Cases which have departed from the "voyage" rule will be found, without exception I think, to have related to ships engaged in other than ocean voyages, as for instance, harbor tugs, coastwise vessels, transportation on the Great Lakes, and comparatively small craft plying local waters. The voyage rule contemplates that at the end of each voyage liens that have arisen during its course should be promptly enforced before the ship departs on another voyage, if there is opportunity to the claimant to so enforce it by libel. As indicated in the opinion of Judge Smith for the Court of Appeals for the Fourth Circuit in the case above cited, the application of the voyage rule presupposes that the voyages are separated "by an appreciable length of time". While this is necessarily still true with respect to transatlantic or other similar ocean voyages, it is obviously not so with respect to the much shorter and more frequent voyages of harbor craft and merely coastwise vessels or other comparatively local transportation. To meet the necessities of such particular local conditions and to accord with the customary business practice locally prevailing it has been found necessary to substitute a rule of priorities other than the voyage rule, and the tendency seems to have been to adopt, as the period allowed prior to the filing of the libel for preferential claims arising therein, a period which can be regarded as a reasonable time for the extension of credit. Thus for New York harbor craft, that period has been fixed at 40 days, and in Puget Sound at 90 days; while on the Great Lakes, where the rigor of winter generally interrupts navigation, the period has been fixed as the navigating season, and thus claims arising during such a particular season are preferred over those of a prior season. More recently, apparently by analogy to this so-called season rule, a rule of priority has been applied by which liens arising in a particular calendar year are given priority over those arising in a prior year; and in a number of cases this latter rule, the so-called "calendar" year rule, has been applied to vessels engaged in coastwise commerce. The Interstate No. 1, supra, 290 F. at page 934. About twenty years ago, in a series of three cases in this court, Judge Coleman applied this latter calendar year rule to small craft locally engaged. While there seems to be no case in the Supreme Court dealing with this particular subject, it seems clearly established in the First Circuit (The Interstate No. 1, supra, 290 F. at page 934) that the voyage rule still applies with respect to "vessels engaged in commerce on the ocean." And it is, I think, likewise, the rule announced in this Fourth Circuit in the case of T+he Steam Dredge A, 122 C.C.A. 527, 204 F. 262, 264 (1912), although on what appears to have been a factually unsatisfactory record, the rule actually applied in the case of a ship apparently engaged in coastwise trade was the so-called calendar year rule.

In the instant case the Commissioner's report expresses his preference for the *voyage* rule but actually applied the *calendar year* rule. It is important, however, to note that in doing so he found that in effect both the voyage rule and the calendar year rule would produce the same actual result with respect to payment of the liens. This was true because the ship made four voyages, one in the later months of 1946 and the remaining three in 1947; and the fund for distribution was sufficient to pay in full all the allowed lien claims arising in 1947, leaving a balance for a percentage distribution of less than 10% to the lien claims arising in connection with the first voyage in 1946. It was, therefore, unnecessary in applying the voyage rule, to distinguish between claims arising on the second, third and fourth voyages as to respective priority. In particular figures the Commissioner thus allowed for prior payment claims for supplies and other necessaries arising on the last three voyages in the aggregate amount of $291,921.68, all to be paid in full from the fund, while those arising in 1946 and to be deferred to the former amounted to $423,950.13, of which the balance due Todd Shipyards represents nearly 90%.

Counsel for Todd and the few other claimants whose liens arose in connection with the first voyage, vigorously protest the correctness of the classification made by the Commissioner. In the first place they point out that in the cases applying the so-called calendar year rule the expression sometimes used by the court is the "year" rule and that, therefore, the period of time referred to should be considered a twelve-month period preceding the date of the libel; but as to this an examination of most if not all of the cases referred to shows from the facts involved that claims allowed (with only trivial exceptions, if any) were those which arose during the calendar year in which the libel was filed; and I have found no case which establishes a twelve month period for the classification of preferred and deferred lien claims.

The next argument advanced is that by reason of changed conditions with respect to ocean voyages which are now generally of much shorter duration than when the voyage rule was established, and since means of communication between the owner and the master of the ship, possibly in a foreign port, are more rapid because of the facilities of cable and radio, the voyage rule should be regarded as obsolete and a different new rule substituted therefor. In support of this contention particular reference is made to the view expressed by Robinson on Admiralty, p. 427, in which that generally excellent author, after referring to the season rule prevailing with regard to shipping on the Great Lakes, and the 90–day rule for credit in navigation in Puget Sound said:

"It is questionable how much further the application of this principle can be carried and to what jurisdictions it extends. But it is sufficient here to point out that for short trips the voyage rule is no longer a test and has given place to rules in which there are local variances. Even where the longer voyages of ocean steamers are concerned, the courts have ceased to apply a technical interpretation of the term 'voyage' and talk in terms of years.

"The year is considered representative of the voyage. This shows a tendency, even in the case of larger vessels, to apply a time measured by a *reasonable period of credit* rather than voyage. Passenger liners today make the transatlantic run in less than a week so that the larger steamship companies in a certain measure are beset with the same problem which faced harbor craft at an earlier date. Judge Brown in the Gratitude ante, note 181, remarked of the 40 day rule: 'It accords in some degree with the period of modern (1890) voyages.' "

However, an examination of the four cases mentioned in the note documenting this view fails to show that any of them related to transatlantic or other ocean voyages. Two of the cases were among those decided some twenty years ago by Judge Coleman and which have been above referred to. They related to small craft locally navigating the Chesapeake Bay.

While counsel for the particular exceptants concede that there is no definite judicial authority in support of their contention they urge that, as the decided cases present such variable rules for determining priorities, some new and definite rule should now be established, and further urge that the new rule to be adopted should be the year rule as they contend it should be understood, that is, that all liens arising in a period of one year prior to the libel should rank pari passu; or, in other words that the period of a year as "a reasonable period of credit" should be established as the test rather than that of the voyage.

My conclusion of law is that the voyage rule still prevails despite greater rapidity of transportation and communication. The reasons which originally gave rise to the voyage rule still exist even though their importance in some respects may have been lessened. Many ocean voyages are still of several months' duration and there is still at times the most imperative need that a ship in a port far distant from the owner should have the ability to obtain repairs and supplies on the credit of the ship itself. This ability to obtain such credit would obviously be much impaired if a long prior claim originating in connection with a previous voyage, as in this case, and amounting to a sum much larger than the sale value of the ship, were to rate equally with the supplies or repairs on the last voyage, imperatively needed to keep the ship a "going concern", and to enable it to return to its home. * * *

With regard to the argument that the court should establish a new rule with respect to priorities and lien claimants, it is sufficient to say that I would not feel warranted in doing so, as I find, the voyage rule is still the established one for ocean voyages.   Nor do I think this case presents in its factual situation a proper one for the establishment of the new twelve-months rule which is advocated.   I will add that while I have concluded that the voyage rule must be observed here, I do not think, apart from it, the facts of the case would justify the application of the calendar year rule. If we were to disregard the voyage rule and accept in lieu thereof as a test, a reasonable period of credit, the facts of the particular case do not furnish an adequate basis for determining what this period should be.   Should it be forty days as a possible inference from what Judge Brown said in the case of The Gratitude above quoted, or two months for a transatlantic liner, or six months as the calendar year rule has in effect been applied by the Commissioner's report, or a year or at least eight months as contended for by the exceptants?   While the calendar year rule, analogized to the season rule, may be fairly applicable to the smaller craft navigating locally only, the court is not in possession of sufficient information in this case with respect to conditions in general affecting transatlantic or ocean voyages to say what period of time should be regarded as reasonable.   Change in the law in this respect and in the establishment of such a definite period, if to be made at all, should be made only after the fullest possible information of all relevant conditions which ordinarily could be brought to the attention of a legislative body with full powers of investigation.   While it may be entirely appropriate and desirable for a court dealing with a particular local situation, as for instance affecting the New York harbor or Puget Sound or the Great Lakes or the Chesapeake Bay, to lay down a general rule that is locally applicable, it is a far more difficult and wider question to determine such a rule for ocean voyages which, in many cases, may involve navigation extending around the globe.

* * *

NOTE

The future of the "voyage" rule has been spoken of as "obscure."   Gilmore and Black, *The Law of Admiralty* 750 (1975), where it is pointed out that the "season" or "calendar year" rule has been applied quite generally in cases involving coastwise or Gulf of Mexico shipping, and of all cases since 1940, *The City of Athens* is the only case involving ocean shipping.

The City of Tawas

District Court, Eastern District of Michigan, 1880.
3 Fed. 170.

■ BROWN, D.J.   The subject of marshalling liens in admiralty is one which, unfortunately, is left in great obscurity by the authorities.   Many of the rules deduced from the English cases seems inapplicable here.   So, also, the principles applied where the contest is between two or three libellants would result in great confusion in cases where 50 or 60 libels are filed against the same vessel. The American authorities, too, are by no means harmonious, and it is scarcely too much to say that each court is a law unto itself.

The order in which liens are paid depends upon four contingencies: (1) The relative merit of the claims; (2) the time at which the claim accrued; (3) the date at which proceedings are commenced for its enforcement; (4) the date of the decree. The practice has grown up in this district, sanctioned by the long acquiescence of the bar, of classifying claims as follows: (1) Seamen's wages; (2) claims for towage and for necessaries furnished in a foreign port; (3) claims for supplies and materials furnished at the home port, for which a lien is given by the state law; (4) mortgages.

Bottomry bonds being unknown on the lakes, no question has ever arisen here with regard to their relative rank. That claims for wages should be paid in preference to all others, except the costs of sale of the ship keeper, and of storage and dockage while the vessel is in the hands of the marshal, and excepting also subsequent salvage, it is well settled in all the districts. Whether one claim is entitled to priority over another of equal rank, by reason of the libel being first filed or decree being first obtained upon it, is a matter of very considerable doubt—at least in cases of contract.

Nearly if not all claims against this vessel accrued during the years 1875 and 1876, and the first exception of the dry dock company proceeds upon the theory that claims in the third class accruing in 1876—that is, for repairs furnished in the home port—should rank claims of the second class, for towage services rendered in 1875. Claims of the same class are sometimes ordered put in the inverse order in which they accrue. This, I believe, is invariably observed in the case of bottomry bonds, the last being put first, and the first last. Maclachlan on Merchant Ship. 652. In some cases it is said that necessaries furnished on the last voyage should be paid in preference to those furnished for a former voyage, and the rule certainly seems a reasonable one as applied to long voyages upon the ocean, but wholly inapplicable to the daily or weekly trips made by vessels upon the lakes. I regard it, however, as a reasonable modification of the general practice that claims of equal rank should be paid *pro rata*; that each year should be considered as a voyage, and that claims accruing the last year should be paid in preference to claims of the same rank accruing the year before, each season of navigation here being separated from the preceding season by four months of inaction. This will encourage diligence in the prosecution of claims, and prevent the proceeds of sale from being absorbed by dilatory creditors. But I know of no authority or principle which would justify the court in ordering a claim of an inferior rank to be paid prior to claims of a superior rank, on the ground that the latter accrued the year before the former, unless the defense of stale claim is pleaded in the libel. Maclachlan, 652. I think, therefore, the first exception is not well taken.

* * *

NOTE

The "season rule" created by Judge Brown became the uniform rule on the Great Lakes and has been adopted in a number of other areas, sometimes modified to a "calendar year rule" where shipping goes on the year around. See Gilmore and Black, *Law of Admiralty* 745 (1975). In the New York Harbor area, the priority period is 40 days. See Proceeds of the Gratitude, 42 Fed. 299 (S.D.N.Y.1890), in which the rule was created by Judge Addison Brown, and The Samuel Little, 137 C.C.A. 136, 221 Fed. 308 (2d Cir.1915), in which it was recognized by the Second Circuit. Other cases are collected in Gilmore and Black, supra, at p. 605. The rule is not applied to craft operating to points on Long Island Sound. In re New England Transp. Co., 220 Fed. 203 (D.Conn.1914). It has been held, however, that harbor craft that make occasional trips out of the harbor are governed by the 40 day rule. The Interstate No. 2, 290 Fed. 1015, 1923 A.M.C. 1128 (D.N.J.1922). A 90 day rule has been created for the Seattle Harbor and Puget Sound area. See The Edith, 217 Fed. 300 (W.D.Wash.1914).

It has been held that the 40 day period is a single priority period, and that all liens of the same rank dating from more than forty days are to share *pro rata*. The Interstate No. 1, 290 Fed. 926, 1923 A.M.C. 1118 (2d Cir.1923), cert. denied 262 U.S. 753, 43 S.Ct. 701, 67 L.Ed. 1216.

The Home

United States District Court, Western District of Washington, 1946.
65 F.Supp. 94, 1946 A.M.C. 585.

■ Bowen, District Judge. The libelant Bank filed this libel in rem against the respondent vessel seeking judgment on a promissory note and to foreclose a preferred ship mortgage securing its payment recorded April 28, 1944. Intervening libelant, Sunde & d'Evers Co., has intervened with its claim for debt and maritime liens for ship's supplies, some of which were furnished to the vessel in 1944 prior to the recording of the mortgage and some of which were furnished subsequent to the recording of the mortgage in 1944 and 1945. The other intervening libelants assert similar claims for ship's supplies and work and repairs furnished to the vessel subsequent to the recording of the mortgage in 1944 and 1945.

The money items sued for by libelant include the principal and interest now due on the promissory note, the costs of suit and also a reasonable sum to be allowed as libelant's attorney's fees under the provisions of the promissory note and the mortgage securing the note. Libelant further asks to have all of these sums paid out of the proceeds of the foreclosure sale of the vessel and her equipment before any portion of any of the claims of intervenors are paid, with the possible exception of that portion of the Sunde & d'Evers claim comprising a preferred maritime lien which covers supplies furnished to the vessel prior to the recording of the mortgage.

As to the amount of such preferred maritime lien claim, however, there is some dispute because Sunde & d'Evers did not, until a few days before the trial, undertake to allocate as between new and old items of the account certain part payments. Then that creditor did attempt to allocate such part payments to the items of the account furnished subsequent to the recording of the mortgage in order thereby to leave a larger amount protected by the preferred maritime lien covering the items supplied before the recording of the mortgage. It is contended by some of the parties that allocation of such part payments to the oldest items of the account is to be presumed in the absence of proof of intention to the contrary formed on the part of the creditor or debtor before the action was commenced.

But that contention cannot prevail here. Unlike the situation where only unsecured claims are involved, the law presumes that a creditor, like Sunde & d'Evers, having two claims, one secured by a first rank security and the other by a lower rank security, intends to allocate such part payments as are received to the payment of the claim with the lower rank security, in the absence of proof of a contrary intention. Restatement of the Law, Contracts, Sec. 394(1)(b)(ii), Page 743, and Illustration 5, Page 746; Washington Grocery Co. v. Citizens' Bank, 132 Wash. 244, 231 P. 780 (1925); Field v. Holland, 10 U.S. (6 Cranch.) 8, 3 L.Ed. 136 (1810).

Sunde & d'Evers Co. will, therefore, be paid $270.47 the full amount of its preferred maritime lien for all items supplied prior to the recording of the mortgage. As to the balance of its account, it will be on the same basis as other lien claimants subsequent to the mortgage.

Another question is whether the Ship Mortgage Act, 46 U.S.C.A. §§ 911, 921 et seq., permits maritime liens inferior to the lien of the mortgage to participate in a fund set aside from the sale proceeds to meet a preferred maritime lien. In this connection it is contended by some of the intervenors that before the enactment of the Ship Mortgage Act a lien later in time was prior in rank and that, unless the Ship Mortgage Act is to be regarded as changing that rule, the liens here arising subsequent to the mortgage should in their bids for prior payment displace the earlier statutory superior lien claim of the preferred maritime lien, once the fund is set aside from the proceeds of the sale of the vessel to meet the preferred maritime lien.

Respecting that contention, lien relationship before the Ship Mortgage Act does not compare with such relationship after the Act because in respect to the statutory mortgage and preferred maritime lien those relationships are not alike. It would seem clear that to allow lien claims arising later than the mortgage to participate in any fund taken out of the sale proceeds ahead of the mortgage for satisfying the preferred maritime lien would defeat the very purpose and provisions of the statute which expressly protects the preferred maritime lien. If the preferred maritime lien should not be paid ahead of the mortgage out of the proceeds of the sale, no matter for what reason, the provision of the statute intending that result would not be carried out and the statute would be violated. The Court, therefore, denies the right of other lien claimants to participate in any fund realized for the payment of the preferred maritime lien of Sunde & d'Evers Co. for items of supplies furnished to the vessel prior to the recording of the mortgage.

It has also been questioned whether under this ship mortgage the indebtedness secured thereby it to include a reasonable sum to be fixed by the Court as an attorney's fee for libelant's proctor. Upon this question counsel cite only one case, namely, The John Jay, 15 F.Supp. 937 (D.C.Pa. 1936), which decided that, as between the mortgagee and the mortgagor, the mortgage lien secured the contingent amount of attorney's fees as a part of the mortgage indebtedness where the mortgage securing the indebtedness was evidenced by a promissory note containing a provision for the payment of reasonable attorney's fees to be fixed by the Court in case of mortgage foreclosure. No cases were cited where junior incumbrancers objected to attorney's fees, undetermined before the Court's decision, becoming a part of the senior mortgage indebtedness; but in this state, mortgages on land securing indebtedness evidenced by notes which in turn in language similar to that here provide for the payment of reasonable attorney's fees to be fixed by the Court are usually held to include such attorney's fee obligation within the mortgage debt protection of the mortgage lien. Cutler v. Keller, 88 Wash. 334, 153 P. 15, L.R.A. 1917C,1116 (1915). No reason appears why the same rule should not apply in the case of preferred ship mortgages with attorney's fee and costs provisions like those in the mortgage and note here. An attorney's fee for libelant in the sum of $350 is reasonable and will be allowed and shall have the same lien rank as the principal mortgage indebtedness.

It is agreed by the parties that in this case maritime liens for supplies arising in a later year shall take priority over those created in an earlier year, and that all of such liens of any one year shall have the same rank and be paid pro rata out of any funds applicable to liens of their respective class. This agreement of course does not apply to the statutory preferred maritime lien of Sunde & d'Evers for supplies furnished prior to the recording of the mortgage.

The proceeds of the foreclosure sale will be paid out in accordance with the following priorities:

1. Taxable costs, including taxable clerk's fees, taxable marshal's fees for serving process and conducting the foreclosure sale, a proctor's fee of $20 for each party except libelant, and an appearance for each party.

2. To Sunde & d'Evers Co. for its preferred maritime lien for supplies furnished prior to recording the mortgage, in the sum of $270.47.

3. To University National Bank (by its correct name) in the sum of $3,015.67 plus $0.8773 per day from February 26, 1946, to the date of entry of decree, plus $350 for its proctor's fee.

4. 1945 claims pro-rated on the following basis:

to Seattle Ship Supply	$194.19
Atlas Engine Co.	429.56
Fred Rowe	234.17

5. 1944 claims subsequent to mortgage pro-rated on the following basis:

to Sunde & d'Evers Co.	$60.63

Seattle Ship Supply 22.34
Fisheries Supply Co. 357.83
Fred Rowe 17.42

* * *

NOTE

Note the second paragraph of 46 U.S.C.A. § 31326(b), added to former § 951 in 1954, and providing in part that a foreign preferred mortgage is subordinate to a maritime lien for necessaries provided in the United States See Gulf Oil Trading Co. v. Creole Supply, 596 F.2d 515, 1979 A.M.C. 585 (2d Cir.1979), in which the holder of a Bahamian mortgage in default continued to release funds for the operation of the vessels and after it called the loan permitted the vessels to depart the United States and then arrested the vessels in the Dominican Republic, released them on the condition that they go to the Bahamas, and rearrested them in the Bahamas, where it foreclosed its mortgage. The supplier of bunkers that had made it possible for the vessel to leave the United States, and as a consequence made it possible for the mortgagee to avoid the priority of supply liens under § 951, sued the mortgagee to impose a constructive trust on the freights and proceeds of sale of the vessels. The court of appeals held that whatever lien the supplier may have had was extinguished by the Bahamian judgment, but ordered entry of a judgment in personam for unjust enrichment.

Section (b)(2) subordinates a foreign mortgage to the lien of American suppliers only when the supplies are delivered in the United States. Thus the foreign preferred mortgage has priority over the liens of American suppliers where the supplies are delivered to the vessel in a foreign port, even where the contract is negotiated in the United States and calls for payment there. Mobil Sales and Supply Corp. v. Panamax Venus, 804 F.2d 541 (9th Cir.1986).

D.   EXTINGUISHMENT OF LIENS

1.   DESTRUCTION OF THE RES

Walsh v. Tadlock

United States Circuit Court of Appeals, Ninth Circuit, 1939.
104 F.2d 131, 1939 A.M.C. 1278, cert. denied 308 U.S. 584, 60 S.Ct. 107, 84 L.Ed. 489 (1939).

Interpleader proceedings by an insurance company against Matt J. Walsh and Frank E. Garbutt, doing business under the firm name and style of Garbutt–Walsh, M.G. Tadlock and others, to determine the right to the proceeds of a marine insurance policy. From the judgment rendered, Matt J. Walsh and Frank E. Garbutt, doing business under the firm name and style of Garbutt–Walsh, appeal.   * * *

■ HEALY, CIRCUIT JUDGE. The earlier history of this litigation is related in Security Trust & Savings Bank of San Diego v. Walsh, 91 F.2d 481 (9 Cir.1937). The present appeal involves the division of the proceeds of an insurance policy.

Appellee Tadlock was the owner of the fishing vessel Yellowtail. Appellee Security Trust & Savings Bank of San Diego was the holder of a mortgage on the vessel as security for the payment of an instalment note in excess of $9,000, made October 22, 1934. The mortgage required the owner to keep the boat insured at all times in a company to be selected by the bank, for an amount at least equal to the sum remaining unpaid on the indebtedness. In October, 1935 the owner procured a policy of insurance on the boat in the sum of $7,000, payable to Tadlock and the bank as their respective interests might appear. The term of the policy was for one year.

Between the 23rd of December, 1935, and the end of January, 1936, appellants Garbutt–Walsh made certain repairs on the boat and furnished materials and equipment for the same at the instance and request of the owner, of the reasonable value of $4,358.06. The trial court found that while this work was in progress the appellants instructed a firm of insurance brokers to procure for them insurance coverage on the vessel in the amount of $1,800. The brokers obtained temporary coverage in that amount. Thereafter, as the proof shows, they contacted the company which had written the outstanding policy in favor of the owner and the bank and requested a separate policy in the amount of $1,800, naming appellants as payees. After some investigation concerning values, the company agreed to write insurance on the boat in the additional amount of $1,000 only, but insisted on combining this with the original coverage in a single policy. Thereupon the brokers, with the consent of the mortgagee bank, procured the issuance of a new policy in the amount of $8,000, the $7,000 policy previously written being canceled. The substitute policy provided coverage for one year from February 5, 1936. Loss was made payable to Tadlock, the bank and appellants, "as their respective interests may appear."

On February 22, 1936, the Yellowtail burned and sank at sea, becoming a total loss. Subsequently the insurer interpleaded the named beneficiaries and deposited the proceeds of the policy, less an unpaid premium, in the registry of the court. After a trial on the cross demands of the beneficiaries the court made findings and conclusions to the effect that the appellee bank was entitled to seven-eighths of the net proceeds of the insurance and the appellants to one-eighth. The seniority of the latter's maritime lien on the boat was recognized, but it was determined that by the cancellation of the original policy and the issuance of the new one it was intended by all parties concerned, including the insurance company, that the insurance protection of the mortgagee bank should continue as before in the amount of $7,000, and that the insurance protection of appellants should be limited to the amount by which the coverage had been increased. The proof is ample that such was the arrangement ultimately made by appellants' brokers, and the decree must be affirmed.

With the total destruction of the vessel the liens thereon were of necessity extinguished. 38 C.J.S. 1247. These liens did not attach to the proceeds of the insurance, nor did appellants' lien on the boat per se entitle them to participate in the division of the insurance money. A.M. Bright Grocery Co. v. Lindsey, 225 F. 257 (D.C.Ala.1915); Place et al. v. Norwich & N.Y. Transp. Co., 118 U.S. 468, 6 S.Ct. 1150, 30 L.Ed. 134 (1885); White

v. Gilman, 138 Cal. 375, 71 P. 436 (1903). Their right to do that was dependent on the contract of insurance. Alexander v. Security–First Nat. Bank, 7 Cal.2d 718, 62 P.2d 735 (1936); Corder v. McDougall, 216 Cal. 773, 16 P.2d 740 (1932); Davis v. Phoenix Ins. Co., 111 Cal. 409, 43 P. 1115 (1896); Newark Fire Ins. Co. v. Turk, 6 F.2d 533, 43 A.L.R. 496 (3 Cir.1925). The interests of the named payees were not described in the policy, either as to nature or as to amount, nor was the order of payment specified. In the absence of any showing to the contrary the loss-payable clause of the policy may be construed as requiring a division in proportion to the respective insurable interests of the payees, or as giving a preferred status to the claimant having a superior lien on the boat. However, the circumstances attendant upon the procurement of this policy were such as to disclose an intention to limit appellants' interest in it to a definite sum. * * *

Affirmed.

NOTE

It is to be noted that in Walsh v. Tadlock, the vessel was sunk and for all that appears was never raised. Therefore, there was nothing left to which the lien could adhere. When the vessel sinks and part of it is raised, of course the lien adheres to the part. Thus in Chapman v. The Engines of Greenpoint, 38 Fed. 671 (S.D.N.Y. 1889), it was held that liens on a vessel attached to the engines when they were all that was salvaged from the wreck. When a vessel is dismantled and reassembled, the pre-existing liens are not discharged. Dann v. Dredge Sandpiper, 222 F.Supp. 838, 1964 A.M.C. 472 (D.Del.1963). In The Sandpiper the dredge was towed on navigable waters while in marine service. Later it was dismantled and transported overland to an inland pond where it was employed in nonmaritime work. While thus situated it was seized by the marshal to enforce the towage lien. Similarly, when a vessel to which a maritime lien had attached was permanently moored and used as a restaurant, it was held that the question that was to be asked was whether it was engaged in maritime service at the time the services were rendered, not whether it was so engaged at the time of seizure. See Arques Shipyards v. The Charles Van Damme, 175 F.Supp. 871, 1959 A.M.C. 1570 (N.D.Cal.1959).

Is there a point at which the vessel ceases to be such for the purpose of foreclosing a lien? Suppose, for example, that the engine in the *Chapman* case had been used in the construction of a different vessel. Would a supply lien on the previous vessel attach to the new one? See Srodes v. The Collier, 22 Fed.Cas. 1019, No.13–272 (W.D.Pa.1861), aff'd 22 Fed.Cas. 1025 (No. 13,272A) (W.D.Pa.1861). Is it important whether the new vessel is owned by the owner of the previous vessel? Cf. The McLaughlin v. Dredge Gloucester, 230 F.Supp. 623, 1964 A.M.C. 2124 (D.N.J.1964).

2.   JUDICIAL SALE

South Carolina State Ports Authority v. Silver Anchor, S.A., (Panama)

United States Court of Appeals, Fourth Circuit, 1994.
23 F.3d 842, 1994 A.M.C. 2463.

■ MURNAGHAN, CIRCUIT JUDGE:

On appeal are two consolidated actions, both brought by the South Carolina Ports Authority ("the SPA"): an *in personam* action against Orestes G. "Rusty" Christophides and a Panamanian company, Silver Anchor, S.A., for breach of an oral contract; and an *in rem* action against Silver Anchor's vessel, M/V Levant Fortune (formerly known as the Valiant), for enforcement of a maritime lien. The district court dismissed the *in personam* action for lack of subject matter jurisdiction and granted summary judgment to the defendant vessel in the in *rem action*. The SPA now appeals.

* * *

III

In the in rem action against the M/V Levant Fortune (formerly the Valiant), the district court granted the defendant vessel's motion for summary judgment, finding that the Greek judicial sale of the Valiant had extinguished the maritime lien asserted by the SPA. Reviewing the district court's ruling *de novo*, we affirm.

The present case is squarely controlled by our precedent in Gulf & Southern Terminal Corp. v. S.S. President Roxas, 701 F.2d 1110 (4th Cir.), cert. denied, 462 U.S. 1133, 103 S.Ct. 3115, 77 L.Ed.2d 1369 (1983). In *President Roxas*, we stated that a judicial sale of a vessel by a court of a sovereign nation will extinguish a maritime lien if (1) the foreign court had personal jurisdiction over the lien-holder; (2) the foreign court acted in a valid in rem proceeding; or (3) the foreign court's proceedings were sufficiently similar to an in rem proceeding to make its decree recognizable by and binding on the American courts. In *President Roxas*, we specifically held that a Mexican bankruptcy court's decree had extinguished an existing maritime lien. We noted that the S.S. President Roxas had been an asset of the bankrupt, under the control and proper jurisdiction of the Mexican court, and that the Mexican court had provided adequate notice to the world that the vessel was being sold free of liens and encumbrances. Therefore, we recognized the validity of the Mexican court's decree. Without the broad international recognition of such foreign judicial sales, we explained, a purchaser could never anticipate what additional claims might be asserted in other countries with different laws. See id. at 1111–12.

In the present case, the district court properly concluded that the Greek court also employed procedures virtually identical to those denominated as an *in rem* proceeding under American law. The vessel was seized by a creditor holding a specific property right in the vessel (i.e., the ship's mortgage). Creditors holding the equivalent of maritime liens, including the SPA, were allowed to intervene. And the ship was sold free and clear of liens and encumbrances under Greek law.[7] Given the similarities between the Greek proceedings and an American *in rem* proceeding, the defendant

---

7. Indeed, as the court below noted, the SPA received greater protection in the Greek court than the President Roxas plaintiff received in the Mexican bankruptcy court: the SPA participated fully in the Greek proceeding and is apparently now entitled to substantial proceeds from the sale that followed.

vessel was entitled to judgment as a matter of law under our *President Roxas* test.

The SPA attempts to distinguish *President Roxas* on the ground that Greece—unlike Mexico—is a signatory to the "Brussels Convention," the International Convention Relating to the Arrest of Sea–Going Ships, May 10, 1952, 439 U.N.T.S. 193. In attempting to argue that Greece's status as a signatory to the Brussels Convention is legally relevant here, the SPA relies almost entirely upon the Fifth Circuit's decisions in Perez & Compania (Catalunia) v. M/V Mexico I, 826 F.2d 1449, 1450–51, and Belcher Co. v. M/V Maratha Mariner, 724 F.2d 1161, 1163–65 (5th Cir.1984). The SPA's reliance on those cases is misplaced. Under the controlling Fourth Circuit precedent, the relevant question is not whether a country has signed the Brussels Convention, but rather whether it affords lienholders procedural and substantive protections sufficiently similar to those available in an American *in rem* proceeding. See *President Roxas*, 701 F.2d at 1111–1112. Moreover, even under the Fifth Circuit law, the SPA's *in rem* claim against M/V Levant Fortune apparently would be barred by the Greek judicial sale. See, e.g., Crescent Towing & Salvage Co. v. M/V ANAX, Civ. A. No. 93–0675, 1993 WL 293274, 1993 U.S.Dist. LEXIS 10613 (E.D.La.1993) (applying Fifth Circuit law and holding that the judicial sale of the defendant vessel in *Greece* pursuant to *Greek* law, as ordered by a *Greek* court with jurisdiction, had extinguished a maritime lien that an American company against the vessel). Therefore, we affirm the district court's grant of summary judgment.[8]

IV

Accordingly, we affirm the district court's judgment with regard to the *in rem* claim * * *

NOTE

The general proposition that a judicial sale in an action in rem confers title on the purchaser free of all maritime liens has been taken as given since The Trenton, 4 Fed. 657 (E.D.Mich.1880). And this is so even though the lienholders have absolutely no notice. Thorsteinsson v. M/V Drangur, 891 F.2d 1547 (11th Cir. 1990). Applying this principle, see Tamblyn v. River Bend Marine, Inc., 837 F.2d 447 (11th Cir.1988). There it was held that a chattel mortgage with an interest in the vessel received all the notice due him when a lienholder caused publication of notice in a newspaper of general circulation in the district, but when the chattel

---

8. The defendant-appellee argues in the alternative that the Greek judicial sale extinguished the SPa's maritime lien because the SPA submitted itself to the *personal* jurisdiction of the Greek court. *See President Roxas*, 701 F.2d at 1111 (stating that a judicial sale of a vessel by a foreign court extinguishes a maritime lien if that court had personal jurisdiction over the lienholder). Because we

have concluded that the Greek proceedings were sufficiently similar to an American in rem proceeding, we need not address that alternative argument.

We also do not address the SPA's appeal from the denial of its motion to amend its complaint in the *in personam* case to reassert and *in rem* claim, as our decision renders the motion moot.

mortgagee reduced his claim on the vessel to a money judgment, his mortgage did not merge into the judgment and he did not become an unsecured creditor.

For a cautious view of the recognition of a judicial sale in a foreign court as discharging a pre-existing American supplier's lien, see Crescent Towing & Salvage Co., Inc. v. M/V Anax, 40 F.3d 741, 1995 A.M.C. 1106 (5th Cir.1994) reversing a summary judgment based upon a Greek decree foreclosing a mortgage executed and recorded in St. Vincent and the Grenadines, in a proceeding at which the holder of the mortgage bought in the vessel on a discount equalling its claim, and sold it to the claimant for $10. The Fifth Circuit indicated that under ordinary principles governing summary judgments, the party setting up a foreign sale as a defense must show "that the sale was conducted pursuant to a valid *in rem* proceeding in the foreign forum, and that under the law of that forum the judicial sale would have transferred title free and clear of all encumbrances."

Sale of the vessel in a proceeding in the state court to foreclose a common law lien, within the jurisdiction of the state under the *Rounds* case, supra at p. 155, does not extinguish maritime liens. See The Winnebago, 205 U.S. 354, 27 S.Ct. 509, 51 L.Ed. 836 (1907); The Gazelle, 10 F.Cas. 127 (D.Mass.1858). Neither does sale to enforce a state forfeiture under the doctrine of C.J. Hendry Co. v. Moore, supra p. 147. See Bard v. The Silver Wave, 98 F.Supp. 271, 1951 A.M.C. 1079 (D.Md.1951).

3.   RELEASE OF VESSEL ON BOND

Hawgood & Avery Transit Co. v. Dingman

United States Circuit Court of Appeals, Eighth Circuit, 1899.
36 C.C.A. 627, 94 Fed. 1011.

These are appeals from two decrees in admiralty rendered in proceedings against the steamer Belle P. Cross. On December 14, 1896, Gustave Herman, Ralph E. Herman, and Edward G. Ashley filed a libel in the court below against this steamer, her engine, boilers, tackle, apparel, and furniture. This libel was in the usual form, except that it contained an allegation that, after the supplies on account of which it was filed had been furnished, the owner of the vessel had taken her engine, boilers, and machinery out of her hull, and had placed them in the steam tug G.A. Tomlinson. A monition issued on the libel, and the marshal arrested the hull of the Belle P. Cross, and also her engine, boilers, and machinery, which he found in the G.A. Tomlinson. On March 8, 1897, the appellant the Hawgood & Avery Transit Company petitioned the court for an appraisal of the engine, boilers, and machinery in the Tomlinson. An appraiser was appointed, and an appraisal thereof was made pursuant to a stipulation signed by the transit company, and all those who had then filed libels against the steamer Belle P. Cross, or its engine, boilers, and machinery. This stipulation recited that it was made "for the purpose of fixing a value thereto, and to enable said property to be released under the provisions of rule 17 of this court and the statute in such case made and provided." The appraiser fixed the value of the engine, boilers, and machinery at $2,000. The transit company executed and filed a bond for this amount for the benefit of "whom it may concern," conditioned that if that company should abide by all the orders of the court, and pay the amount awarded by the final decree, the bond should be void. Upon the filing of this bond, and on March 10, 1897, the engine, boilers, and machinery were released and surrendered to the transit company pursuant to an order of the court to that effect. But the hull of the steamer Belle P. Cross remained in the possession of the marshal. After this release, and on April 3, 1897, the Inter–Ocean Coal & Coke Company filed an intervening libel against the Belle P. Cross and her boilers, engine, and machinery, and caused the engine, boilers, and machinery to be again arrested in the Tug Tomlinson under a monition issued upon this libel. On September 4, 1897, the Barry Towing & Wrecking Company, which had succeeded to the title of the transit company, filed a claim for this engine, these boilers, and this machinery, and gave a bond in the sum of $2,329.66 to R.T. O'Connor, the marshal of the district, which recited the filing of the intervening libel and the seizure of the engine, boilers, and machinery thereunder, and was conditioned that the wrecking company should abide by and perform the decree of the court in relation to the claim of the coal and coke company. On September 11, 1895, the wrecking company filed an answer to the intervening libel, in which it set forth the prior proceedings, which we have detailed, alleged that it had bought the engine, boilers, and machinery for value, and without notice, on April 1, 1897, that it was the owner thereof, and that the release of March 10, 1897, discharged this property from all maritime liens. Meanwhile the hull of the steamer Belle P. Cross had been condemned and sold, and the proceeds of the sale, which were only $310, had been paid into the registry of the court. Upon the final hearing the court below entered two decrees, one to the effect that the money in the registry of the court and the proceeds of the bond of the transit company of March 4, 1897, should be distributed among those who had filed their libels prior to March 10, 1897, and the other to the effect that N.J. Trodo, who had become the assignee of the coal and coke company, should have summary judgment for $1,333.53 and interest, the amount of that company's claim, against the Barry Towing & Wrecking Company and the sureties upon its bond of September 4, 1897. From these decrees the transit company and the wrecking company have appealed. * * *

■ SANBORN, CIRCUIT JUDGE (after stating the facts as above) delivered the opinion of the court.

The questions presented in this case turn upon the legal effect of the discharge of the engine, boilers, and machinery upon the appraisal and bond on March 10, 1897. If that discharge released this property from the maritime liens of those who had not then filed their libels in the court below, the decrees were erroneous; but if it left these liens unimpaired, and discharged the property from the liens of those who were then parties to the proceedings only, they were right. The theory of the appellants is that the bond of March 4, 1897, became a substitute for the engine, boilers, and machinery as to all who claimed maritime liens upon this property, whether they had presented their liens in the court below or not when the bond was given and the machinery was released. Upon this theory they insist that the court erred in refusing to include the Inter–Ocean Coal & Coke Company, or its assignee, and the Hawgood & Avery Transit Company, among the distributees of the proceeds of that bond, although neither of them had filed any libel against or leaded any lien upon the machinery or the vessel when this bond was given, and they contend that the seizure of the machinery under the subsequent libel of the coal and coke company and the decree that the wrecking company and the sureties on its bond shall pay the claim of that company are erroneous, because, as they say, the machinery was discharged of all maritime liens by the substitution of the earlier bond in its place on March 10, 1897. When a ship which has been arrested under a libel is released upon an appraisal and a deposit, or a bond, or a stipulation, not given under the limited liability act, the deposit or bond or stipulation is substituted for the vessel as to all those who have then filed their libels and become parties to the proceedings but as to no other parties. The proceeds of the deposit, bond, or stipulation inure to the benefit of those who were parties to the proceeding when the release was made. But they inure to the benefit of no others. The vessel is discharged from the liens of these parties, and from their liens only. Lienholders who have not filed their libels, and have not become parties to the proceeding when the ship is discharged, may not be permitted to share in the proceeds of the deposit or bond or stipulation, and their liens are neither detached nor affected by the release. The vessel returns to the claimant subject to the maritime liens of all who were not parties to the proceeding before the discharge was made, and they may libel and arrest her to enforce their liens to the same extent and with the same effect as though she had never been seized before. Rev.St. Secs. 940, 941; Adm.Rules, 11, 26; The Langdon Cheves, 2 Mason 58, 14 F.Cas. 1111 (1819); The Union, 4 Blatchf. 90, 24 F.Cas. 535 (1857); The Antelope, 1 Ben. 521, 1 F.Cas. 1041 (1867); The Haytian Republic, 57 F. 508, 509; Id., 154 U.S. 118, 14 S.Ct. 992, 38 L.Ed. 930 (1893); The Oregon, 158 U.S. 186, 15 S.Ct. 804, 39 L.Ed. 943 (1895).

If the transit company in the case at bar had claimed both the hull and the machinery of the steamer, and had procured the appraisal and given the bond for the entire res, and the vessel and machinery had both been discharged thereunder, the right of the coal and coke company to subsequently libel her and to enforce its lien by seizure and sale of every part of the vessel and of the machinery could not have been successfully questioned under these authorities. The reason for this rule is that the maritime lien of that company had attached to every part of the ship and to every part of her machinery before any libel was filed against her, and the acts of third parties in seizing her and releasing her on an appraisal and bond could not affect the right and lien of this company in its absence, and without its consent. On this ground all the authorities are that, if the entire thing had been libeled and discharged here, the lien of the coal and coke company would have remained untouched. How, then, could a discharge of a part of this thing have a greater effect than the release of the whole? Every reason which tends to support the lien of the absent holder when the entire thing is discharged pleads with equal cogency for its maintenance when only a part is released. The lien attaches to every part as much as to the whole. If one-half, two-thirds, or any other portion of the res is destroyed, the maritime lien still adheres to the remnant that has escaped, and no persuasive reason occurs to us why it should not hold as firmly every part which has been released from a seizure made by strangers to pay their debts. Any other rule would permit the first libelants and the owner to destroy the value of the liens of all others by an appraisal and discharge of the valuable part of the thing seized, leaving as in this case, nothing but a worthless remnant for their satisfaction. Every consideration of reason and of equity demands that the same rule should apply to a discharge of a part which governs the release of the whole. Our conclusion is that a release to a claimant under an appraisal and stipulation or bond, not made under the limited liability act, of a part of the res seized under a libel in admiralty, has the same effect upon the liens upon the part released that a discharge of the entire res under a like appraisal and stipulation or bond would have had upon the liens upon the whole thing.

The result of this conclusion is that there was no error in the decree of the court below. The coal and coke company was not entitled to share in the distribution of the proceeds of the bond given by the transit company on March 4, 1897, as the claimant of the engine, boilers, and machinery, because it had not filed its libel when they were discharged under that bond. The transit company had no right to share in the proceeds of that bond as the assignee of the maritime lien of the Phenix Iron Works, because it had not filed any libel to enforce that lien, nor had it pleaded the same, or made any claim upon it in any way, when the engine, boilers, and machinery were discharged under that bond on March 10, 1897. The course of the transit company was this: It appeared on March 5, 1897, and filed a claim for the engine, boilers, and machinery, in which it alleged that it was the owner thereof. On March 6, 1897, it filed a petition for leave to intervene, in which it pleaded that it had an interest in the vessel by reason of a mortgage. But it was not until May 8, 1897, that it first presented to the court below the claim that it had a maritime lien which it had derived from the Phenix Iron Works. The engine, boilers, and machinery had then been discharged under the bond of March 4, 1897, and it was too late for the transit company to present a claim to share with the libelants who were parties to the cause on March 10, 1897, in the proceeds of a bond which they had secured for their own benefit. Not only this, but the transit company was prevented from asserting such a claim as against those libelants by the fact that it had induced them to accept its bond, and to return to it the engine, boilers, and machinery, by its silence regarding the maritime lien it now urges, and by its positive averment in its claim to the property that it was the owner of it. Chase v. Driver, 92 F. 780. Moreover, the transit company did not present its claim to enforce this maritime lien in a libel or a cross-libel. It merely pleaded it in its answer. When the machinery was released by the order of March 10, 1897, it undoubtedly went back to this company, subject to all the maritime liens that had not been presented to the court below before the property was discharged. That company might have filed a libel or a cross libel, and it might have caused this machinery to be arrested upon the maritime lien it now presses. But it could not have acquired any right to enforce that lien, or to share in the distribution of the proceeds of the engine, boilers, and machinery, or in the proceeds of a bond or a stipulation taken for them by other parties, by simply setting it forth in its answer. Respondents in a libel suit are required to file a cross libel, to take out process, and have it served in the usual way, if they have maritime liens which they desire to enforce. Ward v. Chamberlain, 21 How. 572, 574 (1858). The coal and coke company pursued the proper and legal course to enforce its lien. After the machinery had been released from the liens of all the libelants who had appeared in court before March 10, 1897, it caused the engine, boilers, and machinery to be arrested upon a monition issued upon a libel against the ship and its machinery, which it filed subsequent to that date. The decree of the court below that its lien existed, and that the wrecking company and its sureties were liable upon the bond which they gave to abide by and perform the decree upon this libel, was in accordance with the rules and principles of law to which we have referred, and both the decrees below must be affirmed. It is so ordered.

4. Reduction of Claim to Judgment in Personam

Pratt v. United States

United States Court of Appeals, First Circuit, 1964.
340 F.2d 174, 1967 A.M.C. 1302.

■ Bailey Aldrich, Ct. J. This is an appeal from the granting of a summary judgment resulting in dismissal. Pratt, the appellant, received personal injuries on December 19, 1958, while a seaman aboard the F/V Sylvester F. Whalen, hereafter vessel, owned by Sylvester F. Whalen, Inc., hereafter owner. He sued the owner *in personam* in the state court in March 1959, in separate counts, under the Jones Act, 46 U.S.C.A. § 688, and because of unseaworthiness of the vessel, and for maintenance and cure. In December, 1960, he executed a general release of all claims for $3,000. The insurance policy written by the insurer defending the suit contained a $250 deductible clause, and the owner refusing to advance this sum towards the settlement, the release was voided. Instead, the insurer paid Pratt $2750 and took a covenant "to forbear to institute or press legal proceedings or in any other way make any other demand or claim against the said [insurer] * * * provided, however * * * that any and all rights and claims against the owners * * * are expressly reserved to me." Pratt continued with his suit against the owner, and in October 1962 recovered a single judgment in the amount of $8694 plus costs. This judgment is unsatisfied.

In February, 1963, the United States, a holder of a preferred mortgage on the vessel, brought a libel *in rem* in the district court to foreclose. Flood, assignee of various lienors, intervened, and so did Pratt. Pratt sought recovery *de novo* under the Jones Act ($25,000), for injury due to unseaworthiness ($25,000) and for maintenance and cure ($5,000). Alternatively he sought satisfaction of his judgment. The court ruled against him on all counts. Since he seeks to intervene as of right an appeal lies. International Mortgage & Investment Corp. v. Von Clemm, 301 F.2d 857 (2 Cir.1962).

With respect to the Jones Act the opinion of the district court pointed out that the three-year statute had run, and that, in any event, no maritime lien ever attached on account of that cause of action so as to permit a proceeding *in rem,* 46 U.S.C.A. § 688, 45 U.S.C.A. § 56, Plamals v. The Pinar Del Rio, 277 U.S. 151, 48 S.Ct. 457, 72 L.Ed. 827, 1928 A.M.C. 932 (1928). Pratt does not contest this. Unfortunately, at least superficially it compounds his troubles. Appellees, *viz.,* the United States and Flood, not unnaturally assert that all of Pratt's claims merged in the judgment, that the judgment, the more particularly because it includes a claim on which he concededly cannot recover, can support no lien, but that it destroyed the liens which previously existed. Pratt contends that he may still enforce his original liens in full or, alternatively, to the extent that the judgment represents a permitted recovery. The resolution of these issues is complicated by the fact that on the face of the judgment it cannot be told whether Pratt prevailed on one count, or two counts or three counts.[1]

Whether a judgment may create a new lien,[2] or, to some extent, is entitled to the benefit of the lien applicable to the original cause of action,[3] does not arise because appellees, the only parties presently interested in the vessel,[4] are not in privity with the owner to the extent that the judgment may be pleaded against them. Baun v. Ethel G., 125 F.Supp. 835, 15 Alaska 283, 1955 A.M.C. 374 (D.C.Alaska, 1954); Boston, 8 F. 628 (C.C.Pa.

---

1. Strictly Pratt could not have recovered, as distinguished from prevailed, on three counts, because the Jones Act count and the unseaworthiness count were, of course, in substance for the same cause of action, Baltimore S.S. Co. v. Phillips, 274 U.S. 316, 47 S.Ct. 600, 71 L.Ed. 1069, 1927 A.M.C. 946 (1927). Hence the judgment would be the same on its face whether the court had found for Pratt on the merits on the Jones Act count and against him on the unseaworthiness count, or vice versa, or in his favor on both. With respect to maintenance and cure Pratt presently alleges no dates, and since such recovery is not normally prospective, Calmar S.S. Corp. v. Taylor, 303 U.S. 525, 58 S.Ct. 651, 82 L.Ed. 993, 1938 A.M.C. 341 (1938); Farrell v. United States, 336 U.S. 511, 515–516, 69 S.Ct. 709, 93 L.Ed. 850, 1949 A.M.C. 613 (1949), the original suit may not have encompassed what he is presently seeking. See Farrell v. United States, supra, 336 U.S. 511, 515–516, 69 S.Ct. 711, 709–710, 93 L.Ed. 850, 1949 A.M.C. at 620.

2. We find no case suggesting that it does. Such a holding would seem inconsis-

tent with the principles upon which maritime liens depend. See Dampskibsselskabet Dannebrog v. Signal Oil & Gas Co., 310 U.S. 268, 280, 60 S.Ct. 937, 84 L.Ed. 1197, 1940 A.M.C. 647 (1940); Piedmont & George's Creek Coal Co. v. Seaboard Fisheries Co., 254 U.S. 1, 9, 41 S.Ct. 1, 65 L.Ed. 97 (1920); Todd Shipyards Corp. v. City of Athens, 83 F.Supp. 67, 76, 1949 A.M.C. 572 (D.C.Md.1949), aff'd sub nom. Acker v. City of Athens, 177 F.2d 961, 1950 A.M.C. 282 (4 Cir., 1949).

3. See Restatement, Judgments, sec. 47, comment d; Steinhardt v. Russian Orthodox, Catholic Mut. Aid Soc., 366 Pa. 222, 77 A.2d 393 (1951); Ulrich v. Lincoln Realty Co., 180 Or. 380, 168 P.2d 582, 175 P.2d 149 (1946); cf. Standard Oil Co. v. Y–D Supplies Co., 288 Mass. 453, 193 N.E. 66 (1934). But cf. Stapp v. Swallow, 22 Fed.Cas. p. 1082 (No. 13,305)(S.D.Ohio, 1858). If a judgment is so entitled it would raise subsidiary questions which, also, we need not consider.

4. The vessel has been sold for considerably less than appellees' liens, and the fund is now the sole *res.*

1881). In other words, so far as the present parties are concerned, Pratt's alternate claim on the judgment itself cannot be sustained. The question must be whether he is precluded as a result of these prior proceedings from going against the vessel on his counts for unseaworthiness and for maintenance and cure.

The court, without going behind the face of the judgment,[5] held that because of the election provision in the Jones Act[6] Pratt had made an election with respect to the unseaworthiness claim when he commenced his civil action in the state court and prosecuted it to final judgment. We believe this a misconception. If Pratt had initially brought only an unseaworthiness claim he could have done so simultaneously in two suits, one on the civil side,[7] and one in rem. McAfoos v. Canadian Pacific Steamships, Ltd., 243 F.2d 270, 1957 A.M.C. 982 (2 Cir.1957). See also Continental Grain Co. v. Barge FBL–585, 364 U.S. 19, 80 S.Ct. 1470, 1961 A.M.C. 1 (1960). The Jones Act election provision has given rise to a number of rulings, not all reconcilable,[8] but no court, prior to the court below, has held that it caused an unsatisfied *in personam* judgment in favor of a seaman to become a binding election. We do not believe Congress had this restrictive intent. The statute's primary purpose was to give seamen a remedy on the civil side of the court, i.e., with jury, without requiring diversity of citizenship. McCarthy v. American Eastern Corp., fn. 8, supra. We regard the phrase "at his election" solely in this sense of optional additional relief and not as imposing special limitations upon the choice.[9] Rather, the question should be what are the normal consequences of selecting one remedy instead of another.

5. On the record there was an indication of a factual issue as to what was covered by the judgment. This would prevent a summary dismissal if such issue were presently relevant.

6. "Any seaman who shall suffer personal injury in the course of his employment may, at his election, maintain an action for damages at law [in the district court] with the right of trial by jury, * * *." 46 U.S.C.A. § 688.

7. In view of Romero v. International Terminal Operating Co., 358 U.S. 354, 79 S.Ct. 468, 3 L.Ed.2d 368, 1959 A.M.C. 832 (1959), he could not have brought that separate action on the civil side of the federal court in the absence of diversity. In other words, the Jones Act election provision would not have been applicable at all.

8. In McCarthy v. American Eastern Corp., 175 F.2d 724, 726, 1953 A.M.C. 1864, 1868 (3 Cir.1949), in holding that a seaman could go to the jury on a Jones Act count and a count for unseaworthiness the court referred to the Jones Act "election" as one between a jury trial and a suit in admiralty. This caused the Second Circuit to enlarge its prior narrower view. Balado v. Lykes Bros. S.S. Co., 179 F.2d 943, 1950 A.M.C. 609 (2 Cir.1950). These decisions have led some courts to hold that an election between the civil and admiralty remedy occurred by the filing of the first suit. Murphy v. American Barge Line Co., 93 F.Supp. 653, 1951 A.M.C. 145 (W.D.Pa.1950); Jonassen v. Norwegian American Line, Inc., 105 F.Supp. 510, 1952 A.M.C.1146 (S.D.N.Y.1952). Jonassen must be taken to be overruled by McAfoos v. Canadian Pacific Steamships, supra, and we believe, properly so. See also Stalker v. Southeastern Oil Delaware, Inc., 103 F.Supp. 436 (D.C.Del.1951).

9. In fact Congress was peculiarly solicitous with regard to seamen's Rights under the Jones Act, providing as a special feature that, as in FELA cases, a suit brought in the state court could not be removed by the defendant. Pate v. Standard Dredging Corp., 193 F.2d 498, 1952 A.M.C. 287 (5 Cir.1952).

Although it has been held that a judgment *in personam* does not prevent a subsequent action against the owner's interest in the vessel *in rem,* generally, Henry S., 4 F.Supp. 953, 1933 A.M.C. 1401 (E.D.Va.1933), or at least under special circumstances, Burns Bros. v. Central R.R. of New Jersey, No. 42, 202 F.2d 910, 1953 A.M.C. 718 (2 Cir.1953), that is not this case. Whatever strength there may be in the fiction that the vessel is a separate entity, but cf. Ruiz Pichirilo v. Guzman, 290 F.2d 812, 1961 A.M.C. 1588 (1 Cir.1961), rev'd on other gr'ds 369 U.S. 698, 1962 A.M.C. 1142, in the case at bar Pratt is truly pursuing different interests. If we were to follow the analogy of joint obligors, a judgment in a joint action *in personam* precludes a further action against one individually. But an "election" to sue one of them individually generally does not preclude, even when it ripens into judgment, a separate action against the others. Lovejoy v. Murray, 70 U.S. 1, 18 L.Ed. 129 (1865); Reynolds v. New York Trust Co., 188 Fed. 611, 616, 39 L.R.A.N.S. 391 (1 Cir.1911); Cameron v. Kanrich, 201 Mass. 451, 87 N.E. 605 (1909); Restatement, Judgments, sec. 94.

A lienor is not, of course, a joint owner, and hence a true joint obligor. Nonetheless his interest is on the block so far as liability incurred by the vessel is concerned, although because of the original obligation to him he has in effect a right over against the owner. In other words, a maritime lienor is an obligor to the extent of his interests to a subsequent[10] 7 lienor, but an indemnitee with respect to the owner. Following the rules which generally apply in situations involving joint obligors between whom there is a duty of indemnification we are led to the following conclusions: (1) that by going against the owner alone Pratt was not barred from proceeding against the interests of other joint obligors, such as appellees, even by the rendition of judgment in the first action; (2) that if the judgment had been in favor of Pratt there was insufficient privity between the owner and appellees to enable the judgment to be used against the latter, cases supra; (3) but that if the judgment had been in favor of the owner, mutuality does not apply and appellees could have taken advantage of it. This last is so whether the owner is regarded simply as an indemnitor, see Restatement, Judgments, sec. 96(1)(a), or as an agent for the lienors. Id., sec. 99; see Adriaanse v. United States, 184 F.2d 968, 1950 A.M.C. 1987 (2 Cir.1950), cert. den. 340 U.S. 932, 71 S.Ct. 495, 95 L.Ed. 673, 1951 A.M.C. 582; Bruszewski v. United States, 181 F.2d 419, 1950 A.M.C. 750 (3 Cir.1950), cert. denied 340 U.S. 865, 71 S.Ct. 87, 95 L.Ed. 632; Developments in the law—Res Judicata, 65 Harv.L.Rev. 818, 862–863 (1952). Furthermore, a decision that a plaintiff may recover a certain amount is a decision that he cannot recover more. We therefore reach the additional conclusion (4) that appellees may use the judgment as a maximum limitation on Pratt's present recovery for the causes of action covered by the judgment. Restatement, Judgments, sec. 96(1), (b); Propeller East, 8 Fed.Cas., p. 265 (No. 4,251), 9 Ben. (U.S.) 76, N.D.N.Y.1877. If a question arises as to the

---

10. That questions of priority are not always simple, see National Shawmut Bank v. Winthrop, 134 F.Supp. 370, 1955 A.M.C. 2089 (D.C.Mass.1955).

interpretation of the judgment the burden should be upon appellees, who are in the position of relying on it.

The foregoing sufficiently sustains, also, Pratt's position with respect to maintenance and cure, and we need not reach certain special contentions with respect to that count.[11]

We turn, finally, to the effect of the covenant not to sue or to make a claim against the insurer, the only question in the case governed by state law, and one not reached by the district court. Since we find it hard to conceive how Pratt ever had any right to sue the insurer as such,[12] but must assume that the agreement for which the insurer paid had an intended business purpose, McMahon v. Monarch Life Ins. Co., 186 N.E.2d 827, 345 Mass. 261, 264 (1962); Restatement, Contracts, sec. 236(a); we naturally conclude that it was designed to protect the insurer's interests in some manner. Clearly it did not, and could not, as a matter of contract protect the insurer from liability to the owner, against whom Pratt's rights were expressly reserved.[13] The insurer's other interests were presumably in the vessel itself, or more exactly in the rights of the mortgagee, and possibly other lienors. The covenant did not in terms reserve Pratt's rights to proceed against the vessel. It may be wondered what value it would be to the insurer if this reservation were to be unreservedly implied. If the insurance protects the separate interests of lienors, and Pratt is free to foreclose, such a proceeding will result in a claim over against the insurer in spite of the covenant.

The question whether the covenant should be construed to permit the present action seems to us one of fact. We do not think it resolved by the circumstance that the superseded release had expressly discharged the vessel and the covenant did not. Since by the latter Pratt expressly reserved his rights against the owner it would be natural for this reservation to include, by implication, his rights against the owner's interest in the ship. To have reiterated the full discharge of the vessel would have been unduly restrictive. Consequently we suggest that it may be inappropriate to retrospect the release. Rather, the emphasis should be on whether the

---

11. We disagree with appellee's view that maintenance and cure will not support a preferred lien. 46 U.S.C.A. § 953(a). This right is, in effect, a part of the seaman's wages. Pacific S.S. Co. v. Peterson, 278 U.S. 130, 137, 49 S.Ct. 75, 73 L.Ed. 220, 1928 A.M.C. 1932, 1938 (1928); Turner v. Wilson Line of Mass. Inc., 242 F.2d 414, 417, 1957 A.M.C. 740 (1 Cir.1957); Sperbeck v. A.L. Burbank & Co., 190 F.2d 449, 452, 1952 A.M.C. 655 (2 Cir.1951).

12. The policy was not introduced, nor its terms described, but direct action is normally only by statute. See Note, Direct Action Statutes: Their Operation and Conflict-of-Law Problems, 74 Harv.L.Rev. 357 (1960).

13. We can only assume, and, indeed, do readily assume, that the insurer felt that by his failure to contribute to the advantageous settlement, the owner lost his rights against it. Even if the policy contained no express provision the insured should have a duty, which it failed to perform, corresponding to the insurer's obligation to pay its share of a reasonable offer of settlement. Murach v. Massachusetts Bonding & Ins. Co., 339 Mass. 184, 158 N.E.2d 338 (1959). See generally, Keeton, Liability Insurance and Responsibility for Settlement, 67 Harv.L.Rev. 1136 (1954).

express reservation in the covenant to sue the owner included the right to make claim against the interests of others.

Appellees' defense of laches we will not consider in advance of the district court. Czaplicki v. Hoegh Silvercloud, 351 U.S. 525, 534, 76 S.Ct. 946, 100 L.Ed. 1387, 1956 A.M.C. 1465, 1471 (1956).

Judgment will be entered vacating the judgment of the district court insofar as it granted summary judgment against appellant on his second and third causes of action and dismissed said counts, but otherwise affirming the judgment of the district court. Further proceedings to be in accordance with this opinion. Appellant to recover his costs in this court.

5. WAIVER

Newport News Shipbuilding & Dry Dock Co. v. S.S. Independence

United States District Court, Eastern District of Virginia, 1994.
872 F.Supp. 262, 1995 A.M.C. 1644.

■ ROBERT DOUMAR, D.J.

This matter comes before the Court on defendants' motion to vacate the arrest of the *S.S. Independence* in the *in rem* action named above. For the reasons outlined below, defendants' motion is denied.

Factual and Procedural Background

In or around March, 1994, defendants began seeking bids for repair work on the *S.S. Independence*, a cruise ship registered in the United States. Prior to submitting its bid, plaintiff did several shipchecks of the *Independence* to ascertain the nature and extent of the work necessary, and ultimately submitted a bid of $19,923,889.00, on or about April 4, 1994. Because the bid exceeded the amount budgeted for the project, defendants reduced the scope of the work to be done on the *Independence*. Plaintiff was hired to do the work at a contract price of $12,428,500, pursuant to a Renovation Contract dated April 29, 1994. Both Tenneco, Inc., plaintiff's parent corporation, and The Delta Queen Steamboat Co. (now "American Classic Voyages Co."), defendants' parent, issued guaranties for the performance of each of their subsidiaries under the Renovation Contract.

The Renovation Contract required (1) that the *Independence* be delivered to dry dock in Newport News on or before July 19, 1994, and (2) that work be completed on the Independence by September 21, 1994, so that defendants could meet her cruise obligations in the month of October. The contract also stipulated that time was of the essence. On July 18, 1994, defendants delivered the *Independence* to plaintiff. Almost immediately, plaintiff alleges, the shipowner began issuing change orders; ultimately, plaintiff contends, about 500 change orders were logged. Defendants counter that the contract required plaintiff to perform all essential changes, and all nonessential changes that would not impact upon the redelivery date for the vessel, and that therefore such orders were contemplated in the Renovation Contract.

On October 4, 1994, plaintiff filed a complaint with this court. In Count I of the complaint, the plaintiff lodged a claim for $29,756,090 in *rem* against the *S.S. Independence* for repairs constituting maritime necessaries within the meaning of the Federal Maritime Lien Act under general maritime law. In Count II, an action *in personam* for breach of contract, the plaintiff alleged that, with changes, plaintiff performed more than $29,765,090.00 worth of work on the *Independence*. Plaintiff alleged that these changes were so substantial as to constitute a cardinal change in the Renovation Contract—the equivalent of a breach of the contract by defendants.

Plaintiff also contended that defendants refused to pay the 95% of the base contract price due at the time the complaint was filed. Plaintiff asked the Court for an *in rem* maritime lien and arrest of the *Independence*. Plaintiff further requested that the Court assert jurisdiction over the *in personam* breach of contract action against the shipowner, but that the claim be stayed pending arbitration of the dispute pursuant to an arbitration requirement in the Renovation Contract. On October 4, 1994, this Court issued an arrest order for the S.S. Independence, and appointed plaintiff substitute custodian for the Independence. On October 7, 1994, the Court ordered the Independence released predicated on the Undertaking in Lieu of Arrest signed by the parties, which, pursuant to Local Rule of Admiralty (c)(1), substituted the sum of $29,756,090 (placed in escrow) for the vessel. On October 27, 1994, defendants filed a motion to vacate the appointment of substitute custodian and the order substituting Local Rule (c)(1) undertaking for the vessel under arrest, or in the alternative, for substitute or reduced security.

On November 2, 1994, because defendants had not filed their responsive pleadings, plaintiff petitioned the court for a default judgment. On November 3, 1994, a default was entered against defendants. However, defendants' answer was also filed (subject to defect) on November 3, 1994.[1] On that same day, defendants filed a counterclaim against plain tiff and a third-party complaint against Tenneco, Inc., plaintiff's parent corporation. On November 9, 1994, the Court heard defendants' motion to vacate the arrest of the S.S. *Independence* or, in the alternative, to lower the amount of the security held in escrow. The Court lowered the security from $29,756,090 to $20,000,000 and reserved judgment on the motion to vacate the arrest, and specifically, on the issue of whether plaintiff was entitled to a maritime lien. That motion is now ripe for consideration by the Court.

Analysis

1.   Motion to Vacate Arrest

Rule E(4)(f) of the Supplemental Federal Rules of Civil Procedure for Admiralty and Maritime Claims governs the procedure for release from

---

1. Plaintiff's motion for default judgment was denied by the Court on December 5, 1994.

arrest. It states in relevant part, "Whenever property is arrested or attached, any person claiming an interest in it shall be entitled to a prompt hearing at which the plaintiff shall be required to show why the arrest or attachment should not be vacated. . . ."

The parties agree that the plaintiff carries the burden of showing that the arrest should not be vacated, but differ on the onerousness of that standard. Defendants cite Marubeni America Corp. v. M/V Unity, 802 F.Supp. 1353, 1356 (D.Md.1992), as standing for the proposition that plaintiff bears a heavy burden. While the court in *Marubeni* recognized the hardship that an arrest of the vessel placed on the shipowner, and stated that "the party seeking to arrest a vessel must carry the burden of showing why the arrest or attachment should not be vacated," the court did not explicitly state that the burden was a heavy one. The court said only that the burden must be carried by the plaintiff.

Plaintiff argues that the plaintiff need only show "probable cause" to arrest. See Amstar Corp. v. S/S Alexandros T., 664 F.2d 904, 912 (4 Cir.1981). In Mujahid v. M/V Hector, 1991 WL 254121, 1991 U.S. App. LEXIS 28445, *4 (4 Cir.1991)(unpublished opinion), the Fourth Circuit adopted the reasoning of the Third Circuit in Salazar v. Atlantic Sun, 881 F.2d 73, 79 (3 Cir.1989), explaining that at a post-arrest hearing, the plaintiff need only show reasonable grounds for obtaining an arrest warrant for a vessel. The reasonable grounds/probable cause standard translates roughly to requiring that plaintiff show entitlement to a maritime lien. *Amstar Corp.*, 664 F.2d at 912.

This Court agrees that plaintiff need show only probable cause for arrest of a vessel, and will evaluate the arrest of the S.S. *Independence* under that standard. To carry its burden, then, plaintiff must establish that it was entitled to a maritime lien, and that therefore it had reasonable grounds or probable cause to arrest the S.S. *Independence*.

2. Entitlement to Maritime Lien

Plaintiff asserts its entitlement to a maritime lien pursuant to the Maritime Lien Act, 46 U.S.C. § 31342(a), which states in relevant part,

> (a) . . . a person providing necessaries to a vessel on the order of the owner or a person authorized by the owner—
>
> > (1) has a maritime lien on the vessel;
> >
> > (2) may bring a civil action in rem to enforce the lien; and
> >
> > (3) is not required to allege or prove in the action that credit was given to the vessel.

The term "necessaries" includes repairs, supplies, towage and the use of a dry dock or marine railway, and has been interpreted broadly to include any goods and services necessary for a vessel's continued operation. Farrell Ocean Services, Inc. v. United States, 681 F.2d 91, 92–93 (1 Cir.1982); 46 U.S.C. § 31301(4). The lien arises "from the moment of the service or occurrence that provides its basis." 1 T. Schoenbaum, *Admiralty and Maritime Law*, § 9–1, at 490 (2d ed. 1994); Equilease Corp. v. M/V

Sampson, 793 F.2d 598, 602 (5 Cir.), cert. denied, Fred S. James & Co. v. Equilease Corp., 793 F.2d 598, 602 (5 Cir.), cert. denied, Fred S. James & Co. v. Equilease Corp., 479 U.S. 984, 107 S.Ct. 570, 93 L.Ed.2d 575 (1986)(explaining that "[t]he lien arises when the debt arises...."); Trinidad Foundry & Fabricating, Ltd. v. M/V K.A.S. Camilla, 776 F.Supp. 1558, 1559 (S.D.Fla.1991), aff'd, 966 F.2d 613 (11 Cir.1992)(stating that a maritime lien "arise[s] at the moment of repair to the vessel").

An action to enforce a maritime lien *in rem* against a vessel is distinct from an action for breach of contract brought against a shipowner *in personam*. The primary right at stake in the first is the right to be compensated for services rendered; in the second, it is the right to receive the benefit of one's bargain. S.E.L. Maduro (Florida), Inc. v. M/V Antonio De Gastaneta, 833 F.2d 1477, 1482 (11 Cir.1987). To enforce its maritime lien under Count I of the complaint against the *S.S. Independence*, then, plaintiff need not prove the elements of the breach of contract action. Instead, plaintiff must show:

(1) that plaintiff performed services on the vessel;

(2) that charges for those services were reasonable;

(3) that services were "necessaries," as defined by 46 U.S.C. § 31301(4); and

(4) that the person who placed the order had the real, apparent or statutorily presumed authority to do so.

Id.

First, it is undisputed that the plaintiff performed services on the vessel; defendants admit that, at this juncture, they owe more than $13 million to the plaintiff for services rendered. Second, "necessaries," as discussed above, include "repairs, supplies, towage, and the use of a dry dock or marine railway." Since this controversy centers around repairs provided to the *S.S. Independence* while in dry dock, it is clear that at least some necessaries were provided by the plaintiff. Third, it is undisputed that the agent for defendant Great Hawaiian Properties who placed the order had the authority to do so. Finally, the Court has some doubts as to whether the original amount claimed by the plaintiff, substituted for the vessel, and placed in escrow (more than $29 million) reflected reasonable charges for necessaries as required by parts 2 & 3 of the test (as part of that figure reflected profits and charges for delay). Nonetheless, the Court finds that the reduced escrow of $20 million is, considering the scope of the work performed by the plaintiff, a reasonable amount to secure the necessary services performed and to substitute for the ship. Therefore, the Court finds that plaintiff has satisfied the test for showing entitlement to a maritime lien.

Defendants have raised a number of defenses to the enforcement of the statutory lien arising under the Renovation Contract, including lack of existence of a current debt, and failure to exhaust administrative procedures and remedies provided in the contract. Additionally, defendants assert that plaintiff waived its right to a maritime lien. As explained above, however, the contract claims are in personam claims and are distinct from the in rem claim contested here, and the contractual defenses are therefore inapplicable.[2] Only the waiver argument carries any weight.

The Maritime Lien Act does not preclude the waiver of the right to obtain a lien. 46 U.S.C. § 31305. Waiver can be either express or by implication. W.A. Marshall & Co. v. S.S. President Arthur, 279 U.S. 564, 568, 49 S.Ct. 420, 421, 73 L.Ed. 846 (1929). However, "waiver is not favored, and the courts will require a clearly manifested intention to forgo the lien." 1 T. Schoenbaum, *Admiralty and Maritime Law*, § 9–7, at 512 (2d ed 1994), citing Nacirema Operating Co. v. The S.S. Al Kulsum, 407 F.Supp. 1222 (S.D.N.Y.1975). In fact, "a presumption arises that one furnishing [necessaries] to a vessel acquires a maritime lien...." *Equilease*, 793 F.2d at 605; General Electric Credit & Leasing Corp. v. Drill Ship Mission Exploration, 668 F.2d 811, 814 (5 Cir.1982); but see Itel Containers International Corp. v. Atlanttrafik Express Service Ltd., 982 F.2d 765, 768 (2 Cir.1992)("As a general rule, maritime liens are disfavored by the law."). The party attacking the lien under a waiver theory bears the burden of presenting clear and affirmative proof that the lien was waived. Ramsay Scarlett & Co., Inc. v. S.S. Koh Eun, 462 F.Supp. 277, 285 (E.D.Va.1978).

Defendants contend that (1) plaintiff expressly waived its right to a lien in the Renovation Contract; (2) plaintiff impliedly waived its lien by accepting defendants' corporate guaranty for contract performance; and (3) plaintiff waived its right to a lien by failing to reserve that right when it contracted to accept defendants' corporate guaranty.

Part III, § 6 of the Renovation Contract states,

> Shipyard shall discharge any and all liens asserted by suit or other filings against the Vessel by any vendor, subcontractor or employee of Shipyard for payment of any purchase price or wage for Contract Work items furnished by Shipyard, except any such liens as are contested in good faith by Shipyard and for which Shipyard provides any required bond or other security.

The vice president of plaintiff Newport News Shipbuilding signed the complaint in this proceeding. Defendants characterize that action as a suit by an employee against the vessel, which must be discharged by plaintiff, as set forth in Part III, § 6 of the Renovation Contract. Going forward with obtaining the lien, defendants argue, is a breach of the contract. However, as the Court indicated during oral argument, to claim that a corporate officer acting on behalf of the corporation (for instance, by executing and authorizing the filing of a complaint) is acting on behalf of himself, as

---

2. Defendants rely heavily on Veverica v. Drill Barge Buccaneer No. 7, 1974 AMC 26, 488 F.2d 880 (5 Cir.1974) to support their argument that plaintiff had no right to enforce its lien until payment was due and owing and until contractual arrangements had been honored. Despite whatever weight this case may carry, however, defendants miss the crucial point: that the lien asserted by plaintiff is a statutory rather than a contractual lien, and that the provisions of the Renovation Contract, in the absence of a waiver of the right to a statutory lien, do not govern the operation of the statutory lien.

contemplated by Part III, § 6, of the Renovation Contract, is specious. The Court rejects the argument that plaintiff violated an express lien waiver by filing the complaint in this action.[3]

Secondly, defendants argue that plaintiff waived its lien by accepting defendants' corporate guaranty. In *S.S."President Arthur"*, the Supreme Court recognized that making alternative security arrangements could serve to waive a lien for necessaries. 279 U.S. at 570–71. Citing that case, defendants assert that reliance on other sources to secure performance under the Renovation Contract also served to waive the lien.

However, it should be recognized that "... *The President Arthur* did not open the door very wide. Lienors have been favoured in the U.S. and in consequence a waiver of lien has required clear, overt acts, when it was not express." Tetley, *Maritime Liens and Claims*, at 510 (1985). Moreover, "... the taking of other security has usually not been held to be a waiver of the lien." Id. at 512. To overcome the presumption in favor of a lien, the defendant must show that the plaintiff relied solely on the corporate guaranty and took affirmative actions that manifested plaintiff's clear and purposeful intention to forgo the lien. *Equilease Corp.*, 793 F.2d at 606; *Farrell Ocean Services, Inc.*, 681 F.2d at93–94; *General Electric Credit & Leasing Corp*, 668 F.2d at 814. The Court finds that the acceptance of a corporate guaranty in this instance was standard procedure for both parties to this contract, and was not the type of clear, overt, and purposeful act necessary to waive a lien.

Finally, defendants contend that because plaintiff has not expressly reserved the right to a lien, it has waived that right. Defendants rely on Dampskibsselskabet Dannebrog v. Signal Oil & Gas Co., 310 U.S. 268, 277, 60 S.Ct. 937, 942, 84 L.Ed. 1197 (1940) to support this proposition. However, that case, in the course of summarizing an earlier case's holding, states only that where the right to a lien was expressly reserved, no waiver would be found. It does not require that plaintiff expressly reserve the right to a lien.

In fact, if the Court followed the defendants' logic, a ship repair facility would almost never be entitled to a maritime lien. In every instance in which necessaries are provided to a ship, an authorized individual must authorize the ship repair facility to provide services or make repairs. That authorization, whether oral or written, is necessarily a contract. Most contracts for the repair of vessels are small in nature and involve small shipyards which operate primarily on an oral basis and do not rely on written contracts prepared by experienced attorneys. If in every such contract the provider of services was required to expressly reserve its right to a maritime lien, the protections afforded by the Federal Maritime Lien Act would be eviscerated, especially in cases involving small ship repair operations like those described above. Accordingly, the Court rejects the

---

3. The Court makes no finding as to whether Part 111, § 6 of the Renovation Contract constitutes an express waiver of a maritime lien, for even if the section did waive contractual liens, plaintiff would still be entitled to a statutory lien, as discussed above.

defendants' argument that failure to expressly reserve the right to a maritime lien amounts to a waiver of the lien. The shipyard can waive such a right, but it must clearly and unequivocally do so.

Plaintiff has shown its entitlement to a maritime lien, and plaintiff therefore had probable cause to arrest the vessel. Defendants have not shown by clear and affirmative proof that plaintiff waived its right to a maritime lien. Therefore, the motion to vacate the arrest of the *S.S. Independence* is denied. Conclusion The defendants' motion to vacate the arrest of the *S.S. Independence* is denied.

Conclusion

The defendant's motion to vacate the arrest of the S.S. *Independence* is denied.

N O T E

The taking of collateral security does not constitute a waiver of a lien. See Point Landing, Inc. v. Alabama Dry Dock & Shipbuilding Co., 261 F.2d 861, 1959 A.M.C. 148 (5th Cir.1958). See also The Crustacea, supra, p. 486.

For a case in which a lienholder relinquished his lien by contract in consideration of an immediate payment of part of the claim, retaining a claim under Chapter XI of the Bankruptcy Act, see American A. & B. Coal Corp. v. Leonardo Arrivabene, S.A., 280 F.2d 119, 1962 A.M.C. 2666 (2d Cir.1960).

6. LACHES

Usher v. M/V Ocean Wave

United States Court of Appeals, Ninth Circuit, 1994.
27 F.3d 370, 1994 A.M.C. 2143.

■ PER CURIAM:

On December 27, 1988 Robert Usher was injured while working as a longshoreman aboard the M/V *Yuhoh* (now the M/V *Ocean Wave*). On November 12, 1991, two years and eleven months later, Robert Usher and his wife Kristi filed this action *in rem* against the *Ocean Wave* seeking damages for Robert's physical injuries and Kristi's loss of consortium. The district court dismissed both claims as barred by laches and Kristi's claim on the additional ground there was no maritime lien and therefore no *in rem* jurisdiction for a claim of loss of consortium. The Ushers argue the court erred in (1) applying the doctrine of laches rather than the three-year limitations provided in 46 U.S.C. app. § 763a and in (2) concluding it had no *in rem* jurisdiction over Kristi Usher's maritime claim for loss of consortium. We reverse and remand.

Before 1980, there was no uniform statute of limitations for maritime claims. Claims for personal injuries at sea were governed by the three year period provided in the Jones Act, 46 U.S.C. App. § 688. Claims for death on the high seas, whether in personam or in rem, were governed by the two-year period provided in former 46 U.S.C. App. § 763.[1] Other claims, including claims for injuries occurring within state territorial waters, were governed by the equitable doctrine of laches. King v. Alaska Steamship Co., 431 F.2d 994, 996 (9 Cir.1970). In 1980, Congress adopted § 763a, providing a uniform three year statute of limitations for maritime personal injury and wrongful death claims. The district court concluded, and *Ocean Wave* argues, § 763a was intended to apply only to in personam actions and the timeliness of *in rem* actions is still to be determined by application of the doctrine of laches.

"A court's objective when interpreting a federal statute is to ascertain the intent of Congress and to give effect to legislative will." Turner v. McMahon, 830 F.2d 1003, 1007 (9 Cir.1987)(citations and internal quotations omitted). The language and legislative history of § 763a indicate Congress intended the three–year limitations period established by that section to apply to all maritime personal injury claims, including *in rem* actions previously governed by the doctrine of laches.

The words of § 763a are general. They draw no distinction between suits in personam and in rem:

> Unless otherwise specified by law, a suit for recovery of damages for personal injury or death, or both, arising out of a maritime tort, shall not be maintained unless commenced within three years from the date the cause of action accrued.

46 U.S.C. App. § 763a.

The legislative history affirms Congress's intention to establish a uniform period of limitations for all suits on maritime torts,[2] and to end reliance on the doctrine of laches.[3] "The stated intent of the legislation is to provide a uniform statute of limitations period for *all* maritime torts. In particular, Congress was concerned with eliminating the uncertainty caused by reliance upon the doctrine of laches to set the time limit for bringing the suit . . ." Friel v. Cessna Aircraft Co., 751 F.2d 1037,1038 (9

---

1. This statute applied only where death occurred outside a state's territorial waters.

2. See H.R. Rep. No. 96–737, 96th Cong., 2nd Sess. 1 (1980), reprinted in 1980 U.S.C.C.A.N. 3303 ("The purpose of the legislation is to establish a uniform national statute of limitations for maritime torts"); 123 Cong. Rec. 2591 (1980)(statement of Rep. Murphy)("The bill . . . would establish a uniform statute of limitation for actions seeking compensation for injury or death resulting from a maritime tort"); id. at 2592 (statement of Rep. Dornan)("The purpose of [the bill] is to establish a uniform statute of limitations for maritime torts."). See also H.R. Rep. No. 96–737, 96th Cong., 2nd Sess. at 4; 1980 U.S.C.C.A.N. at 3306 (Departmental Report, Secretary of Transportation)(The bill is

"to provide for a uniform national three-year statute of limitations in actions to recover damages for personal injury or death, arising out of a maritime tort . . .").

3. Cong. Rec. S26,884 (1980)(statement of Sen. Cannon)("By establishing a uniform 3–year statute of limitation for personal injury or death arising out of a maritime tort, [the bill] would eliminate the 'laches' issue and therefore end existing confusion"). See also H.R. Rep. No. 96–737, 96th Cong., 2nd Sess. at 3; 1980 U.S.C.C.A.N. at 3305 (Departmental Report, U.S. Department of Justice)("The bill would apply a specific 3–year statute of limitation to those maritime tort actions currently governed by the doctrine of laches").

Cir.1985)(citation omitted)(emphasis in original). Sponsors of the legislation in both the House and the Senate identified applications of the
"indefinite common law" doctrine of laches to some personal injury claims
as the source of the uncertainty, inconsistency and unpredictability leading
to forum shopping and presentation of stale claims which the uniform
statute of limitations was designed to eliminate. 123 Cong. Rec. 2591–92
(Feb. 11,1980), (statements by Rep. Murphy and Rep. Dornan); Cong. Rec.
526,884 (1980)(statement by Senator Cannon). Excepting *in rem* proceedings from the uniform statute of limitations would have perpetuated the
problem the statute was expressly changed to eliminate.

It follows that the Ushers' personal injury claims are not subject to the
doctrine of laches, but rather to the three–year limitations period established by § 763a. The authorities on which *Ocean Wave* relies are not to
the contrary. Induron Corp. v. M/V AIGIANIS, 1990 AMC 1398 (D.N.J.
1989), was not a personal injury action. Trivizas v. Tanjong Shipping Co.,
1982 AMC 2520 (S.D.N.Y.1982), was brought before § 763a was passed.

II

In Sea-Land Services, Inc. v. Gaudet, 414 U.S. 573, 94 S.Ct. 806, 39 L.Ed.2d
9 (1974), the Supreme Court held the right to bring a maritime action for
wrongful death under Moragne v. States Marine Lines, 398 U.S. 375, 90
S.Ct. 1772, 26 L.Ed.2d 339 (1970), see G. Gilmore & C. Black, *The Law of
Admiralty*, § 9–20 n.95 ("No doubt the action for wrongful death under the
general maritime law created by [*Moragne*] carries lien status"), encompasses the right of a decedent's widow to recover for loss of consortium,
and the Fifth Circuit has treated as within its *in rem* jurisdiction actions
brought under *Gaudet*. See Sincere Navigation Corp. v. United States, 547
F.2d 255 (5 Cir.1977)(No suggestion of problem with *in rem* jurisdiction
over claim for loss of consortium in wrongful death action); Matter of S/S
Helena, 529 F.2d 744 (5 Cir.1976)(same).

Recognition of a lien for claims under *Gaudet* is consistent with this
court's statement that " '[t]he only liens recognized today are those created
by statute and those historically recognized in maritime law.' " Melwire
Trading Co. v. M/V Cape Antibes, 1987 AMC 1217, 1219, 811 F.2d 1271,
1273 (9 Cir.)(citations omitted), amended on other grounds, 1990 AMC 608,
830 F.2d 1083 (9 Cir.1987). Courts have long recognized liens in connection with maritime personal injury claims generally, The Anaces, 93 Fed.
240 (4 Cir.1899); The Christobal Colon, 44 Fed. 803, 804 (E.D.Pa.1890);
The General De Sonis, 179 Fed. 123, 126 (W.D.Wash.1910); Gilmore &
Black at § 9–20 n.95, and *Gaudet* makes clear a claim for loss of consortium due to wrongful death fits squarely within the category of maritime
personal injury claims. In American Export Lines v. Alvez, 446 U.S. 274,
276, 100 S.Ct. 1673, 1674, 64 L.Ed.2d 284 (1980), the Supreme Court
extended the right of recovery for loss of consortium to the wife of a
longshoreman who was injured but not killed, and the Fifth Circuit has
recognized the existence of a maritime lien for such claims. See Mallard v.
Aluminum Co. of Canada, 634 F.2d 236, 239 n.2 (5 Cir.1981)(Reversing

dismissal of *in rem* action for loss of consortium under *Alvez*).   Allowing lien for claims under *Alvez* is appropriate for the same reasons allowing a lien for claims under *Gaudet* is appropriate.   Both claims are for compensation for physical injuries and the right to such compensation has long been protected by a lien under general maritime law.

Denying such a lien would be contrary to the premise of *Alvez* that claims for loss of consortium arising out of fatal and non–fatal injuries are to be treated equally under maritime law.   In recognizing a cause of action for loss of consortium based on non–fatal injuries, the Court pointed out that general maritime law provides the basis for recovery or both personal injury and wrongful death, and concluded "there is no apparent reason to differentiate between fatal and nonfatal injuries in authorizing the recovery of damages."   446 U.S. at 281.[4]   Similarly, since maritime law provides a lien to protect a widow's right under maritime law to recover for loss of consortium due to the wrongful death of her husband, there is no apparent justification for denying the same protection for loss of consortium due to injuries not resulting in death.

Melwire Trading Co. and Hunley v. Ace Maritime Corp., 927 F.2d 493 (9 Cir.1991), are not to the contrary.   *Melwire Trading Co.* merely refused to recognize a lien for breach of a shipping contract where the breach caused no physical damages to the cargo.   811 F.2d at 1274.   Robert Usher, in contrast, suffered physical injuries historically recognized as a basis for recovery under maritime law.   Similarly, Hunley refused to extend the lien to a claim for punitive damages on the ground that the lien "is only as security for actual damages for the wrong done, for which the ship herself is bound to make compensation."   927 F.2d at 496 (quoting The William H. Bailey, 103 Fed. 799 (D.Conn.1900), aff'd, 111 Fed. 1006 (2 Cir.1901)).   Kristi Usher, in contrast, claims compensation for actual damage she suffered—loss of consortium—due to the injuries suffered by Robert Usher.

Ocean Wave suggests the Fifth Circuit's statement in Overstreet v. Water Vessel Norkong, 706 F.2d 641 (5 Cir.1983), that "[w]e are urged to expand an ancient remedy to accommodate a new right," Id. at 642, implies the lien should not be recognized for claims under *Alvez*. However, *Overstreet* addressed only whether the wife of an injured seaman could intervene in an action against the vessel.   In affirming the denial of the wife's motion to intervene, the court specifically left open whether a maritime lien was available in connection with her claim for loss of consortium.   Id. at 645.   We recognize that a maritime lien is an extraordinary remedy which should be allowed sparingly because it "is not a matter of public record," *Melwire Trading Co.*, 811 F.2d at 1274, and attaches to the vessel without

---

4.   *Ocean Wave* offers the comment that the "continued vitality of *Alvez* is doubtful" in light of the Supreme Court's recent holding in Miles v. Apex Marine Corp., 498 U.S. 19, 111 S.Ct. 317, 112 L.Ed.2d 275 (1990), that families of seamen have no maritime cause of action for loss of consortium because remedies for torts against seamen are now governed exclusively by the Jones Act, but *Ocean Wave* does not rely on this speculation as a ground for refusing to recognize a maritime lien in connection with the claim for loss of consortium which presently exists under *Alvez*.

notice. However, this is a characteristic of all maritime liens. Secrecy alone does not justify allowing the remedy for some types of maritime personal injury claims but not for others that are indistinguishable by reason or authority.

Reversed and remanded.

NOTE

In actions in personam § 763a is applied whether the action is brought under the admiralty jurisdiction, or diversity. Mendez v. Ishikawajima–Harima Heavy Industries Co., Ltd., 52 F.3d 799, 1995 A.M.C. 1233 (9th Cir.1995), reversing the dismissal of a longshore worker's suit under the one-year state tort statute.

Prior to the enactment of § 763(a), Jones Act cases were subject to the three-year FELA statute of limitations, but actions for unseaworthiness were ruled by laches. Since these two claims are traditionally brought in the same action, this disparity in treatment produced some confusion. Section 763a has gone a long way to eliminate such confusion. Are there still pockets? A claim for damages for wrongful refusal to pay maintenance and cure sounds in tort and is governed by the three-year statute of limitations. A claim for maintenance and cure, on the other hand, is considered contractual and is governed by laches. See Lightfoot v. F/V ARCTIC STORM, 1994 A.M.C. 2460, 1994 WL 615113 (W.D.Wash.1994).

The statute applies only to personal injuries. Collision cases remain governed by laches. See, e.g., Windjammer Cruises, Inc. v. Paradise Cruises, Ltd., 1994 A.M.C. 1282, 1993 WL 732431 (D.Hawai'i 1993), in which it was held that an action by one cruise line against another arising out of an incident in which two cruise ships backed into each other was not barred although it was brought four years after the occurrence and two years after the analogous statute of limitations. The court found that the defendants showed no prejudice.

A class action for wages and penalty wages charging a fraudulent scheme under which the employer deducted 10% of seamen's wages for foreign taxes charged for working off their coasts, when no such taxes existed and no money payed, was governed by laches and a delay of six months was not unreasonable. Guenther v. Sedco, Inc., 866 F.Supp. 786, 1995 A.M.C. 1083 (S.D.N.Y.1994).

And laches still rule service contracts. See, e.g., Galehead, Inc. v. M/V Fratzis M., 1994 A.M.C. 1160, 1994 WL 251192 (S.D.Fla.1994), an action against a vessel for services provided on the unauthorized order of a charterer was permitted after two years, although in the meanwhile the vessel had been sold to an innocent purchaser. The court found that the supplier had diligently sought to collect its debt. Due to the circumstances, however, it used its discretion to deny prejudgment interest.

In addition to 46 U.S.C.A. § 763a, there are several admiralty statutes of limitation.

COGSA claims for loss or damage to goods shipped must be brought within one year after the goods are delivered or ought to have been delivered. 46 U.S.C.App. § 1303(d).

Salvage claims must be brought within two years from the date on which the assistance or salvage was rendered. 46 U.S.C.App. § 730.

Actions in rem of certain fishermen on law arrangements must be brought within six months after the sale of the fish. 46 U.S.C.A. § 10602. And contract clauses similarly limiting the time for suits in personam have been upheld. Fuller v. Golden Age Fisheries, 14 F.3d 1405, 1994 A.M.C. 1275 (9th Cir.1994).

Suits against the United States under the Suits in Admiralty Act and the Public vessels Act must be brought within two years. 46 U.S.C.App. § 745.

Where the doctrine of laches applies, the court looks to applicable state or foreign statutes of limitation as an initial measure of the period before a claim in admiralty is barred by laches. See, e.g., The S.S. Percy Jordan, 1968 A.M.C. 2195 (S.D.N.Y.1968), where the court held that the measure in a case against underwriters to enforce undertakings to pay general average contributions against cargo delivered in Japan would be the one year Japanese statute of limitations, not the three or six year statutes of New York. The court went on to state:

"Of course, the Japanese statute is to be applied only as an analogy, and we must now consider whether or not plaintiff has been guilty of laches. Since suit was commenced six months after the end of the one-year period, the burden is upon the plaintiff to demonstrate both a reasonable excuse for its own delay as well as the absence of prejudice to the defendant. Larios v. Victory Carriers, Inc., 316 F.2d 63, 1963 A.M.C. 1704 (2d Cir.1963). Plaintiff here argues that the delay of eighteen months after the completion of the general average adjustment and six months after expiration of the limitations period was reasonable because during that entire time the parties and counsel were conferring and exchanging correspondence concerning the validity of the assessment of contributions against defendants. Much of that correspondence is attached to the motion papers. From the letters dated May 23, 1966, September 1, 1966, March 27, 1967, and August 28, 1967, it seems clear that there is at least an issue of fact as to whether the delay was reasonable. Proof of what transpired in the interstices between these letters would be particularly helpful. Furthermore, as to the question of prejudice to defendants, it seems that most, if not all, of the witnesses who will be able to testify on the circumstances of the voyage giving rise to the general average, as well as the general average adjusters, are within the control of the plaintiff and can be produced.

"As a general rule, the question of laches is essentially one of fact addressed to the discretion of the trial court. Gardner v. Panama R. Co., 342 U.S. 29, 72 S.Ct. 12, 96 L.Ed. 31, 1951 A.M.C. 2048 (1951); Molnar v. Gulfcoast Transit Co., 371 F.2d 639, 1967 A.M.C. 1925 (5th Cir.1967); McConville v. Florida Towing Corp., 321 F.2d 162, 1963 A.M.C. 1456 (5th Cir.1963). Where, as here, the motion papers indicate a genuine question of fact and there is a substantial possibility that the party having the burden of proof on delay and prejudice will be able to sustain it, determination of the issue should await trial. Alberts v. American President Lines, Ltd., 207 F.Supp. 666 (S.D.N.Y.1962)."

7. FORECLOSURE OF MARITIME LIENS AFTER INITIATION OF INSOLVENCY PROCEEDINGS

United States v. LeBouf Bros. Towing Co., Inc.

United States District Court, Eastern District of La., 1985.
45 B.R. 887, 1985 A.M.C. 1956.

■ MOREY L. SEAR, D.J.:

The United States brought this action *in rem* against four vessels owned by defendant, LeBouf Bros. Towing Co., Inc. ("LeBouf") to foreclose on a preferred ship mortgage. Two vessels were arrested in December of 1983 and two in January of 1984. On August 16, 1984, I granted partial summary judgment in favor of the United States recognizing the preferred ship mortgage.

On motion of the United States, I ordered on September 21, 1984 that the vessels be sold as soon as practicable. Sale of the vessels was scheduled for November 8, 1984. However, on November 5, 1984, LeBouf filed a petition in the Bankruptcy Court of this district for reorganization under Chapter 11 of the Bankruptcy Code and filed into the record of this case a notice of automatic stay provided in section 362(a) of the Bankruptcy Code, 11 U.S.C. sec. 362(a).

Thereafter, LeBouf moved that the order of sale be revoked in light of the automatic stay. The United States opposed the stay and argued that the sale should proceed. Nevertheless, it agreed on November 7, 1984 that the sale should be continued until after both parties had the opportunity to submit memoranda on the effect of the automatic stay under the Bankruptcy Code on this admiralty proceeding.

The United States argues that the vessels should be sold pursuant to my order and offers several theories in support of its argument. The government first contends that the bankruptcy court and the district court have concurrent jurisdiction over the vessels in this case, and the question of which court should exercise jurisdiction over the vessels is properly resolved on the theory of first come, first served. In other words, the United States asserts that because the district court was the first court to exercise jurisdiction over LeBouf's boats, it alone should exercise its jurisdiction over them, disregard the automatic stay and order that the sale of the boats proceed. In the alternative, the United States maintains that even if the automatic stay is effective, the reference by the district court of the LeBouf reorganization proceeding to the bankruptcy judge should be withdrawn and the stay as to LeBouf's vessels revoked.[1]

LeBouf contends that the United States' theory of first come, first served is incorrect and that the automatic stay pursuant to sec. 362 of the Bankruptcy Code prevents the sale of its boats from proceeding. LeBouf also argues that neither the reference nor the stay should be revoked because there has been no showing that the interests of the United States will not be properly protected in the bankruptcy proceeding.

I. *Stays Under the Bankruptcy Act of 1898*

Under the Bankruptcy Act of 1898, as amended, whether a district court could continue to exercise jurisdiction over the property of a debtor after initiation of an action in a bankruptcy court was dependent on whether the bankruptcy action was for liquidation, or reorganization or arrangement of

---

1. Pursuant to section 104(a) of the Bankruptcy Amendments and Federal Judgeship Act of 1984, Pub.L. No. 98–353, 1984 U.S.Code Cong. & Ad.News (98 Stat.) 340 (to be codified at 28 U.S.C. sec. 157(a)), and the Order of Reference of Bankruptcy Cases and Proceedings of this district, all cases arising under the Bankruptcy Code are referred automatically to the bankruptcy judges.

the debtor.   The Act provided that approval of a petition for reorganization operated as an automatic stay of any prior pending bankruptcy, mortgage foreclosure, equity receivership or lien enforcement proceeding.   Section 148 of the Bankruptcy Act, 11 U.S.C. sec. 548 (repealed October 1, 1979). The Act also permitted the bankruptcy court to stay these proceedings prior to approval of a petition for reorganization.   See sec. 113 of the Bankruptcy Act, 11 U.S.C. sec. 513 (repealed October 1, 1979).   At least one district court in an admiralty proceeding involving a debtor's property respected the automatic stay arising from a bankruptcy court's approval of the debtor's petition in a reorganization case.   In re J.S. Gissel & Co., 238 F.Supp. 130 (S.D.Tex.1965).   See generally Landers, The Shipowner Becomes a Bankrupt, 39 U.Ch.L.Rev. 490, 509 (1972).

Section 11 of the Act provided that:

> "A suit which is founded upon a claim from which a discharge [in bankruptcy] would be a release, and which is pending at the time of the filing of a petition by or against him, shall be stayed until an adjudication or dismissal of the petition."   11 U.S.C. sec. 29 (repealed October 1, 1979).

In contrast to the automatic stay under sec. 148 of the Act, this stay was not automatic.   It required the debtor to seek an order from the district court specifically enjoining the prosecution of the suit.   This automatic provision applied with equal force to liquidation and arrangements proceedings.   See sec. 314 of the Bankruptcy Act, 11 U.S.C. sec. 714 (repealed October 1, 1979).   Nevertheless, where the action in the bankruptcy court was for liquidation of the debtor, the first court to exercise jurisdiction over the debtor's property continued to exercise jurisdiction— notwithstanding the later filing of a bankruptcy petition.

For example, in Wong Shing v. M/V Mardina Trader, 564 F.2d 1183 (5 Cir.1977), the Fifth Circuit considered the decision of the district judge in the Canal Zone to sell a vessel in disregard of a temporary restraining order issued by the District Court for the Northern District of Illinois.   The ship had been arrested in the Canal Zone on June 6, 1974 and on July 15, 1974, the Canal Zone court ordered that it be sold on July 30, 1974.   A trustee for the benefit of the creditors of the ship's owners was appointed, apparently by the Illinois District Court, on July 13, 1974.   The Illinois court, on motion of the trustee, issued on July 29, 1974 a temporary order restraining the United States Marshal in the Canal Zone from selling the vessel. The Canal Zone court, however, ordered the United States Marshal to disregard the order and to proceed with the sale.   The Fifth Circuit affirmed, finding that the Illinois court lacked jurisdiction over the vessel to restrain its sale:

> "When a court of competent jurisdiction takes possession of property through its officers, that property is withdrawn from the jurisdiction of all other courts.   Where the jurisdiction of a court, and the right of a plaintiff to prosecute his suit in it, have attached, that right cannot be arrested or taken away by proceedings in another court."   Id. at 1188.

The result reached—that the stay did not prevent the sale—was consistent with the existing case law.

A more accurate portrayal of the jurisprudence under the Bankruptcy Act, however, is Atlantic Richfield Co. v. Good Hope Refineries, Inc., 1980 AMC 470, 604 F.2d 865 (5 Cir.1979).   In that case, the Fifth Circuit reviewed the Florida district court's decision to proceed with determination of the merits of an *in rem* admiralty action despite the order of the United States District Court for the District of Massachusetts issued in an arrangement proceeding which enjoined the prosecution of actions against GHR.[2] The admiralty action was to assert a lien against cargo for demurrage.   The Fifth Circuit found that the *res* at issue was a bond issued by the surety and that the admiralty court had limited the action before it to determine the liability of the surety on the bond.   Because the surety's bond was never property of the bankrupt or its estate, the Fifth Circuit held that it was not property protected by the stay order.

The Fifth Circuit discussed stay orders issued in bankruptcy actions and concluded that admiralty proceedings involving the debtor's property were stayed only where the bankruptcy proceeding was an arrangement or reorganization and not a liquidation.   The court observed that because the goal of a reorganization is "to achieve the continuation of the debtor's enterprise * * * it is essential to marshal [in the bankruptcy court] all assets of that business necessary to its rehabilitation whether or not those assets are subject to liens."   Id. 1980 AMC at 473–74, 604 F.2d at 869. The court found that because liquidation of a debtor involves only liquidation of the debtor's estate and distribution of the assets, there was no similar need to have the entire liquidation accomplished by the bankruptcy court.   Thus, the court found that the practice of first come, first served applied in liquidations not because the bankruptcy court lacked jurisdiction over the property, but because the practice was:

> "a practical means of resolving the conflict between courts of concurrent jurisdiction by allowing the court that first secures custody of the property to proceed with the action without interference."   Id. 1980 AMC at 473, 604 F.2d at 869 (emphasis added).

Distinguishing between liquidations and reorganizations in this way, however, ignores that the goal of bankruptcy law regarding liquidation is to ensure a fair distribution of the debtor's assets.   If a court proceeds with an *in rem* admiralty action after a petition for liquidation has been filed, the rights of the debtor's creditors may not be adequately represented in the admiralty action.   Indeed, if a vessel were sold in an admiralty action, the plaintiff could potentially recover a greater proportion—perhaps even 100 percent—of his claim against the debtor than could other secured or unsecured creditors.   Holders of claims cognizable in admiralty would effectively be granted a priority in the liquidation of the debtor superior even to that of the holders of other secured claims.

2.   An "arrangement" proceeding was provided for under Chapter 11 of the Bankruptcy Act of 1898 and was designed primarily to permit extension of the time for payment by the debtor of his unsecured debts. The provision of Chapter 11 of the Act, together with those of Chapters 10 (pertaining to reorganizations) and 12 (real property arrangements) were consolidated in the 1978 Bankruptcy Code as Chapter 11 (reorganizations).

II.   *Stays Under the Bankruptcy Code, 11 U.S.C. Sec. 101 et seq.*

The disparity between treatment of liquidations and reorganizations existing under the Bankruptcy Act was eliminated by the Bankruptcy Reform Act of 1978 which established the Bankruptcy Code.   The plain language of the automatic stay provision of the Bankruptcy Code applies equally to liquidations and reorganizations:

> "[A] petition filed under [the Bankruptcy Code] * * * [o]perates as a stay, applicable to all entities, of—
>
>> (1) the commencement or continuation, including the issuance or employment of process, of a judicial, administrative, or other action or proceeding against the debtor that was or could have been commenced before the commencement of the case under this title, or to recover a claim against the debtor that arose before the commencement of the case under this title;
>>
>> (2) the enforcement, against the debtor or against property of the estate, of a judgment obtained before the commencement of the case under this title;
>>
>> * * *
>>
>> (4) any act to create, perfect, or enforce any lien against property of the estate."   11 U.S.C. sec. 362(a).

Moreover, the Reports of the House and Senate Judiciary Committees evidence the intent of Congress that the automatic stay apply to all actions automatically.   The Senate Report provides that "the scope of [the stay] is broad.   All proceedings are stayed, including arbitration, administrative and judicial proceedings."   S.Rep. (Judiciary Committee) No. 989, 95th Cong., 2d Sess., reprinted in 1978 U.S.Code Cong. & Ad.News 5836.

The House Report declares a similar intent:

> "The automatic stay is one of the fundamental debtor protections provided by the bankruptcy laws.   It gives the debtor a breathing spell from his creditors.   It stops all collection efforts, all harassment, and all foreclosure actions.   It permits the debtor to attempt a repayment or reorganization plan, or simply to be relieved of the financial pressures that drove him into bankruptcy.

> "The automatic stay also provides creditor protection.   Without it, certain creditors would be able to pursue their own remedies against the debtor's property.   Those who acted first would obtain payment of the claims in preference to and to the detriment of other creditors.   Bankruptcy is designed to provide an orderly liquidation procedure under which all creditors are treated equally.   A race of diligence by creditors for the debtor's assets prevents that.

> "Subsection (a) defines the scope of the automatic stay, by listing the acts that are stayed by the commencement of the case.   The commencement or continuation, including the issuance of process, of a judicial, administrative, or other proceeding against the debtor that was or could have been commenced before the commencement of the bankruptcy case is stayed under paragraph (1).   The scope of this paragraph is broad.   All proceedings are stayed, including arbitration, license revocation, administrative,

and judicial proceedings. Proceedings in this sense encompass civil actions as well, and all proceedings even if they are not before government tribunals." H.Rep. (Judiciary Committee) No. 595, 95th Cong., 2d Sess., reprinted in U.S.Code Cong. & Ad.News 6296–97.

Congress certainly intended, and the statute clearly provides, that the automatic stay effected by sec. 362 prevent all post-petition executions on a debtor's property; consequently the sale of LeBouf's boats in this action cannot proceed.

III. *Withdrawal of Reference*

The Bankruptcy Amendments and Federal Judgeship Act of 1984, Pub.L. No. 98–3531, 1984 U.S.Code Cong. & Ad.News (98 Stat.) 333 (to be codified in scattered sections of 28 U.S.C. and 11 U.S.C.)(the "1984 Amendments"), amended, *inter alia,* the provisions of title 28 United States Code regarding jurisdiction of bankruptcy proceedings. Section 157(d) of title 28 United States Code now provides that a district court may for cause remove from the bankruptcy court any part of a case or proceeding referred pursuant to sec. 157(a). 1984 Amendments, sec. 104(a)(to be codified as 28 U.S.C. sec. 157). The United States argues that cause to remove LeBouf's boats from the bankruptcy proceeding is demonstrated here by the conflict in jurisdiction over the ships between this court and the bankruptcy court. This argument suggests a misunderstanding on the part of the government as to the source of the bankruptcy court's jurisdictional authority. A conflict of jurisdiction presupposes two independent jurisdictional authorities. Under the 1984 Amendments, the district courts "have original and exclusive jurisdiction of all cases under title 11" and the bankruptcy court is merely a unit of the district court exercising that court's authority pursuant to 28 U.S.C. secs. 151 and 157. See 1984 Amendments, sec. 101(a)(to be codified at 28 U.S.C. sec. 1334(a)). Consequently, the bankruptcy court has no jurisdictional authority independent of this court; hence, there is no conflict of jurisdiction in this case.[3]

Furthermore, there would have been no jurisdictional conflict even if LeBouf had filed its petition for reorganization in another district. First, if I still had jurisdiction over LeBouf's boats after the bankruptcy action were filed, I would nevertheless be required to abide by the automatic stay effected by sec. 362 of the Bankruptcy Code. Second and more important, 28 U.S.C. sec. 1334 was amended by the 1984 Amendments so that the district court in the district in which a title 11 case is commenced has "exclusive jurisdiction of all of the property, wherever located, of the debtor. * * *" 1984 Amendments, sec. 101(a)(to be codified at 28 U.S.C. sec. 1334(d)). I would therefore have had no jurisdiction over the boats and thus there could have been no conflict of jurisdiction. The United States has not demonstrated any cause for me to withdraw this court's reference of LeBouf's title 11 case to the bankruptcy court.

3. In any case, if I were to withdraw the reference to the bankruptcy judge of Le-Bouf's reorganization proceeding, I would consider the matter under the bankruptcy jurisdiction of the district court and apply applicable bankruptcy law.

IV. *Relief From the Stay*

The United States next argues that it is entitled to relief from the automatic stay effected by sec. 362 because LeBouf has failed to provide the government with adequate protection for the value of its interest in LeBouf's property. Section 362 provides, in relevant part:

> "On request of a party in interest and after notice and a hearing, the Court shall grant relief from the stay provided under subsection (a) of this section, such as by terminating, annulling, modifying, or conditioning such stay—(1) for cause, including the lack of adequate protection of an interest in property of such party in interest; or (2) with respect to a stay of an act against property [under subsection (a) of this section], if—(A) the debtor does not have an equity in such property; and (B) such property is not necessary to an effective reorganization." 11 U.S.C. sec. 362(d)(language in brackets added by the 1984 Amendments).

Although the case law is sparse, it would seem that the better reading of the statute prior to the 1984 Amendments was that "the Court" to which it refers was the bankruptcy court and not the district court unless, of course, the reference to the bankruptcy court had been revoked. See In re Robintech, Inc., 35 B.R. 688 (Bkrtcy.Ala.1983). The 1984 Amendments provide that the bankruptcy court is merely a unit of the district court composed of the bankruptcy judges of the district. See 1984 Amendments, sec. 104(a)(to be codified at 28 U.S.C. sec. 151). Consequently, "the court" to which the statute refers should be interpreted to mean the unit of the district court known as the bankruptcy court. Moreover, the notice and hearing for which the statute provides are apparently intended not only to allow the debtor the opportunity to be heard, but also the other creditors. It is the bankruptcy judge that has LeBouf's other creditors before him. The arguments of the United States for relief from the stay therefore are more properly directed to him.

N O T E

See In re Louisiana Ship Management, Inc., 761 F.2d 1025, 1985 A.M.C. 2667 (5th Cir.1985), in which the court of appeals granted mandamus to declare void the sale of a vessel to satisfy a maritime lien held after the claimant filed for a voluntary Chapter 11 bankruptcy. The court of appeals held that the filing of the petition automatically stayed the sale (11 U.S.C.A. § 362(a)(5)), and vested exclusive jurisdiction over the property in the district court in which the Title 11 proceeding was pending.

Cf. Morgan Guaranty Trust Co. of New York v. Hellenic Lines, Ltd., 585 F.Supp. 1227, 1984 A.M.C. 2409 (S.D.N.Y.1984), decided before the effective date of the 1984 Bankruptcy Amendments, in which the court drew a distinction between a Chapter 11 reorganization and a Chapter 7 liquidation, in its effect upon an in rem proceeding under the admiralty jurisdiction. It believed that in the former the need for concentrating control of the petitioner's assets outweighed the interests of admiralty and therefore the admiralty court would stay its hand. In the case of a liquidation, however, it believed that the matter was governed by the doctrine of custodia legis, that is to say that a res will be administered by the court first acquiring in rem jurisdiction.

Some decisions applied the custodia legis doctrine even in the case of the Chapter 11 petition. See McDermott, Inc. v. M/V ANGELA BRILEY, 1984 A.M.C. 1331 (D.Miss.1984). This view is clearly wrong under *Louisiana Ship Mgt.,* is it not?

Although both *LeBouf Bros.* and *Louisiana Ship Mgt.,* involved Chapter 11 proceedings, neither 11 U.S.C.A. § 362(a)(5) nor 28 U.S.C.A. § 1334(d) makes any distinction between chapters of the Act. Note, however, that the latter vests exclusive jurisdiction over the property in the district court in which the Title 11 proceeding is pending, not in the "bankruptcy court," this distinction having been eliminated by the 1984 Amendments. Nevertheless, the court in *LeBouf Bros.* found transfer to the bankruptcy unit of the district court the efficient procedure.

The preference for considering all claims, terrestrial or maritime, in one proceeding once the debtor is insolvent that is evident in the present bankruptcy Act has been extended by comity to foreign bankruptcy proceedings. See, e.g., Cunard S.S. Co. v. Salen Reefer Services AB, 773 F.2d 452, 1986 A.M.C. 163 (2d Cir.1985), in which the court of appeals affirmed the district court's order vacating an attachment under Supplemental Rule B(1) of the assets of a Swedish bankrupt to satisfy a London arbitration award.

CHAPTER 13

CARRIAGE OF PASSENGERS

INTRODUCTORY NOTE

As the steamboat has given way to the railroad, and the railroad and ocean liner to the automobile and airplane, the volume of litigation in American courts produced by mass transportation of passengers by water has dwindled to practically nothing. The void has been filled to a large extent, however, by the growth of pleasure boating and pleasure cruises.

For some reason not altogether apparent, the duties of a carrier to his passengers, unlike the duties of a carrier to his shipper, has never been the subject of comprehensive statutory definition. It has long been held that a contract to carry a passenger by water is a maritime contract, by analogy to a contract for carriage of goods. "The Court held that a vessel carrying passengers for hire stands on the same footing of responsibility as one carrying merchandise, the passage money in the former case being the equivalent for the freight in the latter; that the vessel, as well as her owner, is responsible for a breach of a contract with a passenger in respect to his passage and for the damage resulting therefrom; that the owner is clearly liable; and that, in an analogy to the principles which make the vessel liable for a breach of contract of affreightment of merchandise, she should also be held liable for a breach of a passenger contract." The Aberfoyle, 1 Blatchf. 360, 1 Fed.Cas. 35 (C.C.N.Y.1848). See also The Pacific, 1 Blatchf. 569, 18 F.Cas. 935 (C.C.N.Y.1850), in which Judge (later Justice) Nelson elaborates on this theme. In *The Pacific* it was held that a person who had contracted for passage and found that the accommodations were not in compliance with the contract could refuse to come on board and could maintain a libel in rem for breach of the contract of carriage. When the theory of the liability of the vessel in rem for breach of an executory contract of affreightment was later repudiated by the Supreme Court (see discussion in *Pacific Export,* p. 417, supra), the lien under an unexecuted contract for carriage of passengers fell with it. See, e.g., Acker v. The City of Athens, 177 F.2d 961, 1950 A.M.C. 282 (4th Cir.1949). Gilmore & Black point out that the result in The City of Athens was that lien claims ate up the entire available fund and $500,000 in claims by the holders of dishonored tickets went begging. Law of Admiralty 749 (2d ed. 1975).

How far can one carry the analogy between carriage of goods and carriage of passengers? In *The Yankee Blade* (quoted by Mr. Justice McReynolds in *Pacific Export*), for example, the lien of cargo on vessel and vessel on cargo are spoken of as mutual and reciprocal. Although this analogy can be worked out with baggage, can we give the vessel owner a lien on the passenger? Post *Pacific Export* decisions on the question of carrier liability to passengers do not address the problem, probably because the breach of a carrier's duty to his passenger has been held to constitute a maritime tort, which quite clearly imports a lien.

Kornberg v. Carnival Cruise Lines, Inc.

United States Court of Appeals, Eleventh Circuit, 1984.
741 F.2d 1332, 1985 A.M.C. 826, cert. denied 470 U.S. 1004, 105 S.Ct. 1357, 84 L.Ed.2d 379 (1985).

■ RONEY, CIRCUIT JUDGE:

Plaintiffs, Albert and Laura Kornberg, filed a class action suit against Carnival Cruise Lines seeking damages allegedly caused by the failure of the sanitary system of the TSS *Tropicale* during a one-week cruise in the Caribbean. The district court denied class action certification on the grounds that the class was not sufficiently numerous and that plaintiffs were not typical of the class. On Carnival's motion for summary judgment, the court dismissed plaintiffs' suit as barred by certain disclaimers in their contract of passage. We reverse the summary judgment for a trial on the merits. As to the denial of class certification, we vacate and remand for further consideration on the ground that the reasons of the denial are insufficient.

Depositions and documentary discovery revealed that the *Tropicale* did indeed suffer problems with its sanitary system on the cruise in question as well as on two earlier cruises. The extent and duration of the breakdowns, however, were a matter of dispute. Eighteen percent of the passengers filling out a questionaire on the *Tropicale* complained about the toilets. Plaintiffs' toilet was particularly troublesome, and required individual servicing by the crew.

Plaintiffs alleged diversity of citizenship as the jurisdictional basis of this suit. Since the complained of injury occurred upon a ship in navigable waters, admiralty jurisdiction is also present and maritime law governs the outcome of the suit. Kermarec v. Compagnie Generale Transatlantique, 358 U.S. 625, 628, 79 S.Ct. 406, 408, 3 L.Ed.2d 550 (1959).

A ship, as a common carrier, owes a special duty to its passengers.

> A contract for passage by water implies something more than ship room and transportation. It includes reasonable comforts, necessaries, and kindness * * *. It is the duty of the common carrier by water to provide his passengers with comfortable accommodations * * * unless there is a contract to the contrary or a fair understanding to the contrary; and the carrier must subject his passengers to no suffering or inconvenience which can be avoided by reasonable care and effort.

Defrier v. The Nicaragua, 81 F. 745 (S.D.Ala.1897)(cite omitted); see Chicago, D. & G.B. Transit Co. v. Moore, 259 F. 490 (6th Cir.), cert. denied, 251 U.S. 553, 40 S.Ct. 118, 64 L.Ed. 411 (1919); The Oregon, 133 F. 609, 617–18 (9th Cir.1904). As an aspect of this duty, the ship's agent must tell prospective passengers when the comfortable staterooms have been filled so that they can make an informed decision on whether they wish to travel in the ship's less desirable accommodations. Sparks v. The Sonora, 22 F.Cas. 883, 885 (N.D.Cal.1859)(No. 13,212).

A breach of the carrier's duty is a "maritime tort." The Williamette Valley, 71 F. 712, 714–15 (D.C.Cal.1896); see The Vueltabajo, 163 F. 594 (S.D.Ala.1908). A carrier by sea, however, is not liable to passengers as an insurer, but only for its negligence; *Kermarec,* 358 U.S. at 632, 79 S.Ct. at 410; Liverpool and G.W. Steam Co. v. Phenix Insurance Co., 129 U.S. 397, 440, 9 S.Ct. 469, 471, 32 L.Ed. 788 (1889). The Ninth Circuit phrased the issue in a case involving a ship's accommodations as "whether the officers and agents of the vessel were guilty of negligence in overcrowding her with passengers, in failing to keep the vessel in a cleanly condition, and in failing to supply the vessel and the libelants with a sufficient quantity of wholesome food and provisions for the voyage." *The Oregon,* 133 F. at 618.

Carnival attempts to avoid the duties imposed on a carrier by sea relying on certain disclaimers presented in each passenger's contract of passage. These disclaimers read:

4. The Carrier shall not be liable for any loss of life or personal injury or delay whatsoever wheresoever arising and howsoever caused even though the same may have been caused by the negligence or default of its servants or agents. No undertaking or warranty is given or shall be implied respecting the seaworthiness, fitness or condition of the Vessel.

14. If the performance of the proposed voyage is hindered or prevented (or in the opinion of the Carrier or the Master is likely to be hindered or prevented) by war, hostilities, blockade, ice, labor conflicts, strikes on board or ashore, Restraint of Rules or Princes, breakdown of the Vessel, congestion, docking difficulties, or any other cause whatsoever * * * the passenger and his baggage may be landed at the port of embarkation or at any port or place at which the responsibility of the Carrier shall cease and this contract shall be deemed to have been fully performed. * * *

Paragraphs 4 and 14 contain a disclaimer of liability for negligence, a disclaimer of any warranty of seaworthiness, and a disclaimer of liability for interruption of full performance of the cruise. Each disclaimer will be addressed separately.

As a general rule, conditions or limitations in a contract for passage are valid if the ticket provides adequate notice of them. Carpenter v. Klosters Rederi A/S, 604 F.2d 11, 13 (5th Cir.1979). Many courts have enforced time limitations for bringing of suit and liability limitations for damage to luggage which were printed on passenger tickets. See Anno., Federal View as to Effect of Conditions Appearing on Back or Margin of Passenger's Ticket for Ocean Voyage, 5 ALR Fed. 394. Carnival, however, has cited no cases upholding such broad disclaimers as involved in this case.

Of the three disclaimers, the disclaimer of liability for negligence appears to be the most applicable to this suit. Yet, for good reason Carnival does not rely on this disclaimer. 46 U.S.C.A. § 183c expressly invalidates any contract provision purporting to limit a ship's liability for negligence to its passengers.

> It shall be unlawful for the manager, agent, master, or owner of any vessel transporting passengers between ports of the United States or between any such port and a foreign port to insert in any rule, regulation, contract, or agreement any provision or limitation (1) purporting, in the event of loss of life or bodily injury arising from the negligence or fault of such owner or his servants, to relieve such owner, master, or agent from liability. * * *

Id. Even prior to 1936, the year § 183c was enacted, such provisions were held to be void under common law as against public policy. Liverpool and G.W. Steam Co. v. Phenix Insurance Co., 129 U.S. 397, 441, 9 S.Ct. 469, 471, 32 L.Ed. 788 (1889).

Carnival relies most heavily on the disclaimer of the implied warranty of seaworthiness. This reliance is misplaced for two reasons. First, the disclaimer does not pertain to Carnival's traditional duties as a common carrier. Second, if the disclaimer can be construed as a waiver of Carnival's duties it is void as against public policy.

The warranty of seaworthiness is a term of art in the law of admiralty. The warranty imposes a form of absolute liability on a sea vessel. It originally applied to the carriage of cargo and was later extended to cover seamen's injuries. See generally Mitchell v. Trawler Racer, Inc., 362 U.S. 539, 80 S.Ct. 926, 4 L.Ed.2d 941 (1960); Chamlee, The Absolute Warranty of Seaworthiness: A History and Comparative Study, 24 Mercer L.Rev. 519 (1972). A ship's passengers are not covered by the warranty. Gibboney v. Wright, 517 F.2d 1054, 1059 (5th Cir.1975). The disclaimer of the warranty of seaworthiness could not reasonably be interpreted as waiving Carnival's duty to provide adequate accommodations to its passengers when the doctrine of seaworthiness does not apply to passengers. Any claim the passenger plaintiffs have can not be based on unseaworthiness, so any waiver of unseaworthiness would be irrelevant.

Even if Carnival's disclaimer of the warranty of seaworthiness did extend to its duty to provide adequate accommodations to its passengers, the disclaimer would undoubtedly be void as against public policy. A sea carrier's ability to disclaim its responsibilities is not unlimited. As the Supreme Court stated in Liverpool and G.W. Steam Co. v. Phenix Insurance Co., 129 U.S. 397, 9 S.Ct. 469, 32 L.Ed. 788 (1889):

> [T]he law does not allow a public carrier to abandon altogether his obligations to the public, and to stipulate for exemptions which are unreasonable and improper, amounting to an abnegation of the essential duties of his employment.

129 U.S. at 441, 9 S.Ct. at 472. See also The Oregon, 133 F. at 630 (sea carrier cannot avoid liability for its duty to keep ship clean); Lawlor v. Incres Nassau Steamship Line, 161 F.Supp. 764, 767 (D.Mass.1958)(ship which contracts to take passengers on a cruise which stops in various foreign ports cannot disclaim duty to provide safe shuttle service into the ports because such service is an essential part of the voyage).

It should be beyond debate that provision of an adequate sanitary system on a passenger boat is an "essential function" for which a sea carrier cannot disclaim responsibility.

Moreover the act complained of here, a failure to warn, involves negligent conduct and thus under § 183c cannot be avoided by contract. In a recent maritime case, this Court discussed whether the law of warranty covers the duty of a manufacturer to warn a purchaser of defects in a product.

> Whatever the merits of adopting a rule that views defects in a product as part of the parties' bargain and thus within the law of sales, it is much less tenable to presume that the buyer has bargained away the manufacturer's obligation to warn of defects that later come to the manufacturer's attention. A duty to warn of a product's defects of which the seller becomes aware goes not to the quality of the product that the buyer expects from the bargain, but to the type of conduct which tort law governs as a matter of social and public policy.

Miller Industries v. Caterpillar Tractor Co., 733 F.2d 813, 818 (11th Cir.1984). See W. Prosser, Law of Torts § 92 (4th ed. 1971); cf. Seas Shipping Co. v. Sieracki, 328 U.S. 85, 94–95, 66 S.Ct. 872, 877–878, 90 L.Ed. 1099 (1946)(duty of shipowner to provide seaworthy ship is not created by contract). Although *Miller Industries* involved the law of sales, the principle discussed there would seem to apply with equal force to this case.

The third disclaimer which releases Carnival from its obligation to perform the voyage is clearly not directed at the carrier's duty to provide adequate accommodations. For this reason, we need not address the enforceability of this disclaimer.

Since none of Carnival's three disclaimers apply in this case, the district court erred in granting summary judgment to Carnival.

Denial of Class Action

* * *

The district court's orders decertifying the class action and denying class action are vacated and remanded. On remand, the court should determine whether plaintiffs have met the other requirements for a class action listed in Rule 23. See Long v. Sapp, 502 F.2d 34, 43 (5th Cir.1974).

Reversed in part; Vacated in part and remanded.

NOTE

In *Kornberg,* Judge Roney adverts to the special duty of a carrier of passengers to provide "comfortable accommodations * * * unless there is a contract to the contrary or a fair understanding to the contrary * * *," quoting from the *Defrier* case, and holds that negligent breach of this "special duty" is a maritime tort. What difference does it make whether it is a tort or a breach of contract? Does the validity of the disclaimers asserted in defense depend upon this characterization? Notice that in *Liverpool and G.W. Steam Co.,* the authority given for the unenforceability of a common carrier's disclaimer of liability for its own negligence, the libel was for breach of a contract for carriage of cargo. In The Williamette Valley, cited by the court for the tort characterization of breach of a carrier's duty, the contract of carriage called for carriage partly on land and partly on water. The court avoided the necessity for ruling on whether the contract was maritime for jurisdictional purposes by finding the conduct of the vessel's purser tortious. In The Vueltabajo, the other authority named in *Kornberg* for the tort characterization, the defendant was not a common carrier, and the court held that the plaintiff was not a passenger who was owed a carrier's duty. Cf. The M/V Floridian, reproduced at p. 475, supra, in which it was held that an action for breach of the carrier's duties under COGSA resulting in cargo damage sounds in tort, and therefore the lien of a consignee is a preferred lien. Would the same be true of the passenger's claim in *Kornberg*?

The *Kornberg* court indicated that the clause of the cruise ticket purporting to exculpate the operator from liability for negligence was unenforceable under 46 U.S.C.A. § 183c. The disclaimer of liability for injury produced by unseaworthiness the court treated as either supererogatory, inasmuch as the carrier does not warrant the seaworthiness of the vessel to a passenger, or in the event that the intention was to absolve the carrier from all responsibility for the condition of the ship, as overreaching and void as against public policy. Disclaimers regarding the condition of the vessel clearly cannot be read as protecting the carrier from liability for loss of life or bodily injury of a passenger in cases in which the condition is produced by the negligence of the carrier and its servants, without doing violence to § 183c.

It should be noted that § 183c proscribes only contractual provisions purporting to relieve the owner, master, or agent from liability "in the event of loss of life or bodily injury." Was *Kornberg* a suit for "loss of life or bodily injury" within the coverage of § 183c, or were the plaintiffs, so to speak, merely discommoded?

And such provisions are proscribed only to the extent that they purport to disclaim or lessen liability for such loss of life or bodily injury as is caused by the negligence or fault of the owner or his servants. In this connection it is necessary to inquire into (1) the scope of duty of the owner, and (2) the question of who are its servants. First, as to the scope of duty of the owner:

§ 183c has been held applicable only to common carriers, and only while the parties stand in the relationship of carrier and passenger. Chervy v. Peninsular & Oriental Steam Nav. Co., 364 F.2d 908, 1966 A.M.C. 2260 (9th Cir.1966), cert. denied 385 U.S. 1007, 87 S.Ct. 714, 17 L.Ed.2d 546 (1967). In *Chervy,* a passenger who had left the vessel but returned that evening as a guest was held bound by an exculpatory clause in the boarding pass.

The duties of a carrier of passengers is not strictly limited to the vessel. Note, e.g., Lawler v. Incres Nassau Steamship Co., mentioned in *Kornberg,* holding that the vessel owner that has contracted to take passengers on a cruise which stops at various ports cannot disclaim the duty to provide the passengers with a safe means of getting into the ports and back to the vessel. Cf. Duluth Superior Excursions, Inc. v. Makela, 623 F.2d 1251, 1950 A.M.C. 2518 (8th Cir.1980), upholding admiralty jurisdiction in an action by a passenger on an excursion advertized as a "booze cruise" who was run into by an automobile operated by a fellow passenger when he was leaving the area at which the passengers were landed. Could the carrier disclaim this sort of floating dram shop liability? Note that for the purposes of jurisdiction the status of the injured party as a passenger is irrelevant. What about the liability of the cruise carrier for injury to passengers while ashore at one of the ports of call? See Lohman v. Royal Viking Lines, 1981 A.M.C. 1104 (D.Colo.1980) in which a claim for damages sustained by a tour passenger who was run down by a motorcycle on the island of Bali was dismissed on summary judgment based on a clause in the contract of carriage disclaiming responsibility for injuries incurred during shore excursions. The court found such a disclaimer valid under both Norwegian and Colorado law. Was there any basis for application of the Colorado law? With *Lohman* cf. Taylor v. Costa Lines, Inc., 441 F.Supp. 783, 1978 A.M.C. 1254 (E.D.Pa.1977), denying summary judgment in an action for injury in a taxi accident during a shore excursion on a pleasure cruise.

Second, as to who are the servants of the owner:

In *Lohman,* supra, it was argued by the vessel owner, as an alternative defense, that if the injury was caused by negligence of the conductor of the shore excursion, the conductor was an independent contractor and therefore absent a showing that the vessel owner had been negligent in the selection of the conductor it could not be held liable. In view of the determination that the disclaimer was valid, the court did not reach this issue. In *Taylor,* the court held that the independent contractor issue could not be determined on summary judgment since there were disputed questions of control and agency. But when an independent contractor is treated as a member of the crew, the vessel owner has been held liable for the contractor's intentional infliction of emotional distress. Muratore v. M/S Scotia Prince, 845 F.2d 347, 1993 A.M.C 2933 (1st Cir.1988)(photographer who was a subcontractor of a shipboard concessionaire).

The independent contractor defense has been permitted in a number of cases in which a suit against the cruise carrier based upon malpractice of the ship's doctor. See Cummiskey v. Chandris, S.A., 895 F.2d 107 (2d Cir.1990), holding that the vessel owner is not vicariously liable for the negligence of the ship's doctor, without mention of disclaimer. And see Barbetta v. S/S Bermuda Star, 848 F.2d 1364 (5th Cir.1988), indicating that negligence in selecting a competent doctor would be a basis of liability, but the vessel owner is not vicariously liable for the doctor's negligence whether the doctor is an employee, or technically an independent contractor. Nevertheless, disclaimers are sometimes included in the ticket. See, e.g., Bowns v. Royal Viking Lines, Ltd., 1977 A.M.C. 2159 (S.D.N.Y.1977)("The Carrier shall not be liable for death, injury, Illness, * * * or fault or neglect of * * * ship's doctor". Does such a clause add anythinger? Remember that if the doctor is an employee of the vessel owner, the clause is invalid.)

The *Kornberg* court states that "[a]s a general rule, conditions or limitations in a contract for passage are valid if the ticket provides adequate notice of them." The *Carpenter* case, cited for this proposition, enforced a ticket provision imposing a one year time limit to the institution of suits for loss of life or bodily injury. Such a contract stipulation is impliedly recognized as enforceable by § 183b, to the extent there provided. This section also assumes the enforceability of a time limit, not less than 6 months, for giving notice of claim. Such limits are generally enforced when the carrier has given the passenger adequate notice of their existence. Schrader v. Royal Caribbean Cruise Line , Inc., 952 F.2d 1008 (8th Cir.1991)(limitation of time for suit); Lousararian v. Royal Caribbean Corp., 951 F.2d 7 (1st Cir.1991)(same). Boyles v. Cunard Line, 1994 A.M.C. 1631 (S.D.N.Y.1994), enforcing 6–month notice limitation in suit charging failure to live up to promise to provide "spa at sea" (with state-of-the-art exercise equipment).

The small print problem has been tenacious. For a discussion of what must be done to bring the time limitations to the attention of the passenger, see Shankles v. Costa Armatori, S.P.A. 722 F.2d 861, 1984 A.M.C. 2772 (1st Cir.1983), enforcing the limitation, and Barbachym v. Costa Line, Inc., 713 F.2d 216, 1984 A.M.C. 1484 (6th Cir.1983), declining to enforce it.

Reasonable communication of a time limit for suit was made to the passenger where there was a notice in boxed off red print on the fifth page of the ticket, which was the same page that gave the fare and date of departure, directing passenger's attention to terms and conditions on the following pages, the limitations language was plain and unambiguous, even though it was one of 28 terms and conditions and neither the limitations provision nor the preceding notice was in lettering as bold or as large as the warning pertaining to the marking of luggage and completion of embarcation cards. Spataro v. Kloster Cruise, Ltd., 894 F.2d 44 (2d Cir.1990).

The fact that two passengers shared one ticket folder did not preclude the holding that the warning was reasonably communicated. Marek v. Marpan Two, Inc., 817 F.2d 242 (3d Cir.1987), cert. denied 484 U.S. 852, 108 S.Ct. 155, 98 L.Ed.2d 110 (1987), followed in Hodes v. S.N.C. Achille Lauro ed Altri–Gestione, 858 F.2d 905, cert. denied sub nom. Hodes v. Lauro Lines, S.R.L., et al., 490 U.S. 1001, 109 S.Ct. 1633, 104 L.Ed.2d 149 (1989). Cf. Muratore v. M/S Scotia Prince, supra, holding that when a master ticket is issued to a tour group, the warning must be given to each member.

In cases other than those involving loss of life or bodily injury, there is no statutory prohibition of exculpatory clauses or limits on liability. In the case of loss of baggage, however, the Supreme Court held in The Kensington, 183 U.S. 263, 22 S.Ct. 102, 46 L.Ed. 190 (1902) that an exception in a passenger ticket disclaiming liability in excess of 250 francs (about $50 at the time), unless the baggage was shipped as cargo (under the Harter Act), and affording no alternative of increasing the limitation "by an adequate and reasonable proportional payment" was void. The Court observed that it was not necessary to decide whether the Harter Act applied to contracts to carry passengers and their baggage, the cause of loss being improper stowage which under the Act, if applicable, would make the carrier liable. It has generally been assumed, however, that neither the Harter Act, nor the COGSA applies to baggage shipped on a passenger ticket. Limitations on liability for loss of baggage that provide the passenger who wishes more protection with the opportunity to declare the value and pay a reasonable charge for the added protection have generally been upheld. See, e.g., Hecht v. Cunard Line, 1982 A.M.C. 656 (S.D.N.Y.1981), in which a $100 limitation was upheld in a case in which the plaintiff alleged a loss of $250,000 in jewels. According to the pleadings she had placed the jewels in the ship safe until shortly before she was scheduled to disembark, when she had removed them and placed them in one of her pieces of luggage which remained in her locked stateroom until she left the vessel. The requirement that jewelry must be given to the purser for safekeeping has been upheld. Avis v. Cunard S.S. Co., 1958 A.M.C. 2453 (Cir.Ct.Mich.1958). Limitations requiring that an action for loss of baggage must be filed within 6 months have been treated as valid. Morak and Morak v. Costa Armatori S.P.A. Genova, 1982 A.M.C. 1859 (E.D.N.Y.1981); Miller v. International Freighting Corp., 97 F.Supp. 60, 1951 A.M.C. 944 (S.D.N.Y.1951). As in the case of time limitations on suit for loss of life or bodily injury, the fine print problem has arisen. See Cada v. Costa Line, Inc., 547 F.Supp. 85 (N.D.Ill.1982), applying the *Silvestri* standard in denying summary judgment based on a provision for a 6 months limit on baggage claims.

Choice of law provisions in passenger tickets are not against public policy and are enforced when reasonable. For a reverse twist on the subject, see Milanovich v. Costa Crociere S.p.A., 954 F.2d 763 (D.C.Cir.1992), in which a one-year limit on the time for bringing suit, valid under U.S. law, was held invalid under incorporated Italian law.

Forum selection clauses are also enforced when reasonable. See Carnival Cruise Lines, Inc. v. Shute, 499 U.S. 585, 111 S.Ct. 1522, 113 L.Ed.2d 622 (1991). Forum selection clauses generally are discussed in Chapter 8, subchapter C, at p. 306, above. *Shute* was distinguished in Effron v. Sun Line, 857 F.Supp. 1079, 1994 A.M.C. 2726 (S.D.N.Y.1994), where the court declined to enforce a fine print clause in a ticket for a South American cruise requiring suit in Greece.

Rainey v. Paquet Cruises, Inc.

United States Court of Appeals, Second Circuit, 1983.
709 F.2d 169, 1983 A.M.C. 2100.

■ VAN GRAAFEILAND, CIRCUIT JUDGE:

John Crews Rainey appeals from a judgment of the United States District Court for the Southern District of New York, Sweet, J., which dismissed appellant's complaint at the close of a bench trial. Appellant had sought to recover damages from Nouvelle Compagnie De Paquetvots, CIE., the owner/operator of the cruise ship M.S. *Mermoz* for injuries sustained by him while a passenger on the ship. For the reasons that follow, we affirm.

Appellant's injuries did not result from the type of occurrence usually associated with a ship at sea. Instead, appellant tripped over a stool while "exuberantly" dancing the "Lindy" in the ship's discotheque. The district court found that the seas were calm and that it "has not been suggested, even inferentially, that it was the ship's motion that caused the stool to be on the dance floor." Because there was no evidence as to how the stool got where it was or how long it had been there, the district court concluded that the defendant was not negligent. Appellant contends that the district court erred in making this determination in that it did not hold appellee to a higher standard than that of reasonable care under the circumstances. We disagree.

We have stated on a number of occasions that an ocean carrier must exercise a very high degree of care for the safety of its passengers. See, e.g., Moore v. American Scantic Line, Inc., 121 F.2d 767, 768 (2d Cir.1941). Respected commentators long have contended, however, that "[t]echnically the 'high degree' instruction is incorrect as a matter of principle * * *." "What is required", they say, "is merely the conduct of the reasonable man of ordinary prudence under the circumstances, and the greater danger, or the greater responsibility, is merely one of the circumstances, demanding only an increased amount of care." Prosser, The Law of Torts § 34, at 181 (4th ed. 1971); see 2 Harper & James, *The Law of Torts,* § 16.13, at 946 n. 13 (1956). In some instances, reasonable care under the circumstances may be a very high degree of care; in other instances, it may be something less. In Pratt v. North German Lloyd S.S. Co., 184 F. 303 (2d Cir.1911), plaintiff fell on a wet deck. The trial court charged that the defendant was bound to exercise reasonable care under the circumstances but refused to charge that the shipowner owed plaintiff "very great care". The Court of Appeals said in affirming:

> "We think the charge was right. 'Very great care' is an unmeaning phrase, and the jury in determining what was reasonable care with reference to the circumstances would necessarily determine whether it was great or very great. Such expressions as 'the utmost care' or 'the highest degree of care' and so forth are appropriate to the seaworthiness or roadworthiness of the vehicle of transportation, or to things inherently dangerous."

Id. at 304.

There is no sound reason to require that a carrier exercise a high degree of care for those trifling dangers which a passenger meets "in the same way and to the same extent as he meets them daily in his home or in his office or on the street, and from which he easily and completely habitually protects himself." Livingston v. Atlantic Coast Line R. Co., 28 F.2d 563, 566 (4th Cir.1928)(citing Bassell v. Hines, 269 F. 231, 232 (6th Cir.1920)). In Valeri v. Pullman Co., 218 F. 519 (S.D.N.Y.1914), then District Judge Augustus Hand held that the defendant, while serving food in its buffet car, "[differed] in no wise from any other person keeping a restaurant," id. at 520, and its obligation was to "exercise the reasonable care of a prudent man in furnishing and serving food," id. at 524.

In McLean v. Triboro Coach Corp., 302 N.Y. 49, 51, 96 N.E.2d 83 (1950), Judge Fuld wrote that negligence generally is defined as the failure to use "the care which the law's reasonably prudent man should use under the circumstances of a particular case." "That being so", he wrote, "it may well be asked whether it is ever practicable for one to use more care than one reasonably can * * *." He suggested that the Court reexamine those decisions which hold that a carrier owes a "high", a "very high" or the "highest" degree of care in transporting its passengers. New York courts since have adopted what this Court has termed "the logical view" that there can be only one degree of care, i.e., reasonable care under the circumstances. Gerard v. American Airlines, Inc., 272 F.2d 35, 36 (2d Cir.1959). See Thomas v. Central Greyhound Lines, 6 A.D.2d 649, 652–53, 180 N.Y.S.2d 461 (1958); Gallin v. Delta Air Lines, Inc., 106 Misc.2d 477, 480–81, 434 N.Y.S.2d 316 (1980). See also Basso v. Miller, 40 N.Y.2d 233, 386 N.Y.S.2d 564, 352 N.E.2d 868 (1976).

A number of other states take the same "logical view", see Elliot, Degrees of Negligence, 6 S.Cal.L.Rev. 91, 124–27 (1933), and it has been adopted by the Supreme Court in the field of admiralty. In Kermarec v. Compagnie Generale Transatlantique, 358 U.S. 625, 79 S.Ct. 406, 3 L.Ed.2d 550 (1959), the Court was called upon to decide whether a shipowner owed a lesser duty of care to a licensee than it did to an invitee. The Court held that "the owner of a ship in navigable waters owes to all who are on board for purposes not inimical to his legitimate interests the duty of exercising reasonable care under the circumstances of each case." Id. at 632, 79 S.Ct. at 410. See also Scindia Steam Navigation Co. v. De Los Santos, 451 U.S. 156, 163–64 n. 10, 101 S.Ct. 1614, 1620 n. 10, 68 L.Ed.2d 1 (1981).

The Fifth Circuit appears to be the only one which squarely has considered whether the reasonable-care-under-the-circumstances rule of *Kermarec* is applicable in passenger cases, and it has answered in the affirmative. See Gibboney v. Wright, 517 F.2d 1054, 1059 (5th Cir.1975); Tullis v. Fidelity and Casualty Co., 397 F.2d 22, 23–24 (5th Cir.1968).[1] We have not yet confronted the issue. The only passenger injury case in our Court since *Kermarec* was Alpert v. Zim Lines, 370 F.2d 115 (2d Cir.1966). There, plaintiff, a 63 year old cruise ship passenger, with a patent pre-existing infirmity which caused her to limp, was injured when rough seas caused the ship to lurch as she was rising from a chair. The single question briefed and argued was whether the defendant had sufficient constructive notice of plaintiff's disability so that summary judgment in the defendant's favor should not have been granted. The defendant did not dispute that, if it knew that plaintiff had physical disabilities, it was required to exercise such higher degree of care—including giving special assistance—as was reasonably necessary to insure plaintiff's safety in view of her disabilities. Id. at 116. We held that there were genuine issues as to material facts, including the state of the weather, and that, therefore, summary judgment was improper.

In the instant case, the district court cited *Kermarec* in support of its holding, and the applicability of that case is now before us. Following the lead of the Fifth Circuit, we hold that the *Kermarec* rule of reasonable care under the circumstances is applicable in passenger cases. The extent to which the circumstances surrounding maritime travel are different from those encountered in daily life and involve more danger to the passenger, will determine how high a degree of care is reasonable in each case. In the absence of any proof that appellee had actual or constructive notice of the presence of the stool, a condition in no way peculiar to maritime travel, the district court did not err in dismissing the complaint. See Demgard v. United States, 94 F.Supp. 309, 310 (S.D.N.Y.1950); Dann v. Compagnie Generale Transatlantique, 45 F.Supp. 225, 226 (E.D.N.Y.1942).

Finding no merit in appellant's remaining contentions, we affirm.

■ OAKES, CIRCUIT JUDGE (concurring):

I concur in the basic proposition that as a matter of law the *standard* of care is no different for a carrier than it is for anyone else—the duty is one of reasonable care under the circumstances. See 2 F. Harper & F. James, The Law of Torts § 16.14 (1956). The circumstances of each case of course vary, and the greater the degree of the carrier's control or the lesser the degree of the passenger's control over the factors causative of the injury, the easier it is to find negligence. Thus, the phrase "highest degree of care" and its variations are useful only insofar as they call a jury's attention to the relative extent of control exercised or exercisable by the carrier so as to prevent or avoid an accident. Where the trier of fact is a judge to whom negligence is a familiar concept, any phrase suggesting

---

1. The Eighth Circuit appears to have adopted the rule without comment. See Uri-

an v. Milstead, 473 F.2d 948, 951 (8th Cir. 1973).

degrees of care owed is at best superfluous, at worst confusing. This being a non-jury case, with the carrier not being charged with, e.g., causing the ship to veer suddenly for no reason, but rather being charged with negligence in permitting a dance floor to have a foreign obstacle on it, concealed by its size, the composition of the floor and the semi-darkness, to talk in terms of degrees of care owed makes no sense whatsoever. The vessel owner or carrier in this situation is in no different position from that of a possessor of land as to licensees and invitees, Restatement (Second) of Torts §§ 342, 343, 343A (1965).

Applying that standard to this case, I agree that the trial judge's finding of no negligence was not clearly erroneous. While the judge, inadvertently I think, referred to the stool on the disco dance floor as three feet high when the only evidence was that it was twelve inches to eighteen inches high, he was careful to distinguish situations in which either by lack of supervision of the dance floor, failure to inspect it, or even the motion of the vessel in the sea, the stool came, was placed, or remained upon the dance floor, thereby causing injury. The judge did not explicitly consider the possibility that the stool was placed on the dance floor during the movies that were shown in the discotheque before the dancing started—a plausible inference given the fact that there were about twelve such stools, regularly used for such purpose—and that it might well have been negligent for the vessel's employees to fail to inspect the dance floor and remove any remaining stools before turning the lights out for disco dancing. But this inference was by no means a necessary one from the facts proved at trial, though I believe it quite permissible; one suspects that counsel, instead of being able to adduce facts from ship personnel, passengers or other sources developing this, his appellate theory of the case, was required to rely upon the "highest duty of care" legal concept, such as it is. Be this as it may, as the trier of fact Judge Sweet was left, in his words, with the limited question whether "the mere presence [of the stool] at an isolated moment in time, without any further evidence of how it got there or how long the stool was on the dance floor" constituted negligence. Since he could not properly find that it was negligent *per se* to have a movable stool in a discotheque, even on a ship on the high seas, he quite understandably found no negligence. I cannot fault him on this, though another trier of fact might have concluded otherwise. I therefore concur in the judgment.

N O T E

It is a settled matter that a vessel owner does not warrant the seaworthiness of a vessel to a passenger. In Tittle v. Aldacosta, 544 F.2d 752, 1978 A.M.C. 112 (5th Cir.1977), Judge Brown refers to this as the "curious anomaly that a bag of coffee beans fares better than a non crew member fare paying passenger." See also Gibboney v. Wright, 517 F.2d 1054, 1975 A.M.C. 2071 (5th Cir.1975), where the favored object is "a bale of cotton." Are these statements hyperbolic? Remember that unlike the warranty to a seaman, the carrier's warranty to the shipper of cargo extends no further than the point at which the vessel breaks ground, and for a century the carrier has been free to limit his obligation to due diligence; if the vessel is unseaworthy through want of diligence on the part of the owner, wouldn't the owner be liable to a passenger whose injury was caused by the unseaworthy condition? See, e.g., Kornberg v. Carnival Cruise Lines, reproduced at p. 583, supra (toilets not working); Stanga v. McCormick Shipping Corp., 268 F.2d 544, 1959 A.M.C. 1666 (5th Cir.1959)(fall on defective stair). See also 46 U.S.C.A. § 491, derived from R.S. 4493, discussed in Judge Ross's concurring opinion in The Oregon, 133 Fed. 609, 636 (9th Cir.1904). Further, under COGSA, the carrier is not liable for cargo damage caused by negligent navigation or management of the vessel. By contrast, the passenger injured as a consequence of faulty navigation may sue. See, e.g., Loc–Wood Boat & Motors, Inc. v. Rockwell, 245 F.2d 306 (8th Cir.1957)(pilot negligence); The Miss New York, 1941 A.M.C. 569 (S.D.N.Y.1941)(collision). By its terms, 46 U.S.C.A. § 182 (the Fire Statute) has no application to actions for personal injury. See Petition of Chadade Steamship Co., Inc. (The Yarmouth Castle) 266 F.Supp. 517, 1967 A.M.C. 1843 (S.D.Fla.1967). And 46 U.S.C.A. § 183(b) requires the posting of a minimum limitation fund in respect of personal injury claims.

The courts have not been uniform in their statements about the applicable standard of care. In Liverpool & G. W. Steam Co. v. Phenix Ins. Co., 129 U.S. 397, 440, 9 S.Ct. 469, 471, 32 L.Ed. 788 (1889), which was not a passenger case, the Supreme Court spoke of the law governing the carriage of passengers as "exacting the highest degree of care and diligence." "Highest degree" appears in some more recent cases. E.g., Moore–McCormack Lines, Inc. v. Russak, 266 F.2d 573, 1959 A.M.C. 1372 (9th Cir.1959). There a passenger slipped on a moist spot on the dance floor, the evidence suggesting that it was produced by a grape thrown by another passenger who was dancing with a fruit bowl on her head in imitation of Carmen Miranda. See also Harrison Boat House, Inc., 1980 A.M.C. 2383 (E.D.Va. 1979), aff'd per curiam 1982 A.M.C. 361 (unpublished opinion)("*highest degree,*" citing *Liverpool & G.W.*).

In Allen v. Matson Nav. Co., 255 F.2d 273, 1958 A.M.C. 1434 (9th Cir.1958), case in which a passenger slipped and fell on a stair landing, the court stated that the carrier had a duty "to exercise extraordinary vigilance and the highest skill" in protecting the safety of its passengers, and the adjective "extraordinary" appears in Traub v. Holland–America Line, 278 F.Supp. 814, 1967 A.M.C. 1161 (S.D.N.Y.1967). There a passenger was injured in a fall when the toilet flush handle broke off in her hand.

In some other cases the standard has been referred to as "high." See, e.g., Stanga v. McCormick Shipping Corp., 268 F.2d 544, 1959 A.M.C. 1666 (5th Cir.1959). In Alpert v. Zim Lines, 370 F.2d 115, 1967 A.M.C. 14 (2d Cir.1966), in which a passenger who was frail and walked with some difficulty was injured in getting up from a deck chair, the court of appeals stated that the standard was "high," and then quoted the language from *Allen,* supra.

In the Fifth Circuit, see Gibboney v. Wright, supra, a case in which the two sons of a person who was operating a 30 foot racing sloop were injured while on board with their father, and Tittle v. Aldacosta Lim. Proc., supra. In both, the court states the standard as ordinary care. See also Tullis v. Fidelity and Casualty Co. of New York, 397 F.2d 22, 1968 A.M.C. 1451 (5th Cir.1968), in which the plaintiff was a fishing tool supervisor being transported to and from a drilling rig in a crew boat. In Roberts v. Offshore Logistics Services, Inc., 1983 A.M.C. 107 (E.D.La.1980), Judge Hebe read such cases to establish a rule for a private carrier of passengers, preserving the "high" standard of care in the case of a common carrier.

In Hays v. Carnival Cruise Lines, 1982 A.M.C. 2658 (M.D.Fla.1982), the court read the Fifth Circuit cases more broadly, adopting an ordinary care standard. In the particular case it taxed the vessel with 25% negligence in an action by a cruise passenger who was five feet five inches tall, weighed 180 pounds, and had a history of back trouble, when she was injured playing a deck game in which two persons straddled a horizontal pole four feet above the deck (which was covered with a mattress) and tried to knock each other off with pillows.

No negligence was found in Huff v. Italian Line, 1967 A.M.C. 2366 (S.D.N.Y. 1967) in which a passenger sued for negligence of the ship barber in dying her hair. The court found photographs of plaintiff's hair unimpressive in view of testimony that she had attended the ship "gala" the evening after she had visited the barber.

Independent of the description of the standard of care, whether ordinary, high, or highest, questions remain about the duties of a water carrier to its passengers. The fact that the passenger aboard ship is confined to the premises and wholly dependent upon the carrier and its employees necessarily imposes upon the carrier a wider range of duties than might be expected in less restricted quarters. Thus the carrier has the duty of providing reasonably safe methods of embarking and disembarking. See, e.g., Scheel v. Conboy, 551 F.2d 41, 1977 A.M.C. 344 (4th Cir.1977); Tittle v. Aldacosta, supra; Gryar v. Odeco, 1982 A.M.C. 143 (E.D.La. 1981).

A common carrier, at least, has been held to be liable for injury to passengers through the intentional torts of their servants. Thus a cruise line was held liable for the rape of a passenger by a crew member. Morton v. De Oliveira and Carnival Cruise Lines, Inc., 984 F.2d 289, 1993 A.M.C. 843 (9th Cir.1993), and for intentional infliction of emotional harm in an action by a passenger who awoke to find a steward fondling the private parts of her sleeping room mate. Nadeau v. Costley, 634 So.2d 649, 1994 A.M.C. 2810 (Fla.Dist.Ct.App.1994). See New Jersey Steam–Boat Co. v. Brockett, 121 U.S. 637, 7 S.Ct. 1039, 30 L.Ed. 1049 (1887). See also Norris, The Law of Maritime Personal Injuries, § 97 (3d ed. 1975).

The carrier also has a duty to protect a passenger from injury inflicted by a fellow passenger, but a violation of this duty is based on negligence. See Colavito v. Gonzales, 1983 A.M.C. 1378 (S.D.Tex.1981)(two of the servants of the carrier were present when one passenger struck another, but the court held that they were not negligent in failing to anticipate it).

CHAPTER 14

CARRIAGE OF GOODS

A. CONTRACTS OF AFFREIGHTMENT

1. COMMON AND PRIVATE CARRIERS

In the carriage of goods, on land as well as on water, a distinction is made between a common carrier, one who holds himself out as ready to carry for anyone who offers, and a private carrier who contracts with individual freighters but does not offer his services to the public. The common carrier has been looked upon as engaging in a public employment and over the years has been subjected to a high level of public regulation. A private carrier, or so-called contract carrier, has been less regulated, leaving the parties somewhat more free to work out their arrangements in their individual contracts. Private carriers by land were spoken of as comparatively rare in 1914. See Dobie on Bailments and Carriers 298 (1914). While a common carrier need not operate on any fixed schedule, e.g., a taxicab, since the owner offers generally to the public to go anywhere within its zone of operation, most commercial vessels are engaged either in a voyage to a designated place, offering to carry goods or passengers to that place, or they are available for hire not to anybody to go anywhere, as the taxicab, but to the freighter who offers the owner or operator a sufficient inducement to transport the cargo to a destination of the freighter's choosing. Such a vessel is referred to as an ocean tramp. The question as to whether a vessel is engaged in common carriage is a matter of proof. See, e.g., United States v. Stephen Brothers Line, 384 F.2d 118, 1968 A.M.C. 1635 (5th Cir.1967). There the question arose in connection with the requirement that common carriers file a schedule of tariffs under the Shipping Act of 1916 (46 U.S.C.A. § 817(b)) under which ocean tramps are specifically excluded from the definition of common carriers by water in foreign commerce (§ 801). The carrier claimed that it maintained no definite schedules and simply solicited freight from shippers and freight forwarders. The court found, however, that the vessel came and went between Miami and the Dominican Republic "with a regularity almost matching the Staten Island Ferry" and that the customs manifests "reflected hundreds of shipments of a wide variety of cargo running the gamut from automobiles, buses, groceries, gas ranges, freezers to veils and hat linings."

At common law a distinction was made between common and private carriage as to the duty of the carrier for the care of the cargo. The common carrier was an insurer except insofar as the loss or damage resulted from act of God or the Queen's enemies, or from the inherent vice of the goods or the act of the freighter.   The private carrier, on the other hand, was merely a bailee for hire, held to a standard of reasonable care. Dobie, supra, 298.   At one time it was doubted that this distinction held true in the case of carriage by water.   See, e.g., the opinion of Brett, J. (later Lord Esher) in In re Nugent v. Smith, 1 C.P.D. 19 (1876), where it is stated "The true rule is that every shipowner or master who carries goods on board his ship for hire, is in the absence of express stipulation to the contrary, subject by implication * * * to the liability of an insurer, except as to act of God or the Queen's enemies * * * not because he is a common carrier, but because he carries goods in his ship for hire."   This statement was repudiated by Chief Justice Cockburn in the same case in the Court of Appeal.   1 C.P.D. 423 (1876).   The case is discussed in Scrutton on *Charter Parties* 202–204 (1964).

The level of liability at common law is not very important, however, because, it will be noted, even Lord Esher excepted the case in which the contract of affreightment contained express provisions to the contrary. Since contracts for private carriage, with the exception of lighterage, were almost invariably embodied in written instruments, the shipowner's liability was rarely governed by common law principles.   Indeed, the same may be said of contracts for public carriage.   The important question, then, is the extent to which these contracts are confined by the law.

2.   CHARTER PARTIES

Pacific Employers Ins. Co. v. M/V Gloria

United States Court of Appeals, Fifth Circuit, 1985.
767 F.2d 229.

■ THORNBERRY, CIRCUIT JUDGE:

This case arises out of a shipment of bagged soybean meal from New Orleans, Louisiana, to Puerto Limon, Costa Rica.   When the cargo arrived in Puerto Limon, tallies of the cargo showed that some of the bags were wet, some torn and slack, and some shortlanded.   Plaintiffs-appellees brought two admiralty actions under the Carriage of Goods by Sea Act, 46 U.S.C. § 1300, et seq. (West 1975)("COGSA"), in which they sought to recover for the cargo damage, slackage, and shortage.   The district court consolidated the two actions.   The plaintiffs were: Cargill, Inc. ("Cargill"), the shipper of the cargo; Ternerina, S.A., Central Agricola De Cartago, S.A., Fabrica De Alimentos Para Animales, and Industria National De Alimentos Gibbons, S.A., the Costa Rican consignees and receivers of the cargo; and Pacific Employers Insurance, the cargo underwriter.   Pursuant to a stipulation of the parties, Pacific Employers Insurance was subrogated to the rights of the owners of the cargo.

The plaintiffs sought recovery against the M/V GLORIA, Aquarius, Ltd., and Transportacion Maritima Mexicana, S.A.   The defendant M/V GLORIA is a three-hatch bulk and general cargo vessel of Liberian registry owned by the defendant Aquarius, Ltd. ("Aquarius").   The GLORIA was under a long-term time charter to the defendant Transportacion Maritima Mexicana, S.A. ("TMM").

For the voyage in issue, TMM entered into a voyage charter with Greenwich Marine, Inc. ("Greenwich"), a subsidiary of plaintiff Cargill. Greenwich was not an original defendant in the action but was tendered as a party defendant by Aquarius and TMM pursuant to Fed.R.Civ.P. 14(c). Aquarius and TMM also filed third-party actions against Greenwich seeking contribution and indemnity.

Cargill entered into contracts to sell soybean meal to certain parties in Costa Rica. Pursuant to these contracts Cargill engaged Greenwich to find a vessel to carry the soybean meal from New Orleans to Puerto Limon, Costa Rica. Greenwich then entered into a voyage charter of the M/V GLORIA for this purpose. Loading of the bagged soybean meal began in New Orleans on August 5, 1980. Rogers Terminal and Shipping Corp. ("Rogers Terminal") was responsible for bagging, clerking, tallying, and stowing the cargo. Rogers Terminal completed stowage on August 11, and seven bills of lading covering the cargo were issued by "ROGERS TERMINAL & SHIPPING CORPORATION, AS AGENTS BY AUTHORITY OF THE MASTER." Each bill of lading indicates that the cargo was being shipped in apparent good order by Cargill, shipper's weight, quantity and quality, unknown. Further, each bill of lading incorporated the terms of the voyage charter party and the provisions of the Carriage of Goods by Sea Act. Cargill subsequently negotiated the bills of lading.

The GLORIA sailed from New Orleans on August 11 and arrived in Puerto Limon on August 16. Tallies of the cargo conducted by employees of the Puerto Limon Port Authority (the Japdeva) disclosed that the discharged cargo contained wet and torn bags and that the cargo was slack and short. Subsequently, the owners of the cargo and the cargo underwriter, as subrogee, brought this action to recover for the alleged damage, slackage, and shortage. Only the cargo carried under bills of lading 1, 2, 3, 5, and 7 is at issue in this litigation.

The defendants-appellants, Aquarius and TMM, brought Greenwich into the action as a defendant to the main demand and as a third-party defendant to their claims for contribution and indemnity. The district court ordered that the third-party action by TMM against Greenwich be stayed pending arbitration as required by the voyage charter party. The parties then agreed to submit the case to the district court on written briefs, depositions, exhibits, and proposed findings of fact and conclusions of law. No oral evidence was taken.

On January 26, 1984, the district court entered judgment in favor of plaintiffs and against the GLORIA, *in rem,* and Aquarius and TMM, *in personam,* in the amount of $59,540.24 plus legal interest from the date of judicial demand. In a written opinion the district court found that the vessel, Aquarius, and TMM were carriers under COGSA and that Greenwich was not a carrier. The court also found that plaintiffs established a *prima facie* case against the carriers for recovery of the cargo damage, slackage, and shortage, and that defendants failed to rebut the plaintiffs' evidence.   On February 23, the district court entered an amended judgment dismissing the claims against Greenwich.   Aquarius and TMM appeal from the judgment and the amended judgment.

The issues before us are (1) whether the district court erred in entering judgment *in rem* against the M/V GLORIA;   (2) whether the district court's findings that Aquarius and TMM were carriers under COGSA and that Greenwich was not a carrier are clearly erroneous;   (3) whether the court erred in holding that the carriers were liable to the plaintiffs for the cargo damage, shortage, and slackage;   and (4) whether the court erred in dismissing the claims against Greenwich.   We vacate the *in rem* judgment because we conclude that the district court did not acquire jurisdiction over the vessel, and we vacate the dismissal of TMM's third-party claim against Greenwich.   In all other respects we affirm the judgment and amended judgment of the district court.

I.   THE JUDGMENT IN REM

The district court entered judgment *in rem* against the M/V GLORIA. Because we find that the district court did not have the power to exercise jurisdiction over the vessel we vacate that judgment.

* * *

II.   COGSA CARRIERS

Plaintiffs may recover under COGSA only from the "carriers" of the cargo. COGSA defines "carrier" to include "the owner or the charterer who enters into a contract of carriage with a shipper."   46 U.S.C. § 1301(a). Accordingly, the plaintiffs must establish that a party defendant executed a contract of carriage.   *Associated Metals,* 484 F.2d at 462.   COGSA defines a "contract of carriage" as follows:

> The term "contract of carriage" applies only to contracts of carriage covered by a bill of lading or any similar document of title, insofar as such document relates to the carriage of goods by sea, including any bill of lading or any similar document as aforesaid issued under or pursuant to a charter party from the moment at which such bill of lading or similar document of title regulates the relations between a carrier and a holder of the same.

46 U.S.C. § 1301(b).   The district court found that TMM and Aquarius entered into a contract of carriage with Cargill and thus were carriers under COGSA, and that Greenwich did not enter into a contract of carriage as defined by the Act and thus was not a carrier.

Appellants challenge the district court's findings.   The findings will not be overturned unless they are clearly erroneous:

> In reviewing a judgment of a trial court, sitting without a jury in admiralty, the Court of Appeals may not set aside the judgment below unless it is clearly erroneous.   * * * A finding is clearly erroneous when "although there is evidence to support it, the reviewing court on the entire evidence is left with a definite and firm conviction that a mistake has been committed."

Daniels Towing Service, Inc. v. Nat Harrison Associates, Inc., 432 F.2d 103, 105 (5th Cir.1970)(quoting McAllister v. United States, 348 U.S. 19, 20, 75 S.Ct. 6, 8, 99 L.Ed. 20 (1954)).   The fact that this case was submitted to the district court without oral testimony does not affect our standard of review:

> If the district court's account of the evidence is plausible in light of the record viewed in its entirety, the court of appeals may not reverse it even though convinced that had it been sitting as the trier of fact, it would have weighed the evidence differently.   Where there are two permissible views of the evidence, the factfinder's choice between them cannot be clearly erroneous.   United States v. Yellow Cab Co., 338 U.S. 338, 342, 70 S.Ct. 177, 179, 94 L.Ed. 150 (1949); see also Inwood Laboratories, Inc. v. Ives Laboratories, Inc., 456 U.S. 844, 102 S.Ct. 2182, 72 L.Ed.2d 606 (1982).

> This is so even when the district court's findings do not rest on credibility determinations, but are based instead on physical or documentary evidence or inferences from other facts.

Anderson v. City of Bessemer City, North Carolina, 470 U.S. 564, 105 S.Ct. 1504, 1512, 84 L.Ed.2d 518 (1985).

TMM

The bills of lading were issued by Rogers Terminal and were signed: "ROGERS TERMINAL & SHIPPING CORPORATION, AS AGENTS BY AUTHORITY OF THE MASTER."   The district court found that in issuing the bills of lading, Rogers Terminal acted as agent for TMM and therefore TMM entered into a contract of carriage.   TMM contends that this finding is clearly erroneous.   We disagree and hold that there was sufficient evidence before the district court to support its finding.   The voyage charter party entered into by TMM and Greenwich was incorporated into the bills of lading and provided, in part, that:

> Owners [TMM] to instruct their New York bank to advise Owners' agents at loading port immediately freight received by cable that freight payment has been received and Owners to instruct their agents to release Bill/s of Lading immediately on receipt of such advice.   If release of Bill/s of Lading should be delayed, the Owners shall pay interest at one per cent over the New York Prime Rate on Bill/s of Lading date/s, on the cost and freight value of the cargo from the day on which the freight payment is received by the Owners' New York bank until the day on which the Bill/s of Lading are actually released by the Owners' agents.

The evidence before the district court did not clearly disclose for whom Rogers Terminal acted when it issued the bills of lading.   Under the voyage charter party, Greenwich was obligated to appoint and employ stevedores at the loading port.   Rogers Terminal performed stevedoring services in New Orleans.   However, the National Cargo Bureau's Certificate of Loading, issued after loading of the GLORIA was completed, stated, "AGENT— ROGERS TERMINAL & SHIPPING CO.—T.M.M. CHARTERING."   Moreover, the charter party states that TMM and/or its agents would be responsible for issuance of the bills of lading.   The master of the GLORIA testified by deposition that he authorized Rogers Terminal to issue the bills of lading on his behalf. He also testified, however, that it was his belief that Rogers Terminal was acting on behalf of Greenwich.

The district court considered all of the evidence before it, and, relying primarily on the voyage charter party provision that TMM would issue the bills of lading upon payment of freight by Greenwich, the court found that the bills were issued by TMM through its agent, Rogers Terminal. The district court's finding, in light of the conflicting evidence, is not clearly erroneous and we affirm the holding that TMM entered into a contract of carriage with respect to the soybean cargo and is thus a carrier under the provisions of COGSA.

Greenwich

The district court held that Greenwich was not a COGSA carrier because Greenwich did not issue the bills of lading and did not otherwise enter into a contract of carriage with Cargill. The court found that "Greenwich acted simply on behalf of the shipper in finding a vessel to carry the cargo and paying the appropriate freight." Greenwich did not enter into a contract that was "covered by a bill of lading or any similar document of title." See 46 U.S.C. § 1301(b).

In addition to contending that Greenwich issued the bills of lading, appellants argue that Greenwich is a COGSA carrier because the bills of lading were issued in connection with the voyage charter and because, under the voyage charter party, Greenwich was responsible for loading, stowage, and discharge—duties which COGSA places on the carrier. See 46 U.S.C. § 1303(2). First, we note that the voyage charter party merely states, "Charterers to appoint and employ stevedores at loading port/s," and "Charterers/Receivers Stevedores to be employed at discharging port/s." The charter party is not so explicit as appellants would have us believe. Moreover, even if Greenwich bore the responsibility under the voyage charter party for loading, stowage, and discharge, we do not believe this fact, alone, would make Greenwich a COGSA carrier. In Demsey & Associates v. S.S. SEA STAR, 461 F.2d 1009 (2d Cir.1972), the time charterer issued bills of lading in connection with a voyage charter. The court held that the time charterer was a COGSA carrier but that the voyage charterer was not. The court further held that the fact that the charter party required the voyage charterer to load, stow, and discharge the cargo created a duty running from the voyage charterer to the time charterer but did not affect the time charterer's obligations under COGSA and did not operate to make the voyage charterer a COGSA carrier. Id. at 1018–1019. We agree with the Second Circuit and we affirm the district court's finding that Greenwich is not a COGSA carrier.

Aquarius

Appellants also argue that the district court erred by finding that Aquarius is a COGSA carrier. Since appellees' causes of action were based on COGSA, there can be in personam liability against the vessel owner only if the owner is a carrier. Associated Metals, 484 F.2d at 462. Appellants contend that Aquarius did not enter into a contract of carriage and did not become bound by the bills of lading merely because they were signed "by authority of the master."

"A contract of carriage with an owner may either be direct between the parties, or by virtue of a charterer's authority to bind the owner by signing bills of lading 'for the master.'" *Matter of Intercontinental Properties Management, S.A.*, 604 F.2d 254, 258 n. 3 (4th Cir.1979). Appellees argue that the bills of lading were issued by Rogers Terminal—TMM's agent—with the actual authority of the vessel owner and that Aquarius is therefore bound. The circumstances under which the vessel owner may be bound by the bills of lading were well-stated by the First Circuit in EAC Timberlane v. Pisces, Ltd., 745 F.2d 715 (1st Cir.1984):

> Generally, when a bill of lading is signed by the charterer or its agent "for the master" with the authority of the shipowner, this binds the shipowner and places the shipowner within the provisions of COGSA. E.g., Gans S.S. Line v. Wilhelmsen (The Themis), 2 Cir.1921, 275 F. 254, 262; Tube Products of India v. S.S. Rio Grande, 1971, S.D.N.Y., 334 F.Supp. 1039, 1041; see generally Bauer, Responsibilities of Owner and Charterer to Third Parties—Consequences under Time and Voyage Charters, 49 Tul. L.Rev. 995, 997–1001 (1975). When, however, a bill of lading is signed by the charterer or its agent "for the master" but without the authority of the shipowner, the shipowner is not personally bound and does not by virtue of the charterer's signature become a COGSA carrier. E.g., Associated Metals and Minerals Corp. v. S.S. Portoria, 5 Cir.1973, 484 F.2d 460, 462; Demsey & Associates, Inc. v. S.S. Sea Star, 2 Cir.1972, 461 F.2d 1009, 1015.

Id. at 719. Aquarius' liability depends on the effect of the signature caption "by authority of the master." In order to determine the effect we must examine Rogers Terminal's authority to sign on behalf of the master and the master's authority to bind Aquarius. See Yeramex International v. S.S. TENDO, 595 F.2d 943, 946 (4th Cir.1979).

The district court's finding that the master authorized Rogers Terminal to issue the bills of lading on his behalf is not clearly erroneous. The captain of the GLORIA testified by deposition that he "gave Rogers Terminal an undertaking that they should sign the bills of lading." Appellants presented no conflicting evidence. This case is therefore unlike those cited by appellants in which there was no evidence that the master authorized the charterer or its agent to sign on his behalf. See Demsey & Associates v. S.S. SEA STAR, 461 F.2d 1009, 1012–15 (2d Cir.1972); Thyssen Steel Corp. v. S.S. ADONIS, 364 F.Supp. 1332, 1335 (S.D.N.Y. 1973); United Nations Children's Fund v. S/S NORDSTERN, 251 F.Supp. 833, 838 (S.D.N.Y.1965).

We must next determine whether the master had actual authority to bind the vessel owner to the terms of the bills of lading. The charter party between Aquarius and TMM contained the following provisions:

> 8. [T]he Captain shall prosecute his voyages with the utmost despatch, and shall render all customary assistance with ship's crew and boats. The Captain (although appointed by the Owners), shall be under the orders and directions of the Charterers [TMM] as regards employment and agency;

and Charterers are to load, stow, and trim and discharge the cargo at their expense under the supervision of the Captain, who is to sign Bills of Lading for cargo as presented, in conformity with Mate's or Tally Clerk's receipts.

Rider 37. If required by Charterers and/or their Agents, Master to authorize Charterers or their Agents to sign Bills of Lading on his behalf in accordance with mates and/or tally clerks receipt with out prejudice to this Charter Party.

We hold that Rider 37 to the charter party empowered the master to authorize TMM's agent to sign the bills of lading and thereby bind Aquarius. The case cited by appellants, Yeramex International v. S.S. TENDO, 595 F.2d 943 (4th Cir.1979), is distinguishable. In *Yeramex* the charter party between the vessel owner and the time charterer contained a provision identical to clause 8 above. It also contained a provision that stated, in part: "Charterers shall indemnify Owners from all consequences arising out of Master or agents signing Bills of Lading in accordance with Charterers' instructions, or from complying with any orders or directions of Charterers in connection therewith." Id. at 947. The court in *Yeramex* found that under the provisions of the charter party the charterer assumed exclusive responsibility for handling of cargo and for issuance of bills of lading. The court further stated:

> "In particular, we think all authority conferred by these provisions upon the vessels' masters for bills of lading issued by [time charterer] was authority which flowed, in fact, from [the time charterer] as principal to the masters as its agents, rather than as authority granted to [the time charterer] from the masters as the traditional personal agents of the owner. * * * No authority in fact existed for [the time charterer] to bind the owner to the terms of the bill of lading as a contracting party, and no liability *in personam* under COGSA will lie against the owner in favor of third parties."

Id. at 948. The Aquarius/TMM charter party did not contain a provision requiring TMM to indemnify Aquarius from all consequences arising out of the master or agents signing bills of lading. Moreover, Rider 37 to the charter party contains an express authorization that was not present in the *Yeramex* charter party. The district court's findings that TMM was authorized to bind Aquarius to the terms of the bills of lading and that Aquarius is a COGSA carrier are not clearly erroneous.

III. COGSA LIABILITY

* * *

IV. DISMISSAL OF CLAIMS AGAINST GREENWICH

Pursuant to Federal Rule of Civil Procedure 14(c), appellants tendered Greenwich to the plaintiffs as a party defendant to the main demand. Aquarius and TMM also brought third-party claims for contribution and indemnity against Greenwich. Greenwich moved for a stay of all of the claims against it. The district court granted the stay only as to the claims of TMM for indemnity and contribution. The stay was granted pending arbitration in New York pursuant to an arbitration clause in the voyage charter party.   The stay was denied as to all other claims.   In its amended judgment the district court dismissed all of the claims against Greenwich. Defendants appeal the dismissal of each claim.

Appellants argue that their demand that there be judgment in favor of one or more of the plaintiffs and against Greenwich should not have been dismissed.   The argument is based solely on appellants' claim that Greenwich is a COGSA carrier.   Since the district court's finding that Greenwich was not a carrier is not clearly erroneous, it was not error to dismiss the claim.

We agree with appellants that the district court erred by dismissing TMM's claims for indemnity and contribution.   These claims were stayed pending arbitration and the stay had not been lifted.   We vacate the judgment of dismissal of TMM's third-party claims against Greenwich.

Aquarius' third-party claims were not stayed.   Since there was no contractual privity between Aquarius and Greenwich, Aquarius' claims must be based on the negligence or actual fault of Greenwich.   By stipulation, the parties submitted the entire case to the court on written briefs, depositions, and other documentary evidence in the record.   That record contains *no* affirmative evidence of fault on the part of Greenwich.   Since Aquarius failed to present any evidence in support of its claims, it was not error for the district court to dismiss.

CONCLUSION

For the above-stated reasons, we VACATE the *in rem* judgment against the M/V GLORIA and we VACATE the judgment of dismissal in favor of third-party defendant Greenwich and against TMM.   In all other respects, we AFFIRM the judgment and amended judgment of the district court.

Complaint of Admiral Towing and Barge Co.

United States Court of Appeals, Fifth Circuit, 1985.
767 F.2d 243.

■ ALVIN B. RUBIN, CIRCUIT JUDGE:

* * *

I

We condense the complex facts to those essential to understanding the issues.   The claims arise out of the stranding of a barge, the CHRISTINA F, off San Juan, Puerto Rico while in the tow of the tug ADMIRAL.   This caused the loss of the tug, the barge, and the cargo aboard the barge.   The tug was owned by Great Lakes Towing Corporation.   Great Lakes had chartered it, purportedly bareboat, to its wholly-owned subsidiary, Admiral Towing, under a charter that required Admiral Towing to insure the tug. Admiral Towing had time chartered the ADMIRAL to Seatrain Intermodal Services Corporation (Intermodal).

The barge, CHRISTINA F, was owned by Bulk Food Carriers, Inc., which later transferred title to Mu–Petco Shipping, Inc., neither being a party to this action. It was bareboat chartered to Intermodal, making Intermodal the time charterer of the tug and bareboat charterer of the barge. Intermodal entered into charters of space aboard the CHRISTINA F to two of its affiliated corporations, both common carriers, Seatrain International S.A. (International) and Seatrain Gitmo, Inc. (Gitmo), which transported cargo in containers. Gitmo issued bills of lading for cargo destined for United States ports and International issued bills of lading for cargo destined for other ports.

The bareboat charter of the tug from Great Lakes to Admiral Towing defines the terms "owner" (Great Lakes) and "charterer" (Admiral Towing) to include "any affiliated and/or subsidiary company listed in Part II," but lists no other affiliated companies. It requires Admiral Towing to obtain insurance "to completely protect the owner from any and all liability * * * arising out of the operation of the vessel under this charter." The tug time charter from Admiral Towing to Intermodal, however, identifies Admiral Towing as "owner" and Intermodal as "charterer." It requires "the Owner" to provide insurance on "the vessel" (the tug but not the tow) and in clause 15 requires the "charterer" to carry "Hull and Cargo insurance on the tow and the cargo respectively to the full extent of their respective values, [and] P & I insurance in amounts satisfactory to the Owner" of the tug. It also requires the charterer to "provide for waiver of subrogation against the Owner of the tug, it being the intent hereof that any claims for damages or loss of the tow, or the cargo thereon shall be borne by the appropriate marine underwriters insuring its said tow and cargo, without recourse against the Owner, or the tug."

Through William Bennett, an employee of its insurance broker, Intermodal obtained insurance for the barge. Bennett obtained a hull policy on the barge with an oral commitment from the underwriter to issue the policy with a waiver of subrogation, which was issued in writing only after the accident. The written policy endorsement reads: "the bareboat charterer [of the barge, i.e., Intermodal] has given a full release to the tug and, consequently, there shall be no rights of subrogation against the tug and/or its *owners*."[1] Bennett also obtained P & I insurance to cover the liability of Intermodal as bareboat charterer of the barge. Because the P & I underwriter, The Club, would not agree to waive subrogation against the tug owner as provided in the tug time charter, Bennett obtained, at additional cost, a policy called "Shipowners' Liability to Cargo" [SOL], which provides coverage for claims for loss of cargo with a waiver of subrogation against the tug ADMIRAL in accordance with the time charter of that tug.

The underwriters paid claims for the loss of the barge, the containers, the cargo, and asserted their rights as subrogees of those claims. The insured parties asserted claims for their deductible portions of the losses.

---

1. Emphasis added.

Admiral Towing was not liable to either Intermodal or its hull underwriter for loss of the barge because these parties had, in the tug time charter and accompanying hull policy endorsement, waived subrogation against the tug and its "owner," Admiral Towing. Intermodal and its insurers, however, contend that Great Lakes, as the legal owner of the tug ADMIRAL, is independently liable for the damages resulting from the stranding of the barge because the bareboat charter between Great Lakes and Admiral Towing was not valid, Great Lakes knew of the tug's unseaworthiness and failed to cure it, and Great Lakes was, therefore, independently negligent.

The district court found that the vessels had been grounded as a result of the tug's negligence and unseaworthiness. It concluded, however, that the bareboat charter was valid and exonerated Great Lakes from liability for Admiral Towing's faults. It found that Great Lakes was not independently negligent and not liable for the unseaworthiness of the tug.

The district court held that, although Great Lakes and Admiral Towing were parent and subsidiary, had a close operating relationship, and Great Lakes had "considerable domination" over Admiral Towing, Great Lakes had divested itself of the "possession, command and navigation of the vessel" sufficiently to constitute Admiral Towing its bareboat charterer.[2] It found that the alleged officers and employees of Admiral Towing were indeed acting on behalf of Admiral Towing even though one officer was the president of both corporations and there was some evidence of Great Lakes' control of these persons. It concluded that the president of Great Lakes had no knowledge of the tug's unseaworthiness and that the persons responsible for the stranding were all employees of Admiral Towing, not Great Lakes.

II

Intermodal points out evidence that would support the conclusion that these persons were Great Lakes' employees. But this simply does not suffice. Unless we have the "definite and firm conviction" that the district court has erred, we must accept its factual conclusions.[3] The record contains ample evidence to support the trial court's findings and, as required by Federal Rule of Civil Procedure 52(a), we give "due regard * * * to the opportunity of the trial court to judge of the credibility of the witnesses." As an appellate court, we sit with limited powers and defined duties. We do not retry facts although we may correct manifest error.

The demise or bareboat charter is, as Gilmore and Black have said, "not a documentary choice for the *conduct* of the business of shipping; it is rather an instrument for vesting in one person most of the incidents of ownership in a capital asset of that business—the ship—while another retains the general ownership and the right of reversion."[4] If a vessel is

---

2. See Guzman v. Pichirilo, 369 U.S. 698, 699, 82 S.Ct. 1095, 1096, 8 L.Ed.2d 205, 207 (1962).

3. E.g., O'Toole v. New York Life Ins. Co., 671 F.2d 913, 914 (5th Cir.1982).

4. G. Gilmore and C. Black, *The Law of Admiralty* 239 (2d ed. 1975), quoted with

chartered bareboat, the owner may escape liability in personam for the condition or management of the vessel at least in some circumstances. The owner therefore "has the burden of establishing the facts which give rise to such relief."[5] While we closely examine the circumstances[6] to determine whether the owner has so far relinquished "possession, command, and navigation" of the vessel as to be "tantamount to, though just short of, an outright transfer of ownership,"[7] the district court's findings of fact remain embossed by the clearly erroneous rule.

The district court's findings are not impugned by inconsistent evidence. There is no evidence that Admiral Towing did not have the power to hire all of the crew members or to navigate the tug wherever it wished. Great Lakes did not share in the profits of the vessel but received only the stated charter fee. It would, therefore, be pointless to pursue the analogy urged by the appellants, that of comparing the tests used to establish the liability of a general employer for acts of its employee.[8]

Michael Chicarel was the port captain for the tug. The district court found that he was an employee solely of Admiral Towing and hence that Great Lakes was neither liable for his acts nor charged with his knowledge. The district court noted that Great Lakes advanced Chicarel's salary although the court did not mention that Great Lakes filed an Internal Revenue wage statement form (W–2) stating that it was Chicarel's employer. The court did find, however, that Chicarel at the time of the casualty was attending solely to Admiral's business, and Admiral's only business was the ocean tow under way. All of Chicarel's thirty years experience was in vessel operations on salt water and he had no training for operations on the Great Lakes and performed no services for Great Lakes. He had been employed by Admiral because the president of Admiral (who was also the President of Great Lakes) wanted him to represent Admiral in its operations in the Atlantic Ocean and Gulf of Mexico. These facts scarcely mandate the conclusion that it was clear error to regard Chicarel as the sole employee of Admiral Towing.

For these reasons, we accept the finding that Great Lakes had relinquished control of the tug to Admiral Towing. While the validity of the bareboat charter is a question of law, on which we have carte blanche to correct error, that conclusion is based on subsidiary findings of fact that are the basic province of the district court. Accepting these fact findings, the bareboat charter from Great Lakes to Admiral Towing was valid. We also affirm the district court's findings that Admiral employees were responsible for the stranding and that Great Lakes had no knowledge of the tug's unseaworthiness and was not independently negligent.

approval in Deal v. A.P. Bell Fish Co., 674 F.2d 438, 440 (5th Cir.1982).

5. Guzman v. Pichirilo, supra n. 2, 369 U.S. at 700, 82 S.Ct. at 1097, 8 L.Ed.2d at 208.

6. E.g., Deal v. A.P. Bell Fish Co., 674 F.2d 438, 441 (5th Cir.1982).

7. Guzman v. Pichirilo, supra n. 2, 369 U.S. at 699–700, 82 S.Ct. at 1096, 8 L.Ed.2d at 207.

8. See Kiff v. Travelers Insurance Company, 402 F.2d 129 (5th Cir.1968).

Because the bareboat charter protects Great Lakes from all claims by all appellants, we need not review the district judge's alternative finding that the waiver of subrogation provisions in the tug time charter and accompanying hull policy endorsement, read together, protected Great Lakes, as an "owner" of the tug, from subrogation claims brought by Intermodal and its insurer.

III

Seatrain Gitmo and Seatrain International and their P and I insurers (all of whom we shall for convenience call the Seatrain interests, since their positions are identical) seek to recover from Great Lakes and Admiral Towing the damages they sustained as a result of the loss of the cargo and containers.   Great Lakes, of course, is insulated from all liability for the reasons discussed in part II.   Clause 15 of the tug time charter, as we have mentioned above, obligated the "charterer" to carry "cargo insurance * * * on the * * * cargo" and to provide for waiver of subrogation against the owner of the tug, stating that it is "the intent hereof that any claims for damages or loss of the tow, or the cargo thereon shall be borne by the appropriate marine underwriters insuring its said tow and cargo, without recourse against the Owner, or the tug."   The "charterer" is defined as only Intermodal.   For this reason, the Seatrain interests assert, Intermodal's obligation to secure a waiver of subrogation did not bind Gitmo and International, their insurers did not waive subrogation against Admiral Towing or the tug, and all are, therefore, free to assert claims against Admiral Towing and the tug.

The district court found that, at the time the tug time charter was executed, the parties intended that Intermodal, which was also the bareboat charterer of the barge, would be the cargo carrier bearing liability under the Carriage of Goods by Sea Act[9] (COGSA) for loss of or damage to cargo on board the barge.   In reliance on that assumption, Admiral Towing required that only Intermodal obligate itself to provide a waiver of subrogation.   Without notice to Admiral Towing, and for their own business reasons, the Seatrain entities decided that Gitmo and International would become the COGSA carriers and issue the bills of lading to cargo interests. "The Seatrain entities cannot be permitted," the court concluded, "to take advantage of their unilateral action to defeat Admiral's rights [to waiver of subrogation] under the charter party."

These findings of fact as to the parties' intentions must be accepted, for they have support in the record.[10]   The parties intended the cargo carrier, who would alone have COGSA liability, to assume that liability and obtain appropriate insurance and the waiver of subrogation against the tug and its owner.   Once the arrangements with Gitmo and International were completed, Intermodal had no exposure to liability for the loss of cargo. We find no error in the district court's findings that Intermodal executed

---

9.   46 U.S.C. §§ 1300 et seq.

10.   Pullman–Standard v. Swint, 456 U.S. 273, 102 S.Ct. 1781, 72 L.Ed.2d 66 (1982).

the tug time charter party on behalf of its affiliates, who would actually carry the cargo, and indeed acted as agent for all the Seatrain entities when time chartering the tug and bareboat chartering the barge, both of which would serve the affiliated cargo carriers.   When Intermodal's affiliates became the cargo carriers, replacing Intermodal, they therefore assumed their affiliate's responsibilities under the tug time charter party, including the obligation to obtain their P and I insurers' waiver of subrogation against the tug and its owner, Admiral Towing.[11]   Clause 15 states the parties' intention "that any claims for * * * loss of * * * cargo * * * shall be borne by the appropriate marine underwriters * * * without recourse against the Owner or the tug."   To impose liability on the owner of the tug as a result of the unilateral space arrangements made by the charterer would defeat the intent expressed in the tug time charter.

That Gitmo and International were separate corporations engaged in common carriage by water, and that Intermodal's business was equipment and terminal operations, do not undermine the district court's findings. There is no evidence that these facts were made known to Admiral Towing when the charter was made.   The district court simply held that all three of the Seatrain interests—Intermodal, Gitmo and International—were obligated to obtain waivers of subrogation.

IV

Admiral Towing cross appeals the allowance against it of the subrogation claims asserted by the P & I insurers of Gitmo and International for recovery of amounts paid to the cargo carriers under the policies.   As the district court recognized, these P & I underwriters had refused to waive subrogation.   It does not follow, however, that they should be allowed subrogation against the tug or its owner.   Any claim by any insurer arose solely out of its rights as subrogee of the insured party.

Subrogation was first recognized as a right in equity to prevent the unjust enrichment of a party who owed a claim that had been satisfied by another party.[12]   Later the equitable right was preserved and sometimes extended by incorporating it into the contract between the claim-debtor and the party who, although not ultimately liable for the claim, satisfied it. Whether subrogation is equitable or conventional or both, the subrogee does not obtain redress in its own right but only as successor to the rights of the subrogor.[13]   Accordingly, a subrogee can obtain no greater rights than its subrogor had.[14]   This principle, applied by us in Liberty Mutual

11. E.g., Restatement (Second) of Agency § 186 (1958), and authorities cited therein.

12. G. Palmer, The Law of Restitution § 1.5(b) at 21 (1978), and authorities cited therein.

13. J. Appleman, Insurance Law and Practice § 4102 at 367 (1972), and authorities cited therein; Couch on Insurance § 61:36 at 118–119 (2d ed. 1983).

14. *Appleman,* id., § 4102 at 368; Standard Marine Ins. Co. v. Scottish Metropolitan Assur. Co., 283 U.S. 284, 51 S.Ct. 371, 75 L.Ed. 1037 (1931); Phoenix Insurance Co. v. Erie and Western Transp. Co., 117 U.S. 312, 6 S.Ct. 750, 29 L.Ed. 873 (1886); Liberty Mut. Ins. Co. v. Gulf Oil Corp., 559 F.Supp. 777, 782 (E.D.La.1983), aff'd, 725 F.2d 293 (5th Cir.1984).

Insurance Company v. Gulf Oil Corporation,[15] a Louisiana diversity case, is imminent in the concept of subrogation, the right to assert the claim of another. If Gitmo and International, the subrogor-insureds, were barred from asserting claims against Admiral Towing, their insurer-subrogees could not surmount that barrier. The P and I underwriters therefore could not assert subrogation claims against Admiral Towing or the tug.

None of the appellants, then, may assert claims against Admiral Towing or the tug. We therefore pretermit discussing whether Admiral Towing might have obtained indemnification from the Seatrain entities for any amounts paid to the P and I underwriters of Gitmo and International had they been entitled to subrogation.

V

The tug time charter, as recited above, required the "charterer" (Intermodal, and, through the agency principles discussed in Part III, International and Gitmo) to carry cargo insurance to the full extent of its value, P and I insurance "in amounts satisfactory to the Owner" of the tug, and to "provide for waiver of subrogation against the Owner of the tug, it being the intent hereof that any claims for damages or loss of the tow, or the cargo thereon shall be borne by the appropriate marine underwriters insuring its said tow and cargo, without recourse against the Owner, or the tug." The district court found, and we agree, that this language required the Seatrain entities "to procure an insurance policy which would be primarily responsible for payment of claims asserted by Cargo for which the carrier was liable without recourse against the tug." The contract, according to the court, amounted to an agreement by the charterer to obtain insurance to protect the tug and its owner from liability to cargo. This finding as to the parties' intent, supported by the language of the contract and testimony in the record, is not to be disturbed on appeal.[16]

The Seatrain entities did not obtain property insurance on the cargo, as warranted, although they argue that it was not feasible for them to insure property they did not own. Further, Intermodal was unable to obtain P and I insurance with a waiver of subrogation against the tug or its owner. The district court therefore properly allowed Admiral Towing indemnification against the Seatrain entities, in the event of future claims by cargo, for their failure to hold Admiral Towing harmless from liability to cargo.

The district court found that Intermodal had procured SOL policies to cover its failure to procure the insurance required by the tug time charter. Gitmo and International were later added as additional insureds under the first SOL policy. The policies waived subrogation against the tug and its owner, as provided in the time charter of the Tug Admiral, and were issued "to cover the contractual legal liability of the Assured for loss and/or damage * * * to cargo, * * * not recoverable from cargo interests, assumed by Charterers under the Charter Party between vessel Owners and the

---

15. Id.   **16.** Supra n. 10.

Assured's hereunder." The district court's finding, which we affirm because supported by the record, was that the SOL policies were intended to insure Intermodal against liability for breach of its contractual obligation to hold the tug and its owner harmless from cargo claims. The court therefore properly held that the SOL policies would cover the Seatrain entities' liability on any indemnification claims asserted by Admiral Towing.

The district court held, however, that Admiral Towing could not proceed directly against the SOL underwriters under the Puerto Rican direct action statute. Because Admiral Towing's indemnification claims arise from the Seatrain entities' breach of contractual obligations, and not from tortious activity, we agree that the direct action was not available.[17]

VI

For the reasons given, we AFFIRM the judgment of the district court insofar as it denies appellants' claims against Great Lakes, Admiral Towing, and the tug ADMIRAL. We REVERSE the judgment allowing the P and I underwriters of Gitmo and International to assert subrogation claims against the tug and Admiral Towing. We AFFIRM the judgment allowing Admiral Towing indemnification against the Seatrain entities for cargo claims and holding that the SOL policies insure the Seatrain entities against this liability. We AFFIRM the judgment denying Admiral Towing a direct action against the SOL underwriters.

All costs are to be assessed against the appellants and the cross appellees, and to be recovered in full by the Great Lakes and Admiral interests.

N O T E

Charter parties are usually used for conveying the right to use an entire vessel. ← Instrument
They are also used, however, to convey the right to use a portion of a vessel. Such an instrument is called a space charter. See Cargill Ferrous Intern. v. M/V ARCTIC CONFIDENCE, 1995 A.M.C. 1782, 1994 WL 97787 (E.D.La.1994). The term was derived from the medieval Latin *carta partita,* which Scrutton translates, "an instrument written in duplicate on a single sheet and then divided by indented edges so that each part fitted the other." Scrutton on *Charter Parties* 3, n. 16 (1984). Molloy referred to it as "all one in the Civil Law with an Indenture at the Common Law." 1 De Jure Maritimo 369 (9th Ed. 1769).

Although the term "charter party" referred to a type of sealed instrument, under present day usage "charter" and sometimes "charter party" is used to mean the agreement rather than the instrument, and while contracts for the use of vessels of large value usually will be written, such contracts may be oral, giving rise to the term "oral charter party," which appears to be, oddly enough, an unwritten

---

17. Cf., Deutsche–Schiffahrtsbank A.G. v. A. Bilbrough and Co., 563 F.Supp. 1307, 1309 (E.D.La.1983); Taylor v. Fishing Tools, Inc., 274 F.Supp. 666, 673 (E.D.La.1967); Pennsylvania Fire Ins. Co. v. Underwriters at Lloyd's, 140 So.2d 212, 215 (La.App. 4th Cir. 1962); Ramos v. Continental Insurance Company, 493 F.2d 329 (1st Cir.1974).

contract in writing.   Cf. Valero Refining, Inc. v. M/T Lauberhorn, 813 F.2d 60 (5th Cir.1987).

Is there some point at which a contract for the use of a vessel falls outside the complexities of the maritime law of charter parties.   What about rental of a small boat?   Cf. Craine v. United States, 722 F.2d 1523, 1984 A.M.C. 2997 (11th Cir.1984), in which the court entertained an action under the Federal Tort Claims Act for wrongful death, claiming negligence in failure to warn the renter of a fourteen foot boat with oars and an outboard motor.   The death occurred on the Chatahoochee River in Columbus, Georgia, when the boat was swept over a dam. No mention is made of admiralty jurisdiction, and there is no discussion of the question of whether the Chatahoochee is navigable water of the United States at the point of the disaster.   Assuming that it was, would the proper remedy be the Suits in Admiralty Act?   Would the rental agreement constitute a bareboat charter?

In general, of course, the charterer is liable for negligent damage to the vessel during the term of the charter.   It has been held, however, that when the charterer negligently overloaded a barge and it sank, while it was liable for the sinking of the barge, it was not liable for the damages that occurred when a salvage team that was lifting coils of wire off the sunken barge with a crane dropped a coil onto the barge. Federal Barge Lines, Inc. v. Granite City Steel Div. of National Steel Corp., 809 F.2d 497 (8th Cir.1987).

Demise Charters

Where the vessel is delivered to the charterer and the charterer operates it as if it were the owner, the transaction is called a demise, or demise charter. Sometimes the charterer leases only the vessel, providing its own master and crew.   This transaction is called a "bareboat" charter.   Under some demise charters, the owner's master and crew remain with the vessel as borrowed servants.   See Federal Barge Lines, Inc. v. SCNO Barge Lines, Inc., 711 F.2d 110, 1984 A.M.C. 2625 (8th Cir.1983).   In either case, however, the owner gives up possession and control, and the charterer treats the vessel as his own.   Thus it is often referred to as an "owner pro hac vice."   Scrutton characterizes a demise charter as a contract for the hire of a chattel, governed by the common law of hire.   Op.cit., 50.

Since the contract places the possession and use in the charterer and the owner retains only a right to the price or "hire" and the right to return of the vessel at the end of the term, the provisions to be found in a demise charter concern themselves largely with protecting the bargain of the parties.   Thus we find clauses that deal with the delivery and redelivery of the vessel, duties with respect to its maintenance, provisions dealing with the respective duties of the owner and the charterer to procure insurance.   There is a specimen bareboat charter party in 2B Benedict (7th Ed. 1985) Form No. 4–1.

Generally speaking, since the vessel is no longer operated by the owner, the owner is not personally liable for the torts of the charterer.   *Federal Barge Lines,* supra.   Nor, generally, on the contracts of the charterer.   See Cactus Pipe & Supply Co. Inc. v. M/V Montmartre, 756 F.2d 1103, 1985 A.M.C. 2150 (5th Cir.1985). There is no way, however, to escape certain kinds of liens on the vessel under the rule in *The Barnstable.*   Industria Nacional Del Papel, CA. v. M/V Albert F., 730 F.2d 622, 1985 A.M.C. 1437 (11th Cir.1984), cert. denied 469 U.S. 1037, 105 S.Ct. 515, 83 L.Ed.2d 404 (1984).   And there is authority for the proposition that the owner remains personally liable for damages to a seaman injured as a result of the unseaworthiness of the vessel, even if the unseaworthiness developed after the delivery of the vessel under a bareboat charter.   Baker v. Raymond Int'l, Inc., 656

F.2d 173, 1982 A.M.C. 2752 (5th Cir.1981), cert. denied 456 U.S. 983, 102 S.Ct. 2256, 72 L.Ed.2d 861 (1982).

The demise of a vessel need not be memorialized by a written instrument, and in the case of lighters and barges sometimes is not.

Time Charters and Voyage Charters

When the arrangement between the charterer and the owner or whoever at the time is operating the vessel, is for the services of the vessel and crew, the contract is not a demise. Sometimes such a contract is for a period of time, usually called a time charter. Sometimes it is for a single voyage, in which event it is generally called a voyage charter. There are hybrid types. See Scrutton on Charter Parties 51 (19th Ed. 1984). Frequently at a given time a vessel is operated under layers of charters. See, e.g., *The M/V Montmartre*, supra: "Before the carriage of the cargo in issue, Orient bareboat chartered the MONTMARTRE to Eternity Navigation Co., S.A. (Eternity), in September, 1976. Eternity, as bareboat charter owner, time chartered the vessel to Iino Kaiun Kaisha, Ltd. (Iino). Iino in turn time chartered the MONTMARTRE to Canadian Forest Navigation Co., Ltd (Canadian) in June 1979. In July, 1979, Canadian Voyage chartered the MONTMARTRE to Seanav International Co. (Seanav). Seanav in turn voyage chartered the vessel to Corinth."

Under a time or voyage charter, the master and crew remain the servants of the owner, or of the demise charterer, and therefore the owner or owner pro hac vice remains in general liable to third parties for their torts, and the charterer, other than a demise charterer, normally is not liable for the torts of the master and crew. Thus a time charterer was held to owe passengers no per se duty of safe access. Forrester v. Ocean Marine Indemnity Co., 11 F.3d 1213, 1994 A.M.C. 2993 (5th Cir.1993). But the charterer is held liable for negligence in the exercise of its control of the vessel under the charter. In Randall v. Chevron U.S.A., 13 F.3d 888, 1994 A.M.C. 1217 (5th Cir.1994), modified 22 F.3d 568, 1944 A.M.C. 2492 (5 Cir.1994), for example, the time charterer was held liable for injuries on a crew boat that was sent out in unfavorable weather. Further, under the charter party, the charterer may be charged with responsibilities in connection with, e.g., the loading of the vessel. See Finora Company, Inc. v. Amitie Shipping, Ltd., 54 F.3d 209 (4th Cir.1995), holding the time charterer and not the owner liable for damage to cargo done by stowaways who presumably boarded the ship at the port of loading. American Home Assurance Co. v. M/V Sletter, 43 F.3d 995, 1995 A.M.C. 1160 (5th Cir.1995).

But absent special provision, the duty to load, stow, and discharge cargo falls on the owner. Wong Wing Fai Co., S.A. v. United States, 840 F.2d 1462 (9th Cir.1988). There it was held that the obligation to pay charter hire ceased when the purpose of the charter was frustrated when the vessel was commandeered by fleeing Vietnamese soldiers following the fall of south Vietnam.

And in general, the owner warrants the seaworthiness of the vessel to the charterer and when a breach of the warranty causes cargo damage, the cargo may sue the owner directly. Siderius, Inc. v. M.V. Amilla, 880 F.2d 662 (2d Cir.1989).

Both the owner and the charterer may be liable for cargo damages but if so, only one can avail himself of the $500 limit. Thyssen, Inc. v. S/S Eurounity, 21 F.3d 533, 1994 A.M.C. 1638 (2d Cir.1994).

Time and particular voyage charters voyage are often contracts of carriage. They need not be, of course, for a vessel may be chartered for purposes other than transportation of cargo. It might be chartered for carriage of passengers, for example, or for fishing, or sailing, or any of a myriad of possible uses. The contract will vary, of course, depending on the contemplated use. In the case of charters used in carriage of goods, the standard terms vary somewhat depending upon the particular trade. A large number of specimens is gathered together in volumes 2B and 2C of Benedict on *Admiralty* (7th Ed. 1985).

There is a readable discussion of the common terms of charter parties in Chapter IV of Gilmore and Black, *Law of Admiralty,* including a clause by clause analysis of the Uniform General Charter 1922 ("Gencon").

3.   TUG AND TOW

Agrico Chemical Co. v. M/V Ben W. Martin

United States Court of Appeals, Fifth Circuit, 1981.
664 F.2d 85, 1985 A.M.C. 563.

■ ALVIN B. RUBIN, CIRCUIT JUDGE:

A barge loaded with liquid nitrogen fertilizer capsized. The parties involved in supplying and moving the barge concede their liability to the owner of the cargo but each contends that the other was liable for the loss. Based on what we consider to be a misconstruction of the contractual relationship between the parties, the district court found only one party at fault. We find both negligent, apportion the liability equally between them, and remand for further proceedings.

Agrico Chemical Company manufactures and sells various chemical products, including 32% liquid nitrogen fertilizer (urea ammonium nitrate or UAN), which it manufactures at a plant near Tulsa, Oklahoma. Agrico contracted with Brent Towing Company to provide the marine services and equipment necessary to transport Agrico's products on a continuing basis. During October 1977, Agrico advised Brent that, pursuant to the contract, it had more than 5000 tons of UAN to be moved from its Oklahoma plant to Westwego, Louisiana. Brent assigned two of its barges to the task and engaged Logicon's tow boat, the M/V GREENVILLE, to tow the barges on a mills-per-ton-mile basis, the usual way in which it engaged a tow. Brent concedes that its contract with Agrico was not a charter but a contract of affreightment. Logicon provided the tug and crew, arranged and paid for insurance, paid the expenses of the trip and was compensated in the same manner in which a taxi would be paid.

Agrico then informed Brent that it wished to move an additional 3,000 tons of UAN. Brent had no other barge available, so Malcolm Gunter, Brent's traffic manager, communicated with Herman Pardue, Logicon's port captain, seeking sufficient space on a Logicon barge to move the additional cargo.

Pardue informed Gunter that the Logicon 2702, a 27,000 barrel, single-skinned barge, was available and could be added to the GREENVILLE's tow. * * *

The interior of the Logicon barge consisted of ten cargo tanks, five on each side of a centerline bulkhead. The centerline bulkhead was liquid-tight only at the number one (forward-most) port and starboard tanks; that part of the bulkhead separating cargo compartments two through five contained "baffles" or openings that permitted liquid to flow between the port and starboard tanks. Diesel fuel is lighter than water, and the barge can be loaded almost to its top with diesel fuel without causing the barge to be overloaded. UAN, however, is so much heavier than water that the vessel is down to its draft line when loaded with a much smaller volume of UAN than of diesel fuel. Thus, there is more empty space in the cargo tanks, leaving more room for the liquid to shift when the barge is loaded with UAN rather than with diesel fuel. When the heavier fluid, UAN, shifts from one side of the barge to another, the stability of the barge is threatened.

* * *

* * * When the barge arrived at Agrico's plant, two Brent tankermen, experienced in handling UAN, began loading. Bland testified that he suggested to the tankermen the order the tanks should be filled. After four hours of loading, the 2702 began to list. One of Brent's tankermen then sought out Bland, who informed the Brent tankerman of the nature of the bulkheads, which permitted the cargo to shift from one side to the other. The district judge found that "[w]ith this knowledge [Brent's employees] continued with the loading, and with the advice and counsel, and at times the assistance, of Mr. Bland the matter was completed."

Loading the barge required twelve hours to complete. The Brent tankermen then left. The barge was afloat and appeared to be stable and level. "[A] little after" the Brent tankermen left, and before the tow commenced, however, the barge began to roll. Captain Jacobs telephoned Pardue for instructions, then directed Bland to get the barge leveled off so the tow could begin. Bland put pumps on the barge and transferred some of the cargo from the first compartment to the other compartments, thus, of course, altering the distribution of the cargo. The barge was left tied up overnight, and the tow commenced the next morning.

The GREENVILLE towed the three barges, including the two Brent barges and the Logicon barge, to Greenville, Mississippi. There the barges were tied up, and the GREENVILLE went into dry dock for a wheel change. * * *

On the morning of November 12, the crew of the M/V GREENVILLE was attempting to make up the tow so that it could continue the downriver voyage. The GREENVILLE was brought outside Logicon 2702 and was being used to slide the barge forward when the barge began to roll and then suddenly capsized.

Agrico sued only Logicon and its vessels. Logicon filed a third-party complaint against Brent seeking indemnity or contribution, and also seeking the damages suffered by its barge. After an evidentiary hearing on liability issues only, the district judge held that the arrangement between

Brent and Logicon constituted a charter, and that Brent was functioning as a stevedore in loading the 2702. The court noted that as a stevedore Brent owed a duty of workmanlike performance to Logicon and that Brent's tankermen had committed a breach of this duty in continuing to load the barge after they knew of the openings in the centerline bulkhead. "[I]t was Brent's duty at that time * * * to discontinue the loading of the barge and thereby avoid an unseaworthy condition in connection therewith."

* * *

* * * The key issue, about which the other determinations revolve, is the nature of the contract between Brent and Logicon, for that determines the rights and duties of each. Accordingly, we first examine that question.

I

Barges are vessels, but of a peculiar kind. A. Parks, Law of Tug, Tow and Pilotage 4 (1971). Lacking power and usually crew, barges depend upon another vessel, a tug, for movement. A contract for a tug to move a barge is one of towage. The tug is neither a bailee nor an insurer of the tow. See Southwestern Sugar and Molasses Co. v. River Terminals Corp., 360 U.S. 411, 418 n. 6, 79 S.Ct. 1210, 1215 n. 6, 3 L.Ed.2d 1334, 1341 n. 6 (1959); Nat G. Harrison Overseas Corp. v. American Tug Titan, 516 F.2d 89, 94 (5th Cir.1975), as modified, 520 F.2d 1104 (5th Cir.1975); Humble Oil & Refining Co. v. Tug Crochet, 422 F.2d 602, 606 (5th Cir.1970); First Mississippi Corp. v. Fielder Towing Co., 469 F.Supp. 1080, 1084 (N.D.Miss. 1979). The tug is, however, obliged to use "'such reasonable care and maritime skill as prudent navigators employ for the performance of similar service.'" First Mississippi Corp., 469 F.Supp. at 1084, quoting from, Stevens v. The White City, 285 U.S. 195, 202, 52 S.Ct. 347, 350, 76 L.Ed. 699, 703 (1932).

A towage contract, imposing the duties we have described, arises when one vessel is employed to expedite the movement of another. A. Parks, supra, at 22. If, however, the tug is engaged to do more than merely tow another's vessel, the contract is considered one for the movement of the tow and its contents, a contract of affreightment, subject to the more exacting duties applicable to those who undertake as carriers to transport cargo. See Southwestern Sugar and Molasses Co. v. River Terminals Corp., 360 U.S. 411, 417 n. 6, 79 S.Ct. 1210, 1215 n. 6, 3 L.Ed.2d 1334, 1341 n. 6 (1959)(a common carrier is liable "without proof of negligence, for all damage to the goods transported by it," but liability in the normal tug-tow relationship has not been held to extend this far). Thus, "when a tug and barge are owned by the same person (or when either the tug or barge is bareboat-chartered to the same person) and are utilized, by contract, to tow cargo from one point to another, the contract is one of affreightment and not towage." A. Parks, supra at 22. Sacramento Navigation Co. v. Salz, 273 U.S. 326, 328, 47 S.Ct. 368, 369, 71 L.Ed. 663, 664 (1927); Continental Grain Co. v. American Commercial Barge Line Co., 332 F.2d 26, 27 (7th Cir.1964).

The owner of a barge may, like the owners of other vessels, agree by contract to allow another to use it. This contract, usually called a charter party or charter, may assume a variety of forms. If full possession and control of the vessel is turned over to the charterer, the contract is a demise or bareboat charter. The primary obligation of the owner under such a charter is to furnish a vessel in seaworthy state when it is delivered to the charterer. G. Gilmore & C. Black, *The Law of Admiralty* 241 (2d ed. 1975). The charterer is regarded as the owner of the vessel for the period of the charter and is responsible for the vessel's operation. Id. at 242.

A "bareboat" or demise charter requires "complete transfer of possession, command, and navigation of the vessel from the owner to the charterer." Gaspard v. Diamond M. Drilling Co., 593 F.2d 605, 606 (5th Cir.1979). A demise is "tantamount to, though just short of, an outright transfer of ownership." Guzman v. Pichirilo, 369 U.S. 698, 700, 82 S.Ct. 1095, 1096, 8 L.Ed.2d 205, 208 (1962). It need not, however, be in writing.

A vessel may, of course, be chartered in some other fashion, for example for a single voyage ("voyage charter"), or for a fixed period of time ("time charter"). Typically in the case of conventional vessels, the owner remains in control during such charters, and provides the master and crew. Because barges lack power and usually have no crew, contracts for the mere use of a barge are usually bareboat, A. Parks, supra, at 394, although this is not inevitable. The owner may not only charter the barge but may also provide a tow and remain in control of the barge.

Whatever the nature of the vessel, the rules concerning responsibility for its operation are the same. If the owner retains control, he remains liable for all damages arising out of its operation whether the charter be only for a single voyage ("voyage charter") or for a fixed time ("time charter"). If the charter is a demise, the charterer is responsible. The charter may describe the duties of the parties and provide for the shifting of risks between them, but, in general, control entails responsibility for fault.

Thus, if the Logicon–Brent agreement for use of the Logicon barge was a bareboat charter and the agreement to tow that barge was a contract of towage, Logicon would be liable only if it were negligent in towage or if it failed to provide a seaworthy vessel. If, however, their arrangement was a contract of affreightment for the benefit of Agrico, primary liability to Agrico for damage to its cargo rests on Logicon. A. Parks, supra, at 24.

The agreement between Agrico and Brent was certainly a contract of affreightment, as it was declared to be by the district court. The contract between Brent and Logicon to tow Brent's two barges from Oklahoma to Louisiana was equally clearly a towage contract. As to Agrico, the cargo owner, Brent was responsible for the delivery of the cargo. Brent in turn could look to Logicon only for reasonable diligence in towage. The agreement by Logicon to supply and to tow the third barge is more difficult to characterize. We look to its terms to determine whether the arrangement should be considered two separate contracts, one a barge charter, the other a towage contract, or whether the terms for the use of the barge made that agreement an affreightment contract.

The district court found that

> the nature of the contract was one of charter rather than a contract of affreightment. That is, for the period of time necessarily involved in the shipment, that the barge was made available to Brent for that purpose. * * * [T]he barge was then placed in the tow of the vessel which was to transport the other two barges to the plaintiff's plant in Oklahoma in order to receive the cargo that was to be transported by Brent under its contract of affreightment with [Agrico].

The district court made only one other factual finding of any possible relevance to the issue: that Brent's tankermen were in control of the loading process and that Brent was, therefore, a stevedore.

The terms of the oral agreement between Gunter, representing Brent, and Pardue, representing Logicon, all point away from bareboat charter. The bareboat charter is not a device for the conduct of the business of shipping but is instead an instrument designed to vest in one person most of the incidents of ownership in a capital asset of that business, a vessel, while another retains its general ownership and the right of reversion. G. Gilmore & C. Black, supra at 239. The bareboat charterer typically is required to carry insurance on the vessel as well as protection and indemnity insurance and crew insurance. See A. Parks, supra, at 406 (The Standard Form of Bareboat Charter, ¶ 4). Though not essential, a survey of the vessel on delivery and redelivery is customary to determine the condition of the vessel at the beginning of the charter and its condition at the end, so as to fix responsibility for and limit disputes about damage during the charter. Because the charter is for the use of the boat bare, the compensation is for the furnishing only of that asset. The term for a bareboat charter would not be for a single, short voyage. Indeed, the usual single voyage charter or charter for a limited period of time provides for control by the owner. A. Parks, supra at 394.

Payment for the Logicon was to be made on the basis of mills-per-ton-mile, a measure that included compensation both for furnishing towing and for use of the barge. Such a measure is inherently inconsistent with the concept of the charter bare of a dumb barge. There was testimony that such payment is typical of affreightment contracts. Both the master who had control of the barge and the crew were Logicon's employees. Logicon was responsible for insurance. No survey was made or contemplated either on delivery or redelivery.

Thus Logicon had "possession, command and navigation" of the barge under an agreement to transport it from one port to another. See Guzman v. Pichirilo, 369 U.S. 698, 699, 82 S.Ct. 1095, 1096, 8 L.Ed.2d 205, 208 (1962); Reed v. United States, 78 U.S. (11 Wall) 591, 600–01, 20 L.Ed. 220, 222–23 (1871); Anderson v. United States, 450 F.2d 567, 572 & n. 15 (5th Cir.1971), cert. denied, 406 U.S. 906, 92 S.Ct. 1608, 31 L.Ed.2d 816 (1972); Stockton Sand & Crushed Rock Co. v. Bundensen, 148 F.2d 159 (9th Cir.1945). But see The Independent, 122 F.2d 141 (5th Cir.1941)(holding no contract of affreightment when a barge was chartered for $500 a month and the charterer then contracted with the owner to tow the barge on a short trip for $50). We conclude that the contract between Brent and Logicon was a contract of affreightment whereby Brent subcontracted with Logicon to perform part of its duties under its own affreightment contract with Agrico.[2]

II

* * *

Application of these principles to the present case leads to a readily predictable result. Brent was negligent in loading the cargo. As a stevedore, Brent violated its duty of workmanlike performance. Logicon, however, was negligent in considering that mere redistribution of the UAN would correct the barge's condition, in taking the barge in tow while it was unstable, in unhitching it at Greenville, and, perhaps, in even supplying the barge without warning of its hidden quality that made it unsuitable for this cargo.[4]

We deem it unnecessary to remand for fault-apportionment.[5] The fault appears to have been equal and damages to the cargo and the barge should be divided between Logicon and Brent.

The judgment of the district court is reversed and the case is remanded for further proceedings consistent with this opinion.

NOTE

In Stevens v. The White City, 285 U.S. 195, 52 S.Ct. 347, 76 L.Ed. 699, 1932 A.M.C. 468 (1932), the Court notes that some vessels, such as barges and canal boats, are built without motive power and with a view of receiving their propelling force from other sources, while others, though having motive power, often employ auxiliary power to assist them in moving about harbors and docks. In either case a contract to supply the needed motive power is a contract for towage, and the Court suggests no distinction between these situations in stating the rule that a contract of towage does not make the tug a common carrier or a bailee of the tow. But if the rationale for this result lies in the ultimate control of the owner of the towed vessel and its master and crew, should such a distinction be made? See Robinson, *Admiralty*, 666, 667 (1939). And see B. Turecamo Towing Corp. v. United States, 125 F.2d 1001, 1942 A.M.C. 254 (2d Cir.1942), Clark, J., concurring. For illustrations of cases under contracts to tow dumb barges or similar vessels that are in fact placed under the exclusive control of the tug, in which it has been indicated that receipt in

---

2. In view of this conclusion, we need not consider whether the Logicon 2702 was unseaworthy, or what Logicon's duty would have been as tower of a barge bareboat chartered to another.

4. That the sinking occurred when the vessel was not actually engaged in movement is purely circumstantial. The barge was under Logicon's control and was in the course of the downstream tow. Stevens v. East–

West Towing Co., 649 F.2d 1104, 1109 (5th Cir.1981)(The "warranty of workmanlike performance extend[s] to all towing operations including preparations necessary and incident to the actual towing of the barge.").

5. See Levin v. Mississippi River Fuel Corp., 386 U.S. 162, 169–70, 87 S.Ct. 927, 932, 17 L.Ed.2d 834 (1967).

good order and failure to deliver, or delivery in a damaged condition, create a prima facie case of negligent towage, see Parks, *The Law of Tug, Tow, and Pilotage,* 19–23 (2d Ed. 1982).   After stating the rule of The White City as "of great comfort to towboat companies," the author cites cases following this general rule, adding somewhat ruefully, "While the statement of the principle is relatively simple and clear, application to specific fact situations may pose monumental headaches for the towboat owner."

The White City is criticized by the Canadian Federal Court, Trial Division, where it is referred to as a strange decision, explanable mainly by its age.   Fraser River Pile & Dredge, Ltd. v. Empire Tug Boats, Ltd., T–1631–93, 1995 A.M.C. 1558 (Can.Fed.T.D.1995).

In a number of cases it has been held that a towage contract implies a warranty of workmanlike service.   See, e.g., Dillingham Tug v. Collier Carbon & Chemical Corp., 707 F.2d 1086, reproduced below, in which it was held that a tug that had lost its tow through negligence is liable for the value of the tow in an action for maritime tort, and has also breached its warranty of workmanlike service, and therefore may not recover its towage fees under a clause providing that such fees "shall be deemed earned * * * upon commencement of the voyage even though at any stage of the venture thereafter the barge or tug be lost * * *," nor recover fees that it had paid for passage through the Panama Canal prior to the loss of the tow. Parks takes sharp exception to reading a warranty of workmanlike service into towage contracts.   Op. cit. at 29.   Among other arguments he points out that the existence of such an implied warranty would cast doubt upon the right of the negligent tug to limit liability, a matter discussed in chapter 17, infra.   He also warns that it would "create confusion in the industry which has come to rely upon the principle that damage actions under towage contracts are *ex delicto* and not *ex contractu.*"   Id.   As to *Dillingham,* of course, there is no way in which an action for towage fees could be characterized as *ex delicto.*   The warranty of workmanlike service in the context of property damage has been rejected as incompatible with the standard of care set forth in The White City. Cargill, Inc. v. C & P Towing Co., Inc., 1991 A.M.C. 101, 1990 WL 270199 (E.D.Va.1990), aff'd 943 F.2d 48, 1992 A.M.C. 392 (4th Cir.1991), rejecting the theory of implied warranty.

It is sometimes stated that the party contracting for towage warrants the seaworthy condition of the tow.   See, e.g., King Fisher Marine Service, Inc. v. NP Sunbonnet, 724 F.2d 1181, 1183, 1984 A.M.C. 1769 (5th Cir.1984).   Is this an accurate statement?   If a tow sinks in calm weather and for no apparent reason, there is a presumption that it sinks because it is unseaworthy, and not through the fault of the tug.   Consolidated Grain & Barge Co. v. Marcona Conveyor Corp., 716 F.2d 1077, 1081, 1985 A.M.C. 117 (5th Cir.1983).

Dillingham Tug & Barge Corp. v. Collier Carbon & Chem. Corp.

United States Court of Appeals, Ninth Circuit, 1983.
707 F.2d 1086, 1984 A.M.C. 1990, cert. denied 465 U.S. 1025, 104 S.Ct. 1280, 79 L.Ed.2d 684 (1984).

■ KENYON, DISTRICT JUDGE:

All four parties to this action appeal from the district court's decision in this case.   We affirm in part and reverse in part, 548 F.Supp. 691.

FACTUAL AND PROCEDURAL BACKGROUND

* * *

Union purchased the barge *Columbia* in the spring of 1976. Union wished to have the *Columbia* ocean towed from Galveston, Texas, to Portland, Oregon. The *Columbia* had been built as an inland barge, and Union intended to use it as an inland barge, but it was necessary to modify it somewhat so that it could survive the ocean tow. Union retained N & S to perform the naval architectural and marine engineering services necessary to allow the barge to make the ocean tow. N & S originally proposed that a hopper cover be built for the barge, to prevent it filling with water. However, this would have been very expensive, and so Union asked N & S if the barge could survive an ocean voyage without the hopper cover. N & S advised Union that it could, if the tie-down devices on the barge were strengthened.

Union's underwriters required the barge to be surveyed by a designated surveyor or salvage association. Union hired Salvage to perform the necessary survey. Salvage determined that the barge was seaworthy for the proposed tow, and issued the survey certificate required by Union's underwriters. As part of their survey, Salvage reviewed the calculations performed by N & S. Salvage also made recommendations for the tow, *inter alia*, that the maximum speed should be restricted to eight knots through the water, that the crew should check the barge periodically to insure that it was not taking on water, and that if it was, the water should be pumped out.

Union hired Dillingham to perform the tow. The towing contract required Dillingham to give "due regard" to Salvage's recommendations. The towing contract also required Union to maintain Hull and Machinery insurance on the barge to its full value naming Dillingham as an additional assured with loss payable to Union. The contract further required a waiver of subrogation against Dillingham, and stated that Union would look only to the insurance for recovery for any loss or damage to the barge. The *Columbia* was placed on Union's fleet Hull and Machinery policy, with the required waiver of subrogation against Dillingham, but also with a $1,000,000 deductible. The parties dispute whether Dillingham was informed of this deductible before or after the commencement of the tow, and the trial judge made no finding of fact on this issue.

The tow commenced on January 29, 1977. By the time the barge reached the Panama Canal, several feet of water had accumulated in the barge's hopper, but the towing crew did not pump it out. After leaving the Canal, the tow consistently exceeded the recommended speed of eight knots. On February 25, the tow encountered heavy seas, speed was reduced at this time, but the barge continued to take on water. After some time, and several speed reductions, the captain of the tug decided to head for Bahia Ballenas to pump out the barge. Bahia Ballenas was over one hundred miles away at this point, and the tug had to head into the northwesterly seas to reach it, while the port of Bahia Santa Maria was only about twenty miles away, and was due east of the tug and tow. Eventually, the captain changed course for Bahia Santa Maria, but it was too late, the straps on the barge gave way, the cargo tanks broke off the barge, and the barge was lost.

The trial court found that Dillingham, Salvage and N & S were liable for the loss of the *Columbia,* and apportioned their fault for the loss at 60%, 20% and 20% respectively. The Court further found that Union's recovery should be reduced by $1,000,000 for its failure to fully insure the barge, and that each defendant would be liable for its proportionate fault only.

DISCUSSION

I. Effect of the Insurance Provision in the Towage Contract Between Dillingham and Union.

The towing contract entered into between Dillingham and Union contained a clause providing that Union would insure the *Columbia* to its full value with Hull and Machinery insurance. The insurance policy was to name Dillingham as an additional assured, with a waiver of right of subrogation against Dillingham. The provision also required Union to look solely to its insurance for the recovery of any loss or damage to the barge.

Union argues that this provision is invalid under Bisso v. Inland Waterways Corp., 349 U.S. 85, 75 S.Ct. 629, 99 L.Ed. 911 (1955). In *Bisso* the Supreme Court held that exculpatory provisions in towing contracts were invalid. Union argues that the insurance provision in this contract is merely an indirect exculpatory clause, since it effectively seeks to shield Dillingham from any liability for the loss of the barge.

The Supreme Court's holding in *Bisso* was based on two public policy factors. The Court wished to discourage negligence by making wrongdoers pay for damage they cause, and the Court also wished to protect those in need of goods and services from being overreached by others who have the power to drive hard bargains.[1] *Bisso* dealt with a pure exculpatory clause. That is not the case herein, though, and the public policy factors key to the holding in *Bisso* do not carry the same weight in the case of an insurance provision like the one at hand. In fact, there are public policy considerations in favor of such provisions.

The Fifth Circuit has previously considered this issue in several cases.[2] In Fluor Western, Inc. v. G & H Offshore Towing Co., 447 F.2d 35 (5th Cir.1971), cert. denied, 405 U.S. 922, 92 S.Ct. 959, 30 L.Ed.2d 793 (1972), a cargo owner had been required to get insurance under a provision similar to the one in question. The court held that the provision was valid, finding several distinctions between it and the exculpatory provision in *Bisso*.

---

1. *Bisso*, supra, 349 U.S. at 91, 75 S.Ct. at 632.

2. The only other circuit which has considered this question found an insurance provision to be unenforceable, saying it had not been bargained for, without giving further explanation. PPG Industries v. Ashland Oil Co., 592 F.2d 138 (3d Cir.1978), cert. denied, 444 U.S. 830, 100 S.Ct. 58, 62 L.Ed.2d 38 (1979).

First, the court stated that there was no absolute exculpation under the provision; if the cargo owner couldn't collect from the insurer he could sue the tower. Union argues that this distinguishes the present case, because the provision appears to eliminate any suits against the tower, whether the insurer pays or not. However, this is not at issue in this case; Union was paid by its insurers for the full value of the barge, minus the $1,000,000 deductible. Whether the provision could shield Dillingham from liability in the absence of such a payment need not be determined.

The *Fluor Western* court went on to note that the contract containing the insurance provision did not bind the underwriters; they bound themselves in a separate agreement, and it was they who would have to bear the loss. The court did not see how any overreaching in the towing industry could have affected the underwriters. The only possible adhesiveness in the contract with regard to the cargo owner was the requirement that he pay the premiums for the insurance, but the court found that public policy was not concerned with which party paid for the insurance.

Fluor Western was followed in Twenty Grand Offshore, Inc. v. West India Carriers, Inc., 492 F.2d 679 (5th Cir.), cert. denied, 419 U.S. 836, 95 S.Ct. 63, 42 L.Ed.2d 63 (1974). The court again noted that the provision in question did not shield the tower from all liability; he could still be liable for loss of use of the barge, or injuries to third persons. Similarly, in the case at hand, the Hull and Machinery insurance obtained would not have paid for loss of use, or injuries to third persons, so it did not shield Dillingham from all liability. Union notes that in *Twenty Grand* there were mutual insurance provisions; since both parties had to insure one another. Union claims that fact distinguishes the present case. However, in BASF Wyandotte Corp. v. Tug Leander, Jr., 590 F.2d 96 (5th Cir.1979), the court explicitly held that such mutuality was not required for the enforcement of such a provision.

We believe that the reasoning of the Fifth Circuit is sound, and that it is not against public policy to enforce an insurance provision in a towage contract. Furthermore, it is economically efficient to allow the enforcement of such provisions. The parties to a towage contract with such a provision are effectively insuring themselves under one policy against any loss due to the fault of either one of them, instead of each obtaining separate policies for this purpose. A single policy can be obtained cheaper than two individual policies. In the event of a loss, the same insurance company pays for the loss, despite who is at fault.

Union argues that even if such provisions are not invalid per se, this one should be held invalid because Union produced uncontradicted evidence of overreaching in the towing industry regarding such provisions. The trial judge found that there was no monopoly in the towing industry, and that there had been no overreaching by Dillingham. The evidence to which Union refers was testimony by an employee of Dillingham that he couldn't recall ever negotiating a contract without such a provision (RT 270–271), and that other major towing companies also used such provisions (RT 272–273). Union also relies on the testimony by a Union employee that Dillingham refused to delete the provision from the contract (RT 532–3, 1937–8). This evidence does not justify a finding that the trial court was clearly erroneous. We uphold the trial court's finding that Union failed to meet their burden of establishing the existence of overreaching.

Having decided that the insurance provision in the towage contract should be enforced, we must determine what effect it has in this case. While finding that the insurance provision was enforceable, the trial judge still allowed Union to collect from Dillingham for its negligence in losing the *Columbia*. We find this to be error.

Normally, the right to sue a party responsible for a loss passes to an insurer once the insurer has paid for the loss. The trial court found that in this case, since a right of subrogation against Dillingham had been waived, and the insurer could therefore not sue Dillingham, the right to sue Dillingham remained with Union. The trial judge went on to rule that, under the collateral source rule, Union's recovery against Dillingham would not be reduced by the amount it had received from its insurer.

We disagree with the trial court's ruling for two reasons. First, the insurance provision in question explicitly provided that Union would look "solely to its Hull and Machinery insurance for the recovery of any loss or damage to the Barge." To allow Union to collect from Dillingham for its negligence violates this provision, which we have found to be enforceable. Second, the collateral source rule only applies to money received from "wholly independent" sources. Union was required to purchase the insurance for Dillingham's benefit. Presumably, Dillingham gave up something in return. Therefore, the insurance payment was not a source wholly independent of Dillingham. In conclusion, to the extent that Union has been paid for its loss by its insurer, Union cannot now collect from Dillingham.

Since the policy under which Union insured the *Columbia* had a $1,000,000 deductible, Union's insurer did not pay for the full value of the barge. The trial court found that Union breached its agreement to insure the barge for its full value by insuring it with a $1,000,000 deductible, and concluded that Union therefore became a self insurer for this $1,000,000. We agree. Union argues that Dillingham either agreed to the deductible, or waived any objection to it. The contract provided that "[Union] shall maintain * * * insurance on the barge to its full value in form and amount satisfactory to [Dillingham]". Union argues that "full value" merely meant last dollar coverage and did not rule out a deductible. While some deductible might have reasonably been anticipated under the contract, we do not believe that insuring the barge for half its value was insuring it to "full value".

* * *

CONCLUSION

The judgments as to Salvage and N & S are reversed. As between Union and Dillingham, the insurance provision at issue is enforceable. Union is responsible for the $1,000,000 deductible under the policy. We reverse the district court, however, as to Dillingham's liability for the amount which the insurer paid Union; Union must look solely to its insurer for recovery. Finally, the district court correctly found that Dillingham was not entitled to collect its towing fees from Union, but erred in awarding Dillingham its Panama Canal fees.

Affirmed in part and reversed in part.

NOTE

As noted in *Dillingham Tug,* the Supreme Court in *Bisso* in 1955, held that a clause in a contract of towage that purported to place the risk of negligent towage on the tow is void as against public policy. See also Boston Metals Co. v. The Winding Gulf, 349 U.S. 122, 75 S.Ct. 649, 99 L.Ed. 933 (1955). Prior to the decisions in *Bisso* and *The Winding Gulf*, the matter was in doubt. See Robinson on Admiralty 670–673 (1939). Four years later, in Southwestern Sugar and Molasses Co. v. River Terminals Corp., 360 U.S. 411, 79 S.Ct. 1210, 3 L.Ed.2d 1334 (1959), the Court held that when the contract of towage incorporated by reference a tariff on file with the ICC, the tariff providing that when shipments were transported in barges furnished by the shipper such barges would be handled at the shipper's risk whether loss or damage to them was caused by negligence or otherwise, the court of appeals should not declare the tariff invalid per se, but should proceed to hear other points raised on the appeal from the district court and if these proved insufficient to dispose of the case, should hold the appeal in abeyance until the ICC had had a chance to rule on the validity of the tariff. The opinion was written by Justice Harlan, who had dissented in *Bisso*. The Chief Justice and Justices Black and Douglas dissented. There was enough in the opinion in *Southwestern Sugar* to cause some hopes that *Bisso* had been materially weakened. In Crescent T. & S. Co. v. Dixilyn Drilling Corp., 303 F.2d 237, 1963 A.M.C. 831 (5th Cir.1962), the Fifth Circuit read it to carve out of the *Bisso* rule contracts dealing with situations in which there are (1) peculiar hazards and the methods of guarding against them are uncertain, and (2) no economic duress. On appeal, however, the Supreme Court reversed per curiam, Justice Harlan writing a short opinion in which he observed that he thought that *Bisso* was wrongly decided but that as long as the decision stood, the *Southwest Sugar* exception should be limited to the case of administrative regulation. Dixilyn Drilling Corp. v. Crescent Towing & Salvage Co., 372 U.S. 697, 83 S.Ct. 967, 10 L.Ed.2d 78 (1963).

In M/S Bremen v. Zapata Off–Shore Co., 407 U.S. 1, 92 S.Ct. 1907, 32 L.Ed.2d 513 (1972), without reexamining the *Bisso* rule, the Court held that it did not reflect so important a national policy at to lead the courts to refuse to give effect to a clause in an ocean towing contract providing for litigation in England, where the exoneration clause would be enforced.

The insurance clause enforced in *Dillingham* above represented a response to *Bisso*.

4.   BILLS OF LADING

The bill of lading serves three distinct purposes. In commercial dealing it is an instrument of title to the goods shipped and may be negotiated to transfer title, or employed as security in the financing of the shipment.

For a discussion of this feature, see Knauth, *Ocean Bills of Lading,* 373, et seq. (1953). Where an instrument purporting to be a bill of lading, but in fact fabricated or forged, is used as security for a loan, is the matter maritime in character? See Societe Generale v. Federal Ins. Co., 856 F.2d 461 (2d Cir.1988), applying the UCC and New York common law without mention of the maritime law.

It is also used as a receipt for the goods delivered to the carrier, serving as evidence of the quantity and condition of goods. Prior to the passage of the Pomerene Bills of Lading Act, 49 U.S.C.A. §§ 81–124, in 1916, a distinction was drawn between the effect of the bill in proving quantity on the one hand, and condition on the other. It was held that the master had no authority to issue a bill of lading for goods in fact not loaded, so the bill was not binding in this respect. Since the master did have authority to state the condition, however, such a statement in the bill would be binding. The Act provides that the carrier shall count or weigh the goods and makes him liable on the bill whether any goods are loaded or not. If the goods are in fact loaded by the shipper, however, and described in the bill of lading only by a statement of marks or labels, or by a statement that the goods "are said to be" of a certain kind or quantity, or it is stated in the bill of lading that packages "are said to" contain goods of a certain kind or quantity or in a certain condition, the carrier may insert a "shipper's weight, load and count" clause and will not be liable for shortage. See 49 U.S.C.A. §§ 100–102. As to condition, of course the bill of lading normally reads "in apparent good order," and refers to external condition of goods the carrier is in no position to examine. See 2A Benedict on Admiralty (7th ed. 1985) § 33. And see Commodity Service Corp. v. Hamburg–American Line, 354 F.2d 234, 1966 A.M.C. 65 (2d Cir.1965). There the court affirmed a judgment for defendant in a case seeking damages for deterioration of a cargo of perishable pork shipped as "fatbacks," holding that since the shipper was in a better position to determine the condition of cargo at the time of loading than the carrier, his failure to submit proof was fatal, the recitation in the bill of lading relating only to external condition.

See Greenburg v. Puerto Rico Maritime Shipping Authority, 835 F.2d 932 (1st Cir.1987), holding that where the cargo is perishable and its condition cannot adequately be gauged by external appearance, a clean bill of lading is not sufficient and the shipper must present other evidence.

And see Tenneco Resins, Inc. v. Davy Intern., AG, 881 F.2d 211 (5th Cir.1989), holding that the carrier had no duty to inspect individual drums that were tendered to its agent stacked in three tiers, and therefore was not liable for water damage attributed to discharge on an open dock when umbrella symbols had been stenciled on the heads of the drums rather than in their customary place on the sides.

When a bill of lading contains no carrier reservations about the condition of the goods, it usually satisfies the requisite proof that the carrier received the goods in good condition for purposes of presenting the prima facie case for cargo damage. Acwoo Intern. Steel Corp. v. Toko Kaiun Kaish, Ltd., 840 F.2d 1284 (6th Cir.1988). In the particular case, however, it was held that a bill of lading with a rust clause in it is not a "clean bill of lading."   See 46 U.S.C.A. § 1303(3) and (4).

While the clean bill establishes, prima facia, the good condition of the goods when delivered to the carrier, it does not help to establish the other end of the prima facie case, that they were damaged when delivered, and failure of the consignee to give notice of damage within three days of delivery creates, under COGSA, a presumption that they were delivered in good condition.   46 U.S.C.A. § 1303(6).   See Crisis Transportation Co. v. M/V Erlangen Exp., 794 F.2d 185 (5th Cir.1986).

Finally, the bill of lading serves as a memorial of the underlying affreightment contract.   It is to be noted that in private carriage the bill of lading, so long as it remains in the hands of the shipper, is not the contract of carriage, the shipper being party to the underlying charter party, and in case of conflict in terms, the charter party controls.   Albert E. Reed & Co. v. M/S Thackeray, 232 F.Supp. 748, 1965 A.M.C. 958 (N.D.Fla.1964). When the vessel is not under charter, however, the bill of lading is considered a part of the contract and the parties are bound by its terms. Cases are collected in Benedict, supra, § 34.

B. THE HARTER ACT

The Carib Prince

(Wuppermann v. The Carib Prince)
Supreme Court of the United States, 1898.
170 U.S. 655, 18 S.Ct. 753, 42 L.Ed. 1181.

The Carib Prince, an iron and steel steamer, was built in England in the spring of 1893, for the carriage of passengers and freight.   She was fitted with a peak tank, triangular in shape, extending from the bottom of the ship to the between deck, the tank being intended to hold water to be used as ballast in trimming the ship.   * * *

On September 14, 1892, * * * On August 31, 1893, while the vessel was * * * lying in the port of Trinidad, loading for a voyage to New York, a number of cases of bitters were delivered on board, consigned to J.W. Wuppermann.   They were placed in the No. 1 hold.   The bill of lading delivered to the consignor contained the following exceptions:

"The act of God, the queen's enemies, pirates, robbers, restraints of princes, rulers, and people, loss or damage from heat or fire on board, in hulk or craft or on shore, explosion, steam, accidents to or latent defects in hull, tackle, boilers, and machinery, or their appurtenances, jettison, barratry, any act, neglect, or default whatsoever of pilots, masters, or crew in the management or navigation of the ship, quarantine, collision, stranding, and all and every other dangers and accidents of the seas, rivers, or steam navigation, of whatever nature or kind, always excepted."

The ship left Trinidad on August 31, 1893, stopped for a short time at Grenada, just north of the Island of Trinidad, and from the latter port proceeded direct to New York. After leaving Grenada, and on the night of the 3d of September, by direction of the captain, the peak ballast tank referred to, and which adjoined the compartment in which the cases of bitters were stored, was filled with sea water. This was done for the purpose of trimming the ship, which was several feet lower at the stern than she was forward. The next morning, or the second morning after, it was discovered that the water from the peak tank was escaping through a rivet hole into the No. 1 hold, the head of one of the rivets having been forced off. To recover the damage occasioned to the goods in question by the water which had thus gotten into the No. 1 hold, Mrs. Wuppermann filed her libel.

■ MR. JUSTICE WHITE delivered the opinion of the Court.

* * * The district court and the circuit court of appeals held that the sole cause of the accident was a latent defect in a rivet from which the head had come off, leaving a hole through which the water poured in and upon the merchandise of the libelant. This defective condition of the rivet was found to have been caused by the fact that the quality of iron had been injured during the construction of the vessel by too much hammering, so that it became brittle and weak, rendering it unfit to sustain the reasonable pressure caused by filling the tank with water while at sea, and consequently caused the vessel to be unseaworthy at the time the bills of lading were issued and the goods were received on board * * *.

As, after a careful examination of the evidence, we conclude that it does not clearly appear that the lower courts erred in their conclusion of fact, we accept as indisputable the finding that the Carib Prince was unseaworthy at the time of the commencement of the voyage in question, by reason of the defect in the tank above referred to.

Upon this premise of fact, the first question which arises for solution is this: Did the exceptions in the bill of lading exempting the shipowner "from loss or damage from * * * accidents to or latent defects in hull, tackle, boilers, and machinery or their appurtenances," operate to relieve him from damages caused by the state of unseaworthiness existing at the inception of the voyage, and at the time the bill of lading was signed? This question is no longer open, as it is fully answered in the negative by the decision in The Caledonia, 157 U.S. 124, 15 S.Ct. 537 (1895). In that case the damage sought to be recovered had been caused by the breaking of the shaft of the steamer by reason of a latent defect which existed at the commencement of the voyage. The exemption from liability, which was there asserted to exist, was predicated on a provision in the bill of lading relieving the owner from "loss or damage * * * from delays, steam boilers and machinery, or defects therein." It was held that the clause in question operated prospectively only, and did not relate to a condition of unseaworthiness existing at the commencement of the voyage, and that it must be construed as contemplating only a state of unseaworthiness arising during the voyage. The principle upon which the ruling rested was that clauses exempting the owner from the general obligation of furnishing a seaworthy vessel must be confined within strict limits, and were not to be extended by latitudinarian construction or forced implication so as to comprehend a state of unseaworthiness, whether patent or latent, existing at the commencement of the voyage. The rule thus announced in *The Caledonia* but expressed the doctrine stated by Lord Selbourne in Steel v. Steamship Co., 3 App.Cas. 72, that the exceptions in a bill of lading ought, if in reason it be possible to do so, to receive "a construction not nullifying and destroying the implied obligation of the shipowner to provide a ship proper for the performance of the duty which he has undertaken." The fact that the exempting clause in the present case refers to latent defects, while that passed on in The Caledonia embraced defects generally, does not take this case out of the control of the general rule laid down in *The Caledonia*. The decision in The Caledonia was based, not on the particular character of the defects there referred to, but on the general ground that, unless there were express words to the contrary, the language of the exempting clause would not be held to apply to defects, whether patent or latent, existing when the voyage was commenced; in other words, that, where the owner desires the exemption to cover a condition of unseaworthiness existing at the commencement of the voyage, he must unequivocally so contract. An illustration of such contract was found in The Laertes, 12 Prob.Div. 187, referred to in the opinion in *The Caledonia*. In that case the bill of lading stipulated, not merely against latent defects, but against all such defects existing at the time of the shipment.

The condition of unseaworthiness found to exist not being then within the exceptions contained in the bill of lading, it remains only to consider whether under the facts disclosed by the record, aside from the exceptions in the bill of lading, the shipowner was liable for the damages caused by the unseaworthy condition of the ship. The contention is that, as the owner exercised due diligence to make the ship seaworthy, he was consequently not liable, because, under the present state of the law, a shipowner is no longer under the obligation to furnish a seaworthy ship, but only to exercise due diligence to do so. The radical change in the duties and obligations of shipowners which this proposition involves is asserted to arise from the statute of February 13, 1893 (27 Stat. 445), commonly described as the "Harter Act." The proposition rests on the assumed meaning of the second and third sections of that act. The second section is as follows:

* * * [46 U.S.C.A. § 191, See Statute and Rule Supplement]

Now, it is patent that the foregoing provisions deal, not with the general duty of the owner to furnish a seaworthy ship, but solely with his power to exempt himself from so doing by contract, when the particular conditions exacted by the statute obtain. Because the owner may, when he has used due diligence to furnish a seaworthy ship, contract against the obligation of seaworthiness, it does not at all follow that, when he has made no contract to so exempt himself, he, nevertheless, is relieved from furnishing a seaworthy ship, and is subjected only to the duty of using due diligence. To make it unlawful to insert in a contract a provision exempting from seaworthiness where due diligence has not been used cannot by any sound rule of construction be treated as implying that where due diligence has been used, and there is no contract exempting the owner, his obligation to furnish a seaworthy vessel has ceased to exist. The fallacy of the construction relied on consists in assuming that, because the statute has forbidden the shipowner from contracting against the duty to furnish a seaworthy ship unless he has been diligent, thereby the statute has declared that without contract no obligation to furnish a seaworthy ship obtains in the event due diligence has been used. And the same fallacy is involved in the contention that this construction is supported by the third section of the act. The third section is as follows:

* * *

The exemption of the owners or charterers from loss resulting from "faults or errors in navigation or in the management of the vessel," and for certain other designated causes, in no way implies that, because the owner is thus exempted when he has been duly diligent, thereby the law has also relieved him from the duty of furnishing a seaworthy vessel. The immunity from risks of a described character, when due diligence has been used, cannot be so extended as to cause the statute to say that the owner when he has been duly diligent is not only exempted in accordance with the tenor of the statute from the limited and designated risks which are named therein, but is also relieved, as respects every claim of every other description, from the duty of furnishing a seaworthy ship. These considerations dispose of all the questions arising on the record.

The decrees rendered both in the circuit court of appeals and in the district court must therefore be reversed and the case be remanded to the district court for further proceedings in conformity with this opinion.

And it is so ordered.

■ MR. JUSTICE BROWN, with whom was MR. JUSTICE BREWER, dissented.

May v. Hamburg–Amerikanische Packetfahrt Aktiengesellschaft

(The Isis)
Supreme Court of the United States, 1933.
290 U.S. 333, 54 S.Ct. 162, 78 L.Ed. 348.

■ MR. JUSTICE CARDOZO delivered the opinion of the Court.

The assignee of cargo owners filed libels against the respondent, the owner of the Isis, to recover moneys deposited as security for general average contributions, the deposit being exacted by the respondent as a condition of delivery.

The Isis, a vessel of about 7,000 tons, sailed from loading ports on the Pacific Coast with cargo destined for Bremen, Hamburg and Antwerp. She was then seaworthy in hull and gear, and fitted in all respects for the intended voyage. In the Weser River, not far from Bremen, Germany, her first port of discharge, she stranded by reason of negligent navigation with damage to her rudder stock and also to the rudder blade. Aided by tugs, she continued up the river to Bremen, disclosing, as she moved, a tendency to sheer to starboard. On arrival at that port, she discharged her Bremen cargo, and there was then an inspection of the damage. The rudder stock had been twisted about 45 degrees. To ascertain the condition of the blade, the vessel was put in a dry dock and kept there a few hours. The examiners reported that the blade was intact. In fact, the lower part of it was bent to starboard to the extent of about five degrees. The inspection was after dark with the bottom of the rudder still under water. The two counts below have concurred in a finding that the use of reasonable care would have caused the bend to be discovered.

The head office of the owner at Hamburg was notified of the mishap to the vessel before she landed at Bremen, and the marine superintendent was sent to meet her. The superintendent, Reichenbacher, and the master of the vessel, Krueger, consulted, along with others, as to what ought to be done. Bremen had adequate facilities for the making of complete repairs, but it would have taken about two weeks to make them. To save time and expense to the vessel and her cargo, the decision was made to send her to Hamburg about seventy miles away, the cargo still aboard. Before a start was made, the rudder was lashed amidships so as to be incapable of motion. The vessel then set forth in the towage of three tugs, one of them in front and one on either side. No harm befell for a distance of about six miles. Then, at or near the junction of the Weser and Lesum Rivers, the pilot in control changed her course to starboard in order to pass a vessel coming up. There is a finding that her navigation at this point was unskillful and negligent, in that she was driven at too high a speed and too close to the edge of the channel. In all events, in passing she made a sheer to starboard which the tugs and her engines were unable to control. She was stranded hard and fast amidships on a sand spit near the bank.

[The vessel was towed back to Bremen where it was repaired. The cargo was transshipped to Antwerp. The Bills of lading contained a Jason Clause entitling the vessel owner to general average contribution despite the fact that the peril occasioning the general average expense was produced by the fault of the vessel. See p. 725, infra. The cargo maintained that the vessel was unseaworthy when it left Bremen with the defective rudder and that therefore the owner had breached the condition held necessary to invoke the provisions of the Harter Act that would entitle it to rely upon the Jason Clause. The Court held that the duty to use due diligence to provide a seaworthy vessel was met on the Pacific Coast and that therefore the vessel was entitled to contribution to the expenses of the first stranding. As to the second, however, it held that the vessel having been returned to the owners officials at Bremen, a new duty arose to use due diligence to make it seaworthy before sending it up the river.]

* * *

The respondent, claiming the benefit of a conditional exemption, has the burden of proof that the condition was fulfilled * * * We are unwilling to say in opposition to the finding of the Court of Appeals that the burden has been borne * * *.

The respondent insists that a vessel may be seaworthy though she is navigated by tugs. No doubt that is true where the rudder is capable of use. This is far from saying that the risk to the cargo is not appreciably increased if the rudder is out of commission and so incapable of giving aid when an emergency arises. There is no need to go beyond the pages of this record for proof that this is so. Witnesses for the respondent tell us that a vessel with her rudder lashed may be towed without risk if the speed of the tugs is slow, less than seven kilometers an hour. They admit that the useless rudder becomes a source of danger if the speed of the tugs is higher, seven kilometers or more. We turn to the findings of the commissioner approved by the district court. From these it appears that the Isis was proceeding, when she sighted the upbound steamer, at a speed of more than eight kilometers an hour. Not only that, but the commissioner has found that she was navigated at too high a speed and too close to the edge of the channel, and that because of these errors she stranded a second time. The speed and place would in all likelihood have been harmless if she had been navigating the river with her steering gear in order * * *.

The rudder * * * was not merely useless and disabled. By reason of the bend of five degrees, it was positively harmful at least to some extent. * * *

We think the cumulative effect of the evidence that the rudder was disabled and that there was a bend of five degrees is to exact of us a holding that the respondent has failed to sustain the burden of establishing due diligence in making the ship seaworthy for her voyage down the Weser.

If due diligence was not used in creating a seaworthy condition, the question to be determined is the need of a causal relation between the defect and the ensuing loss. * * *

The statute, aided by the contract, gives the shipowner a privilege upon his compliance with a condition. If he would have the benefit of the privilege, he must take it with the attendant burden. There would be no end to complications and embarrassments if the courts were to embark upon an inquiry as to the tendency of an unseaworthy defect to aggravate the risk of careless navigation. Little can be added on this point to what has been said so well by Learned Hand, J., in a case already cited. The Elkton, 49 F.2d 700, 1931 A.M.C. 1040 (2 Cir.1931). The barrier of the statute would be sufficient, if it stood alone, to overcome the claim of privilege. It is reinforced, however, by the barrier of contract. The Harter Act, as we have seen, would not impose upon the cargo a duty to share in general average contribution if the Jason Clause or an equivalent were not embodied in the bill of lading or contract of affreightment. The owners of this cargo have stated the conditions on which they are willing to come in and pay their share of the expenses. A court should be very sure that the literal meaning is not the true one before subtracting from conditions that are clear upon their face.

We are told that the provisions of the Harter Act, 46 U.S.C.A. §§ 190–195, will lead to absurdity and hardship if an unseaworthy condition is to take away from the carrier an exemption from liability for the negligence of its servants in the management of the vessel without a causal relation between the defect and the disaster. Extreme illustrations are set before us, as where there is a loose rivet in the deck, or a crack in a hatch cover, or one less messboy than required. Seaworthiness of the vessel becomes, it is said, a whimsical condition if exemption is lost through defects so unsubstantial. We assume for present purposes that the nature of the defects brought forward as illustrations is sufficient to condemn a vessel as unfitted for her voyage. Even if that be so, the argument for the respondent loses sight of the value of a uniform rule that will put an end to controversy where the causal relation is uncertain or disputed. Particularly is there need of such a test where the carrier asks to be relieved from liability for conduct which without the benefit of the statute would be an actionable wrong. The maritime law abounds in illustrations of the forfeiture of a right or the loss of a contract by reason of the unseaworthiness of a vessel, though the unseaworthy feature is unrelated to the loss. The law reads into a voyage policy of insurance a warranty that the vessel shall be seaworthy for the purpose of the voyage. There are many cases to the effect that, irrespective of any relation of cause and effect, the breach of the warranty will vitiate the policy. What is implied is a condition, and not merely a covenant, just as here there is not a covenant, but a condition of exemption. * * *

The distinction is apparent between suits such as this where the unseaworthiness of a vessel is merely a condition of exemption and suits where the unseaworthiness of a vessel is the basis of a suit for damages. In cases of the latter order there can be no recovery of damages in the absence of a causal relation between the loss and the defect. Unseaworthiness viewed as a condition of exemption stands upon a different footing from unseaworthiness viewed as a subject of a covenant.

We are thus brought to the conclusion that the shipowner was not relieved by the Harter Act from the negligence of the pilot in the navigation of the vessel, and that for like reasons the cargo owners are not chargeable with general average contributions.

The decree is reversed and the cause remanded for further proceedings in accordance with this opinion.

■ MR. JUSTICE MCREYNOLDS and MR. JUSTICE BUTLER think that the court below was right and its decree should be affirmed.

NOTE

The Harter Act represented an obvious compromise between the positions of carriers and shippers, hewing a line between the English law permitting freedom of contract and the American law holding exculpatory clauses against public policy.

See Yiannopoulos, Bills of Lading and the Conflict of Laws: Validity of "Negligence" Clauses in England, 37 Det.L.J. 199 (1959); Yiannopoulos, Conflicts Problems in International Bills of Lading: Validity of "Negligence" Clauses, 18 La. L.Rev. 609 (1958). The particular compromise that was reached, imposing a duty on the carrier to use due diligence to provide a seaworthy vessel and to provide proper stowage and care for the cargo, but permitting him to contract out of operational negligence during the voyage, proved a workable one and by 1910 it was adopted in the acts of Australia, New Zealand, and Canada. The drive for international uniformity in treatment of shipment under bills of lading that followed World War I and the American part in the development of the Hague Rules of 1921 and the Hague Convention of 1924 are set forth in some detail in Knauth, *Ocean Bills of Lading* 118 et seq. (1953).

The British ratified the convention in 1924 with the adoption of the Carriage of Goods by Sea Act, 14 & 15 Geo. 5, c. 22. See Scrutton on *Charter Parties* 393 (1964). American shipping interests bickered over the text of the convention and it was not until a dozen years later that it was given effect by the passage in 1936 of the Carriage of Goods by Sea Act, 49 Stat. 1207–1213 (1936), 46 U.S.C.A. §§ 1300–1315. Knauth indicates that a combination of British impatience evidenced by threats to repeal the Act of 1924 unless other nations gave effect to the convention, coupled with the restrictive interpretation of the Harter Act in *The Isis* were prods to American action.

The Harter Act was not repealed. By its terms COGSA applies only to foreign commerce, leaving the Harter Act applicable to bills of lading in domestic carriage. Note, however, that § 1312 of the act provides that the act may be made applicable to bills of lading in the domestic trade by containing an "express statement" to the effect that they are subject to the act. This so-called "coastwise option" is often included in bills of lading. No provision is made in the act for subjecting charter parties to the act, but it is often done, and in view of the fact that exceptions in charter parties are generally upheld, there appears no reason to suppose that the parties may not operate under COGSA. For reasons that will be made apparent later, COGSA may not be incorporated by reference in a contract of towage that does not qualify as a contract of affreightment.

C. COVERAGE OF HARTER AND COGSA

Caterpillar Overseas, S.A. v. S.S. Expeditor

United States Court of Appeals, Second Circuit, 1963.
318 F.2d 720, 1963 A.M.C. 1662.

■ STERRY R. WATERMAN, CT. J. Caterpillar Overseas, S.A. appeals from a final decree in admiralty denying recovery in its action against American Export Lines, Inc. for damage to cargo. The decree was entered in the United States District Court for the Southern District of New York, METZNER, D.J., 1963 A.M.C. 1670, where jurisdiction was based upon 28 U.S.C.A. § 1333.

On December 30, 1959, Caterpillar shipped two tractors from New York to Tripoli, Libya, on appellee's vessel, the S.S. Expeditor. Because the vessel's draft was too deep for a berth at the port of Tripoli, the ship anchored, upon arrival, in the Tripoli harbor. There the tractors were transferred from the S.S. Expeditor, by use of her tackle operated by stevedores, to the deck of a steel lighter which was secured by lines to the ship. The lighter had been hired and the stevedores employed by W.E. Rippon & Sons, appellee's agent in Tripoli for many years. The lighterage was billed to the consignee of the cargo, but, as permitted by the bill of lading, the consignee was neither consulted by the ship's agent concerning the use of the lighter nor notified of the arrival of the ship.

After the tractors had been placed on the deck of the lighter and chocked, and while the stevedores were lifting a sling load of additional cargo from the ship's hold, the lighter listed toward the ship and the two tractors were cast overboard. They were subsequently raised and deposited on the quay in a damaged condition.

At the trial below, American Export Lines sought to escape liability by setting up three exculpatory clauses in the bill of lading,[1] the net effect of which was to excuse the carrier from any liability for loss or damage to the goods when they were not in its actual custody, or when they had been "discharged" onto a wharf or lighter. Moreover, American Export denied that it was negligent in the handling of appellant's cargo. Caterpillar sought to establish defendant's negligence by offering proof that the lighter was unseaworthy and that it was given only a perfunctory examination by American Export's agents before use. Caterpillar also maintained that the exculpatory clauses in the bill of lading, relied upon by appellee, were void under Section 1 of the Harter Act, 46 U.S.C.A. § 190 et seq., or Section 3(a) of the Carriage of Goods by Sea Act (COGSA), 46 U.S.C.A. § 1300 et seq. The district court ruled that the Harter Act and COGSA were inapplicable to the facts of this case, gave effect to the exculpatory clauses of the bill of lading, and held that American Export was not liable for the damage to appellant's cargo. We reverse and remand with instructions that a decree be entered in favor of libellant, Caterpillar Overseas, S.A.

Under the general law of maritime carriage, public carriers of goods by sea were absolutely responsible for their safe arrival, subject to certain common law exceptions not here relevant. The Propeller Niagara v. Cordes, 62 U.S. 7, 16 L.Ed. 41 (1858); Carver, *Carriage of Goods by Sea* 3–20 (9th ed. 1952). During the Nineteenth Century ship-owners sought to limit their stringent liabilities for loss or damage to cargo by inserting exculpatory clauses in their bills of lading. Some of these clauses exempted the carrier from liability for loss due to particularly-described perils and causes. Others went so far as to relieve the carrier from liability for the

---

1. Clause 1: "The Carrier shall not be liable in any capacity whatsoever for * * * loss of or damage to the goods occurring while the goods are not in the actual custody of the Carrier."

Clause 4: "When the goods are discharged from the ship, as herein provided, they shall be at their own risk and expense; such discharge shall constitute complete delivery and performance under this contract and the Carrier shall be freed from any further responsibility."

Clause 12: "All lighterage and use of craft in discharging shall be at the risk and expense of the goods."

results of his own negligence. Because of the superior bargaining position of the carriers, shippers of goods were largely powerless to avoid the proliferation of these exceptions to liability, and bills of lading became contracts of adhesion forced upon shippers by carriers. See generally Gilmore & Black, *The Law of Admiralty* 119 et seq. (1957); Note, 27 Texas L.Rev. 525 (1949).

In 1893 Congress sought to eliminate these abuses by enacting the Harter Act, 46 U.S.C.A. § 190 et seq. Section 1 of the Act provides that:

"It shall not be lawful for the * * * owner of any vessel transporting * * * property from or between ports of the United States and foreign ports to insert in any bill of lading * * * any clause, * * * whereby it * * * shall be relieved from liability for loss or damage arising from negligence, fault, or failure in proper loading, stowage, custody, care, or proper delivery of * * * property committed to its * * * charge. Any and all words or clauses of such import inserted in bills of lading * * * shall be null and void and of no effect."

Section 2 declares of no effect any attempt to lessen, weaken or avoid the obligations of the owner to exercise due diligence properly to make the vessel seaworthy. In 1936, the Harter Act was supplanted, in large part, by the Carriage of Goods by Sea Act, 46 U.S.C.A. § 1300 et seq., which reaffirmed the carrier's liability for loss or damage to cargo caused by its own negligence. COGSA's coverage however, extends only to the period, in foreign commerce, "from the time when the goods are loaded on to the time when they are discharged from the ship." 46 U.S.C.A. § 1301(e). Harter remained applicable, therefore, to the period between the discharge of cargo from the vessel and its proper delivery. Gilmore & Black, supra at 126.

Under general maritime law, a port to port contract of carriage ordinarily requires the carrier to deliver goods into the possession of the consignee, or at least to place the goods upon a fit wharf at the port of destination. See Tan Hi v. United States, 94 F.Supp. 432, 1951 A.M.C. 127 (N.D.Cal.1950); Titania, 131 F. 229, 230 (2 Cir.1904); The Mary Washington, 16 Fed.Cas. 1006 (C.C.Md.1865). This duty of proper delivery is not, of course, co-terminous with the duty to transport, Isthmian Steamship Co. v. California Spray–Chemical Corp., 300 F.2d 41, 46, 1962 A.M.C. 1474 (9 Cir.1960); nor is it affected by the allocation of costs between carrier and shipper. Ibid. Thus the carrier remains liable for negligence even if, as here, the goods are required to be off-loaded in the harbor and carried to shore by means of a lighter, and even if it is agreed that the shipper shall bear the costs of lighterage. Under Section 1 of the Harter Act, therefore, Clauses 1 and 12 of the present bill of lading, taken by themselves, would appear to be void insofar as they attempt to shift the risk of lighterage to the goods.

Appellee relies primarily, however, upon Clause 4 of its bill of lading which purports to make *delivery* of the goods, and thus the termination of the carrier's statutory and contractual liability, concurrent with *discharge of the cargo* from the vessel, wherever that discharge may take place:

"4. In any situation whatsoever and wheresoever occurring * * * which in the judgment of the Carrier or the Master is likely to give rise to * * * delay or difficulty in arriving, discharging at or leaving the port of discharge or the usual or agreed place of discharge in such port, * * * the Carrier or the Master * * * may discharge the goods into depot, lazaretto, craft, or other place; or * * * may discharge and forward the goods by any means * * *. The Carrier or the Master is not required to give notice of discharge of the goods or the forwarding thereof as herein provided. When the goods are discharged from the ship, as herein provided, they shall be at their own risk and expense; such discharge shall constitute complete delivery and performance under this contract and the Carrier shall be freed from any further responsibility. * * * "(Emphasis supplied.)

The purpose of the clause is apparent. By equating "discharge" with "delivery" the carrier seeks to eliminate the operation of the Harter Act upon foreign trade. By fiat it seeks to secure immunity from liability which no combination of mere exculpatory clauses could achieve. All of this it purports to accomplish in the name of a freedom of contract which Congress, in enacting Harter and COGSA, found to be largely fictional in view of the disparate positions of the parties.

The Harter Act does not define "proper delivery," however. It remains to be determined, therefore, whether such a delivery may be accomplished by the mere discharge of goods from the vessel, wherever that discharge may take place.

In Isthmian Steamship v. California Spray–Chemical Corp., 290 F.2d 486, 1961 A.M.C. 2476 (9 Cir.1961), on reargument, 300 F.2d 41, 1962 A.M.C. 1474 (9 Cir.1962), cargo was discharged from the carrier's vessel, in the harbor at Alexandria, Egypt, to a lighter for oncarriage to the dock. In an action for damage to the cargo while it was on the lighter the carrier's defense was based upon two bill of lading clauses which authorized the carrier to effect "delivery" of the cargo by discharging it onto lighters "at the risk and expense of the goods * * * without any responsibility whatsoever." Holding the clauses void under Section 1 of the Harter Act, the Ninth Circuit ruled that "proper delivery" under the Act, in the absence of port customs and regulations to the contrary, constitutes delivery at a fit and customary wharf. See Morris v. Lamport & Holt, Ltd., 54 F.2d 925, 926, 1931 A.M.C. 1926 (S.D.N.Y., 1931); aff'd per curiam, 57 F.2d 1081, 1932 A.M.C. 1011 (2 Cir.1932); North American Smelting Co. v. Moller S.S. Co., 204 F.2d 384, 386, 388, 1953 A.M.C. 1380 (3 Cir.1953); Remington Rand, Inc. v. American Export Lines, 132 F.Supp. 129, 1955 A.M.C. 1789 (S.D.N.Y.1955).

On the facts of this case we are not required to determine whether proper delivery under a port to port contract of maritime carriage may only be made by discharge onto a fit wharf. On the contrary, we should suppose, for example, that in a case where the consignee owns his own lighter and has his own stevedores, the Harter Act would not prohibit a properly drafted agreement providing for delivery of goods by discharge onto the consignee's lighters. Here, however, the lighter was not selected by the shipper nor by the consignee of the goods, but by the carrier. Under these circumstances, proper delivery requires, at the very least, the selection of, and the discharge of the goods onto, a fit and safe lighter. See The Tangier, 64 U.S. 28, 16 L.Ed. 412 (1859). This obligation, for the negligent performance of which the carrier bears full responsibility, might be found as an implied term of the bill of lading before us; but insofar as the lighterage clauses have been construed by both the parties and the Court below so as to relieve the carrier of this duty, we are constrained to hold the clauses null and void under Section 1 of the Harter Act.[2]

At the trial below appellant established *a prima facie case* for recovery by showing that its goods were received in damaged condition at the port of destination. Schnell v. Vallescura, 293 U.S. 296, 304, 55 S.Ct. 194, 79 L.Ed. 373, 1934 A.M.C. 1573 (1934); Schroeder Bros. Inc. v. Saturnia, 226 F.2d 147, 149, 1955 A.M.C. 1935 (2 Cir.1955); Gilmore & Black, *The Law of Admiralty,* 162–63 (1957). Appellant further established that the damage was not due to the operation of the lighter during oncarriage from the vessel to the dock, for the Court below found that appellant's tractors were cast overboard while goods were still being off-loaded onto the lighter and while the lighter was secured by lines to the ship.

Upon this showing, American Export Lines had the burden of proving that the loss was due to an excepted cause under its bill of lading. Because of the invalidity of Clauses 1, 4 and 12, however, American Export could only rely upon Section 4(2)(q) of COGSA (incorporated into the present bill of lading by agreement of the parties) which provides:

"4(2) Neither the carrier nor the ship shall be responsible for loss or damage arising or resulting from—

* * *

"any other cause arising without the actual fault and privity of the carrier and without the fault or neglect of the agents or servants of the carrier, but the burden of proof shall be on the person claiming the benefit of this exception to show that neither the actual fault or privity of the carrier nor the fault or neglect of the agents or servants of the carrier contributed to the loss or damage."

We hold that appellee failed below to sustain this burden of proof. The trial court found that the lighter careened in fair weather and a calm sea, and, as appellee failed to advance any explanation of this occurrence, a

---

2. Caterpillar argues, as an alternative ground for reversing the judgment below, that its tractors were not "discharged" at the time they were cast overboard, because the loading of the lighter was not fully completed before the accident occurred. See Remington Rand, Inc. v. American Export Lines, Inc., 132 F.Supp. 129, 137, 1955 A.M.C. 1789 (S.D.N.Y.1955); Hoegh Lines v. Green Truck Sales, Inc., 298 F.2d 240, 1962 A.M.C. 431 (9 Cir.1962), cert. denied 371 U.S. 817, 83 S.Ct. 31, 9 L.Ed.2d 58, 1963 A.M.C. 1646. We find it unnecessary, however, to rule on this issue. If injury to the goods occurred before their discharge from the vessel, Section 3(2) of COGSA would invalidate any agreement purporting to shield the carrier from liability for negligence in the handling of the goods. If the goods were discharged but not delivered at the time of the injury, Section 1 of the Harter Act would control.

presumption of unseaworthiness arose which appellee failed to rebut. Commercial Molasses Corp. v. New York Tank Barge Corp., 314 U.S. 104, 111–12, 62 S.Ct. 156, 86 L.Ed. 89, 1941 A.M.C. 1697 (1941); The Jungshoved, 290 F. 733, 1923 A.M.C. 630 (2 Cir.1923), cert. denied 263 U.S. 707, 44 S.Ct. 35, 68 L.Ed. 517. This presumption gained support from Caterpillar's affirmative proofs tending to show that the lighter had a holed side plate and warped tank top lids and no gaskets, which permitted water to enter the lighter's tanks and thereby to render it unstable.

Although a presumption of actual unseaworthiness did not preclude American Export Lines from providing that it exercised due care in *attempting* to select a seaworthy lighter, little such evidence was forthcoming. Appellee's agent, a stevedore foreman, allegedly took a 5 or 10 minute walk over the deck of the lighter, prior to the tractors' off-loading, but no attempt was made to ascertain whether water was in the lighter's tanks and no inspection was made of the lighter's sides. Upon such a factual showing we hold that a finding of due care in the selection of the lighter could not be sustained.

Reversed and remanded.

N O T E

In making the Carriage of Goods by Sea Act applicable only from "tackle to tackle," did Congress create a line drawing problem similar to the jurisdictional line at the edge of the sea? Would COGSA apply if the goods were on the end of a crane that was located on a lighter, having been lifted from the hold of the ship? Remember O'Keeffe v. Atlantic Stevedoring Co., p. 96, supra. In Hoegh v. Green Truck Sales, Inc., 298 F.2d 240, 1962 A.M.C. 431 (9th Cir.1962), it was held that the COGSA $500 per package limit of liability applied in such a situation, the court observing that it attached no significance to the fact that the lighters were provided by the shipper and that substitute tackle was used. Judge Solomon noted that in Knauth, *Ocean Bills of Lading* 145 (1953), it is stated that if substitute tackle is used the cargo is discharged as soon as it is lifted from the hold of the vessel, but noted also that Knauth cited no cases.

Although provision is made for extending COGSA to coastwise The voyage ends for these purposes when the cargo is delivered. In Hiram Walker & Sons, Inc. v. Kirk Line, R.B. Kirkconnell & Bro., Ltd., 963 F.2d 327, 1993 A.M.C. 965 (11th Cir.1992), it was held that a stevedore who spilled 5,000 gallons of Tia Maria attempting to lift the container above a tank truck and pour it into the top opening, was still covered by the Himalaya clause in the bill of lading, when the bill of lading required actual change of custody and it was found that a delivery receipt had been issued in error.

When COGSA is applicable through inclusion of an express statement in the bill of lading, there is no express provision for its application to the loading-unloading phase. It has been stated that § 1311 precludes application of any clause that conflicts with Harter. Uncle Ben's International Div. of Uncle Ben's Inc. v. Hapag–Lloyd Aktiengesellschaft, 855 F.2d 215 (5th Cir.1988). In the particular case, however, it was held that the COGSA one year statute of limitations does not conflict with Harter. Cf. Gamma–10 Plastics, Inc., 32 F.3d 1244, 1995 A.M.C. 909 (8th Cir.1994), holding that notice of such an extension must be given the shipper.

It has also been held that the limitation of liability provision does not conflict with Harter and thus may be extended to loading and unloading under a Himalaya clause. Wemhoener Pressen v. Ceres Marine Terminals, Inc., 5 F.3d 734, 1993 A.M.C. 2842 (4th Cir.1993).

When COGSA does not apply ex proprio vigore but is made applicable by inclusion in the bill of lading, the body of law interpreting COGSA will be applied. State Establishment for Agr. Product Trading v. M/V Wesermunde, 838 F.2d 1576 (11th Cir.1988), cert. denied sub nom. United Kingdom Mut. S.S. Assurance Ass'n. (Bermuda) Ltd. v. State Establishment for Agricultural Product Trading, 488 U.S. 916, 109 S.Ct. 273, 102 L.Ed.2d 262 (1988), in which the court of appeals held that a clause in a charter party requiring arbitration in a foreign country with no contacts with the transaction would not be enforced when the bill of lading contained a clause applying COGSA.

When COGSA was made applicable by a clause in a charter party the cargo owners were precluded from recovery of damages due to delay occasioned by a collision taking place before the cargo was loaded aboard, since the occurrence was one for which the carrier would not be liable under COGSA (navigation and management of the vessel). Mathiesen v. M/V Obelix, 817 F.2d 345 (5th Cir.1987), cert. denied sub nom. Unimills B.V. and Margarine Verkaufs Union GmbH v. Statistix Shipping, N.V., 484 U.S. 898, 108 S.Ct. 234, 98 L.Ed.2d 192 (1987).

Delivery of the goods without collecting the bill of lading has been held to be misdelivery and a breach of the contract of carriage. Barretto Peat, Inc. v. Luis Ayala Colon Sucrs., Inc., 896 F.2d 656 (1st Cir.1990). See also Unimac Company, Inc. v. C.F. Ocean Service, Inc., 43 F.3d 1434, 1995 A.M.C. 1484 (11th Cir.1995).

In addition to exempting from its coverage the period prior to loading and after unloading, COGSA provides in terms that it does not apply to carriage of live animals and carriage of goods under a contract that calls for stowage on deck, if the goods are actually so carried (§ 1301(c)). The Harter Act exempts live animals from the provisions of §§ 190 and 193, presumably to permit special individual contracts for carriage of such cargo, leaving the contracts subject to §§ 191 and 192. See Knauth, supra, 237.

Knauth suggests that because COGSA does not provide in terms that the Harter Act is preserved as to bills of lading calling for on deck shipment, as it is preserved in § 1311 as to the period before loading and after discharge, there "would seem to be no positive legislative expression to preclude the shipper and carrier from voluntarily contracting that the provisions of the 1936 Act shall govern their 'tackle to tackle' relations in respect of deck cargo." Knauth, supra, 236. In Blanchard Lumber Co. v. S.S. Anthony II, 259 F.Supp. 857, 1967 A.M.C. 103 (S.D.N.Y.1966), Judge Levet noted the passage in Knauth, but held that the Harter Act was applicable in a case in which an effort had been made to cut liability below the Harter standard by specifying that the contract should be governed by the Canadian law.

Clauses in a bill of lading providing for litigation in a particular country have been held to violate the COGSA. Indussa Corp. v. S.S. Ranborg, 377 F.2d 200, 1967 A.M.C. 589 (2d Cir.1967)(en banc). But both "the reasoning and conclusion" of *Indussa* were recently rejected by the Supreme Court in Vimar Seguros y Reaseguros, S.A. v. M/V Sky Reefer, 515 U.S. ___, 115 S.Ct. 2322, 132 L.Ed.2d 462, 1995 A.M.C. 1817 (1995), holding that a clause requiring arbitration in a foreign country does not violate § 1303(8). Justice O'Connor wrote a separate opinion to indicate that the ruling should not be extended to foreign litigation clauses. To what extent do you read The M/V Sky Reefer to leave this open?

It should be noted that the exception clause in COGSA dealing with on deck shipment covers only "cargo which by the contract of carriage is stated as being carried on deck and is so carried." Thus, of course, a carrier may not reduce his legal responsibility by moving the cargo up on the deck. When the bill of lading is a "clean" bill, it is presumed that carriage will be below decks, though port customs to the effect that packaged freight will be carried on deck have been given effect. See St. John's N.F. Shipping Corp. v. S.A. Companhia Geral Commercial do Rio de Janeiro, 263 U.S. 119, 44 S.Ct. 30, 68 L.Ed. 201 (1923).

Baggage

In The Kensington, 183 U.S. 263, 22 S.Ct. 102, 46 L.Ed. 190 (1902), the Supreme Court held that an exception in a passenger ticket disclaiming liability in excess of 250 francs (about $50 at the time), unless the baggage was shipped as cargo (under the Harter Act), and affording no alternative of increasing the limitation "by an adequate and reasonable proportional payment" was void. The Court observed that it was unnecessary to decide whether the Harter Act applied to contracts to carry passengers and their baggage, the cause of loss being improper stowage which under the act would make the carrier liable. It has generally been assumed, however, that neither the Harter Act nor the COGSA apply to baggage that is shipped under a passenger ticket. For a discussion of the cases in the lower courts, see Robinson on *Admiralty* 566 (1939).

Contract limitations on liability for luggage providing for declaration and increase of limits upon proportional payment have been upheld. See The Leviathan, 4 F.Supp. 918, 1933 A.M.C. 1394 (E.D.N.Y.1933). Other reasonable contract stipulations have also been enforced. See, e.g., Avis v. Cunard S.S. Co., 1958 A.M.C. 2453 (Cir.Ct.Mich.1958), where it was held that a regulation to the effect that passengers must not put jewelry in their baggage and making provision for its receipt and safekeeping by the purser is not void as against public policy. Six months limitations on the bringing of actions respecting baggage claims have been upheld. Miller v. International Freighting Corp., 97 F.Supp. 60, 1951 A.M.C. 944 (S.D.N.Y.1951); De Pontet v. Italian Line (N.Y.Sup.Ct.App.Term 1967) 1967 A.M.C. 1168 (action to recover for mink stole stolen out of locked baggage area dismissed as brought two weeks late, despite fine print of clause).

D.   CARRIER'S RESPONSIBILITIES

1.   SEAWORTHINESS

International Navigation Company v. Farr & Bailey Manufacturing Company

Supreme Court of the United States, 1901.
181 U.S. 218, 21 S.Ct. 591, 45 L.Ed. 830.

[The petitioner was consignee of twenty bales of burlap shipped under a bill of lading. The burlap was stowed in a compartment of the lower steerage deck. The compartment contained only one tier of cargo, two or three feet high, so that there was easy access to the ports. Four or five days after the vessel broke ground, water was discovered in the compartment, and when the hatches were opened a day or two later it was discovered that the covers of the ports were unfastened and open and that one admitted water freely as the vessel rolled. There was no severe weather and no accident was known to have happened to the vessel. The ports in the compartment had been inspected the day before the vessel sailed and were believed to have been closed. Several hours elapsed between the inspection and the time at which the vessel sailed. The petitioner's burlap was damaged by the water.]

■ Mr. Chief Justice Fuller delivered the opinion of the court.

Counsel for petitioner states that the question raised on this record is: "Was the Indiana unseaworthy at the time of beginning her voyage from Liverpool to Philadelphia, or was the failure to securely fasten the port covers and keep them fastened a fault or error in the management of the vessel under the exemption of the 'Harter act?' "

The courts below concurred in the conclusion that the Indiana was unseaworthy when she sailed because of the condition of the porthole, but the district judge on the reargument felt constrained to yield his individual convictions to the rule he understood to have been laid down in The Silvia, 171 U.S. 462, 19 S.Ct. 7, 43 L.Ed. 241 (1898).

The Silvia was decided, as all these cases must be, upon its particular facts and circumstances. The case is thus stated by Mr. Justice Gray, who delivered the opinion of the court:

"The Silvia, with the sugar in her lower hold, sailed from Matanzas for Philadelphia on the morning of February 16, 1894. The compartment between decks next the forecastle had been fitted up to carry steerage passengers, but on this voyage contained only spare sails and ropes and a small quantity of stores. This compartment had four round ports on each side, which were about 8 or 9 feet above the water line when the vessel was deep-laden. Each port was 8 inches in diameter, furnished with a cover of glass ⅝ of an inch thick, set in a brass frame, as well as with an inner cover or dummy of iron. When the ship sailed the weather was fair, and the glass covers were tightly closed, but the iron covers were left open in order to light the compartment should it become necessary to get anything from it, and the hatches were battened down, but could have been opened in two minutes by knocking out the wedges. In the afternoon of the day of sailing, the ship encountered rough weather, and the glass cover of one of the ports was broken, whether by the force of the seas or by floating timber or wreckage was wholly a matter of conjecture, and the water came in through the port, and damaged the sugar."

And again:

"But the contention that the Silvia was unseaworthy when she sailed from Matanzas is unsupported by the facts. The test of seaworthiness is whether the vessel is reasonably fit to carry the cargo which she has undertaken to transport. The portholes of the compartment in question were furnished both with the usual glass covers and with the usual iron shutters or dead lights; and there is nothing in the case to justify an inference that there was any defect in the construction of either. When she began her voyage, the weather being fair, the glass covers only were shut, and the iron ones were left open for the purpose of lighting the compartment. Although the hatches were battened down they could have been taken off in two minutes, and no cargo was stowed against the ports so as to prevent or embarrass access to them in case a change of weather should make it necessary or proper to close the iron shutters. Had the cargo been so stowed as to require much time and labor to shift or remove it in order to get at the ports, the fact that the iron shutters were left open at the beginning of the voyage might have rendered the ship unseaworthy. *But as no cargo was so stowed, and the ports were in a place where these shutters would usually be left open for the admission of light, and could be speedily got at and closed if occasion should require, there is no ground for holding that the ship was unseaworthy at the time of sailing.*"

In the present case the compartment in which the burlaps were stowed was used exclusively as a cargo hold; the glass and iron covers were intended to be securely closed before any cargo was received; the persons whose duty it was to close them or see that they were closed supposed that that had been properly done; and the hatches were battened down with no expectation that any more attention would be given to the port covers during the voyage; but in fact the port was not securely covered, and there was apparently nothing to prevent the influx of water, even under conditions not at all extraordinary, the port being only 2 or 3 feet above the water line.

We are of the opinion that the difference in the facts between the two cases was such that the court of appeals was at liberty to reach a different result in this case from that arrived at in The Silvia. The latter decision simply demonstrated the justness of Lord Blackburn's observation in Steel v. State Line S.S. Co., L.R. 3 App.Cas. 72, that the question whether a ship is reasonably fit to carry her cargo must be "determined upon the whole circumstances and the whole evidence."

* * *

[The Court went on to reject the argument that despite the fact of unseaworthiness the condition arose from an error in management within the Harter Act exemption, and similarly to reject the argument that the owner is responsible for the provision of a proper structure and equipment, and for the diligence of his "shore" personnel, but is not responsible for the negligence of his "sea" personnel though the negligence result in unseaworthiness before breaking ground. Ed.]

NOTE

The duty to use due diligence is limited by § 1303(1) to "before or at the beginning of the voyage." As to when the voyage "begins," see The Del Sud (Mississippi Shipping Co. v. Zander & Co.), 270 F.2d 345, 1959 A.M.C. 2143 (5th Cir.1959), vacated as moot 361 U.S. 115, 80 S.Ct. 212, 4 L.Ed.2d 148 (1959). There it was held by a divided court of appeals that a vessel that was engaged in maneuvering away from the dock with the aid of tugs had begun its voyage, despite the fact that two lines were still connected to the pier. The vessel was damaged when it came in contact with the concrete facing of the dock, leaving a twelve inch fracture in a shell plate. When the vessel reached its next port of call there was enough water in the bilge to put the master on notice, but apparently he thought it was rain water and there was no inspection for damage. Cargo argued that whether or not the vessel had left on its voyage at the time of the accident the failure to inspect at the first port of call was a failure to use due diligence. The court held that unlike The Isis, the vessel was not returned to her owners' marine superintendent and that as to the original cargo the negligence of the master was negligence in "management of the ship," also excused under the act. As to cargo loaded at the first port of call, however, the master was a servant of the owner and the owner was liable for his want of due diligence to make the vessel seaworthy for *that* voyage.

The question of what constitutes due diligence is, of course, a matter of fact and governed by the clearly erroneous rule. Schade v. National Surety Corp., 288 F.2d 106, 1961 A.M.C. 1225 (2d Cir.1961). Compare Peter Paul, Inc. v. Rederi A/B Pulp (The Christer Salen), 258 F.2d 901, 1958 A.M.C. 2377 (2d Cir.1958), with States S.S. Co. v. United States (The Pennsylvania), 259 F.2d 458, 1958 A.M.C. 1775 (9th Cir.1957). In each case a fully welded vessel cracked in half during a voyage. In the former it was held that there was no want of due diligence. Against the argument that because this sort of vessel is likely to be "notch brittle," the master should have required extensive tests, Judge Moore observed, "While a master is presumed to know the general characteristics of his ship, he is not required to possess the combined knowledge of a naval architect and a metallurgist." In the latter, a twenty foot crack had developed during the previous voyage and had been repaired. The court held that the owner was on notice the vessel was crack sensitive and should not have scheduled her for service in cold water where this feature would be accentuated. Compare in the same fashion M/S *Black Heron,* infra p. 631, and the Farrandoc (Canada Exch.1967) 1967 A.M.C. 1451. In the former the mistaken turning of a valve so as to put water into the cargo instead of into a ballast tank was excused as an error in management. In the latter, upon a finding that although the engineer was licensed, he was new to the ship and had not been instructed about the vessel's peculiar valve system, it was held that due diligence had not been used.

Evidence was sufficient to establish due diligence when the damage was alleged to have been caused by sea water from leaky hatch covers and the owner had had the vessel subjected to classification society's testing for watertightness only a few weeks before and the tests involved water pressures much greater than those encountered at sea. Fireman's Fund Ins. Cos. v. M/V Vignes, 794 F.2d 1552 (11th Cir.1986). But compliance with classification Society's survey does not necessarily establish due diligence to make the vessel seaworthy under COGSA. Louis Dreyfus Corp. v. 27,946 Long Tons of Corn, 830 F.2d 1321 (5th Cir.1987). In the particular case lack of due diligence was found in failure to correct light and shaft markings after warning by manufacturer's service engineer.

See Federazione Italiana Dei, Corsorzi Agrari v. Mandask Compania De Vapores, 388 F.2d 434, 1968 A.M.C. 315 (2d Cir.1968), where the court relied upon a presumption to the effect that a vessel that sinks in calm seas and fair weather is unseaworthy.

Of course COGSA may be incorporated into a charter party, either in toto or specific clauses. When only a part of the Act is incorporated, there are obvious problems of interpretation. See, e.g., U.S. v. M/V Marilena P., 433 F.2d 164, 1969 A.M.C. 1155 (4th Cir.1969). There the United States entered into a time charter for transportation of military supplies to Viet Nam. The charter party incorporated Paragraphs (1), (2), and (3) of § 1304. The crew of the vessel refused to go to Viet Nam and walked off. The United States sued for damages for breach, including costs of unloading a portion of the cargo that had been loaded when the refusal occurred. The vessel owner defended under § 1304(2), absolving the owner from loss or damage arising from "(j) Strikes or lockouts or stoppage or restraint of labor from whatever cause * * *." The government contended that since under § 1301, COGSA applies only from loading to unloading, and only to damages to the cargo, the provisions of § 1304(2)(j), as incorporated in the charter party, were to be construed as so limited. The court held that the failure to incorporate § 1301 left the provisions of g § 1304(1), (2), and (3) applicable according to their terms. To the contention that the vessel was rendered unseaworthy, it answered that the owner, who had offered double wages and otherwise attempted to deal with the crew, had used due diligence. Judge Winter dissented.

In cases in which the charter party does not incorporate COGSA, normally the terms of the charter party will be enforced. While clauses waiving the implied warranty of seaworthiness are very strictly construed, if they are clear they are enforceable. See, e.g., A. Kemp Fisheries, Inc. v. Castle & Cooke, Inc., Bumble Bee Seafoods Div., 852 F.2d 493 (9th Cir.1988).

2. CARE AND CUSTODY OF CARGO

Knott v. Botany Worsted Mills

Supreme Court of the United States, 1900.
179 U.S. 69, 21 S.Ct. 30, 45 L.Ed. 90.

■ MR. JUSTICE GRAY delivered the opinion of the court:

* * *

The Portuguese Prince was a British vessel belonging to a line trading between New York and ports in the River Plata, Brazil, and the West Indies, loading and discharging cargo and having a resident agent at each port. The bills of lading of the wool, signed at Buenos Ayres December 21, 1894, gave her liberty to call at any port or ports to receive and discharge cargo, and for any other purpose whatever; and purported to exempt the carrier from liability for "negligence of masters or mariners;" "sweating, rust, natural decay, leakage, or breakage, and all damage arising from the goods by stowage, or contact with, or by sweating, leakage, smell, or evaporation from, them;" "or any other peril of the seas, rivers, navigation, or of land transit, of whatsoever nature or kind; and whether any of the perils, causes, or things above mentioned, or the loss or injury arising therefrom, be occasioned by the wrongful act, default, negligence, or error in judgment of the owners, masters, officers, mariners, crew, stevedores, engineers, and other persons whomsoever in the service of the ship, whether employed on the said steamer or otherwise, and whether before or after or during the voyage, or for whose acts the shipowner would otherwise be liable; or by unseaworthiness of the ship at the beginning or at any period of the voyage, provided all reasonable means have been taken to provide against such unseaworthiness." Each bill of lading also contained the following clause: "This contract shall be governed by the law of the flag of the ship carrying the goods, except that general average shall be adjusted according to York–Antwerp Rules 1890."

The facts of the case are substantially undisputed. The bales of wool of the libellants were taken on board at Buenos Ayres, December 21–24, 1894, and were stowed on end, with proper dunnage, between decks near the bow, and forward of a temporary wooden bulkhead, which was not tight. The vessel, after touching at other ports, touched on February 19, 1895, at Pernambuco, and there took on board 200 tons of wet sugar (from which there is always drainage), which was stowed, with proper dunnage, between decks, aft of the wooden bulkhead. At that time the vessel was trimmed by the stern, and all drainage from the sugar flowing aft, was carried off by the scuppers, which were sufficient for the purpose when the vessel was down by the stern, or on even keel in calm weather. There was no provision for carrying off the drainage in case it ran forward. She discharged other cargo at Para; and on March 10, when she left that port, she was 2 feet down by the head. She continued in this trim until she took on additional cargo at Port of Spain, where the error in trim was corrected, and she left that port on March 18, loaded 1 foot by the stern. It was agreed by the parties that there was no damage to the wool by sugar drainage until she was trimmed by the head at Para; that the wool was damaged, by sugar drainage finding its way through the bulkhead and reaching the wool, at Para, or between Para and Port of Spain, and not afterwards; that, after she was again trimmed by the stern at Port of Spain, none of the drainage from the sugar found its way forward; and that the court might draw inferences.

Upon the facts of this case there can be no doubt that the ship was seaworthy, and that the damage to the wool was caused by drainage from the wet sugar through negligence of those in charge of the ship and cargo. The questions upon which the decision of the case turns are two:

First. Whether this damage to the wool was "loss or damage arising from negligence, fault, or failure in proper loading, stowage, custody, care, or proper delivery" of cargo, within the 1st section of the Harter act; or was "damage or loss resulting from faults or errors in navigation or in the management of said vessel," within the 3d section of that act.

Second. Do the words, in the 1st section, "any vessel transporting merchandise or property from or between ports of the United States and foreign ports," include a foreign vessel transporting merchandise from a foreign port to a port of the United States?

* * *

We fully concur with the courts below that the damage in question arose from negligence in loading or stowage of the cargo, and not from fault or error in the navigation or management of the ship, for the reasons stated by the district judge, and approved by the circuit court of appeals, as follows:

"The primary cause of the damage was negligence and inattention in the loading or stowage of the cargo, either regarded as a whole, or as respects the juxtaposition of wet sugar and wool bales placed far forward. The wool should not have been stowed forward of the wet sugar, unless care was taken in the other loading, and in all subsequent changes in the loading, to see that the ship should not get down by the head. There was no fault or defect in the vessel herself. She was constructed in the usual way, and was sufficient. But on sailing from Para she was a little down by the head, through inattention, during the changes in the loading, to the effect these changes made in the trim of the ship and in the flow of the sugar drainage. She was not down by the head more than frequently happens. It in no way affected her seagoing qualities; nor did the vessel herself cause any damage to the wool. The damage was caused by the drainage of the wet sugar alone. So that no question of the unseaworthiness of the ship arises. The ship herself was as seaworthy when she left Para as when she sailed from Pernambuco. The negligence consisted in stowing the wool far forward, without taking care subsequently that changes of loading should not bring the ship down by the head. I must therefore regard the question as solely a question of negligence in the stowage and disposition of cargo, and of damage consequent thereon, though brought about by the effect of these negligent changes in loading on the trim of the ship. * * * The change of trim was merely incidental, the mere negligent result of the changes in the loading, no attention being given to the effect on the ship's trim, or on the sugar drainage. * * * Since this damage arose through negligence in the particular mode of stowing and changing the loading of cargo, as the primary cause, though that cause became operative through its effect on the trim of the ship, this negligence in loading falls within the first section. The ship and her owner must therefore answer for this damage, and the third section is inapplicable." * * *

The remaining question is whether the first section of the Harter act applies to a foreign vessel on a voyage from a foreign port to a port in the United States.

* * *

NOTE

See Elia Salzman Tobacco Co. v. S.S. Mormacwind, 371 F.2d 537, 1967 A.M.C. 277 (2d Cir.1967)(damage to cargo of tobacco through use of improper dunnage and failure to ventilate); States Marine Corp. of Delaware v. Producers Cooperative Packing Co., 310 F.2d 206 (9th Cir.1962)(canned goods and dried fruit turned out "damp, stained, dented, rusty and mouldy"). In *States Marine* the court indicated that the libellant's case requires an ordinary preponderance of the evidence and the findings of the trial court will not be set aside unless clearly erroneous. See also Columbus Co. v. Shore, 276 F.2d 93, 1961 A.M.C. 2557 (5th Cir.1960), where proof of a refrigerator breakdown during loading and the out turning of a cargo of bananas in a ripened condition supported a judgment for negligent carriage when no evidence of care for the cargo was given in rebuttal.

E.   EXCEPTED PERILS

1.   ACT OF GOD

Mamiye Bros. v. Barber Steamship Lines

United States Court of Appeals, Second Circuit, 1966.
360 F.2d 774, 1966 A.M.C. 1165.

■ HENRY J. FRIENDLY, CT. J.   These libels, consolidated for trial before Judge Wyatt in the District Court for the Southern District of New York, see 241 F.Supp. 99, 1966 A.M.C. 1175 (S.D.N.Y.1965), were brought to recover for damage to cargo on Pier 5, Bush Terminal, Brooklyn.   The cause of the damage was a flooding of the pier due to storm surge and wave action created by Hurricane Donna which struck New York harbor in the early afternoon of Monday, September 12, 1960.   The pier was 10' above mean low water, as against 9' required by the New York City, but the unusually high level of the water covered the floor to a considerable height.[1]   Some of the cargo was inbound, having been unloaded on or before Friday, September 9, from the M/V Toreador, the M/V Tatra and the M/V Turandot; other cargo was outbound, having been delivered on or before September 9 for shipment on the Turandot and the Tatra.   The respondent shipowners impleaded Atlantic Stevedoring Co., the pier operator, which carried the burden of the defense.   After trial Judge Wyatt dismissed the libels on the ground that the loss was attributable to an "Act of God" within the meaning of the Carriage of Goods by Sea Act, 46 U.S.C.A. § 1304(2)(d).[2]   In a thorough opinion, he recognized that under the statute the carriers and pier operator were liable for damage to the cargo caused by their negligence and had the burden of showing either freedom from negligence or that the loss could not have been prevented by the exercise of reasonable care.   He held, however, that in view of the Weather Bureau estimates as to the probable course of the hurricane they had not been negligent.   On appeal no one challenges his analysis of the governing legal principles; the attack by the cargo owners is on the correctness of his conclusion that the burden of negating negligence was satisfied.

[Judge Wyatt's analysis follows.]

* * *

---

1.   According to Judge Wyatt's calculations, all cargo on the floor of the pier would have been in 8″ to 9″ of water, and cargo on a single pallet in 2″ to 3″, but wave action must have raised the water level on the pier as high as 36″. 241 F.Supp. at 115, 1966 A.M.C. at 1197.

2.   The court held that under the agreements of carriage COGSA was to determine rights and duties with respect to both inbound and outbound goods on the pier. 241 F.Supp. at 105–6, 1966 A.M.C. at 1181–1184. This decision is not here challenged.

3.   *The Act of God exception and the burden of persuasion on the issue of negligence*

It must next be determined whether the burden of persuasion as to the issue of negligence rests on libellants or on respondents.

The matter is not without difficulty.

Respondents have pleaded, as an affirmative defense, in substance that Hurricane Donna was an "Act of God."   These precise words are not used in the answers but there are general expressions ("* * * a cause or causes for which neither the Carriers nor the vessels are liable * * *") which are sufficient to raise the point, made more explicit in the brief for respondents (pp. 17–24).

The Act of God exception to liability of the carrier or bailee exists under general maritime law (Carver, *Carriage of Goods By Sea* (10th ed.) 10–13) and under COGSA (46 U.S.C.A. § 1304(d)).

The definition of "Act of God" in the present context seems generally to include, as an essential element, that the damage from the natural event could not have been prevented by the exercise of reasonable care by the carrier or bailee.

In the Majestic, 166 U.S. 375, 17 S.Ct. 597, 41 L.Ed. 1039 (1897) the Court referred with approval to the definition of Chancellor Kent, as follows (p. 386):

"The act of God, said Chancellor Kent (2 Kent, Comm. p. 597), means 'inevitable accident, without the intervention of man and public enemies'; and again (volume 3, p. 216), that 'perils of the sea denote natural accidents peculiar to that element, which do not happen by the intervention of man, nor are to be prevented by human prudence.'   A *'casus fortuitus'* was defined in the civil law to be *'Quod damno fatali contingit, cuivis diligentissimo possit contingere.'*   It is a 'loss happening in spite of all human effort and sagacity.'   The words 'perils of the sea' may, indeed, have grown to have a broader signification than 'the act of God,' but that is unimportant here."

Judge McGohey appears to have assumed that an "act of God" is not only one which causes damage but one as to which reasonable precautions could not have prevented damage.   In Moran Transportation Corp. v. N.Y. Trap Rock Corp., 194 F.Supp. 599, 602, 1961 A.M.C. 1836, 1840 (S.D.N.Y. 1961) Judge McGohey said:

"Hurricane Hazel was not an Act of God.   At Tomkins Cove it was neither so sudden nor so violent that Trap Rock's experienced men who had not less than twenty-four hours' warning could not have taken precautions to guard against it."

The definition quoted by Judge Inch with approval in Empress of France, 49 F.2d 291, 1931 A.M.C. 392 at 393 (E.D.N.Y.1930) is this:

"By 'act of God' is meant some inevitable accident which cannot be prevented by human care, skill, or foresight, but results from natural causes, such as lightning, tempests, floods, and inundations."

The exception for "perils of the sea" is very like in principle to that for an act of God. The former has been defined in The Giulia, 218 F. 744, 746, 134 C.C.A. 422 (1914) as follows:

"Perils of the seas are understood to mean those perils which are peculiar to the sea, and which are of an extraordinary nature or arise from irresistible force or overwhelming power, and which cannot be guarded against by the ordinary exertions of human skill and prudence."

This definition has been cited with approval. R.T. Jones Lumber Co. v. Roen S.S. Co., 270 F.2d 456, 1960 A.M.C. 46 at 49 (2 Cir.1959). The significance for present purposes is in that part of the definition which makes an essential element of the exception that the perils "cannot be guarded against by the ordinary exertions of human skill and prudence."

Gilmore and Black, cited above, first deal with the "perils of the sea" exception which they define (at 140) as follows:

"* * * a fortuitous action of the elements at sea, of such force as to overcome the strength of the well-found ship or the usual precautions of good seamanship. Thus, in a sense, the absence of negligence as a concurring cause may be said to enter into the very definition of a sea peril, so that, in order to establish an exception under this clause, the ship would have to establish freedom from negligence."

They then turn to act of God and refer (at 141) to the language of an old English case, Nugent v. Smith, 1 C.P.D. 423, 444 [1876], defining act of God as follows:

"* * * a mere short way of expressing this proposition. A common carrier is not liable for any accident as to which he can show that it is due to natural causes directly and exclusively, without human intervention, and that it could not have been prevented by any amount of foresight and pains and care reasonably to be expected from him."

The authors then note (at 141–42): "* * * absence of human negligence or fault as a concurring cause is a part of the definition of the 'Act of God.'"

The first definition of "Act of God" given in 1 Bouvier's *Law Dictionary* Rawle's Third Revision (8th Rawle ed.) p. 116 is:

"Any accident due to natural causes directly and exclusively without human intervention, such as could not have been prevented by any amount of foresight and pains, and care reasonably to have been expected."

And the following statement is from Carver, *Carriage of Goods By Sea* (10th ed.) 10:

"The meaning of 'act of God' in this relation has given rise to much discussion and difference of opinion. The result of this seems to be that to enable us to describe a casualty as arising from an act of God it must have two essential features. First, it must have occurred independently of human action; man must have been purely passive. Secondly, it must have been an event which the shipowner could not have avoided, or guarded against, by any means which he could reasonably be expected to use."

It seems accepted on all sides that a shipper makes out a prima facie case against a carrier or bailee by showing merely that the goods were not turned out in as good condition as when delivered by or for the shipper. The carrier or bailee must then bring the loss within an "exception" to his liability established by law or contract. Gilmore and Black, cited above, at 162–163.

It would seem therefore to follow that the Act of God exception by definition cannot be established unless and until the carrier or bailee shows that the loss could not have been prevented by reasonable care and foresight. This logic would mean that in the case at bar the burden is on respondents to show the exercise by them of reasonable care or, to put it another way, that the damage could not have been prevented by the exercise of reasonable care.

The Majestic, above, is authority for this view. The Court approved the award of damages against a ship where luggage of passengers was wet by water and where the ship pleaded act of God. The Court said (166 U.S. at 386):

"* * * the question still remains, on the doctrine of implied exceptions, whether the injury here was by the act of God, for which the company was not liable. The burden in this respect is on the carrier."

The burden meant that the carrier had to show that the damage could not have been prevented by reasonable care. The Court said (166 U.S. at 388):

"In our opinion, the steamship company failed to show that the accident was one which could not have been prevented by human effort, sagacity, and care * * *."

Citing *Majestic* as authority and referring to the common law rule, Carver, cited above, has this to say in discussing the act of God exception (at 12):

"What is needful is that the causes of the event shall have been so far beyond what could reasonably be foreseen, or, if they might have been foreseen, shall have been so far irresistible that no foresight or endeavor of man, reasonably to be expected, would have prevented their operation.

"It is not enough for the shipowner to show that the loss arose from natural, as distinguished from human, causes, and to leave it to the other side to show that there was some want of precaution or care on his part; he must himself show affirmatively that the causes were such that no reasonable amount of precaution and care would have enabled him to avoid or guard against them."

There is authority in England that the burden of proof as to negligence in respect of all the COGSA exceptions (46 U.S.C.A. § 1304(2)(a) through (g)) is on the ship (Gosse Millard v. Canadian Government Merchant Marine, 2 K.B. 432, 436–437 [1927]). The act of God exception was not specifically mentioned.

In discussing the effect of COGSA on burden of proof, Carver, above, does not treat specifically the act of God exception but, criticizing the Gosse

Millard decision, seems to say that the cargo should have the burden of proof as to negligence in connection with nearly all the COGSA exceptions. Carver, cited above, at 185–186.

Gilmore and Black, cited above, seem to state clearly that under COGSA the carrier has the burden of persuasion as to negligence in an act of God situation. They say (at 163; emphasis supplied):

"Once the damage is established, the carrier, it would seem, has two main lines of possible escape. He may take up the burden of establishing that the loss falls within 4(2)(a) to (p) [which includes act of God as (d)]. If he does this successfully, then either (as in 4(2)(a)) he is exonerated regardless of his negligence; or (as in 4(2)(c) [perils of the sea; analogous to act of God]) *he will, in effect, already have established his own freedom from negligence as a part of the process of bringing himself under the exception;* or, if the exception he has brought himself under is one to which his own contributing fault would disentitle him, the burden will shift to the shipper to prove the carrier's negligence or other fault."

There are, on the other hand, old decisions which indicate that when act of God is pleaded and the natural event shown, the burden is on the shipper to prove negligence in failing to take precautions. Examples are Clark v. Barnwell, 53 U.S. 272, 280, 13 L.Ed. 985 (1851); Taney, C.J., and Wayne, J. (dissenting); Memphis & C. Railroad Co. v. Reeves, 77 U.S. 176, 190 (1869). Judge Friendly has in effect put the first of these cases to one side on its facts Lekas & Drivas, Inc. v. Goulandris, 306 F.2d 426, 431, 1962 A.M.C. 2366, 2374 (2 Cir.1962):

"The respondents in Clark v. Barnwell had not only established a peril of the sea as a cause but had negated all others; libellants in that case not merely failed to sustain a burden, but no evidence of negligence 'is found in the record,' 53 U.S. at 283."

The authority of the two old Supreme Court cases has been virtually destroyed by later decisions.

Schnell v. Vallescura, 293 U.S. 539, 58 S.Ct. 83, 79 L.Ed. 645, 1934 A.M.C. 1573 (1934) is important in this connection. Onions were delivered on board ship in Spain in good condition but were turned out in New York "damaged by decay." The ship pleaded no liability because there was an exception relieving the ship of liability for decay and further because the damage was caused by "perils of the sea," a defense very like that of Act of God. The evidence indicated that damage to the onions was caused (a) by closing hatches in heavy weather (a peril of the sea) and (b) by keeping the hatches closed in fair weather (negligence). This Court concluded that since the ship had failed to prove (and could not prove) how much of the damage was due to the peril of the sea, the cargo could recover for the full damage. 43 F.2d 247, 1929 A.M.C. 1409 (S.D.N.Y.1929). The Court of Appeals reversed (70 F.2d 261, 1934 A.M.C. 573 (2 Cir.1934)) because all the damage was from decay and thus *prima facie* shown to be within a specific exception for decay; therefore the cargo had the burden of proof to show that the exception was not conclusively established by showing that the decay in whole or in part was caused by negligence of the ship.   Since the cargo could not show what part of the damage was due to negligence, the ship was left "excused" 70 F.2d at 263, 1934 A.M.C. at 576.   The Supreme Court unanimously reversed, holding that the burden was upon the carrier to bring himself within an exception; that this was true with respect to exceptions implied in law such as "act of God or the public enemy" (293 U.S. at 304, 1934 A.M.C. at 1576); that it was also true in respect of exceptions agreed upon in the bill of lading; that the burden is placed on the carrier because he is a "bailee" who has "an extraordinary duty" and usually has peculiar knowledge of those facts relied upon to relieve him of the duty; and that the law "annexes a condition" to the exceptions "that they shall relieve the carrier from liability for loss from an excepted cause only if in the course of the voyage he has used due care to guard against it." (293 U.S. at 304, 1934 A.M.C. at 1576).   The Court took note of such cases as Clark v. Barnwell, above, and Memphis & Charleston Railroad Co. v. Reeves, above, and in this connection said (293 U.S. at 304–305, 1934 A.M.C. at 1577):

"It is commonly said that when the carrier succeeds in establishing that the injury is from an excepted cause, the burden is then on the shipper to show that that cause would not have produced the injury but for the carrier's negligence in failing to guard against it.   Such we may assume the rule to be, at least to the extent of requiring the shipper to give evidence of negligence where the carrier has sustained the burden of showing that the immediate cause of the loss or injury is an excepted peril."

On its face, this language would not affect the analysis here made because, by definition, the carrier does not establish the "excepted cause" of act of God unless freedom from negligence in "failing to guard against it" is itself shown.

But, assuming the quoted language to refer to negligence with reference to an act of God exception, the Supreme Court appears to be limiting the old decisions to this effect: if a *prima facie case* of due care is made out by the ship, then the burden of *going forward* with evidence of negligence is on the shipper and (inferentially) the burden of *persuasion* is left on the ship.   Cf. Alliance Assurance Co. v. United States, 252 F.2d 529, 535 (2 Cir.1958).

A note appearing in the Texas Law Review discusses Vallescura and other cases and says:

"* * * if the burden of the ship is to show that the *cause* of the injury was, for instance, a peril of the sea, it cannot be satisfied without a corresponding exclusion of any other cause, including that of negligence.

"If this is the case, under the causal type exception, can there really be a shifting burden?   It would seem that if the ship actually carried the burden laid on her in Clark v. Barnwell, i.e., showed the damage to have been in actuality the result of an excepted cause, such showing would *ipso facto,* leave the shipper without a case.

"To cloud such an analysis, however, two further problems arise. One is the question of *separate* concurring causes, each of which was responsible for part of the damage. This will be discussed later. Another is the theory that although the loss be caused by a peril of the sea, the shipper may still recover by showing that the use of diligence on the part of the ship would have avoided the effects of the peril. It would seem, however, that analytically, an attempt by the cargo to make such a showing would be in the nature of a rebuttal of the causation element of the ship's primary burden—if (under the bill of lading exception) that burden contains a causation element. The diverse effects of 'cause' and 'effect' type exceptions appear. As before stated, in the 'cause' type case, the question of proximate cause of the damage must be put in issue first by the ship, as part of its case for the excepted cause. Therefore, it would seem that an attempt by the shipper to show the efficiency of another cause (negligence) must be in the nature of a rebuttal and of meeting the requirement that he 'go forward' with some showing of negligence, in order to prevent an instructed verdict." Note, Cargo Damage at Sea: The Ship's Liability, 27 Tex.L.Rev. 525, 533 (1949).

The length of this discussion may well have been unnecessary in view of very plain language in a recent Supreme Court decision, Missouri Pac. R.R. Co. v. Elmore & Stahl, 377 U.S. 134, 84 S.Ct. 1142, 12 L.Ed.2d 194, rehearing denied 377 U.S. 984, 84 S.Ct. 1880, 12 L.Ed.2d 752 (1964), quoting and citing *Vallescura*. The Supreme Court said (377 U.S. at 138):

"Accordingly, under federal law, in an action to recover from a carrier for damage to a shipment, the shipper establishes his *prima facie case* when he shows delivery in good condition, arrival in damaged condition, and the amount of damages. Thereupon, the burden of proof is upon the carrier to show both that it was free from negligence and that the damage to the cargo was due to one of the excepted causes relieving the carrier of liability."

The case dealt with a railway carrier but, unless the provisions of COGSA can be said to be to the contrary (which seems not possible), the language seems applicable to maritime cargo claims.

For the reasons indicated, the conclusion is that respondents have the burden of persuasion that damage from Hurricane Donna could not have been guarded against by reasonable care on their part.

* * *

[After finding that it could not, the decree was made for respondents, dismissing the libels on the merits.]

NOTE

See also Petition of United States, 425 F.2d 991, 1970 A.M.C. 2034 (5th Cir.1970).

On the "restraint of princes," see Lekas & Drivas, Inc. v. Goulandris, 306 F.2d 426, 1962 A.M.C. 2366 (2d Cir.1962). There a vessel was about to depart Greece for the United States with a cargo of, inter alia, soft cheese. Before the vessel left for what was to have been a Gibraltar crossing in October, the Italians attacked Greece and the vessel was ordered to join a convoy for Port Said and thereafter follow the instructions of the British Admiralty.   In May, she finally arrived in New York via the Cape of Good Hope.   The cheese had been removed from the vessel in Aden because of necessary repairs there, and when it was reloaded "had begun to develop a certain odor."   By the time it arrived in New York, a surveyor found it "melted with a terrible stench, and worthless."   Cargo contended that despite the "restraint" as cause of the direction and length of the voyage, the carrier had violated § 1303(2) by not selling the cheese in Aden.   Judge Friendly held that the carrier having shown "restraint of princes" as a cause, it was not obligated to prove compliance with § 1303(2).   The burden rested with the cargo to demonstrate failure to care for the cargo.   This is the distinction, he noted, between exceptions (a) through (p) in § 1304(2) and exception (q).   "To hold that when a carrier has shown that the loss arose as a consequence of restraint of princes, § 4(2)(g), it still has the burden of negating any other fault or neglect of its agents or servants would be to read the qualification of (q) into (a)–(p), although Congress did not put it there."

Cf.   Sedco, Inc. v. S.S. Strathewe, 800 F.2d 27 (2d Cir.1986)—when a vessel en route from to Dubai to the United States was requisitioned by the British Government, and went to Malta to tranship cargo, its negligence in handling the cargo was not excused as "restraint of princes."

2.   PERILS OF THE SEA

The Vallescura

Supreme Court of the United States, 1934.
293 U.S. 296, 55 S.Ct. 194, 79 L.Ed. 373, 1934 A.M.C. 1573.

■ MR. JUSTICE STONE delivered the opinion of the Court.

Petitioners brought suit in admiralty in the District Court for Southern New York, to recover damages for injury to a shipment of onions on respondent's steamship Vallescura from Spain to New York City.   The onions, receipt of which in apparent good condition was acknowledged by the bill of lading, were delivered in New York damaged by decay.   The vessel pleaded as a defense an exception, in the bill of lading, from liability for damage by "decay" and "perils of the seas," and that the damage "was not due to any cause or event arising through any negligence on the part of the vessel, her master, owner or agents."

On the trial there was evidence that the decay was caused by improper ventilation of the cargo during the voyage, and that the failure to ventilate was due in part to closing of the hatches and ventilators made necessary by heavy weather, and in part to the neglect of the master and crew in failing to keep them open at night in fair weather.   The District Court entered an interlocutory decree, adjudging that the libelants recover the amount of damage sustained by them, caused by closing the hatches and ventilators during good weather, and appointing a special commissioner to ascertain and compute the amount of damage.   43 F.2d 247.

The commissioner, after hearing evidence found that it was impossible to ascertain how much of the damage was due to want of ventilation in fair weather and how much to want of it in bad. But, after comparing the periods during which the ventilators were negligently closed with those during which they were open or properly closed, he stated: "It would seem, therefore, that the greater part of the damage must have been due to improper shutting of the hatches and ventilators." He concluded that as the vessel had failed to show what part of the damage was due to bad weather, the petitioner should recover the full amount of the damage. The District Court, accepting the report of the commissioner as presumably correct, as required by Admiralty Rule 43½, 286 U.S. 572 (28 U.S.C.A. § 723), found no basis for rejecting its conclusions and gave judgment to libelants accordingly. The Court of Appeals for the Second Circuit, reversed, 70 F.2d 261, holding that as the damage was within the clause of the bill of lading exempting the vessel from liability for decay, the burden was on petitioner to show what part of the damage was taken out of the exception, because due to respondent's negligence.

* * * No formal findings were made, but in directing entry of the interlocutory decree, and after reviewing the evidence and commenting on the fact that the hatches and ventilators had been kept closed at night in fair weather, a circumstance which the trial judge declared established negligence in the care and custody of the cargo, he stated: "Thus it appears that this notoriously perishable cargo of Spanish Onions (The Buckleigh, 31 F.2d 241, 1929 A.M.C. 449, 450 (2 Cir.1929)), was deprived of all ventilation during the nighttime, regardless of the state of the weather. Such treatment was obviously ruinous and must have caused substantial damage." We have no doubt that this was intended to be a finding that negligence in failing to provide proper ventilation was the cause of some of the damage and that, as such, it was adequately supported by evidence. The commissioner and the court below assumed it to be such and we so accept it.

The failure to ventilate the cargo was not a "fault or error in navigation or management" of the vessel, from the consequences of which it may be relieved by section 3 of the Harter Act of February 13, 1893, § 3, c. 105, 27 Stat. 445; section 192, tit. 46, U.S.C. (46 U.S.C.A. § 192). The management was of the cargo, within the meaning of sections 1 and 2 of the act (46 U.S.C.A. §§ 190, 191), and not of the vessel, to which section 3 relates. Oceanic Steam Nav. Co. v. Aitken (The Germanic), 196 U.S. 589, 597, 25 S.Ct. 317, 49 L.Ed. 610 (1905); Knott v. Botany Worsted Mills, 179 U.S. 69, 73, 74, 21 S.Ct. 30, 45 L.Ed. 90 (1900); The Jean Bart, 197 F. 1002, 1006 (D.C.Cal.1912). Hence, we pass to the decisive question whether, in view of the presumptions which aid the shipper in establishing the vessel's liability under a contract for carriage by sea, it was necessary for the petitioners to offer further evidence in order to recover the damage which they have suffered. If, in the state of the proof which the record exhibits, recovery depends upon their ability to produce evidence which would enable the court to separate the amount of damage attributable to respondent's negligence from that attributable to the unavoidable failure to ventilate in bad weather, they have failed to do so and judgment must go against them. But if respondent can relieve itself from liability only by showing what part of the damage was due to sea peril, in that bad weather prevented ventilation, judgment must go against it for the full damages.

In general the burden rests upon the carrier of goods by sea to bring himself within any exception relieving him from the liability which the law otherwise imposes on him. This is true at common law with respect to the exceptions which the law itself annexed to his undertaking, such as his immunity from liability for act of God or the public enemy. See Carver, Carriage by Sea (7th Ed.) c. I. The rule applies equally with respect to other exceptions for which the law permits him to stipulate. Clark v. Barnwell, 12 How. 272, 280, 13 L.Ed. 985 (1851); Rich v. Lambert & Bro., 12 How. 347, 357, 13 L.Ed. 1017 (1851); Propeller Niagara v. Cordes, 21 How. 7, 29, 16 L.Ed. 41 (1858); The Maggie Hammond, 9 Wall. 435, 459, 19 L.Ed. 772 (1869); The Edwin I. Morrison, 153 U.S. 199, 211, 14 S.Ct. 823, 38 L.Ed. 688 (1894); The Folmina, 212 U.S. 354, 361, 29 S.Ct. 363, 53 L.Ed. 546, 15 Ann.Cas. 748 (1909). The reason for the rule is apparent. He is a bailee intrusted with the shipper's goods, with respect to the care and safe delivery of which the law imposes upon him an extraordinary duty. Discharge of the duty is peculiarly within his control. All the facts and circumstances upon which he may rely to relieve him of that duty are peculiarly within his knowledge and usually unknown to the shipper. In consequence, the law casts upon him the burden of the loss which he cannot explain or, explaining, bring within the exceptional case in which he is relieved from liability. See Bank of Kentucky v. Adams Express Co., 93 U.S. 174, 184, 23 L.Ed. 872 (1876); Chicago & Eastern Illinois R. Co. v. Collins Produce Co., 249 U.S. 186, 192, 193, 39 S.Ct. 189, 63 L.Ed. 552 (1919); New York C. Railroad Co. v. Lockwood, 17 Wall. 357, 379, 380, 21 L.Ed. 627 (1873).

To such exceptions the law itself annexes a condition that they shall relieve the carrier from liability for loss from an excepted cause only if in the course of the voyage he has used due care to guard against it. Liverpool & G. W. Steam Co. v. Phenix Insurance Co., 129 U.S. 397, 438, 9 S.Ct. 469, 32 L.Ed. 788 (1889); Compania De Navigacion La Flecha v. Brauer, 168 U.S. 104, 117, 18 S.Ct. 12, 42 L.Ed. 398 (1897). This rule is recognized and continued in the first section of the Harter Act (46 U.S.C.A. § 190), which makes it unlawful to insert any clause in a bill of lading whereby the carrier shall be relieved of liability for negligence.

It is commonly said that when the carrier succeeds in establishing that the injury is from an excepted cause, the burden is then on the shipper to show that that cause would not have produced the injury but for the carrier's negligence in failing to guard against it. Such we may assume the rule to be, at least to the extent of requiring the shipper to give evidence of negligence where the carrier has sustained the burden of showing that the immediate cause of the loss or injury is an excepted peril. Clark v. Barnwell, 12 How. 272, 280, 13 L.Ed. 985 (1851); Memphis & C. Railroad Co. v. Reeves, 10 Wall. 176, 189, 190, 19 L.Ed. 909 (1869); Western

Transportation Co. v. Downer, 11 Wall. 129, 134, 20 L.Ed. 160 (1870); The Victory & The Plymothian, 168 U.S. 410, 423, 18 S.Ct. 149, 42 L.Ed. 519 (1897); Cau v. Texas & Pacific Ry. Co., 194 U.S. 427, 432, 24 S.Ct. 663, 48 L.Ed. 1053 (1904); The Malcolm Baxter, 277 U.S. 323, 334, 48 S.Ct. 516, 72 L.Ed. 901 (1928).

But this is plainly not the case where the efficient cause of the injury for which the carrier is prima facie liable is not shown to be an excepted peril. The Mohler, 21 Wall. 230, 234, 22 L.Ed. 485 (1874); The Edwin I. Morrison, supra, 153 U.S. 199, 14 S.Ct. 823, 38 L.Ed. 688 (1894). If he delivers a cargo damaged by causes unknown or unexplained, which had been received in good condition, he is subject to the rule applicable to all bailees, that such evidence makes out a prima facie case of liability. It is sufficient, if the carrier fails to show that the damage is from an excepted cause, to cast on him the further burden of showing that the damage is not due to failure properly to stow or care for the cargo during the voyage. Rich v. Lambert, supra, 12 How. 347, 13 L.Ed. 1017 (1851); The Maggie Hammond, supra, 9 Wall. 435, 19 L.Ed. 772 (1869); Jahn v. The Folmina, 212 U.S. 354, 361, 29 S.Ct. 363, 53 L.Ed. 546, 15 Ann.Cas. 748 (1909); Chesapeake & Ohio Ry. Co. v. A.F. Thompson Manufacturing Co., 270 U.S. 416, 422, 423, 46 S.Ct. 318, 70 L.Ed. 659 (1926).

Here the stipulation was for exemption from liability for a particular kind of injury, decay. But the decay of a perishable cargo is not a cause; it is an effect. It may be the result of a number of causes, for some of which, such as the inherent defects of the cargo, or, under the contract, sea peril making it impossible to ventilate properly, the carrier is not liable. For others, such as negligent stowage, or failure to care for the cargo properly during the voyage, he is liable. The stipulation thus did not add to the causes of injury from which the carrier could claim immunity. It could not relieve him from liability for want of diligence in the stowage or care of the cargo.

It is unnecessary for us to consider whether the effect of the clause is to relieve the carrier from the necessity, in the first instance, of offering evidence of due diligence in caring for a cargo received in good condition, and delivered in a state of decay. See The Hindoustan, 67 F. 794, 795 (2 Cir.1895); The Patria, 132 F. 971, 972 (2 Cir.1904); Loma Fruit Co. v. International Navigation Co., Ltd., 11 F.2d 124, 125 (2 Cir.1926); The Gothic Star, 4 F.Supp. 240, 241 (D.C.N.Y.1933). For here want of diligence in providing proper ventilation is established and it is found that the failure to ventilate has caused the damage. It is enough that the clause plainly cannot be taken to relieve the vessel from bringing itself within the exception from liability for damage by sea peril where the shipper has carried the burden of showing that the decay is due either to sea peril, in that bad weather prevented ventilation, or to the vessel's negligence. Where the state of the proof is such as to show that the damage is due either to an excepted peril or to the carrier's negligent care of the cargo, it is for him to bring himself within the exception or to show that he has not been negligent. The Folmina, supra.

Similarly, the carrier must bear the entire loss where it appears that the injury to cargo is due either to sea peril or negligent stowage, or both, and he fails to show what damage is attributable to sea peril.   * * *

The vessel in the present case is in no better position because, upon the evidence, it appears that some of the damage, in an amount not ascertainable, is due to sea peril.   That does not remove the burden of showing facts relieving it from liability.   If it remains liable for the whole amount of the damage because it is unable to show that sea peril was a cause of the loss, it must equally remain so if it cannot show what part of the loss is due to that cause.   Speyer v. The Mary Belle Roberts, supra; The Rona, 5 Asp. 259, 262; Carver, Carriage by Sea (7th Ed.) § 78, p. 114.

Since the respondent has failed throughout to sustain the burden, which rested upon it at the outset, of showing to what extent sea peril was the effective cause of the damage, and as the petitioners are without fault, no question of apportionment or division of the damage arises.

Reversed.

NOTE

It is to be noted that a hurricane may be pleaded as a "peril of the sea" as well as an "act of God."   See, e.g., J. Gerber & Co. v. S.S. Sabine Howaldt, 437 F.2d 580, 1971 A.M.C. 539 (2d Cir.1971), in which it was held that a vessel was seaworthy and vessel owner was not liable when hurricane force winds in December in North Atlantic resulted in cross-seas that wrenched and twisted the vessel, forcing up the hatch covers and letting in water that damaged the cargo.

Rust damage to steel was held to result from a peril of the sea when it was established by expert testimony that the damage occurred from sweating, that there is no way to prevent steel from sweating when it is transported from a cold to a warm place except to ventilate it, and that in the circumstances ventilation would have exacerbated the problem by exposing the steel to additional rusting from exposure to salt water.   Associated Metals and Minerals Corp. v. Etelae Suomin Laiva, 858 F.2d 674 (11th Cir.1988).

Destruction of a cargo container and its contents during adverse weather conditions when it was properly stored on deck was held to be within the "perils of the sea" exception in Taisho Marine & Fire Ins. Co., Ltd. v. M/V Sea–Land Endurance, 815 F.2d 1270 (9th Cir.1987).

3. FIRE

Westinghouse Elec. Corp. v. M/V Leslie Lykes

United States Court of Appeals, Fifth Circuit, 1984.
734 F.2d 199, 1985 A.M.C. 247, cert. denied 469 U.S. 1077, 105 S.Ct. 577, 83 L.Ed.2d 516 (1984).

■ JOHN R. BROWN, CIRCUIT JUDGE:

This is a suit by a shipper of cargo against an ocean carrier for damage to cargo resulting from a fire aboard ship.   * * *

Facts and Decision Below

In August of 1976, Westinghouse Electric Corp. (*Cargo*) shipped several large electric rotors aboard the SS LESLIE LYKES (LESLIE) owned by Lykes Brothers Steamship Co., Inc. (Carrier). The LESLIE was an ocean-going steamship used to transport break-bulk or general cargo.

* * *

Among the cargo stowed in the No. 3 LTD were bales of cotton. Cotton is flammable and, if ignited, is very difficult to extinguish. Baled cotton can smolder indefinitely, even under water, because there is a source of oxygen within the cotton fibers themselves. Between the starboard bulkhead and the cotton was a stow of drill pipe running fore and aft. The pipe stow was secured properly by chains, which were tightened by turnbuckles.

* * *

At 2315 hours on August 31, 1976, a clanking noise was heard by members of the crew, which they believed at the time had come from the No. 4 hold. No attempt was made by the crew to investigate the clanking sound at that time, even though there was access into No. 4. At the time the noise was heard, the vessel was still sailing in rough seas.

At 1212 hours on the following day, roughly twelve and one-half hours after the clanking was heard, smoke was observed from the bridge by Captain Metcalf, master of the vessel, coming from the kingpost forward of the No. 3 hold. The smoke detector system indicated that a fire was in the No. 3 LTD. Although an access way was provided in No. 3 hold, access could not be obtained into No. 3 LTD because bags of flour had been stowed over the manhole cover in No. 3 upper tween deck. * * *

Captain Metcalf ordered the release of 24 bottles of CO_2 into No. 3 LTD, in accordance with the directions provided by the manufacturer of the CO_2 system. * * *

Soon after the introduction of CO_2, the smoke abated, as indicated by the smoke detector. Neither the smoke detector nor the kingpost ventilator revealed any indication of smoke from September 1st until the opening of the No. 3 weatherdeck hatch at El Ferrol on September 8.

* * *

While at sea, Captain Metcalf discussed the events taking place with Lykes' managing personnel at New Orleans by radiotelephone each day, from the time fire was first detected. He considered and followed some suggestions for fighting the fire made by Lykes' vice-president in charge of maintenance and repair, Joseph Bernstein.

Mr. Lucian Castro, then a supervisory port engineer for Lykes in New Orleans, was sent to meet the vessel at El Ferrol for the purpose of rendering the master any assistance and advice that he could. Castro was sent because he was considered to be knowledgeable and experienced in cotton fires. Castro prepared himself for the journey and task by reviewing the stowage plan for the voyage, the vessel's CO_2 system, and bringing available foam and other chemicals for extinguishing cotton fires.

When the vessel arrived at El Ferrol on September 6 at about 1818 hours, Captain Metcalf held an informal meeting in his cabin to discuss what action would be taken. Numerous Spanish firefighting authorities and port officials, including representatives of the Spanish Navy and the Navy's firefighting school, were present. Also attending were Castro and the ship's chief engineer.

Captain Metcalf decided at the conclusion of the meeting that an access hole would be cut in the bulkhead between No. 3 and No. 4 holds, at the point of highest temperature. This was done in order to see into the No. 3 LTD, inspect the status of the fire and, if necessary, fight the fire from its own level through the access hole.

The access hole was cut in the same location on the bulkhead where the steam lance holes had been drilled, beneath an athwartship walkway which ran along the forward bulkhead in No. 4 hold. * * *

After the fire was extinguished and the holds were emptied of water, a turnbuckle securing one of three chains surrounding the pipe stow in the starboard side of No. 3 LTD was found to have been broken. The remaining two chains securing the starboard pipe stow were unbroken and still held the stow intact.

Cargo brought an action against Carrier for damage to its cargo, and Carrier asserted the defense of the Fire Statute,[2] which was preserved and incorporated into the Carriage of Goods By Sea Act.[3] The District Court

2. The Fire Statute provides:

No owner of any vessel shall be liable to answer for or make good to any person any loss or damage, which may happen to any merchandise whatsoever, which shall be shipped, taken in, or put on board any such vessel, by reason or by means of any fire happening to or on board the vessel, unless such fire is caused by the design or neglect of such owner.

46 U.S.C. § 182.

3. The Carriage of Goods By Sea Act provides:

(2) Neither the carrier nor the ship shall be responsible for loss or damage arising or resulting from—

* * *

(b) *Fire,* unless caused by the actual fault or privity of the carrier;

46 U.S.C. § 1304(2)(b).

The Carriage of Goods By Sea Act specifically incorporates and carries forward the terms of the Fire Statute. Even more important, COGSA § 1308 expressly provides that other provisions of the Act (see, e.g., § 1303(1), (2)) shall not affect the rights and obligations of the Carrier under the Fire Statute (§ 182).

The provisions of this chapter shall not affect the rights and obligations of the carrier under the provisions of the Shipping Act, 1916, or under the provisions of sections 175, 181 to 183, and 183b to 188 of this title or any amendments thereto; or under the provisions of any other enactment for the time being in force relating to the limitation of the liability of the owners of seagoing vessels.

46 U.S.C. § 1308.

It has long been held that the COGSA fire exemption and the Fire Statute exemption are the same, e.g., Complaint of Ta Chi Navigation (Panama) Corp., 677 F.2d 225, 228 (2d Cir.1982), except that COGSA extends to the "carrier," not just the "owner" as in the Fire Statute. See 2A Benedict on *Admiralty* § 147 (7th ed. 1983).

explained that, under the reasoning of Sunkist Growers v. Adelaide Shipping Lines, Ltd., 603 F.2d 1327 (9th Cir.1979), the Carrier may not be exonerated under the Fire Statute unless he first bears the burden of proving that he used due diligence to provide a seaworthy ship or that any unseaworthy condition did not cause the fire and resulting damage. Pursuing this approach, the District Court concluded

> that Lykes failed to exercise due diligence in providing a seaworthy vessel in its stowing bags of flour over the manhole access way to No. 3 lower tween deck. The manhole was not fit for its intended use, and as a result, rendered the LESLIE LYKES unseaworthy. This unseaworthy condition was a proximate cause of the fire and resulting damage to the cargo. * * * Thus, under the holding *Sunkist Growers* Lykes would be barred from asserting the fire defense.

* * *

Proof Under the Fire Statute

* * *

Once the Carrier shows that the loss or damage was caused by fire, the burden of proof shifts back onto Cargo to prove that the fire was "*caused by the design or neglect*" of the shipowner. Thus, the burden is on the Cargo to identify by a preponderance of the evidence the cause of the fire, and also to establish that the cause was due to the "actual fault or privity" of the Carrier. Comment, The Elements of the Burden of the Proof under the Carriage of Goods By Sea Act, 12 Colum.J.Trans.L. 289, 298 (1973); *Thede,* supra, 45 Tul.L.Rev. at 985; 2A Benedict on Admiralty § 143 (7th ed. 1983)(citing cases); Fidelity– Phenix Fire Ins. Co. v. Flota Mercante Del Estado, 205 F.2d 886, 887 (5th Cir.1953); Complaint of Ta Chi Navigation (Panama) Corp., 677 F.2d 225, 228 (2d Cir.1982); Asbestos Corp. v. Compagnie De Navigation, 480 F.2d 669, 672–73 (2d Cir.1973). See Blasser Bros. v. Northern Pan–American Line, 628 F.2d 376, 382 (5th Cir.1980); Nitram, Inc. v. Cretan Life, 599 F.2d 1359, 1373 (5th Cir.1979). Moreover, Cargo's burden is not satisfied by proving that the fire was caused by the negligence of the master or crew. "Neglect of such owner" means personal neglect of the owner, or, in case of a corporate owner, negligence of its managing officers or agents. Earle & Stoddart, Inc. v. Ellerman's Wilson Line, Ltd., 287 U.S. 420, 424–25, 53 S.Ct. 200, 200–01, 77 L.Ed. 403 (1932); Alfa Romeo, Inc. v. SS Torinita, 499 F.Supp. 1272, 1282 (S.D.N.Y.1980), aff'd, 659 F.2d 1057 (2d Cir.1981); Complaint of Caldas, 350 F.Supp. 566 (E.D.Pa.1972), aff'd, 485 F.2d 680 (3d Cir.1973).

Not following this time honored approach, the District Court instead[4] emphasized the Ninth Circuit's decision in Sunkist Growers, Inc. v. Ade-

---

4. The District Court declared:

The burden which the carrier must meet under this interpretation is that it exercised due diligence in providing a seaworthy ship or that any unseaworthi-

ness was not attributable to lack of due diligence. *Sunkist Growers, Inc.,* supra.

Under the Ninth Circuit's interpretation, if the carrier fails to establish that it acted in accordance with 46

laide Shipping Lines, Ltd., 603 F.2d 1327 (9th Cir.1979), cert. denied, 444 U.S. 1012, 100 S.Ct. 659, 62 L.Ed.2d 640 (1980), and held that the burden of proof is on the Carrier to show that it exercised due diligence to provide a seaworthy ship as a precondition to invoking the defense of § 1304(2)(b) and the Fire Statute.   603 F.2d at 1336.

We need not look far upward to reject the Ninth Circuit's construction of the Fire Statute.   In Earle & Stoddart v. Ellerman's Wilson Line, 287 U.S. 420, 53 S.Ct. 200, 77 L.Ed. 403 (1932), the very same argument was made and squarely rejected by the Supreme Court.   There the Court explained:

> But the Act does not purport to create any general duty on the part of shipowners.   Its requirement of due diligence is imposed as a condition of securing immunity from liability for certain kinds of losses, like those due to errors in navigation or management.   That the provisions of the Harter Act do not refer to liability for losses arising from fire is made clear by § 6 which declares that the Act "shall not be held to modify or repeal §§ 4281, 4282, and 4283 of the Revised Statutes,"—§ 4282 being the fire statute. The *courts have been careful not to thwart the purpose of the fire statute by interpreting as "neglect" of the owners the breach of what in other connections is held to be a non-delegable duty.*

287 U.S. at 427, 53 S.Ct. at 201 (emphasis added).   Because of this positive directive and the underlying policy of the Fire Statute, we join in the Second Circuit's recent emphatic rejection of *Sunkist:*

> When Congress wanted to put the burden of proving freedom from fault on a shipowner claiming the benefit of an exemption, it specifically said so.   See 46 U.S.C. § 1304(2)(q).   The *Sunkist* court would read the language of subsection (q) into subsection (b), "although Congress did not put it there."   See Lekas & Drivas, Inc. v. Goulandris, supra, 306 F.2d [426] at 432 [(2d Cir.1962)].   This Court has not put it there either.   We adhere to our prior holdings that, if the carrier shows that the damage was caused by fire, the shipper must prove that the carrier's negligence caused the fire or prevented its extinguishment.   If on remand the shipper fails to meet this burden, the action must be dismissed.

Complaint of Ta Chi Navigation (Panama) Corp., 677 F.2d 225, 229 (2d Cir.1982).   * * *

* * * Moreover, COGSA expressly provides that the obligation of the Carrier under § 1303(1) to exercise due diligence to make the ship seaworthy, or under (2) to properly load, handle, stow and care for cargo shall not affect the rights of the Carrier under the Fire Statute.   46 U.S.C. § 1308, see note 3, supra.   Thus, clear authority compels our rejection of *Sunkist* and its interpretation of the Fire Statute that imposes an obligation of due diligence to make seaworthy on the shipowner and relieves the Cargo of its

---

U.S.C. § 1303, or that failure to do so did not cause the fire and resulting damage, the carrier is barred from asserting the fire exemptions as a defense.   *Sunkist Growers, Inc.,* supra.   If the carrier does meet that burden, then the burden shifts to Cargo to prove that the fire was caused by the "design or neglect" or the "fault or privity" of the carrier.

burden of proof on privity and fault causation. Both Congress[5] and the Supreme Court have made it clear that the Fire Statute is to be applied broadly, and the exception to the defense for fires "caused by the design or neglect of such owner" must be viewed narrowly. E.g. Providence & New York S.S. Co. v. Hill Mfg. Co., 109 U.S. 578, 3 S.Ct. 379, 27 L.Ed. 1038 (1883). In that case the Court stated that if the Fire Statute "is administered with a tight and grudging hand, construing every clause most unfavorably against the shipowner, and allowing as little as possible to operate in his favor, the law will hardly be worth the trouble of its enactment." Id. at 589, 3 S.Ct. at 386. * * *

Design or Neglect of Such Owner

Accepting, *arguendo,* the trial court's finding that the cause of the fire was the covering of the manhole leading to No. 3 LTD with sacks of flour, and that such stowage was negligent in this case, we reject the Court's conclusion that such stowage was brought about by the "design or neglect" of the shipowner so as to overcome the fire defense.

> The District Court reasoned as follows: The uncontroverted testimony established that the cargo layout section in Lykes' head office in New Orleans was responsible for confecting the stowage plan for Lykes voyages. The vessel was loaded pursuant to that plan. The stowage plan for Voyage 64 indicates that bags of flour were to be stowed "all over" in the No. 3 upper tween deck, blocking the manhole to the accessway ladder in the No. 3 lower tween deck. The Court finds that Lykes' management knew or should have known of this practice. *It is the carrier's responsibility to make sure the vessel is properly loaded. 46 U.S.C. § 1303(2).* The Court concludes that the stowage of the bags of flour over the manhole was attributable to the management level of Lykes. Consumers Import Company v. Zosenjo, [320 U.S. 249] 64 S.Ct. 15 [88 L.Ed. 30] (1943). (Emphasis supplied).

Although we may accept the facts recited in this passage as supported by the record, we disagree with the Court's legal conclusions. It is plain that while asserting an alternative analysis on burden of proof, the Judge once again put primary reliance on the erroneous reasoning of *Sunkist* in his ruling on "design or neglect."

Although the District Court paid heed to the *Earle & Stoddart* holding on who bears the burden of proof, it ignored the Supreme Court's ruling in *Earle & Stoddart* on *what the cargo must prove.* The italicized sentence in the foregoing quotation demonstrates that the District Court reasoned that the failure of the Carrier to "make sure the vessel is properly loaded * * *

---

5. Congress has devised a very detailed scheme for the burden of proof in maritime cargo cases, see generally Comment, The Elements of the Burden of Proof Under the Carriage of Goods by Sea Act, 12 Colum.J.Trans.L. 289 (1973), that deliberately achieves a "ping pong" sort of shifting of the burden. 46 U.S.C. § 1304(2). Nitram, Inc. v. Cretan Life, 599 F.2d 1359, 1373 (5th Cir.1979).

As explained above, if the carrier satisfies his burden of showing loss by fire, the carrier will be exonerated if the cargo is unable to substantiate that it was caused by the "design or neglect" of the owner.

[under] 46 U.S.C. § 1303(2)" leads to the conclusion "that the stowage * * * was attributable to the management level of Lykes," and thus within Lykes' "design or neglect." If *Sunkist* were acceptable, this would be correct, because improper stowage constitutes unseaworthiness, and this would deprive the owner of the Fire Statute exemption under *Sunkist*. 603 F.2d at 1335–36.

However, the Supreme Court's opinion in *Earle & Stoddart* refutes *Sunkist* not only as to who bears the burden of proof, but also on what the cargo must prove to take the case out of the fire exemption. The cargo in *Earle & Stoddart* contended "that the [Fire] statute does not confer immunity where the fire resulted from unseaworthiness existing at the commencement of the voyage and * * * discoverable by due diligence." 287 U.S. at 425–26, 53 S.Ct. at 200–01. The Court flatly rejected this position, declaring: "The courts have been careful not to thwart the purpose of the fire statute by interpreting as 'neglect' of the owners the breach of what in other connections is held to be a non-delegable duty." 287 U.S. at 427, 53 S.Ct. at 201.

This admonition is directly applicable here. The District Court interpreted as "neglect" *of the owners* the improper stowage of cargo by lower-level employees, which in a non-fire COGSA context would be a non-delegable duty of the carrier properly to load, stow and care for the cargo. 46 U.S.C. § 1303(2); Agrico Chemical Co. v. S.S. Atlantic Forest, 620 F.2d 487, 489 (5th Cir.1980), aff'g 459 F.Supp. 638, 647 (E.D.La.1978). In a COGSA case involving a defense other than fire, the Carrier is liable for the negligence of its servants or agents in the loading, handling, stowing, carrying, caring for, or discharging the cargo. Id. The District Court cited (see the quotation supra) Consumers Import Company v. Zosenjo, 320 U.S. 249, 64 S.Ct. 15, 88 L.Ed. 30 (1943), in support of like reasoning in the context of the Fire Statute.

Actually, *Consumers Import* is directly contrary to the District Court's reasoning. There the Supreme Court pointed out:

> The cause of the fire is found to be negligent stowage of the fish meal, which made the vessel unseaworthy. The negligence was that of a person employed to supervise loading to whom responsibility was properly delegated and who was qualified by experience to perform the work. No negligence or design of the owner or charterer is found.

> * * *

> Since "neglect of the owner" means his personal negligence, or in case of a corporate owner, negligence of its managing officers and agents as distinguished from that of the master or subordinates, the findings below take the case out of the only exception provided by statute.

320 U.S. at 250, 252, 64 S.Ct. at 16, 17. This holding in *Consumers Import* is particularly compelling in this case for two reasons. First, it is the Supreme Court's most recent word on the Fire Statute. Second, the negligence was, as in this case, by shore-based persons who were delegated the task of designing and planning the stowage. Because the delegees were

not managerial agents with a broad range of responsibility in the corporation and because they were "qualified by experience to perform the work," such negligence was not the "design or neglect" of the owner.

* * *

* * * Thus, it is clear that under the Fire Statute the negligence of corporate subordinates is not as the District Court assumed, "attributable" to the "managing officers and agents" either by respondeat superior or by the concept of non-delegable duties.[6]

In this case, the evidence showed only that the stowage plan called for the manhole to be covered with sacks of flour and that the stowage plan had been prepared in the Lykes cargo layout department in New Orleans. As demonstrated above, the burden of proof was on the cargo to show that this stowage decision was within the "design or neglect" of the "managing officers and agents as distinguished from the master or subordinates" of Lykes. See supra p. 4172. Despite this burden, Cargo failed to present any evidence as to who within the layout department prepared this cargo plan and which, if any, supervisors checked and approved this person's work. There was no evidence of how many persons worked in this department, the various job categories and their corresponding spheres of authority, or the structure of the hierarchy leading from the layout personnel to the highest officers of the corporation. Nor was there any evidence that anyone with a broad range of authority in Lykes knew that cargo which might require access during the voyage was being stowed in No. 3 LTD and that the manhole leading to that compartment was being covered by cargo.[7] Nor was there evidence of negligence in hiring an incompetent.

6. Of course, there may be "design or neglect" if the owner negligently hired a person to perform a task for which he is incompetent. E.g., Skibs A/S Jolund (American Smelting & Refining Co. v. Black Diamond S.S. Corp.), 250 F.2d 777 (2d Cir.1957); United States v. Charbonnier, 45 F.2d 174 (4th Cir.1930)(president of shipping corporation hired incompetent engineer even though not favorably impressed by interview). However, even in such cases, the negligence in hiring must be personal to a managing agent of the corporation.

7. Cargo raises a great hue about the stowage of cotton bales without open access during the voyage as being a violation of Coast Guard regulations. The regulations are somewhat unclear. Although access for inspection during the voyage is generally a requirement for stowage of "dangerous articles," see 46 C.F.R. § 146.02-12 (1975), a broad category including "hazardous articles," see id. at § 146.03-8, which in turn includes cotton, see id. at § 146.27-1(c), in § 146.27-100, special, detailed regulations have been promulgated for the stowage of cotton. 46 C.F.R. § 146.27-25. These extensive regulations particularly on cotton do not contain a requirement of access during the voyage. Because of the peculiar danger of fire, the regulations require a CO_2 or steam smothering system and also require that the hatch be closed and covered by tarpaulins to make a tight seal. Id. at § 146.27-25(b)(6)(c). These requirements were fulfilled in this case.

Perhaps because of this ambiguity, the District Court made no finding on any violation of Coast Guard regulations. However, we point out that if there had been a violation of safety regulations, this would not deprive the shipowner of its defense under the Fire Statute, unless Cargo proved that the shipowner or his managing agents were personally negligent in causing the violation that caused the fire damage. Fidelity–Phenix Fire Ins. Co. v. Flota Mercante Del Estado, 205 F.2d 886 (5th Cir.1953), cert. denied, 346 U.S. 915, 74 S.Ct. 275, 98 L.Ed. 411; Auto-

Without such evidence showing a broad range of corporate authority in a person involved in the stowage decision, the District Court could not properly conclude that the improper stowage was within the personal "design or neglect" of the corporate owner. The evidence was only that some employee or employees in the layout department designed the stowage in this case. This is not sufficient to defeat the Carrier's defense under the Fire Statute. * * *

The Firefighting Effort: Quenching the Claim

This brings us to the purported cross-appeal by Cargo from the District Court's finding that, whether or not the firefighting effort was negligent, it was not attributable to the shipowner, because the Master retained control of the decision-making in the foreign port. * * *

A Carrier may be liable for fire damage where the "design or neglect" of the owner prevented extinguishment of the fire once it had begun. E.g., Complaint of Ta Chi Navigation (Panama) Corp., 677 F.2d 225, 228 (2d Cir.1982). Carrier liability on this basis has generally been predicated on failure to provide adequate firefighting equipment and training, or a failure by management level employees to use a clear opportunity and available means to put out the fire. See Asbestos Corp. v. Compagnie De Navigation, 480 F.2d 669 (2d Cir.1973); American Mail Line, Ltd. v. Tokyo Marine & Fire Ins. Co., 270 F.2d 499, 501 (9th Cir.1959); Fidelity–Phenix Fire Ins. Co. v. Flota Mercante Del Estado, 205 F.2d 886, 889 (5th Cir.1953); Great Atlantic & Pacific Tea Co. v. Brasileiro, 159 F.2d 661, 664 (2d Cir.1947).

In this case, there is no contention that the LESLIE did not have a complete, properly working system of firefighting equipment or that it was not used. Cargo challenged the specific tactics used to extinguish the fire after the vessel was moored in a foreign port. The District Court found that the Master, although listening to advice from Spanish port authorities, the Spanish naval firefighting school officials and shore-based Lykes em-

mobile Ins. Co. v. United Fruit Co., 224 F.2d 72 (2d Cir.1955); Complaint of Caldas, 350 F.Supp. 566 (E.D.Pa.1972), aff'd 485 F.2d 678 (3d Cir.1973).

Cargo also makes much of an isolated portion of the Master's testimony in which he stated that the covering at times of access manholes was not uncommon throughout the shipping industry. The Master explained that access during the voyage is not needed for certain cargos, and that leaving an access passage in a stow of cargo above a manhole might create an unnecessary hazard of instability in the cargo. Cargo argues that this testimony shows that the covering of manholes with cargo was so widespread as to be known by all, including the Lykes managers. The District Court did not make any finding

that the Lykes management knew that access to cargo requiring inspection during the voyage was routinely being blocked on Lykes ships. To the contrary, the District Court found that the particular stowage decision in this case was made in the cargo layout department, and thus the particular decision was "attributable" to management. Indeed, the Master's testimony was so general as to state only the equivalent of what is in the Coast Guard regulations: that access is required for certain types of cargo, but not for others. See 46 C.F.R. § 146.02–12(a)(1975). There is absolutely no evidence that Lykes management knew or should have known of a general practice among its subordinates of blocking access to stows of *cotton,* or to any other cargos to which open access is required.

ployees, retained and exercised actual ultimate control over the firefighting effort on his ship. The tactical decisions of the Master, the Court held, were not attributable to the owner. Thus, the District Court did not reach the issue of whether the elaborate firefighting effort was negligent.[10]

* * *

* * * If the Master's decision were negligent, such negligence would not be attributable to the owner under the Fire Statute nor under the District Court's finding, which we affirm.

The owner is not liable for a master's negligence in fighting fires, unless the supervision exercised by the owner is also negligent. E.g., Great Atlantic & Pacific Tea Co. v. Brasileiro, 159 F.2d 661, 664 (2d Cir.1947). Cf., Craig v. Continental Insurance Co., 141 U.S. 638, 639, 12 S.Ct. 97, 98, 35 L.Ed. 886 (1891)(acts of owner's envoy, who took command of vessel, were not within "privity or knowledge" of owner). Thus, in this case, where the Master retained decision-making authority, and was operating in a foreign port and needing to accommodate the concerns of foreign port officials and yet act expeditiously, the question of the owner's liability for the firefighting effort narrows to whether the owner was negligent in not insisting that the Master take a different course of action and relieving him of his command if he refused. The District Court's finding that the Master's actions were not attributable to the owner states in different words that management level employees did not know of any obviously unwise course of action taken by the Master that would require the owner to rigidly overrule the Master's "good faith latitude in professional judgment" by relieving him of his command. Vela, 231 F.2d at 819. The evidence was to the contrary. The Master safely brought the vessel with the cargo fire through heavy weather in the North Atlantic and into a safe harbor. The crew was saved, as was the vessel, and most of the cargo. After the fire, the voyage was completed. Thus, we find no error in the District Court's findings that, even if some aspect of the firefighting were negligent, such negligence would not be attributable to the owner.

In summary, we hold that the Carrier is exonerated from liability for the fire and water damage in this case by the Fire Statute. The interlocutory judgment is reversed, the cross-appeal is affirmed, and the case remanded for further proceedings.

Reversed in Part, Affirmed in Part.

---

10.   The District Court explained:

The Court does not feel that suggestions made by Mr. Bernstein nor active assistance on the part of Mr. Castro constitute control such as to attribute the firefighting endeavors to Lykes' management. The Court finds, therefore, that the actions taken in an effort to extinguish the fire were taken pursuant to the orders of Captain Metcalf.

Hence, the Court does not reach the contention of cargo that the carrier was negligent in actually fighting the fire because the Court had concluded that Captain Metcalf made the decisions relating to the method of fighting the fire, which decisions are not attributable to the carrier. Great Atlantic and Pacific Tea Co. v. Brasileiro, 159 F.2d 661 (2d Cir.1947).

NOTE

As indicated in *Westinghouse* above, *Sunkist Growers* received very little support from judges or commentators. See Calamari, The Eternal Conflict Between Cargo and Hull: The Fire Statute—A Shifting Scene, 55 St. Johns L.Rev. 417 (1981). For a supportive view, see Comment, The Allocation of the Burden of Proof in Marine Fire Damage cases., 50 U.Chi.L.Rev. 1146 (1983).

The Ninth Circuit has adhered to its view on the issue of the burden of proof of due diligence to provide a seaworthy vessel as a condition to invocation of the Fire Statute and § 1304(2)(b). See Complaint of Damodar Bulk Carriers Ltd., 903 F.2d 675, 683 (9th Cir.1990). There, however, it emphasized the fact that the decisions applying *Sunkist Growers* have been cases in which the fire was determined to be caused by the unseaworthiness, and do not hold that unseaworthiness without causal connection with the damage precludes reliance on the Fire Statute, nor alter the burden the plaintiff must shoulder in demonstrating "actual fault and privity of the carrier."

In *Westinghouse,* the assumption is indulged that § 1304(2)(b) merely extends the protection of § 192 to carriers who would not qualify as owners under the latter, leaving the substance of the immunity unchanged. See court's footnote 3. See also Gilmore & Black, *Law of Admiralty* § 3–31 (1975).

4. ERRORS IN MANAGEMENT

Firestone Synthetic Fibers Co. v. M/S Black Heron

United States Court of Appeals, Second Circuit, 1963.
324 F.2d 835, 1964 A.M.C. 42.

■ PER CURIAM. Libellant, Firestone Synthetic Fibers Company, appeals from a decree dismissing a libel against respondents for water damage to a shipment of machinery. 1963 A.M.C. 253.

The damage occurred when water ballast was introduced through an error of the chief officer into a deep tank in which libellant's cargo was stored rather than into a deep tank that had been kept empty to permit ballasting. One vent of one of the deep tanks was clogged with the residue of tallow transported on a prior voyage. The chief officer, intending to ballast through the other vent of that tank, by-passed it by mistake and inserted the hose in a vent of the deep tank in which libellant's cargo was stored.

Libellant contends that the vessel was unseaworthy because of a crack in the port steer strake plate and the loading of the vessel so that it had an eight foot drag (both allegedly rendering the heavy seas more dangerous) and because of the clogged condition of the vent. Libellant further contends that, since the unseaworthiness of the vessel provided the occasion for the error of pumping the ballast into the wrong tank, it was a concurrent cause of the damage for which the ship is liable. Walter Raleigh, 1952 A.M.C. 618 (S.D.N.Y.1951), aff'd sub nom. Union Carbide & Carbon Corp. v. United States, 200 F.2d 908 (2 Cir.1953). The district judge found that the ship was seaworthy and that the damage was caused by the chief officer's error in management for which, under the Carriage of

Goods by Sea Act, 46 U.S.C.A. § 1304(2)(a)(1958),[1] the ship was not responsible. See General Foods Corp. v. Mormacsurf, 276 F.2d 722, 1960 A.M.C. 1103 (2 Cir.), cert. denied 364 U.S. 822, 1961 A.M.C. 288 (1960). We affirm.

Under the Carriage of Goods by Sea Act, 46 U.S.C.A. § 1304(2)(a)(1958), the defense of error in management is not conditioned, as it is under the Harter Act, 46 U.S.C.A. § 192 (1958), on a showing of seaworthiness or due diligence to make the vessel seaworthy. Isbrandtsen Co. v. Federal Ins. Co., 113 F.Supp. 357, 1952 A.M.C. 1945 (S.D.N.Y.1952), aff'd per curiam, 205 F.2d 679, 1953 A.M.C. 1033 (2 Cir.), cert. denied 346 U.S. 866, 74 S.Ct. 106, 98 L.Ed. 377 (1953). Therefore once the carrier has brought forth evidence establishing the defense of error in management the burden is on the shipper to show that the ship was unseaworthy and that the damage was caused by such unseaworthiness. See Isbrandtsen Co. v. Federal Ins. Co., supra.

In the trial below the shipper's own expert admitted that, despite the clogged after vent and the other alleged conditions of unseaworthiness, the ship was seaworthy if the forward vent was unclogged. Neither side produced evidence relative to the state of the forward vent. Thus the shipper failed to sustain its burden of showing unseaworthiness, and the court properly found for the respondent.

Affirmed.

NOTE

In circumstances akin to those in *M/S Black Heron,* unseaworthiness was found in the fact that the error was occasioned by indistinct markings on the pipe outlets. Hydaburg Co–op. Ass'n v. Alaska S. S. Co., [The Coastal Rambler], 404 F.2d 151, 1969 A.M.C. 363 (9th Cir.1968).

The "error in navigation" exception is most generally relied upon in cases of collision or stranding (e.g., The Isis, supra), so that the question becomes one of whether the collision was attributable to lack of due diligence to make the vessel seaworthy. See Cia. Atlantica Pacifica, S.A. v. Humble Oil & Refining Co. (M/V Clydewater), 274 F.Supp. 884, 1967 A.M.C. 1474 (D.C.Md.1967), for a discussion of the interrelationship between these defenses. Following the reasoning of Judge Friendly in *Lekas & Drivas,* supra, p. 616, the court held that when the respondent undertook to show that the stranding took place through an error in navigation he did not undertake the burden of negativing all other causes, or of proving due diligence to make the vessel seaworthy. It is up to the libellant, then, to demonstrate that the stranding was produced by unseaworthiness. Then, if the respondent wishes to rely upon the due diligence exception, the act puts on him the burden of demonstrating it.

---

1. "(2) Neither the carrier nor the ship shall be responsible for loss or damage arising or resulting from—

(a) Act, neglect, or default of the master, mariner, pilot, or the servants of the carrier in the navigation or in the management of the ship;" 46 U.S.C.A. § 1304(2)(a)(1958).

In Mississippi Shipping Co. v. Zander & Co. (The Del Sud), 270 F.2d 345, 1959 A.M.C. 2143 (5th Cir.1959), judgment vac'd as moot 361 U.S. 115, 80 S.Ct. 212, 4 L.Ed.2d 148 (1959), a vessel maneuvering away from the dock, but still connected to the dock by two lines, came into contact with the concrete facing of the dock, leaving a 12 inch fracture in a shell plate through which water entered during the voyage, damaging cargo. The cargo conceded that had water rushed right in, there would be no liability because the "error in navigation" exception provided for in § 1304(2)(a) is not restricted in time. It argued, however, that the voyage had not begun and therefore failure to have the ship surveyed and repair the damage was a want of due diligence to make the ship seaworthy. A split court of appeals held that the voyage had begun, despite the remaining lines to the dock, and reversed a judgment for cargo. The case was ultimately settled, however, and the Supreme Court vacated the judgment of the court of appeals as moot.

In Hershey Chocolate Corp. v. The Mars, 172 F.Supp. 321 (E.D.Pa.1959), aff'd 273 F.2d 617, 1961 A.M.C. 1727 (3d Cir.1960), the cargo was damaged by sweat explained by the failure properly to ventilate, explained in turn by storm conditions. The cargo argued that the master could have gone around the storm rather than through it. The court held that this error, if any, was an error in navigation, and excused under the act.

5. OTHER CAUSES WITHOUT FAULT OR NEGLECT

Tubacex, Inc. v. M/V Risan

United States Court of Appeals, Fifth Circuit, 1995.
45 F.3d 951, 1995 A.M.C 1305.

■ JOHNSON, CIRCUIT JUDGE:

Shipper brought action under COGSA[1] to establish carrier's liability for damage to cargo. The district court granted summary judgment in favor of carrier, however, finding that the carrier had successfully made out a defense under 46 U.S.C. § 1304(2)(q) by showing that the damage was caused by the actions of the shipper's agents and without the fault or negligence of the carrier. Finding no error, we AFFIRM.

I. Facts and Procedural History

In December of 1990, Tubacex, Inc., contracted with Forest Lines, Inc. (hereinafter "FLI"), to ship a load of seamless rolled steel tubes from Bilbao, Spain, to New Orleans, Louisiana, and Houston, Texas. This was loaded aboard an FLI lash barge[2] and FLI issued to Tubacex bills of lading which were "clean."[3] This barge was to be loaded aboard the next available FLI mother vessel to call at Bilbao, Spain.

1. Carriage of Goods by Sea Act, 46 U.S.C. §§ 1300 et seq.

2. A lash barge is a type of barge that may be loaded on a larger ship called a mother vessel. The mother vessel collects the loaded barges and unloads them at various ports of destination. The loaded barges may then be moved to waters that the mother vessel cannot reach or unloaded at that port without the need for special equipment.

3. This signifies that no damage to the cargo was noted at the time of the issuance of the bills of lading.

Tubacex believed that such a vessel would be available in January of 1991. However, in January, FLI informed Tubacex that the next mother vessel that would call at Bilbao would be in April of 1991. Facing other deadlines for the cargo, Tubacex decided to make other arrangements. Hence, Tubacex demanded that the cargo be unloaded so that it could be shipped by other means. On February 7, 1991, a stevedore chosen and hired by Tubacex unloaded the cargo from the FLI barge. This unloading procedure took place during inclement weather and the cargo was stored in the open air, while wet, for several days until it was loaded aboard the vessel M/V RISAN. The bills of lading issued by Jugoslavenska Oceanska Plovidba (Jugooceanija) at that time noted some damage to the cargo.[4] Subsequently, Tubacex brought the instant action against FLI[5] in redress of the damage caused to the cargo. FLI filed a motion for summary judgment requesting that the district court find, in pertinent part, that:

1. The damage was caused by Tubacex's agents and not by FLI. Thus, FLI is exempt from liability under 46 U.S.C. § 1304(2)(i), and

2. There is no evidence to show that FLI in any way caused the damage. Therefore, FLI is exempt from liability under 46 U.S.C. § 1304(2)(q).

Initially, the district court denied this motion. However, FLI filed a motion for reconsideration of its summary judgment which the district court granted finding that FLI had successfully made out a defense under 46 U.S.C. § 1304(2)(q). The district court entered final judgment on March 25, 1994, and Tubacex has timely appealed.

II. DISCUSSION

A. Standard of Review

In determining whether a district court properly granted summary judgment, this Court must review the record under the same standards that guided the district court. Walker v. Sears, Roebuck & Co., 853 F.2d 355, 358 (5th Cir.1988). Under those standards, we will only affirm a summary judgment if we conclude that "there is no genuine issue of [sic] as to any material fact and that the moving party is entitled to a judgment as a matter of law." Fed.R.Civ.P. 56(e).

The party that moves for summary judgment bears the initial burden of identifying those portions of the pleadings and discovery on file, together with any affidavits, which it believes demonstrates the absence of a genuine issue of material fact. Celotex Corp. v. Catrett, 477 U.S. 317, 323, 106 S.Ct. 2548, 2553, 91 L.Ed.2d 265 (1986). If the moving party fails to meet this burden, the motion must be denied, regardless of the nonmovant's response. If the movant does meet this burden, however, the nonmovant must go beyond the pleadings and designate specific facts showing that

---

4. The damage noted was that some of the pipes were bent and that the pipes were partly wet and had some surface rust.

5. Tubacex also brought suit against the M/V RISAN, in rem, and against Jugo-oceanija in personam. Jugooceanija answered but was eventually dismissed from the suit and jurisdiction was never obtained over the M/V RISAN.

there is a genuine issue for trial. Id.; Anderson v. Liberty Lobby, Inc. 477 U.S. 242, 250, 106 S.Ct. 2505, 2511, 91 L.Ed.2d 202 (1986). If the nonmovant fails to meet this burden, then summary judgment is appropriate.

B. COGSA Generally

Both parties agree that this dispute is governed by COGSA, which regulates the rights and liabilities arising out of the carrier's issuance of a bill of lading with respect to cargo damage or loss. Quaker Oats Co. v. M/V Torvanger, 734 F.2d 238, 240 (5th Cir.1984), cert. denied 469 U.S. 1189, 105 S.Ct. 959, 83 L.Ed.2d 965 (1985). To enforce their respective rights under COGSA "'litigants must engage in the ping-pong game of burden-shifting mandated' by sections 1303 and 1304 of the Act." Sun Co., Inc. v. S.S. Overseas Arctic, 27 F.3d 1104, 1109 (5th Cir.1994)(quoting Nitram, Inc. v. Cretan Life, 599 F.2d 1359, 1373 (5th Cir.1979)). Initially, a shipper plaintiff establishes a prima facie case by proving that the cargo for which the bill of lading was issued was loaded in an undamaged condition, and discharged in a damaged condition. Socony Mobil Oil Company v. Texas Coastal and International, Inc., 559 F.2d 1008, 1010 (5th Cir.1977); United States v. Central Gulf Lines, 974 F.2d 621, 628 (5th Cir.1992), cert. denied, ___ U.S. ___, 113 S.Ct. 1274, 122 L.Ed.2d 669 (1993). For the purpose of determining the condition of the goods at the time of receipt by the carrier, the bill of lading serves as prima facie evidence that the goods were loaded in the condition therein described. 46 U.S.C. § 1304(4); Blasser Bros., Inc. v. Northern Pan–American Line, 628 F.2d 376, 381 (5th Cir.1980).

Once the shipper has presented a prima facie case, the burden shifts to the carrier to prove that it either exercised due diligence to prevent the damage or that the loss was caused by one of the exceptions set out in section 1304(2) of COGSA. *Sun Oil Company*, 27 F.3d at 1109; Tenneco Resins Inc. v. Davy International, AG, 881 F.2d 211, 213 (5th Cir.1989). If the carrier rebuts the shipper's prima facie case with proof of an excepted cause listed in section 1304(2)(a)(p), the burden returns to the shipper to establish that the carrier's negligence contributed to the damage or loss. *Quaker Oats*, 734 F.2d at 238. Then, if the shipper is able to establish that the carrier's negligence was a contributory cause of the damage, the burden switches back to the carrier to segregate the portion of the damage due to the excepted cause from that portion resulting from the carrier's own negligence. *Nitram*, 599 F.2d at 1373.

In addition to the excepted causes listed in section 1304(2)(a)(p), a carrier may rebut a shipper's prima facie case by relying on the catchall exception in section 1304(2)(q). This section provides that the carrier may exonerate itself from loss from any cause other than those listed in section 1304(2)(a)-(p) by proving that the loss or damage occurred "without the actual fault and privity of the carrier...." 46 U.S.C. § 1304(2)(q). The burden on the carrier under this section, however, is more than merely a burden of going forward with evidence, but rather it is a burden of persuasion with the attendant risk of non-persuasion. *Quaker Oats*, 734

F.2d at 241. Hence, under this section, the burden of proof does not switch back to the shipper, but rather "judgment must hinge upon the adequacy of the carrier's proof that he was free from any fault whatsoever contributing to the damage of the goods entrusted to his carriage." Id.

C. Availability of Defenses Under Section 1304(2)(i) and (q)

In the case at bar, the district court determined that Tubacex successfully made out a prima facie case by providing the clean bills of lading issued by FLI and showing damage to the goods. In response, FLI raised defenses under section 1304(2)(i) and (q)[6] arguing that it did not cause the damage to the cargo, but rather the damage was caused during the unloading by the actions of the stevedore that was hired by, and under the control of, Tubacex.

Tubacex contends, however, that these section 1304(2) defenses are unavailable to FLI because the damage to the goods herein arose out of the unloading of the pipe. In making this argument, Tubacex notes that section 1303(2) states that "[t]he carrier shall properly and carefully load, handle, stow, carry, keep, care for, and discharge the goods carried." Further, Tubacex contends that these duties are nondelegable because the statute goes on to provide that "[a]ny clause, covenant, or agreement in a contract of carriage" which seeks to relieve the carrier for liability for the duties provided in this section will not be valid. 46 U.S.C. § 1303(8)(emphasis added). Relying on these two sections, Tubacex argues that the nondelegability of the carrier's loading and unloading duties overrides any defense that might apply under section 1304(2) when the damage is caused during the performance of those tasks.

We disagree with Tubacex's melding of these provisions. COGSA was designed to void overreaching clauses inserted by carriers in bills of lading unreasonably limiting the carrier's liability. Siderius, Inc. v. M/V Ida Prima, 613 F.Supp. 916, 920 (S.D.N.Y.1985); see also Encyclopaedia Britannica v. S.S. Hong Kong Producer, 422 F.2d 7, 11–12 (2d Cir.1969), cert. denied, 397 U.S. 964, 90 S.Ct. 998, 25 L.Ed.2d 255 (1970); Calmaquip Engineering West Hemisphere Corp. v. West Coast Carriers, Ltd., 650 F.2d 633, 639 (5th Cir.1981). Section 1303(8) embodies this purpose by invalidating "any clause, covenant or agreement in a contract of carriage" which seeks to relieve the carrier of liability for the duties assigned to the carrier under the statute. However, in this case, there is no overreaching contract provision in the bill of lading that the carrier is resorting to in order to exonerate itself.

---

6. Section 1304(2) provides that neither the carrier nor the ship shall be responsible for damage to the cargo arising or resulting from—

(1) Act or omission of the shipper or owner of the goods, his agent or representative ; or

(q) Any other cause arising without the actual fault and privity of the carrier and without the fault or neglect of the agents or servants of the carrier . . .

Instead, the carrier is relying on two defenses, section 1304(2)(i) and (q), specifically extended to carriers under the Act itself.   We see no conflict in the statute with applying these two defenses even to the nondelegable duties of the carrier.   Other federal courts have done so without comment. See Aunt Mid, Inc. v. Fjell–Oranje Lines, 458 F.2d 712 (7th Cir.), cert. denied, 409 U.S. 877, 93 S.Ct. 130, 34 L.Ed.2d 131 (1972)(upholding carrier's section 1304(2)(i) defense in a case involving the proper stowage of perishable cargo); Jefferson Chemical Co. v. M/T GRENA, 413 F.2d 864 (5th Cir.1969)(affirming trial court's finding that shipper assumed risk by not requiring shipment of propylene glycol in lined or stainless steel tanks); Puerto Rican–American Ins. & Co. v. Sea–Land Service, Inc., 653 F.Supp. 396 (D.P.R.1986)(upholding carrier's section 1304(2)(i) defense where the shipper stowed the car to a height exceeding the underlying boxes' capacity).

Most instructive, though, is the Second Circuit's opinion in Associated Metals & Minerals Corp. v. M/V ARKTIS SKY, 978 F.2d 47 (2d Cir.1992). In that case, the cargo was damaged when it shifted during the voyage. Even though this damage arose from the handling and stowage of the cargo, a nondelegable duty of the carrier under section 1303(2), the carrier sought to exonerate itself on the basis of a FIOS clause[7] in the bill of lading.   The district court ruled in favor of the carrier, but the Second Circuit reversed holding that contract terms shifting liability for the duties of the carrier set out in section 1303(2) were barred by the nondelegable provisions of section 1303(8).   Id. at 51.   Even so, our sister circuit went on to explain that the carrier could escape liability under the defense provided in section 1304(2)(i) "by carrying its burden of proof that the damage did not occur because of its own acts."   Id. at 52.

Proving that the loss herein did not occur because of its own acts is exactly what FLI has attempted to do.   Like the M/V ARKTIS SKY court, we find that while section 1303(8) would bar a provision in the bill of lading shifting liability for the duties set out in section 1303(2), it does not bar a defense under section 1304(2)(i) or (q) that attempts to prove that the damage did not occur through any act of the carrier or its agents.

D.   Application of Section 1304(2)(q)

The district court found that FLI had met its burden under section 1304(2)(q) to show that no act or omission of FLI had caused the damage to the pipes, but rather the damage was caused by the acts of Tuba or its agents.   To that end, FLI has presented summary judgment evidence in the form of affidavits to establish that the damage to the cargo was caused during the offloading.   These affidavits relate that the unloading took place during inclement weather and that, during the unloading, some of the bundles of pipe unloosened causing bending or damage to the pipe.   Also, the pipe was stored in the open air, while wet, for several days before it was loaded onto the vessel that would transport it.   Finally, FLI's affidavits established that the stevedore that accomplished the unloading was hired

7.   "Free in and out, stowed" clause.

by, and under the complete control of, Tubacex.[8] In response, Tubacex presented no evidence that FLI caused the damage.

In determining whether it was appropriate to grant summary judgment on these facts, it is again useful to consider M/V ARKTIS SKY, 978 F.2d 47. In that case, the carrier attempted to meet its burden under section 1304(2)(i) by showing the loading and stowing was done by the shipper's agent. Id. at 51. However, the appellate court noted that there was evidence that it was the custom for the master and his chief mate to exercise total control over all stowage operations and that the chief mate had personally signed the lashing statement with the notation that the lashing and stowing had been performed under his instructions and to his satisfaction. Id. That was sufficient, the court found, to raise a genuine issue of material fact as to whether any action of the carrier contributed to the loss thus defeating summary judgment. Id. at 52.

In contrast to the M/V ARKTIS SKY, there is no evidence to conflict with FLI's affidavits that the damage was caused by the actions of the stevedores hired by Tubacex. Therefore, Tubacex has failed to designate specific facts demonstrating the existence of a genuine issue of material fact on this issue. Accordingly, the district court was correct in granting summary judgment. *Celotex*, 477 U.S. at 323, 106 S.Ct. at 2553.

III

CONCLUSION

For the reasons stated above, the judgment of the district court is AF-FIRMED.

N O T E

With *Tubacex*, cf. Quaker Oats Co. v. M/V Torvanger, 734 F.2d 238, 1984 A.M.C. 2943 (5th Cir.1984). There the shipper was shipping tetrahydrofuran. The cargo was in three tanks and when it arrived the contents of one tank had a peroxide content above commercially acceptable levels. The court found that tetrohydrofuran has a natural tendency to create peroxide, especially if exposed to oxygen unless it is chemically inhibited. The carrier introduced testimony that the tanks had been injected with a nitrogen blanket as a safeguard to exposure to exposure against oxygen and that the nitrogen blanket had been inspected periodically with "due diligence," and that a water content analysis performed on arrival in Texas showed

---

8. In Agrico Chemical Co. v. S/S ATLANTIC FOREST, 459 F.Supp. 638 (E.D.La. 1978), aff'd 620 F.2d 487 (5th Cir.1980), a carrier attempted to make out a § 1304(2)(q) defense by arguing that the towing company, which the *carrier* had hired, was an independent contractor. Accordingly the carrier argued that the towing company's actions, which caused the damage, were not its own actions of one of its agents. The trial court rejected this argument, though, finding that the carrier could not insulate from liability for its nondeligable duties under § 1303(2) by use of independent contractors. Id. at 489. That case is distinguishable from the case at bar, though. In the instant case, Tubacex, the shipper, and not FLI, the carrier, hired the independent contractor. FLI was not trying to delegate away its nondeligable duties. Instead, Tubacex was reasserting its control over the cargo.

the "blanket" to be intact. The court of appeals reversed a judgment for the carrier, indicating that the duty of the carrier under the Q clause is to demonstrate not only what it did no avoid the cargo loss or damage, but also to produce evidence of the cause of the loss.

F. DAMAGES; LIMITATION

Minerais U.S. Inc., Exalmet Div. v. M/V Moslavina

United States Court of Appeals, Fifth Circuit, 1995.
46 F.3d 501, 1995 A.M.C. 1209.

■ DUHE, CIRCUIT JUDGE:

Defendant Turner Marine Bulk, a New Orleans stevedore, negligently commingled two lots of ferrochrome that Plaintiff Minerais U.S. Inc. was importing for resale in the United States. Minerais had purchased 700 metric tons (MT) high grade ferrochrome and 1000 MT low grade ferrochrome; 250 MT high grade ferrochrome escaped damage, and the remaining 450 MT high grade and the 1000 MT low grade ferrochrome were commingled. None of the combined material fell within the higher grade, and Plaintiff was forced to downgrade 450 MT high grade material to low grade for purposes of resale. This appeal concerns only the issue of damages.

The district court awarded damages based on wholesale values of the material (i.e., wholesale value of 450 MT high grade ferrochrome minus wholesale value of 450 MT low grade ferrochrome), finding that Plaintiff failed to establish the fair market value as the appropriate measure of damages. Holding that Plaintiff adequately established fair market values, we reverse and remand for application of the market-value rule using retail values as specified herein.

I. The Market–Value Rule.

The market-value rule requires that damages be calculated using market values *at the time the cargo is discharged*. Such a damage award places the injured cargo owner in the same position it was in before the damage. The market-value rule makes the cargo claimant whole by awarding him the difference between the fair market value of the undamaged cargo and the fair market value of the cargo as damaged on the date of discharge at the port of destination. Cook Indus., Inc. v. Barge UM–308, 622 F.2d 851. 854 (5th Cir.1980).

Nothing in *Illinois Central Railroad v Crail* compels use of the wholesale price rather than retail. See Illinois Cent. R.R. v. Crail, 281 U.S. 57, 64–65, 50 S.Ct. 180, 181, 74 L.Ed. 699 (1930)("[The market-value rule] may be discarded and other more accurate means [to measure the loss] resorted to, if, for special reasons, it is not exact or otherwise not applicable.")(awarding wholesale value of lost shipment). *Illinois Central* was a shortage-in-delivery case, not a damaged-goods case; where cargo is downgraded but not completely destroyed, this Court has held the market-value rule to be both a convenient and accurate means of measuring damages. *Cook Indus.*, 622 F.2d at 855–56. We hold the rule provides an accurate measure of damages in this case as well.

A. Fair Market Value of Undamaged Cargo.

In June 1990, when the shipment was discharged in New Orleans, the average market price of high grade ferrochrome was $1.15 per pound of contained chromium, according to *Metals Week* (a weekly publication), which was found by the district court to be the most reliable evidence of the market price. Published market quotations of bulk commodities provide simple proof of market value and damages so as to support application of the market-value rule. See 2 Thomas J. Sehoenbaum, *Admiralty and Maritime Law* § 10–36 (2d ed. 1994); see also Amstar Corp. v. M/V ALEXANDROS T., 472 F.Supp. 1289, 1294 (D.Md.1979), aff'd, 664 F.2d 904 (4th Cir.1981). Further, Minerais' retail sales price in August 1990 corroborated *Metals Week* by establishing $1.15 per pound of chromium as the retail price. The market value of high grade ferrochrome at the time of the arrival of the shipment was thus adequately established at $1.15 per pound of chromium.

B. Fair Market Value of Cargo as Damaged.

The 450 MT damaged cargo after commingling was indistinguishable from the 1000 MT low grade ferrochrome with which it was mixed. *Metals Week* did not list a price for low grade ferrochrome at the time of discharge of the shipment, because there was no established market for it at the time. Minerais ordered the low grade to test the market for it. Minerais sold the 1450 MT low grade product in varying quantities over several months and the price varied over those few months. The district court declined to rely on a retail price in part because of the declining market and in part because it was unclear which resale accounted for the 450 MT downgraded material.

We hold that the sales price close in time to the discharge date is nevertheless sufficient to establish the market value of the downgraded product at the time of discharge. Some of the low grade material sold at $.99 per pound chromium in June and July 1990 as shown by two invoices (for sales of 160 MT and 400 MT). These contemporaneous sales provide sufficient evidence from which to apply the market-value rule. See Standard Oil Co. v. Southern Pac. Co., 268 U.S. 146, 155, 45 S.Ct. 465, 466–67, 69 L.Ed. 890 (1925)(recognizing "contemporaneous sales of like property in the way of ordinary business" as one manner of establishing market value); cf. Holden v. S.S. Kendall Fish, 395 F.2d 910, 913 (5th Cir.1968)(requiring that damages be calculated at the time of delivery, because the carrier "is not and should not be the guarantor of the ups and downs of commodity prices"). We have no reason to factor in the varying prices of low grade ferrochrome over the ensuing months. Regardless of the fact that Plaintiff intended to introduce only a limited quantity of low grade ferrochrome into the United States market, the sale of 560 MT low grade product for $.99 per pound chromium near the time of delivery provides adequate proof of the fair market value of all of the downgraded product (only 450 MT) at the time of discharge.

II. Conclusion.

Applying the general measure of the shipper's recovery, ie., the difference in market values before and after damage to the damaged cargo, will accurately compensate Plaintiff. Plaintiff having provided sufficient evidence of fair market values of both high and low grade ferrochrome at the time of delivery, we remand for calculation of damages under the market-value rule using the June 1990 retail values.

REVERSED and REMANDED.

N O T E

When damaged goods are repaired, normally the damage is calculated on the difference between the value of the cargo in good condition at the place where it arrived or should have arrived and its fair market value in the condition in which it did arrive. It should no be calculated on the cost of restoring damaged cargo to its undamaged condition. Kanematsu–Gosho, Ltd. v. M/T Messiniaki Aigli, 814 F.2d 115 (2d Cir.1987). As noted in *Minerais* above, this is not an invariable rule. See Texport Oil Co. v. M/V Amolyntos, 11 F.3d 361, 1994 A.M.C 815 (2d Cir.1993), in which a cargo of gasoline from was contaminated by coal residue in the hold of a vessel and was discharged darkened in color, making it less marketable as clear gasoline. At considerable expense the discolored gas was blended with clear gas and eventually sold at the ordinary price. The court denied damages for the diminution in market price, but allowed incidental expenses incurred in the more expensive blending process that was necessary because of the discoloration.

The determination of the market value of flower bulbs in the damage surveyor's report was not displaced by plaintiff's concession that he sometimes gave good customers better prices. Van der Salm Bulb Farms, Inc. v. Hapag Lloyd, AG, 818 F.2d 699 (9th Cir.1987).

In computing damages in cargo damage cases, the collateral source rule is applied. In *Texport Oil*, above, for example the court rejected any objection based on the fact that the losses were insured. See Thyssen, Inc. v. S/S Eurounity, 21 F.3d 533, 1994 A.M.C 1638 (2d Cir.1994).

Hayes–Leger Associates, Inc. v. M/V Oriental Knight

United States Court of Appeals, Eleventh Circuit, 1985.
765 F.2d 1076.

■ KRAVITCH, CIRCUIT JUDGE:

This case presents the recurring issue of how to apply the limitation-of-liability clause contained in section 4(5) of the Carriage of Goods by Sea Act (COGSA), 46 U.S.C. § 1304(5), to goods shipped in containers. Section 4(5) limits a carrier's and vessel's liability for goods damaged in transportation to "$500 per package * * *, or in case of goods not shipped in packages, per customary freight unit," unless the shipper explicitly declares a higher value. Here, five containers' worth of woven baskets and rattan goods were damaged while being carried aboard two vessels. The district court held that the goods were shipped in "packages," that none of the "packages" was worth more than $500, and that the defendant carrier and vessels thus were liable for the entire amount of damage sustained. On appeal, the defendants argue that the goods were not shipped in "packages," that the "customary freight unit" for such goods is the container itself, and that therefore the award of damages should have been limited to $500 per container, or $2,500. We affirm in part, reverse in part, and remand for further proceedings.

I. FACTS AND PROCEDURAL HISTORY

Plaintiff Hayes–Leger Associates, Inc. ("Hayes–Leger"), d/b/a Mainly Baskets, was the consignee of five containers' worth of woven baskets and rattan goods shipped from the Philippines in July, 1981, aboard the M/V Oriental Knight and the M/V Pacific Dispatcher. Hayes–Leger opened the sealed containers upon their delivery, only to discover that the goods had been severely damaged. Testing revealed that the damage had been caused by salt water entering each of the containers through holes or other defects.

Hayes–Leger commenced five separate actions in federal district court against the carrier, the vessels, the shipper, and various charterers, managers, and agents for the cargo. The five cases were consolidated and tried before the court. At trial, Hayes–Leger presented evidence that (1) the bills of lading under which the goods were shipped were "clean" and contained no exceptions as to the goods or the containers, (2) the containers were defective upon receipt, (3) when the containers were opened, the goods were discovered to be damaged, (4) the goods were damaged by salt water, (5) Hayes–Leger's vice president previously had observed the loading of similar goods by the supplier in the Philippines, and (6) in nine years of dealing with the same supplier, Hayes–Leger had never received damaged goods such as those in the instant case. The defendants presented no evidence.

The district court ruled that Hayes–Leger had made out a *prima facie* case of liability under COGSA, 46 U.S.C. §§ 1300–1315, and Terman Foods, Inc. v. Omega Lines, 707 F.2d 1225 (11th Cir.1983),[1] and that the defendants had failed to meet their corresponding burden of proof.[2] The court

---

1. Under the Carriage of Goods by Sea Act * * * the plaintiff establishes a prima facie case by proving the carrier received the cargo in good condition but unloaded it in a damaged condition at its destination. * * * A clean bill of lading is prima facie evidence that the carrier received the goods it describes. * * * It creates a rebuttable presumption the goods were delivered to the carrier in good condition and thus satisfies that element of the plaintiff's prima facie case.

Id. at 1227 (citations omitted).

2. Once the [plaintiff] presents a prima facie case, the burden shifts to the carrier to prove either that it exercised due diligence to prevent the damage by properly handling, stowing, and caring for the cargo in a seaworthy ship, 46 U.S.C.A. §§ 1303(1) and (2), or

therefore held the defendants liable for the damage to the goods. The court also found that the total amount of damage was $29,121.91,[3] and that prejudgment interest at the rate of 14% was appropriate.[4]

Finally, the court rejected the defendants' argument that section 4(5) of COGSA, 46 U.S.C. § 1304(5), limited their liability. The court adopted the Second Circuit's definition of a COGSA "package": "[A] class of cargo, irrespective of size, shape or weight, to which some packaging preparation for transportation has been made, which facilitates handling but which does not necessarily conceal or completely enclose the goods." *Aluminios Pozuelo, Ltd. v. S. S. Navigator*, 407 F.2d 152, 155 (2d Cir.1968). Applying this definition to the facts of the case before it, the court found that:

> the goods in question were prepared for shipping in each case in the manner customarily used for these types of goods. Specifically, the larger pieces of furniture were tied together in pairs, their arms and legs wrapped in paper, and separated from other items with cardboard; the trays were stacked and tied together as were the magazine racks and woven wreaths; the basket sets or individual baskets of the same size not shipped in sets were pre-grouped and tied together with string, rattan or plastic and then stacked inside the containers in groups, usually in groups or [sic] two to five; and the decorative ducks and chickens and other miscellaneous items were individually wrapped or boxed. Virtually every item or piece was prepared for shipment in some fashion.

The court held that the goods were shipped in "packages," and that the applicable COGSA liability limitation was "$500 per package." Because the court also found that none of the "packages" in the containers was worth more than $500, judgment was entered in favor of Hayes–Leger, and against the defendants, in the amount of $39,284.44, including prejudgment interest, plus costs.

II. DISCUSSION

The sole issue on appeal is whether the district court failed to properly apply section 4(5) of COGSA, 46 U.S.C. § 1304(5).[5] The defendants

---

that the harm resulted from one of the excepted causes listed in 46 U.S.C.A. § 1304(2). * * * Only if the carrier is able to rebut the [plaintiff's] prima facie case by proving that it falls within one of the exceptions does the burden of proof then shift back to the [plaintiff] to show the carrier's negligence was, at the least, a concurrent cause of the loss. Id. at 1227 (citations omitted).

3. The damage to each shipment was as follows:

Shipment # 1: 223 chairs damaged but recouped; 26 chairs destroyed; total loss $2,094.47

Shipment # 2: 228 baskets damaged but recouped; 247 baskets destroyed; total loss $3,165.33

Shipment # 3: 553 baskets destroyed; total loss $8,006.42

Shipment # 4: 55 pieces of furniture damaged but recouped; 638 baskets destroyed; total loss $7,332.47

Shipment # 5: 643 wreaths and 200 baskets destroyed; total loss $8,523.22

4. The interest, computed from the date of arrival of each container through the date of judgment, totalled $10,162.53.

5. 46 U.S.C. § 1304(5) provides, in pertinent part:

(5) Neither the carrier nor the ship shall in any event be or become liable for any loss or damage to or in connection with the transportation of goods in an

contend that the goods were not shipped in "packages," and that the applicable COGSA liability limitation should have been $500 "per customary freight unit." According to the defendants, the "customary freight unit" for such goods is the container itself, and the award of damages therefore should have been limited to $500 per container, or $2,500.

As noted by the court below, the term "package" as used in section 4(5) has no legislatively supplied definition. Rather, the task of defining and applying the term has fallen to the courts. The advent of containerized shipping has exacerbated this problem, requiring the courts to resolve such issues as whether a container itself may constitute a COGSA "package," and whether and to what extent various kinds of goods placed within a container constitute separate "packages."

In Allstate Insurance Co. v. Inversiones Navieras Imparca, C.A., 646 F.2d 169 (5th Cir. Unit B 1981),[6] this circuit's predecessor discussed the application of section 4(5) to goods shipped in containers. There, the goods consisted of 100 stereo receivers, each packed in an individual carton, and several hundred digital clock radios, packed in 241 cartons with an average of six radios in each carton. The bill of lading described the cargo as "One 20′ Container With 341 Cartons," and "One 20′ Container said to contain electronic equipment radio apparatus." All of the cartons were missing upon arrival. The district court held that the container itself was the "package" for purposes of COGSA, and limited recovery to $500.

On appeal, the former Fifth Circuit reversed. The court adopted the view of the Second Circuit, which previously had held:

> [W]hile * * * there might be some instances where a container might be the package, e.g., when the shipping documents * * * gave the carrier no information as to the contents, * * * at least when what would ordinarily be considered packages are shipped in a container supplied by the carrier and the number of such units is disclosed in the shipping documents, each of those units and not the container constitutes the "package" referred to in § 4(5).

Mitsui & Co. v. American Export Lines, Inc., 636 F.2d 807, 817 (2d Cir.1981). The former Fifth Circuit concluded that, because the number of packages within the container had been disclosed to the carrier in the bill of lading, "each package or unit within the container constitutes one 'package' for purposes of COGSA's $500 limitation of liability." *Allstate*, 646 F.2d at 172–73.

---

amount exceeding $500 per package lawful money of the United States, or in case of goods not shipped in packages, per customary freight unit, unless the nature and value of such goods have been declared by the shipper before shipment and inserted in the bill of lading. This declaration, if embodied in the bill of lading, shall be prima facie evidence, but shall not be conclusive on the carrier.

6. The *Allstate* decision was rendered on May 26, 1981. The Eleventh Circuit, in the *en banc* decision Bonner v. City of Prichard, 661 F.2d 1206, 1209 (11th Cir.1981), adopted as precedent decisions of the former Fifth Circuit rendered prior to October 1, 1981.

The *Allstate* rule, then, is that "if a shipper places its packages of goods in a container furnished by the carrier and discloses the number of packages in the container to the carrier in the bill of lading or otherwise, each package or unit within the container constitutes one package for purposes of COGSA's five hundred dollar limitation of liability." Vegas v. Compania Anonima Venezolana De Navegacion, 720 F.2d 629, 630 (11th Cir.1983). But what if the bill of lading fails to disclose to the carrier the number of packages in the container? The Second Circuit recently faced this problem in Binladen BSB Landscaping v. M.V. "Nedlloyd Rotterdam", 759 F.2d 1006 (2d Cir.1985). There, the court identified four basic principles for applying section 4(5) to containerized shipments. First, "the touchstone of our analysis should be the contractual agreement between the parties, as set forth in the bill of lading." Id. at 1012. Second, the term "package" means "the result of some 'preparation [of the cargo item] for transportation * * * which facilitates handling but which does not necessarily conceal or completely enclose the goods.'" Id. (quoting Aluminios Pozuelo Ltd. v. S. S. Navigator, 407 F.2d 152, 155 (2d Cir.1968)). Third, since a container is functionally part of the vessel, a container cannot be a COGSA "package" absent "a clear agreement between the parties to that effect, [and] at least so long as 'its contents and the number of packages or units are disclosed.'" Id. at 1013 (quoting Mitsui & Co., Ltd. v. American Export Lines, Inc., 636 F.2d 807, 821 (2d Cir.1981)). Fourth, and finally, "absent an agreement in the bill of lading as to packaging of the cargo, goods placed in containers and described as not separately packaged will be classified as 'goods not shipped in packages.'" Id.

The net effect of these principles can be summarized in the following two rules: (1) when a bill of lading discloses the number of COGSA packages in a container, the liability limitation of section 4(5) applies to those packages; but (2) when a bill of lading lists the number of containers as the number of packages, and fails to disclose the number of COGSA packages within each container, the liability limitation of section 4(5) applies to the containers themselves. See id. at 1013–16. Recognizing that the second rule might be considered a departure from prior law, the Second Circuit applied it prospectively only. For bills of lading prepared prior to the date of the *Binladen BSB Landscaping* decision, the court held that the "goods not shipped in packages" liability limitation would apply to such situations. See id. at 1016.

In our view, these two rules represent a reasonable method for applying section 4(5) to the developing area of containerized shipping. As the Second Circuit noted, the rules comport with the 1968 Brussels Protocol[7]

7. The 1968 Brussels Protocol to Amend the International Convention for the Unification of Certain Rules of Law Relating to BILLS OF LADING, which has been adopted by some 17 countries, provides, in pertinent part:

Where a container, pallet or similar article of transport is used to consolidate goods, the number of packages or units enumerated in the bill of lading as packed in such article of transport shall be deemed the number of packages or

and provide much-needed certainty. See id. at 1013. Uniformity is also an important consideration, since vessels often travel between different jurisdictions. We therefore adopt the rules announced by the Second Circuit in *Binladen BSB Landscaping*. Like the Second Circuit, however, we apply the second rule, under which containers may be treated as COGSA "packages" if the bills of lading so provide, prospectively only. For bills of lading prepared prior to the date of this decision, we will apply the "goods not shipped in packages" limitation to such situations.

Turning to the instant case, we begin by examining the five relevant bills of lading. The first bill of lading, dated June 30, 1981, listed the number of packages as "TWO THOUSAND SIX HUNDRED FORTY ONE PCS. ONLY." The goods were described as "2.641 PCS. WOVEN BASKETS AND RATTAN FURNITURES." The second bill of lading, dated July 20, 1981, listed the number of packages as "ONE CONTAINER ONLY." The goods were described as "1 CONTAINER SAID TO CONTAIN: 3,542 PCS. WOVEN BASKETS AND RATTAN FURNITURES." The other three bills of lading contained listings and descriptions identical to those in the first bill of lading, except for the numbers.[8]

The second bill of lading, dated July 20, 1981, is governed by the second *Binladen BSB Landscaping* rule. Because the bill of lading listed "ONE CONTAINER ONLY" as the number of packages, and did not otherwise disclose to the carrier the number of packages within the container,[9] the shipment must be treated as one of "goods not shipped in packages." We therefore reverse the district court's award of full damages for the goods shipped under the second bill of lading. Because the district court did not determine the "customary freight unit" for the goods,[10] we remand for such a determination and the entry of a revised damage award.

units for the purpose of this paragraph as far as these packages or units are concerned. Except as aforesaid such article of transport shall be considered the package or unit.

Id. at Article 2, paragraph (c); see 6 M. Cohen, Benedict on Admiralty, Document No. 1–2, at page 1–26 (7th ed. 1984).

8. The third bill of lading, dated July 26, 1981, listed the number of packages as "THREE THOUSAND FORTY FIVE PCS. ONLY," and described the goods as "3,045 PCS. WOVEN BASKETS AND RATTAN FURNITURES." The fourth bill of lading dated August 7, 1981, listed the number of packages as "TWO THOUSAND FOUR HUNDRED THIRTY ONE PCS. ONLY," and described the goods as "2,431 PCS. WOVEN BASKETS AND RATTAN FURNITURES." The fifth bill of lading, dated August 16, 1981, listed the number of packages as "TWO THOUSAND ONE HUNDRED FORTY SIX PCS. ONLY," and described the

goods as "2,146 PCS. WOVEN BASKETS AND RATTAN FURNITURES."

9. The bill of lading described the goods as "3,542 PCS." of baskets and furniture. This description was insufficient to indicate to the carrier that the goods were "packaged." As the Second Circuit explained in *Binladen BSB Landscaping,* if the shipper intends to rely on the description portion of the bill of lading to disclose to the carrier the number of COGSA "packages" in a container, that description must indicate "the number of items qualifying as packages (i.e., connoting preparation in some way for transport), such as 'bundles,' 'cartons,' or the like." Id. at 1013–14.

10. Because the court below determined that the goods were shipped in "packages," it never reached the defendants' argument that the "customary freight unit" is the container itself. The "customary freight unit" is a question of fact that varies from

The remaining four bills of lading pose a different problem. These four bills of lading purported to treat each piece of woven baskets and rattan furniture as a separate COGSA "package." The district court found, however, that each piece was *not* a separate "package," but rather that the pieces were grouped together into "packages," each "package" containing anywhere from one to several pieces.[11] In short, we are faced with four bills of lading that purported to disclose to the carrier the number of packages in each container, but did so inaccurately. Cf. Binladen BSB Landscaping, 759 F.2d at 1014 n. 7 (reserving question "whether our conceptual definition of a package may impose limits on the types of items that parties may agree to treat as packages").

In resolving this problem, we are influenced by two considerations. First, there are important reasons for requiring the shipper to disclose, fully and accurately, the number of packages in a container. As the Second Circuit noted in *Binladen BSB Landscaping*:

> The ability of the shipper and carrier to contract fairly for the division of liability between themselves depends in turn on disclosure of the relevant information about the packaging of the goods being shipped. The shipper retains the power to protect itself by stating in plain terms on the bill of lading the number of COGSA packages being shipped. Any other interpretation would prevent the carrier from accurately assessing its potential liability at the time it contracts to transport the goods.

Id. at 1016. Inaccurate disclosure, like non-disclosure, may expose a carrier to unforeseen liability.

On the other hand, whether inaccurate disclosure will lead to unforeseen carrier's liability depends on whether the shipper has *overstated* or *understated* the number of COGSA packages in the container. Where, as in *Binladen BSB Landscaping*,[12] the shipper has *understated* the number of packages, the carrier faces "liability that might vary by orders of magnitude depending on the exact packaging of goods inside a sealed

contract to contract, see Croft & Scully Co. v. M/V Skulptor Vuchetich, 664 F.2d 1277, 1282 (5th Cir.1982), and the resolution of such purely factual issues is not the proper role of an appellate court. See Binladen BSB Landscaping, 759 F.2d at 1016 (citing Pullman–Standard v. Swint, 456 U.S. 273, 291–92, 102 S.Ct. 1781, 1791–92, 72 L.Ed.2d 66 (1982), and remanding for determination of "customary freight unit" by district court).

11. The court found that the larger pieces of furniture were "tied together in pairs," the trays, magazine racks, and wreaths were "stacked and tied together," the baskets were "pre-grouped and tied together * * * and then stacked inside the containers in groups, usually in groups or [sic] two to five," and the decorative ducks and chickens were "individually wrapped or boxed."

12. In *Binladen BSB Landscaping,* the bills of lading listed the number of containers as the number of packages. In reality, each container contained thousands of individually potted plants. The Second Circuit held:

> When a bill of lading specifies the number of containers but does not reveal the number of packages inside, the only certain figure known to both parties is the number of containers shipped. In such event the carrier cannot be charged with knowledge of whether the container is filled with packages, with unpackaged goods, or with some combination. The carrier should not be expected to assume the risk inherent in such uncertainty. * * *

Id. at 1015.

container, even though this information was not revealed to it by the bill of lading." Id. at 1015. The best approach in such a case is to limit the carrier's liability based on the number of packages stated in the bill of lading. See Nemeth v. General S.S. Corp., Ltd., 694 F.2d 609, 613–14 (9th Cir.1982).

Where, as here, however, the shipper has *overstated* the number of COGSA packages, the carrier is *not* exposed to unforeseen liability. Rather, because the carrier must assume that a sealed container holds as many packages as the shipper claims it does, the carrier actually is exposed to *less* liability than anticipated. Although the carrier certainly cannot be held liable based on the number of packages stated in the bill of lading, it is reasonable to apply the "$500 per package" liability limitation to the actual number of packages in the container. We therefore hold that, where the shipper *overstates* the number of packages in a container, the COGSA liability limitation should be applied to the actual number of packages in the container.

In the instant case, the district court properly applied the COGSA liability limitation to the actual number of packages in the container. Furthermore, we agree with the court below that the proper definition of a COGSA "package" is the one stated in the *Aluminios Pozuelo, Ltd.* case. See id. at 155. Our final inquiry is whether the court correctly determined that the goods were shipped in "packages." We conclude that the court did not err in making this determination.[13] As the court noted, all of the goods were "prepared for shipment in the normal manner in which goods of this kind are prepared," and "were in fact wrapped, tied, or bound together in distinct groups and packed inside the containers." Such preparation satisfied the *Aluminios Pozuelo, Ltd.* standard. We thus hold that the district court properly awarded full damages for the goods shipped under the first, third, fourth, and fifth bills of lading.

III. CONCLUSION

In light of the foregoing discussion, we hereby AFFIRM the judgment of the court below in part, but REVERSE the award of full damages for the goods shipped under the second bill of lading and REMAND for further proceedings consistent with this opinion.

NOTE

In Mitsui & Co., Ltd. v. American Export Lines, Inc., 636 F.2d 807, 1981 F.2d 807, 1981 A.M.C. 331 (2d Cir.1981), there is an extensive and valuable discussion by Judge Friendly of the text, legislative history, and policy considerations behind the package limitation provision.

Independent of the container problem, there remains the question of what "package" means. If a large piece of equipment is bolted to skids, is it a package? Aluminios Pozuelo, Ltd. v. S.S. Navigator, 277 F.Supp. 1008, 1968 A.M.C. 741

---

13. Hayes–Leger contends that the district court's finding must be upheld unless "clearly erroneous," see Fed.R.Civ.P. 52(a), while the defendants argue for plenary review. Because we would uphold the district court's finding under either standard of review, we need not resolve this dispute.

(S.D.N.Y.1967), aff'd 407 F.2d 152 (2d Cir.1968)(yes); Hartford Fire Ins. Co. v. Pacific Far East Line, Inc., 491 F.2d 960, 1974 A.M.C. 1475 (9th Cir.1974)(no). There the court observed, "[since no specialized or technical meaning was ascribed to the word 'package,' we must assume that Congress had none in mind and intended that this word be given its plain, ordinary meaning.]"

What is the "plain, ordinary" meaning of "package"? Suppose the shipper packs each unit separately and then ties them together. See Standard Electrica, S.A. v. Hamburg Sudamerikanische Dampfschiffahrts–Gesellschaft, 375 F.2d 943, 1967 A.M.C. 881 (2d Cir.1967). There the court of appeals held that a "pallet" containing six cardboard containers each of which contained 40 television tuners constituted a package and the liability was limited to $500 per pallet. Cf. Yang Machine Tool Co. v. Sea–Land Service, Inc., 58 F.3d 1350 (9th Cir.1995), in which a large machine too large to be put in a standard 40 foot enclosed container was shipped on a "flat rack," a metal pallet with no sides or top, to which the machine, in two parts, was secured with steel bands. It was held that this constituted two packages.

Suppose that in *Yang Machine*, the machine had been left in one piece and wheeled aboard without the "flat rack." See Henley Drilling Co. v. McGee, 36 F.3d 143, 1995 A.M.C. 173 (1st Cir.1994), in which a drilling rig was shipped in this fashion and disappeared en route. The court of appeals noted that it could not really be called a package, but held that when shipped for a lump sum freight charge, it constituted a single customary freight unit (CFU).

If a container is not deemed to be a COGSA package, a clause in the bill of lading limiting liability to $500 per container is invalid. See Leather's Best, Inc. v. S.S. Mormaclynx, 451 F.2d 800, 1971 A.M.C. 2383 (2d Cir.1971); David Crystal, Inc. v. Cunard S.S. Co., 339 F.2d 295 (2d Cir.1964). In both cases it was also held that the clause being void under COGSA, it did not "spring to life" after discharge of the cargo. In *S.S. Mormaclynx*, however, Judge Friendly observed that clauses limiting the liability to $500 per container for losses before and after discharge are effective, citing The Ansaldo San Giorgio I v. Rheinstrom Bros. Co., 294 U.S. 494, 496–497, 55 S.Ct. 483, 484–485, 79 L.Ed. 1016, 1019–1020 (1935), so long as the shipper is permitted to place a higher value on the goods at a higher rate. It is to be noted that the Harter Act does not contain a limitation of liability provision. See also Antilles Ins. Co. v. Transconex, 862 F.2d 391 (1st Cir.1988).

Such clauses are rather strictly construed. See Toyomenka, Inc. v. S.S. Tosaharu Maru, 523 F.2d 518, 1975 A.M.C. 1820 (2d Cir.1975). There it was held that a clause extending the benefit of the package limitation to "all servants, agents and independent contractors * * * used or employed by the Carrier" did not apply to a pier guard service hired as an independent contractor by the stevedore.

G.   DEVIATION

General Elec. Co. Intern. v. S.S. Nancy Lykes

United States Court of Appeals, Second Circuit, 1983.
706 F.2d 80, 1984 A.M.C. 2403, cert. denied 464 U.S. 849, 104 S.Ct. 157, 78 L.Ed.2d 145 (1983).

■ LUMBARD, CIRCUIT JUDGE:

* * *

I

The basic facts are not in dispute. On April 16, 1978, three locomotive cabs manufactured by GE were loaded onto the deck of the Nancy Lykes in New Orleans pursuant to a bill of lading which provided for shipment to Keelung, Taiwan. The locomotive cabs were 56 feet long, 10 feet wide, 13 feet high, and weighed between 50 and 52 tons. The bill of lading, which incorporated the provisions of COGSA, allowed the locomotive cabs, which could not be stowed below deck because of their great bulk, to be secured and stowed on deck. The bill of lading also contained in paragraph 3 a standard "liberties" clause, which defined the scope of the voyage as including "usual, customary, or advertised ports, whether herein named or not, and ports in or out of the advertised, geographical, or usual route or order," and specifically allowed the vessel to "call at any port * * * [to] take fuel oil * * *."

Kobe, Japan was to be the Nancy Lykes' first port of call in the Far East, with an estimated arrival date of May 11, 1978. Prior to departure of the vessel from the Gulf Coast, Lykes decided to send the Nancy Lykes to the port of San Pedro to obtain the more than 12,000 barrels of bunker fuel ("bunkers") necessary to complete the voyage to Kobe.

San Pedro, approximately 2,900 miles north of the Panama Canal, was not an advertised port on the Nancy Lykes' published itinerary, and the decision to send the vessel there was never communicated to GE or otherwise made known to the shipping community. Lykes acknowledges that in making the decision to send the Nancy Lykes to San Pedro, it never considered any factor other than the advantage of less expensive fuel prices that had become available at that port in early 1978, and it concedes that there was an ample supply of slightly more expensive bunker fuel at New Orleans and at other ports on the Nancy Lykes' route from the Gulf to the Panama Canal.

In fact, the Nancy Lykes had never before bunkered at San Pedro while voyaging from the Gulf Coast to the Far East, and of Lykes' forty or more vessels, only two had ever previously stopped at San Pedro solely to take on bunker fuel during such a voyage: the S.S. Dolly Thurman on March 22, 1978 and the S.S. Brinton Lykes on March 30, 1978. Moreover, although at least 30 of GE's locomotive cabs had previously been transported by Lykes' vessels to the Far East, GE was not informed of the routes taken by these vessels and had no knowledge whether they called at ports other than those specified in their published itineraries.

Pursuant to Lykes' instructions, the Nancy Lykes, after transiting the Panama Canal, voyaged to San Pedro and there obtained 12,877 additional barrels of bunker fuel. On May 4, 1978, the vessel departed San Pedro on a route that took it to the north of that port and soon encountered rough waters and gale force winds which measured between 8 and 10 on the Beaufort Scale.[2] At 0430 on May 5, 1978, two of the three locomotive cabs

---

2. In relevant part, the Beaufort Scale is as follows:

Beaufort Number	Knots	Wind Speed in Miles Per Hour
8	34–40	39–46
9	41–47	47–54
10	48–55	55–63

broke their lashings and were washed overboard within three minutes of each other. The loss occurred at 34° N to 35° N and 121° W, a position close to the California coast. Having suffered no major structural damage, the vessel completed its voyage to the Far East.

Pursuant to its agreement with the Taiwan Railway Administration, the purchaser of the locomotive cabs, GE was required to replace the lost cabs at a cost of $1,709,000, which included $71,000 for ocean freight to Taiwan.

II

Finding that the Nancy Lykes had engaged in an unreasonable deviation by bunkering at San Pedro, Judge Lasker held Lykes liable for the loss of the locomotive cabs on the basis of § 4(4) of COGSA, 46 U.S.C. § 1304(4) (1976) * * * This section clearly implies that any *unreasonable* deviation is to be treated as a breach of COGSA and the contract of carriage. * * *

A. *Effect of the Liberties Clause*

Lykes argues that in light of the broad liberties clause contained in paragraph 3 of the bill of lading, the Nancy Lykes' call for bunkers at San Pedro cannot under any circumstances be considered a breach of COGSA or the contract of carriage. In relevant part, the liberties clause provided:

> The scope of the voyage herein contracted for shall include usual, customary, or advertised ports, whether herein named or not, and ports in or out of the advertised, geographical, or usual route or order, even though in proceeding thereto the ship may sail beyond the port of discharge, or in a direction contrary thereto, * * * or depart from the direct or customary route. The ship may call at any port * * * [to] take fuel oil, * * * and all of the foregoing are included in the contract voyage.

* * *

Even before COGSA was enacted in 1936, it was well settled that liberties clauses, though broad in language, were limited in scope. See, e.g., The Willdomino, 300 F. 5, 18 (3d Cir.1924), aff'd sub nom. The Willdomino v. Citro Chemical Co., 272 U.S. 718, 47 S.Ct. 261, 71 L.Ed. 491 (1927); The Blandon, 287 F. 722, 725 (S.D.N.Y.1922). Because liberties clauses refer to the voyage contemplated by the parties, and not to a different voyage determined unilaterally by the carrier, these clauses have long been interpreted to give the carrier only a limited right to deviate when such a deviation is reasonable under all the circumstances. * * *

We agree, therefore, with Judge Lasker that liberties clauses must be construed to permit only reasonable deviations and that the presence of such a clause in the bill of lading did not give Lykes any deviation rights beyond those allowed by § 4(4) of COGSA.

B. *The Question of Deviation*

We also agree with Judge Lasker that the Nancy Lykes' call for bunkers at San Pedro constituted a deviation. As Judge Lasker found, San Pedro was never advertised as a port of call in the vessel's published itinerary and was not on the ordinary trade routes from the Panama Canal to Kobe and the Far East. This finding was confirmed by the testimony of Lykes' own weather routing expert. Moreover, Judge Lasker found that at least for vessels operating on scheduled liner services such as the Nancy Lykes, bunkers at that time were normally obtained only at ports advertised in the vessel's itinerary.[3]

Lykes acknowledges that a deviation results when a vessel " 'wander[s] or stray[s] * * * from the customary course of the voyage,' " Spartus Corp. v. S.S. Yafo, 590 F.2d 1310, 1313 (5th Cir.1979)(quoting G.W. Sheldon & Co. v. Hamburg Amerikanische Packetfahrt–Actien–Gesellschaft, 28 F.2d 249, 251 (3d Cir.1928)); see also G. Gilmore & C. Black, supra, at 177, but argues that the Nancy Lykes' bunkers call at San Pedro was not a deviation from the usual routes on the ground that the vessel's course from San Pedro in fact merged with and followed the northernmost customary route when the vessel reached mid-ocean at 170 W to 180 W. We disagree.

Lykes' contention not only disregards Judge Lasker's finding with respect to the bunkering customs of liner services, but ignores the fact that San Pedro and the site of the casualty are close to 120W, and at that point the vessel was approximately 600 miles and 1320 miles north, respectively, of the northernmost and southernmost customary routes from the Canal to the Far East.[4] * * *

Also lacking merit is Lykes' contention that the prior bunkers calls at San Pedro in March 1978 of two of its vessels, the Dolly Thurman and the Brinton Lykes, rendered that stop customary for vessels voyaging from the Gulf to the Far East. A course will only be considered customary when the route is *"established and by all means published to the world."* W.R. Grace & Co. v. Toyo Kisen Kabushiki Kaisha, 12 F.2d 519, 521 (9th Cir.)(emphasis supplied), cert. denied, 273 U.S. 717, 47 S.Ct. 109, 71 L.Ed. 856 (1926); see also *The Frederick Luckenbach,* supra, 15 F.2d at 243. Certainly, the bunkers calls at San Pedro of these two Lykes vessels on Gulf to Far East voyages do not make that stop customary. There is no evidence that the previous bunkers calls at San Pedro of the Dolly Thurman and the Brinton Lykes were made known to GE or generally published to the shipping community, and it is undisputed that GE did not know that such a stop was planned for the Nancy Lykes. Cf. Hostetter v. Park, 137 U.S. 30, 40,

3. The district court found that the evidence established that liner services, as opposed to "tramp" ventures, hold themselves to a high degree of schedule exactness upon which the shipping community relies. Thus, liners do not seek bunkers at ports not advertised since such a diversion would normally delay the vessel.

4. San Pedro and the site of the loss are in the region of 33° N to 35° N and 118° W to 121° W. At 120° W, the northernmost and southernmost customary routes from the Canal to the Far East are near 25° N and 13° N respectively.

11 S.Ct. 1, 4, 34 L.Ed. 568 (1890)(call at a port will not be a deviation where such stop is either revealed to the shipper or generally made known to the shipping community); *The Frederick Luckenbach, supra,* 15 F.2d at 243 (same). Beyond doubt, therefore, a call at San Pedro solely for bunkers on a Gulf Coast to Far East voyage was not customary at the time of the Nancy Lykes' voyage.[5]

C. *The Reasonableness of the Deviation*

The reasonableness of the Nancy Lykes' deviation from the customary route depends on an assessment of all the surrounding circumstances. * * * Judge Lasker found that the Nancy Lykes, by stopping at San Pedro rather than voyaging directly from the Panama Canal to the Far East, was assured, no matter what route was taken to the Far East from San Pedro, of passing through regions north of 30° N and near the California coast in which there was a known and increased risk of encountering adverse weather during the springtime months. In so finding, Judge Lasker accepted GE's evidence which showed that the customary routes to the Far East were generally calmer during springtime and thus that the risk of unfavorable weather conditions would have been significantly reduced had the vessel not deviated. Judge Lasker also found that Lykes should have been forewarned of the dangers of deviating to San Pedro by the experiences of the Dolly Thurman and the Brinton Lykes which, in calling at San Pedro in the early springtime, had encountered bad weather on courses to and from that port respectively. These findings are supported by the record and are not clearly erroneous.

We agree with Judge Lasker that, under all the circumstances, the Nancy Lykes' deviation to San Pedro to obtain inexpensive bunkers was unreasonable. In The Waalhaven, 36 F.2d 706 (2d Cir.1929), cert. denied, 281 U.S. 747, 50 S.Ct. 352, 74 L.Ed. 1159 (1930), a pre-COGSA case, we held that the vessel was liable for cargo damage resulting from a deviation taken to obtain inexpensive bunker fuel when the carrier's decision to deviate knowingly exposed the vessel without justification to the dangerous ice fields which caused the casualty. * * * In another pre-COGSA case, *The Frederick Luckenbach, supra,* the court held the vessel liable for damage to cargo caused by a hurricane encountered on the course of a deviation when the deviation, the purpose of which was merely to discharge cargo, took the vessel on "a course which involved well-known difficulties and dangers of navigation, all of which would have been avoided by taking the direct and usual course. * * *"[6] 15 F.2d at 243. These cases suggest

5. The record indicates that soon after the Nancy Lykes' voyage, Lykes and other liner services, seeking to take advantage of the lower fuel prices offered at San Pedro, began to advertise San Pedro as a port of call on Gulf to Far East voyages. Indeed, by June 1981, Lykes' vessels had made over 100 stops at San Pedro on such voyages. Of course, these later developments have no bearing on whether a customary route to San Pedro in fact existed at the time of the Nancy Lykes' voyage.

6. Lykes attempts to undercut the pertinence of *The Frederick Luckenbach* by noting that the court there focused on the construction to be given to liberties clauses and held the vessel liable to all but one of the shippers only after determining that none of

that a deviation is unreasonable, thereby breaching the contract of carriage, when, in the absence of significant countervailing factors, the deviation substantially increases the exposure of cargo to foreseeable dangers that would have been avoided had no deviation occurred. See also G. Gilmore & C. Black, supra, at 179 ("The carrier * * * is always subject to the § 3(2) [of COGSA, 46 U.S.C. § 1303(2)(1976)]duty to care for and carry the goods properly, and his decision on a route would seem to be improper and unreasonable whenever it is made in disregard of that duty."). We conclude, therefore, that the Nancy Lykes' deviation to San Pedro, which subjected the cargo to a known and substantially increased probability of adverse weather for the sole purpose of allowing Lykes to realize fuel cost savings, was unreasonable.

III

Lykes argues that even if the Nancy Lykes engaged in an unreasonable deviation, thereby breaching the contract of carriage and § 4(4), Lykes is nonetheless entitled to limit its liability to $500 per package pursuant to the terms of § 4(5) of COGSA, 46 U.S.C. § 1304(5)(1976). We agree with Judge Lasker that Lykes is liable for the full amount of the loss.

Section 4(5) of COGSA reads in relevant part:

> Neither the carrier nor the ship shall in any event be or become liable for any loss or damage to or in connection with the transportation of goods in an amount exceeding $500 per package lawful money of the United States, * * * unless the nature and value of such goods have been declared by the shipper before shipment and inserted in the bill of lading.[7]

It is undisputed that, prior to COGSA's enactment, an unreasonable deviation, whether geographic or otherwise, deprived the carrier of all liability limitations on the ground that such deviations ousted the contract of carriage and made the carrier fully responsible for the cargo as an insurer. * * * In the first post-COGSA case to address this issue, Judge Weinfeld determined that, at least where the loss was causally related to the deviation, COGSA was not intended to change the existing law, and accordingly he held that an unreasonable deviation deprives the carrier of

the liberties clauses in the bills of lading, with the exception of one which was similar to the liberties clause in the instant case, was broad enough to authorize a deviation from the usual course. See 15 F.2d at 244. We believe, however, that the court's holding of liability is relevant to our examination of the reasonableness of the Nancy Lykes' deviation, especially in light of our conclusion in part II.A. that all liberties clauses only allow reasonable deviations.

7. Section 4(5) of COGSA applies in this case not as a matter of law but as a matter of contract. Because the bill of lading issued to Lykes expressly provided for carriage of cargo on deck, the locomotive cabs are not in fact "goods" covered by § 4(5). See COGSA § 1(c), 46 U.S.C. § 1301(c)(1976)("The term 'goods' includes goods, wares, merchandise, and articles of every kind whatsoever, except * * * cargo which by the contract of carriage is stated as being carried on deck and is so carried."). However, since the provisions of COGSA are fully incorporated in the instant bill of lading, § 4(5) is applicable as a contractual term. See Jones v. The Flying Clipper, 116 F.Supp. 386, 388 (S.D.N.Y.1953)("[The bill of lading] defines the rights, duties, exemptions, and limitations of the parties, whether imposed by statute or the result of voluntary agreement.").

the benefit of section 4(5)'s liability limitation. Jones v. The Flying Clipper, 116 F.Supp. 386, 388–90 (S.D.N.Y.1953). Explicitly adopting the rule of *The Flying Clipper,* we have held that "it is the law of this Circuit that any * * * unreasonable deviation from the contract of carriage will deprive the carrier of * * * [the § 4(5)]statutory limitation of liability." DuPont de Nemours International S.A. v. S.S. Mormacvega, supra, 493 F.2d at 100 n. 9; see also Encyclopaedia Britannica, Inc. v. S.S. Hong Kong Producer, 422 F.2d 7, 18 (2d Cir.1969), cert. denied, 397 U.S. 964, 90 S.Ct. 998, 25 L.Ed.2d 255 (1970). Other circuits are in accord. Nemeth v. General Steamship Corp., supra, 694 F.2d at 612–13 (9th Cir.); Spartus Corp. v. S.S. Yafo, supra, 590 F.2d at 1316–17 (5th Cir.). But see Atlantic Mutual Insurance Co. v. Poseidon Schiffahrt, 313 F.2d 872, 874–75 (7th Cir.), cert. denied, 375 U.S. 819, 84 S.Ct. 56, 11 L.Ed.2d 53 (1963).

Lykes urges us to abandon *The Flying Clipper* rule on the ground that modern marine insurance has eliminated the need for depriving the carrier of the benefit of the liability limitation. One of the underlying reasons for the traditional rule affirmed in *The Flying Clipper* was that the shipper lost its insurance coverage when the vessel deviated. *The Flying Clipper,* supra, 116 F.Supp. at 389; see also G. Gilmore & C. Black, supra, at 181–82. Lykes argues that because modern marine insurance policies usually contain clauses which provide that the risks of deviation are covered, see G. Gilmore & C. Black, supra, at 182, there is no longer any justification for the rule. See also Singapore Navigation Co. v. Mego Corp., 540 F.2d 39, 45 (2d Cir.1976)(Oakes, J., dissenting). We disagree.

Unlike ordinary risks of shipping such as negligence in the stowage or handling of cargo or lack of due diligence in making the vessel seaworthy, unreasonable deviations are "fundamental breach[es] which go[ ]to the very essence of the undertaking," *The Flying Clipper,* supra, 116 F.Supp. at 390, since they expose cargo to "unanticipated and additional risks." Id. at 389; cf. Nemeth v. General Steamship Corp., supra, 694 F.2d at 613 ("[m]ere negligence in the stowage or handling of cargo * * * might be considered an inherent risk of shipping"). It follows that a deviation which unjustifiably exposes cargo to unanticipated risks is such a serious breach of the contract of carriage that the carrier must be deprived of the protection of the § 4(5) liability limitation. See Nemeth v. General Steamship Corp., supra, 694 F.2d at 613.

Indeed, exposing carriers which engage in unreasonable deviations to the risk of full liability has the salutary effect of discouraging such deviations. On the other hand, to allow carriers to limit their liability when an unreasonable deviation causes damage to cargo not only would weaken the carrier's primary duty of care to cargo under § 3(2) of COGSA, 46 U.S.C. § 1303(2)(1976), but would render meaningless the § 4(4) distinction between reasonable and unreasonable deviations. See Mitsui & Co. v. American Export Lines, Inc., 636 F.2d 807, 815 (2d Cir.1981). Such a result is not warranted. See id. ("In interpreting § 4(5), courts must * * * take a critical look at any proposed construction * * * that would reduce a carrier's liability below reasonable limits."). We see no reason, therefore, to abandon a rule the ultimate effect of which is to preserve and enforce the underlying policies of COGSA.

Affirmed.

Yutana Barge Lines v. Northland Services

United States District Court, Western District of Washington, 1983.
574 F.Supp. 1003, 1985 A.M.C. 1499.

■ BEEKS, SENIOR DISTRICT JUDGE.

Plaintiff Yutana Barge Lines (Yutana) is an Alaska corporation which maintains an office and does business in the State of Washington and plaintiff Shelver is its president. Defendant Northland Corporation is a Washington corporation engaged in the business of water transportation of cargo between Seattle, Washington and various ports in Alaska. On October 14, 1980, defendant accepted Yutana's 25–foot vessel, in apparent good order and condition, for carriage from St. Michael, Alaska to Seattle, Washington. Defendant provided insurance on said cargo in accordance with its open marine cargo insurance policy, Policy No. DER & W 2871. Said vessel, secured to a wooden platform, was stowed on the deck of Barge DT 160. Tug TAURUS towed DT 160 with Barge TAZLINA in tandem tow southbound from St. Michael. Barge DT 160 was the smaller of the two barges and it was defendant's practice in tandem tow to place the smallest barge first in the tow. On or about November 15, 1980, near Yakutat, in the Gulf of Alaska, the tug and tow encountered a severe storm, which is common to the area during the period of time involved. The master of TAURUS cut said barges adrift whereupon DT 160 capsized resulting in the total loss of the vessel being transported.

Plaintiffs bring this action to recover the value of the lost cargo. Trial, limited to the issue of liability, was held on September 27, 1983.

* * *

BREACH OF CONTRACT

Plaintiff knew that the cargo was to be stowed on the deck of a barge and that the barge was to be towed to destination, but plaintiff did not consent by bill of lading or otherwise to transportation by tandem tow. It is well recognized that a tandem tow is far more dangerous than a single tow because of the increased risk of loss or damage to cargo.[1] See, Tugs, Towboats, and Towing, 166–68 (1967), by Edward M. Brady, an eminent

---

1. The general weather conditions in the Gulf of Alaska indicate the inexpediency of tandem tows. The Gulf of Alaska, with its rim of coastal mountain ranges, catches the frequent storms that move in from the southwest. Winds of fifty to sixty knots are not unusual and may occur in any month of the year. Williwaws are especially dangerous winds which are known to be sudden, violent, and unpredictable and frequently occur in the area involved. See In re New England Fish Co., 465 F.Supp. 1003, 1007 n. 4 (W.D.Wash.1979); 9 United States Coastal Pilot, published by the United States Coast Guard.

authority on towage. Such an increase of risk constitutes an unreasonable deviation. See generally, St. Johns N.F. Shipping Corp. v. S.A. Companhia, 263 U.S. 119, 44 S.Ct. 30, 68 L.Ed. 201 (1923); Nemeth v. General S.S. Corp., 694 F.2d 609 (9th Cir.1982). In connection with its operations as a common carrier, defendant confirms this conclusion by fixing its own standard of carriage in an open marine cargo insurance policy which defendant arranged with a group of marine underwriters which enabled defendant to insure shippers against marine risks. This policy contained a specific warranty of transportation only by single tow in the Gulf of Alaska beyond Cape Spencer between October 15 and April 1 annually. Defendant contends that said warranty applies only to northbound shipments. The court, however disagrees that the warranty is so limited and the court construes the warranty to mean in the Gulf of Alaska irrespective of direction. It is significant that the published tariff rates are the same for both northbound and southbound shipments. In any event, defendant, by agreeing to a warranty of single tow transportation, implicitly recognized the increase of risk of loss or damage to cargo transported by tandem tow.

It has long been held that a common carrier by water is required to stow cargo underdeck, and unless the shipper agrees prior to the commencement of the voyage, the carrier may not stow otherwise even though the bill of lading makes the place of stowage optional with the carrier. St. Johns N.F. Shipping Corp. v. S.A. Companhia, 263 U.S. 119, 124–25, 44 S.Ct. 30, 31, 68 L.Ed. 201 (1923); Jones v. Flying Clipper, 116 F.Supp. 386, 389–91 (S.D.N.Y.1953). In *St. Johns,* the Supreme Court held that, absent an express contract providing for on deck stowage, a clean bill of lading amounts to a positive representation that the goods would receive under-deck stowage. The court reasoned that stowage on deck exposes the cargo to greater risks than the shipper had bargained for, and that the increased risk of loss or damage resulting from such on deck stowage was an unreasonable deviation which made the carrier an insurer. Id.

St. Johns and *Nemeth* illustrate the principle that an increase of risk of loss or damage to cargo, without the knowledge and consent of the shipper, constitutes an unreasonable deviation. It is apparent that transporting cargo by tandem tow substantially increases the risks of loss or damage to said cargo. Such an increase of risk is an unreasonable deviation which creates an insurer's liability on part of the carrier for resulting loss or damage. Furthermore an unreasonable deviation deprives the carrier of the protection of both contractual and statutory liability limitations. Nemeth v. General S.S. Corp., 694 F.2d 609, 612–13 (9th Cir.1982). The theory behind depriving the carrier of the protection of liability limitations is that a deviation subjects the cargo to risks the shipper did not anticipate. Id. The shipper had the right to assume that the carrier would not deviate and thereby subject the cargo to other than the known risks inherent in a single tow. Since such an unreasonable deviation deprives the carrier of contractual and statutory limitations of liability, the court holds that defendant may not rely upon its (1) time-bar,[2] (2) package/customary

---

2. All claims for shortage of entire shipments shall be waived and no suit shall be maintained to recover therefor unless instituted within two (2) years after the day of

freight unit limitation,[3] and peril of the sea[4] defenses. Furthermore, by such deviation, defendant, with full knowledge of the single tow warranty, not only made itself an insurer, but also voided the insurance policy it arranged for plaintiff.

BENEFIT OF INSURANCE

Defendant also contends that it is entitled to the benefit of plaintiffs' insurance pursuant to Tariff No. 20, Rule No. 7, ¶ 18, entitled "Benefit of Insurance."[5]   It is undisputed that Shelver entered into a loan and trust receipt with the Insurance Company of North America for $16,825.20.   It has long been recognized that a loan receipt based upon a payment equal to the amount of the loss does not affect the right of the assured to sue as the proper party in interest.   Luckenbach v. W.J. McCahan Sugar Refining Co., 248 U.S. 139, 148, 39 S.Ct. 53, 55, 63 L.Ed. 170 (1918).   Accordingly, the court holds that defendant's benefit of insurance provision is inapplicable.

Defendant contends that it is entitled, by virtue of Tariff No. 20, Rule No. 7, ¶ 7,[6] to offset the freight due for the shipment in question against any recovery of plaintiffs.   The court holds that the carrier's right to the recovery of freight was forfeited by its unreasonable deviation.   Finally, defendant's contention that its underwriters on its Open Marine Cargo Policy are necessary parties to this action is also without merit.

arrival of the vessel at port of discharge named herein, or in case of her nonarrival, within six (6) months from the day of her scheduled arrival at said port. No suit or proceeding to recover for or upon any claim or demand shall be maintained against the Carrier or vessel, or owner thereof, unless commenced within six (6) months after delivery of the goods to the Carrier, and the lapse of such period shall be deemed a complete bar to recovery in any suit or proceeding not sooner commenced. * * * Defendant's Tariff No. 20, Rule 7, ¶ 20.

Defendant also contends that plaintiffs' claims are barred by the doctrine of laches. Laches consists of two elements: inexcusable delay in commencing the action and prejudice resulting to the other party from such delay. Sea Quest Marine, Inc. v. Cove Shipping, Inc., 474 F.Supp. 164, 167 (W.D.Wash.1979). Inasmuch as defendant has not introduced any evidence of prejudice, and the court finds that any delay in commencing the action was not unreasonable or inexcusable, defendant's contention that plaintiffs' claim is barred by laches is rejected.

3.   In case of any loss or damage to, or in connection with, goods exceeding in actual value $500 lawful money of the United States, per package or, in case of goods not shipped in packages, per customary freight unit, the value of the goods shall be deemed to be $500 per package or per unit. * * * Defendant's Tariff No. 20, Rule 7, ¶ 19.

4.   46 U.S.C. § 192 (Harter Act).

5.   In case of any loss and/or damage for which the Carrier shall be liable, the Carrier shall, to the extent of such liability, have the full benefit of any insurance that may have been effected upon the goods or against said loss or damage, and as will also of any payment to insured by underwriters repayable only out of recovery against Carrier, notwithstanding the underwriters are not obligated to make such payment.

6.   Full freight to destination, whether intended to be prepaid or collect at destination, and all advance charges are due and payable to the Carrier upon receipt of the goods by the latter and shall be deemed fully and irrevocably earned, vessels or goods lost or not lost at any stage of the entire transit, or if there shall be a forced interruption or abandonment of the voyage at a port of distress or elsewhere. * * *

If the parties cannot agree on the amount of damages prior to December 16, 1983, the court will set the matter down for hearing.

This Memorandum of Decision shall constitute the court's findings of fact and conclusions of law pursuant to Rule 52(a) of the Federal Rules of Civil Procedure.

N O T E

The doctrine of deviation is derived from the law of marine insurance. The salient features of deviation as a defense in a suit on an insurance policy are described in 3 Kent, *Commentaries on American Law* 312–318 (1832). A short statement derived in part from Kent, appears in Sawyer, *Shipmaster's Guide*, 224–236 (1840). By way of introductory definition Sawyer observes, "Deviation means *voluntary departure, without necessity,* or any *reasonable cause* from the regular, and usual course of the specific voyage insured; or it is a varying of the voyage; and it matters not whether the risk is increased or diminished thereby; the effect in either case being the same—to terminate the responsibility of the underwriters. It is necessary to insert in every policy of insurance, the place of the ship's departure, and also of her destination, unless she be insured on time. Hence it is a condition on the part of the insured, that the ship shall pursue the most direct course of which the nature of the case will admit, to arrive at the destined port. If this be not done, and there be no special agreement to allow the ship to go to certain places out of the usual track, or if there be no just cause assigned for such a deviation, the underwriter is no longer bound by his contract. Nor is it at all material whether the loss be or be not, actually in consequence of the deviation; for the insurers are in no case answerable for any subsequent loss, in whatever place it happens, or to whatever cause attributed." For application of these principles, see, e.g., Kettell v. Wiggin, 13 Mass. 68 (1816). There the vessel was insured for a voyage from Gibraltar to ports in the United States, with liberty to stop in the Cape de Verd Islands to take on a cargo of salt. When it arrived at the Isle of May, there was a queue of 17 vessels in the port and the wait for its turn would be four to five weeks. The governor of the Islands indicated to the master that if he would sail to two of the other islands for a load of provisions, when he returned the vessel would be loaded right away, ahead of the other ships. This was done and the vessel was loaded. Being itself short of provisions and water, it stopped at one of the other islands for such, and while it was there it was attacked by banditti and carried off. The master succeeded in recapturing it, but later it was seized by a British man-o-war and lost. Justice Parker observed:

"But it was confidently insisted that, as the effect of this expedition at the request of the governor was to shorten the duration of the voyage, by enabling the master to obtain his cargo much sooner than he otherwise could, it ought to be considered as done for the benefit of all concerned, and not as amounting to a deviation.

"But masters have not a right to speculate, in this manner, upon the possible advantages of pursuing a rout which does not belong to the voyage. They are to pursue the usual course, and let the consequences fall where they may. In this case the master probably thought he was advancing the interests of his employers, of the underwriters, and of all concerned, by getting his vessel loaded several weeks sooner than would have been his turn: and yet it is almost certain that his very success, in being able to commence his homeward voyage so soon, was the cause of the disaster which befell his vessel. Certainly, had he arrived at St. Jago a week later, he would have avoided the immediate cause of the loss." 13 Mass. at 72–73.

The doctrine of deviation has been held to apply to private as well as public carriage. See Close v. Anderson, 442 F.Supp. 14, 1978 A.M.C. 959 (W.D.Wash. 1977). What about a contract to carry passengers? See Kelly v. S/S "Queen Elizabeth 2", 1986 A.M.C. 349, 1985 WL 2051 (S.D.N.Y.1985).

The development of deviation as a predicate to carrier liability is traced in Friedell, The Deviating Ship, 32 Hastings L.J. 1535 (1981). The relationship between the underlying principles of the traditional maritime law and the COGSA provision is discussed in Morgan, Unreasonable Deviation under COGSA, 9 J.Mar.L. & Com. 481 (1978). See also Gilmore & Black, *Law of Admiralty,* 176–183. In The Deviating Ship, supra, Professor Friedell also touches upon deviation under the Visby Amendments to the Hague Rules and the Hamburg Rules.

Gilmore & Black argue that the COGSA provision can be read to substitute for the insurer's liability of the general maritime law a liability only for loss causally connected with the deviation. This argument is bottomed to a certain extent on the text of COGSA but rests also on the opinion that the "insurer" rule is not justifiable today, since the risk of deviation can be insured against. Cf. Wabco Trade Co. v. Great Am. Ins. Co., 508 F.Supp. 94, 1981 A.M.C. 876 (S.D.N.Y.1980), rev'd on other grounds 663 F.2d 369 (2d Cir.1981).

In Singapore Nav. Co., S./A. v. Mego Corp., 540 F.2d 39, 1976 A.M.C. 1512 (2 Cir.1976), the loss was occasioned by stranding due to a navigational error. The vessel was prevented from unloading at east coast ports of the United States. The bill of lading was construed to require, in this eventuality, that it be unloaded at the nearest Canadian port. Instead it proceeded to Detroit. The district court found that the trip to Detroit subjected the cargo to additional risks in the Seaway passage and the necessity for taking on a compulsory pilot. The court of appeals expressly rejected these findings but nevertheless concluded that there was a causal connection. What was it? When there is a localized incident such as a stranding or a collision, and it occurs while the vessel is off its normal course, is there always a causal connection?

Note that the question of whether there is a deviation depends upon the delineation of the voyage. When the vessel has aboard cargo taken on in different ports, it may be that steering a particular course may be a deviation as to some cargo, and not as to other cargo. See, e.g., Delphinus Maritima, S.A., 1982 A.M.C. 796 (S.D.N.Y.1982). In this connection, as noted in The S.S. Nancy Lykes above, liberties clauses in the bill of lading, however broad the language, are construed to permit only reasonable deviation. For example the liberty "to proceed by any route" in a Taiwan/New York Bill of lading bill of lading would not be construed to permit the carrier to arrange for shipment of a cargo of umbrellas across the United States by rail. Berkshire Fashions, Inc. v. M.V. Hakusan II, 954 F.2d 874, 1992 A.M.C. 1171 (3d Cir.1992). But a shipper can agree to a particular deviation. See Caterpillar Overseas, S.A. v. Marine Transport Inc., 900 F.2d 714 (4th Cir.1990), where the shipper consented to having his cargo taken from one port to another by truck.

The doctrine of deviation has been applied to both common and private carriage. cases covered by the COGSA deviation is not a separate cause of action and must be pleaded as an aspect of a claim under COGSA. Konica Business Machines v. SEA–LAND CONSUMER, 1993 A.M.C. 25 (C.D.Cal.1992). Under COGSA a "reasonable" deviation is not the basis for carrier liability. Professor

Friedell argues from principle that the carrier should be held responsible if the deviation increased the risk and the loss could be attributed to a risk of the sort that was increased. Is this because a deviation that does not increase the risk is "reasonable"? Or is it because a deviation that does not increase the risk cannot be said to be causally related to the loss?

Departure from the customary route occasioned by press of weather, or to avoid privateers, or under some such similar compulsion was not considered a deviation under the law of marine insurance, nor is it considered an unreasonable deviation under the COGSA. E.g., in Lekas & Drivas, Inc. v. Goulandris, p. 616, supra, if the change in route from an Atlantic crossing to a trip around the Cape of Good Hope, passing through Aden were construed to be a deviation, there would be an obvious connection between it and the loss of a cargo of soft cheese. Similarly, when a vessel on its way from Dubai to Houston was requisitioned by the British Government under its war powers, its proceeding to Malta for the purpose of transhipping its cargo was reasonable, and did not deprive it of its limitation of liability under COGSA. Sedco, Inc. v. S.S. Strathewe 800 F.2d 27 (2d Cir.1986). But cf. Spartus Corp. v. SS/Yafo, 590 F.2d 1310, 1979 A.M.C. 2294 (5th Cir.1979), in which it was held that an Israeli vessel with a cargo bound for New Orleans, was guilty of an unreasonable deviation when it proceeded to Mobile and offloaded the New Orleans cargo to take on military cargo for Israel. The court found that the fact that the deviation came within the presumption set up in the statute and the fact that it was in compliance with the order of the Israeli government did not rebut the presumption.

There may be more than one route that is customary. Held to be reasonable was the choice of a great circle route from Korea to Panama that was recommended by most publications and taken by most masters. Miller Yacht Sales, Inc. v. M.V. OCEAN FRIEND, 1994 A.M.C. 2493 (S.D.N.Y.1993).

The doctrine of deviation in the law of marine insurance related to the definition of the voyage as the measure of the insurer's undertaking. The defense of deviation sometimes related to a geographical departure from the agreed upon or customary route, but not always. Delay in the prosecution of the voyage was considered a deviation. See, e.g., Oliver v. Maryland Ins. Co., 11 U.S. (7 Cranch) 487, 3 L.Ed. 414 (1812)(remaining in port 40 days without sufficient justification), and any other voluntary departure from the terms of the policy stipulating the voyage. See Maryland Insurance Co. v. LeRoy, 11 U.S. (7 Cranch) 26, 3 L.Ed. 257 (1812)(under a voyage policy covering a trading voyage to African ports, with liberty of touching at the Cape de Verds, on her return passage, "for stock and to take in water," the underwriters were discharged when the master took on four jack-asses, the Court construing the term "stock" in the policy to mean smaller animals). In an opinion by Justice Johnson, the Court observed:

"The discharge of the underwriters from their liability, in such cases, depends, not upon any supposed increase of risk, but wholly upon the departure of the insured from the contract of insurance. The consequences of such violation of the contract are immaterial to its legal effect, as it is, *per se,* a discharge of the underwriters, and the law attaches no importance to the degree, in cases of voluntary deviation; necessity alone can sanction a deviation, in any case; and that deviation must be strictly commensurate with the *vis major* producing it."

With the extension of the doctrine of deviation to contracts of carriage, it was early recognized that the term, while possibly originally descriptive of geographical departure from the prescribed or customary route, embraces at least some other departures from the terms of the contract. See The Indrapura, 171 Fed. 929

(D.Or.1909), in which it was held that placing a vessel in dry dock after loading cargo, for the purpose of painting its bottom, without marine necessity, constituted a deviation and rendered the owner liable for loss of the cargo in a fire occurring while the vessel was in the dry dock, thus depriving the owner of the protection of the fire statute.

Can the decision in *The Indrapura* be read as a delay case, much like *Oliver?* See also Allstate Ins. Co. v. International Shipping Corp., 1982 A.M.C. 1763 (S.D.Fla.1981), in which removing a cargo of aluminum extrusions from trailers and storing it outdoors on pallets and changing the voyage date without notifying the shipper was held to be a deviation.

Also held to be a deviation has been the stowage on deck of cargo shipped under a clean bill of lading. See St. Johns N.F. Shipping Corp. v. S.A. Companhia Geral Commercial do Rio de Janeiro, 263 U.S. 119, 44 S.Ct. 30, 68 L.Ed. 201 (1923). See also Encyclopaedia Britannica v. S.S. Hong Kong Producer, 422 F.2d 7 (2d Cir. 1969). To what extent can this holding be analogized to the decisions like *Le Roy* in which the taking on of cargo not provided for in the insurance contract was held to excuse the insurer from liability? Have recent technological changes in the design of vessels and the manner of stowage made the *St. Johns* rule obsolete? See O'Connell Machinery Co., Inc. v. M.V. Americana, 797 F.2d 1130 (2d Cir.1986). In the particular case, where the vessel was equipped with eight on-deck bays for deck storage, there were space limitations at the time the machine was presented for loading, as well as safety and loading difficulties, custom in the port permitted on-deck storage of flat-racks, and the cause of the slippage and fall of the machine was packaging, not stowage, the court of appeals held that there was no unreasonable deviation within the Act. And see Whitehead, Deviation: Should the Doctrine Apply to On–Deck Carriage?, 6 Maritime Lawyer 37 (1981).

If cases like *The Indrapura* and *St. Johns* do not relate strictly speaking to geographical departures, is it possible to reframe the definition of "deviation" to refer to deviation from the terms of the contract, rather than deviation from the voyage? Would this sort of redefinition make every breach of the contract of carriage a deviation? Or is it possible to single out some failures to perform and some advertent acts that constitute a deviation, and some that do not? On what basis? Some of the cases refer to a "fundamental" breach of the terms of the contract. See, e.g., S. Hong Kong Producer, *supra*. *For discussion of the doctrine of "fundamental breach of contract," see Parks, The Law of Tug, Tow, and Pilotage, 97 et seq. (2d Ed.1982).*

If there are "fundamental" terms implied in the contract of carriage the breach of which will constitute a "deviation," other than dispatch, the customary route, stowage below deck, and tandem towing, what are they? Suppose the cargo owner alleged systematic theft on the part of the officers and crew of the vessel. See Italia Di Navigazione, S.P.A v. M.V. Hermes I, 724 F.2d 21, 1984 A.M.C. 1676 (2d Cir.1983), holding no. What about gross negligence in failing to provide a seaworthy vessel? See Iligan Integrated Steel Mills, Inc. v. S.S. John Weyerhaeuser, 507 F.2d 68, 1975 A.M.C. 33 (2d Cir.1974), holding no. And see American Express v. U.S. Lines, 1979 A.M.C. 218 (N.Y.Sup.Ct.1978), a state court case, in which the court held that failure of the carrier to provide special security did not constitute a deviation such as would preclude the application $500 package limitation when two cases of travellers's checks, worth $483,000 were taken by armed robbers from a crib on carrier's pier prior to loading. For discussion of the doctrine of "quasi deviation," as nongeographic deviation is sometimes called, see Knauth, Ocean Bills of Lading 2511 (1953); 2A Benedict on Admiralty § 123 (7th Ed.1984).

Issuing an incorrect bill of lading has been held to deprive the carrier of the package limitation. Allied Chemical International Corp. v. Companhia de Navega-cao Lloyd Brasileiro, 775 F.2d 476, 1986 A.M.C. 826 (2d Cir.1985).

And failure to keep a refrigeration system constantly in operation has been thought to be so likely a deviation as to preclude summary judgment. Agfa-Gevaert, Inc. v. S/S TFL ADAMS, 596 F.Supp. 338, 1986 A.M.C. 411 (S.D.N.Y.1984).

It has been held that non-delivery does not constitute a deviation, and also misdelivery. See Unimac Company, Inc. v. C.F. Ocean Service, Inc., 43 F.3d 1434, 1995 A.M.C. 1484 (11th Cir.1995)

Restowage of cargo en route is not a deviation. Yang Machine Tool Co. v. Sea-Land Service, Inc., 58 F.3d 1350 (9th Cir.1995). SPM Corp. v. M/V's Ming Moon, 965 F.2d 1297, 1992 A.M.C. 2409 (3d Cir.1992), in which restowage at intermediate ports of call is spoken of as a common practice.

And failure to follow discharge instructions to shipper's stevedore that were not contained in the bill of lading did not constitute a deviation. Rockwell Intern. Corp. v. M/V Incotrans Spirit, 998 F.2d 316, 1994 A.M.C. 71 (5th Cir.1993).

In both *S.S. Nancy Lykes* and *Yutana Barge Lines,* above, it was held that limitation of liability provisions in the contract of carriage, or in the Act, were nullified by the deviation. As noted in the former, this is the view of the Second, Fifth, and Ninth Circuits, but rejected in the Seventh. There is district court authority in the Sixth that sides with the view of the Seventh. Professor Friedell suggests that the rule of the Second and Fifth circuits (now joined by the Ninth) had its genesis in a misreading of the legislative history. Op.Cit., 1561.

In *Yutana Barge Lines,* note that the contractual time limit on suit was also nullified. What about the one year limitations period in 46 U.S.C.A. § 1303(6)? Holding that the one year period is not ousted, Bunge Edible Oil Corp. v. M/V Torm Rask and Fort Steele, 949 F.2d 786, 1992 A.M.C. 2227 (5th Cir.1992). The *Bunge* decision was noted in *Unimac* supra, but finding no unreasonable deviation, the court found it unnecessary to address the matter. See Corat Int'l, Inc. v. Saudi National Lines, 439 So.2d 1035, 1984 A.M.C. 1268 (Fla.App.1983), aff'd per cur. 1984 A.M.C. 1274 (Fla.D.C.App.3d 1983) and Francosteel Corp. v. N.V. Neder-landsch Amerikaansche, Stoomvart–Maatschappij, 249 Cal.App.2d 880, 57 Cal.Rptr. 867, 1967 A.M.C. 2440 (1967). But Cf. Allstate Ins. Co. v. International Shipping Corp., 1982 A.M.C. 1763 (S.D.Fla.1981); Cerro Sales Corp. v. Atlantic Marine Enterprises, Inc., 403 F.Supp. 562, 1976 A.M.C. 375 (S.D.N.Y.1975).

And deviation does not deprive the carrier of a forum selection clause. North River Ins. Co. v. Fed Sea/Fed Pac Line, 647 F.2d 985, 1982 A.M.C. 2963 (9th Cir.1981).

While the breach of contract that constitutes a deviation is referred to as a "fundamental" breach, it is still merely a breach of contract, and does not subject the carrier to punitive damages. Thyssen, Inc. v. S.S. Fortune Star, 777 F.2d 57 (2d Cir.1985). If deviation is firmly locked into the breach of contract, and cannot be characterized as tort, does this mean that a failure in the duty to cargo under COGSA not sufficiently fundamental to constitute a deviation may import a lien superior to the claim based on deviation? Cf. Oriente Commercial, Inc. v. M/V Floridian, reproduced at p. 475, supra.

CHAPTER 15

SALVAGE

A. PROPERTY THE SUBJECT OF SALVAGE

Provost v. Huber

United States Court of Appeals, Eighth Circuit, 1979.
594 F.2d 717.

■ VAN SICKLE, DISTRICT JUDGE.

The Appellant Provost brings this timely appeal from an order of the district court[1] which dismissed his complaint and first amended complaint for lack of subject matter jurisdiction. The action was brought under the admiralty or maritime jurisdiction of the federal courts, and sought a salvage award. The district court, in ruling upon Appellee Huber's Rule 12(b)(1) motion, found lacking a nexus with traditional maritime activity and dismissed the action upon that ground.[2]

The basic facts of this novel case are undisputed. From the allegations of the complaints (original and amended) and the affidavits submitted by the parties in connection with the motion to dismiss, it appears that Huber purchased a two-story frame house in Bayfield County, Wisconsin, with the purpose in mind of moving the structure from the mainland to a lot on Madeline Island situated in Lake Superior. Huber hired a housemover to transport the building and contents by truck-trailer over the frozen surface of Lake Superior. The move was attempted in March of 1977 and, at a point approximately three-fourths of the way to the island, the truck, trailer, house and contents broke through the ice.

While the house was partially submerged in the waters of Lake Superior, Huber was approached by an individual who represented himself to be an underwater contractor and who suggested that the structure be sunk to the bottom of the lake to preserve and protect it from ice damage until such time that it could be raised when weather permitted. Huber and his insurer agreed to the plan and the house was thereupon lowered to the lake bottom by placing sandbags on the floor.

---

1. Honorable Harry H. MacLaughlin, United States District Court, District of Minnesota.

2. The district court, in considering the Defendant's Rule 12(b)(1) motion to dismiss,

reached his decision after "* * * a full review of the record of the case, including the Amended Complaint, the accompanying affidavits, and the memoranda and arguments of counsel, * * *"

In May of 1977 the Plaintiff and a second diver (not a party to this litigation) were approached by Mr. Edward Erickson (the underwater contractor who had lowered the structure to the lake bed). After the situation concerning the submerged house was discussed, the Plaintiff and his fellow diver agreed to assist in retrieving the building, although no specific terms of compensation were reached. Plaintiff spent about sixty hours of underwater work removing sandbags from the floor of the house. While Plaintiff was recharging his air tanks and absent from the jobsite, Erickson commenced to raise the structure. That attempt resulted in the house breaking up to the point of total destruction. Erickson retrieved substantially all of the pieces and disposed of them in a landfill at a cost of $500.00 to the Defendant and his insurer.

Prior to the move in March of 1977, the Defendant secured insurance on the structure (but not the contents) in the sum of $20,000.00. It is unclear from the record, but we may safely assume for purposes of this decision, that the insurer paid the full amount of the policy limits.

Some time after the unsuccessful attempt to retrieve the house intact from the bottom of Lake Superior, the Plaintiff billed the Defendant for $500.00 for his services rendered. The bill remains unpaid, and this suit claiming a maritime salvage of $10,000.00 followed.

As stated above, the district court dismissed Plaintiff's action for lack of a nexus with traditional maritime activity. This Court recently, in Shows v. Harber, 575 F.2d 1253 (1978) determined the necessity of such nexus in maritime cases. The Supreme Court has established that proposition in tort actions brought under the admiralty jurisdiction, Executive Jet Aviation, Inc. v. Cleveland, 409 U.S. 249, 93 S.Ct. 493, 34 L.Ed.2d 454 (1972), and the same has been fixed for salvage cases, Cope v. Vallette Dry-Dock Co., 119 U.S. 625, 7 S.Ct. 336, 30 L.Ed. 501 (1887).

In *Cope* the Supreme Court, at page 627, 7 S.Ct. at page 337, rejected a salvage claim in connection with a floating drydock on the basis that "no structure that is not a ship or vessel is a subject of salvage." "Vessel" is defined at 1 U.S.C., Section 3, as "every description of water craft or other artificial contrivance used, or capable of being used, as a means of transportation on water." The short answer to Appellant's assertion that the tractor-trailer being used to carry the house was a vessel within the meaning of maritime law because it was transporting the structure over water is that such transportation was on ice, not water, and that immediately upon the transporter breaking through the ice, it sank to the bottom of the lake. By no stretch of the imagination can we equate a multi-wheeled device, designed and built for the purpose of transportation over a hard, defined surface—such as roads, highways, and even ice—with a vessel or ship as those terms are used in maritime law.

The Appellant argues that even if the transporter cannot be considered a vessel, the house is still the proper subject of salvage, thereby bringing this action with the admiralty jurisdiction of the federal courts. In support of this assertion the Appellant cites, inter alia, Broere v. Two Thousand One Hundred Thirty–Three Dollars, 72 F.Supp. 115 (E.D.N.Y.1947), wherein the court found that money found on a human body floating on navigable waters was a proper subject of salvage. The distinguishing feature found in *Broere,* however, and the determinant for finding admiralty jurisdiction, was the fact that, prior to his death, the individual concerned had embarked upon a maritime adventure. In the instant case we do not and cannot find that, prior to breaking through the ice and submerging, the house had embarked upon a "maritime" adventure. In other words, circumstances attending the placement of property in or upon navigable waters must be considered and are decisive when dealing with the question of admiralty jurisdiction and salvage. The fact that certain property may be the proper subject of salvage, standing alone, does not confer admiralty jurisdiction upon the federal courts. A nexus with traditional maritime activities must still be shown.

We recognize that cases decided since *Cope,* supra, have broadened the somewhat restrictive view therein enunciated by the Supreme Court as to what may properly be the subject of maritime salvage. For example, the Second Circuit concluded in Lambros Seaplane Base v. The Batory, 215 F.2d 228 (1954), that a seaplane down at sea is subject to the maritime law of salvage. *Lambros* is distinguishable on the ground that a seaplane—as opposed to a wheeled land vehicle—is designed and used for taking off of, flying over, and landing upon a water surface. Also, the district court in Colby v. Todd Packing Co., 77 F.Supp. 956, 12 Alaska 1 (D.Alaska, 1948), allowed a salvage claim involving floating fish trap frames found adrift. The distinguishing feature in *Colby* is obvious: Fish trap frames are designed to float upon and be transported across a water surface.

We conclude, upon the facts present in this case, that the district court was correct in dismissing the action for lack of a nexus with traditional maritime activities.

Affirmed.

NOTE

In *Provost,* the court distinguishes the case from *Lambros* on the ground that "a seaplane—as opposed to a wheeled land vehicle—is designed and used for taking off of, flying over, and landing upon a water surface." Suppose a land based airplane crashes in water. Are the pieces floating in the water a subject of marine salvage? See Mark v. South Continental Ins. Agency and One Cessna 411, 1978 A.M.C. 519 (D.P.R.1976), in which the court upheld the jurisdiction. Judge Pesquera observed that "as long as it is property that may be considered to have been lost in navigable waters from which it was salved, for the benefit of the owner, this Court has jurisdiction over the subject matter."

The 1989 Salvage Convention, which has been ratified by the Senate but has not yet gone into effect because the requisite number of nations (fifteen) have not as yet ratified it, defines a "salvage operation" as "any act or activity undertaken to assist a vessel or any other property in danger in navigable waters or any other waters whatsoever," and defines "property" as "any property not permanently and intentionally attached to the shoreline." Would saving the house in Provost v.

Huber qualify under these definitions? Would they cover the rescue of a piano during the Johnstown flood?

In Pelaez, Salvage—a New Look at an Old Concept, 7 J.Mar.L. & Comm. 505 (1976), it is suggested that in salvage cases the courts have been too fixed in their focus upon the nature and situs of the property, and argued that rescue and salvage in which it is necessary to employ marine resources should qualify. One example Professor Pelaez gives is the situation in which persons and property on a fixed oil drilling platform are in peril and the only source of succor will be vessels. Professor Palaez later suggested that Provost v. Huber might be illustrative of the same principle. See 7A Moore's Federal Practice ¶.275[3] (1994–95 Supp.) 281. Article 3 of the 1989 Convention provides that the Convention "shall not apply to fixed or floating platforms or to mobile offshore drilling units when such platforms or units are on location engaged in the exploration, exploitation or production of seabed mineral resources." Does Article 3 encourage or discourage such an expansion of the traditional law of salvage as is suggested by Professor Palaez?

B. WHO MAY BE A SALVOR?

Mason v. The Blaireau

Supreme Court of the United States, 1804.
6 U.S. (2 Cranch.) 240, 2 L.Ed. 266.

This was an appeal from a decree of the circuit court of the United States for the district of Maryland, in a cause of salvage instituted by the master, officers and crew of the British ship Firm, against the French ship Blaireau and her cargo, which came in collision with a Spanish sixty-four gun ship, was seriously injured, and was abandoned on the high seas by her officers and all her crew except one man, Thomas Toole, who was left on board, either by accident or design. Toole also filed a libel in which he alleged that being compelled by force to remain on board, he cut away the anchors and the bowsprit, which had been carried away, but was hanging by the stays, thus relieved the bows, got her before the wind and hoisted a signal of distress. The next day she was boarded by the ship Firm, bound on a voyage from Lisbon to Baltimore, of the actual burden of five hundred tons, and of the value of $10,000, with a cargo of salt of the value of $4,000, and having on board one of her charterers, the master, mate and thirteen hands all told, including two apprentices and a boy; 2,000£ was insured on The Firm and her freight. The Blaireau and her cargo produced, net, $60,-272.68.

Upon taking possession of The Blaireau she had about four feet of water in her hold, and could not have swum more than twelve hours longer. There was great risk and peril in taking charge of her. She was brought into the Chesapeake Bay after a navigation of nearly three thousand miles, by six persons who went on board of her from The Firm, and the man who was found on board. Part of her cargo was taken out to lighten her forward, and put on board The Firm; and part of it shifted aft. The Blaireau was navigated by the people of The Firm without boat or

effort

anchors. She was obliged to be pumped in fair weather by all hands, every two, three, or four hours, half an hour at a time, and in blowing weather every hour, a quarter of an hour at a time. Her bow was secured by coverings of leather, copper and sheet lead, nailed on, and pitch and turpentine in large quantities poured down hot between the planks and the coverings. The labor of working The Blaireau by the men on board was great and severe, and they had frequently thought of abandoning her, but fortunately persevered. She was a slight built vessel, and constructed without knees, and was very weak. The forestay was gone, and the foremast was secured by passing a large rope through the hawse holes and securing it to the foremast head. It was the opinion of several experienced sea captains that the bringing in The Blaireau was a service of great risk and peril, and nearly desperate, and such as they would not have undertaken.

* * *

■ Marshall, C.J., delivered the opinion of the court.

In this case a preliminary question has been made by the counsel for the plaintiffs, which ought not to be disregarded. As the parties interested, except the owners of the cargo of The Firm, are not Americans, a doubt has been suggested respecting the jurisdiction of the court, and upon a reference to the authorities, the point does not appear to have been ever settled. These doubts seem rather founded on the idea, that upon principles of general policy, this court ought not to take cognizance of a case entirely between foreigners, than from any positive incapacity to do so. On weighing the considerations drawn from public convenience, those in favor of the jurisdiction appear much to overbalance those against it, and it is the opinion of this court that whatever doubts may exist in a case where the jurisdiction may be objected to, there ought to be none where the parties assent to it.

The previous question being disposed of, the court will proceed to consider the several cases which have grown out of the libel filed in the district court.

Captain of The Firm

The first to be decided is that of the captain of The Firm, who, by the sentence of the circuit court, was declared to have forfeited his right to salvage, by having embezzled a part of the cargo of The Blaireau.

The fact is not contested, but it is contended that the embezzlement, proved in the cause, does not affect the right of the captain to salvage.

The arguments in support of this position shall very briefly be reviewed. It is insisted that the embezzlement was made after the vessel was brought into port, and this seems to be considered as a circumstance material to the influence which the embezzlement ought to have in the case. So far as respects the fact, the evidence is that the articles were brought on board The Firm when The Blaireau was found at sea, and the fraud was detected in the port of Baltimore. When the concealment took place does not appear, but it would be straining very hard to presume that it took place after arriving in port. It is not, however, perceived that this need be the subject of very minute inquiry, since the fact must have occurred before he parted with the possession acquired by the act, on the merit of which his claim for salvage is founded.

It is also stated, that this court has no jurisdiction of the crime committed by the captain, and cannot notice it even incidentally.

If it was intended merely to prove that this court could not convict Captain Mason of felony, and punish him for that offense, there certainly could never have been a doubt entertained on the subject; but when it is inferred from thence, that the court can take no notice of the fact, the correctness of the conclusion is not perceived. It is believed to be universally true, that when a claim of any sort is asserted in court, all those circumstances which go to defeat the claim, and to show that the person asserting it has not a right to recover, may and ought to be considered. The real question, therefore, is whether the claim for salvage is affected by the act of embezzlement; and if it is, the incapacity of this court to proceed criminally against the captain, forms no objection to their examining a fact which goes to the very foundation of his right.

The legal right of the salvors is insisted on, and it is said, that in trover for the ship and cargo by the owners, salvage would be allowed to those who had rendered the service, and then openly converted them to their own use.

Yet the jury, trying the action, would determine on the right to salvage, and would inquire into any fact which went to defeat that right.

Whatever shape, then, may, be given to the question, it still resolves itself into the inquiry, whether the embezzlement of part of the cargo does really intermingle itself with, and infect the whole transaction in such a manner as to destroy any claim founded on it.

The counsel for this plaintiff contends, that the merits of Captain Mason, as a salvor, are not impaired by the act charged upon him, because a crime is no offset against a debt, and the claim for salvage is in nature of a debt.

This leads to an inquiry into the principles on which salvage is allowed. If the property of an individual on land be exposed to the greatest peril, and be saved by the voluntary exertions of any persons whatever; if valuable goods be rescued from a house in flames, at the imminent hazard of life by the salvor, no remuneration in the shape of salvage is allowed. The act is highly meritorious, and the service is as great as if rendered at sea. Yet the claim for salvage could not, perhaps, be supported. It is certainly not made. Let precisely the same service, at precisely the same hazard, be rendered at sea, and a very ample reward will be bestowed in the courts of justice.

If we search for the motives producing this apparent prodigality, in rewarding services rendered at sea, we shall find them in a liberal and enlarged policy. The allowance of a very ample compensation for those services, (one very much exceeding the mere risk encountered, and labor employed in effecting them,) is intended as an inducement to render them, which it is for the public interests, and for the general interests of humanity to hold forth to those who navigate the ocean. It is perhaps difficult on any other principle to account satisfactorily for the very great difference which is made between the retribution allowed for services at sea and on land; neither will a fair calculation of the real hazard or labor, be a foundation for such a difference; nor will the benefit received always account for it.

If a wise and humane policy be among the essential principles which induce a continuance in the allowance of that liberal compensation which is made for saving a vessel at sea, we must at once perceive the ground on which it is refused to the person whose conduct ought to be punished instead of being rewarded. That same policy which is so very influential in producing the very liberal allowances made by way of salvage, requires that those allowances should be withheld from persons who avail themselves of the opportunity furnished them by the possession of the property of another to embezzle that property. While the general interests of society require that the most powerful inducements should be held forth to men to save life and property about to perish at sea, they also require that those inducements should likewise be held forth to a fair and upright conduct with regard to the objects thus preserved. This would certainly justify the reduction of the claim to a bare compensation on the principles of a real *quantum meruit*; and the losses in the cargo, which may be imputed to the captain, would balance that account, if, as is contended by his counsel, the court could not, on principles generally received, consider the act of embezzlement as a total forfeiture of all right to salvage.

But the case of a mariner, who forfeits his right to wages by embezzling any part of the cargo, is precisely in point. That case stands on the same principles with this, and is a full authority for this, since it cannot be denied that the right to salvage is forfeited by the same act that would forfeit the right to wages.

In the case of Mr. Stevenson, the fact is not clearly ascertained. If the embezzlement was fixed upon him, he as well as the captain ought to forfeit his salvage. But it is not fixed. Yet there are circumstances in the case, which, if he stands acquitted of the charge of unfairness, do certainly so implicate him in that of carelessness as to destroy his pretensions to superior compensation, and reduce his claim to a level with that of a common mariner.

The decree of the circuit court being approved so far as respects Captain Mason and Mr. Stevenson, the general rate of salvage allowed by that decree is next to be considered.

Taking the whole subject into consideration, the court is disposed to reduce the rate of salvage, and to allow about two fifths instead of three fifths to the salvors. The vessel and cargo will then be really charged in consequence of the savings produced by the forfeiture of the captain's claim, and the reduction of those of the mate and Mr. Christie, with not more than one third of the gross value of the property.

In the distribution of this sum, the court does not entirely approve the decree which has been rendered in the circuit court.

The proportion allowed the owners of The Firm and her cargo is not equal to the risk incurred, nor does it furnish an inducement to the owners of vessels to permit their captains to save those found in distress at sea, in any degree proportioned to the inducements offered to the captains and crew. The same policy ought to extend to all concerned, the same rewards for a service designed to be encouraged, and it is surely no reward to a man, made his own insurer without his own consent, to return him very little more than the premium he had advanced.

The common course of decisions, too, has established a very different ratio for the distribution of salvage money, and the court is of opinion that those decisions are founded on substantial considerations.

The owners of the vessel and cargo, in this case, will be allowed one third of the whole amount of salvage decreed, which third is to be divided between them in the proportion established in the district court, it being, in our opinion, very clear, that the owner of the vessel continued to risk the freight after as much as before the assent of Mr. Christie to the measures necessary for saving The Blaireau. That assent could only be construed, to charge him with the hazards to be encountered by the cargo, and not to vary the contract respecting the freight.

The proportions established by the decree of the circuit court between those who navigated The Firm, and those who navigated The Blaireau, and between the individuals in each ship, are all approved with this exception. The case exhibits no peculiar merits in Mr. Christie, and, therefore, his allowance is not to exceed that of a seaman on board that vessel.

On the rights of Toole and the apprentices, this court entirely concurs in opinion with the district and circuit courts.

There was certainly no individual who assisted in bringing in The Blaireau, that contributed so much to her preservation as Toole. Every principle of justice, and every feeling of the heart, must arrange itself on the side of his claim.

But it is contended, that the contract he had entered into bound him to continue his endeavors to bring the vessel into port, and that the principles of general policy forbid the allowance of salvage to a mariner belonging to the ship which has been preserved.

The claims upon him, on the ground of contract, are urged with a very ill grace indeed. It little becomes those who devoted him to the waves to set up a title to his further services. The captain, who was intrusted by the owner with power over the vessel and her crew, had discharged him from all further duty under his contract, as far as any act whatever could discharge him, and it is not for the owner now to revive this abandoned claim.

Those principles of policy which withhold from the mariners of a ship their wages on her being lost, and which deny them salvage for saving their ship, however great the peril may be, cannot apply to a case like this. There is no danger that a single seaman can be induced, or enabled, by the prospect of the reward given to Toole, to prevail on the officers and crew of a vessel to abandon her to the mercy of the waves for the purpose of entitling the person who remains in her to salvage, if she should be fortunately preserved.   * * *

Upon these principles the following decree is to be entered:

"This cause came on to be heard on the transcript of the record of the circuit court, and was argued by counsel, on consideration whereof, this court doth reverse the sentence of the circuit court, so far as the same is inconsistent with the principles and opinions hereinafter stated:

"This court is of opinion that too large a proportion of the net proceeds of the ship Blaireau and her cargo has been allowed to the salvors, and that $21,400 is a sufficient retribution for the service performed, which sum is decreed to the claimants, except Captain Mason, whose rights are forfeited by embezzling a part of the cargo, in full of their demands. In distributing the sum thus allowed, this court is of opinion that the owners of The Firm and her cargo ought to receive one third of the whole amount thereof, of which one third the proportion of the owner of the vessel ought to be to that of the owner of the cargo, as the value of the vessel, and freight is to the value of the cargo; that is, as 18 to 4.

"It is further the opinion of the court, that the remaining two thirds of the salvage allowed, ought to be divided between those who navigated both The Firm and The Blaireau, excluding Captain Mason, in the proportions directed by the circuit court, with this exception, that the sum to be received by Charles Christie is to be the same with that received by a seaman on board The Blaireau.

"In every thing not contrary to the principles herein contained, the decree of the circuit court is affirmed, and the cause is remanded to the said circuit court to be further proceeded in, according to the directions given. The parties are to pay their own costs."

NOTE

Certain classes of people are generally excluded from salvage awards on the ground that they have acted out of duty. The first of these is a member of the crew of a salved vessel. In The Tashmoo, 48 F.2d 366, 1931 A.M.C. 48 (D.N.Y.1930), a workaway serving as a pantryman and paid 30 cents a month was denied an award though at some personal risk he had devoted two days of almost ceaseless labor in repairing the ship's radio so that it could signal for help. The court distinguished *The Blaireau* on the ground that there the vessel had been abandoned and therefore Thomas Toole was relieved of whatever duty he had to his employer. Norris lists only four exceptions to the rule that a member of the crew may not be salvors of his own vessel. They are: (1) abandonment by all or all except the salvors in circumstances that show conclusively that the abandonment is absolute; (2) Where the master has unmistakeably discharged the seaman from the service of the shipowner; (3) after shipwreck and total loss of the vessel; and (4) recapture of a vessel after it has been captured by a hostile power. *The Law of Salvage* 81 (1958).

This strict rule against self-salvage has been justified on a number of grounds, among them the possibility that salvage awards to the crew of a salved vessel might encourage crews to create salvage situations. See The Clarita and The Clara, 90 U.S. (23 Wall.) 1, 23 L.Ed. 146 (1874). See Gilmore and Black, *Law of Admiralty* 541 (1975). Both Gilmore and Black and Kennedy, *Civil Salvage* 25 (1958) treat the rule against self-salvage as part of the broader requirement that salvage be voluntary

Others usually denied salvage awards on the ground that they act under compulsion of duty are passengers, firemen, pilots, and similar persons. The rule against awards to such persons is less rigid that it is in the case of crew members. See Gilmore and Black, *Law of Admiralty* 543 (1975), where the authors observe, "The dividing line between 'duty' and 'no duty' is, of course, drawn through the customary twilight zone of obscurity; the cases suggest that presumptions run heavily against claimants so situated." See S.C. Loveland Co., Inc. v. Barge Arlington, 1982 A.M.C. 704 (W.D.La.1980), in which a $50,000 award was made to a municipal fire department for salvaging a foundering barge, when the fire boat had no duty to render assistance.

33 U.S.C.A. § 367 required a vessel involved in a collision to stand by until it is sure that the other vessel does not need assistance. In In re Sun Oil Co. (M/T Maumee Sun), 342 F.Supp. 976 (S.D.N.Y.1972), aff'd 474 F.2d 1048 (2d Cir.1973), a collision between the Maumee Sun and the American Pilot, later adjudged to have been caused by the fault of the Maumee Sun, left the prow of the American Pilot driven into the hull of the Maumee Sun. Instead of taking steps to separate the two vessels, the American Pilot lashed the two together until the cargo of the Maumee Sun had been salvaged. In denying a salvage award, the district court found that the lashing of the ships was undertaken for the safety of the American Pilot, and accordingly was not a voluntary service to the Maumee Sun. It also held that since § 367 placed the American Pilot under a statutory duty to stand by and render assistance, the assistance could not be voluntary for salvage purposes. The court of appeals affirmed on the first ground and declined to address the effect of former § 367 on the right of the crew to recover for salvage services. The text of 46 U.S.C.A. § 2303, which replaces § 367, substitutes for the language "to render to the other vessel, her master, crew, and passengers (if any) such assistance as may be practicable and as may be necessary in order to save them from any danger caused by the collision," the following: "render necessary assistance to each individual affected to save that affected individual from danger caused by the marine casualty." Does this eliminate the preexisting duty problem. How about life salvage?

Nicholas E. Vernicos Shipping Co. v. United States

United States Court of Appeals, Second Circuit, 1965.
349 F.2d 465, 1965 A.M.C. 1673.

■ HENRY J. FRIENDLY, CT. J. The United States appeals from a judgment of the District Court for the Southern District of New York, 223 F.Supp. 116, 1964 A.M.C. 1222 (D.C.N.Y.1963), awarding the owners of two Greek tugs an amount equal to three months' expenses of maintenance, to wit, $24,098.70, and the crews an amount equal to three months' wages, to wit, $5,577.60, for salvage services to two store ships of the Sixth Fleet at Piraeus in 1956. In this court the Government wisely has not disputed, as it apparently did below, 1964 A.M.C. at 1227, 223 F.Supp. at 119–20, that libellants in fact rendered salvage services rather than mere towage. Its points on appeal are the overruling of its defense of sovereign immunity, the making of an award to the crew, an allegedly excessive amount.

* * * [Portions of the opinion dealing with suits against the United States by Greek citizens have been omitted]

(2) The United States attacks the award to the crews as violating what it claims to be a rule of the admiralty prohibiting such awards to the employees of professional salvors; it also says that if there is to be any award, three months wages are too much.

The law as to who may participate in a salvage award and in what proportions has undergone a sea change. "Primitive salvage law allowed nothing to the owner as such, on the ground that the award was made as an inducement to individuals to risk their lives at sea. Owners who had not personally participated in the salvage began to be allowed to share during the nineteenth century, as ship values increased * * *. At first the lion's share was reserved to the crew, with the owner getting a third or a fourth. As values continued to increase the proportion was reversed; today when a salvage service is performed by anything larger than a fishing smack the owner receives more than the crew." Gilmore & Black, *Admiralty* (1957), sec. 8–11, pp. 467–68.

The Government's claim that the crews of the Vernicos Manos and the Kentavros should receive nothing is rested on the basis that since crews of professional salvors are hired for the precise purpose of rendering salvage, they lack the "voluntary" character universally held requisite for a salvage award, see Gilmore & Black, supra, sec. 8–4; Norris, supra, secs. 68–87; Kennedy, *Civil Salvage,* 24–97 (4th ed., McGuffie, 1958). Conceptually their position differs somewhat from that of the crew of the salvaged vessel, already in the ship's pay and inclined to save the ship in their own interest, or public employees of the Coast Guard or local fire department, acting in the line of official duty. Despite the differences in status, there is the argument that the crew of a salvage vessel have already engaged themselves to do this very work, usually at a regular salary.

Authority on the precise issue appears surprisingly scanty. In Resolute, 168 U.S. 437, 441, 18 S.Ct. 112, 113, 42 L.Ed. 533 (1897), Mr. Justice Brown said in the course of discussing a quite different issue that "it has sometimes been held that, if such [salvage] services are rendered by seamen in the employ of a wrecking tug, or by a municipal fire department, no lien arises, for the very reason that the men are originally employed for the very purpose of rescuing property from perils of the sea or loss by fire"; no citations to the holdings were given and we note the word "sometimes." In Cetewayo, 9 F. 717, 719 (E.D.N.Y.1881), Judge Benedict made a salvage award to the crew of a wrecking vessel; however, he stressed that "wrecking does not necessarily include salving" and that there was no proof that the vessel had ever before earned a salvage award during the libellants' service. A square statement to the effect urged by the Government was made in Arakan, 283 F. 861 (N.D.Cal.1922), but only as dictum supporting a liberal award to the owners on the basis that this would be all the salved vessel would have to pay. In W.E. Rippon v. United States, 1964 A.M.C. 2695 (S.D.N.Y.1963), Judge Croake upheld the position here taken by the United States, and the issue was not pressed on the appeal to this court, 1966 A.M.C. 153, 348 F.2d 627 (2 Cir.1965). The many other cases cited by the Government are relevant only in that awards were there made to the owners of salving vessels without discussion of any award to the crew. By contrast, Glengyle, P. 97, 104 [1898], aff'd, A.C. 519 [1898], confirmed an award to the "owners, masters, and crews" of two quite professional salvage vessels, again without any consideration of the issue.

Turning from the inconclusive precedents to the equities, we likewise find a number of imponderables. Whether the crew of a professional salvor has been paid compensation by its employer covering the risks of salvage will depend upon the particular facts, for fixed wages may be less in the expectation that the crew will receive salvage awards or more on the assumption that only the employer collects and collects somewhat more to offset his increased wage costs. One might guess that the greater the proportion of salvage work carried on by the ship, the more likely it is that the risk element has been absorbed by the employer and the crew more fully compensated through wages for salvage dangers—but local custom may be to the contrary. Also, to the degree that the employer is a professional salvor, it may be thought that the actual danger to the crew is attenuated, and the need for special inducement from any source is reduced, by the experience and specialized equipment of the employer himself.

Applying these considerations to the facts, Vernicos testified that although the activity of his company (and apparently also of the owner of the Kentavros) was "mainly salvage business," the tugs engaged in the collateral activity of "deep sea towage and harbor towage, this because otherwise it is impossible to maintain a salvaging station in Greece owing to the limited number of cases which we have in our area." There is no evidence that the wages of the crews of the two tugs were more than those paid to tug crews at Piraeus generally—indeed Vernicos testified they were lower than those paid to the crews of port tugs. However, he also stated he paid no bonus to the crews for salvage operations "because they are professional salvage crews." The willingness of the crews to work for standard tug wages or less may or may not reflect a hope of awards from salved vessels even though their employer would not pay them a bonus out of his award; the record is silent on Greek practice on this score.

We are not convinced that, even in the case of crews engaged in nothing but professional salvage, the law has hardened to the degree the Government argues. Although the considerations urged by the Government weigh against the crew's claims, circumstances may arise in which the conscience of the admiralty may be moved in favor of making a modest award. Doing this would heighten the incentive of such crews—although, of course, it would also serve that purpose in the case of the ship's own crew or of public employees to whom it is clear that no award may be made save for exceptions not here relevant. Circumstances that were appealing in the instant case were the high value of the salved vessels, the crews' receipt of wages corresponding to those on port tugs, and the existence of some peril; if the weather had worsened and the naval vessels could not be held, the tugs could have been forced between them and the power plant, which was only 375 feet east of the initial mooring and even nearer to the vessels when the tugs first appeared. See 223 F.Supp. at 117, 1964 A.M.C. at 1223.

On the other hand, the award of three months' wages was excessive. The very factors which the judge considered to support a similar basis for calculating the award to the owners—payment for stand-by service and the speculative nature of salvage operations—make it inappropriate for the crews, who received their agreed wages whether or not opportunity for salvage occurred and regardless of the results. Award of the equivalent of a month's wages for less than a day's work would be most liberal.

(3) In fixing the award to the owners the judge took account of the large value of the salved vessels; of the peril to which they were still exposed even though the most extreme hazard had abated before the tugs arrived; of the value of the tugs, $142,000; of the promptness of their response and the skill and efficiency displayed; of such hazards as they underwent; and of the relatively short time consumed. Finding that the case represented a "low order" of salvage, he nevertheless thought a liberal award was merited because of the owners' character as professional salvors—theirs being the only salvage tugs in Greece according to Vernicos' testimony. To arrive at a measure he took three months' expenses, with resulting awards of $13,274.34 for the Vernicos Manos and of $10,824.36 for the Kentavros.

There is no force either in the Government's claim that this in part duplicated the awards to the crews or in libellants' argument that if we eliminate or reduce the latter, we should correspondingly increase the owners' awards or permit the district court to do so. Although crew wages were an item in both calculations, the theory was entirely different—in the one case, a method for calculating a bonus; in the other a basis for determining the compensation properly payable for the owner's stand-by costs and the aleatory nature of his business. Whether the award nevertheless was not excessive is another matter. The Government argues that libellants are less deserving because the tugs were not reserved exclusively for salvage work; but there is nothing to show that, despite these other assignments, the libellants did not maintain on station at Piraeus a number of tugs adequate to meet the reasonable needs of shipping in that harbor. The record contains no evidence how often the libellants' vessels were able to earn salvage or in what amounts. In view of the traditional principle of liberality in awards to professional salvors, Lamington, 86 F. 675 (2 Cir.1898); *Glengyle* supra, a substantial award was warranted. However, for reasons similar to those recently expounded by our brother Moore in W.E. Rippon & Son v. United States, supra, we think the award was overly

reduced to
2 months
expenses for
each
vessel

generous, and direct that it be reduced to the equivalent of two months' expenses for each vessel.

The decree is modified by reducing the awards to the shipowners to two months' expenses and the awards to the crews to the equivalent of one month's wages and is affirmed as so modified.

N O T E

But when contract salvor's superintendent brought his own equipment aboard and performed services his employer had contracted to perform, he was not entitled to a personal salvage award. Nunley v. M/V Dauntless Colocotronis, 863 F.2d 1190, 1993 A.M.C. 1676 (5th Cir.1989).

C.   SALVAGE SITUATIONS; PERIL

Faneuil Advisors, Inc. v. O/S Sea Hawk

United States Court of Appeals , First Circuit, 1995.
50 F.3d 88, 1995 A.M.C. 1504.

■ STAHL, CIRCUIT JUDGE.

Plaintiff-appellant, Faneuil Advisors, Inc. ("Faneuil"), appeals the district court's order subordinating Faneuil's preferred ship mortgage on the O/S Sea Hawk to the salvage claim of intervenor-appellee Portsmouth Harbor Towing ("PHT"). Because the district court predicated its order on a misunderstanding of the applicable law, we reverse.

I.

BACKGROUND

The Sea Hawk is a forty-five foot Hatteras sport-fishing boat built in 1974. David Kinchla, its owner during the time relevant to this case, purchased the boat in January 1988. In August, 1988, Kinchla granted a first preferred ship mortgage on the Sea Hawk to Atlantic Financial Federal Savings and Loan Association ("Atlantic"), which held Kinchla's $148,000 note executed in association with his purchase of the boat. Atlantic eventually went into receivership and was taken over by the Resolution Trust Corporation ("RTC"). On April 23, 1993, Faneuil purchased Kinchla's note and the preferred ship mortgage on the Sea Hawk from the RTC as part of a pool of fifty-six non-performing boat loans for a total price of $1,516,000.

As Kinchla's mortgage was making it through the receivership netherworld, Kinchla was losing his grip on the Seahawk. He stopped making payments on his note in May 1991 and filed a Chapter 11 bankruptcy petition on January 6, 1992. On June 3, 1992, the Sea Hawk broke loose from its mooring in the Hampton–Seabrook harbor ("Hampton Harbor") and drifted until it became snagged near the Hampton River Bridge. Harbormaster William J. Cronin, an employee of the New Hampshire State Port Authority, enlisted the aid of the U.S. Coast Guard, which towed the boat to the state pier in Hampton Harbor. Cronin contacted Kinchla, but Kinchla told Cronin that he had abandoned his interest in the boat and that the mortgage-holder intended to foreclose on it. Cronin testified at his deposition (which was admitted in evidence) that he attempted to reach the mortgage-holder but had no success, apparently due to the RTC receivership.[1] Because the state has no facility of its own at Hampton Harbor to store a boat as large as the Sea Hawk—the state pier being a busy, commercial fishing pier—Cronin arranged for one Ray Gilmore to take custody of the boat until its ownership could be sorted out, explaining to Gilmore that he would have a possessory lien on the boat for reasonable towing and storage fees.

On July 15, 1992, shortly after 5 a.m., Kinchla and his son attempted to retake possession of the Sea Hawk by surreptitiously removing it from Gilmore's mooring in the harbor and towing the vessel under the Hampton River Bridge and out to sea. They did not request an opening of the drawbridge, however, and in attempting to maneuver the Sea Hawk under the bridge, lost control of it in the current. The Sea Hawk slammed broadside into a bridge support, damaging the vessel's hull, and then slid under the bridge stern-first, damaging the boat's bridge-superstructure and outrigger tuna poles. The Coast Guard soon intercepted the Kinchlas and took them and the Sea Hawk back to the state pier. Kinchla told Harbormaster Cronin that his attorney had advised him to retake the boat; both Kinchla and his son were turned over to the police and Kinchla was arrested. Gilmore wanted no further involvement with the Sea Hawk, leaving Cronin once again with the problem of what to do with the beleagured boat.

Here the tales diverge. Steven Holt, one of PHT's partners, testified that Cronin contacted him and asked if PHT would tow the boat to Portsmouth, New Hampshire, and store it safely in dry storage. Holt claimed that, in a conference call with the Coast Guard, Cronin specifically told Holt that this would be a "salvage job." Cronin testified that he could not remember with whom he spoke at PHT, whether he mentioned the word "salvage," or even whether the topic of PHT's compensation ever came up. Cronin testified that in his mind, this was a tow job. In any event Holt accepted the task, and he and his son went to Hampton to bring back the Sea Hawk. Both Holt and Cronin inspected the boat and determined that it was in no danger of sinking despite the damage that it had just sustained.[2] Holt and his son then towed the boat out to open ocean and up the coast to Portsmouth Harbor, a two-and-one-half-hour trip.

Initially, PHT stored the boat at Patton's Yacht Yard in Eliot, Maine. Because PHT was paying for this storage out of its own pocket, however, and, ostensibly, for insurance reasons, PHT soon moved the Sea Hawk to its own dock in Portsmouth, where Holt and his partner, Walter Dunfey,

---

1. The record does not indicate exactly when Atlantic went into receivership.

2. Indeed, Holt was prepared to place his eleven-year-old son aboard the Sea Hawk

to help steer it on the trip back to Portsmouth, but changed his plans after determining that the Sea Hawk has lost its steering.

actively maintained the boat and performed some repairs. PHT attempted to contact the mortgage-holder on several occasions to establish their claim, but were unable to locate definitely any party claiming an interest in the boat.[3] PHT never brought an action to foreclose its claimed salvage lien.

Finally, on October 26, 1993, with the bankruptcy court's permission, Faneuil filed a complaint in the district court initiating this **in rem** proceeding against the Sea Hawk to foreclose its mortgage. Federal marshals arrested the vessel on December 2, 1993, and moved it to dry storage in Newington, New Hampshire. PHT intervened in January 1994 asserting its salvage lien. The Sea Hawk was sold at auction on April 22, 1994, yielding $32,537.20 after deductions for *custodia legis* expenses. That amount was placed in escrow, pending resolution of PHT's and Faneuil's competing claims to the sale proceeds. The amount due under Faneuil's mortgage at the time of the trial was $177,676; PHT claimed expenses of $24,606 plus attorney's fees of $6,279.04, or a total of $30,-885.04, in addition to a claimed salvage award of 20% of the value of the vessel.[4] Following a one-day bench trial, the district court held that, under the law of admiralty and the federal statutory scheme for disbursing proceeds from a foreclosure sale of a vessel, PHT had a valid salvage claim that had priority over Faneuil's preferred ship mortgage, and also that, because it had expended much time and effort in preserving the Sea Hawk while Faneuil's purchase was "a pig in a poke," the equities dictated that PHT should recover first. Finding all of PHT's expenses reasonable, the district court awarded PHT $32,885,[5] exhausting the sale proceeds. Faneuil now appeals, arguing that the district court erred in ruling that PHT had a claim for salvage or any other claim that should prime Faneuil's mortgage.[6]

II.

DISCUSSION

A. *Standard of Review*

We may not set aside the district court's factual findings unless they are clearly erroneous. * * *

3. On February 10, 1993, an attorney for PHT sent a letter to Prentiss Properties of Dallas, Texas, which assembled the loan documents for the RTC's pool of assets that Faneuil purchased, informing it of PHT's "salvage and storage claim." Faneuil apparently received this letter at some point, because it included it in the motion for relief from the automatic stay it filed in Kinchla's bankruptcy proceeding in the fall of 1993.

4. PHT's requested expenses included $1,205 in towing and repairs and $23,101 in marina charges, calculated at $1 per day per foot, or approximately $1,400 per month for sixteen months of storage. Great Bay Marina, which stored the Sea Hawk for the U.S.

Marshal pending the foreclosure sale, charged a total of $900 for a period of approximately five months.

5. This is $2,000 more than claimed. The court's mathematical error was apparently induced by PHT's trial brief, which contained the same $2,000 error.

6. Faneuil attacks on appeal other aspects of the district court's ruling, in particular its failure to make specific findings justifying the amount of PHT's salvage award. Our holding as to Faneuil's primary issue on appeal obviates the need for any discussion on those other issues.

B. The Statutory Scheme

* * * [The court explains that under Ship Mortgage Act of 1920, presently codified as 46 U.S.C. §§ 30101–31343, if the towing and storage represents merely the provision of necessaries to the vessel, they are primed by the mortgage, but if they constitute salvage, the mortgage claim imports a "preferred maritime lien" under the Act, and prime the mortgage.]

C. The Law of Salvage

The admiralty doctrine of salvage, which rewards volunteers who save ships from dangers at sea, is an equitable doctrine that dates back to the Romans. *Wijsmuller*, 702 F.2d at 337. To establish a salvage claim, PHT must prove three elements: " '1. A marine peril. 2. Service voluntarily rendered when not required as an existing duty or from a special contract. 3. Success in whole or in part, or service [contributing] to such success' " Clifford v. M/V Islander, 751 F.2d 1, 5 (1st Cir.1984)(Quoting The Sabine, 101 U.S. (11 Otto) 384, 25 L.Ed. 982 (1879)). In this case Faneuil contends that PHT's claim for salvage must fail because the Sea Hawk was never in "marine peril," which, as we stated in *Clifford*.

> occurs when a vessel is exposed to any actual or apprehended danger which might result in her destruction. "All services rendered at sea to a vessel in distress are salvage services. It is not necessary ... that the distress should be immediate and absolute; it will be sufficient if, at the time the assistance is rendered, the vessel has encountered any damage or misfortune which might possibly expose her to destruction if the services were not rendered." Reasonable apprehension of peril, whether actual or not, is enough.

751 F.2d at 5–6 (quoting M. Norris, The Law of Salvage § 63, at 97). Marine peril has been found to exist in a variety of circumstances, including where a vessel had run aground on a rocky ledge, *Wijsmuller*, 702 F.2d 333; was adrift with no power within a short distance of the coast, The Plymouth Rock, 9 F. 413 (S.D.N.Y.1881); was docked but was close to a fire, The John Swan, 50 F. 447 (S.D.N.Y.1892); was on course at sea but where its crew was stricken with yellow fever, Williamson v. The Alphonso, 30 F.Cas. 4 (C.C.Mass.1853). On the other hand, courts have found no marine peril where a vessel had been holed but was secured in calm weather and was not sinking. *Clifford*, 751 F.2d 1; had drifted out to sea during a hurricane but subsequently come to rest and held fast on a mooring in calm waters, Phelan v. Minges, 170 F.Supp 826 (D.Mass.1959); was adrift as a result of bad weather but could have returned to port under its own power once the weather cleared, The Viola, 52 F. 172 (C.C.Pa. 1892), aff'd, 55 F. 829 (3d Cir.1893).

PHT does not contend , and the district court did not find, that the damaged Sea Hawk was unseaworthy or in immediate danger of sinking when PHT took possession took possession of it at the state pier on July 15, 1992. The district court apparently predicated its finding that PHT had satisfied its burden with regard to "marine peril" on the fact that the Sea Hawk was essentially an orphaned vessel, and *eventually* "would have sunk or deteriorated to the point that it would have been a derelict or worthless hulk" had PHT not volunteered as guardian:[8]

> The peril was not immediate or absolute. Events as already related by this court showed that there was actual apprehension, though not of actual danger. Gilmore had washed his hands and would not longer deal with the Sea Hawk. Cronin, who seems to need a mnemonic, wanted an immediate solution so he would be freed of an untoward situation. The Coast Guard did what it had to do and disembarked from the scene.... But for PHT as heretofore stated and its expensive remedial action there is no doubt in the court's mind that the boat would have deteriorated and become valueless.

Faneuil Advisors v. Sea Hawk [sic], No. 93–549–L, 1994 WL 484380, at *4 (D.N.H.1994).

In holding that these circumstances constituted a reasonable apprehension of marine peril, the district court misreads the salvage cases holding that marine peril need not be immediate or absolute. While it is true that the threat need not be *imminent*, see, e.g., Williamson v. The Alphonso, F.Cas. No. 17749, the cases make apparent that the threat must be something more than the inevitable deterioration that any vessel left untended would suffer; otherwise ordinary maintenance, repairs and storage—i.e., "necessaries"—could easily give rise to salvage liens if a vessel's owner were particularly negligent in caring for his or her boat. Such a result could hardly be squared with the intent of the Ship Mortgage Act.

[handwritten margin note: Threat must be Something more than eventual deterioration]

Moreover, in stating that it had "no doubt" that the Sea Hawk would have become a worthless hulk without PHT's intervention, the district court glossed over an important fact: once the Sea Hawk was intercepted by the Coast Guard and delivered to Cronin at the state pier, the boat was in the custody of the State of New Hampshire, which certainly had the authority, and perhaps the duty to remove the vessel from the harbor and store it in a safe location. See, e.g., N.H.Rev.Stat.Ann. § 271–A:8 (1987)(giving harbormasters authority, *inter alia*, "to require the removal of vessels if necessity or an emergency arises"); N.H.Rev.Stat.Ann. §§ 270–B.1 to -B:7 (1987)(giving director of safety services or representative authority to impound or order the removal and storage of abandoned boats and imposing lien on such boats for all reasonable charges associated therewith). As already stated, the Sea Hawk was in no imminent danger of sinking. We fail to see how such a boat, in the safe custody of a state officer with statutory authority to provide for its safekeeping, can possibly

---

8. PHT advances other possible bases for a finding that marine peril existed: Cronin's testimony that he feared that Kinchla might return and try to steal the boat again or, even worse, that he might sink it for insurance proceeds, and that therefore Cronin had to remove the boat out of Hampton Harbor. This argument is preposterous. First, Kinchla had just been arrested for trying to retake the boat; he was not likely to make another attempt anytime soon. Sec-

ond, even if another attempt by Kinchla to seize his boat would have been unlawful, it would not necessarily have posed any grave peril to the *boat*. Third, Cronin's concern about Kinchla sinking the boat for insurance seems entirely unfounded: Kinchla was more than a year behind in his mortgage payments on the boat and the record contains no indication that Kinchla was any more punctual in paying insurance premiums.

be said to be facing "marine peril," or how any such peril could reasonably be apprehended.

The district court stated that Cronin "wanted an immediate solution so he would be freed of an untoward situation." Id. This is not marine peril; it is mere inconvenience, and the state cannot transform an unwanted tow and store job into a salvage job simply by declaring it to be such (if that is in fact what Cronin attempted to do, as Holt's testimony suggests). We have scoured the salvage cases and located not a single one in which a seaworthy vessel in the safe possession of the state was found to be in marine peril. Thus we hold that the district court's finding that there was reasonable apprehension of marine peril incorporated clearly erroneous factual assumptions and was predicated on an erroneous understanding of the applicable law. We hold that, under these circumstances, PHT has failed to prove marine peril or reasonable apprehension thereof, and therefore it has failed to prove an essential element of its salvage claim.

D.   The District Court's alternative Holding.

We have also considered whether PHT might be entitled to recover on the basis of the district court's implicit alternative ground for its holding—namely, that "[i]t is not fair or equitable that the plaintiff should reap the benefits bestowed on the Sea Hawk by [PHT] when it contributed nothing to its well being." *Faneuil Advisers,* 1994 WL 484380, at *4. Nevertheless, the statutory scheme permits no contrary conclusion: Congress clearly intended to afford holders of preferred ship mortgages considerable protections against irresponsible actions by ship owners, and the exceptions to their priority status are explicitly spelled out. See 46 U.S.C. §§ 31301(5), 31326(b)(1). A lien for necessaries, even one obtained by a state or its agent under state law, is not among those exceptions. In fact any argument that such a lien may have priority would appear to be entirely foreclosed by 46 U.S.C. § 31307: "This chapter supersedes any State statute conferring a lien on a vessel to the extent the statute establishes a claim to be enforced by a civil action in rem against the vessel for necessaries."[9]

While the results we reach may appear harsh, the priority scheme simply allows for no judicial reordering on expansive notions of equity where the mortgage holder has engaged in no inequitable conduct that might justify subordination of his claim. See Maryland National Bank v. The Vessel Madam Chapel, 46 F.3d 895, 901–902 (9th Cir.1995)(holding that equitable subordination generally requires inequitable conduct by mortgagee and reversing order that subordinated preferred ship mortgage). It may well be that other doctrines might supply some basis for relief in cases such as this one. But no such argument has been made on appeal,

---

9. That a state statutory lien is superseded should come as no surprise; not even the federal government's claims against a vessel are given special dispensation from the priority scheme. See General Electric Credit Corp. v. Oil Screw Triton, VI, 712 F.2d 991, 995 (5th Cir.1983) (holding that government's claim for expenses in capturing and preserving vessel seized for violation of narcotics laws—incurred before ship came within court's custody—could not be classified as *custodia legis* expenses, and thus were primed by preferred ship mortgage).

and this is hardly a case for us to attempt to find a basis on which to remand in order to explore issues that have never been raised.

CONCLUSION

For the foregoing reasons, the order of the district court is

Reversed.   Costs to appellant.

N O T E

A vessel need not be in extremis to be in peril, however.   In Beach Salvage Corp. v. The Cap't. Tom and Tom R. Jr., 201 F.Supp. 479, 1961 A.M.C. 2244 (S.D.Fla.1961) the court awarded salvage in a case in which two shrimp boats were stranded on the beach, observing that any vessel aground on the beaches of northern Florida is in danger even if the weather conditions are presently favorable.   On the other hand, a vessel may be in relatively bad condition and still be in no danger.   See, e.g., The J.C. Pfluger, 109 Fed. 93 (N.D.Cal.1901) where the vessel had lost "mainmast and mizzen topmast, fore-topsail, and fore royal yard," all carried away in a "squall of great violence," and was held to be in no danger in view of the fact that she had come about 200 miles with a "foresail, fore-topmast staysail, spanker, and jibs" and the services touted as salvage consisted of towing her in a dead calm for the last 12 miles.

D.   ACTS CONSTITUTING SALVAGE SERVICES

Saint Paul Marine Transp. Corp. v. Cerro Sales Corp.

United States Court of Appeals, Ninth Circuit, 1974.
505 F.2d 1115, 1975 A.M.C. 503.

■ SPENCER WILLIAMS, DISTRICT JUDGE. Early in the morning of June 23, 1968 the crew of the SS North America, a small Liberian tramp freighter, abandoned its flaming vessel approximately 600 miles east-southeast of Honolulu.   The ship's $1,850,000 cargo of copper concentrates bound for South America belonged to appellant Cerro Sales.   The U.S. Coast Guard picked up the crew's distress signal and at approximately 1515 (HST) directed the M/V St. Paul, a huge Liberian bulk carrier to proceed some 30 miles to render assistance to the disabled vessel.   The St. Paul swept the area for some time, rescued 22 survivors and then turned its attention to saving the ship.

Crewmen from St. Paul under the leadership of Second Mate Anastasio boarded the North America that afternoon and again the next day.   While the testimony is conflicting as to what happened on the respective days, it is clear that they extinguished several small fires, cleared the decks of burning material, closed several open doors, and on the second trip rigged an emergency towing wire from the North America's bow to the St. Paul's stern.   The towing attempt was discontinued when the line snapped.   On

June 24th the St. Paul obtained Coast Guard permission to leave and proceed to Honolulu, where the North America's crew was put ashore.

The Hawaiian tug Malie, engaged by owners of the North America, left Honolulu June 28th, reached the distressed ship five days later, took it in tow and returned with it to Honolulu. The North America was sold as scrap but the $1.85 million cargo was saved intact.

The district court, in an opinion reported at 332 F.Supp. 233 (D.Haw. 1971), granted plaintiff a salvage award of $200,000, 65% to go to the vessel St. Paul and her owners with the remaining 35% to go to the officers and the crew. An extra $1000 was granted to Second Mate Anastasio and $500 to each other member of the boarding party.

Cerro Sales appeals the decision on six grounds: (1) all the actions of the vessel St. Paul were taken for the purpose of rescuing the crew of the North America—not for saving property—and therefore, the St. Paul and the non-boarding crew members are not entitled to a property award; (2) the master and crew are not parties to this purported class action; (3) plaintiffs did not sustain the burden of proving their activities saved the North America and her cargo; (4) the St. Paul, having voluntarily abandoned the North America, is precluded from a salvage award; (5) the district court erred in refusing to reopen the case to take testimony from a witness after a decision was entered; and (6) the amount of the award was unreasonable in relation to the services performed.

) The Award to the Owner and Non–Boarding Crew Members

Appellant contends only crew members who went aboard the North America performed salvage acts with respect to the North America's cargo and this precludes the St. Paul's owner and the non-boarding crew members from sharing in the salvage award. This position is contrary to established admiralty law. All who render service in a salvage operation may share in an award. Each individual need not actively participate by manning the small boats, boarding the salved vessel or fighting fires. Norris, The Law of Salvage § 48. Every man's duties on the salving ship contribute to the property salvage and the law extends a portion of the award to even a "scullion in the galley peeling potatoes while the actual salvage work is going on." The Centurion, 1 Ware 490 (D.Me.1839). See also The Norden, 1 Spinks 185 (1853); The Barge Ulak, 1924 A.M.C. 1500 (S.D.N.Y.1924).

Similarly, the owner of the salving vessel need not personally participate in the salvage service to receive an award. Norris, supra, § 57; The Blackwall, 77 U.S. 1, 10 Wall. 1, 19 L.Ed. 870 (1869); The Camanche, 75 U.S. 448, 8 Wall. 448, 19 L.Ed. 397 (1869); Sears v. S.S. American Producer, 1972 A.M.C. 1647 (N.D.Cal.1972); Conolly v. SS Karina II, 302 F.Supp. 675 (E.D.N.Y.1969).[1]

---

1. Appellant also points out that proceeding to the disabled ship, rescuing survivors, searching for lost crew members and transporting the survivors to Honolulu were actions directed at "life salvage." If this was all that had been done by the St. Paul, plain-

2) Class Action Requirements

This action was properly maintained by the St. Paul on its own behalf and on the behalf of the master and crew and is not subject to Federal Rule of Civil Procedure 23.

Admiralty courts have long accepted the obvious judicial economy in maritime representative suits to allow owners of salving vessels to sue on behalf of the master and crew although judgments in such suits do not provide complete theoretical protection to the defendants. The Camanche, supra, at 470–77, 2 Benedict, Law of American Admiralty § 247. See 1 Benedict, supra, § 123, The Lowther Castle, 195 F. 604 (D.N.J.1912); The Neptune, 277 F. 230 (2d Cir.1921).[2]

4) Defense and Abandonment

Appellant had the burden of proving the affirmative defense of abandonment. If a potential salvor does abandon a distressed vessel, it is precluded from any award. The abandonment, however, must be voluntary, absolute and of such nature that indicates an absence of all further interest in the property or an indifference to whether it will be saved or not. The Loch Garve, 182 F. 519 (9th Cir.1910); The City of Puebla, 153 F. 925 (N.D.Cal. 1907); The Strathnevis, 76 F. 855 (D.Wash.1896); The Angeline Anderson, 34 F. 925 (D.N.Y.1888); The Khio, 46 F. 207 (C.C.Md.1891); The Aberdeen, 27 F. 479 (E.D.N.Y.1885); The Tolomeo, 7 F. 497 (S.D.Fla.1881). Therefore, if a salving vessel, after doing all it can and having contributed to the salvage of the vessel, finds it impossible to continue and complete the entire salvage, the doctrine of abandonment does not apply. The Fisher's Hill, 1953 A.M.C. 2037 (S.D.N.Y.1953), rev'd sub nom. Lago Oil and Transport Co. v. United States, 218 F.2d 631 (2d Cir.1955); Atlantic Transport Co. v. United States, 42 F.2d 583 (Ct.Cl.1930); The Strathnevis, supra. The District Court found that the St. Paul had not abandoned the North America, and in view of the evidence of the attempted (though unsuccessful) tow, the boarding of the vessel, the extinguishment of deck fires, clearing of burning material, closing of open doors, notification to the Coast Guard of the North America's position and the St. Paul's remaining on station until authorized to depart, it cannot be said that such a finding is clearly erroneous.[3]

---

tiffs would be limited to an action against the tug Malie for a share of its property award under 46 U.S.C. § 729. The fire fighting and closing of doors were directed at saving the cargo and have given the owner and the non-boarding crew members a right to participate in any salvage award. See St. Paul v. Cerro Sales, 313 F.Supp. 377 (D.Hawaii 1970).

2. The Advisory Committee on the Federal Rules of Civil Procedure, commenting on the merger of admiralty and civil practice, treated representative marine salvage suits

under Rule 17(a) and not under Rule 23. See 7A Moore's Federal Practice ¶ .55(3).

3. The defendant suggests the plaintiff should have attempted more than one tow, searched below deck for water leaks and additional fires, rigged navigational running lights and left a crew to stand watch until a salvage tug arrived. A suggested course of conduct made with the benefit of "20–20" hindsight does not alter an appellate court's standard of review over district court factual determinations.

Refusal to Reopen Testimony

* * *

Factual Support for the District Court's Findings

Defendant vigorously asserts the record does not support the district court's determination that the firefighting and the closing of certain apertures significantly contributed to the salvage of the vessel and her cargo.[4]   The record contains over 850 pages of reporter's transcripts, two depositions of witnesses upon written interrogatories and four depositions on oral interrogatories along with innumerable photographs, log books and transcriptions of radio messages.   Additionally, the circumstances surrounding the presentation of evidence were somewhat unusual given the international composition of the crew, numerous language difficulties, and the time-lag between the accident, when the statements were taken and the trial.

The trier of fact has the duty to sift through the inconsistencies of testimony, to weigh the credibility of witnesses and to resolve any ambiguities in the evidence.   The scope of appellate review is a narrow one limited to setting aside findings of fact only when they are clearly erroneous.   Federal Rule of Civil Procedure 52(a);   Guzman v. Pichirilo, 369 U.S. 698, 82 S.Ct. 1095, 8 L.Ed.2d 205 (1962).

The trial court found that (1) a crew from the St. Paul boarded the North America June 23rd, (2) a second party went aboard on June 24th, (3) crew members closed open doors and portholes,[5] (4) the North America's stern was down and her freeboard was less than normal, (5) the crew extinguished numerous fires on the deck, hatch covers and threw burning debris into the sea, and (6) but for these activities the North America would have sunk.

The district court relied quite heavily on the testimony of John Walsh, plaintiff's expert witness,[6] in making its award.   Answering a hypothetical question, Walsh testified that, in his opinion, two series of acts performed

---

4.   The district court correctly discounted all activities directed at life salvage from its consideration of the property salvage award and also noted that the "bare attempt" to tow the North America had not contributed to the ultimate salvage of the cargo.

5.   Defendant belatedly objects that certain statements made by Seaman DiColo were inadmissible hearsay and therefore, improperly considered by the district court. Counsel must make and preserve his record at the trial level and may not present new objections on appeal.   The record clearly shows that defendant waived any objection to the admissibility of the statement on two occasions.   Reporter's Transcript at Pages 12 and 147.

6.   "Probably the most significant evidence presented came from Mr. John Walsh, an expert witness presented by plaintiff, and one of three surveyors who surveyed the North America upon her arrival at Honolulu. Mr. Walsh has impressive credentials and presented himself and his testimony in a manner most persuasive upon the Court." See 332 F.Supp. 233, at 237–238 (D.Hawaii 1971).

by the St. Paul's crew saved the ship.[7] He concluded that without the firefighting action by the crew, the fire would have spread to the No. 5 hatch and the after accommodation house. The hold under No. 5 hatch would then have been open to sea water.[8] If the after accommodation house had burned, the portholes below decks would have disintegrated and have been open to the sea. As noted, these portholes were partially submerged when the North America reached Honolulu. Therefore, but for the firefighting actions, sea water would have flowed into both the aft-hold of the ship and into the after accommodation house through the open portholes. Walsh emphasized that had either one or both of these events occurred, the North America would have sunk.[9]

Walsh also testified that, independent of the fire-fighting, the closing of open doors and portholes contributed to the ultimate salvage of the cargo. The stern was down when the salvage tug Malie reached the North America, her freeboard was less than normal and the surveyors ultimately found approximately 15 feet of water in the engine spaces. Walsh persuaded the court that any sea water that had been kept out of the ship could well have been the overbalancing amount that would have sunk her. When the salvors closed the doors and portholes, they prevented the awash deck conditions and the lack of freeboard from reaching a critical point thus keeping the North America afloat until the salvage tug reached her.

This expert opinion, obviously persuasive to the district court, is properly supported by facts in the record. The determination that the St. Paul's crew saved the defendant's cargo is therefore not clearly erroneous.

The Size of the Award

Of the $200,000 awarded, $130,000 (65%) went to the St. Paul and her owners, [including $15,000 for reimbursement of costs and expenses], and $70,000 went to the officers and crew. Appellant argues this award is

---

7. Plaintiff asked Walsh to assume the following facts before giving his expert opinion:

    (1) a boarding party had gone aboard the North America,

    (2) members of that party had extinguished the following small fires:

        (a) debris fires in the area between No. 4 and No. 5 hatches,

        (b) small fires in the after area of No. 4 hatch,

        (c) other fires in the area of No. 3 hatch,

    (3) threw burning boards and other items overboard from the areas around both No. 3 and No. 4 hatches,

    (4) neither No. 5 hatch cover was damaged by fire nor the after accommodation house was damaged by fire,

    (5) the aft portholes were partially submerged before the vessel reached Honolulu, and

    (6) the North America had a freeboard of less than normal when she was towed to safety in Honolulu.

The testimony of the various witnesses, although varying to some degree, placed all the above facts before the court.

8. Walsh testified that this would have caused the aft end to submerge and/or increase the "probability of a decisive free-surface area in No. 4 hold," (i.e. cause the North America to roll heavily in a very sluggish manner allowing the sea to break over the open deck).

9. Reporter's Transcript Page 360.

"grotesquely excessive" in relation to the labor expended and the risks incurred.

The Supreme Court has suggested the following criteria for determining an appropriate salvage award: (1) the labor expended by the salvors in rendering the salvage services, (2) the promptitude, skill and energy displayed in rendering the service and saving the property, (3) the risk incurred by the salvors in securing the property from its peril, (4) the value of the property saved, (5) the degree of danger from which the property was rescued, and (6) the value of the property employed by the salvors and the danger to which the property was exposed. The Blackwall, 77 U.S. 1, 13–14, 10 Wall. 1, 19 L.Ed. 870 (1869).

These guidelines have weathered the storms of the past century. See *Norris*, supra, at 386 (1958); Seaman v. Tank Barge OC601, 325 F.Supp. 1206, 1208–1209 (S.D.Ala.1971). An inspection of the district court's opinion in this case indicates that in making the award he applied factors analogous to these guidelines.

The St. Paul, her master and crew performed in careful, seamanlike fashion while boarding the burning ship, fighting the fires, sealing off the lower spaces and attempting to tow the North America; they willingly exposed themselves to considerable danger by boarding a burning, disabled vessel under the threat of continuing explosions. The danger of collision between the two ships during the abortive towing operation was extremely high due to the North America's short tow line. The salvaged property had a stipulated value of $1.85 million and was in imminent danger of being lost when the North America was saved. The St. Paul, carrying a cargo valued at $750,000, was worth over $4 million.[10]

Appellant further contends that any dangers to which the St. Paul and her cargo were exposed during the unsuccessful towing attempt must be disregarded when determining the size of the award.[11] Admiralty courts award property salvage as a matter of public policy to induce future potential salvors to assume the inconvenience and unknown risk inherent in every salvage effort.[12]

---

10. Statistical comparisons, while not dispositive, can be helpful. The owners of the St. Paul received a $130,000 award or less than 3% of the combined value of the St. Paul and its cargo that had been exposed to risk of loss during the salvage operation.

The $200,000 salvage award is approximately 11% of the value of appellant's cargo that would have been lost but for the St. Paul and her crew.

11. Merritt & Chapman Derrick & Wrecking Co. v. United States, 274 U.S. 611, 47 S.Ct. 663, 71 L.Ed. 1232 (1926), cited by defendant, does not support its position. In that case, a vessel, lying next to a blazing pier, was cooled by an overflow of water that had been directed at the pier fire. The Supreme Court refused to allow a salvage award on the grounds that any aid to the ship was both unrequested and merely incidental.

12. Waterman SS Corporation v. Dean, 171 F.2d 408 (4th Cir.1948), cert. denied 337 U.S. 924, 69 S.Ct. 1168, 93 L.Ed. 1732 (1949); The Kia Ora, 252 F. 507 (4th Cir.1918); United States v. Aslaksen, 281 F. 444 (6th Cir.1922); The Varzin, 180 F. 892, aff'd 185 F. 1007 (2d Cir.1910); The Philah, 19 F.Cas. 494 (D.Fla.1857). See also, Dize v. Steel Barge Beverley, 247 F.Supp. 968, 973 (E.D.Va.1965).

The question thus becomes whether, as a matter of public policy, the courts should consider only the risks inherent in a ship's good faith attempts at rescue that are actually shown to have contributed to the rescue.[13]

The evidence indicates the St. Paul's master, although apprehensive of the risks involved, told his owners he would attempt to tow the North America to safety.[14] He sent members of his crew aboard the North America to extinguish the fires and to rig the ship for towing. These activities were interrelated portions of the salvage operation which, *in toto*, saved the cargo. Portions of that successful salvage may not be discounted when figuring the size of the award. To do so would discourage future salvors from attempting similar acts when given the opportunity to render assistance and frustrate the policy underlying marine salvage awards.

It would be unwise to accept appellant's totally unsupported premise that unsuccessful efforts contained within the context of an overall successful salvage operation may not be considered. A successful salvage must be viewed as one continuum from beginning to end. Any other rule would require courts to make speculative and unreasonable dissections of complex, multi-faceted salvage operations. By way of example, if defendant's rule were applied to the plaintiff's activities in this action, the trial court would be required to determine the quantum of risk and the contribution to the ultimate salvage of each extinguished fire, each closed porthole and question whether each man who boarded the disabled ship successfully extinguished a fire or closed a crucial door. This type of determination has not been required to date and nothing warrants the implementation of such a restrictive rule.

However, the $15,000 reimbursement for costs, included in the owner's $135,000 award, was erroneously computed on an alleged three-day effort during the salvage operation. The St. Paul was only engaged for 25.5 hours and the $3,840.00 daily cost estimate was unrefuted. The award for costs will therefore be reduced to $4,070.40.

The judgment of the district court is affirmed with the reduction of the owner's share to $124,070.40.

■ Eugene A. Wright, Circuit Judge (concurring):

I concur in Judge Williams' opinion with the following additional comments concerning the issue of abandonment.

As Judge Williams points out, if the distressed ship is ultimately saved, the general rule that an abandoning salvor forfeits a salvage award does not preclude an award simply because the salvor does not complete the task of saving the distressed ship. See The Fisher's Hill, 1953 A.M.C. 2037 (S.D.N.Y.), rev'd sub nom. on other grounds Lago Oil and Transport Co. v.

---

13. Success is a prerequisite to any salvage award. Courts will not reward any efforts, however meritorious, if the property is not ultimately saved. However, the St. Paul and her crew *were* successful in saving both the ship and her copper cargo.

14. See Exhibits P–5(a), P–16, P–37, P–41, and P–42.

United States, 218 F.2d 631 (2d Cir.1955); Atlantic Transport Co. v. United States, 42 F.2d 583 (Ct.Cl.1930); The Strathnevis, 76 F. 855 (D.Wash.1896), and cases cited therein. Appellant argues that in these cases mechanical disability or weather conditions rendered further salvage efforts *impossible,* whereas no similar circumstances accompanied *St. Paul's* departure from the disabled *North America.* *St. Paul* was simply unable to take *North America* safely in tow.

The purpose of salvage awards and the abandonment rule dictate that we reject the contention that an award for a partial salvage be predicated upon the physical *impossibility* of further effort. Salvage awards encourage mariners to aid ships in distress. See Atlantic Transport Co. v. United States, supra, 42 F.2d at 589. Similarly, the abandonment rule encourages those who do aid distressed vessels to maximize their efforts and to discourage them from quitting the salvage before doing all that reasonably can be done. But where more cannot reasonably be accomplished and the distressed ship is ultimately saved, it serves no purpose to deny an award.

Indeed, a contrary rule would discourage potential salvors from giving assistance if they thought that they could not complete the salvage by towing the distressed ship to port. Significantly for this case, the disincentive to give partial assistance to the best of one's ability does not depend on whether the obstacle to further aid is physical impossibility or, as here, impracticality due to the relative values of the vessels and the risks involved. We should not insert such dissuasion into the law.

The reasoning of the court in Atlantic Transport Co. v. United States, id., did not depend on the fact that further salvage efforts were physically impossible:

> Where a vessel is in distress, in peril and danger, as here, or where the sea is rough and the weather unfavorable and the wind high, or where other facts which usually attend a vessel in distress exist, there is always a risk and danger in rendering assistance. It is easier for another vessel to stay out of the way or to pass by and not attempt to render assistance than it is to undertake the risk of doing so and incur a risk of injury to itself and a possible loss of life and cargo in connection with the effort. It has therefore been the policy of the courts, in order to encourage salvaging and the saving of life and property at sea, to be liberal in the matter of salvage where the vessel has made an honest effort to be of assistance or has joined with others in doing so, whether its efforts resulted in the final saving of the vessel or not, provided the failure of final success was not due to any lack of honest effort and willing purpose to assist. * * * "It is not necessary, in order to establish a claim to salvage, that the salvor should actually complete the work of saving the property at risk. It is sufficient if he endeavor to do so, and his efforts have a *causal* relation to the eventual preservation of it."

The court's reasoning supports an award under the circumstances of this case.

Of course, the salvor must show that it did what it reasonably could do and that his effort had "a causal relation to the eventual preservation of" the ship. But this is a factual question to be resolved by the trier of fact.

The district court apparently agreed with appellees that *St. Paul* "made an honest effort to be of assistance," that she did all that she reasonably could do under the circumstances, and that she did not "abandon" *North America*. I cannot conclude that this finding is "clearly erroneous."

■ HUFSTEDLER, CIRCUIT JUDGE (dissenting):

The crew of the Saint Paul performed ably and courageously in rescuing crewmen from the North America and in boarding her later in an attempt to salvage the vessel and her cargo. But our admiration for the men of the Saint Paul is not a substitute for evidence that the efforts of the boarding parties meaningfully contributed to the ultimately successful salvage by the tug Malie.

The key district court findings were that the boarding parties closed doors and portholes in the after accommodations and that without that action seawater would have entered the vessel through these apertures in such quantities that the vessel could have sunk before the Malie reached her. No one testified that anyone closed portholes. The porthole finding is based solely on DiColo's unsworn statement in Italian annexed to his deposition. The Italian statement was accompanied by an English translation that does not mention portholes. Porthole closing entered the case for the first and only time when plaintiff's in-court translator was trying to interpret DiColo's unsworn statement. Of course, the DiColo statement was inadmissible hearsay even if the translator correctly interpreted it, a dubious assumption under the circumstances. Plaintiffs do not question its hearsay character; rather, they argue that defendant waived objection when it failed to object upon the initial offer of the document. The document was offered, along with a number of other documents, under a single number before any testimony was taken. Defendant's counsel reserved the right to correct the translation. After plaintiff's translator testified, defendant's counsel moved to strike the unsworn statement, and the motion was denied. The motion should have been granted. On these facts, no predicate exists for a waiver of the hearsay objection.

Testimony is in the record that the boarders closed one or more of the poop house doors. For two reasons the door closing episode cannot sustain the district court's further finding that the boarding crew's activities contributed to salvaging the vessel: first, neither the plaintiff's expert nor the court attempted to decide what effect door closing would have had on the vessel if portholes had not also been closed;[1] second, no substantial evidence, direct or circumstantial, supported an inference that the amount of water that was prevented from entering the vessel through the closing of one or more doors in the poop house could have been enough to sink the vessel.

---

1. Mr. Walsh, the plaintiff's expert witness, based his opinion that the plaintiff's efforts contributed to the salvage upon hypothetical questions. When the facts in a hypothetical are not supported by the record, the foundation for the expert's opinion obviously collapses.

Entirely apart from these deficiencies in the evidence, the Saint Paul is foreclosed from any recovery because she abandoned the North America. The Saint Paul conducted vigorous and successful efforts in rescuing the crew of the North America. In contrast, her attempt, after the crew were rescued, to salvage the vessel was brief, sporadic, and ineffectual. She did not have adequate equipment to make more than a passing try to salvage the North America. After her insufficient towline parted, she gave up any further salvage operations and left. Her departure was voluntary; she was not dismissed, superseded, or disabled by her salvage attempt. She is not to be criticized for deciding that the risks to herself were too great to undertake any further salvage efforts, but neither is she entitled to a salvage award after she voluntarily abandoned the North America. The district court's finding that she did not abandon the vessel is unsupported by the record and is thus clearly erroneous.

The important purposes served by salvage awards and the abandonment rule are impaired, not promoted, by permitting those whose contributions to ultimate salvage are as slight as those performed by the Saint Paul to share in the salvage award. Heroic efforts to salvage are not likely to be made by salvors knowing that any ultimate bounty will be shared handsomely with any potential salvage claimant who made any fleeting effort toward salvage.

I have no occasion to reach any of the other issues. I would reverse.

NOTE

Given the requisite peril, anything that aids in the extrication of the vessel can constitute a salvage service. Perhaps the limiting case is South American S.S. Co. v. Atlantic Towing Co. 22 F.2d 16 (5th Cir.1927). In that case a steamship, listing badly because of a shift in cargo, was on its way in to Savannah. A tug was sent out to meet it and offered its services to tow it in. The steamship rejected the services and continued on its way. The tug took soundings and finding the water shallow, overtook the steamship and warned it that it was approaching shallow water, advising a change of course. The advice was taken and the steamship made the harbor without damage. If it had proceeded along its original course, it would have been certain to go ashore. Of course the service rendered in the *South American S.S.* case was accomplished without any great danger to the salvaging vessel. Sometimes, however, services that appear peripheral to salvage may be very dangerous. See, e.g., Petition of the United States, 229 F.Supp. 241, 1963 A.M.C. 1469 (D.Or.1963). There a fishing boat, having crossed Gray's Harbor Bar, turned back to render assistance to a Coast Guard vessel that was in difficulty. The skipper of the Coast Guard vessel requested the fishing boat to contact the Coast Guard station by radio. She did. In the course of its mission of aid, however, the fishing boat capsized with a loss of two men.

When the vessel is derelict, or on the bottom, the usual salvage act is to bring it in or raise it and bring it in. In such cases the disputation is often between several parties each claiming to have aided in the process. See *Schooner Brindicate II,* infra, p. 696.

E.   NECESSITY FOR REQUEST

Merritt & Chapman Derrick & Wrecking Co. v. United States

Supreme Court of the United States, 1927.
274 U.S. 611, 47 S.Ct. 663, 71 L.Ed. 1232.

■ MR. JUSTICE BUTLER delivered the opinion of the Court.

Plaintiff in error sued under the Tucker Act, c. 359, 24 Stat. 505, upon a claim for salvage on account of service alleged to have been rendered the Steamship Leviathan owned by the defendant in error. United States v. Cornell Steamboat Co., 202 U.S. 184, 189, 26 S.Ct. 648, 50 L.Ed. 987 (1906). On defendant's motion the court, May 7, 1925, dismissed the petition on the ground that it fails to state a cause of action. The case is here on writ of error to that court. J. Homer Fritch, Inc. v. United States, 248 U.S. 458, 39 S.Ct. 158, 63 L.Ed. 359 (1919).

The petition alleges the following. August 24–25, 1921, at Hoboken, there was a fierce and extensive fire on Pier 5. The Leviathan lay bow in at the south side of Pier 4. She could not be towed out. She had only a skeleton crew, and it would have required a large number to man her and many hours of preparation to get up sufficient steam and move her by means of her own engines. The fire started at half after six in the evening and was not extinguished until seven in the morning. A part of the time it covered the whole length of Pier 5, the bulkhead and adjacent houses. The wind was from the south and tended to carry the fire across the slip and onto the Leviathan. Her port side was considerably scorched, and several times fire broke out on her superstructure. Ammunition was stored in a building near the bulkhead, and the possibility of an explosion added to the danger. Plaintiff's steamers Commissioner and Chapman Brothers were powerful boats, specially built, equipped and manned for salvage and fire fighting service. The former from seven until half after nine in the evening and the latter from about seven in the evening until seven in the morning continuously fought the fire. They played heavy streams of water on the burning pier where the fire threatened the Leviathan. And, by way of conclusion, it is stated that "The service was a direct aid and benefit to the steamer Leviathan in preventing the spread of flames from Pier 5 to that vessel, and had it not been for the said service great damage to, if not total loss of, the said steamship would have resulted." Limiting the general statement by the specific, in accordance with the context, (United States v. Union Pacific R. Co., 169 F. 65, 67 (8 Cir.1909) and cases cited) the substance of the allegation is that plaintiff in error, by preventing the spread of the fire from the pier to the Leviathan, rendered her direct aid and benefit.

There is no claim that the Leviathan, or any one in her behalf, requested or accepted assistance from plaintiff in error, or that its fireboats played any water on that vessel or did anything to extinguish fire thereon or to give her any assistance other than that involved in fighting the fire on and about Pier 5. The distance between the Leviathan and that fire is not stated, and there is nothing to indicate that she did not have adequate protection from other sources. Indeed, the circumstances disclosed by the petition rather tend to show that she did not need any assistance from plaintiff in error.

While salvage cannot be exacted for assistance forced upon a ship (The Bolivar v. The Chalmette, 1 Woods C.C. 397), her request for or express acceptance of the service is not always essential to the validity of the claim. It is enough if under the circumstances any prudent man would have accepted. The Annapolis (In the Privy Council), Lushington 355, 375. Plaintiff in error claims as a volunteer salvor going at his own risk to the assistance of the ship on the chance of reward in case of success, and not as one employed rendering service for pay according to his effort or the terms of his contract. The Sabine, 101 U.S. 384, 390, 25 L.Ed. 982. It did not communicate with or enter into the service of the Leviathan. Its fireboats did not put water upon her. The fires that started on her were put out by other means. All effort of plaintiff in error was put forth directly for the purpose of extinguishing fire at and about Pier 5 and to save property not at all relating to the Leviathan. The elimination of that fire contributed mediately to her safety. But, whatever the aid or benefit resulting to her, it was incidental and indirect for which, in the absence of request for or acceptance of the service, a claim for salvage cannot be sustained. *The Annapolis,* supra; The City of Atlanta, 56 F. 252, 254 (2 Cir.1893); The San Cristobal, 215 F. 615 (6 Cir.1914); Id. 230 F. 599 (5 Cir.1916).

Judgment affirmed.

F.   Conduct Forfeiting a Salvage Award

M/T Norseman

United States District Court, District of Puerto Rico, 1967.
1967 A.M.C. 1531.

■ Pierson M. Hall, D.J. * * *

Conclusions of Law

1.   This Court has jurisdiction over the parties and subject matter of this action.

2.   To sustain a claim for marine salvage, a plaintiff must prove that he voluntarily rendered services which preserved, or contributed to the preservation of, imperiled marine property. Blackwall, 77 U.S. 1, 12, 19 L.Ed. 870 (1869).

3. Where a number of groups combine their efforts to salve property, the Court must determine the value of each individual contribution to the overall effort. The fact that certain salvors either cannot or do not claim salvage inures to the benefit of the owners of the salved property, and does not increase the fair proportion of the claiming salvors. Dize v. Steel Barge Beverley, 247 F.Supp. 968, 973, 1965 A.M.C. 1886 (E.D.Va.1965), and cases there cited.

4. In the case at bar, it is apparent that those primarily responsible for putting out the fires on the *Norseman* were United States Coast Guard personnel from the cutter *Sagebrush*. Indeed, there is no persuasive evidence that the efforts of the plaintiffs and intervenor had any significant effect on the fires. Plaintiffs and the intervenor did perform certain intermittent services prior to the time the *Norseman* returned to Commonwealth's pier. In the absence of misconduct on their part, the Court would have to evaluate their contribution within the context of the total salvage effort. However, defendants have pleaded the defense of salvors' misconduct. Accordingly the Court must determine, at the threshold of the case, whether plaintiffs and the intervenor were guilty of such misconduct as to work a forfeiture of any salvage award or *quantum meruit* compensation, to which they might otherwise be entitled.

5. While honest salvors are liberally rewarded, the law also requires of salvors "the most scrupulous fidelity," Island City, 66 U.S. 121, 130, 17 L.Ed. 70 (1861). Salvors who embezzle any distressed property forfeit not only an award for salvage, but, by way of penalty for their fraud, quantum meruit compensation for their services. Island City, supra; Mason v. Blaireau, 6 U.S. 240, 266 (1804); Bello Corrunes, 19 U.S. 152, 173, 5 L.Ed. 229 (1821); Danner v. United States, 99 F.Supp. 880, 884–885, 1951 A.M.C. 1495 (S.D.N.Y.1951).

6. "Salvors are responsible for the reasonable care of the property which they take in charge," Bremen, 111 F. 228, 234 (S.D.N.Y.1901). Accordingly salvors are under a duty to obtain additional assistance, if the circumstances permit and they are not competent to deal with the peril by themselves. Similarly, salvors must not unreasonably refuse assistance from other, better equipped vessels, Yan–Yean, 8 P.D. 147, 149–150 (1883); or make false statements or misrepresentations "in order to secure the salvage work," Norris, *The Law of Salvage* (1958) at page 215; Pocomoke, 173 F. 94 (S.D.N.Y.1909)(claim for salving a barge disallowed on showing that salving tugs misrepresented to barge instructions received from barge's own tug). Salvor's misconduct in these regards will, in a sufficiently aggravated case, forfeit their right to any award.

7. Salvors also forfeit any award if it appears that they have persistently and deliberately exaggerated their services. Relatively slight errors or exaggerations are excused, if not "so flagrant as to warrant the inference of bad faith or of fraudulent misrepresentation," Bremen, supra, at 111 F. 239. In the cited case, Judge Addison Brown went on to observe, in words fully applicable to the present plaintiffs and intervenor:

"To this an exception should be made as respects the testimony of Capt. Blake of the Mattie, and of all the witnesses for the Volunteer except the pilot. The effort of these witnesses was evidently to make their services appear to have been rendered from the very beginning, whereas there can be no doubt from other testimony and circumstances that those tugs did not join the Bremen until about 7 p.m. For boldness and persistent effrontery of false statement I have seldom met the equal of Capt. Blake's testimony, and for this reason I must disallow him any share of the award to the Mattie." 111 F. at p. 239.

8. The evidence in this case establishes that the plaintiffs and intervenor were guilty of each of the several kinds of misconduct described above. They looted the Norseman and her lifeboats. They actively misled the Coast Guard concerning conditions on the Norseman. Finally, they have consistently attempted to mislead this Court as to the extent and effect of their services to the Norseman and her cargo. The plaintiffs and the intervenor all participated in this aggravated misconduct, to such a degree that any award to which any of them might otherwise have been entitled must be forfeited.

9. The services of plaintiffs and the intervenor in towing the Norseman from Commonwealth's pier to anchorage in Guayanilla harbor, and thereafter towing the vessel from the harbor to where she stranded on the reef, would not in any event be compensable in salvage. These actions did not benefit efforts to fight the fires on the Norseman, and were taken to preserve shore and harbor facilities. Services rendered to preserve property other than the marine property before the Court cannot form the basis of a salvage award. Cope v. Vallette Dry Dock Co., 119 U.S. 625, 7 S.Ct. 336, 30 L.Ed. 501 (1887). However, even if these towing services were compensable in salvage, or on the basis of *quantum meruit,* the compensation would be forfeited by reason of their misconduct.

10. The complaint and the complaint in intervention must be dismissed, with costs to the defendants.

G.   Rival Salvors

Schooner Brindicate II

(Dominguez v. Schooner Brindicate II)

United States District Court, District of Puerto Rico, 1962.
204 F.Supp. 817, 1962 A.M.C. 1659.

■ Calvert Magruder, Acting U.S.D.J. These two cases were consolidated for trial, because they involve competing salvage claims against the same vessel, namely, the Schooner Brindicate II. Though the registered owner of the Brindicate II was served by publication, he did not appear or put in any claim to the vessel. Thereafter, by court order, the schooner was sold by the marshal of the court for the sum of $3000. The marshal expended $43.75 in connection with the sale so that there is now on hand in the registry of the court $2956.25 to be divided between the competing sets of salvors. This amount is not enough to go around, considering the value of the salvage services as given by the salvors.

The result is that the salvors in Adm. 5–60 are reduced to the necessity of contending that the other group of salvors is entitled to no salvage award at all in view of their membership in the Coast Guard Auxiliary.

I think that this contention is wholly unsound. The Coast Guard Auxiliary is a civilian organization administered by the Coast Guard under the direction of the Secretary of the Treasury. 14 U.S.C.A. § 821. These members of the Coast Guard Auxiliary were not assigned by competent Coast Guard authority to any specific duty with reference to the salvage of this schooner. It may well be that regular members of the Coast Guard cannot claim for salvage operations conducted by them because they could not say that that which was their legal duty to do was a voluntary risking of their safety in salvage operations. It is provided in 14 U.S.C.A. § 831, reading in part as follows, that:

"No member of the Auxiliary, solely by reason of such membership, shall be vested with, or exercise, any right, privilege, power, or duty vested in or imposed upon the personnel of the Coast Guard or the Reserve, except that any such member may, under applicable regulations, be assigned specific duties, which, after appropriate training and examination, he has been found competent to perform, to effectuate the purposes of the Auxiliary."

It certainly would be contrary to good public policy, and to the wording of the Act of Congress, if members of the Coast Guard Auxiliary, by the mere fact of such membership, would be disentitled to claim a salvage award for services they voluntarily undertook and rendered when they were not acting as members of the Coast Guard by designation from competent Coast Guard authority. This is borne out, I believe, by the regulations covering the Coast Guard Auxiliary to be found in 33 C.F.R. pp. 7–11 (1949), (Supp. 1961 pp. 9–11).

There is no doubt that the Schooner Brindicate II was discovered as a derelict by the two salvors Quintin Lugo Suarez and Antonio Valentin, of Adm. 5–60, on March 16, 1960. This discovery, however, does not give them any priority in the salvage award. When these two fishermen discovered the schooner, a derelict, off the harbor of Aguirre, on the south coast of Puerto Rico, they repaired to the Club Nautico in Aguirre and called the police to report what they had found. The police officer told the salvors to wait, that he was sending an "emissary" to go and tend to the vessel. Thereafter, Mr. Enrique Girod, one of the salvors in Adm. 4–60, appeared. Mr. Girod owned a cabin cruiser about 23 feet long. This motorboat did not thereby become a public vessel, although Girod was a member of the Coast Guard Auxiliary, for the reason that the vessel was never utilized as a public vessel to engage in specific salvage services, so far as any Coast Guard authorities were concerned. 14 U.S.C.A. § 826.

The caretaker of the yacht club reported the presence of the derelict to Dr. Alberto Dominguez, who brought along with him to the yacht club, Mr. Eric S. Williams, who was a patient in Dr. Dominguez' dentist's chair at the time. Dr. Dominguez, Mr. Girod, and Mr. Williams formed a joint venture to salvage the vessel though they did not file their libel for salvage against the vessel until April 4, 1960.

The two groups of salvors proceeded to the derelict, the first in Mr. Girod's vessel and the second in the fishing boat. There was some conflict on the testimony as to whether Mr. Valentin or Mr. Williams first went aboard the schooner. I am inclined to resolve this conflict in favor of Mr. Williams, for Mr. Girod's vessel was surely faster than the fishing boat and arrived at the scene first. The seas were rough at the time and it was quite a feat to get aboard the schooner. It was conceded by Dr. Dominguez' testimony that from the time Mr. Valentin boarded the schooner, at about 2:30 p.m. until 5:00 p.m. of the same day he performed some useful and helpful services in connection with the salvage operation. At 5:00 p.m. Mr. Valentin and his companion left, stating that they had some fish on board which had to be sold before it spoiled.

Although the salvors in Adm. 5–60 were not seen again, the schooner after arriving at the port of Aguirre was grounded in the mud and the salvors in Adm. 4–60 had particular difficulty in floating her again. I cannot find evidence of any alleged misconduct on the part of these salvors. The cargo which consisted of bags of cement was a complete loss and had to be dumped to loosen the schooner from the mud where it had become grounded. The three salvors in Adm. 4–60 gave evidence of actual expenses incurred in the salvage operations, which expenses did in fact exceed the fund which is to be distributed. We find it unnecessary to go into the validity of these claims for expenditures as salvage claims, though we are in agreement with counsel for the salvors in Adm. 5–60 that no claims for expenditures should be recognized as valid which postdated the time when the marshal of the United States District Court took charge of the vessel pursuant to the libel for salvage filed by the salvors.

The salvors in Adm. 4–60 state that the court should enter a decree "allowing to the co-salvors Quintin Lugo Suarez and Antonio Valentin a token payment for the assistance they gave during the first few hours of the salvage and which assistance was terminated by them before the vessel was actually safely docked."

I think it would be fair to award to the salvors in Adm. 5–60 the sum of $400.00 for their relatively brief share in the salvage operations, and to award the balance of the amount in the registry of the court to the salvors in Adm. 4–60.

A decree will be entered to that effect.

The Acara

(Rickard v. Pringle)

United States District Court, Eastern District of New York, 1968.
293 F.Supp. 981, 1968 A.M.C. 1008.

■ MATTHEW T. ABRUZZO, D.J.

* * *

Plaintiff Had a Right to Salvage the Propeller of the Derelict "Acara"

Public policy is to encourage volunteers in the salvage of derelict, abandoned or distressed property. For this reason salvage awards in generous amounts have traditionally been given to successful salvors. See Blackwall, 77 U.S. 1, 13, 19 L.Ed. 870 (1869); Anderson v. Edam, 13 F. 135 (E.D.N.Y.1882).

"Salvage awards are not intended merely as compensation for work and labor performed. Public policy intends them as rewards in the nature of a bounty to encourage voluntary services by seamen and others to save imperiled lives, ships and their cargoes." Burke v. U.S., 96 F.Supp. 335, 1951 A.M.C. 1137 (S.D.N.Y.1951).

That the Acara which sunk in 1902, was a derelict is without question in fact and law. Rowe v. Brig, Judge Story, 20 F.Cas. 1281, 1282 [1 Cir.1818]. Tubantia, 18 Lloyds L.Report 158 [Admiralty Div.1924].

The Plaintiff Rickard, as the first salvor to commence salvage operations on the propeller of the Acara had the right to do so since:

"When a ship or property has been abandoned or when it has been temporarily left, and is in a disabled or damaged condition so as to require assistance, one who in good faith takes possession as a salvor, is not an interloper or trespasser * * *."

Norris, *Law of Salvage,* sec. 136, p. 228.

Plaintiff as First Salvor is Entitled to Sole Possession of the Salvaged Propeller

The Complaint, which is now deemed admitted, clearly shows that the Plaintiff discovered the propeller of the Acara, made investigation, spent various monies for the purpose of salvaging this propeller, and began salvage operations, placing floating buoys at the scene of said salvage operations. After approximately ten months he successfully detached and removed the propeller from the Acara and left the wreck temporarily to "engage machinery for the purpose of lifting to the surface and transporting the blades of the propeller which were of great size and weight."

It is evident that Plaintiff was successfully prosecuting the salvage operation and did not abandon it at any time and thus was entitled to the rights of a first salvor legally in possession. Since the Acara had rested on the ocean floor in an abandoned state for sixty years, ownership of the salvaged propeller would vest by operation of law in Rickard, as the first finder lawfully and fairly appropriating it and reducing it to possession, with intention to become its owner.   See Clythia, 1960 A.M.C. 1774; 1 C.J.S. "Abandonment," sec. 9, p. 18.

Defendants Wrongfully Interfered With the Plaintiff–Salvor's Possession of the Propeller of the "Acara" and Have no Rights in the Said Propeller

Paragraphs Fourteenth and Fifteenth of the Complaint completely cover the fact that the Plaintiff was engaged in salvage work on the propeller, had not abandoned his salvage operation, and that the Defendants, with full knowledge of this, and with knowledge that Plaintiff was temporarily absent, acting in concert, did remove the said propeller and appropriate same to their own use, selling the same and dividing the proceeds from the said sale among themselves, destroying the fruits of Plaintiff's labor.

A strong inference can readily be drawn from the facts stated in the Complaint that the Defendants' conduct indicated that they must have been watchful of the Plaintiff's efforts, for they readily pounced upon this propeller at a time when they saw that the plaintiff had temporarily departed from his salvage operation.   It wasn't coincidental that the Defendants were at the site where the Plaintiff was working on this wreck, at the time that they moved in with their boat and attached lines to the propeller and dragged it to Freeport, since when they started to drag the propeller they could see from the buoys that someone had been working there.

With respect to abandoned property, the first salvors have possession of the distressed property with which no one can interfere, and the admiralty courts will protect the rights of the first salvor legally in possession whose right of possession has been wrongfully interfered with.

The rule respecting dispossession of one salvor by another was stated in the Edilio, as follows:

> "It is well settled, upon just principles, that as between two sets of salvors, if it appears that the claim of a set of salvors to a share in the salvage reward is based upon the dispossession, against their will, of other persons who were at the time continuously engaged in salving the vessel in distress, and who were willing themselves to persevere in the service which they had begun, the court allows the claim only, if it is clearly proved that the first salvors had not any fair prospect of success.   In the absence of such proof, the burden of which lies upon the second set of alleged salvors, the court holds the dispossession to be wrongful and treats the subsequent service rendered by the wrongdoers as inuring wholly to the benefit of those who have been dispossessed, and not as entitling the wrongdoers to any share in the salvage award."   246 F. 470, 474 (E.D.N.C.1917).

Judge Betts in *The John Gilpin*[1] commented that those beginning a salvage service and who are successfully prosecuting it are entitled to the sole possession of the property.   If they are interrupted or intercepted in

---

1.   Fed.Case 7345 (S.D.N.Y.1845).

the work by others who complete the salvage service and bring in the salved property, the first salvors will, nevertheless, be regarded as the meritorious salvors.

The Plaintiff is clearly entitled to a decree in his favor.

Conclusions of fact and of law and a decree must be submitted to this Court within twenty days, in accordance with this decision.

NOTE

In the last few decades development of more sophisticated equipment has led to substantial investment in efforts to raise vessels long resting on the bottom. A number of such ventures have brought to the surface gold and other valuable property dating to the days of Colonial Spain. These ventures have produced a considerable amount of litigation. Since the stakes are very high, the "rival salvor" problem is potentially troublesome. See Treasure Salvors, Inc. v. Unidentified Wrecked and Abandoned Sailing Vessel, 640 F.2d 560, 1981 A.M.C. 1857 (5th Cir.1981), in which a salvor which in 1971 had brought up an anchor from the Spanish ship Nuestra Señora de Atocha, which sank in 1622 and since that time had continued with its salvage operations, bringing up gold, silver, and artifacts, sought an injunction to prevent operations of a rival organization in the vicinity of its operation, contending that its discovery of the location of the remains of The Atocha gave it a property interest in the wreck. The court of appeals upheld a preliminary injunction against operation of the rival in an area 2,500 yards on either side of a line drawn between two points contained in the salvor's description of the wreck site, but in order to spread a resolution of the merits modified the injunction to limit it to 90 days after the issuance of the mandate of the court of appeals.

H. AMOUNT OF AWARD; DISTRIBUTION; LIFE SALVAGE

Trico Marine Operators, Inc. on its own Behalf and on Behalf of the M/V Manatee River and M/V Wolf River v. Dow Chemicalco. and Security Pacific Leasing, Inc.

United States District Court, Eastern District Louisiana, 1992.
809 F.Supp. 440, 1993 A.M.C. 1042 (E.D.La.1992).

■ EDITH BROWN CLEMENT, D.J.

Defendant's motion for partial summary judgment on the issue of averted liability was decided this date on memoranda. For the reasons stated below, defendant's motion is granted, but the Court will hear evidence on the plaintiff's skill and efforts in protecting the environment

I. Background

On November 3, 1990, the M/V Lisa C, owned by Childress Co., Inc., was engaged in towing the barges DC 310, DC 373 and DC 371 through the Corpus Christi, Texas. The barges were chartered to defendant Dow

Chemical Company and owned by Defendant Security Equipment Leasing, Inc. Due to rough seas, the Lisa C. and the tow, which was loaded with benzene, broke up. The Coast Guard sent out a distress call to any vessels in the vicinity to assist in the recapture of the barges. Six vessels, including two owned by plaintiff Trico Marine Operators, Inc. and one owned by plaintiff Sea Mar Operators, Inc., responded to the call and rounded up the barges. Two other vessels attempted to render assistance, but were unsuccessful.

Plaintiffs contend that, in addition to rescuing the vessels and their cargo, they prevented an environmental disaster. They contend their salvage operation prevented any benzene from escaping from the barges and causing damage to the environment. They seek and award for the averted liability that the defendants would have faced, including statutory liability under the Comprehensive Environmental Response, Compensation and Liability Act (CERCLA), 42 U.S.C. § 9601 *et seq.*, and the Oil Pollution Act (OPA), 33 U.S.C. § 2701 *et seq.*

II.   Salvage Law Principles

A.   *Traditional Salvage Award Criteria and the Environmental Incentive Problem*

There is no precise formula for determining an appropriate salvage award, as each case must be evaluated according to its own circumstances. Allseas Maritime, S.A. v. M/V Mimosa, 812 F.2d 243, 245–46, 1987 A.M.C. 2515, 2516–17 (5th Cir.1987). American courts have traditionally applied the six criteria set out by the Supreme Court in The Blackwall, 77 U.S. (10 Wall.) 1 (1869):

> (a) the degree of danger from which the salvaged property was saved—
>
> (b) the salvaged property's value—
>
> (c) the risk incurred by the salvors—
>
> (d) the salvor's promptitude, skill and energy—
>
> (e) the value of the salvor's property put at risk—
>
> (f) the salvor's time and labor

Allseas Marine, 812 F.2d at 245–46, 1987 A.M.C. at 2517. Because the reward is based on the salvor's rescue of property belonging to the shipowner, the award is limited to "the value of the property saved after all of the appropriate factors are taken into account including risk to the salvor." Id. 812 F.2d at 246. This ceiling is commonly referred to as "the *Blackwall* principle."

Commentators have noted that an award based on the above criteria, and limited by the *Blackwall* principle, might not provide an adequate incentive for potential salvors to undertake salvage operations to protect the environment. See Binney, Protecting the Environment with Salvage Law: Risks, Rewards, and the "1989 Salvage Convention." 65 Wash. L.Rev. 639. Possible remedies to this problem are to (1) recognize liability salvage[2], and/or (2) add an additional criterion to the *Blackwall* list (environmental protection).[3] To effectuate either of these policies, it may also be necessary to (1) discard the *Blackwall* principle, or (2) allow a limited exception to the *Blackwall* principle where the salvor rescues property of little value but prevents significant environmental damage or other liability. These options are discussed below.

B. *Allseas Maritime and Liability Salvage*

In *Allseas Marine,* the Fifth Circuit addressed the issue of recovery for averted liability. The court recognized that "traditional salvage law does not reward a salvor for saving the shipowner from liability for damages to other ships, oil rigs, or other nearby property." Id. 812 F.2d at 247, 1987 A.M.C. at 2520. In dicta, however, the Court noted that there was "considerable merit" to the "position that salvors should be compensated for liability avoided." Id. 812 F.2d at 247, 1987 A.M.C. at 2520. The Court declined to consider an award for averted liability because of the Limitation of Liability Act, 46 U.S.C. §§ 183–188, which ordinarily permits shipowners to limit their liability to the value of their vessel(s) and cargo:

> Thus, even though the *Mimosa* might have caused millions of dollars of damage to nearby oil rigs, its owner could not have been required to pay more than the salvage value of the *Mimosa*. Had the *Mimosa* not been salved, but crashed into a rig, the owner would still have lost only the value of the *Mimosa*, and that averted loss is already considered in the salvage award calculation.

Id. The Court went on to criticize the "anachronistic survival of the Limitation of Liability Act." Id.

In a petition for rehearing, the plaintiff called the court's attention to a report by a maritime board indicating that the crew of the salved vessel acted negligently. The court held that it was too late (at the appellate level) for the plaintiff to present evidence that the shipowner was not entitled to limit its liability:

> the issue of the *Mimosa's* negligence was not pressed below and therefore not adequately developed. We cannot try this issue on appeal.

Juniper Shipping, Ltd. v. Vizier Offshore Towing, Inc., 820 F.2d 130, 130, 1987 A.M.C. 2523, 2523 (5th Cir.1987). In denying the petition for rehearing, the court made it clear that the reason for not considering averted liability was the Limitation of Liability Act:

> We denied an allowance based on [averted liability] because the owner could limit his liability to the value of the *Mimosa* and the salvage award had already accounted for the saving of that value. While the *Taroze Vizier* challenged the owner's ability to limit liability, we found no evidence

2. At least one commentator has expressed support for liability salvage. Note, Calculating and Allocating salvage liability, 99 Harv.L.Rev., 1896, 1904 (1986).

3. Another commentator contends that liability salvage would create too many problems of proof, but advocates that environmental concerns be taken into account in determining salvage awards, as outlined in the 1989 Convention on salvage. Binney, 65 WALR (WESTLAW) at 6–8. The 1989 Convention is discussed below.

in the record of negligence by the *Mimosa* that would prevent it from limiting liability.

Id. Thus, if not for the shipowner's right to limit liability, the Fifth Circuit presumably would have required the district court to consider averted liability.[4]

C.   *Other Recent Decisions*

The court is aware of two other recent decisions discussing the possibility of liability salvage. Both courts denied the salvor a recovery based on averted liability. Hendricks v. Tug Gordon Gill, 737 F.Supp. 1099, 1104, 1989 A.M.C. 1960, 1966 (D.Alaska 1989); Westar Marine Serv. v. Heerema Marine Contractors, 621 F.Supp. 1135, 1140–41 (C.D.Cal.1985). Both cases involved foreign parties, and, thus, were governed by the Brussels Convention of 1910, which did not allow for recovery based on averted liability.

D.   *The 1989 Convention on Salvage*

The 1989 Convention on Salvage seeks to replace the Brussels Convention of 1910. The 1989 Convention has been ratified by the U.S. Senate, but has not taken effect yet because it has not yet been ratified by the required number (15) of nations.[5]

Although the 1989 Convention is not in force, it represents an important statement of salvage law by the world's maritime nations which has been signed by the President and ratified by the Senate. Both sides in this litigation have cited the 1989 Convention in support of their position on liability salvage.

Article 13 of the Convention provides that one of the factors to consider in determining the salvage award is "the skill and efforts of the salvors in preventing or minimizing damage to the environment" (the other factors listed in Article 13 are similar to the *Blackwall* list). However, the award cannot exceed the value of the salved vessel and cargo. Thus, "the Convention incorporates the *Blackwall* principle, but adds a new factor"—environmental protection. Pell, "International Convention on Salvage," S.Exec.Rep. No. 102–17, 102nd Cong., 1st Sess. (1991).

Article 14 of the Convention provides that a salvor who prevents environmental damage may recover "special compensation" in the amount of up to 200% of his expenses where that amount would exceed the amount of a conventional salvage award under Article 13. Thus a salvor who has salved a vessel of little value, but has prevented environmental damage, may recover in excess of the value of the property saved.

---

4. It is not clear why the *Allseas Maritime* court did not consider awarding compensation for averted liability up to the value of the property saved.

5. Once in force, it would appear that the 1989 Convention would apply to the case at bar. Unlike the 1910 Convention, it does not contain a provision precluding its application to purely domestic disputes. See 1989 Convention, Article 2; Gaskell, "The 1989 Salvage Convention and the Lloyd's Open Form (LOF) Salvage Agreement 1990," 16 Tul.Mar.L.J., 23 (1991).

The 1989 Convention contains no mention of the concept of liability salvage, as the concept was rejected in the negotiations leading up to the Convention. See Gaskell, 16 Tu.Mar.L.J. at 7 n. 16 (1991).

E. *Lloyd's Open Form*

Lloyd's of London's Open Form Salvage Agreement (LOF), a standard salvage contract form, represents another important authority on salvage awards. Recent revisions to the form reflect a growing international consensus that salvage awards should encourage environmental protection. Gaskell, 16 Tul.Mar.L.J. at 10–11.

The 1990 revision required salvors to use their "best endeavors" to prevent oil escaping from a vessel. It also provided the first exception to the no cure-no pay rule: if a salved vessel is a tanker laden with oil, owners must pay the salvor's expenses plus up to fifteen percent, even if the vessel and cargo are lost. LOF 1980, Clause 1(a). The 1990 revision incorporates Articles 13 and 14 of the 1989 Convention, giving them contractual effect. LOF 1990, Clause 2. Neither revision recognizes liability salvage.

III.   Analysis

As noted above, the *Allseas Maritime* court rejected liability salvage because it was inconsistent with the Limitation of Liability Act. The defendants in this case have instituted a separate limitation proceeding in Corpus Christi. Thus if defendants prevail in their petition for limitation, their common law tort liability will be limited to the value of their values and cargo.

Plaintiffs point out that defendant's liability could have exceeded the value of their vessels and cargo under CERCLA, which provides for environmental liability notwithstanding the Limitation of Liability Act. 42 U.S.C. § 9607(h).[6] Consequently the Limitation of Liability Act does not necessarily preclude an award based on averted liability in this case.

Although the Court is not constrained by the Limitation of liability Act, as the *Allseas Maritime* court was, the Court does not adopt a rule of averted liability. In light of the rejection of liability salvage in the 1989 Convention and LOF 1990, the Court declines to follow the *Allseas Maritime* dicta suggesting that salvors should be compensated for liability avoided, and instead will apply the rule set forth in those documents. Thus, the Court will add an additional factor to the *Blackwall* list—"skill and efforts of the salvors in preventing or minimizing damage to the environment."

Adding this factor (1) will require the Court to hear evidence detailing the plaintiff's skill and efforts in protecting the environment and (2) may result in an enhanced award, as if the Court had recognized the concept of liability salvage. The difference is that the Court will not need to make an inherently speculative determination of the defendant's averted liability,

---

6.   Plaintiffs also rely on the Oil Pollution Act (OPA), which has no application here because the barges were carrying benzene, not oil.

but instead will consider the plaintiff's skill and efforts in protecting the environment as a seventh subjective factor in calculating the appropriate award.

The Court need not consider whether to (1) discard the *Blackwall* ceiling, adopt a rule of "special compensation" such as that described in Article 14 of the 1989 Convention, because the value of the vessels and cargo in this case is more than sufficient to compensate the salvors for their efforts. However, there is considerable merit to the position that an exception to the *Blackwall* ceiling should be made where the value of the property saved is inadequate to compensate the salvors for their efforts in protecting the environment.

IV.   Conclusion

For the reasons stated above, it is ordered that defendant's motion for partial summary judgment on averted liability is granted.

NOTE

The 1989 Convention, as the court in *Trico* notes, adds environmental concerns as an additional factor in computing the amount of a salvage award, but continues to limit the total award to the value of the property salved. Id. Article 13(1)(b), and (3). When the award under Article 13 is insufficient, the salvor who has prevented or minimized damage to the environment is entitled to special compensation *"from the owner of that vessel."* Thus the owner of the cargo may never be called upon to pay to salvors an award in excess of the value of the cargo. But the convention does not preclude the possibility that the owner of the vessel from pursuing any right of recourse it may have against the cargo owner or others. Art. 14(6).

Article 16, dealing with life salvage, provides that "[a] salvor of human life, who has taken part in the services rendered on the occasion of the accident giving rise to salvage" is entitled to "a fair share of the payment awarded to the salvor for salving the vessel or other property *or preventing or minimizing damage to the environment."* Thus it appears that anything awarded as "special compensation" under Article 14 must be shared with life salvors under Article 16.

Would the adoption of the theory of averted liability be more generous to salvors who protect the environment than the added criterion approach, or less?

The student who is curious about the amounts in salvage cases will find that as Appendix E, beginning on p. 553 of Norris, *The Law of Salvage,* there is a chart that gives the value of the salved property, the value of the salving vessel, the place, the time involved, the amount of the award, and a thumbnail description of the case, for all American salvage awards.

The location and successful salvage of the remains of a number of seventeenth century ships containing gold, silver, and other valuable property had brought with it not only the problem of rival salvors, discussed earlier, but also the basis for salvage awards in the case of the raising of the cargo of a vessel that has been on the bottom for 300 years. There has been some disposition to apply the law of finds to such a situation. See Treasure Salvors, Inc. v. Unidentified Wrecked and Abandoned Sailing Vessel, 569 F.2d 330, 1978 A.M.C. 1404 (5th Cir.1978)(Treasure Salvors I). And see Treasure Salvage: The Admiralty Court "Finds" Old Law, 28 Loy.L.Rev. 1126–45 (1982). In such a case, if no claimant appears, it is perhaps easy to treat the property as abandoned. In the case of the Atocha the only contestants were the salvors and the government. Suppose that Juan Carlos, Rey de Espana, had filed a claim. When is a shipload of gold and silver abandoned in a way that will strip the owner of his interest?

Such considerations apart, the application of the law of finds has created some problems. In Treasure Salvors, Inc. v. Unidentified Wrecked and Abandoned Sailing Vessel, 640 F.2d 560, 1981 A.M.C. 1857 (5th Cir.1981)(Treasure Salvors III), in remanding the case for a determination of the rights of the plaintiff in the wreck observed:

> "Although cases involving the principles of the law of finds are few and far between, we think that a basic principle emerges with some clarity from the cases which have considered problems similar to the one presented here. Persons who actually reduce lost or abandoned objects to possession and persons who are actively and ably engaged in efforts to do so are legally protected from others, whereas persons who simply discover such property, but do not undertake to reduce it to possession, are not. This principle reflects a very simple policy—the law acts to afford protection to persons who actually endeavor to return lost or abandoned goods to society as an incentive to undertake such expensive and risky ventures; the law does not clothe mere discovery with an exclusive right to the discovered property because such a rule would provide little encouragement to the discoverer to pursue the often strenuous task of actually retrieving the property and returning it to a socially useful purpose and yet would bar others from attempting to do so.

> "These cases also suggest that determining property rights in lost or abandoned objects, some equitable considerations come into play in determining the legal protection afforded a finder For example, in Eads v. Brazelton, the court noted that the location of the wreck was well known. Although Brazelton had marked the site, it did not appear that Eads had relied on those markings in finding the wreck. Thus the court did not think that Brazelton's actions in marking the site represented such an investment of skill and effort that equity would suggest that he be afforded some special protection or priority in the conduct of salvage operations on the vessel. In Rickard v. Pringle, by contrast, the court suggested that Pringle had relied on Rickard's bouys and markers in order to find the propeller. Thus the court may well have influenced not only by the extent of Rickard's salvage endeavors, but also by some notion of unjust enrichment * * * "

If the law of finds is applied, is it to be created as a maritime law of finds or is the court to borrow it from the common law? See Chance v. Certain Artifacts Found and Salvaged, 606 F.Supp. 801, 1985 A.M.C. 609 (S.D.Ga.1984) in which the court applied the "embeddedness" exception to the common law of finds to deny the finder a property interest in artifacts taken from the wreck of a Confederate raider that sank in 1863. And on the Union side, see Hatteras, Inc. v. U.S.S. Hatteras, 1984 A.M.C. 1094 (S.D.Tex.1981), in which the court held that the wreck of a civil war vessel could not be treated as abandoned property because the United States can abandon its property only pursuant to statutory authority.

With the cases that have relied, at least in the alternative, on the law of finds, cf. Platoro Ltd., Inc. v. Unidentified Remains of a Vessel, Etc., 695 F.2d 893, 1984 A.M.C. 2288 (5th Cir.1983), cert. denied 464 U.S. 818, 104 S.Ct. 77, 78 L.Ed.2d 89 (1983), involving artifacts from The Espiritu Santo, a Spanish vessel that sank in 1555. As in the other Spanish gold cases there were no claimants appearing as successors in interest to the original owners. The contest was, then, between the salvors and the state. The court left the artifacts with the state, but affirmed a salvage award in the value of the property salved, less the expense the state had been to in cleaning and preserving them.

SAVING LIFE AT SEA

As pointed out in *The Shreveport*, above, under the Salvage Act of 1912 persons who save lives are entitled to a fair share of any salvage award made to those who save property. Pure "life salvage" goes uncompensated.

What about the case in which the same salvor saves both life and property? Is an extra amount added for the saving of life? How would such an amount be computed. See The Bremen, 111 Fed. 228 (S.D.N.Y.1901). A fire originating in a cotton storage facility swept the pier and set the Bremen and two other ships afire. The crew of the Bremen had barely time to disengage the vessel, close her ports and bulkheads, warn those who were below deck, and jump into the water or run to the end of the burning pier. Some 26 tugs claimed to have performed salvage services to the Bremen, including rescuing crew members, towing the vessel away from the pier, and putting out the fire. In determining the amounts awarded to the various tugs, the court declined to make any special allowance for taking crew members from the Bremen onto tugs that had already come alongside. It indicated that the peril to the crew members trapped below decks was a factor to be considered in determining the merit of the salvage service, but it was of the opinion that this was part of the general salvage service. In the case of four tugs that had been on the scene early and picked up crewmen from the end of the burning pier and from the water, however, it made an allowance of approximately $25 a head.

In Markakis v. S/S Volendam, 486 F.Supp. 1103, 1980 A.M.C. 915 (S.D.N.Y. 1980), the master and crew of a cruise vessel sued for salvage of its disabled sister ship. The salving vessel had taken on board the 368 passengers, some of the crew, about 1,000 pieces of luggage, and a considerable quantity of provisions, and had towed the disabled vessel to safe waters, whence it was towed into port by a tug. The court found that the service was a salvage service of a low grade, and referred the question of amounts to a special master. It indicated in a footnote that when the life salvors and the salvors of property are identical, they are not entitled to an added amount because they saved lives as well as property. Adopting the report of the master, the court ultimately awarded one and a half month's pay to the crewmen who actually participated in the transfer of passengers and goods, and allowed those who did not participate, $50 apiece. The total award was approximately $127,000.

The *Markakis* footnote is the subject of sharp criticism in Friedell, Salvage and the Public Interest, 4 Cardozo Law Rev. 431, 443 (1983). Professor Friedell cites a number of pre-statute cases in which the courts have enhanced a salvage award on the ground of the saving of lives. In an earlier article, Compensation and Reward for Saving Life at Sea, 77 Mich.L.Rev. 1218 (1979), Professor Friedell expressed himself as critical of the whole doctrine limiting the law of salvage to situations in which property is saved. Others have taken the same critical position. See, e.g., Jarett, The Life Salvor Problem in Admiralty, 63 Yale L.J. 779 (1954).

While much of the criticism of a rule that "puts property above human life" has taken a moral tone, Professor Bockrath in The American Law of Salvage, 7 Jour. of Mar.Law & Comm. 207 (1975), takes a more sanguine view of the matter. "No doubt history, religion, judicial inertia, and pure change all have contributed to the fact that law has shown more concern with property than with life. This should not, however, compel the conclusion that the failure is solely with the law. It is a simple if unsavory fact that people in general revere property over persons." The Bockrath article has an interesting discussion of the problem of measuring awards for saving life.

Should the judicial award mechanism, an important feature of the law of civil salvage, be viewed as a general instrument for encouraging desirable behavior, of course saving life is just one possible avenue of growth. See the draft Convention on Salvage of the Comite Maritime Internationale (Montreal, 1981). Under Article 3–3 of the draft convention provision is made for compensating salvors who have acted to protect the environment but whose reward under the normal compensation would be less than their expenses as defined in the article. The draft convention did not expand the liability for life salvage. For discussion of the positions taken by the delegates on this topic, see Salvage and the Public Interest, supra.

If the problem of compensation for saving life at sea can not comfortably be integrated into the law of salvage, are there other approaches. In Peninsular & Oriental Steam Navigation Co. v. Overseas Oil Carriers, Inc., 553 F.2d 830 (2d Cir.1977), a crewman aboard the Overseas Progress was stricken by chest pains. It was suspected that he had suffered a heart attack and since the Overseas Progress did not have a doctor aboard, the officers took care of the seaman as best they could, while the master sent out a radio message calling for responses from all ships in the vicinity. Three vessels answered the call. Of these the Canberra, a British passenger vessel was closest, and was faster than the Overseas Progress, and therefore could take the stricken seaman to facilities on shore in less time. Further, the Canberra itself carried a hospital with a fully equipped operating room and medical personnel able to give the seaman immediate attention. In view of these circumstances, the master of the Overseas Progress sent a second radio message, explaining the situation and requesting that the Canberra rendezvous with it. In an action against the owner of the Overseas Progress for the cost of the medical services rendered to the stricken seaman, and for expenses incurred in changing its route and increasing its speed to effect the rendezvous, the district court gave judgment for the doctor's services, but found that the claim of the Canberra was in the nature of a claim for "pure life salvage," not maintainable under the maritime law. The court of appeals reversed, holding that the Overseas Progress had a duty under the maritime law to provide the stricken seaman with maintenance and cure, which includes medical attention, and that the Canberra, by picking up and treating the seaman and taking him to shore facilities, had saved the Overseas Progress from resort to the more expensive alternative of diverting to the nearest adequate shoreside facility; thus an action in quasi-contract lay for the reasonable value of the services. It noted that in some circumstances the "reasonable value" might be measured by the market value of the services, but in the instant case found that the Canberra was the only possible provider of the services and therefore the value would be measured by its cost in departing from its route, increasing its speed, and providing the medical treatment.

In Salvage and the Public Interest, supra, Professor Friedell refers to the *Peninsula & Oriental* case as "potentially explosive." To what extent does the liability in quasi-contract depend upon a request for the services? To what extent upon the duty of the vessel owner to provide maintenance and cure? Would it apply, for example, to the rescue of passengers from life boats? See Complaint of Ta Chi Nav. (Panama) Corp., S.A., 583 F.Supp. 1322 (S.D.N.Y.1984), applying the doctrine to crew members rescued from life boats, but relying, in part, on later instructions from the owner. To what extent must it depend upon liability for damage that would have occurred?

To what extent is pure life salvage a real problem? In Salvage in the Public Interest, supra, Professor Friedell notes that his inquiry by letter disclosed that in England, where provision is made for life salvage claims, there has not been a life salvage case in 20 years. See also Hill, *Maritime Law* 185 (1981) "Life salvage independent of property is a rare occurrence and reported cases this century are almost, if not entirely, non-existent."

Warshauer v. Lloyd Saboudo S.A.

United States Circuit Court of Appeals, Second Circuit, 1934.
71 F.2d 146, 1934 A.M.C. 864.[1]

■ Swan, Circuit Judge. This is an action at law by the plaintiff Warshauer, a citizen of the United States and a resident of New York City, against an Italian corporation which owned and operated the steamship Conte Biancamano. In substance the complaint alleges that on the afternoon of October 31, 1931, the plaintiff and a companion were adrift on the high seas in a disabled motorboat, without gasoline and without food, when the defendant's steamer passed within hailing distance; that he exhibited a recognized signal of distress and requested the steamer to come to his assistance, and the defendant's servants on said steamer, particularly its operating personnel, clearly observed his signals of distress, but refused to heed them or to stop and take the plaintiff aboard, although they could have done so without peril to themselves or their vessel; that two days later the plaintiff was rescued by a Coastguard cutter. In the meantime and in consequence of the exposure and deprivations to which he was subjected by the failure of the defendant's steamship to render the requested aid, the plaintiff suffered permanent physical injuries for which, together with the attendant pain and subsequently incurred medical expenses, he demands damages. On motion to dismiss, equivalent to a demurrer, the District Court held the complaint insufficient, and the correctness of this ruling is the issue presented by this appeal.

Argument of counsel has taken a wider range than the precise issue presented by the pleadings requires. The question chiefly debated was whether the common law or the law of the sea recognizes the existence of a legal duty coextensive with the universally admitted moral duty to rescue a stranger from peril, when this can be done without risk to the one called upon for help. This interesting problem we pass by as unnecessary to the decision, as did the District Court.[2]

---

1. Cert. denied 293 U.S. 610, 55 S.Ct. 140, 79 L.Ed. 700 (1934).

2. Most of the authorities gathered by the industry of the respective counsel are cited below.

In support of the view that the common law does not compel active benevolence to a stranger whose plight the defendant has neither occasioned nor aggravated, see Am. L.Inst., Restatement of Torts (Proposed Final

Draft No. 2) § 192; Ames, Lectures on Legal History, 435, 450; Buch v. Amory Mfg. Co., 69 N.H. 257, 44 A. 809, 76 Am.St.Rep. 163 (1898); Union Pac. Ry. Co. v. Cappier, 66 Kan. 649, 72 P. 281, 69 L.R.A. 513 (1903); Allen v. Hixson, 111 Ga. 460, 36 S.E. 810 (1900); King v. Interstate Consol. Ry., 23 R.I. 583, 51 A. 301, 70 L.R.A. 924 (1902); Griswold v. Boston & Maine Ry. Co., 183 Mass. 434, 67 N.E. 354 (1903); Herd v. Wearsdale

The precise issue is whether a shipowner is liable for damages to a stranger in peril on the high seas to whom the ship's master has failed to give aid. This situation, it may be noted, involves no personal dereliction of a moral duty by the person sought to be held to respond in damages. Such dereliction was that of the master, and only by applying the doctrine of respondeat superior can it be imputed to the ship's owner; moral obliquity is not imputed to one personally innocent. It is conceded that no authority can be found which has imposed legal liability on the owner in such circumstances. Dicta adverse to liability are contained in Saunders v. The Hanover, Fed.Cas. No. 12,374 and United States v. Knowles, Fed.Cas. No. 15,540. Cf. Harris v. Penn. R.R. Co., 50 F.2d 866 (4 Cir.1931); Cortes v. Baltimore Insular Line, 287 U.S. 367, 377, 53 S.Ct. 173, 77 L.Ed. 368 (1932). The absence of specific precedent, however, is no insuperable barrier, for the law of the sea can grow by judicial decision no less than the common law. See Cain v. Alpha S.S. Corp., 35 F.2d 717, 722 (2 Cir.1929). But a court should be slow to establish a new legal principle not in harmony with the generally accepted views of the great maritime nations.

Their views on this subject are disclosed in the International Salvage Treaty, which was drafted by representatives of more than twenty nations, meeting at Brussels in 1910, and to which both Italy and the United States are parties. 37 Stat. 1658, 1672. Articles 11 and 12 of the treaty relate to the matter under consideration and read as follows:

"Article 11.

"Every master is bound, so far as he can do so without serious danger to his vessel, her crew and passengers, to render assistance to everybody, even though an enemy, found at sea in danger of being lost.

"The owner of the vessel incurs no liability by reason of contravention of the foregoing provision.

"Article 12.

"The High Contracting Parties whose legislation does not forbid infringements of the preceding article bind themselves to take or to propose to their respective legislatures the measures necessary for the prevention of such infringements. * * * "

Steel Corp., 3 K.B. 771 [1913], aff'd A.C. 67 [1915].

A tendency toward a more liberal view is indicated in the following cases: Cardozo, Paradoxes of Legal Science, 25; Pound, Law and Morals, 72; Wagner v. International Ry. Co., 232 N.Y. 176, 133 N.E. 437, 19 A.L.R. 1 (1921); Brandon v. Osborne Garrett & Co., 1 K.B. 548 [1924]; Wilkinson v. Kinneil Cannel Co., 34 Scot.L.R. 533; Waters v. Taylor Co., 218 N.Y. 248, 112 N.E. 727, L.R.A.1917A, 347 (1916); Hollaran v. City of New York, 168 App.Div. 469, 153 N.Y.S. 447 (1915); Gibney v. State of New York, 137 N.Y. 1, 33 N.E. 142, 19 L.R.A. 365, 33 Am.St.Rep. 690 (1893); Muhs v. Fire Ins. Salvage Corp., 89 App.Div. 389, 85 N.Y.S. 911 (1904); Depue v. Flatau, 100 Minn. 299, 111 N.W. 1, 8 L.R.A.,N.S., 485 (1907); Southern R.R. Co. v. Sewell, 18 Ga.App. 544, 90 S.E. 94 (1916); Pate v. Steamboat Co., 148 N.C. 571, 62 S.E. 614 (1908); Kimber v. Gas Light & Coke Co., 1 K.B. 439 [1918]; Queen v. Instan, 1 Q.B. 450 [1893].

The treaty was ratified by the United States in 1912, to become effective on March 1, 1913. In the meantime Congress passed legislation in fulfillment of the obligation imposed by article 12 of the treaty. Section 2 of the Act of Aug. 1, 1912, provides as follows (37 Stat. 242, 46 U.S.C.A. § 728):

"Sec. 2. That the master or person in charge of a vessel shall, so far as he can do so without serious danger to his own vessel, crew, or passengers, render assistance to every person who is found at sea in danger of being lost; and if he fails to do so, he shall upon conviction, be liable to a penalty of not exceeding $1,000 or imprisonment for a term not exceeding two years, or both."

The appellant contends that the declaration in article 11 that the shipowner "incurs no liability by reason of contravention" of the master's obligation to render assistance refers only to criminal liability of the owner. Such an interpretation would seem a most unlikely meaning. Unless it was intended to cover civil liability, no reason is apparent for mentioning the shipowner's exemption from liability. It is almost inconceivable that criminal responsibility should be imputed to an owner who had not directed the dereliction of his agent. In the United States, at least, imputed crime is substantially unknown. A penal statute is construed to apply only to the class of persons to whom it specifically refers. Field v. United States, 137 F. 6, 8 (8 Cir.1905). The same principle should be equally applicable to the construction of a treaty. Hence if the first sentence of article 11 refers only to the master's public duty, breach of which is to be enforced by the criminal law, there was no need to express the owner's exemption from responsibility. If, however, the master's liability may be civil as well as criminal, then the provision referring to the owner serves a purpose and clearly relieves him from civil liability.

It is further urged that the treaty is not self-executing, that article 11 is no more than an expression of policy and by the very terms of article 12 requires legislation to carry it into effect (Cf. Foster v. Neilson, 2 Pet. 253, 314, 7 L.Ed. 415 (1829)), and that Congress in enacting such legislation dealt only with the criminal liability of the master, leaving untouched the civil liability of both master and owner, so that no implication can be drawn, either from the treaty or the statute, that civil liability does not exist. On the contrary, the argument proceeds, the enactment of a criminal statute for the protection of a class creates a right of civil action in a member of the class who is caused harm by an infraction of the statute. Texas & Pac. Ry. Co. v. Rigsby, 241 U.S. 33, 39, 36 S.Ct. 482, 60 L.Ed. 874 (1915). Granting all this, the appellant advances no further than to establish a cause of action against the violator of the criminal statute; that is, the master. He must still prove that the master's breach of duty is imputable to his employer. It is at this point that the absence of precedent and the declaration of the treaty against liability on the part of the owner stands in his way. As a declaration of the views of the great maritime nations, the treaty needs no "implementation" by legislation. We are not

at liberty to make new law in the face of that declaration. See article 15 of
the Treaty (37 Stat. 1672).

Judgment affirmed.

NOTE

A foreign flag vessel operating in international waters is not subject to 46 U.S.C.A.
§ 728. Peninsular & O. Steam Nav. Co. v. Overseas Oil Carriers, 418 F.Supp. 656,
1976 A.M.C. 1505 (S.D.N.Y.1976), reversed on other grounds 553 F.2d 830 (2d
Cir.1977).

What if the vessel, despite the absence of criminal penalties under § 728, does
go to the rescue. Is it entitled to recover its expenses in doing so in an action based
on unjust enrichment? In the *Peninsular & O.* case, above, it was held that no
action would lie for the amount of fuel consumed, but when the aiding vessel was
called because of the illness of a passenger and the passenger was taken aboard and
treated in the aiding vessel's hospital, the aided vessel would be liable for these
medical services since it had a duty to provide medical services under the circumstances.

In Caminiti v. Tomlinson Fleet & American S.S. Co., 1981 A.M.C. 201
(N.D.Ohio 1979), it was held that the survivors of persons who drowned after going
overboard from their pleasure boat could maintain an action against the owners of
two vessels that negligently failed to rescue them. The court was of the opinion
that the rule in *Warshauer* did not preclude the issue because there the parties were
each from a different signatory of the 1910 Convention, while in *Caminiti* both
parties were citizens of the United States. Feeling itself thus free to decide, the
court held that the doctrine of respondeat superior applies to the duty imposed
upon the master under 46 U.S.C.A. § 2304, then § 728. It found analogies in cases
in which crewmen or passengers have gone overboard, and indicated that in view of
the federal courts' "leading role in formulating flexible and fair remedies in the
maritime law," it felt no qualms in going beyond the decided cases.

Note that the proviso in Article 15, of the 1910 Brussels Convention excluding
from the provisions of the Convention cases "[w]here all the persons interested
belong to the same State as the court trying the case" does not appear in the 1989
Convention. Would this be significant in a case like *Caminiti*?

I. SALVAGE CONTRACTS

The Elfrida

Supreme Court of the United States, 1898.
172 U.S. 186, 19 S.Ct. 146, 43 L.Ed. 413.

This was a libel in rem by the firm of Charles Clarke & Co., of Galveston,
Texas, against the British steamship Elfrida, to recover the sum of $22,000,
with interest and costs, claimed to be due them for services rendered in the
performance of a salvage contract with the master, to release the Elfrida,
then stranded near the mouth of the Brazos River.

The principal averments of the answer were, in substance, that the
agreement was signed by the master under a mutual mistake of fact, or by

mistake on his part, which libellants took advantage of, as to the danger in which the vessel was, and that it was improvidently made for an excessive compensation without a proper understanding by him of the vessel's alleged freedom from danger; that the master had been prevented from carrying out his instructions to accept a tender made, if lower impossible, by information of the cable being conveyed to the salvors before the master saw it; that the parties were not upon an equal footing; that libellants made an unreasonable bargain with the master because of the stress of the situation and that of his vessel, and acted collusively with other salvors in obtaining from him the agreement. * * *

■ MR. JUSTICE BROWN, after stating the case, delivered the opinion of the court.

But a single question is presented by the record in this case: Was the contract with the libellants of such a character, or made under such circumstances, as required the court to relieve the Elfrida against the payment of the stipulated compensation?

We are all of opinion that this question must be answered in the negative. Salvage services are either (1) voluntary, wherein the compensation is dependent upon success; (2) rendered under a contract for a per diem or per horam wage, payable at all events; or (3) under a contract for a compensation payable only in case of success.

The first and most ancient class comprises cases of pure salvage. The second is the most common upon the Great Lakes. The third includes the one under consideration. Obviously where the stipulated compensation is dependent upon success, and particularly of success within a limited time, it may be very much larger than a mere quantum meruit. Indeed, such contracts will not be set aside unless corruptly entered into, or made under fraudulent representations, a clear mistake or suppression of important facts, in immediate danger to the ship, or under other circumstances amounting to compulsion, or when their enforcement would be contrary to equity and good conscience. Before adverting to the facts of this particular case, it may be well to examine some of the leading authorities where salvage contracts have been set aside and compensation awarded in proportion to the merit of the services.

In the case of The North Carolina, 40 U.S. (15 Pet.) 40, 10 L.Ed. 653 (1841), the master of a vessel which had struck upon one of the Florida reefs was improperly, if not corruptly, induced to refer the amount of salvage to the arbitrament of two men, who awarded thirty-five per cent of the vessel and cargo. The court found that under the circumstances the master had no authority to bind his owners by the settlement; that the settlement was fraudulently made, and that the salvors, by their contract, had forfeited all claims to compensation even for services actually rendered.

In The Tornado, 109 U.S. 110, 3 S.Ct. 78, 27 L.Ed. 874 the owners of three steam tugs which had pumping machinery were employed by the master and agent of a ship sunk at a wharf in New Orleans, with a cargo on board, to pump out the ship for a compensation of $50 per hour for each boat, "to be continued until the boats were discharged." When the boats were about to begin pumping, the United States marshal seized the ship and cargo upon a warrant on a libel for salvage. After the seizure the marshal took possession of the ship and displaced the authority of the master, but permitted the tugs to pump out the ship. After they had pumped for about eighteen hours, the ship was raised and placed in a position of safety. The tugs remained by the ship, ready to assist her in case of need, for twelve days, but their attendance was unnecessary, and not required by any peril of ship or cargo. In libels of intervention, in the suit for salvage, the owners of the tugs claimed each $50 per hour for the whole time, including the twelve days, as salvage. The court held that as the contract was to pump out the ship for an hourly compensation, the right of the steam tugs to compensation must be regarded as having terminated when the ship and cargo were raised, and that, as the marshal seized the ship as the tugs began to pump her out, the authority of the master was displaced, and the boats must be regarded as having been discharged under any fair interpretation of the contract. Standing by for a period of twelve days was found to have been unnecessary, and not required by any peril to the Tornado or her cargo. The case was not one where the contract was set aside as inequitable, though found to be so, but where it had been completed by pumping out the ship and the supersession of the master. See, also, Bondies v. Sherwood, 63 U.S. (22 How.) 214, 16 L.Ed. 238 (1859) where the court overruled an attempt on the part of the salvors to repudiate their contract as unprofitable and recover on a quantum meruit.

These are the only cases in our reports in which the question of nullifying a salvage contract was squarely presented, although there is in the case of Post v. Jones, 60 U.S. (19 How.) 150, 160, 15 L.Ed. 618 (1856) an expression of the court to the effect that "courts of admiralty will enforce contracts made for salvage service and salvage compensation, where the salvor has not taken advantage of his power to make an unreasonable bargain; but they will not tolerate the doctrine that a salvor can take the advantage of his situation, and avail himself of the calamities of others to drive a bargain; nor will they permit the performance of a public duty to be turned into a traffic of profit." Indeed it may be said in this connection that the American and English courts are in entire accord in holding that a contract which the master has been corruptly or recklessly induced to sign will be wholly disregarded. The Theodore, Swab., 351; The Crus. V., Lush. 583; The Generous, L.R. 2 Ad. 57, 60.

The intimations of this court have been followed except in very rare instances by the subordinate courts. Thus, in the case of The Agnes I. Grace, 49 F. 662 (5 Cir.1892); s.c., 2 U.S.App. 317, a schooner bound for Port Royal, South Carolina, put into Tybee Roads under stress of weather. She came up on the sands in an exceedingly perilous condition. The ground was treacherous and dangerous, and while lying there she was exposed to the full force of the sea and winds. A tow boat company offered its services, and a contract was entered into to pay the sum of $5000 as salvage. A portion of the cargo, amounting to $7000, was saved, as well as the schooner, which was sold for $5030, probably about one half her value. The contract was sustained. The court put its decision upon the ground that the case could not be considered as belonging to that class "where the master being upon the high seas or an uninhabited coast, at a distance from all other aid, is absolutely helpless and without power to procure assistance other than that offered, and is compelled in consequence to make a hard and inequitable contract. He was within easy reach of Savannah, where, had he desired to assume the risk for his owners, he could have procured lighters and other tugs to render the service."

The cases in these courts are too numerous for citation, but it is believed that in nearly all of them the distinction is preserved between such contracts as are entered into corruptly, fraudulently, compulsorily or under a clear mistake of facts, and such as merely involve a bad bargain, or are accompanied with a greater or less amount of labor, difficulty or danger than was originally expected. * * *

In most of the cases where the contract was held void the facts showed that advantage was taken of an apparently helpless condition to impose upon the master an unconscionable bargain. Brooks v. Steamer Adirondack, 2 F. 387 (2 Cir.1880); The Young America, 20 F. 926 (3 Cir.1884); The Don Carlos, 47 F. 746 (9 Cir.1891).

It must be admitted that some of these courts have exercised a wide discretion in setting aside these contracts, and have laid down the rule that they are to be closely scrutinized, and will not be upheld when it appears that the price agreed upon by the master is unreasonable or exorbitant. We do not undertake to say that these cases were improperly decided upon their peculiar facts, but we are unable to assent to the general proposition laid down in some of them that salvage contracts are within the discretion of the court, and will be set aside in all cases where, after the service is performed, the stipulated compensation appears to be unreasonable. If such were the law, contracts for salvage services would be of no practical value, and salvors would be forced to rely upon the liberality of the courts.

Nor is such a contract objectionable, when prudently entered into, upon the ground that it may result more or less favorably to the parties interested than was anticipated when the contract was made. A person may lawfully contract against contingencies; in fact, the whole law of insurance is based upon the principle that, by the payment of a small sum of money, the insured may indemnify himself against the possibility of a greater loss; or, by the expenditure of a trifling amount to-day in the way of premium, his family may receive a much larger sum in case of his subsequent death. If there were ever any doubt with respect to the validity of such contracts it was long since removed by the universal concurrence of the courts, and an enormous business has grown up all over the world upon the faith of their validity. Indeed, nearly every contract for a special undertaking or *job* is subject to the contingencies of a rise or fall in the price of labor or materials, to the possibility of strikes, fires, storms, floods, etc., which may render it unexpectedly profitable to one party or the other.

We do not say that to impugn a salvage contract such duress must be shown as would require a court of law to set aside an ordinary contract; but where no such circumstances exist as amount to a moral compulsion, the contract should not be held bad simply because the price agreed to be paid turned out to be much greater than the services were actually worth. The presumptions are in favor of the validity of the contract, The Helen & George, Swabey, 368; The Medina, 2 P.D. 5, although in passing upon the question of compulsion the fact that the contract was made at sea, or under circumstances demanding immediate action, is an important consideration. If when the contract is made the price agreed to be paid appears to be just and reasonable in view of the value of the property at stake, the danger from which it is to be rescued, the risk to the salvors and the salving property, the time and labor probably necessary to effect the salvage, and the contingency of losing all in case of failure, this sum ought not to be reduced by an unexpected success in accomplishing the work, unless the compensation for the work actually done be grossly exorbitant.

* * *

The facts in this case are somewhat peculiar, and, in entering into the contract, unusual precautions were taken. On October 5, the Elfrida in entering the river grounded by the stern about midchannel, her bow drifting over toward the west jetty. Her crew were unable to get her off, either upon that or the following day, when, owing to the sea rising, she was carried over the jetty and a very considerable distance further onto the beach (about 600 feet), where she remained in seven or eight feet of water, gradually working inward and making a bed for herself in the sand, which had a tendency to bank up about her bows. She appears to have been at no time in imminent peril, but her situation could have been hardly without serious danger, unless she were released before a heavy storm came on, which might have broken her up or driven her so far ashore that her rescue would have been impossible. It was shown that in previous years a number of vessels had gone ashore in this neighborhood, several of which were lost by bad weather coming on. In other cases the difficulty of getting them off had been very largely increased by similar causes. The testimony shows that while the Elfrida lay there the wind was at times blowing a gale with the rough sea in which the ship strained and bumped heavily. On Saturday the 6th, the day of her final stranding, the master having given up his idea of getting her off with her own anchors, telegraphed his owners and also Lloyds' agent at Galveston, who appear to have sent Mr. Clarke, one of the libellants, down on Sunday evening. He offered to undertake the relief of the ship for what the court would allow him. This offer the master declined. About the same time Mr. Sorley, Lloyds' agent, came down to the vessel, saw her situation, remained there two days, and advised the master to invite bids for her relief. He obtained two bids, one for $24,000 and one made by the libellants for $22,000, and on the advice of Sorley and of his owners, Pynam, Bell & Co., of Newcastel-on-Tyne, with whom he kept in constant communication by cable, he accepted libellants' bid, and a contract was entered into, whereby they agreed to float the

Elfrida and place her in a safe anchorage, and to complete the job within twenty-one days from date. The master agreed to pay therefor the sum of $22,000, but reserved the right to abandon the ship in lieu of this amount. At the request of the owners he also inserted a further stipulation that if the libellants should fail to float the ship and place her in a position of safety within twenty-one days, they should receive no compensation whatever for the work performed, or the labor, tools or appliances furnished. This contract was made at Velasco on October 15. Clarke proceeded at once to get ready a wrecking outfit, consisting of a tugboat and schooner, with fifteen or sixteen men, went to the wreck, and spent about two days planting anchors and connecting cables from them to the winches of the ship. The tugboat took no part in the actual relief of the vessel, which was effected by the aid of the anchors and the steamer's engines, although after the Elfrida was afloat she drifted against the west jetty and the tug hauled her off.

For the work actually done the stipulated compensation was undoubtedly very large, and if the validity of the contract depended alone upon this consideration, we should have no hesitation in affirming the decree of the Circuit Court of Appeals; but the circumstances under which the contract was made put the case in a very different light. In the first place, the libellants offered to get the vessel off for such salvage as the court should award, but the master declined the proposition, and, acting under the advice of Lloyds' agent and of Moller & Co., the owners' agents at Galveston, invited bids for the service. This certainly was a very proper step upon his part, and there is no evidence showing any collusion between the bidders to charge an exorbitant sum. The conditions imposed upon the libellants were unusual and somewhat severe. Their ability to get her off must have depended largely upon the continuance of good weather. Their ability to get her off within the time limited was even more doubtful, and yet under their contract they were to receive nothing—not even a quantum meruit—unless they released her and put her in a place of safety within twenty-one days. Further than this, if in getting her off, or after she had been gotten off, she proved to be so much damaged that she was not worth the stipulated compensation, the master reserved the right to abandon her.

We give no weight to the advice of Pynam, Bell & Co., her owners, to enter into the contract, since in the nature of things they could have no personal knowledge of her situation, or of the possibility of relieving her; but it shows that her master, though a young man and making his first voyage as master, acted with commendable prudence. He took no step without the advice of his owners and that of the underwriters' agent at Galveston, Mr. Sorley, who was a man over seventy years of age, perfectly honest, and of large experience in these matters. Sorley visited the vessel, saw her situation, and advised an acceptance of the bid. The value of the ship is variously estimated at from $70,000 to $110,000, but the sum for which she was insured 18,000£ or $90,000, may be taken as her approximate value. Under the stringent circumstances of this contract, we do not think it could be said that an agreement to pay one quarter of her value if released could be considered unconscionable, or even exorbitant, and unless the fact that it proved to be exceedingly profitable for the libellants is decisive that it was unreasonable, it ought to be sustained.   For the reasons above stated we think that the disproportion of the compensation to the work done is not the sole criterion.   Very few cases are presented showing a contract entered into with more care and prudence than this, and we are clear in our opinion that it should be sustained.   Had the agreement been made with less deliberation or pending a peril more imminent our conclusion might have been different.

The decree of the Circuit Court of Appeals must therefore be reversed and the case remanded to the District Court for the Eastern District of Texas with directions to execute its original decree.

N O T E

The fact that the owner of a salving vessel enters into a contract with the vessel salved cannot bind the crew of the salving vessel.   They may seek an award in any event.   See Bergher v. General Petroleum Co., 242 Fed. 967 (N.D.Cal.1917).   There the court held that the contract would be binding as between the parties and if it reflected an amount that was a fair award for the services of both salving vessel and its crew, the owner would have to share the amount with his crew.   In the *Bergher* case, however, the evidence was to the effect that the charge under the contract was no more than the actual value of the use of the vessel at charter rates.   Under those circumstances, it was held that the award to the crew would have to be paid by the vessel salved.   See Norris, *The Law of Salvage* §§ 172–179 (1958).

But when the Coast Guard entered into a contract with a firm to provide equipment and manpower to remove water, slops, and oil from a vessel disabled in the Mississippi River by collision with a submerged barge, the vice president and general manager of the firm, who had obtained pumps and put them to use could not treat himself as a an individual salvor when his services were the same that the Coast Guard had contracted for.   The court of appeals rejected the argument that on Friday night, Saturday, and Monday he was acting as vice president of the contracting party, but on Sunday evening and dawn on Monday he was an individual salvor, finding the distinction "simply too fine."   Nunley v. M/V Dauntless Colocotronis, 863 F.2d 1190, 1993 A.M.C. 1676 (5th Cir.1989).

CHAPTER 16

GENERAL AVERAGE

LAWS OF OLERON
ART. VIII

If a vessel be laden to sail from Bordeaux to Caen, or any other place, and it happens that a storm overtakes her at sea, so violent, that she cannot escape some of the cargo overboard for lightening the vessel, and preserving the rest of the lading, as well as the vessel itself, then the master ought to say, *Gentlemen, We must throw part of the goods overboard;* and if there are no merchants to answer him, or if those that are there approve of what he says by their silence, then the master may do as he thinks fit; and if the merchants are not pleased with his throwing over any part of the merchandize, and forbid him, yet the master ought not to forbear casting out so many of the goods as he shall see to be for the common good and safety; he and the third part of his mariners making oath on the Holy Evangelists, when they arrive at their port of discharge, that he did it only for the preservation of the vessel, and the rest of the lading that remains yet in her. And the wines, or other goods, that were cast overboard, ought to be valued or prized according to the just value of the other goods that arrive in safety. And when these shall be sold, the price or value thereof ought to be divided livre a livre among the merchants. The master may compute the damage his vessel has sustained, or reckon the freight of the goods thrown overboard at his own choice. If the master does not make it appear that he and his men did the part of able seamen, then neither he nor they shall have anything. The mariners also ought to have one tun free, and another divided by cast of the dice, according as it shall happen, and the merchants in this case may lawfully put the master to his oath.

ART. IX

If it happen, that by reason of much foul weather the master is like to be constrained to cut his masts, he ought first to call the merchants, if their be any aboard the ship, and such as have goods and merchandize in the vessel, and to consult them, saying, *Sirs, it is requisite to cut down the mast to save the ship and lading, it being in this case my duty.* And frequently they also cut their mooring cables, leaving behind them their cables and anchors to save the ship and her lading; all which things are reckoned and computed *livre* by *livre,* as the goods are that were cast overboard. And when the vessel arrives in safety at her port of discharge, the merchants ought to pay the master their shares or proportions without delay, or sell or pawn the goods and employ the money he raises to satisfy by it the same, before the said goods be unlade out of the said ship: but if he lets them go, and there happens controversies and debates touching the premises, if the master observes collusion therein, he ought not to suffer, but is to have his complete freight, as well for what goods were thrown overboard as for what he brought home.

A.   GENERAL AVERAGE SACRIFICES

Barnard v. Adams

Supreme Court of the United States, 1850.
51 U.S. 270, 13 L.Ed. 417, 10 How. 270.

■ MR. JUSTICE GRIER delivered the opinion of the court.

The plaintiffs below, Joseph Adams and others, brought this action against Charles Barnard and others, in the Circuit Court of New York, to recover contribution in general average for the loss of their vessel called the Brutus, on board of which certain goods were shipped, and consigned to the plaintiffs in error, and delivered to them on their promise to pay, provided contribution were justly due.

As the facts of the case were not disputed, it will be proper to state them in connection with the instructions given by the court, in order to avoid any mistake or misconception which might arise in construing the terms of mere abstract propositions without relation to the facts on which they were based.

On the 8th of October, 1843, the ship Brutus was lying at anchor, at the usual place of mooring vessels in the outer roads at Buenos Ayres, about seven miles from the shore. The width of the river at that place, between Buenos Ayres and Colonia on the opposite shore, is about fifteen miles. The Brutus had taken her cargo on board for New York, consisting of nutria skins, dry hides, horns, and jerked beef. The master was on shore, and she was in charge of the first mate, with a crew consisting of twelve persons in all. On the 7th, a gale had commenced, which on the 8th had become dangerous. About four o'clock next morning the ship began to drag her anchors, and the small bower anchor was let go. About nine o'clock in the evening, the gale increasing, the best bower anchor parted with a loud report. About ten o'clock, the small bower parted, and the ship commenced drifting broadside with the wind and waves. Endeavors were then made to get the ship before the wind, which failed, on account of the chains keeping her broadside to the sea, which was making a breach over her fore and aft. The chains were then slipped, and the vessel got before the wind, two men were put to the wheel, and one to the lead, and it was determined "to run the ship ashore for the preservation of the cargo and the lives of the crew." It was now about eleven o'clock at night when the ship was got before the wind and under command of the helm. The shore next to Buenos Ayres side, toward which the ship had been drifting, had banks and shallows extending out some three or four miles. If the vessel had been driven on these by the tempest, she would have been wrecked and lost, together with the cargo and crew. On the Colonia side of the river were sunken rocks several miles from the shore. "For the purpose of saving the cargo and crew anyhow, and possibly the ship," she was steered up the river, inclining a little towards the Buenos Ayres side, with the intention of running her on shore at a convenient place. After they had proceeded up the river about ten miles, the mate discovered from the flashes of lightning that the vessel was approaching a point called St. Isidro, off which he perceived something black which he supposed to be rocks, and "being afraid," or "thinking it impossible to get by" this point without being wrecked and lost, he directed the course of the vessel to be changed towards the shore, where he had seen what he supposed to be a house, but which turned out to be a large tree. About midnight the vessel struck the beach and the rudder was knocked away. The foresail was then hauled up, but the staysail was let remain to keep her head straight, and she continued to work herself up until daylight. The place where she was stranded was a level beach about two hundred yards above ordinary low-water mark. The ship was not wrecked, or broken up, though somewhat damaged, and the cargo was not injured. The master chartered the bark Serene, and transferred the cargo to her. But it was found that, with the means to be obtained in that vicinity, it would have cost more than the ship was worth to get her off the beach. She was therefore sold. The Serene afterwards arrived safely at New York, under command of Captain Adams, former master of the Brutus. In transshipping the jerked beef from the Brutus to the Serene, a portion of it got wet, and when it arrived at the port of New York it was all found to be worthless.

On these facts the court instructed the jury as follows:—

1. "The evidence on the subject of the stranding consists in the uncontradicted and unimpeached testimony of a single witness. He was the acting master of the vessel at the time of the loss in question. He states that when the vessel was without any means of resisting the storm, and her going ashore upon a rocky and more dangerous part of the shore was, in his opinion, inevitable, he did intentionally and for the better security of the property and persons engaged in the adventure, give her a direction to what he supposed to be, and what proved to be, a part of the shore where she could lie more safely. These facts, if credited by you, constitute in judgment of law, a voluntary sacrifice of the vessel, and for such sacrifice the plaintiffs are entitled to recover in general average."

This instruction forms the subject of the first exception, and raises the most important question in the case.

The apparent contradiction in the terms of this instruction has evidently arisen from a desire of the court to give the plaintiffs in error, on the argument here, the benefit of the negation of their own proposition, viz., that if the loss of the vessel by the storm was inevitable, the stranding could not be a voluntary "sacrifice entitling the plaintiffs to contribution." It is because the form in which this proposition is stated is equivocal and vague, when applied to the case before us, that the negation of it appears to

be contradictory in its terms. The court should, therefore, not be understood as saying, that, if the jury believed the peril which was avoided was "inevitable," or that if the jury believed that the imminent peril was not avoided, they should find for the plaintiffs. But rather, that if they believed there was an imminent peril of being driven "on a rocky and dangerous part of the coast," when the vessel would have been inevitably wrecked, with loss of ship, cargo, and crew, and that this immediate peril was avoided by voluntarily stranding the vessel on a less rocky and dangerous part of the coast, whereby the cargo and crew were saved uninjured, then they should find for the plaintiffs. Looking at the admitted facts of this case in connection with the instruction given, it is plain that the jury could not have understood the court to mean anything else.
* * *

The law of general average has its foundation in equity. The principle, that "what is given for the general benefit of all shall be made good by the contribution of all," is recommended, not only by its equity, but also by its policy, because it encourages the owner to throw away his property without hesitation in time of need.

In order to constitute a case for general average, three things must concur:—

1st. A common danger; a danger in which ship, cargo, and crew all participate; a danger imminent and apparently "inevitable," except by voluntarily incurring the loss of a portion of the whole to save the remainder.

2d. There must be a voluntary jettison, jactus, or casting away, of some portion of the joint concern for the purpose of avoiding this imminent peril, pericula imminentis evitandi causa, or, in other words, a transfer of the peril from the whole to a particular portion of the whole.

3d. This attempt to avoid the imminent common peril must be successful.

It is evident from these propositions, that the assertion so much relied on in the argument, namely, "that if the peril be inevitable there can be no contribution," is a mere truism, as the hypothesis of the case requires that the common peril, though imminent, shall be successfully avoided. Those who urge it must therefore mean something else. And it seems, when more carefully stated, to be this, "that if the common peril was of such a nature, that the 'jactus,' or thing cast away to save the rest, would have perished anyhow, or perished 'inevitably,' even if it had not been selected to suffer in place of the whole, there can be no contribution." If this be the meaning of this proposition, and we can discover no other, it is a denial of the whole doctrine upon which the claim for general average has his foundation. For the master of the ship would not be justified in casting a part of the cargo into the sea, or slipping his anchor, or cutting away his masts, or stranding his vessel, unless compelled to it by the necessity of the case, in order to save both ship and cargo, or one of them, from an imminent peril which threatened their common destruction. The necessity of the case must compel him to choose between the loss of the whole and part; but, however metaphysicians may stumble at the assertion, it is this forced choice which is necessary to justify the master in making a sacrifice (as it is called) of any part for the whole. Hence the answer of every master of a vessel, when examined, will be, "I considered the destruction of both ship and cargo 'inevitable,' unless I had thrown away what I did." "The goods thrown away would have gone to the bottom anyhow." If the case does not show that the jettison was "indispensable," in order to escape the common peril, the master would himself be liable for the loss consequent therefrom. It is for this reason, that the ordinances of Marseilles require that the master should have a consultation with the supercargo and crew as to the absolute necessity of the measure, and as evidence that it was not done through the vain fears, cowardice, or imprudence of the master. But the right to contribution is not made to depend on any real or presumed intention to destroy the thing cast away, but on the fact that it had been selected to suffer the peril in place of the whole, that the remainder may be saved. The anchor lost by voluntarily slipping the cable may be recovered, the goods jettisoned may float to the shore and be saved, and yet, if the anchor or goods had not been cast away, they would have been "inevitably" lost and there would have been a total loss of both ship and cargo. * * *

Why, then, should there be a difference in principle, where the cargo is damaged or lost by being cast into the sea, and the ship saved, and the case where the ship is damaged or lost by a voluntary stranding, or by being cast on the land and the cargo saved, is a question which has never yet been satisfactorily answered. In fact, we do not understand the counsel to contend for the doctrine of salva navi, or that the Brutus was not entitled to contribution because she could not be got afloat at a less cost than her value. The principle on which the counsel relied is that enunciated in the opinion of the court in Walker v. United States Ins. Co., 11 Serg. & R. (Pa.) 61 (1824). "It is not enough," says the learned judge, "that there be a deliberate intent to do an act which may or may not lead to a loss; there must be a deliberate purpose to sacrifice the thing at all events, or at the very least to put it in a situation in which the danger of eventual destruction would be increased."

But, as we have already seen, the intention to destroy the jactus, or thing exposed to loss or damage for the benefit of the whole, makes no part of the hypothesis upon which the right of contribution is founded. Indeed, the speciousness of this assertion seems to have its force from the use of the word "sacrifice" in its popular and tropical, instead of its strict or technical meaning. The offering of sacrifices was founded on the idea of vicarious suffering. And when it is said of the jactus, that it is sacrificed for the benefit of the whole, it means no more than that it is selected to undergo the peril, in place of the whole, and for the benefit of the whole. It is made (if we may use another theological phrase) the "scape-goat" for the remainder of the joint property exposed to common destruction. * * *

The common peril, which in this case was sought to be avoided, was shipwreck, or the destruction of vessel, cargo, and crew. The ship lay at anchor; she was assailed by a violent tempest, her cables broken, her anchors gone, and she was being driven by the force of the gale broadside upon the shallows extending three miles out from the shore at Buenos Ayres. In order to save the cargo and crew, it is determined to put on sail, and run up the river to find a safe place to strand the vessel. They proceed ten miles up the river, when they encounter another peril at Point St. Isidro. To avoid being wrecked on the rocks, the course of the vessel is immediately changed, and she is steered directly for the shore, and run upon a sandy beach, where she is left high and dry by the tide. The cargo is saved without injury, but the ship is on the land, where she is comparatively valueless, on account of the expense which must be incurred to replace her in her element. By the will and directions of the master, she has become the victim, and borne the loss, that the cargo might escape from the common peril. It is true she has not been wrecked or lost, as she inevitably would, had she been driven on the flats at Buenos Ayres by the tempest, or been foundered on the rocks off Point St. Isidro, but she has voluntarily gone on shore, which was death to her, while it brought safety to the cargo. And we are of opinion she has the same right to demand contribution that the owners of the cargo would have had against her, had it been cast into the sea to insure her safety.

There is therefore no error in the instruction given by the court below on this point. * * *

The judgment of the Circuit Court is therefore affirmed.

■ [The dissenting opinion of Mr. Justice Daniel is omitted.]

NOTE

The case of voluntary stranding has been the subject of much doubt and diversity of opinion over the years. Lowndes and Rudolf state that the desirability of achieving some common rule was pointed up by the fact that not only were the decisions in England and the United States inconsistent, but differences existed in the views of the courts in France, Holland, Italy, Germany, and Scandinavia. Under the Glascow Resolutions of 1860, a general rule was stated that stranding should not give rise to general average but might be on "clear proof of special facts." The York Rules of 1864 stated plainly that there was to be no general average when "a ship is intentionally run on shore because she is sinking, or driving on shore or rocks." With some change in language this provision appears in the York Antwerp Rules of 1877 and 1890. In 1924 Rule V was amended to delete the language "sink or" and the 1924 rule was carried forward into the 1950 rules. The 1950 rule reads:

> "When a ship is intentionally run on shore, and the circumstances are such that if that course were not adopted she would inevitably drive on shore or on rocks, no loss or damages caused to the ship, cargo and freight or any of them by such intentional running on shore shall be made good as general average, but loss or damage incurred in refloating such a ship shall be allowed as general average.

"In all other cases where a ship is intentionally run on shore for the common safety, the consequent loss or damage shall be allowed as general average."

What are the arguments to be made for permitting the vessel owner to charge cargo for general average contribution in the case of a voluntary stranding? What was the assumption behind the pre–1924 rule that no contribution could be had when the ship would certainly either sink or strike the rocks in any event? How voluntary a sacrifice for the common venture is it to choose between certainly sinking or being dashed on the rocks, and grounding the vessel in the most opportune place? But as Lowndes and Rudolf point out, General Average 373 (1948), the whole theory of general average is that there will be a voluntary act to choose the lesser peril. They suggest that the stranding of a vessel to avoid sinking is a classic case for general average.

Rule 5 of the 1994 version of the York–Antwerp Rules reads:

When a ship is intentionally run on shore for the common safety, whether or not she might have been driven on shore, the consequent loss or damage to the property involved in the common maritime adventure shall be allowed in general average.

The phrase "to the property involved in the common maritime adventure" was added in 1994. Was it aimed purely at clarification? Should the liability of the owner for damage to shore structures be included?

Ralli v. Troop

Supreme Court of the United States, 1895.
157 U.S. 386, 15 S.Ct. 657, 39 L.Ed. 742.

■ MR. JUSTICE GRAY, after stating the case, delivered the opinion of the court.

The law of general average, coming down to us from remote antiquity, is derived from the law of Rhodes, through the law of Rome, and is part of the maritime law, or law of the sea, as distinguished from the municipal law, or law of the land.

The typical case is that mentioned in the Rhodian law preserved in the Pandects of Justinian, by which, if a jettison of goods is made in order to lighten a ship, what is given for the benefit of all is to be made good by the contribution of all. Cavetur ut, si levandae navis gratia jactus mercium factus est, omnium contributione sarciatur, quod pro omnibus datum est. Dig. 14, 2, 1, 1.

Another case of general average, put in the Pandects, and the only one, beside jettison, mentioned in the Judgments of Oleron, or in the Laws of Wisby, is the cutting away of a mast to save ship and cargo. Dig. 14, 2, 1, 4; Oleron, arts. 8, 9; Wisby, arts. 7, 11, 14.

The distinction between voluntary and compulsory sacrifice is well illustrated by another case stated in the Pandects, recognized in the earliest English case on general average, and approved in all the books, in which money voluntarily paid by the master to ransom the ship and cargo from pirates is to be contributed for; but not so, as to goods or money forcibly taken by pirates. Dig. 14, 2, 1, 5; Hicks v. Palington, (32 Eliz.) Moore, 297.

In the courts of England and America, general average has not been restricted to the cases put by way of illustration in the Rhodian and Roman laws; but it has never been extended beyond the spirit and principle of those laws. * * *

As the right to general average may be considered as resting not merely on implied contract between the parties to the common adventure, but rather on the established law of the sea, in the light of and subject to which all owners of ships and cargoes undertake maritime adventures, so the authority of the master may be treated as resting either on implied contract of the parties, or on the duty imposed upon him by the law, as incident to his station and office, to meet the necessity created by an emergency which could not be foreseen or provided for, and to prevent the property in his custody and control from being left without protection and care.

Sir William Scott, speaking of the powers and duties of the master, said: "Though in the ordinary state of things he is a stranger to the cargo, beyond the purposes of safe custody and conveyance, yet in cases of instant and unforeseen and unprovided necessity, the character of agent and supercargo is forced upon him, not by the immediate act and appointment of the owner, but by the general policy of the law; unless the law can be supposed to mean that valuable property in his hand is to be left without protection and care. It must unavoidably be admitted, that in some cases he must exercise the discretion of an authorized agent over the cargo, as well in the prosecution of the voyage at sea, as in intermediate ports, into which he may be compelled to enter." * * *

At the present day, since voyages are longer, and merchants seldom go with their goods, there is the greater reason that upon the captain, selected for his skill and courage, and for his fitness to command the whole adventure, and to decide promptly and justly in cases of emergency, and better acquainted than any one else with the qualities and condition of the ship, and with the nature and stowage of her cargo, should rest the authority and the duty, in case of imminent peril, first taking such advice as he sees fit, to determine finally, so far as concerns the mutual relations of those interested in the maritime adventure, the time and the manner of sacrificing part of the adventure to secure the safety of the rest. * * *

If the master does not exercise reasonable skill and judgment and courage in sacrificing goods for the benefit of the adventure, the master and the owner of the ship are each liable to the owner of the goods sacrificed. Barnard v. Adams, 10 How. 270, 304, 13 L.Ed. 417 (1850); Lawrence v. Minturn, 17 How. 100, 110, 15 L.Ed. 58 (1854). * * *

In case of the master's death, disability or absence, no doubt, the mate or other chief officer of the vessel may succeed to the authority of the master, in this as in other respects. The Ann C. Pratt, 10 N.Y.Leg.Obs. 193; 1 Curtis, 340, and 18 How. 63. * * *

There is no case, in England or America, before the one at bar, in which a sacrifice made by a stranger, in no way connected with the navigation of the ship, or with the control or the care of the ship and cargo, as a distinct maritime adventure, has been held to give a right to contribution in general average.

There can be no general average, unless there has been a voluntary and successful sacrifice of part of the maritime adventure, made for the benefit of the whole adventure, and for no other purpose, and by order of the owners of all the interests included in the common adventure, or the authorized representative of all of them. The safety of any property, on land or water, not included in that adventure, can neither be an object of the sacrifice, nor a subject of the contribution. * * *

In none of the cases cited by the appellees, was property, sacrificed to put out a fire, by direction of others than the master or mate of a ship, adjudged to be a general average loss. * * *

The members of a fire department, or other persons, under the command of municipal officers of a port, and not under the employment and direction of the master of the ship, are simply executing a public duty, and are not acting, by any implication of contract or of law, for or in behalf of the owners of the ship and cargo. The Mary Frost, 2 Woods 306 (1876); The Cherokee, 31 F. 167, 170 (D.C.S.C.1887); Wamsutta Mills v. Old Colony Steamboat Co., 137 Mass. 471 (1884).

* * *

The leading facts found by the Circuit Court are as follows: The vessel, when the cargo in her hold took fire, was moored in the port of Calcutta, and near other vessels, as is shown by the finding of fact that, as soon as the mate sounded the alarm of fire, "from sixty to seventy men from the crews of the neighboring vessels" came to his assistance, bringing their buckets with them, as well as a force-pump "from a ship near by," and poured water into the hold. Afterwards, the port authorities came with fire-engines, and took the direction of the vessel, and were found by the master, when he returned on board, in charge of her. The port authorities pumped steam and water from their engines into the hold, and moved the vessel from her moorings and put her aground. The master does not appear to have objected to their taking charge of and moving the ship, and any objection on his part would have been futile, for it was clearly within their powers as conservators of the port. The master successfully removed part of the cargo, and desired, and believed it to be prudent and feasible, to remove more. But the port authorities forbade and prevented his doing so, because of the danger of increasing the fire, and, acting upon their own judgment, extinguished the fire by scuttling the vessel, whereby she became a wreck, not worth repairing. The master, being then permitted by the port authorities to resume charge of the vessel, saved the rest of the cargo in a damaged condition.

If the course desired and proposed by the master had been followed, the injuries, either to the cargo or to the ship, or to both, might have been different from those caused by the measures taken by the port authorities; and the difference in the property sacrificed might have affected the adjustment of contribution in general average.

The Circuit Court, indeed, has found, as facts, that "the measures taken by the mate before the port authorities took charge of the ship, and those subsequently taken by the port authorities, were the best available to extinguish the fire, and to save greater loss upon the cargo." But it is not found whether the motive and purpose of the port authorities was to save this vessel and her cargo, or to save other vessels and property in the port; whereas, in order to constitute a general average, the sole object of the sacrifice must appear to have been to save this vessel and cargo. Moreover, by the law of general average, the question what measures were the best and most prudent, the most feasible and available to extinguish the fire, or, in other words, what part of the maritime adventure should be sacrificed, and in what manner, for the safety of the rest of the adventure, was to be determined by the master at the time of the emergency; and his determination, faithfully and reasonably made, was, so far as affects the right of mutual contribution between the parties to the adventure, not to be overruled by the municipal authorities at the time, or by the court long afterwards. * * *

A sacrifice of vessel or cargo by the act of a stranger to the adventure, although authorized by the municipal law to make the sacrifice for the protection of his own interests, or of those of the public, gives no right of contribution, either for or against those outside interests, or even as between the parties to the common adventure.

The port authorities are strangers to the maritime adventure, and to all the interests included therein. They are in no sense the agents or representatives of the parties to that adventure, either by reason of any implied contract between those parties, or of any power conferred by law over the adventure as such.

They have no special authority or special duty in regard to the preservation, or the destruction, of any vessel and her cargo, as distinct from the general authority and the general duty appertaining to them as guardians of the port, and of all the property, on land or water, within their jurisdiction.

Their right and duty to preserve or destroy property, as necessity may demand, to prevent the spreading of a fire, is derived from the municipal law, and not from the law of the sea.

Their sole office and paramount duty, and, it must be presumed, their motive and purpose, in destroying ship or cargo, in order to put out a fire, are not to save the rest of a single maritime adventure, or to benefit private individuals engaged in that adventure; but to protect and preserve all the shipping and property in the port, for the benefit of the public.

In the execution of this office, and in the performance of this duty, they act under their official responsibility to the public, and are not subject to be controlled by the owners of the adventure, or by the master of the vessel as their representative.

In fine, the destruction of the J.W. Parker by the act of the municipal authorities of the port of Calcutta was not a voluntary sacrifice of part of a maritime adventure for the safety of the rest of that adventure, made, according to the maritime law, by the owners of vessel or cargo, or by the master as the agent and representative of both. But it was a compulsory sacrifice, made by the paramount authority of public officers deriving their powers from the municipal law, and the municipal law only; and therefore neither gave any right of action, or of contribution, against the owners of property benefited by the sacrifice, but not included in the maritime adventure, nor yet any right of contribution as between the owners of the different interests included in that adventure.   * * *

Decree reversed, claim of general average for loss or damage by the acts of the port authorities disallowed, and case remanded to the Circuit Court for further proceedings consistent with this opinion.

■ Mr. Justice Brown, with whom concurred Mr. Justice Harlan, dissenting.

I am compelled to dissent from the opinion of the court in this case. I find myself unable to escape the conviction that a person who has lawful possession of a vessel, and exercises the authority of a master over it, either by appointment or consent of the owner, or by operation of law, is to be considered the master pro hac vice, and competent to bind the vessel or her cargo by all acts within the scope of his apparent authority.

There is in this case a failure to find an important fact, namely, whether the action of the port authorities was taken in the interest of the ship and cargo alone, or in the interest of other neighboring property exposed to the conflagration.   * * *

Speaking for myself, I think the case should have been remanded for a further finding upon this point, since it is quite possible these facts might be considered as having a bearing upon the result. The opinion, however, is put upon the broad ground that the sacrifice must not only be for the benefit of the common adventure, but must be made by some one specially charged with the control and safety of that adventure, and must not be caused by the compulsory act of others, whether private parties or public authorities. To this I am unable to give my assent.   * * *

That damage done by pumping in water, or by scuttling and sinking the ship and extinguishing a fire, is a subject of general average contribution is now too well settled both in England and in this country to be longer a question of doubt, although the practice was formerly the other way. There is no disagreement upon this point. That there must be a common danger in which ship, cargo, and crew all participate; that the sacrifice must be necessary, or at least made in the exercise of a reasonable judgment that it was necessary; and that it must be voluntary, is also admitted. But whether the water be pumped in by the crew, or by a fire-engine stationed on shore, is quite immaterial, as was held in Nelson v. Belmont, 5 Duer 10 (1855); aff'd 21 N.Y. 36; Gregory v. Orrall, 8 F. 287

(C.C.Mass.1881); The Roanoke, 46 F. 297 (D.C.Wis.1891); S.C., 53 F. 270 (D.C.Wis.1892), and 59 F. 161 (D.C.Wis.1893); Stewart v. West India & c. Steamship Co., L.R. 8 Q.B. 88.

But if the master be engaged in extinguishing a fire by pumping in water, and the damage thereby done subjects the property saved to a general average contribution, I fail to see why he should lose his right to such contribution, if the port authorities, acting under a local ordinance, interfere and take possession of the vessel, and do exactly what he was engaged in doing, but more efficiently and expeditiously. It was for the interest of all parties that the fire should be extinguished as quickly as possible, and if the port authorities had more efficient means for such purposes than the master, and therefore interfered to assist him, it seems to me he should not lose his right to contribution. * * *

N O T E

Assuming that the sacrifice is made by, or on the order of a person who represents the common adventure, it must be made to avert a common peril threatening the adventure. A classic case taking a hard-nosed view of this requirement is Dabney v. New England Mut. Marine Ins. Co., 14 Allen (Mass.) 300 (1867). The saga was as follows. The Fredonia, loaded with fruit and oil, came upon another vessel, the Gratitude, that had suffered severe damage from a storm. It accompanied the Gratitude for three days and on the third day the mate of the Gratitude came aboard the Fredonia and stated to the master that his ship was in a sinking condition and that the pumps had been going for seven days and the passengers and crew were worn out with pumping. He asked the master to take off the women and children. At first he said he would not do it, that they would perish if they came aboard, but later when the mate and several passengers begged him to save their lives and it appeared that the forward pumps had given out and the ship was soon to sink, he agreed to take them if they would bring provisions and water, which they promised to do. Three hundred and twenty came aboard the Fredonia from the Gratitude. There was room for one hundred and fifty persons to stand on the deck. To make room for them, a portion of the cargo had to be jettisoned. In a split opinion, the court held that the purpose of the jettison was to save the lives of the passengers and crew of The Gratitude, not to save the common venture, that is, the Fredonia and its cargo. The dissenting judges were impressed by the fact that had the passengers been taken aboard first and the cargo jettisoned to preserve the stability of the vessel, there would have been a general average act. Accordingly they would have treated it as proximately caused by the necessities of navigation and would have allowed it as average.

Rule III of the York–Antwerp Rules (1974), provides that damage to the vessel or the cargo in extinguishing a fire on board is a general average sacrifice, whether the damage is done by "water or otherwise," including damage by grounding or scuttling the vessel. The rule excepts, however, "damage by smoke or heat, however caused."

Rule III of the 1950 version of the rules did not contain the smoke and heat exception, but contained a clause as follows: "except that no compensation shall be made for damage to such portions of the ship and bulk cargo, or to such separate packages of cargo, as have been on fire." The exception of damage to separate packages was added in the Rules of 1877, and that of damage to "portions of the ship and bulk cargo" in 1890. Rule III of the 1890 Rules was copied verbatim in the 1924 and 1950 versions. The exception of damage to packages and portions that have been on fire appears to have been in accord with the case law in both the United States and Great Britain. See Lowndes & Rudolf, General Average (9th ed. 1964) [published as Vol. 7 of the collection British Shipping Laws], 79. It appears to be a practical rule designed to govern cases in which it will be difficult if not impossible to tell what damage was done by the fire, and what by the water. Lowndes & Rudolf point out, however, that some unfairness exists under such a rule because there are cases in which such damage can be determined, and exclusion of contribution for damage by water to packages that have been on fire, while packages that inevitably would have been on fire but for the water applied to those actually on fire are included, is not strictly logical.

Of course the determination of what is a package for the purposes of Rule III (1950) presents the same difficulties we have seen in connection with the application of 46 U.S.C.A. § 1303(6), the COGSA $500 a package limitation of liability. See p. 680, supra. What is a "portion" of bulk cargo, or a "portion" of the vessel is also a problem. In the case of bulk cargo does it mean only the grains of wheat or lumps of coal that have been on fire, or the portion stored in a particular hold or part of the vessel? In Greenshields, Cowie & Co. v. Stephens & Sons [1908], 1 K.B. 51, aff'd [1908] A.C. 431, the cargo was coal and it was stowed in four separate holds. The coal in three of four of the holds caught fire by spontaneous combustion. Some of it burned and some of it was damaged by water used to put out the fire. General average was sought by the shipper and resisted on the ground that "portion" in the premises meant the coal stowed in a particular hold. In rejecting this argument the Court of Appeal noted that had the vessel not been constructed with divisions into separate holds and the cargo had been all in one mass there would be no general average. Such an interpretation would also, it felt, make general average of damage to the vessel rarely, if ever, available. It held, therefore, that the phrase was to be interpreted as meaning the "portion" actually on fire. What do you suppose the general average adjusters did, count out the cargo lump by lump?

To the extent that the 1974 Rules come to be included in bills of lading, the "smoke, heat" exception appears to change the present rule. See Starlight Trading, Inc. v. S.S. San Francisco Maru, 1974 A.M.C. 1523 (S.D.N.Y.1974). There it was thought necessary to seal the hold in which fire broke out when the fire was fought with CO_2, resulting in smoke damage that very probably would not have occurred if the hold had not been sealed. Judge Knapp rejected the contention that the 1974 amendment was declarative of the existing law. Concededly damage from smoke or heat from the fire would not be general average losses, however, and the 1974 version is another effort to eliminate difficult line drawing. See Reliance Marine Ins. Co. v. New York & C. Mail S.S. Co., 77 Fed. 317 (2d Cir.1896), distinguished in *The San Francisco Maru*, in which it was held that the owner of a cargo of tobacco was not entitled to general average contributions for damage to the cargo from smoke carried into the cargo by steam used to put out a fire when if the steam had not been used no part of the vessel would have been free from the "pervasive effects of smoke."

The 1994 version transposes the sentence, substituting "smoke however caused or by heat of the fire" for "smoke or heat however caused." How much tinkering does it take to get a rule right?

B. IMMINENT PERIL

The West Imboden

(Ravenscroft v. United States)

United States District Court, Eastern District of New York, 1936.
1936 A.M.C. 696, aff'd 88 F.2d 418 (2d Cir.1937).

■ CAMPBELL, D. J. This suit was filed on September 17, 1932 and purports to be based upon the amendment of June 30, 1932 to the Suits in Admiralty Act of 1920, 46 Mason's U.S.C. § 745. It relates to certain shipments of cotton made on respondent's S. S. West Imboden from Texas City, Texas, in the latter part of December 1919, to Liverpool, England, where the vessel arrived on, or about January 20, 1920.

The libel alleges two causes of action, the first in the ordinary cargo damage form, and the second for general average contribution.

* * *

The shipments of cotton herein referred to were duly * * * delivered to the said steamship West Imboden and to the respondent, in * * * good order and condition * * * to be transported by the said steamship West Imboden and by the respondent from the * * * port of Texas City to the port of Liverpool, England in accordance with the terms of the * * * bills of lading.

Thereafter the said steamship West Imboden having said cotton on board and being employed as a merchant vessel, sailed from the port of Texas City, Texas and arrived on or about January 30, 1920, at the port of Liverpool, England, and there made delivery of the shipments referred to in the stipulation filed herein, and some of the said merchandise was damaged and not in the like good order and condition as when shipped and as when delivered to the said steamship * * * West Imboden and to respondent.

On January 27, 1920, a hurricane broke, and the vessel was compelled to stop on account of inability to steer. During all of this heavy weather, the superstructure and boats sustained damage. During the storm of the 27th at 2:25 p.m., the deck above the No. 2 hold was found to be hot, and when rain and heavy seas fell on same, it caused vapor and steam to rise. The hatches were not opened, and from the above indication, the master and officers concluded there was a fire in the said hold, and steam and water was injected into the hold. By 6:00 o'clock p.m. the deck was cool.

The vessel arrived at Liverpool and anchored in the River Mersey on January 30, 1920. At this time, the deck was locally warm, and upon the recommendation of the surveyor from the Liverpool Salvage Association (engaged by the United States Shipping Board), who had boarded the vessel, further steam was injected into this hold. All due efforts were made by the ship's agents at Liverpool, to procure, through the harbor authorities, a berth at which the vessel could discharge her cargo at the earliest practicable moment. As soon as one was allocated by the authorities, she was moved to a closed berth where the discharge of Nos. 1 and 3 hatches was commenced, leaving No. 2 hold isolated, and under slight upper steam pressure. She was not permitted to discharge the No. 2 hold at this closed berth because of port regulations which prohibited the discharging of a hold in which fire existed, or was suspected, at a closed berth. After discharge from her other holds had been completed, she was moved to an open berth where the No. 2 hold was partly discharged, and when it became evident that there was no fire in the hold the discharge of this hold was completed, at a closed berth. On March 1, 1920 the hatches of No. 2 hold were opened, and as discharge proceeded, it was found that no fire had ever existed among the cargo stowed therein. A steam pipe in the hold was found to be broken near the deck, from which steam had escaped and heated the deck plating near No. 2 hatch. Cotton belonging to the libellants upon being taken from the hold, was found to be damaged by the steam and water injected as above stated.

I will now consider the second cause of action.

Under this cause of action libellants seek a decree against the respondent for the amount of the contributions which they would have received had a general average been stated.

This suit is predicated on the amendment of June 30th, 1932 to the Suits in Admiralty Act, and to be sustained it must be "based upon a cause of action whereon a prior suit in admiralty, or an action at law, or an action under the Tucker Act" was commenced.

The original suit was a suit for cargo damage based on the contract of carriage. There was no allegation in the petition to the Court of Claims of any claim on general average nor was any recovery on that theory sought on the trial before the Court of Claims.

The attempt to recover on that theory is first made in this action more than twelve years after the alleged damage occurred.

While it is true that it has been held that recovery might be had on a claim for general average although it is not specifically alleged in the libel, Dupont De Nemours & Co. v. Vance, 60 U.S. 162, 15 L.Ed. 584 (1856); Eugenia J. Diacakis, 22 F.2d 461, 1923 A.M.C. 305 (D.C.N.Y.1923), it seems clear to me that it was not the intent of Congress, in the amendment supra, to permit the introduction, twelve years after the event, of a cause of action never presented before. What Congress did intend was to give a day in court, on the merits, to those litigants who were deprived of it by what was considered the technicality of the *Johnson* and *Lustgarten* cases.

The case at bar was fully tried and decided by the Court of Claims without any mention of any rights of libellants under general average, and what they are entitled to try under that amendment is what they tried before the Court of Claims. This amendment was considered in Adders v.

United States, 5 F.Supp. 457, 460, 1933 A.M.C. 1554 (D.C.N.Y.1933), aff'd 70 F.2d 371, 1934 A.M.C. 511 (2 Cir.1934); Phoenix Ins. Co. v. United States, 3 F.Supp. 112, 113, 1933 A.M.C. 308 (D.C.Conn.1932).

The burden rests upon libellants to establish the right to sue the United States. Schillinger v. United States, 155 U.S. 163, 166, 15 S.Ct. 85, 39 L.Ed. 108 (1894); The Harrisburg, 119 U.S. 199, 214, 4 S.Ct. 140, 30 L.Ed. 358 (1886); The Isonomia, 285 F. 516, 520, 1923 A.M.C. 132 (2 Cir.1923).

No fire existed on the West Imboden.

On behalf of libellants but one case is cited, Wordsworth, 88 Fed. 313, but that case is not in point, as in that case there was an actual peril to cargo, the master being merely mistaken as to its degree.

The bills of lading in the case at bar provide that general average shall be according to the York–Antwerp Rules.

See appendix in Arnould on *Marine Insurance and General Average,* 10th Ed., p. 1709.

"Damage done to a ship and cargo or either of them by water or otherwise, including damage by beaching or scuttling a burning ship in extinguishing a fire on board the ship, shall be made good as general average. * * *"

The rule is limited to acts done to extinguish a fire, and not a supposed fire, and this rule is in accordance with the recognized definitions of general average. Ralli v. Troop, 157 U.S. 386, 15 S.Ct. 657, 39 L.Ed. 742 (1895).

See Stevenson on *Average,* p. 8, with reference to Jettison:

"But it is said that in all cases of a sacrifice for the general good there must be a sufficient cause. For if Jettison (e.g.) be made on a false alarm, it cannot be said that the Jettison procured the safety of the vessel. Jettison cannot therefore, in this case give rise to contribution."

No allowance can be made in general average for any damage if such additional damage was caused by reason of action taken after the ship reached Liverpool.

There was no fire, and if the action taken be deemed that of the master, then what I have already said applies. If the action taken was that of the port authorities of Liverpool, such action is not a general average act.

The contention that libellants are equitably estopped to assert their second cause of action requires no extended argument.

Respondent first contended and now denies that it was a case for general average and libellants first contended it was not and now contend it was a case for general average, but the fact remains that although respondent returned the general average securities it had received, it did so as to libellants (except as to but one of them) on receiving general average guarantees.

The respondent's contention that libellants are equitably estopped to assert the second cause of action is not sustained.

A decree may be entered in favor of the respondent dismissing the libel on the merits with costs.

Settle decree on notice.

Submit proposed findings of fact and conclusions of law in accordance with this opinion for the assistance of the court as provided by Rule 46½ of the Admiralty Rules and the Admiralty Rules of this Court.

NOTE

It is not usually as easy to tell in retrospect whether or not there was a peril. See, e.g., Navigazione Generale Italiana v. Spencer Kellogg & Sons, Inc. (The S.S. Minicio). In the *Minicio,* the vessel sought general average contribution for damages and expenses in getting it off a bar on which it was stranded. In answer to the argument that no danger existed, the court observed, "Indeed when a vessel is stranded she and her cargo are practically always in a substantial peril." One of the cases relied upon in *The Minicio* was Lawrence v. Minturn, 58 U.S. (17 How.) 100, 15 L.Ed. 58 (1854), in which the Court noted that the jettison involved was actually made when the sea was smooth and the ship in no immediate danger. It went on to say that the particular cargo could be jettisoned only at great risk when there was any considerable sea and to hold that the master would have to wait until a storm would in effect prohibit any sacrifice at all. Suppose, however, an approaching storm leads the master to jettison the cargo in calm seas and the storm does not materialize. Is this situation covered by The West Imboden? Rule A of the York Antwerp Rules of 1950 provides:

> There is a general average act when, and only when, any extraordinary sacrifice or expenditure is intentionally and reasonably made or incurred for the common safety for the purpose of preserving from peril the property involved in a common maritime adventure.

This language was not changed in either the 1974 or the 1994 version. Gilmore and Black refer to The West Imboden as "hard," observing "A 'purpose of preserving from peril' surely may exist, even though a mistake may be made as to the existence of the peril." Since the text of Rule A (1950) is unchanged from rules of 1924, The West Imboden is in effect an interpretation of the present York–Antwerp Rule. Note that the English rule is to the same effect. See Lowndes & Rudolf on *General Average* 349 (1948). Note that in The West Imboden, the court distinguishes The Wordsworth, 88 Fed. 313 (S.D.N.Y.1898), on the ground that there, there *was* a peril, but the *degree* of peril was misapprehended and the sacrifice later proved to be unnecessary. The forepeak tank had been found full of water and the master believed the reason to be a leak in the shell plating. Accordingly, he opened the sluices and let the water run back into the engine room where the pumps would take care of it, damaging some of the cargo in the process. It turned out that there was no leak in the shell plating and the water had entered the tank through the hawse pipes and it was unnecessary to open the sluices. Lowndes and Rudolf did not mention The West Imboden, but read The Wordsworth as inconsistent with the English cases.

A discernible modern tendency toward relaxation of the requirement of imminent peril is discussed by Judge Feinberg in Eagle Terminal Tankers v. Ins. Co. of U.S.S.R., reproduced in subchapter E, infra.

C.   COMMON ADVENTURE

S. C. Loveland Co. v. United States

United States District Court, Eastern District of Pennsylvania, 1962.
207 F.Supp. 450, 1963 A.M.C. 260.

■ ALLAN K. GRIM, SR., D. J.   Libellant contracted with the government (the Navy) to transfer by barge five picket boats from Salisbury, Maryland, to the Norfolk Naval shipyard at Portsmouth, Virginia.   In 1952 libellant's tug Gertrude Loveland sailed from Salisbury down Chesapeake Bay, towing behind her two barges with the five picket boats aboard, three in the front barge, Loveland 33, and two in the rear barge, Loveland 32.   During the voyage the tug left the proper channel and ran aground.   When the tug grounded, the barges, having no means of stopping, kept moving.   The first barge, Loveland 33, rammed the grounded tug and was rammed in turn by the second barge, Loveland 32.   The collision damage to Loveland 33 caused her to leak, and the tug, having gotten herself off the ground, pushed 33 aground to keep her from sinking.[1]

After the accident the tug, leaving Loveland 33 grounded, proceeded to tow Loveland 32 to Portsmouth.   Shortly thereafter temporary repairs were made to Loveland 33 and another tug towed her to Portsmouth.   The picket boats on the barges, constituting the cargo, were not damaged.

Under these facts the parties have stipulated that:

"17.   The facts present a situation to which the principles of general average apply."

Under this stipulation the only problem before the court is how much libellant is entitled to under the principles of general average contribution.

The parties have stipulated that the reasonable cost of the repairs to Loveland 33 for her collision damage alone was $5,000 and that the reasonable cost of the repairs to Loveland 33 due to her grounding was $2,500.

---

1. The parties have stipulated that 33 was run aground to prevent sinking, although the captain of the tug, who was the only witness on the question of whether or not she would have sunk, testified in his deposition:

"Q. If you had not run # 33 ashore, she would have sunk, right? A. I would say she would have went decks to the water.

"Q. Could you have towed her in that condition? A. No sir.

"Q. But you did say that it would have continued to float, right? A. I think she would have continued to float."

There is no evidence in the case as to whether or not 33's cargo, three picket boats, would have been damaged if 33 had sunk "decks to the water."

General average is defined in The Star of Hope, 76 U.S. 203, 19 L.Ed. 638 (1870), at page 228:

"General average contribution is defined to be a contribution by all the parties in a sea adventure to make good the loss sustained by one of their number on account of sacrifices voluntarily made of part of the ship or cargo to save the residue * * * or for extraordinary expenses necessarily incurred by one or more of the parties for the general benefit of all the interests embarked in the enterprise * * *

"Common justice dictates that where two or more parties are engaged in the same sea risk, and one of them, in a movement of imminent peril, makes a sacrifice to avoid the impending danger or incurs extraordinary expenses to promote the general safety, the loss or expenses so incurred shall be assessed upon all in proportion to the share of each in the adventure."

In the present case, the "extraordinary expense" incurred "to promote the general safety" of the two parties, namely the government (owner of the cargo) and the Loveland Company, was the damage caused to Loveland 33 by the grounding, by which she was prevented from sinking and by which her cargo of three picket boats was saved. The damage resulting from the collisions was not the sacrifice made for the benefit of the rest, but the fact that gave rise to the need for sacrifice.

The expense incurred resulting from repairs to the barge due to its damage from grounding "shall be assessed upon all in proportion to the share of each in the undertaking." *The Star of Hope,* supra. Respondent contends that its share in the undertaking was the five picket boats and that they all should be taken into consideration as part of the undertaking and that the tug and both barges should be taken into consideration as libellant's part of the undertaking. Libellant, on the other hand, contends that only the value of Loveland 33 and its cargo of three picket boats should be taken into consideration, on the ground that only they were in peril. If libellant's contention were adopted respondent's liability would be increased considerably over its liability if respondent's contention were adopted.

On the question of damages the present case seems to be controlled by Sacramento Navigation Co. v. Salz, 273 U.S. 326, 47 S.Ct. 368, 71 L.Ed. 663, 1927 A.M.C. 397 (1927). In the *Salz case* the Sacramento Navigation Co. agreed to transport certain barley for Salz on a barge. The barge was towed by a Sacramento steamship in accordance with the terms of a contract of affreightment. The steamship was operated negligently and caused the barge to collide with another ship so that the barley was swamped and destroyed. Salz sued to collect the value of his barley. The defense was that the situation was controlled by section 3 of the Harter Act, 46 U.S.C.A. § 192, which provides:

"If the owner of any vessel transporting merchandise or property to or from any port in the United States of America shall exercise due diligence to make the said vessel in all respects seaworthy and properly manned, equipped, and supplied, neither the vessel, her owner or owners, agent, or charterers, shall become or be held responsible for damage or loss resulting from faults or errors in navigation or in the management of said vessel. * * * "

Salz contended that the Harter Act did not apply, since the negligence causing the injury was that of the steamship and the "vessel transporting" the cargo was in fact the barge, a separate vessel. The Supreme Court held, however, that for the purposes of the Act the barge and steamship together constituted "the effective instrumentality" for performing the contract between the parties (which the Court determined to be a contract of affreightment rather than a contract of towage) and that the Act applied to relieve the navigation company of liability.

Although the Harter Act is not involved in the present case, the question arises of whether the tug and barges should be considered as separate vessels or as one. On this issue the facts of the present case are analogous to those of the *Salz case* and on that basis the tug and barges must be considered as one. Hence, for purposes of general average contribution, there must be taken into consideration the value, just before the collision, of the tug and two barges, and the value of the entire cargo: the five picket boats.

Libellant places great reliance on The J. P. Donaldson, 167 U.S. 599, 17 S.Ct. 951, 42 L.Ed. 292 (1897), for the proposition that there can be no general average contribution against a tug for damage to, or loss of, a tow of barges. In that case the owner of a tug contracted to tow two barges from Buffalo to Bay City, Michigan. On Lake Michigan a storm arose, and in order to prevent the tug from being driven ashore, her master cut the tow lines. The tug was saved, but the barges were lost. The Supreme Court held that on these facts the tug was not liable in general average for the loss of the barges because "the right of contribution is limited to the particular ship and cargo, and the sacrifice of one ship for the safety of another does not give rise to any claim of general average," 167 U.S. at p. 602. This case is factually distinguishable from the case at bar, however, in the ownership of the vessels and in the type of contract involved. In the *Donaldson case* one party owned the tug and another the barges, and the contract was by A to tow the barges of B. Here tug and barges were all owned by libellant and the contract was not to tow barges but a contract of affreightment. The fact that the freight consisted of picket boats, which are themselves vessels, is totally immaterial.

The *Salz case,* supra, which deals with a similar factual and contractual situation, governs the present case. The *Donaldson case* is clearly distinguishable.

In accordance with the stipulation of the parties an interlocutory decree will be entered in favor of libellant for general average contribution for the grounding damage to the barge Loveland 33, the amount of grounding damage being $2,500. In determining the general average contribution there shall be taken into account the value of the entire cargo of five picket boats and the value of the tug Gertrude Loveland and both barges. The determination of values and resultant contribution shall be referred to a commissioner if the proctors for the parties are unable to agree thereon between themselves within 30 days after the entry of the interlocutory decree. The collision damage of $5,000 to Loveland 33 will not be included in the calculation of the liability of respondent.

NOTE

S.C. Loveland, although spoken of by Gilmore & Black as "eminently correct," is criticized in Parks, *The Law of Tug, Tow, and Pilotage,* 646–647 (2d Ed. 1982). Parks states that few persons who write about general average would agree with Gilmore & Black. If one pictures the master of the tug as one in charge of the enterprise, tug and tow, there is no trouble in viewing the pushing of the Loveland 33 aground as an intentional grounding within the *Barnard* rule, viewing the barge and its cargo as a unit, but was the act designed to avoid a danger common to the enterprise? The original damage to the Loveland 33 was occasioned by the accidental grounding of the tug, and the resulting collision, neither of which was a general average sacrifice. The Tug and the Loveland 32 were not in danger by virtue of the condition of the Loveland 33. On what basis, then, can the grounding be viewed as a sacrifice of the property of one to save the property of the rest?

With *S.C. Loveland,* cf. Northland Navigation Co., Ltd. v. Patterson Boiler Works, Ltd. [1983] 2 F.C. 59, 1985 A.M.C. 465. In *Northland,* a tug and tow encountered heavy seas, with water breaking over the stern of the tug, flooding the bilge, and entering the engine room. The engine began to shudder. At this juncture the tow line was cut and the tug headed for shelter. The next morning the barge was found aground. After a number of unsuccessful attempts to free the barge, it was declared a constructive total loss and abandoned to its underwriters, and efforts were begun to unload the cargo. Several such efforts failed, but ultimately the vessel shifted fortuitously into a position making it possible to unload the entire cargo. The carrier and owner of the tow (parent and subsidiary corporations) sued the shipper and owner of the cargo for general average contribution to the "extraordinary expenditures" incurred in the efforts to salvage the barge and cargo.

The Canadian court in Vancouver considered the case as it stood on three different dates. First, it indicated that since the tug and tow were both in some danger of going down, the act of cutting the barge adrift, knowing that it would either sink or strand, could be characterized as a general average sacrifice. It did not pursue this matter further, however, except to note that on the subject of the liability of a tug to contribute in general average when its tow had been cut away and the tow and its cargo lost there was no direct English or Canadian authority, and to call attention to *The J.P. Donaldson* in the United States, holding so.

Second, it took up the period between the stranding and the abandonment of the barge to its underwriters. Although the stranding was not a general average act, there being no indication that it was or could have been run aground apurpose, once the vessel was stranded there was a common danger that barge and cargo would be lost. Therefore, while there was no general average sacrifice, the extraordinary expenses made to save the barge and its cargo constituted general average expenditures. Since the common danger that occasioned these expenditures was one not shared by the tug, it was not required to contribute.

Finally, after the abandonment of the barge to the underwriters, the court found no further common danger. Thus the extraordinary expenses (salvage) of the cargo was a particular charge to cargo.

Is the result in *Northland* based upon the separation of the tug from the tow and its cargo prior to the general average expenditure? Cf. Ellerman Lines v. Gibbs, [1984] 1 C.F. 411, 1984 A.M.C. 2579 (Fed.Ct.Trial Div., Ottawa 1983), in which the court indicated that even if it be assumed that cargo must contribute in general average to the costs of repair of a condition discovered while the vessel was in its berth at a port of call, a shipper who had paid the freight in full had a right to demand delivery of cargo at an intermediate port and the carrier could not exact as a condition the signing of a "non-separation of interest agreement." No contribution was sought from the owners of cargo delivered in due course at that port. See also Walthew v. Mavrojami, 5 L.R.Ex. 116 (1870), which the *Northland* court found analogous. There the vessel stranded and its cargo was removed to a safe place, and it was held that subsequent extraordinary expenditures to float the vessel were not general average expenditures. The facts of the *Ellerman* case are given in greater detail on p. 798, infra.

Or does general average adjust itself to the breadth of the risk? In other words, while all interests are still part of the voyage is it possible to have a general average act in averting a peril to some interests that is no peril to others, or to excuse a particular interest from contribution where it did not share the peril? For example, suppose that a number of shippers have goats on board and it becomes apparent that unless some of the goats are thrown overboard the health of all the goats will suffer, but there is no danger to the vessel. If the goats of A are thrown over and the goats of B, C, and D are delivered healthy, can A obtain contribution from B, C, and D? If so, will the vessel interest have to go into the average?

There are also instances when cargo, or particular cargo, incurs expenses not in the interest of preserving the vessel.Rule XVII provides that deduction shall be made from the value of the property of "all extra charges incurred in respect thereof subsequent to the general average act, except such charges as are allowed in general average." See, e.g., Ultramar Canada, Inc. v. Mutual Marine Office, Inc., 1994 A.M.C. 2409 (Can. Fed. Tr. Div.1994) in which $818,097.62 in charges for heating and removing a cargo of oil, which had almost solidified in cold weather, was deducted, leaving a contributive value of $30,518.37. The $818,097.62 was charged to the cargo individually.

In cases like *Ultramar* in which there was a $2,000,000 contract salvage bill for the ship and cargo, and after the ship was towed in it was declared a constructive total loss, it may occur that the vessel's owner's expenditures in connection with a general average act will exceed the total contributory values. The court indicated that in such a case the universally acknowledged rule is that the owner must bear the excess.

D.   PERIL THE RESULT OF NEGLIGENCE

The Jason

Supreme Court of the United States, 1912.
225 U.S. 32, 32 S.Ct. 560, 56 L.Ed. 969.

"Statement of Facts

"The facts upon which the questions arise are these:

"On July 30, 1904, the Norwegian Steamship Jason while bound on a voyage from Cienfuegos, Cuba, to New York, with general cargo, including 12,000 bags of sugar, consigned to Arbuckle Brothers, and insured with the Insurance Company of North America, stranded off the south coast of Cuba, through the negligence of her navigators. The steamship was seaworthy and was properly manned, equipped and supplied.

"The vessel was relieved from the strand on August 9 as the result of sacrifices by jettison of 2,042 bags of sugar (1,657 bags being the property of Arbuckle Brothers), of sacrifices and extraordinary expenditures voluntarily made or incurred by the shipowner through the master, and of the services of salvors specially employed. Said sacrifices and expenditures were necessary to relieve ship, cargo and freight from common peril. She then completed her voyage, and made delivery of the remainder of her cargo to the several consignees at New York on their executing an average bond for the payment of losses and expenses which should appear to be due from them, provided they were stated and apportioned by the adjusters 'in accordance with established usages and laws in similar cases.'

"The bills of lading for all of the Jason's cargo contained the following provision:

" 'General average payable according to York–Antwerp Rules, and as to matters not therein provided for according to usages of port of New York.

" 'If the owner of the ship shall have exercised due diligence to make said ship in all respects seaworthy and properly manned, equipped and supplied, it is hereby agreed that in case of danger, damage or disaster resulting from fault or negligence of the pilot, master or crew, in the navigation or management of the ship, or from latent or other defects, or unseaworthiness of the ship, whether existing at time of shipment or at beginning of the voyage, but not discoverable by due diligence, the consignees or owners of the cargo shall not be exempted from liability for contribution in General Average, or for any special charges incurred, but with the shipowner shall contribute in General Average, and shall pay such special charges, as if such danger, damage or disaster had not resulted from such fault, negligence, latent or other defect or unseaworthiness.'

"Both parties pleaded the bills of lading as constituting the contract of carriage.

"A general average adjustment was afterwards made in New York by Johnson & Higgins, adjusters appointed in the average bond. Both parties presented their claims to the adjusters for sacrifices made by them respectively for the common benefit and safety of the adventure. The adjusters allowed in the General Average account the compensation of the salvors, the sacrifices of cargo, and the sacrifices and extraordinary expenditures of the shipowner, and each of the interests was credited with such amounts as had been paid by it for the common benefit. * * *

"The adjustment and apportionment of General Average, so made, showed a balance due from Arbuckle Brothers of $5,060.24, which the latter refused to pay. The grounds of such refusal were that the stranding resulted from the ship's negligence, and that the general average clause, above quoted, contained in the bills of lading is invalid.

"The original libel was filed by the owner of the Jason against Arbuckle Brothers and its guarantor, the Insurance Company of North America, to recover this amount.

"Arbuckle Brothers and the Insurance Company of North America filed a cross libel to recover the sum of $3,506.50, which they alleged would be due them on an adjustment of the general average losses, if the shipowner's losses and sacrifices were excluded from the General Average account by reason of the fact that the stranding was caused by negligence of the ship's navigators. They claimed that the shipowner's sacrifices and extraordinary expenditures, made for the common benefit and safety of the adventure after the stranding, should not be allowed in the adjustment. If said sacrifices and expenditures should be excluded from the adjustment and the value of the ship should be taken account of as a contributory interest, the adjustment would show a balance in favor of Arbuckle Brothers.

"The District Court made a decree dismissing both libels, from which decree both parties duly appealed to this Court.

"Questions Certified

"Upon the facts above set forth the questions of law concerning which this Court desires the instruction of the Supreme Court are:

"1. Whether the general average agreement above quoted from the bills of lading is valid, and entitles the shipowner to collect a general average contribution from the cargo owners, under the circumstances above stated, in respect of sacrifices made and extraordinary expenditures incurred by it subsequent to the stranding for the common benefit and safety of ship, cargo and freight.

"2. Whether, in view of the provisions of the third section of the Harter Act the cargo owners, under the circumstances above stated, have a right to contribution from the shipowner for sacrifices of cargo made subsequent to the stranding, for the common benefit and safety of ship, cargo and freight?

"3. Where the cargo owners, under the circumstances above stated, can recover contribution from the shipowner in respect of general average sacrifices of cargo, without contributing to the general average sacrifices and expenditures of the shipowner made for the same purpose. * * *"

■ MR. JUSTICE PITNEY, after stating the case as above, delivered the opinion of the court.

That the facts present a case of general average within the meaning of the clause embodied in the bills of lading is entirely clear. There was a common, imminent peril involving ship and cargo, followed by a voluntary and extraordinary sacrifice of property (including extraordinary expenses), necessarily made to avert the peril, and a resulting common benefit to the adventure. * * *

The principal controversy is upon the question of the validity of the agreement that if the shipowner "shall have exercised due diligence to make said ship in all respects seaworthy, and properly manned, equipped and supplied," then, in case of danger, damage, or disaster resulting from (inter alia) negligent navigation, the cargo-owners shall not be exempted from liability for contribution in general average, but with the shipowner shall contribute as if such danger, damage, or disaster had not resulted from negligent navigation. The facts show that the shipowner had fulfilled the condition imposed upon him by this clause; that is, he had "exercised due diligence to make said ship in all respects seaworthy and properly manned, equipped and supplied." The question presented for solution turns upon the effect of the third section of the act of Congress approved February 13, 1893, c. 105, 27 Stat. 445 (U.S.Comp.Stat., 1901, p. 2946), known as the Harter Act, and of the decision of this court in the case of The Irrawaddy, 171 U.S. 187, 18 S.Ct. 831, 43 L.Ed. 130 (1898).

Prior to the Harter Act it was established that a common carrier by sea could not by any agreement in the bill of lading exempt himself from responding to the owner of cargo for damages arising from the negligence of the master or crew of the vessel. Liverpool & G. W. Steam Co. v. Phenix Ins. Co., 129 U.S. 397, 438, 9 S.Ct. 469, 32 L.Ed. 788 (1889); following New York C. Railroad Co. v. Lockwood, 84 U.S. (17 Wall.) 357, 21 L.Ed. 627 (1873).

But of course the responsibilities of the carrier were subject to modification by law, and with respect to vessels transporting merchandise from or between ports of the United States and foreign ports they were substantially modified by the Harter Act. * * *

In the case now before us it is argued in behalf of the shipowner that since by the third section of the Harter Act he is absolved from responsibility for the negligence of his master and crew under the circumstances existing, there is nothing in the policy of the law to debar him from bargaining with the owners of cargo for a participation in the general average contribution. In behalf of the cargo-owners it is insisted that the construction placed upon the legislation in question by this court in The Irrawaddy, 171 U.S. 187, 18 S.Ct. 831, 43 L.Ed. 130 (1898), leaves the shipowner still disabled from making an agreement with the cargo-owners for a participation with them in general average contributions resulting from negligent navigation or management of the ship by its master and crew.

* * * In reaching this result the courts below have, as we think, misconceived the effect of the language used by Mr. Justice Shiras, speaking for this court, in The Irrawaddy, and have given to that decision an import quite beyond its legitimate scope. In that case there was no agreement between shipowner and cargo-owner respecting general average, nor respecting the consequences of a stranding or other peril that might result from the negligence of the master or crew of the vessel. * * *

The point of the decision in The Irrawaddy (and as an authority the case goes no further), is, that while the Harter Act relieved the shipowner from liability for his servant's negligence, it did not of its own force entitle him to share in a general average rendered necessary by such negligence.

* * *

In our opinion, so far as the Harter Act has relieved the shipowner from responsibility for the negligence of his master and crew, it is no longer against the policy of the law for him to contract with the cargo-owners for a participation in general average contribution growing out of such negligence; and since the clause contained in the bills of lading of the Jason's cargo admits the shipowner to share in the general average only under circumstances where by the act he is relieved from responsibility, the provision in question is valid, and entitles him to contribution under the circumstances stated.

The second question is whether, under the like circumstances, the cargo-owners can recover contribution from the shipowner for sacrifices of cargo made subsequent to the stranding, for the common benefit and safety of ship, cargo and freight. * * *

Having already held that the general average clause contained in the bill of lading is valid as against the cargo-owner, it follows ex necessitate that it is valid in his favor; indeed, no ground is suggested for disabling the shipowner from voluntarily subjecting himself or his ship to liability to respond to the cargo in an action or in a general average adjustment, for the consequences of the negligence of his master or crew, even though by the Harter Act he is relieved from responsibility for such negligence. Therefore we have only to determine whether by the language of the general average clause the cargo-owners are entitled to contribution from the ship for sacrifices of cargo made subsequent to the stranding for the common benefit and safety. The language is that in the circumstances presented "the consignees or owners of the cargo shall not be exempted from liability for contribution in general average, or for any special charges incurred, but with the shipowner shall contribute in general average, and shall pay such special charges, as if such danger, damage or disaster had not resulted from such default, negligence," etc. This language clearly imports an agreement that the shipowner shall contribute in general average. The opposite view would render the clause inconsistent with the principles of equity and reciprocity upon which the entire law of general average is founded.

The foregoing considerations compel a negative answer to the third question. In view of the valid stipulations contained in the bill of lading, it would be a contradiction of terms to permit the cargo-owners to recover contribution from the ship in respect of general average sacrifices of cargo, without on their part contributing to the general average sacrifices and expenditures of the shipowner made for the same purpose. This would not be general average contribution, the essence of which is that extraordinary sacrifices made and expenses incurred for the common benefit and safety are to be borne proportionately by all who are interested.

Our conclusion, accordingly, is that of the questions certified to us by the Circuit Court of Appeals, the first question should be answered in the affirmative, the second question should be answered in the affirmative, and the third question should be answered in the negative, and it is so ordered.

NOTE

Present day "Jason clauses" read:

> "In the event of accident, danger, damage, or disaster, before or after commencement of the voyage, resulting from any cause whatsoever, whether due to negligence or not, for which, or for the consequence of which, the Carrier is not responsible, by statute, contract, or otherwise, the cargo, shippers, consignees, or owners of the cargo shall contribute with the Carrier in general average to the payment of any sacrifices, losses or expenses of a general average nature that may be made or incurred and shall pay salvage and special charges incurred in respect of the cargo."

Such a clause is to be interpreted in the light of the Carriage of Goods by Sea Act. It has been held, for example, that despite its conclusion in the bill of lading, there is no right to contribution in general average for sacrifices made necessary by unseaworthiness if the vessel owner did not use due diligence to provide a seaworthy vessel at groundbreaking. Deutsche Shell Tanker Gesellschaft v. Placid Refining Co., 993 F.2d 466, 1993 A.M.C. 2141 (5th Cir.1993); Orient Mid–East Lines, Inc. v. A Shipment of Rice, 496 F.2d 1032, 1974 A.M.C. 2593 (5th Cir.1974). See also Todd Shipyards Corp. v. United States, 391 F.Supp. 588, 1975 A.M.C. 753 (S.D.N.Y.1975).

What if the bill of lading does not include a Jason clause? Is the rule of *The Irrawaddy* still good law? See American Home Assurance Co. v. L & L Marine Service, Inc., 688 F.Supp. 502, 1989 A.M.C. 684 (E.D.Mo.1988), aff'd in part, vac'd in part 875 F.2d 1351, 1989 A.M.C. 1817 (8th Cir.1989); Manhattan Oil Transportation Co. v. M/V Salvador, 1976 A.M.C. 134 (S.D.N.Y.1975); Todd Shipyards Corp. v. United States, supra.

E.   EXTRAORDINARY EXPENSE AS GENERAL AVERAGE

Eagle Terminal Tankers, Inc. v. Insurance Co. of U.S.S.R.

United States Court of Appeals, Second Circuit, 1981.
637 F.2d 890, 1981 A.M.C. 137.

■ FEINBERG, CHIEF JUDGE:

* * *

I

According to the record now before us, Eagle's general average claim arose in the following manner. On December 30, 1975, the S. S. Eagle Courier left Port Arthur, Texas, bearing some 26,000 metric tons of grain destined for Leningrad. At 7:45 on the evening of January 13, 1976, as the ship was maneuvering off the English coast to pick up a pilot, the first assistant engineer advised the officer on watch that he had felt a bump. Visibility was good, with only light winds, but nothing could be seen in the water near the ship at the time. The ship continued sailing toward Rotterdam, its next scheduled port of call. By 3:00 P.M. the next day, metallic scraping noises could be heard coming from the stern. The ship successfully completed its voyage, however, reaching a mooring buoy at Rotterdam two and a half hours later. Shortly thereafter, divers hired by the ship's captain conducted an underwater examination of the ship. Their report disclosed extensive damage to the propeller; among other things, the propeller's blades were bent and the propeller itself appeared to have shifted aft from the tailshaft. When turned, the propeller produced a scouring noise. This damage was serious enough, as defendant has conceded, to make repairs necessary before the voyage could be resumed. Accordingly, after a portion of the cargo was unloaded and the ship placed in drydock, the propeller shaft was replaced and a spare propeller installed. The cargo was then reloaded and the ship continued on to Leningrad, discharging its cargo there between February 9 and February 23.

Eagle declared a general average, seeking contribution for expenses arising from the Rotterdam repairs from the ship's underwriters and from defendant as insurer of the cargo. The expenses covered by the statement of general average included the costs of unloading and reloading the cargo in connection with the drydocking, as well as the costs of maintaining the ship's crew and officers during the repair period. Defendant's assessed share of these expenses totalled $126,951.61. When defendant refused to pay, Eagle brought this suit in the district court.

In May 1980, Judge Knapp granted defendant's motion for summary judgment on the ground that no general average situation existed in the circumstances of this case. 489 F.Supp. 920 (S.D.N.Y.1980). Specifically, Judge Knapp found that the ship had not been threatened by any "peril," as required under traditional principles of the law of general average and under the York–Antwerp Rules of 1950, which apply to this case in accordance with the terms of the voyage charter party.[1] Noting that the damage was discovered only after the ship was safely moored, Judge Knapp concluded that "[t]he vessel could have remained moored indefinitely at Rotterdam without incurring the slightest peril to itself or its cargo." Id. at 923. That the voyage could not have been completed without the repairs was deemed "irrelevant." Id. Eagle appeals from this judgment.

II

Resolution of the issues posed by this appeal requires an understanding of the history and content of both the law of general average and the York–Antwerp Rules. We turn first to the former.

---

1. Clause 2 of the voyage charter party, dated November 15, 1975, provided:

General Average shall be payable according to York/Antwerp Rules, 1950, and to be settled in New York.

General Average

The central principle of the law of general average is that "[w]hat is given, or sacrificed, in time of danger, for the sake of all, is to be replaced by a general contribution on the part of all who have been thereby brought to safety." R. Lowndes & G. Rudolf, The Law of General Average and the York–Antwerp Rules ¶ 1 (10th ed. J. Donaldson, C. Staughton, D. Wilson 1975)(Vol. 7 of British Shipping Laws). In this country, the principle was defined in fuller terms in the early case of Barnard v. Adams, 51 U.S. (10 How.) 270, 303, 13 L.Ed. 417 (1850):

> In order to constitute a case for general average three things must concur:—
>
> 1st. A common danger; a danger in which ship, cargo, and crew all participate; a danger imminent and apparently "inevitable," except by voluntarily incurring the loss of a portion of the whole to save the remainder.
>
> 2d. There must be a voluntary jettison, *jactus,* or casting away, of some portion of the joint concern for the purpose of avoiding this imminent peril, *pericula imminentis evitandi causa,* or, in other words, a transfer of the peril from the whole to a particular portion of the whole.
>
> 3d. This attempt to avoid the imminent common peril must be successful.

This formula still describes the classic general average case, but it is too narrow to encompass the full range of such cases recognized today. Two ways in which the *Barnard* formula has been liberalized are of special relevance to this appeal.

First, general average is not limited to cases involving a literal "voluntary jettison" or "casting away"; other "sacrifices" made to save the common venture may also give rise to a right of contribution from the benefited parties. As the Supreme Court observed in another leading case, The Star of Hope, 76 U.S. (9 Wall.) 203, 228, 19 L.Ed. 638 (1869):

> Losses which give a claim to general average are usually divided into two great classes: (1.) Those which arise from sacrifices of part of the ship or part of the cargo, purposely made in order to save the whole adventure from perishing. (2.) *Those which arise out of extraordinary expenses incurred for the joint benefit of ship and cargo.*

(Citation omitted; emphasis added.) This category of "extraordinary expenses" has long been recognized to include the costs incurred by a ship's interruption of its voyage to enter a port or similar shelter for repairs necessary for the safe completion of the venture. In Hobson v. Lord, 92 U.S. (2 Otto) 397, 23 L.Ed. 613 (1876), for example, a ship had been badly damaged in a collision at sea, "and being in distress, and unable to prosecute her voyage by reason of such injuries, she proceeded to the port of Callao," her intended port of call. Id. at 400. Extensive repairs were made, requiring the discharge of the ship's cargo; "the repairs, though they were of a permanent character, were necessary to enable the ship to prosecute her voyage to its termination." Id. at 401. In holding the costs of these repairs to be subject to general average, the Court stated:

>   Where the disaster occurs in the course of the voyage, and the ship is
> disabled, the necessary expenses to refit her to go forward create an equity
> to support * * * a claim [for proportionate contribution], just as strong as
> a sacrifice made to escape [an imminent sea] peril, if it appears that the
> cargo was saved, and that the expenses incurred enabled the master to
> prosecute the voyage to a successful termination.

Id. at 405.   The recoverable expenditures included not only the cost of the
repairs, but also wages and provisions "during the consequent and necessary *interruption* of the voyage, occasioned by the disaster."   *Id.* at 407
(emphasis in original).   These principles, as will be seen below, were
subsequently codified in the York–Antwerp Rules.

    The second direction of liberalization of *Barnard's* strict definition of
general average acts has involved the degree of "peril" necessary to render
sacrifice or extraordinary expenses recoverable.   The early cases uniformly
speak, as does *Barnard,* of "imminent" or "impending" peril threatening
the ship.   In *The Star of Hope,* for example, a fire aboard a ship carrying
gunpowder and "large quantities of spirituous liquors" caused "[g]reat
alarm," which "increased as the impending peril became more imminent."
76 U.S. (9 Wall.) at 225–26.   The master decided to seek shelter in an
unfamiliar bay, sailing in without a pilot and as a result grounding the ship
on a reef.   The grounding created a leak in the hull; the water that poured
in extinguished the fire but made it necessary to return the ship to its
previous port of call for repairs.   The Supreme Court held that the
expenses of the repairs could be recovered as general average costs.   See
also Columbian Insurance Co. v. Ashby & Stribling, 38 U.S. (13 Pet.) 331,
338, 10 L.Ed. 186 (1839)("[T]he ship and cargo should be placed in a
common imminent peril.   * * * Hence, if there was no imminent danger or
necessity for the sacrifice, as if the jettison was merely to lighten a ship too
heavily laden, by the fault of the master, in a tranquil sea, no contribution
was due."); E. Congdon, General Average 11 (1952)(citing cases).

    It is clear that the law of general average continues to require a
showing of peril.[2]   But in this century, perils less than "imminent" have
been recognized as sufficient to create a general average situation.   Writing
for this court in 1937, Judge Augustus Hand expressed this changing view:

>   There must be fair reason to regard a vessel in peril in order to require
> a contribution in general average.   While the courts in some cases have
> used expressions indicating that both in general average and in salvage
> cases it is essential that the property at risk be subject to an immediately
> impending danger, we think the "imminency" of the peril is not the critical
> test.   *If the danger be real and substantial, a sacrifice or expenditure made
> in good faith for the common interest is justified, even though the advent of
> any catastrophe may be distant or indeed unlikely.*

---

2. See, e.g., Aktieselskabet Cuzco v.
The Sucarseco, 294 U.S. 394, 401, 55 S.Ct.
467, 470, 79 L.Ed. 942 (1935); G. Gilmore &
C. Black, *The Law of Admiralty* § 5–6 at 254
(2d ed. 1975); L. Buglass, Marine Insurance
and General Average in the United States,
122–23 (1973); E. Congdon, supra, at 11.

Navigazione Generale Italiana v. Spencer Kellogg & Sons, 92 F.2d 41, 43 (2d Cir.), cert. denied, 302 U.S. 751, 58 S.Ct. 271, 82 L.Ed. 580 (1937)(emphasis added). See also Shaver Transportation Co. v. Travelers Indemnity Co., 481 F.Supp. 892, 897–98 (D.Or.1979); Todd Shipyards Corp. v. United States, 391 F.Supp. 588, 590 (S.D.N.Y.1975); United States v. Wessel, Duval & Co., 123 F.Supp. 318, 328 (S.D.N.Y.1954)(denying general average recovery in absence of evidence of "substantial peril, either present or probable in the future"). The concern underlying this more flexible view of "peril" is that the master should not be discouraged from taking timely action to avert a threat to the safety of the ship and its cargo.[3] The critical issue, then, in the modern law of general average is the seriousness of the danger created by an accident or peril at sea rather than its immediacy.

York-Antwerp Rules

Although the principles of the law of general average discussed above are relevant to this case, more immediately significant is their codification in the York–Antwerp Rules. As already indicated, see note 1 supra, these Rules were made applicable to the voyage of the Eagle Courier by the terms of the voyage charter party. A brief description of the development of the Rules will be helpful.

The movement to achieve some sort of international consensus on basic principles of general average began in Great Britain in 1860 as a response to concern over the costs, confusion, and abuses resulting from diverse national approaches to the question. The end result of many years of discussion and several conferences was the promulgation of the York–Antwerp Rules of 1890 by the Conference of the Association for the Reform and Codification of the Law of Nations (later the International Law Association). The Conference, attended by representatives of shipping and insurance interests in the United Kingdom, France, Germany, Belgium, Denmark, and the United States, adopted a set of eighteen rules designed to resolve specific, common problems of general average rather than to set out a comprehensive approach to the subject. The Rules came rapidly to be accepted as a standard code of practice by shippers in virtually all maritime states, although the original objective of uniformity through national legislation based on the Rules was not met. See generally R. Lowndes & G. Rudolf, supra, ¶¶ 481–508; Felde, General Average and the York–Antwerp Rules, 27 Tulane L.Rev. 406, 427–29 (1953).

Pressures for revision of some of the Rules and their expansion to deal with new problems led to the convening of another conference following World War I. This conference produced the York–Antwerp Rules of 1924,

---

3. See R. Lowndes & G. Rudolf, supra, ¶ 51:

Although the peril must be real, "it is not necessary that the ship should be actually in the grip, or even nearly in the grip, of the disaster that may arise from a danger. It would be a very bad thing if shipmasters had to wait until that state of things arose in order to justify them doing an act which would be a general average act."

(Quoting from Vlassopoulos v. British & Foreign Marine Ins. Co. (The "Makis"), [1929] 1 K.B. 187, 199).

consisting of twenty-three "numbered" rules dealing with specific questions (mostly based on the Rules of 1890), as well as seven new "lettered" rules setting out more general definitions and principles of general average. The 1924 Rules met with general approval in the maritime states, including, it appears, the Soviet Union, see Felde, supra, 27 Tulane L.Rev. at 432–33.   However, several provisions of the new Rules were strenuously opposed by shippers, insurers, and other maritime interests in the United States, which devised contractual formulas providing for only selective application of the Rules.   See R. Lowndes & G. Rudolf, supra, ¶ 510.

Following World War II, the International Law Association undertook a new effort to achieve universally acceptable Rules.   Representatives from thirteen countries, including the United States, met in 1949 to consider further revisions.   The results were the York–Antwerp Rules of 1950, the Rules of particular interest in the present case.   The principal modification introduced in 1950 was the addition of the following "Rule of Interpretation" at the beginning of the Rules:

> In the adjustment of general average the following lettered and numbered Rules shall apply to the exclusion of any Law and Practice inconsistent therewith.

> *Except as provided by the numbered Rules, General Average shall be adjusted according to the lettered Rules.*

(Emphasis added.)   The new Rule thus gave priority to the numbered Rules, making it clear that "if the facts support a claim in general average under the numbered rules, it matters not that there has been no general average act within the meaning of Rule A."   R. Lowndes & G. Rudolf, supra, ¶ 548 at 256.

Added at the request of the British delegation, the new Rule was designed to overrule the interpretation of the 1924 Rules rendered in the case of Vlassopoulos v. British & Foreign Marine Insurance Co., [1929] 1 K.B. 187.   This decision, which "upset all preconceived ideas" on the relationship between the lettered and numbered Rules, see R. Lowndes & G. Rudolf, supra, ¶ 511 at 247, ¶ 545 at 255–56, held that the numbered Rules were merely specific examples of types of general average situations, subordinate to the principles set forth in the lettered Rules.   To overcome the "embarrassment" this decision caused in commercial circles, id. ¶ 511 at 248, shippers began inserting a new contractual provision, known as the "Makis Agreement" (after the ship involved in *Vlassopoulos*), which made clear that recourse would be had to the lettered Rules only when none of the numbered Rules was applicable.   The new Rule of Interpretation formalized this Agreement by incorporating its substance into the body of the Rules.

The 1950 Rules achieved the widespread acceptance sought by the sponsors of the 1949 Conference.   In the United States, the Rules were approved by the Maritime Law Association in May 1950.   See 1950 A.M.C. 895; L. Buglass, supra, at 119.   In 1974, the Rules were further amended in respects not directly relevant here,[4] see R. Lowndes & G. Rudolf, supra, at ¶¶ 518–24.

We see no reason not to give the Rules full effect in this case, in accordance with the agreement between the parties. Although they have not been formally sanctioned on an intergovernmental basis, and thus lack the force of law, the Rules reflect an important consensus of the international shipping industry and merit "full judicial cognizance," see 2 Benedict on *Admiralty* § 183 at 13–14 (7th ed. 1975), at least insofar as they do not conflict with statutory or other policies of equal or greater importance. See Sea–Land Service, Inc. v. Aetna Insurance Co., 545 F.2d 1313, 1315 n. * (2d Cir.1976).

III

Against this background, we can now look more closely at the arguments made in this case. Appellant Eagle's central contention is that the district court erred by applying one of the lettered Rules, Rule A, to the facts presented here and by ignoring the numbered Rules. Rule A provides:

> There is a general average act when, and only when, any extraordinary sacrifice or expenditure is intentionally and reasonably made or incurred for the common safety for the purpose of preserving from peril the property involved in a common maritime adventure.

The district court concluded that no "purpose of preserving from peril" had been shown, since the ship was safely moored when the damage was discovered and "could forever have remained at its Rotterdam mooring without being subject to any dangers except those incident to old age." 490 F.Supp. at 923. The judge thus held that no general average act had occurred.

The district court's error, appellant contends, lay in its failure to consider the applicability of two of the numbered rules addressed to precisely the type of situation involved here. Specifically, appellant points to Rule X(b), which provides:

> (b) The cost of handling on board or discharging cargo, fuel or stores, whether at a port or place of loading, call or refuge, shall be admitted as general average when the handling or discharge was necessary for the common safety *or to enable damage to the ship caused by sacrifice or accident to be repaired, if the repairs were necessary for the safe prosecution of the voyage.*

(Emphasis added.) Appellant also cites Rule XI(b), a related provision:

> (b) When a ship shall have entered or been detained in any port or place in consequence of accident, sacrifice or other extraordinary circumstances which render that necessary for the common safety, *or to enable damage to the ship caused by sacrifice or accident to be repaired, if the repairs were necessary for the safe prosecution of the voyage,* the wages and maintenance of the master, officers and crew reasonably incurred during the extra period of detention in such port or place until the ship shall or

---

4. But see note 7 infra.

should have been made ready to proceed on her original voyage, shall be admitted in general average. * * *

Fuel and stores consumed during the extra period of detention shall be admitted as general average, except such fuel and stores as are consumed in effecting repairs not allowable in general average.

Port charges incurred during the extra period of detention shall likewise be admitted as general average except such charges as are incurred solely by reason of repairs not allowable in general average.

(Emphasis added.) If, as appellant contends, these two Rules govern on the facts of this case, then they must be given precedence over the language of Rule A in conformity with the Rule of Interpretation discussed above.

Rules X(b) and XI(b), which in substance date back to the original 1890 Rules, do appear to contemplate contribution in general average toward expenses that might not qualify under Rule A. This is particularly evident in the alternative basis of recovery set out in the numbered Rules: recovery of expenses incurred "to enable damage to the ship caused by sacrifice or accident to be repaired, if the repairs were necessary for the safe prosecution of the voyage" (the safe prosecution clause). Under this clause, repairs necessary for the safe continuation of the voyage can be deemed general average acts, even if they would not be so regarded under Rule A alone. Buglass gives the following explanation:

[T]he York/Antwerp Rules adopted and legalized the so-called "artificial general average" or "general average by agreement" in the numbered rules by admitting as general average port of refuge expenses incurred not only consequent on putting into port "for the common safety," but also while detained at a port of loading or call undergoing repairs necessary for the safe prosecution of the voyage. [Knut] Selmer, a Norwegian authority, rationalizes this by reasoning that it is not the *actual* danger but rather the *eventual* danger that might arise during the subsequent part of the voyage which gave rise to the claim for general average contribution. In short, the principles laid down by Rule A are greatly modified; it is sufficient that a situation has arisen in which the further prosecution of the voyage might entail actual danger for vessel and cargo. * * *

It seems clear * * * that under the York/Antwerp Rules, as long as a peril does exist, not only need it not be imminent, it is permissible that it be merely anticipated; and presumably, as in other general average matters, the opinion of the master will not be lightly challenged. In practice a situation of reasonable apprehension, although not of actual danger, is sufficient.

L. Buglass, supra, at 123–24. In effect, then, the safe prosecution clause is to be read not as eliminating the requirement of peril but as presuming its presence in cases where, because of accident or sacrifice, a voyage cannot safely be resumed without repairs. Such a presumption is entirely consistent with the modern interpretation of the peril requirement in *Navigazione Generale,* supra, which, as noted above, involves only a showing of "real and substantial" danger even though ultimate catastrophe "may be distant or indeed unlikely." Lowndes and Rudolf agree that the safe prosecution clause "is a notable example of the occasions where those who supported completion of the adventure as the basis of general average prevailed over those who supported the common safety." R. Lowndes & G. Rudolf, supra, ¶ 692.[5] We believe that this interpretation of Rules X(b) and XI(b) gives proper effect to their language and purpose.

Under this view of the Rules, we are satisfied that this record establishes a prima facie general average claim. Although the ship here had not lost its propeller, cf. note 5 supra, the record shows that it had been seriously damaged and that its condition was deteriorating. As indicated above, the damage report revealed that the propeller "had backed down the taper of the tailshaft by about 250 mm and the top of the taper was clearly visible." As we read these facts, the ship's condition, allegedly as the result of an accident at sea, presented a "real and substantial" danger of loss or complete incapacitation of the propeller—and consequent peril—if the ship had still been at sea or if it returned to sea without repairs. Defendant implicitly recognizes this threat by conceding the necessity of the repairs prior to the resumption of the voyage. Under these circumstances, we believe the requirements for a prima facie claim under Rules X(b) and XI(b) have been satisfied.[6]

We are aware of the different view of these Rules taken by the Fifth Circuit in Orient Mid–East Lines v. A Shipment of Rice, 496 F.2d 1032, 1038–39 (5th Cir.1974), cert. denied, 420 U.S. 1005, 95 S.Ct. 1447, 43 L.Ed.2d 763 (1975). But we respectfully disagree with the assumption in

---

5. The authors do, however, play down to some extent the distinction between the common safety and safe prosecution clauses, asserting that "[t]he degree of *damage* to the ship necessary to meet the requirements of the expression is the same as—no less than—would be necessary to endanger the 'common safety' of the adventure if the vessel were at sea." As an example of the requisite "damage," the authors cite the loss of a propeller at sea, rendering a ship "unfit to encounter the ordinary perils of the sea." Id. ¶ 692 at 330. Under such circumstances, they note, "once within a port where repairs can be effected, safety will have been attained"; the safe prosecution clause "merely provides for a situation in port which, if the ship were at sea, would endanger the common safety." Id.

This interpretation appears to reflect a narrower reading of the safe prosecution clause than that contained in the previous edition of the same work, which asserted that the clause "contemplates repairs to avert a frustration of the adventure and is to be contrasted with repairs 'necessary for the common safety' which is concerned with physical safety." R. Lowndes & G. Rudolf, The Law of General Average ¶ 708 at 350 (9th ed. J. Donaldson, C. Ellis, C. Staughton

1964). The earlier edition also specifically recognized that the safe prosecution clause would permit general average contribution under circumstances "which would *not* be a general average act either at common law or under Rule A unless incurred for the common safety or as a direct consequence of a general average act." Id. ¶ 671 at 336.

The change in emphasis in the 10th edition may reflect a recent trend toward tightened definition of general average acts. See, e.g., R. Lowndes & G. Rudolf (10th edition), supra, ¶ 694 at 331, noting that at the 1974 Conference to amend the Rules "some effort was made to reduce the incidence of general average costs by increasing the stringency of the criteria by which it should be determined whether a general average situation exists." But see G. Gilmore & C. Black, supra, § 5–16 at 271.

6. Compare Empire Stevedoring Co. v. Oceanic Adjusters, Ltd., 315 F.Supp. 921 (S.D.N.Y.1970), a case whose facts are similar to those here and in which the validity of the general average claim appears to have been assumed without consideration of the issue of peril.

that case that "Rules X and XI are limited to actions taken 'for the common safety,' "id. at 1039—an assumption that overlooks the alternative basis of recovery set forth in the safe prosecution clause. We note, in any event, that the primary basis of the court's decision was not the inapplicability of the Rules to the facts there but its finding that general average recovery was unavailable in any event because the damage had been incurred in the process of making the ship seaworthy. Id. at 1038.

Moreover, we see no basis here for the concern voiced in *Orient Mid–East Lines,* id. at 1039, over the possibility of conflict between the Rules and the Carriage of Goods by Sea Act (COGSA), 46 U.S.C. §§ 1300 et seq. In particular, we note that the record before us presents no issues of negligence or unseaworthiness, which might implicate COGSA policies with respect to limitations of liability, see 46 U.S.C. § 1303(8).

IV

In light of these considerations, we conclude that the district court erred in relying solely on Rule A to the exclusion of Rules X(b) and XI(b). Giving the latter precedence, as required by the Rule of Interpretation, we are persuaded that Eagle presented a valid prima facie claim.

Of course, we are concerned here with the grant of summary judgment; our holding is merely that a claim has been stated, not that it has been proved. Eagle still bears the burden of showing that the requirements of the Rules have been satisfied. See Rule E of the 1950 Rules, providing that "[t]he onus of proof is upon the party claiming in general average to show that the loss or expense claimed is properly allowable as general average." See also L. Buglass, supra, at 130. Thus, for example, appellant must show that the damage requiring repair was the result of an "accident," rather than a latent defect attributable to the ship's unseaworthiness.[7] We express no views on this or any other factual issue that may arise at trial.

The judgment is reversed and the case remanded for further proceedings.

NOTE

With *Eagle Terminal Tankers,* cf. Ellerman Lines, Ltd. v. Gibbs, Nathaniel (Canada) Ltd., [1984] 1 C.F. 411, 1984 A.M.C. 2579 (Fed.Ct., Trial Div., Ottawa, 1983). A vessel carrying cargo consigned to Montreal and Toronto, discovered, four days after its arrival in Montreal, that there its main engine had been damaged. The shippers of freight consigned to Toronto were notified that the vessel would be repaired in Montreal, that this would take one and a half months, and the carrier offered to forward the cargo to Toronto by other vessel if the cargo owners would enter into a

---

7. It is worth noting in this connection two amendments to the numbered Rules adopted in 1974 designed to make clear that damage must have been incurred as the result of accident during the voyage. An amendment to Rule X(b) qualified the availability of contribution under that rule by excluding "cases where the damage to the ship is discovered at a port or place of loading or call without any accident or other extraordinary circumstance connected with such damage having taken place during the voyage." Rule XI(b) was similarly amended by the addition of a provision to the same effect. See R. Lowndes & G. Rudolf, supra, ¶¶ 694, 729–30.

"non-separation of interest" agreement, preserving the right of the vessel owner to general average. The cargo owners refused to do so and sued for release of the cargo in Montreal. The court ordered the cargo released, leaving the question of general average undetermined, and the vessel owner brought suit for contribution to the general average claim.

Although the York–Antwerp Rules and the New Jason Clause were included in the shipping documents, counsel agreed that "there was nothing in these provisions which would be of any assistance in determining the issues before the Court and that they may therefore be ignored." Returning to the general maritime law of general average, the court observed:

"In the case of the Royal Mail steam Packet Company Limited v. The English Bank of Rio de Janeiro, Limited [(1865) 34 L.J.Q.B. 233, 242] which has been frequently referred to with approval, we find the following passages at pages 370 and 371 of the report:

'I take it to be settled now that the circumstances which impose a liability in the nature of general average must be such as to imperil the *safety* of the ship and cargo and not merely such as to impede the successful prosecution of the particular voyage: Svensden v. Wallace * * *; Harrison v. Bank of Australasia * * * I take it also to be settled that if the cargo as a whole be landed and in safety the expenses of getting the ship afloat incurred thereafter are not general average: Job v. Langton * * *, a case with which Moran v. Jones * * * has been supposed to conflict, but which does not seem to me, so far as principles are concerned, to be open to that observation * * *

'These principles, though they deal with different epochs, so to speak, in the chain of events which give rise to general average, the first dealing with the state of things at the commencement of the liability, and the other with a state of things at which the liability has terminated, have this in common. Both point to the necessity, in order to establish a case of general average, for the existence of common danger of destruction at the moment when the liability is incurred. This necessity is laid down as the cardinal element necessary to establish a general average contribution, Arnould on *Insurance*, p. 917 (1st ed.), p. 934 (2nd ed.), where the learned author says, 'all which is ultimately saved out of the whole adventure, i.e., ship, freight, and cargo, contributes to make good the general average loss, *provided it have been actually at risk at the time such loss was incurred, but not otherwise,* because if not at risk at the time of the loss, it was not saved thereby * * *'.

"I consider this to be good law in Canada today. Several United States cases were referred to by counsel and it is clear that the same principle, that there must be actual risk or peril for a general average situation to arise, has been consistently applied.

"In the case at bar, the damage to the engine was discovered in the Port of Montreal some four days after the ship had put into port. Neither the ship nor the cargo was in peril at the time. The actions stands to be dismissed on that ground alone."

The court went on to hold that even if there were a general average expenditure, the cargo consigned to Toronto had a right to pay the full freight and insist upon delivery of the cargo in Montreal, and upon discharge, the cargo would no longer be liable to contribute in general average. This alternative ground for the decision was based in large part on the American cases. See The Julia Blake, 107 U.S. (17 Otto) 418, 431, 2 S.Ct. 692, 702, 27 L.Ed. 595 (1883).

F.   NOTE ON SALVAGE EXPENSES AS GENERAL AVERAGE

Rule VI of the York Antwerp Rules of 1994 provides:

Rule VI—Salvage Remuneration

(a) Expenditures incurred by the parties to the adventure in the nature of salvage, whether under contract or otherwise, shall be allowed in general average provided that the salvage operations were were carried out for the purpose of preserving from peril the property involved in the common maritime adventure.

Expenditures allowed in general average shall include any salvage remuneration in which the skill and efforts of the salvors in preventing or minimising damage to the environment such as is referred to in Art.13 ¶1(b) of the International convention on salvage, 1989 have been taken into account.

(b) Special compensation payable to a salvor by a shipowner under Art. 14 of the said convention to the extent specified in ¶ 4 of that Article or under any other provision similar in substance shall not be allowed in general average.

The second two paragraphs of Rule VI were added in 1990 and carried over into the 1994 version to adjust the practice in general average to the changes in the International Convention on salvage discussed above in chapter 10. These provisions deal with a salvage award, permitting inclusion of the total amount of the award, including whatever might be attributable to criterion (1)(b) of Article 13 of the Convention, but not to include amounts assessed against the vessel as special compensation under Article XIV. See also Rule C, excluding "damages or expenses incurred in respect of damage to the environment."

The easiest case to conceptualize is that of a disabled vessel that is towed to a port of refuge, with its cargo aboard. Unless the vessel is in peril, the towing services will not be salvage services; thus whenever there is salvage the expenditure meets the peril requirement for purposes of general average. If the master obtains the salvage services by contract and pays for them, every requirement for a general average expenditure is met. See, e.g., International Adjusters, Ltd. v. M.V. MANHATTAN, 405 F.Supp. 1293 (S.D.N.Y.1975), in which the court indicated that assessment of general average contributions to cargo after stranding caused by navigational error required partial unloading to refloat the vessel, was proper.

But is the peril that will convert services into salvage more or less than the peril or common danger that is required for general average. See Containerschiffsreedei T.S. Columbus New Zealand v. Corporation of Lloyd's, 1981 A.M.C. 60 (S.D.N.Y.1980). There there was an engine room fire at sea and the master entered into a salvage agreement with a sister ship to tow the vessel to port, and settled the salvage claim for $350,000. The court enforced general average contribution by the cargo, but found that since the fire had been put out before the towage was effected, the towage did not constitute salvage; accordingly it allowed the vessel interest of only $120,000 in general average expenditure.

It is to be noted that the 1974 Rule states specifically that expenses incurred "on account of salvage, whether under contract or otherwise" shall be allowed "to the extent that the salvage operations were undertaken for the purpose of preserving from peril the property involved in a common maritime adventure." It is explicit in this language that *some* salvage other than contract salvage may be allowed as general average. Lowndes and Rudolf take the position that, "salvage charges," defined in the Marine Insurance Act of 1906 as "the charges recoverable under maritime law by a salvor independent of contract," can never constitute general average expenditures. Op. Cit., at 243. The reason for this is stated to be that the rule in the law of salvage is that the property benefitted is alone charged with the salvage recovered, "and thus each interest incurs a liability on its own account but not for the common safety." Id.

Cf. Amerada Hess Corp. v. S/T Mobil Apex, 602 F.2d 1095, 1979 A.M.C. 2406 (2d Cir.1979), in which, after a fire and explosion on a vessel tied up at the pier, the master accepted the offer of a tug to tow it away from the pier for the safety of the vessel and its crew, and later settled the tug's claim for salvage for $40,000. The court held that the expenditure was a general average expenditure. It mentioned the statement in Lowndes and Rudolf, but noted that the authors cited no judicial authority. Is the decision irreconcilable with the position taken by Lowndes and Rudolf? Does the fact that the amount was settled and paid by the carrier take it out of the term "salvage charges" as used by Lowndes and Rudolf?

Suppose that the salvor was given a salvage award based upon the criteria used in such cases, each interest being charged with the salvage of his property. How would this be readjusted in a general average?

Lowndes and Rudolf point out some other problems in connection with the edge between salvage and general average. They take the position that prior to the 1974 Rules the salvage of a derelict could not easily be fitted into the theory of general average because the payment of the salvage award in such a case cannot be looked upon as an intentional act taken by the master for the common safety. They go on to say that for a different reason they do not believe that even under the 1974 Rules salvage of a derelict can be treated as a general average expense; the vessel having been abandoned, there is no longer any common venture.

There is also to be accounted for the phrase in Rule VI of the 1974 Rules, "to the extent that the operations were undertaken for the purpose of preserving from peril the property involved in a common maritime adventure." The problem is illustrated by Northland Navigation Co., Ltd. v. Patterson Boiler Works, Ltd., discussed in the note following *S.C. Loveland,* above.

CHAPTER 17

COLLISION

A. FAULT

1. INSCRUTABLE FAULT AND THE INEVITABLE ACCIDENT

The Jumna

United States Circuit Court of Appeals, Second Circuit, 1906.
149 Fed. 171, 79 C.C.A. 119.

On appeal and cross-appeal from a decree of the District Court for the Southern District of New York dismissing the libel and cross-libels and deciding that the collision between barge No. 19, in tow of the tug Gypsum King, and the steamship Jumna, and the subsequent collision of said barge and the schooner Gypsum Emperor with the New Haven Railroad's pier No. 38, East river, was the result of inevitable accident.

■ COXE, CIRCUIT JUDGE. It is conceded on all hands that, except in a few unimportant details, the facts are fully and accurately stated in the opinion of the district judge. He has carefully considered the conflicting theories of fault and has reached the conclusion that negligence has not been established as to any of the vessels participating in the collision. To arrive at this result it was necessary for him to determine several disputed questions of fact regarding which it is sufficient to say that in many instances he was unquestionably right and in no instance is the finding so clearly against the preponderance of proof as to warrant us in setting it aside.

For instance, was the Jumna's hawser sufficient and in proper condition? Was the tow of the Gypsum King properly made up? Did the McCaldin Brothers make proper effort to reach the port side of the Jumna? Did the Dalzell put a sudden strain on the hawser?

In each of these instances the district judge found against the asserted negligence and we think the weight of testimony sustains these findings. Like him we are unable to localize the blame for the collision. We had some doubt as to whether the tugs in charge of the Jumna, and particularly the McCaldin Brothers, can be exculpated but, after an examination of the testimony, we incline to the opinion that they did everything which could be reasonably expected of them and that the McCaldin Brothers started to make fast to the port quarter of the Jumna as soon as the latter cleared the pier and it was possible to get around her stern.

The judge of the District Court has found that the collision was the result of an inevitable accident. Such an accident usually happens when it is not possible to prevent it by the exercise of due care, caution and nautical skill. It is generally, though not invariably, attributed to an act of God, as where a tremendous tempest arises, such as devastated Galveston a few years ago, or more recently destroyed the shipping in the harbor of Havana. So, where a dense fog or falling snow obstructs the vision, where a gale and high seas unite to make navigation difficult, or where a severe storm is prevailing upon a dark night, a collision happening in such circumstances, the colliding vessels exercising the care, skill and caution required by prudent navigation, would be attributed to inevitable accident. Such accidents usually occur when safe navigation is rendered impossible from causes which no human foresight can prevent; when the forces of nature burst forth in unforeseen and uncontrollable fury so that man is helpless, and the stoutest ship and the most experienced mariner are at the mercy of the winds and waves.

In admiralty law, however, the phrase has a more comprehensive meaning. It is not necessary that the accident should be the result of a vis major. If no negligence can be imputed to either vessel there is a presumption that they are navigating in a lawful manner and where no fault can be shown the accident may be said to be inevitable.

In the case of The Morning Light, 2 Wall. 550, 17 L.Ed. 862 (1864), Mr. Justice Clifford, quoting Dr. Lushington, says (page 561 of 2 Wall. [17 L.Ed. 862]):

"Inevitable accident must be considered as a relative term, and must be construed not absolutely but reasonably with regard to the circumstances of each particular case. Viewed in that light, inevitable accident may be regarded as an occurrence which the party charged with the collision could not possibly prevent by the exercise of ordinary care, caution, and maritime skill."

In the case of The Grace Girdler, 7 Wall. 196, 19 L.Ed. 113 (1868) the Supreme Court says:

"Inevitable accident is where a vessel is pursuing a lawful avocation in a lawful manner, using the proper precautions against danger, and an accident occurs. The highest degree of caution that can be used is not required. It is enough that it is reasonable under the circumstances."

The test is, could the collision have been prevented by the exercise of ordinary care, caution and maritime skill? In the case at bar we are unable upon the testimony before us to specify any particular fault, to put our finger upon any act or omission and assert that to it the accident was attributable. Fault may exist, but we are unable to discover it; it is inscrutable. Where the evidence is so conflicting that it is impossible to determine to what direct and specific acts the collision is attributable, it is a case of damage arising from a cause that is inscrutable. The Fern and The Swann, Newb. 158, Fed.Cas.No.8,588 (1854). Whether the case at bar be thus classified, or whether it be held to come within the admiralty definition of inevitable accident is not material; in either event the loss

must be borne by the party on whom it falls.

In the early administration of the maritime law in this country the damages were divided in cases of inscrutable fault precisely as in cases where both vessels were in fault. The John Henry, 3 Ware, 264, Fed.Cas. No.7,350 (1860); The Sciota, 2 Ware (Dar. 359) 360, Fed.Cas.No.12,508 (1847); The Fern and The Swann, supra. The question has now been definitely decided by a vast preponderance of authority that there can be no recovery or partial recovery unless fault be affirmatively shown. The Clara, 102 U.S. 200, 26 L.Ed. 145 (1880); The Breeze, 6 Ben. 14, Fed.Cas. No.1,829 (1872); The Grace Girdler, supra; The Sunnyside, 91 U.S. 208, 215–216, 23 L.Ed. 302 (1875).

As we all concur in the conclusion that the case at bar falls within one of these categories, the decree should be affirmed with costs.

N O T E

There is a distinction to be drawn between cases like The Jumna and The Worthington, 19 Fed. 836 (E.D.Mich.1883)(cases of "inscrutable fault"), on the one hand, and cases in which the accident is produced by a *vis major* ("inevitable accident") on the other. Gilmore and Black point out that the term "inevitable" accident includes, in addition to incidents produced by a *vis major,* cases in which it is determined that both vessels were proceeding with due care and the incident occurred anyway. *Law of Admiralty,* 486–488 (1975).

Cases of "inscrutable fault" like The Jumna and The Worthington, on the surface of the matter, appear to be implicit in any system of liability based on fault; they represent, simply, a failure of proof. In maritime collision cases, however, they do not occur very often. This is so because the showing of fault in collision cases is aided by a number of evidentiary presumptions. When a vessel under power collides with a vessel at anchor, it is presumed that the fault lies with the powered vessel. The Oregon, 158 U.S. 186, 15 S.Ct. 804, 39 L.Ed. 943 (1895).

Suppose that the anchored or moored vessel was moored in the wrong place, or was not properly lighted. In Gaspar v. United States, 460 F.Supp. 656, 1979 A.M.C. 2232 (D.Mass.1978) it is stated that in such circumstances there is no presumption of fault. See Creole Shipping v. Diamandis Pateras, 554 F.2d 1348, 1977 A.M.C. 1648 (5th Cir.1977), in which the court of appeals declined to decide this question. Would it be more accurate to say that a showing of fault rebuts the presumption?

A presumption of fault also attaches to a manned vessel that runs into a stationary object, like a pier or a bridge. See, e.g., City of Boston v. S.S. Texaco Texas, 773 F.2d 1396, 1986 A.M.C. 676 (1st Cir.1985); Bunge Corp. v. M/V Furness Bridge, 558 F.2d 790, 1977 A.M.C. 2109 (5th Cir.1977).

Is a drawbridge a stationary object for these purposes? See Trinidad Corp. v. Commonwealth of Massachusetts, 1984 A.M.C. 260 (Mass.Sup.Ct.1983), holding no.

Suppose the stationary object is under water. Should there be any presumption of fault? See, e.g., See Peoples Natural Gas Co. v. Ashland Oil, Inc., 604 F.Supp. 1517, 1985 A.M.C. 3000 (W.D.Pa.1985). Or should it depend on whether the moving vessel should know that it is there? In AT & T v. Steuart, 1978 A.M.C. 1680 (D.Md.1977), the presumption was applied to a vessel that grounded on a known submerged cable in a river, located outside the main navigational channel. And so with a charted reef. Exxon Co. v. Sofec, Inc., reproduced in part beginning on p. 774, infra.

A similar presumption applies when a drifting vessel collides with an anchored one (or moored one). See James v. River Parishes Co., Inc., 686 F.2d 1129 (5th Cir.1982). Or a vessel drags its anchor and collides with another vessel. Neptune Maritime Co. v. Vessel Essi Camilla, 562 F.Supp. 14, 1982 A.M.C. 1836 (E.D.Va. 1982), aff'd 714 F.2d 132, 1984 A.M.C. 2983 (4th Cir.1983). But suppose 130 vessels broke from their moorings during one night and went floating down the Mississippi. The "Great Barge Breakaway" is described in Nunley v. M/V Dauntless Colocotronis, 863 F.2d 1190, 1993 A.M.C. 1676 (5th Cir.1989).

For discussion of the effect of such a presumption, whether merely shifting the burden of going forward or shifting the burden of persuasion, cf. Pennsylvania R. Co. v. S.S. Marie Leonhardt, 320 F.2d 262, 264, 1964 A.M.C. 1507 (3d Cir.1963)(burden of going forward) with Bunge Corp. v. M/V Furness Bridge, supra (burden of persuasion). In James v. River Parishes Co., supra, the Fifth Circuit applied the rule in *Bunge* to the presumption of fault in the case of a drifting ship. The Third Circuit/Fifth Circuit conflict is noted in City of Boston v. SS Texaco Texas, 599 F.Supp. 1132, 1985 A.M.C. 1870 (D.Mass.1984), but because the court found the cause of the allision was mistranslation of the pilot's orders to the helmsman, and found the vessel responsible for the pilot's negligence (under a pilotage clause), it did not find it necessary to take sides on the issue of the continuing effect of presumptions of fault. To the effect that the adoption of the Federal Rules of Evidence did not alter or modify the substantive burden and presumptions established in the federal maritime law, see Self v. Great Lakes Dredge & Dock Co., 832 F.2d 1540 (11th Cir.1987), cert. denied sub nom. Great Lakes Dredge & Dock Co. v. Chevron Transport Corp., 486 U.S. 1033, 108 S.Ct. 2017, 100 L.Ed.2d 604 (1988).

For discussion of the significance of the moving vessel/stationary object fault presumption in a case in which the vessel has petitioned for limitation of liability, see Matter of Texaco, Inc., 570 F.Supp. 1272, 1985 A.M.C. 1650 (E.D.La.1983).

Although a vessel has a duty to avoid swells when passing another vessel, when a vessel is not injured by the swell there is no presumption of liability for injury when the swell causes unusual movement of a properly moored vessel, causing a person standing on the deck to fall. Maxwell v. Hapag–Lloyd Aktiengesellschaft Hamburg, 862 F.2d 767 (9th Cir.1988).

Given the unpredictability of wind and weather, cases involving the "inevitable accident" arise with some frequency. They arise most frequently in storms of great force. See, e.g., Twery v. Houseboat Jilly's Yen, 267 F.Supp. 722, 1968 A.M.C. 453 (S.D.Fla.1967), in which a houseboat secured to a dock in Indian Creek canal opposite the Eden Rock Hotel in Miami Beach broke loose from its moorings during Hurricane Betsy. Finding that the Jilly's Yen was properly secured under the circumstances and that the storm was one of unusual force, the court held that the damage caused by the vessel was the result of an Act of God. See also Massman–Drake and Connecticut Fire Ins. Co. v. Towboat M/V Hugh C. Blaske, 289 F.Supp. 700, 1968 A.M.C. 1981 (E.D.La.1968). A heavy burden rests on the shipowner to demonstrate that the ship's breaking loose was inevitable. See, e.g., Tidelands Barge No. 5 (Boudin et al. v. J. Ray McDermott & Co.) 281 F.2d 81, 1961 A.M.C. 1457 (5th Cir.1960), in which the court of appeals reversed the district court's finding of "inevitable accident" in a case in which a barge had broken loose from its moorings during Hurricane Audrey on the ground that when the hurricane approached the barge should have been taken from the dock at Cameron, La., a sea-flat and mud-flat area, and moored in Lake Charles. See also Hercules Carriers Lim. Proc., 1982 A.M.C. 2888 (M.D.Fla.1982), in which the vessel, which collided with a bridge, was held at fault because of the negligent failure of the compulsory pilot in not dropping anchor during a rainstorm when visibility dropped to 500 feet.

Another circumstance that seems to produce "inevitable accident" defenses is an unexpected and unexplained sheer. See, e.g., The S.S. Andros Tower (Maroceano Co. Naviera S.A. v. Los Angeles), 193 F.Supp. 529, 1961 A.M.C. 1573 (S.D.Cal.1961). But with the sheer as with the collision with a stationary object, or the drifting vessel, there is a heavy presumption to be overcome. See, e.g., Martha Anne–Ceara (Atkins v. Lorentzen), 328 F.2d 66, 1964 A.M.C. 2331 (5th Cir.1964). See also Seacarriers Maritime Co. v. M/T Stolt Jade, 823 F.Supp. 1311, 1994 A.M.C. 191 (E.D.La.1993)(heavy weather, poor visibility, and seas with a strong set to the west were not an act of God, since the vessel should have been heavily ballasted).

In some cases a vessel colliding with a moored vessel or with a stationary object has been able to rebut the presumption of fault by undertaking to prove that it was proceeding in the exercise of all due care. In other cases the vessel that has collided with a moored vessel or allided with a shore structure has been able to demonstrate that it was proceeding without fault and the incident was the fault of a third party. See, e.g., United States v. Compania Peruana De Vapores, 1985 A.M.C. 1208, 1984 WL 1483 (D.Or.1984), in which the defendant vessel was in the hands of an experienced pilot who took evasive action to avoid collision with a small boat and despite all possible reasonable steps to avoid the accident allided with a Coast Guard facility.

The question of whether a vessel is navigating at the time of a collision, and thus that the vessel that struck it is not solely liable under the presumption of fault when a moving vessel strikes a stationery one is a matter of fact. See United Overseas Export Lines, Inc. v. Medluck Compania Maviera, S.A., 785 F.2d 1320 (5th Cir.1986).

See American Petrofina Pipeline Co. v. M/V Shoko Maru, 837 F.2d 1324 (5th Cir.1988), in which the court found that either (1) no collision took place, or (2) the vessel had presented sufficient evidence to rebut the presumption, even though owner did not present the master or crew members as witnesses.

For other presumptions that have been applied in collision cases, see Griffin on *Collisions* § 153 (1949).

2. THE RULES OF NAVIGATION

The determination of fault in collision cases is made somewhat easier in maritime collision cases by the fact that the duties and obligations of vessels are regulated more or less comprehensively by rules that have the force of statute.

The International Regulations For Preventing Collisions at Sea, 1972. The Convention on the International Regulations for Preventing Collisions at Sea, 1972, designated in 33 U.S.C.A. § 1602 as the "International Regulations," but are often referred to as the "COLREGS," was proclaimed effective July 15, 1977. The COLREGS are printed following 33 U.S.C.A. § 1602.

Rule 1 of the COLREGS provides that the rules apply to all vessels upon the high seas and in all waters connected therewith navigable by seagoing vessels.

The Inland Navigational Rules. The Inland Navigational Rules (33 U.S.C.A. §§ 2001 through 2073), were enacted effective December 24, 1981, superseded three different sets of rules governing navigation on territorial waters; the Navigation Rules for the Great Lakes and their Connecting and Tributary Waters (33 U.S.C.A. §§ 241 through 295), known as the "Great Lakes Rules," the Navigation Rules for Red River of the North and Rivers Emptying into Gulf of Mexico and Tributaries (33 U.S.C.A. §§ 301 through 356), known as the "Western Rivers Rules," and the Navigation Rules for Harbors, Rivers, and Inland Waters (33 U.S.C.A. §§ 151 through 232), known as the "Inland Rules" and applicable generally where the other two sets were not.

The Pilot Rules. In addition to the four sets of rules set out in the statutes, the Code empowers the Commandant of the United States Coast Guard to promulgate pilot rules which are published in the Federal Register and when not in conflict with the statutory rules have the force and effect of statutes. See 33 U.S.C.A. §§ 157, 243, 253. There are three sets of pilot rules. Since the boundaries of coastal and inland waters are drawn in a fashion so that vessels under pilot are within the area of application of the Inland Rules, there is no necessity for international pilot rules. The three sets apply, then, in the territory covered by the three sets of rules governing territorial waters, The Inland Pilot Rules, The Great Lakes Pilot Rules, and The Western Rivers Pilot Rules.

Local Ordinances and Regulations. With regard to such local matters as mooring and anchorage, local statutes, ordinances, and regulations are binding insofar as they do not conflict with the federal statutory rules and Pilot Rules. See Griffin on *Collisions* § 153 (1949).

Customs. Local customs sometimes receive judicial recognition. On the Mississippi, for example, the custom is to permit the ascending vessel to run the points and the descending vessel to run the bends. See The John D. Rockefeller, 272 Fed. 67 (4th Cir.1921), cert. denied 256 U.S. 693, 41 S.Ct. 535, 65 L.Ed. 1175; Birney R.—Katherine H., 198 F.Supp. 515, 1962 A.M.C. 916 (E.D.La.1961). See also Bulkcrude—Newport (New York Trap Rock Corp. v. Red Star Towing and Transp. Co.), 1962 A.M.C. 2323 (S.D.N.Y.1961)(existence of custom having force of law calling upon vessel stemming the tide to let the other by at Hell Gate rejected by the court); Pioneer Mart, 1968 A.M.C. 1411 (D.C.Z.1968)(custom and usage of Panama Canal in handling lightly loaded vessels approved by the court).

The rules of navigation are relatively comprehensive, covering lights and shapes, sound signals and conduct in restricted visibility (the fog rules), steering and sailing rules, and sound signals for vessels in sight of one another. Of special interest is Rule 2 of both the COLREGS and the Inland Rules, which reads:

Rule 2. Responsibility.

(a) Nothing in these Rules shall exonerate any vessel, or the owner, master, or crew thereof, from the consequences of any neglect to comply with these Rules or of the neglect of any precaution which may be required by the ordinary practice of seamen, or by the special circumstances of the case.

(b) In construing and complying with these Rules due regard shall be had to all dangers of navigation and collision and to any special circumstances, including the limitations of the vessels involved, which may make a departure from these Rules necessary to avoid immediate danger.

These "special circumstance" provisions, which carry forward provisions that appeared in the former International and Inland Rules as Rules 27 and 29, and in the other sets under slightly different numbers, lend some flexibility to the Rules by providing that when safety requires it departure from the specific rules is not a fault, and indeed may be required (Rule 2(b)), and further, that the fact of compliance does not excuse failure to take other precautions (Rule 2(a)). See Griffin on Collisions § 228 (1949). The force and effect of these provisions is discussed in the Note on p. 815, infra.

3. THE RULE OF THE PENNSYLVANIA

Hellenic Lines, Ltd. v. Prudential Lines, Inc.

United States Court of Appeals, Fourth Circuit, 1984.
730 F.2d 159, 1984 A.M.C. 2713.

■ CHAPMAN, CIRCUIT JUDGE:

* * *

I

The Hellenic and the Atlantico collided on May 6, 1981 at approximately 0700 hours. The approximate position of the collision was 36° 15′ North Latitude and 75° 34′ West Longitude. Although both vessels incurred substantial structural damage, the collision did not result in the loss of life.

The district court made numerous findings of fact, which are summarized below.

Both vessels were equipped with radar. Atlantico had both a starboard and a port radar but both radars were faulty and found to be functionally inoperable at the time of the collision. The Hellenic carried only one radar but it was fully operable at the time of the collision.

The Hellenic was en route from Savannah, Georgia, to Baltimore, Maryland and the Atlantico was en route from Newport News, Virginia, to Charleston, South Carolina. At 0640, the Hellenic was proceeding on a course of 338° true at a speed of 14 knots in restricted visibility, and the Atlantico was proceeding on what its radar showed to be a course of 161° at a speed of 18 knots in restricted visibility. Weather was calm, with intermittent fog, limiting visibility to 500 to 1000 feet.

Chief Mate Konstantinos T. Rentas was the watch officer on the bridge of the Hellenic from 0400 until the time of the collision. At 0640,[1] Rentas

---

1. The testimony of Hellenic Lines' expert, Captain Robert Slack, states that the clock on the Atlantico was one and one half minutes behind the clock on the Hellenic.

observed a radar contact forward of the ship's beam at a distance of 12 miles, approximately 10 ° off the starboard of the Hellenic. At 0645, he ordered the course of the Hellenic changed to port from 338° to 330° to increase the passing distance between the vessels.

Approximately two minutes before the collision, the boatswain, who had been assigned as lookout on the starboard bridge wing of the Hellenic, heard two whistles from an approaching vessel. Approximately one minute before the collision, Rentas observed that the oncoming vessel was less than one mile from the Hellenic and that it was approaching the Hellenic on the starboard beam. At this point Rentas ordered a full port turn but it was too late to prevent the collision.

The crew of the Atlantico first observed the Hellenic on radar at 0650 when Paul Ticer, the second mate, observed a target at a distance of five miles and bearing 8° to 10° on what he believed was his port bow. The district court found, and Prudential Lines does not dispute, that this assessment was incorrect because the readings were taken from the Atlantico's unreliable starboard radar. The district court found that the Hellenic was actually about 5° to 7° on the Atlantico's starboard bow.

At approximately 0653, Captain Nicholas Tittonis ordered the Atlantico to change course four degrees to what he believed was 165°. From 0654 to 0659, Captain Tittonis ordered several small course changes to the starboard.

At approximately 0659, the Hellenic became visible to the occupants of the Atlantico's bridge. About 35 seconds before the collision Captain Tittonis ordered the rudder hard right and the engines stopped.

The district court found that, in the minutes before the collision, neither vessel attempted to communicate with the other and the Hellenic failed to sound any fog signals. The court also found that neither vessel slackened its speed, although both vessels were proceeding in restricted visibility.

The district court concluded that sixty percent of the fault for the collision was attributable to Prudential Lines for its failure to outfit the Atlantico with functional radar and that twenty percent was attributable to Prudential for the failure of the Atlantico to reduce its speed. The court apportioned the remaining twenty percent to Hellenic Lines for the failure of the Hellenic to reduce its speed.

Finally, the court allowed Hellenic Lines to limit its liability to the value of its interest in the Hellenic and her freight, pursuant to 46 U.S.C. § 183 (1976), because the court found that the cause of the collision attributable to the Hellenic was not within the privity or knowledge of Hellenic Lines.

The times used in this opinion are taken from the opinion of the district court, and that opinion does not state whether it employed Atlantico or Hellenic time.

II

Prudential attacks both the district court's apportionment of liability between the two parties and the court's holding that Hellenic was entitled to a limitation of liability. We will address first the apportionment of liability between the parties.

Appellant argues that the court below erred in three instances by failing to assign fault to Hellenic Lines for the Hellenic's violations of the 72 Colregs. First, it asserts the district court erred in not finding the Hellenic at fault for her admitted failure to sound fog signals in violation of Rule 35(a) of the 72 Colregs.

There is no dispute that the Hellenic neglected to give fog signals in the minutes before the collision and that this omission was a violation of Rule 35(a). The only dispute is whether the district court properly applied the "Pennsylvania Rule" in determining that there was no causal relationship between the collision and the Hellenic's failure to give fog signals.

The "Pennsylvania Rule" is derived from The Pennsylvania, 86 U.S. (19 Wall) 125, 22 L.Ed. 148 (1873):

> When * * * a ship at the time of a collision is in actual violation of a statutory rule intended to prevent collisions * * * the burden rests upon the ship of showing not merely that her fault might not have been one of the causes, or that it probably was not, but that it could not have been.

The district court concluded that Hellenic Lines had met its burden under the "Pennsylvania Rule" of showing that the absence of fog signals could not have contributed to the collision. Our review of the record convinces us that this finding is not clearly erroneous. There was expert testimony before the court that in the circumstances of this case, the sounding of a fog signal by the Hellenic would not have provided the Atlantico with any warning of the presence and location of another ship which had not already been provided by the Atlantico's radar, even though the radar was defective.

III

Prudential contends that the district court should have found the Hellenic at fault for failing to make proper use of its radar, as required by Rule 7 of the 72 Colregs. Rule 7(b) states that "proper use shall be made of radar equipment if fitted and operational, including long range scanning to obtain early warning of risk of collision and radar *plotting*, or *equivalent systematic observation* of detected objects." (emphasis added)

Although it is clear from the evidence that Chief Mate Rentas did not employ plotting in tracking the position of the Atlantico, the district court found that the Hellenic had not violated Rule 7 because Rentas employed a method of observation known as "parallel indexing" which the court found to be "equivalent systematic observation" within the meaning of Rule 7.

We hold that "parallel indexing" is not "equivalent systematic observation" to radar plotting, because it is not *equivalent* or reasonably equal to radar plotting. Hellenic's own expert, Captain Slack, testified that "parallel indexing" was not equivalent to radar plotting because "parallel index-ing" does not give the relative motion, course and speed of the other vessel. It provides only the closest point of approach. A system that does not provide information as to the course, speed and relative motion of an approaching vessel cannot be the *equivalent* of a system that does.

No court has yet addressed the question of what constitutes "equiva-lent systematic observation." However, A. Cockcroft & J. Lameijer, who assisted in drafting the 72 Colregs, are authors of A Guide to the Collision Avoidance Rules, 2d edition (1976) which was introduced into evidence at the request of the trial judge, and state at page 56 of this text:

> *Plotting or equivalent systematic observation*
>
> Even continuous observation by a competent person is unlikely to be accepted as proper use of radar to obtain early warning of risk of collision if the bearings and distances of approaching vessels are not taken at regular intervals and carefully evaluated by *plotting* or by some *equivalent* method. (Emphasis added).

Knight's Modern Seamanship, which has been the standby of mariners for generations, in its 16th edition (1977) states at page 566:

> The radar plot required by the International Rules includes a radar deflection plotter fitted over the scope, as well as plotting directly on the scope. "Systematic observation" includes the plotting teams used on most naval vessels as well as computerized collision avoidance systems which process radar bearings and range data and display information on a cathode ray tube.

The trial court found that there was no violation of Rule 7 because watch officer Rentas was competent to plot. However, it is clear from Rentas' own testimony that he did not plot and he testified that he did not know how to plot. Accordingly, we find that the district court was clearly in error when it found that the Hellenic did not violate Rule 7 by failing to make proper use of its radar. The Hellenic violated Rule 7 because its "parallel indexing" does not qualify as "equivalent systematic observation" under the Rule.

IV

Prudential's final argument against the district court's apportionment of fault is that the court erred in not holding the Hellenic to be in violation of Rule 19(d)(i) of the 72 Colregs for its two left turns in the minutes before the collision. Rule 19 regulates the conduct of vessels not in sight of one another when navigating in restricted visibility. The applicable portion of the rule states as follows:

> (d) A vessel which detects by radar alone the presence of another vessel shall determine if a close-quarters situation is developing and/or risk of collision exists. If so, she shall take avoiding action in ample time, provided that when such action consists of an alteration of course, so far as possible the following shall be avoided:
>
> (i) An alteration of course to port for a vessel forward of the beam, other than for a vessel being overtaken;

It is clear from the record that the Hellenic detected the Atlantico's presence through the use of radar alone and that the Hellenic altered course to port twice during the time before the collision, once at 0645 by 8° and once immediately before the collision. The district court excused the first turn to port because it found that a "close quarters" situation was not developing and because it interpreted the rule as not prohibiting left turns but only advising against them. The district court excused the second turn because it was made "in extremis" and because it was made too late to be a cause of the collision.

Initially we consider the district court's determination that a close quarters situation was not developing. What constitutes close quarters is not defined in Rule 19 and must be determined in each case primarily upon the location of the vessels and the space in which they have to maneuver. See A. Cockcroft & J. Lameijer, A Guide To The Collision Avoidance Rules p. 129 (2d ed. 1976). Although the district court made no specific finding on what distance constituted close quarters in this case, it is clear from the fact that a collision occurred and the testimony of Captain Slack that any passing distance under two miles is close quarters in a fog.

The district court found that the two vessels were set up to pass at a distance of two miles when the Hellenic made its first turn to port. The only evidence which supports this finding is the testimony of Chief Mate Rentas of the Hellenic that the Atlantico appeared on the spot on his radar scope which indicated a passing distance of two miles at the time he ordered the first left turn at 0645. On the other hand, both the testimony of Captain Slack and the district court's own amended finding of fact No. 50 support the conclusion that the passing distance between the vessels was significantly less than two miles at 0645. Captain Slack stated that the passing distance between the two vessels was 1.1 miles after the Hellenic's first left turn. Since the parties agree that the effect of the 8° port turn was to increase the passing distance between the vessels, Captain Slack's testimony establishes that the passing distance at the time the turn was made was less than one mile. The district court's amended finding of fact states that the two vessels would have passed at a distance of 1.1 miles if they had maintained the courses they were pursuing before the Hellenic's left turn. This finding is particularly significant because it is inconsistent with the court's other finding that the vessels were set up to pass at a distance of two miles before the port turn. These two inconsistent findings indicate that the district court was confused on this crucial issue of whether a close quarters situation existed. We should therefore give less weight to the court's finding on this issue.

In light of the district court's confusion on the close quarters issue and the strong evidence that the vessels were in a close quarters situation at 0645, we are forced to conclude the court's finding that close quarters did not exist was clearly erroneous. Since the vessels were in close quarters, we must consider the meaning of Rule 19(d)(i) and whether it prohibits or only advises against port turns.

The district court interpreted the language "so far as possible" found in Rule 19 to excuse Hellenic's left turn because, the alternative, a starboard turn across the bow of the Atlantico, would have "exceeded the bounds of good seamanship." We find two problems with this interpretation. First, the district court's finding that a starboard turn at 0645 would have exceeded the bounds of good seamanship was based on the testimony of Captain Slack to that effect. However, Captain Slack's testimony was in response to hypothetical questions posed by the district court and Hellenic Lines' attorney which required Captain Slack to assume that the passing distance between the vessels was two miles. Since we have concluded that the passing distance must have been less than two miles, Captain Slack's testimony, and the district court's conclusion based on that testimony carries no weight.

The second problem with the district court's interpretation of the phrase "so far as possible" is that it has the effect of making Rule 19(d)(i) advisory instead of mandatory. Rule 19(d)(i) has been interpreted by four different courts and each has interpreted the language to prohibit port turns for vessels navigating in close quarters, in restricted visibility and not in sight of one another. Alkmeon Naviera, S.A. v. M/V Marina L, 633 F.2d 789 (9th Cir.1980); Amoco Transport Company v. S/S Mason Lykes, 550 F.Supp. 1264 (S.D.Tex.1982); The Roseline, 2 Lloyd's List L.R. 410 (Q.B. 1981); The Sanshin Victory, 2 Lloyd's List L.R. (Q.B.1980).

We agree with the reasoning of these courts that Rule 19(d)(i) should be interpreted to mean that alterations of course to port should be avoided in situations where a vessel has room to maneuver and a choice of which way to turn to avoid a risk of collision. When vessels are maneuvering in close quarters, there is not usually time for each vessel to observe the action of the other and adjust its course accordingly. A vessel must be able to anticipate the actions of an oncoming vessel if it is to adequately adjust its course to avoid the risk of collision. The intent of the rule is expressed well in the following language from *The Roseline:*

> I cannot condemn too strongly any alteration of course to port when a ship which is not in sight is approaching from ahead. Whether action is taken to avoid a close-quarters situation which is seen to be developing or to remove a risk of collision which already exists, an alteration of course to port should be avoided.

2 Lloyd's List L.R. at 417.

The entire purpose of the Colregs and particularly of its Rule 19 will be lost if it is construed to be advisory rather than mandatory. These are internationally adopted rules which are to control in ships of all nations. They must be enforced if they are to serve any useful purpose, and they must be enforced uniformly. The captain of a ship, regardless of the ship's country of registration or its port of call or the language of its crew, must be able to rely upon other ships complying with these Colregs and never turning to port when it is forward of the beam of another vessel and in a close-quarters situation. The rule is the same and must be enforced whether the ships are off the coast of North Carolina or off the coast of Borneo.

Because the Hellenic's first port turn was made when the two vessels were in close quarters and at a time when the Hellenic could have taken other action to avoid a risk of collision, we conclude that this turn to port violated Rule 19(d)(i). Since it is clear that this violation was a contributing cause of the collision,[2] the district court should have considered it as a fault of Hellenic when it was apportioning responsibility for the collision.

Appellant also argues that the Hellenic should have been held at fault for its second port turn made in the final seconds before the collision. The evidence clearly supports the district court's finding that this turn did not contribute to the collision. The uncontradicted testimony of Captain Slack was that this last turn to port was made at a time when no action by the Hellenic could have avoided the collision. Accordingly, we affirm the district court's refusal to assign fault for this second turn.

V

We now turn to a consideration of the limitation of Hellenic Lines liability.
* * *

CONCLUSION

We remand the case to the district court for a reconsideration of the apportionment of fault between the parties and its limitation of Hellenic's liability in accordance with our holding that the Hellenic was in violation of Rule 19(d)(i) of the 72 Colregs and that Hellenic's use of "parallel indexing" did not comply with Rule 7(b).

Remanded.

N O T E

The Pennsylvania, 86 U.S. (19 Wall.) 125, 22 L.Ed. 148 (1873), applied in *Hellenic Lines* above, involved a collision on the high seas between two British ships, the Steamboat Pennsylvania and the bark Mary Troop. The collision took place in a heavy fog. The Pennsylvania was proceeding too fast for the circumstances, and the bark, contrary to the provisions of the British Merchant Shipping Act, was ringing a bell instead of sounding a fog horn. When the lookout on the Pennsylvania heard the bell on the starboard side, the helm of the Pennsylvania was first ported, then put to starboard, but before the steamboat had moved her length (341 feet), it struck the bark. The bark was cut in half and sank. Mr. Justice Strong delivered the opinion of the court. In holding the accident attributable to mutual fault, he observed:

"Concluding, then, as we must, that the bark was in fault, it still remains to inquire whether the fault contributed to the collision, whether in any degree

---

2. The Hellenic's only alternative to a turn to port at 0645 was a turn to starboard which would have put the Atlantico on its port side. Our earlier discussion has established that there is no evidence to support the district court's finding that a starboard turn would have exceeded the bounds of good seamanship.

it was the cause of the vessels coming into a dangerous position. It must be conceded that if the fault could have had nothing to do with the disaster, it may be dismissed from consideration. The liability for damages is upon the ship whose fault caused the injury. But when, as in this case, a ship at the time of the collision is in actual violation of a statutory rule intended to prevent collisions it is no more than a reasonable presumption that the fault, if not the sole cause, was at least a contributory cause of the disaster. In such a case the burden rests upon the ship of showing not merely that her fault might not have been one of the causes, or that it probably was not, but that it could not have been * * *"

The rule of *The Pennsylvania*, it is to be noted, was stated as a rule applicable to a violation of a *statutory* rule intended to prevent collisions. A violation of a custom may constitute a fault. See, e.g., Valley Towing Service, Inc. v. SS American Wheat, 618 F.2d 341, 1981 A.M.C. 436 (5th Cir.1980), in which the court of appeals remanded for a determination of whether the descending vessel was in violation of the Mississippi River point-bend custom and assign some weight to such violation in determining the percentage of each vessel's fault. And see Stevens v. F/V Bonnie Doon, 655 F.2d 206, 1982 A.M.C. 294 (9th Cir.1981), apportioning the fault 70–30 when both vessels were without lookout but one was not observing the fishing circles custom. But the rule of The Pennsylvania does not apply to failure to observe the point-bend custom. See Canal Barge Co., Inc. v. China Ocean Shipping Co., 579 F.Supp. 243, 1985 A.M.C. 731 (E.D.La.1984), aff'd 770 F.2d 1357 (5th Cir.1985).

What is "statutory" for the purposes of *The Pennsylvania* rule? The Inland Rules obviously are, and the COLREGS plainly have the force of statute. What about rules, like the Pilot Rules that are not statutes but are adopted pursuant to statute? Cf. Peoples Natural Gas Co. v. Ashland Oil, Inc., 604 F.Supp. 1517 (W.D.Pa.1985), in which it was held that the presumption of causation under *The Pennsylvania* applied to plaintiff failure to bury its pipeline four feet below the riverbed, as required by its Corps of Engineers permit.

One of the troublesome areas in the application of the rule in The Pennsylvania has been relationship between the rule and those of the rules of navigation that are cautionary in character, so that violation is determined only in reference to the circumstances. A case in point was Rule 29 of the former Inland Rules (Article 29 of the International Rules), which provided:

"Nothing in these rules shall exonerate any vessel, or the owner, master or crew thereof, from the consequences of any neglect to carry lights or signals, or of any neglect to keep a proper lookout, or of any neglect of any precaution which may be required by the ordinary practice of seamen, or by the special circumstances of the case."

There was a difference of opinion on the question of whether Rule 29 placed on the vessel an additional statutory duty. Second circuit cases held that failure to have a proper lookout was a statutory violation. See Dwyer Oil Transport Co. v. Tug Matton, 255 F.2d 380, 1961 A.M.C. 406 (2d Cir.1958). The same position was taken by the Seventh Circuit in Florida East Coast Railway Co. v. Revilo Corp., 637 F.2d 1060, 1982 A.M.C. 643 (5th Cir.1981). In the Fifth Circuit, see The Union Reliance—Berean, 364 F.2d 769, 1966 A.M.C. 1653 (5th Cir.1966). There the contention was made that appellee had violated Rule 29 by failure to keep a proper lookout. The court did not quite meet that contention, observing that The Pennsylvania does not place a burden upon the faulted vessel to demonstrate that "its fault could not, by any stretch of the imagination, have a causal connection to the collision, no matter how speculative, improbable or remote." The Fourth Circuit view of the matter was explained in Anthony v. International Paper Co., 289 F.2d 574, 1961 A.M.C. 1890 (4th Cir.1961):

> "It has been held in a number of decisions in the Second and Fifth Circuits that failure to have a proper lookout is a statutory fault or, in any event, is such a grave default in careful navigation as to impose upon the ship the same obligation as rests upon one which has been guilty of a statutory fault [citing cases].

> "In our view the violation of the duty, although a serious one, is not a statutory fault with the extreme consequences imposed by *The Pennsylvania* rule. The purpose of article 29, which refers to the negligence of a vessel to keep a proper lookout, was not to make an addition to the statutory rules of navigation theretofore set out, but to make certain that compliance with those rules would not excuse the failure of the ship to comply with the other well known rules of good seamanship which exist irrespective of statute."

The court went on to say that it did not minimize the duty to have a proper lookout and to hold that in such a case the failure to maintain proper lookout would "give rise to a strong inference that it contributed to the accident and to impose upon the vessel the heavy burden to show by clear and convincing evidence that it did not so contribute."

The particular question of the statutory nature of the failure to maintain a lookout under Rule 29 of the Inland Rules and Article 29 of the International Rules prior to the adoption of the COLREGS in 1977 and the present Inland Rules in 1981, is no longer with us. The general precautionary language of old Rule 29 now appears solo in Rule 2(a), and the language with regard to maintenance of a lookout is made a statutory obligation under Rule 5.

> Every vessel shall at all times maintain a proper look-out by sight and hearing as well as by all available means appropriate in the prevailing circumstances and conditions so as to make a full appraisal of the situation and of the risk of collision.

Thus, though this rule clearly makes the duty statutory, is the determination whether it has been violated so tied to the circumstances surrounding the collision as to reduce very materially the importance of the presumption imposed by *The Pennsylvania*? See, e.g., Capt'n Mark v. Sea Fever Corp., 692 F.2d 163, 1983 A.M.C. 2651 (1st Cir.1982). Cf. Marcona Corp. v. Oil Screw Shifty III, 615 F.2d 206, 1981 A.M.C. 468 (5th Cir.1980), decided under former Rule 49. The court of appeals observed, "There is no absolute duty to maintain a lookout or signal other vessels during the final stages of mooring. Absent a fixed requirement, the question of whether these precautions are necessary 'is one of fact to be determined from all the circumstances on the basis of common prudence.'"

Prior to 1975 it was the practice in maritime collision cases in which two or more vessels were found to be at fault to apportion the damages in moieties, that is to say that each vessel found to be at fault was charged with the damages of each of the others at fault divided by the number of such vessels. Thus in the two vessel collision, each paid half the damages of the other. The moieties rule and its abrogation is treated beginning on p. 854, infra. To some large extent, does this not account for the importance of rule of *The Pennsylvania* in judicial decisions on the allocation of fault?

How important is it in the present day practice in which fault is apportioned? See Tug Ocean Prince, Inc. v. United States, 584 F.2d 1151, 1978 A.M.C. 1786 (2d

Cir.1978): "The 'Pennsylvania rule' is still alive and well today. That rule's vitality and force were not in any degree affected by United States v. Reliable Transfer Co., * * * which overruled *The Pennsylvania* only insofar as it abolished the Mutual Fault–Equal Contribution rule and substituted a new rule requiring liability for collision damage to be allocated proportionately to the comparative degree of fault."

To the extent that the rule will result in the characterization of most collision cases as mutual fault cases, this appears to be so. Indeed, is it not true that in a system in which the damages are apportioned on the basis of fault one would expect less pressure against application of the rule of *The Pennsylvania*? Does the fact that the court must assign a percentage figure to each fault make the application of *The Pennsylvania* presumption unnecessary? Some thought so, at least in cases in which both sides are guilty of fault. See Claim of Gypsum Carrier, 465 F.Supp. 1050, 1063, 1979 A.M.C. 1311 (S.D.Ga.1979).

4. Supervening Negligence, the Major–Minor Fault Rule, and the Last Clear Chance

Exxon Company v. Sofec, Inc.

United States Court of Appeals, Ninth Circuit, 1995.
54 F.3d 570, 1995 A.M.C. 1521, cert.granted ___ U.S. ___, 116 S.Ct. 493, 133 L.Ed.2d 419.

■ Thomas G. Nelson, Ct.J.:

Overview

Exxon Shipping Co. and Exxon Company U.S.A. (collectively, "Exxon") appeal the district court's judgment following a bench trial in Exxon's admiralty action seeking damages for loss of its tanker, the Exxon *Houston*, and costs of oil spill cleanup and loss of cargo. Exxon maintains that the failure of a Single Point Mooring System ("SPM") manufactured by defendant Sofec and sold by defendants Pacific Resources, Inc. and associated corporations (collectively, "HIRI"[1]) was the actual and proximate cause of its losses. The district court found in Phase One of a bifurcated proceeding that Exxon's negligence superseded any damage caused by the failure of the SPM, and was the sole proximate cause of the *Houston's* stranding. On appeal, Exxon argues that the district court improperly bifurcated the proceedings and that the doctrine of superseding cause has no application to cases in admiralty. We affirm the district court's order.

Facts

This case arises from the stranding of the *Exxon Houston* on March 2, 1989, near the Island of Oahu, several hours after she broke away from an SPM owned and operated by defendants HIRI. The *Houston*, a steam propulsion oil tanker weighing over 72,000 dead weight tons, was engaged

---

1. We follow the district court's designation of the defendant corporations, which include Pacific Resources, Inc., Hawaiian In-dependent Refinery, Inc., PRI Marine, Inc., and PRI International, Inc., as "HIRI."

in delivering oil via two floating hoses into HIRI's submerged pipeline, pursuant to a contract between Exxon and defendant Pacific Resources International, Inc. ("PRII"), when a heavy southern storm (locally termed a Kona storm) caused a break in the chafe chain linking the vessel to the SPM. As the vessel drifted, the two oil hoses broke away from the SPM. Because the hoses were bolted to the ship rather than secured by more readily detachable safety locks, a long (800 feet) length of one hose remained attached to the ship, and interfered with her ability to maneuver.

While the parting of the first hose did not cause a significant threat to the Houston, the parting and partial sinking of the second, longer hose, weighed down by a heavy piece of spool torn from the SPM, threatened to foul the ship's propeller. The parting of the second hose at approximately 1728,[2] designated as the "breakout" or "breakaway," is the initiating point in time for events covered in the Phase One trial.

Immediately after the breakout, the Coast Guard contacted the *Houston* to see whether she needed assistance, but because he was advised assistance vessels would not arrive within two hours, Captain Coyne refused the offer, thinking the problem would be resolved within that time. Captain Coyne did not thereafter request assistance from the Coast Guard. During the two hours and forty-one minutes following the breakout, the *Houston's* Captain, Kevin Coyne, took the ship through a series of phases described in some detail in the district court's findings of fact. These phases are summarized in the following paragraphs.

At about 1740, Captain Coyne attempted to anchor, dropping a single anchor which paid out one shot (90 feet) of chain. On the basis of expert testimony, the district court found that Captain Coyne failed to follow standard maritime practice, which would have involved releasing five to six shots of chain to hold the ship under the circumstances. The *Houston* had twelve shots of chain available for each of her two anchors. After this attempt to anchor failed, Captain Coyne made no further efforts to anchor the *Houston* before she stranded, although the district court found there were numerous places en route he could safely have done so.

By 1803, the small assist vessel *Nene* was able, with the assistance of the *Houston*, to get control of the end of the second hose so that it was no longer a threat to the larger ship. Captain Coyne controlled the *Nene's* movements as necessary to coordinate with the *Houston's* movements. Between 1803 and 1830, Captain Coyne maneuvered the *Houston* out to sea and away from shallow water.

Between 1830 and 2009, the time of stranding, the district court found that Captain Coyne made a series of ill-advised moves. Perhaps most significant was his failure to plot the ship's position on the chart between 1830 and 2004. Rather than plotting fixes of the vessel's position at regular intervals, Captain Coyne relied after 1830 entirely on parallel

---

2. The equivalent local time was 5:28 p.m. In keeping with the record, we refer to   nautical time in this opinion.

indexing, a supplemental technique which, according to Exxon's Navigation and Bridge Organization Manual ("Navigation Manual"), "does not relieve the ship's officer of the duty to frequently plot the position of the ship on the chart by means of navigational fixes." Without a fix, Captain Coyne was unable to make effective use of the chart to check for hazards.

Between 1830 and 1947, the crews of the *Houston* and the *Nene* worked to disconnect the second hose from the *Houston*. This was accomplished by 1947. The *Houston's* port crane collapsed in the process, taking the crane operator's seat with it onto the deck. The second mate went below to attend to the crane operator, who was in shock, leaving Captain Coyne alone on the bridge at 1948. Although the Navigation Manual requires that at least two officers be present on the bridge at all times, Captain Coyne did not call upon any of the other available officers to join him until 2000. The district court found that if the bridge had been properly manned, the stranding danger would have been avoided.

Finally, at 1956, Captain Coyne made a disastrous final turn to the right (toward the shore) which resulted in the ship's stranding. Given that the Kona storm was threatening to push the vessel into shore, it is not clear why the Captain chose to turn right instead of continuing to back out safely to sea, or turning to port, away from the coast. Both options were viable. The district court found Captain Coyne's explanations for his decision unconvincing. Because he had not taken fixes, Captain Coyne apparently was unaware of the ship's position until he ordered Third Mate Spiller to do so at 2004. Third Mate Spiller testified that, on seeing the 2004 fix on the chart, Captain Coyne uttered an expletive and immediately ordered an increased speed. Moments later the ship ran aground on a reef near the shore.

Procedural History

In April, 1990, Exxon filed its complaint in admiralty against HIRI and Sofec (the manufacturer of the SPM) for the loss of its ship and cargo, and for oil spill cleanup costs. HIRI filed a third-party complaint against Bridon Fibres and Plastics, Ltd. ("Bridon"), and Griffin Woodhouse, Ltd. ("Griffin").[3] On June 3, 1992, Griffin moved to bifurcate the trial. All defendants joined the motion. The district court granted the motion on July 31, 1992, limiting the first phase of the trial to the issue of causation with respect to the *Houston's* grounding, leaving the issue of causation with respect to the breakout for Phase Two.

After conducting a bench trial in admiralty between February 9, 1993, and March 3, 1993, the district court found that Captain Coyne's (and by imputation, Exxon's) extraordinary negligence was the sole proximate and superseding cause of the *Houston's* grounding. Exxon filed an appeal on June 16, 1993, which was dismissed for lack of a final judgment. Following motions by Bridon and Exxon, the district court entered a final motion precluding all of Exxon's claims for loss of the vessel on April 20, 1994. We

---

3. A third company which was dismissed without prejudice.

have jurisdiction over Exxon's subsequent timely appeal pursuant to 28 U.S.C. § 1291, and we affirm the judgment.

Analysis

A. *Applicability of superseding cause in admiralty.*

The district court's conclusions of law are reviewed de novo. Havens v. F/T Polar Mist, 996 F.2d 215, 217 (9th Cir.1993). Exxon argues that the Supreme Court's holding in United States v. Reliable Transfer Co., 421 U.S. 397, 95 S.Ct. 1708, 44 L.Ed.2d 251 (1975), replacing the historical divided damages rule in favor of comparative negligence in admiralty cases, vitiates the use of concepts such as intervening force and superseding cause. In *Reliable Transfer*, the Court rejected the rule whereby damages were divided equally between or among negligent vessels (usually in collision cases) regardless of the degree of fault attributable to each. 421 U.S. at 397, 411. In concluding, the Court stated that:

> [W]hen two or more parties have contributed by their fault to cause property damage in a maritime collision or stranding, liability for such damages is to be allocated among the parties proportionately to the comparative degree of their fault, and that liability for such damages is to be allocated equally only ... when it is not possible fairly to measure the comparative degree of their fault.

Id. at 411. In the wake of *Reliable Transfer*, the circuits have considered with sometimes conflicting results the issue of whether superseding cause may still be used to attribute fault in admiralty cases. In Hercules, Inc. v. Stevens Shipping Co., 765 F.2d 1069 (11th Cir.1985), on which Exxon relies, the Eleventh Circuit appears to have held the doctrine of superseding cause inapplicable in the maritime context after *Reliable Transfer*. Rejecting appellee's argument that its negligence was not a proximate cause of the accident in question, the *Hercules* court stated:

> The doctrines of intervening cause and last clear chance, like those of "major-minor" and "active-passive" negligence, operated in maritime collision cases to ameliorate the ... so-called "divided damages" rule [rejected by the Supreme Court in *Reliable Transfer*].... Under a "proportional fault" system, no justification exists for applying the[se] doctrines.... Unless it can truly be said that one party's negligence did not in any way contribute to the loss, complete apportionment ... is the proper method for calculating and awarding damages in maritime cases.

765 F.2d at 1075. While *Hercules* was understood by the Eighth Circuit to reject the role of superseding cause altogether in maritime cases, Lone Star Industries, Inc. v. Mays Towing Co., Inc., 927 F.2d 1453, 1458 (8th Cir.1991), it is not entirely clear whether in rejecting intervening cause the Eleventh Circuit meant merely to reject "normal intervening cause" as defined by Restatement (Second) of Torts ("Restatement") § 443, or whether it meant also to reject "superseding cause" as defined by Restatement § 440.[4] Given that the *Hercules* court explicitly ruled that appellee's

---

4. Section 440 of the Restatement (Second) of Torts defines superseding cause as: an act of a third person or other force which by its intervention prevents

underlying actions were a proximate cause (as well as a cause in fact) of the damage, it is plausible that the court would not have ruled out a defense based on superseding cause as the sole proximate cause of the damage.

It is not necessary to resolve here whether the Eleventh Circuit has proscribed the use of superseding cause in admiralty. Several other circuits, most importantly this one, have affirmed the continuing viability of superseding cause in the maritime context. In Hunley v. Ace Maritime Corp., 927 F.2d 493, 497 (9th Cir.1991), we held that an intervening force supersedes prior negligence where the subsequent actor's negligence was "extraordinary" (defined as "neither normal nor reasonably foreseeable"). Thus, a ship's failure to stand by and offer assistance to the sinking vessel with which she had collided was deemed the sole proximate cause of injury to a rescuing vessel's crewman, even though both of the colliding vessels were causes-in-fact of the collision. 927 F.2d at 496–97. Accordingly, we held the departing vessel "solely responsible" for the injuries of the seaman aboard the rescuing vessel. 927 F.2d at 498. See also Protectus Alpha Navigation Co. v. North Pac. Grain Growers, 767 F.2d 1379,1384 (9th Cir.1985)(indicating in dicta that application of the principle of superseding cause in a a maritime case "would not have been improper."); Nunley v. M/V Dauntless Colocotronis, 727 F.2d 455, 466 (5 Cir.1984)(en banc)(indicating that superseding cause might come into play in admiralty), cert. denied, 469 U.S. 832, 105 S.Ct. 120, 83 L.Ed.2d 63 (1984); Donaghey v. Ocean Drilling & Exploration Co., 974 F.2d 646, 652 (5th Cir.1992)(holding

the actor from being liable for harm to another which his antecedent negligence is a substantial factor in bringing about.

Comment b adds:

A superseding cause relieves the actor from liability, irrespective of whether his antecedent negligence was or was not a substantial factor in bringing about the harm.

Section 441 defines intervening force as:

one which actively operates in producing harm to another after the actor's negligent act or omission has been committed.

Section 443 on "normal intervening force" states that:

[t]he intervention of a force which is a normal consequence of a situation created by the actor's negligent conduct is not a superseding cause of harm....

Section 442 lays out factors for determining whether an intervening force is a superseding cause:

(a) the fact that its intervention brings about harm different in kind from

that which would otherwise have resulted from the actor's negligence;

(b) the fact that its operation or the consequences thereof appear after the event to be extraordinary rather than normal in view of the circumstances existing at the time of its operation;

(c) the fact that the intervening force is operating independently of any situation created by the actor's negligence, or, on the other hand, is or is not a normal result of such a situation;

(d) the fact that the operation of the intervening force is due to a third person's act or to his failure to act;

(e) the fact that the intervening force is due to an act of a third person which is wrongful toward the other and as such subjects the third person to liability to him;

(f) the degree of culpability of a wrongful act of a third person which sets the intervening force in motion.

Restatement (Second) of Torts §§ 44042 (1965).

that "the doctrine of superseding negligence in maritime cases . . . retains its vitality"); *and cf. Lonestar*, 927 F.2d at 1458–60 (rejecting the *Hercules* approach and applying superseding cause in a case involving ordinary (as opposed to extraordinary) negligence).

We hereby reaffirm that superseding cause may act to cut off liability for antecedent acts of negligence in admiralty cases where the superseding cause is the result of extraordinary negligence. We therefore hold that the district court did not "disobey" *Reliable Transfer* in employing the concept of superseding cause in this case.

* * *

Conclusion

We hold the district court did not err in finding Captain Coyne's extraordinary negligence to be the sole proximate and superseding cause of the damage to the *Houston*, and we affirm.

NOTE

The use of a pair of tongs in excess of their rating in an effort to change a frozen safety valve was not a superseding cause of injury to a seaman struck by the tong when it failed such as would insulate the manufacturer of the valve in causing the valve to be frozen. Conoco v. Varco International, Inc., 974 F.2d 646, 1994 A.M.C. 512 (5th Cir.1992).

The major-minor fault rule developed as a mitigating factor in the application of the moieties rule for apportionment of damages. See the discussion in United States v. Reliable Transfer Co., Inc., reproduced on p. 859, infra. In the President Grant the court indicates that *Reliable Transfer* did not exactly repudiate the major-minor fault rule. It was not exactly supportive of it either—vide "But this escape valve, in addition to being inherently unreliable, simply replaces one unfairness with another. That a vessel is primarily negligent does not justify its shouldering all responsibility, nor excuse the slightly negligent vessel from bearing any responsibility at all."

The doctrine of the last clear chance was developed in the common law as a means of mitigating the harshness of the doctrine that contributory negligence served as an absolute bar to recovery. See Prosser, *Law of Torts*, Ch. 11, § 66 (1971). In connection with its application in maritime cases, Judge Friendly observed in Petition of Kinsman Transit Co., 338 F.2d 708, 1964 A.M.C. 2503 (2d Cir.1964):

> "Although it might have been thought that the less severe consequences attributed to contributory negligence by the admiralty would have prevented the last clear chance doctrine from entering maritime law, see The Norman B. Ream, 252 F. 409, 414 (7th Cir.1918), a number of factors dictated otherwise. One was the influence of English cases in the common law courts involving collisions in territorial waters; another was the manning of the Court of Appeal and the House of Lords and of both trial and appellate admiralty tribunals in this country with lawyers whose principal training was in the common law; a third, no longer applicable in England since the Brussels Rules for apportioning damages in proportion to fault were adopted by the Maritime Conventions Act, 1 & 2 Geo. V, c. 57, § 1(1)(1911), but highly influential here—is that the

doctrine selectively applied, has helped to overcome results of the equal division principle which are sometimes quite as shocking as those for the common law bar for contributory negligence—especially in cases where reliance by a relatively innocent plaintiff on the 'major-minor fault' exception has been thought to be barred by the rule of The Pennsylvania, 86 U.S. (19 Wall) 125, 22 L.Ed. 148 (1874), that a party to a collision who has violated a statutory rule of navigation may not escape liability except on proof that the violation could not have contributed to the accident * * *.''

"However the case would stand at common law, the last clear chance doctrine, not very satisfactory at best, has been utilized in admiralty quite selectively, to free a claimant from the consequences of a rather low degree of negligence in creating a dangerous situation of which the party whose activity led to the damage was well aware and which he could easily have overcome."

The authority on the subject since the decision in *Reliable Transfer* suggests that the doctrine of the last clear chance, like the doctrine of the major-minor fault, ceased to be a feature of the allocation of fault in maritime collision cases after the adoption of the proportional fault rule in *Reliable Transfer*. See Hercules, Inc. v. Stevens Shipping Co., 765 F.2d 1069 (11th Cir.1985); Whitney S.S. Co. v. United States, 747 F.2d 69, 1985 A.M.C. 493 (2d Cir.1984); Getty Oil Co., Inc. v. S.S. Ponce de Leon, supra, 555 F.2d at 333.

5.   ERRORS IN EXTREMIS

The Bywell Castle

Court of Appeal, 1879.
L.R. 4 Prob.Div. 219.

* * *

■ JAMES, L. J. Upon the point which is first to be considered, namely, whether the Princess Alice was in fault or not, we have the direct finding of the Judge of the Court of Admiralty, and of the Trinity Masters who assisted him, they finding in distinct terms that the Princess Alice was once in a parallel course with the Bywell Castle, red light to red light, and that if their respective courses had been continued they would have passed at a safe distance from each other; but that when a very short distance, variously stated at from 100 to 400 yards, intervened between the two vessels, the master of the Princess Alice ordered the helm to be put starboard by which he brought his vessel athwart the bows of the Bywell Castle. That was the finding of the judge and the Trinity Masters, who heard all the evidence, and all the comments made, and many of the defences that have been suggested to us on the evidence. They came to that conclusion, and it would require a great deal to satisfy me, that we, sitting as a Court of Appeal, could, on any considerations suggested to us, overrule that finding. My own opinion, moreover, is that the evidence is in support of it. Then with regard to the general conduct of the Princess Alice—on which I have not heard a comment made in support of her—the Court says: "It appears to us, moreover, that the Princess Alice was navigated in a careless and reckless manner, without due observance of the regulations respecting look-out and speed." That is not to be questioned. Therefore upon the first issue, whether the Princess Alice was to blame, there can be no doubt that we must affirm the judgment of the Court below. The judge of the Court below then says that the Bywell Castle "appears to have been navigated with due care and skill till within a very short time of the collision," and I understand our assessors to agree with those in the Court below, that all the manoeuvres of the Bywell Castle up to the time of the collision were executed with due care and skill. Then there comes the very last thing that occurred on the part of the Bywell Castle, which is that she, in the very agony, just at the time when the two ships were close together, hard a-ported. The judge and both of the Trinity Masters were of opinion that that was a wrong manoeuvre. I understand our assessors to agree in that conclusion, but they advise us that it could not, in their opinion, have had the slightest appreciable effect upon the collision. That view, if adopted by us, and I think that it should be adopted, would be sufficient to dispose of the case upon the question of contributory negligence. But I desire to add my opinion that a ship has no right, by its own misconduct, to put another ship into a situation of extreme peril, and then charge that other ship with misconduct. My opinion is that if, in that moment of extreme peril and difficulty, such other ship happens to do something wrong, so as to be a contributory to the mischief, that would not render her liable for the damage, inasmuch as perfect presence of mind, accurate judgment, and promptitude under all circumstances are not to be expected. You have no right to expect men to be something more than ordinary men. I am therefore of opinion that the finding of the Court below, that the Bywell Castle was, for the purposes of the suit, to be considered to blame, must be overruled, and that the Princess Alice was alone to blame.

■ BRETT, L. J. In this case the Admiralty Court has found that both ships were to blame, and there are, practically, cross appeals. * * *

I cannot indeed have a doubt that the Princess Alice was in the wrong. She was in the wrong for not keeping on the port side of the Bywell Castle, having once got there, and she was also in the wrong in going at the time at full speed; therefore she was twice in the wrong. Then, if that be so, of course she was still more wrong, if, instead of easing her starboard helm, she kept on that helm, and if she did ease, she was still more wrong in putting the helm again to starboard. If she was on the port side of the Bywell Castle, by her wrong act she put the Bywell Castle's captain into an extreme difficulty, in being close to him shewing him a green light on his port bow. The next question is whether the Bywell Castle being put into that difficulty did what was wrong. It is said that she did so in two instances. But what is the wrong that the Court is bound to find she did? Not merely that she did a wrong thing, but that she was guilty of a want of that care or skill which she ought to have shewn under such difficult circumstances. I am clearly of opinion that when one ship, by her wrongful act, suddenly puts another ship into a position of difficulty of this kind, we cannot expect the same amount of skill as we should under other circumstances. The captains of ships are bound to shew such skill as persons of their position with ordinary nerve ought to shew under the circumstances. But any Court ought to make the very greatest allowance for a captain or pilot suddenly put into such difficult circumstances; and the Court ought not, in fairness and justice to him, to require perfect nerve and presence of mind, enabling him to do the best thing possible. What the pilot did was to give the orders to stop and to put the helm hard a-port; and the order to stop was carried out. He says that he gave the order not only to stop, but to reverse. I agree that if he had time to do it he ought to have done it. There was some dispute as to who did give the order, and it is said that if he did give the order it was not obeyed. But whichever order was given we must consider the circumstances. He was not called upon to give the order to stop and reverse until the other ship had done the wrong thing. Where did she do it? She did it close to him, and the first order was to stop or to stop and reverse, the next to put the helm a-port. Whichever it was, the Court has not found that there was any wrong order as to the stopping or reversing, though it has found that the order to port was wrong. We are, however, advised that the order to put the helm hard a-port had no practical effect as to the collision. If that be so, of course it follows that the last wrongful act of the Princess Alice was done so near to the other that it was impossible by any manoeuvre to avoid the collision. If the fact of ordering the helm hard a-port had no effect upon the collision, it is immaterial whether it was given or not. Even if it had an effect and was wrong, we have come to the conclusion that the captain of the Bywell Castle was suddenly put into an extremely difficult position, and assuming that a wrong order was given, that it ought not under the circumstances to be attributed to him as a thing done with such want of nerve and skill as entitles us to say that by negligence and want of skill the Bywell Castle contributed to the accident. Therefore, though agreeing with all the other findings as to the Princess Alice, we must come to a different opinion as to the last finding, the result of which is that we must hold the Princess Alice solely to blame.

■ Cotton, L. J. * * * Even if the collision had not been unavoidable at the time when the helm of the Bywell Castle was put hard a-port, I should not have held that vessel liable. For in my opinion the sound rule is, that a man in charge of a vessel is not to be held guilty of negligence, or as contributing to an accident, if in a sudden emergency caused by the default or negligence of another vessel, he does something which he might under the circumstances as known to him reasonably think proper; although those before whom the case comes for adjudication are, with a knowledge of the facts, and with time to consider them, able to see that the course which he adopted was not in fact the best. In this case, though to put the helm of the Bywell Castle hard a-port was not in fact the best thing to be done, I cannot hold that to do so was under the circumstances an act of negligence on the part of those who had charge of that vessel.

Judgment for the Bywell Castle.

NOTE

The error in extremis doctrine has been applied in many American cases, as far back as The Genessee Chief, 53 U.S. (12 How.) 443, 13 L.Ed. 1058 (1851). Cases are collected in Griffin on *Collisions* §§ 233–235 (1949). The application of the rule is necessarily vague. See Gilmore and Black 491 (1975). "Even *in extremis* a vessel's master is supposed to act with a level head and upon judgments wrought of long experience * * * *" U.S. v. M/V Wuerttemberg, 330 F.2d 498, 1964 A.M.C. 1098 (4th Cir., 1964). When collision is imminent enough, maneuvers patently wrong have been excused. In Deep Sea Tankers, Ltd. Rincon Hills v. Long Branch, 258 F.2d 757, 1959 A.M.C. 28 (2d Cir.1958), the pilot gave an order that the helm be put hard right and the helmsman put it hard left. The court, in excusing the disobedience of the order, held that the helmsman's action was a natural reaction when faced with running down a car float. In U.S. v. Panama Transp. Co., 253 F.2d 758, 1958 A.M.C. 830 (2d Cir.1958), a vessel was exonerated though it made a hard right turn immediately before collision with a vessel that had deviated from the prescribed course by failing to make allowance for a 2–knot current. In Rederi A/B Soya v. S.S. Grand Grace, 369 F.2d 159, 1967 A.M.C. 344 (9th Cir.1966), failure to move out of the way was excused when action was called for only seconds or minutes before the collision.

It is to be noted that the doctrine *in extremis* is related to the provisions of Rule 2(b), which excuses a vessel from following the Rules when special circumstances demand action to avoid a collision. The cases often raise the issue of the point of time at which special action should be taken. When a vessel is aware of the danger and waits too long to act, it will not be excused on the ground that at the time it did act it was *in extremis*. See, e.g., *Wuerttemberg—Swerve,* supra. There the master "needlessly elected a close passage in fog, knowing the Wuerttemberg was rapidly closing, apparently on a collision course, when, by a turn into safe waters to the right, she could have avoided all risk of collision." On the other hand it was held that former Rule 27 did not permit premature maneuvers by the burdened vessel. If it fails to hold its course and speed until evasive action is called for, it was in violation of former Rule 21. Darby—Soya Atlantic, 330 F.2d 732, 1964 A.M.C. 898 (4th Cir.1964). If it does hold its course in compliance with Rule 21 until it was *in extremis,* the question becomes one of whether it has waited too long, in violation of Rule 27. See Vagabond—Myab III (Harry B. Luke v. Howard S. Hirsch), 287 F.Supp. 75, 1968 A.M.C. 338 (S.D.N.Y.1968), in which it was held that a sailing vessel being overtaken by a steam vessel was correct in holding its speed and course and its last minute turning into the wind was excused as an error *in extremis.*

And see Pentelikon v. Verdi, 438 F.2d 854, 1971 A.M.C. 584 (2d Cir.1971). There the privileged vessel sounded a danger signal and held its course until the last minute, when it maneuvered to avoid the collision. At this juncture the burdened vessel maneuvered wrongly. The district court divided the damages on the ground that the privileged vessel should have acted to avoid the collision and the burdened vessel's last faulty maneuver was "in extremis." The court of appeals reversed, holding that the privileged vessel after giving a danger warning was correct in maintaining its course and if the last fault of the burdened vessel was to be excused as "in extremis," the behavior of the privileged vessel, occurring at the same time, was perforce also excusable.

A vessel relying on the "in extremis" rule must be free from fault until the emergency arose. See Bucolo, Inc. v. S/V Jaguar, 428 F.2d 394, 1970 A.M.C. 2379 (1st Cir.1970), in which an inbound vessel, after observing an outbound vessel change to a crossing course sounded only one blast instead of a danger signal which might have alerted oncoming vessel, though they were then only 50 yards and five seconds apart. And see Matter of G & G Shipping Co., 767 F.Supp. 398, 1994 A.M.C. 170 (D.P.R.1991) abrupt turn to port during head to head port to port passing was not excused as an error in extremis when the vessel was proceeding with an unlicensed helmsman who was left alone at the wheel from time to time while the captain, who served as lookout, did paper work, the helmsman was inadequate as a lookout, and the captain failed to make proper use of the radar.

B.   DAMAGES

1.   COMPUTATION OF DAMAGES

Howard Olson v. Marine Leopard

United States Court of Appeals, Ninth Circuit, 1966.
356 F.2d 728, 1966 A.M.C. 1064.

■ FREDERICK G. HAMLEY, CT. J.   This is an admiralty cause arising out of the collision between the S.S. Howard Olson and the S.S. Marine Leopard, on May 14, 1956. As a result of that collision the Howard Olson, which was in ballast, was sunk and the Marine Leopard and its cargo were damaged. The Howard Olson was owned by Oliver J. Olson & Co. (Olson), and the Marine Leopard is owned by Luckenbach Steamship Company, Inc. (Luckenbach). The owners of cargo aboard the Marine Leopard are referred to herein as Cargo.

The issues of fault were tried early in 1957, and an interlocutory decree was entered on September 13, 1957, finding both vessels at fault. In that decree it was also found that the owners of the Howard Olson were not in privity to its faults. This latter finding entitled the owners of the Howard Olson to limit their liability in accordance with the provisions of the Limitation of Shipowners' Liability Act, Rev.Stat. § 4283 (1875), as amended, 46 U.S.C.A. § 183 (1964). The interlocutory decree was affirmed by this court. Oliver J. Olson & Co. v. Luckenbach S.S. Co., 279 F.2d 662, 1960 A.M.C. 1230 (9 Cir.1962).

Pursuant to a provision of the interlocutory decree which was not challenged on the prior appeal, the causes were referred to a commissioner to take testimony and ascertain the value of the Howard Olson immediately before the collision, and at the end of her voyage, together with the freight pending for the voyage, and the freight lost as a result of the collision. The commissioner was also directed to ascertain the damages sustained by the various claimants. All questions in respect to the division of damages, the application of the statutes for limitation of liability, priorities, and distribution of the limitation fund were reserved for decision by the court.

All items of damage referred to the commissioner were settled by stipulation, or otherwise disposed of, except the valuation of the Howard Olson. Hearings were had on that issue resulting in a report by the commissioner valuing the vessel at $430,000 immediately prior to the collision. The commissioner's report was confirmed by the district court and a final decree was thereafter entered. Luckenbach and Cargo have appealed.

Luckenbach contends that the district court erred in overruling Luckenbach's exceptions to the commissioner's report valuing the Howard Olson at $430,000. In these exceptions, as restated in Luckenbach's opening brief on appeal, it is asserted that the commissioner erred in several different respects in fixing that valuation. Some of these exceptions have to do with the factors upon which the commissioner premised his valuation, and others pertain to the rejection or disregard of certain evidence produced by Luckenbach.

Before discussing these contentions, an account of the history and characteristics of the Howard Olson will be helpful. This vessel was of a type known as a "Laker," having been built on the Great Lakes in 1917 for a cost of $983,171.05. The Howard Olson was a steel-riveted, single screw vessel with engines astern. She was 4,100 D.W.T., 2477 gross tons, 261 feet overall length and 43 feet 6 inches overall beam. She had a lumber carrying capacity of approximately 2,100,000 feet board measure.

Olson purchased the vessel in 1946 for $116,000. At that time she was, in the opinion of underwriters, in condition to be classed A–1 with the American Bureau of Shipping. In 1950 she was equipped with radar worth $5,644. In 1952, diesel cranes were installed on the vessel at a cost of $69,000. Olson maintained the vessel in excellent condition. In February, 1956, three months before she was lost, plate renewals were effected costing $33,000. An expert expressed the opinion that the condition of the vessel in 1956 was such that she could have operated nine more years without incurring major repair.

The Howard Olson had certain characteristics which well suited her for the coastwise lumber trade conducted by Olson. Among these features were the placement of her engines astern, the radar and diesel crane equipment, large hatches and square, boxlike holds. The vessel was comparatively inexpensive to operate, requiring a crew of only twenty-nine men. All of these features, taken together, contributed to her high record of average daily earnings as compared to the Karen and Barbara Olson, operated by the same owner. The Howard Olson, as a domestic-built and documented vessel, had coastwise privileges pursuant to Rev.Stat. sec. 4132 (1875), as amended, and 41 Stat. 999 (1920), as amended, 46 U.S.C.A. §§ 11, 883 (1964).

The Howard Olson was engaged in carrying packaged lumber from deepwater ports in Washington and Oregon to Southern California and returning in ballast. There was evidence to the effect that while other vessels in the Olson fleet were to be replaced by barges, the Howard Olson, because of her special features, was not to be replaced. On the other hand, there was also evidence to the effect that for several months prior to the collision the owner had been trying to sell the Howard Olson. Moreover, after that vessel was lost, Olson made no effort to replace her with another freighter but, in accordance with the trend in the coastwise trade, turned exclusively to barges.

Holding that the market value of the Howard Olson in May, 1956, could not be determined because there was no relevant market, the commissioner primarily used reproduction cost depreciated in reaching a valuation of $430,000. The commissioner thus accepted the opinion testimony of Andrew E. Allen, chief engineer for Todd Shipyards Corporation, and Leroy T. Kanapaux, an employee of Frank S. Martin & Sons, ship surveyors and appraisers. Kanapaux, whose testimony was principally relied upon, fixed the reproduction cost of the Howard Olson at $2,949,540. Depreciation was predicated upon the so-called Martin Scale which is a declining balance depreciation of five percent reduced over the years. This produced a figure of $399,013.77, to which Kanapaux added the depreciated cost of the cranes ($33,720.71), for a total reproduction cost depreciated of $432,734.48. This method of determining the reproduction cost depreciated of the Howard Olson was not challenged.

The commissioner also took into account evidence that the Howard Olson was insured for $495,000, plus twenty-five percent or a total of $618,000 in the event of total loss. The commissioner also noted that the vessel's earning record was "impressive," and that, over her expectable life, she would have returned far more to her owner than her reproduction depreciated valuation. The commissioner indicated, however, that he did not consider these matters of insured value or earnings to be conclusive on valuation, but only as indicating that these factors could in no way cause him to reduce the experts' reproduction depreciated valuation.

Luckenbach questions the propriety of basing valuation of the Howard Olson on reproduction cost depreciated, in view of the other evidence of valuation in the record.

The principles governing the allowance of damages for the total loss of a vessel in a collision at sea are comprehensively set forth in Standard Oil Co. of New Jersey v. Southern Pacific Co., 268 U.S. 146, 155–56, 45 S.Ct. 465, 467, 69 L.Ed. 890, 1925 A.M.C. 779, 782 (1925).[1] As there stated, the

---

1. In the *Standard Oil Co.* case the Supreme Court said:

"It is fundamental in the law of damages that the injured party is entitled to compensation for the loss sustained. Where property is destroyed by wrongful act, the owner is entitled to its money equivalent, and thereby to be put in as good position pecuniarily as if his property had not been destroyed. In case of total loss of a vessel, the measure of damages is its market value, if it has a market value, at the time of destruction. Baltimore, 75 U.S. (8 Wall.) 377, 385, 19 L.Ed. 463 (1869). Where there is no market value such as is established by contemporaneous sales of like property in the way of ordinary business, as in the case of merchandise bought and sold in the market, other evidence is resorted to. The value of the vessel lost properly may

be taken to be the sum which, considering all the circumstances, probably could have been obtained for her on the date of the collision; that is, the sum that in all probability would result from fair negotiations between an owner willing to sell and a purchaser desiring to buy. Brooks–Scanlon Co. v. United States, 265 U.S. 106, 123, 44 S.Ct. 471, 68 L.Ed. 934, 1924 A.M.C. 856 (1923). And by numerous decisions of this Court it is firmly established that the cost of reproduction as of the date of valuation constitutes evidence properly to be considered in the ascertainment of value [citing cases]. The same rule is applied in England [citing cases]. It is to be borne in mind that value is the thing to be found and that neither cost of reproduction new, nor that less depreciation, is the measure or sole guide. The ascertainment of value is not controlled by artificial rules. It is

measure of damages to be applied is the market value of the lost ship, if it has a market value at the time of destruction. Market value, as the Court indicated, is value "* * * such as is established by contemporaneous sales of like property in the way of ordinary business, as in the case of merchandise bought and sold in the market, * * *." See, also, Barton v. Borit, 316 F.2d 550, 552 (3 Cir.1963). Other evidence of value, such as reproduction cost depreciated, may be resorted to only where no market value can be established.

Luckenbach asserts that evidence was presented of contemporaneous sales of comparable vessels and that the commissioner's determination of the value of the Howard Olson should therefore have been based upon that evidence, rather than evidence of reproduction cost depreciated.

According to the undisputed evidence, two sister ships owned by Olson, the Barbara Olson and the Karen Olson, were sold in November, 1956, for $205,000 each. These vessels were sold to foreign buyers for foreign operations. While these sales were made six months after the loss of the Howard Olson, there was undisputed testimony that, by November, 1956, the market for ships had risen approximately twenty percent above the market in May, 1956.

There was also testimony that each of these vessels was generally equivalent to the Howard Olson. All three vessels had coastwide privileges. The Barbara and Karen Olson were regularly surveyed and maintained in class A–1 with the American Bureau of Shipping, whereas the Howard Olson was not maintained in class. Luckenbach's experts testified that lack of classification would reduce the value of the Howard Olson by $30,000 as compared to classified vessels.

The Barbara and Karen Olson were not equipped with diesel cranes of the kind which were installed on the Howard Olson at a cost of $69,000. The Howard Olson may also have had other special features which made it of more value than the Barbara or Karen. However, on September 1, 1955, Olson offered all three vessels for sale at the same price, i.e., $250,000 each, or $675,000 for the three.

The commissioner made no finding that the three vessels were not generally comparable, or that the date of the sale of the Barbara and Karen, taking into consideration testimony concerning the rising market, was too far removed from the date of the Howard Olson's loss. Instead, the commissioner rejected this evidence on two other grounds which we now consider.

First, the commissioner stated in his report that according to the evidence, Olson, in November, 1956, no longer had use for the Barbara and Karen Olson and was replacing them with barges. The party liable for the loss of the Howard Olson in May of 1956, the commissioner stated, "* * * can take no advantage from these circumstances."

not a matter of formulas, but there must be a reasonable judgment having its basis in a proper consideration of all relevant facts. Minnesota Rate Cases, 230 U.S. 352, 434, 33 S.Ct. 729, 57 L.Ed. 1511 (1913)."

But the fact that Olson decided to replace these vessels with barges does not constitute grounds to disallow evidence of their sales. Presumably every owner who sells a vessel has a reason for doing so. Unless the sale is in the nature of a forced liquidation, and that was not the case here, the reason which motivates the seller is wholly irrelevant in utilizing the sale price as a measure of the market value of a comparable ship.

Second, the commissioner stated in his report that the sale of the Barbara and Karen Olson to foreign buyers does not tend in any way to prove a fair open market in the United States for coastwise privilege vessels.

In our opinion, the fact that the buyers of the Barbara and Karen Olson were foreign, and desired the vessels for foreign service, is without significance. The vessels were sold in the United States, presumably for the highest price obtainable. If a domestic operator had desired the Barbara and Karen Olson because of their coastwise privileges, he might have paid more; the fact that no domestic buyer appeared proves only that coastwise privileges no longer added value to these ships.

We hold that the commissioner's reasons, referred to above, for rejecting the sale of the Barbara and Karen Olson as evidence of the market value of the Howard Olson in May, 1956, were insufficient. This is not to say that the commissioner was necessarily required to equate the value of the Howard Olson to the sale price of the Barbara and Karen Olson. Variances in physical and operative characteristics might warrant some differentiation in values; however, it must also be considered that, in the fall of 1955, Olson did not differentiate in values in offering all three ships for sale.

Luckenbach also offered evidence concerning ten foreign vessels on the market in the months preceding and following the collision. The commissioner initially rejected evidence concerning five of the foreign vessels as being dissimilar. Under the evidence, however, the remaining five vessels were all similar to the Howard Olson in the 1956–1957 period. We refer to the S.S. Kalle, S.S. Sileno, S.S. Parame, S.S. Merida and S.S. Dagenham. These vessels were sold at various times between April 1956 and July, 1957, for prices ranging from $137,200 to $196,000.

Olson could not have utilized any of these vessels as a replacement for the Howard Olson because none of them had or could obtain coastwise privileges. On this ground the commissioner struck all the evidence pertaining to the sale of the five foreign flag vessels referred to above, in determining the value of the Howard Olson. In taking this action the commissioner apparently relied upon the decision of this court in President Madison, 91 F.2d 835 (9 Cir.1936), 1937 A.M.C. 1375.

In *President Madison*, it was held that the district court did not err in failing to predicate the value of a vessel lost in a collision upon her market value. The vessel in question, the Harvester, was a sternwheeler of shallow draft, sturdy enough for use on Puget Sound yet small enough to negotiate the Skagit River where she was mainly utilized. It appeared from the evidence that no other ship could be secured which would answer the purpose for which the Harvester was designed. Under these circumstances, this court held that the trial court's conclusion that the Harvester had no market value was well substantiated by the evidence.[2]

Even in those cases where a market value cannot be established other evidence of value resorted to is to be of a kind which will establish the sum "* * * which, considering all the circumstances, probably could have been obtained for her on the date of the collision * * *." Standard Oil, supra, 268 U.S. at 155, 1925 A.M.C. at 782.

The fact that no domestic buyer bought the Barbara Olson or the Karen Olson, both of which had coastwise privileges, indicates that these privileges added no appreciable marketable value to those vessels, or to the Howard Olson. Hence, even disregarding the intangible character of those privileges, as compared to the physical characteristics which rendered the Harvester unique in the President Madison case, the fact that the five foreign registry vessels did not have those privileges is immaterial.

In our opinion, the commissioner erred in excluding the evidence pertaining to the sale of these five vessels, and in failing to consider that evidence in determining the market value of the Howard Olson. Considering this evidence and the evidence relating to the sale of the Barbara and Karen Olson, the commissioner had ample evidence regarding generally contemporaneous sales of similar vessels on which to predicate a finding of the Howard Olson's market value. It was therefore error for the commissioner to turn from evidence of market value to that tending to show reproduction cost depreciated in valuing the Howard Olson.

---

2. In *President Madison*, this court said, in part (91 F.2d at 844, 1937 A.M.C. at 1391 (1937)):

"It is urged that the market value test is not whether other vessels can be purchased in the open market to replace the one which is lost, but rather whether the lost vessel could have been used in other services to a sufficient extent to find purchasers. So it is said that, although a Columbia River stern wheeler could not have been used on the Puget Sound–Skagit River route, the Harvester nevertheless could have been sold for use on the Columbia River.

"This argument overlooks the economic reasons for the market value test and for substituting other criteria when that fails. If the Harvester had been sold for Columbia River service, she would have commanded a price measurable to vessels in that service. Her peculiarities—broad beam, exceptionally shallow draft, and other special features—

would not have been reflected in the price commanded by the vessel in a market where these features were unnecessary and superfluous. Such a price could not give the owner, who needs these special features for his trade, the value of what he had lost."

President Madison, in our opinion, does not represent a holding that the market value test is whether other vessels can be purchased in the open market to replace the one which is lost. This would run counter to the principles announced in Standard Oil Co. v. Southern Pacific Co., 268 U.S. 146, 155–56, 45 S.Ct. 465, 69 L.Ed. 890, 1925 A.M.C. 779, 785 (1925), wherein no such replacement factor was injected. "Market value" denotes what it fairly may be believed that a purchaser in fair market conditions would have given. United States v. Miller, 317 U.S. 369, 374, 63 S.Ct. 276, 87 L.Ed. 336 (1942); New York v. Sage, 239 U.S. 57, 61, 36 S.Ct. 25, 60 L.Ed. 143 (1915).

In the final decree Luckenbach was required to pay into the limitation fund created by Olson, in addition to the principal amount of $30,673, seven percent interest thereon from May 14, 1956, until paid. On this appeal, Luckenbach urges that in a mutual-fault collision such as this, it is unworkable and unfair to award interest from the date of the collision. Apparently agreeing that such an interest award is, absent special circumstances, warranted in a single-fault collision, such as President Madison, Luckenbach points out that in the case of a mutual-fault collision, there must necessarily be a balancing of damages between the two shipowners before it can be determined who is the judgment creditor and who is the judgment debtor. The award of interest back to the date of the collision, Luckenbach argues, therefore represents an abuse of discretion.

In view of the disposition we have made of the valuation issue, it seems highly unlikely that Luckenbach will be charged any interest in the revised final decree which must be entered. We therefore refrain from a discussion of this point.

Luckenbach and Cargo both contend that the district court erroneously allocated the death and personal injury claims. All claims for death and personal injury arising from the collision were settled by Luckenbach and Olson for $181,432. Each shipowner, according to a written agreement, advanced one-half of this sum to effect settlement. The agreement provided:

"Should it be finally adjudicated that either party making advances for such settlements was not under legal liability to make payment to claimants, then such advances shall be immediately refunded by the party held liable to make such payment."

In its final decree, the district court ordered Luckenbach to reimburse Olson for the $90,716 advanced by Olson pursuant to the settlement agreement. In so doing, the district court stated that "* * * in accordance with his rights of limitation Oliver J. Olson & Co. is adjudged to have been under no legal obligation to pay any amount to the death and personal injury claimants. * * *" The $90,716 was then added to Luckenbach's collision damages and accordingly decreased the offset payable to Olson for the benefit of Cargo in the limitation proceeding.

Cargo asserts that despite Olson's right to limit liability, Olson nevertheless remained legally obligated to pay death and personal injury claims from a sixty dollar per ton fund provided for in 49 Stat. 1479 (1936), 46 U.S.C.A. § 183(b)(1964).[3] Olson urges affirmance of the district court

---

3. The 1936 amendment to Rev.Stat., sec. 4283, 46 U.S.C.A. § 183(b), provides as follows:

"(b) In the case of any seagoing vessel, if the amount of the owner's liability as limited under subsection (a) of this section is insufficient to pay all losses in full, and the portion of such amount ap-

plicable to the payment of losses in respect of loss of life or bodily injury is less than $60 per ton of such vessel's tonnage, such portion shall be increased to an amount equal to $60 per ton, to be available only for the payment of losses in respect of loss of life or bodily injury. If such portion so increased is insuffi-

order contending that the prior appeal in this case resulted in a holding that it was not liable to make payments to third party claimants.

In the prior appeal, this court held that Olson was entitled to limit its liability for damages resulting from the collision and for death and personal injury claims. Oliver J. Olson & Co. v. Luckenbach S.S. Co., 279 F.2d 662, 671–73, 1960 A.M.C. 1230, 1244 (9 Cir.1960). This was not an adjudication absolving Olson of liability. Olson's liability remained unchanged, although the amount recoverable became subject to the limiting provision of section 183.

With regard to cargo claimants, it is conceivable that Olson's obligation to pay can be limited to zero under section 183(a). However, in the case of death and personal injury claimants, this result is avoided by section 183(b) which establishes a sixty dollar per ton fund for the benefit of these claimants. The Howard Olson's tonnage was 2477, giving her an exposure of $148,620 to death and personal injury claims ($60 × 2477). Despite Olson's right to limit liability, death and personal injury claimants, had they retained their claims, would have been entitled to recover at least $148,620 from Olson.[4]

Olson advanced $90,716 as its share of the settlement arrangement. This sum was well within the limits of Olson's sixty dollar per ton fund; there is no conflict between the settlement agreement and the limitation of liability invoked by Olson. The fact that Olson was found to be entitled to limit liability did not amount to an adjudication that it was under no legal liability to pay within the meaning of the valid settlement agreement.

Olson argues that the sixty dollar per ton fund is designed to insure payment to death and personal injury claimants where no other source of recovery is available. And, in this case, since Luckenbach has not limited its liability, Olson contends that Luckenbach is primarily liable for these claims.

In a single-ship accident, it is true that the sixty dollar per ton fund will not be created unless the limitation fund under section 183(a) proves insufficient to satisfy the claims. However, it does not follow that the limiting ship in a mutual fault collision can avoid liability altogether at the expense of the non-limiting ship. Liability of the shipowners to third party claimants in a mutual-fault collision is joint and several; and the fact that a limiting ship may have to resort to a sixty dollar per ton fund does not alter the nature of its liability.

---

cient to pay such losses in full, they shall be paid therefrom in proportion to their respective amounts."

4. The section 183(b) fund is available only in the case of a "seagoing vessel." Section 183(f) limits the term "seagoing vessel" by listing several types of vessels which are not to be included in that term. Olson urges that these exceptions together with excerpts from the legislative history indicate that sec-

tion 183(b) was not intended to increase the liability of a nonpassenger-carrying vessel to its crew members. We do not agree. The restriction of section 183(b) to passenger-carrying vessels only, would be an unwarranted limitation of that statute. See In re Petition of the Dodge, Inc., 282 F.2d 86, 89, 1961 A.M.C. 233, 238 (2 Cir.1960); 3 Benedict, *Admiralty,* sec. 475 (6th ed. 1940).

The purpose of section 183(b) is to assure some recovery to death and personal injury claimants; there is no indication that it was also intended to alter established admiralty concepts by allowing a limiting ship to avoid primary liability in a mutual-fault collision case. Olson had no right to be reimbursed for the payments advanced to settle claims for which it was legally liable. The district court erred in reallocating the death and personal injury claims and invalidating the private settlement agreement. See In re Petition of the Dodge, Inc., 282 F.2d 86, 1961 A.M.C. 233 (2 Cir.1960).[5]

Cargo argues that the district court failed to recognize and apply the principle that the admiralty divided damages rule prevails over any limitation statute until after the balance is struck. More specifically, Cargo asserts that the full amount of the cargo damage claims against the Howard Olson should have been included in its damages before the balance of damages of the Howard Olson and the Marine Leopard was struck. Instead, the district court, adopting the view of Luckenbach and Olson, ruled that the cargo damage should not be included in the division. This resulted in a division based primarily on hull damage, and reduced the single liability of Luckenbach to Olson which creates the limitation fund out of which Cargo could realize on its claims against Olson.

The problem thus posed involves the interplay, in mutual-fault cases, between section 3 of the Harter Act, 27 Stat. 445 (1893), 46 U.S.C.A. § 192 (1964), relieving a vessel owner, under indicated circumstances, from liability for loss or damage to the vessel's cargo, and Rev.Stat. § 4283(a)(1875), 46 U.S.C.A. § 183(a)(1964), limiting the liability of a vessel owner for loss or destruction, by collision, of another vessel or its cargo to the amount or value of the interest of such owner and her freight then pending. Also involved is the rule of law, first announced in O'Brien v. Miller, 168 U.S. 287, 18 S.Ct. 140, 42 L.Ed. 469 (1897), that, in applying the latter statute, the limiting vessel's (Howard Olson's) claim against the non-limiting ship (Marine Leopard), to the extent that it represents the loss

---

5. Reversal of the district court decree in regard to the death and personal injury claims makes it necessary to provide for the possible distribution of the limitation fund. This fund should be divided, pro rata, between the cargo claims and the death and personal injury claims paid by Olson. Since Olson has paid its share of these claims, the proportion of the limitation fund allocated to death and personal injury claims can be retained by Olson. The difference between this sum and the $90,000 actually paid to claimants, represents the contribution from Olson's sixty dollar per ton fund.

Cargo suggests that under the equitable doctrine of marshalling, the death and personal injury claimants should be remanded to the sixty dollar per ton fund, leaving the limitation fund of section 183(a) entirely to cargo claimants. We do not think that this is a proper case for the application of the principle of marshalling assets. Both the wording of section 183(b) and its legislative history make it clear that death and personal injury claimants are to share pro rata in the limitation fund and only when their proportion fails to satisfy their claims will they be remanded to the sixty dollar per ton fund. See H.R. No. 2517, 74th Cong., 2nd Sess. (1936).

Of course, this problem of distribution of the limitation fund will arise only if Luckenbach, after the final division of damages, is ordered to pay Olson a sum which represents Olson's interest in the Howard Olson.

of its interest in the vessel, is still an interest in the vessel which is subject to liability.

Olson has been granted limited liability and therefore will not have to pay the full amount of Cargo's claim. The extent to which Olson must respond in damages to Cargo can only be determined after the size of the limitation fund is established; until that time, Cargo's claim is too speculative to warrant inclusion in the division of damages. Only those damage items which have been paid or will be certainly payable are includible. Luckenbach Steamship Co. v. United States, 315 F.2d 598, 604, 1963 A.M.C. 1940 (2 Cir.1963).

If these claims were nevertheless included, the result would be to circumvent Luckenbach's complete exclusion from liability to its own cargo, accomplished under the Harter Act. This is true because, to the extent that cargo claims were included in Olson's damages before striking the balance, Luckenbach would be required to pay fifty percent thereof for the purposes of the limitation fund.[6] See In re Petition of the Dodge, Inc., 282 F.2d 86, 89, 1961 A.M.C. 233, 236 (2 Cir.1960).

Cargo relies upon language to be found in North Star, 106 U.S. 17, 1 S.Ct. 41, 27 L.Ed. 91 (1882). But, as Cargo concedes, *North Star* did not involve any cargo or other third-party claims. The decisional language to which Cargo points must be read in the light of that fact, which distinguishes *North Star* from the case before us. Chattahoochee, 173 U.S. 540, 19 S.Ct. 491, 43 L.Ed. 801 (1899), also relied upon by Marine Leopard Cargo, was concerned with the question of recoupment by the non-carrying shipowner for amounts actually payable to the cargo interests. The non-carrying ship in that case had not limited its liability and was liable to pay cargo the full amount of its loss.

In Weyerhaeuser S.S. Co. v. United States, 372 U.S. 597, 83 S.Ct. 926, 10 L.Ed.2d 1 (1963), 1963 A.M.C. 846, cited by Cargo, the issue was the propriety of including in the collision damages of Weyerhaeuser, for division purposes, a personal injury settlement it had made with a member of the crew of the other colliding vessel. The crewman was precluded by statute from recovering from his vessel's owner, the United States.[7] There was no question of measuring the amount of money actually paid in settlement of the seaman's claim.

We agree with Luckenbach that the thrust of these decisions is simply that statutes governing the carrier's relations or liabilities to its own crew members or to its own cargo have no application to the non-carrier's claim for collision damages to the extent that such damages represent actual payment by the non-carrier or definite future payment of claims made

---

6. Although this result was condoned in Chattahoochee, 173 U.S. 540, 19 S.Ct. 491, 43 L.Ed. 801 (1899), it is a result which has not been reached in a case such as ours involving limited liability on the part of the non-carrying vessel.

7. The statute involved was the Federal Employees Compensation Act, which stood in the way of the seaman's recovering from the owner of the vessel on which he was employed.

against it by the carrier's crew or cargo. No such problem is involved in the case before us; the invocation of limited liability by the non-carrier renders its damages, the amount payable to Cargo, uncertain and wholly contingent upon recovery of a sum representing an interest in the Howard Olson.

We conclude that the district court did not err in the respect claimed by Marine Leopard Cargo.

Cargo next argues that the district court erroneously treated the item of interest on the general average disbursements.

Cargo acknowledges that when a vessel is under average, a party who incurs extraordinary expenses necessary to keep the vessel going is entitled to collect from the other parties to the voyage interest on their proportion of such extraordinary expenses. The shipowner's proportion of the interest on general average disbursements is a proper item of its collision damages. However, Cargo asserts, an anomaly and an absurdity is created where the interest on general average disbursements is allowed as a separate item of loss and interest is also allowed on all damages as in the present case. General average interest was allowed at the rate of five percent, and interest on all damages was allowed at the rate of seven percent.

In our opinion this treatment of interest accords with well-settled practice and is correct. See Moore–McCormack Lines v. Esso Camden, 141 F.Supp. 742, 1956 A.M.C. 2018 (S.D.N.Y.) mod. on other grounds, 244 F.2d 198, 202, 1957 A.M.C. 971 (2 Cir.1957). As the Court of Appeals there pointed out, the award of general average interest cannot be considered interest on damages. It is payment for the use of money which was necessary to keep the ship under way. Interest on a shipowner's general average disbursements is for a fixed period in the past and has thus been liquidated. As such, it stands no differently than any other items of general average expense.

Finally, Cargo argues, the district court abused its discretion in failing to award costs to the prevailing Cargo claimants.

No party prevailed in this litigation. As for Cargo, it set out to prove mutual fault of the vessels and to defeat Olson's right to limitation. Cargo won on the fault issue but lost on the limitation issue. The district court did not abuse its discretion in declining to award costs to Marine Leopard Cargo.

Reversed and remanded for further proceedings consistent with this opinion.

Compania Pelineon De Navegacion, S.A. v. Texas Petroleum Co.

United States Court of Appeals, Second Circuit, 1976.
540 F.2d 53, 1976 A.M.C. 1245.

■ BRIEANT, DISTRICT JUDGE.   Plaintiff-appellant, Compania Pelineon De Navegacion, S.A. ("Pelineon"), as owner of the chartered petroleum tanker

S.S. *Capetan Mathios* ("the Mathios"), seeks to review a final judgment entered in the Southern District of New York upon oral decision and written findings following a bench trial. The trial court awarded plaintiff damages in the total amount of $75,258.05, including interest, arising out of loss of use of the vessel, and directed that each party bear its own costs.

On September 29, 1972 at Tumaco, Colombia, while under a long-term time charter to Gulf Oil Corporation ("Gulf") the Mathios was being maneuvered into a sea berth by a pilot employed by defendant-appellee Texas Petroleum Company. In part due to the negligence of Texaco employees, not disputed here, her propeller became fouled in the chain of a buoy marking the berth. As a result of this allision, the vessel suffered severe physical damage, also not in issue on this appeal.

an allision

In the days immediately following the allision, the vessel was examined at Tumaco by an American Bureau of Shipping ("ABS") surveyor who observed that, among other damage, the fair water cone was missing but nevertheless issued a certificate of seaworthiness on October 3, 1972. The Mathios resumed trading under the Gulf charter. A new fair water cone was ordered with drydocking to be scheduled as soon as the needed repair part became available.

Soon after leaving Tumaco, the vessel experienced some vibration and operating difficulties. The owner and charterer agreed that a mutually convenient time to accomplish this yard repair would be in late March and early April, 1973. When the fair water cone became available, the Mathios entered drydock at Hoboken, New Jersey, on March 29, 1973, some four months prior to her next scheduled drydocking and overhaul, which had been originally planned following charter expiry.

In drydock, it was discovered for the first time that the vessel had been rendered unseaworthy by the occurrence at Tumaco. The needed repairs being accomplished, together with certain unrelated owner's repairs, the Mathios returned to the charterer's service on April 19, 1973.

On June 28, 1973, Gulf exercised its option under the charter-party to extend the charter by a period equal to all the off-hire time experienced by the Mathios during the charter. The off-hire extension included 25.179 days due to the aforementioned drydocking at Hoboken.

Between April and October, 1973, the market rates for voyage charters, and to a lesser extent for time charters, soared. On October 6, 1973, an Arab–Israeli war broke out. For a brief time thereafter, market rates remained high, but with the advent of oil embargoes by Mid–East oil producers, the demand for tankers fell sharply, along with the market rate for charter hire of tankers. The lower market rates began in the third week of October and remained depressed for some time thereafter.

The parties stipulated in the pre-trial order that the vessel "would have completed its charterparty commitment and all extensions, except that related to the Tumaco casualty, by on or about October 30, 1973. The vessel came off charter after all extensions on November 24, 1973."

would have come off charter on Oct. 30, 1973

Assigned as error on this appeal are (A) denial of recovery for loss of profit in excess of the rate under the existing time charter for that period by which the charter term was extended as a result of the allision; (B) denial of recovery for four (4) days loss of profit out of the repair period, found by the trial court to be attributable to unrelated owner's work; and (C) denial of an award of costs to the prevailing party. We discuss these claims in the order listed.

(A) The trial court held Pelineon's damages for loss of the use of the vessel as a result of the Tumaco incident should be measured by the net profits lost under the charterparty in effect at that time, holding:

> "[P]laintiff in effect seeks to have defendant pay twice for a single wrong. The off-hire provision in the charterparty is a contractual provision between plaintiff and the charterer. Plaintiff well knew that any off-hire time could be added to the charter term, and that plaintiff would be paid at the agreed rate for any off-hire period added. Plaintiff's attempt to recover hypothetical profits from defendant over and above those amounts actually contracted and paid under the charterparty has never before been awarded in similar circumstances, and this Court finds and holds it to be inequitable under well accepted equitable principles in Admiralty."

Relying on Skou v. United States, 478 F.2d 343 (5th Cir.1973) the court below held that the applicable measure of damages in determining lost profits is the charter rate less costs and expenses saved by the owner when the vessel was not in active service under the charter. The court found that Pelineon earned $2,179.36 net profit per day under the charterparty, which had been entered into in September 1969, and extended by an addendum dated May 28, 1971, at a rate of $3.85 per deadweight ton per month.

The court found plaintiff's calculation of lost profits to be highly speculative and "based on questionable assumptions of unforeseeable facts."

In this we find error. Demurrage, loss of profits from loss of the use of a vessel, traditionally has been an item of damage in maritime tort law. However, "demurrage will only be allowed when profits have actually been, or may be reasonably supposed to have been, lost, and the amount of such profits is proven with reasonable certainty." The Conqueror, 166 U.S. 110, 125, 17 S.Ct. 510, 516, 41 L.Ed. 937 (1897).

In Petition of Kinsman Transit Company, 338 F.2d 708, 724 (2d Cir.1964), cert. denied sub. nom. Continental Grain Co. v. City of Buffalo, 380 U.S. 944, 85 S.Ct. 1026, 13 L.Ed.2d 963 (1965), this Court observed that

> "[t]he weight of authority in this country rejects the limitation of damages to consequences foreseeable at the time of the negligent conduct when the consequences are 'direct,' and the damage, although other and greater than expectable, is of the same general sort that was risked."

Pelineon's damage here was plainly damage of the "same general sort that was risked."

Under the circumstances presented here, the magnitude of this damage, in addition to the fact of damage itself, was foreseeable. It was foreseeable that damage to the vessel would result in loss of use, and hence lost profits. It was also foreseeable that the vessel would be operating under time charter nearly complete as to term, with provision for off-hire extension. Ironically, the very charterparty agreement between Pelineon and Gulf was a form contract, amended as to matters not relevant here, used by appellee's parent company, Texaco. It was also foreseeable that the off-hire extension provision would be invoked by the charterer only if it were commercially advantageous to do so. The off-hire extension provision would be advantageous to the charterer if, at the time the charterparty would otherwise have expired, the market price for tankers had risen.

It is clear that if defendant had not negligently caused the accident, necessitating drydock repair and the attendant delay and off-hire extension, Pelineon would have been able to earn additional profits during the time when the Gulf charter had to be extended at the old rate. We, therefore, reject the argument that these profits were too remote a consequence or too unforeseeable to be recoverable.

[handwritten margin note: would have made more money had it not had to be extended at the old / lower rate]

The uncertainty regarding the damages in this case is only as to their amount.

> "The rule which precludes the recovery of uncertain damages applies to such as are not the certain result of the wrong, not to those damages which are definitely attributable to the wrong and only uncertain in respect of their amount." Story Parchment Co. v. Paterson Co., 282 U.S. 555, 562, 51 S.Ct. 248, 250, 75 L.Ed. 544 (1931).

It is not required that damages be proved with mathematical exactness provided that there is reasonable data from which the amount of damages can be ascertained with reasonable certainty, "and the party who has caused the loss may not insist on theoretical perfection." Entis v. Atlantic Wire & Cable Corporation, 335 F.2d 759, 763 (2d Cir.1964).

We hold that plaintiff-appellant is entitled to recover its net damages representing the reasonable current market value of the loss of use of the Mathios for that portion of the drydock period attributable to repairs necessitated by the Tumaco allision, not limited by the Gulf time charter rate. The amount of such damages must be determined on remand. For purposes of computing the amount on remand, we express no opinion at this time as to whether it is appropriate to assume, as appellant does, that upon the termination of the Gulf charter, the Mathios would of necessity be withdrawn from the long term time charter market, and become available for short term spot voyage charters, and therefore whether the relevant rate is that then prevailing for time or spot charters.

We believe that, upon this record, such profits may be determined without regard to any possible overlap period.[1] The stipulated facts

---

1. Paragraph 8 of the charterparty provided in relevant part:

"Notwithstanding the provisions of Clause 3 hereof [the clause fixing the term], should the vessel be upon a voy-

previously quoted from the pretrial order show that the parties have agreed as to the precise length of the extension caused by the period off-hire, and also the date on which the vessel would have come off charter but for the Tumaco casualty. Whatever allowance which would have to be made for underlap or overlap has been eliminated from the computation by the parties' agreement as to the exact date of redelivery to the owner but for the appellee's negligence.

(B) Plaintiff-appellant also disputes the disallowance by the trial court of four (4) days off-hire at the Hoboken drydock attributable to owner's repairs. As to the exclusion of this time in computing lost profits, the trial court was correct. After the Tumaco allision, the Mathios was found seaworthy by ABS although it was recommended that collision damage be reexamined at the next regular drydock period. The vessel continued her operations thereafter. Awaiting a repair part, Pelineon scheduled drydocking for a time convenient to owner and charterer. The trial court found that this scheduling was planned so as to move ahead the next regularly scheduled drydock period by a few months. At the time that the drydocking was scheduled, Pelineon did not know that the vessel was in fact unseaworthy. Accordingly, the evidence justified the holding below that the vessel may recover lost profits only for that portion of the Hoboken repair period by which Tumaco collision repairs extended the time which the owner's routine repairs required. See Skibs A/S Dalfonn v. S/T Alabama, 373 F.2d 101 (2d Cir.1967); The Pocahantas, 109 F.2d 929, 931 (2d Cir.), cert. denied sub nom. Eagle Transport Co. v. United States, 310 U.S. 641, 60 S.Ct. 1088, 84 L.Ed. 1409 (1940).

(C) Since no reason was given for denying appellant the ordinary taxable costs as the prevailing party below, we also reverse on this point.

While the trial court has discretion under Rule 54(d), F.R.Civ.P., to allow or disallow costs, such discretion is not to be exercised arbitrarily. Trans World Airlines, Inc. v. Hughes, 515 F.2d 173 (2d Cir.1975), cert. denied 424 U.S. 934, 96 S.Ct. 1147, 47 L.Ed.2d 341 (1976). Upon remand the district court may determine upon the present record or additional submissions whether appellant has done anything to deserve imposition of the penalty of denial of costs.

This action is remanded to recompute plaintiff-appellant's damages consistently with the foregoing, and ascertain whether costs should be allowed in the district court. In all other respects, the judgment appealed from is affirmed, with costs to appellant in this Court.

Since it appears that Judge Boldt is not designated or available in the Southern District of New York at this time, our remand shall issue to the transferor Judge, Hon. Robert J. Ward, in accordance with local IAC Rule 12 of that district.

age at expiry of the period of the charter, Charterer shall have the use of the vessel at the same rate and conditions for such extended time as may be necessary for completion of the round voyage on which she is engaged and her return to a port of redelivery as provided by this charter."

NOTE

1. Valuation

One starts with the principle that the vessel is a total loss, the loss is represented by its fair market value. See, e.g., Barton v. Borit, 316 F.2d 550, 1969 A.M.C. 216 (3d Cir.1963), where the court of appeals held that the district court erred in valuing a 40 foot catamaran built in Portugal the year before for $12,500 on the basis of depreciated replacement cost in the Virgin Islands (found by the court to be $23,000 plus $2,500 for sails and miscellaneous equipment) without first investigating whether there was a market for this sort of vessel.

If there is no market for vessels of the sort involved, a variety of evidence may be considered and the figure must be "a reasonable judgment" having its basis in a proper consideration of all relevant facts. Standard Oil Co. v. Southern Pacific Co., 268 U.S. 146, 156, 45 S.Ct. 465, 467, 69 L.Ed. 890 (1925).

Try this one out:

The tug Huntington was involved in an allision with a bridge in 1976, and petitioned for limited liability, and in order to determine the amount of the limitation fund, it was necessary to determine the value of the vessel. The following figures were adduced before the commissioner:

Original purchase price in 1951	$ 393,000
Title transferred in intercompany transaction in 1970s ...	65,600
Petitioner's claim as to value	75,000
Petitioner's insurance on tug	250,000
Evidence as to reconstruction cost in 1976	1,150,000
Book value in 1976	40,668
Operational profit/loss during 1976	59,000 (loss)

The commissioner fixed the value at $112,000. On hearing before the district court one sale of a tug of relevant age was adduced. This was the tug Sea Traveller, whose purchaser testified that he paid $99,500 and insured it for $185,000. The Huntington and the Sea Traveller compared as follows:

	Huntington	**Sea Traveller**
Age	25 years	22 years
Length	91 feet	68 feet
Gross tons	144	93
Net tons	98	63
Engines	1,280 H.P. Single Screw	680 H.P. Twin Screw

The greater power of the Huntington would make it possible to push larger barges, but the two engines of the Sea Traveller would make it more maneuverable and, in case of engine trouble, more reliable.

The district court fixed the value at $135,000. It arrived at this figure by taking the ratio of purchase price to insured value of the Sea Traveller and applying this to the insured valuation of the Huntington. The claimant appealed, arguing on appeal, inter alia, that the valuation was too low. What result? Red Star Barge Line, Inc. v. Nassau County Bridge Authority, 683 F.2d 42, 1982 A.M.C. 2588 (2d Cir.1982).

What of a vessel purchased for a particular purpose? Should the unique value to the purchaser be reflected in the appraisal? In King Fisher Marine Service v. NP Sunbonnet, 724 F.2d 1181, 1984 A.M.C. 1769 (5th Cir.1984), the plaintiff purchased a barge for use as a platform for a drydock, paying $30,000 on the open market, and hired defendant to tow it to its place of operation. On the way across the Gulf of Mexico the barge sank though the negligence of the tug. The plaintiff then was able to find another barge suitable for the purpose. He purchased this barge, too, for $30,000, but it had a hole in it and repair of the hole cost $202,996.75.

See B.V. Bureau Wijsmuller v. United States, 487 F.Supp. 156, 1979 A.M.C. 1979 (S.D.N.Y.1979) on the valuation (in the particular case for salvage cases) of special purpose naval vessels.

What if a vessel is determined to be a constructive total loss and is made useable by temporary repairs and then is involved in a second collision. In Barge BA–1041 (Hewlett v. Tug Evelyn), 283 F.Supp. 917, 1968 A.M.C. 1422 (E.D.Va. 1968), a barge was determined to be worth less than the cost of repairs and was taken over by the salvor. Later it was repaired at a cost of about $1,000 and put in use. It was involved in another collision in which it did not sink but acquired a large dent in the side. The district court held that since it would still float and was worth nothing, no damages would be awarded. The court of appeals reversed, Judge Haynesworth dissenting. Hewlett v. Barge Bertie, 418 F.2d 654, 1969 A.M.C. 2238 (4th Cir.1969).

The Weak Boat Doctrine. Since vessels are subject to "ordinary contacts of navigation," it is held that when a vessel is old, weak, and unseaworthy its loss through "ordinary contacts" is not compensable. See, e.g., The John E. Berwind, 270 Fed. 569 (2d Cir.1920). In Kookum II—Montauk, 358 F.2d 485, 1966 A.M.C. 881 (2d Cir.1966), it was argued that small pleasure craft are "weak" without being old and unseaworthy and therefore their owners may not recover for damages occasioned, in the particular case, when a yacht was nudged by a tug, doing $2,213.88 in damage. The court rejected this argument.

2. The Cost of Repairs

When a vessel is not a total loss, the owner is entitled to the cost of restoring it to the condition in which it was just prior to the collision. Freeport Sulphur Co. v. S/S Hermosa, 526 F.2d 300, 304 (5th Cir.1976). Damages are measured by the diminution of the value of the property. Stevens v. F/V Bonnie Doon, 731 F.2d 1433, 1985 A.M.C. 363 (9th Cir.1984). It is not necessary that repairs actually be made. See, e.g., Complaint of Hercules Carriers, Inc., 614 F.Supp. 16 (M.D.Fla. 1984), where estimated repair costs were awarded in respect to damage to a bridge, though the owners elected to replace the old span.

There is a detailed description of the charges in connection with the repair of a ship in Diesel Tanker Ira S. Bushey v. Tug Bruce A. McAllister, 1995 A.M.C. 806, 1994 WL 320328 (S.D.N.Y.1994).

Where parts replaced in the course of repairs were in good working order prior to the accident, the vessel liable for the damage ordinarily is not permitted a credit against its liability for the enhanced value of the repaired vessel because of the substitution of new parts for old. The Baltimore, 75 U.S. (8 Wall.) 377, 19 L.Ed. 463 (1869). When the parts were not in good working order at the time of the collision, however, depreciation has been allowed. See, e.g., Exner Sand and Gravel Corp. v. Maher Stevedoring Corp., 1955 A.M.C. 2286 (D.N.J.1955). And when land structures have been damaged, reduction in damages to reflect depreciation or "new for old" allowances have been granted. See Pizani v. M/V Cotton Blossom, 669 F.2d 1084, 1088 (5th Cir.1982), where it is stated as a general proposition that "a defendant cannot be held liable * * * for the cost of repairs that enhance the value of the damaged property compared with its pretort condition." See also Seaboard

Air Line RR Co. v. Marine Industries, Inc., 237 F.Supp. 10, 1966 A.M.C. 1552 (E.D.S.C.1964). See also Patterson Terminals, Inc. v. S.S. Johannes Frans, 209 F.Supp. 705, 1962 A.M.C. 2623 (E.D.Pa.1962), in which 50% deterioration and 20% for betterment through repair was allowed against the cost of repairing a breasting dolphin attached to a pier when the court found that the dolphin was in a deteriorated condition. With Patterson Terminals compare City of New Orleans v. American Commercial Lines, Inc., 662 F.2d 1121, 1982 A.M.C. 1296 (5th Cir.1981), affirming the district court in finding that a nine year old fender system damaged when struck by a barge had not deteriorated and refusing to reduce damages on the basis of depreciation.

Suppose that the owner makes the repairs himself. See Greer v. United States, 1975 A.M.C. 1672 (M.D.Fla.1975) in which the district court allowed $4 an hour for the owner's time. In English Whipple Sailyard, Ltd. v. Ardent, 459 F.Supp. 866, 1980 A.M.C. 1096 (W.D.Pa.1978), the owner was allowed $10 an hour. When the repairs are made by the owner of the injured property, should the damages include an allowance for profit? See Boh Bros. Constr. Co. v. M/V Tag Along, 577 F.2d 303, 1979 A.M.C. 797 (5th Cir.1978).

When extensive repairs are made after a collision, it is the owner who has the burden of showing which repairs were made necessary by the accident. See, e.g., Pizani v. M/V Cotton Blossom, supra, 669 F.2d at 1088–1089.

In Stevens Institute of Technology v. United States, 396 F.Supp. 986, 1975 A.M.C. 997 (S.D.N.Y.1975) the vessel involved in the collision was a dead ship that was to be converted into a dormitory. What repairs would be allowed?

Temporary Repairs.—When temporary repairs are necessary to facilitate the use of a damaged vessel until major repairs can be undertaken, they are allowed. See, e.g., Dominican Maritime, S.A. v. M/V Inagua Beach, 572 F.2d 892, 1978 A.M.C. 1552 (1st Cir.1978).

Duty To Minimize Damages.—The owner of a damaged vessel is called upon to have repairs made with due regard to minimizing the cost, and if the charges for repair services are excessive, the court might make its own determination. See, e.g., The Robert Hadden, 68 Fed. 1017 (S.D.N.Y.1895).

But it has been held that a subsidized vessel can have repairs made in the United States rather than in the Orient when one of the conditions of the subsidy is that repairs be made in the United States when conditions permit, the court observing that to take the vessel to Japan for repairs would not be minimizing damages in view of the fact that the offending vessel would be liable for the loss of subsidy income. Illinois—Union Star, 378 F.2d 356, 1967 A.M.C. 1725 (9th Cir. 1967).

The burden to show failure to minimize damages lies with the defendant. See Sutton River Services v. Inland Tugs Co., 1985 A.M.C. 858, 1984 WL 1462 (S.D.Ill.1984).

3. Economic Loss

Owner's Loss of Profits.—When a vessel is a total loss, the owner is entitled to the net freight pending. The net is calculated by deducting the anticipated expenses from the gross freight. See Urubamba—Tug Coot, 171 F.Supp. 735, 1959 A.M.C. 2505 (S.D.N.Y.1959), where net freight was denied, no evidence being offered of anticipated expenses. The court observed that it could not determine that any profit would have been made from the gross freight of $1,000.

Claim for lost income from allision may not be disallowed merely because the claimant fails to prove specific contract was lost because the vessel was out of commission for repairs. Parker Towing Co. v. Yazoo River Towing, Inc., 794 F.2d 591 (11th Cir.1986).

But ordinarily when the vessel is a total loss the owner is not compensated for loss of the use of the vessel as an item of damages, though where it is not possible to determine the fair market value, capitalized future earnings, as represented by a charter, may be evidence of value. See King Fisher Marine Service, Inc. v. NP Sunbonnet, 724 F.2d 1181, 1984 A.M.C. 1769 (5th Cir.1984); A & S Transp. Co., Inc. v. Tug Fajardo, 688 F.2d 1, 1983 A.M.C. 10 (1st Cir.1982); Alkmeon Naviera, S.A. v. M/V Marina L, 633 F.2d 789, 1982 A.M.C. 153 (9th Cir.1980).

When the vessel is not lost, the owner is entitled to be compensated for lost profits. This means loss of profits on the casualty voyage and also detention damages. For an example of the complications that beset the calculation of both, see Delta S.S. Lines v. Avondale Shipyards, Inc., 747 F.2d 995, 1985 A.M.C. 2554 (5th Cir.1985), in which the calculations are clearly explained.

Evidence was sufficient to show that the vessel was worth more than the cost of repairs and therefore was not a constructive total loss and therefore vessel owner was entitled for damages for loss of use. Ryan Walsh Stevedoring Co., Inc. v. James Marine Services, Inc. 792 F.2d 489 (5th Cir.1986).

Is there something unique about the loss of the use of a vessel? Suppose that a vessel were to damage a bridge belonging to a steel mill, and the bridge were the only way of transporting hot ore from the mill to the mainland, and as a consequence of the damage to the bridge the mill lost three days' production while the bridge was being repaired? See National Steel Corp. v. Great Lakes Towing Co., 574 F.2d 339, 1979 A.M.C. 369 (6th Cir.1978).

In lieu of lost profits for the period of detention the court may allow the cost of obtaining a substitute vessel. See The Emma Kate Ross, 2 C.C.A. 55, 50 Fed. 845 (3d Cir.1892). On the subject of working other vessels of the owner overtime to substitute for the one undergoing repairs, see Brooklyn Eastern District Terminal v. United States, 287 U.S. 170, 53 S.Ct. 103, 77 L.Ed. 240 (1932). The allowance of the cost of employing one's own vessel as a substitute presents, of course, a different problem of calculating the amount to be allowed as a loss. See, e.g., The Priscilla, 55 F.2d 32 (1st Cir.1932), in which the vessel was being repaired for a period of 21 days, and the owner used other vessels belonging to him on all days save 8, for which he chartered a vessel.

Because detention damages are allowed, it is important that repairs be made when they will result in the least lost time for the vessel. Thus it has been held that if the owner unreasonably lays the vessel up for repairs instead of waiting until the time when it is scheduled for drydocking for its annual overhaul, detention damages will not be allowed. See Hellenic Lines, Ltd. v. S.S. Union Metropole, 206 F.Supp. 383, 1966 A.M.C. 326 (E.D.Va.1962). Cf. Waterman S.S. Corp. v. Chrysanthi, 1965 A.M.C. 474 (S.D.N.Y.1964), where it was held reasonable to proceed with repairs although a survey found the vessel seaworthy, when the annual overhaul was scheduled in May and to wait would subject the vessel to the rigors of winter weather in the Atlantic. When the vessel is made unseaworthy it has been held that the repairs may be made immediately even if drydocking for other repairs has already been scheduled. S.S. Clarke's Wharf, 1960 A.M.C. 2106 (S.D.N.Y.1960)(commissioner's report).

Loss of the use of a vessel for purely recreational purposes has been held not compensable. The Conquerer, 166 U.S. 110, 17 S.Ct. 510, 41 L.Ed. 937 (1897). And despite the dictum by Justice Cardozo in Brooklyn Eastern District Terminal v. United States, 287 U.S. 170, 175, 53 S.Ct. 103, 104, 77 L.Ed. 240 (1932), characterizing the statement on the matter in The Conquerer as dictum, and suggesting a contrary rule, the lower courts have generally thought themselves bound by The Conquerer. E.g., Snavely v. Lang, 592 F.2d 296, 1979 A.M.C. 1011 (6th Cir.1979). See Nordasilla Corp. v. Norfolk Shipbuilding & Drydock Corp., 1982 A.M.C. 99 (E.D.Va.1981), aff'd without opin. 679 F.2d 885 (4th Cir.1982), cert. denied 459 U.S. 861, 103 S.Ct. 135, 74 L.Ed.2d 115 (1982), in which the district court expresses itself as "reluctant."

Economic Loss to Persons other than the Owner.—In Robins Dry Dock and Repair Co. v. Flint, 275 U.S. 303, 48 S.Ct. 134, 72 L.Ed. 290 (1927), the Supreme Court held that a time charterer of a vessel that had been put in dry dock for repairs, had no cause of action for loss of time under the charter against the repairer arising out of negligent damage to the vessel in the course of the repairs. The nature and extent of the rule in *Robins Dry Dock* has been a question much agitated. As related to collision damages, the question has usually been raised when the collision has blocked a waterway, or damaged a shore structure and persons who have a contractual or public right to use the waterway or the shore structure sue for damages for interference with their right to use.

Of the first variety was Kingston Shipping Co., Inc. v. Roberts, 667 F.2d 34, 1982 A.M.C. 2705 (11th Cir.1982), cert. denied 458 U.S. 1108, 102 S.Ct. 3487, 73 L.Ed.2d 1369 (1982). After a collision with the S.S. Capricorn, the United States Coast Guard buoy tender Blackthorn sank in the main ship channel of the port of Tampa and as a consequence deep draft vessels were unable to enter or leave until the wreckage was cleared away, which took 26 days. When the owners of The Capricorn petitioned for exoneration or limitation of liability, a number of the owners of the vessels whose arrival or departure had been delayed claimed for damages. The *Robins* rule was applied.

For a similar case in which there was a stranding rather than a collision, see Akron Corp. v. M/T Cantigny, 706 F.2d 151, 1984 A.M.C. 2969 (5th Cir.1983). There the vessel stranded in the Mississippi River as it attempted to negotiate the sharp exit turn into the Gulf of Mexico, and vessel owners sued for damages attendant to the ensuing delay. The *Robins* rule was applied.

And for another change that can be rung on this theme, see Getty Refining and Marketing Co. v. MT. Fadi B., 766 F.2d 829, 1985 A.M.C. 2579 (3d Cir.1985), in which the owner of a marine terminal sought to recover damages caused by the fact that the vessel, while unloading at the terminal pier, developed a crack in its deck and hull and had to remain at the pier for several days, thus subjecting the terminal to demurrage it was obligated to pay other vessels that were scheduled to dock at the pier, but couldn't. The *Robins* rule was applied here, too.

Of the second variety was Louisville & Nashville Railroad Co. v. M/V Bayou Lacombe, 597 F.2d 469, 1980 A.M.C. 2914 (5th Cir.1979). The vessel collided with a bridge across the Tennessee River and the L & N, which had a contractual right of way over the bridge, sued for loss of its right of way, which required the rerouting of its trains. The *Robins* rule was applied. Compare *The M/V Bayou Lacombe* with National Steel Corp. v. Great Lakes Towing Co., supra. Should the result turn on who owns the bridge?

On this issue see PPG Industries, Inc. v. Bean Dredging, et al., 447 So.2d 1058, 1986 A.M.C. 197 (La.1984). The M/V Bayou Lacombe was explained and applied in Texas Eastern Transmission Corporation v. McMoRan Offshore Exploration Co., 863 F.2d 355 (5th Cir.1989), cert. denied sub nom. Marathon Oil Co. v. McMoRAN Offshore Exploration Co., 493 U.S. 937, 110 S.Ct. 332, 107 L.Ed.2d 321 (1989), in which the court of appeals rejected the argument of an oil Company that it had "a proprietary interest" or "functional control and possession" of a pipe line injured in the repositioning of a drilling rig.

See In re Bethlehem Steel Corp., 631 F.2d 441, 1980 A.M.C. 2122 (6th Cir.1980), cert. denied 450 U.S. 921, 101 S.Ct. 1370, 67 L.Ed.2d 349 (1981), in which the Louisiana Supreme Court held that a utility customer of the owner of a natural gas pipeline negligently injured by a dredge could not maintain an action against the owner of the dredge. Judge Calogero observed in dissent, "Bean was dredging the waterway that ran right along the side of PPG's plant. There were signs along the waterway warning of the existence of the gas pipeline and cautioning against dredging in the area. There were also maps of the water bottom showing the pipelines. At the time Bean negligently dredged through the waterway, there could have been no doubt to anyone that the pipeline in question was providing PPG with its fuel to run its plant. The damages suffered by PPG were not *unforeseen,* at least as far as added fuel costs go."

In connection with the same event a different plaintiff sued in the United States district court charging that the interruption of the gas supply occasioned by the damage to the pipeline caused physical damage to its plant and from this it sustained economic loss. See Consolidated Aluminum Corp. v. C.F. Bean Corp., 1986 A.M.C. 203 (W.D.La.1984): "If this court were writing on a clean slate, we might depart from established tort principles and sympathetically allow consolidated some recovery here. However, it seems that Consolidated suffered physical damages from the gas-interruption solely because of the fragileness of the aluminum-making process. Alternatively, other industries suffering power interruption are not as adversely affected. Perhaps Consolidated's 'physical damages argument' against the *Robins Dry Dock* rule is merely a 'distinction without a difference' as plaintiff argues." The court of appeals thought not and reversed, 772 F.2d 1217 (5th Cir.1985).

Are there other possible chinks in the *Robins Dry Dock* armor? In Union Oil Company v. Oppen, 501 F.2d 558 (9th Cir.1974), a case arising out of an offshore oil spill, it was held that commercial fishermen could sue for economic loss attributable to the negligent spill. The majority discuss both California and admiralty cases; Judge Eli dissassociated himself from the discussion of the admiralty law since the case had been briefed and argued on the basis of the law of California. If *Oppen* can be viewed as a statement of the admiralty law, does the liability stem from a pollution exception? Or does it stem from a commercial fisherman exception?

In Carbone v. Ursich, 209 F.2d 178, 1954 A.M.C. 169 (9th Cir.1953), fishermen on a lay arrangement were permitted to recover damages against another vessel and its owners who had negligently fouled their net, causing the loss of the fish and damage to the net. Damages were allowed both for loss of the fish in the net but for the prospective catch during the time necessary to repair the net. *Carbone* was one of the cases relied upon in *Oppen.*

Following out the pollution exception, see State of Louisiana ex rel Guste v. M/V Testbank, 752 F.2d 1019, 1985 A.M.C. 1521 (5th Cir.1985)(en banc) appeal pending. There the court of appeals affirmed the dismissal of an action by vessel owners suing for loss due to delay attributable to a collision in which a chemical spill resulted in the closing of the Mississippi River Gulf outlet for two weeks. The court reserved the question of whether commercial fishermen could sue.

In Lloyd's Leasing Ltd. v. Conoco, 868 F.2d 1447 (5th Cir.1989), cert. denied sub nom. Lucas v. Lloyd's Leasing, 493 U.S. 964, 110 S.Ct. 405, 107 L.Ed.2d 371 (1989), businessmen in an area in which oil from an offshore spill washed ashore attempted to supply the physical damage required in the *Robins* formulation by alleging that people who walked on the oily beaches tracked the oil into their places of business. Two members of the panel were of the opinion that this effort failed because of a lack of predictability. Judge Higgenbotham was of the opinion that it would have been better to apply the M/V Testbank rule and to hold that this was not the sort of direct injury that the rule contemplates.

And see Barber Lines A/S v. M/V Donau Maru, 764 F.2d 50, 1985 A.M.C. 2600 (1st Cir.1985). A ship prevented from docking at a nearby berth and thereby forced to discharge cargo at another pier at a higher cost because of an oil spill in the harbor, had no cause of action against the vessel responsible for the spill.

Following out the commercial fisherman exception, if any, see, in the Ninth Circuit, Jones v. Bender Welding and Machine Works, Inc., 581 F.2d 1331, 1979 A.M.C. 1300 (9th Cir.1978), in which it was held that negligent design of an engine causing the disabling of a commercial fishing vessel gives rise to a cause of action for lost profits, though there was no physical damage. And in such a case the liability rests on products liability and not negligence. Emerson G.M. Diesel, Inc. v. The Alaskan Enterprise, 732 F.2d 1468, 1985 A.M.C. 2069 (9th Cir.1984). Extending this principle, see Miller Industries v. Caterpillar Tractor Co., 733 F.2d 813, 1984 A.M.C. 2559 (11th Cir.1984), permitting such an action by crew members working on a lay arrangement for loss of their share of the catch.

On the assumption that the owner of the vessel may sue, is the standing of the crew entitled to a share of the catch premised on their being commercial fishermen, or is it more easily explained on the ground that they are partners in the injured enterprise. See, e.g., Amoco Transport Co. v. S/S Mason Lykes, 768 F.2d 659, 1986 A.M.C. 563 (5th Cir.1985), holding that the cargo called upon to pay double freight as a result of a both to blame collision has a cause of action for the added freight against each of the colliding vessels.

The charterer of a vessel who has cargo on board may sue to recover damages occasioned by a collision involving the carrying vessel despite the absence of physical damage to the cargo. See Mathiesen v. M/V Obelix, 817 F.2d 345 (5th Cir.1987), cert. denied sub nom. Unimills B.V. and Margarine Verkaufs Union GmbH v. Statistix Shipping N.V., 484 U.S. 898, 108 S.Ct. 234, 98 L.Ed.2d 192 (1987). In the M/V Obelix, damage was sought for storage charges occasioned by delay that was caused by a collision occurring before the cargo was loaded, and the action was held to be precluded by the *Robins Drydock* rule.

4. Punitive Damages

While punitive damages are sometimes awarded in maritime cases, as for example where the vessel is put in the hands of an unfit master, ordinarily the vessel owner will not be liable for punitive damages grounded on the negligent conduct of the master and crew. See United States Steel Corp. v. Fuhrman (Cedarville—Topdalsford), 407 F.2d 1143, 1969 A.M.C. 252 (6th Cir.1969).

In cases in which the owner wilfully violates the duty to maintain a safe and seaworthy ship, punitive damages may be awarded. Self v. Great Lakes Dredge & Dock Co. , 832 F.2d 1540 (11th Cir.1987), cert. denied sub nom. Great Lakes Dredge and Dock Co. v. Chevron Transport Corp., 486 U.S. 1033, 108 S.Ct. 2017, 100 L.Ed.2d 604 (1988), remanding for findings. But punitive damages are not awarded against the owner for the acts of the master, and a time charterer who does not furnish the master and crew is no liable for punitive damages. Matter of P & E Boat Rentals, Inc., 872 F.2d 642 (5th Cir.1989).

5. Interest and Costs

Interest on a judgment for money in an action under the admiralty and maritime jurisdiction, like any other judgment for money in a civil action in the federal court is governed by 28 USC § 1961, which provides that interest begins to run upon entry of the judgment. Gele v. Wilson, 616 F.2d 146, 1981 A.M.C. 462 (5th Cir.1980); Kotsopoulos v. Asturia Shipping Co., 467 F.2d 91, 95 (2d Cir.1972).

The Supreme Court has had recent occasion to explore the basis for award of prejudgment interest. It reiterated the general principle that prejudgment interest is to be awarded absent unusual circumstances and held that it is not to be denied either on the basis that there was a good faith dispute over liability, or that the party seeking interest was disproportionately at fault. City of Milwaukee v. Cement Division, National Gypsum Co., 515 U.S. ___, 115 S.Ct. 2091, 132 L.Ed.2d 148 (1995).

See discussion in Alkmeon Naviera, S.A. v. M/V Marina L, supra, 633 F.2d at 797–798. There it is stated that generally special circumstances exist only when the party seeking interest has (1) unreasonably delayed in prosecuting his claim, (2) made a bad faith estimate of its damages that precluded settlement, or (3) not sustained any actual damage. See Matter of Bankers Trust Co., 658 F.2d 103, 1982 A.M.C. 1098 (3d Cir.1981), cert. denied 456 U.S. 961, 102 S.Ct. 2038, 72 L.Ed.2d 485 (1982). In Bunge Corp. v. American Commercial Barge Line Co., 630 F.2d 1236, 1242, 1980 A.M.C. 2981 (7th Cir.1980), it is stated that the prejudgment interest is generally awarded from the date of the collision. But suppose that the judgment includes damages for loss of use. Would addition of prejudgment interest constitute double payment. See Stevens v. F/V Bonnie Doon, 731 F.2d 1433, 1437–1438, 1985 A.M.C. 363 (9th Cir.1984).

2. Apportionment of Damages, the Moieties Rule

The Woodrop–Sims

2 Dod 83 (1815).

■ Sir William Scott.—This is one of those unfortunate cases in which the entire loss of a ship and cargo has been occasioned by two vessels running foul of each other.

There are four possibilities under which an accident of this sort may occur. In the first place, it may happen without blame being imputable to either party; as where the loss is occasioned by a storm, or any other *vis major*: In that case, the misfortune must be borne by the party on whom it happens to light; the other not being responsible to him in any degree.— Secondly, a misfortune of this kind may arise where both parties are to blame; where there has been a want of due diligence or of skill on both sides: In such a case, the rule of law is, that the loss must be apportioned between them, as having been occasioned by the fault of both of them.—

Thirdly, it may happen by the misconduct of the suffering party only; and then the rule is, that the sufferer must bear his own burden. Lastly, it may have been the fault of the ship which ran the other down; and in this case the injured party would be entitled to an entire compensation from the other. * * *

Vanderplank v. Miller

1 W & M 169 (1828).

The action was brought against the owners of a ship called the Robert and Ann, for negligence in the navigation of it, whereby it ran foul of a small vessel called the Louisa, on board of which there were goods of the plaintiffs, and sunk the vessel, and thereby destroyed the goods.

The evidence showed, that the Louisa was at anchor, waiting for the tide to carry her up the river Thames, and that the Robert and Ann coming rather suddenly on her in rounding a corner of the river ran foul of her, and sunk her. There was evidence to show that the Robert and Ann, if carefully and skilfully navigated, might have avoided the Louisa; but there was also evidence, that the whole crew of the Louisa were below at the time of the accident; and that if any of them had been on deck, they might, by a slight shifting of the position of the Louisa as she lay at anchor, have avoided the shock of the Robert and Ann, and the accident would not have happened. The plaintiffs, therefore, contended that the accident happened by the fault of the crew of the Robert and Ann; the defendants that it was the negligence of the persons aboard the Louisa.

■ LORD TENTERDEN, C.J., in summing up to the jury, said,—The question is, Whether you think that the accident was occasioned by the want of care on the part of the crew of the Robert & Ann? If there was want of care on both sides, the plaintiffs cannot maintain their action: to enable them to do so, the accident must be attributed solely to the fault of the defendant.

1 Conkling, Admiralty 300

(1848).

When there has been a want of diligence or skill on both sides, the settled rule of the general maritime law is that the loss must be apportioned between the parties in equal moieties. This is the established doctrine of the English High Court of Admiralty, and it was solemnly recognized by the House of Lords in the case of Hay v. Le Nerve, an appeal from the judgment of the Court of Session in Scotland, in which it was also held that each party should pay his own costs. It is laid down as unquestionable, by Mr. Justice Story and by Chancellor Kent, and is stated, also without dissent, by Mr. Justice Catron, and by the late Judge Hopkinson; but it is not the rule of the English common law, and I am not aware that it has been applied in any court of common law, or even in the admiralty, in this country. But as it is the business of the American courts of admiralty to administer the maritime law, it may be presumed that they will consider themselves bound to enforce this in common with its other rules. The common law rule is that if the plaintiff, in a suit to recover damages arising from collision, is shown to have been in any degree at fault, he is entitled to no remuneration. This state of the law has of course led, in England, as it may do in this country, to this remarkable result: that what is regarded in one court as an injury entitling the sufferer to redress, is, by another court of the same country, possessing a concurrent jurisdiction, held to furnish no title to remuneration. In the case above cited, decided in the House of Lords, the value of the cargo of the ship sunk and lost was included in the estimate on which the apportionment was made.

The justice of this rule of *equal* apportionment between two culpable vessels, has been severely questioned; and considering the great disparity in the degree of culpability which may well happen to be, and often is attributable to the respective parties, the rule must be conceded to be extremely defective, as a means for the attainment of particular justice. But its experience and substantial equity, as a general rule, though it has been aptly called a *rusticum judiciam,* have been vindicated and maintained by very able writers, and by the highest judicial authorities, on account of the difficulty of determining the comparative measure of blame chargeable upon each party, and the tendency of the rule to insure vigilance on the part of those who have charge of both large and of small vessels. [footnotes omitted]

NOTE

The anomaly that Conkling saw in the English cases was, as he suggested it might be, imported into the American law. Some half a century later the Supreme Court held that when a collision case was tried on the law side of the court, contributory negligence operated as a bar. Belden v. Chase, 150 U.S. 674, 14 S.Ct. 264, 37 L.Ed. 1218 (1893). While the case has never been specifically overruled, it is to be remembered that the same was true of personal injury actions (see Kalleck v. Deering, p. 366, supra), and it has been held that the law court, federal or state, must apply the maritime law in a maritime case under the saving to suitors clause. See, e.g., Chelentis v. Luckenbach, supra, p. 375. In Pope & Talbot, Inc. v. Hawn, 346 U.S. 406, 74 S.Ct. 202, 98 L.Ed. 143 (1953), the Supreme Court affirmed an apportioned damage award in a civil case, and the Second Circuit has read the *Pope and Talbot* decision to require the application of the apportioned damage rule in all cases of maritime collisions. Nygren v. American Boat Cartage, Inc., 290 F.2d 547, 1961 A.M.C. 2032 (2d Cir.1961).

It should be noted that contrary to the implication of Lord Tenterden's instruction in *Vanderplank,* negligence of the crew of a vessel is not imputed to the cargo. Thus in a mutual fault collision, the owner of the cargo on each vessel may recover against the other vessel. See United States v. Farr Sugar Corp., 191 F.2d 370, 1951 A.M.C. 1435 (2d Cir.1951).

Until 1975, the equally divided damages rule continued to operate in much the same fashion described by Conkling in 1848, much criticized but generally followed. In N.M. Paterson & Sons, Ltd. v. City of Chicago, 209 F.Supp. 576, 1962 A.M.C. 2215 (N.D.Ill.1962), Judge Minor noted the fact that the requirement of equal apportionment had never been announced by the Supreme Court, and reviewing the criticism of the rule by Judge Learned Hand in his dissent in Ulster Oil Transportation Corp. v. Matton No. 20, 210 F.2d 106 (2d Cir.1954), and by Judge Frank by way of dictum in his opinion in Ahlgren v. Red Star Towing Co., 214 F.2d 618, 1954 A.M.C. 1504 (2d Cir.1954), and calling attention to the fact that in The Margaret, 30 F.2d 923, 1929 A.M.C. 1 (3d Cir.1928), the Third Circuit had first apportioned on a three-fourths/one fourth basis, and then modified its decree to apply the equal moieties rule, observing that while it was still of the opinion that it had power to depart from equal moieties it was experiencing growing doubts as to whether it was respectfully following the rule applied from time to time by the Supreme Court, he apportioned the damages on a one third/two thirds basis in a case involving a collision between a vessel and a city-owned drawbridge. In March of 1963, Judge Zirpoli of the Northern District of California indicated his agreement with Judge Minor and applied a seventy-five/twenty-five formula to a case involving a collision between two vessels. In October of the same year the Court of Appeals for the Seventh Circuit reversed the decree in N.M. Paterson & Sons Ltd. v. City of Chicago, 324 F.2d 254, 1963 A.M.C. 2471 (7th Cir.1963), holding that the negligence of the city in operation of the bridge was the sole fault in the case. While the holding of want of fault on the part of the vessel made consideration of Judge Minor's ruling on apportionment of damages unnecessary, Judge Castle, for an unanimous court, took occasion to state that the decision below was incorrect in this respect as well.

The criticism of the divided damages rule continued. See Gulf Atlantic Transp. Co. v. The F. L. Hayes, 144 F.Supp. 147, 1958 A.M.C. 1322 (E.D.Pa.1956), Elna II– Mission San Francisco (Petition of Oskar Tiedemann & Co.), 289 F.2d 237, 1961 A.M.C. 1878 (3d Cir.1960). And see Pioneer—Wallschiff, 164 F.Supp. 421, 1958 A.M.C. 2511 (E.D.Mich.1958), in which the court found with obvious satisfaction that the accident occurred in Canadian waters and applying the comparative negligence rule under Canadian law, apportioned the damages on a ninety-five percent/five percent basis.

When more than two vessels are at fault in a collision, the damages were apportioned equally among them. The Eugene F. Moran, 212 U.S. 466, 29 S.Ct. 339, 53 L.Ed. 600 (1909)(four vessels at fault—damages split in fourths); Atlantic Pipe Line v. Philadelphia, 366 F.2d 780, 1967 A.M.C. 502 (3d Cir.1966)(three vessels—thirds); Booth S.S. Co. v. Dalzell No. 2, 1966 A.M.C. 2615 (S.D.N.Y. 1966)(same). When there are two or more faulted vessels and one without fault, the innocent interest may libel any or all of the faulted vessels and when it singles out one enforce its decree for full damages against it alone. The Atlas, 93 U.S. (3 Otto) 302, 23 L.Ed. 863 (1876). When this is done, the vessel paying the damages may later sue for contribution from the other vessels at fault. See, e.g., Erie R.R. Co. v. Erie and Western Transportation Co., 204 U.S. 220, 27 S.Ct. 246, 51 L.Ed. 450 (1907); The Ira M. Hedges, 218 U.S. 264, 31 S.Ct. 17, 54 L.Ed. 1039 (1910). Under Rule 14(h) of the F.R.C.P., preserving the substance of former Admiralty Rule 56, the defendant in an action identified as maritime under Rule 9(h) "may bring in a third-party defendant who may be wholly or partly liable, either to the plaintiff or to the third-party plaintiff, by way of remedy over, contribution, or otherwise on account of the same transaction, occurrence, or series of transactions or occurrences. In such a case the third-party plaintiff may also demand judgment against the third-party defendant in favor of the plaintiff, in which event the third-party defendant shall make his defenses to the claim of the plaintiff as well as to that of the third-party plaintiff in the manner provided in Rule 12 and the action shall proceed as if the plaintiff had commenced it against the third-party defendant as well as the third-party plaintiff.'' Accordingly, the vessel named in the initial action may bring in the other vessels allegedly at fault. See, e.g., National Iranian Tanker Co. v. Tug Dalzell No. 2, 284 F.Supp. 451, 1966 A.M.C. 2615 (S.D.N.Y.1966).

An innocent interest, either a vessel or cargo, involved in a collision in which more than one vessel is held at fault, may recover a judgment against the faulted vessels jointly and severally. In The Alabama and The Game–Cock, 92 U.S. (2 Otto) 695, 23 L.Ed. 763 (1875), for example, cargo aboard a tow was damaged in a collision held to be the fault of its tug and a second ship. The tug was valued at $10,000, the other vessel, $100,000. Cargo interests libeled both vessels. The district court rendered a decree against both in solido. The court of appeals reversed, dividing the loss ($80,000) between them in moieties, relying on earlier English and American authorities. In reversing, the Supreme Court held that while splitting the damage was appropriate when both halves could be collected, the split damages rule is not to be applied if the result will make it impossible for the innocent interest to collect.

The same principle has been applied where one of several faulted vessels or interests limits liability and as a result the innocent interest is unable to collect that vessel's share of the damage. The deficiency is apportioned among the remaining tortfeasors. See, e.g., Petition of Kinsman Transit Corp., 338 F.2d 708, 1964 A.M.C. 2503 (2d Cir.1964).

When a tug and tow are in collision, the whole flotilla is regarded as one unit for the application of the moieties rule, the tug being regarded as ''the dominant mind.'' The cases are collected in Gilmore and Black, *Law of Admiralty* 425 (1957). When there is an independent fault on the part of the tow, however, as when a barge is improperly lighted, the vessel thus at fault shares the liability. See, e.g., Horton & Horton v. The Robert E. Hopkins, 269 F.2d 914, 1959 A.M.C. 1681 (5th Cir.1959).

Mechanics of Divided Damages

When damage is limited to the interests of the owners of the vessels involved in a collision, the application of the divided damages rule is fairly simple. In The North Star, 106 U.S. 17, 1 S.Ct. 41, 27 L.Ed. 91 (1882), referred to in *Howard Olson— Marine Leopard*, supra, the Supreme Court stated the rule thus: ''Each vessel being liable for half the damage done to both, if one suffered more than the other, the difference should be equally divided, and the one which suffered least should be decreed to pay one-half of such difference to the one which suffered most, so as to equalize the burden.'' In that case two vessels, The Ella Warley and The North Star were involved in a mutual fault collision. The former sank and was a total loss. The latter sustained considerable damage. The owners of The Ella Warley argued that the rule should be applied to make each party liable to the other for half of his damages. Since The Ella Warley's owners could limit their liability to the value of the vessel after the collision (zero)(see Chapter 21, Limitation of Liability, infra), the result would be that they could collect their half damages and not pay The North Star's half. The Court found this contention ''startling.''

The application of the rule to collisions involving innocent interests is somewhat more complex. It has already been pointed out that the liability of the parties at fault to innocent interests is joint and several. When such an interest, an innocent vessel, cargo, personal injury claimants, for example, collects from one of the faulted vessels, the amount becomes an item of damage to the party paying it and is to be included as such in striking the balance between the faulted vessels. In this connection it should be noted that contrary to the intimation in Lord Tenterden's instructions in Vanderplank v. Miller, the negligence of the carrying vessel is not imputed to its cargo or passengers. See The Washington and The Gregory, 76 U.S. (9 Wall.) 513, 19 L.Ed. 787 (1869); Robinson on *Admiralty* § 116 (1939). The amount in personal injury claims is not determined on the basis of the divided damage rule, but according to the doctrine of comparative negligence generally applied in personal injury cases in the admiralty. The damages to a crew member injured in the collision will depend, then, upon his personal contributory negligence. See Wright v. Cion Corp. Peruna Desvaspores, 171 F.Supp. 735, 1959 A.M.C. 2505 (S.D.N.Y.1959), where the owner and captain of one of the faulted vessels, killed in the collision, was determined to be 70% negligent, and the mate was charged with none. The court held that judgments on behalf of third parties, e.g., the mate, would be included in the damages for purposes of striking the balance under the divided damages rule.

Under the Harter Act and the Carriage of Goods by Sea Act (see chapter on Carriage of Goods), a carrier is not ordinarily liable for damage to cargo occasioned by faulty navigation. This created a dilemma when the cargo recovered full damages against the non-carrying vessel. Either the non-carrying vessel would be deprived of its balance under the divided damages rule, or the carrier would be deprived of half the benefit of its bargain with the cargo interest. The Supreme Court, in The Chatahoochee, 173 U.S. 540, 19 S.Ct. 491, 43 L.Ed. 801 (1899), resolved the dilemma by holding that the payments to cargo may be included in striking the balance. The carriers countered by including a clause in the bill of lading providing that the cargo would indemnify the carrier for amounts it was required to pay because of the inclusion of the damage in the balance. In United States v. Atlantic Mutual Ins. Co. (Nathaniel Bacon—Esso Belgium), 343 U.S. 236, 72 S.Ct. 666, 96 L.Ed. 907 (1952), this "both to blame clause" was declared to be a violation of the Harter Act. The Court found it anomalous that the cargo owner could be required to give up half of the amount that it had a right to collect from the third-party tortfeasor. Both to blame clauses have continued to be included in charters, however, and there is recent authority upholding their validity when no bill of lading is issued and the contract deemed to be a contract for private carriage. American Union Transport, Inc. v. United States, 1976 A.M.C. 1480 (N.D.Cal.1976).

3. ABROGATION OF THE MOIETIES RULE

United States v. Reliable Transfer Co., Inc.

Supreme Court of the United States, 1975.
421 U.S. 397, 95 S.Ct. 1708, 44 L.Ed.2d 251, 1975 A.M.C. 541.

■ MR. JUSTICE STEWART delivered the opinion of the Court.

More than a century ago, in The Schooner Catharine v. Dickinson, 58 U.S. (17 How.) 170, 15 L.Ed. 233, this Court established in our admiralty law the rule of divided damages. That rule, most commonly applied in cases of collision between two vessels, requires the equal division of property damage whenever both parties are found to be guilty of contributing fault, whatever the relative degree of their fault may have been. The courts of every major maritime nation except ours have long since abandoned that rule, and now assess damages in such cases on the basis of proportionate fault when such an allocation can reasonably be made. In the present case we are called upon to decide whether this country's admiralty rule of divided damages should be replaced by a rule requiring, when possible, the allocation of liability for damages in proportion to the relative fault of each party.

I

On a clear but windy December night in 1968, the *Mary A. Whalen,* a coastal tanker owned by the respondent Reliable Transfer Company, embarked from Constable Hook, New Jersey, for Island Park, New York, with a load of fuel oil. The voyage ended, instead, with the vessel stranded on a sand bar off Rockaway Point outside New York harbor.

The *Whalen's* course led across the mouth of the Rockaway Inlet, a narrow body of water that lies between a breakwater to the southeast and the shoreline of Coney Island to the northwest. The breakwater is ordinarily marked at its southernmost point by a flashing light maintained by the Coast Guard. As, however, the *Whalen's* captain and a deckhand observed while the vessel was proceeding southwardly across the Inlet, the light was not operating that night. As the *Whalen* approached Rockaway Point about half an hour later, her captain attempted to pass a tug with a barge in tow ahead, but, after determining that he could not overtake them, decided to make a 180 degree turn to pass astern of the barge. At this time the tide was at flood, and the waves, whipped by northwest winds of gale force, were eight to ten feet high. After making the 180 degree turn and passing astern of the barge, the captain headed the *Whalen* eastwardly, believing that the vessel was then south of the breakwater and that he was heading her for the open sea. He was wrong. About a minute later the light structure on the southern point of the breakwater came into view. Turning to avoid rocks visible ahead, the *Whalen* ran aground in the sand.

The respondent brought this action against the United States in a federal district court, under the Suits in Admiralty Act, 46 U.S.C. § 741 et seq., and the Federal Tort Claims Act, 28 U.S.C. § 1346 et seq., seeking to recover for damages to the *Whalen* caused by the stranding. The District Court found that the vessel's grounding was caused 25% by the failure of the Coast Guard to maintain the breakwater light and 75% by the fault of the *Whalen.* In so finding on the issue of comparative fault, the court stated:

> "The fault of the vessel was more egregious than the fault of the Coast Guard. Attempting to negotiate a turn to the east, in the narrow space between the bell buoy No. 4 and the shoals off Rockaway Point, the Captain set his course without knowing where he was. Obviously, he would not have found the breakwater light looming directly ahead of him within a minute after his change of course, if he had not been north of the point where he believed he was.

> "Equipped with look-out, chart, searchlight, radio-telephone, and radar, he made use of nothing except his own guesswork judgment. After * * * turning in a loop toward the north so as to pass astern of the tow, he should have made sure of his position before setting his new 73° course. The fact that a northwest gale blowing at 45 knots with eight to ten foot

seas made it difficult to see, emphasizes the need for caution rather than excusing a turn into the unknown. * * *"

The court held, however, that the settled admiralty rule of divided damages required each party to bear one-half of the damages to the vessel.[1]

The Court of Appeals for the Second Circuit affirmed this judgment. 2 Cir., 497 F.2d 1036. It held that the trial court "was not clearly erroneous in finding that the negligence of both parties, in the proportions stated, caused the stranding." Id., at 1037–1038. And, although "mindful of the criticism of the equal division of damages rule and * * * recogniz[ing] the force of the argument that in this type of case division of damages in proportion to the degree of fault may be more equitable," id., at 1038, the appellate court felt constrained to adhere to the established rule and "to leave doctrinal development to the Supreme Court or to await appropriate action by Congress." Ibid.

We granted certiorari, 419 U.S. 1018, 95 S.Ct. 491, 42 L.Ed.2d 291, to consider the continued validity of the divided damages rule.[2]

1. The operation of the rule was described in The Sapphire, 85 U.S. (18 Wall.), 51, 56, 21 L.Ed. 814:

"It is undoubtedly the rule in admiralty that where both vessels are in fault the sums representing the damage sustained by each must be added together and the aggregate divided between the two. This is in effect deducting the lesser from the greater and dividing the remainder. * * * If one in fault has sustained no injury, it is liable for half the damages sustained by the other, though that other was also in fault."

Similarly, in The North Star, 106 U.S. 17, 22, 1 S.Ct. 41, 45, 27 L.Ed. 91, the rule was thus stated:

"[A]ccording to the general maritime law, in cases of collision occurring by the fault of both parties, the entire damage to both ships is added together in one common mass and equally divided between them, and thereupon arises a liability of one party to pay to the other such sum as is necessary to equalize the burden."

See also, e.g., White Oak Transportation Co. v. Boston, Cape Cod & New York Canal Co., 258 U.S. 341, 42 S.Ct. 338, 66 L.Ed. 649; The Eugene F. Moran, 212 U.S. 466, 29 S.Ct. 339, 53 L.Ed. 600.

It has long been settled that the divided damages rule applies not only in cases of collision between two vessels, but also in cases like this one where a vessel partly in fault is damaged in collision or grounding because of the mutual contributing fault of a non-vessel party. Atlee v. Northwestern Union Packet Co., 88 U.S. (21 Wall.) 389, 22 L.Ed. 619 (barge struck pier because of mutual fault of barge and of pier owner); White Oak Transportation Co. v. Boston, Cape Code & New York Canal Co., 258 U.S. 341, 42 S.Ct. 338, 66 L.Ed. 649 (steamship ran aground in canal because of joint negligence of steamship and canal company). See also G. Gilmore & C. Black, *The Law of Admiralty* §§ 7–17, 522–523 (2d ed. 1975).

2. The Government's petition for certiorari presented the single question whether the admiralty rule of equally divided damages should be replaced by the rule of damages in proportion to fault. The respondent did not file a cross-petition for certiorari, but it now argues that the Government was solely at fault and requests an increase of the judgment in its favor to the full amount of its damages. However, absent a cross-petition for certiorari, the respondent may not now challenge the judgment of the Court of Appeals to enlarge its rights thereunder. Morley v. Maryland Casualty Co., 300 U.S. 185, 190, 57 S.Ct. 325, 327, 81 L.Ed. 593; United States v. American Railway Express Co., 265 U.S. 425, 435, 44 S.Ct. 560, 563, 68 L.Ed. 1087. Moreover, even if it could be argued that respondent's challenge of the factual findings could be taken as an argument in support of the judgment, see Stern, When to Cross–Appeal or Cross–Petition—Certainty

II

The precise origins of the divided damages rule are shrouded in the mists of history.[3] In any event it was not until early in the 19th century that the divided damages rule as we know it emerged clearly in British admiralty law. In 1815, in The Woodrop–Sims, 2 Dods. 83, 165 Eng.Rep. 1422, Sir William Scott, later Lord Stowell, considered the various circumstances under which maritime collisions could occur and stated that division of damages was appropriate in those cases "where both parties are to blame." 2 Dods., at 85, 165 Eng.Rep., at 1423. In such cases the total damages were to be "apportioned between" the parties "as having been occasioned by the fault of both of them." Ibid. Nine years later the divided damages rule became settled in English admiralty law when the House of Lords in a maritime collision case where both ships were at fault reversed a decision of a Scottish court that had apportioned damages by degree of blame, and, relying on *The Woodrop–Sims,* ordered that the damages be divided equally. Hay v. LeNeve, 2 Shaw's Scotch App.Cas. 395 (1824).

It was against this background that in 1854 this Court adopted the rule of equal division of damages in The Schooner Catharine v. Dickinson, 58 U.S. (17 How.) 170, 15 L.Ed. 233. The rule was adopted because it was then the prevailing rule in England, because it had become the majority rule in the lower federal courts, and because it seemed the "most just and equitable, and * * * best [tended] to induce care and vigilance on both sides, in the navigation." Id., at 177–178. There can be no question that subsequent history and experience have conspicuously eroded the rule's foundations.[4]

---

or Confusion?, 87 Harv.L.Rev. 763, 774 (1974), the findings of fact with respect to comparative negligence were concurred in by both the District Court and the Court of Appeals, and the respondent could not in this case meet its heavy burden under the "two-count rule." Graver Mfg. Co. v. Linde, 336 U.S. 271, 275, 69 S.Ct. 535, 537, 93 L.Ed. 672. See Berenyi v. Immigration Director, 385 U.S. 630, 635, 87 S.Ct. 666, 669, 17 L.Ed.2d 656.

3. Most commentators have traced the rule back to Article XIV of the Laws of Oleron, promulgated in about 1150 A.D., which provided that in cases of collision between a ship under way and another at anchor, the damages would be divided equally between the owners of the two vessels, so long as the captain and crew of the ship under way swore under oath that the collision was accidental. See, e.g., Marsden, 4 British Shipping Laws, Collisions at Sea § 119 (11th ed. 1961). See also Staring, Contribution and Division of Damages in Admiralty and Maritime Cases, 45 Calif.L.Rev. 304 (1957).

Other maritime nations enacted provisions similar to Article XIV during the same period, with slight variations in the scope of the rule and the principle of division. Marsden, supra, §§ 119–125. "The principle * * * underlying the rule seems to have been that collision was a peril of the sea—a common misfortune to be borne by all parties, either equally or ratably according to their interests at risk." Id., § 140.

4. The Court has acknowledged the continued existence of the divided damages rule in at least two recent cases. See Weyerhaeuser S. S. Co. v. United States, 372 U.S. 597, 603, 83 S.Ct. 926, 929, 10 L.Ed.2d 1; Halcyon Lines v. Haenn Ship Ceiling & Refitting Corp., 342 U.S. 282, 284, 72 S.Ct. 277, 279, 96 L.Ed. 318. But in neither case did the Court have occasion to re-examine the rule or to appraise the validity of its underpinnings or the propriety of its present application. The Court granted certiorari in Union Oil Co. of California v. The San Jacinto, 409 U.S. 140, 93 S.Ct. 368, 34 L.Ed.2d 365, to reconsider the divided damages rule, but did

It was true at the time of *The Catharine* that the divided damages rule was well entrenched in English law. The rule was an ancient form of rough justice, a means of apportioning damages where it was difficult to measure which party was more at fault. See 4 Marsden, British Shipping Laws, Collisions At Sea, §§ 119–147 (11th ed., 1961); Staring, Contribution and Division of Damages in Admiralty and Maritime Cases, 45 Calif.L.Rev. 304, 305–310 (1957). But England has long since abandoned the rule[5] and now follows the Brussels Collision Liability Convention of 1910 that provides for the apportionment of damages on the basis of "degree" of fault whenever it is possible to do so.[6] Indeed, the United States is now virtually alone among the world's major maritime nations in not adhering to the Convention with its rule of proportional fault[7]—a fact that encourages transoceanic forum shopping. See G. Gilmore & C. Black, *The Law of Admiralty* 529 (2d ed. 1975).

While the lower federal courts originally adhered to the divided damages rule, they have more recently followed it only grudgingly, terming it "unfair,"[8] "illogical,"[9] "arbitrary * * * archaic and frequently unjust."[10] Judge Learned Hand was a particularly stern critic of the rule. Dissenting in National Bulk Carriers, Inc. v. United States, 183 F.2d 405, 410 (C.A.2), he wrote: "An equal division [of damages] in this case would be plainly unjust; they ought to be divided in some such proportion as five to one. And so they could be but for our obstinate cleaving to the ancient rule which has been abrogated by nearly all civilized nations." And Judge Hand had all but invited this Court to overturn the rule when, in an earlier opinion for the Second Circuit Court of Appeals, he stated that "we have no power to divest ourselves of this vestigial relic; we can only go so far to close our eyes to doubtful delinquencies." Oriental Trading & Transp. Co.

not reach the issue because of our conclusion that one of the vessels involved in that case was totally free of contributing fault.

5. Maritime Conventions Act, 1911, 1 & 2 Geo. 5, c. 57, § 1.

6. Article 4 of the Convention provides in part: "If two or more vessels are in fault the liability of each vessel shall be in proportion to the degree of the faults respectively committed. Provided that if, having regard to all the circumstances, it is not possible to establish the degree of the respective faults, or if it appears that the faults are equal, the liability shall be apportioned equally."

7. We are informed by the Government that the following jurisdictions have ratified or adhere to the Brussels Convention on Collision Liability: Argentina, Australia, Austria, Belgium, Brazil, Canada, Danzig, Denmark, Egypt, Estonia, Finland, France, Germany, Great Britain, Greece, Haiti, Hungary, Iceland, India, Ireland, Italy, Japan, Latvia, Mexico, Newfoundland, New Zealand, Netherlands, Nicaragua, Norway, Poland, Portugal, Romania, U.S.S.R., Sweden, Switzerland, Turkey, Uruguay, and Yugoslavia. See 6 Knauth's Benedict on *Admiralty* (7th ed. 1969), at 38–39. See also J. Griffin, The American Law of Collision 857 (1949); Staring, Contribution and Division of Damages in Admiralty and Maritime Cases, 45 Calif.L.Rev. 304, 340–341 (1957); Tank Barge Hygrade v. The Gatco NJ, 250 F.2d 485, 488 (C.A.3).

8. Ahlgren v. Red Star Towing and Transp. Co., 214 F.2d 618, 620 (C.A.2).

9. Marine Fuel Transfer Corp. v. The Ruth, 231 F.2d 319, 321 (C.A.2).

10. Tank Barge Hygrade v. The Gatco NJ, 250 F.2d 485, 488 (C.A.3). See also Mystic S. S. Corp. v. M/S Antonio Ferraz, 498 F.2d 538, 539 n. 1 (C.A.2); Petition of Oskar Tiedemann and Co., 289 F.2d 237, 241–242 (C.A.3); In re Adams' Petition, 237 F.2d 884, 887 (C.A.2); Luckenbach S. S. Co. v. United States, 157 F.2d 250, 252 (C.A.2).

v. Gulf Oil Corp., 173 F.2d 108, 111. Some courts, even bolder, have simply ignored the rule. See J. Griffin, The American Law of Collision, 564 (1949); Staring, Contribution and Division of Damages in Admiralty and Maritime Cases, 45 Calif.L.Rev. 304, 341–342 (1957). Cf. The Margaret, 30 F.2d 923 (C.A.3).

It is no longer apparent, if it ever was, that this solomonic division of damages serves to achieve even rough justice.[11] An equal division of damages is a reasonably satisfactory result only where each vessel's fault is approximately equal and each vessel thus assumes a share of the collision damages in proportion to its share of the blame, or where proportionate degrees of fault cannot be measured and determined on a rational basis. The rule produces palpably unfair results in every other case. For example, where one ship's fault in causing a collision is relatively slight and her damages small, and where the second ship is grossly negligent and suffers extensive damage, the first ship must still make a substantial payment to the second. "This result hardly commends itself to the sense of justice any more appealingly than does the common law doctrine of contributory negligence * * *." G. Gilmore & C. Black, *The Law of Admiralty* 528 (2d ed. 1975).

And the potential unfairness of the division is magnified by the application of the rule of The Pennsylvania, 86 U.S. (19 Wall.) 125, 22 L.Ed. 148, whereby a ship's relatively minor statutory violation will require her to bear half the collision damage unless she can satisfy the heavy burden of showing "not merely that her fault might not have been one of the causes, or that it probably was not, but that it *could not have been.*" Id., at 136 (emphasis added). See O/Y Finlayson–Forssa A/B v. Pan Atlantic S.S. Co., 259 F.2d 11, 22 (C.A.5); In The New York Marine No. 10, 109 F.2d 564, 566 (C.A.2). See also Griffin, The American Law of Collisions § 202 (1949).

The Court has long implicitly recognized the patent harshness of an equal division of damages in the face of disparate blame by applying the "major-minor" fault doctrine to find a grossly negligent party solely at fault.[12] But this escape valve, in addition to being inherently unreliable,

---

11. It is difficult to imagine any manner in which the divided damages rule would be more likely to "induce care and vigilance" than a comparative negligence rule that also penalizes wrongdoing, but in proportion to measure of fault. A rule that divides damages by degree of fault would seem better designed to induce care than the rule of equally divided damages, because it imposes the strongest deterrent upon the wrongful behavior that is most likely to harm others.

12. See, e.g., The City of New York, 147 U.S. 72, 85, 13 S.Ct. 211, 216, 37 L.Ed. 84:

"Where fault on the part of one vessel is established by uncontradicted testimony, and such fault is, of itself, sufficient to account for the disaster, it is not enough for such vessel to raise a doubt with regard to the management of the other vessel. There is some presumption at least adverse to its claim, and any reasonable doubt with regard to the propriety of the conduct of such other vessel should be resolved in its favor."

See also The Victory and the Plymouthian, 168 U.S. 410, 18 S.Ct. 149, 42 L.Ed. 519; The Umbria, 166 U.S. 404, 17 S.Ct. 610, 41 L.Ed. 1053; The Oregon, 158 U.S. 186, 15 S.Ct. 804, 39 L.Ed. 943; The Ludvig Holberg, 157 U.S. 60, 15 S.Ct. 477, 39 L.Ed. 620.

simply replaces one unfairness with another.   That a vessel is primarily negligent does not justify its shouldering all responsibility, nor excuse the slightly negligent vessel from bearing any liability at all.   See Tank Barge Hygrade v. The Gatco New Jersey, 250 F.2d 485, 488 (C.A.3).   The problem remains where it began—with the divided damages rule:

> "[T]he doctrine that a court should not look too jealously at the navigation of one vessel, when the faults of the other are glaring, is in the nature of a sop to Cerberus.   It is no doubt better than nothing; but it is inadequate to reach the heart of the matter, and constitutes a constant temptation to courts to avoid a decision on the merits."   National Bulk Carriers, Inc. v. United States, 183 F.2d 405, 410 (L. Hand, J., dissenting).

The divided damages rule has been said to be justified by the difficulty of determining comparative degrees of negligence when both parties are concededly guilty of contributing fault.   The Max Morris, 137 U.S. 1, 12, 11 S.Ct. 29, 32, 34 L.Ed. 586.   Although there is some force in this argument, it cannot justify an equal division of damages in every case of collision based on mutual fault.   When it is impossible fairly to allocate degrees of fault, the division of damages equally between wrongdoing parties is an equitable solution.   But the rule is unnecessarily crude and inequitable in a case like this one where an allocation of disparate proportional fault has been made.   Potential problems of proof in some cases hardly require adherence to an archaic and unfair rule in all cases.   Every other major maritime nation has evidently been able to apply a rule of comparative negligence without serious problems, see Mole & Wilson, A Study of Comparative Negligence, 17 Corn.L.Q. 333, 346 (1932);   In re Adams' Petition, D.C., 125 F.Supp. 110, 114, aff'd, 2 Cir., 237 F.2d 884, and in our own admiralty law a rule of comparative negligence has long been applied with no untoward difficulties in personal injury actions.   See, e.g., Pope & Talbot, Inc. v. Hawn, 346 U.S. 406, 409, 74 S.Ct. 202, 204, 98 L.Ed. 143. See also Merchant Marine ("Jones") Act, 46 U.S.C. § 688;   Death on the High Seas Act, 46 U.S.C. § 766.

The argument has also been made that the divided damages rule promotes out-of-court settlements, because when it becomes apparent that both vessels are at fault, both parties can readily agree to divide the damages—thus avoiding the expense and delay of prolonged litigation and the concomitant burden on the courts.   It would be far more difficult, it is argued, for the parties to agree on who was more at fault and to apportion damages accordingly.   But the argument is hardly persuasive.   For if the fault of the two parties is markedly disproportionate, it is in the interest of the slightly negligent party to litigate the controversy in the hope that the major-minor fault rule may eventually persuade a court to absolve it of all liability.   And if, on the other hand, it appears after a realistic assessment of the situation that the fault of both parties is roughly equal, then there is no reason why a rule that apportions damages would be any less likely to induce a settlement than a rule that always divides damages equally. Experience with comparative negligence in the personal injury area teaches that a rule of fairness in court will produce fair out-of-court settlements.[13] But even if this argument were more persuasive than it is, it could hardly be accepted. For, at bottom, it asks us to continue the operation of an archaic rule because its facile application out of court yields quick, though inequitable, settlements, and relieves the courts of some litigation. Congestion in the courts cannot justify a legal rule that produces unjust results in litigation simply to encourage speedy out-of-court accommodations.

Finally, the respondent suggests that the creation of a new rule of damages in maritime collision cases is a task for Congress and not for this Court.[14] But the judiciary has traditionally taken the lead in formulating flexible and fair remedies in the law maritime and "Congress has largely left to this Court the responsibility for fashioning the controlling rules of admiralty law." Fitzgerald v. United States Lines Co., 374 U.S. 16, 20, 83 S.Ct. 1646, 1650, 10 L.Ed.2d 720. See also Moragne v. States Marine Lines, 398 U.S. 405 n. 17, 90 S.Ct. 1790; Kermarec v. Compagnie Generale Transatlantique, 358 U.S. 625, 630–632, 79 S.Ct. 406, 409–410, 3 L.Ed.2d 550. No statutory or judicial precept precludes a change in the rule of divided damages, and indeed a proportional fault rule would simply bring recovery for property damage in maritime long since established by Congress for personal injury cases. See the Jones Act, 46 U.S.C. § 688.[15]

As the authors of a leading admiralty law treatise have put the matter:

> "[T]here is no reason why the Supreme Court cannot at this late date 'confess error' and adopt the proportional fault doctrine without Congressional action. The resolution to follow the divided damages rule, taken 120 years ago, rested not on overwhelming authority but on judgments of fact and of fairness which may have been tenable then but are hardly so today. No 'vested rights,' in theory or fact, have intervened. The regard for

---

13. The rule of comparative negligence applicable to personal injury actions in our maritime law, see The Jones Act, 46 U.S.C. § 688, Death on the High Seas Act, 46 U.S.C. § 766, does not appear to discourage the negotiation of settlements in such litigation. It has been reported, for example, that of the marine personal injury cases involving a federal question that were terminated in fiscal year 1974, only 9.6% ever reached trial. Annual Report of the Director of the Administrative Office of the United States Courts, Table C4, at 429 (1974).

14. The respondent also relies on the fact that the Senate has twice failed to ratify the Brussels Convention with its proportional fault rule. It is urged that this inaction indicates "grave doubt" in Congress that rejection of the divided damages rule will further justice. But even if we could find guidance in such "negative legislation." Moragne v. States Marine Lines, 398 U.S. 375, 405 n. 17, 90 S.Ct. 1772, 1790, 26

L.Ed.2d 339, it appears that the Senate took no action with respect to the Convention not because of opposition to a proportional fault rule, but because of the Convention's poor translation and the opposition of cargo interests to the provision which would prevent cargo from recovering in full from the noncarrying vessel by eliminating joint and several liability of vessels for cargo damage. See H. Baer, Admiralty Law in the Supreme Court 414–415 (2d ed. 1969); Staring, Contribution and Division of Damages in Admiralty and Maritime Cases, 45 Calif.L.Rev. 304, 343 (1957). See also Note, 64 Yale L.J. 878 (1955).

15. This Court, in other appropriate contexts, has not hesitated to overrule an earlier decision and settle a matter of continuing concern, even though relief might have been obtained by legislation. See Burnet v. Coronado Oil & Gas Co., 285 U.S. 393, 406 n. 1, 52 S.Ct. 443, 447, 76 L.Ed. 815 (Brandeis, J., dissenting)(collecting cases).

'settled expectation' which is the heart-reason of * * * *stare decisis* * * * can have no relevance in respect to such a rule; the concept of 'settled expectation' would be reduced to an absurdity were it to be applied to a rule of damages for negligent collision. The abrogation of the rule would not, it seems, produce any disharmony with other branches of the maritime law, general or statutory." G. Gilmore & C. Black, *The Law of Admiralty* 531 (2d ed. 1975)(footnote omitted).[16]

The rule of divided damages in admiralty has continued to prevail in this country by sheer inertia rather than by reason of any intrinsic merit. The reasons that originally led to the Court's adoption of the rule have long since disappeared. The rule has been repeatedly criticized by experienced federal judges who have correctly pointed out that the result it works has too often been precisely the opposite of what the Court sought to achieve in *The Schooner Catharine*—the "just and equitable" allocation of damages. And worldwide experience has taught that that goal can be more nearly realized by a standard that allocates liability for damages according to comparative fault whenever possible.

We hold that when two or more parties have contributed by their fault to cause property damage in a maritime collision or stranding, liability for such damage is to be allocated among the parties proportionately to the comparative degree of their fault, and that liability for such damages is to be allocated equally only when the parties are equally at fault or when it is not possible fairly to measure the comparative degree of their fault.

Accordingly, the judgment before us is vacated and the case is remanded for further proceedings consistent with this opinion.

It is so ordered.

Judgment vacated and case remanded.

---

16. See also Donovan, Mutual Fault– Half Damage Rule—A Critical Analysis, 41 Ins.Coun.J. 395 (1974); Allbritton, Division of Damages in Admiralty—A Rising Tide of Confusion, 2 Journal of Maritime Law and Commerce 322 (1971); Jackson, The Archaic Rule of Dividing Damages in Maritime Colli- sions, 19 Ala.L.Rev. 263 (1967); Staring, su- pra, 45 Calif.L.Rev., at 304; Mole & Wilson, A Study of Comparative Negligence, 17 Corn. L.Q. 333 (1932); and Huger, The Proportion- al Damage Rule in Collisions at Sea, 13 Corn. L.Q. 531 (1928).

CHAPTER 18

Tort Law in General

INTRODUCTORY NOTE

In The Plymouth, 70 U.S. (3 Wall.) 20, 26, 18 L.Ed. 125 (1865), it was stated that "[e]very species of tort, however occurring, and whether on board a vessel or not, if upon the high seas or navigable waters, is of admiralty cognizance." At the time The Plymouth was decided, it was generally thought that in an action under the saving to suitors clause the court would apply the common law, state or federal, as the case might be. And this was thought to be so until the decisions in *Jensen* and *Chelentis*, reproduced in Chapter 11 above. See Mr. Justice Holmes' observations concerning *The Max Morris* and Belden v. Chase on page 375. So long as the plaintiff could avail himself of the common law rule by exercising his option under the savings to suitors clause, in personam actions in the admiralty were of very little significance except in those cases in which the federal courts fashioned a rule in admiralty more favorable to the plaintiff than the rule at common law. In The Max Morris, 137 U.S. 1, 11 S.Ct. 29, 34 L.Ed. 586 (1890), for example, the Supreme Court rejected the common law rule of contributory negligence as a bar in personal injury cases, building on the divided damages rule employed in the admiralty in collision and some non-collision property damage cases.

With the decisions in *Jensen* and *Chelentis* (Chapter 11 above), the maritime law as developed in the federal courts became the rule of decision in all actions within the admiralty and maritime jurisdiction, and with the advent of *Erie* the maritime tort jurisdiction has become one of the relatively few areas in which one can observe the federal courts applying an essentially common law decisional process. Despite the broad language of The Plymouth, the locational limitation on the admiralty and maritime jurisdiction in tort cases resulted in limiting such cases very largely to the claims of those involved in some fashion in the shipping industry, either as operator, customer, or workman. Thus the vast bulk of maritime tort cases have been, and still are, industrial accident cases, or actions by shippers or passengers, plus, in recent years, a significant number of cases arising out of the operation of pleasure boats.

As courts charged with the development by common law process of the general law of maritime torts, the federal courts appear to have followed in large measure the same principles that have emerged in terrestrial tort law, to the extent that they are compatible with a fairly large body of statute law that has developed in the maritime area. Because of the fact that such a large proportion of the maritime tort litigation has been in connection with industrial accidents, some tort doctrines developed in the state courts and generally regarded as settled have emerged as cases of novel impression in admiralty after many years.   See, e.g., Byrd v. Byrd, 657 F.2d 615 (4 Cir.1981), in which the court of appeals rejects the common law rule precluding interspousal actions in tort as obsolete.   This lag has tended to be longest in areas in which common law rules have been changed in the states by statute and Congress has not followed suit.   See Chapter 20 for discussion of maritime actions for wrongful death.

Leathers v. Blessing

Supreme Court of the United States, 1882.
105 U.S. (15 Otto) 626, 26 L.Ed. 1192.

■ MR. JUSTICE BLATCHFORD delivered the opinion of the court.

This is an appeal by the respondents in a suit in admiralty *in personam* from the decree therein.   Leathers was the master of the steamboat "Natchez," and he and the other respondent were the owners of that vessel.   The suit was brought in the District Court to recover damages for personal injuries received by Blessing, the libellant, on board of that vessel, and he had a decree in that court against the respondents *in personam,* and as owners of the vessel, and *in solido,* for $5,758.50, with five per cent interest from judicial demand till paid, and costs of suit.   The respondents appealed to the Circuit Court.   That court found the following facts: "1. That on the twenty-sixth day of December, A.D. 1873, the defendant therein, Thomas P. Leathers, was the master, and he and Mary Meeha, wife of Anthony Pauly, were the owners of the steamboat 'Natchez.'   2. That about 1 o'clock P.M. of said day the said steamboat 'Natchez' was lying at the wharf on the Mississippi, near the foot of Canal Street, in the city of New Orleans, securely moored to said wharf, and with at least one of her gang-planks out and resting on the shore, which afforded ingress and egress between the lower deck of said steamboat and the wharf.   3. That on the day and at the hour above mentioned the said steamboat had recently arrived at the port of New Orleans from a trip up the Mississippi River, having on board a large number of bales of cotton, and that the trip of said steamboat was completed, but her cargo was still to be discharged.   4. That a part of said cargo of cotton was stowed on the forward deck several tiers high, and a passageway was left from the end of the gang-plank to the foot of the stairs.   This passageway was covered with bales of cotton piled on the bridging, and persons on shore who desired to go to the cabin or office of the steamboat could only do so by going along this passageway to the stairs, and up the stairs to the cabin and office.   5. That, after the landing of said boat, and after her gang-plank had been run ashore, so that persons could go from shore to said steamboat, the libellant went aboard of said steamboat, along said gang-plank, with the purpose of going up into her cabin or to her office.   6. That the master and officers of said steamboat were accustomed to permit persons expecting to find on said steamboat freight consigned to them, as soon as she had landed, and her gang-plank was out, to go aboard of her to examine the manifest or transact any other business with her master or officers.   7.   That the libellant had business on said steamboat when he went aboard of her as aforesaid, he was expecting a consignment of cotton-seed by said steamboat, and went aboard to ascertain whether it had arrived.   8.   That, when libellant was going through said passageway, and when near the foot of the stairs, on his way to the cabin or office of said steamboat, a bale of cotton fell from the upper part of said passageway against and upon the leg and ankle of libellant, causing a compound fracture of the bones of his ankle and leg.   9.   That said bale of cotton was carelessly and negligently stowed, and was left in such a position that it was liable to fall upon persons going along said passageway to the foot of the stairs of said steamboat, and its position was known to the master of said steamboat.   10.   That libellant was in no manner negligent or in fault, whereby he contributed to his said injury.   11.   That the fracture of libellant's leg and ankle was such as to render amputation of his leg necessary, and his leg had to be and was amputated in consequence of the injury sustained by him as aforesaid.   12. That, at the time of his injury aforesaid, the libellant was thirty-eight years of age, and was earning in his business, which was buying cotton-seed, as agent for the Louisiana Oil Company, the sum of $750 per year.   13. That, at the time of said injury, the libellant was in good health, with a good character for sobriety and integrity.   14.   That, in consequence of the injury sustained by him as aforesaid, the costs and expenses incurred by libellant for treatment, surgical services, and in and about his care and cure, amounted to the sum of seventeen hundred and seven dollars and fifty cents.   15.   That the other damage resulting to libellant from said injury, consequent upon loss of time and the permanent disability caused by the loss of his leg, amounted to the sum of four thousand dollars." As a conclusion of law from the foregoing facts, the court found that the libellant ought to recover from the respondents the aggregate amount of said costs, expenses, and damage, with interest thereon, as additional damage, from the date of judicial demand, and it gave a decree in favor of libellant against the respondents for the said sum of $5,707.50, with interest at the rate of five per cent per annum from the date of judicial demand till paid, and costs of suit.   From that decree this appeal was taken by the respondents.

The only question raised by the appellants is as to whether the suit was one of admiralty jurisdiction in the District Court.   They maintain that jurisdiction of the case belonged exclusively to a court of common law. Attention is directed to the facts that the Circuit Court did not find that the libellant was an officer, seaman, passenger, or freighter, or that he had any connection with the vessel or any business upon her or about her, except that when he went on board of her he was expecting a consignment of cotton-seed by her, and went on board to ascertain whether it had arrived; and that the vessel had fully completed her voyage and was securely moored at the wharf at the time the accident occurred.   It is urged that the case is one of an injury received by a person not connected with the vessel or her navigation, through the carelessness or neglect of another person, and that the fact that the person guilty of negligence was at the time in control of a vessel which had been previously engaged in navigating waters within the jurisdiction of the admiralty courts of the United States, cannot give jurisdiction to such courts.

Although a suit might have been brought in a common-law court for the cause of action sued on here, the District Court, sitting in admiralty, had jurisdiction of this suit. The vessel was waterborne in the Mississippi River at the time, laden with an undischarged cargo, having just arrived with it from a voyage. The findings sufficiently show that her cargo was to be discharged at the place where she was moored. Therefore, although the transit of the vessel was completed, she was still a vessel occupied in the business of navigation at the time. The facts, that she was securely moored to the wharf, and had communication with the shore by a gang-plank, did not make her a part of the land or deprive her of the character of a water-borne vessel.

The findings state that the master and officers of the vessel were accustomed to permit persons expecting to find on the vessel freight consigned to them, as soon as she had landed and her gang-plank was out, to go on board of her to examine the manifest or transact any other business with her master or officers; that the libellant had business on her when he went on board of her under the circumstances set forth in the findings; that he was expecting a consignment of cotton-seed by her; and that he went on board to ascertain whether it had arrived. These findings show that not only did the libellant go on board for a purpose proper in itself, so far as he was concerned, but that he went substantially on the invitation of those in control of the vessel. It is not found that he knew of the custom referred to, but it is found that he was acting in accordance with such custom, and it is not found that he did not know of such custom. With the added fact that his business was that of buying cotton-seed, it is properly to be inferred that he went on board to inquire whether the vessel had brought the cotton-seed which he was expecting, because he knew of such custom. This makes the case one of invitation to the libellant to go on board in the transaction of business with the master and officers of the vessel, recognized by them as proper business to be transacted by him with them on board of the vessel at the time and place in question. Under such circumstances, the relation of the master and of his co-owner, through him, to the libellant, was such as to create a duty on them to see that the libellant was not injured by the negligence of the master. On the facts found there was a breach of that duty by the negligence of the master, constituting a maritime tort, of which the District Court had jurisdiction in this suit. Not only does the jurisdiction of courts of admiralty in matters of tort depend entirely on locality, but since the case of Waring v. Clarke (5 How. 441, 464)(1847) the exception of *infra corpus comitatus* is not allowed to prevail. Nor is the term "tort," when used in reference to admiralty jurisdiction, confined to wrongs or injuries committed by direct force, but it includes wrongs suffered in consequence of the negligence or malfeasance of others, where the remedy at common-law is by an action on the case. Phila., Wil., & Balt. Railroad Co. v. Phil. & Havre de Grace Steam Towboat Co., 23 id. 209, 214, 215.

The decree of the Circuit Court will be affirmed, with costs and interest on the principal sum of $5,707.50 decreed by the Circuit Court, to be computed at the rate of five per cent per annum from the date of judicial demand in the District Court, till paid; and it is

So ordered.

Orient Mid–East Lines v. Bowen

United States District Court, Southern District of New York, 1966.
255 F.Supp. 627, 1966 A.M.C. 623.

■ JOHN F.X. McGOHEY, D.J.   General Motors Corporation filed an exception to the libel on the ground that the facts alleged do not state a claim within the admiralty and maritime jurisdiction.[1] The libel charges General Motors with inducing the breach of an affreightment contract between the libellant and the respondent Alfred E. Bowen Corp. [Bowen]. The libellant contends that General Motors prevented Bowen, its freight forwarder, from shipping certain dump trucks, the subjects of the affreightment contract, thereby causing libellant's vessel, the S. S. Orient Liner, to sail light, resulting in damages to the libellant of $38,808. Libellant also claims $250,000 as exemplary damages.

General Motors, admitting that the test for the exercise of admiralty jurisdiction in this circuit is whether the injury relates to the operation of a vessel plying navigable waters,[2] nonetheless contends that its alleged interference was not a maritime tort. The contention is rejected. It is clear that the inducement of a breach of a maritime contract which causes a light sailing is indeed a maritime tort.[3] The facts alleged here state a claim cognizable in admiralty under 28 U.S.C.A. § 1333.[4]

1. The pass contained the following language. "The person accepting this pass in consideration thereof assumes all risks of accidents, and expressly agrees that the Compagnie Generale Transatlantique shall not be held liable under any circumstances whether by negligence of their employees, or otherwise, for any injury to his person or for any loss or injury to his property." The district judge instructed the jury that this attempted disclaimer could have no effect unless it had been made known to Kermarec. The evidence showed that Kermarec had not seen the pass. By its verdict the jury implicitly found that Kermarec had not been informed of the language appearing on it. Since that finding is not disputed here, we need not consider what effect the attempted disclaimer would have had if Kermarec had been aware of it. See Moore v. American Scantic Line, Inc., 121 F.2d 767 (2 Cir.1941). Compare 46 U.S.C.A. § 183c.

2. See Castillo v. Argonaut Trading Agency, Inc., 156 F.Supp. 398, 1958 A.M.C. 1422 (S.D.N.Y.1957).

3. See Poznan, 276 F. 418, 433–434 (S.D.N.Y.1921), where L. Hand, J., arrived at the same conclusion by an application of the more stringent traditional test of locus delicti. See also Khedivial Line, S.A.E. v. Seafarers' International Union, 278 F.2d 49, 52, 1960 A.M.C. 795 (2 Cir.1960) [dictum]; Upper Lakes Shipping Ltd. v. International Longshoremen's Assoc., 33 F.R.D. 348 (S.D.N.Y.1963); Cocotos S.S. of Panama, S.a. v. Sociedad Maritima Victoria, S.a., 146 F.Supp. 540, 545, 1956 A.M.C. 397 (S.D.N.Y. 1956) [dictum]. Cf. Castillo v. Argonaut Trading Agency, Inc., supra.

4. The attempted distinction on the grounds that this tort did not actually prevent a sailing is not persuasive.

Accordingly, the respondent's exception to the libel for lack of admiralty and maritime jurisdiction is overruled.

So ordered.

Kermarec v. Compagnie Generale Transatlantique

Supreme Court of the United States, 1959.
358 U.S. 625, 79 S.Ct. 406, 3 L.Ed.2d 550.

■ MR. JUSTICE STEWART delivered the opinion of the Court.

On November 24, 1948, the respondent's vessel, the S.S. Oregon was berthed at a pier in the North River, New York City. About noon on that day Joseph Kermarec came aboard to visit Henry Yves, a member of the ship's crew. The purpose of the visit was entirely personal, to pay a social call upon Yves and to give him a package to be delivered to a mutual friend in France. In accordance with customary practice permitting crew members to entertain guests aboard the vessel, Yves had obtained a pass from the executive officer authorizing Kermarec to come aboard.[1] As he started to leave the ship several hours later, Kermarec fell and was injured while descending a stairway.

On the theory that his fall had been caused by the defective manner in which a canvas runner had been tacked to the stairway, Kermarec brought an action for personal injuries in the District Court for the Southern District of New York, alleging unseaworthiness of the vessel and negligence on the part of its crew. Federal jurisdiction was invoked by reason of the diverse citizenship of the parties, and a jury trial was demanded.

The district judge was of the view that the substantive law of New York was applicable. Accordingly, he eliminated the unseaworthiness claim from the case and instructed the jury that Kermarec was "a gratuitous licensee" who could recover only if the defendant had failed to warn him of a dangerous condition within its actual knowledge, and only if Kermarec himself had been entirely free of contributory negligence.[2]

---

1. The pass contained the following language: "The person accepting this pass in consideration thereof assumes all risks of accidents, and expressly agrees that the Compagnie Generale Transatlantique shall not be held liable under any circumstances whether by negligence of their employees, or otherwise, for any injury to his person or for any loss or injury to his property." The district judge instructed the jury that this attempted disclaimer could have no effect unless it had been made known to Kermarec. The evidence showed that Kermarec had not seen the pass. By its verdict the jury implicitly found that Kermarec had not been informed of the language appearing on it. Since that finding is not disputed here, we need not consider what effect the attempted disclaimer would have had if Kermarec had been aware of it. See Moore v. American Scantic Line, Inc., 121 F.2d 767 (2 Cir.1941). Compare 46 U.S.C.A. § 183c.

2. "With respect to the first issue of fact, namely, the alleged negligence of the defendant, you must bear in mind that the owner of a ship such as the defendant is subject to liability for bodily harm caused to a gratuitous licensee, such as the plaintiff, by any artificial condition on board the ship, only if both of the following conditions are present: (1) if the defendant knows of the unsafe condition and realizes that it involves an unreasonable risk to the plaintiff and has reason to believe that the plaintiff will not

The jury returned a verdict in Kermarec's favor. Subsequently the trial court granted a motion to set the verdict aside and dismiss the complaint, ruling that there had been a complete failure of proof that the shipowner had actually known that the stairway was in a dangerous or defective condition. A divided Court of Appeals affirmed. The opinion of that court does not make clear whether affirmance was based upon agreement with the trial judge that New York law was applicable, or upon a determination that the controlling legal principles would in any event be no different under maritime law. 245 F.2d 175 (1957). Certiorari was granted to examine both of these issues. 355 U.S. 902, 78 S.Ct. 335, 2 L.Ed.2d 259 (1957).

The District Court was in error in ruling that the governing law in this case was that of the State of New York. Kermarec was injured aboard a ship upon navigable waters. It was there that the conduct of which he complained occurred. The legal rights and liabilities arising from that conduct were therefore within the full reach of the admiralty jurisdiction and measurable by the standards of maritime law. See The Plymouth, 3 Wall. 20, 18 L.Ed. 125 (1865); Philadelphia, W. & B.R. Co. v. Philadelphia & Havre de Grace Steam Tugboat Co., 23 How. 209, 215, 16 L.Ed. 433 (1859); The Commerce, 1 Black 574, 579, 17 L.Ed. 107 (1861); The Rock Island Bridge, 6 Wall. 213, 215, 18 L.Ed. 753 (1867); The Belfast, 7 Wall. 624, 640, 19 L.Ed. 266 (1868); Leathers v. Blessing, 105 U.S. 626, 630, 26 L.Ed. 1192 (1882); The Admiral Peoples, 295 U.S. 649, 651, 55 S.Ct. 885, 886, 79 L.Ed. 1633 (1935). If this action had been brought in a state court, reference to admiralty law would have been necessary to determine the rights and liabilities of the parties. Carlisle Packing Co. v. Sandanger, 259 U.S. 255, 259, 42 S.Ct. 475, 476, 66 L.Ed. 927 (1922). Where the plaintiff exercises the right conferred by diversity of citizenship to choose a federal forum, the result is no different, even though he exercises the further right to a jury trial. Whatever doubt may once have existed on that score was effectively laid to rest by Pope & Talbot, Inc., v. Hawn, 346 U.S. 406, 410–411, 74 S.Ct. 202, 204, 98 L.Ed. 143 (1953). It thus becomes necessary to consider whether prejudice resulted from the court's application of the substantive law of New York.

In instructing the jury that contributory negligence on Kermarec's part would operate as a complete bar to recovery, the district judge was clearly

discover the condition or realize the risk; and (2) if the defendant invites or permits the plaintiff to enter or remain upon the ship without exercising reasonable care either to make the condition reasonably safe or to warn the plaintiff of the condition and risk involved therein.

"In short, in order that the plaintiff recover in this case, he must establish by a fair preponderance of the evidence that the defendant knew of the unsafe condition and invit-

ed the plaintiff aboard without either correcting the condition or warning him of it.

* * *

"In connection with damages, if you find that the plaintiff's injuries were the proximate result of the defendant's negligence and the plaintiff's own contributory negligence, even in the slightest degree, then the plaintiff cannot recover at all."

in error. The jury should have been told instead that Kermarec's contributory negligence was to be considered only in mitigation of damages. The Max Morris, 137 U.S. 1, 11 S.Ct. 29, 34 L.Ed. 586 (1890); Pope & Talbot, Inc. v. Hawn, 346 U.S. 406, 408–409, 74 S.Ct. 202, 204, 98 L.Ed. 143 (1953). It is equally clear, however, that this error did not prejudice Kermarec. By returning a verdict in his favor, the jury necessarily found that Kermarec had not in fact been guilty of contributory negligence "even in the slightest degree."

The district judge refused to submit the issue of unseaworthiness to the jury for the reason that an action for unseaworthiness is unknown to the common law of New York. Although the basis for its action was inappropriate, the court was correct in eliminating the unseaworthiness claim from this case. Kermarec was not a member of the ship's company, nor of that broadened class of workmen to whom the admiralty law has latterly extended the absolute right to a seaworthy ship. See Mahnich v. Southern S.S. Co., 321 U.S. 96, 64 S.Ct. 455, 88 L.Ed. 561 (1944); Seas Shipping Co. v. Sieracki, 328 U.S. 85, 66 S.Ct. 872, 90 L.Ed. 1099 (1946); Pope & Talbot, Inc., v. Hawn, 346 U.S. 406, 74 S.Ct. 202, 204, 98 L.Ed. 143 (1953). Kermarec was aboard not to perform ship's work, but simply to visit a friend.

It is apparent, therefore, that prejudicial error occurred in this case only if the maritime law imposed upon the shipowner a standard of care higher than the duty which the district judge found owing to a gratuitous licensee under the law of New York. If, in other words, the shipowner owed Kermarec the duty of exercising ordinary care, then upon this record Kermarec was entitled to judgment, the jury having resolved the factual issues in his favor under instructions less favorable to him than should have been given.[3] Stated broadly, the decisive issue is thus whether admiralty recognizes the same distinctions between an invitee and a licensee as does the common law.

It is a settled principle of maritime law that a shipowner owes the duty of exercising reasonable care towards those lawfully aboard the vessel who are not members of the crew. Leathers v. Blessing, 105 U.S. 626, 26 L.Ed. 1192 (1882); The Max Morris, 137 U.S. 1, 11 S.Ct. 29, 34 L.Ed. 586 (1890); The Admiral Peoples, 295 U.S. 649, 55 S.Ct. 885, 79 L.Ed. 1633 (1935).[4] But this Court has never determined whether a different and lower standard of care is demanded if the ship's visitor is a person to whom the label "licensee" can be attached. The issue must be decided in the performance of the Court's function in declaring the general maritime law, free from inappropriate common-law concepts. The Lottawanna, 21 Wall. 558, 22 L.Ed. 654 (1874); The Max Morris, 137 U.S. 1, 11 S.Ct. 29, 34

3. The record clearly justifies a finding that the canvas runner was defectively tacked to the stairway, and that this caused a dangerous condition of which the shipowner's agent would have known in the exercise of ordinary care. By its verdict, the jury found that much and more.

4. Cf. The Osceola, 189 U.S. 158, 23 S.Ct. 483, 47 L.Ed. 760 (1903).

L.Ed. 586 (1890).[5]

The distinctions which the common law draws between licensee and invitee were inherited from a culture deeply rooted to the land, a culture which traced many of its standards to a heritage of feudalism. In an effort to do justice in an industrialized urban society, with its complex economic and individual relationships, modern common-law courts have found it necessary to formulate increasingly subtle verbal refinements, to create subclassifications among traditional commonlaw categories, and to delineate fine gradations in the standards of care which the landowner owes to each.[6] Yet even within a single jurisdiction, the classifications and subclassifications bred by the common law have produced confusion and conflict.[7] As new distinctions have been spawned, older ones have become obscured. Through this semantic morass the common law has moved, unevenly and with hesitation, towards "imposing on owners and occupiers a single duty of reasonable care in all the circumstances."[8]

For the admiralty law at this late date to import such conceptual distinctions would be foreign to its traditions of simplicity and practicality. The Lottawanna, 21 Wall. 558, at 575, 22 L.Ed. 654 (1874). The incorporation of such concepts appears particularly unwarranted when it is remembered that they originated under a legal system in which status depended almost entirely upon the nature of the individual's estate with respect to real property, a legal system in that respect entirely alien to the law of the sea.[9] We hold that the owner of a ship in navigable waters owes

---

5. Where there is no impingement upon legislative policy. Cf. United States v. Atlantic Mut. Ins. Co., 343 U.S. 236, 72 S.Ct. 666, 96 L.Ed. 907 (1952); Halcyon Lines v. Haenn Ship Corp., 342 U.S. 282, 72 S.Ct. 277, 96 L.Ed. 318 (1952).

6. Random selection of almost any modern decision will serve to illustrate the point. E.g., Chicago G.W.R. Co. v. Beecher, 150 F.2d 394 (licensee by express invitation; licensee by implied invitation; bare licensee).

7. For example, the duty of an occupier toward a licensee under the law of New York, which the District Court thought applicable in the present case, appears far from clear. Compare Fox v. Warner–Quinlan Asphalt Co., 97 N.E. 497, 498, 204 N.Y. 240, 245, (1912); Mendelowitz v. Neisner, 179 N.E. 378, 379, 258 N.Y. 181, 184, (1932); Paquet v. Barker, 293 N.Y.S. 983 (2d Dept.) 250 App.Div. 771, (1937); Byrne v. New York C. & H. R. R. Co., 10 N.E. 539, 104 N.Y. 362, (1887); Higgins v. Mason, 174 N.E. 77, 79, 255 N.Y. 104, 109, (1931); Ehret v. Village of Scarsdale, 199 N.E. 56, 60, 269 N.Y. 198, 208, (1936); Mayer v. Temple Properties, 122 N.E.2d 909, 911–913, 307 N.Y. 559, 563–564, (1954); Friedman v. Berkowitz, 136 N.Y.S.2d 81, 206 Misc. 889, (1954).

8. See Chief Judge Clark's dissenting opinion in the Court of Appeals. 245 F.2d 175, at 180. A survey here of the thousands of judicial decisions in this area during the last hundred years is as unnecessary as it would be impossible. A recent critical review is to be found in 2 Harper and James. The Law of Torts, c. xxvii, *passim* (1956). See also, Prosser, Business Visitors and Invitees, 26 Minn.L.Rev. 573; Marsh, The History and Comparative Law of Invitees, Licensees and Trespassers, 69 L.Q.Rev. 182, 359.

9. This is not to say that concepts of status are not relevant in the law of maritime torts, but only that the meaningful categories are quite different. Membership in the ship's company, for example, a status that confers an absolute right to a seaworthy ship, is peculiar to the law of the sea. Such status has now been extended to others aboard "doing a seaman's work and incurring a seaman's hazards." Seas Shipping Co. v. Sieracki, 328 U.S. 85, at 99, 66 S.Ct. 872, at page 880, 90 L.Ed. 1099 (1946).

to all who are on board for purposes not inimical to his legitimate interests the duty of exercising reasonable care under the circumstances of each case.[10] It follows that in the present case the judgment must be vacated and the case remanded to the District Court with instructions to reinstate the jury verdict and enter judgment accordingly.

It is so ordered.

NOTE

In *Kermarec,* it was held that the owner of a vessel in navigable waters "owes to all who are on board for purposes not inimical to his legitimate interests the duty of exercising reasonable care under the circumstances of each case."

A group of Sunday curious who boarded a vessel without invitation were held to be within the *Kermarec* exception in Johnson v. Mobile Towing & Wrecking Co., 224 F.Supp. 811, 1964 A.M.C. 686 (S.D.Ala.1963), aff'd 339 F.2d 205, 1965 A.M.C. 1271 (5 Cir.1964). But see Taylor v. Alaska Rivers Nav. Co., 391 P.2d 15, 1965 A.M.C. 1073 (Alaska 1964), applying the attractive nuisance doctrine when a barge owner knew or ought to have known that the arrival of a barge in a remote village would be an exciting event. In fact the children were released from school so that they could go to see it.

In Ryder v. United States, 373 F.2d 73, 1968 A.M.C. 418 (4 Cir.1967), it was held that the United States was not liable to a passenger on a small pleasure craft who was injured in the process of boarding a Navy seaplane to exchange beer for food. The court found that she was on the seaplane for purposes inimical to the owner's interest.

Does a finding that takes the injured person out of the *Kermarec* standard relieve the vessel owner of all duty of care whatsoever? See Garrett v. United States Lines, Inc., 574 F.2d 997, 1978 A.M.C. 2373 (9 Cir.1978), in which it was held that the United States had discharged whatever "slight" duty of care it had to an inebriated seaman who contrary to instructions insisted upon entering a Navy launch being used to transport seamen to and from shore leave. In Buchanan v. Stanships, Inc., 744 F.2d 1070 (5th Cir.1984), the court describes the standard of care of a stowaway as "humane treatment," citing Norris, *The Law of Seamen,*

---

10. The inconsistent and diverse results reached by courts which have tried to apply to the facts of shipboard life common-law distinctions between licensees and invitees reinforce the conclusion here reached. As to a seaman crossing another vessel to reach the pier, see Radoslovich v. Navigazione Libera Triestina, S.a., 72 F.2d 367 (2 Cir.1934)(invitee); Aho v. Jacobsen, 249 F.2d 309 (1 Cir.1957)(licensee); Anderson v. The E.B. Ward, Jr., 38 F. 44 (C.C.1890)(invitee); Griffiths v. Seaboard Midland Petroleum Corp., 1933 A.M.C. 911 (D.C.Md.1933)(invitee); see also Lauchert v. American S.S. Co., 65 F.Supp. 703 (D.C.1946)(licensee). As to a guest of a passenger, see McCann v. Anchor Line, 79 F.2d 338 (2 Cir.1936)(invitee); Zaia v. "Italia" Societa Anonyma di Navigazione,

87 N.E.2d 183, 324 Mass. 547 (1949)(licensee); The Champlain, 270 N.Y.S. 643, 151 Misc. 498, 1934 A.M.C. 25 (1934)(invitee). See also Metcalfe v. Cunard S.S. Co., 16 N.E. 701, 147 Mass. 66 (1888)(licensee).

The English courts appear to have differentiated between an invitee and a licensee in cases of personal injury on shipboard, without critical inquiry. See, e.g., Smith v. Steele, L.R. 10 Q.B. 125 (1875) and Duncan v. Cammell Laird & Co., Ltd., [1943] 2 All E.R. 621. These distinctions have after thorough study (Law Reform Committee, Third Report, Cmd. No. 9305 (1954)) been eliminated entirely from the English law by statutory enactment. Occupiers' Liability Act. 1957, 5 and 6 Eliz. 2, c. 31.

§ 667 & n. 15. In *Buchanan,* the court of appeals remanded the case for a determination of whether the deceased actually was a stowaway.

Does it follow from the language in *Kermarec* quoted above that the duty to "all who are on board" is the same? Compare with the decision in *Rainey* Judge Pope's statement that a passenger carrier has a duty "to exercise extraordinary vigilance and the highest skill to secure the safe conveyance of his passengers."   Allen v. Matson Navigation Co., 255 F.2d 273, 1958 A.M.C. 1343 (9 Cir.1958).   Is there a difference in the standard of care that depends upon whether the vessel is a common carrier or a private carrier? Cf. Roberts v. Offshore Logistics Services, Inc., 1983 A.M.C. 107 (E.D.La.1980), in which the court made a finding that the defendant was a private carrier and applied the *Kermarec* standard, distinguishing the cases that have started a high standard for common carriers.

Lewis v. Timco, Inc.

United States Court of Appeals, Fifth Circuit, 1984.
736 F.2d 163, 1985 A.M.C. 1185.

■ Politz, Circuit Judge:

This case was returned to the panel by the en banc court, 716 F.2d 1425 (5th Cir.1983), for our determination whether Alfred Lewis' conduct constituted 50% of the total negligence proximate to his accident. On our initial consideration we did not reach this question, concluding instead that the rule of comparative negligence was not applicable in a strict products liability case by a longshoreman. 697 F.2d 1252 (5th Cir.1983). Sitting en banc this court vacated the panel opinion in part and held "that the trial court was correct in its decision that the maritime principle of comparative fault is applicable in maritime cases that urge strict liability for defects in products." 716 F.2d at 1427.

At the outset, to the extent deemed necessary we reinstate the prior panel opinion except insofar as it may be modified by this opinion or is inconsistent with the teachings of the majority opinion of the en banc court. The pertinent facts are detailed in the panel opinion, 697 F.2d 1253–54. We set forth only a factual summary for purposes of the present opinion, with emphasis on those facts considered critical to the question we address today—to what extent did Lewis' acts or omissions proximately contribute to his accident.

Lewis was part of a crew furnished by his employer, Timco, Inc., to work on the jackup drilling barge VICKSBURG in the coastal waters of Louisiana. Lewis was assigned to operate the hydraulic tongs used in the "make-up" of tubing joints being run into a well with a "fishing tool" to retrieve an obstruction dropped into the drilling hole. Lewis was inexperienced as a tong operator, having regularly worked tongs on only one prior occasion. That earlier assignment totaled approximately 25 hours including travel time to and from the work site. Other than that, his experience was limited to relieving tong operators, for a few minutes at a time, when they ate or went to the restroom. Lewis' education was limited; he left school in the eighth grade because of economic necessity. He previously worked at various jobs which required only manual labor or limited skills.

When Lewis reported to work on the fateful tour of duty a computerized control unit supplied by Rebel Rentals, Inc. to monitor the torque applied to the tubing joints would not work with the original tongs supplied. Rebel Rentals dispatched a set of Hillman–Kelley Model 500 C tubing tongs manufactured by Joy Manufacturing. These tongs were involved in the accident. At the time of the accident the Timco crew, under the supervision of an employee of Edwards Rental and Fishing Tools, Inc., was setting up to begin the "fishing operation" to retrieve the obstruction.

Hydraulic power tongs are large mechanical wrenches with internal cams that rotate jaws around tubings and casings so that they may be assembled or dismantled. Generally, power tongs have "dead man switches," a safety device which immediately stops the operation of the tongs when the throttle is released. The Hillman–Kelley 500 C tongs did not have this safety feature. Instead, these tongs were designed to free the tubing when the throttle was released. This automatic indexing feature required that two switches be set properly. When these controls were not synchronized, the tongs would not stop upon release of the throttle. The tongs would continue to turn unless restrained by a tight "snubbing line." A snubbing line is a cable which anchors the suspended tongs to the rig platform, stabilizing the tongs. If the snubbing line is not sufficiently taut, it may fail to restrain the tongs and the operator may be caught between the snubbing line and the tubing. That was Lewis' fate. He released the throttle but the tongs did not stop. The tongs continued to turn, and Lewis was crushed between the snubbing line and the tubing and sustained serious and permanently disabling injuries.

The district court found that the "tongs had a design defect in that a control setting could be imposed which would cause them to continue operating even when the throttle was released." These defects "rendered the tongs unnecessarily dangerous to normal use." In addition, the district court found that the representative of Rebel Rentals knew that Lewis was experiencing difficulty because the controls were not coordinated but did not instruct Lewis on the proper manner of operating the tongs. Incredibly, instead of setting the tongs' controls properly, or cautioning Lewis about the dangers of improper settings, the representative gave Lewis a hammer and an oil can and told him to strike the controls to force the release of the tubing. In addition, the trial court found that the representative of Edwards Rental who was in direct supervision of the fishing operation, a man with broad experience in oilfield work, observed Lewis's difficulty in operating the tongs, was aware of the danger posed by the slack in the snubbing line, but said or did nothing to assist or warn the inexperienced Lewis.

The district court found Lewis negligent for "attempting to make up the fishing tool joint without adjusting the length of the snubbing line." The record reflects that Lewis made an effort to reset the snubbing line when the fish tool operator directed that the assembly of the fishing tool and joints be done in the "mouse hole," an opening slightly closer to the anchoring post of the snubbing line than the drilling hole. This repositioning caused slack to develop in the snubbing line. When Lewis got a tool and started to adjust the snubbing line he was told by the Timco driller, his immediate superior, that they were behind on the job and did not have time to adjust and re-adjust the snubbing line. He was told to get on with his work. The message was pungent and clear; Lewis obeyed. Shortly thereafter, when Lewis attempted to disengage the tongs the throttle would not release, the tool continued to turn, and Lewis was crushed against the tubing by the snubbing line.

After a bench trial the district court assigned responsibility for the tragic accident 40% to the manufacturer, Joy Manufacturing, 40% to the power tong owner, Rebel Rentals, and 20% to the fishing operator, Edwards Rental. The court then found that Lewis' failure to tighten the snub line contributed 50% to the accident and reduced his quantum by one-half, resulting in a net recovery of $343,027.22.

Discussion

The sole issue on this remand to the panel is whether the trial court clearly erred in determining that Lewis was 50% at fault in the accident causing his injuries. In a maritime appeal the appellant has the burden, when challenging a factual finding, to show that the district court was clearly erroneous. McAllister v. United States, 348 U.S. 19, 75 S.Ct. 6, 99 L.Ed. 20 (1954); Noritake Co., Inc. v. M/V Hellenic Champion, 627 F.2d 724 (5th Cir.1980). Questions of negligence in admiralty cases are treated as factual issues, and are thus subject to the clearly erroneous standard. Valley Towing Service, Inc. v. S/S American Wheat, Freighters, Inc., 618 F.2d 341 (5th Cir.1980). After an exhaustive study of the record, including multiple readings of some parts, we are persuaded beyond peradventure that the trial court's finding is clearly erroneous in fact and involves an erroneous application of law.

The record supports all factual findings other than the extent of Lewis' negligence.[1] We are not prepared to say that a 40% allocation to Joy

---

1. The relevant findings of fact and conclusions of law are:

* * *

13. The accident was caused by the fact that the tongs did not shut off automatically when Lewis released the throttle combined with the fact that the snubbing line had too much slack in it. The tongs failed to disengage because the two separate control devices were not synchronized.

15. The tongs had a design defect in that a control setting could be imposed which would cause them to continue op-

erating even when the throttle was released. Although the instructional manual for the tongs pointed out the necessity for synchronizing the controls, it gave no warning of the severe hazard created by failing to synchronize, nor was there any such warning on the tool itself. These design deficiencies in the tongs and the instructions accompanying them rendered the tongs defective and unreasonably dangerous to the operator. Additionally, Joy was negligent in furnishing tongs with these defects which it knew or should have known

Manufacturing for placing an unreasonably dangerous product on the market, a 40% allocation to Rebel Rentals for negligently supplying a product it knew or should have known was unreasonably dangerous and for not preventing its use in a dangerous manner, and a 20% allocation to Edwards Rental for negligent supervision and instructions is clearly erroneous.[2] We accept those findings and assignments.

We are persuaded, however, that the evidence simply does not support the conclusion that Lewis' actions equaled the combined fault of the tong manufacturer, the tong owner and the fishing operation supervisor.   In an employment situation, in determining whether a worker acted reasonably in encountering a risk, we examine, *inter alia,* the following criteria:

> (1) relative knowledge of the danger by the supervising employee and the injured employee; (2) relative control over the employee's situation; (3) the degree to which the employee's conduct is voluntary on his part; (4) alternatives available to the employee; (5) obviousness of the danger; and (6) relative ability to eliminate the danger.

Martinez v. United States Fidelity and Guaranty Company, 423 So.2d 1088, 1090 (La.1982).

rendered the tongs unnecessarily dangerous to normal use.

16.   Timco and many other companies which operated tongs routinely disconnected linkage so that the 500 C tong would disengage even if the controls were not synchronized.   The Rebel representative on the rig had knowledge of this practice.   This knowledge by the Rebel representatives should have made it obvious to them why Lewis was experiencing difficulty in disengaging the tongs; this knowledge of the operation of the Rebel tong and observation of plaintiff's problem with the tong made it imperative that the Rebel representatives instruct plaintiff on the proper manner of operating the tong.   I find that the Rebel representatives observed the persistent problems Mr. Lewis encountered in disengaging the tongs and were negligent in failing to instruct him as to the proper method of synchronizing the controls.

17.   Mr. Larry Franks was the representative of Edwards on the rig and was in direct charge of the fishing operation in which plaintiff was participating at the time of his accident.   Mr. Franks had broad experience in oilfield work.   While it was plaintiff's primary responsibility as operator of the tong to adjust the snub line, Mr. Franks also should have been

aware of the fact that the snub line was too long and I find that Mr. Franks was negligent in failing to advise plaintiff to shorten the snub line.

18.   Although the Atwood crew observed plaintiff's difficulty in operating the tongs, they had no peculiar knowledge of the nature of the problem.

Considering the obvious nature of the danger inherent in operating the tong with the snub line too long and the fact that the operations were being directly supervised by Mr. Franks, I find no fault on the part of Atwood or its employees under the standard established by 33 U.S.C. § 905(b).

19.   The plaintiff failed to establish that the Home representative had knowledge of the difficulty with the operation of the tongs or that the snub line was too long. Accordingly, I find no negligence on the part of Home.

2.   These are not, necessarily, the results we would have reached were we the fact-finders, see e.g. Western Beef, Inc. v. Compton Inv. Co., 611 F.2d 587 (5th Cir. 1980); we say no more than there is evidence to support these findings and we are not left with a definite and firm conviction that a mistake has been committed.   Pullman v. Swint, 456 U.S. 273, 102 S.Ct. 1781, 72 L.Ed.2d 66 (1982).

Lewis, an untutored, poorly experienced, unlettered workman, operated unfamiliar, defective tongs with a slack snubbing line as he was ordered to do by his supervisor. The record firmly establishes Lewis' inexperience. On his second regular assignment as a tong operator he was required to use a set of tongs which the district court found to be "defective and unreasonably dangerous to the operator." He had never operated such tongs before. He did not comprehend why the controls would not work properly. When his superiors and the Rebel Rentals representative observed his problem in getting the tongs to stop and release the tubing their response was to give him an oil can and a hammer to use in forcing the controls. No one properly set the controls. No one told Lewis how to set the automatic indexer. No one warned of the danger. No one tried to help. When Lewis moved to adjust the slack in the snub line caused by the movement over to the mouse hole he was admonished by his supervisor not to delay further their activities by adjusting that line. Lewis, newly promoted to tong operator, was concerned about losing his new job unless he followed his orders. We are in accord with an early expression of the Louisiana Supreme Court in Lee v. Powell Bros. & Sanders Co., 126 La. 51, 52 So. 214, 216 (La.1910), holding that:

> the servant is relieved of the imputation of contributory negligence for obeying an order of his master, or of his master's representative, which exposes him to danger, "unless the risk is so great, or the danger so obvious or glaring that no prudent person, in a like situation, would undertake it, even when ordered to do so by his employer." Thompson, Com.Neg. (2d Ed.) § 5379.

Lewis should have removed the slack from the snubbing line. That act, viewed with the unerring visual acuity of $^{20}\!/_{20}$ hindsight, was careless, and it was involved in the occurrence of this sad accident. But what is its legal effect in that rig operation setting? Considering the legal fault of the other parties—the strict liability of the manufacturer of an unreasonably dangerous product, the blatant negligence of the power tong owner, and the negligence of the fishing operation supervisor—Lewis' contribution wanes into insignificance. Under the prevailing circumstances, it cannot be said that Lewis' willingness and efforts to operate unfamiliar tongs without adequate training, briefing or supervision, and his obeisance to an order from his superiors to desist from his efforts to tighten the snub line, were unreasonable acts constituting negligence. We find and hold as a matter of fact and law that Lewis was guilty of no proximate act of negligence. Accordingly, no reduction in quantum is appropriate.

The judgment of the district court is AFFIRMED except insofar as it assesses Lewis with 50% comparative negligence. In that respect the judgment is REVERSED and RENDERED, and the matter is returned to the district court for entry of a judgment consistent herewith.

NOTE

The court declined to rehear Lewis v. Timco en banc a second time. See 744 F.2d 94 (Table). The en banc decision, at 716 F.2d 1425, noted in the opinion in *Timco* above contains a thorough discussion of the pros and cons of wedding strict liability and comparative fault. See also Owen & Moore, Comparative Negligence in a Maritime Products Liability Case, 43 La.L.Rev. 1543–1548 (1983).

Outside the area of products liability the apportionment of damages in respect of fault has been an important principle of the tort law. Collision damages were apportioned by moieties from very early times, and some early American personal injury cases followed the collision cases by analogy. In The Max Morris, 137 U.S. 1, 11 S.Ct. 29, 34 L.Ed. 586 (1890), the Supreme Court made it clear that in personal injury cases in admiralty the common law rule of contributory negligence as a bar was not to be followed, leaving open the question of whether damages were to be divided as in collision cases, or apportioned on some other basis. Since that time the practice has been to reduce the award in proportion to the percentage of contributory fault. See, e.g., Pope & Talbot v. Hawn, 346 U.S. 406, 74 S.Ct. 202, 98 L.Ed. 143 (1953), although it has been pointed out that the Supreme Court has never set forth a rule of comparative negligence. See Owen & Moore, Comparative Negligence in Maritime Personal Injury Cases, 43 La.L.Rev. 941, 943 (1983).

Ocean Barge Transp. Co. v. Hess Oil Virgin Islands Corp.

United States Court of Appeals, Third Circuit, 1984.
726 F.2d 121, 1984 A.M.C. 1979.

■ JAMES HUNTER, III, CIRCUIT JUDGE:

This products liability case arose from the collapse of a crane boom onto the deck of the barge Pavel. The owner and operator of the barge, Ocean Barge Transport Company ("Ocean Barge"), sued the crane's owner-operator, Hess Oil Virgin Islands Corporation ("HOVIC"), and its manufacturer, Mintec/International ("Mintec"), in the District Court of the Virgin Islands, alleging admiralty jurisdiction. After a trial to the bench, the judge concluded that the crane was defective and that Mintec was wholly liable for Ocean Barge's injuries. Mintec appeals. Because we believe that the trial judge erred in his application of the principles of strict liability, we will vacate the judgment below and remand the case.

I

In 1977, HOVIC contracted to purchase from Mintec a sulphur loading facility for HOVIC's St. Croix refinery. The facility, which included the crane, was designed to load sulphur from land to ships via conveyors. Mintec contracted to design and pre-package the facility and to supervise its installation. HOVIC was responsible for the daily operation, repair and maintenance of the facility.

On November 20, 1978, the Pavel arrived at the sulphur loading dock of HOVIC's St. Croix refinery to be loaded with sulphur. After the loading had been completed, and as the crane's boom was being lifted up towards its stowed position, the boom collapsed onto the Pavel causing extensive property damage.

On November 22, 1978, personnel from HOVIC and Mintec met to determine the cause of the accident. It was agreed that two of the four steel bolts which fastened one side of the hoist drum assembly to the pillow block base[1] came loose immediately before the accident. It was also agreed that this loosening caused the hoist drum assembly, which was designed to raise and lower the boom by winding and unwinding cable, to be pulled from both the cradle and the pillow block base to which it had been attached. The hoist cable was then able to unwind, allowing the boom to descend rapidly onto the deck of the Pavel. No agreement, however, could be reached on the critical issue of why the two bolts came loose. HOVIC contended that the bolts came loose because of a defect in the crane, while Mintec argued that the entry of a foreign object into the gear box exerted the pressure which caused the loosening.

Ocean Barge originally brought suit only against HOVIC, alleging negligence. HOVIC then filed a third-party complaint against Mintec, proceeding under alternative theories of strict liability and negligence, alleging that the crane had been defectively designed. Ocean Barge subsequently amended its complaint to assert a direct claim against Mintec based upon the allegations set forth in the HOVIC third-party complaint.

The trial lasted from March 15, 1982 to March 19, 1982. After the trial, the judge concluded, "Because the evidence concerning the failed bolts strongly suggests a defect in the design and/or assembly of the machinery at issue, *Mintec bears a substantial burden in seeking to establish that an affirmative act and/or omission on the part of the operators* of the machinery (HOVIC or its agents) was the sole proximate cause of the accident." (emphasis added). Finding that Mintec had adduced no evidence conclusively establishing HOVIC's negligence, the trial judge held Mintec wholly liable for Ocean Barge's damages of $41,415.30. He also found that HOVIC was not at fault and that Ocean Barge was not contributorily negligent. The judge subsequently awarded attorney's fees in favor of Ocean Barge and HOVIC, and against Mintec.

Mintec appeals from this judgment. We believe that the trial judge erred in inferring the existence of a defect solely from the fact of the bolts' failure and consequently in not requiring plaintiff to meet its burden of negating other reasonable explanations for the failure. Accordingly, we will reverse the judgment below and remand the case.

II

Initially, we note that this action is within the admiralty jurisdiction of the district court.[2] We note also that it is no longer seriously contested that

---

1. Although a precise definition of "pillow block base" cannot be derived from the factual record in this case, it is clear that this item is an integral part of the mechanism supporting the hoist drum assembly.

2. The two-part test of Executive Jet Aviation, Inc. v. City of Cleveland, 409 U.S.

249, 268, 93 S.Ct. 493, 504, 34 L.Ed.2d 454 (1972), requires (1) a maritime locality of the injury, and (2) a "significant relationship" between the wrong and traditional maritime activity. In this case, the crane's boom fell on the Pavel while the barge was afloat on navigable waters. The maritime locality re-

"the legal theories of strict liability in tort now so prevalently applied on land can be applied to suits in admiralty." Pan–Alaska Fisheries, Inc. v. Marine Construction & Design Co., 565 F.2d 1129, 1134 (9th Cir.1977); see also Lewis v. Timco, Inc., 697 F.2d 1252 (5th Cir.1983); Lindsay v. McDonnell Douglas Aircraft Corp., 460 F.2d 631, 635 (8th Cir.1972); Schaeffer v. Michigan–Ohio Navigation Co., 416 F.2d 217, 221 (6th Cir. 1969). Section 402A of the Restatement (Second) of Torts has been embraced in federal maritime law as the best expression of this doctrine as it is generally applied. See, e.g., Pan–Alaska Fisheries, 565 F.2d at 1134; Lindsay, 460 F.2d at 636; Ohio Barge Line, Inc. v. Dravo Corp., 326 F.Supp. 863, 865 (W.D.Pa.1971); Soileau v. Nicklos Drilling Co., 302 F.Supp. 119, 127 (W.D.La.1969). The doctrine of strict liability in tort is therefore properly applicable in this admiralty case.

III

With those guidelines established, we turn to the determinative issue in this case: whether the trial judge correctly applied the principles of strict liability.[3] He did not. The judge inferred that the crane was defective solely from the fact that its bolts failed. Without more, however, this explanation for the failure was no more likely than other explanations—such as HOVIC's negligence—reasonably raised by the evidence. The judge erred in failing to require the plaintiff to establish by a preponderance of the evidence that a defect existed and in imposing a "substantial burden" upon the defendant "to establish that an affirmative act and/or omission on the part of the operators of the machinery (HOVIC or its agents) was the sole proximate cause of the accident."

It is undisputed that a plaintiff proceeding under Section 402A of the *Restatement* bears the burden of proving that the product was defective. See, e.g., Dalton v. Toyota Motor Sales, Inc., 703 F.2d 137, 140 (5th Cir.1983)(applying Louisiana law); Lantis v. Astec Industries, Inc., 648 F.2d 1118, 1120 (7th Cir.1981)(applying Indiana law); Fabian v. E.W. Bliss Co., 582 F.2d 1257, 1260 (10th Cir.1978)(applying New Mexico law). A plaintiff may meet this burden by pointing to some specific dereliction by the manufacturer in constructing or designing the product. But he need not. Courts have been very sensitive to the danger that "[t]here would be little gain to the consuming public if the courts would establish a form of recovery with one hand and take it away with the other by establishing impossible standards of proof." *Lindsay,* 460 F.2d at 639. Of course a

quirement is thus clearly satisfied. The "nexus" requirement is also satisfied; the loading of cargo for transport by water is certainly a traditional maritime activity.

3. At points, Mintec argues that the trial judge could not have been proceeding under § 402A of the *Restatement* because the judge made no findings that the product was "unreasonably dangerous" or that it reached the user "without substantial change in the condition in which it is sold." While we agree that the trial judge's findings of fact were not as detailed or specific as is desirable, we are nonetheless convinced that the judge applied strict liability principles in finding Mintec liable. The judge's assumption that liability flowed directly from a showing of defect and causation clearly indicates that he was proceeding under strict liability theory.

defect, like any other fact, may be proven entirely by circumstantial evidence. See, e.g., Barris v. Bob's Drag Chutes & Safety Equipment, Inc., 685 F.2d 94, 101 (3d Cir.1982)(applying Pennsylvania law); Farner v. Paccar, Inc., 562 F.2d 518, 522 (8th Cir.1977)(applying South Dakota law); Stewart v. Ford Motor Co., 553 F.2d 130, 137 (D.C.Cir.1977)(applying District of Columbia law); Franks v. National Dairy Products Corp., 414 F.2d 682, 685–87 (5th Cir.1969) (applying Texas law). More important, however, the plaintiff need not even prove a specific defect; he may discharge his burden by showing an unexplained occurrence and eliminating all reasonable explanations for the occurrence other than the existence of a defect. See, e.g., Lindsay, 460 F.2d at 638–40; Daleiden v. Carborundum Co., 438 F.2d 1017, 1022 (8th Cir.1971); Greco v. Bucciconi Engineering Co., 407 F.2d 87, 89–90 (3d Cir.1969). Pennsylvania's "malfunction theory," see Sochanski v. Sears, Roebuck & Co., 689 F.2d 45, 50 (3d Cir.1982), is simply a specific application of these general rules of proof. Under this theory "[a] malfunction may itself, *in the absence of abnormal use and reasonable secondary causes,* be sufficient evidence of a defect to make the existence of a defect a jury question." Knight v. Otis Elevator Co., 596 F.2d 84, 89 (3d Cir.1979)(emphasis added). It is incumbent upon the plaintiff to negate other reasonable explanations for the malfunction because "[e]vidence of a malfunction * * * is not a substitute for the need to establish that the product was defective. A malfunction is evidence that a defect existed and eliminates only the need to identify a specific failure." *Sochanski,* 689 F.2d at 50. See also Paoletto v. Beech Aircraft Corp., 464 F.2d 976, 982 (3d Cir.1972). Thus, the malfunction theory in no way relieves the plaintiff of the burden of proving a defect: it simply allows him to show that a defect is the most likely explanation for an accident by eliminating other reasonable explanations. See Stewart, 553 F.2d at 137; Wojciechowski v. Long–Airdox Division of Marmon Group, Inc., 488 F.2d 1111, 1116–17 (3d Cir.1973); *Franks,* 414 F.2d at 685–87. The plaintiff still must satisfy the burden of proving that a defect is the most likely cause of the accident, and therefore must negate the likelihood of other reasonable causes.

In this case, the evidence fairly suggested two explanations for the failed bolts: the failure could have resulted either from a defect or from HOVIC's negligent operation or maintenance.[4] The plaintiff bore the burden of negating the latter explanation for the failure in order to prove indirectly the existence of a defect. The judge, however, did not require the plaintiff to meet this burden. Instead he inferred a defect from the failed bolts and held that Mintec bore the burden of establishing HOVIC's negligence. In not holding the plaintiff to its burden of proof, the judge erred.

Accordingly, we will reverse the judgment of the district court, and remand this case for proceedings consistent with this opinion. We do not

---

4. We note that both Ocean Barge and HOVIC introduced evidence tending to rebut the explanation that HOVIC had negligently operated or maintained the crane. We take no position upon the sufficiency of that evidence to satisfy the plaintiff's burden.

reach the question of whether a court in the Virgin Islands can grant attorney's fees generally in federal question cases or in this admiralty case because there is no longer a prevailing party here. The award of attorneys' fees will be vacated.

NOTE

The application of principles of strict liability in tort in maritime products liability cases where injury occurs on navigable waters has been recognized by the Supreme Court, at least where there exists a maritime nexus. East River S.S. Corp. v. Transamerica Delaval, 476 U.S. 858, 106 S.Ct. 2295, 90 L.Ed.2d 865. In *East River S.S.*, the bareboat charterer of four oil tankers brought an action against a subcontractor of the shipbuilder who designed and manufactured turbines that were to be the main propulsion units of the tankers, but malfunctioned due to design and manufacturing defects. The plaintiffs sought damages for the cost of repairing the turbines and for income lost while they were out of service. The Court found maritime location in the fact that the malfunction occurred on the high seas, and without deciding whether maritime nexus is a requirement of admiralty jurisdiction of an action for a tort occurring on the high seas, recognized that if there is such a requirement it was met, inasmuch as the vessels were engaged in maritime commerce, "a primary concern of admiralty law."

It went on to note that products liability based on negligence has been a part of the admiralty law for over forty years and approved a growing number of court of appeals cases that have held that strict liability is also a part of the admiralty law, but declined to extend the concepts of products liability in the maritime law, whether based on strict liability or on negligence, to embrace cases in which only the "product" itself is damaged, rejecting both a minority rule allowing recovery for damage to the "product" even absent an unusual risk of harm, and intermediate positions that would make liability turn upon the person sustaining the damage or the level of risk created by the defendant's acts.

In creating a federal admiralty rule precluding tort liability for defects in design and manufacture when the injury is maritime and purely economic, the Court left the injured party in such a case to his contract remedy for breach of warranty. It noted that in a case such as *East River S.S.* the contract (to provide and install a turbine in connection with the building of a vessel) was not maritime and an action sounding in contract would not be within the admiralty jurisdiction and would be governed by state law.

Cf. Miller Industries v. Caterpillar Tractor Co., 733 F.2d 813, 1984 A.M.C. 2559 (11th Cir.1984) in which the court of appeals affirmed a judgment for a vessel owner for economic loss due to the malfunction of an engine installed in a new fishing vessel and for crew members for loss of their share of the lost catch. Because the court found negligence, it found it unnecessary to address the question of strict liability or breach of warranty. In *East River S.S.* the Court noted the *Miller* decision and others allowing recovery, suggesting that they seem to have been based upon a special solicitude for fishermen. It did not rule on the fisherman exception.

East River Steamship has been applied to a defect in the manufacture of the hydraulic system of a fishing boat which caused a fire that resulted in the loss of the boat, her equipment, and catch. The whole boat was treated as the product and recovery for the hull, skiff, net, fuel, spare parts, and miscellaneous equipment was denied, but recovery on the theory of strict liability was allowed for the loss of the "other property," including skiff, net, fuel, spare parts and miscellaneous equipment, and for crew losses, rescue costs and cash, together with the catch. Saratoga Fishing Co. v. Marco Seattle Inc., 69 F.3d 1432 (9th Cir.1995).

NOTE ON INDEMNITY AND CONTRIBUTION

From among the alternatives described in the Restatement (Second) of Torts on the question of settlement with one or more tortfeasors, the Supreme Court has selected the proportional fault rule. See McDermott, Inc. v. AmClyde and River Don Castings, Ltd., 511 U.S. ___, 114 S.Ct. 1461, 128 L.Ed.2d 148, 1994 A.M.C. 1521 (1994).

The Court pointed out that the proportional fault rule on settlement is compatable with the rule of joint and several liability.

M. Muratore v. M/S Scotia Prince

United States Court of Appeals, First Circuit, 1988.
845 F.2d 347, 1993 A.M.C. 2933.

■ HECTOR M. LAFFITTE, D.J.:

* * *

V. Punitive Damages

[After finding no error in the award of compensatory damages] We, however, take a different tack as to the award for punitive damages. We commence with the proposition that punitive damages may be awarded in maritime tort actions where defendant's actions were intentional, deliberate or so wanton and reckless as to demonstrate a conscious disregard of the rights of others. See The Amiable Nancy, 16 U.S. (3 Wheat.) 546 (1818); Protectus Alpha Navigation Co. v. North Pacific Grain Growers, Inc., 767 F.2d 1379, 1385 (9 Cir.1985); Complaint of Merry Shipping, Inc., 650 F.2d 622, 624–25 & n. 9 (5 Cir.1981); rehearing denied sub nom. Dyer v. Merry Shipping Co., Inc., 659 F.2d 1079 (5 Cir.1981); In Re Marine Sulphur Queen, 460 F.2d 89, 105 (2 Cir.1972), cert. denied, 409 U.S. 982, 93 S.Ct. 318, 34 L.Ed.2d 246 (1972); Robinson v. Pocahontas, Inc., 477 F.2d 1048, 1051–52 (1 Cir.1973); Pino v. Protection Maritime Ins. Co., Ltd., 490 F.Supp. 277, 281 (D.Mass.1980).[5] The purpose served for awarding exemplary damages to a fully compensated plaintiff is to punish defendant and to deter others from engaging in like manner. Lake Shore & M.S.R Co. v. Prentice, 147 U.S.101 (1893); Prosser, supra at 7–9. An

---

5. Awards for punitive damages have been under much controversy. See generally, Prosser, supra at 11–13. In fact, pending before the Supreme Court is whether a $1.6 million punitive damages award violates the excessive fines clause of the Eighth Amendment. *Bankers Life & Casualty Co. v. Crenshaw*, No. 85–1765. See ABA Journal, *The Constitutionality of Punitive Damages*, December 1, 1987. In our case, Prince had moved to alter the judgment before the lower court on the ground that it violated the First Amendment. Prince, however, did not raise this issue of the constitutionality of punitive damages, and therefore, that particular issue is not before this Court

award of punitive damages is within the sound discretion of the trial court unless clearly erroneous. *Marine Sulphur Queen*, 460 F.2d at 105.

The issue faced in this case is whether or not the district court clearly erred in awarding punitive damages against defendant carrier for the intentional infliction of emotional distress committed by the photographers against plaintiff-passenger. Prince asserts that there is no evidence in the record to support the district court's conclusion that Prince knew of the conduct of the photographers, or ratified it. We agree.

When a principal has neither authorized nor ratified the conduct of her servant, the courts are split on whether to hold the principal liable for punitive damages. A majority of courts have awarded punitive damages against corporations or principals for the tortious acts of their agents regardless of approval or ratification. American Society of Mechanical Engineers, Inc. v. Hydrolevel Corp., 456 U.S. 556, 575 n. 14 (1982)(citing Prosser, supra at 12). The rationale for this view is that it is in accordance with agency law that holds principals liable when their agents commit a tortious act with apparent authority. Id. at 566. A significant minority of courts following the Supreme Court decision in Lake Shore & M.S.R. Co. v. Prentice, 147 U.S. 101 (1893), have held that a master cannot be held liable for the acts of her agent when the master has neither authorized nor ratified such conduct.[6] Prosser, supra at 12. This position is followed by the Restatement (Second) of Torts in § 909.[7] Under the Restatement (Second) standard, punitive damages award is appropriate in circumstances where the principal authorizes or ratifies the agent's act or if the agent is employed in a managerial capacity and was acting within the scope of employment. Unlike *Lake Shore*, the Restatement (Second) standard would place liability on a master when a servant was in a "managerial capacity" performing within the scope of his or her employment regardless of the master's authorization or ratification. Protectus Alpha Navigation Co., 767 F.2d at 1386; Thyssen, Inc. v. S.S. Fortune Star, 777 F.2d 57, 67 (2 Cir.1985). This is a matter of first impression in this Circuit. We decide it as one of federal admiralty law. Although we understand the district court's reasons for choosing the majority view expressed in Goddard U (Srand Trunk Ry., 57 Me. 202, 223–28 (1869)), we believe that a more limited view should be taken. The *Lake Shore* rule is the "touchstone." The rationale for this rule is to ensure that punitive damages are

---

6. The Supreme Court mentioned in a footnote that the Court may have deviated from the trend of the late 1900s in deciding *Lake Shore*, 147 U.S. 101. *American Society of Mechanical Engineers*, Inc., 456 U.S. at 575 n. 14.

7. Section 909 of the Restatement (Second) of Torts states:

Punitive damages can properly be awarded against a master or other principal because of an act by an agent if, but only if,

(a) the principal or a managerial agent authorized the doing and the manner of the act, or

(b) the agent was unfit and the principal or a managerial agent was reckless in employing or retaining him, or (c) the agent was employed in a managerial capacity and was acting in the scope of employment, or

(d) the principal or a managerial agent of the principal ratified or approved the act.

awarded against the guilty offender. Hence, "(a) principal, ... though of course liable to make compensation for injuries done by his agent within the scope of his employment, cannot be held liable for exemplary or punitive damages merely by reason of wanton, oppressive or malicious intent on the part of the agent." 147 U.S. at 107–108. We do not decide today whether, as other circuits apparently believe, *Lake Shore* should be expanded to encompass the Restatement (Second) outlook. Whether this Court applies Lake Shore's strict "complicity rule" or the more relaxed standard in § 909 of the Restatement (Second) to this case, the result is the same. Plaintiff cannot be awarded punitive damages. Under the strict complicity rule, the court must determine whether or not there was knowledge or ratification on the part of the principal. In the present case, the record is barren of any evidence to demonstrate Prince's knowledge or ratification of the photographers' misconduct. In fact, both Giuseppe Ravenna, the Hotel Manager, and Henk Pols, the President and General Manager, of Prince testified at trial that they had no prior knowledge of the photographers' activities. After the Hotel Manager learned of the photographers' behavior, he insisted that the photographers apologize to plaintiff. He also sent a memorandum to his superiors stating that he had severely reprimanded the photographers. There was no showing that the photographers had indulged in such antics on prior occasions, or that, because of some "track record," a reasonably conscientious charterer would have had reason to suspect that they would harass passengers on this voyage. Punitive damages cannot be imposed upon Prince since plaintiff did not show that Prince approved or ratified the outrageous conduct of the photographers. It would be unfair to punish the charterer when it was not aware actually or constructively of its staff's misconduct and had not encouraged such misconduct.

Under the *Restatement (Second)* standard, a principal may be held liable if the agent was employed in a managerial capacity and acting under the scope of employment or there was authorization, ratification or approval by the principal. For instance, in *Protectus Alpha*, 767 F.2d 1379, the Ninth Circuit recently upheld a punitive damages award against a shipowner. In that case, a fire broke out aboard the defendant's vessel. When the flames were being brought under control by the local firefighters and Coast Guard, the dock foreman cast off the ship without consulting the firefighters and in disregard of the Fire Department's order. In applying the *Restatement (Second)* standard, the court determined that a dock foreman clearly held a managerial position and the dock foreman committed the tortious conduct while he was acting within the scope of his employment. 767 F.2d at 1386. The court, because of these facts, concluded that the shipowner would be liable for punitive damages regardless of corporate authorization or ratification.[8] In the case at hand, the photographers

---

8. But see McGuffie v. Transworld Drilling Co., 625 F.Supp. 369 (W.D.La.1985)(explicitly rejecting reasoning of *Protectus Alpha* in favor of *Lake Shore* strict complicity theory).

obviously did not occupy a managerial position and therefore Prince cannot be held liable for punitive damages.

In this particular case, Prince cannot be held liable because (1) it neither authorized nor ratified the photographers' misbehavior, (2) it had no reason to suspect—and was not aware of—such misconduct until after the fact, (3) it took appropriate action once it learned what had transpired, and (4) the photographers were not managerial agents.

The judgment awarding compensatory damages is affirmed. The award for punitive damages is vacated. Each party to bear its own costs. The case is remanded for the entry of a revised judgment consistent with this opinion.

NOTE

The practice in collision cases to award prejudgment interest except in "special circumstances" is applicable, as well, in non-collision cases. See, e.g., Vance v. American Hawaii Cruises, Inc., 789 F.2d 790 (9th Cir.1986), an action brought by a bedroom steward on a cruise ship in which prejudgment interest was denied and the court of appeals reversed and remanded for a statement of special circumstances.

See Ingram River Equipment, Inc. v. Pott Industries, Inc., 816 F.2d 1231 (8th Cir.1987)(award of prejudgment interest in judgment on maritime tort claim vacated on remand to the court of appeals by the Supreme Court after the decision in *East River*, despite the affirmance of the judgment for damages on a theory of breach of warranty under state law.)

The finding of peculiar circumstances justifying the denial of prejudgment interest is reviewed on a clearly erroneous standard, the failure to award interest on the basis of abuse of discretion. Orduna S.A. v. Zen–Noh Grain Corp., 913 F.2d 1149 (5th Cir.1990)(reversing refusal to award prejudgment interest).

CHAPTER 19

MARITIME LAW OF INDUSTRIAL ACCIDENTS

A. SEAMEN

1. WHO IS A SEAMAN

Chandris, Inc. v. Latsis

Supreme Court of the United States, 1995.
—— U.S. ——, 115 S.Ct. 2172, 132 L.Ed.2d 314.

■ JUSTICE O'CONNOR delivered the opinion of the Court.

This case asks us to clarify what "employment-related connection to a vessel in navigation," McDermott International, Inc. v. Wilander, 498 U.S. 337, 355, 111 S.Ct. 807, 817, 112 L.Ed.2d 866 (1991), is necessary for a maritime worker to qualify as a seaman under the Jones Act, 46 U.S.C.App. § 688(a). In *Wilander*, we addressed the type of activities that a seaman must perform and held that, under the Jones Act, a seaman's job need not be limited to transportation-related functions that directly aid in the vessel's navigation. We now determine what relationship a worker must have to the vessel, regardless of the specific tasks the worker undertakes, in order to obtain seaman status.

I

In May 1989, respondent Antonios Latsis was employed by petitioner Chandris, Inc., as a salaried superintendent engineer. Latsis was responsible for maintaining and updating the electronic and communications equipment on Chandris' fleet of vessels, which consisted of six passenger cruise ships. Each ship in the Chandris fleet carried between 12 and 14 engineers who were assigned permanently to that vessel. Latsis, on the other hand, was one of two supervising engineers based at Chandris' Miami office; his duties ran to the entire fleet and included not only overseeing the vessels' engineering departments, which required him to take a number of voyages, but also planning and directing ship maintenance from the shore. Latsis claimed at trial that he spent 72 percent of his time at sea, App. 58; his immediate supervisor testified that the appropriate figure was closer to 10 percent, id, at 180.

On May 14, 1989, Latsis sailed for Bermuda aboard the *S.S. Galileo* to plan for an upcoming renovation of the ship, which was one of the older vessels in the Chandris fleet. Latsis developed a problem with his right eye

844

on the day of departure, and he saw the ship's doctor as the *Galileo* left port. The doctor diagnosed a suspected detached retina but failed to follow standard medical procedure, which would have been to direct Latsis to see an ophthalmologist on an emergency basis. Instead, the ship's doctor recommended that Latsis relax until he could see an eye specialist when the *Galileo* arrived in Bermuda two days later. No attempt was made to transport Latsis ashore for prompt medical care by means of a pilot vessel or helicopter during the 11 hours it took the ship to reach the open sea from Baltimore, and Latsis received no further medical care until after the ship arrived in Bermuda. In Bermuda, a doctor diagnosed a detached retina and recommended immediate hospitalization and surgery. Although the operation was a partial success, Latsis lost 75 percent of his vision in his right eye.

Following his recuperation, which lasted approximately six weeks, Latsis resumed his duties with Chandris. On September 30, 1989, he sailed with the *Galileo* to Bremerhaven, Germany, where the vessel was placed in drydock for a 6–month refurbishment. After the conversion, the company renamed the vessel the *S.S. Meridian*. Latsis, who had been with the ship the entire time it was in drydock in Bremerhaven, sailed back to the United States on board the *Meridian* and continued to work for Chandris until November 1990, when his employment was terminated for reasons that are not clear from the record.

In October 1991, Latsis filed suit in the United States District Court for the Southern District of New York seeking compensatory damages under the Jones Act, 46 U.S.C.App. § 688, for the negligence of the ship's doctor that resulted in the significant loss of sight in Latsis' right eye. The Jones Act provides, in pertinent part, that "[a]ny seaman who shall suffer personal injury in the course of his employment may, at his election, maintain an action for damages at law, with the right of trial by jury. . . ." The District Court instructed the jury that it could conclude that Latsis was a seaman within the meaning of the statute if it found as follows:

> "[T]he plaintiff was either permanently assigned to the vessel or performed a substantial part of his work on the vessel. In determining whether Mr. Latsis performed a substantial part of his work on the vessel, you may not consider the period of time the *Galileo* was in drydock in Germany, because during that time period she was out of navigation. You may, however, consider the time spent sailing to and from Germany for the conversion. Also, on this first element of being a seaman, seamen do not include land-based workers." App. 210.

The parties stipulated to the District Court's second requirement for Jones Act coverage—that Latsis' duties contributed to the accomplishment of the missions of the Chandris vessels. Id., at 211. Latsis did not object to the seaman status jury instructions in their entirety, but only contested that portion of the charge which explicitly took from the jury's consideration the period of time that the *Galileo* was in drydock. The jury returned a verdict in favor of Chandris solely on the issue of Latsis' status as a seaman under the Jones Act. Id., at 213.

Respondent appealed to the Court of Appeals for the Second Circuit, which vacated the judgment and remanded the case for a new trial. 20 F.3d 45 (1994). The court emphasized that its longstanding test for seaman status under the Jones Act required " 'a more or less permanent connection with the ship,' " Salgado v. M.J. Rudolph Corp., 514 F.2d 750, 755 (C.A.2 1975), a connection that need not be limited to time spent on the vessel but could also be established by the nature of the work performed. The court thought that the alternate formulation employed by the District Court (permanent assignment to the vessel or performance of a substantial part of his work on the vessel), which was derived from Offshore Co. v. Robison, 266 F.2d 769, 779 (C.A.5 1959), improperly framed the issue for the jury primarily, if not solely, in terms of Latsis' temporal relationship to the vessel. With that understanding of what the language of the *Robison* test implied, the court concluded that the District Court's seaman status jury instructions constituted plain error under established circuit precedent. The court then took this case as an opportunity to clarify its seaman status requirements, directing the District Court that the jury should be instructed on remand as follows:

> "[T]he test of seaman status under the Jones Act is an employment-related connection to a vessel in navigation. The test will be met where a jury finds that (1) the plaintiff contributed to the function of or helped accomplish the mission of, a vessel; (2) the plaintiff's contribution was limited to a particular vessel or identifiable group of vessels; (3) the plaintiff's contribution was substantial in terms of its (a) duration or (b) nature; and (4) the course of the plaintiff's employment regularly exposed the plaintiff to the hazards of the sea." 20 F.3d, at 57.

Elsewhere on the same page, however, the court phrased the third prong as requiring a substantial connection in terms of both duration *and* nature. Finally, the Court of Appeals held that the District Court erred in instructing the jury that the time Latsis spent with the ship while it was in drydock could not count in the substantial connection equation. Id., at 55–56. Judge Kearse dissented, arguing that the drydock instruction was not erroneous and that the remainder of the charge did not constitute plain error. Id., at 58.

* * *

II

* * *

A

In *Wilander*, decided in 1991, the Court attempted for the first time in 33 years to clarify the definition of a "seaman" under the Jones Act. Jon Wilander was injured while he worked as a foreman supervising the sandblasting and painting of various fixtures and piping on oil drilling platforms in the Persian Gulf. His employer claimed that he could not qualify as a seaman because he did not aid in the navigation function of the vessels on which he served. Emphasizing that the question presented was narrow, we considered whether the term "seaman" is limited to only those maritime workers who aid in a vessel's navigation.

After surveying the history of an "aid in navigation" requirement under both the Jones Act and general maritime law, we concluded that "all those with that 'peculiar relationship to the vessel' are covered under the Jones Act, regardless of the particular job they perform," 498 U.S., at 354, 111 S.Ct., at 817, and that "the better rule is to define 'master or member of a crew' under the LHWCA, and therefore 'seaman' under the Jones Act, solely in terms of the employee's connection to a vessel in navigation," ibid. Thus, we held that, although "[i]t is not necessary that a seaman aid in navigation or contribute to the transportation of the vessel, . . . a seaman must be doing the ship's work." Id, at 355, 111 S.Ct., at 817. We explained that "[t]he key to seaman status is employment-related connection to a vessel in navigation," and that, although "[w]e are not called upon here to define this connection in all details, . . . we believe the requirement that an employee's duties must 'contribut[e] to the function of the vessel or to the accomplishment of its mission' captures well an important requirement of seaman status." Ibid.

Beyond dispensing with the "aid to navigation" requirement, however, *Wilander* did not consider the requisite connection to a vessel in any detail and therefore failed to end the prevailing confusion regarding seaman status.

B

Respondent urges us to find our way out of the Jones Act "labyrinth" by focusing on the seemingly activity-based policy underlying the statute (the protection of those who are exposed to the perils of the sea), and to conclude that anyone working on board a vessel for the duration of a "voyage" in furtherance of the vessel's mission has the necessary employment-related connection to qualify as a seaman. Brief for Respondent 12–17. Such an approach, however, would run counter to our prior decisions and our understanding of the remedial scheme Congress has established for injured maritime workers. A brief survey of the Jones Act's tortured history makes clear that we must reject the initial appeal of such a "voyage" test and undertake the more difficult task of developing a status-based standard that, although it determines Jones Act coverage without regard to the precise activity in which the worker is engaged at the time of the injury, nevertheless best furthers the Jones Act's remedial goals.

Our Jones Act cases establish several basic principles regarding the definition of a seaman. First, "[w]hether under the Jones Act or general maritime law, seamen do not include land-based workers." *Wilander*, supra, at 348, 111 S.Ct., at 814; see also Allbritton, Seaman Status in *Wilander's* Wake, 68 Tulane L. Rev. 373, 387 (1994). Our early Jones Act decisions had not recognized this fundamental distinction. In International Stevedoring Co. v. Haverty, 272 U.S. 50, 47 S.Ct. 19, 71 L.Ed. 157 (1926), we held that a longshoreman injured while stowing cargo, and while aboard but not employed by a vessel at dock in navigable waters, was a seaman covered by the Jones Act. Recognizing that "for most purposes, as the word is commonly used, stevedores are not 'seamen,' " the Court nevertheless concluded that "[w]e cannot believe that Congress willingly would have allowed the protection to men engaged upon the same maritime duties to vary with the accident of their being employed by a stevedore rather than by the ship." Id., at 52, 47 S.Ct., at 19. Because stevedores are engaged in "a maritime service formerly rendered by the ship's crew," ibid (citing Atlantic Transport Co. of W.Va. v. Imbrovek, 234 U.S. 52, 62, 34 S.Ct. 733, 735, 58 L.Ed. 1208 (1914)), we concluded, they should receive the Jones Act's protections. See also Uravic v. F. Jarka Co., 282 U.S. 234, 238, 51 S.Ct. 111, 112, 75 L.Ed. 312 (1931); Jamison v. Encarnacion, 281 U.S. 635, 639, 50 S.Ct. 440, 442, 74 L.Ed. 1082 (1930). In 1946, the Court belatedly recognized that Congress had acted, in passing the LHWCA in 1927, to undercut the Court's reasoning in the *Haverty* line of cases and to emphasize that land-based maritime workers should not be entitled to the seamen's traditional remedies. Our decision in Swanson v. Marra Brothers, Inc., 328 U.S. 1, 7, 66 S.Ct. 869, 872, 90 L.Ed. 1045 (1946), acknowledged that Congress had expressed its intention to "confine the benefits of the Jones Act to the members of the crew of a vessel plying in navigable waters and to substitute for the right of recovery recognized by the *Haverty* case only such rights to compensation as are given by [the LHWCA]." See also South Chicago Coal & Dock Co. v. Bassett, 309 U.S. 251, 257, 60 S.Ct. 544, 547–548, 84 L.Ed. 732 (1940). Through the LHWCA, therefore, Congress "explicitly den[ied] a right of recovery under the Jones Act to maritime workers not members of a crew who are injured on board a vessel." *Swanson*, supra, at 6, 66 S.Ct., at 871. And this recognition process culminated in *Wilander* in the Court's statement that, "[w]ith the passage of the LHWCA, Congress established a clear distinction between land-based and sea-based maritime workers. The latter, who owe their allegiance to a vessel and not solely to a land-based employer, are seamen." 498 U.S., at 347, 111 S.Ct. at 813.

In addition to recognizing a fundamental distinction between land-based and sea-based maritime employees, our cases also emphasize that Jones Act coverage, like the jurisdiction of admiralty over causes of action for maintenance and cure for injuries received in the course of a seamen's employment, depends "not on the place where the injury is inflicted ... but on the nature of the seaman's service, his status as a member of the vessel, and his relationship as such to the vessel and its operation in navigable waters." *Swanson* supra, at 4, 66 S.Ct., at 871. Thus, maritime workers who obtain seaman status do not lose that protection automatically when on shore and may recover under the Jones Act whenever they are injured in the the service of a vessel, regardless of whether the injury occurs on or off the ship. In O'Donnell v.Great Lakes Dredge & Dock Co., 318 U.S. 36, 63 S.Ct. 488, 87 L.Ed. 596 (1943), the Court held a shipowner liable for injuries caused to a seaman by a fellow crew member while the former was on shore repairing a conduit that was a part of the vessel and that was used for discharging the ship's cargo. We explained: "The right of recovery in the Jones Act is given to the seaman as such, and, as in the case of maintenance and cure, the admiralty jurisdiction over the suit depends not on the place where the injury is inflicted but on the nature of the service and its relationship to the operation of the vessel plying in navigable waters." Id., at 42–43, 63 S.Ct., at 492. Similarly, the Court in *Swanson* emphasized that the LHWCA "leaves unaffected the rights of members of the crew of a vessel to recover under the Jones Act when injured while pursuing their maritime employment whether on board ... or on shore." 328 U.S., at 7–8, 66 S.Ct., at 872. See also Braen v. Pfeifer Oil Transp. Co., 361 U.S. 129, 131–132, 80 S.Ct. 247, 249. 4 L.Ed.2d 191 (1959).

Our LHWCA cases also recognize the converse: land-based maritime workers injured while on a vessel in navigation remain covered by the LHWCA, which expressly provides compensation for injuries to certain workers engaged in "maritime employment" that are incurred "upon the navigable waters of the United States," 33 U.S.C. § 903(a). Thus, in Director OWCP v. Perini North River Associates, 459 U.S. 297, 103 S.Ct. 634, 74 L.Ed.2d 465 (1983), we held that a worker injured while "working on a barge in actual navigable waters" of the Hudson River, Id. at 300, n. 4, 103 S.Ct., at 638, n. 4, could be compensated under the LHWCA, Id. at 324, 103 S.Ct., at 651. See also Parker v. Motor Boat Sales, Inc., 314 U.S. 244, 244–245, 62 S.Ct. 221, 222, 86 L.Ed. 184 (1941)(upholding LHWCA coverage for a worker testing outboard motors who "was drowned when a motor boat in which he was riding capsized"). These decisions, which reflect our longstanding view of the LHWCA's scope, indicate that a maritime worker does not become a "member of a crew" as soon as a vessel leaves the dock.

It is therefore well settled after decades of judicial interpretation that the Jones Act inquiry is fundamentally status-based: land-based maritime workers do not become seamen because they happen to be working on board a vessel when they are injured, and seamen do not lose Jones Act protection when the course of their service to a vessel takes them ashore. In spite of this background, respondent and Justice STEVENS suggest that any maritime worker who is assigned to a vessel for the duration of a voyage—and whose duties contribute to the vessel's mission—should be classified as a seaman for purposes of injuries incurred during that voyage. See Brief for Respondent 14; *post*, at 1 (STEVENS, J., concurring in the judgment). Under such a "voyage test," which relies principally upon this Court's statements that the Jones Act was designed to protect maritime workers who are exposed to the "special hazards" and "particular perils" characteristic of work on vessels at sea, see, e.g., *Wilander*, supra, at 354, 111 S.Ct., at 817, the worker's activities at the time of the injury would be controlling.

The difficulty with respondent's argument, as the foregoing discussion makes clear, is that the LHWCA repudiated the *Haverty* line of cases and established that a worker is no longer considered to be a seaman simply because he is doing a seaman's work at the time of the injury. Seaman status is not coextensive with seamen's risks. See, e.g., Easley v. Southern Shipbuilding Corp., 965 F.2d 1, 4–5 (C.A.5 1992), cert. denied, 506 U.S.

1050, 113 S.Ct. 969, 122 L.Ed.2d 124 (1993); Robertson 93 (following "the overwhelming weight of authority in taking it as given that seaman status cannot be established by any worker who fails to demonstrate that a significant portion of his work was done aboard a vessel" and acknowledging that "[s]ome workers who unmistakably confront the perils of the sea, often in extreme form, are thereby left out of the seamen's protections" (footnote omitted)). A "voyage test" would conflict with our prior understanding of the Jones Act as fundamentally status-based, granting the negligence cause of action to those maritime workers who form the ship's company. *Swanson*, supra, at 4–5, 66 S.Ct., at 871; *O'Donnell*, supra, at 42–43, 63 S.Ct., at 492.

* * *

To say that our cases have recognized a distinction between land-based and sea-based maritime workers that precludes application of a voyage test for seaman status, however, is not to say that a maritime employee must work *only* on board a vessel to qualify as a seaman under the Jones Act. In Southwest Marine, Inc. v. Gizoni, 502 U.S. 81, 112 S.Ct. 486, 116 L.Ed.2d 405 (1991), decided only a few months after *Wilander*, we concluded that a worker's status as a repairman, one of the enumerated occupations encompassed within the term "employee" under the LHWCA, 33 U.S.C. § 902(3), did not necessarily restrict the worker to a remedy under that statute. We explained that, "[w]hile in some cases a ship repairman may lack the requisite connection to a vessel in navigation to qualify for seaman status, . . . not all ship repairmen lack the requisite connection as a matter of law. This is so because '[i]t is not the employee's particular job that is determinative, but the employee's connection to a vessel.'" *Gizoni*, supra, at 89, 112 S.Ct., at 492 (quoting *Wilander*, 498 U.S., at 354, 111 S.Ct., at 817) (footnote omitted). Thus, we concluded, the Jones Act remedy may be available to maritime workers who are employed by a shipyard and who spend a portion of their time working on shore but spend the rest of their time at sea.

Beyond these basic themes, which are sufficient to foreclose respondent's principal argument, our cases are largely silent as to the precise relationship a maritime worker must bear to a vessel in order to come within the Jones Act's ambit. We have, until now, left to the lower federal courts the task of developing appropriate criteria to distinguish the "ship's company" from those members of the maritime community whose employment is essentially land-based.

C

The Court of Appeals for the First Circuit was apparently the first to develop a generally applicable test for seaman status. In Carumbo v. Cape Cod S.S. Co., 123 F.2d 991 (C.A.1 1941), the court retained the pre-*Swanson* view that "the word 'seaman' under the Jones Act did not mean the same thing as 'member of a crew' under the [LHWCA]," id., at 994. It concluded that "one who does any sort of work aboard a ship in navigation is a 'seaman' within the meaning of the Jones Act." Id., at 995. The phrase "member of a crew," on the other hand, the court gave a more restrictive meaning.   The court adopted three elements to define the phrase that had been used at various times in prior cases, holding that "[t]he requirements that the ship be in navigation; that there be a more or less permanent connection with the ship; and that the worker be aboard primarily to aid in navigation appear to us to be the essential and decisive elements of the definition of a 'member of a crew.'"   Ibid.   Cf. *Senko*, supra, at 375, 77 S.Ct., at 418 (Harlan, J.,dissenting)("According to past decisions, to be a 'member of a crew' an individual must have some connection, more or less permanent, with a ship and a ship's company"). Once it became clear that the phrase "master or member of a crew" from the LHWCA is coextensive with the term "seaman" in the Jones Act, courts accepted the *Carumbo* formulation of master or member of a crew in the Jones Act context.   See Boyd v. Ford Motor Co., 948 F.2d 283 (C.A.6 1991); Estate of Wenzel v. Seaward Marine Services, Inc., 709 F.2d 1326, 1327 (C.A.9 1983); Whittington v. Sewer Constr. Co., 541 F.2d 427, 436 (C.A.4 1976); Griffith v. Wheeling Pittsburgh Steel Corp., 521 F.2d 31, 36 (C.A.3 1975), cert. denied, 423 U.S. 1054, 96 S.Ct. 785, 46 L.Ed.2d 643 (1976); McKie v. Diamond Marine Co., 204 F.2d 132, 136 (C.A.5 1953). The Court of Appeals for the Second Circuit initially was among the jurisdictions to adopt the *Carumbo* formulation as a basis of its seaman status inquiry, see Salgado v. M.J. Rudolph Corp., 514 F.2d, at 755, but that court took the instant case as an opportunity to modify the traditional test somewhat (replacing the "more or less permanent connection" prong with a requirement that the connection be "substantial in terms of its (a) duration and (b) nature"), 20 F.3d, at 57.

The second major body of seaman status law developed in the Court of Appeals for the Fifth Circuit, which has a substantial Jones Act caseload, in the wake of Offshore Co. v. Robison, 266 F.2d 769 (C.A.5 1959).   At the time of his injury, Robison was an oil worker permanently assigned to a drilling rig mounted on a barge in the Gulf of Mexico.   In sustaining the jury's award of damages to Robison under the Jones Act, the court abandoned the aid in navigation requirement of the traditional test and held as follows:

> "[T]here is an evidentiary basis for a Jones Act case to go to the jury: (1) if there is evidence that the injured workman was assigned permanently to a vessel ... or performed a substantial part of his work on the vessel; and (2) if the capacity in which he was employed or the duties which he performed contributed to the function of the vessel or the accomplishment of its mission, or to the operation or welfare of the vessel in terms of its maintenance during its movement or during anchorage for its future trips." Id., at 779 (footnote omitted).

Soon after *Robison*, the Fifth Circuit modified the test to allow seaman status for those workers who had the requisite connection with an "identifiable fleet" of vessels, a finite group of vessels under common ownership or control.   Braniff v. Jackson Avenue–Gretna Ferry, Inc., 280 F.2d 523, 528 (1960).   See also *Barrett*, 781 F.2d, at 1074; Bertrand v. International Mooring & Marine, Inc., 700 F.2d 240 (C.A.5 1983), cert. denied, 464 U.S.

1069, 104 S.Ct. 974, 79 L.Ed.2d 212 (1984). The modified *Robison* formulation, which replaced the Carumbo version as the definitive test for seaman status in the Fifth Circuit, has been highly influential in other courts as well. See Robertson 95; Miller v. Patton–Tully Transp. Co., 851 F.2d 202, 204 (C.A.8 1988); Caruso v. Sterling Yacht & Shipbuilders, Inc., 828 F.2d 14, 15 (C.A.11 1987); Bennett v. Perini Corp., 510 F.2d 114, 115 (C.A.1 1975).

While the *Carumbo* and *Robison* approaches may not seem all that different at first glance, subsequent developments in the Fifth Circuit's Jones Act jurisprudence added a strictly temporal gloss to the Jones Act inquiry. Under Barrett v. Chevron, U.S.A., Inc., supra, if an employee's regular duties require him to divide his time between vessel and land, his status as a crew member is determined "in the context of his entire employment" with his current employer. Id., at 1075. See also Allbritton, 68 Tulane L.Rev., at 386; *Longmire*, 610 F.2d, at 1347 (explaining that a worker's seaman status "should be addressed with reference to the nature and location of his occupation taken as a whole"). In *Barrett*, the court noted that the worker "performed seventy to eighty percent of his work on platforms and no more than twenty to thirty percent of his work on vessels" and then concluded that, "[b]ecause he did not perform a substantial portion of his work aboard a vessel or fleet of vessels, he failed to establish that he was a member of the crew of a vessel." 781 F.2d, at 1076. Since *Barrett* the Fifth Circuit consistently has analyzed the problem in terms of the percentage of work performed on vessels for the employer in question—and has declined to find seaman status where the employee spent less than 30 percent of his time aboard ship. See, e.g., Palmer v. Fayard Moving & Transp., Corp., 930 F.2d 437, 439 (C.A.5 1991); Lormand v. Superior Oil Co., 845 F.2d 536, 541 (C.A.5 1987), cert. denied, 484 U.S. 1031, 108 S.Ct. 739, 98 L.Ed.2d 774 (1988); cf. Leonard v. Dixie Well Service & Supply, Inc., 828 F.2d 291, 295 (C.A.5 1987); Pickle v. International Oilfield Divers, Inc., 791 F.2d 1237, 1240 (C.A.5 1986), cert. denied, 479 U.S. 1059, 107 S.Ct. 939, 93 L.Ed.2d 989 (1987).

Although some courts of appeals have varied the applicable tests to some degree, see, e.g., Johnson v. John F. Beasley Constr. Co., 742 F.2d, at 1062–1063, the traditional *Carumbo* seaman status formulation and the subsequent *Robison* modification are universally recognized, and one or the other is applied in every federal circuit to have considered the issue. See Bull, Seaman Status Revisited: A Practical Guide To Status Determination, 6 U.S.F.Mar.L.J. 547, 562–572 (1994)(collecting eases). The federal courts generally require at least a significant connection to a vessel in navigation (or to an identifiable fleet of vessels) for a maritime worker to qualify as a seaman under the Jones Act. Although the traditional test requires a "more or less permanent connection" and the *Robison* formulation calls for "substantial" work aboard a vessel, "this general requirement varies little, if at all, from one jurisdiction to another," id., at 587, and "[t]he courts have repeatedly held that the relationship creating seaman status must be substantial in point of time and work, and not merely sporadic." Id. at 587–588.

D

From this background emerge the essential contours of the "employment-related connection to a vessel in navigation." *Wilander*, 498 U.S., at 355, 111 S.Ct., at 817, required for an employee to qualify as a seaman under the Jones Act. We have said that, in giving effect to the term "seaman," our concern must be "to define the meaning for the purpose of a particular statute" and that its use in the Jones Act "must be read in the light of the mischief to be corrected and the end to be attained." *Warner*, 293 U.S., at 158, 55 S.Ct., at 48. Giving effect to those guiding principles, we think that the essential requirements for seaman status are twofold. First, as we emphasized in *Wilander*, "an employee's duties must 'contribut[e] to the function of the vessel or to the accomplishment of its mission.'" 498 U.S., at 355, 111 S.Ct., at 817 (quoting *Robison*, 266 F.2d, at 779). The Jones Act's protections, like the other admiralty protections for seamen, only extend to those maritime employees who do the ship's work. But this threshold requirement is very broad: "[a]ll who work at sea in the service of a ship" are eligible for seaman status. 498 U.S., at 354, 111 S.Ct., at 817.

Second, and most important for our purposes here, a seaman must have a connection to a vessel in navigation (or to an identifiable group of such vessels) that is substantial in terms of both its duration and its nature. The fundamental purpose of this substantial connection requirement is to give full effect to the remedial scheme created by Congress and to separate the sea-based maritime employees who are entitled to Jones Act protection from those land-based workers who have only a transitory or sporadic connection to a vessel in navigation, and therefore whose employment does not regularly expose them to the perils of the sea. See 1B A. Jenner, Benedict on Admiralty, § lla, pp. 2–10.1 to 2–11 (7th ed. 1994)("If it can be shown that the employee performed a significant part of his work on board the vessel on which he was injured, with at least some degree of regularity and continuity, the test for seaman status will be satisfied" (footnote omitted)). This requirement therefore determines which maritime employees in *Wilander's* broad category of persons eligible for seaman status because they are "doing the ship's work," 498 U.S., at 355, 111 S.Ct., at 817, are in fact entitled to the benefits conferred upon seamen by the Jones Act because they have the requisite employment-related connection to a vessel in navigation .

It is important to recall that the question of who is a "member of a crew," and therefore who is a "seaman," is a mixed question of law and fact. Because statutory terms are at issue, their interpretation is a question of law and it is the court's duty to define the appropriate standard. *Wilander*, 498 U.S., at 356, 111 S.Ct., at 818. On the other hand, "[i]f reasonable persons, applying the proper legal standard, could differ as to whether the employee was a 'member of a crew,' it is a question for the jury." Ibid. See also *Senko*, 352 U.S., at 374, 77 S.Ct., at 417 (explaining that "the determination of whether an injured person was a 'member of a crew' is to be left to the finder of fact" and that "a jury's decision is final if it has a reasonable basis"). The jury should be permitted, when determining whether a maritime employee has the requisite employment related connection to a vessel in navigation to qualify as a member of the vessel's crew, to consider all relevant circumstances bearing on the two elements outlined above.

In defining the prerequisites for Jones Act coverage, we think it preferable to focus upon the essence of what it means to be a seaman and to eschew the temptation to create detailed tests to effectuate the congressional purpose, tests that tend to become ends in and of themselves. The principal formulations employed by the Courts of Appeals—"more or less permanent assignment" or "connection to a vessel that is substantial in terms of its duration and nature"—are simply different ways of getting at the same basic point: the Jones Act remedy is reserved for sea-based maritime employees whose work regularly exposes them to "the special hazards and disadvantages to which they who go down to sea in ships are subjected." *Sieracki*, 328 U.S., at 104, 66 S.Ct., at 882 (Stone, C.J., dissenting). Indeed, it is difficult to discern major substantive differences in the language of the two phrases. In our view, "the total circumstances of an individual's employment must be weighed to determine whether he had a sufficient relation to the navigation of vessels and the perils attendant thereon." Wallace v. Oceaneering, Int'l, 727 F.2d 427, 432 (C.A.5th., 1984). The duration of a worker's connection to a vessel and the nature of the worker's activities, taken together, determine whether a maritime employee is a seaman because the ultimate inquiry is whether the worker in question is a member of the vessel's crew or simply a land-based employee who happens to be working on the vessel at a given time. Although we adopt the centerpiece of the formulation used by the Court of Appeals in this case—that a seaman must have a connection with a vessel in navigation that is substantial in both duration and nature—we should point out how our understanding of the import of that language may be different in some respects from that of the court below. The Court of Appeals suggested that its test for seaman status "does not unequivocally require a Jones Act seaman to be substantially connected to a vessel" in terms of time if the worker performs important work on board on a steady, although not necessarily on a temporally significant, basis. 20 F.3d, at 53. Perhaps giving effect to this intuition, or perhaps reacting to the temporal gloss placed on the *Robison* language by later Fifth Circuit decisions, the court phrased its standard at one point as requiring a jury to find that a Jones Act plaintiff's contribution to the function of the vessel was substantial in terms of its duration *or* nature. Id., at 57. It is not clear, which version ("duration or nature" as opposed to "duration and nature") the Court of Appeals intended to adopt for the substantial connection requirement—or indeed whether the court saw a significant difference between the two. Nevertheless, we think it is important that a seaman's connection to a vessel in fact be substantial in both respects.

We agree with the Court of Appeals that seaman status is not merely a temporal concept, but we also believe that it necessarily includes a temporal element. A maritime worker who spends only a small fraction of his working time on board a vessel is fundamentally land-based and therefore not a member of the vessel's crew, regardless of what his duties are. Naturally, substantiality in this context is determined by reference to the period covered by the Jones Act plaintiff's maritime employment, rather than by some absolute measure. Generally, the Fifth Circuit seems to have identified an appropriate rule of thumb for the ordinary case: a worker who spends less than about 30 percent of his time in the service of a vessel in navigation should not qualify as a seaman under the Jones Act. This figure of course serves as no more than a guideline established by years of experience, and departure from it will certainly be justified in appropriate cases. As we have said, "[t]he inquiry into seaman status is of necessity fact specific; it will depend on the nature of the vessel and the employee's precise relation to it." *Wilander*, 498 U.S., at 356, 111 S.Ct., at 818. Nevertheless, we believe that courts, employers, and maritime workers can all benefit from reference to these general principles. And where undisputed facts reveal that a maritime worker has a clearly inadequate temporal connection to vessels in navigation, the court may take the question from the jury by granting summary judgment or a directed verdict. See, e.g., *Palmer*, 930 F.2d, at 439.

On the other hand, we see no reason to limit the seaman status inquiry, as petitioners contend, exclusively to an examination of the overall course of a worker's service with a particular employer. Brief for Petitioners 14–15. When a maritime worker's basic assignment changes, his seaman status may change as well. See *Barrett*, 781 F.2d, at 1077 (Rubin, J., dissenting)("An assignment to work as a crew member, like the voyage of a vessel, may be brief, and the *Robison* test is applicable in deciding the worker's status during any such employment"); *Longwire*, 610 F.2d, at 1347, n. 6. For example, we can imagine situations in which someone who had worked for years in an employer's shoreside headquarters is then reassigned to a ship in a classic seaman's job that involves a regular and continuous, rather than intermittent, commitment of the worker's labor to the function of a vessel. Such a person should not be denied seaman status if injured shortly after the reassignment, just as someone actually transferred to a desk job in the company's office and injured in the hallway should not be entitled to claim seaman status on the basis of prior service at sea. If a maritime employee receives a new work assignment in which his essential duties are changed, he is entitled to have the assessment of the substantiality of his vessel-related work made on the basis of his activities in his new position. See *Cheavens*, 64 Tulane L.Rev., at 389 390. Thus, nothing in our opinion forecloses Jones Act coverage, in appropriate cases, for Justice STEVENS' paradigmatic maritime worker injured while reassigned to "a lengthy voyage on the high seas," post, at 2198. While our approach maintains the status-based inquiry this Court's earlier cases contemplate, we recognize that seaman status also should not be some immutable characteristic that maritime workers who spend only a portion of their time at sea can never attain.

III

One final issue remains for our determination: whether the District Court erred in instructing the jurors that, "[i]n determining whether Mr. Latsis performed a substantial part of his work on the vessel, [they could] not consider the period of time the *Galileo* was in drydock in Germany, because during that time period she was out of navigation." We agree with the Court of Appeals that it did.

The foregoing discussion establishes that, to qualify as a seaman under the Jones Act, a maritime employee must have a substantial employment-related connection to a vessel in navigation. See *Wilander,* supra, at 354–355, 111 S.Ct., at 817. Of course, any time Latsis spent with the *Galileo* while the ship was out of navigation could not count as time spent at sea for purposes of that inquiry, and it would have been appropriate for the District Court to make this clear to the jury. Yet the underlying inquiry whether a vessel is or is not "in navigation" for Jones Act purposes is a fact-intensive question that is normally for the jury and not the court to decide. See Butler v. Whiteman, 356 U.S. 271, 78 S.Ct. 734, 2 L.Ed.2d 754 (1958)(per curiam); 2 M. Norris, Law of Seamen, § 30.13, p. 363 (4th ed. 1985)("Whether the vessel is in navigation presents a question of fact to be determined by the trier of the facts. When the case is tried to a jury the fact question should be left to their consideration if sufficient evidence has been presented to provide the basis for jury consideration"). Removing the issue from the jury's consideration is only appropriate where the facts and the law will reasonably support only one conclusion, Anderson v. Liberty Lobby, Inc., 477 U.S. 242, 250–251, 106 S.Ct. 2505, 2511, 91 L.Ed.2d 202 (1986), and the colloquy between the court and counsel does not indicate that the District Court made any such findings before overruling respondent's objection to the drydock instruction. See Tr. 432. Based upon the record before us, we think the court failed adequately to justify its decision to remove the question whether the *Galileo* was "in navigation" while in Bremerhaven from the jury.

Under our precedent and the law prevailing in the circuits, it is generally accepted that "a vessel does not cease to be a vessel when she is not voyaging, but is at anchor, berthed, or at dockside," DiGiovanni v. Traylor Bros., Inc., 959 F.2d 1119, 1121 (CA1)(en banc), cert. denied, 506 U.S. 827, 113 S.Ct. 87, 121 L.Ed.2d 50 (1992), even when the vessel is undergoing repairs. See *Butler,* supra, at 271, 78 S.Ct., at 734; *Senko,* 352 U.S., at 373, 77 S.Ct., at 417; *Norris, supra,* at 364 ("[A] vessel is in navigation ... when it returns from a voyage and is taken to a drydock or shipyard to undergo repairs in preparation to making another trip, and likewise a vessel is in navigation, although moored to a dock, if it remains in readiness for another voyage" (footnotes omitted)). At some point, however, repairs become sufficiently significant that the vessel can no longer be considered in navigation. In West v. United States, 361 U.S. 118, 80 S.Ct. 189, 4 L.Ed.2d 161 (1959), we held that a shoreside worker was not entitled to recover for unseaworthiness because the vessel on which he was injured was undergoing an overhaul for the purpose of making her seaworthy and therefore had been withdrawn from navigation. We explained that, in such cases, "the focus should be upon the status of the ship, the pattern of the repairs, and the extensive nature of the work contracted to be done." Id., at 122, 80 S.Ct., at 192. See also United New York & New Jersey Sandy Hook Pilots Association v. Halecki, 358 U.S. 613, 79 S.Ct. 517, 3 L.Ed.2d 541 (1959); *Desper*, 342 U.S., at 191, 72 U.S., at 218. The general rule among the Courts of Appeals is that vessels undergoing repairs or spending a relatively short period of time in drydock are still considered to be "in navigation" whereas ships being transformed through "major" overhauls or renovations are not. See Bull, 6 U.S.F.Mar.L.J., at 582 584 (collecting cases).

Obviously, while the distinction at issue here is one of degree, the prevailing view is that "major renovations can take a ship out of navigation, even though its use before and after the work will be the same." McKinley v. All Alaskan Seafoods, Inc., 980 F.2d 567, 570 (C.A.9 1992). Our review of the record in this case uncovered relatively little evidence bearing on the *Galileo's* status during the repairs, and even less discussion of the question by the District Court. On the one hand, the work on the Chandris vessel took only about six months, which seems to be a relatively short period of time for important repairs on oceangoing vessels. Cf. id., at 571 (17–month-long project involving major structural changes took the vessel out of navigation); Wixom v. Boland Marine & Manufacturing Co., 614 F.2d 956 (C.A.5 1980)(similar 3–year project); see also *Senko*, supra, at 373, 77 S.Ct., at 417 (noting that "[e]ven a transoceanic liner may be confined to berth for lengthy periods, and while there the ship is kept in repair by its 'crew'"—and that "[t]here can be no doubt that a member of its crew would be covered by the Jones Act during this period, even though the ship was never in transit during his employment"). On the other hand, Latsis' own description of the work performed suggests that the modifications to the vessel were actually quite significant, including the removal of the ship's bottom plates and propellers, the addition of bow thrusters, overhaul of the main engines, reconstruction of the boilers, and renovations of the cabins and other passenger areas of the ship. See App. 93–94. On these facts, which are similar to those in McKinley, it is possible that Chandris could be entitled to partial summary judgment or a directed verdict concerning whether the *Galileo* remained in navigation while in drydock: the record, however, contains no stipulations or findings by the District Court to justify its conclusion that the modifications to the *Galileo* were sufficiently extensive to remove the vessel from navigation as a matter of law. On that basis, we agree with the Court of Appeals that the District Court's drydock instruction was erroneous.

Even if the District Court had been justified in directing a verdict on the question whether the *Galileo* remained in navigation while in Bremerhaven, we think that the court's charge to the jury swept too broadly. Instead of simply noting the appropriate legal conclusion and instructing the jury not to consider the time Latsis spent with the vessel in drydock as time spent with a vessel in navigation, the District Court appears to have prohibited the jury from considering Latsis' stay in Bremerhaven for any purpose. In our view, Latsis' activities while the vessel was in drydock are at least marginally relevant to the underlying inquiry (whether Latsis was a seaman and not a land-based maritime employee). Naturally, the jury would be free to draw several inferences from Latsis' work during the conversion, not all of which would be in his favor. But the choice among such permissible inferences should have been left to the jury, and we think the District Court's broadly worded instruction improperly deprived the jury of that opportunity by forbidding the consideration of Latsis' time in Bremerhaven at all.

IV

Under the Jones Act, "[i]f reasonable persons, applying the proper legal standard, could differ as to whether the employee was a 'member of a crew,' it is a question for the jury." *Wilander*, 498 U.S., at 356, 111 S.Ct., at 818. On the facts of this case, given that essential points are in dispute, reasonable factfinders could disagree as to whether Latsis was a seaman. Because the question whether the *Galileo* remained "in navigation" while in drydock should have been submitted to the jury, and because the decision on that issue might affect the outcome of the ultimate seaman status inquiry, we affirm the judgment of the Court of Appeals remanding the case to the District Court for a new trial.

On remand, the District Court should charge the jury in a manner consistent with our holding that the "employment-related connection to a vessel in navigation" necessary to qualify as a seaman under the Jones Act, id., at 355, 111 S.Ct., at 817, comprises two basic elements: the worker's duties must contribute to the function of the vessel or to the accomplishment of its mission, and the worker must have a connection to a vessel in navigation (or an identifiable group of vessels) that is substantial in terms of both its duration and its nature. As to the latter point, the court should emphasize that the Jones Act was intended to protect seabased maritime workers, who owe their allegiance to a vessel, and not land-based employees, who do not. By instructing juries in Jones Act cases accordingly, courts can give proper effect to the remedial scheme Congress has created for injured maritime workers.

It is so ordered.

■ JUSTICE STEVENS, with whom JUSTICE THOMAS and JUSTICE BREYER join, concurring in the judgment.

The majority has reached the odd conclusion that a maritime engineer, injured aboard ship on the high seas while performing his duties as an employee of the ship, might not be a "seaman" within the meaning of the Jones Act. This decision is unprecedented. It ignores the critical distinction between work performed aboard ship during a voyage—when the members of the crew encounter "the perils of the sea"—and maritime work performed on a vessel moored to a dock in a safe harbor. In my judgment, an employee of the ship who is injured at sea in the course of his employment is always a "seaman." I would leave more ambiguous, shorebound cases for another day. Accordingly, though I concur in the Court's disposition of this case, returning it to the District Court for a new trial, I disagree with the standard this Court directs the trial court to apply on remand.

I

The Jones Act,[1] 46 U.S.C.App. § 688, provides, in part, "[a]ny seaman who shall suffer personal injury in the course of his employment may, at his election, maintain an action for damages at law." In this case, it is undisputed that respondent, Antonios Latsis, was injured in the course of his employment. When the injury occurred, he was on board the steamship Galileo, a vessel in navigation in the Atlantic Ocean. He was therefore exposed to the perils of the sea; indeed, as the Court of Appeals correctly noted, "his injury was the result of such a peril." [2] Respondent was not a mere passenger; he was performing duties for his employer that contributed to the ship's mission. In common parlance, then, he was a member of the crew of the *Galileo*. I think these facts are sufficient to establish that respondent was, as a matter of law, a "seaman" within the meaning of the Jones Act at the time of his injury. Although the character of Latsis' responsibilities before the voyage began and after it ended would be relevant in determining his status if he had been injured while the ship was in port, they have no bearing on his status as a member of the *Galileo's* crew during the voyage.

This conclusion follows, first, from the language of the Jones Act and of the Longshore and Harbor Workers' Compensation Act (LHWCA), 33 U.S.C. § 901, *et seq.* The latter, a federal workers' compensation scheme for shore-based maritime workers, exempts any "master or member of a crew of any vessel," 33 U.S.C. § 902(3)(G-a formulation that, we have held, is coextensive with the term "seaman" in the Jones Act). McDermott International, Inc. v. Wilander, 498 U.S. 337, 347, 111 S.Ct. 807, 813, 112 L.Ed.2d 866 (1991). In ordinary parlance, an employee of a ship at sea who is on that ship as part of his employment and who contributes to the ship's mission is both a "seaman" and a "member of [the] crew of [the] vessel." Indeed I am not sure how these words can reasonably be read to exclude such an employee. Surely none of the statutory language suggests that the individual must be a member of the ship's crew for longer than a single voyage.

2.   THE TRADITIONAL SEAMEN'S REMEDIES

The Osceola

Supreme Court of the United States, 1903.
189 U.S. 158, 23 S.Ct. 483, 47 L.Ed. 760.

This was a libel *in rem* filed in the District Court for the Eastern District of Wisconsin, in admiralty, against the propeller Osceola, to recover damages

---

1. The "Jones Act" is actually § 33 of the Merchant Marine Act, 1020, 41 Stat. 1007.

2. "Latsis's employment did expose him to the perils of the sea—in fact, his injury was the result of such a peril in the sense that while on board a seaman is very much reliant upon and in the care of the ship's physician. If that physician is unqualified or engages in medical malpractice, it is just as much a peril to the mariner on board as the killer wave, the gale or hurricane, or other dangers of the calling." 20 F.3d 45, 55 (C.A.2 1994).

for a personal injury sustained by one Patrick Shea, a seaman on board the vessel, through the negligence of the master.

The case resulted in a decree for the libellant, from which an appeal was taken by the owners to the Circuit Court of Appeals, which certified to this court certain questions arising upon the following statement of facts:

"The owners had supplied the vessel with a movable derrick for the purpose of raising the gangways of the vessel when in port, in order to discharge cargo. The appliance was in every respect fit and suitable for the purpose for which it was intended and furnished to be used, and at the time of the injury was in good repair and condition. The gangways which were to be raised by the derrick were each about ten feet long lengthwise of the ship, about seven feet high and weighed about 1050 pounds. In the month of December, 1896, the vessel was on a voyage bound for the port of Milwaukee, and when within three miles of that port, and while in the open lake, the master of the vessel ordered the forward port gangway to be hoisted by means of the derrick, in order that the vessel might be ready to discharge cargo immediately upon arrival at her dock. At this time the vessel was proceeding at the rate of eleven miles an hour against a head wind of eight miles an hour. Under the supervision of the mate, the crew, including the appellee Patrick Shea, who was one of the crew, proceeded to execute the order of the master. The derrick was set in place to raise the gangway. As soon as the gangway was swung clear of the vessel, the front end was caught by the wind and turned outward broadside to the wind, and by the force of the wind was pushed aft and pulled the derrick over, which in falling struck and injured the libellant. The negligence, if any there was, consisted solely in the order of the master that the derrick should be used and that the gangway should be hoisted while the vessel was yet in the open sea when the operation might be impeded and interfered with by the wind. The mate and the crew in executing the orders of the master of the vessel acted in all respects properly, and were guilty of no negligence in the performance of the work. The libel charged negligence upon the owners of the vessel in 'requiring and permitting the work of unshipping said gangway to be done while the said vessel was at sea and running against the wind.' The owners were not present upon the vessel, nor was the master a part owner of the vessel. It is contended that the vessel and its owners are liable for every improvident or negligent order of the captain in the course of the navigation or management of the vessel."

The questions of law upon which that court desired the advice and instruction of the Supreme Court are—

"First. Whether the vessel is responsible for injuries happening to one of the crew by reason of an improvident and negligent order of the master in respect of the navigation and management of the vessel.

"Second. Whether in the navigation and management of a vessel, the master of the vessel and the crew are fellow servants.

"Third. Whether as a matter of law the vessel or its owners are liable to the appellee, Patrick Shea, who was one of the crew of the vessel, for the injury sustained by him by reason of the improvident and negligent order of the master of the vessel in ordering and directing the hoisting of the gangway at the time and under the circumstances declared; that is to say, on the assumption that the order so made was improvident and negligent."

* * *

■ MR. JUSTICE BROWN, after making the foregoing statement, delivered the opinion of the court.

In the view we take of this case we find it necessary to express an opinion only upon the first and third questions, which are in substance whether the vessel was liable *in rem* to one of the crew by reason of the improvident and negligent order of the master in directing the hoisting of the gangway for the discharge of cargo, before the arrival of the vessel at her dock, and during a heavy wind. As this is a libel *in rem* it is unnecessary to determine whether the owners would be liable to an action *in personam,* either in admiralty or at common law, although cases upon this subject are not wholly irrelevant.

1. If the rulings of the District Court were correct, that the vessel was liable *in rem* for these injuries, such liability must be founded either upon the general admiralty law or upon a local statute of the State within which the accident occurred. As the admiralty law upon the subject must be gathered from the accepted practice of courts of admiralty, both at home and abroad, we are bound in answering this question to examine the sources of this law and its administration in the courts of civilized countries, and to apply it, so far as it is consonant with our own usages and principles, or, as Mr. Justice Bradley observed in The Lottawanna, 88 U.S. (21 Wall.) 558, 22 L.Ed. 654 (1874), "having regard to our own legal history, Constitution, legislation, usages, and adjudications."

By Article VI of the Rules of Oleron, sailors injured by their own misconduct could only be cured at their own expense, and might be discharged; "but if, by the master's order and commands, any of the ship's company be in the service of the ship, and thereby happened to be wounded or otherwise hurt, in that case they shall be cured and provided for at the cost and charges of the said ship." By Article 18 of the Laws of Wisbuy, "a mariner being ashore in the master's or the ship's service, if he should happen to be wounded, he shall be maintained and cured at the charge of the ship," with a further provision that, if he be injured by his own recklessness, he may be discharged and obliged to refund what he has received. Practically the same provision is found in Article 39 of the Laws of the Hanse Towns; in the Marine Ordinances of Louis XIV, Book III, Title 4, Article 11; and in a Treatise upon the Sea Laws, published in 2 Pet. Admiralty Decisions. In neither of these ancient codes does there appear to be any distinction between injuries received accidentally or by negligence, nor does it appear that the seaman is to be indemnified beyond his wages and the expenses of his maintenance and cure. We are also left in the dark as to whether the seaman in such a case has recourse to the ship herself or is remitted to an action against the owners.

By the modern French Commercial Code, Art. 262, "seamen are to be paid their wages, and receive medical treatment at the expense of the ship, if they fall sick during a voyage, or be injured in the service of the vessel." Commenting upon this article, Goirand says in his commentaries upon the French Code, that "when a sailor falls ill before the sailing of the vessel, he has no right to his wages; if he becomes ill during the voyage, and from no fault of his own, he is paid his wages, and tended at the expense of the ship, and if he is left on shore, the ship is also liable for the expense of his return home;" and under Article 263 "the same treatment is accorded to sailors wounded or injured in the service of the ship. The expenses of treatment and dressing are chargeable to the ship alone, or to the ship and cargo, according to whether the wounds or injuries were received in the service of the ship alone, or that of the ship and cargo."

Similar provisions are found in the Italian Code, Article 363; the Belgian, Article 262; the Dutch, Articles 423 and 424; the Brazilian, Article 560; the Chilian, Article 944; the Argentine, Article 1174; the Portuguese, Article 1469; the Spanish, Articles 718 and 719; the German, Articles 548 and 549. In some of these codes, notably the Portuguese, Argentine and Dutch, these expenses are made a charge upon the ship and her cargo and freight, and considered as a subject of general average. By the Argentine Code, Article 1174, the sailor is also entitled to an indemnity beyond his wages and cure in case of mutilation; and by the German Code he appears to be entitled to an indemnity in all cases for injuries incurred in defence of his ship; and by the Dutch Code, the sailor, if disabled, is entitled to such damages as the judge shall deem equitable. In all of them there is a provision against liability in case of injuries received by the sailor's willful misconduct.

Except as above indicated, in a few countries, the expense of maintenance and cure do not seem to constitute a privilege or lien upon a ship, since by the French Code, Article 191, classifying privileged debts against vessels, no mention is made of a lien for personal injury. The other Continental and South American codes do not differ materially from the French in this particular. Probably, however, the expenses of maintenance and cure would be regarded as a mere incident to the wages, for which there is undoubtedly a privilege.

By the English Merchants' Shipping Act, 17 & 18 Vict. chap. 104, sec. 228, subd. 1, "if the master or any seaman or apprentice receives any hurt or injury in the service of the ship to which he belongs, the expense of providing the necessary surgical and medical advice, with attendance and medicines, and of his subsistence until he is cured, or dies, or is brought back to some port in the United Kingdom, if shipped in the United Kingdom, or if shipped in some British possession to some port in such possession, and of his conveyance to such port, and the expense (if any) of his burial, shall be defrayed by the owner of such ship, without any deduction upon that account from the wages of such master, seaman, or apprentice."

These provisions of the British law seem to be practically identical with the Continental codes. In the English courts the owner is now held to be liable for injuries received by the unseaworthiness of the vessel, though not by the negligence of the master, who is treated as a fellow servant of the seamen. Responsibility for injuries received through the unseaworthiness of the ship is imposed upon the owner by the Merchants' Shipping Act of 1876, 39 & 40 Vict. chap. 80, section 5, wherein in every contract of service, express, or implied, between an owner of a ship and the master or any seaman thereof, there is an obligation implied that all reasonable means shall be used to insure the seaworthiness of the ship before and during the voyage. Hedley v. Pinkney & c. Steamship Co., 1894, App.Ca. 222, an action at common law. Beyond this, however, we find nothing in the English law to indicate that a ship or its owners are liable to an indemnity for injuries received by negligence or otherwise in the service of the ship. None such is given in the Admiralty Court Jurisdiction Act of 1861, although it seems an action in admiralty will lie against the master *in personam* for an assault committed upon a passenger or seaman. The Agincourt, 1 Hagg.Adm. 271; The Lowther Castle, 1 Hagg.Adm. 384. This feature of the law we have ourselves adopted in general admiralty rule 16, declaring that "in all suits for assault or beating on the high seas, or elsewhere within the admiralty and maritime jurisdiction, the suit shall be *in personam* only." In England the master and crew are also treated as fellow servants, and hence it would follow that no action would lie by a member of the crew against either the owners or the ship for injuries received through the negligence of the master. Hedley v. Pinkney & c. Steamship Co., 1894, App.Ca. 222. It is otherwise, however, in Ireland, Ramsay v. Quinn, Irish Rep. 8 C.L. 322, and in Scotland, where the master is regarded as a vice principal. Leddy v. Gibson, 11 Ct.Sess.Cases, 3d Ser., 304.

The statutes of the United States contain no provision upon the subject of the liability of the ship or her owners for damages occasioned by the negligence of the captain to a member of the crew; but in all but a few of the more recent cases the analogies of the English and Continental codes have been followed, and the recovery limited to the wages and expenses of maintenance and cure. The earliest case upon the subject is that of Harden v. Gordon, 2 Mason, 541, in which Mr. Justice Story held that a claim for the expenses of cure in case of sickness constituted in contemplation of law a part of the contract for wages, over which the admiralty had a rightful jurisdiction. The action was *in personam* against the master and owner for wages and other expenses occasioned by the sickness of the plaintiff in a foreign port in the course of the voyage, all of which were allowed. The question of indemnity did not arise in this case, but the court held that upon the authority of the Continental codes and by its intrinsic equity there was no doubt of the seaman's right to the expenses of his sickness.

This case was followed in The Brig George, 1 Sumner, 151 (1 Cir.1832) and in Reed v. Canfield, 1 Sumner, 195 (1 Cir.1832). Though the last case did not involve the question of indemnity, Mr. Justice Story, in delivering the opinion, remarked that "the sickness or other injury may occasion a temporary or permanent disability; but that is not a ground for indemnity from the owners. They are liable only for expenses necessarily incurred for the cure; and when the cure is completed, at least so far as the ordinary medical means extend, the owners are freed from all further liability. They are not in any just sense liable for consequential damages. The question, then, in all such cases is, what expenses have been virtually incurred for the cure."

The question of indemnity, however, was fully considered by Judge Brown of the Southern District of New York in The City of Alexandria, 17 F. 390 (D.C.N.Y.1883) which was an action *in rem* for personal injuries received by the cook in falling through the fore hatch into the hold; and it was held that upon common law principles the claim could not be sustained, as the negligence through which the accident occurred was that of fellow servants engaged in a common employment. The court, however, went on to consider whether the negligence, upon the recognized principles of maritime law, entitled the libellant to compensation from the ship or her owners in cases not arising from unseaworthiness. After going over the Continental codes, the cases above cited and a few others, Judge Brown came to the conclusion that he could find "no authority in the ancient or modern codes, in the recognized text-books, or the decisions on maritime law, for the allowance of consequential damages resulting from wounds or hurts received on board ship, whether arising from ordinary negligence of the seaman himself, or of others of the ship's company. Considering the frequency of such accidents, and the lasting injuries arising from them in so many cases, the absence of any authority holding the vessel liable, beyond what has been stated, is evidence of the strongest character that no further liability under the maritime law exists."

The general rule that a seaman receiving injury in the performance of his duty is entitled to be treated and cured at the expense of the ship was enforced in The Atlantic, Abbott's Adm. 451 (1849) though it was said in this case and in Nevitt v. Clarke, 1 Olcott, 316 (1843) that the privilege of being cured continues no longer than the right to wages under the contract in the particular case. In The Ben Flint, 1 Abb.U.S. 126, 1 Biss. 562 (1867) the claim to be cured at the expense of the ship is held to be applicable to seamen employed on the lakes and navigable rivers within the United States. See also Brown v. Overton, 1 Sprague, 462 (1859); Croucher v. Oakman, 85 Mass. (3 Allen) 185 (1861); Brown v. The Bradish Johnson, 1 Woods, 301 (1873).

In The Edith Godden, 23 F. 43 (1885) the vessel was held liable *in rem* for personal injuries received from the neglect of the owner to furnish appliances adequate to the place and occasion where used. In other words, for unseaworthiness. This is readily distinguishable from the previous case of The City of Alexandria, 17 F. 390 (2 Cir.1883) and is in line with English and American authorities holding owners to be responsible to the seamen for the unseaworthiness of the ship and her appliances. In The Titan, 23 F. 413 (2 Cir.1885) the ship was held liable to a deck hand, who was injured by a collision occasioned partly by fault of his own vessel. The question of general liability was not discussed but assumed. In the case of The Noddleburn, 28 F. 855 (9 Cir.1886) the question of jurisdiction was not pressed by counsel, but merely stated and submitted. The case is put upon the ground that, as the accident was occasioned by the master knowingly allowing a rope to remain in an insecure condition, the vessel was consequently unseaworthy. In Olson v. Flavel, 34 F. 477 (9 Cir.1888) libellant was allowed to recover damages for personal injury suffered by him while employed as mate, but if there were any negligence on the part of the respondent, it appears to have been in not providing proper appliances, so that the case was one really of unseaworthiness. In the case of The A. Heaton, 43 F. 592 (1 Cir.1890) a seaman was allowed to recover consequential damages for negligence of the owners in not providing suitable appliances, although in the opinion, which was delivered by Mr. Justice Gray, he seems to assume the right of the seaman to recover against the masters or owners for injuries caused by their willful or negligent acts. The case however was one of injuries arising from unseaworthiness, although the learned judge in his discussion does not draw a distinction between the cases arising from the unseaworthiness of the ship and the negligent act of the master. It is interesting to note that in The Julia Fowler, 49 F. 277 (D.C.N.Y.1892) a seaman, employed in scraping the main mast on a triangle surrounding the mast, was allowed to recover for the breaking of the rope which held the triangle, and precipitated libellant to the deck; while in a case almost precisely similar, Kalleck v. Deering, 161 Mass. 469 (1894) the owners were held not to be liable for an injury caused by the negligence of the mate in constructing the triangle and ordering the seaman to use it. In The Frank and Willie, 45 F. 494 (D.C.N.Y.1891) the ship was held liable to a sailor who was injured by the negligence of the mate in not providing safe means for discharging the cargo. As the opinion was delivered by Judge Brown, who was also the author of the opinion in The City of Alexandria, 17 F. 390 (D.C.N.Y.1883) the case can be reconciled with that upon the ground that the question was really one of unseaworthiness and not of negligence.

Upon a full review, however, of English and American authorities upon these questions, we think the law may be considered as settled upon the following propositions:

1. That the vessel and her owners are liable, in case a seaman falls sick, or is wounded, in the service of the ship, to the extent of his maintenance and cure, and to his wages, at least so long as the voyage is continued.

2. That the vessel and her owner are, both by English and American law, liable to an indemnity for injuries received by seamen in consequence of the unseaworthiness of the ship, or a failure to supply and keep in order the proper appliances appurtenant to the ship. Scarff v. Metcalf, 107 N.Y. 211 (1887).

3. That all the members of the crew, except perhaps the master, are, as between themselves, fellow servants, and hence seamen cannot recover

for injuries sustained through the negligence of another member of the crew beyond the expense of their maintenance and cure.

4. That the seaman is not allowed to recover an indemnity for the negligence of the master, or any member of the crew, but is entitled to maintenance and cure, whether the injuries were received by negligence or accident.

It will be observed in these cases that a departure has been made from the Continental codes in allowing an indemnity beyond the expense of maintenance and cure in cases arising from unseaworthiness. This departure originated in England in the Merchants' Shipping Act of 1876, above quoted, Couch v. Steel, 3 El. & Bl. 402; Hedley v. Pinkney & c. Co., 7 Asp.M.L.C. 135; 1894, App.Cas. 222, and in this country, in a general consensus of opinion among the Circuit and District Courts, that an exception should be made from the general principle before obtaining, in favor of seamen suffering injury through the unseaworthiness of the vessel. We are not disposed to disturb so wholesome a doctrine by any contrary decision of our own.

It results that the first and third questions must be answered in the negative.

NOTE

For a discussion of the background of *The Osceola* and contemporary reaction to the decision, see Lucas, Flood Tide: Some Irrelevant History of the Admiralty, 1964 Sup.Ct.Rev. (Kurland, Ed.) 249, 262–284.

3. MAINTENANCE AND CURE

Warren v. United States

Supreme Court of the United States, 1951.
340 U.S. 523, 71 S.Ct. 432, 95 L.Ed. 503.

■ MR. JUSTICE DOUGLAS delivered the opinion of the Court.

Petitioner seeks in this suit maintenance and cure from the United States, as owner of S.S. Anna Howard Shaw. Petitioner was a messman who went ashore on leave while the vessel was at Naples in 1944. He and two other members of the crew first did some sightseeing. Then the three of them drank one bottle of wine and went to a dance hall, where they stayed an hour and a half, dancing. There was a room adjoining the dance hall that overlooked the ocean. French doors opened onto an unprotected ledge which extended out from the building a few feet. Petitioner stepped to within 6 inches of the edge and leaned over to take a look. As he did so, he took hold of an iron rod which seemed to be attached to the building. The rod came off and petitioner lost his balance and fell, breaking a leg.

The District Court awarded maintenance.[1]   75 F.Supp. 210, 76 F.Supp. 735.   The Court of Appeals disallowed it.   179 F.2d 919.   The case is here on certiorari.

The Shipowners' Liability Convention, proclaimed by the President Sept. 29, 1939, 54 Stat. 1693, provides in Art. 2:

> "1.   The shipowner shall be liable in respect of—
>
> "(a) sickness and injury occurring between the date specified in the articles of agreement for reporting for duty and the termination of the engagement;
>
> "(b) death resulting from such sickness or injury.
>
> "2.   Provided that national laws or regulations may make exceptions in respect of:
>
> "(a) injury incurred otherwise than in the service of the ship;
>
> "(b) injury or sickness due to the wilful act, default or misbehaviour of the sick, injured or deceased person;
>
> "(c) sickness or infirmity intentionally concealed when the engagement is entered into."

Petitioner's argument is twofold.   He maintains first that under paragraph 1 a shipowner's duty to provide maintenance and cure is absolute and that the exceptions specified in paragraph 2 are not operative until a statute is enacted which puts them in force.   He argues in the second place that, even if paragraph 2 is operative without an Act of Congress, his conduct was not due to a "wilful act, default or misbehaviour" within the meaning of that paragraph.   An *amicus curiae* argues that the injury was not received "in the service of the ship" within the meaning of Paragraph 2(a) of Art. 2.

There is support for petitioner's first point in the concurring opinion of Chief Justice Stone in Waterman Steamship Corp. v. Jones, 318 U.S. 724, 738, 63 S.Ct. 930, 937, 87 L.Ed. 1107 (1943).[2]   But we think the preferred

---

1.   Petitioner sued the United States as owner and American South African Line, Inc. as the general agent and operator.   The District Court dismissed the libel as to the United States and held the general agent liable under Hust v. Moore–McCormack Lines, 328 U.S. 707, 66 S.Ct. 1218, 90 L.Ed. 1534 (1946).   During the pendency of the appeal by the general agent and the cross-appeal by petitioner, Fink v. Shepard S.S. Co., 337 U.S. 810, 69 S.Ct. 1330, 93 L.Ed. 1709 (1949) was decided.   Accordingly the decree against the general agent was reversed and the Court of Appeals considered the case on the merits against the United States.

2.   Chief Justice Stone relied on the report of the Secretary of State to the President on the need for legislation implementing the Convention.   The Secretary said in part:

"Many of the provisions of the convention are considered to be self-executing, and there would appear to be no need to repeat verbatim the language of the convention in a statute to make it effective.   Some of the articles of the convention, however, after stating the general rule, provide that national laws may make specified exceptions thereto.   If this Government is to be excepted from certain obligations of the convention or alterations in our present practice, it is necessary to do so affirmatively by statute."   H.R.Rep. No. 1328, 76th Cong., 1st Sess. 6.

The Secretary had the following to say about Article 2: "Section 4 follows the exceptions in article 2 of the convention which sets forth the risks covered in the entire convention. * * * Paragraph 1 of article 2 of the convention was not incorporated in the bill

view is opposed. Our conclusion is that the exceptions permitted by paragraph 2 are operative by virtue of the general maritime law and that no Act of Congress is necessary to give them force.

The language of paragraph 2, in its ordinary range of meaning, easily permits that construction. It is "national laws or regulations" which may make exceptions. The term law in our jurisprudence usually includes the rules of court decisions as well as legislative acts. That was held in Erie R. Co. v. Tompkins, 304 U.S. 64, 58 S.Ct. 817, 82 L.Ed. 1188 (1938), to be true of the phrase "the laws of the several states" as used in the first Judiciary Act. 1 Stat. 73, § 34. No reason is apparent why a more restricted meaning should be given "national laws or regulations." The purpose of the Convention would not be served by the narrow meaning. This Convention was a product of the International Labor Organization.[3] Its purpose was to provide an international system of regulation of the shipowner's liability. That international system was aimed at providing a reasonable average which could be applied in any country.[4] We find no suggestion that it was designed to adopt a more strict standard of liability than that which our maritime law provides. The aim indeed was not to change materially American standards but to equalize operating costs by raising the standards of member nations to the American level.[5] If the Convention was designed to make absolute the liability of the shipping industry until and unless each member nation by legislative act reduced it, we can hardly believe some plain indication of the purpose would not have been made. Much of this body of maritime law had developed through the centuries in judicial decisions. To reject that body of law and start anew with a complete code would be a novel and drastic step. Under our construction the Convention provides a reasonable average for international application. The definition of the exception itself helps provide the average, leaving the creation of the exceptions to any source of law which the member nations recognize. That view serves the purpose of the Convention and conforms to the normal meaning of the words used. Our conclusion is that both

---

because of the belief (1) that it is self-executing in that it establishes liability, although no definite amount is provided; and (2) that it will not be held by the courts to conflict with present law in this country." Id., p. 6.

The implementing legislation was passed by the House, 84 Cong.Rec. 10540, but not by the Senate. See Hearings, Subcommittee of the Committee on Commerce, U.S. Senate, on H.R. 6881, 76th Cong., 3d Sess.; S.Doc. 113, 77th Cong., 1st Sess.; 87 Cong.Rec. 7434.

3. See Fried, Relations Between the United Nations and the International Labor Organization, 41 Am.Pol.Sci.Rev. 963; Dillon, International Labor Conventions (1942); Shotwell, The Origins of the International Labor Organization (1934).

The United States became a member of the International Labor Organization on August 20, 1934. See U.S. Treaties, Treaty Series, No. 874.

4. See International Labor Conference, Proceedings, Thirteenth Sess. (1929), 131.

5. The report of the Secretary of State recommending ratification of the Convention emphasized that the treaty (1) would not materially change American legal standards and (2) would raise standards of member nations to the American level and thus equalize operating costs. S.Exec.Rep. 8, 75th Cong., 3d Sess. 3.

paragraph 1 and paragraph 2 of Art. 2 state the standard of liability which legislative and decisional law define in particularity.

The District Court held that petitioner's degree of fault did not bar a recovery for maintenance and cure. The Court of Appeals thought otherwise. The question is whether the injury was "due to the wilful act, default or misbehaviour" of petitioner within the meaning of Art. 2, paragraph 2(b) of the Convention. The standard prescribed is not negligence but wilful misbehavior. In the maritime law it has long been held that while fault of the seaman will forfeit the right to maintenance and cure, it must be "some positively vicious conduct—such as gross negligence or willful disobedience of orders." The Chandos, 6 Sawy. 544, 549–550 (1880); The City of Carlisle, 39 F. 807, 813 (1889); The Ben Flint, 1 Biss. 562, 566 (1867). And see Reed v. Canfield, 1 Sumn. 195, 206 (1832). In Aguilar v. Standard Oil Co., 318 U.S. 724, 731, 63 S.Ct. 930, 934, 87 L.Ed. 1107 (1943) we stated the rule as follows: "Conceptions of contributory negligence, the fellow-servant doctrine, and assumption of risk have no place in the liability or defense against it. Only some wilful misbehavior or deliberate act of indiscretion suffices to deprive the seaman of his protection."

The exception which some cases have made for injuries resulting from intoxication (see Aguilar v. Standard Oil Co., supra, p. 731, notes 11 and 12) has no place in this case. As the District Judge ruled, the amount of wine consumed hardly permits a finding of intoxication. Petitioner was plainly negligent. Yet we would have to strain to find the element of wilfulness or its equivalent. He sought to use some care when he looked down from the small balcony, as evidenced by his seizure of the iron bar for a handhold. His conduct did not measure up to a standard of due care under the circumstances. But we agree with the District Court that it was not wilful misbehavior within the meaning of the Convention.

Finally it is suggested that the injury did not occur "in the service of the ship," as that term is used in paragraph 2(a) of Art. 2 of the Convention. We held in Aguilar v. Standard Oil Co., supra that maintenance and cure extends to injuries occurring while the seaman is departing on or returning from shore leave though he has at the time no duty to perform for the ship. It is contended that the doctrine of that case should not be extended to injuries received during the diversions of the seaman after he has reached the shore. Mr. Justice Rutledge, speaking for the Court in the *Aguilar* case, stated the reasons for extending maintenance and cure to shore leave cases as follows (pp. 733–734):

> "To relieve the shipowner of his obligation in the case of injuries incurred on shore leave would cast upon the seaman hazards encountered only by reason of the voyage. The assumption is hardly sound that the normal uses and purposes of shore leave are 'exclusively personal' and have no relation to the vessel's business. Men cannot live for long cooped up aboard ship, without substantial impairment of their efficiency, if not also serious danger to discipline. Relaxation beyond the confines of the ship is necessary if the work is to go on, more so that it may move smoothly. No master would take a crew to sea if he could not grant shore leave, and no crew would be taken if it could never obtain it. * * * In short, shore leave

is an elemental necessity in the sailing of ships, a part of the business as old as the art, not merely a personal diversion.

"The voyage creates not only the need for relaxation ashore, but the necessity that it be satisfied in distant and unfamiliar ports. If, in those surroundings, the seaman, without disqualifying misconduct, contracts disease or incurs injury, it is because of the voyage, the shipowner's business. That business has separated him from his usual places of association. By adding this separation to the restrictions of living as well as working aboard, it forges dual and unique compulsions for seeking relief wherever it may be found. In sum, it is the ship's business which subjects the seaman to the risks attending hours of relaxation in strange surroundings. Accordingly it is but reasonable that the business extend the same protections against injury from them as it gives for other risks of the employment."

This reasoning is as applicable to injuries received during the period of relaxation while on shore as it is to those received while reaching it. To restrict the liability along the lines suggested would be to whittle it down "by restrictive and artificial distinctions" as attempted in the *Aguilar* case. We repeat what we said there, "If leeway is to be given in either direction, all the considerations which brought the liability into being dictate it should be in the sailor's behalf." 318 U.S. at 735.

Reversed.

■ MR. JUSTICE JACKSON and MR. JUSTICE CLARK dissent on the ground that the injuries were not sustained in the service of the ship. Aguilar v. Standard Oil Co., 318 U.S. 724, 63 S.Ct. 930, 87 L.Ed. 1107 (1943) held a seaman to be in the ship's service while going to or from the ship over premises at which the ship docked, even if the purpose of being ashore was leave from duty. The route of access was not the choice of the seaman, and access to the ship was held essential to the ship's service. But the choice of places of refreshment and varieties of entertainment are the sailor's own. Unless his employment is a policy of accident insurance while on leave, recovery cannot be sustained in this case. That might be a wise rule of law but we think it one that should depend on legislation.

■ MR. JUSTICE FRANKFURTER, dissenting.

We brought this case here because it involved construction of the Shipowners' Liability Convention, 54 Stat. 1693. As to that, I agree with the Court that the Convention does not afford any basis for libellant's claim. Assuming that Article 2 of the Convention is self-executing, a matter which I do not now have to decide, the exceptions permitted by paragraph 2 of that Article are operative by virtue of the general maritime law. But I am unable to agree that we should reverse the Court of Appeals on its application of the proper standard to the facts.

The District Judge gave this description of what happened:

"Libellant was a messman aboard the S.S. 'Anna Howard Shaw.' On October 30, 1944, while the vessel was in the Bay of Naples, Italy, libellant left on shore leave. In company with the ship's carpenter and another messman, he went sightseeing. They came to the waterfront town of Bagnoli (referred to by libellant as Magnolia). The group stopped at various stores and at one such place they bought a small bottle of wine which they divided among them. About three miles down the shore from where they had landed from a motor lifeboat, they stopped at a dance hall and stayed an hour and a half or so. Libellant says he was dancing most of the time, and drank only one additional glass of wine.

"After a time libellant entered another room and approached a large window overlooking the sea, and he says the sight of the waves breaking upon the rocks some thirty-five feet below intrigued him. The French doors of this window extended to the level of the floor and he observed a sort of wholly unprotected ledge or balcony, which extended out from the building some two and a half or three feet. There was no railing of any sort and the slightest misstep or unsteadiness was almost sure to precipitate libellant. In any event, it was a perilous undertaking to go out upon this balcony and one even more perilous to lean over the edge to get a better view of the rocks and waves immediately below. But this is what libellant did. When he came to a position where the toes of his shoes were six inches from the edge, he leaned over, at the same time taking hold of a rod about one-half inch in circumference, which was apparently affixed to the building to his right. He merely took a casual glance at this rod and makes no claim to have done more. It looked like a 'lightning arrester or something of that type.' Whether the fastenings such as they were had been weakened by bombs and shell fire, which had otherwise marked the buildings in the vicinity to some extent, does not appear. Nor does the testimony disclose the purpose which this rod served. As he grasped it, and leaned over the edge, the rod came off and libellant lost his balance and fell. A similar ledge or balcony on one of the windows below broke his fall or he would have sustained injuries far more serious than a broken leg. This fall and its consequences are the basis for his suit for maintenance and cure." 75 F.Supp. 210, 213.

The District Judge concluded that libellant had not acted "in reckless disregard of safety." 75 F.Supp. at 216. The Court of Appeals for the Second Circuit unanimously reversed. It thought that

"In the case at bar, the risk of serious injury or even death if the seaman should fall over the cliff, was obvious; and the requisite degree of care correspondingly higher. In the face of evident danger, the care which Warren took was very slight—a mere casual glance at the rod which he thought to be a 'lightning arrester or something of that type.' We think that a man who acts as he did under circumstances of danger does not show even a minimal degree of regard for the consequences of his act. Unless his ship is to be an insurer of his safety, he cannot recover against her." 179 F.2d 919, 922.

I do not think the judgment of the Court of Appeals that the libellant's conduct was a "deliberate act of indiscretion," Aguilar v. Standard Oil Co., 318 U.S. 724, 731, 63 S.Ct. 930, 934, 87 L.Ed. 1107 (1943) should be disturbed.

Koistinen v. American Export Lines, Inc.

City Court of City of New York, Trial Term, 1948.
194 Misc. 942, 83 N.Y.S.2d 297.

■ CARLIN, JUSTICE. The plaintiff, a seaman, rated as a fireman and watertender, on the S.S. John N. Robins, was injured while on shore leave in the port of Split, Yugoslavia, on February 3rd, 1946; he went ashore about noon; in the exercise of a seaman's wonted privilege he resorted to a tavern where he drank one glass of wine like to our familiar port; thereafter in the course of a walk about town he visited another liquid dispensary where he quaffed two glasses of a similar vintage; there he met a woman whose blandishments, prevailing over his better sense, lured him to her room for purposes not particularly platonic; while there "consideration like an angel came and whipped the offending Adam out of him"; the woman scorned was unappeased by his contribution and vociferously remonstrated unless her unregarded charms were requited by an accretion of "dinner" (phonetically put); the court erroneously interpreted the word as showing that the woman had a carnivorous frenzy which could only be soothed by the succulent sirloin provided at the plaintiff's expense; but it was explained to denote a pecuniary not a gastronomic dun; she then essayed to relieve his pockets of their monetary content but without the success of the Lady that's known as Lou in Service's Spell of the Yukon where the man from the creeks, unlike plaintiff, was not on his toes to repel the peculation; completely thwarted the woman locked plaintiff in her room whereupon he proceeded to kick the door while he clamored for exit; not thus persuasive, he went to the window which was about six to eight feet above the ground and while there contemplating departure he was quickened to resolution by the sudden appearance of a man who formidably loomed at the lintels; thus, tossed between the horns of a most dire dilemma to wit, the man in the doorway and the window, the plaintiff eyeing the one with the duller point, elected the latter means of egress undoubtedly at the time laboring under the supposition that he was about to be as roughly used as the other man in a badger game; parenthetically it may be observed that it is a matter of speculation for contemporary commentators as well as for discussion by the delegates to U.N. how the refinements of that pastime came to penetrate the ferruginous arras of Yugoslavia especially as the diversion is reputed to be of strictly capitalistic American origin. So the plaintiff thus confronted leaped from the window and sustained injuries which hospitalized him in Yugoslavia and the United States; during the extensive period of his incapacitation his wages and hospital bills were paid by defendant; the only question confronting the court is his claim for maintenance over a period of thirty-six days. The defendant resists the claim on the foregoing facts contending that it is founded in immorality * * * This brings us to a consideration of the peculiar circumstances under which plaintiff met with his injuries; do they militate against the recovery of maintenance from the defendant? No authority with an analogous state of facts was cited by either side; the defendant contends that as the plaintiff did not accompany the woman to her room for heavenly contemplation his leap from the window was tainted with his original immoral intent and, therefore, he is not entitled to sue for maintenance. While it is true that there was a gross degree of culpability in the original purpose of the plaintiff for which he went to the woman's room it cannot be consistently argued that plaintiff, having abandoned that purpose before consummation and having sought to conserve his safety as well as the life of a good sailor, was acting in continuance of the initial immoral intent; in the court's opinion the proximate cause of plaintiff's leap from the window was not his original intent but was the concurrence of the locked door from which he sought egress and the subsequent looming threat of the man with the menacing mien; the expedition of plaintiff's violent fear outran the pauser, reason, causing him in the exercise of an erroneous judgment to jump rather than drop to the ground which undoubtedly would have been a safer means in view of the comparatively short space he had to negotiate for escape. Under the circumstances the window was the only solution presented to plaintiff in his emergency; at least he cannot be condemned for so conjecturing despite his starting on the wrong moral foot in the first instance; again the ticklish situation which confronted plaintiff immediately before his leap was not a reasonably foreseeable consequence of his original intention. It may be argued that the foregoing pronouncement is obiter dicta but the court holds that it is consistent with the law enunciated by more respectable authority; as heretofore intimated no case cited in the briefs of either side squares analogously in its facts with those presented to the court in this case; though of novel impression it does not fall without well defined principles found in the decisions. In Ellis v. American Hawaiian S.S. Co., 165 F.2d 999 (9 Cir.1948) a seaman on shore leave was not found to be definitely intoxicated from the consumption of three bottles of beer and his diving into a swimming pool was not construed as willful or gross misconduct; nor does the court find in the present case that the drinking of three glasses of wine rendered plaintiff intoxicated; nor did his jump from the window denote inebriation; to hold otherwise would argue strongly against his ability to choose the means of escape and would indict him for an error of judgment which is not the law against one who chooses in an emergency one means of safety when another might have been more conducive to that end. See Maguire v. Barrett, 223 N.Y. 49, 55, 119 N.E. 79, 80 (1918); Lewis v. Long Island R.R. Co., 162 N.Y. 52, 62, 56 N.E. 548, 551 (1900); Laidlaw v. Sage, 158 N.Y. 73, 89, 90, 52 N.E. 679, 684, 685, 44 L.R.A. 216 (1899). Peculiarly the plaintiff chose the only means of escape even though it resulted in his injuries; had he elected to go out the door with the threatening man, there barring the way, his injuries reasonably might have been more dire and serious than those sustained by his jump from the window; at least he's still alive. In the Anna Howard Shaw case, supra, the seaman is held to be entitled to maintenance unless his injury resulted from some wilful misbehavior or deliberate act of indiscretion; gross negligence according to the rule of this case would deprive the seaman of maintenance. As appears from the foregoing it may be argued that plaintiff's immoral indiscretion first put him in the woman's room but it did not impel him to jump from the window; that was occasioned by the barred door with the man thereat menacingly looming; nor did the Anna Howard Shaw case hold that the seaman on shore leave was so intoxicated as to constitute wilful misbehavior prejudicial to his right to maintenance and cure. Quoting from the Anna Howard Shaw case, supra, 75 F.Supp. at page 213 which cited Aguilar v. Standard Oil Co., of New Jersey, 318 U.S.

724, 63 S.Ct. 930, 87 L.Ed. 1107 (1943) it is said "A seaman, injured in the service of his ship, is entitled to maintenance at its expense. * * * 'Only some wilful misbehavior or deliberate act of indiscretion suffices to deprive' him of maintenance, the 'traditional instances' being 'venereal disease and injuries received as a result of intoxication.'" See also Nowery v. Smith, 69 F.Supp. 755 (D.C.Pa.1946) affirmed 161 F.2d 732 (3 Cir.1947); Moss v. Alaska Packers Ass'n, 70 Cal.App.2d Supp. 857, 160 P.2d 224 (1945). In Boulton v. Moore, 14 F. 922, 926 (1882) the court said regarding seamen "As 'wards' of the court, they are treated with the tenderness of a guardian" and consistent with that principle is the decision in Aguilar v. Standard Oil Co. of New Jersey, 318 U.S. 724, 63 S.Ct. 930, 934, 87 L.Ed. 1107, 1943 A.M.C. 451 (1943) in holding that the shipowner is liable for maintenance and cure to a seaman the court said "Only some wilful misbehavior or deliberate act of indiscretion suffices to deprive the seaman of his protection. * * * The traditional instances are venereal disease and injuries received as a result of intoxication, though on occasion the latter has been qualified in recognition of a classic predisposition of sailors ashore. Other recent cases however disclose a tendency to expand these traditional exceptions". In other words the courts have been liberal in their attitude toward seamen who receive injuries on shore leave through their notorious penchants not stemming from intoxication or deliberate acts of indiscretion; neither is established in the present case under the facts adduced. The plaintiff in the court's opinion is entitled to recover. The question remaining is how much; cases have been cited which have variously held a range for maintenance between $2.50 to $4.00 a day; this court in the case of Proctor v. Sword Line, Inc., 83 N.Y.S.2d 288 (Misc. 1948) held that $5.20 a day was a reasonable allowance for maintenance; considering the costs of living and lodging under the standards prevailing in the recent times involved in this claim which differ no whit from those obtaining now, the court adheres to its prior determination that $5.20 a day is a fair and reasonable allowance for maintenance. Motions by defendant upon which decision was reserved to dismiss the complaint are denied with exceptions to defendant. Judgment for plaintiff against defendant for $187.20 for thirty-six days of maintenance at $5.20 a day. As findings of fact and conclusions of law were waived at the trial let the clerk enter judgment accordingly. Ten days' stay and thirty days to make a case is granted defendant after service upon its attorneys of the judgment herein with notice of entry. Exhibits may be had at chambers.

NOTE

The decisions in *Warren* and *Koistenen* deal with two separate limitations on eligibility for award of maintenance and cure. The first is the requirement that the injury or illness occur while the seaman is in the service of the ship. In *Warren* the majority is able to rely on Mr. Justice Rutledge's observations in the *Aguilar* case respecting the importance of shore leave in the life of a seaman who lives a close life aboard. Both Warren and Koistenen were "blue water" seamen on shore leave in foreign parts. Suppose that the vessel was in its home port. Should the same principles apply? Should a distinction be drawn between an articled seaman and an unarticled seaman? The articled seaman is under the command of the master and "on call". See Rose v. Bloomfield S.S. Co., 162 F.Supp. 576, 1953 A.M.C. 2261 (E.D.La.1958), in which the seaman had signed foreign articles on January 21, on a ship scheduled to leave port on January 23. On January 23, while on shore leave, he was struck by a taxicab while running for a bus. And in Smith v. United States, 167 F.2d 550, 1848 A.M.C. 761 (4th Cir.1948), the seaman was injured in an automobile accident leaving the home of a friend with whom he had spent his first night on shore leave after the arrival of the vessel in port.

In cases involving unarticled seamen, the requirement that the injury or illness occur while the seaman is in the service of the vessel is followed more literally. See, e.g., Keeping v. Dawson, 262 F.2d 868, 1959 A.M.C. 388 (1st Cir.1959). On the night of his day off following service on the ship (a fishing vessel), plaintiff was taken with a violent headache and admitted to the hospital. The court of appeals affirmed denial of maintenance and cure absent a showing that the plaintiff was at the time subject to call. To the same effect, see Foret v. Co–Mar Offshore Corp., 508 F.Supp. 980 (E.D.La.1981). The plaintiff in *Foret* was hired as a relief captain at a daily rate. He received permission to leave the ship on personal business. On the way back on his motorbike he collided with an automobile. It was held that he was not in the service of the vessel. Cf. Macedo v. F/V Paul & Michelle, 868 F.2d 519 (1st Cir.1989), in which a fisherman was awarded maintenance and cure in respect of an accident occurring on a pleasure jaunt on Sunday when he could have been called upon to sail on the day of the accident. Similar is Moran v. Bay State Trawler, 4 Mass.App.Ct. 764, 358 N.E.2d 473 (1976). There it was held that a fisherman severely burned at a friend's house during a two day free time between fishing voyages was entitled to maintenance and cure on a showing that he was subject to recall and had left word where he could be located on shore if he were needed.

Even in the case of an articled seaman, there are some limits. In Hokanson v. Maritime Overseas Corp., 1974 A.M.C. 948, 1974 WL 948 (E.D.La.1974), the plaintiff was hired as a relief mate during the vessel's stay in New Orleans. He lived in the vicinity of New Orleans and for a week worked on the vessel during the day and went home at night. Subsequently he was hired as chief mate and signed overseas articles. Nevertheless he continued to go home at night. On the third night after signing articles, he fell through the ceiling from his attic to the room below and injured his leg. The court found that he was not obligated to remain at home or stay in communication with the vessel, nor to keep himself physically and mentally alert to return to the vessel if necessary and undertake the duties aboard, and held that the defendant had overcome the prima facie case made out by showing that the seaman was injured or fell ill while under articles.

The other limitation is that the injury or illness was not, in the words of the Shipowner's Liability Convention, "due to the wilful act, default or misbehavior of the sick, injured or deceased person." In *Koistenen,* suppose the lady's friends had caught Koistenen and *they* had broken his leg. Would that circumstance have altered the outcome? Suppose that she had fully performed her obligations under their agreement and his injuries had been inflicted in a general affray that took place when he revealed that he was unable to pay the amount that she thought that they had agreed upon. See Matthews v. Gulf & South American S.S. Co., 226 F.Supp. 555 (E.D.La.1964), aff'd per curiam 339 F.2d 702 (5th Cir.1964).

In Thomas D. Dailey v. Alcoa S.S. Co., Inc., 219 F.Supp. 601 (E.D.La.1963), aff'd 337 F.2d 611 (5th Cir.1964), the seaman signed on the ship at 2:45 P.M. and then went ashore to enjoy "one last evening of drinking at one of his old haunts in

New Orleans." At a little past midnight he fell off the bar stool and was injured. For cases involving assorted affrays, drunken or otherwise, see Prendis v. Central Gulf S.S. Co., 330 F.2d 893, 1963 A.M.C. 1157 (4th Cir.1963); Watson v. Joshua Hendy Corp., 245 F.2d 463, 1957 A.M.C. 2367 (2d Cir.1957); Jones v. United States, 232 F.Supp. 585, 1964 A.M.C. 955 (E.D.Va.1964). For a case involving more passive drunkenness see Palmer v. Waterman S.S. Corp., 52 Wash.2d 604, 328 P.2d 169, 1962 A.M.C. 253 (1958)(where a returning seaman was helped half way down a ladder and fell the other half).

When the action for maintenance and cure is brought under the savings to suitors clause, should the issue of wilful misconduct go to the jury? it has been held that the issue of, e.g., intoxication, must be put to the jury but that the question of whether, under the circumstances, it constitutes wilful misconduct is a matter of law. See Garay v. Carnival Cruise Line, Inc., 904 F.2d 1527 (11th Cir.1990), cert. denied 498 U.S. 1119, 111 S.Ct. 1072, 112 L.Ed.2d 1178 (1991), in which a seaman sustained head injuries when he fell down a stair three hours after he returned to the ship from shore where he had consumed four to six beers within the space of two hours. The court of appeals found that although the evidence of intoxication was not strong, the jury could that the seaman was intoxicate. It found, however, that intoxication was regularly tolerated on the vessel and was not, therefore, wilful misconduct. See also Connolly v. Farrell Lines, Inc., 268 F.2d 653, 1960 A.M.C. 1068 (1st Cir.1959), cert. denied 361 U.S. 902, 80 S.Ct. 208, 4 L.Ed.2d 158 (1959).

The misconduct disqualification applies to disease as well as injury. Thus it has been held that a seaman is not entitled to maintenance and cure for hypertension caused by excessive drinking. Blouin v. American Export Isbrandtsen Lines, 319 F.Supp. 1150, 1970 A.M.C. 712 (S.D.N.Y.1970). And maintenance and cure has generally been denied for treatment for venereal disease. Ressler v. States Marine Lines, Inc., 517 F.2d 579, 1975 A.M.C. 819 (2d Cir.1975). Bringing the doctrine up to date, see Bynum v. Premier Cruise Lines, Ltd., 1994 A.M.C. 2185, 1994 WL 617067 (M.D.Fla.1994) denying maintenance and cure to a seaman with H.I.V. who acknowledged prior male and female sexual contacts on the ground that he had incurred his disability through vices and wilful misconduct and not in the service of the ship.

Fraud

Intentional misrepresentation or concealment of medical facts from an employer while applying for work has been held to be a ground for denying maintenance and cure when they are related to the injury for which the employee seeks the maintenance and cure. See Wactor v. Sparton Transp. Corp., 27 F.3d 347 (8th Cir.1994). See also McCorpen v. Central Gulf S.S. Corp., 396 F.2d 547 (5th Cir.), cert. denied 393 U.S. 894, 89 S.Ct. 223, 21 L.Ed.2d 175 (1968). Cf. Omar v. Sea–Land Service, 813 F.2d 986 (9th Cir.1987), in which it was held that a messman who had slipped on a greasy alley floor was entitled to maintenance and cure despite the fact that he was subsequently disciplined by the Coast Guard for fraud in obtaining his able bodied seaman's certificate. The court conceded cases holding that fraud in concealing conditions that are the basis for the claim has been held to constitute a defense.

Reimbursement

An employer who has paid maintenance and cure to an employee injured by a third person, may recover the amount from the tortfeasor. See Bertram v. Freeport McMoran, Inc., 35 F.3d 1008, 1995 A.M.C. 707 (5th Cir.1994). In *Bertram*, in an action under the Jones Act, the employer had been exonerated, the seaman had been held 60% negligent, and a platform owner and a contractor had each been held 20% negligent. The two were charged each 50% of the amount of maintenance and cure.

Farrell v. United States

Supreme Court of the United States, 1949.
336 U.S. 511, 69 S.Ct. 707, 93 L.Ed. 850.

■ MR. JUSTICE JACKSON delivered the opinion of the Court.

Petitioner, a seaman, brought suit in admiralty to recover damages under the Jones Act, 41 Stat. 1007, 46 U.S.C. § 688, and maintenance, cure and wages under maritime law. The issue of negligence was decided against him by both courts below and the claim is abandoned here. Petition for certiorari to review other issues was granted. 335 U.S. 869.

I. Maintenance and Cure

The facts which occasion maintenance and cure for this seaman are not in dispute. The claimant, 22 years of age and in good health, was a member of the Merchant Marine. He was in the service of the S.S. James E. Haviland, a merchant vessel owned and operated by the United States as a cargo and troop ship. On February 5, 1944, she was docked at Palermo, Sicily, and Farrell was granted shore leave which required his return to the ship by 6 p.m. of the same day. He overstayed his leave and about eight o'clock began, in rain and darkness, to make his way to the ship. He became lost and was misdirected to the wrong gate, by which he entered the shore-front area about a mile from where the ship lay moored. The area generally was blacked out but petitioner's companion, forty or fifty feet away, saw him fall over a guard chain into a drydock which was lighted sufficiently for night work then in progress. Farrell was grievously injured.

He was treated without expense to himself in various government hospitals until June 30, 1944, when he was discharged at Norfolk, Virginia, as completely disabled. He is totally and permanently blind and suffers post-traumatic convulsions which probably will become more frequent and are without possibility of further cure. From time to time he will require some medical care to ease attacks of headaches and epileptic convulsions. The court below concluded that the duty of a shipowner to furnish maintenance and cure does not extend beyond the time when the maximum cure possible has been effected. Petitioner contends that he is entitled to maintenance as long as he is disabled, which in this case is for life.

Admittedly there is no authority in any statute or American admiralty decisions for the proposition that he is entitled to maintenance for life. But an argument is based upon the ancient authority of Cleirac, Jugmens d'Oleron, Arts. 6 and 7 and notes by Cleirac; Consolato del Mare, cc. 182, 137; 2 Pard Coll. Mar. 152; to which American authorities have paid considerable respect. See Story, Circuit Justice, in Reed v. Canfield, Fed.Cas. No. 11,641, p. 429. A translation of the note relied upon reads:

"If in defending himself, or fighting against an enemy or corsairs, a mariner is maimed, or disabled to serve on board a ship for the rest of his life, besides the charge of his cure, he shall be maintained as long as he lives at the cost of the ship and cargo. Vide the Hanseatic law, art. 35." 1 Peters' Admiralty Decisions (1807), Appendix, p. xv.

Article 35 of the Laws of the Hanse Towns referred to reads:

"ART. XXXV. The seamen are obliged to defend their ship against rovers, on pain of losing their wages; and if they are wounded, they shall be healed and cured at the general charge of the concerned in a common average. If anyone of them is maimed and disabled, he shall be maintained as long as he lives by a like average." Ibid., p. civ.

We need not elaborate upon the meanings or weight to be given to these medieval pronouncements of maritime law. As they show, they were written when pirates were not operatic characters but were real-life perils of the sea. When they bore down on a ship, all was lost unless the seaman would hazard life and limb in desperate defense. If they saved the ship and cargo, it was something in the nature of salvage and for their sacrifice in the effort a contribution on principles of average may have been justly due. Perhaps more than humanitarian considerations, inducement to stand by the ship generated the doctrine that saving the ship and her cargo from pirates entitles the seaman to lifelong maintenance if he is disabled in the struggle.

But construe the old-time law with what liberality we will, it cannot be made to cover the facts of this case. This ship was not beset but was snug at berth in a harbor that had capitulated to the United States and her allied forces six months before. No sea rovers, pirates or corsairs appeared to have menaced her. It is true that the ship was engaged in warlike operations and was a legitimate target for enemy aircraft or naval vessels, which made her service a war risk, but at that time and place no enemy attack was in progress or imminent. Even if we pass all this and assume the ship always to have been in potential danger and in need of defense, this seaman at the time of his injury had taken leave of her and he is in no position to claim that he was a sacrifice to her salvation. Far from helping to man the ship at the moment, he was unable to find her; he was lost ashore and not able adequately to take care of himself. However patriotic his motive in enlisting in the service and however ready he may have been to risk himself for his country, we can find no rational basis for awarding lifetime maintenance against the ship on the theory that he was wounded or maimed while defending her against enemies.

It is claimed, however, even if the basis for a lifetime award does not exist, that he is entitled to maintenance and cure beyond the period allowed by the courts below. This is based largely upon statements in the opinion of the Court in Calmar Steamship Corp. v. Taylor, 303 U.S. 525, 58 S.Ct. 651, 82 L.Ed. 993 (1938). There the question as stated by the Court was whether the duty of a shipowner to provide maintenance and cure for a seaman falling ill of an incurable disease while in its employ, extends to the payment of a lump-sum award sufficient to defray the cost of maintenance and cure for the remainder of his life. The Court laid aside cases where incapacity is caused by the employment and said, "We can find no basis for saying that, if the disease proves to be incurable, the duty extends beyond a fair time after the voyage in which to effect such improvement in the seaman's condition as reasonably may be expected to result from nursing, care, and medical treatment. This would satisfy such demands of policy as underlie the imposition of the obligation. Beyond this we think there is no duty, at least where the illness is not caused by the seaman's service."

It is claimed that when the Court reserved or disclaimed any judgment as to cases where the incapacity is caused "by the employment" or "by the seaman's service" it recognized or created such cases as a separate class for a different measure of maintenance and cure. We think no such distinction exists or was premised in the *Calmar* case. In Aguilar v. Standard Oil Co., 318 U.S. 724, 63 S.Ct. 930, 87 L.Ed. 1107 (1943) the Court pointed out that logically and historically the duty of maintenance and cure derives from a seaman's dependence on his ship, not from his individual deserts, and arises from his disability, not from anyone's fault. We there refused to look to the personal nature of the seaman's activity at the moment of injury to determine his right to award. Aside from gross misconduct or insubordination, what the seaman is doing and why and how he sustains injury does not affect his right to maintenance and cure, however decisive it may be as to claims for indemnity or for damages for negligence. He must, of course, at the time be "in the service of the ship," by which is meant that he must be generally answerable to its call to duty rather than actually in performance of routine tasks or specific orders.

It has been the merit of the seaman's right to maintenance and cure that it is so inclusive as to be relatively simple, and can be understood and administered without technical considerations. It has few exceptions or conditions to stir contentions, cause delays, and invite litigations. The seaman could forfeit the right only by conduct whose wrongful quality even simple men of the calling would recognize—insubordination, disobedience to orders, and gross misconduct. On the other hand, the master knew he must maintain and care for even the erring and careless seaman, much as a parent would a child. For any purpose to introduce a graduation of rights and duties based on some relative proximity of the activity at time of injury to the "employment" or the "service of the ship," would alter the basis and be out of harmony with the spirit and function of the doctrine and would open the door to the litigiousness which has made the landman's remedy so often a promise to the ear to be broken to the hope.

Nor is it all clear to us what this particular litigant could gain from introduction of the distinction for which contention is made. If we should concede that larger measure of maintenance is due those whose injury is caused by the nature of their employment, it would seem farfetched to hold it applicable here. Claimant was disobedient to his orders and for his personal purposes overstayed his shore leave. His fall into a drydock that was sufficiently lighted for workmen to be carrying on repairs to a ship therein was due to no negligence but his own. These matters have not been invoked to forfeit or reduce his usual seaman's right, but it is difficult to see how such circumstances would warrant enlargement of it. We hold that he is entitled to the usual measure of maintenance and cure at the ship's expense, no less and no more, and turn to ascertainment of its bounds.

The law of the sea is in a peculiar sense an international law, but application of its specific rules depends upon acceptance by the United States. The problem of the sick or injured seaman has concerned every maritime country and, in 1936, the General Conference of the International Labor Organization at Geneva submitted a draft convention to the United States and other states. It was ratified by the Senate and was proclaimed by the President as effective for the United States on October 29, 1939. 54 Stat. 1693. Article 4, paragraph 1, thereof, provides: "The shipowner shall be liable to defray the expense of medical care and maintenance until the sick or injured person has been cured, or until the sickness or incapacity has been declared of a permanent character."

While enactment of this general rule by Congress would seem controlling, it is not amiss to point out that the limitation thus imposed was in accordance with the understanding of those familiar with the laws of the sea and sympathetic with the seaman's problems.

The Department of Labor issued a summary of the Convention containing the following on this subject: "The shipowner is required to furnish medical care and maintenance, including board and lodging, until the disabled person has been cured or the disability has been declared permanent." Robinson, *Admiralty,* p. 300.

Representatives of the organized seamen have recognized and advised Congress of this traditional limitation on maintenance and cure. When Congress has had under consideration substitution of a system of workmen's compensation on the principles of the Longshoremen's and Harbor Workers' Compensation Act, 44 Stat. 1424, as amended, 33 U.S.C.A. §§ 901–950, organized seamen, as we have heretofore noted, have steadfastly opposed the change. Hust v. Moore–McCormack Lines, 328 U.S. 707, 715, 66 S.Ct. 1218, 1222, 90 L.Ed. 1534 (1946). In doing so the legal representative of one maritime union advised the Committee on Merchant Marine of the House of Representatives that maintenance extended during "(a) the period that a seaman receives treatment at a hospital either as an in-patient or an out-patient; and (b) during a period of convalescence, and until the maximum cure is obtained."[1] Another representative, after defining it to include hospitalization, said, "In addition a seaman is entitled to recover maintenance while outside of the hospital until his physical condition becomes fixed."[2]

1. Hearings before the House Committee on Merchant Marine and Fisheries, 76th Cong., 1st Sess., on H.R. 6726 and H.R. 6881, p. 83.

2. Id., p. 131.

That the duty of the ship to maintain and care for the seaman after the end of the voyage only until he was so far cured as possible, seems to have been the doctrine of the American admiralty courts prior to the adoption of the Convention by Congress,[3] despite occasional ambiguity of language or reservation as to possible situations not before the court. It has been the rule of admiralty courts since the Convention.[4]

Maintenance and cure is not the only recourse of the injured seaman. In an appropriate case he may obtain indemnity or compensation for injury due to negligence or unseaworthiness and may recover, by trial before court and jury, damages for partial or total disability. But maintenance and cure is more certain if more limited in its benefits. It does not hold a ship to permanent liability for a pension, neither does it give a lump-sum payment to offset disability based on some conception of expectancy of life. Indeed the custom of providing maintenance and cure in kind and concurrently with its need has had the advantage of removing its benefits from danger of being wasted by the proverbial improvidence of its beneficiaries. The Government does not contend that if Farrell receives future treatment of a curative nature he may not recover in a new proceeding the amount expended for such treatment and for maintenance while receiving it.

The need of this seaman for permanent help is great and his plight most unfortunate. But as the evidence has afforded no basis for supplying that need by finding negligence, neither does the case afford a basis for distortion of the doctrine of maintenance and cure. This seaman was in the service of the United States and extraordinary measures of relief while not impossible are not properly addressed to the courts.

II. Wages

The two courts below have held the petitioner entitled to wages until the completion of the voyage at the port of New York on March 28, 1944. The petitioner contends that he has a right to wages for twelve months from December 16, 1943, the date he joined the vessel. The articles of the Haviland, signed by petitioner, were on a printed form which left a vacant space subject to the following footnote: "Here the voyage is to be described, and the places named at which the ship is to touch; or, if that cannot be done, the general nature and probable length of the voyage is to be stated, and the port or country at which the voyage is to terminate." [The Haviland's articles, for security reasons during the war, did not describe the voyage in such terms but provided, "from the Port of Philadelphia, to A point in the Atlantic Ocean to the eastward of Phila. and thence to such ports and places in any part of the world as the Master may direct or as may be ordered or directed by the United States Government or any department, commission or agency thereof * * * and back to a final port of

3. See, for example, The Wensleydale, 41 F. 829 (2 Cir.1890); The Bouker No. 2, 241 F. 831 (2 Cir.1917); Skolar v. Lehigh Valley R. Co., 60 F.2d 893 (5 Cir.1932); The Point Fermin, 70 F.2d 602 (5 Cir.1934).

4. See, for example, Lindgren v. Shepard S.S. Co., 108 F.2d 806 (2 Cir.1940); The Josephine & Mary, 120 F.2d 459 (1 Cir.1941); Luksich v. Misetich, 140 F.2d 812 (9 Cir. 1944).

discharge in the United States, for a term of time not exceeding 12 (Twelve) calendar months." It is not questioned that the general custom in ships, other than the coastwise trade, is to sign on for a voyage rather than for a fixed period. But it is contended that the last clause of this contract obligated the petitioner to serve for twelve calendar months, irrespective of the termination of the voyage, and therefore gave him the right to wages for a similar period. The contract is not an uncommon form and complied with war-time requirements as to voyage contracts.[5] We think, in the light of the custom of the industry and the condition of the times, there is nothing ambiguous about it and that it obligated the petitioner only for the voyage on which the ship was engaged when he signed on and that, when it terminated at a port of discharge in the United States, he could not have been required to reimbark for a second voyage. The twelve-month period appears as a limitation upon the duration of the voyage and not as a stated period of employment. We think the court below made no error in determining the wages.

For the reasons set forth, the judgment is

Affirmed.

◼ MR. JUSTICE DOUGLAS, with whom MR. JUSTICE BLACK, MR. JUSTICE MURPHY and MR. JUSTICE RUTLEDGE concur, dissenting.

I. *Wages.*—The articles bound Farrell to a voyage on the vessel which was en route to "a point in the Atlantic Ocean to the eastward of Phila. and thence to such ports and places in any part of the world as the Master may direct or as may be ordered or directed by the United States Government or any department, commission or agency thereof * * * and back to a final port of discharge in the United States, for a term of time not exceeding 12 (Twelve) calendar months." If this were a coastwise voyage, there would be little question that Farrell could recover his wages for the entire twelve-month period. See Enochasson v. Freeport Sulphur Co., 7 F.2d 674, 675 (5 Cir.1925); Jones v. Waterman S.S. Corp., 155 F.2d 992, 996 (3 Cir.1946). I agree with Judge Kirkpatrick that the principle of those cases is likewise applicable to foreign voyages. Shields v. United States, 73 F.Supp. 862, 866 (D.C.Pa.1947). Any difference is not apparent. In each the seaman binds himself for the period. The obligations to pay wages should be coterminous with that responsibility. Enochasson v. Freeport Sulphur Co., supra. The number of voyages made is therefore immaterial. It is the extent of the voyage that could be demanded that is controlling.

II. *Maintenance and Cure.*—Calmar S.S. Corp. v. Taylor, 303 U.S. 525, 58 S.Ct. 651, 82 L.Ed. 993 (1938) involved maintenance and cure[1] for an incurable disease which manifested itself during the seaman's employment but was not caused by it. The Court held that the shipowner's liability ended when the seaman was cured as far as possible, reserving the

---

5. 7 Fed.Reg. 2477.

1. Maintenance includes food and lodging; and cure means care. The Bouker No. 2, 241 F. 831, 835.

question whether a different rule would apply if the incapacity arose from the employment. P. 530. The question reserved is now presented, for an injury received on returning to a ship from shore leave is plainly incurred in the service. Aguilar v. Standard Oil Co., 318 U.S. 724, 63 S.Ct. 930, 87 L.Ed. 1107 (1943); Reed v. Canfield, Fed.Cas. No. 11,641. Justice Story was of the view that the ship remained liable until the cure was completed. Reed v. Canfield, supra. That was in 1832. Intervening decisions in the lower courts qualified that view. It was held that the right to maintenance and cure extended to a reasonable time beyond the end of the voyage.[2] The problem of what was a reasonable time remained. The test adopted by the Court is that it extends through the period when the maximum cure within the reach of medical science has been achieved.

But that test is not sufficiently discriminating.

Even though a maximum cure has been effected, two entirely different states of being may result when the injured man is left totally disabled.

(1) He may be totally disabled but no longer in need of medical aid to care for the condition created by the injury nor without means of providing maintenance. That is not the present case, at least so far as medical care is concerned. And we need not determine what rights to maintenance and cure one so situated has.

(2) One injured in the service of a ship may not only be permanently disabled after reaching the point of maximum cure. He may also be in need of future medical aid to sustain that condition and be without means of maintenance. These needs may extend to end of life. That is the present case, at least so far as medical care is concerned.[3] In this situation payments to give continuing needed care of wounds have been allowed, even though a maximum cure has been effected. The Josephine & Mary, 120 F.2d 459, 462, 464 (1 Cir.1941). Cf. Saunders v. Luckenbach Co., 262 F. 845, 847 (2 Cir.1920).

In the present case an award for maintenance and cure to cover a six-month period after discharge from the hospital was allowed. Nevertheless even though Farrell's expenses of care may be continuing, the district court judge refused any further award. I do not believe that these future expenses should be any less a charge on the ship than past expenses. To

---

2. *The Bouker No. 2,* supra; The Mars, 149 F. 729 (3 Cir.1907); The Eastern Dawn, 25 F.2d 322 (3 Cir.1928); The Troy, 121 F. 901 (2 Cir.1903); Geistlinger v. International Mercantile Marine Co., 295 F. 176 (2 Cir. 1924).

3. The District Court said:

"He will continue to have these spells and to have pain in the area of the fracture. He will need treatment and medical care from time to time and probably some care for the rest of his life.

He was always a healthy individual before his accident and never showed any signs of epilepsy before then. The medical testimony also shows that his condition of blindness is permanent, that in all likelihood his convulsive attacks will continue, and possibly become more frequent, and without any possibility of a further cure. The attacks and headaches mentioned will require some care from time to time whenever they persist."

conclude as the Court now does that they are not is to ignore in part the salutary policy supporting the doctrine of maintenance and cure.

Maintenance and cure is an ancient doctrine. It reflects in part the concern which the state has had from an early date in a poor and improvident class of workers. See Mr. Justice Story in Harden v. Gordon, Fed.Cas. No. 6,047. It also recognizes the imperative necessity of the nation to maintain in peace and war a merchant marine. If men are to go down to the sea in ships and face the perils of the ocean, those who employ them must be solicitous of their welfare. Maintenance and cure is an inducement on the part of masters and owners to be solicitous of the health, safety, and welfare of seamen while they are in the service. It gives a degree of security, though injury or sickness be incurred. It gives service in the merchant marine a dignity equal to the important function it performs. It reflects "the great public policy of preserving this important class of citizens for the commercial service and maritime defence of the nation." Id. at p. 483.

Accordingly, the injuries of seamen arising out of the service were made a charge against the enterprise to the extent at least of maintenance and cure. Their maintenance and cure was indeed part of the cost of the business. It is nonetheless a legitimate cost though the expense continues beyond the time when a maximum cure has been effected.[4]

NOTE

The holding in *Farrell* was explicated in Vella v. Ford Motor Co., 421 U.S. 1, 95 S.Ct. 1381, 43 L.Ed.2d 682, 1975 A.M.C. 563 (1975), where the Court held that the duty to provide maintenance and cure extends to the point at which there has been a good faith determination that the condition has reached maximum cure. In *Vella*, testimony at the trial indicated that the condition of the plaintiff was untreatable from the moment of the accident, and the Supreme Court held that no prior determination of the point of maximum cure having been made, the plaintiff was entitled to maintenance and cure up until the testimony was given at the trial.

When a seaman is injured on one vessel and then receives maintenance and cure from several successive vessels on which he serves, the owners of the latter may recover their payments from the vessel on which the seaman was injured. Gore v. Clearwater Shipping Corp., 378 F.2d 584, 1968 A.M.C. 396 (3d Cir.1967). It is held, however, that where the initial injury was not produced through either negligence or unseaworthiness, and the injury is "heightened" by the subsequent service, the vessels involved should make equal contribution to the cost of mainte-

---

4. The Shipowners' Liability Convention of 1936, 54 Stat. 1693, does not require a contrary result. Article 4, cl. 1, provides:

"The shipowner shall be liable to defray the expense of medical care and maintenance until the sick or injured person has been cured, or until the sickness or incapacity has been declared of a permanent character."

But Art. 12 contains a power to depart from that standard in this type of case. It provides:

"Nothing in this Convention shall affect any law, award, custom or agreement between shipowners and seamen which ensures more favourable conditions than those provided by this Convention."

nance and cure. Gooden v. Sinclair Refining Co., 378 F.2d 576, 1968 A.M.C. 210 (3d Cir.1967).

And when the injury or illness that creates the duty to pay maintenance and cure is caused solely or partly by a third person, the employer is entitled to indemnity or contribution, as the case may be, from the third party tortfeasor. Adams v. Texaco, Inc., 640 F.2d 618, 1982 A.M.C. 1004 (5th Cir.1981). And a suit for contribution in proportion to fault is not subject to the settlement bar rule, since the seaman's claims for maintenance and cure are separate from his claims for personal injury. Liberty Seafood Limitation Procs., 38 F.3d 755, 1995 A.M.C. 1142 (5th Cir.1994).

Computation of Wages

As pointed out by the dissenters in *Farrell*, unearned wages are payable to the end of the period of employment. See, e.g., Flores v. Carnival Cruise Lines, 47 F.3d 1120, 1995 A.M.C. 1360 (11th Cir.1995), in which unearned wages were paid a cabin steward on cruise vessels for the balance of a contract period of a year after illness forced him ashore.

In *Flores*, the plaintiff's contract called for a salary of $45 a month, payable every two weeks, plus tips, which were not guaranteed but which had averaged $800 a week during the period he served under the first contract, and $600 under the second. Judge Carnes observed, "The remedy has served its purposes well over the centuries. Until recently, no luxury cruise ships, no cabin stewards, and no system of compensation through tips from passengers existed to complicate the disabled seaman's simple right to recover wages." On policy, the court allowed average tips.

Amounts paid for maintenance are not subtracted from full past and future wages. The reason is explained in Rodriguez Alvarez v. Bahama Cruise Line, Inc., 898 F.2d 312, 316 (2d Cir.1990). "Because free food and lodging is a component of the seaman's compensation apart from wages ... an injured seaman would be less than whole if a ship operator were free to elect between providing maintenance and or furnishing lost wages." Judge Oakes added that earlier authority in the circuit precluded an action for damages, including lost wages and a second action for "maintenance, cure, and wages" in which the same wages were included in the ad damnum. See footnote 1 in *Rodriguez Alvarez*.

Vaughan v. Atkinson

Supreme Court of the United States, 1962.
369 U.S. 527, 82 S.Ct. 997, 8 L.Ed.2d 88.

■ Opinion of the Court by MR. JUSTICE DOUGLAS, announced by MR. JUSTICE BRENNAN.

This is a suit in admiralty brought by a seaman to recover (a) maintenance and cure and (b) damages for failure to pay maintenance and cure.[1] The District Court, while disallowing the claim for damages, granted maintenance, less any sums earned by the libellant during the period in question. 200 F.Supp. 802. The Court of Appeals affirmed, Chief Judge Sobeloff

[handwritten margin note: Suit for m/c & damages for failure to pay m/c]

---

1. Claims for damages for the illness and for wages, disallowed below, are not presented here.

dissenting. 291 F.2d 813. The case is here on a writ of certiorari. 368 U.S. 888.

Libellant served on respondents'[2] vessel from November 26, 1956, to March 2, 1957, when he was discharged on termination of a voyage. On March 7, 1957, he reported to a United States Public Health Service Hospital for examination and was admitted on March 18, 1957, as an inpatient, and treated for suspected tuberculosis. On June 6, 1957, he was discharged to an outpatient status and he remained in that status for over two years. On August 25, 1959, he was notified that he was fit for duty as of August 19, 1959.

The hospital records show a strong probability of active tuberculosis. The Master furnished libellant a certificate to enter the hospital on his discharge, March 2, 1957. Though libellant forwarded to the owner's agent an abstract of his clinical record at the hospital in 1957, the only investigation conducted by them was an interrogation of the Master and Chief Engineer, who stated that the libellant had never complained of any illness during his four months' service. The owner made no effort to make any further investigation of libellant's claim for maintenance and cure, and according to the findings did not bother even to admit or deny the validity of that claim. Nearly two years passed during which libellant was on his own. Ultimately he was required to hire an attorney and sue in the courts to recover maintenance and cure, agreeing to pay the lawyer a 50% contingent fee. Even so, the District Court held that no damages for failure to furnish maintenance and cure had been shown. In its view such damages are payable not for attorney's fees incurred but only when the failure to furnish maintenance and cure caused or aggravated the illness or other physical or mental suffering.

The District Court first allowed maintenance at the rate of $8 a day from June 6, 1957, to February 18, 1959. Since libellant during that period had worked as a taxi driver, the District Court ordered that his earnings be deducted from the amount owed by respondents. Subject to that credit, the order also provided that maintenance at $8 per day be continued until such time as the libellant reached the maximum state of recovery. The District Court allowed in addition 6% interest for each week's maintenance unpaid. Subsequently the District Court extended the maintenance to cover the period from March 7, 1957, to March 17, 1957, and from February 18, 1959, through August 25, 1959, these later awards being without interest.

The Court of Appeals denied counsel fees as damages, relying on the conventional rule that in suits for breach of contract the promisee is not allowed that item in computing the damages payable by the promisor. And the Court of Appeals, following Wilson v. United States, 229 F.2d 277 (2 Cir.1956) and Perez v. Suwanee S.S. Co., 239 F.2d 180 (2 Cir.1957) from the Second Circuit, held that a seaman has the duty to mitigate damages

---

2. The owner was American Waterways Corp., and National Shipping & Trading Corp. was its agent, both being respondents. Respondent Atkinson was the Master.

and that since "the purpose of maintenance and cure is to make the seaman whole," "he will get something more than he is entitled to" unless his earnings during the period are deducted.   291 F.2d, at 814, 815.

We disagree with the lower courts on both points.

I

Equity is no stranger in admiralty; admiralty courts are, indeed, authorized to grant equitable relief.   See Swift & Co. v. Compania Caribe, 339 U.S. 684, 691–692, 70 S.Ct. 861, 866, 94 L.Ed. 1206 (1950) where we said, "We find no restriction upon admiralty by chancery so unrelenting as to bar the grant of any equitable relief even when that relief is subsidiary to issues wholly within admiralty jurisdiction."

Counsel fees have been awarded in equity actions, as where Negroes were required to bring suit against a labor union to prevent discrimination. Rolax v. Atlantic Coast Line R. Co., 186 F.2d 473, 481 (4 Cir.1951).   As we stated in Sprague v. Ticonic Nat. Bank, 307 U.S. 161, 164, 59 S.Ct. 777, 779, 83 L.Ed. 1184 (1939) allowance of counsel fees and other expenses entailed by litigation, but not included in the ordinary taxable costs regulated by statute, is "part of the historic equity jurisdiction of the federal courts."   We do not have here that case.   Nor do we have the usual problem of what constitutes "costs" in the conventional sense.   Cf. The Baltimore, 75 U.S. 377, 19 L.Ed. 463, 8 Wall. 377 (1869).   Our question concerns damages.   Counsel fees were allowed in The Apollon, 22 U.S. 362, 6 L.Ed. 111, 9 Wheat. 362, 379 (1824) an admiralty suit where one party was put to expense in recovering demurrage of a vessel wrongfully seized. While failure to give maintenance and cure may give rise to a claim for damages for the suffering and for the physical handicap which follows (The Iroquois, 194 U.S. 240, 24 S.Ct. 640, 48 L.Ed. 955 (1904)), the recovery may also include "necessary expenses."   Cortes v. Baltimore Insular Line, 287 U.S. 367, 371, 53 S.Ct. 173, 174, 77 L.Ed. 368 (1932).

In the instant case respondents were callous in their attitude, making no investigation of libellant's claim and by their silence neither admitting nor denying it.   As a result of that recalcitrance, libellant was forced to hire a lawyer and go to court to get what was plainly owed him under laws that are centuries old.   The default was willful and persistent.   It is difficult to imagine a clearer case of damages suffered for failure to pay maintenance than this one.[3]

II

Maintenance and cure is designed to provide a seaman with food and lodging when he becomes sick or injured in the ship's service; and it extends during the period when he is incapacitated to do a seaman's work and continues until he reaches maximum medical recovery.   The policy

---

3. Whether counsel fees in the amount of 50% of the award are reasonable is a matter on which we express no opinion, as it was not considered by either the District Court or the Court of Appeals.

underlying the duty was summarized in Calmar S.S. Corp. v. Taylor, 303 U.S. 525, 528, 58 S.Ct. 651, 653, 82 L.Ed. 993 (1938):

> "The reasons underlying the rule, to which reference must be made in defining it, are those enumerated in the classic passage by Mr. Justice Story in Harden v. Gordon, Fed.Cas. No. 6047 (C.C.): the protection of seamen, who, as a class, are poor, friendless and improvident, from the hazards of illness and abandonment while ill in foreign ports; the inducement to masters and owners to protect the safety and health of seamen while in service; the maintenance of a merchant marine for the commercial service and maritime defense of the nation by inducing men to accept employment in an arduous and perilous service."

Admiralty courts have been liberal in interpreting this duty "for the benefit and protection of seamen who are its wards." Id., at 529. We noted in Aguilar v. Standard Oil Co., 318 U.S. 724, 730, 63 S.Ct. 930, 933, 934, 87 L.Ed. 1107 (1943) that the shipowner's liability for maintenance and cure was among "the most pervasive" of all and that it was not to be defeated by restrictive distinctions nor "narrowly confined." Id., at 735. When there are ambiguities or doubts, they are resolved in favor of the seaman. Warren v. United States, 340 U.S. 523, 71 S.Ct. 432, 95 L.Ed. 503 (1951).

Maintenance and cure differs from rights normally classified as contractual. As Mr. Justice Cardozo said in Cortes v. Baltimore Insular Line, supra, 371, the duty to provide maintenance and cure[4] "is imposed by the

---

4. It derives from Article VI of the Laws of Oleron, 30 Fed.Cas. 1171, 1174:

> "If any of the mariners hired by the master of any vessel, go out of the ship without his leave, and get themselves drunk, and thereby there happens contempt to their master, debates, or fighting and quarrelling among themselves, whereby some happen to be wounded: in this case the master shall not be obliged to get them cured, or in any thing to provide for them, but may turn them and their accomplices out of the ship; and if they make words of it, they are bound to pay the master besides: but if by the master's orders and commands any of the ship's company be in the service of the ship, and thereby happen to be wounded or otherwise hurt, in that case they shall be cured and provided for at the costs and charges of the said ship."

Justice Story, in holding that maintenance and cure was a charge upon the ship, said concerning its history:

> "The same principle is recognised in the ancient laws of Wisbuy (Laws of Wisbuy, art. 19), and in those of Oleron, which have been held in peculiar respect by England, and have been in some measure incorporated into her maritime jurisprudence. The Consolato del Mare does not speak particularly on this point; but from the provisions of this venerable collection of maritime usages in cases nearly allied, there is every reason to infer, that a similar rule then prevailed in the Mediterranean. Consolato del Mare, cc. 124, 125; Boucher, Consulat de la Mer, cc. 127, 128. Molloy evidently adopts it as a general doctrine of maritime law (Molloy, b. 2, c. 3, § 5, p. 243); and two elementary writers of most distinguished reputation have quoted it from the old ordinances without the slightest intimation, that it was not perfectly consonant with the received law and usage of England. Abb.Shipp. p. 2, c. 4, § 14; 2 Brown, Adm. 182–184. There is perhaps upon this subject a greater extent and uniformity of maritime authority, than can probably be found in support of most of those principles of commercial law, which have been so successfully engrafted into our jurisprudence within the last century." Harden v. Gordon, 11 Fed.Cas. 480, 483.

law itself as one annexed to the employment. * * * Contractual it is in the sense that it has its source in a relation which is contractual in origin, but given the relation, no agreement is competent to abrogate the incident."

In Johnson v. United States, 333 U.S. 46, 68 S.Ct. 391, 92 L.Ed. 468 (1948) we held that a seaman who while an outpatient was living on his parents' ranch without cost to himself was not entitled to maintenance payments. There maintenance and cure was wholly provided by others. Here the libellant was on his own for nearly two years and required to work in order to survive. It would be a sorry day for seamen if shipowners, knowing of the claim for maintenance and cure, could disregard it, force the disabled seaman to work, and then evade part or all of their legal obligation by having it reduced by the amount of the sick man's earnings. This would be a dreadful weapon in the hands of unconscionable employers and a plain inducement, as Chief Judge Sobeloff said below (291 F.2d at 820), to use the withholding of maintenance and cure as a means of forcing sick seamen to go to work when they should be resting, and to make the seamen themselves pay in whole or in part the amounts owing as maintenance and cure. This result is at war with the liberal attitude that heretofore has obtained and with admiralty's tender regard for seamen. We think the view of the Third Circuit (see Yates v. Dann, 223 F.2d 64, 67 (3 Cir.1955)) is preferable to that of the Second Circuit as expressed in Wilson v. United States and Perez v. Suwanee S.S. Co., supra, and to that of the Fourth Circuit in this case.

Reversed.

■ MR. JUSTICE FRANKFURTER took no part in the decision of this case.

■ MR. JUSTICE WHITE took no part in the consideration or decision of this case.

■ MR. JUSTICE STEWART, whom MR. JUSTICE HARLAN joins, dissenting.

I agree with the Court that whether earnings received by a disabled seaman prior to his maximum medical recovery are to be credited against the shipowner's obligation for maintenance is an issue which should not be resolved by a mechanical application of the rules of contract law relating to mitigation of damages. But I cannot agree that in this case the petitioner's earnings should not have been set off against the maintenance owed to him. Nor can I agree with the Court's conclusion that the petitioner is entitled as a matter of law to damages in the amount of the counsel fees expended in his suit for maintenance and cure.

The duty to provide maintenance and cure is in no real sense contractual, and a suit for failure to provide maintenance or cure can hardly be equated, therefore, with an action for breach of contract. "The duty * * * is one annexed by law to a relation, and annexed as an inseparable incident without heed to any expression of the will of the contracting parties." Cortes v. Baltimore Insular Line, 287 U.S. 367, 372, 53 S.Ct. 173, 174, 77 L.Ed. 368 (1932). Moreover, if the seaman's accountability for earnings were to be determined solely by reference to damage mitigation principles of contract law, the breach of the shipowner's duty to pay maintenance would become crucial, since without such a breach on his part no duty to mitigate would arise.[1] The assignment of such a dispositive role to the shipowner's failure to perform his obligation would create an unwarranted incentive for refusing to perform it.

The issue should be decided, rather, with reference to the scope of the duty which the admiralty law imposes. The obligation of a shipowner, irrespective of fault, to provide maintenance and cure to a seaman injured or taken ill while in the ship's service has lost much of its original significance in this era of relaxed unseaworthiness and negligence concepts. But the obligation is of ancient origin,[2] first recognized in our law in Harden v. Gordon, 11 Fed.Cas. 480, No. 6,047, and Reed. v. Canfield, 20 Fed.Cas. No. 11,651,426.[3] The duty was historically imposed in order to alleviate the physical and financial hardships which otherwise would have beset a sick or injured seaman put ashore, perhaps in a foreign port, without means of support, or hope of obtaining medical care. See Harden v. Gordon, supra, at 483 (Story, J.). The law of the sea sought to alleviate these hardships, partly for humanitarian reasons, and partly because of the strong national interest in maintaining the morale and physical effectiveness of the merchant marine. Calmar S.S. Corp. v. Taylor, 303 U.S. 525, 528, 58 S.Ct. 651, 653, 82 L.Ed. 993 (1938).

But "[t]he duty does not extend beyond the seaman's need." Calmar S.S. Corp. v. Taylor, supra, at 531. It ends absolutely when a point of maximum medical recovery has been reached. Id., at 530; Farrell v. United States, 336 U.S. 511, 69 S.Ct. 707, 93 L.Ed. 850 (1949). And when the seaman has not incurred expense, the shipowner has no obligation to make payment.[4] Thus a seaman hospitalized without expense in a marine hospital is not entitled to maintenance and cure for that period. Calmar S.S. Corp. v. Taylor, supra, at 531. Nor must the shipowner pay maintenance to a seaman who convalesces at the home of his parents without incurring expense or liability for his support. Johnson v. United States, 333 U.S. 46, 50, 68 S.Ct. 391, 393, 394, 92 L.Ed. 468 (1948).

---

1. McCormick, *Damages,* §§ 158–160; Restatement, Contracts, § 336(1); 5 Corbin, *Contracts,* § 1041.

2. The earliest codifications of the law of the sea provided for medical treatment and wages for mariners injured or falling ill in the ship's service. These early maritime codes are, for the most part, reprinted in 30 Fed.Cas. 1171–1216. See Arts. VI and VII of the Laws of Oleron, 30 Fed.Cas. 1174–1175; Arts. XVIII, XIX, and XXXIII of the Laws of Wisbuy, 30 Fed.Cas. 1191, 1192; Arts. XXXIX and XLV of the Laws of the Hanse Towns, 30 Fed.Cas. 1200; and Title Fourth, Arts. XI and XII, of the Marine Ordinances of Louis XIV, 30 Fed.Cas. 1209. These provisions may also be found reprinted in 2 Norris, The Law of Seamen, § 537. Other provisions rather similar to the present maintenance and cure remedy may be found in the Ordinances of Trani, Art. X, 4 Black Book of the Admiralty (Twiss' ed. 1876) 531; The Tables of Amalphi, Art. 14, 4 Black Book of the Admiralty (Twiss' ed. 1876) 13.

3. See Gilmore and Black, *Admiralty,* 253.

4. See Stankiewicz v. United Fruit S.S. Corp., 229 F.2d 580 (2 Cir.1956); Williams v. United States, 228 F.2d 129 (4 Cir.1956); Dodd v. The M/V Peggy G., 149 F.Supp. 823 (5 Cir.1957); Nunes v. Farrell Lines, Inc., 129 F.Supp. 147 (D.C.Mass.1955), affirmed as to this point, 227 F.2d 619 (1955); Ballard v. Alcoa S.S. Co., Inc., 122 F.Supp. 10 (D.C.Ala. 1954); Gilmore and Black, *Admiralty,* 266; 2 Norris, *The Law of Seamen,* § 568.

Since the limited purpose of maintenance is to make the seaman whole, it would logically follow that there should be no such duty for periods when the seaman, though not yet at the point of maximum cure, either does in fact obtain equivalently gainful employment or is able to do so.[5] Moreover, no rule which keeps able workers idle can be deemed a desirable one.[6] But there are countervailing policies involved in resolving the issue. The adequate protection of an injured or ill seaman against suffering and want requires more than the assurance that he will receive payments at some time in the indefinite future. Payments must be promptly made, at a time contemporaneous to the illness or injury. And for this reason the maintenance remedy should be kept simple, uncluttered by fine distinctions which breed litigation, with its attendant delays and expenses. See Farrell v. United States, 336 U.S. 511, 516, 69 S.Ct. 707, 709, 93 L.Ed. 850 (1949). A shipowner should therefore not be encouraged to withhold maintenance payments in the hope that economic necessity will

5. Similarly, there is generally no duty to make payments for cure if marine hospital service is available, and a seaman seeks hospitalization elsewhere. United States v. Loyola, 161 F.2d 126 (9 Cir.1947); United States v. Johnson, 160 F.2d 789 (9 Cir.1947); Marshall v. International Mercantile Marine Co., 39 F.2d 551 (2 Cir.1930); Zackey v. American Export Lines, Inc., 152 F.Supp. 772 (2 Cir. 1957); Benton v. United Towing Co., 120 F.Supp. 638 (D.C.Cal.1954). See Kossick v. United Fruit Co., 365 U.S. 731, 737, 81 S.Ct. 886, 891, 6 L.Ed.2d 56 (1961); Calmar S.S. Corp. v. Taylor, 303 U.S. 525, 531, 58 S.Ct. 651, 654, 82 L.Ed. 993 (1937). In exceptional circumstances, however, where adequate treatment is not available at a marine hospital, expenses incurred for hospitalization elsewhere may be chargeable to the shipowner. Williams v. United States, 133 F.Supp. 319 (D.C.Va.1955) aff'd, 228 F.2d 129 (4 Cir. 1956).

6. Actual earnings during a period prior to maximum cure have been allowed as an offset against maintenance payments in many reported cases, usually without discussion. Rodgers v. United States Lines Co., 189 F.2d 226 (4 Cir.1951); Inter Ocean S.S. Co. v. Behrendsen, 128 F.2d 506 (6 Cir.1942); Loverich v. Warner Co., 118 F.2d 690 (3 Cir.1941); Colon v. Trinidad Corp., 188 F.Supp. 97 (2 Cir.1960); Scott v. Lykes Bros. S.S. Co., 152 F.Supp. 104 (D.C.La.1957); Benton v. United Towing Co., 120 F.Supp. 638 (D.C.Cal.1954) aff'd, 224 F.2d 558 (1955); Steinberg v. American Export Lines Inc., 81 F.Supp. 362 (D.C.Pa.1948); Burch v. Smith, 77 F.Supp. 6 (D.C.Pa.1948); The Eastern

Dawn, 25 F.2d 322 (3 Cir.1928). In Wilson v. United States, 229 F.2d 277 (2 Cir.1956), the court held, after discussion, that the shipowner should be permitted to offset potential earnings, the seaman having failed to establish that he could not have secured work. The seaman had done some work during the period, and had not sought maintenance for the days he was actually employed. The same court subsequently ruled that under *Wilson* a recuperating seaman must account for actual earnings. Perez v. Suwanee S.S. Co., 239 F.2d 180 (2 Cir.1957).

In three cases setoff of actual earnings has been denied. In Yates v. Dann, 124 F.Supp. 125 (D.C.Del.1954) the district judge found that the seaman had been "in need" throughout the whole period and should not be "penalized" because he returned to work. The case was reversed on other grounds, 223 F.2d 64 (1955) the court sustaining the ruling of the District Court on this point with the statement that "the circumstance that appellee was forced by financial necessity to return to his regular employment is not legally a bar to his recovery." 223 F.2d, at 67. See also Hanson v. Reiss Steamship Co., 184 F.Supp. 545, 550 (D.C.Del.1960) ("Liability for maintenance and cure does not necessarily cease when the injured person obtains gainful occupation where such employment is compelled or induced by economic necessity."); Meirino v. Gulf Oil Corp., 170 F.Supp. 515, 517 (D.C.Pa.1959)("The fact that libellant returned to work because of economic necessity while he was in need of medical care and attention does not deprive him of his right to maintenance and cure.").

force the seaman back to work and thereby reduce the shipowner's liability. Moreover, maintenance payments are designed to meet the living expenses of the seaman until maximum cure is reached. The ultimate goal is the recovery of the seaman, and this requires the avoidance of pressures which would force him to obtain employment which hinders his recovery.[7]

The need for prompt payment and the desirability of avoiding any rule which might force a seaman back to work to the detriment of his recovery might well require that no compulsion to seek employment be placed on a convalescing seaman, and that a setoff be allowed only with respect to actual, as opposed to potential, earnings. But this question is not presented by the record before us. Similarly, it may well be that a seaman should not be held to account for actual earnings to a shipowner whose dereliction in making payments compels the seaman, as a matter of economic necessity, to obtain gainful employment. But that question is not presented by the present case either, for there is no showing here that the seaman's return to work was brought on by economic necessity. So far as the record before us indicates, the petitioner's return to work was completely voluntary, and not the result of the shipowner's failure to pay maintenance. Holding the seaman accountable for his earnings in such circumstances carries out the basic purpose of making the seaman whole, and creates neither an undue incentive for withholding payments, nor pressure compelling a premature return to work. I therefore think that the District Court and the Court of Appeals were right in holding that the petitioner was not entitled to maintenance for the period during which he was gainfully employed as a taxicab driver.[8]

The second issue presented in this case is whether the petitioner should have been awarded damages in the amount of the counsel fees incurred in bringing his action for maintenance and cure. The Court held in Cortes v. Baltimore Insular Line, supra, at 371, that "[i]f the failure to give maintenance or cure has caused or aggravated an illness, the seaman has his right of action for the injury thus done to him, the recovery in such circumstances including not only necessary expenses, but also compensation for the hurt." But neither the *Cortes* decision, nor any other that I have been able to find, furnishes a basis for holding as a matter of law that a seaman forced to bring suit to recover maintenance and cure is also

---

7. A seaman whose condition is actually aggravated by reason of the shipowner's dereliction in making maintenance and cure payments may of course seek damages above and beyond the maintenance and cure payments due. Cortes v. Baltimore Insular Line, 287 U.S. 367, 53 S.Ct. 173, 77 L.Ed. 368 (1932). But the availability of this remedy does not detract from the importance of avoiding the harmful effects of a premature return to work.

8. I would, however, remand the case to the District Court for recomputation of its award. Maintenance is a day-by-day concept, and in my view maintenance should be reduced or denied only as to days during which the petitioner was gainfully employed. Instead, the District Court computed the total amount of maintenance due, and then deducted the total amount earned by the petitioner. Compare Perez v. Suwanee S.S. Co., 239 F.2d 180 (2 Cir.1957) with Wilson v. United States, 229 F.2d 277 (2 Cir.1956). See the full discussion of this aspect of the problem in Note, 37 N.Y.U.L.Rev. 316, 320–321.

entitled to recover his counsel fees. *Cortes* dealt with compensatory damages for a physical injury, and the opinion in that case contains nothing to indicate a departure from the well-established rule that counsel fees may not be recovered as compensatory damages. McCormick, Damages, § 61.

However, if the shipowner's refusal to pay maintenance stemmed from a wanton and intentional disregard of the legal rights of the seaman, the latter would be entitled to exemplary damages in accord with traditional concepts of the law of damages. McCormick, Damages, § 79. While the amount so awarded would be in the discretion of the fact finder, and would not necessarily be measured by the amount of counsel fees, indirect compensation for such expenditures might thus be made. See Day v. Woodworth, 54 U.S. (13 How.) 363, 371, 14 L.Ed. 181 (1851). On this issue I would accordingly remand the case to the District Court, so that the circumstances which motivated the respondents' failure to make maintenance payments could be fully canvassed.

NOTE

Other forms of income have been treated similarly. See, e.g., Morel v. Sabine Towing & Transp. Co., Inc., 669 F.2d 345, 1984 A.M.C. 1318 (5th Cir.1982), holding that accumulated leave time is not to be deducted from maintenance. See also Gauthier v. Crosby Marine Service, Inc., 752 F.2d 1085, 1985 A.M.C. 2477 (5th Cir.1985), in which it was held that amounts paid by Blue Cross–Blue Shield under a policy paid for by the seaman are not to be deducted. In Shaw v. Ohio River Co., 526 F.2d 193, 1976 A.M.C. 1164 (3d Cir.1975), it was held that payments under a non-occupational disability policy provided for under the labor contract were not to be credited against the duty to pay maintenance and cure, since the payments could be looked upon as wages. In the case of amounts paid under a Blue Cross–Blue Shield policy paid for by the employer, however, the court of appeals held that case was governed by the general principle that the employer is not liable to pay for maintenance and cure that has been provided to the employee without charge.

When 90% of the Accident and Sickness portion the Plan and 100% of the Major Medical portion were funded by the employer, the court of appeals expressed doubt that the district court was correct in holding that payments from the Plan were a collateral source, but affirmed on the alternative ground that the issue had not been timely raised, Davis v. Odeco, Inc., 18 F.3d 1237 (5th Cir.1994).

The same medical expenses cannot be recovered as damages and as "cure." Colburn v. Bunge Towing, Inc., 883 F.2d 372 (5th Cir.1989).

Maintenance payments are payable only when there have been actual expenditures or the employee has incurred actual liabilities. The employee makes a prima facie case by showing the actual expenditures he found it necessary to incur, and his own testimony as to the reasonable cost of room and board is enough to support an award, but an award made without any indication of record that any expenditures were actually incurred will be reversed. Curry v. Fluor Drilling Services, Inc., 715 F.2d 893 (5th Cir.1983). It is a purely personal right and does not embrace the cost of maintaining other members of the family. See Macedo v. F/V Paul & Michelle, supra, in which the court of appeals reversed an award , and commented in passing that the district court erred in computing it on the figures supplied on the household expenses of the seaman and his wife, despite an attempt to establish the fact that the wife was a "light" eater.

For a long period maintenance was usually granted in a flat daily amount, sometimes viewed as customary, sometimes fixed in the union contract. Eight dollars a day is the figure used in a great many cases. For a collection of cases and the amounts awarded, see Norris, 2 *The Law of Seamen*, § 607 (3d Ed.1970), and 1984 Cumulative Supp. Recent cases indicate that the amount allowed should be related to actual cost in the community. See Wood v. Diamond M Drilling Co., 691 F.2d 1165, 1983 A.M.C. 2959 (5th Cir.1982), cert. denied 460 U.S. 1069, 103 S.Ct. 1523, 75 L.Ed.2d 947 (1983), holding that $30 was not excessive. And see Autin v. Otis Engineering Corp., 641 F.2d 197, 1982 A.M.C. 601 (5th Cir.1981), in which the plaintiff put on expert testimony by an economist to establish the cost of board. In Billy Joe Bell v. Zapata Haynie Corp., 855 F.Supp. 152, 1995 A.M.C. 785 (W.D.La. 1994), the court declined to determine on summary judgment whether $15 a day is so grossly inadequate as to justify an award of punitive damages.

There has been sharp disagreement over the question whether the rate can be set by union contract. The First, Sixth, and Ninth Circuits have held that a union contract rate is binding. Macedo v. F/V Paul & Michelle, 868 F.2d 519, 522 (1st Cir.1989); Al–Zawkari v. American S.S. 871 F.2d 585 (6th Cir.1989); Gardiner v. Sea–Land Service,Inc., 786 F.2d 943 (9th Cir.1986), cert. denied 479 U.S. 924, 107 S.Ct. 331, 93 L.Ed.2d 303 (1986). In the Third Circuit it is held that the collective bargaining agreement is not controlling. Barnes v. Andover Co., 900 F.2d 630 (3d Cir.1990). Following *Barnes* in the Second Circuit, see Brown v. United States, 882 F.Supp. 1424, 1995 A.M.C. 1801 (S.D.N.Y.1995). In the Fifth Circuit it has been held that the right to maintenance and cure and to unearned wages cannot be waived in an employment contract, but has not reached the issue of the rate. Dowdle v. Offshore Express, Inc., 809 F.2d 259 (5th Cir.1987).

Turning to the other issue decided in Vaughan v. Atkison, the award of attorney's fees in an action for maintenance and cure can be distinguished from a suit to recover damages flowing from failure to provide maintenance and cure. Such suits were entertained before the Jones Act. See The Iroquois, cited by the majority in Vaughan v. Atkison, above at p. 885. And they were recognized as a basis for a suit under the Jones Act. See Cortes v. Baltimore Insular Line, cited at the same place. This distinction continues to be recognized. See, e.g., Gaspard v. Taylor Diving & Salvage Co., 649 F.2d 372, 1982 A.M.C. 2875 (5th Cir.1981), cert. denied 455 U.S. 907, 102 S.Ct. 1252, 71 L.Ed.2d 445 (1982), affirming a judgment of $45,000 Jones Act damages in respect of an accident to a diver, and $296,000 for employer's failure to provide him with decompression treatments after notice that he was suffering from decompression illness.

Under Vaughan v. Atkison, attorney's fees may be awarded when the failure to provide maintenance and cure is unreasonable under the circumstances. See Catrakis v. Nautilus Petroleum Carriers Corp., 427 F.Supp. 255, 1977 A.M.C. 1980 (S.D.N.Y.1977). Plaintiff was a ship's officer who was the victim of an unprovoked assault by a member of the crew during shore leave in a foreign country. The court characterized the refusal as "callous" and awarded interest and a 40% attorney's fee. Award of attorney's fees was affirmed on a finding that the refusal was "arbitrary and capricious" in Deisler v. McCormack Aggregates Co., 54 F.3d 1074 (3d Cir.1995).

For cases in which it has been held that the refusal was not unreasonable, see, e.g., Bergeron v. Lionel Mire, 1982 A.M.C. 1203 (E.D.La.1981), in which the seaman was given maintenance at $8 a day in respect of a siege of hepatitis, but attorney's fees were denied. The court found that the employer had not acted arbitrarily since there was at the time a strong speculative possibility that plaintiff's illness was caused by his smoking marijuana cigarettes, although there was a failure of proof of wilful misconduct. And where the seaman did not inform his employer of a continuing problem until several years had elapsed, there could be no liability for capricious refusal to pay. Harrell v. Dixon Bay Transp. Co., 718 F.2d 123, 1985 A.M.C. 2407 (5th Cir.1983).

See also Harper v. Zapata Off–Shore Co., 741 F.2d 87, 1985 A.M.C. 979 (5th Cir.1984), in which the court declined to hold that payment of the customary $8 a day constituted an unreasonable refusal to pay adequate maintenance, although at the trial the district court fixed the figure at $40.

The question whether the holding in Vaughn v. Atkinson justifies an award of punitive damages as well as attorney's fees in cases charging unreasonable refusal to pay maintenance and cure has remained unsettled. It was held in the First and Fifth Circuits that punitive damages could be awarded for a failure to provide maintenance and cure that is "callous and recalcitrant, arbitrary and capricious, or willful, callous, and persistent." Robinson v. Pocahontas, Inc., 477 F.2d 1048 (1st Cir.1973); Holmes v. J.Ray McDermott & Co., 734 F.2d 1110, 1985 A.M.C. 2024 (5th Cir.1984). The Second Circuit read **Vaughn** to permit award of punitive damages only to the extent of the amount of attorney's fees. Kraljic v. Berman Enterprises, Inc., 575 F.2d 412, 1978 A.M.C. 1297 (2d Cir.1978). Superimposed on this difference of opinion is the decision in Miles v. Apex Marine Corp., 498 U.S. 19, 111 S.Ct. 317, 112 L.Ed.2d 275 (1990), precluding the award of punitive damages in actions for the wrongful death of a seaman under the general maritime law. See Ch. 20, infra. The Ninth Circuit has rejected the contention that **Miles** controls, but read **Vaughn** to preclude punitive damages. Glynn v. Roy Al Boat Mgt. Corp., 57 F.3d 1495 (9th Cir.1995). The Fifth has held itself bound by **Holmes**, but indicated that in light of **Miles**, the issue should be reexamined en banc. Guevara v. Maritime Overseas Corp., 34 F.3d 1279, 1995 A.M.C. 321 (5th Cir.1994).

REJECTION OF MEDICAL CARE

Until 1981, the United States Public Health Service Hospitals provided free medical care for merchant seamen, and it was held that an arbitrary refusal of treatment at such a hospital without cause would forfeit the right to maintenance and cure. See Kossick v. United Fruit Co., 365 U.S. 731, 737, 81 S.Ct. 886, 891, 6 L.Ed.2d 56 (1961). But if the care available at the Public Health Hospital was inadequate, the seaman could seek care from a private physician. See Kratzer v. Capital Marine Supply, Inc., 645 F.2d 477, 1982 A.M.C. 2691 [DRO] (5 Cir.1981). Where the forfeiture rule was applied it was held, however, that the seaman forfeited only so much as he forewent by declining treatment. Thus if he turned down outpatient treatment at the Public Health Hospital and was attended by his own physician, he would forfeit his cure without necessarily forfeiting his maintenance. See Pelotto v. L & N Towing Co., 604 F.2d 396, 1981 A.M.C. 1047 (5th Cir.1979).

The Public Health Hospitals no longer provide such free care. See Omnibus Budget Reconciliation Act of 1981, Act of August 13, 1981, §§ 986–988, Pub.L. 97–35, 95 Stat. 603–604. Provision was made for continued care in some "pipe line" cases. See discussion in Jones v. Reagan, 748 F.2d 1331, 1985 A.M.C. 944 (9th Cir.1984), cert. denied 472 U.S. 1029, 105 S.Ct. 3505, 87 L.Ed.2d 636 (1985). It has been held that refusal to accept treatment by a private doctor designated by the employer does not stand on the same footing, and maintenance and cure can be claimed if there is no determination that the private physician chosen by the seaman provided more unnecessary or expensive treatment than the designated physician would have supplied. Caulfield v. AC & D Marine, Inc., 633 F.2d 1129, 1982 A.M.C. 1033 (5th Cir.1981).

The question arises whether refusal to accept free medical care under various public health programs, such as medicare, forfeits maintenance and cure. In Moran Towing & Transportation Co. v. Lombas, 843 F.Supp. 885 (S.D.N.Y.1994). aff'd 58 F.3d 24 (2d Cir.1995), it was held that a seaman who had been placed on disability and therefore was eligible for medicare could not demand "cure" on the ground that his surgeon refused to waive co-payment without investigating whether a surgeon was available who would waive co-payment.

The question of acceptance of free care at the Public Health facilities apart, it has been held that wilful refusal of medical treatment may forfeit maintenance and cure. See Coulter v. Ingram Pipeline, Inc., 511 F.2d 735, 1975 A.M.C. 826 (5th Cir.1975), although in that case the court declined to exact a forfeiture based upon an obese longshoreman's inability without more adequate supervision to stay on a 1,500 calorie diet.

4.   THE WARRANTY OF SEAWORTHINESS

A.   WHAT CONSTITUTES UNSEAWORTHINESS

Hughes v. ContiCarriers and Terminals, Inc.

United States Court of Appeals, Seventh Circuit, 1993.
6 F.3d 1195, 1994 A.M.C. 436.

■ EASTERBROOK, CIRCUIT JUDGE.

River towboats push rather than pull their cargo. M/V CONTI-KARLA, built in 1980, was designed to push fleets of fifteen or more barges on the Mississippi. Maneuvering a chain of barges, with power from far astern, is possible only if the barges are lashed tightly with steel cables, to each other and to the towboat. Cables between the bow or face of the towboat and the closest barge are called facewires. Towboats sit low in the water, while barges may ride higher, especially if unladen. To prevent it from driving under the barges, a towboat has a pair of sturdy pillars, usually called towknees, rising above its blunt prow. * * *

[T]here is a narrow walkway 2 to 3½ feet wide between the vessel's cabin and the water. Crew who must work outside may hold onto the banisters attached to the cabin. Like most modern towboats, the CONTI-KARLA also is equipped with a safety line around its perimeter. The nylon line begins at the towknee and runs through upright stanchions around the vessel. The stanchions may be lowered in order to get the safety line out of the way when members of the crew need to work nearby, so that the men won't constantly be stepping over the line—a hazard as well as an inconvenience. Parts of the lines come down when the towboat is coupling or uncoupling from the barges, when the crew is connecting or disconnecting fuel or water hoses, or taking on supplies, and so on.

On June 28, 1986, the CONTI-KARLA unfaced from her tow of barges so that she could refuel. The procedure entails taking the barges to a fleeting area and removing the facewires that join the towboat to the closest barge. These heavy steel cables are too rigid to take up on a winch and spindle, so the crew of the towboat places the cables in the long walkways between the cabin and the water. (The CONTI-KARLA is 115 feet from stem to stern, so there is plenty of room.) After unfacing from the barges, the CONTI-KARLA docked three miles away to take on fuel and water. The CONTI-KARLA'S port side adjoined the dock. While unfacing from the barges and tying up at dock, the CONTI-KARLA was under the command of Captain Oscar Bechard. At noon that day command passed to Rex W. Hughes, the pilot, who was in charge of the next watch. (The CONTI-KARLA carried two full complements, alternating in service, so that it could operate 24 hours a day.)

When Hughes began his watch, the CONTI-KARLA was securely tied to the dock. The weather was sunny and calm. Hughes noticed that the section of the safety line from the starboard towknee to the first stanchion was down. It had been lowered during the unfacing, and the crew had not put it back up. Hughes shouted to one of the seamen to put the line back in position. Apparently the seaman did not hear the order. Instead of using the vessel's intercom to repeat the command, or walking closer to the seaman, Hughes decided to restore the safety line himself. As he was walking toward the line he tripped over the facewires and fell overboard.

Hughes filed this suit under the law of admiralty and the Jones Act, 46 U.S.C.App. § 688. The maritime action was based on the requirement that the vessel be seaworthy. The Jones Act claim asserted that the employer was negligent. A jury, answering special interrogatories, determined that the vessel was seaworthy and that its owner, ContiCarriers and Terminals, Inc., had not been negligent. The district court granted judgment for Hughes on the admiralty claim notwithstanding the verdict, 753 F.Supp. 221 (N.D.Ill.1990), and later awarded damages of $813,000, Hughes v. ContiCarriers and Terminals, Inc., 1992 WL 32882. The judge reasoned that because the doctrine of unseaworthiness is a species of liability without fault, any injury on the vessel is compensable: "The concept of absolute liability in these areas unlimited by growing concern in employer-employee relations in industry for dictates of comparative and relative negligence, has justly been found to be and is in fact grounded in fundamental fairness." 753 F.Supp. at 225. Yet admiralty does not include a workers' compensation program parallel to the Longshore and Harbor Workers' Compensation Act, which covers dock workers. Seamen did not give up the tort measure of damages and receive broader coverage in return. Although the doctrine of unseaworthiness entails liability without fault, there must still be a defect in the vessel. "The standard is not perfection, but reasonable fitness; not a ship that will weather every conceivable storm or withstand every imaginable peril of the sea, but a vessel reasonably suitable for her intended service." Mitchell v. Trawler Racer, Inc., 362 U.S. 539, 550, 80 S.Ct. 926, 933, 4 L.Ed.2d 941 (1960). See also Morales v. Galveston, 370 U.S. 165, 170, 82 S.Ct. 1226, 1229, 8 L.Ed.2d

412 (1962); Seas Shipping Co. v. Sieracki, 328 U.S. 85, 94–95, 66 S.Ct. 872, 877, 90 L.Ed. 1099 (1946). A seaman must show that an unsafe condition on the vessel caused his injury; dispensing with the need to prove that some "fault" led to this condition does not dispense with the need to establish that there was one.

Portions of the district court's opinion suggest that Hughes' own inept effort to restore the safety line was the unsafe condition: "Whether this condition, which the plaintiff had sought in an incorrect way to correct, was purposefully or accidentally left that way by the captain of the vessel when he went off duty, his failure to correct it was the tug's failure, and the failure of the pilot when coming on duty to use safe methods in correcting it, were also the ship's failures and improprieties." 753 F.Supp. at 228. Hughes does not defend the conclusion that his own errors support recovery; his negligence not only is not attributed to the vessel but also could be the basis for reducing an award otherwise justified. Socony-Vacuum Oil Co. v. Smith, 305 U.S. 424, 431, 59 S.Ct. 262, 266, 83 L.Ed. 265 (1939); Chotin Transportation, Inc. v. United States, 819 F.2d 1342, 1354 (6th Cir.1987); van Nijenhoff v. Bantry Transportation Co., 791 F.2d 26, 27 (2d Cir.1986); Norris, *The Law of Seamen* § 27:19 (4th ed. 1985). That is to say, admiralty recognizes the doctrine of comparative fault, which would be destroyed (and the system converted to one of workers' compensation) if the sailor's negligence were imputed to the vessel.

Hughes' own theory is that both the facewires and the guard lines were in an unsafe condition—the facewires because they were so worn that burrs entangled his leg and caused him to lose his balance, and the guard line because it was down, so that he could not grab something to stop the fall. The jury rejected these submissions, and we must now take the evidence in the light most favorable to the verdict. Atlantic & Gulf Stevedores, Inc. v. Ellerman Lines, Ltd., 369 U.S. 355, 358–59, 82 S.Ct. 780, 782–83, 7 L.Ed.2d 798 (1962); Tennant v. Peoria Ry., 321 U.S. 29, 35, 64 S.Ct. 409, 412, 88 L.Ed. 520 (1944). Several witnesses testified that the facewires were in good condition, looped and bent (thick steel cables do not lie straight and flat after they have been bent and subjected to tension) but not burred. Hughes insisted that they were inordinately worn and frayed, with projections that would snag passing trousers, but the jury did not have to accept this evidence. Thus Hughes' claim depends on the fact that the safety line was down. The crew properly took it down while unfacing from the barges and, all witnesses agreed, should have put it back up before leaving the fleeting area. According to Hughes, this supplies the necessary unsafe condition.

If Hughes had fallen overboard while the towboat was under way, he would have a solid argument. But he did not; he fell while the vessel was at rest. Evidence at trial conflicted on the question whether a vessel at dockside is unsafe when the safety lines are down. Hughes and his witnesses testified that safety depends on the lines being up unless the crew is then performing an operation (such as unfacing from the barges) that requires them to be down. ContiCarriers presented substantial contrary evidence. We mention only some of it.

Its star witness was retired Admiral Owen Siler. Between 1971 and 1974 Admiral Siler was District Commander of the Second Coast Guard District, which supervises inland navigation. Later he became Commandant of the Coast Guard. Admiral Siler testified that safety lines need not be up when a towboat is docked, and that there are good reasons for having them down—crew members moving back and forth in the vicinity otherwise would step over them, or put them up and down frequently, with greater risks than leaving them down. Admiral Siler stated explicitly that the CONTI-KARLA tied up at dock with the safety lines down, was a "reasonably safe" place to work. ContiCarriers' experience reinforces this conclusion: several of its employees testified that the safety lines regularly are left down while its vessels are docked, yet in the history of the company (which operates 10 towboats) no one other than Hughes has fallen overboard.

ContiCarriers' general manager, with 30 years' experience in the industry (including almost every position from deckhand on up), testified that because the safety line can pose a danger while the crew is performing work with the facewires or in port, many towboats do not have such lines near the bow. Other witnesses gave similar testimony. A jury would have been entitled to discount this testimony, which came from ContiCarriers' managers and employees (and from an expert witness in ContiCarriers' pay), but the jury was also entitled to accept it—as it did.

Appellate judges ought not say that as; a matter of law the views of the former Commandant of the Coast Guard on a matter of maritime safety are unacceptable. Especially when the Admiral's testimony accords with the opinions of other appellate judges who have held that a safety line is unnecessary when a vessel is moored or in calm waters.

> Seaworthiness is a relative term; a vessel may have that quality in port, and yet be wholly unfit for rough water; and to say that the ship was unseaworthy because she had no handrail up, while lying alongside a wharf discharging cargo, is merely untrue.

Hanrahan v. Pacific Transport Co., 262 F. 951, 952 (2d Cir.1919)(citation omitted). See also Lester v. United States, 234 F.2d 625, 628 (2d Cir.1956)(motionless vessel seaworthy despite lack of guard rails required by contract); Newport News Shipbuilding & Dry Dock Co. v. Watson, 19 F.2d 832, 833 (4th Cir.1927)(hand railing around deck house makes vessel seaworthy; outer hand railing would unduly interfere with operations).

Another route to the same conclusion does not depend on the relative worth of the testimony. The stanchions and safety lines were constructed so that the lines could be taken down and put back up. Unfacing from the barges is an appropriate occasion for having the line down. Hughes concedes that the crew properly took the line down at the fleeting area. The condition of "safety line down" thus does not automatically make the vessel unseaworthy. It means only that the line must be put back up. That is exactly what Hughes was trying to do when he fell. Hughes was not walking along the edge of the vessel, oblivious to the lack of a safety line; he did not rely on an apparently sound piece of equipment that failed. In Villers Seafood Co. v. Vest, 813 F.2d 339 (11th Cir.1987), a ladder collapsed because the pins securing it in place had been removed, unbeknownst to the person trying to climb. Equipment that injures a sailor ignorant of its defect presents problems distinct from ours. Hughes knew full well about the condition of the line (and of the facewires). Given his concession that the towboat does not become unseaworthy the instant the line drops, and given the implication that putting the line back up is an ordinary task for the crew—one that can be performed in reasonable safety when done properly—Hughes needed to show that it was more hazardous to restore the line in port than at the fleeting area. He did not try to do so, probably because he recognizes that it is less risky to handle the safety line while the towboat is lashed to a dock than when it is in open water. A captain might accept the greater risk of putting the safety line back up in the fleeting area in order to obtain the increase in safety that the line would provide while the towboat was in transit to the dock. A seaman who fell overboard while the vessel was underway thus would have a legitimate complaint. But Hughes did not fall victim to that risk. He was injured while trying to put the line back up. And that operation is not unacceptably risky.

To put this slightly differently, someone had to bear whatever risk inheres in raising the safety line while the facewires are on deck. The timing of the operation affected who bore the risk—a sailor on the morning watch, or a sailor on the afternoon watch—but did not increase the level of risk to the person moving the safety lines. Cf. William M. Landes & Richard A. Posner, *The Economic Structure of Tort Law* 237–39 (1987). Both crews have seamen experienced in handling stanchions and safety lines, and the task is no riskier when done in the afternoon than in the morning. Hughes increased that risk by acting carelessly. As the district court observed, Hughes was carrying a case, so that he had only one hand free to move the line and balance himself, and he approached the stanchion the wrong way. (Hughes testified that he did not approach the stanchion from the proper direction because he was concerned that he would soil his shirt passing under a radio antenna.) That increase in risk is Hughes' own responsibility; it shows that he went about the task in an unsafe way, not that the task or vessel was unsafe. Cargo should be lashed during a storm yet may be unlashed in calm waters; a seaman who injured his back while stooping to lash a barrel at dockside could not argue that the ship was unseaworthy because the cargo should have been tied down at sea by someone else. Just so here. The jury's verdict should not have been disturbed.

The judgment is reversed. On remand the district court shall enter judgment on the jury's verdict.

■ Cummings, Circuit Judge, dissenting.

Even if the events leading up to Hughes' accident are viewed in a light most favorable to ContiCarriers, the jury's verdict cannot stand because at the time of Hughes' accident the CONTI-KARLA lacked a rope guard rail, and this condition made it unseaworthy as a matter of law. I therefore respectfully dissent from the majority's opinion.

It is well established that a missing safety device can make a ship unfit for its intended use and hence unseaworthy. Villers Seafood Co., Inc. v. Vest, 813 F.2d 339, 342 (11th Cir.1987); Skipper v. Amerind Shipping Corp., 230 F.Supp. 253 (D.La.1964)(slack safety rope); Scarberry v. Ohio River Co., 217 F.Supp. 189 (D.W.Va.1963)(defective handrail). At the time of Hughes' accident protective safety lines had not been in place for hours. Furthermore, ContiCarriers never tried to justify why these lines were down when the CONTI-KARLA sailed from where it "fleeted" its barges to the oil dock. Undisputed testimony at trial established that the safety lines should have been raised once the CONTI-KARLA was underway. One witness implied that when a boat is on a short refueling trip between tows it is not "underway"—but this is hair-splitting. The majority hints that a towboat would be unseaworthy if someone fell overboard when the boat was sailing and the safety lines were down for no reason. Therefore the critical question is whether it matters that Hughes' accident occurred after the towboat arrived at the refueling dock.

In this case it should make no difference that Hughes fell overboard after the vessel had come to a stop. Once ContiCarriers breached a plain, undisputed duty to raise the safety line when the ship was underway, it should be held liable for injuries resulting from that breach until the safety defect was cured. The majority suggests that once the CONTI-KARLA moored against a dock, it was no longer unsafe to have the safety lines down. This is true for the dock-side line—but false for the river-side line that would have prevented Hughes' fall. No witness suggested that the starboard (i.e. river-side) line needed to be down for port-side refueling. This line should have been in position when Hughes fell because it should have been raised before the CONTI-KARLA sailed to the dock. There are simply no facts that would allow a jury to find that the starboard line was properly down at the time of Hughes' accident, or that the line's lowered position did not cause his injuries. "[E]ven though the equipment furnished for [a] particular task is itself safe and sufficient, its misuse by the crew renders the vessel unseaworthy." Waldron v. Moore–McCormack Lines, Inc., 386 U.S. 724, 727, 87 S.Ct. 1410, 1412, 18 L.Ed.2d 482.

The CONTI-KARLA was unseaworthy as a matter of law because a vital safety device was missing from a hazardous deck area, and it would have prevented the injury if in place. Villers, 813 F.2d at 342; Comeaux v. T.L. James & Co., Inc., 666 F.2d 294, 299 (5th Cir.1982), modified 702 F.2d 1023; Oliveras v. American Export Isbrandtsen Lines, Inc., 431 F.2d 814, 816 (2d Cir.1970); Gibbs v. Kiesel, 382 F.2d 917, 919 (5th Cir.1967). ContiCarriers should not avoid liability merely because its boat was docked at the time of the accident. Sweeney v. American Steamship Co., 491 F.2d 1085, 1089 (6th Cir.1974).

This result is supported by Villers, 813 F.2d at 339, which reviewed an unseaworthiness claim where pins designed to secure a ladder were removed, resulting in injury to the plaintiff when he climbed the ladder. The court granted the plaintiff judgment as a matter of law "If a ship's equipment breaks under normal use, the logical inference that follows is that the equipment was defective. * * * The same presumption arises when a safety device is removed from a ship's equipment resulting in the type of accident which the safety device was designed to prevent." *Villers*, 813 F.2d at 342. This means that Hughes is also entitled to judgment as a matter of law, for here the safety lines were removed and this resulted in an accident which the lines were designed to prevent. Contrary to the majority's view, *Villers* does not turn on a seaman's knowledge of a defect that causes his injury. It does not matter that Hughes was trying to fix a defect whereas the *Villers* plaintiff was caught unaware, for ship owners may be held liable when seamen attempt to repair a known defect that renders a vessel unseaworthy.

Comeaux, 666 F.2d at 299.

The majority also argues that raising the CONTI-KARLA'S safety lines when the boat is docked is no more dangerous than raising the lines as soon as the facewires are stowed on deck. While this may be true, it is irrelevant because Hughes would not have had to risk raising the starboard line if it had been properly in place when he began his watch. After today's decision the sloppy practice of sailing to refuel with safety lines lowered is given a false imprimatur of economic rationality. For even if the isolated risks of raising the line in the morning or the afternoon are equivalent, the overall risks of one practice or the other are not the same. When towboats sail with safety lines down, the risk of injury to the crew increases, and since it is no more costly to raise safety lines as soon as barges are fleeted, our rule should encourage behavior that produces less aggregate risk.

Finally, the majority suggests that Hughes' own negligent acts led to his injury. This discussion serves to make today's result appear more just, but it ignores admiralty's maxim that "a seaman's duty to protect himself is slight." Ceja v. Mike Hooks, Inc., 690 F.2d 1191, 1193 (5th Cir.1982). The trial judge's well-reasoned opinion granting Hughes judgment notwithstanding the verdict should be affirmed.

Usner v. Luckenbach Overseas Corp.

Supreme Court of the United States, 1971.
400 U.S. 494, 91 S.Ct. 514, 27 L.Ed.2d 562, 1971 A.M.C. 277.

■ MR. JUSTICE STEWART delivered the opinion of the Court.

The petitioner, a longshoreman employed by an independent stevedoring contractor, was injured while engaged with his fellow employees in loading cargo aboard the S.S. *Edgar F. Luckenbach*. He brought this action for damages against the respondents, the owner and the charterer of the ship, in a federal district court, alleging that his injuries had been caused by the ship's unseaworthiness.

In the course of pretrial proceedings the circumstances under which the petitioner had been injured were fully disclosed, and they are not in dispute. On the day in question the ship lay moored to a dock in New Orleans, Louisiana, receiving cargo from a barge positioned alongside. The loading operations were being performed by the petitioner and his fellow longshoremen under the direction of their employer. Some of the men were on the ship, operating the port winch and boom at the No. 2 hatch. The petitioner and others were on the barge, where their job was to "break out" the bundles of cargo by securing them to a sling attached to the fall each time it was lowered from the ship's boom by the winch operator. The loading operations had been proceeding in this manner for some time, until upon one occasion the winch operator did not lower the fall far enough. Finding the sling beyond his reach, the petitioner motioned to the flagman standing on the deck of the ship to direct the winch operator to lower the fall farther. The winch operator then lowered the fall, but he lowered it too far and too fast. The sling struck the petitioner, knocking him to the deck of the barge and causing his injuries. Neither before nor after this occurrence was any difficulty experienced with the winch, boom, fall, sling, or any other equipment or appurtenance of the ship or her cargo.

The respondents moved for summary judgment in the District Court, upon the ground that a single negligent act by a fellow longshoreman could not render the ship unseaworthy. The District Court denied the motion, but granted the respondents leave to take an interlocutory appeal under 28 U.S.C. § 1292(b).[1] The United States Court of Appeals for the Fifth Circuit allowed the appeal and, reversing the District Court, directed that the respondents' motion for summary judgment be granted. 413 F.2d 984. It was the appellate court's view that " '[i]nstant unseaworthiness' resulting from 'operational negligence' of the stevedoring contractor is not a basis for recovery by an injured longshoreman." 413 F.2d, at 985–986. We granted certiorari, 397 U.S. 933, 90 S.Ct. 940, 25 L.Ed.2d 114, because of a conflict among the circuits on the basic issue presented.[2]

---

1. 28 U.S.C. § 1292(b) provides as follows:

"When a district judge, in making in a civil action an order not otherwise appealable under this section, shall be of the opinion that such order involves a controlling question of law as to which there is substantial ground for difference of opinion and that an immediate appeal from the order may materially advance the ultimate termination of the litigation, he shall so state in writing in such order. The Court of Appeals may thereupon, in its discretion, permit an appeal to be taken from such order, if application is made to it within ten days after

the entry of the order: *Provided, however, That* application for an appeal hereunder shall not stay proceedings in the district court unless the district judge or the Court of Appeals or a judge thereof shall so order."

2. Compare Candiano v. Moore–McCormack Lines, 382 F.2d 961 (C.A.2); Alexander v. Bethlehem Steel Corp., 382 F.2d 963 (C.A.2); Cleary v. United States Lines Co., 411 F.2d 1009 (C.A.2); and Venable v. A/S Det Forenede Dampskibsselskab, 399 F.2d 347 (C.A.4), with Grigsby v. Coastal Marine Service, 412 F.2d 1011 (C.A.5), and Tim v. American President Lines, 409 F.2d 385 (C.A.9).

The development in admiralty law of the doctrine of unseaworthiness as a predicate for a shipowner's liability for personal injuries or death has been fully chronicled elsewhere, and it would serve no useful purpose to repeat the details of that development here.[3] Suffice it to recall that from its humble origin as a dictum in an obscure case in 1922,[4] the doctrine of liability based upon unseaworthiness has experienced a most extraordinary expansion in a series of cases decided by this Court over the last 25 years.[5] The Court's decisions in some of those cases have been severely questioned, by dissenting Justices and by others, on the basis of history, reason, and logic.[6] The present case, however, offers no occasion to re-examine any of our previous decisions. We may accept it as fully settled that a shipowner's liability for an unseaworthy vessel extends beyond the members of the crew and includes a longshoreman like the petitioner.[7] We may accept it as settled, too, that the shipowner is liable though the unseaworthiness be transitory,[8] and though the injury be suffered elsewhere than aboard the ship.[9] But these propositions do not dispose of the case before us. For the

3. See Mitchell v. Trawler Racer, 362 U.S. 539, 80 S.Ct. 926, 4 L.Ed.2d 941; id., at 550, 80 S.Ct., at 933 (Frankfurter, J., dissenting); see also G. Gilmore & C. Black, *The Law of Admiralty* 315–332 (1957); Tetreault, Seamen, Seaworthiness and the Rights of Harbor Workers, 39 Cornell L.Q. 381.

4. Carlisle Packing Co. v. Sandanger, 259 U.S. 255, 42 S.Ct. 475, 66 L.Ed. 927. There it was said, "[W]e think the trial court might have told the jury that without regard to negligence the vessel was unseaworthy when she left the dock * * * and that if thus unseaworthy and one of the crew received damage as the direct result thereof, he was entitled to recover compensatory damages." 259 U.S., at 259, 42 S.Ct. at 477.

5. Mahnich v. Southern S.S. Co., 321 U.S. 96, 64 S.Ct. 455, 88 L.Ed. 561; Seas Shipping Co. v. Sieracki, 328 U.S. 85, 66 S.Ct. 872, 90 L.Ed. 1099; Pope & Talbot, Inc. v. Hawn, 346 U.S. 406, 74 S.Ct. 202, 98 L.Ed. 143; Alaska Steamship Co. v. Petterson, 347 U.S. 396, 74 S.Ct. 601, 98 L.Ed. 798; Rogers v. United States Lines, 347 U.S. 984, 74 S.Ct. 849, 98 L.Ed. 1120; Boudoin v. Lykes Bros. S. S. Co., 348 U.S. 336, 75 S.Ct. 382, 99 L.Ed. 354; Crumady v. The J. H. Fisser, 358 U.S. 423, 79 S.Ct. 445, 3 L.Ed.2d 413; Mitchell v. Trawler Racer, 362 U.S. 539, 80 S.Ct. 926; Atlantic & Gulf Stevedores v. Ellerman Lines, 369 U.S. 355, 82 S.Ct. 780, 7 L.Ed.2d 798; Gutierrez v. Waterman S. S. Corp., 373 U.S. 206, 83 S.Ct. 1185, 10 L.Ed.2d 297; Waldron v. Moore–McCormack Lines, 386 U.S. 724, 87 S.Ct. 1410, 18 L.Ed.2d 482.

6. See, e.g., Mahnich v. Southern S. S. Co., supra, 321 U.S., at 105, 64 S.Ct., at 460 (Roberts, J., joined by Frankfurter, J., dissenting); Seas Shipping Co. v. Sieracki, supra, 328 U.S., at 103, 66 S.Ct., at 882 (Stone, C. J., joined by Frankfurter and Burton, JJ., dissenting); Pope & Talbot, Inc. v. Hawn, supra, 346 U.S., at 419, 74 S.Ct., at 210 (Jackson, J., joined by Reed and Burton, JJ., dissenting); Alaska Steamship Co. v. Petterson, supra (Burton, J., joined by Frankfurter and Jackson, JJ., dissenting): Mitchell v. Trawler Racer, supra, 362 U.S., at 550, 80 S.Ct., at 933 (Frankfurter, J., joined by Harlan and Whittaker, JJ., dissenting); Gutierrez v. Waterman S.S. Corp., supra 373 U.S. at 216, 83 S.Ct., at 1191 (Harlan, J., dissenting); Waldron v. Moore–McCormack Lines, supra, 386 U.S., at 729, 87 S.Ct., at 1413 (White, J., joined by Harlan, Brennan, and Stewart, JJ., dissenting).

See also G. Gilmore & C. Black, *The Law of Admiralty* 315–332 (1957); Tetreault, Seamen, Seaworthiness, and the Rights of Harbor Workers, 39 Cornell L.Q. 381.

7. Seas Shipping Co. v. Sieracki, 328 U.S. 85, 66 S.Ct. 872.

8. Crumady v. The J.H. Fisser, 358 U.S. 423, 79 S.Ct. 445; Mitchell v. Trawler Racer, 362 U.S. 539, 80 S.Ct. 926.

9. Gutierrez v. Waterman S.S. Corp., 373 U.S. 206, 83 S.Ct. 1185.

question here goes to the very definition of what unseaworthiness is and what it is not.

A major burden of the Court's decisions spelling out the nature and scope of the cause of action for unseaworthiness has been insistence upon the point that it is a remedy separate from, independent of, and additional to other claims against the shipowner, whether created by statute[10] or under general maritime law.[11] More specifically, the Court has repeatedly taken pains to point out that liability based upon unseaworthiness is wholly distinct from liability based upon negligence.[12] The reason, of course, is that unseaworthiness is a *condition,* and how that condition came into being—whether by negligence or otherwise—is quite irrelevant to the owner's liability for personal injuries resulting from it.

We had occasion to emphasize this basic distinction again in Mitchell v. Trawler Racer, 362 U.S. 539, 80 S.Ct. 926. There the unseaworthy condition causing the plaintiff's injury was a ship's rail made slippery by the presence of fish gurry and slime. The trial judge had instructed the jury that the shipowner could be held liable for this unseaworthy condition only upon a finding that the slime and gurry had been on the ship's rail for a time long enough for the respondent to have learned about it and to have removed it. The Court of Appeals affirmed the judgment for the defendant shipowner, holding that at least with respect to "an unseaworthy condition which arises only during the progress of the voyage," the shipowner's obligation "is merely to see that reasonable care is used under the circumstances * * * incident to the correction of the newly arisen defect." 265 F.2d 426, 432. We reversed the judgment, holding that the trial and appellate courts had been wrong in confusing liability for negligence with liability for unseaworthiness. What has evolved in our case law, we said, is the "complete divorcement of unseaworthiness liability from concepts of negligence." 362 U.S. at 550, 80 S.Ct. at 933.

Trawler Racer involved the defective condition of a physical part of the ship itself. But our cases have held that the scope of unseaworthiness is by no means so limited. A vessel's condition of unseaworthiness might arise from any number of circumstances. Her gear might be defective,[13] her appurtenances in disrepair,[14] her crew unfit.[15] The number of men assigned to perform a shipboard task might be insufficient.[16] The method of

---

10. E.g., the Jones Act, 41 Stat. 1007, 46 U.S.C. § 688. The petitioner in the present case was fully covered, of course, by the provisions of the Longshoremen's and Harbor Workers' Compensation Act, 33 U.S.C. § 901 et seq.

11. E.g., maintenance and cure. See Calmar S.S. Corp. v. Taylor, 303 U.S. 525, 58 S.Ct. 651, 82 L.Ed. 993; Waterman S.S. Corp. v. Jones, 318 U.S. 724, 63 S.Ct. 930, 87 L.Ed. 1107; Farrell v. United States, 336 U.S. 511, 69 S.Ct. 707, 93 L.Ed. 850; Warren v. United States, 340 U.S. 523, 71 S.Ct. 432, 95 L.Ed. 503.

12. E.g., Seas Shipping Co. v. Sieracki, 328 U.S. 85, 94, 66 S.Ct. 872, 877; "[T]he liability is neither limited by conceptions of negligence nor contractual in character."

13. Mahnich v. Southern S.S. Co., 321 U.S. 96, 64 S.Ct. 455.

14. Seas Shipping Co. Sieracki, 328 U.S. 85, 66 S.Ct. 872.

15. Boudoin v. Lykes Bros. S.S. Co., 348 U.S. 336, 75 S.Ct. 382.

16. Waldron v. Moore–McCormack Lines, 386 U.S. 724, 87 S.Ct. 1410.

loading her cargo, or the manner of its stowage, might be improper.[17]   For any of these reasons, or others, a vessel might not be reasonably fit for her intended service.

What caused the petitioner's injuries in the present case, however, was not the condition of the ship, her appurtenances, her cargo, or her crew,[18] but the isolated, personal negligent act of the petitioner's fellow longshoreman.   To hold that this individual act of negligence rendered the ship unseaworthy would be to subvert the fundamental distinction between unseaworthiness and negligence that we have so painstakingly and repeatedly emphasized in our decisions.[19]   In *Trawler Racer,* supra, there existed a condition of unseaworthiness, and we held it was error to require a finding of negligent conduct in order to hold the shipowner liable.   The case before us presents the other side of the same coin.   For it would be equally erroneous here, where no condition of unseaworthiness existed, to hold the shipowner liable for a third party's single and wholly unforeseeable act of negligence.   The judgment of the Court of Appeals is affirmed.

It is so ordered.

Judgment of Court of Appeals affirmed.

■ Mr. Justice Douglas, with whom Mr. Justice Black and Mr. Justice Brennan concur, dissenting.

While petitioner was working on a barge loading cargo into a hatch of the ship, he was injured as a result of the negligent operation of a winch.   The winch was part of the ship and the winch operator was a member of the crew of stevedores.   The injury was caused by a lowering of a sling, which carried the cargo, too quickly and too far.

Prior to the 1970 Term the judgment denying recovery would have been reversed, probably out of hand.   We held in Mahnich v. Southern S.S. Co., 321 U.S. 96, 64 S.Ct. 455, 88 L.Ed. 561, that the obligation of an owner to furnish a seaworthy ship extends to seaworthy appliances.   We also held that the owner was not insulated from liability by the "negligent failure" of

---

17.   A. & G. Stevedores v. Ellerman Lines, 369 U.S. 355, 82 S.Ct. 780; Gutierrez v. Waterman S.S. Corp., 373 U.S. 206, 83 S.Ct. 1185.

18.   No member of the ship's crew was in any way involved in this case.

19.   The petitioner's reliance upon our summary *per curiam* reversal of a judgment for the shipowner in Mascuilli v. United States, 387 U.S. 237, 87 S.Ct. 1705, 18 L.Ed.2d 743, is misplaced.   There a longshoreman had been killed during a loading operation aboard a Government vessel when, under the strain of the opposing pull of two winches, a heavy shackle parted, recoiled, and struck him.   The petition for certiorari posed three questions: (1) Did a prior unseaworthy condition come into play by the

tightline condition?   (2) Did the negligent handling of proper equipment by the longshoremen create a dangerous condition rendering the vessel unseaworthy?   (3) Was the vessel unseaworthy because the longshoremen were not "equal in disposition and seamanship to the ordinary men in the calling," as was found in Boudoin v. Lykes Bros. S.S. Co., 348 U.S. 336, 75 S.Ct. 382?

Our *per curiam* reversal cited two cases: Mahnich v. Southern S.S. Co., 321 U.S. 96, 64 S.Ct. 455, and Crumady v. The J.H. Fisser, 358 U.S. 423, 79 S.Ct. 445.   *Mahnich* involved a defective rope, *Crumady* a defective winch.   It seems evident, therefore, that it was the first question posed by the petition for certiorari to which the Court gave an affirmative answer.

his officers or members of the crew to furnish seaworthy appliances. Id., at 101, 64 S.Ct. at 458. In *Mahnich,* the staging from which the seaman fell was an unseaworthy appliance because of the defective rope with which it was rigged. There was sound rope on board but defective rope was used. The fact that the mate and boatswain were negligent in selecting defective rope was held to be no defense.

In Crumady v. The J.H. Fisser, 358 U.S. 423, 79 S.Ct. 445, 3 L.Ed.2d 413, a winch was not inherently defective as was the rope in *Mahnich.* But it was used in a way which made it unsafe and dangerous for the work at hand. While the rigging would take only three tons of stress, the cutoff of the winch, "its safety device," was set at twice that limit. Id., at 427, 79 S.Ct. at 447–448. And so the rope sling broke and injured the seaman. The vessel which paid the damages was allowed to recover over from the stevedores whose negligence with the winch made the vessel pro tanto unseaworthy.

In Mascuilli v. United States, 387 U.S. 237, 87 S.Ct. 1705, 18 L.Ed.2d 743, negligent use of a winch in a loading operation so obviously made the vessel *pro tanto* unseaworthy that we reversed out of hand a judgment of no liability, citing *Mahnich* and *Crumady.*

What we said in Mitchell v. Trawler Racer, 362 U.S. 539, 550, 80 S.Ct. 926, 933, 4 L.Ed.2d 941, about the "complete divorcement of unseaworthiness liability from concepts of negligence" related to a condition which made the vessel not "reasonably suitable for her intended service." Yet alongside that conventional type of unseaworthiness there developed the concept of unseaworthiness resulting from operational negligence.

Indeed, the doctrine of operational negligence which causes unseaworthiness has had a sturdy growth. Chief Justice Stone, writing for the Court in *Mahnich,* showed that this doctrine goes at least as far back as The Osceola, 189 U.S. 158, 23 S.Ct. 483, 47 L.Ed. 760, decided in 1903. See 321 U.S., at 101–104, 64 S.Ct. at 458–460. The intervening decision of Plamals v. Pinar Del Rio, 277 U.S. 151, 48 S.Ct. 457, 72 L.Ed. 827, which looked the other way, was decided in 1928. It was around that case that Justices Roberts and Frankfurter turned their dissent, saying that unless the Court followed precedent "the law becomes not a chart to govern conduct but a game of chance; instead of settling rights and liabilities it unsettles them." 321 U.S., at 112, 64 S.Ct. at 463. They added:

> "Respect for tribunals must fall when the bar and the public come to understand that nothing that has been said in prior adjudication has force in a current controversy." Id., at 113, 64 S.Ct. at 463.

Justices Roberts and Frankfurter bitterly expressed that view in *Mahnich* when *Pinar Del Rio* was overruled—a freak decision not in keeping with the mainstream of the law that had come before.

Changes in membership do change decisions; and those changes are expected at the level of constitutional law. But when private rights not rooted in the Constitution are at issue, it is surprising to find law made by new judges taking the place of law made by prior judges.

Up to today operational negligence has been one sturdy type of unseaworthiness.* I would let it continue as the prevailing rule unless Congress in its wisdom changes it.

■ MR. JUSTICE HARLAN, dissenting.

Past decisions of this Court have expanded the doctrine of unseaworthiness almost to the point of absolute liability. I have often protested against this development. See, e.g., the cases cited by the Court, ante, at 516 n. 6. But I must in good conscience regard the particular issue in this case as having been decided by Crumady v. The J.H. Fisser, 358 U.S. 423, 79 S.Ct. 445, 3 L.Ed.2d 413 (1959), even if prior decisions did not inexorably point to that result. As my BROTHER DOUGLAS states, *Crumady* cannot justly be distinguished from the case before us. Much as I would welcome a thoroughgoing re-examination of the past course of developments in the unseaworthiness doctrine, I fear that the Court's action today can only result in compounding the current difficulties of the lower courts with this area of the law.

N O T E

In an action tried to a jury, the question of seaworthiness is a question of fact for the jury. See Jordan v. United States Lines, Inc., 738 F.2d 48 (1st Cir.1984), affirming a jury verdict for the defendant despite evidence that the vessel's machinery was not functioning perfectly. And see Valm v. Hercules Fish Products, Inc., 701 F.2d 235, 1983 A.M.C. 2585 (1st Cir.1983), affirming a judgment on a verdict for the defendant despite the contention that the court below must necessarily find that the ship was unseaworthy by reason of a rusty winch, when plaintiff had failed to move for a directed verdict on the issue of unseaworthiness. This being the case it is difficult to state just what condition will render a vessel unseaworthy.

Just what condition will render a vessel unseaworthy is difficult to state, of course, since the question is one of fact for the jury. Compare Haughton v. Blackships, Inc., 334 F.Supp. 317, 1971 A.M.C. 1654 (S.D.Tex.1971), rev'd on other grounds 462 F.2d 788 (5th Cir.1972) in which it was held that the vessel was unseaworthy because of the presence of snow and ice that had fallen and formed the day before with Tate v. A/B Svenska Amerika Linein, 331 F.Supp. 854, 1971 A.M.C. 1223 (E.D.La.1970), aff'd per curiam 435 F.2d 172 (5th Cir.1970) in which slippery, damp walking boards in the hatch caused by two sudden rain showers were held not to render the vessel unseaworthy when the hatches were covered as fast as possible.

---

* The Second Circuit adopted the view that while one act of operational negligence would not make a vessel unseaworthy, unseaworthiness did result if the negligent act was incident to a continuous course of operation as where a wrong hatch cover was used, Grillea v. United States, 232 F.2d 919, but not by an isolated act as where a boom was carrying a dangerous stress due to a negligent act. Puddu v. Royal Netherlands S.S. Co., 303 F.2d 752. The difference in the two cases was stated as follows:

"A ship is not unseaworthy because it has glass in a window which might be broken. The injuries of a seaman who negligently breaks such a glass are not the result of unseaworthiness, nor are the injuries of a seaman who is cut by the falling glass. But injury incurred in stepping on the broken glass does result from unseaworthiness." Id., at 757.

It is clear, however, that it may consist of a sloppy condition, such as that involved in *Mitchell,* failure to provide serviceable tools or equipment (see Michalic v. Cleveland Tankers, Inc., 364 U.S. 325, 81 S.Ct. 6, 5 L.Ed.2d 20 (1960)), failure to provide safety devices such as proper railings (Salem v. United States Lines, 370 U.S. 31, 82 S.Ct. 1119, 8 L.Ed.2d 313 (1962)), a latent defect in a piece of equipment, even if the equipment is not supplied by the vessel (Alaska S.S. Co. v. Petterson, infra, p. 1010), or it can consist of a dangerous method of operating otherwise seaworthy equipment (Crumady v. J.H. Fisser, infra, p. 1011; Mascuilli v. United States, 387 U.S. 237, 87 S.Ct. 1705, 18 L.Ed.2d 743 (1967)). It can consist, for example, of ordering a three man job to be done by two. Waldron v. Moore–McCormack Lines, Inc., 386 U.S. 724, 87 S.Ct. 1410, 18 L.Ed.2d 482 (1967). There the jury had found that the order was not negligent. The majority of the Supreme Court, in an opinion by Mr. Justice Black, held that the plaintiff was entitled also to present his theory of unseaworthiness to the jury and reversed for that purpose. Mr. Justice White, joined by Justices Harlan, Brennan, and Stewart, dissented. They agreed that a negligent order can result in an unseaworthy condition, but since this order was found by the jury to be non-negligent, they could not see how the resulting work method could be unseaworthy. Where the order is found to be negligent, ordinarily it is unnecessary to determine whether or not it created an unseaworthy condition. See, e.g., Blevins v. United States, 1983 A.M.C. 2168 (D.Md.1983). There are examples of unseaworthiness produced by the bellicose nature of a crew member who assaults another. See Boudoin v. Lykes Bros. S.S. Co., 348 U.S. 336, 75 S.Ct. 382, 99 L.Ed. 354 (1955). Seamen are allowed a generous measure of rowdiness before they make their ship unseaworthy. In Walters v. Moore–McCormack Lines, Inc., 309 F.2d 191, 1962 A.M.C. 2556 (2d Cir.1962), for example, the Second Circuit affirmed a directed verdict for the vessel owner in a case in which the plaintiff was attacked by a man thirty pounds heavier than he was, was hit with a karate blow that dropped him to the floor and there he was leaped upon and subjected to a beating that left him to be carried off in a stretcher. Judge Friendly dissented. The cases in which recovery is had seem to be cases in which either the assailant has a history of unprovoked brutality or where the assault is with a deadly weapon. See, e.g., Smith v. Lauritzen, 356 F.2d 171, 1966 A.M.C. 1424 (3d Cir.1966), where the plaintiff had been attacked with a cargo hook. See also Clevenger v. Star Fish & Oyster Co., 325 F.2d 397, 1964 A.M.C. 27 (5th Cir.1963), where the Fifth Circuit held as a matter of law that the vessel was unseaworthy because of an attack upon the plaintiff in which he was stabbed in the back with a devil's fork. For a rerun, see Claborn v. Star Fish & Oyster Co., Inc., 578 F.2d 983, 1979 A.M.C. 636 (5th Cir.1978) cert. denied 440 U.S. 936, 99 S.Ct. 1281, 59 L.Ed.2d 494 (1979). Similarly, in Calcagni v. Hudson Waterways Corp., 603 F.2d 1049, 1979 A.M.C. 1728 (2 Cir.1979), an officer's use of a wrench instead of his fists in an attack on a seaman rendered the vessel unseaworthy. It has been stated by the Second Circuit, however, that the mere fact that a seaman attacks another with a knife does not make the vessel unseaworthy. See Gerald v. United States Lines Co., 368 F.2d 343, 1967 A.M.C. 17 (2d Cir.1966). Indeed in an action by a captain who had been stabbed in the stomach the court of appeals affirmed a judgment for the defendant when the testimony indicated that the captain had cursed, ill-fed, and abused his crew, and especially his assailant, who was, the court found, "a quiet, peaceful, efficient seaman." Id. See also Mears v. American Export Lines, Inc., 457 F.Supp. 846, 1979 A.M.C. 395 (S.D.N.Y. 1978).

The conduct of seamen is not to be measured by the standard of conduct for ordinary men ashore. Thus the fact that a seaman has had five fist fights during his 30–year career does not render the vessel unseaworthy. Kirsch v. United States, 450 F.2d 326 (9th Cir.1971).

What is the effect of the *Usner* decision on the law governing actions brought by seamen? In the usual case in which the *Grillea* problem arises in such an action, the negligence involved is that of a fellow seaman. If this is so, the injured party may sue under the Jones Act. If there is doubt as to whether the case is one for breach of the warranty to provide a seaworthy vessel or one for negligence, of course he may plead both. Is the only effect of *Usner* to eliminate the case such as *Mahnich* in which the plaintiff has let the statute of limitations under the Jones Act run? Note that the action under the Jones Act must be brought in personam. This means that in the instantaneous negligence case the seaman will have no lien. Are there other possibilities? Suppose that the vessel were in the course of being unloaded and the negligence were that of the employees of the stevedore?

B. WHAT VESSELS ARE WARRANTED SEAWORTHY

The first "prong" of the test stated in *Chandris* for determining seaman status was that there be a vessel in navigation. (p. 888, supra). Generally, then, if the structure is not a vessel in navigation, since persons who work upon it are not seamen, they cannot maintain an action for maintenance and cure, for breach of the warranty of seaworthiness, or for negligence under the Jones Act. In the period between the decision in Seas Shipping Co. v. Sieracki (discussed at p. 967, below) and the 1972 amendments to the Longshore and Harborworkers' Compensation Act, longshoremen and harbor workers who did "the work of a seaman" were held to be beneficiaries of the warranty of seaworthiness, though not seamen for purposes of the Jones Act, or for the purposes of maintenance and cure. Such "seamen pro hac vice," in particular, repairmen, often, indeed usually, working aboard during periods during which the vessel was laid up for repairs.

In West v. United States, 361 U.S. 118, 80 S.Ct. 189, 4 L.Ed.2d 161 (1959), a "Liberty" ship from the era of World War II, consigned to the "mothball fleet" at Norfolk, Virginia, where it remained for several years with its pipes, boilers, and tanks completely drained and an oil preservative injected through them to prevent rusting, was towed to the repair docks of an independent contractor for overhaul and reactivation. There one of the contractor's shore-based employees was injured through a condition that the contractor had been hired to correct. The Supreme Court held that under the circumstances the owner (the United States) did not warrant the seaworthiness of the vessel. *West* was followed by Roper v. United States, 368 U.S. 20, 82 S.Ct. 5, 7 L.Ed.2d 1 (1961). There another "mothballed" Liberty ship was loaded with grain for storage. Two years later it was towed back to the loading facility for unloading and in the course of unloading an employee of the grain company was injured through a defective part of the grain company's unloading equipment. The district court found as a fact that the vessel was not in navigation and the Supreme Court refused to overturn this finding. There is a good discussion of *West* and *Roper* by Judge Wisdom in Watz v. Zapata Off–Shore Company, 431 F.2d 100, 1970 A.M.C. 2307 (5th Cir.1970).

With the 1972 amendments to the LHWCA, eliminating the longshore-man's and harborworker's action for breach of warranty of seaworthiness, the importance of the *"West-Roper"* rule, sometimes called the "dead ship" doctrine, was much reduced. Does anything remain of it? In Dean v. United States, 418 F.2d 1236, 1970 A.M.C. 796 (9th Cir.1969), it was held that a naval vessel undergoing very extensive repairs, was out of service despite the fact that the crew continued to be housed and fed aboard and the vessel remained in commission. The injury was to an employee of the shipyard. Would the result have been the same if a member of the crew had been injured? In *Dean* the court stated that "no reasonable person could have believed, at the times in question, That the Toluga was a ship 'in navigation' so that the government was then holding its vessel, or pump room No. 2 thereof, out to Dean or anyone else as 'seaworthy.'"

5. ACTION FOR NEGLIGENCE UNDER THE JONES ACT

A. "ANY SEAMAN"

for: Choice of law in Jones Act/ general maritime law actions is irrelevant to SMJ determinations

Nicol v. Gulf Fleet Supply Vessels, Inc.

United States Court of Appeals, Fifth Circuit, 1984.
743 F.2d 289, 1985 A.M.C. 2669.

■ GEE, CIRCUIT JUDGE:

"As a moth is drawn to the light, so is a litigant drawn to the United States." Smith Kline and French Laboratories, Ltd., et al. v. Block [1983] 2 All E.R. 72, 74 (C.A.1982)(Denning, M.R.). Today's litigant is David Nicol, a Scottish deep-sea diver, who was drawn to the United States District Court for the Eastern District of Louisiana seeking to recover for personal injuries he suffered off the coast of Abu Dhabi while working aboard an American tugboat for his Liberian employer. When considering two Gulf Fleet pre-trial motions filed in 1982, one to dismiss and the other for partial summary judgment, the district court decided that the laws of the United States do not govern Nicol's various claims brought under the Jones Act and general maritime law. Because he found that foreign law applies to this case, the district judge dismissed the action for failure to state a claim upon which relief can be granted. From there he proceeded to dismiss for mootness another Gulf Fleet motion for summary judgment filed in 1981 which he thought was being reurged on the ground of *forum non conveniens*. We reverse and remand for further consideration by the district court of issues that our opinion will indicate.

I. Nicol's Injury

David Nicol, a domiciliary of the environs of Edinburgh in Scotland, was injured approximately 45 miles off the coast of Abu Dhabi[1] in late 1979

---

1. The Emirate of Abu Dhabi is also known as Abu Zaby. It is one of several independent Arab states forming the federa-tion known as the United Arab Emirates

Employer

while aboard the M/V GULF QUEEN II, a tugboat flying the American flag and owned by Gulf Fleet Western, Inc., a Delaware corporation.[2] Nicol was employed as a diver by CCC Underwater Engineering, Ltd., a Liberian corporation. He and his fellow divers lived and worked off the lay barge GERALDINE, a vessel believed to be owned by the National Petroleum Company of Abu Dhabi (N.P.C.C.) and used to lay pipelines in the Zakum Oil Field off the coast of Abu Dhabi. The M/V GULF QUEEN II frequently assisted the lay barge GERALDINE in replacing pendant wires.[3] Nicol

what he was → doing

temporarily boarded the M/V GULF QUEEN II to help replace a pendant wire, an operation which required the assistance of the divers from the lay barge GERALDINE. Nicol was injured when a piece of equipment that was welded to the stern of the M/V GULF QUEEN II broke loose, striking

Injury

him and knocking him into the sea. His physician's deposition testimony indicates that he lost about 30 percent of the use of his right arm, wrist, and hand. The evidence is uncontroverted that Nicol can never again work as a diver.

No one disputes that an American company, Gulf Fleet Western, owned the M/V GULF QUEEN II when the accident happened. The charter arrangements were a little more complicated. The record is not entirely consistent on the details, but there is evidence to indicate that Gulf Fleet Middle East, Inc.,[4] a Panamanian corporation, bareboat-chartered the tug from Gulf Fleet Western. Gulf Fleet Abu Dhabi, a joint venture between Gulf Fleet Middle East and local Arab interests organized under the laws of Abu Dhabi, then bareboat-chartered the vessel from Gulf Fleet Middle East. Finally, Gulf Fleet Middle East time-chartered the M/V GULF QUEEN II to N.P.C.C. These charters were in effect when Nicol was injured.

*Bareboat charter -
- absolute control of vessel
- can put own crew on it*

(U.A.E.). The other states are Al Fujayrah, Ash Shariquh, Dubayy (or Dubai), Ras al Khaymuh, Ujman and Umm al Qaywayn. Each emirate has a city or town of that same name. The city of Abu Dhabi is the federation's capital, while Dubai is the largest city and a leading Persian Gulf port. The federal government handles the U.A.E.'s foreign affairs, while the ruler, or emir, of each state controls its internal affairs. The U.A.E. is located at the base of the Persian Gulf and is bordered by the Gulf, Oman, Saudi Arabia, and Qatar. Iran is located directly north across the Gulf from the U.A.E.

  2. The M/V GULF QUEEN II was sold to Gulf Fleet Middle East, Inc. in 1983.

  3. A pendant wire is used to attach a floating, surface marker buoy to a large anchor block on the ocean floor. These anchor blocks were an integral part of the system whereby the lay barge GERALDINE propelled itself through the water during the course of pipe laying operations. The divers

from the lay barge GERALDINE boarded the M/V GULF QUEEN II to replace pendant wires approximately 26 times during the four months preceding Nicol's mishap.

  4. Although Gulf Fleet Middle East is a Panamanian corporation, it is ultimately 100% owned by an American company. According to the 10K Statement of Houston Natural Gas in the record for that company's fiscal year ended July 31, 1980, Gulf Fleet Marine Corporation is a Louisiana corporation that is a wholly-owned subsidiary of Potts Industries. In turn, Potts Industries is a wholly-owned subsidiary of Houston Natural Gas. Gulf Fleet Marine Corporation likewise owns Gulf Fleet Western, a Delaware corporation, and Gulf Mississippi International, S.A., a Panamanian corporation. Gulf Mississippi International, S.A., in turn owns Gulf Fleet Middle East, Inc., a Panamanian corporation.

II.   The Light is Extinguished

Nicol filed suit in late 1980.   About a year later, after extensive discovery, the defendants filed a motion to dismiss for lack of subject matter jurisdiction or alternatively, to dismiss based on the doctrine of *forum non conveniens*.   The motion was summarily denied in December of 1981 without written reasons.   The case had been set for trial in mid-December of that year, but the matter was continued on the court's own motion.   The trial was rescheduled to begin in the spring of 1982, but was again continued, this time on the defendants' motion.   The defendants filed two more motions in December of 1982.   The first was entitled "Motion to Dismiss or, Alternatively, for Summary Judgment" and the defendants' reasons for bringing the motion were stated in a legal memorandum accompanying their motion.   In the memorandum the defendants reurged their arguments concerning lack of subject matter jurisdiction because foreign law should apply to Nicol's case, but a discussion of *forum non conveniens* is nowhere to be found.[5]   The second motion requested partial summary judgment, contending in an accompanying memorandum that Nicol's claims do not fall under the Jones Act and that he is not entitled to invoke the doctrine of unseaworthiness.   Again, *forum non conveniens* is nowhere mentioned.   Three days before trial was to begin in January of 1983, the case was continued to the end of May on the court's motion.   Then, in April, the district judge ordered that the first of the defendants' motions filed the previous December be treated as a motion for summary judgment and granted it.   He did so presumably because he decided that foreign law applies and, the plaintiff having made no claim under foreign law, the complaint should be dismissed for failure to state a claim under Rule 12(b)(6) of the Federal Rules of Civil Procedure.[6]   Then the judge stated in his order, "IT IS FURTHER ORDERED that the defendants' Motion for Summary Judgment on the grounds of *forum non conveniens* is DENIED AS MOOT."   The problem with this adjudication of mootness is that the only motion based on *forum non conveniens* was made and denied back in 1981.[7]   The judge must have assumed that the defendants were

---

5.   The cases cited in the accompanying legal memorandum were *forum non conveniens* controversies, but the defendants' stated reason for urging dismissal or summary judgment was lack of subject matter jurisdiction.

6.   In granting summary judgment, the district judge apparently relied upon the following footnote in Chiazor v. Transworld Drilling Co., Ltd., 648 F.2d 1015, 1020 n. 7 (5th Cir.1981), cert. denied, 455 U.S. 1019, 102 S.Ct. 1714, 72 L.Ed.2d 136 (1982).

The plaintiffs here asserted a claim based only upon the Jones Act, DOHSA, and the general maritime law of the United States; they failed to assert a claim under Nigerian law.   Once the dis-

trict court determined that American law as not applicable, it could have properly dismissed the case pursuant to Federal Rule of Civil Procedure 12(b)(6) for failure to state a claim upon which relief can be granted, and, if deposition and affidavits were considered, have granted a summary judgment under Rule 56.   See de Alvarez v. Creole Petroleum Corp., 613 F.2d 1240 (3d Cir.1980).   See also H. Watson, Applicable Law in Suits by Foreign Offshore Oil Workers, 41 La.L.R. 827, 828–29 (1981).

7.   Unless, perhaps, a motion based on *forum non conveniens* was made in open court, but no such motion appears anywhere in the written record.

reurging their 1981 motions in their entirety, even though they said they were not, and despite their failure to mention *forum non conveniens* in their December 1982 filings. As for the defendants' motion for partial summary judgment based on the Jones Act and unseaworthiness, it appears from the record that it was never ruled upon. In any event, it was clear to Nicol that the United States court had sent him elsewhere, and he appeals to us.

III. Jurisdiction: An Incomplete Analysis

Our most recent pronouncement regarding the standard of review for choice of law in Jones Act/general maritime law cases is contained in Koke v. Phillips Petroleum Co., 730 F.2d 211, 218 (5th Cir.1984):

> Before dismissing a case for *forum non conveniens,* a court must first determine whether American or foreign law governs that claim. Bailey v. Dolphin International, Inc., 697 F.2d 1268, 1274 (5th Cir.1983). This Court has held that, if American law applies, a federal court should retain jurisdiction. Fisher v. Agios Nicolaos V, 628 F.2d 308, 315 (5th Cir.1980), cert. denied sub nom., Valmas Brothers Shipping, S.A. v. Fisher, 454 U.S. 816, 102 S.Ct. 92, 70 L.Ed.2d 84 (1981). But see Piper Aircraft Co. v. Reyno, 454 U.S. 235, 260, 102 S.Ct. 252, 268, 70 L.Ed.2d 419 (1981). If foreign law applies, however, the court may dismiss if there is a more convenient forum available. De Oliveira v. Delta Marine Drilling Co., 707 F.2d 843, 845 (5th Cir.1983). While the choice of law is subject to our *de novo* review, the court's dismissal for *forum non conveniens* will be disturbed "only if its action constitutes a clear abuse of discretion." *Bailey,* 697 F.2d at 1274.

Before the district judge, the parties in Nicol's case appear to have confused subject matter jurisdiction with *forum non conveniens* and thus to have led him into error. The district judge's order is couched strictly in terms of choice of law. In Romero v. International Terminal Operating Co., 358 U.S. 354, 359, 79 S.Ct. 468, 473, 3 L.Ed.2d 368, 374–75 (1959), Justice Frankfurter recognized that the question whether subject matter jurisdiction exists is often confused with whether the complaint states a cause of action. Nicol argues that the Jones Act affords him a right of recovery for the injuries he suffered in the course of his employment.[8] For

---

8. On the date Nicol was injured, the Jones Act, 46 U.S.C. § 688 (1976), provided:

> *Any seaman who shall suffer personal injury in the course of his employment* may, at his election, maintain an action for damages at law, with the right of trial by jury, and in such action all statutes of the United States modifying or extending the common-law right or remedy in cases of personal injury to railway employees shall apply; and in case of the death of any seaman as a result of any such personal injury the personal representative of such seaman may maintain an action for damages at law with the

right of trial by jury, and in such action all statutes of the United States conferring or regulating the right of action for death in the case of railway employees shall be applicable. *Jurisdiction in such actions shall be under the court of the district in which the defendant employer resides or in which his principal office is located.*

(Emphasis added.) The Jones Act was amended in 1982 as follows:

> (a) Application of railway employee statutes; jurisdiction.

Jones Act purposes, Nicol alleges that his "employer"[9] was any one or all of the Gulf Fleet companies named as the defendants.

Such assertion alone is sufficient to empower the District Court to assume jurisdiction over the case and determine whether, in fact, the Act does provide the claimed rights. "A cause of action under our law was asserted here, and the court had power to determine whether it was or was not well founded in law and in fact." Lauritzen v. Larsen, 345 U.S. 571, 575, 73 S.Ct. 921, 924, 97 L.Ed. 1254, 1262.

Romero, 358 U.S. at 359, 79 S.Ct. at 473, 3 L.Ed.2d at 375. The district judge in Nicol's case did not address whether, for example, Nicol is a Jones Act seaman or whether the Gulf Fleet companies might fall under the Jones Act as "employers" given the facts of this case. Thus, he did not rule on whether his court has the *power* to determine Nicol's claims under the Jones Act, nor did he determine whether Nicol states a valid cause of

Any seaman who shall suffer personal injury in the course of his employment may, at his election, maintain an action for damages at law, with the right of trial by jury, and in such action all statutes of the United States modifying or extending the common-law right or remedy in cases of personal injury to railway employees shall apply; and in case of death of any seaman as a result of any such personal injury the personal representative of such seaman may maintain an action for damages at law with the right of trial by jury, and in such action all statutes of the United States conferring or regulating the right of action for death in the case of railway employees shall be applicable. Jurisdiction in such actions shall be under the court of the district in which the defendant employer resides or in which his principal office is located.

(b) Limitation for certain aliens; applicability in lieu of other remedy.

(1) No action may be maintained under subsection (a) of this section or under any other maritime law of the United States for maintenance and cure for damages for the injury or death of a person who was not a citizen or permanent resident alien of the United States at the time of the incident giving rise to the action if the incident occurred—

(A) while that person was in the employ of an enterprise engaged in the exploration, development, or production of off-shore mineral or energy resources—including but not limited to drilling, mapping, surveying, div-

ing, pipelaying, maintaining, repairing, constructing, or transporting supplies, equipment or personnel, but not including transporting those resources by (a) vessel constructed or adapted primarily to carry oil in bulk in the cargo spaces; and

(B) in the territorial waters or waters overlaying the continental shelf of a nation other than the United States, its territories, or possessions. As used in this paragraph, the term "continental shelf" has the meaning stated in article I of the 1958 Convention on the Continental Shelf.

(2) The provisions of paragraph (1) of this subsection shall not be applicable if the person bringing the action establishes that no remedy was available to that person—

(A) under the laws of the nation asserting jurisdiction over the area in which the incident occurred; or

(B) under the laws of the nation in which, at the time of the incident, the person for whose injury or death a remedy is sought maintained citizenship or residency.

46 U.S.C.A. § 688 (Supp.1984). Congress, however, did not make these amendments retroactive and they do not apply to Nicol's accident.

9. He specifically alleged that he was "an employee or borrowed servant or employee pro hac vice of" the five Gulf Fleet defendants.

action under the Act. He determined only that foreign law applies, the first prong in a *forum non conveniens* assessment. Similarly, the district court never discussed its jurisdiction over this case in terms of American general maritime law, nor was the validity of Nicol's cause of action questioned under general maritime law.[10] It is clear from *Romero* that choice of law in Jones Act/general maritime law cases is relevant only to the doctrine of *forum non conveniens* and has nothing to do with subject matter jurisdiction. Thus, the district judge had taken only the first step in a *forum non conveniens* analysis when he dismissed Nicol's case. Consequently he erred, perhaps in finding that American law does not apply and surely in failing to complete the *forum non conveniens* assessment suggested by Gulf Oil Corporation v. Gilbert, 330 U.S. 501, 67 S.Ct. 839, 91 L.Ed. 1055 (1947), and its progeny.[11]

IV. Choice of Law

As the case must be remanded, and since the record is silent regarding several of the pertinent factors governing choice of law, we conclude that the interests of justice would be best served by vacating the district court's order in that regard also. We discuss these briefly for such aid as we may be to the trial judge.

Any analysis of choice-of-law in an injured seaman's action must begin with the Supreme Court's decisions in Lauritzen v. Larsen, 345 U.S. 571, 73 S.Ct. 921, 97 L.Ed. 1254 (1953), and Hellenic Lines, Ltd. v. Rhoditis, 398 U.S. 306, 90 S.Ct. 1731, 26 L.Ed.2d 252 (1970). Those cases set forth eight factors to be employed in deciding choice-of-law in maritime tort claims: (1) place of the wrongful act; (2) law of the flag; (3) allegiance or domicile of the injured; (4) allegiance of the defendant shipowner; (5) place of contract; (6) inaccessibility of foreign forum; (7) law of the forum; and (8) shipowner's base of operations.

Lauritzen and *Rhoditis* also provide guidance as to the weight and significance to be accorded each factor. As to the place of the wrongful act, *Lauritzen* counsels that while the law of the place where the acts giving rise to liability occurred is a commonly accepted solution to the choice of law dilemma, it is of limited application to shipboard torts and is usually modified by the law of the flag. *Lauritzen*, 345 U.S. 571 at 583–84, 73 S.Ct. at 928–929, 97 L.Ed. 1254 at 1268. The opinion implies that this is particularly so when the tort is committed on the high seas. Regarding the law of the flag:

> Perhaps the most venerable and universal rule of maritime law relevant to our problem is that which gives cardinal importance to the law of the flag. Each state under international law may determine for itself the conditions on which it will grant its nationality to a merchant ship, thereby

---

10. *Romero* held that a federal district court has pendent jurisdiction on the law side of its docket over causes brought under United States general maritime law when such causes are joined with Jones Act claims. 358 U.S. at 378, 79 S.Ct. at 484, 3 L.Ed.2d at 387.

11. E.g., Chiazor v. Transworld Drilling Co., 648 F.2d 1015 (5th Cir.1981).

accepting responsibility for it and acquiring authority over it. Nationality is evidenced to the world by the ship's papers and its flag. * * *

It is significant to us here that the weight given to the ensign overbears most other connecting events in determining applicable law. As this Court held in United States v. Flores, supra (289 U.S. at [137] 158 [53 S.Ct. 580 at 585, 77 L.Ed. 1086]), and iterated in Cunard S.S. Co. v. Mellon, supra (262 U.S. [100] at 123 [43 S.Ct. 504 at 507, 67 L.Ed. 894]):

> "And so by comity it came to be generally understood among civilized nations that all matters of discipline and all things done on board which affected only the vessel or those belonging to her, and did not involve the peace or dignity of the country, or the tranquillity of the port, should be left by the local government to be dealt with by the authorities of the nation to which the vessel belonged as the laws of that nation or the interests of its commerce should require. * * *"

Lauritzen, 345 U.S. at 584–585, 586, 73 S.Ct. at 929–930, 97 L.Ed. at 1269.

Nicol's accident occurred approximately 45 miles off the coast of Abu Dhabi in the Zakum field. The parties present conflicting affidavits as to whether the Zakum field is within the territorial waters of the Emirate of Abu Dhabi.[12] On remand, the court should resolve the dispute. It does appear to be undisputed that the M/V GULF QUEEN II flew the flag of the United States in 1979, a factor that, even standing alone, can be paramount in suggesting a choice of American law. *Koke,* 730 F.2d at 218.

Nicol is a British subject. *Lauritzen* points out that there is a long standing rule that for jurisdictional purposes the nationality of the vessel is attributed to all her crew. On the other hand, "each nation has a legitimate interest that its nationals and permanent inhabitants be not maimed or disabled from self-support." *Lauritzen,* 345 U.S. at 586, 73

---

12. We suspect that 45 miles offshore is too far out to be within the territorial waters of Abu Dhabi for purposes of civil jurisdiction over a maritime tort. Information supplied to this Court by the United States Department of State indicates that between 1970 and August 1980, Abu Dhabi claimed a territorial sea of three nautical miles (approximately 3.45 miles) and no additional contiguous zone. While different countries claimed territorial seas of differing breadths in 1979, most coastal states adhered to territorial seas of no more than 12 miles. L. Henkin, R. Pugh, O. Schachter and H. Smit, International Law Cases and Materials 311 (1980). See also: Convention on the Territorial Sea and the Contiguous Zone, *opened for signature* Apr. 29, 1958, 15 U.S.T. 1606, T.I.A.S. No. 5639, 516 U.N.T.S. 205, arts. 20, 24 (zone of the high seas contiguous to the territorial sea of a state may not extend beyond 12 miles from the baseline from which the breadth of the territorial sea is measured; coastal states may not exercise civil jurisdiction beyond pre-

venting infringement of its customs, fiscal, immigration, or sanitary regulations within its contiguous zone); Convention on the High Seas, *opened for signature* Apr. 29, 1958, 13 U.S.T. 2312, T.I.A.S. No. 5200, 450 U.N.T.S. 82, art. 1 (high seas means all parts of the sea not included in the territorial sea of a state).

According to our information received from the Department of State, the U.A.E. declared an exclusive economic zone of unlimited breadth in August of 1980. But generally a state may use its exclusive economic zone only for purposes of exploiting natural resources; its civil jurisdiction over a claim such as Nicol's does not extend beyond its territorial waters into the exclusive economic zone. See Informal Composite Negotiating Text, Third U.N. Conference on the Law of the Sea, A/CONF.62/WP./10/Rev. 2 (11 April 1980), arts. 55–58 reprinted in L. Henkin, R. Pugh, O. Schachter & H. Smit, International Law Cases and Materials 378–79 (1980).

S.Ct. at 930, 3 L.Ed.2d at 1270. *Lauritzen* did not go further with this discussion because the nationality of the seaman and the flag were the same under its facts.   Here, Nicol was not a regular member of the crew of the M/V GULF QUEEN II, and certainly Great Britain has an interest that Nicol not be added to her public relief rolls.   Thus, Nicol's nationality for purposes of the *Lauritzen* instructions is probably British, but the fact that legally he may have been a temporary member of the tug's crew may lessen the effect of the "injured's domicile" factor in this case.

Gulf Fleet Western, owner of the M/V GULF QUEEN II in 1979, is undeniably an American company.   Thus, the "allegiance of the defendant shipowner" factor points to the application of American law.

The Supreme Court accorded little weight to the place of contract. *Lauritzen*, 345 U.S. at 588, 73 S.Ct. at 931, 97 L.Ed. at 1271.   In *Lauritzen*, as in this case, the seaman did not seek to recover anything due under the contract or damages for its breach.   Justice Jackson stated that if contract law is to be considered at all, the law which contracting parties intended to apply should govern.   In any event, Justice Jackson's majority did not think the place of contract a substantial influence in the choice between competing laws to govern a maritime tort.   Id.   In the case before us, we know little about Nicol's contract with his Liberian employer, if, indeed, he had one.   There is certainly insufficient information in the record to attempt a determination of what law the parties intended to govern any employment contract Nicol may have had.   And even if adequate information were at hand, Nicol's accident did not take place on his Liberian employer's property, nor does the diver seek to recover damages pursuant to his employment contract.   Even so, on remand the court may wish to determine what law governs Nicol's contract, weak though that influence on its decision may be.

As to the accessibility of a foreign forum in this case, the parties introduced conflicting affidavits on whether Nicol could bring an action in Abu Dhabi.[13]   No one has introduced any evidence on the question of whether the courts of Scotland, Liberia, or Panama might be available to the plaintiff.   Because no party has adequately proved the law of Abu Dhabi or that of any other possible foreign forum, we are unable to consider it.

The purpose of the *Lauritzen* "law of the forum" factor is to assure that a case will be treated in the same way under the appropriate law regardless of the fortuitous circumstances which often determine the forum.   The Supreme Court emphasized that the mere ability to serve

---

13.   The plaintiff's expert says that the Abu Dhabi court would apply American law. He states that Abu Dhabi would not have jurisdiction over companies not organized under the laws of Abu Dhabi or the U.A.E.   The defendants' expert opines that Nicol could recover from his employer under the laws of Abu Dhabi, but does not address whether any of the Gulf Fleet companies would be considered Nicol's employer in the courts of the U.A.E.   Based on the parties' submissions as to the law of Abu Dhabi, we are unable to say one way or the other whether Nicol has either a cause of action or jurisdiction over the defendants in Abu Dhabi.

American process on the defendants is not enough to impose the law of an American forum on them if it would not otherwise apply. Id., 345 U.S. at 590–592, 73 S.Ct. at 932–933, 97 L.Ed.2d at 1272–73. Thus, we doubt that this factor is of much weight.

Finally, *Rhoditis* teaches that a defendant's American base of operations can be sufficient to support the application of American law. The reasoning of *Rhoditis* was based principally upon the shipowner corporation's American base of operations, but mention was also made of the vessel's frequent calls at American ports. We must consider the base of operations of both the shipowner and the vessel. See Fajardo v. Tidewater, Inc., 707 F.2d 858, 862 (5th Cir.1983); see also Diaz v. Humboldt, 722 F.2d 1216 (5th Cir.1984). It is undisputed that Gulf Fleet Western's base of operations is in Louisiana, and it may well be that the base of operations of the bareboat charterer(s) is also there.[14] The M/V GULF QUEEN II made her maiden voyage from New Orleans in 1977, and it is clear that the vessel would have returned to New Orleans in 1978 had extensive repairs not necessitated cancelling the remaining voyage when the tug reached Greece.[15] Thus, it appears that the "base of operations" factor weighs in favor of the application of American law, but it may be of little weight because the day-to-day activities of the tug were probably directed by the time charterer (N.P.C.C.) in Abu Dhabi, and a case can be made for a U.A.E. base of operations for the bareboat charterers.

Lauritzen and *Rhoditis* were intended to apply to ocean-going vessels generally, true maritime vessels that ply the seas as an integral part of the shipping industry. Where these vessels are concerned, Gilmore and Black states:

> American law will * * * be applied in actions brought on account of injuries suffered on American-flag ships, whether the plaintiffs are American or foreign, resident or non-resident, seamen, harbor-workers, passengers, guests or, for that matter, pirates. By taking out registry in this country, the shipowner consents in effect to the application of the law of the United States. This proposition has seemed so self-evident that it appears never to have been questioned.

G. Gilmore & C. Black, *The Law of Admiralty* at 477 (2d Ed.) (1975).

It has now been questioned in this Circuit, however, in the context of drilling rigs. *Koke,* 730 F.2d 211; De Oliveira v. Delta Marine Drilling Co., 707 F.2d 843 (5th Cir.1983)(law of the flag not considered); Chiazor v. Transworld Drilling Co., Ltd., 648 F.2d 1015 (5th Cir.1981), cert. denied 455 U.S. 1019, 102 S.Ct. 1714, 72 L.Ed.2d 136 (1982)(law of the flag not considered). Beginning with *Chiazor* in this Circuit, the suggestion is

---

14. Gulf Fleet Abu Dhabi is one-half owned by Gulf Fleet Middle East, a company in which 100% of the stock is owned by Americans. Gulf Mississippi International, S.A., is also wholly owned by Americans. See generally Baker v. Raymond International, Inc., 656 F.2d 173 (5th Cir.1981), cert. de-nied, 456 U.S. 983, 102 S.Ct. 2256, 72 L.Ed.2d 861 (1982).

15. The M/V GULF QUEEN II was towing the dredge JIM BEAN from the Middle East to New Orleans on orders from Louisiana.

made that the *Lauritzen/Rhoditis* choice of law factors should be applied differently to offshore drilling rigs or vessels so intimately connected with one or just a few such rigs that they remain stationary or move only short distances infrequently. *Koke,* 730 F.2d 211; *De Oliveira,* 707 F.2d 843; Bailey v. Dolphin International, Inc., 697 F.2d 1268 (5th Cir.1983); Vaz Borralho v. Keydril Co., 696 F.2d 379 (5th Cir.1983); Zekic v. Reading & Bates Drilling Co., 536 F.Supp. 23 (E.D.La.1981), modified 680 F.2d 1107 (5th Cir.1982). In these drilling rig cases, factors such as the place of the wrong, the domicile of the injured, and the place of contract take on greater significance. *Chiazor,* 648 F.2d at 1019. Thus, the court must analyze the activities of the M/V GULF QUEEN II to determine whether it is to weigh the eight factors in the traditional *Lauritzen/Rhoditis* manner or under the drilling rig variation.

Drilling rig cases, such as this? [handwritten margin note]

The defendants here insist that their tugboat has been engaged in oil operations in the Middle East almost exclusively since 1977, necessitating the application of the drilling rig rules. But the record establishes the tug's presence in New Orleans, Ras Shakheir (Egypt) and Port Said (Egypt) in 1977; Ras Shakheir; Dubai (U.A.E.); Piraeus (Greece); and "Jubail"[16] in 1978; and two states in the U.A.E. in 1980. The vessel has not been engaged exclusively off the coast of Abu Dhabi since its maiden voyage in 1977. It is also clear that a Gulf Fleet entity out of New Orleans ordered the tug to tow another vessel to the United States in 1978, although the mission was reassigned to another tug when the M/V GULF FLEET II had to put in for extensive repairs on the way. The tug is self-propelled and moves about freely. It is not engaged in the sole service of one drilling rig in a fixed location or even a small number of drilling rigs in close proximity. Accordingly, we are not so clear as was the trial court that the M/V GULF QUEEN II is not a true blue-water vessel and that the district court's analysis should not have proceeded under *Chiazor* and its progeny, but rather under the traditional *Lauritzen/Rhoditis* reasoning. On the remand that we direct, the court should re-examine these questions.

Vacated and Remanded.

B.   IN THE COURSE OF HIS EMPLOYMENT

McAleer v. Smith

United States Court of Appeals, First Circuit, 1995.
57 F.3d 109, 1995 A.M.C. 2174

■ STAHL, CIRCUIT JUDGE:

Plaintiffs-appellants appeal from the district court's grant of summary judgment to defendant-appellee in this admiralty case. We affirm.

---

16. "Jubail," or Jubayl, could be either a port city in Lebanon or another port city in Saudi Arabia sometimes known as Al Jubail or Al Jubayl. The record suggests that the Jubail it refers to is the Saudi Arabian one, but it makes little difference for our purposes.

I

BACKGROUND

On June 3, 1984, the Tall Ship S/V MARQUES, a participant in the Cutty Sark International Tall Ships Race between Bermuda and Nova Scotia, encountered a violent squall about eighty miles northeast of Bermuda. Almost without warning, and within seconds of starting to take on water, the vessel sank with the loss of nineteen of the twenty-eight persons on board, including the plaintiffs' decedents and the defendant's decedent, the vessel's master or captain, Stuart A. Finlay. Plaintiffs' decedents, James F. McAleer and Thomas A. Lebel, were on board under the auspices of a sailing program run by the American Sail Training Association ("ASTA"), which had arranged for six sail trainees to crew for the MARQUES during the race.

Plaintiffs brought claims against defendant for unseaworthiness under the general maritime law; for negligence under the Jones Act, 46 U.S.C.App. § 688; for negligence under the general maritime law; and for wrongful death under the Death on the High Seas Act, 46 U.S.C.App. §§ 761–768 ("DOHSA"). The district court granted summary judgment to defendant, holding that defendant could not be liable for unseaworthiness because Finlay was not an owner of the MARQUES, McAleer v. Smith, 818 F.Supp. 486, 494 (D.R.I.1993); for negligence under the Jones Act, because Finlay did not employ plaintiffs' decedents, id. at 493–94; for negligence under the general maritime law, because such claims cannot be brought by seamen against masters, id. at 496; or under DOHSA, because DOHSA is a derivative cause of action requiring the existence of another claim not existent here, id. at 496–97. From that judgment this appeal followed.[1]

II

DISCUSSION

A. Standard of Review

As always, we review a district court's grant of summary judgment de novo and, like the district court, review the facts in the light most favorable to the nonmoving party. See, e.g., Lareau v. Page, 39 F.3d 384, 387 (1st Cir.1994). Summary judgment is appropriate when "the pleadings, depositions, answers to interrogatories, and admissions on file, together with the affidavits, if any, show that there is no genuine issue as to any material fact and that the moving party is entitled to a judgment as a matter of law." Fed.R.Civ.P. 56(c).

---

1. The district court granted defendant's motion for summary judgment on April 8, 1993. The district court nonetheless held a trial to determine damages because it had entered default judgments against the co-owners of the Marques, see McAleer v. Smith, 860 F.Supp. 924, 930, n.10 (D.R.I.1994). On October 18, 1994, the district court entered judgments of $403,246.57 for Lebel and $322,597.25 for McAleer against the co-owners and entered final judgments in favor of defendants in the instant appeal and other defendants.

B. Unseaworthiness

Shipowners are liable to indemnify seamen[2] for injuries "caused by the unseaworthiness of the vessel or its appurtenant appliances and equipment." Seas Shipping Co. v. Sieracki, 328 U.S. 85, 90, 66 S.Ct. 872, 875, 90 L.Ed. 1099 (1946)(citing The Osceola, 189 U.S. 158, 23 S.Ct. 483, 47 L.Ed. 760 (1903)). Unseaworthiness "is essentially a species of liability without fault.... It is a form of absolute duty." Id. at 94–95, 66 S.Ct. at 877; see also Grant Gilmore & Charles L. Black, Jr., *The Law of Admiralty* § 6–41, at 393 (2d ed. 1975). Shipowners may not delegate their duty to provide a seaworthy ship. *Sieracki*, 328 U.S. at 94 n. 11, 66 S.Ct. at 877 n. 11. Plaintiffs concede that Finlay did not own the MARQUES, which was co-owned by Mark Shirley Portal Litchfield and Robin Patrick Cecil–Wright, the sole principals in the China Clipper Company, an unincorporated holding company that held title to the MARQUES. Plaintiffs argue, however, that Finlay is nonetheless liable for unseaworthiness because he was an owner *pro hac vice*.

An "owner *pro hac vice*" of a vessel is "one who 'stands in the place of the owner for the voyage or service contemplated and bears the owner's responsibilities, even though the latter remains the legal owner of the vessel.'" Matute v. Lloyd Berm. Lines, Ltd., 931 F.2d 231, 235 n. 2 (3d Cir.)(quoting Aird v. Weyerhaeuser S.S. Co., 169 F.2d 606, 610 (3d Cir. 1948), cert. denied, 337 U.S. 959, 69 S.Ct. 1521, 93 L.Ed. 1758 (1949)), cert. denied, 502 U.S. 919, 112 S.Ct. 329, 116 L.Ed.2d 270 (1991). In effect, for liability purposes, an owner *pro hac vice* is treated as a shipowner. See Reed v. The Yaka, 373 U.S. 410, 412–13, 83 S.Ct. 1349, 1351–52, 10 L.Ed.2d 448 (1963); see generally Gilmore & Black, *The Law of Admiralty* § 4–23, at 242. Thus, an owner *pro hac vice* may be liable for the unseaworthiness of a vessel. See *Reed*, 373 U.S. at 412–13, 83 S.Ct. at 1351–52. In general, if there is an owner *pro hac vice*, the title owner will be absolved of personal liability (except for defective conditions that existed before the owner *pro hac vice* took control of the vessel). See Ramos v. Beauregard, Inc., 423 F.2d 916, 917–18 (1st Cir.), cert. denied, 400 U.S. 865, 91 S.Ct. 101, 27 L.Ed.2d 104 (1970); see generally Thomas J. Schoenbaum, *Admiralty and Maritime Law* 5–3, at 168 (1987).

Admiralty cases have recognized only two types of owners *pro hac vice*: demise, or bareboat, charterers and captains of fishing vessels operated under agreements, called "lays." A demise charterer is "one who contracts for the vessel itself and assumes exclusive possession, control, command and navigation thereof for a specified period," Stephenson v. Star–Kist Caribe, Inc., 598 F.2d 676, 679 (1st Cir.1979), in contrast to a time or voyage charterer who "contracts not for the vessel itself but for a specific service of the vessel, such as carriage of goods, which is rendered by the

---

2. For the purposes of this summary judgment motion, we assume *arguendo*, as Judge Selya did for other MARQUES sail trainees in Heath v. American Sail Training Ass'n, 644 F.Supp. 1459, 1468 (D.R.I.1986)(Selya,J.), that plaintiff's decedents were seamen despite the fact that they were unpaid (indeed, themselves paying for the privilege of being on board as trainees).

owner's master and crew." Id. Demise charters are created when "the owner of the vessel completely and exclusively relinquish[es] possession, command, and navigation thereof to the demisee. [They are] therefore tantamount to, though just short of, an outright transfer of ownership. However, anything short of such a complete transfer is a time or voyage charter party or not a charter party at all." Guzman u Pichirilo, 369 U.S. 698, 699–700, 82 S.Ct. 1095, 1096, 8 L.Ed.2d 205 (1962)(internal quotation and citations omitted); see generally Gilmore & Black, *Law of Admiralty* § 4–21, at 240. While demise charterers may be liable for unseaworthiness as owners *pro hac vice*, see *Reed*, 373 U.S. at 412–13, 83 S.Ct at 1351–52, time or voyage charterers may not be, see *Stevenson*, 598 F.2d at 679; *see also Rodriguez v. McAllister Bros., Inc.*, 736 F.2d 813, 815 (1st Cir.1984). The mere fact that a time or voyage charterer " 'has some control over the master . . . [or] selects the routes to be taken or the cargo to be carried does not make him the owner *pro hac vice.*' " *Stephenson*, 598 F.2d at 681 (quoting *Fitzgerald v. A.L. Burbank & Co.*, 451 F.2d 670, 676 (2d Cir.1971))(alterations in *Stephenson*).

Captains of vessels operated under, which are agreements under that which the participating fishermen share the catch, may also be liable as owners *pro hac vice*. See Cromwell v. Slaney, 65 F.2d 940, 941 (1st Cir.1933). Such situations are similar to demise charters, for a fishing lay captain will only be found to be an owner *pro hac vice* if the captain employs the members of the crew and controls all the operations of the vessel, both in purchasing supplies for the voyage, in determining where he will fish, how long, and in disposing of the catch and settling all the bills. Id.

Plaintiffs cite no case, and we have found none, outside the context of a fishing lay that accords a master status as an owner *pro hac vice.* In fact, many of our cases find an owner liable precisely *because* the owner (rather than, say, the time charterer) provided the master and crew, id. *Stephenson,* 598 F.2d at 680. As a general rule, we think that masters are not owners *pro hac vice* because a master, despite having control over the vessel, exercises that control on behalf of the the owner. Cf. 46 U.S.C. § 10101(1)(defining "master" as "the individual having command of a vessel"); 46 U.S.C. § 10101(2)(defining "owner" as "the person to whom the vessel belongs").

Plaintiffs argue, however, that even if masters are not generally considered to be owners *pro hac vice*, Captain Finlay had responsibilities for and interests in the MARQUES beyond those of an ordinary master that render him liable as an owner *pro hac vice*. In particular, plaintiffs point out that Finlay had full operational control of the MARQUES, except that he had to report itinerary changes to the owners; that Finlay drew the ship's regulations for both mates and crew members, and that everyone on board was required to "read" his orders; that Finlay's contract with the MARQUES's owners designated him as "self-employed"; that Finlay was engaged in promoting the business of the MARQUES, such as charters and cruises, for which he was paid a commission in addition to his monthly base pay;[3] that Finlay was required to solicit contributions towards expenses and was obligated whenever possible to negotiate directly with suppliers to obtain free or discounted supplies in exchange for publicity or other recompense arrangements; that Finlay was a founding member and chief instructor of the Antiguan Maritime School and expected to use the MARQUES as a training ship to train young Antiguans in seamanship; and that the "Ship's regulations" provided that one person, the captain, was solely responsible for the safety of the ship and those on board. Plaintiffs also point out that their decedents had no contract with the MARQUES's actual owners but only with ASTA and Finlay, and make much of the fact that Finlay had the right to direct and control plaintiff's decedents in the performance of their duties as sail trainees and the right to fire and/or remove them from the ship.

We fail to see how these facts convert Finlay into an owner *pro hac vice*. In determining that Finlay was not an owner *pro hac vice*, we are mindful not only of the law of agency, but also of the fact that time charterers, who may exercise large amounts of control over the vessels they charter, are not subject to liability for unseaworthiness, see *Stephenson*, 598 F.2d at 679. While we take plaintiffs' arguments in turn, even considered cumulatively we do not think they support Finlay being considered an owner *pro hac vice*. While Finlay did exercise operational control over the MARQUES, that control is inherent in being a master; it does not convert Finlay into an owner *pro hac vice*. Similarly, drawing up the ship's regulations and giving orders are part and parcel of a master's duties; such activities do not accord Finlay status as an owner *pro hac vice*. That Finlay was designated as "self-employed" also does not make him an owner *pro hac vice*. Despite being "self-employed," Finlay still functioned as an agent of the owners; he did not assume control of the MARQUES in his own right and, accordingly, cannot be said to have stood in the place of the owner. We also do not think that the fact that Finlay was to receive a commission for business he brought to the MARQUES makes him an owner *pro hac vice*, any more than a salesman paid a commission for his sales or a businessman paid a bonus for business brought in or money saved would become an owner of the business. Similarly, that Finlay was required to negotiate with suppliers does not make him an owner *pro hac vice*; rather, it was just one of the duties imposed on him by the MARQUES's actual owners. There is no evidence that Finlay was to share in any savings generated by these negotiations. Indeed, the owners were responsible for all expenses associated with the MARQUES, including those incurred by captains for generating business or negotiating for supplies.

Nor do we think that Finlay's role in the Antiguan Maritime School converts him into an owner *pro hac vice*. While at some point in the future this may have brought some business to the MARQUES, thus being mutually beneficial for both Finlay and the owners of the MARQUES, there

---

3. Although he received 1000 British pounds sterling per month while the MARQUES was at sea and 500 pounds per month while ashore, plaintiffs also argue that Finlay was not a salaried employee.

is no evidence that Finlay had actually brought such business to the MARQUES or that arrangements for such a venture had actually been made. Nor is there any evidence to suggest that Finlay had entered into any sort of partnership with the owners of the MARQUES regarding the school; the implication, therefore, is that Finlay would have received his standard commission for bringing business to the MARQUES if in fact he ever brought such business from the school.

The fact that the Ship's Regulations provided that the captain was solely responsible for the safety of the ship and those on board does not make Finlay liable for the ship's unseaworthiness, because a shipowner's duty to provide a seaworthy ship is nondelegable. See *Sieracki*, 328 U.S. at 94 n. 11, 66 S.Ct. at 877 n. 11. Holding Finlay to be an owner *pro hac vice* because the Ship's Regulations made him solely responsible for the safety of the ship would defeat the rule of nondelegability, for it would absolve the owners of liability for unseaworthiness. See *Ramos*, 423 F.2d at 917–18 (holding that owner could not be "liable for unseaworthy conditions arising after he has parted with control over his vessel under a demise charter" and that "a shipowner cannot escape liability by delegating partial control of his vessel to an independent contractor").

That plaintiffs' decedents had no contact with the MARQUES's owners, but only with ASTA and Finlay, does not convert Finlay into an owner *pro hac vice*. Finlay played no part in hiring plaintiffs' decedents or in arranging with ASTA to have paying sail trainees on board. Finlay was not to share in the profits from the owners' arrangement with ASTA, nor in any profits from the vessel's participation in the tall ships race. That Finlay had authority over plaintiffs' decedents is not indicative of status as an owner *pro hac vice*, for any master would necessarily have such authority over his crew.

To the extent that plaintiffs argue that Finlay was a partner or co-venturer with the MARQUES's owners, the undisputed facts make clear, as the district court noted, that Finlay had no ownership interest in the vessel, did not share in the profits from the vessel's operations, and had no control over the vessel's itinerary beyond the operational control necessarily assumed by a captain. The marketing and commission arrangement raises no inference of a partnership. Because plaintiffs have not produced facts that give rise to an inference that Finlay was either an owner *pro hac vice* or a partner in the MARQUES, summary judgment was properly granted to defendant on plaintiffs' unseaworthiness claims.

C. The Jones Act

Congress passed the Jones Act in 1920 to abrogate the Supreme Court's holding in The Osceola, 189 U.S. 158, 175, 23 S.Ct. 483, 487, 47 L.Ed. 760 (1903), that seamen could not recover under the general maritime law for the negligence of the master or crew. See generally Gilmore & Black, *The*

Law of Admiralty § 1920, at 325–28. The Jones Act[4] provides a remedy to a "seaman" injured (or killed) "in the course of his employment." 46 U.S.C.App. § 688. The Jones Act remedy is available only against the seaman's employer. Cosmopolitan Shipping Co. v. McAllister, 337 U.S. 783, 787 n. 6, 69 S.Ct. 1317, 1320 n. 6, 93 L.Ed. 1692 (1949). Accordingly, plaintiffs can recover against defendant under the Jones Act only if Finlay was plaintiffs' decedents' employer.

Plaintiffs contend that if their decedents "were employees of anyone," they were employees of Captain Finlay. We do not agree. Although Finlay exercised authority over plaintiffs' decedents, he did so only as an agent of the owners, and not on his own behalf. Cf. *Matute*, 931 F.2d at 236 (Holding that a time charterer was not a seaman's employer when "[t]he owner ..., *through the ship's captain*, hired Matute [the seaman] and eventually terminated him. It set the amount of Matute's wages and was responsible for paying him. The captain supervised Matute in his position as oiler.")(emphasis added). Finlay had nothing to do with arranging with ASTA for the sail trainees to be on board the MARQUES; accordingly, he cannot be said to have "hired" them in any sense. Nor was Finlay to receive any benefit from having the sail trainees on board; rather, monies paid by the sail trainees went to the owners of the MARQUES, with a small amount reserved by ASTA to cover its expenses.

In arguing that Finlay should be held to be plaintiffs' decedents' employer, plaintiffs rely on many of the same reasons they relied on in arguing that Finlay was an owner *pro hac vice*. We need not re-analyze those reasons here because they do not indicate that Finlay was an employer any more than they indicate that he was an owner *pro hac vice*. Accordingly, the district court properly granted summary judgment to defendant on plaintiffs' Jones Act claims.

D. Negligence Under General Maritime Law.

Plaintiffs argue that they are entitled to recover from defendant for negligence under the general maritime law on two separate theories. First, plaintiffs argue that they have such a cause of action if their decedents, as sail trainees who each paid $750 to crew on the MARQUES, are found to be passengers rather than seamen. Second, plaintiffs argue that if their decedents were seamen, they nevertheless may maintain a cause of action

---

4. The Jones Act provides:

Any seaman who shall suffer personal injury in the course of his employment may, at his election, maintain an action for damages at law, with the right of trial by jury, and in such action all statutes of the United States modifying or extending the common law right or remedy in cases of personal injury to railroad employees shall apply; and in the case of the death of any seaman as a result of any such personal injury the personal representative of such seaman may maintain an action for damages at law with the right of trial by jury, and in such action all statutes of the United States conferring or regulating the right of action for death in the case of railway employees shall be applicable. Jurisdiction in such actions shall be under the court of the district in which the defendant employer resides or in which his principal office is located.

46 U.S.C.App. § 688.

for negligence against the master under the general maritime law. We consider these arguments in turn.

1. Recovery as Passengers

Plaintiffs now urge that because their decedents paid to crew on the MARQUES, they may be considered passengers rather than seamen and so have a cause of action against the master for negligence under the general maritime law. Defendant argues, however, that plaintiffs never made this argument to the district court, and that in fact plaintiffs fought hard to establish that their decedents were seamen, as recovery for unseaworthiness and under the Jones Act is limited to seamen.

When asked at oral argument whether plaintiffs had raised this argument in the district court, plaintiffs' counsel referred the court to a portion of plaintiffs' memorandum of law opposing defendant's motion for summary judgment. In turning to plaintiffs' memorandum, the most applicable statement we could find reads, "A general maritime claim for negligence exists no matter what the status of Finlay was, even if he were found not to be an owner *pro hac vice.*" We do not view this statement as preserving a claim stemming from plaintiffs' decedents' possible status as passengers. In fact, in another portion of their memorandum, plaintiffs cited Judge Selya's opinion in Heath v. American Sail Training Ass'n, 644 F.Supp. 1459, 1463 (D.R.I.1986)(Selya, J.)(dealing with claims by other sail trainees killed in same accident), for the proposition: "It is established that the ASTA trainees were considered to be part of the permanent crew and divided into duty watches." Because plaintiffs did not raise any claims stemming from the possible passenger status of their decedents in the district court, we will not consider them on appeal. See, e.g., Focus Investment Assocs., Inc. v. American Title Ins. Co., 992 F.2d 1231, 1240 n. 12 (1st Cir.1993).

2. Recovery as Seamen

Plaintiffs argue that, even if their decedents are considered to have been seamen,[5] they nonetheless may maintain a cause of action against the master for negligence under the general maritime law. Deciding whether they are right requires us to examine the history of negligence under the general maritime law.

As a general matter, anyone who is the victim of a maritime tort is entitled to bring an action in admiralty. See, e.g., Pope & Talbot, Inc. v. Hawn, 346 U.S. 406, 413–14, 74 S.Ct. 202, 207–08, 98 L.Ed. 143 (1953) (business invitees may bring a cause of action for negligence); cf. United NY & NJ Sandy Hook Pilots Ass'n. v. Halecki, 358 U.S. 613, 617–18, 79 S.Ct. 517, 519–20, 3 L.Ed.2d 541 (1959)("the owner of a ship in navigable waters owes to all who are on board for purposes not inimical to his legitimate interests the duty of exercising reasonable care"). Seamen,

---

5. Defendant does not contest the seaman status of plaintiffs' decedents for pur- poses of the summary judgment motion.

however, were traditionally barred from exercising this remedy with respect to injuries caused by "the negligence of the master, or any member of the crew." *The Osceola*, 189 U.S. at 175, 23 S.Ct. at 487; see also Gilmore & Black, *The Law of Admiralty* 6–21, at 328. Congress, in response to the rule of *The Osceola* passed the Jones Act in order to give seamen "the same rights to recover for negligence as other tort victims. It follows, therefore, that, if plaintiff is a seaman, he can recover under the Jones Act; if he is not a seaman, he can recover under the general maritime law." Gilmore & Black, *The Law of Admiralty* 6–21, at 328–318–29. Thus, it appears that the general maritime law affords seamen no right to recover for injuries caused by a negligent master or crew member, but that they may recover for such injuries from their employer under the Jones Act.

Plaintiffs make several arguments in an attempt to get around the rule that seamen have no general maritime cause of action for injuries caused by the negligence of the master or crew. First, plaintiffs cite Cerqueira v. Cerqueira, 828 F.2d 863 (1st Cir.1987); Stoot v. D & D Catering Serv., Inc., 807 F.2d 1197 (5th Cir.), cert. denied, 484 U.S. 821, 108 S.Ct. 82, 98 L.Ed.2d 44 (1987); Mahramas v. American Export Isbrandtsen Lines, Inc., 475 F.2d 165 (2d Cir.1973); and Favaloro v. S/S Golden Gate, 687 F.Supp. 475 (N.D.Cal.1987), which they construe to grant seamen a cause of action for negligence under the general maritime law. Upon examining each of these cases, however, we find them distinguishable.

In *Cerqueira*, we allowed the equitable owner of a boat to sue his brother, the legal title owner of the boat, for simple negligence, positing that jurisdiction seemed proper on the basis of the court's general maritime jurisdiction. *Cerqueira*, 828 F.2d at 866. We did not, however, consider the plaintiff to be a "seaman," nor do we think a shipowner would generally be accorded seaman status. Thus, while *Cerqueira* may be read to provide a cause of action for negligence under the general maritime law, it does not support plaintiffs' argument that seamen are entitled to bring such an action for injuries arising from the negligence of the master or crew. In *Stoot*, the Fifth Circuit considered the claim of a seaman injured during an altercation with the vessel's cook, who was employed by the defendant, an independent contractor providing catering services on board the vessel. The Fifth Circuit held that the catering company could not be held vicariously liable for the cook's intentional tort because it was committed outside the scope of her employment. *Stoot*, 807 F.2d at 1200. In so holding, however, the Fifth Circuit stated that the catering company could have been held vicariously liable to the seaman for its employee's wrongful acts if the employee had been acting in the course and scope of her employment. Id. at 1199. Based on this, plaintiffs argue that seamen may assert a cause of action for negligence under the general maritime law against independent contractors. Plaintiffs further argue that because Finlay's contract designated him as "self-employed," he should be treated as an independent contractor and his estate should be liable for his negligence under the general maritime law. We need not decide whether we would follow the *Stoot* dictum granting seamen a cause of action against third parties for negligence under the general maritime law because we do not consider Finlay to have been a third party of the type envisioned by *Stoot*. Although his contract did designate him as "self-employed," Finlay did not function as an independent contractor, but rather as an employee and agent of the owners of the MARQUES. Even if Finlay was an independent contractor, however, we would hesitate to extend *Stoot* to negligence actions under the general maritime law by seamen against their independent-contractor masters, especially in light of the Supreme Court's holding that seamen cannot recover for the negligence of the master or crew under the general maritime law, see *The Osceola*, 189 U.S. at 175, 23 S.Ct. at 487. *Mahramas* involved a hairdresser working aboard a cruise ship who was employed by the owner of the on-board beauty salon (not the shipowner) and who was injured when the ladder in her cabin allegedly gave way. *Mahramas*, 475 F.2d at 167. We fail to see how this case provides a claim under the general maritime law against the master for negligence. To the extent that plaintiff argues that *Mahramas* granted the plaintiff a general maritime cause of action for negligence against her independent-contractor employer (and therefore, by extension, that plaintiffs should have a general maritime cause of action for negligence against Finlay, since he was "self-employed"), we think that contention is belied by the case; the court did not consider the plaintiff's employer's liability for negligence under the general maritime law, but only under the Jones Act. See id. at 172, 23 S.Ct. at 485–86. *Favaloro* involved claims brought by the estates of fishermen killed when the defendant tanker collided with and sank their fishing boat. To the extent that it recognizes a cause of action for negligence under the general maritime law, *Favaloro* does not support the inference that such claims may be brought by a seaman against the master of his own vessel, for it deals only with claims against a colliding vessel and the crew. See *Favaloro*, 687 F.Supp. at 477. Thus, all of the cases relied upon by plaintiffs are distinguishable from the instant case.

As a second basis for finding that seamen may maintain an action against their masters for negligence under the general maritime law, plaintiffs rely on the "Seamen's Act of 1915," which provided: "In any suit to recover damages for any injury sustained on board vessel or in its service seamen having command shall not be held to be fellow-servants with those under their authority." See 46 U.S.C.App. § 688 (1975) historical note. Plaintiffs argue that this abolishes the fellow-servant rule, which the Supreme Court had referred to in *The Osceola*, 189 U.S. at 175, 23 S.Ct. at 487, by stating:

> we think the law may be considered as settled upon the following propositions:
>
> 3. That all the members of the crew, except, perhaps, the master, are, as between themselves, fellow servants, and hence seamen cannot recover for injuries sustained through the negligence of another member of the crew beyond the expense of their maintenance and cure.

(Emphasis added.) Plaintiffs conclude that because Congress abolished the fellow-servant rule, seamen may recover from their master for negligence under the general maritime law. We do not agree. *The Osceola* barred seamen from suing their master or fellow crew members not because of the fellow-servant rule, but rather because the general maritime law did not provide seamen with a cause of action for such negligence:

> we think the law may be considered as settled upon the following propositions:
>
> > 4. That the seaman is not allowed to recover an indemnity for the negligence of the master, or any member of the crew.

Id.; see Chelentis v. Luckenbach S.S. Co., 247 U.S. 372, 384, 38 S.Ct. 501, 503–04, 62 L.Ed. 1171 (1918)(characterizing the Seamen's Act of 1915 as "irrelevant" and holding that shipowners may not be held liable for the negligence of the crew); Gilmore & Black, *The Law of Admiralty* § 6–20, at 32526 (describing Congress's abolition of the fellow-servant rule as an ill-fated attempt to abrogate *The Osceola*). We do not think the Seamen's Act of 1915, now itself abrogated by the Jones Act, provided seamen with a cause of action against a master for negligence under the general maritime law. We note that Kennedy v. Gulf Crews, Inc., 750 F.Supp. 214, 215–16 (W.D.La.1990), the only other case that we know of to consider whether a master may be liable to a seaman for negligence under the general maritime law, rejected a similar argument by the plaintiff and held that a seaman does not have a cause of action against his master for negligence. Cf. California Home Brands, Inc. v. Ferreira, 871 F.2d 830, 834–35 (9th Cir.1989)(holding that the Jones Act did not operate to make negligent crew members liable to their employers for damages paid to other seamen under the Jones Act because crew members cannot sue each other for negligence). We hold that the general maritime law does not afford seamen a cause of action for negligence against masters. Accordingly, summary judgment was properly granted to defendant on plaintiffs' counts for negligence under the general maritime law.

E.   DOHSA

Plaintiffs argue that they are entitled to recover against defendant under DOHSA, which provides:

> Whenever the death of a person shall be caused by wrongful act, neglect, or default occurring on the high seas ... the personal representative of the decedent may maintain a suit for damages ... for the exclusive benefit of the decedent's wife, husband, parent, child, or dependent relative against the vessel, person, or corporation which would have been liable if death had not ensued.

46 U.S.C App. § 761. The district court held that DOHSA does not create any substantive rights, but merely provides a cause of action against a party "which would have been liable if death had not ensued." See *McAleer*, 818 F.Supp. at 496. We agree. Plaintiffs assert no theory of recovery against defendant: they may not recover against defendant under the general maritime law for unseaworthiness, under the Jones Act for negligence, or under the general maritime law for negligence. Accordingly, there is no basis under which Finlay or his estate "would have been liable"

to plaintiffs' decedents if they were still living. Thus, summary judgment was properly granted to defendant for plaintiff's claims under DOHSA.

III

CONCLUSION

In conclusion, summary judgment was properly granted to defendant because (1) Finlay was not an owner *pro hac vice* of the MARQUES and so was not liable for unseaworthiness; (2) Finlay was not the employer of plaintiff' decedents and so was not liable under the Jones Act; (3) plaintiffs did not argue below that they were not seamen and therefore were entitled to sue a master for negligence under the general maritime law; (4) seamen may not bring a cause of action against a master for negligence under the general maritime law; and (5) plaintiffs may not recover under DOHSA because they assert no theory of recovery under which Finlay or his estate would have been liable to plaintiffs' decedents if they were still living. In light of our holding, we need not consider plaintiff's request for us to transfer the case to the District of Massachusetts.

Affirmed

NOTE

The requirements for seaman status are discussed above in subchapter A. The statute creates a cause of action of the seaman "who shall suffer personal injury in the course of his employment." The only reference to the identity of the defendant comes in the venue provision, which is placed in the district in which the "defendant employer" resides or in which his principal office is located. The FELA, which is incorporated by the Act, is more explicit. It imposes the duties on "ever common carrier by railroad" and makes it liable to "any person suffering injury while he is employed by such carrier" in interstate commerce. These provisions, taken together, have been read to indicate that the Jones Act applies only to actions between a seaman and his employer. In Cosmopolitan Shipping Co. v. McAllister, 337 U.S. 783, 69 S.Ct. 1317, 93 L.Ed. 1692, 1949 A.M.C. 1031 (1949), in which the issue was whether a seaman serving on a vessel owned by the United States was an employee of the United States, and as such limited to compensation under the FECA, or by a "general agent" of the United States under a World War "general agency" contract, and as such a Jones Act seaman. The Supreme Court held that the United States was the employer and stated "We have no doubt that, under the Jones Act, only one person, firm, or corporation can be sued as an employer." In 1973, in Mahramas v. American Export Isbrandtsen Lines, Inc., 475 F.2d 165, 1973 A.M.C. 587 (2d Cir.1973), it was held that a hairdresser on a cruise vessel, who was required to have seaman's papers and sign ship's articles but was employed by a concessionaire and took orders from the concessionaire' supervisor on the ship, and who claimed to be injured by defective equipment in her quarters, could not maintain an action under the Jones Act against the owner of the vessel, because the owner was not her employer, nor against the concessionaire, because it did not own or control the vessel. Judge Oakes dissented. For the view that *Cosmopolitan* is not dispositive of the question, and highly critical of the majority view in *Mahramas*, see Gilmore & Black, Law of the Admiralty, § 6–21(a)(1975). In a case like *Mahramas*, what is the result of the decision that the Jones Act does not apply? What is the basis for an action against the vessel owner? Against the concessionaire?

The question of whether the plaintiff is a seaman and the question of employment are sometimes related. Suppose a college professor is given free passage and meals on two cruises in return for giving topical lectures to passengers on board. Is she a seaman? Is she an employee of the vessel owner, or did she purchase her passage "in kind"? See Anderson v. Cunard, 1995 A.M.C. 1499 (E.D.La.1995), holding her to be a passenger. See also Bach v. Trident Steamship, Inc., 920 F.2d 322, 1991 A.M.C. 928 (5th Cir.1991), vacated for reconsideration in light of Wilander, and reaffirmed on remand, 947 F.2d 1290, 1992 A.M.C. 643 (5th Cir. 1991), holding that a compulsory river pilot is not a seaman because he lacks continuing connection with a single vessel or a fleet of vessels. Judge Brown dissented both times. With Bach, compare Evans v. United Arab Shipping Co. S.A.G., 4 F.3d 207, 1993 A.M.C. 2705 (3d Cir.1993), in which the majority declined to determine whether a compulsory pilot is a seaman, but held that even if a seaman he is not an employee of the vessel owner for purposes of the Jones Act. See also Stoller v. Evergreen International (U.S.A.) Corp., 1993 A.M.C. 258 (N.D.Cal.1992)(port pilot employed by the City not a Jones Act seaman on piloted vessel, and the city is his Jones Act employer). If the pilot is not a seaman, or is a seaman but not an employee, what is he?

The statement in *Cosmopolitan* that a seaman may have only one Jones Act employer at the same time has been taken as a given. It is implicit in *McAleer* above. And see Wolsiffer v. Atlantis Submarines, Inc., 848 F.Supp. 1489, 1994 A.M.C. 1476 (D.Hawai'i 1994), Wolsiffer was employed by Atlantis, which provides submarine tours, as a deck hand, co-pilot, and crewman. Atlantis chartered the M/V Voyager, which belonged to Ecoscapes and entered into a contract under which Ecoscapes would ferry passengers out to the buoy where the submarine was moored, and back. The contract provided that one Atlantis employee would work on The Voyager and aid in the ferrying activities. Wolsiffer was chosen, and on one of the ferrying voyages, while they were mooring the vessel, the captain of The Voyager ordered Wolsiffer to jump from the vessel to the dock to help moor the vessel. He jumped and was injured. It was held that he could bring the action against both employers but could recover only against one. In the particular case the plaintiff was held to be a borrowed servant, exonerating Atlantis. For a recapitulation of the indicia of an employer-employee relationship such as will support an action under the Jones Act, see Guidry v. South Louisiana Contractors, Inc., 614 F.2d 447 (5th Cir.1980). Guidry is quoted in Schoenbaum, Admiralty and Maritime Law, § 5–6, n.18 (1987).

Does the rule that the seaman must have only one Jones Act employer extend to the determination of liability of parent and subsidiary corporations? See Penny v. United Fruit, 869 F.Supp. 122, 1995 A.M.C. 652 (E.D.N.Y.1994), reading the Second Circuit rule as holding "no". See Williams v. McAllister Bros., Inc., 534 F.2d 19, 21, 1976 A.M.C. 558, 561 (2d Cir.1976), cited in *Penny*.

Colon v. Apex Marine Corp.

United States District Court for the Dist. of R.I., 1993.
832 F.Supp. 508.

■ LAGUEUX CHIEF JUDGE.

This matter is now before the Court on a motion filed by defendants Apex Marine Corporation c/o Westchester Shipping Company, Westchester Marine, Inc., and Westchester Marine Shipping Co., Inc. (the Apex defendants) for summary judgment on Count I of the complaint which alleges a claim under the Jones Act. For the reasons stated below, the motion is granted.

I. *Background*

This suit arises from a knifing incident on December 23, 1987, involving crew members of the S/T Charleston on authorized shore leave in Providence, Rhode Island. Plaintiff Daniel Colon was an engineer aboard the vessel, while Victor DeJesus and Michael McCarthy were able bodied seamen. Those three members of the crew left the S/T Charleston separately during the afternoon or evening of December 23, 1987. While they had not planned to meet ashore, after finding themselves in the same bar by happenstance they chose to share a taxi in their travels to other bars. Between 9:30 and 10:00 p.m. the sailors were in a bar known as Tillies King Cocktail Lounge, playing videogames and drinking. At approximately 10:30P.M. an altercation broke out between DeJesus and Michael, in which the bartender and plaintiff intervened to restrain the two men. When the combatants were released, DeJesus again attacked McCarthy, who retreated behind plaintiff. The Coast Guard Hearing record outlines the subsequent events. "In an effort to bring the fight to a halt and to calm [DeJesus], Colon put out his hands in a gesture of peace and told DeJesus to calm down. At that point [DeJesus] pulled out his knife and stabbed Colon in the side. Colon fell to the floor and DeJesus pursued McCarthy about the lounge...." Plaintiff's Exhibit "A" at P. 6. Plaintiff was transported to Rhode Island Hospital to undergo surgery for a laceration to his spleen.

McCarthy had reported prior threats made to him by DeJesus to officers of the S/T Charleston. On about four occasions McCarthy, assigned to work with DeJesus, had criticized DeJesus' laziness and asked him to do his share of the work. On these occasions DeJesus became verbally abusive, and threatened McCarthy with a knife.

Plaintiff filed this suit in December 1990 seeking to recover damages from the Apex defendants under the Jones Act (Count I), and from Vertigo, Inc., doing business as Tillies King, under the Rhode Island Liquor Liability Act (Count II). Plaintiff claims that because the officers aboard the ship were aware of DeJesus' behavior on prior occasions, the Apex defendants are liable for the injuries plaintiff received at Tillies King Cocktail Lounge. The Apex defendants move for summary judgment, on the grounds that there is no evidence that they were negligent, and that plaintiff was not injured in the course of his employment as required by the Jones Act. The parties engaged in oral argument on March 10, 1993, and the matter was taken under advisement. It is now in order for decision.

II. *Discussion*

A. Motion for Summary Judgment

Rule 56(c) of the Federal Rules of Civil Procedure sets forth the standard for ruling on a summary judgment motion:

> The judgment sought shall be rendered forthwith if the pleadings, depositions, answers to interrogatories, and admissions on file, together with the affidavits, if any, show that there is no genuine issue as to any material fact and that the moving party is entitled to a judgment as a matter of law.

In determining whether summary judgment is appropriate, the court must view the facts on the record and all inferences therefrom in the light most favorable to the nonmoving party. Continental Casualty Co. v. Canadian Universal Ins. Co., 924 F.2d 370, 373 (1st Cir.1991). Additionally, the moving party bears the burden of showing that no evidence supports the nonmoving party's position. Celotex Corp. v. Catrett, 477 U.S. 317, 325, 106 S.Ct. 2548, 2554, 91 L.Ed.2d 265 (1986). In order for the Apex defendants to prevail on their motion, they must show that no genuine issue of material fact exists to support plaintiffs case. The motion can then be granted if, as a matter of law, defendants are entitled to judgment in their favor.

B.   The Jones Act

The Jones Act provides, in relevant part, that "any seaman who shall suffer personal injury in the course of his employment may, at his election, maintain an action for damages at law, with the right of trial by jury...." 46 U.S.C. § 688.

Prior to 1920, when Congress passed the Jones Act, an injured seaman was entitled to receive wages and expenses of maintenance and cure, essentially financial support for as long as necessary to effect the highest degree of recovery possible, but could not recover damages for personal injury caused by negligence of the shipowner or captain. See The Osceola, 189 U.S. 158, 172–73, 23 S.Ct. 483, 485–86, 47 L.Ed. 760 (1903). The Jones Act granted seamen injured in the course of their employment because of shipowner negligence the right to recover damages. See Merchant Marine Act of 1920, ch. 250, § 33, 41 Stat. 988, 1007 (codified at 46 U.S.C. § 688). In this case, plaintiff claims that the Apex defendants may be held liable in negligence for the attack, on shore in a bar, by his fellow crew member DeJesus.

Two issues are raised by the motion for summary judgment: whether the Apex defendants were negligent in retaining DeJesus as a seaman aboard the S/T Charleston after notice of his violent propensities, and whether plaintiff was injured in the "course of employment" as required for recovery under the Jones Act.

1.   Negligence

The Apex defendants argue that they can not be found negligent because they did not know of any dangerous propensities on the part of DeJesus, and they did not have control over the premises where plaintiff was injured.

Plaintiff counters that because McCarthy had reported the prior incidents with DeJesus, the Apex defendants had, or should have had, knowledge of DeJesus' "violent propensity." Possession of that knowledge made harm caused by DeJesus foreseeable, and triggered a duty to protect the crew. Plaintiff argues that this duty to protect the crew makes the Apex defendants liable even for an injury in a bar during shore leave.

Under general maritime law recovery for an assault of this type (one crew member on another) is possible under theories of either unseaworthiness or shipowner negligence. See Benedict on Admiralty, § 31 et seq. The unseaworthiness approach involves a showing that the assailant was a sufficient danger to the crew as to violate the shipowner's absolute duty to maintain a seaworthy vessel. Id.; Kratzer v. Capital Marine Supply, Inc., 490 F.Supp. 222, 229 (M.D.La.1980), aff'd 645 F.2d 477 (5th Cir.1981)(citing Mitchell v. Trawler Racer, Inc., 362 U.S. 539, 80 S.Ct. 926, 4 L.Ed.2d 941 (1960)). That theory has not been argued before this Court.

The theory of shipowner negligence, on the other hand, requires plaintiff to establish one of the following: "1) that the assault was committed by the plaintiff's superior for the benefit of the ship's business; 2) that the master or ship's officers failed to prevent the assault when it was foreseeable." Benedict on Admiralty, at 3–242. See Wiradihardja v. Bermuda Star Line, Inc., 802 F.Supp. 989, 993 (S.D.N.Y.1992). Plaintiff was not assaulted by a superior, foreclosing that branch of negligence recovery.

Under a foreseeability of harm theory, liability is established by showing that the shipowner breached its duty of providing for the crew's reasonable safety. Such liability can arise when "(1) the assailant is a person of known vicious character, and (2) the shipowner knew or should have known of the crew member's violent propensities." Wiradihardja, 802 F.Supp. at 993 (citations omitted). See also Koehler v. Presque–Isle Transp. Co., 141 F.2d 490, 491 (2d Cir.), cert. denied, 322 U.S. 764, 64 S.Ct. 1288, 88 L.Ed. 1591 (1944)(shipowner liable for damages where "the ship's officers knew, or with ordinary diligence, should have known" of the assailant-employee's character).

The Apex defendants argue that there is no showing that they had sufficient knowledge regarding DeJesus to foresee a danger posed to plaintiff or other crew members. A shipowner can not be found liable for an assault injury where there is no evidence the assailant was a habitual violator of ship discipline or had "engaged in any fights or controversies ... or that he had ever threatened anyone with a knife or other weapon prior to [the assault]." Connolly v. Farrell Lines, Inc., 268 F.2d 653, 655 (1st Cir.), cert. denied 361 U.S. 902, 80 S.Ct. 208, 4 L.Ed.2d 158 (1959). In *Connolly*, the Court held that one assault, without prior threats or violence, was insufficient to establish negligence by the employer. Additionally, in *Connolly*, there was insufficient evidence to find that the assailant possessed "a savage disposition" or "a vicious nature." Id. at 656.

However, in this case plaintiff has presented evidence that previous incidents of violent behavior by DeJesus were reported to superior officers. Whether those reports gave plaintiff's employer sufficient knowledge to foresee a danger to the crew is a question of fact for the jury. Therefore, the motion for summary judgment cannot be granted on this basis.

2. Course of Employment

To recover under the Jones Act, plaintiff must show that he was injured while in the course of his employment. The Apex defendants argue that plaintiff, while away from the ship for his own purposes, was not in the performance of his duties when injured, and thus he was not in the course of his employment.

Plaintiff argues that the scope of "course of employment" under the Jones Act is an expansive one that encompasses injuries suffered on shore leave. Plaintiff relies on Daughenbaugh v. Bethlehem Steel Corp., Great Lakes S.S. Div., 891 F.2d 1199 (6th Cir.1989), in which plaintiffs decedent was a seaman who was returning to the ship from shore leave when he disappeared. His body was found three weeks later floating in the water near the dock. The Sixth Circuit upheld the District Court's determination that Daughenbaugh was acting in the course of employment when he disappeared. The Court stated, "because Daughenbaugh was required to return to the ship before the appointed sailing time, he was acting in the course of his employment when, en route to his [ship], he disappeared on the dock." Id. at 1207.

Daughenbaugh is factually distinguishable from the instant case, because Daughenbaugh was returning to the ship, as required by his duties on board ship, at the time of his death. Plaintiff, on the other hand, was pursuing his own agenda for pleasure at a local bar at the time of his injury. Plaintiff, however, argues that the reasoning used by the Sixth Circuit, applying the standard used under maintenance and cure to Jones Act "course of employment," indicates that plaintiff was acting in the course of employment while in a bar on shore leave.

It is well established that a seaman injured while on shore leave is entitled to maintenance and cure from his employer. In Aguilar v. Standard Oil Co., 318 U.S. 724, 63 S.Ct. 930, 87 L.Ed. 1107 (1943), the United States Supreme Court held that an employer's responsibility for maintenance and cure for a seaman injured in the service of the ship "extends beyond injuries sustained because of, or while engaged in, activities required by his employment." Id. at 732, 63 S.Ct. at 934. The Court reasoned

> To relieve the shipowner of his obligation in the case of injuries incurred on shore leave would cast upon the seaman hazards encountered only by reason of the voyage. The assumption is hardly sound that the normal uses and purposes of shore leave are "exclusively personal" and have no relation to the vessel's business. Men cannot live for long cooped up aboard ship, without substantial impairment of their efficiency, if not also serious danger to discipline. Relaxation beyond the confines of the ship is necessary if the work is to go on, more so that it may move smoothly. No master would take a crew to sea if he could not grant shore leave, and no crew would be taken if it could never obtain it. . . . In short, shore leave is an elemental necessity in the sailing of ships, a part of the business as old as the art, not merely a personal diversion.

Id. at 733–34, 63 S.Ct. at 935. The Court held that Aguilar, who was injured while travelling on the only route between the ship and a public street as he left the vessel for shore leave, was entitled to maintenance and cure. Eight years later, the Court relied on *Aguilar* in holding that a seaman injured in a dance hall while on shore leave was entitled to maintenance and cure. Warren v. United States, 340 U.S. 523, 71 S.Ct. 432, 95 L.Ed. 503 (1951).

Although both *Aguilar* and *Warren* involved recovery for maintenance and cure, the Court in *Daughenbaugh* relied on those cases in its determination of the scope of recovery under the Jones Act. The Court relied on language used by the Supreme Court in Braen v. Pfeifer Oil Transp. Co., 361 U.S. 129, 132–33, 80 S.Ct. 247, 250, 4 L.Ed.2d 191 (1959), indicating that course of employment under the Jones Act is equivalent to the maintenance and cure requirement that a seaman be in service of the ship. In *Braen*, the plaintiff was injured on a catwalk between his vessel and a work barge, while preparing to perform some carpentry work on a raft as ordered by his superior. The Supreme Court reversed the Court of Appeals' denial of recovery under the Jones Act, which apparently was based on the theory that the plaintiff was not a seaman at the time he was injured because the work he was doing was not in furtherance of the navigation of the vessel. 361 U.S. at 131, 80 S.Ct. at 249. The Supreme Court held that even though plaintiff was not on board the vessel, he "was acting 'in the course of his employment' at the time of the injury, for at that moment he was doing the work of his employer pursuant to his employer's orders." Id. at 133, 80 S.Ct. at 250. In its analysis, the Supreme Court cited both *Aguilar* and *Warren* in support of the proposition that the fact that the injury did not occur on the vessel was not controlling. *Braen* 361 U.S. at 132, 80 S.Ct. at 250. The Court stated:

> These two cases were not brought under the Jones Act but involved maintenance and cure. Yet they make clear that the scope of a seaman's employment or the activities which are related to the furtherance of the vessel are not measured by the standards applied to land-based employment relationships. They also supply relevant guides to the meaning of the term 'course of employment' under the Act since it is the equivalent of the 'service of the ship' formula used in maintenance and cure cases.

Id. at 132–33, 80 S.Ct. at 250.

Although not cited by the plaintiff, one court applies the same reasoning as *Daughenbaugh* to sustain Jones Act recovery in circumstances very similar to the case at hand. In Nowery v. Smith, 69 F.Supp. 755 (E.D.Pa. 1946), aff'd, 161 F.2d 732 (3d Cir.1947)(*per curiam*), plaintiff Nowery was injured in a fist fight with the chief engineer of the vessel while he was on shore leave in a bar room at Antilla, Cuba. The district court held that plaintiff was both "on the shipowner's business" for maintenance and cure purposes and "in the course of employment" under the Jones Act when he was injured.[3] The court noted that *Aguilar* involved a different factual situation, but stated:

---

3. The court granted the motion for a new trial on the Jones Act claim because, while there was sufficient evidence to go to the jury on the foreseeability theory, there

it seems to me that it was the occasion for the seaman's absence from the vessel—shore leave—which determined that he was on "the shipowner's business" while he was actually enjoying his shore leave. And if for the purpose of determining the shipowner's liability for maintenance and cure, the seaman is said to be on "the shipowner's business" while on shore leave, I can see no valid reason why, for the purpose of determining the shipowner's liability under the Jones Act, the seaman should not be said to be "in the course of his employment" at the same time. It is a simple question of defining the seaman's status; and I think that the concepts "on the shipowner's business," and "in the course of employment," as they are applied to the seafaring trade, comprehend identical factual situations.

Id. at 757 (footnote omitted).

The court believes that the *Daughenbaugh* and *Nowery* courts' reliance on the dicta in *Braen* is misplaced. *Braen* actually held that the plaintiff "was acting 'in the course of his employment' at the time of the injury for at that moment he was doing the work of the employer pursuant to his employer's orders." 361 U.S. at 133, 80 S.Ct. at 250. In contrast, the Supreme Court has defined the requirement for maintenance and cure much more broadly, stating that for maintenance and cure a seaman must "at the time be 'in the service of the ship,' by which is meant that he must be generally answerable to its call of duty rather than actually in performance of routine tasks or specific orders." *Farrell v. United States*, 336 U.S. 511, 516, 69 S.Ct. 707, 709, 93 L.Ed. 850 (1949). The *Farrell* case is instructive because it contrasts the rights of seamen under the two theories:

In Aguilar v. Standard Oil Co., 318 U.S. 724 [63 S.Ct. 930, 87 L.Ed. 1107], the Court pointed out that logically and historically the duty of maintenance and cure derives from a seaman's dependence on his ship, not from his individual deserts, and arises from his disability, not from anyone's fault. We there refused to look to the personal nature of the seaman's activity at the moment of the injury to determine his right to award. Aside from gross misconduct or insubordination, what the seaman is doing and why and how and how he sustains injury does not affect his right to maintenance and cure, *however decisive it may be as to claims for indemnity or for damages for negligence*.

Id. at 515–16, 69 S.Ct. at 709 (emphasis added).

This Court is not the first to hold that Jones Act course of employment is more limited that the scope of maintenance and cure. In In re Atlass, 350 F.2d 592 (7th Cir.1965), cert. denied, 382 U.S. 988, 86 S.Ct. 551, 15 L.Ed.2d 476 (1966), the Seventh Circuit contrasted the scope of recovery under these two actions in holding that the employer was entitled to exoneration from liability because, inter alia, its seamen were not acting in the course of employment when they returned to the vessel heavily intoxicated. The Court recognized that numerous courts had allowed Jones Act

was no legal basis for the alternate theory presented to the jury, that plaintiff could recover if he was acting "as an officer of the ship." 69 F.Supp. at 758.

recovery for seamen injured while leaving or returning to a ship, but stated:

> Assuming that [the injured seamen] were in the course of their employment while departing from the yacht for the purpose of obtaining their meals and returning thereto in the normal manner, it certainly is a far-fetched idea that they continued in such course when they took to themselves the liberty of spending three near-midnight hours in a tavern consuming intoxicating liquors.

350 F.2d at 597.   Similarly, in Szopko v. Kinsman Marine Transit Co., 426 Mich. 653, 397 N.W.2d 171 (1986), cert. denied, 483 U.S. 1007, 107 S.Ct. 3232, 97 L.Ed.2d 738 (1987), the Michigan Supreme Court held that an intoxicated sailor returning from shore leave was not acting in the course of employment when he slipped on the dock.   The Court rejected application of a maintenance and cure standard, aptly stating, "We cannot ignore the phrase 'in the course of his employment,' because it was intended to mean what it says."   Id., 397 N.W.2d at 175.   It is appropriate that maintenance and cure be afforded an expansive scope, covering all injuries incurred during the term of a seaman's employment. Maintenance and cure is a very different remedy from that of the Jones Act.   It gives shipowners "broad responsibilities for [the] health and safety" of seamen, necessitated by an occupation involving not only significant hazards, but also "constant shuttling between unfamiliar ports." *Aguilar*, 318 U.S. at 727, 63 S.Ct. at 932.   As Justice Story wrote in an early American commentary on maintenance and cure:

> [i]f some provision be not made for [seamen] in sickness at the expense of the ship, they must often in foreign ports suffer the accumulated evils of disease, and poverty, and sometimes perish from the want of suitable nourishment. . . .   On the other hand, if these expenses [the expenses occasioned by perilous diseases] are a charge upon the ship, the interest of the owner will be immediately connected with that of the seamen.   The master will never be tempted to abandon the sick to their forlorn fate. Harden v. Gordon, 2 Mason 541, 11 F.Cas. 480, 483 (C.C.D.Me.1823). Furthermore, the Supreme Court has expressed a policy of making the maintenance and cure remedy as simple as possible.   It has been the merit of the seaman's right to maintenance and cure that it is so inclusive as to be relatively simple, and can be understood and administered without technical considerations.   It has few exceptions or conditions to stir contentions, cause delays, and invite litigations. . . .   [T]he master knew he must maintain and care for even the erring and careless seaman, much as a parent would a child.   For any purpose to introduce a graduation of rights and duties based on some relative proximity of the activity at time of injury to the "employment" or the "service of the ship," would alter the basis and be out of harmony with the spirit and function of the doctrine and would open the door to the litigiousness which has made the landman's remedy so often a promise to the ear to be broken to the hope.

Farrell, 336 U.S. at 516, 69 S.Ct. at 709–10.   Such concerns do not apply to the Jones Act, which is not intended to be a form of insurance for an ill seaman, and necessarily involves sometimes complicated issues of fault. Lastly, this case is distinguishable from the many cases holding that a seaman returning from shore leave via a customary route is acting in the course of his employment, because in those cases the injury is related to the seaman's duty to return to the ship at a particular time. See *Daughenbaugh*, 891 F.2d at 1206 ("Thus, because Daughenbaugh was required to return to the ship before the appointed sailing time, he was acting in the course of his employment when, en route to the M/V Foy, he disappeared on the dock."); Marceau v. Great Lakes Transit Corp., 146 F.2d 416, 418 (2d Cir.), cert. denied, 324 U.S. 872, 65 S.Ct. 1018, 89 L.Ed. 1426 (1945)("The plaintiff was acting under orders when he returned to the ship."). Plaintiff here was pursuing his own private interests when he was injured. He was in the company of his fellow crew members by his own choice in that cocktail lounge. When plaintiff intervened in the dispute between DeJesus and McCarthy, he was not performing a duty that was assigned to him either explicitly or implicitly as an engineer on the S/T Charleston. He had no obligation of any kind to the vessel, its officers or owners to get involved in that altercation. Therefore, on the undisputed facts in this case, plaintiff was not acting "in the course of his employment" as a matter of law at the time of his injury.

III.   *Conclusion*

For the reasons stated above, the Apex defendants' motion for summary judgment on Count I is hereby granted. No judgment shall enter until all issues in this case are resolved. It is so ordered.

NOTE

Closer to the interests of the employer but still not within the scope of employment is Hamilton v. Seariver Maritime, Inc., 1995 WL 133335, 1995 A.M.C. 1639 (E.D.La.1995). There the plaintiff seaman was sent to a firefighting school instead of starting her next assignment. While attending the school, operated by Texas A & M University, she injured her neck and shoulder going through the "smokehouse obstacle course," apparently striking a suspended tire. Are such cases as this more properly considered as raising the question of imputed negligence rather than whether the seaman was injured in the course of his employment?

On the far side, see McClendon v. OMI Offshore Marine Service, 807 F.Supp. 1266, 1993 A.M.C.1786. A caretaker on a tug was not injured in the course of his employment when he was overcome by the fumes while roasting a potatoe laced with mercury in an effort to turn it into gold.

C.   STANDARD OF CARE UNDER THE JONES ACT

Smith v. Trans–World Drilling Co.

United States Court of Appeals, Fifth Circuit, 1985.
772 F.2d 157.

■ ROBERT MADDEN HILL, CIRCUIT JUDGE.

This is an appeal from a judgment denying plaintiff Calvin Smith's claims against defendant Trans–World Drilling Company (Trans–World) for negligence under the Jones Act, 46 U.S.C. § 688, and under the general maritime law of unseaworthiness. We reverse the trial court's denial of Smith's directed verdict motion on the negligence claim, we affirm the trial court's denial of Smith's directed verdict motion on the unseaworthiness claim, and we remand for further proceedings in accordance with this opinion.

I. FACTS

Smith, a roustabout, was injured on June 26, 1982, when he fell while working on Trans–World's drilling rig number forty-seven.[1] Smith fell from a height of ten to twelve feet while descending from an engine room roof on which he had been working, striking his back and head on a concrete deck. After a helicopter transported Smith to a hospital, he underwent three weeks of in-patient treatment and therapy as well as subsequent out-patient treatment.

Smith's fall occurred as he was attempting to cross from the engine room roof to the lower nearby roof of a storage shed. The engine room roof was constructed of several tin panels bolted together on a slight incline to form a peak. The engine room was separated from the storage shed by an open-air gap of thirty-three inches. A twelve inch diameter exhaust pipe extended from the engine room wall about eighteen inches below the edge of the sloping roof across this gap and connected to a large metal tubular muffler unit that rested atop the storage shed's flat roof. There was no railing on the pipe nor on the engine room roof. The supply shed roof had around its edge a forty-five inch high aluminum railing, the top of which was on an even plane with the top of the exhaust pipe.

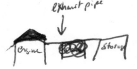

Both parties agree that the exhaust pipe was used by roustabouts to go to and from the engine room roof. According to the uncontradicted testimony of two of Trans–World's witnesses, a fellow roustabout and a crane operator, the exhaust pipe was often so used. The fellow roustabout testified that the exhaust pipe was used as a means of going to or from the engine room roof up to four or five times a week.

Smith's fall occurred as he stepped on the exhaust pipe. At the time, Smith was one of four roustabouts who were removing roof panels from the engine room roof. As it began to rain, they covered the open portion of the roof with a canvas tarp and began to descend by use of the exhaust pipe as a walkway to go from the engine room to the supply shed roof. Smith was the last of the four to descend because he had paused to secure the tarp. When he stepped on the exhaust pipe, Smith fell as he "was reaching for a railing hoping some was there."

Smith filed suit for damages against Trans–World for Jones Act negligence, for unseaworthiness, and for maintenance and cure under the general maritime law. Trans–World denied these claims and affirmatively pleaded that Smith's injuries were caused or contributed to by his own

---

1. The parties stipulated that Smith was a seaman and that the rig, a semisub- mersible mobile offshore drilling rig operating in the Gulf of Mexico, was a vessel.

fault.   At a jury trial after the close of all the evidence, Trans–World moved for directed verdict on the negligence and unseaworthiness claims on the ground of insufficient evidence, and on the maintenance and cure claim on the ground that Smith had reached maximum cure.   Smith then also moved for directed verdict on the negligence, unseaworthiness, and maintenance and cure claims.   The motions were denied.   The jury returned verdicts for Trans–World on the negligence and the unseaworthiness claims, and found that Smith had reached maximum cure.   The jury did not answer the interrogatories as to Smith's contributory negligence or as to damages.   The trial court entered judgment for Trans–World.   Smith did not move for judgment n.o.v. or for new trial.   Smith now appeals the denial of his directed verdict motion on the negligence and unseaworthiness claims.[2]

II.   STANDARD OF REVIEW

A threshold question exists as to whether this Court may examine the evidence for sufficiency notwithstanding Smith's failure to move for judgment n.o.v. under Fed.R.Civ.P. 50(b).   Trans–World argues that such failure precludes examination of the sufficiency of the evidence upon which the jury's verdict was based, and cites Delchamps, Inc. v. Borkin, 429 F.2d 417, 418 (5th Cir.1970).   Trans–World suggests that Smith's motion for directed verdict is inadequate by itself to preserve issues of the sufficiency of the evidence.

We disagree.   While *Delchamps,* as well as the case cited on this point in Delchamps, Parker v. American Oil Co., 327 F.2d 987 (5th Cir.1964), recite the proposition that an appellate court may not test the evidence for sufficiency absent a motion for judgment n.o.v., closer examination reveals that in both cases the verdict loser also failed to move for directed verdict.[3] Both cases recognize that a directed verdict motion, such as the one made by Smith, is adequate to preserve sufficiency of evidence issues on appeal. The prerequisite for testing the sufficiency of the evidence on appeal is a proper motion at trial for a directed verdict.   See, e.g., Coughlin v. Capitol Cement Co., 571 F.2d 290, 297 (5th Cir.1978); Gorsalitz v. Olin Mathieson Chemical Corp., 429 F.2d 1033, 1037–38 (5th Cir.1970), cert. denied, 407 U.S. 921, 92 S.Ct. 2463, 32 L.Ed.2d 807 (1972); 9 C. Wright & A. Miller, Federal Practice and Procedure § 2536 (1971).

We must next determine the proper standard of review of the denial of Smith's directed verdict motion.   This Court, in Springborn v. American Commercial Barge Lines, Inc., 767 F.2d 89, 100 (5th Cir.1985), has now

2.   Smith also asks for a remand for determination of damages on the negligence and unseaworthiness claims, but it is unclear whether Smith challenges the denial of his directed verdict motion on maintenance and cure.   In any event, sufficient evidence at trial supports the jury's finding that Smith had reached maximum cure when Trans– World stopped making maintenance and cure payments.   Smith's own physician, called as a witness by Smith, testified that he had discharged Smith on November 8, 1982, as ready to resume work.

3.   In *Parker,* the Court did not explicitly so state, but cited two authorities which state that the directed verdict motion is crucial.   See 327 F.2d at 988.

determined that the proper standard of review of a seaman's motion for directed verdict on a Jones Act negligence claim is the "reasonable man" standard of *Boeing Co. v. Shipman,* 411 F.2d 365, 374 (5th Cir.1969)(en banc). The *Boeing* standard is also appropriate for a seaman's directed verdict motion on an unseaworthiness claim. See *Springborn,* 767 F.2d at 96; Robin v. Wilson Brothers Drilling, 719 F.2d 96, 98 (5th Cir.1983). Under *Boeing,* Smith would be entitled to a directed verdict if the facts and inferences point so strongly in his favor that reasonable men could not arrive at a contrary verdict.

III. NEGLIGENCE PER SE

Applying this standard of review to the facts presented at trial, we conclude that Trans–World was negligent as a matter of law because its failure to install a railing along the exhaust pipe from which Smith fell constituted negligence *per se.* Five elements of a Jones Act negligence *per se* claim are the following: (1) a violation of Coast Guard regulations, (2) the plaintiff's membership in the class of intended beneficiaries of the regulations, (3) an injury of a type against which the regulations are designed to protect, (4) the unexcused nature of the regulatory violation, and (5) causation. Reyes v. Vantage S.S. Co., Inc., 558 F.2d 238, 242–44 (5th Cir.1977)(Reyes I), modified, 609 F.2d 140 (1980)(Reyes II). Because, as shown below, Smith met these elements, the trial court erred in denying Smith's directed verdict motion.

The first element of the negligence *per se* test, that a violation of Coast Guard regulations occurred, was established at trial by uncontradicted evidence. Coast Guard regulations require mobile drilling rigs to have a railing on at least one side of each "passageway" that is less than six feet wide.[4] As already noted, two of Trans–World's witnesses testified without contradiction that the exhaust pipe was used for passage to and from the engine room roof. Smith and his fellow workers used the pipe for passage from the engine room roof at the time of his fall. We conclude that no reasonable man could find that the pipe was not a "passageway" within the meaning of the regulations. Thus Trans–World violated the regulations.[5]

---

4. Smith's witness George Blann, an expert on maritime safety, testified (without contradiction on *this* issue) that the lack of a railing on the exhaust pipe constituted a violation of safety standards. We take judicial notice of the regulation in question:

Storm rails.

Each unit must have a storm rail in the following locations:

(a) On each deckhouse side that is normally accessible.

(b) On each side of each passageway that is wider than 1.83 meters (6 feet).

(c) On at least one side of each passageway that is less than 1.83 meters (6 feet) wide.

46 C.F.R. § 108.221 (1984).

Although the Coast Guard had certified the rig, this factor is irrelevant given the lack of a factual predicate. There was no evidence in the record suggesting that the Coast Guard was aware of the use of the exhaust pipe as a passageway.

5. Smith also urged that another regulation, requiring a ladder between each "weather deck," was violated. See 47 C.F.R. § 108.167 (1984). However, cross-examination of the expert witness Blann provided

The next two elements, that Smith was an intended beneficiary of the regulations, and that his injury was of the type against which the regulations were intended to protect, are easily met. Railings are to provide safe passageways for workers on the rig, and Smith was a roustabout working on the rig at the time of his accident. The purpose of railings is obviously to prevent falls by persons using passageways, and Smith's injuries were a result of such a fall. It is unreasonable to conclude otherwise than that the regulations were intended to protect a person such as Smith from a fall such as the one he had. See Reyes I, 558 F.2d at 243.

There is no indication in the record that the regulatory violation was excused or otherwise justified. Witnesses for Trans–World testified that work on the engine room roof was routine, and there was no showing of a present emergency or other condition where installation of a railing would have been more dangerous than violation of the regulations. Indeed, Trans–World contends that the railing was not installed only because the exhaust pipe was considered already safe; this reasoning cannot excuse the violation.

Finally, we conclude that, for the purposes of his Jones Act claim, the lack of a railing was a cause of Smith's fall as a matter of law. As the trial court instructed the jury, without objection by either side, the question of causation in a Jones Act claim turns on whether the acts or omissions of Trans–World contributed to Smith's injury in even the slightest degree. See Sanford Brothers Boats, Inc. v. Vidrine, 412 F.2d 958, 962 (5th Cir.1969); see also Reyes II, 609 F.2d at 146 (reaffirming the Reyes I interpretation of *Sanford*). The negligence of Trans–World in failing to provide a railing along the exhaust pipe must have contributed to Smith's fall, because neither side disputed Smith's contention that he was on the exhaust pipe when the fall occurred. For Trans–World to retain its jury verdict, we would have to conclude that the lack of a railing at the precise spot of Smith's fall could not have had the slightest effect in contributing to the cause of the fall. We find that no reasonable man could so conclude.[6] Therefore, we conclude that Trans–World was negligent as a matter of law.

IV. UNSEAWORTHINESS PER SE

Unseaworthiness, like Jones Act negligence, can be the *per se* result of a regulatory violation.[7] See Phipps v. S.S. Santa Maria, 418 F.2d 615, 616–

evidence from which a reasonable man could conclude that the engine room roof was not a "deck."

6. Trans–World would have us conclude that impeachment of Smith's version of the fall produced evidence sufficient to uphold a finding of no causation even under the lenient Jones Act standard. While Trans–World was able to show Smith's memory for numerical information was not perfect (e.g. that he had made at least seven dollars an hour at a previous job instead of six dollars as

he testified at trial) and that he estimated the length of the pipe at five feet when it was actually just under three feet, the cross-examination of Smith reinforced his prior direct and deposition testimony that he was standing on the pipe when he fell.

7. Smith's claim for damages was based on the alternate grounds of negligence and unseaworthiness. He could not recover cumulative damages under both the Jones Act and the general maritime law of unseaworthiness. See McCarty v. Service Contracting,

17 (5th Cir.1969). However, a crucial distinction between the two claims is the differing standard of causation required to find liability. While Jones Act negligence is a legally sufficient cause of injury if it played any part, no matter how small, in bringing about the injury, the plaintiff must meet a more demanding standard of causation in an unseaworthiness claim. See, e.g., Rogers v. Eagle Offshore Drilling Services, Inc., 764 F.2d 300, 304–05 (5th Cir.1985); Landry v. Oceanic Contractors, Inc., 731 F.2d 299, 302 (5th Cir.1984). Unlike the "featherweight" standard of causation in a Jones Act claim, the standard in an unseaworthiness claim is "proximate cause in the traditional sense." Comeaux v. T.L. James & Co., 702 F.2d 1023, 1024 (5th Cir.1983). As the district court instructed the jury without objection by either side, proximate cause means that (1) the unseaworthiness played a substantial part in bringing about or actually causing the injury and that (2) the injury was either a direct result or a reasonably probable consequence of the unseaworthiness. See Alverez v. J. Ray McDermott & Co., Inc., 674 F.2d 1037, 1042–43 (5th Cir.1982).

We conclude that Smith has not met the more demanding burden of showing proximate cause as a matter of law on his unseaworthiness claim. A reasonable juror could have determined that Smith's fall was not a direct result nor a reasonably probable consequence of the lack of a railing on the exhaust pipe. Although Smith was indisputably on the pipe when he fell, and the lack of a railing must have played some part, no matter how slight, in causing the fall, the factual dispute at trial over the exact details of how Smith fell leave us unable to find that proximate cause was established as a matter of law. It is consistent for the same condition or defect to be a legally sufficient cause of an injury on a Jones Act negligence theory of liability but not on an unseaworthiness theory. See *Landry,* 731 F.2d at 302. We therefore hold that the district court's denial of Smith's directed verdict motion on the unseaworthiness claim was correct.

V.   APPELLATE REMEDY

Because Smith failed to move for judgment n.o.v., our role at this juncture is a limited one. We are without power to reverse and render; we may only reverse and remand. See Cone v. West Virginia Pulp and Paper Co., 330 U.S. 212, 217–18, 67 S.Ct. 752, 755–56, 91 L.Ed. 849 (1947); University Computing Co. v. Lykes–Youngstown, 504 F.2d 518, 548 (5th Cir.1974); 5A J. Moore & J. Lucas, Moore's Federal Practice ¶ 50.12 (2d ed. 1985). Because the district court committed no error as to Smith's unseaworthiness or maintenance and cure claims, these issues need not be retried. However, we remand for a new trial on the issues of Jones Act negligence,[8] comparative negligence, and damages.[9]

---

317 F.Supp. 629 (E.D.La.1970). We choose to reach this issue, however, in order to clarify that only the Jones Act claim need be addressed on remand.

8. Although we conclude that the district court should have directed a verdict for Smith, since no motion for judgment n.o.v.

was filed, we have no power under *Cone* to do more than remand this case for what may be "the useless formality of another trial" on the Jones Act liability issue. See Yorkshire Indemnity Co. v. Roosth & Genecov Produc-

---

9. See note 9 on page 946.

The judgment is affirmed in part, and reversed in part and remanded.

NOTE

Imputed Negligence

In Hopson v. Texaco, Inc., 383 U.S. 262, 86 S.Ct. 765, 15 L.Ed.2d 740 (1966), the Supreme Court held that a vesselowner who sent two seamen who were disabled in a foreign port to the United States Consul in a local taxi, were liable under the Jones Act for their injuries sustained in a collision en route. The Court followed Sinkler v. Missouri Pacific R.R. Co., 356 U.S. 326, 78 S.Ct. 758, 2 L.Ed.2d 799 (1958).

Compare *Hopson* with Hamilton v. Seariver Maritime, Inc., noted above in NOTE on p. 940. Since in neither case did the vesselowner have any supervision or control over the "independent contractor," and in neither case was there evidence of direct negligence in selection of the cab driver or the school, what is the difference? In *Hopson* the Court lay emphasis on the fact that the vesselowner was discharging a legal duty to deliver the seamen to the Consul. Does this distinguish the cases? Similarly it has been held that since the vesselowner owes a duty to provide prompt and adequate medical care and therefore is vicariously liable for the negligence of a doctor that it retains. DeCenteno v. Gulf Fleet Crews, Inc., 798 F.2d 138 (5th Cir.1986).

Test out the edges of the doctrine. Suppose that the master has a catered party on board to celebrate the completion of the voyage and the crew is stricken with food poisoning. Suppose the party is held at a famous and expensive restaurant in the port.

Absent contract, the negligence of the vessel owner is not imputed to the independent contractor. In Thornton v. Steiner Products, Ltd., 608 So.2d 508, 1995 A.M.C. 1215 (Fla.App. 3d Dist.1992) it was held that the negligence of the vessel owner was not imputable to the concessionaire in an action by one of its employees who slipped and fell on the deck in an area for which the concessionaire was not responsible.

Scope of Duty

The FELA, which is incorporated by the Jones Act, provides that the carrier shall be liable to its employee injured in the course of his employment through the negligence of its officers, agents, and employees, and also "by reason of any defect or insufficiency, due to its negligence, in its cars, engines, appliances, machinery, track, roadbed, works, boats, wharves, or other equipment." The FELA covered railroad workers rather than seamen. Yet it did make reference to boats and

tion Co., 252 F.2d 650, 657–58 (5th Cir.1958)(citing Garman v. Metropolitan Life Insurance Co., 175 F.2d 24, 28 (3d Cir.1949)). When a motion for judgment n.o.v. is filed under Fed.R.Civ.P. 50(b), the discretion of the district court is called upon to determine in the first instance whether to grant a new trial or to enter judgment. See *Cone,* 330 U.S. at 215–16, 67 S.Ct. at 754–55. When no motion for judgment n.o.v. is filed, then an appellate court is constrained from exercising that discretion which should have been vested in the district court. See id. at 217–18, 67 S.Ct. at 755–56.

9. Smith's failure to move for new trial does not preclude ordering a new trial as a remedy for erroneous denial of his motion for directed verdict on the Jones Act claim. See Gorsalitz v. Olin Mathieson Corp., 429 F.2d 1033, 1038 (5th Cir.1970), cert. denied, 407 U.S. 921, 92 S.Ct. 2463, 32 L.Ed.2d 807 (1972).

wharves. To the extent that railroad carriers operated vessels on navigable waters, what was the relationship between the FELA and the maritime law? Clearly the Act covered only defects or insufficiencies "due to its negligence." The Act was adopted five years after the decision in The Osceola. What does this suggest about the Congressional understanding of the second proposition of The Osceola?

Standard of Care

Neither the FELA nor the Jones Act purports to state what constitutes negligence, either that of its officers, agents or employees, or negligence in failing to provide a safe place to work. The standard for providing a safe place to work has been spoken of high. Dempsey v. Mac Towing, Inc. 876 F.2d 1538 (11th Cir.1989). It has been held that the vesselowner may be negligent in allowing oil to accumulate on the galley deck though the condition was not sufficient to justify a finding of unseaworthiness. Magnussen v. Yak, 73 F.3d 245 (9th Cir.1996). It had been contended that jury verdicts of negligence but no unseaworthiness were inconsistent. And see Boyle v. Pool Offshore Co., a Division of Enserch Corp., 893 F.2d 713 (5th Cir.1990)("In a Jones Act case, the showing required to overturn a jury verdict is even more stringent than in the case of a general negligence claim"); Colburn v. Bunge Towing, Inc., 883 F.2d 372, 375 (5th Cir.1989), quoting from Theriot v. J.Ray McDermott & Co., 742 F.2d 877, 881 (5th Cir.1984).

There are limits. When the injury was caused by high breaking waves and no evidence of negligence was produced, judgment for the defendant was affirmed. Complaint of Hechinger, 890 F.2d 202 (9th Cir.1989), cert. denied, 498 U.S. 848, 111 S.Ct. 136, 112 L.Ed.2d 103 (1990).

It was not negligent to leave chains and equipment temporarily on deck during maintenance when a safe path was left and the injured seaman took an unsafe one. Billedeaux v. Tidex, Inc., 3 F.3d 437, 1994 A.M.C. 1103 (5th Cir.1993).

When there were ladders available, it was not negligent to fail to instruct a veteran seaman that he should use a ladder to reach an object that is out of his reach. As defendant's supervisor put it at the trial, it was common knowledge among experienced seamen that sailors should use ladders instead of climbing because men "are not monkeys." Grover v. American President Lines, 1995 A.M.C.2105 (N.D.Cal.1995).

Similarly, the vesselowner is not negligent in not instructing a seaman that if he needs help he should request it, rather than attempt to do the task himself. Dickens v. United States, 815 F.Supp. 913, 1993 A.M.C. 1647 (E.D.Va.1993).

And in a case in which a seaman was precipitated into the water by an allision between the vessel and a gas line, held not to be the fault of the vessel, it was held that the vesselowner was not negligent for not teaching the seaman how to swim or for failing to require the wearing of flotation devices while on board. McClendon v. OMI, 807 F.Supp. 1266, 1993 A.M.C. 1786 (E.D.Tex.1992).

Causation

The FELA provides that the carrier is liable for injuries occasioned "in whole or in part" through its negligence or the negligence of its officers, agents or employees. This language has been interpreted to mean that it is only necessary to show that the negligence played any role, however small, in causing the injury. This burden to tie the injury to the negligence has often been spoken of as "featherweight."

The significance of the "featherweight" standard is illustrated by Evans v. United Arab Shipping Co. S.A.G., 4 F.3d 207, 1993 A.M.C. 2705 (3d Cir.1993). There a compulsory pilot sued the owner of a vessel on which he was injured for a new injury and for the aggravation of an old neurological injury. The district court rendered judgment in the pilot's favor for damages attributable to the new injury, but found the plaintiff was not an employee of the vesselowner and therefore not entitled to the "featherweight" standard of causation, and that the medical testimony on the issue of aggravation of the old injury did not meet the more stringent standard for actions under the general maritime law. Judge Nygaard dissented.

The reduced standard has sometimes been applied to fill gaps in the facts when seamen disappear from the ship. In Kline v. Maritrans, 791 F.Supp. 455, 1993 A.M.C. 655 (D.Del.1992), a seaman left a gathering of his mates on the vessel, stating that he was going up to the deck to urinate. When he did not return they went to look for him and found him nowhere on the vessel. When his body was discovered six months later, his pants were unzipped. There was no rail at the point at which the crew usually urinated and at the time of the seaman's disappearance there was an accumulation of ice on the deck. Under the Jones Act standard this evidence was sufficient to put the cause of his death to the jury. Even less evidence was adduced in Gaymon v. Quinn Menhaden Fisheries of Texas, Inc., 118 So.2d 42, 1962 A.M.C. 2065 (Fla.App.1960), in which testimony that there were no toilet facilities and the crewmembers were obliged to suspend themselves over the rail, and the decedent was last seen on the vessel and when his body was discovered, he was clad only in an undershirt.

Under even the "featherweight" standard, there are cases in which causation has not been found. See, e.g., Martin v. John W.Stone Oil Distributor, Inc.819 F.2d 547 (5th Cir.1987). There a seaman apparently fell off a vessel and his body was found nine months later. An autopsy indicated that drowning was the cause of death. The court of appeals affirmed a summary judgment for the defendants. Despite the seaman's history of epileptic seizures since childhood, it could not be assumed that his falling off the vessel was caused by a seizure when there was medical testimony that established that a fall a few weeks earlier was not the product of a seizure and the record contained no evidence to explain why he fell.

Contributory negligence

Under the Act, contributory negligence is not a bar but reduces damages. Should the "featherweight" standard of causation which is applied to the evidence in chief also be applied to contributory negligence? Holding that it must, see Bunting v. Sun Company, Inc., 434 Pa.Super. 404, 643 A.2d 1085, 1994 A.M.C. 2754 (Pa.Super. 1994).

D. DAMAGES

Horsley v. Mobil Oil Corp.

United States Court of Appeals, First Circuit,1994.
15 F.3d 200, 1994 A.M.C. 1372.

■ CONRAD K. CYR, CT.J.:

We must decide whether either punitive damages or damages for loss of parental and spousal society allegedly caused by a nonfatal injury to a seaman aboard a vessel in territorial waters are recoverable in an unseaworthiness action under the general maritime law. On plenary review, see Gaskell v. The Harvard Coop. Soc'y, 3 F.3d 495, 497 (1 Cir.1993), we affirm the summary judgment entered against plaintiffs-appellants based on the analysis required under Miles v. Apex Marine Corp., 498 U.S. 19, 1991 AMC 1 (1990).

I. Background

Plaintiffs-appellants Jonathan C. Horsley and his wife, Elizabeth Horsley, allege that he sustained a back injury in the course of his duties aboard a vessel owned by defendant-appellee Mobil Oil Corporation while operating in the territorial waters of the Gulf of Maine. Their unseaworthiness action involves, inter alia, claims for punitive damages by Jonathan C. Horsley; and damages for loss of parental society by their minor son and loss of spousal society by Elizabeth Horsley. The district court entered summary judgment for Mobil on all three claims.[10]

II. Discussion

The Supreme Court has decided that damages for loss of society are not cognizable in a general maritime action for the wrongful death of a seaman, because "[i]t would be inconsistent with [the Supreme Court's] place in the constitutional scheme were we to sanction more expansive remedies in a judicially-created cause of action in which liability is without fault than Congress has allowed in cases of death resulting from negligence." *Miles*, 498 U.S. at 33, 1991 AMC at 11. The Court reasoned that the remedial limitations imposed by Congress in admiralty actions predicated on negligence likewise restrict an admiralty court's power to fashion damages remedies in actions under the general maritime law, such as the present unseaworthiness claim against a vessel where liability may be imposed without establishing fault. See Seas Shipping Co. v. Sieracki, 328 U.S. 85, 94–95, 1946 AMC 698 (1946)(noting unseaworthiness "is essentially a species of liability without v. fault"). Thus, the admiralty court's remedial autonomy is "both direct[ed] and delimit[ed]" by federal statute, *Miles*, 498 U.S. at 27, 1991 A.M.C. at 7 insofar as Congress has spoken directly to the point in issue, id. 498 U.S. at 31, 1991 AMC at 10, citing Mobil Oil Corp. v. Higginbotham, 436 U.S. 618, 625, 1978 AMC 1059, 1065 (1978).

Two statutes are directly relevant to general maritime claims based on fatal injury: the Death on the High Seas Act (DOHSA), 46 U.S.C. app. § 761, et seq., and the Jones Act, 46 U.S.C. app. § 688, both enacted in 1920. DOHSA makes specific provision only for the recovery of damages for *pecuniary* loss. See 46 U.S.C. app. § 762 ("The recovery ... shall be a fair and just compensation for the pecuniary loss sustained by the persons for whose benefit the suit is brought...."). Notwithstanding that the fatal injury at issue in *Miles* did not take place on the high seas, the Supreme Court considered DOHSA indicative of congressional intent in

---

10. Jurisdiction over this interlocutory admiralty appeal is based on 28 U.S.C. 1292(a)(3). See Martha's Vineyard Scuba Headquarters, Inc. v. Unidentified, Wrecked, and Abandoned Steam Vessel, 833 F.2d 1059, 1064, 1988 AMC 1109, 1115 (1st Cir.1987).

cases involving fatal injuries to seamen in territorial waters as well. *Miles*, 498 U.S. at 31, 1991 AMC at 9.

Since the Jones Act does afford a right of action to dependents of seamen fatally injured in territorial waters, it formed the principal focus of inquiry in *Miles*. The Jones Act simply incorporated by reference the remedial scheme established twelve years earlier under the Federal Employee Liability Act (FELA), 46 U.S.C. App. § 688. FELA, the progenitor of all federal liability schemes, simultaneously afforded a uniform cause of action for railroad workers and dispensed with traditional master-and-servant defenses. See generally Rogers v. Missouri Pac. R. Co., 352 U.S. 500 (1957). FELA's language is unhelpful on its face, however, as it simply provides for "damages," without further elaboration. 45 U.S.C. § 51.

This seeming dead-end is averted, nevertheless, by Congress's adoption and incorporation, in the Jones Act, of the remedial scheme previously established under FELA. The courts may assume that Congress, at the time it enacted the Jones Act, was cognizant of the decisional law developed under FELA during the twelve-year interim between the enactment of the two statutes. *Miles*, 498 U.S. at 32, 1991 AMC at 10–11; see generally Cannon v. University of Chicago, 441 U.S. 677, 696–97 (1979)("It is always appropriate to assume that our elected representatives, like other citizens, know the law . . . .").

The *Miles* Court relied extensively on just such a decision, see Michigan Cent. R Co. v. Vreeland, 227 U.S. 59 (1913), which revealed yet another evolutionary layer in the development of wrongful death statutes:

> In [*Vreeland*] the Court explained that the language of the FELA wrongful death provision is essentially identical to that of Lord Campbell's Act, 9 & 10 Vict. ch. 93 (1846), the first wrongful death statute. Lord Campbell's Act also did not limit explicitly the "damages" to be recovered, but that Act and the many state statutes that followed it consistently have been interpreted as providing recovery only for pecuniary loss. *Miles*, 498 U.S. at 32, 1991 AMC at 10 (emphasis added), citing *Vreeland*, 227 U.S. at 69–71. Finally, the Miles Court retraced the development of wrongful death statutes into the Twentieth Century and the meaning of the unelaborated FELA term "damages" became clear:

> > When Congress passed the Jones Act, the *Vreeland* gloss on FELA, and the hoary tradition behind it, were well established. Incorporating FELA unaltered into the Jones Act, Congress must have intended to incorporate the pecuniary limitation on damages as well. We assume that Congress is aware of existing law when it passes legislation. There is no recovery for loss of society in a Jones Act wrongful death action. Id.

Uniformity provided the companion rationale for the *Miles* decision. See Moragne v. States Marine Lines, Inc., 398 U.S. 375, 402, 1970 AMC 967, 988 (1970) "admiralty law should be 'a system of law coextensive with, and operating uniformly in, the whole country.'" (quoting The Lottawanna, 88 U.S. (21 Wall.) 558, 575 (1875)). As noted, damages awarded under DOHSA are restricted to pecuniary loss. *Miles* cautions that the traditional gap-filling function of the admiralty court is to be exercised only in furtherance of the presumed congressional objective of uniformity:

> We no longer live in an era when seamen and their loved ones must look primarily to the courts as a source of substantive legal protection from injury and death; Congress and the States have legislated extensively in these areas. In this era, an admiralty court should look primarily to these legislative enactments for policy guidance. We may supplement these statutory remedies where doing so would achieve the uniform vindication of such policies consistent with our constitutional mandate, but we must also keep strictly within the limits imposed by Congress. *Miles*, 498 U.S. at 27, 1991 AMC at 6–7 (emphasis added). Thus, *Miles* "restore[d] a uniform rule applicable to all actions for the wrongful death of a seaman, whether under DOHSA, the Jones Act, or the general maritime law [,]" by limiting damages in wrongful death actions to the amount of pecuniary loss. *Miles*, 498 U.S. at 33, 1991 AMC at 11.

A. *Damages in Nonfatal-Injury Cases*

The district court relied primarily on Murray v. Anthony J. Bertucci Constr. Co., 1992 AMC 2028, 958 F.2d 127 (5 Cir.), cert. denied, 506 U.S. 865, 1993 AMC 2999 (1992), in holding that *Miles* precludes punitive damages and damages for loss of society under the Jones Act. See also Smith v. Trinidad Corp., 992 F.2d 996 (9 Cir.1993)(adopting Murray reasoning)(per curiam); and Lollie v. Brown Marine Serv., Inc., 1993 AMC 2947, 995 F.2d 1565 (11 Cir.1993)(same). For the reasons discussed below, we agree. Under the analysis obligated by *Miles*, we inquire whether Congress has preempted all interpretive discretion on the part of the admiralty court—as the traditional protector and benefactor of its wards— in extending damages relief for nonpecuniary loss in the present context. At the outset, we note distinctions pertinent to our inquiry. First, since DOHSA is inapplicable to nonfatal injuries sustained by a seaman aboard a vessel operating in territorial waters, it has no direct bearing on the damages remedies presently at issue. Accordingly, whatever direct analogic bearing DOHSA had in *Miles* is diminished in the present context. Second, as concerns the Jones Act, *Vreeland* is inapposite to the availability of damages for nonpecuniary loss in cases involving nonfatal injuries.[11] The Miles methodology takes us beyond *Vreeland*, however.

---

11. At a time when wrongful death statutes were very much the exception, the *Vreeland* court explicitly distanced its analysis from that involved in nonfatal injury cases.

> This [wrongful death] cause is independent of any cause of action the decedent had, and includes no damages which he might have recovered for the injury if he had survived. It is one beyond that which the decedent had—*one proceeding on altogether different principles.*

Vreeland, 227 U.S. at 68 (emphasis added). These "altogether different principles," derived from Lord Campbell's Act, the first wrongful death statute: "It is a liability for the loss and damage sustained by relatives dependent upon the decedent. It is therefore a liability for the pecuniary damage resulting to them, and for that only." Id. In sum, the evidence directly adduced by the *Miles* court is not particularly probative beyond the discreet confines of wrongful death actions.

In Igneri v. Cie. de Transports Oceaniques, 1963 AMC 2318, 323 F.2d 257 (2 Cir.1963), the Second Circuit inquired into the availability of damages for loss of society under the Jones Act and concluded as follows:

> The failure of the Jones Act to confer . . . a right [to loss of society/consortium damages] on the spouse of a seaman cannot be dismissed as an inadvertence. The policy of the Federal Employees Liability Act, the regime which the Jones Act made applicable to seamen, was that the new remedy for the employee was to be exclusive and that claims of relatives recognized by state law were to be abrogated; the FELA had been thus authoritatively construed before the Jones Act was passed.

Igneri, 1963 AMC at 2331, 323 F.2d at 266 (emphasis added), citing *New York Cent. & H. RR. v. Tonsellito*, 244 U.S. 360 (1917)(FELA precludes claim brought by father for "loss of services" of minor son injured in course of employment with railroad). Finally, the thrust of the Supreme Court's holding in *Tonsellito* is that FELA affords a remedy to injured workers—and only to workers, not to their relatives: "Congress having declared when, how far, and to whom carriers shall be liable on account of accidents in the specified class, such liability can neither be extended nor abridged. . . ." New York Cent. & H. R.R., 244 U.S. 360, 362 (1917); see also New York Cent. R.R. v. Winfield, 244 U.S. 147 (1917); Erie R.R. v. Winfield, 244 U.S. 170 (1917). Thus, the *Tonsellito* rationale ineluctably precludes the present claims for damages for loss of parental and spousal society.[12]

Similarly, compelling evidence precludes Jonathan Horsley's claim for punitive damages. "It has been the unanimous judgment of the courts since before the enactment of the Jones Act that punitive damages are not recoverable under" FELA. Miller v. American President Lines, Ltd., 1993 A.M.C. 1217, 1225, 989 F.2d 1450, 1457 (6 Cir.1993)(emphasis added), citing Kozar v. Chesapeake & O. Ry. Co., 449 F.2d 1238, 124043 (6 Cir.1971)(citing cases). Once again, therefore, since the Supreme Court's authoritative interpretation of FELA antedated enactment of the Jones Act, *Miles* mandates the conclusion that punitive damages are not available in an unseaworthiness action under general maritime law.

III. Conclusion

Under the analysis prescribed in Miles v. Apex Marine Corp., 498 U.S. 19, 1991 AMC 1 (1990), an admiralty court may not extend the remedies available in an unseaworthiness action under the general maritime law to include punitive damages or damages for loss of parental or spousal society. Accordingly, the district court judgment must be affirmed.

---

12. No court of appeals recognizes a claim for loss of parental society under general maritime law. *Murray*, 958 F.2d at 132, n.3, 1992 A.M.C. at 2035, citing DeLoach v. Companhia de Navegaccao Lloyd Brasiliero, 782 F.2d 438, 1986 A.M.C. 1217 (3d Cir. 1986), and Madore v. Ingram Tank Ships , Inc., 732 F.2d 475, 1986 A.M.C. 46 (5th Cir. 1984). Moreover, the cognizability of such claims in a minority of states, Prosser & Keeton, Torts § 125 (5th Ed. 1984), would provide no basis under *Miles* for recognizing such a remedy in an action for unseaworthiness—closely akin to a strict liability claim—where it is not even widely available in nonadmiralty actions.

N O T E

See Wadell, Punitive damages in Admiralty, 19 J. of Mar.L. & Com. 65 (1988). The subject of punitive damages for failure to pay maintenance and cure is discussed above in chap. 19–3 above.

Although they might be looked upon as a variety of non-pecuniary damages, it is established that damage for pain and suffering can be recovered under the Jones Act. See Figueroa v. Campbell Industries, 45 F.3d 311, 1995 A.M.C. 793 (9th Cir.1995).

Negligent infliction of emotional harm is recognized as a basis for liability under the F.E.L.A., and hence under the Jones Act. Consolidated Rail Corp. v. Gottshall, 512 U.S. ___, 114 S.Ct. 2396, 129 L.Ed.2d 427, 1994 A.M.C. 2113 (1994), adopting the "zone of danger" test.

Pre-*Gotchall* maritime cases appear to have applied the same test. In Nelson v. Research Corp. of the University of Hawaii, 805 F.Supp. 837, 1993 A.M.C. 2696 (D.Haw.1992), holding that the master of a research vessel required to go to sea with defective bilge pumps and uninsulated equipment could sue under the Jones Act for emotional distress, since he was clearly subject to the the threat of physical harm. See also Gough v. Natural Gas Pipeline Co. of America, 996 F.2d 763, 1993 A.M.C. 2889 (5th Cir.1993), upholding suit for emotional harm when master had to jump overboard when a fireball swept his vessel. With *Nelsen* and *Gough* compare Ainsworth v. Penrod Drilling Corp., 972 F.2d 546, 1994 A.M.C. 1211 (DRO)(5th Cir.1992), dubitante on the question of liability for emotional harm, but finding that even if the "zone of danger" test were adopted, the facts would not support recovery. There was some authority for the requirement of physical contact. See, e.g., Grace v. Keystone Shipping Co., 805 F.Supp. 436, 1994 A.M.C. 290 (E.D.Tex. 1992).

Conceding that under some circumstances actions for emotional harm might be brought under the Jones Act, a seaman who alleged psychiatric problems attributable to a long list of emotionally damaging experiences during a career that included thirty-two voyages on sixteen different vessels failed to show negligence in not anticipating his problems. Puthe v. Exxon Shipping Co., 2 F.3d 480, 1994 A.M.C. 421 (2d Cir.1993).

Prejudgment interest is not permitted in an action at law under the Jones Act. Theriot v. J. Ray McDermott & Co., 742 F.2d 877, 883 (5th Cir.1984). Where the action is joined with a claim of unseaworthiness, and there is a basis for distinguishing damages caused by unseaworthiness from those caused by negligence, prejudgment interest can be awarded on the latter. See Melancon v. Petrostar Corp.,762 F.Supp. 1261, 1992 A.M.C. 521 (W.D.La.1991). And when a maritime claim is joined to a claim under the Jones Act and tried to a jury, the amount of prejudgment interest must be put to the jury. Glynn v. Roy Al Boat Corp., 57 F.3d 1495, 1995 A.M.C. 2022 (9th Cir.1995).

E. WRONGFUL DEATH AND SURVIVAL UNDER THE JONES ACT

The FELA contained both a wrongful death provision and a survival provision. In 1908, when the FELA was enacted, although most states had enacted worker compensation statutes, common law actions against an employer were, in general, subject to the three common law defenses, contributory negligence, the fellow servant defense, and assumption of risk. Since there was no general federal provision for actions for wrongful death, and the plaintiff was left dependent upon the state statutes, the adoption of the FELA, which treated contributory negligence as reducing the damages rather than barring the action, abolished the fellow servant defense altogether, and very sharply limited the application of the doctrine of assumption of risk, reliance on the state wrongful death statutes would have created the risk that such statutes would be construed to apply only in cases in which the cause of action was viable under the State law.   Since the abrogation of the common law defenses had been eliminated in most state through the adoption of worker compensation schemes, theoretically these defenses remained viable in a common law action.   This possibility was forestalled by adding to the FELA a provision for actions for wrongful death that tracked exactly the injury provisions.

In 1920, when the Supreme Court in Chelentis v. Luckenbach forced the Congress into direct creation of a seaman's cause of action against the vesselowner for injury due to negligence of the officers and other crew members, it again raised the possibility that state statutes might be interpreted as inapplicable, it solved the problem by making the FELA applicable, including the wrongful death and survival provisions.   Less enthused by the uniformity cry than the Court in *Jensen* and *Chelentis*, Congress enacted the DOHSA, covering deaths on the high seas, and left in place the rule that actions for wrongful death on domestic waters is governed by the applicable State statute.

The result of this solution of the problem was to leave actions by a seaman for death on the high seas covered by both the Jones Act and the DOHSA, which were somewhat different in their provisions, and actions for death on domestic waters charging negligence covered by the Jones Act, and actions for deaths on domestic waters charging unseaworthiness either covered by the state statute or not at all.   In Lindgren v. United States, 281 U.S. 38, 50 S.Ct. 207, 74 L.Ed. 686 (1930), the Supreme Court held that the Jones Act was preemptive of any action for wrongful death under the state law and since it covered only actions based on negligence, the survivors of a seaman whose death took place on domestic waters had no action for wrongful death based upon unseaworthiness.   This view was reiterated in Gillespie v. United States Steel Corp., 379 U.S. 148, 85 S.Ct. 308, 13 L.Ed.2d 199 (1964).   Despite the decisions in *Lindgren* and *Gillespie*, however, it that the DOHSA applies in an action by a seaman's survivors suing in respect of death of the seaman on the high seas and caused by unseaworthiness.   See Miles v. Apex Marine Corp., chapter 20 below.

The working of these three overlapping solutions and the ultimate creation of a general maritime law cause of action for wrongful death as a fourth, is discussed in Chapter 20 below.

6.   REMEDIES OF GOVERNMENT EMPLOYEES

Civilian employees of the United States are generally covered under the Federal Federal Employees Compensation Act of 1916 (FECA), 5 U.S.C.A. §§ 751 et seq., and may not sue under the Suits in Admiralty Act, the

Public Vessels Act, or the Jones Act. See Johansen v. United States, 343 U.S. 427, 72 S.Ct. 849, 96 L.Ed. 1051 (1952). In Lockheed Aircraft Corporation v. United States, 460 U.S. 190, 103 S.Ct. 1033, 74 L.Ed.2d 911 (1983), the Supreme Court held that the FECA does not directly bar an action for indemnity or contribution against the United States by a third party sued by the government employee. It has been held since, however, that while such an action is not barred, the third-party plaintiff must have a substantive claim against the United States to avoid dismissal. See Walls Industries, Inc. v. United States, 958 F.2d 69, 1993 A.M.C. 1144 (5th Cir.1992), where the cases are collected.

In Eagle–Picher Industries, Inc. v. United States, 846 F.2d 888, 1988 A.M.C. 2058 (3d Cir.1988), cert. denied 488 U.S. 965, 109 S.Ct. 490, 102 L.Ed.2d 527 (1988), the FTCA making the United States liable "in the same manner and to the same extent as a private individual under like circumstances under the law of the place where the act or omission complained of occurred," it could be sued for indemnity or contribution under *Lockheed* for amounts recovered in respect of injuries to a worker in a government shipyard because a private person, as owner of a vessel, could be sued by its employee for negligence under § 5(b) of the LHWCA (46 U.S.C.A. § 905(b)) despite the exclusiveness of its liability as an employer. The court of appeals found this analysis too involved, and reversed, holding that liability could not be predicated upon § 905(b) because § 903(b) specifically excludes federal employees from the coverage of the Act.

Members of the Armed Forces are barred from suing the United States for injuries incurred on active duty by Feres v. United States, 340 U.S. 135, 71 S.Ct. 153, 95 L.Ed. 152 (1950). See Miller v. United States, 42 F.3d 297 (5th Cir.1995); Blakey v. Iowa, 991 F.2d 148 (4th Cir.1993).

B. LONGSHOREMEN AND HARBOR WORKERS

1. HISTORICAL NOTE

The Fellow Servant Doctrine and Maritime Workers

To summarize the legal position of maritime workers following the decision in *The Osceola,* the seaman proper was entitled to maintenance and cure if he was injured or fell ill in the service of the vessel and, except for disabilities produced by his wilful misbehavior, this remedy was not dependent upon negligence, whether of the employer or of his fellow servants. If injury was produced by the unseaworthiness of the vessel he was entitled to full indemnity, at least where the condition was called to the attention of the ship's officers and not corrected. For injuries produced by the mere negligence of the master and other officers, or of his fellow seamen, he had no action in rem in admiralty, and if he sued at common law, or very probably if he sued in personam in the admiralty, he was precluded from recovery by the fellow servant doctrine if the negligence of a member of the ship's company, except, perhaps, the master, was the cause of the injury.

The harborworker was in a less advantageous position in some ways, but perhaps in a more advantageous position in others. Like other land workers he had no right to recover for maintenance and cure, or to recover an indemnity for breach of the warranty to supply a seaworthy vessel. If he worked on a vessel, however, and the owner of the vessel was not his employer, as a business invitee he could recover from the vessel owner for the negligence of *his* servants. In this connection ordinary principles of tort law in master-servant cases were applied—the safe place to work doctrine, the borrowed servant doctrine, the vice-principal doctrine, etc.

With the advent of workmen's compensation plans in the early twentieth century the longshoreman took a step ahead. There appeared to be no reason why the workmen's compensation statutes were not applicable to harborworkers, and they were generally applied. While there are almost no cases on the subject, there is authority rejecting their application to members of the crew of a vessel. See Schuede v. Zenith S.S. Co., 216 Fed. 566 (N.D.Ohio 1914). If the non-applicability of workmen's compensation to crew members may be assumed, 1915 found the seaman one of the few if not the only worker without remedy, above the very limited recovery for maintenance and cure, for injury produced by the negligence of his fellow servant. The railroad worker was covered under the FELA. The land worker and the harbor worker were covered by workmen's compensation. In that year Congress enacted § 20 of the Seamen's Act, providing that "in any suit to recover damages for any injury sustained on board vessel or in its service seamen having command shall not be held to be fellow servants with those under their authority." This is, of course, an extension of the vice-principal doctrine, narrowing, but not eliminating, the fellow servant defense.

In Southern Pacific Co. v. Jensen, reproduced at p. 367, supra, the Supreme Court held that the workmen's compensation statutes could not be applied to an injury to a harborworker when the injury took place within the maritime jurisdiction. This decision was bound to produce trouble, was it not? Mr. Justice McReynolds states that if New York could subject foreign ships coming into her ports to the obligations to conform to its workmen's compensation statute, so could every state to which the vessel travelled. The necessary consequence, he added, would be "destruction of the very uniformity in respect to maritime matters which the Constitution was designed to establish; and freedom of navigation between the States and with foreign countries would be seriously hampered and impeded." The plaintiff in the *Jensen* case was engaged in the loading of a vessel. His job was driving a truck on and off the vessel. The Court noted that (1) the work he was engaged in was maritime in its nature, (2) his employment was a maritime contract, (3) the injuries he received were maritime, and (4) the rights and liabilities of the parties were matters clearly within the maritime jurisdiction. Does (4) follow from (1) and (2), or from (3)? If it follows from (1) and (2), it seems to announce that the right of recovery of all maritime workers, on or off the vessel, is governed by the maritime law and the workmen's compensation statutes could not be applied to workers loading or unloading vessels regardless of the location of the incident producing the injuries.   If it follows from (3), the impact of *Jensen* is limited to excluding liability of the employer for accidents on navigable water.

Did the *Jensen* decision accomplish its purpose?   Did it go too far? Notice that the longshoreman may be employed directly by the vessel owner, or he may be employed by a master stevedore who has contracted to load or unload the vessel.   If he is employed by the vessel and *Jensen* can be said to rest on maritime location of the injury, the vessel owner is not protected against qualification under the State Act, is it?   After all, Jensen could just as easily have sustained injuries on the pier.   On the other hand, if *Jensen* were to be given occupational limits the stated reason for the decision does not seem to apply when the longshoreman is employed by a stevedore, since the liability of the employer would not subject the vessel owner to the burden of complying with various state statutes absent the application of some sort of borrowed servant theory.   In such circumstances the maximum impact of the application of the Act appears to be whatever increased cost might be expected from an increase in the liability of the master stevedore.

These questions were not conclusively settled until 1922.   In State Industrial Commission v. Nordenholt Corp., 259 U.S. 263, 42 S.Ct. 473, 66 L.Ed. 933 (1922), it was held that the workmen's compensation statutes could be applied to accidents to longshoremen injured on the pier.

During the years between *Jensen* and *Nordenholt,* the Court and the Congress had worked out the problem of the fellow servant defense in actions by crew members along other lines.   In the *Chelentis* case, reproduced at p. 382, supra, the Court had emasculated § 20 of the Seamen's Act.   This occurred in 1918, and in 1920 Congress enacted the Jones Act, extending to seamen the provisions of the Federal Employers Liability Act, which in terms eliminated the fellow servant defense.   During the same period it had attempted to extend by statute the application of the State workmen's compensation acts.   This attempt, occurring in 1919, was an amendment to the "saving to suitors" clause, preserving "the rights and remedies under the workmen's compensation law of any state."   Note that this language was broad enough to cover members of the crew of a vessel as well as longshoremen and other harborworkers.   This provision was invalidated the following year in Knickerbocker Ice Co. v. Stewart, 253 U.S. 149, 40 S.Ct. 438, 64 L.Ed. 834 (1920).

In 1922, then, it was clear that the seaman had a remedy for fellow servant negligence under the Jones Act, and that under *Nordenholt* the longshoreman had such a remedy as to injuries on the pier, but that under *Jensen* no such remedy existed if the injury took place on navigable waters. The same year the Congress once again attempted to place longshoremen under the State Acts.   It again amended the "savings to suitors" clause to provide for recovery under the workmen's compensation statutes, this time exempting a master or member of the crew of a vessel.   This was also invalidated in State of Washington v. W. C. Dawson & Co., 264 U.S. 219, 44 S.Ct. 302, 68 L.Ed. 646, 1924 A.M.C. 403 (1924).

Also in 1922, the Court decided Grant Smith–Porter Ship Co. v. Rohde, 257 U.S. 469, 42 S.Ct. 157, 66 L.Ed. 321 (1922). There it was held that the State could apply its workmen's compensation statute to a worker engaged in completing a launched vessel under construction on navigable waters. Unlike the longshoreman, the worker in *Rohde* was engaged in an activity (shipbuilding) that was viewed as essentially local, the contract to build a ship being nonmaritime. The following year the Court declined to apply the *Rohde* doctrine to a worker engaged in the repair of an already completed vessel. Great Lakes Dredge & Dock Co. v. Kierejewski, 261 U.S. 479, 43 S.Ct. 418, 67 L.Ed. 756 (1923). Thus under *Jensen-Rhode* the line was drawn on the essentially maritime nature of the activity involved.

At the close of the first quarter of the twentieth century, these events left the remedies of workers on the water and at the water's edge as follows:

Crew members.—Maintenance and cure and an indemnity for breach of the warranty of seaworthiness of the vessel or its equipment, and an action under the Jones Act for negligence, free of the common law defenses.

Land workers, and workers at the water's edge whose work was only peripherally connected with maritime commerce.—The workmen's compensation remedy under State law.

The Longshoreman and other harborworkers who might be thought not "local" under the *Rohde* doctrine.—Workmen's compensation if injured on land or on the pier, but no remedy for injuries due to fellow servant negligence if the injury took place on the water.

It will be noted that at this point the only gap to be filled in is the accident to a longshoreman or not "local" harborworker injured while on a vessel, or otherwise on navigable waters. In 1926, the Supreme Court filled this gap by applying the Jones Act. International Stevedoring Co. v. Haverty, 272 U.S. 50, 47 S.Ct. 19, 71 L.Ed. 157, 1926 A.M.C. 1638 (1926).

The following year the Congress enacted the Longshoremen's and Harborworkers' Compensation Act. Act of March 4, 1927, c. 509, 44 Stat. 1424.

The Longshore and Harbor Workers' Compensation Act

The Longshoremen's and Harborworkers' Compensation Act of 1927 was a complete compensation scheme for industrial accidents within its coverage. Indeed it was later made applicable to the District of Columbia (Act of May 17, 1928, c. 612, 45 Stat. 600), and to defense bases (See 42 U.S.C.A. §§ 1651–1654. And see Royal Indemnity Co. v. Puerto Rico Cement Corp., 142 F.2d 237, 1944 A.M.C. 672 (1st Cir.1944)). The coverage of the LHWCA proper was limited, however, to the necessities that Congress saw as reasons for its enactment.

It has been pointed out that at the time of the enactment of the LHWCA the problem of providing some method of compensating the injuries of workers at the water's edge had been taken care of in some fashion. Crew members were covered under the Jones Act. All other workers were covered by the State Acts if injured on land (*Nordenholt*). Longshoremen injured on the vessel were covered under the Jones Act (*Haverty*). It was an awkward adjustment, perhaps, but a complete or nearly complete one. This being so, it remains somewhat obscure why the Congress in 1927 should have enacted the LHWCA. It should be remembered, however, that legislative solutions take time in preparation and in assembling support, and once the momentum for reform is generated, perhaps it is difficult to turn it off. It must also be remembered that in 1919 and again in 1922 an effort had been made to embrace all harbor workers in a compensation scheme. Both these attempts had been directed at placing such workers under the State Acts. Such efforts having been thwarted by the *Jensen* doctrine of uniformity within the maritime jurisdiction, except for local employments within the *Rohde* doctrine, it might be supposed that the concern of the Congress was with the bringing of the longshoreman (or non-*Rohde*) worker within a workmen's compensation scheme.

The language of the LHWCA suggests that this is so. Section 902(4) of the Act defined an "employer" as "an employer any of whose employees are employed in maritime employment, in whole or in part, upon navigable waters of the United States." Section 902(3) defined "employee" as excluding the master or any member of the crew of a vessel. Thus any employer *any* of whose employees was employed in maritime employment *on navigable waters* was covered. Section 903 provided:

(a) Compensation shall be payable under this Act [§§ 901 and note–945, 957–950 of this Title] in respect of disability or death of an employee, but only if the disability or death results from an injury occurring upon the navigable waters of the United States (including any dry dock) and if recovery for the disability or death through workmen's compensation proceedings may not validly be provided by State law. No compensation shall be payable in respect of the disability or death of—

(1) A master or member of a crew of any vessel, nor any person engaged by the master to load or unload or repair any small vessel under eighteen tons net; or

(2) An officer or employee of the United States or any agency thereof or of any State or foreign government, or of any political subdivision thereof.

(b) No compensation shall be payable if the injury was occasioned solely by the intoxication of the employee or by the willful intention of the employee to injure or kill himself or another.

The evident purpose of §§ 902 and 903 was to make certain that all workers at the water's edge were covered under either the State Act or the LHWCA, with the application of one or the other to depend upon the location of the accident and the essentially maritime nature of the services being rendered at the time.

The Twilight Zone

The sort of ad hoc determination of which compensation scheme applied to each accident that the Act of 1927 seems to have contemplated was obviously awkward in application.   Read literally, the Act could have resulted in a hiatus, for the limitations expressed in § 903 related not to cases that *were* covered by the State Acts, but to cases in which compensation *may not validly be provided*.   Thus, if the state *could* validly provide for compensation, but *did* not, there would be no coverage at all.   This was more a theoretical than a practical danger inasmuch as the State Acts normally applied to industrial accidents generally and the exclusion of maritime workers stemmed from the *Jensen* decision, not from the State statutes.   To the extent that the *Rohde* line proved to be crooked, however, there was a possibility that absent a strict application of the doctrine of issue preclusion a given applicant might be hoisted by a difference of opinion between the State and federal courts.   How crooked was the *Rohde* line?   Take, for example, Parker v. Motor Boat Sales, Inc., 314 U.S. 244, 62 S.Ct. 221, 86 L.Ed. 184, 1942 A.M.C. 1 (1941).   There the applicant for compensation was an employee of a seller of small boats, maritime supplies, and outboard motors.   He was employed chiefly as a janitor and porter.   Note that a contract to sell a vessel is not a maritime contract, but a contract to repair one is.   Is a contract to sell a new motor for an existing vessel a maritime contract?   If it were an inboard motor and were installed in the boat, it would probably be assimilated to repairs would it not?   But an outboard motor that may be clamped to different boats might be looked upon as separate from the boat.   The claimant, at the time of the subject occurrence, was riding in a boat on the James River near Richmond, Virginia, concededly in navigable waters of the United States.   He and another employee of the employer were engaged in testing one of the employer's motors for which the owner of the boat was a prospective purchaser.   His occupation at the time was assuredly maritime.   Was it "local" under *Rohde?*   He claimed under the LHWCA and the Supreme Court upheld his right to recover, reversing the Fourth Circuit.

Two years later, in Davis v. Department of Labor & Industries, 317 U.S. 249, 63 S.Ct. 225, 87 L.Ed. 246 (1943), the Court made it clear that the State Acts and the LHWCA were not mutually exclusive.   In *Davis* the claimant was engaged in dismantling a bridge over navigable waters.   He was a structural steel worker and at the time of the accident he was working on a barge cutting and stowing steel taken from a bridge.   The Court recognized the difficulties involved in determining whether or not the State Act could be applied and held that in such a "twilight zone" the LHWCA applied despite the possibility that the State Act might also apply.   While this decision might be said to do violence to § 905, providing, in part, "The liability of an employer prescribed in section 4 [§ 904 of this title] shall be exclusive and in place of all other liability of such employer to the employee" except in cases in which the employer fails to secure payment of compensation as required by the Act, it represented a practical adjustment that appeared necessary to the accomplishment of the ends that Congress sought to achieve.

The Calbeck Case

In Calbeck v. Travelers Ins. Co., 370 U.S. 114, 82 S.Ct. 1196, 8 L.Ed.2d 368, 1962 A.M.C. 1413 (1962), the claimant was a welder working on a launched but uncompleted drilling barge, at the time of the accident afloat on navigable waters of the United States. Mr. Justice Brennan, writing for a majority of six (Mr. Justice Frankfurter did not participate and Justices Stewart and Harlan dissented), held that the LHWCA applied. Mr. Justice Brennan lay stress on the fact that the Senate version of the bill originally had contained the language "except employment of local concern and of no direct relation to navigation and commerce," which after a hearing during which two large employer groups and the chairman of the committee had expressed concern lest this language perpetuate the uncertainties of the "maritime but local" distinction, was changed to read as it did in the final version. He admitted that "we are not privy" to the committee deliberations that resulted in the change. He saw in the overall legislative history, however, a congressional concern for two problems, the first to provide compensation for workers excluded by *Jensen* and *Dawson* from coverage under the State workmen's compensation schemes, and the second to eliminate the uncertainty of the "local concern" doctrine. He concluded:

> "We conclude that Congress used the phrase 'if recovery * * * may not validly be provided by State law' in a sense consistent with the delineation of coverage as reaching injuries occurring on navigable waters. By that language Congress reiterated that the Act reached all those cases of injury to employees on navigable waters as to which Jensen, Knickerbocker and Dawson had rendered questionable the availability of a state compensation remedy. Congress brought under the coverage of the Act all such injuries whether or not a particular one was also within the constitutional reach of a state workmen's compensation law." [Footnotes omitted.]

In a companion case, Donovan v. Avondale Shipyards, the Court held that the claim under the LHWCA was not precluded by the fact that the claimant had applied for and received benefits under the State workmen's compensation statute.

Mr. Justice Stewart, joined by Mr. Justice Harlan, dissented. While he indicated that the decision announced a rule that might be a better one, he was convinced that it was not the rule that had been provided for in the statute. Most comment on the case agreed with him. Critical comment is collected in Robertson, Admiralty and Federalism 213, n. 45 (1970). Professor Robertson, in the text, and in an appendix (id. at 304), proffers an elaborate justification for Mr. Justice Brennan's reading of the statutory phrase. The student may judge its success. Note, however, that after discussing numerous permutations, the preferred interpretation turns out to be "if it is possible that recovery not be validly provided by state law." Such an interpretation appears to be a restatement of the twilight zone decisions rather than the position taken by Mr. Justice Brennan in *Calbeck*. As Mr. Justice Stewart pointed out in his *Calbeck* dissent, the case at bar was not one within the area of the confusion the majority decision purported to eliminate inasmuch as the occupation in question had been held subject to State compensation statutes for forty years.

In his dissent, Mr. Justice Stewart observed in passing that if the LHWCA applied to all employee accidents occurring on navigable waters, and as Mr. Justice Brennan intimated had been so applied since the decision in the *Parker* case, there would have been no necessity for the judicial creation of the "twilight zone" in *Davis*. What, then, was left of the doctrine after *Calbeck*? *Davis* was not overruled by the majority. Gilmore and Black state that "[i]t is fair to say that the post-Calbeck consensus came to be that the twilight zone—taking that phrase to mean that there existed an area of concurrent state and federal jurisdiction over injuries on navigable waters—had not been affected by anything in Calbeck." *The Law of Admiralty*, § 6–49 (1975). Writing in 1970, Professor Robertson had taken the position that this was the correct reading of the case. Op. cit., at 219–221, criticizing state court cases to the contrary ("Of course, *Calbeck* clearly stands for the proposition that all of the effects of the mutual exclusivity theory are gone, so that any extension of federal compensation rights worked by that case should have no adverse effect whatsoever as to state claims").

To the extent that the *Jensen* doctrine was designed to protect maritime employers from the burden of qualifying under several different schemes it could be argued that the *Davis* distinction remained necessary as a minimum limit on state power to impose its scheme. Thus the vessel owner whose vessel visits many states is no more inconvenienced by the exclusive application of the State Act than by its concurrent application. On the other hand the extension of the LHWCA to "maritime but local" workers does, as Mr. Justice Stewart noted, make the "twilight zone unnecessary." And if, as Mr. Justice Brennan suggests, the intention of Congress was to eliminate the uncertainties of the *Davis* doctrine, a strict adherence to *Jensen* arguably would have been a better way to do it. This is so because the claimant might seek compensation under the State Act and after litigation of the issue find that he was on the water side of the *Davis* rule. Indeed at the time of the *Calbeck* decision there was district court authority for the proposition that filing a claim for state compensation did not toll the one year limit for the filing of the LHWCA claim under § 913 of the Act. Romaniuk v. Locke, 3 F.Supp. 529, 1933 A.M.C. 113 (S.D.N.Y.1932). Section 913(d) provided:

> "Where recovery is denied to any person, in a suit brought at law or in admiralty to recover damages in respect of injury or death, on the ground that such person was an employee and that the defendant was an employer within the meaning of this Act and that such employer had secured compensation to such employee under this Act, the limitation of time prescribed in subdivision (a) shall begin to run only from the date of termination of such suit."

In the *Romaniuk* case, it was held that the filing of the claim with the state department of labor did not constitute a suit under subdivision (d). In Ayers v. Parker, 15 F.Supp. 447, 1936 A.M.C. 911 (D.Md.1936), it was held that a state court suit based on rejection of a claim under a state workmen's compensation scheme was not a suit that would toll the time under § 913. This view was rejected by the Fifth Circuit. T. Smith & Son, Inc. v. Wilson, 328 F.2d 313 (5th Cir.1964), aff'g 218 F.Supp. 944, 1964 A.M.C. 120 (E.D.La.1963), decided after the *Calbeck* decision. Independent of the time limit under § 913, however, and assuming that after *Calbeck* the injured worker could avoid the issue by filing under the LHWCA in the first place, the risk that an ignorant mistake would postpone if not bar compensation in a worthy case remained. If one assumes the validity of *Jensen,* was preservation of the *Davis* doctrine worth this risk?

Occurrence on Navigable Waters

It has been noted that while in *Jensen* the Court mentioned occurrence on navigable waters as only one of four maritime connections that underlay the necessity for uniform treatment under federal law of liability of the employer of longshoremen for injuries sustained in their employment, in *Nordenholt* it was made clear that the *Jensen* doctrine did not extend to the pier. At the time the water's edge was the measure of the admiralty jurisdiction in tort. See Chapter 3, supra. This line was written into the LHWCA in § 903(a), with the qualifying phrase, "including any dry dock".

In 1948, the admiralty jurisdiction was expanded by statute to cover "damage or injury, to persons or property, caused by a vessel on navigable water, notwithstanding that such damage or injury be done or consummated on land." See Chapter 3, supra.

What impact, if any, would this provision have on the interpretation of the LHWCA? Gilmore and Black state "A possible reading of Calbeck was that Congress had intended the coverage of LHWCA to be coextensive with the limits of admiralty jurisdiction." *The Law of Admiralty,* § 6–49 (1975). They concluded, "If that was what Calbeck meant, it should follow that LHWCA awards were to be made with respect to injuries which occurred on piers and other land areas." In support of this view, they pointed out that maintenance and cure was allowed for injuries received on shore, that Jones Act recoveries were also allowed for shore injuries, and that recovery for unseaworthiness had been permitted when the injury took place on the pier. Further, they found support for the extension of the LHWCA to the pier in the decision of the Court in Avondale Marine Ways, Inc. v. Henderson, 346 U.S. 366, 74 S.Ct. 100, 98 L.Ed. 77, 1953 A.M.C. 1990 (1953). There the Court affirmed, per curiam, a decision of the Fifth Circuit permitting an award when the injury was produced by an explosion of a barge that had been drawn up on a marine railway. The Fifth Circuit had read "any dry dock" in § 903(a) to include the marine railway. The Supreme Court, however, had cited the "twilight zone" cases, without further explicating its decision.

In Marine Stevedoring Corp. v. Oosting, 398 F.2d 900, 1968 A.M.C. 1125 (4 Cir.1968), the Fourth Circuit upheld the authority to make a LHWCA award in a case in which the injury had been produced by the swinging of a draft of cargo attached to the ship's gear, lifting one longshoreman in the air and dropping him on his head and crushing another against a railroad car. Judge Sobeloff read *Calbeck* to quote with approval the circuit decision in De Bardeleben Coal Corp. v. Henderson, 142 F.2d 481, 1944 A.M.C. 773 (5 Cir.1944), in which the court had stated "that Congress intended to exercise to the fullest extent all the power and jurisdiction it had over the subject matter * * * It is sufficient to say that Congress intended the compensation act to have a coverage coextensive with the limits of its authority." Alternatively, he found that assuming a more limited tort jurisdiction the pier accident was brought within that jurisdiction by the Extension Act in 1948.

The view that the Act of 1927 was intended to embrace the full measure of Congressional power under the Constitution must account for the dry dock provision, must it not? Is it possible that Congress was acting under the assumption that the admiralty jurisdiction extended to dry docks in cases in which the accident occurred on land, while not to cases in which the accident occurred on piers?

The *Oosting* case was reversed in Nacirema Operating Co. v. Johnson, 396 U.S. 212, 90 S.Ct. 347, 24 L.Ed.2d 371, 1969 A.M.C. 1967 (1969). In addition to the drydock provision, the Court found convincing indication in the legislative history that the Act was not intended to include pier injuries. The bill had been objected to by the Labor Department on exactly that issue, and the report accompanying the bill had stated quite clearly that it did not cover injuries except those occurring on the vessel or between the pier and vessel and thus on navigable waters.

This is not conclusive, of course, on the question of whether the Congress thought that it was exhausting its jurisdiction. If by judicial construction the admiralty jurisdiction were to be extended beyond navigable waters, it could be held that a statute intended to expand jurisdiction will not be construed to restrict it. What happened to the 20 ton and interstate restrictions written into the Great Lakes Act of 1845 after the general admiralty jurisdiction was extended to such waters in *The Genesee Chief*? See The Eagle, 75 U.S. (8 Wall.) 15, 19 L.Ed. 365 (1868). And see discussion in Robertson, Admiralty and Federalism 117 (1970). But the Supreme Court in *Nacirema* was not prepared to hold that the tort jurisdiction generally extends to the pier, thus no such leap frog interpretation was possible. It went on to indicate that such extension of the jurisdiction as had taken place was effected by the Extension Act of 1948, and that both the terms and history of that Act negatived the suggestion that it was intended to expand the jurisdiction to include injuries other than those that were "caused" by vessels. Since in *Nacirema* the injury in question was "caused" by a vessel inasmuch as the draft of cargo was suspended from the ship's crane, could the action be treated as under the Act? The Court thought not, reading the language "in rem or in personam" and "damage" to "person or property" as bespeaking concern with actions in a court and "wholly at odds with the theory of workmen's compensation."

Mr. Justice Douglas dissented, joined by Justices Black and Brennan. They agreed with Judge Sobeloff's interpretation of the *Calbeck* case, but did not discuss the effect of the Extension Act.

Actions Against Third Persons

Section 933(a) preserved the right of an injured employee covered under the LHWCA to maintain an action against a person other than his employer "or a person or persons in his employ" when such person is liable. Gilmore and Black observe:

> "When LHCA was drafted no thought, presumably, was given to the fact that maritime workers regularly work on premises (i.e., ships) owned by third parties (shipowners) which are temporarily relinquished to the employers (master stevedores) for the carrying out of, say, loading or unloading operations. Thus, the situation of employment-related injuries attributable to the acts of third parties (not employers), exceptional in the context of shore-based industrial employment, is the order of the day in maritime employment. Nevertheless, LHCA routinely followed the state compensation acts in preserving the injured employee's right to sue third parties (as distinct from his employer) outside the framework of the compensation system." *The Law of Admiralty* § 6–46 (1975).

In the context of the state compensation acts, they suggest that the action against third persons was looked upon as an action in tort for negligence, and add the observation that "[i]n the usual conditions of industrial employment the likelihood of employment-related injuries being caused by third-party tortfeasors is of course negligible." While "negligible" is difficult to quantify, is third person liability all that rare? There are many service industries in which employees routinely work on the premises of others are there not? And the not negligible number of employees who drive vehicles on the street are exposed to the negligence of third persons every day. In the setting of the plant or factory of course the chances of third person liability are smaller, but even there the growth of products liability law beyond the requirement of privity leaves open cases in which the injury is produced by defects in the equipment. In such cases strict liability, as well as negligence, may be involved, as it may on construction sites under state scaffold acts. The parallel is not, then, quite so far-fetched as it might seem.

It is to be noted that prior to the enactment of the LHWCA, the maritime worker injured on board a vessel through the negligence of the vessel owner or his employees had a cause of action for negligence. The LHWCA simply preserved such a cause, making provision in § 933 for reimbursement of the employer for his expenditures under the Act by providing that the acceptance of compensation, or failure to bring an action against the third person (§ 933(b)), or the payment of compensation into the fund provided for in § 944 (§ 933(c)), would effect an assignment of the claim to the employer who might sue on it or compromise it (§ 933(d)), retaining enough to make him whole and paying the excess to the employee (§ 933(e)).

Since injuries to workmen in the setting of the longshoreman's work was generally not attributable to the negligence of the shipowner, but rather to the negligence of the servants of his employer, the master stevedore, actions under §§ 905, 933 were not common. There were such cases, however. See, e.g., Colvin v. The Kokusai Kisen Kabushiki Kaisha,

72 F.2d 44, 1934 A.M.C. 1116 (5 Cir.1934); The Meton, 62 F.2d 825, 1933 A.M.C. 291 (5 Cir.1933); Calhoun v. Daly, 18 F.Supp. 1005 (S.D.N.Y.1936), aff'd per curiam 89 F.2d 1004 (2d Cir.1936).

Expansion of the Doctrine of Seaworthiness

Earlier in this chapter the growth of the warranty of seaworthiness has been considered. The history of its growth from what was a limited species of negligence justifying recovery of full indemnity despite the fellow servant defense to an absolute liability in the *Mahnich* case is set forth in Mr. Justice Stewart's opinion in Mitchell v. Trawler Racer, Inc., subchapter 4A supra. Lurking in the background was the decision in International Stevedoring Co. v. Haverty, already discussed, which held that a longshoreman was a seaman under the Jones Act. Thus the stage was set for Seas Shipping Co. v. Sieracki.

Seas Shipping Co. v. Sieracki

The Seaman Pro Hac Vice

Two years after the decision in *Mahnich,* the Court decided Seas Shipping Co. v. Sieracki, 328 U.S. 85, 66 S.Ct. 872, 90 L.Ed. 1099 (1946). In the *Sieracki* case, *Mahnich, Haverty,* and §§ 905 and 933 of the LHWCA were fused into the *Sieracki* doctrine, so called, which extended the warranty of seaworthiness to longshoremen, thus permitting the longshoreman, as a "seaman pro hac vice" to maintain a § 933 action against the vesselowner for full damages when his injury was produced through a shipboard condition despite the absence of negligence on the part of the latter and in spite of the fact that the condition was produced by the negligence of his fellow servants.

Writing for a majority of five (Justice Jackson taking no part and Chief Justice Stone and Justices Frankfurter and Burton dissenting) Mr. Justice Rutledge stated that historically members of the crew had loaded and unloaded ships. In more recent days different persons had been hired for this task, and it had come to be common to contract out the loading and unloading to stevedoring concerns who hired the longshoremen. The duty to maintain a seaworthy vessel, he noted, had been held to be an absolute duty. It was not based in contract and therefore the fact that the longshoremen were employed by someone else did not exclude them from its protection. The seaworthiness doctrine was a humanitarian doctrine designed to protect those who do a ship's work and share the hazards of doing a ship's work. The LHWCA, while depriving the longshoreman of a cause of action against the vesselowner under the Jones Act, since the vesselowner was not his employer, did not deprive him of his traditional remedies under the maritime law.

Turning to the LHWCA, Mr. Justice Rutledge observed:

> "We may take it therefore that Congress intended the remedy of compensation to be exclusive as against the employer [citing Swanson v. Marra Brothers, Inc. and § 905 of the Act]. But we cannot assume, in face of the Act's explicit provisions, that it intended this remedy to nullify or

affect others against third persons. Exactly the opposite is true. The legislation therefore did not nullify any right of the longshoreman against the owner of the ship, except possibly in the instance, presumably rare, where he may be hired by the owner. The statute had no purpose or effect to alter the stevedore's rights as against any but his employer alone. Beyond that consequence, moreover, we think it had none to alter either the basic policy or the rationalization of the *Haverty* decision. Because the recovery under the Merchant Marine Act of 1920 was limited to the employer, the necessary effect of the Longshoremen's and Harbor Workers' Act, likewise so limited, was to substitute its remedy for that provided under the preexisting legislation and the *Haverty* decision's construction of it. There was none to nullify the basic and generally applicable policy of that decision or to affect the validity of its foundations in other applications.

It may be added that, beyond the applicability of these considerations to sustain the stevedore's right of recovery for breach of the owner's obligation of seaworthiness, are others to support the statutory policy of giving his employer recovery over against the owner when the latter's breach of duty casts upon the employer the burden of paying compensation. These may furnish additional reason for our conclusion. With them however we are not immediately concerned.''

In the *Sieracki* case the plaintiff was a winch operator. The winch he operated was controlled by a ten ton boom. One part of a freight car had been lowered into the hold. While the second part, weighing about eight tons, was being put down, the shackle supporting the boom broke, causing the boom and tackle to fall and injure the plaintiff. The case was, then, an optimum one for the application of the doctrine announced. First, while the "history" that had persisted since *Haverty* to the effect that in the past members of the crew had loaded and unloaded vessels was questionable (See Tetreault, Seamen, Seaworthiness, and the Rights of Harbor Workers, 39 Corn.L.Q. 381 (1954)), it is true that winchmen were sometimes provided by the vessel, it being a matter of dispute whether in such a situation he was a fellow servant of the longshoreman. See The Slingsby, 120 Fed. 748 (2d Cir.1903). Second, the unseaworthiness complained of was a basic insufficiency of the equipment of the vessel, provided by the owner. In the *Mahnich* case, however, the seeds for growth had been sown. There the statement had been made that the duty was absolute, and independent of the fact that the "condition" of unseaworthiness might have been characterized as operating negligence. There, it will be remembered, the plaintiff had been injured through the collapse of a staging due to the negligence of the mate in selecting defective rope in rigging it. Mr. Justice Rutledge may not have recognized the implications of *Mahnich* in the context of *Sieracki*. Notice that in the last paragraph quoted above, he seems concerned about placing liability where the breach of duty lies, independent of the employer-employee relationship of the parties. Notice that in *Mahnich* there would be no recovery on a negligence theory, since the statute of limitations under the Jones Act has run. Notice, however, that had the plaintiff in *Mahnich* been a longshoreman in the employ of a master stevedore, clearly he would have his action for negligence under the general maritime law, since the mate was not his fellow servant, and he was at least a business invitee.

Read narrowly, then, *Sieracki* stood for the proposition that the vessel owner warranted the vessel and its equipment to the longshoreman, and insofar as it related to the longshoreman at all, *Mahnich* stood for the proposition that the allegation that a condition that rendered the vessel unseaworthy was produced by the negligence of the ship's company was no defense in an action for the breach of warrant of the seaworthiness of the vessel. But despite the fairly modest change in the law that can be read from these cases when they are confined to their facts, they created three directions of growth. While in *Mahnich* there had been negligence, Mr. Chief Justice Stone had spoken of the duty to provide a seaworthy vessel as "absolute," in the sense that the duty exists independent of a showing of notice or negligence. This aspect of the doctrine has already been discussed. See subchapter 4A supra.

The second growth point of the seaworthiness doctrine as applied to longshoremen lay in the relationship between operating negligence and the doctrine of seaworthiness. The *Mahnich* case itself dealt with equipment of the vessel (rope) that was defective, and Chief Justice Stone's reliance on the statement from *The Osceola* to the effect that a shipowner has a duty "to supply and *keep in order* the proper appliances appurtenant to the ship" [emphasis his], could be read as indicating that he intended no extension of the duty beyond the physical equipment of the ship. The fact that the injury derived from the negligent selection of the rope for the purpose for which it was used, however, led to a possible inference that the negligent use of equipment might be deemed to create an unseaworthy condition.

The third point of possible growth derives from the first and second. If the duty to provide a seaworthy vessel is absolute and unconnected with negligence, and unseaworthiness may result from negligent use of equipment as well as failure to provide safe equipment, does it matter whether the defective equipment belonged to the vessel, or to someone else, or whether the negligence is that of the vesselowner or his servants, or that of someone else?

Ship's Equipment Pro Hac Vice

Alaska S.S. Co. v. Petterson

The first and third of these growth points were developed in Alaska S.S. Co. v. Petterson, 347 U.S. 396, 74 S.Ct. 601, 98 L.Ed. 798, 1954 A.M.C. 860 (1954). There the plaintiff had been injured through the breaking of a block used in loading the vessel. There was no clear evidence as to who provided the block or what caused it to break. The court of appeals assumed that the vesselowner had not furnished the block. Responding to the argument that the master stevedore had furnished it, it stated that the duty to maintain a seaworthy vessel was "nondelegable." As to the want of evidence of what caused the block to break, it held such evidence unnecessary, likening the doctrine to *res ipsa loquitur*.

The vessel had been turned over to a master stevedore for loading and it had been argued that having thus relinquished control, it was not responsible for conditions arising after it was relinquished, relying on a series of cases to that effect in the Second Circuit. The court of appeals rejected this doctrine point blank.

The Supreme Court affirmed per curiam, citing the *Sieracki* case and Pope and Talbot v. Hawn (discussed in another connection later in this note) in which the Court extended the *Sieracki* doctrine to persons engaged in repairing the vessel. Justices Burton, Frankfurter, and Jackson dissented.

This view of the warranty of seaworthiness as both "absolute" and "non-delegable" was reiterated in Rogers v. United States Lines, 347 U.S. 984, 74 S.Ct. 849, 98 L.Ed. 1120, 1954 A.M.C. 1088 (1954), a per curiam reversal of a decision of the Third Circuit dismissing an action predicated on unseaworthiness attributable to defectiveness of a wire furnished by the longshoreman's employer.

Just how far *Petterson* and *Rogers* went to make the vesselowner responsible for equipment brought on board by the master stevedore is obscured somewhat by the fact that in both cases the disposition was per curiam. In both cases the injury was attributable to the failure of equipment that was attached to the ship's gear. In *Petterson* the equipment was a block generally found among the gear of both vessels and stevedores. In *Rogers,* the wire was used as a land fall runner which was hooked up to and used in connection with other rigging in the operation of the vessel's winch. To date the Supreme Court had not had before it a case in which there was a failure on board the vessel of transitory equipment used by a longshoreman.

Negligent Operation as Unseaworthiness

Crumady v. The J.H. Fisser

The second growth point of the *Mahnich-Sieracki* doctrine, the suggestion that negligent use of seaworthy equipment results in an unseaworthy "condition" began in Crumady v. The Joachim Hendrik Fisser, 358 U.S. 423, 79 S.Ct. 445, 3 L.Ed.2d 413, 1959 A.M.C. 580 (1959). The Court took the facts as found by the district court:

"* * * libellant and his fellow employees had placed a double eyed wire rope sling, provided with a sliding hook movable within the eyes thereof, around the two timbers at a location two or three feet from their after ends. The two eyes of the sling were then placed upon the cargo hook of the up-and-down boom runner and a signal given by the stevedore gangwayman to the winchman to 'take up the slack'. The winchman complied with the signal, and during this operation libellant stood clear upon other timbers forming a part of the cargo, within the open square of the hatch. There was some testimony that when the slack was taken up by the winchman, the two timbers slid toward each other in the sling, the timber which had been under the lower edge of the hatch combing moving or commencing to move toward the timber which lay within the open hatch square.   After the slack had been taken up by the winchman, the same signaller called for the 'taking of a strain' upon the cargo runner.   The winchman again responded, the two-part topping lift broke and the head of the up-and-down boom, with its attached cargo and topping-lift blocks, fell to the top of the cargo within the hatch square.

"The topping lift had been rigged in a double purchase and had been supporting the head of the boom.   The wire rope constituting the topping-lift extended from a shackle on the topping-lift block at the cross-tree of the mast, through a block at the boom head, back through the mast block, down the mast, through a block welded to the mast table, and thence around a drum of the winch.   When the boom fell, libellant was knocked down either by the boom itself or its appurtenant tackle, and thus sustained numerous serious and permanently disabling orthopedic and neurological injuries."

The district court's opinion was read by the court of appeals to rest upon the defective condition of the topping lift, brought into play by the stevedores' improper positioning of the boom.   The court of appeals reversed.   It rejected this basis for unseaworthiness and found from the record that the accident had been produced primarily by the negligence of the stevedores in permitting a long and heavy timber to be wedged under the combing of the hatch from which it was being removed, and in having changed, contrary to instructions, the position of the boom, this procedure having caused the topping lift cable to be subjected to "excessive and abnormal strain," causing the cable to break and the boom to fall.   The Supreme Court in turn reversed the decision of the court of appeals not on this ground but on the theory that the servants of the vesselowner had set the cut-off on the winch at six tons when the equipment was rated at three tons.   Mr. Justice Douglas found that the record justified a finding that this rendered the vessel unseaworthy.   The negligence of the stevedores, he found, merely brought this unseaworthiness into play.

In passing the Court noted that in Grillea v. United States, 232 F.2d 919, 1956 A.M.C. 1009 (2d Cir.1956), the Second Circuit had held that stevedores themselves could render a ship pro tanto unseaworthy and make a vessel owner liable for injuries to one of them.   In *Grillea,* the longshoremen had laid the wrong hatch cover over the "pad eye," and a short time later this misposition had resulted in the plaintiff's injury.   Judge Learned Hand had held that the cover had been in its position long enough to create a condition that might be viewed as unseaworthiness, intimating that there is a distinction between contemporaneous negligence that causes an accident, on the one hand, and negligence that produces a condition that is the later cause of an accident, on the other.

Mr. Justice Douglas noted that inasmuch as the decision could be rested on the negligent setting of the cut-off, done by persons who were acting for the ship, it was unnecessary to approve the *Grillea* holding. Justice Harlan, in a dissent in which he was joined by Justices Frankfurter and Whittaker, noted that he believed that the facts of the *Crumady* case were outside the *Grillea* doctrine in any event, since they were "an incident in a continuous operation," not within the *Grillea* formulation.

If one were to agree with the majority in *Crumady* that the setting of the cut-off was negligent and causally related to the injury, a proposition denied by the dissenters and apparently by both lower courts, the decision did not carry liability much if any beyond previous holdings.

The *Grillea* holding that a shipboard condition caused by the negligence of the employees of the master stevedore could render the vessel unseaworthy was followed in many cases in the lower courts despite the Supreme Court's refusal in *Crumady* to "go so far." The time factor proved troublesome, however. See Reid v. Quebec Paper Sales & Transp. Co., 340 F.2d 34, 1965 A.M.C. 112 (2d Cir.1965), where the doctrine is discussed and the cases collected. In *Reid*, when a rest period was called, one of the plaintiff's fellow workers placed an aluminum ladder in the hold to enable the men to come up to the main deck, and held the ladder in place, as it was not secured in any other way. The plaintiff was standing on the cargo in the hold. The worker holding the ladder left it to get a garment for one of the other men. The ladder slid along the hatch combing and fell into the hold, hitting the plaintiff on the head. Judge (now Mr. Justice) Marshall held that whatever the limits of *Grillea*, the district court was correct in holding the vessel unseaworthy, since the accident was not the *sole* product of fellow servant negligence, it having been found that the ladder moved because of the wind. In discussing *Grillea*, however, he observed:

> "In *Grillea*, Judge Hand held that although the libellant and his fellow stevedores 'laid the wrong hatch cover over the pad eye only a short time before he fell, we think enough time had elapsed to result in unseaworthiness.' * * * But there was no explanation why the ship would be any less unseaworthy if the accident occurred the very instant the hatch cover was placed over the 'pad-eye.' "

Elsewhere he observed, "Any extension of the *Grillea* doctrine, if not the doctrine itself, might well become the Trojan horse of the warranty of seaworthiness." Judge Friendly dissented, being of the opinion that the accident was the product of simple negligence of a fellow servant. He found the facts a perfect case for application of Judge Hand's distinction, and observed that courts should not push in a direction that frustrated the purposes of the LHWCA.

In Skibinski v. Waterman S.S. Corp., 360 F.2d 539, 1966 A.M.C. 873 (2d Cir.1966), a case in which it was held that the lowering of a one ton steel ladder by means of an open mouth "S" shaped cargo hook rendered the vessel unseaworthy, since the "use of the apparatus took a substantial amount of time, so that the apparatus became a part of the [ship's] equipment," Judge Friendly again dissented. This time he indicated that in view of the fact that Justice Douglas in *Crumady* had left the whole issue open, declaring that the Court "need not go so far," he was prepared to "scuttle" the whole *Grillea* doctrine that "a momentarily unsafe condition created solely by negligence of stevedores in the course of their work" is a basis for holding the vessel unseaworthy.

In Mascuilli v. United States, 387 U.S. 237, 87 S.Ct. 1705, 18 L.Ed.2d 743, 1967 A.M.C. 1702 (1967), the improper use of a winch caused a shackle to break, producing plaintiff's injuries. The court of appeals had affirmed dismissal of an action for unseaworthiness on a finding that the equipment was seaworthy and the accident produced by the negligence of the stevedoring crew in operating it improperly, and further that the accident was instantaneous. The Supreme Court reversed, per curiam, citing *Mahnich* and *Crumady*. As later proved to be the case in *Mascuilli,* it is not easy to speculate profitably about what the Supreme Court has actually decided in its per curiam decisions in this area. In some quarters, however, the reversal of *Mascuilli* was read as eliminating altogether the "operational negligence" defense. See Candiano v. Moore–McCormack Lines, 382 F.2d 961, 1967 A.M.C. 2312 (2d Cir.1967). There Judge Leonard Moore observed, "Although there is no basis in logic for attributing unseaworthiness to a vessel which is in every respect soundly constructed and completely equipped merely because of the negligence of longshoremen or crew members engaged in an operation on board, the term has been created by judicial fiat and used for all practical purposes for imposing absolute liability on shipowner and stevedore."

In Usner v. Luckenbach Overseas Corp., reproduced at p. 902, supra, the Court rejected the *Candiano* reading of *Mascuilli,* noting that its citation of *Mahnich* and *Crumady* indicated that the per curiam reversal was on the issue of whether a prior unseaworthy condition came into play by the tightline condition.

It has been pointed out that the decision in the *Usner* case will have very little effect on seamen covered by the Jones Act. As will appear later, it is calculated to have little effect on actions by longshoremen and other harbor workers since the 1972 amendments to the LHWCA. The time consumed in filing and prosecuting litigation is often considerable, however, and in cases involving occurrences that took place before the effective date of the 1972 amendments, courts have had to wrestle with its application. Illustrative is Ryan v. Pacific Coast Shipping Co., Liberia, 448 F.2d 525, 1971 A.M.C. 2468 (9th Cir.1971), on certiorari to the Supreme Court at the time of the *Victory Carriers* decision. There a crane operator attempted to straighten out a crooked load of steel pipe by carrying the boom of the crane over and past a gondola car while lowering the load into the car, so that one end of the load would strike the inner side of the car farthest from the vessel and thereby cause the load to turn and straighten. The gondola car tipped over against a car on the adjoining track, crushing a longshoreman between the cars. The Ninth Circuit held that the cause of the accident was an unsafe method of unloading, rendering the vessel unseaworthy. The Supreme Court vacated the judgment in light of *Usner* and *Victory Carriers*. See 404 U.S. 1035, 92 S.Ct. 713, 30 L.Ed.2d 727 (1972). On remand the district court adhered to its original decision.

In this case how do we tell whether this was an unsafe method, or an isolated act of negligence? The district court found that while the method was employed only once, "The procedure employed would have been, in all likelihood, repeated it not for the injury to Ryan." The court of appeals reversed. Ryan v. Pacific Coast Shipping Co., Liberia, 509 F.2d 1054, 1975 A.M.C. 1224 (9th Cir.1975). The majority was impressed by the fact that in the six shifts preceding the accident no such method had been used, and the testimony of the plaintiff that in 20 years of working as a longshoreman he had never seen it used.

Judge Koelsch dissented. He believed that in such cases the only way to handle a doctrine such as the *Usner* doctrine is to place great weight on the district court's findings. Ryan v. Pacific Coast Shipping Co., Liberia, 509 F.2d 1054, 1975 A.M.C. 1224 (9th Cir.1975).

And see Baker v. S.S. Cristobal, 488 F.2d 331, 1974 A.M.C. 36 (5th Cir.1974). There the plaintiff complained of a back injury incurred when he and his co-worker were lifting a pallet weighing 200 to 250 pounds while he was straddling the coupling apparatus at the end of the wagon on to which the pallet was being lifted. In affirming a dismissal of the action the court quoted with approval that statement of the district court that "[a]t the most, it can be said only that, engaged in a plan of operation that was safe, the plaintiff chose to employ a particular method that was unsafe, and this does not render the vessel unseaworthy."

What was the net effect of *Usner?* Gilmore and Black quip that apart from possible jurisprudential implications, "there is much less in Usner than meets the eye." Law of Admiralty 389 (1975). Did it aid Judge Friendly by giving him a more accurate time piece to use in the *Grillea* type cases? Notice that Mr. Justice Marshall, who in *Reid* had warned of letting extensions of the *Grillea* doctrine become a Trojan horse of the warranty of seaworthiness, joined the *Usner* majority. Indeed his vote was necessary.

The Ryan Cycle

Indemnity of the Vessel by the Master Stevedore

In Halcyon Lines v. Haenn Ship Ceiling & Refitting Corp., 342 U.S. 282, 72 S.Ct. 277, 1952 A.M.C. 1, 96 L.Ed. 318 (1952), the Court held that in a case in which a longshoreman injury had been produced partially through the fault of the vesselowner and partially through the fault of the servants of the longshoreman's employer, and the longshoreman brought his action against the vesselowner, the vesselowner could not maintain an action against the longshoreman's employer seeking contribution. In American Stevedores, Inc. v. Porello, 330 U.S. 446, 67 S.Ct. 847, 1947 A.M.C. 349, 91 L.Ed. 1011 (1947), however, it had been recognized that a contract for the provision of stevedoring services could provide for indemnity by the stevedoring contractor. The case was remanded for a consideration of the particular provision in the written contract. In Ryan Stevedoring Co. v. Pan–Atlantic S.S. Corp., 350 U.S. 124, 76 S.Ct. 232, 1956 A.M.C. 9, 100 L.Ed. 133 (1956), it was held that even in the absence of a written provision, every stevedoring contract contains a "warranty of workmanlike service," making the stevedoring company liable over to the vesselowner for amounts the vesselowner is called upon to pay to an injured longshoreman under the *Sieracki* doctrine when the unseaworthiness that formed the basis of the action against the vesselowner was produced through the fault of the contracting stevedoring company.

In the *Ryan* case, the plaintiff had been injured when a roll of pulpboard broke loose and struck him during an unloading operation. The absence of proper wedges and dunnage established the fact that the cargo had been improperly stowed. It had been stowed by a stevedoring company in another port under an agreement, evidenced by letters, to supply all stevedoring services in the port, but without a written contract containing an indemnity clause. The Court held that the warranty of workmanlike service is to be implied in all such contracts, and therefore the stevedoring company was liable over to the vessel owner cast in damages because the vessel was unseaworthy in respect of the proper stowage of its cargo. The Court declined to reexamine the decision in *Halcyon,* and predicated the liability over purely on contractual grounds. In later cases it rejected the contention that the liability rested on a distinction between active, as against passive, or primary, as against secondary, negligence. Weyerhaeuser S.S. Corp. v. Nacirema Operating Co., 355 U.S. 563, 78 S.Ct. 438, 1958 A.M.C. 501, 2 L.Ed.2d 491 (1958). It rejected the contention that it rested upon a direct contractual relation between the negligent party and the vesselowner. Waterman Steamship Corp. v. Dugan & McNamara, Inc., 364 U.S. 421, 81 S.Ct. 200, 1960 A.M.C. 2260, 5 L.Ed.2d 169 (1960). It held that negligence in bringing into play an unseaworthy condition purely the product of earlier negligence of the vesselowner was enough to trigger the warranty. Crumady v. The J.H. Fisser, discussed earlier in another connection. Finally in Italia Societa per Azioni di Navigazione v. Oregon Stevedoring Co., 376 U.S. 315, 84 S.Ct. 748, 1964 A.M.C. 1075, 11 L.Ed.2d 732 (1964) it held that the contracting stevedore was liable over to the vesselowner in a case in which equipment belonging to the stevedore failed through a latent defect.

In short, as the warranty of seaworthiness that would cast the vesselowner grew absolute, so, too, did the warranty of workmanlike service. The result, of course, was to rest on the master stevedore the cost of providing full indemnity to longshoremen injured in loading or unloading ships, despite the limitation of his liability contemplated by the LHWCA in 1927.

In *Ryan,* Mr. Justice Burton states, "The shipowner's claim here also is not a claim for contribution from a joint tortfeasor. Consequently, the considerations which led to the decision in Halcyon Lines v. Haenn Ship Corp. * * * are not applicable * * *" What were the "considerations" that led to *Halcyon?* In his dissent, Mr. Justice Black notes that these considerations were that if the Court allowed contribution the stevedore employer would be called upon to pay part of the judgment, which would "frustrate this [Act's] purpose to protect employers who were subjected to absolute liability by the Act." If this was the purpose, isn't it odd that the Act would be frustrated less by saddling the employer with the full judgment than by requiring him to pay part of it?

But Mr. Justice Burton is correct, is he not, in stating that the considerations that led to the decision in *Halcyon* did not govern *Ryan,* an action against a non-employing stevedoring company? Why was it necessary, however, to draw a distinction between contribution and indemnity under a warranty?

Ultimately these considerations were back before the Court. In Cooper Stevedoring Co., Inc. v. Fritz Kopke, Inc., 417 U.S. 106, 94 S.Ct. 2174, 40 L.Ed.2d 694, 1974 A.M.C. 537 (1974), supra, the vessel was loaded in part in Mobile with palletized crates of cargo. It then proceeded to Houston where longshoremen began loading sacked cargo. The Houston longshoremen had to use the top of the tier of crates loaded in Mobile as a floor on which to walk while stowing the Houston cargo. One of the longshoremen stepped in a gap between the crates and was injured. The injured longshoreman brought his action for unseaworthiness against the owner and the time charterer, and they filed third-party complaints against both the Mobile and Houston stevedores. The district court divided the damages equally between the vessel (treating the various interests in the vessel as one) and the Mobile stevedore. The Mobile stevedore appealed and the vessel cross-appealed, contending that it should have been granted full indemnity. The court of appeals affirmed. The vessel did not seek certiorari on the full indemnity issue, so when the case reached the Supreme Court the only question for consideration was the contribution issue. It held that when the employment factor is absent, the considerations that led to the *Halcyon* decision are wanting, so that contribution is proper.

The Court adhered to the view that in actions involving injury to an employee in which the third party shipowner is the defendant, the shipowner may not seek contribution from the employer. It distinguished the decision in Atlantic Coast Line R. Co. v. Erie Lackawanna R. Co., 406 U.S. 340, 92 S.Ct. 1550, 32 L.Ed.2d 110, 1972 A.M.C. 1121 (1972). There the plaintiff, an employee of a railroad, was working on a car float owned by his employer when he was injured allegedly because of a defective footboard and handbrake on a box car owned by a second railroad. He sued the owner of the box car and it sought contribution from the employing railroad. In *Cooper* the petitioner argued that any protection against payment over and above compensation under the LHWCA was ephemeral, since under the *Yaka* doctrine, (see infra) the injured employee could have sued the employer directly, claiming unseaworthiness. In rejecting this argument, the Court indicated that had this been the case the railroads would not have been joint tortfeasors since the liability for unseaworthiness is absolute. Why is the *Cooper* case different in this regard? There the vessel was found to be unseaworthy.

Navigable Waters Pro Hac Vice

Accidents to Longshoremen and Harbor Workers on Land

It has already been pointed out that the LHWCA Act of 1927 was limited in its application to occurrences on navigable waters. Since the pier is regarded as an extension of the land, it had no application to accidents that occurred on the pier. What of actions under the *Sieracki* doctrine? Under the holding in the *Nordenholt* case, such accidents were governed by the state law, including the state workmen's compensation acts. In 1948, the admiralty jurisdiction was extended to cover actions for damage or injuries "caused by a vessel on navigable water, notwithstanding that such damage or injury be done or consummated on land." See Chapter 3, supra.

In Gutierrez v. Waterman Steamship Corp., 373 U.S. 206, 83 S.Ct. 1185, 1963 A.M.C. 1649, 10 L.Ed.2d 297 (1963), discussed at p. 112, in connection with the application of the Extension Act, the facts were stated as follows by Mr. Justice White:

> "Petitioner, a longshoreman unloading the S.S. Hastings at Ponce, Puerto Rico, slipped on some loose beans spilled on the dock and suffered personal injuries * * *
>
> "The cargo of beans was packed in broken and defective bags, some of which were being repaired by coopers aboard ship during unloading. Beans spilled out of the bags during unloading, including some from one bag which broke open during unloading, and the scattering of beans about the surface of the pier created a dangerous condition for the longshoreman who had to work there. The shipowner knew or should have known that injury was likely to result to persons who would have to work around the beans spilled from defective bags * * * "

The action was in two counts, one for negligence and one for unseaworthiness. The negligence count will be discussed later. As to the unseaworthiness count, Mr. Justice White observed that two questions were raised, "(1) whether the use of defective cargo containers constitutes unseaworthiness, and (2) whether the shipowner's warranty of seaworthiness extends to longshoremen on the pier who are unloading the ship's cargo." As to the first, he indicated that the answer was controlled by such cases as Atlantic & Gulf Stevedores, Inc. v. Ellerman Lines, Ltd., 369 U.S. 355, 82 S.Ct. 780, 1962 A.M.C. 565, 7 L.Ed.2d 798 (1962), in which it was held that defective bands around a bale of burlap cloth would render the vessel unseaworthy, and circuit cases holding that improper stowage constituted unseaworthiness. The second question he treated as one of first impression, though he noted circuit authority on the subject. The court of appeal had held, building on O'Donnel v. Great Lakes Dredge and Dock Co., holding that recovery could be had under the Jones Act when injury took place on land, that unseaworthiness was a tort arising out of maritime "status or relations" and therefore "cognizable by the maritime [substantive] law whether it arises on sea or on land." Mr. Justice White concluded,

> "We agree with this reading of the case law and hold that the duty to provide a seaworthy ship and gear, including cargo containers, applies to longshoremen unloading the ship whether they are standing aboard ship or on the pier."

The decision in *Gutierrez* afforded yet another growth point in the liability of the vesselowner due to defectiveness or negligent use of equipment provided by the master stevedore.   Mr. Justice White, in his discussion of jurisdiction, had indicated that the Extension Act of 1948 conferred jurisdiction whenever the injury was the product of whatever breach of duty the vessel might be charged with.   In discussing the reach of unseaworthiness he indicated that the vessel's warranty extended to the pier because the duty to provide a seaworthy vessel was grounded in status rather than in location.   This led to the possibility that a longshoreman injured by the defective equipment of his employer employed wholly on the pier would cast the vesselowner in damages for unseaworthiness.   The argument could run thus: (1) the longshoreman is a "seaman" protected by the warranty of seaworthiness of the vessel and its equipment, i.e., he is a seaman pro hac vice (*Sieracki*); (2) the vesselowner warrants not only the vessel, but its equipment, including the equipment provided by the master stevedore (*Petterson*); (3) if the injury is produced by the unseaworthiness of the vessel or its equipment, the vessel is liable whether the injury occurred on sea or on land (*Gutierrez*).   The conclusion is that equipment used in loading or unloading the vessel is warranted by the vesselowner whether or not it is integrated into the equipment of the vessel, and whether or not the accident occurs on sea or on land.   See, e.g., Judge Hufstedler's opinion in Gebhard v. S.S. Hawaiian Legislator, 425 F.2d 1303, 1970 A.M.C. 2056 (9th Cir.1970).

So long as the decision in *Gutierrez* is looked upon as an application of the Extension Act of 1948, it was not a startling extension of the law.   One may quarrel with the process by which the bean bags are analogized to pallets to bring them within the concept of "equipment" of the ship.   This was the basis of Mr. Justice Harlan's dissent.   But assuming that they were ship's equipment, the application was a straightforward application of the Act.   The observation that the warranty to the longshoreman was based on status was probably intended merely to indicate that the reason the vessel warranted its seaworthiness to the longshoreman lay in the fact that he was "doing ship's work," not because he was on the ship.   Therefore the injury from the breach did not have to take place on the vessel.   The decision nowhere purported to deal with the *Petterson* kind of case.   Mr. Justice White's discussion of the first question he presented, whether the use of defective cargo containers constituted a breach of the warranty of seaworthiness, would have been total surplusage if he had intended to announce a rule that the "status" of longshoremen carried with it a warranty of all the stevedore's equipment.

Nevertheless between 1963 and 1971 there developed a considerable body of authority to the effect that failure of even purely shore-based equipment provided by the master stevedore was within the vessel's warranty of seaworthiness.   This view was rejected in some cases.   See, e.g., Forkin v. Furness Withy & Co., 323 F.2d 638, 1964 A.M.C. 356 (2d Cir.1963), in which Judge Friendly held, over a dissent by Judge Smith, that a conveyor belt maintained on the pier to establish connection with the vessel was not warranted by the vessel, at least until it had become attached to the vessel.   Cf. Deffes v. Federal Barge Lines, Inc., 361 F.2d 422, 1966 A.M.C. 1415 (5th Cir.1966).

Thus the application of the "status" concept had the potential of expanding the duty of the vessel owner to cover all injuries to longshoremen in the course of the loading or unloading operation, for it has already been seen that pre-*Usner,* the law was developing in the direction of equating operating negligence to unseaworthiness.

This process was cut off by the Supreme Court in Victory Carriers, Inc. v. Law, 404 U.S. 202, 92 S.Ct. 418, 30 L.Ed.2d 383, 1972 A.M.C. 1 (1971). In *Victory Carriers,* the plaintiff was a longshoreman who operated a forklift moving cargo from one point on the pier to another point alongside the vessel, where subsequently it would be hoisted on the vessel by the ship's gear. The forklift belonged to the plaintiff's employer, the stevedore. While he was thus employed the overhead protection rack on the forklift came loose and fell on him. The district court granted summary judgment for the defendant shipowner, and the plaintiff appealed. The Fifth Circuit reversed, relying on the *Sieracki* and *Gutierrez* cases. The Supreme Court in turn reversed. *Gutierrez,* it emphasized, dealt with the *ship's* equipment. *Petterson* and *Rogers* were cases involving injuries in the ship's hold by defective apparatus attached to the ship's gear. Mr. Justice White did not retreat from *Gutierrez,* observing that in that case jurisdiction "was clearly present."

The effect of the *Victory Carriers* decision on the *Petterson-Rogers* doctrine is more difficult to calculate. Mr. Justice White's reference to these cases was brief. "In * * * Petterson and * * * Rogers * * * the Court decided without opinion that an unseaworthiness recovery would be possible to a longshoreman injured by equipment brought aboard ship by the stevedore company. In both these cases, the accident occurred on navigable water: both longshoremen were injured while in the hold of a ship by defective apparatus attached to the ship's gear." Whether he intended to suggest that attachment to the ship's gear was an element of those decisions is a matter for speculation. There is authority, however, for the proposition that attachment of equipment to the vessel is not enough to sustain an action for an accident on the pier. See Jones v. Fruchtreederei Harald, Schuldt & Co., 347 F.Supp. 853, 1973 A.M.C. 1153 (E.D.La.1972), aff'd 476 F.2d 246 (5th Cir.1973), in which it was held that the fact that shore-based equipment was rigged so that control switches were located both aboard the vessel and on shore.

The Longshoreman Hired Directly

Reed v. Steamship Yaka

It will be remembered that in *Sieracki,* Mr. Justice Rutledge stated "We may take it therefore that Congress intended the remedy of compensation to be exclusive as against the employer * * *. The legislation therefore did not nullify any right of the longshoreman against the owner of the ship, except possibly in the instance, presumably rare, where he may be hired by the owner." In Reed v. Steamship Yaka, 373 U.S. 410, 83 S.Ct. 1349, 1963 A.M.C. 1373, 10 L.Ed.2d 448 (1963), this "presumably rare" circumstance arose. In *Reed,* plaintiff was an employee of a bare boat charterer of the vessel. He was engaged in the loading of the vessel when he was injured through the breaking of a pallet being used in the loading. The pallet was furnished by the bare boat charterer, the plaintiff's employer. It broke because of a latent defect in one of its boards. The action was brought in rem on the theory that despite the lack of in personam liability, the action would lie against the ship. The Third Circuit held that neither the vesselowner nor the charterer could be held personally liable and absent personal liability there could be no liability in rem. The Supreme Court granted certiorari to resolve the question of liability in rem absent personal liability, reserved in Guzman v. Pichirilo, 369 U.S. 698, 82 S.Ct. 1095, 1962 A.M.C. 1142, 8 L.Ed.2d 205 (1962). Mr. Justice Black, speaking for a majority of seven, found it unnecessary to reach the question of in rem liability without liability in personam, since he found that under the circumstances of the case the charterer was liable. He conceded that the action was barred by the express terms of the LHWCA. He noted, however, that the Court had held in the *Ryan* series of cases that a master stevedore must ultimately shoulder the liability for the unseaworthiness of the vessel. This being so, he indicated that it would make no economic sense to permit the bare boat charterer to escape liability because he was at the same time employer of the longshoreman. It should be noted that Mr. Justice Black dissented in *Ryan*, decided prior to *The Yaka*, and in *Italia Societa*, decided after *The Yaka*, both times laying the blame for the rape of the LHWCA on the majority. In *The Yaka*, Justices Harlan and Stewart, both in the majority in *Ryan* and *Italia Societa*, dissented, suggesting that Mr. Justice Black had simply repealed a plain provision in the statute. They defended the decision in *Ryan* on the ground that it did *not* contravene any provision of the statute. Who was to blame? Or did it all begin with *Sieracki*? See Judge Friendly's dissent in Skibinski v. Waterman S.S. Co., 360 F.2d 539, 1966 A.M.C. 873 (2d Cir.1966). ("Indeed, I suspect we would have long since revolted against a principle which capriciously imposes liability on a thoroughly well equipped ship if we did not know that in the usual case, where the plaintiff 'seaman' is shore-based, the story will have a happy ending for the ship since liability will rest on her only for a moment and then will be transferred to the stevedoring contractor. By very definition, improper use of ship's equipment triggers the contractor's warranty of workmanlike service, Ryan Stevedoring Co. v. Pan–Atlantic S.S. Corp. * * * the ship regularly impleads the stevedore, and there the burden falls. To me this argues for a restrictive rather than an expansive notion of unseaworthiness in these situations; courts should not strain to use the ship, innocent in every realistic sense, merely as a conduit for imposing on the negligent employer a liability to his employees differing from the absolute but limited one which Congress made exclusive by section 5 of the Longshoremen's and Harbor Workers' Compensation Act * * *. Of course the statute did not impair an injured longshoreman's right against third parties who have wronged him * * *. But proper respect for what Congress was 'driving at', see Johnson v. United States, 163 Fed. 30, 32 (1st Cir.1908)(Holmes, J.), ought to lead judges away from a doctrine which so frustrates the legislative purpose by imposing a

transitory liability on a third party that has turned over a thoroughly
seaworthy vessel to a qualified stevedore. If the benefits under the
Compensation Act are inadequate, the remedy lies in action by Congress,
not in judicial legerdemain which helps one longshoreman but does nothing
for another whose situation would appear similar to everyone except those
lawyers and judges who have had to accustom themselves to the witty
diversities of this branch of the law.'')

The decision in *The Yaka* was reiterated in Jackson v. Lykes Bros.
Steamship Co., 386 U.S. 731, 87 S.Ct. 1419, 1967 A.M.C. 584, 18 L.Ed.2d
488 (1967).

2.   THE LONGSHORE AND HARBOR WORKERS' COMPENSATION ACT

A. COVERAGE

Chesapeake and Ohio Ry. v. Schwalb

Supreme Court of the United States, 1989.
493 U.S. 40, 110 S.Ct. 381, 1989 A.M.C. 2965, 107 L.Ed.2d 278.

■ JUSTICE WHITE delivered the opinion of the Court.

Nancy J. Schwalb and William McGlone, respondents in No. 87–1979, were
employees of petitioner Chesapeake and Ohio Railway Company (C & O),
and were injured while working at petitioner's terminal in Newport News,
Virginia, where coal was being loaded from railway cars to a ship on
navigable waters. Robert T. Goode, respondent in No. 88–127, was injured
while working for petitioner Norfolk and Western Railway Company (N &
W) at its coal loading terminal in Norfolk, Virginia. If respondents'
injuries are covered by the Longshore and Harbor Workers' Compensation
Act (LHWCA or Act), 44 Stat. 1424, as amended, 33 U.S.C. §§ 901–950
(1982 ed. and Supp. V), the remedy provided by that Act is exclusive and
resort may not be had to the Federal Employers' Liability Act (FELA), 35
Stat. 65, as amended, 45 U.S.C. §§ 5140 (1982 ed. and Supp. V), which
provides a negligence cause of action for railroad employees. The Supreme
Court of Virginia held in both cases that the LHWCA was not applicable
and that respondents could proceed to trial under the FELA. We reverse.

I

At the C & O facility, a mechanical conveyor-belt system transports coal
from railroad hopper cars to colliers berthed at the piers. The loading
process begins when a hopper car is rolled down an incline to a mechanical
dumper which is activated by trunnion rollers and which dumps the coal
through a hopper onto conveyor belts. The belts carry the coal to a loading
tower from which it is poured into the hold of a ship. The trunnion rollers
are located at each end of the dumper. Typically some coal spills out onto
the rollers and falls below the conveyor belts during the loading process.
This spilled coal must be removed frequently to prevent fouling of the
loading equipment. Respondents Nancy Schwalb and William McGlone

both worked at C & O's terminal as laborers doing housekeeping and janitorial services. One of their duties was to clean spilled coal from the trunnion rollers and from underneath the conveyor belts. Both also performed ordinary janitorial services at the loading site. McGlone's right arm was severely injured while he was clearing away coal beneath a conveyor belt. Schwalb suffered a serious head injury when she fell while walking along a catwalk in the dumper area. At the time, she was on her way to clean the trunnion rollers.

At N & W's terminal, a loaded coal car is moved to the dumper where it is locked into place by a mechanical device called a "retarder." The dumper turns the car upside down. The coal falls onto conveyor belts and is delivered to the ship via a loader. Respondent Robert Goode was a pier machinist at N & W's terminal. His primary job was to maintain and repair loading equipment, including the dumpers and conveyor belts. Goode injured his hand while repairing a retarder on one of N & W's dumpers. Loading at that dumper was stopped for several hours while Goode made the repairs.

The three respondents commenced separate actions in Virginia trial courts under the FELA. Petitioners responded in each case by challenging jurisdiction on the ground that the LHWCA provided respondents' sole and exclusive remedy. See 33 U.S.C. § 905(a)(1982 ed., Supp. V). All three trial courts held evidentiary hearings and concluded that respondents were employees covered by the LHWCA. The suits were dismissed and respondents appealed. The Supreme Court of Virginia consolidated the appeals of Schwalb and McGlone and reversed the dismissals. 235 Va. 27. 365 S.E.2d 742 (1988).

Relying on one of its earlier decisions, White v. Norfolk & Western R. Co., 217 Va. 823, 232 S.E.2d 807 (1977), the court stated that the key question was whether an employee's activities had a realistically significant relationship to the loading of cargo on ships. 235 Va., at 31, 365 S.E.2d, at 744. Pointing to expressions in our opinion in Northeast Marine Terminal Co. v. Caputo, 432 U.S. 249, 97 S.Ct. 2348, 53 L.Ed.2d 320 (1977), that landward coverage of the LHWCA was limited to the " 'essential elements' " of loading and unloading, the court concluded that "the 'essential elements' standard is more nearly akin to the 'significant relationship' standard we adopted in White" than the broader construction argued by C & O. 235 Va., at 33, 365 S.E.2d, at 745. Applying the *White* standard, the court ruled that employees performing purely maintenance tasks should be treated no differently under the Act than those performing purely clerical tasks and held that Schwalb and McGlone were not covered. The court later dealt with the Goode case in an unpublished order, relying on its decision in Schwalb and reversing the trial court's judgment that an employee who repairs loading equipment is covered by the LHWCA. No. 870252 (Apr. 22, 1988), App. to Pet. for Cert. in No. 88–127, p. 17A.

Because the Supreme Court of Virginia's holding in these cases was contrary to the position adopted by Federal Courts of Appeals, see, e.g., Harmon v. Baltimore & Ohio R. Co., 239 U.S.App.D.C. 239, 244–245, 741

F.2d 1398, 1403–1404 (1984); Sea-Land Services, Inc. v. Director, Office of Workers' Compensation Programs, 685 F.2d 1121, 1123 (C.A.9 1982)(*per curiam*); Hullinghorst Industries, Inc. v. Carroll, 650 F.2d 750, 755, 756 (C.A.5 1981); Garvey Grain Co. v. Director, Office of Workers' Compensation Programs, 639 F.2d 366, 370 (C.A.7 1981)(per curiam); Prolerized New England Co. v. Benefits Review Board, 637 F.2d 30, 37 (C.A.1 1980), we granted certiorari to resolve the conflict. 489 U.S. 1009, 1010, 109 S.Ct. 1116, 103 L.Ed.2d 180 (1989).

II

For the LHWCA to apply, the injured person must be injured in the course of his employment, 33 U.S.C. § 902(2)(1982 ed.); his employer must have employees who are employed in maritime employment. § 902(4); the injury must occur "upon the navigable waters of the United States (including any adjoining pier, wharf, dry dock, terminal building way, marine railway, or other adjoining area customarily used by an employer in loading, unloading, repairing, dismantling or building a vessel)," 33 U.S.C. § 903(a)(1982 ed., Supp. V); and the employee who is injured within that area must be a "person engaged in maritime employment, including any longshoreman or other person engaged in longshoring operations, and any harborworker including a ship repairman, shipbuilder, and ship-breaker, but such term does not include—" certain enumerated categories of employees, § 902(3). It is undisputed that the first three of these requirements are satisfied in these cases. The issue is whether the employees were engaged in maritime employment within the meaning of § 902(3),

The employment that is maritime within the meaning of § 902(3) expressly includes the specified occupations but obviously is not limited to those callings. Herb's Welding, Inc. v. Gray, 470 U.S. 414, 423, n. 9, 105 S.Ct. 1421, 1427, n. 9, 84 L.Ed.2d 406 (1985). P.C. Pfeiffer Co. v. Ford, 444 U.S. 69, 77–78, n. 7, 100 S.Ct. 328, 334, n. 7, 62 L.Ed.2d 225 (1979). The additional reach of the section has been left to the courts sitting in review of decisions made in the Department of Labor. which is charged with administering the Act. In the course of considerable litigation, including several cases in this Court, it has been clearly decided that, aside from the specified occupations, land-based activity occurring within the § 903 situs will be deemed maritime only if it is an integral or essential part of loading or unloading a vessel. This is a sensible construction of § 902(a) when read together with 903(a), particularly in light of the purpose of the 1972 amendments to the LHWCA which produced those sections.

Prior to 1972, the Act applied only to injuries occurring on navigable waters. Longshoremen loading or unloading a ship were covered on the ship and the gangplank but not shoreward, even though they were performing the same functions whether on or off the ship. Congress acted to obviate this anomaly: § 903(a) extended coverage to the area adjacent to the ship that is normally used for loading and unloading, but restricted the covered activity within that area to maritime employment. Pub.L. 92–576, 86 Stat. 1251. There were also specific exclusions in both § 902(3) and

§ 903; those exclusions were expanded in 1984. See Pub.L. 98–426, § 2(a), 98 Stat. 1639.

In Northeast Marine Terminal Co. v. Caputo, supra, we held that the 1972 amendments were to be liberally construed and that the LHWCA, as amended, covered all those on the situs involved in the essential or integral elements of the loading or unloading process. Id., 432 U.S., at 267, 268, 271, 97 S.Ct., at 2359, 2359, 2361. But those on the situs not performing such tasks are not covered. Id., at 267, 97 S.Ct., at 2359. This has been our consistent view. P.C. Pfeiffer Co. v. Ford, supra, held that workers performing no more than one integral part of the loading or unloading process were entitled to compensation under the Act. Id., 444 U.S. at 82, 100 S.Ct., at 337. We also reiterated in Herb's Welding, Inc. v. Gray, supra, that the maritime employment requirement as applied to land-based work other than longshoring and the other occupations named in § 902(3) is an occupational test focusing on loading and unloading. Those not involved in those functions do not have the benefit of the Act. Id., 470 U.S., at 424, 105 S.Ct., at 1427–1428.

In the cases before us, respondents were connected with the loading process only by way of the repair and maintenance services that they were performing when they were injured. There is no claim that if those services are not maritime employment, respondents are nevertheless covered by the LHWCA. See Northeast Marine Terminal Co. v. Caputo, 432 U.S., at 272–274, 97 S.Ct. at 2361–2363. Only if the tasks they were performing are maritime employment are respondents in these cases covered by the Act.

Although we have not previously so held, we are quite sure that employees who are injured while maintaining or repairing equipment essential to the loading or unloading process are covered by the Act. Such employees are engaged in activity that is an integral part of and essential to those overall processes. That is all that § 902(3) requires. Coverage is not limited to employees who are denominated "longshoremen" or who physically handle the cargo. Nor are maintenance employees removed from coverage if they also have duties not integrally connected with the loading or unloading functions. Someone who repairs or maintains a piece of loading equipment is just as vital to and an integral part of the loading process as the the operator of the equipment. When machinery breaks down or becomes clogged or fouled because of the lack of cleaning, the loading process stops until the difficulty is cured. It is irrelevant that an employee's contribution to the loading process is not continuous or that repair or maintenance is not always needed. Employees are surely covered when they are injured while performing a task integral to loading a ship.

Our conclusion that repair and maintenance to essential equipment are reached by the Act is buttressed by the fact that every Court of Appeals to have addressed the issue has arrived at the same result. See the cases cited supra, at 383–384. As evidenced by the amicus brief of the United States filed in these cases, the Secretary of Labor also agrees that such repair and maintenance are engaged in maritime employment within the meaning of § 902(3), and the Benefits Review Board also has consistently taken this view, see, e.g., Wuellet v. Scapose Sand & Gravel Co., 18 BRBS 108, 110–111 (1986); De Robertis v. Oceanic Container Service, Inc., 14 BRBS 284, 286–287 (1981); Cabezas v. Oceanic Container Service, Inc., 11 BRBS 279, 283–288 (1979), and cases cited therein.

III

Applying the standard expressed in our cases, we conclude that each of the respondents is covered by the LHWCA. The Supreme Court of Virginia held that Goode was not covered because in its view repair of equipment essential to the loading process was not maritime employment. This was error. It makes no difference that the particular kind of repair Goode was doing might be considered traditional railroad work or might be done by railroad employees wherever railroad cars are unloaded. The determinative consideration is that the ship loading process could not continue unless the retarder that Goode worked on was operating properly. It is notable that the loading actually was stopped while Goode made the repairs and that one of his supervisors apparently expressed the desire that Goode hurry up so that the loading could continue.

Respondents Schwalb and McGlone also were performing duties essential to the overall loading process. There is testimony in the record that if the coal which spills onto the rollers is not periodically removed, the rollers may become clogged and the dumper will become inoperable. App. 57, 92. The same is true of the coal that falls beneath the conveyor belts. Ibid. Testimony indicated that a buildup of such coal could eventually foul the conveyors and cause them to be shut down. Equipment cleaning that is necessary to keep machines operative is a form of maintenance and is only different in degree from repair work. Employees who are injured on the situs while performing these essential functions are covered by the LHWCA.

IV

For the reasons given above, the judgments of the Supreme Court of Virginia are reversed.

It is so ordered.

■ JUSTICE BLACKMUN, with whom JUSTICE MARSHALL and JUSTICE O'CONNOR join, concurring.

Although I join the opinion of the Court, I write separately to emphasize that I do not understand our decision as in any way repudiating the "amphibious workers" doctrine this Court articulated in Northeast Marine Terminal Co. v. Caputo, 432 U.S. 249, 272–274, 97 S.Ct. 2348, 2361–2363, 53 L.Ed.2d 320 (1977). We hold today that respondents Schwalb, McGlone, and Goode are covered by the LHWCA since they were injured while performing tasks essential to the process of loading ships. In light of *Northeast Marine Terminal Co.*, however, it is not essential to our holding that the employees were injured while actually engaged in these tasks.

They are covered by the LHWCA even if, at the moment of injury, they had been performing other work that was not essential to the loading process.

As the Court explained in *Northeast Marine Terminal Co.*, Congress, in amending the LHWCA in 1972, intended to solve the problem that under the pre–1972 Act employees would walk in and out of LHWCA coverage during their workday, if they performed some tasks over water and other tasks ashore. Congress wanted

> "to provide continuous coverage throughout their employment to these amphibious workers who, without the 1972 Amendments, would be covered only for part of their activity. It seems clear, therefore, that when Congress said it wanted to cover 'longshoremen,' it had in mind persons whose employment is such that they spend at least some of their time in indisputably longshoring operations and who, without the 1972 Amendments, would be covered for only part of their activity." Id., at 273, 97 S.Ct., at 2362.

Later, in P.C. Pfeiffer Co. v. Ford, 444 U.S. 69, 100 S.Ct. 328, 62 L.Ed.2d 225 (1979), we said that the "crucial factor" in determining LHWCA coverage "is the nature of the activity to which a worker may be assigned." Id., at 82, 100 S.Ct., at 337 (emphasis added). Although the employees in Pfeiffer were actually engaged in longshoring work at the time of their injuries, we noted: "Our observation that Ford and Bryant were engaged in maritime employment at the time of their injuries does not undermine the holding of *Northeast Marine Terminal Co.* ... that a worker is covered if he spends some of his time in indisputably longshoring operations." Id., 444 U.S., at 83, n. 18, 100 S.Ct., at 337, n. 18.

To suggest that a worker like Schwalb, McGlone, or Goode, who spends part of his time maintaining or repairing loading equipment, and part of his time on other tasks (even general clean up, or repair of equipment not used for loading), is covered only if he is injured while engaged in the former kind of work, would bring the "walking in and out of coverage" problem back with a vengeance. We said in Northeast Marine Terminal Co. that "to exclude [a worker] from the Act's coverage in the morning but include him in the afternoon would be to revitalize the shifting and fortuitous coverage that Congress intended to eliminate." 432 U.S., at 274, 97 S.Ct., at 2362–2363.

I join the Court's opinion on the specific understanding that it casts no shadow on the continuing validity of *Northeast Marine Terminal Co.*

■ JUSTICE STEVENS, concurring in the judgment.

Had this case arisen in 1977, I would have subscribed to the interpretation of the Longshoremen's and Harbor Workers' Compensation Act that the Supreme Court of Virginia adopted in White v. Norfolk and Western R. Co., 217 Va. 823, 232 S.E.2d 807, cert. denied 434 U.S. 860, 98 S.Ct. 186, 54 L.Ed.2d 133 (1977). I continue to believe that the text of the Act "merely provides coverage for people who do the work of longshoremen and harbor worker—amphibious persons who are directly involved in moving freight onto and off ships, or in building, repairing, or destroying ships," and that the Act's history in no way clouds the text's plain import. See Director,

OWCP v. Perini North River Associates, 459 U.S. 297, 328, 342, 103 S.Ct. 634, 652–653, 660, 74 L.Ed.2d 465 (1983)(STEVENS, J., dissenting). The *White* opinion reaches a similar conclusion. See *White*, 217 Va., at 833, 232 S.E.2d, at 813 (employing a "direct involvement" test).

Yet, as the majority correctly observes, *ante*, at 383–384, the Federal Courts of Appeals have consistently interpreted the Act's status requirement to encompass repair and maintenance workers. That uniform and consistent course of decision has established a reasonably clear rule of law that I feel bound to respect. Cf. Commissioner v. Fink, 483 U.S. 89, 102–103, 107 S.Ct. 2729, 2736–2737, 97 L.Ed.2d 74 (1987)(STEVENS, J., dissenting). I therefore concur in the Court's judgment.

NOTE

In *Schwalb*, all three injured workers were employed to work on the pier. Goode is referred to as a "pier machinest." Schwalb and McGlone were stated to be working at the terminal, "doing housekeeping and janitorial services," including cleaning up spilled coal and also performing "ordinary janitorial services at the loading site." Does it matter that they were terminal employees?

In Etheridge v. Norfolk & Western Ry. Co., 9 F.3d 1087 (4th Cir.1993), a brakeperson employed by the railroad at a railroad terminal, located adjacent to the Elizabeth River in Norfolk, Virginia, where the coal is loaded on vessels, and which receives, processes, and stores railroad cars full of coal until they are ready to be loaded, was held to be engaged in a maritime employment when she was injured pinching a railroad car with a pinchbar to send it down the incline to the ships. The accident occurred in a yard adjacent to the pier, and from all that appears in the opinion, the injured worker was generally employed in the yard. The court of appeals held that since the employment was maritime, the LHWCA was the injured party's exclusive remedy and she could not sue the railroad under the FELA.

But a railroad engineer in a switchyard crew who positioned rail cars for discharge of coal into the vessels and discharge of iron ore from the vessels into the cars, was not engaged in a maritime occupation and therefore came under the FELA and not the LHWCA. Stowers v. Consolidated Rail Corp., 985 F.2d 292, 1993 A.M.C. 2992 (DRO).

In Pittman Mechanical Contractors, Inc. v. Director, OWCP, 35 F.3d 122 (4th Cir.1994), the injured workman was a welder employed by a welding contractor which had contracted to remove an existing pipeline on the pier and replace it with a new one. The pipe line was designed for use in supplying vessels with steam, water, and fuel. During the construction of the new pipeline the pier was closed. The court of appeals found the welder's employment was maritime.

With *Pittman* cf. Weyher/Livsey Constructors , Inc. v. Prevetire, 27 F.3d 985, 1995 A.M.C. 94 (4th Cir.1994), holding that a construction worker engaged in the building of a power plant on the pier was not covered by the LHWCA. *Prevetire* was distinguished in *Pittman* on the ground that the connection between the power plant, constructed to provide electricity for the operation of equipment needed for shipbuilding and ship-repair operations, and the loading and unloading ships was too "tenuated." Judge Sprouse dissented, being of the opinion that the case fell within the *Schwalb* analysis, and even if this were not clear, the "liberality" rule should preclude reversal of the decision of the Director in favor of coverage. In

Prevetire, the "liberal" view lies with upholding the application of the LHWCA because the alternative is the state workmen's compensations Acts, under which, generally the awards are smaller. But what of cases like *Etheridge* and *Stowers*, where the alternative is suit under the FELA?

In *Schwalb*, Justice White states "In these cases before us, respondents were connected with the loading process only by way of the repair and maintenance services that they were performing when they were injured. There is no claim that if those services are not maritime employment, respondents are nevertheless covered by the LHWCA. He did not wish to suggest that it is necessary that the harborworker be engaged in a maritime task when injured, did he? He cites *Caputo*, which is to the contrary. Is it this remark that makes Justices Blackmun, Marshall, and O'Connor cautious? But what of the railroad worker? Does he fall under the FELA in the morning and the LHWCA in the afternoon?"

The situs requirement of the Act has proved less troublesome, but not completely without problems. See Hurston v. Director OWCP, 989 F.2d 1547, 1993 A.M.C. 2477 (9th Cir.1993), holding that a decision of the Director that a structure extending from the land over navigable water, used only for oil collection and treatment met the situs requirement under the Act, despite the fact that it was not used for traditional maritime activity such as the loading and unloading or repair of vessels, was reasonable. Judge Alarcon dissented. "This question of whether the customarily used ... for" phrase in 33 U.S.C. § 903 modifies "adjoining pier" or only "other adjoining area" was discussed but not decided in the *Caputo* case. 432 U.S. 249, 97 S.Ct. 2348, 53 L.Ed.2d 320. In the circumstances of that case the argument that a pier used for stripping and stuffing containers and for storage was outside the situs provision was disposed of by pointing out that the whole terminal was used for the purposes specified in the Act. Cf. Herb's Welding, Inc. v. Gray, 470 U.S. 414, 105 S.Ct. 1421, 84 L.Ed.2d 406, 1985 A.M.C. 1700 (1985), in which the Supreme Court declined to address the question of whether drilling platform, like a pier, is a situs covered by the Act.

In Sea–Land Service, Inc. v. Director, OWCP, 540 F.2d 629, 1976 A.M.C. 1427 (3d Cir.1976) on the day of the accident the employer was engaged in moving its operations from its old facilities to new facilities a mile and a half away. The petitioner was hired as a shuttle driver, moving with a tractor trailer between the two facilities, requiring the traverse of the city streets. He began his day by hitching a trailer to his rig at Berth 52, the old facility, and moved it to Berth 90, the new facility. The evidence sustained the the fact that the trailer had been loaded with cargo off-loaded from a vessel at Berth 52. At Berth 90, he hitched the rig to a container for movement to Berth 52. There was no evidence as to what the container contained, or whether it was received from or was being delivered to a vessel. On the way to Berth 52 the rig turned over on the city street, half a mile from the water and one-third of a mile from the edge of the employer's facility. In an opinion by Judge Gibbons, the court of appeals remanded for exploration of the origin and destination of the container. "Judge Gibbons observed, We recognize that both of these statutory provisions, as amended in 1972, further state that the 'navigable waters' shall include any 'adjoining pier, wharf, dry dock, terminal, building way, marine railway or other adjoining area customarily used by an employer in loading, repairing, or building a vessel.' But we do not construe this enumeration of covered areas to be an exclusive enumeration. Congress was cautious in its language but the fact remains that it intended to expand the scope of the LHWCA to provide a federal workmen's compensation remedy for all maritime employees. We believe that Congress has exercised in full its legislative jurisdiction in admiralty. As long as the employment nexus (status) with maritime activity is maintained, the federal compensation should be available."

Although the LHWCA defines "navigable water" to include the stated shoreside locations, of course it covers accidents on wet water. The *Caputo-Schwalb* definition of "maritime employment" limiting such employment to those specifically named and those that relate to the loading and unloading of ships has been applied only to the faux water. See Director OWCP v. Perini North River Associates, 459 U.S. 297, 103 S.Ct. 634, 74 L.Ed.2d 465, 1983 A.M.C. 609 (1983). There the Court stated the facts as follows:

> "* * * Respondent Perini North River Associates ('Perini') contracted to build the foundation of a sewer treatment plant that extends approximately 700 feet over the Hudson River between 135th and 145th streets in Manhattan. The project required that Perini place large, hollow, circular pipes called caissons in the river, down to embedded rock, fill the caisons with concrete, connect the caissons together above the water with concrete beams, and place precast concrete slabs on the beams. The caissons were delivered by rail to the shore, where they were loaded on supply barges and towed across the river to await unloading and installation."

> "The injured worker, Raymond Churchill, was an employee of Perini in charge of all work performed on a cargo barge used to unload caissons and other materials from the supply barges and set caissons in position for insertion into the embedded rock. Churchill was on the deck of the cargo barge giving directions to a crane operator engaged in unloading a caisson from a supply barge when a line used to keep the caissons in position snapped and struck Churchill."

The Supreme Court held that Churchill was covered by the statute, and in an opinion by Justice O'Connor indicated that a worker injured on wet water who would have come within the coverage of the Act prior to 1972 remains with its coverage, despite a want of "a direct (or substantial) relation to navigation or commerce." She went on to observe, "We consider these employees to be 'engaged in maritime employment' not simply because they are injured in an historically maritime locale, but because they are required to perform their employment duties upon navigable waters." The Court reserved the issue of "whether such coverage extends to a worker injured while transiently or fortuitously upon actual navigable waters, or to a land-based worker injured on land who then falls into actual navigable waters." Justice Rehnquist was of the opinion that all this was unnecessary inasmuch as the work the injured worker was engaged in appeared to be that of a longshoreman. Justice Stevens dissented. The *Perini* rule has been applied in a number of cases. For example, a shoregang employee assigned as a relief cook, injured while ascending the main gangplank of a vessel, was stipulated to be covered in Guilles v. Sea–Land Service, Inc., 12 F.3d 381, 1995 A.M.C. 1223 (2d Cir.1993).

In Fontenot v. AWI, Inc., 923 F.2d 1127 (5th Cir.1991), a "wireline operator" employed as a "pipe recovery specialist" who testified that he spent equal amounts of his time working on shore, on fixed platforms, and on oil exploration and production vessels and was injured injured while unloading his equipment from the deck of a crewboat to the dock, was held to be within the Act. Although the concurring opinion in *Fontenot* emphasized that the court was not deciding the issue, the case was later read to hold that fortuitous presence would suffice. See Randall v. Chevron U.S.A., Inc., 13 F.3d 888, 1994 A.M.C. 1217 (5th Cir.1994), holding that the Act applied in the case of a mechanic killed in the course of his evacuation from a fixed platform in the Gulf of Mexico. How far can we carry this? Would a clerk in a grocery store who was evacuated during a flood be covered under the LHWCA?

To what extent have the 1972 and 1984 amendments made litmus for coverage more reliable? See Sun Ship, Inc. v. Pennsylvania, 447 U.S. 715, 100 S.Ct. 2432, 65 L.Ed.2d 458, 1980 A.M.C. 1930 (1980), in which the Court held that the *Calbeck* principle of overlap between the LHWCA and the State compensation schemes in areas maritime but local left pier injuries within the "twilight zone." The Court observed, "The line that circumscribes jurisdictional compass of the LHWCA—a compound of 'status' and 'situs'—is no less vague than its counterpart in the pre 'twilight zone' *Jensen* era."

The Master and Crew Exclusions

Under § 902(3)(G), the master and members of a crew of a vessel are excluded from the LHWCA. The test for determining who is a master or member of the crew of a vessel for these purposes is the same as the test for determining who is a a seaman under the Jones Act. The remedies are, then, mutually exclusive. McDermott Int'l v. Wilander, 498 U.S. 337, 111 S.Ct. 807, 112 L.Ed.2d 866 (1991). Bundens v. J.E. Brenneman Co., 46 F.3d 292, 1995 A.M.C.1330 (3d Cir.1995). As we have already seen, determination of seaman status for the purposes of the Jones Act and the general maritime law is fact specific and in doubtful cases is a jury question, and even a worker whose occupation is one of those specifically stated in the LHWCA to be covered by the Act can be shown to be a member of the crew of a vessel. 5–a above. The danger of mistake in the choice of remedy is discussed in Schoenbaum, Admiralty and Maritime Law, § 4–4 (1987). Professor Schoenbaum suggests that only when a court has before it both the question of seaman status and the question of coverage under the LHWCA, should the decision bar a later claim under the appropriate Act. When is that?

A petition for benefits, or acceptance of benefits voluntarily paid, does not bar a suit under the Jones Act. Southwest Marine, Inc. v. Gizoni, 502 U.S. 81, 112 S.Ct. 486, 116 L.Ed.2d 405, 1992 A.M.C. 305 (1991). The Court added, "This is so, quite obviously, because the question of coverage has never actually been litigated."

These are the words of collateral estoppel. Are the demands for damages under the Jones Act and benefits under the LHWCA the same claim so that a judgment disposing of either proceeding bars initiation of the other? Is there a difference, in this respect, between bar and merger? If a judgment dismissing an action under the Jones Act on the status issue barred a compensation claim, it would force the kind of election of remedies repudiated in *Gizoni*.

But what of merger? Should an award under the LHWCA in a contested proceeding bar an action under the Jones Act, even if the status issue was not agitated? Or, conversely, should a judgment for the plaintiff in an action under the Jones Act bar a later compensation award even if the issue of seaman status was not contested?

The preclusion doctrines exhibit other vagaries, of course. What of settlements? It has been held that a settlement approved by an administrative law judge is a formal award that bars a Jones Act suit even if the issue of coverage was not litigated in an adversarial proceeding. Sharp v. Johnson Bros. Corp., 973 F.2d 423, 426 (5th Cir.1992). See also Vilanova v. United States, 851 F.2d 1, 5–6 (1st Cir.1958). State law of finality of judgments was also applied in Trico Marine v. Champagne, 1992 A.M.C. 1883, 1992 WL 91928 (E.D.La.1992).

In Figueroa v. Campbell Industries, 45 F.3d 311, 1995 A.M.C. 793 (9th Cir.1995), the Ninth Circuit read the *Gizoni* decision to hold that a harbor worker whose relationship to a ship was close enough to justify a holding that he is a seaman has a dual status and may sue under both Acts, so long as he does not receive double recovery. Because there had been no actual litigation of the coverage issue in the compensation proceedings, the court also rejected the application of collateral estoppel. In *Figueroa*, the injured party received a compensation award for medical expenses, temporary disability, and permanent disability, and in the subsequent action under the Jones Act, sued for pain and suffering.

Persons Hired by the Master to Load,

Unload or Repair Vessels Under Eighteen Tons Net

Section 902(3)(H) also exempts from coverage persons engaged by the master to load or unload or repair any small vessel under eighteen tons net. What was the purpose of this provision. Was it to excuse the owners of small vessels dealing through the master from securing compensation under § 932? In Johnson v. G.T. Elliott, Inc., 152 Va. 121, 146 S.E. 298 (1929), it was stated that § 902(a)(1) leaves such workers where they were before the passage of the LHWCA. Where was that? Are they Jones Act seamen under *Haverty*? Are they "maritime but local" and covered under the State compensation Acts?

Government Employees

Under § 903(b) officers and employees of the United States, or of any state or foreign government, or of any political subdivision thereof are excluded from the coverage of the LHWCA.

The exclusion of employees of the United States reflects the fact that five years before the enactment of the LHWCA Congress had provided for compensation of federal government employees in the Federal Employees Compensation Act of 1916. This Act has been held to be exclusive of suits under the Suits in Admiralty Act, the Public Vessels Act, and the Tort Claims Act. See Chapter 10, supra ... But employees of "nonappropriated fund instrumentalities," such as the service "exchanges" and the Navy's "Ships Stores Ashore," are covered under the LHWCA by virtue of 5 U.S.C.A. § 8171. See Vilanova v. United States, 851 F.2d 1 (1st Cir.1988), cert. denied, 488 U.S. 1016, 109 S.Ct. 811, 102 L.Ed.2d 801 (1989).

It has been supposed that the exclusion of the employees of the States and of foreign states, and their respective subdivisions reflected concerns over sovereign immunity. Gilmore & Black, *Law of the Admiralty*, § 6–46, at 338 (1975). It is held that under § 903(b) the exclusion applies to municipal corporations, and the contention that a home rule city is not a subdivision of the State has been rejected. O'Brien v. City of N.Y., 822 F.Supp. 943, 1994 A.M.C. 787 (E.D.N.Y.1993).

While the effect of the municipal government is to preclude a claim for benefits under the Act, it also frees workers from the exclusive remedy provisions of the Act and leaves them with any other maritime remedies they may have. In Purnell v. Norned Shipping B.V., 804 F.2d 248 (3d Cir.1986), cert. denied sub nom. City of Wilmington v. Wilmington Stevedores, Inc., 480 U.S. 934, 107 S.Ct. 1576, 94 L.Ed.2d 767 (1987), it was held that a personal representative of an employee of the city, serving as a crane operator, could sue a stevedore who was lessee of the crane and also sue his employer, the city, for wrongful death under the maritime law, despite the fact that the exclusive remedy provisions of the state workers' compensation statute purported to preclude the action against the employing city. Cf. Bagrowski v. American Export Isbrandtsen Lines, Inc., 440 F.2d 502 (7th Cir.1971).

Although in Lockheed Aircraft Corp. v. United States, 460 U.S. 190, 103 S.Ct. 1033, 74 L.Ed.2d 911 (1983), it was held that the exclusive remedy provision of the FECA does not preclude a suit for indemnity or contribution brought against the United States by a third person held liable for injury to a federal employee, liability cannot be based upon 46 U.S.C.A. § 905(b), since the LHWCA does not apply to employees of the United States. Eagle–Picher Industries v. United States, 846 F.2d 888 (3d Cir.1988), cert. denied 488 U.S. 965, 109 S.Ct. 490, 102 L.Ed.2d 527 (1988).

In Parden v. Terminal R.Co., 377 U.S. 184, 84 S.Ct. 1207, 12 L.Ed.2d 233 (1964), the Supreme Court held, 5 to 4' that the operation of a railroad in interstate commerce constituted a waiver of the Eleventh Amendment and afforded State consent to be sued under the FELA. Presumably the same is true under the Jones Act.

Intoxication, Intentional Injury, Murder, and Suicide

Section 903(c) provides that no compensation shall be payable "if the injury was occasioned solely by the intoxication of the employee or by the willful intention of the employee to injure or kill himself or another." It has been held that this section does not apply to injury incurred in a good-natured scuffle with a fellow employee. General Accident, Fire & Life Assurance Corp. v. Crowell, 76 F.2d 341 (5th Cir.1935). Note that the injury must be "occasioned solely" by the intentional behavior. While the language does not fit very well the language of suicide, it has been held, quite reasonably, that when the suicide is attributable to depression itself compensable, death benefits are not barred by § 903(b). See Voris v. Texas Employers Ins. Ass'n, 190 F.2d 929 (5th Cir.1951); Terminal Shipping Co. v. Traynor, 243 F.Supp. 915 (D.Md.1965).

When would the injury be caused "solely" by intention of the employee to injure or kill another? Is it when he had it coming. See White v. J.P. Florio & Co., 12 La.App. 508, 126 So. 452 (1930). There it was found that the section precluded coverage when the claimant was shot by a policeman in self defence during an altercation not involving the employer's business.

Or solely by the claimant's intoxication. See Wimmer v. Hoage, 90 F.2d 373 (D.C.Cir.1937). There the deputy commissioner's finding that the assault from which the claimant's injury arose was produced solely by his intoxication. Suppose both parties are drunk. What is the standard to be applied?

Small Vessel Exclusion

Section 903(d) of the LHWCA exempts from coverage facilities used exclusively for the building, repair, or dismantling of small vessels as there defined. Such an exclusion must be certified by the Secretary of Labor. When an employee files a claim and questions the current status of the exclusion, the employer must demand a hearing before an administrative judge and if it loses there, seek review from the Benefits Review Board, and only then seek judicial review. Maxon Marine, Inc. v. Director OWCP, 39 F.3d 144 (7th Cir.1994).

B. THIRD PERSON LIABILITY

Howlett v. Birkdale Shipping Co., S.A.

Supreme Court of the United States, 1994.
___ U.S. ___, 114 S.Ct. 2057, 129 L.Ed.2d 78, 1994 A.M.C. 1817.

■ JUSTICE KENNEDY delivered the opinion of the Court.

Under § 5(b) of the Longshore and Harbor Workers' Compensation Act, 33 U.S.C. § 905(b), a shipowner must exercise ordinary care to maintain the ship and her equipment in a condition so that an expert and experienced stevedore can load and unload cargo with reasonable safety. As a corollary to this duty, the shipowner must warn the stevedore of latent hazards, as the term is defined in maritime law, that are known or should be known to the shipowner. This case requires us to define the circumstances under which a shipowner must warn of latent hazards in the cargo stow or cargo area.

I

The case arrives after a grant of summary judgment to respondent Birkdale Shipping Co., S.A., so we consider the facts in the light most favorable to petitioner Albert Howlett. Howlett, a longshoreman employed in the Port of Philadelphia by stevedore Northern Shipping Co. was injured while discharging bags of cocoa beans from a cargo hold on the *M/V Presidente Ibanez* a ship owned and operated by Birkdale. During the unloading operation, Howlett and three other longshoremen hooked up a draft, or load, of bags stowed on the tween deck of the hold. When the ship's boom lifted the draft out of the hold, an 8 square-foot area of the tween deck was exposed. Howlett, who was standing on surrounding bags, jumped down about three feet to the deck, where he slipped and fell on a sheet of clear plastic that had been placed under the cargo. As a result of his fall, Howlett sustained serious injuries that have disabled him from returning to work as a longshoreman.

Howlett brought suit against Birkdale under § 5(b) of the Act. Both parties agreed that it is customary to lay paper and plywood on a steel deck to protect a stow of cocoa beans against condensation damage. They also agreed that, for purposes of protecting the beans, it was improper to use plastic, which tends to aggravate condensation damage rather than prevent it. Evidence adduced during pretrial proceedings suggested that the independent stevedore engaged by Birkdale to load the beans in Guayaquil, Ecuador, had placed the plastic on the tween deck. Further evidence showed that the vessel had supplied the Guayaquil stevedore with the plastic, along with other material used in stowing cargo, including paper, plywood and dunnage. Howlett claimed that before jumping to the deck he did not see the plastic, which was covered by dirt and debris. He charged that Birkdale was negligent in failing to warn Northern and its longshoremen-employees of this dangerous condition.

The United States District Court for the Eastern District of Pennsylvania granted summary judgment in favor of Birkdale. Relying upon Derr v. Kawasaki Kisen K K, 1988 A.MC 746, 835 F.2d 490 (3 Cir.1987), cert. denied, 486 U.S. 1007, 1988 A.M.C. 2398 (1988), the court held that Howlett, to prevail on his failure-to-warn claim, had to demonstrate that Birkdale had actual knowledge of the hazardous condition, and that the condition was not open and obvious. After reviewing the record, the court concluded that Howlett had failed to present evidence sufficient to sustain his claim. The court declined to infer that Birkdale had actual knowledge of the condition from the fact that it had supplied the Guayaquil stevedore with the plastic, reasoning that "being the supplier of equipment does not necessarily imply knowledge of its intended purpose." App. to Pet. for Cert. 4a. The court further declined to infer actual knowledge from the fact that the members of the vessel's crew were present on the top deck during the loading operation. And even if the Guayaquil stevedore's improper use of plastic had been apparent to the crew, the court continued, "then it readily transpires that this was an open and obvious condition" for which Howlett could not recover. Ibid. The Court of Appeals affirmed without opinion, 1993 AMC 291, 998 F.2d 1003 (3 Cir.1993).

We granted certiorari, 510 U.S. ___ (1994), to resolve a conflict among the Circuits regarding the scope of the shipowners' duty to warn of latent hazards in the cargo stow, an inquiry that depends in large part upon the nature of the shipowners' duty to inspect for such defects. Compare Derr v. Kawasaki Kisen K K, supra (vessel need not inspect or supervise the loading stevedore's cargo operations for the benefit of longshoremen in later ports), with Turner v. Japan Lines, Ltd., 1981 AMC 2223, 651 F.2d 1300 (9 Cir.1981)(vessel must supervise a foreign stevedore's loading operations), cert. denied, 459 U.S. 967, 1983 AMC 2111 (1982).

II

The Longshore and Harbor Workers' Compensation Act, 44 Stat. 1424, as amended, 33 U.S.C. § 901 *et seq.*, establishes a comprehensive federal workers' compensation program that provides longshoremen and their families with medical, disability, and survivor benefits for work-related injuries and death. See generally T. Schoenbaum, Admiralty and Maritime Law § 6–6(1987); Norris, Law of Maritime Personal Injuries §§ 4:11, 4:22–4:29 (4th ed. 1990). The injured longshoreman's employer—in most instances, an independent stevedore, see Edmonds v. Compagnie Generale Transatlantique, 443 U.S. 256, 263–264, 1979 AMC 1167, 1172–73 (1979)—must pay the statutory benefits regardless of fault, but is shielded from any further liability to the longshoreman. See 33 U.S.C. §§ 904, 905(a); Norris, supra, §§ 4:7–4:10.

The longshoreman also may seek damages in a third-party negligence action against the owner of the vessel on which he was injured, and may do so without foregoing statutory compensation if he follows certain procedures. See Estate of Cowart v. Nicklos Drilling Co., 112 S.Ct. 2589, 1992 A.M.C. 2113 (1992). Section 5(b) provides in relevant part:

> In the event of injury to a person covered under this Act caused by the negligence of a vessel, then such person ... may bring an action against such vessel as a third party ..., and the employer shall not be liable to the vessel for such damages directly or indirectly and any agreements or warranties to the contrary shall be void.... The liability of the vessel under this subsection shall not be based upon the warranty of seaworthiness or a breach thereof at the time the injury occurred.

33 U.S.C. § 905(b).

This provision, enacted as part of the extensive 1972 Amendments to the Act, effected fundamental changes in the nature of the third-party action. First, it abolished the longshoreman's pre-existing right to sue a shipowner based upon the warranty of seaworthiness, a right that had been established in Seas Shipping Co. v. Sieracki, 328 U.S. 85, 1946 A.M.C. 698 (1946). Section 5(b) also eliminated the stevedore's obligation, imposed by Ryan Stevedoring Co. v. Pan–Atlantic S.S. Corp., 350 U.S. 124, 1956 A.M.C. 9 (1956), to indemnify a shipowner, if held liable to a longshoreman, for breach of the stevedore's express or implied warranty to conduct cargo operations with reasonable safety. See generally Scindia Steam Navigation Co. v. De Los Santos, 451 U.S. 156, 165, 1981 A.M.C. 601, 608 (1981); G. Gilmore & C. Black, *Law of Admiralty* § 6–57, pp. 449–455 (2d ed. 1975). Other sections of the 1972 Amendments provided for a substantial increase in the statutory benefits injured longshoremen are entitled to receive from their stevedore-employers. See Northeast Marine Terminal Co. v. Caputo, 432 U.S. 249, 261–262, 1977 A.M.C. 1037, 1047 (1977); Gilmore & Black, supra, § 6–46, p. 411; Note, 13 Tul. Mar. L.J. 163, 163–164 (1988). The design of these changes was to shift more of the responsibility for compensating injured longshoremen to the party best able to prevent injuries: the stevedore-employer. See *Scindia Steam,* 451 U.S. at 171, 1981 A.M.C. at 613. Subjecting vessels to suit for injuries that could be anticipated and prevented by a competent stevedore would threaten to upset the balance Congress was careful to strike in enacting the 1972 Amendments.

The question whether Howlett produced evidence sufficient to hold Birkdale liable for his injuries turns on the meaning of the term "negligence" in § 5(b). Because Congress did not "specify the acts or omissions of the vessel that would constitute negligence," the contours of a vessel's duty to longshoremen are "left to be resolved through the 'application of accepted principles of tort law and the ordinary process of litigation.'" Id. 451 U.S. at 165–166, 1981 A.M.C. at 608–09.

The starting point in this regard must be our decision in *Scindia Steam,* which outlined the three general duties shipowners owe to longshoremen. The first, which courts have come to call the "turnover duty," relates to the condition of the ship upon the commencement of stevedoring operations. See 451 U.S. at 167, 1981 A.M.C. at 610. The second duty, applicable once stevedoring operations have begun, provides that a shipowner must exercise reasonable care to prevent injuries to longshoremen in areas that remain under the "active control of the vessel." Ibid. The third duty, called the "duty to intervene," concerns the vessel's obligations with regard to cargo operations in areas under the principal control of the independent stevedore. See 451 U.S. at 177–178, 1981 A.M.C. at 616–17.

The allegations of Howlett's complaint, and the facts adduced during pretrial proceedings, implicate only the vessel's turnover duty. We provided a brief statement of the turnover duty in Federal Marine Terminals, Inc. v. Burnside Shipping Co., 394 U.S. 404, 1969 A.M.C. 745 (1969): A vessel must "exercise ordinary care under the circumstances" to turn over the ship and her equipment and appliances "in such condition that an expert and experienced stevedoring contractor, mindful of the dangers he should expect to encounter, arising from the hazards of the ship's service or otherwise, will be able by the exercise of ordinary care" to carry on cargo operations "with reasonable safety to persons and property." 394 U.S. at 416–417, 1969 A.M.C. at 754 n. 18 (internal quotation marks omitted); see also *Scindia Steam,* 451 U.S.at 167,1981 A.M.C. at 610. A corollary to the turnover duty requires the vessel to warn the stevedore "of any hazards on the ship or with respect to its equipment," so long as the hazards "are known to the vessel or should be known to it in the exercise of reasonable care," and "would likely be encountered by the stevedore in the course of his cargo operations[,] are not known by the stevedore[,] and would not be obvious to or anticipated by him if reasonably competent in the performance of his work." Ibid., citing *Marine Terminals*, supra, 394 U.S. at 416, 1969 A.M.C. at 754 n. 18. Although both components of the turnover duty are related in various respects, Howlett confines his case to an allegation that Birkdale failed to warn that the tween deck was covered with plastic rather than (as is ordinarily the case) paper and plywood.

Most turnover cases brought under § 5(b) concern the condition of the ship herself or of equipment on the ship used in stevedoring operations. See e.g, Bjaranson v. Botelho Shipping Corp., Manila, 1989 A.M.C. 381, 873 F.2d 1204 (9 Cir.1989)(no handhold on coaming ladder); Griffith v. Wheeling–Pittsburgh Steel Corp., 1980 A.M.C. 833, 610 F.2d 116 (3 Cir.1979)(defective hatch covers), remanded, 451 U.S. 965, 1981 A.M.C. 2097, reinstated 1981 A.M.C. 2974, 657 F.2d 25 (3 Cir.1981), cert. denied, 456 U.S. 914, 1982 A.M.C. 2108 (1982); Scalafani v. Moore McCormack Lines, Inc., 1975 A.M.C. 2024, 388 F.Supp. 897 (E.D.N.Y.)(no handrail on platform linking gangway and deck), aff'd without opinion, 535 F.2d 1242 (2 Cir.1975). The turnover duty to warn, however, may extend to certain latent hazards in the cargo stow. This is so because an improper stow can cause injuries to longshoremen, see. e.g., Atlantic & Gulf Stevedores, Inc. v. Ellerman Lines, Ltd., 369 U.S. 355, 1962 A.M.C. 565 (1962); Ryan Stevedoring Co. v. Pan–Atlantic S.S. Corp., 350 U.S. 124, 1956 A.M.C. 9 (1956); Clay v. Lykes Bros. S.S. Co., 1982 A.M.C. 1027, 525 F.Supp. 306 (E.D.La.1981); The Etna, 1942 A.M.C. 489, 43 F.Supp. 303 (E.D.Pa.1942), and thus is among the "hazards on the ship" to which the duty to warn attaches. *Scindia Steam,* 451 U.S. at 167, 1981 A.M.C. at 609.

The precise contours of the duty to warn of latent hazards in the cargo stow must be defined with due regard to the concurrent duties of the stevedore and to the statutory scheme as a whole. It bears repeating that the duty attaches only to latent hazards, defined in this context as hazards that would be neither obvious to nor anticipated by a competent stevedore in the ordinary course of cargo operations. In addition, the vessel's duty to warn is confined to latent hazards that "are known to the vessel or should be known to it in the exercise of reasonable care." Ibid. Absent actual knowledge of a hazard, then, the duty to warn may attach only if the exercise of reasonable care would place upon the shipowner an obligation to inspect for or discover the hazard's existence. See Kirsch v. Plovidba, 1992 A.M.C. 2747, 2752, 971 F.2d 1026, 1029 (3 Cir.1992)("[T]he shipowner's duty to warn the stevedore of hidden dangers necessarily implies a duty to inspect to discover those dangers'').

Howlett, relying upon the *Restatement (Second) of Torts*, § 412 (1965), maintains that a vessel's obligations in this regard are broad. Section 412 provides that an owner of land or chattels who hires an independent contractor must take reasonable steps to "ascertain whether the land or chattel is in reasonably safe condition after the contractor's work is completed." In light of this provision, Howlett argues that "a shipowner, who has hired an independent contractor stevedore to perform the work of loading cargo aboard its ship, has a duty to make 'reasonable' (not continuous) inspections" during and after cargo operations to discover dangerous conditions in the stow. Brief for Petitioner 27.

We decline to adopt Howlett's proposal. As an initial matter, we repeat our caveat that the *Restatement's* land-based principles, "while not irrelevant, do not furnish sure guidance" in maritime cases brought under § 5(b). *Scindia Steam*, 451 U.S. at 168, 1981 A.M.C. at 610 n. 14. On a more fundamental level, Howlett's contention that a vessel must make reasonable inspections, both during and after stevedoring operations, to discover defects in the stow contradicts the principles underlying our decision in *Scindia Steam.* The plaintiff longshoreman in *Scindia Steam,* injured by cargo that fell from a defective winch, alleged that the shipowner should have intervened in the stevedoring operations and repaired the winch before permitting operations to continue. The case thus turned not upon the turnover duty but upon the scope of the vessel's duty to intervene once cargo operations have begun. We held that the duty to intervene, in the event the vessel has no knowledge of the hazardous condition, is limited: "[A]bsent contract provision, positive law, or custom to the contrary," a vessel "has no general duty by way of supervision or inspection to exercise reasonable care to discover dangerous conditions that develop within the confines of the cargo operations that are assigned to the stevedore." 451 U.S. at 172, 1981 A.M.C. at 614.

The rule relieving vessels from this general duty rests upon "the justifiable expectations of the vessel that the stevedore would perform with reasonable competence and see to the safety of the cargo operations." Ibid.; see also Hugev v. Dampskisaktieselskabet Int'l, 1959 A.M.C. 439, 449–50, 170 F.Supp. 601, 609–610 (S.D.Cal.1959), aff'd sub nom. Metropolitan Stevedore Co. v. Dampskisaktieselskabet Int'l, 1960 A.M.C. 591, 274 F.2d 875 (9 Cir.), cert. denied, 363 U.S. 803, 1961 A.M.C. 287 (1960). These expectations derive in part from § 41 of the Act, 33 U.S.C. § 941, which requires the stevedore, as the longshoreman's employer, to provide a "reasonably safe" place to work and to take safeguards necessary to avoid injuries. *Scindia Steam*, 451 U.S. at 170, 1981 A.M.C. at 612. The expectations also derive from indemnity cases decided prior to the 1972 Act, which teach that "the stevedore [is] in the best position to avoid accidents during cargo operations" and that "the shipowner [can] rely on the stevedore's warranty to perform competently." 451 U.S. at 171, 1981 A.M.C. at 613 citing Italia Societa v. Oregon Stevedoring Co., 376 U.S. 315,

1964 A.M.C. 1075 (1964); see also 451 U.S. at 175, 1981 A.M.C. at 616 (safety is "a matter of judgment committed to the stevedore in the first instance"). The stevedore's obligations in this regard may not be diminished by transferring them to the vessel.

Given the legal and practical realities of the maritime trade, we concluded in *Scindia Steam* that imposing a duty upon vessels to supervise and inspect cargo operations for the benefit of longshoremen then on board would undermine Congress' intent in § 5(b) to terminate the vessel's "automatic, faultless responsibility for conditions caused by the negligence or other defaults of the stevedore," 451 U.S. at 168, 1981 AMC at 611 and to foreclose liability "based on a theory of unseaworthiness or nondelegable duty." 451 U.S. at 172, 1981 AMC at 613–14. Agreeing with the Court, Justice Powell further observed that imposing such a duty—in light of the stevedore-employer's right to receive reimbursement for its payment of statutory compensation if a longshoreman prevails in a § 5(b) action against a vessel, see Edmonds v. Compagnie Generale Transatlantique, 443 U.S. at 269–270, 1979 A.M.C. at 1178—would "decrease significantly the incentives toward safety of the party in the best position to prevent injuries." *Scindia Steam*, 451 U.S. at 181, 1981 A.M.C at 621 (concurring opinion); see also *Edmonds*, supra, 443 U.S. at 274, 1979 AMC at 1181 (Blackmun, J., dissenting). It is also worth noting that an injured longshoreman's acceptance of statutory compensation operates as an assignment to the stevedore-employer of the longshoreman's right to bring suit against the vessel, so long as the longshoreman does not sue within six months of accepting compensation. 33 U.S.C. § 933(b). Were we to have accepted the longshoreman's contentions in *Scindia Steam,* we would have run the risk of promoting the kind of collateral litigation between stevedores and vessel (albeit in a different guise) that had consumed an intolerable amount of litigation costs prior to the 1972 Amendments. See Gilmore & Black, supra, § 6–46, p. 411.

The foregoing principles, while taken from *Scindia Steam's* examination of the vessel's duty to intervene, bear as well on the nature of the vessel's turnover duty, and hence on the case before us. We consider first Howlett's view that a vessel must make reasonable inspections during stevedoring operations to ensure a proper stow and to detect any hazards or defects before they become hidden. The beneficiaries of this proposed duty would be longshoremen who unload or otherwise deal with the cargo at later ports. But if, as we held in *Scindia Steam,* a vessel need not supervise or inspect ongoing cargo operations for the benefit of longshoremen then on board, it would make little sense to impose the same obligation for the benefit of longshoremen at subsequent ports. In practical effect, then, adopting Howlett's proposal would impose inconsistent standards upon shipowners as to different sets of longshoremen, and would render much of our holding in *Scindia Steam* an empty gesture.

These concerns are mitigated somewhat when a longshoreman, such as Howlett, works on cargo stowed in a foreign port and undisturbed by longshoremen in a prior American port of call. Foreign longshoremen are not covered by the Act, so requiring vessels to supervise and inspect a foreign stevedore's ongoing operations would not be inconsistent with the precise rule laid down in *Scindia Steam*. This consideration, however, does not support imposing broader duties upon vessels to inspect cargo loading operations in foreign ports. It is settled maritime custom and practice that the stevedore exercises primary control over the details of a cargo operation, see *Oregon Stevedoring*, supra, 376 U.S. at 322–323, 1964 A.M.C. at 1081–82, and we are given no reason to believe that this is any less true in foreign ports than in domestic ports.

That is not to say, of course, that the vessel and her crew remain detached from cargo operations altogether. Most vessels take responsibility, for instance, for preparing a stowage plan, which governs where each cargo will be stowed on the ship. See generally C. Sauerbier & R. Meurn, *Marine Cargo Operations* 217–239 (2d ed. 1985). But it is the stevedore, an independent contractor hired for its expertise in the stowage and handling of cargo, that is charged with actual implementation of the plan. To impose a duty upon vessels to exercise scrutiny over a cargo loading operation to discover defects that may become hidden when the stow is complete would require vessels to inject themselves into matters beyond their ordinary province. See Williams, *Shipowner Liability for Improperly Stowed Cargo: Federal Courts at Sea on the Standard of Care Owed to Off-Loading Longshoremen*, 17 Tul. Mar. L. J. 185, 198–199 (1993), contra Turner v. Japan Lines, Ltd., 651 F.2d at 1304, 1981 A.M.C. at 2229 (vessel "can ensure safety by choosing a reliable foreign stevedore [and] supervising its work when necessary"). The proposed rule would undermine Congress' intent in § 5(b) to eliminate the vessel's nondelegable duty to protect longshoremen from the negligence of others. See *Scindia Steam*, 451 U.S. at 168–169, 1981 A.M.C. at 611.

We next consider Howlett's view that a vessel must make reasonable inspections after the completion of stevedoring operations to discover hazards in the stow. There is good reason to doubt that adopting this rule would have much practical import. Any hazard uncovered by a shipowner who inspects a completed stow would, as a matter of course, be discovered in a subsequent port by a stevedore "reasonably competent in the performance of his work." 451 U.S. at 167, 1981 A.M.C. at 610. As discussed above, shipowners engage a stevedore for its expertise in cargo operations and are entitled to assume that a competent stevedore will be able to identify and cope with defects in the stow. See 451 U.S. at 171, 1981 A.M.C. at 613, Hugev v. Dampskisaktieselskabet Int'l, 1959 A.M.C. at 449–50, 170 F.Supp. at 609–610. Once loading operations are complete, it follows that any dangers arising from an improper stow would be "at least as apparent to the [stevedore] as to the [shipowner]." Atlantic & Gulf Stevedores, Inc. v. Ellerman Lines, Ltd., 369 U.S. at 366, 1962 A.M.C. at 573 (Stewart, J., dissenting). Because there can be no recovery under § 5(b) for a vessel's failure to warn of dangers that would be apparent to a longshoreman of reasonable competence, *Scindia Steam*, supra, 451 U.S. at 167, 1981 A.M.C. at 609, nothing would be accomplished by imposing a duty upon vessels to inspect the stow upon completion of cargo operations. That is reason enough to reject it.

For the purposes of delineating the scope of a shipowner's turnover duty, then, the cargo stow is separate and distinct from other aspects of the ship. When between ports, the vessel and her crew have direct access to (and control over) the ship herself and her gear, equipment and tools. The vessel's responsibilities to inspect these areas of the ship are commensurate with her access and control, bearing in mind, of course, that negligence, rather than unseaworthiness, is the controlling standard where longshoremen are concerned. Because the vessel does not exercise the same degree of operational control over, and does not have the same access to, the cargo stow, her duties with respect to the stow are limited by comparison. See *Robertson v. Tokai Shosen K K,* 655 F.Supp. 152, 154 (E.D.Pa.), aff'd., 1988 A.M.C. 746, 835 F.2d 490 (3 Cir.1987), cert. denied, 486 U.S. 1007, 1988 A.M.C. 2398 (1988).

In sum, the vessel's turnover duty to warn of latent defects in the cargo stow and cargo area is a narrow one. The duty attaches only to latent hazards, defined as hazards that are not known to the stevedore and that would be neither obvious to nor anticipated by a skilled stevedore in the competent performance of its work. *Scindia Steam,* 451 U.S. at 167, 1981 A.M.C. at 609. Furthermore, the duty encompasses only those hazards that "are known to the vessel or should be known to it in the exercise of reasonable care." Ibid. Contrary to Howlett's submission, however, the exercise of reasonable care does not require the shipowner to supervise the ongoing operations of the loading stevedore (or other stevedores who handle the cargo before its arrival in port) or to inspect the completed stow.

III

We turn to the proper disposition of this case. As the Court of Appeals did not issue an opinion, we have before us only the District Court's statement of its reasons for granting summary judgment in favor of Birkdale. The vessel having been under no obligation to supervise and inspect the cargo loading operations, and no other theory for charging the vessel with constructive knowledge having been advanced, the District Court was correct to inquire whether the vessel had actual knowledge of the tween deck's condition. The District Court found it undisputed that there was no actual knowledge. At this stage of the proceedings, however, we cannot conclude that summary judgment can rest on this ground. There is sufficient evidence in the record to support a permissible inference that, during the loading process, some crew members, who might have held positions such that their knowledge should be attributed to the vessel, did in fact observe the plastic on the tween deck. And the District Court's alternate theory that even if some crew members were aware of the condition during loading operations, then the condition also would have been open and obvious to a stevedore during unloading operations, may prove faulty as well, being premised on the state of affairs when the vessel took on cargo, not during discharge at the port where Howlett was injured.

All this does not mean that the vessel is not entitled to summary judgment. Howlett's own witnesses stated that the plastic was visible, even from the top deck, during unloading operations. Howlett must overcome these submissions, for even assuming the vessel had knowledge of the tween deck's condition, he must further demonstrate that the alleged hazard would have been neither obvious to nor anticipated by a skilled and competent stevedore at the discharge port. This contention, however, was not addressed by the District Court and was not explored in detail here. We think it the better course to remand the case to the Court of Appeals so that it, or the District Court, can address in the first instance these and other relevant points upon a review of the entire record made in support of the vessel's motion for summary judgment. For these reasons, the judgment of the Court of Appeals is vacated and the case remanded for further proceedings consistent with this opinion.

Burchett v. Cargill, Inc.

United States Court of Appeals for the Fifth Circuit, 1995.
48 F.3d 173, 1995 A.M.C. 1576.

* * *

III

* * *

Plaintiffs' amended complaint seeks recovery against MEMCO under § 905(b) of the LHWCA, which allows a longshoreman injured as a result of the negligence of a vessel to bring an action for damages against the vessel. 33 U.S.C. § 905(b). Plaintiffs claim that MEMCO's failure to install nonskid surfaces on its hatch covers constitutes actionable negligence under § 905(b).

In Scindia Steam Navigation Co., Ltd. v. De Los Santos, 451 U.S. 156, 1981 AMC 601 (1981), the Supreme Court articulated the scope of a vessel's duty under § 905(b). *Scindia* established that "the primary responsibility for the safety of the longshoremen rests upon the stevedore."[3] Randolph v. Laeisz, 896 F.2d 964, 970 (5 Cir.1990). However, vessel liability may still arise

(1) if the vessel owner fails to warn on turning over the ship of hidden defects of which he should have known.

(2) for injury caused by hazards under the control of the ship.

(3) if the vessel owner fails to intervene in the stevedore's operations when he has actual knowledge both of the hazards and that

---

3. We have held that these principles also apply to LHWCA-covered employees of independent contractors other than steve- dores. Hill v. Texaco, Inc., 674 F.2d 447, 1984 AMC 1558.

the stevedore, in the exercise of "obviously improvident" judgment means to work on in the face of it and therefore cannot be relied on to remedy it.

Pimental v. LTD Canadian Pacific Bul, 1992 AMC 2930, 2932, 965 F.2d 13, 15 (5 Cir.1992).

The district court held that the summary judgment evidence negated a finding of liability under any of the above *Scindia* scenarios. Assuming, without deciding that an injury to longshoreman platform by a piece of a vessel, her gear or equipment can give rise to § 905(b) liability against the vessel owner, we agree with the district court that the summary judgment evidence demonstrates that MEMCO has no liability under *Scindia*.

MEMCO asserts that it cannot be liable under the first *Scindia* duty of failure to warn of a hidden defect because the slippery hatch cover was an open and obvious danger. A defendant generally has not breached its duty to turn over a safe vessel if the defect causing the injury is open and obvious. Id. at 16. The courts have created a narrow exception to this rule where a longshoreman's only options when facing an open and obvious danger are unduly impracticable or time-consuming. Id. The summary judgment evidence reveals that Burchett was aware of the accumulation of-soybean dust and dew on the hatch cover and knew that it would cause the cover to be slippery. In fact, Burchett admitted in his deposition that he had seen a co-worker slip under the same conditions. He further admitted that none of the steel hatch covers he had encountered previously had non-skid surfaces and that he had also seen men slip and fall under similar conditions on fiberglass covers with non-skid surfaces. The summary judgment evidence also does not indicate that Burchett was obliged to climb onto the hatch cover. Burchett testified in his deposition that he climbed onto the hatch cover only because the K–2 crew was shorthanded that day. According to Burchett, a crane operator would not need to climb onto the hatch covers under ordinary circumstances.

For similar reasons, MEMCO cannot be liable under *Scindia's* second scenario, which imposes liability for injury caused by hazards under the vessel owner's control. The vessel has a duty to "exercise due care to avoid exposing longshoremen to harm from hazards they may encounter in areas, or from equipment, under the active control of the vessel during the stevedoring operation." *Scindia*, 451 U.S. at 167, 1981 AMC at 610. The summary judgment evidence showed that the hatch cover was removed from MEMCO's "dumb barge" and stacked on the cover deck of the K–2 by Cargill personnel. No MEMCO personnel were present at any time during the offloading process. The dust accumulated on the cover as a result of Cargill's offloading operation. Cargill also controlled the number of men working on the K–2 cover deck. Thus, MEMCO neither controlled nor created the circumstances leading to Burchett's injury.

As to the third *Scindia* scenario, which imposes on the vessel a duty to intervene, the vessel must have "actual knowledge that it could not rely on the stevedore to protect its employees and that if unremedied the condition posed a substantial risk of danger." *Randolph*, 896 F.2d at 971. As indicated above, MEMCO had no personnel present at the job site who could have had knowledge of any peculiar dangers related to Cargill's unloading operations. See Helaire v. Mobil Oil Co., 1984 AMC 820, 830, 709 F.2d 1031, 1038–39 (5 Cir.1983).

IV

For the reasons stated above, we affirm the judgment of the district court.

NOTE

Subject to narrow exceptions found in the statute, LHWCA is a covered worker's exclusive remedy against his employer for injuries sustained in the course of his employment. See 33 U.S.C. §§ 905(a) and 933(i). These sections do not limit a worker's recourse against a third person whose negligence is the cause of his injury, and the right to pursue both is preserved specifically in § 933(a). Since the potential recovery in an action for damages will frequently exceed the amount of compensation under the Act, actions against third persons are not unusual. E.g., Couch v. Cro–Marine Transport, Inc. 44 F.3d 319, 1995 A.M.C. 1586 (5th Cir.1995), a suit against an onloading stevedore for injuries to an offloading longshoreman charging negligent stowage; Delaney v. Merchants River Transportation, 829 F.Supp. 186, 1994 A.M.C. 1207 (DRO)(W.D.La.1993), against the builder of a barge on which plaintiff was injured.

While §§ 905(a) and 933(a) thus do not purport to limit actions by an injured employee, they do not expand federal jurisdiction. Actions against third persons, then, may be brought in the federal court only if there is admiralty jurisdiction or diversity.

An injured employee may pursue both remedies, but the employer may set off any net recovery in an action for damages against the amount of compensation payable. In cases in which a formal award is made, the recipient can bring suit against the third person tortfeasor at any time within six months after the award. The liability of the employer to pay compensation is reduced by the net amount of any recovery (deducting expenses including attorney's fees) in the action for damages. § 933(f). At this point the cause of action is deemed to be assigned to the employer, who is given ninety days in which to bring suit against the third person. In such a suit the employer sues for the entire amount of damages, retains from any judgment the costs of litigation and the compensation paid and payable, and pays over the balance to the employee. If the employer does not sue within the ninety-day period the cause of action is deemed reassigned to the employee.

Whether the action is maintained by the injured employee or by his employer, a negligent third person is held liable for the entire amount of the employee's damage, discounted for contributory negligence, but not for the negligence of the employer or of his employees. Edmonds v. Compagnie Generale Transatlantique, 443 U.S. 256, 99 S.Ct. 2753, 1979 A.M.C. 1167, 61 L.Ed.2d 521 (1979). And the defendant may not maintain an action against the employer for contribution. This was the law before the 1972 amendments. See Cooper Stevedoring Co. v. Fritz Kopke, Inc., 417 U.S. 106, 94 S.Ct. 2174, 40 L.Ed.2d 694, 1974 A.M.C. 537 (1974). And remains so under the *Edmonds* decision. The four dissenting justices in *Edmonds* pointed out that under this rule, a vessel owner who is passively negligent, is forced to shoulder liability for all the damages, less a reduction for such as may be charged to the plaintiff longshoreman, while the liability of the plaintiff's employer is limited to the amount of compensation, and if there is a recovery against the third person, he may be reimbursed for that.

The employer's right to reimbursement is protected in a number of ways. If the employee brings an action for damages under § 933, he is required to notify the employer of any judgment or any settlement, and may not settle such a suit for less than the amount of compensation without the approval of the settlement by the employer. Failure to give notice or settlement without prior approval results in the termination of the employer's duty to pay compensation. Cowert v. Nicklos Drilling Co., 505 U.S. 469, 112 S.Ct. 2589, 120 L.Ed.2d 379, 1992 A.M.C. 2113 (1992).

While the 1972 amendments did little to change the law relating to actions against third persons generally, but made important changes in the law relating to shipboard injuries of longshoremen and other harbor workers who might be regarded as "doing a seaman's work." The development of the absolute liability of the vessel and its owner for injuries to these "seamen pro hac vice" occasioned by conditions on the vessel, whether created by the ship's company or the negligence of the covered worker's fellow servants, and the shifting of this liability to the covered employer through a warranty of workmanlike service is discussed elsewhere. See Historical Note, beginning on p. 955 supra.

The 1972 amendments preserved the injured employee's action against a vessel on which he was injured for negligence, but provided that such an action may no longer be based on the warranty of unseaworthiness. As a counterweight it provided that the employer paying compensation may not be held liable to the vessel for such damages directly or indirectly, and that every agreement or warranty to the contrary is void. § 905(b). Actions under § 905(b) must be brought in accordance with the provisions of § 933, and are made the exclusive remedy of a covered employee against a vessel, defined in § 902(21), "[u]nless the context requires otherwise," as

> "any vessel upon which or in connection with which any person entitled to benefits under this chapter suffers injury or death arising out of or in the course of his employment, and said vessel's owner, owner pro hac vice, agent, operator, charter or bare boat charterer, master, officer, or crew member."

Does § 905(b) create a cause of action, or limit one? One year before the enactment of the 1972 amendments to the LHWCA, it was held that an action by a longshoreman against the vessel in respect of an injury occurring on the pier through failure of equipment furnished by his employer was not within the admiralty jurisdiction. Victory Carriers, Inc. v. Law, 404 U.S. 202, 92 S.Ct. 418, 30 L.Ed.2d 383, 1972 A.M.C. 1 (1971). At the time the coverage of the LHWCA was limited to navigable water in the literal sense. Can you make a textual case for the view that the broadening of the situs of injuries covered by the Act intended to extend the jurisdiction over § 905(b) cases? The cases in the courts of appeals indicate that no change was effected. See, e.g., Richendollar v. Diamond M Drilling Co., 819 F.2d 124, 1987 A.M.C. 2613 (5th Cir.1987)(en banc). May v. Transworld Drilling Co. , 786 F.2d 1261 (5th Cir.1986), cert. denied 479 U.S. 854, 107 S.Ct. 190, 93 L.Ed.2d 123 (1986). Speaking of an incomplete drilling rig on land and with holes in its hull, the court in *Richendollar* observed, "It was not in or on navigable waters. It was not a vessel within the admiralty jurisdiction of the federal courts under the longstanding jurisdictional rubric, and § 905(b) did not extend that jurisdiction."

But even where the location requirement is satisfied, an absence of maritime nexus will preclude an action under § 905(b). See, e.g., Molett v. Penrod Drilling

Co., 872 F.2d 1221 (5th Cir.1989), cert. denied sub nom. Columbus–McKinnon, Inc. v. Gearench, 493 U.S. 1003, 110 S.Ct. 563, 107 L.Ed.2d 558 (1989); May v. Transworld Drilling Co., supra.

See also Shea v. Rev–Lyn Contracting Co., Inc., 868 F.2d 515 (1st Cir.1989), in which it was held that a worker who fell from a crane that was fastened to a barge while engaged in repairing a drawbridge met the maritime nexus test and could sue the vessel under § 905(b).

Can it be argued that an action under § 905(b) arises under the LHWCA and therefore there is jurisdiction of such an action under 28 U.S.C. § 1331? Cf Garvin v. Alumax of South Carolina, Inc., 787 F.2d 910 (4th Cir.1986), cert. denied 479 U.S. 914, 107 S.Ct. 314, 93 L.Ed.2d 288 (1986), holding that an action against a general contractor whose subcontractor was uncovered (see § 905(a)) arose under federal law. Judge Murnaghan dissented. The Fifth Circuit has agreed with Judge Murnaghan. Griffis v. Gulf Coast Pre–Stress Co., Inc., 850 F.2d 1090 (5th Cir.1988).

Section 902(21) does not define what sort of structure is a vessel—vide "Unless the context requires otherwise, the term 'vessel' means any vessel . . ." Most of the cases have indicated that the very broad definition that appears in 1 U.S.C.A. § 3 is the one to be applied. See Chap. 4 above. Relying on this definition, it was held in McCarthy v. The Bark Peking, 716 F.2d 130, 1984 A.M.C. 1 (2d Cir.1983), cert. denied 465 U.S. 1078, 104 S.Ct. 1439, 79 L.Ed.2d 760 (1984), that a museum vessel on exhibit as an artifact was a vessel for the purposes of §§ 902(21), 905(b). The Bark Peking was followed in Tonnesen v. Yonkers Contracting Co., 847 F.Supp. 12, 1994 A.M.C. 2778 (E.D.N.Y.1994), holding that a crane barge used as a work platform in the building of a bridge, and fixed in place at the work site by steel support legs called spuds, which rendered it immobile so that the crane could operate, was not a vessel in navigation for the purposes of the Jones Act, but was a "vessel" for purposes of § 905(b). Vessels that are permanently moored and used for non-maritime purposes have been held to fall outside §§ 902(21), 905(b). See Kathriner v. Unisea, 975 F.2d 657, 1994 A.M.C. 2787 (9th Cir.1992), holding that a liberty ship permanently moored and used as a fish processing facility was not a "vessel" for purposes of the Jones Act or the LHWCA. The court distinguished The Bark Peking on the ground that there the structure had retained its character as a vessel, while the liberty ship had been converted into a factory and all that remained of the original vessel was the hull.

Since § 933 protects the covered employee's action against third persons generally, and the special provisions of § 905(b) are applicable only to actions against a "vessel," as defined, the injured workman is free to sue other third persons to the extent that he may have a cause of action against them, and a vessel owner sued under § 905(b) may implead such a third person. See, e.g., Barrios v. Pelham Marine, Inc., 796 F.2d 128 (5th Cir.1986), although in the particular case third-party claim was found to be frivolous.

What is the significance of the definition of "vessel" in § 902(21)? Note that under § 933(a) the covered employee may sue any third person whom he determines to be liable in damages. This is true whether the defendant is defined as a "vessel" in § 902(21) or not. E.g., Couch v. Cro–Marine Transport, Inc., supra. Does § 905(b) in conjunction with § 902(21) make the enumerated categories all liable for "vessel" negligence. Cf. Riggs v. Scindia Steam Navigation Co., 8 F.3d 1442,1443 n.2, 1994 A.M.C. 331 (9th Cir.1993)(same standards of care apply to shipowners and time charterers). *Riggs* was vacated by the Supreme Court on another point. See also Carpenter v. Universal Star Shipping, 924 F.2d 1539,1542, 1991 A.M.C. 1555 (9th Cir.1991)("Defendants [owner and time charterer] both concede that they are 'vessels' under LHWCA. As a result both defendants are subject to the duty to avoid negligence that is imposed by § 905(b) of the LHWSA.") Is it plausible that the ship's duties to a longshoreman under *Scindia* and *Howlett* are imposed equally upon its owner, agent, charterer, master, and crew.? Or does the broad definition indicate merely that injury through the negligence of any of them permits an action against such of them as may be liable for "ship's" negligence? The owner is, of course. E.g., Keller v. United States, 38 F.3d 16, 1995 A.M.C. 397 (1st Cir.1994), a suit against the United States for violation of the turnover duty under *Scindia*. And so with a bare boat charterer or owner pro hac vice. See Bjaranson v. Botelho Shipping Corp. Manila, 873 F.2d 1204 (9th Cir.1989).

A time charterer is conceded to be within the § 902(21) definition. See Hines v. British Steel Corp., 907 F.2d 726 (7th Cir.1990). In *Hines*, for example, it was recognized that the time charterer has no general duty to supervise the officers and crew of the vessel and therefore, unless it has assumed such duty, it is not negligent within the *Scindia* formulation. See also Hayes v. Wilh Wilhelmsen Enterprises, Ltd., 818 F.2d 1557 (11th Cir.1987). In both *Hines* and *Hayes* the charter was construed to place no duty to supervise the vessel's unloading that would make it liable in a third-party action permitted by § 905. To the same effect, see Kerr–McGee Corp. v. Ma—Ju Marine Services, Inc., 830 F.2d 1332 (5th Cir.1987); also Moore v. Phillips Petroleum Co., 912 F.2d 789 (5th Cir.1990), in which it was held that a time charterer was not liable for injury on rope swings when as time charterer it had no control over or responsibility for the rope swings.

For a case in which the jury found that both the owner-operator and the time charterer were responsible for the unloading operation and the court of appeals held that neither the owner-operator nor the time charterer would be entitled to indemnity from the other. Woods v. Sammisa Co., Ltd., 873 F.2d 842 (5th Cir.1989).

And even if the duties in connection with loading or unloading are assigned to the vessel owner under the charter, the charterer may in fact exercise sufficient control of the operation to be held for its own negligence and in such circumstances a time charterer is held to the same duty to avoid negligence as is an owner or other person defined as a "vessel" under the section. Carpenter v. Universal Star Shipping, S.A., 924 F.2d 1539 (9th Cir.1991).

Recognizing that normally the time charterer's control of the vessel is limited to the right to determine where it shall go, the court in Randall v. Chevron U.S.A., Inc., 13 F.3d 888, 1994 A.M.C. 1217 (5th Cir.1994), held the owner of a vessel 90% negligent for the negligence of the master and crew and its own negligence in failing properly to equip the vessel with lifesaving equipment and properly instruct the master and crew, and the time charterer 10% for its negligence in ordering the vessel to go out in dangerous weather conditions.

Section 905(b) precludes an action for contribution by a vessel against the employer of a covered workman for sums awarded the workman in an action against the vessel. It is silent on the subject of third-party actions for indemnity or contribution in the case of a third-person tortfeasor not a vessel. It has been held, nevertheless, that such an action will not lie against the employer, despite dicta in Lockheed Aircraft Corp. v. United States, 460 U.S. 190, 103 S.Ct. 1033, 74 L.Ed.2d 911 (1983), that might be read to point in the other direction. Ketchum v. Gulf Oil Corp., 798 F.2d 159 (5th Cir.1986); Drake v. Raymark Indus., Inc., 772 F.2d 1007 (1st Cir.1985), cert. denied sub nom. Raymark Industries, Inc. v. Bath Iron Works Corp., 476 U.S. 1126, 106 S.Ct. 1994, 90 L.Ed.2d 675 (1986).

Section 905(b) provides, in part, that the employer shall not be made liable for the employee's recovery against a vessel as a third party "directly or indirectly," and further that "any agreements or warranties to the contrary shall be void." This eliminates, of course, an action over by the vessel owner against the stevedore/employer predicated upon the warranty of workmanlike service, which was the final connecting arc of the Ryan cycle, discussed in the text above on pp. 973–975. To what extent does the "WWLS" survive in other contexts? For an estimation of its present day "withered" form, see Fontenot v. Mesa Petroleum Co., 791 F.2d 1207 (5th Cir.1986). Liability under an implied WWLS was imposed in the case of injury to a seaman through the negligence of a contractor working on the vessel in Campbell Industries, Inc. v. Offshore Logistics Intern., 816 F.2d 1401 (9th Cir. 1987).

But when the LHWCA is inapplicable, e.g., where the injured party is an employee of a municipal corporation, the right to contribution generally recognized in Cooper Stevedoring has been protected. In Purnell v. Norned Shipping B.V., 804 F.2d 248 (3d Cir.1986), cert. denied sub nom. City of Wilmington v. Wilmington Stevedores, Inc., 480 U.S. 934, 107 S.Ct. 1576, 94 L.Ed.2d 767 (1987), the rule is stated that the availability of a suit for contribution depends upon whether the injured party could sue the person from whom the defendant seeks contribution. In the particular case the plaintiff was personal representative of an employee of a municipal corporation and the defendant was a stevedore lessee of a crane of which the plaintiff's decedent was operator when the crane fell into the ship in the loading of which it was employed. Since the plaintiff had a cause of action against the city for wrongful death under the general maritime law, the stevedore had an action against the city for contribution. For an earlier decision in same case, see 801 F.2d 152 (3d Cir.1986).

The provisions of § 905 precluding an action over against the employer in case of injury to a covered worker and the prohibition of contracts for indemnity or contribution has no application to third-party practice among defendants who are not employers. See Hernandez v. M/V Rajaan, 841 F.2d 582 (5th Cir.1988), cert. denied sub nom. Dianella Shipping Corp. v. Hernandez, 488 U.S. 981, 109 S.Ct. 530, 102 L.Ed.2d 562 (1988), in which a longshoreman sued the vessel owner and the vessel in rem and the defendants impleaded the manufacturer of a winch the malfunction of which was alleged to have caused the precipitation of a 110 pound bag of rice on the head of the plaintiff, together with the manufacturer of the winch's remote control system, the miller who had bagged the rice and chartered the vessel, the navigation district that had provided the vessel with berthing, water, and other necessaries, and others unnamed. The third-party defendants settled the damages issue and continued to participate in the trial on the issue of liability. Conceding that the defendants were not automatically entitled to a credit for the settlement, the court ordered that to avoid double recovery the amount of the settlement be deducted. See also Self v. Great Lakes Dredge & Dock Co., 832 F.2d 1540 (11th Cir.1987), cert. denied sub nom. Great Lakes Dredge & Dock Co. v. Chevron Transport Corp., 486 U.S. 1033, 108 S.Ct. 2017, 100 L.Ed.2d 604 (1988).

Similarly, an action by a ship owner to recover from a stevedore the amount of a settlement with a seaman injured in the off-loading of the vessel is within the admiralty jurisdiction. Cooper v. Loper, 923 F.2d 1045 (3d Cir.1991).

In the converse situation, where the injured party has received compensation and has not sued the vessel, the employer who has paid compensation, or its insurance carrier, may sue the vessel directly in tort for the injury done the employer. So much was established prior to the 1972 revision of the Act. Federal

Marine Terminals, Inc. v. Burnside Shipping Co., Ltd., 394 U.S. 404, 89 S.Ct. 1144, 22 L.Ed.2d 371 (1969). See Ray v. Lykes Bros. S.S. Co., 805 F.2d 552 (5th Cir.1986). It remains so after the revision. Hartford Acc. & Indem. Co. v. Costa Lines Cargo Serv., 903 F.2d 352 (5th Cir.1990). On the other hand, the employer has no cause of action against third persons on a theory of subrogation except by way of statutory assignment under § 903(b). This subsection gives the injured employee an exclusive control of the cause of action for 30 days, and in the event that the employee does not bring suit within that time, assigns the right to the employer for 90 days, at which time it is by the statute reassigned to the employee.

In Reed v. The Steamship Yaka, discussed above in subdivision B–1 above at page 978, the 1927 Act had been read to permit a covered employee injured on a vessel owned by his employer to maintain an action against the employer in its capacity as vessel owner, in effect treating the employer-cum-owner as a third party for these purposes. In Jones & Laughlin Steel Corp. v. Pfeifer, 462 U.S. 523, 103 S.Ct. 2541, 76 L.Ed.2d 768, 1983 A.M.C. 1881 (1983), the Supreme Court held that the doctrine of The Yaka was preserved in the amended statute. Justice Stevens conceded that under the plain meaning of § 905(a) compensation under the Act is the sole remedy against the employer, but read § 905(b), also in its plain meaning, to carve out the exception of the longshoreman hired directly by a vessel owner. Unlike the suit of the covered employee against a third person, the suit under § 905(b) against the "vessel" is the sole exception to the exclusive remedy provision of § 905(a). Thus, unlike the case of the third person suit against a third person, in a *Yaka* type action, it is crucial that in the circumstances the employer be owner, owner pro hac vice, agent, operator, or charterer of a vessel on which or in connection with which the employee received his injuries. Otherwise compensation under the LHWCA is his sole relief from his employer. It is held, for example, that a railroad worker who works in a maritime occupation and is injured in statutory navigable waters, may not sue his employer under the FELA. Etheridge v. Norfolk & Western Railway, 9 F.3d 1087 (4th Cir.1993); Kelly v. Pittsburgh & Conneaut Dock Co., 900 F.2d 89 (6th Cir.1990); Harmon v. Baltimore & Ohio Railroad, 741 F.2d 1398 (D.C.Cir.,1984).

When the structure on which a covered employee is injured is a vessel, and the employer is the owner, owner pro hac vice, agent, or charterer of the vessel, its negligence in that capacity may cast it in damages beyond compensation under the Act. Guilles v. Sea–Land Service, Inc., 12 F.3d 381, 1995 A.M.C. 1223 (2d Cir.1993), an action by a shoregang employee injured on his employer's vessel while assigned to the vessel as a relief cook. But the negligence must be in the discharge of the duties imposed upon it in that capacity. See, e.g., Kerr–Magee, supra, indicating that an employer-time charterer may be liable to the injured employee only if it is negligent in the discharge of its duties as a time-charterer. If the structure is owned by the employer and it is not a "vessel" within § 905(b), however, the covered employee is limited to compensation under the Act. In the case of the third-party tortfeasor not the employer, however, the Act relieves the owner or operator from liability for unseaworthiness but does not protect him further, whether the structure is a vessel or not.

To *the Yaka* exception to § 905(a), there are, in turn, two exceptions. First, if the injured person was employed by the vessel to provide stevedoring services, no action against the vessel is permitted in respect of an injury caused by the negligence of other persons engaged to provide stevedoring services. And, second, if the injured person was employed to perform shipbuilding, repairing or breaking services, and the vessel is owned by his employer, he may not maintain an action against the vessel for negligence. These exceptions are specifically limited to the

Yaka type suit, and have been rather strictly limited to the named categories. See, e.g., Gay v. Barge 266, 915 F.2d 1007 (5th Cir.1990). There the plaintiff had been hired to pump out a barge. The court of appeals held that because the plaintiff was not obviously engaged in "repairing" the barge, the issue of employment status should have been put to the jury.

When the employer of an injured longshoreman is also the owner of the vessel, and has paid benefits under the LSHWCA, and the injured longshoreman sues the vessel under the doctrine of The Yaka, the action is treated as if it had been brought against a third person. Thus the net amount of any judgment or settlement is credited against the liability of the employer for compensation under the Act. See Bundens v. J.E. Brenneman Co., 46 F.3d 292, 1995 A.M.C. 1330 (3d Cir.1995),and it it has been held that so distinct are the "two hats" worn by the defendant as employer and as owner, that it it entitled to enforce a lien on the recovery in the action against the vessel for reimbursement of the amounts paid under the Act. Taylor v. Bunge Corp., 845 F.2d 1323 (5th Cir.1988). In *Bundens*, the court indicated that the role playing would not be taken so far as to hold that § 933(g)(1) requires employee to obtain prior written approval of the employer as employer to a settlement to which it is a party as "vessel," or under § 933(g)(2) give written notice of the settlement.

Since § 933 saves remedies against third-party tortfeasors generally, and § 905(b) relates only to "vessels," the injured workman suing a "vessel" under § 905(b) is free to join other third-parties to the extent that he has a cause of action against them, and the vessel owner sued under § 905(b) may implead such a third-party. See, e.g., Barrios v. Pelham Marine, Inc., 796 F.2d 128 (5th Cir.1986), although in that case the third-party claim was found to be frivolous and sanctions imposed under Rule 11.

The provision in § 905(a) to the effect that if the employer does not carry insurance under the Act the injured employee may sue and in such a suit the employer may not take advantage of the defense of contributory negligence has no application to a suit against a third-party tortfeasor. Roach v. M/V Aqua Grace, 857 F.2d 1575 (11th Cir.1988); Reichert v. Chemical Carriers, Inc., 794 F.2d 1557 (11th Cir.1986).

In a case in which the injury is on land under the old Act (e.g., the pier) and is caused in whole or in part by third persons but involves no vessel, the injured longshoreman can proceed under either the LHWCA or the state law (usually the state workmen's compensation law), but in a case in which the state workmen's compensation law bars relief it has been held that § 905(b) is in no way preemptive and does not create a cause of action against the third-party tortfeasor. Therefore, when the State law precludes an action against a contractor as a "statutory employer," no common law action may be brought against the contractor. Garvin v. Alumax of South Carolina, Inc., 787 F.2d 910 (4th Cir.1986), cert. denied, 479 U.S. 914, 107 S.Ct. 314, 93 L.Ed.2d 288 (1986).

In Roach v. M/V Aqua Grace, 857 F.2d 1575 (11th Cir.1988), state law was applied on the issue of whether the vessel owner who hired a contractor to clean the hull of a vessel functioned in the dual capacity of owner and general contractor.

The Standard of Care under *Scindia* and *Howlett*

Where the vessel owner knows of a hazardous condition on the vessel and knows that the stevedore, in the exercise of an obviously improvident judgment, intends to continue work in spite of the condition, it has a duty under *Scindia* to intervene. See Gay v. Barge 266, 915 F.2d 1007, 1012 (5th Cir.1990). In *Gay* it was held that the barge owner was negligent for failure to intervene when when its employee was using a board as a gangplank.

An unreasonably dangerous condition, and hence a violation of the *Scindia* "turnover" duty was found when an access ladder running from the weather deck of the hatch to the tween deck terminated so close to a second hatch opening, unguarded and uncovered, in which a second ladder, led to the lower hold, and the longshore worker came down the first ladder backward, took her hand off the ladder and took one step and fell down the second opening. Thomas v. Newton International Enterprises, 42 F.3d 1266, 1995 A.M.C. 388 (9th Cir.1994). The court held that the district court did not err in admitting expert testimony by a longshoreman with 29 years of varied experience in the industry that "the presence of an unguarded uncovered deck opening or manhole positioned within two feet of the bottom of an access ladder is an extremely unusual and hazardous condition," and that "it is customary for a vessel to have in place over all deck openings or manholes either a properly functioning manhole cover or a barricade of some sort such as a large piece of plywood or a chain-type railing." With the *Thomas* case compare Keller v. United States, 38 F.3d 16, 1995 A.M.C. 397 (1st Cir.1994), also a ladder case, in which the district court found the defendant's expert more persuasive.

Howlett does not preclude an action against an onloading stevedore as a third person. In such an action the stevedore is not limited to the "vessel's" duties under *Scindia* and *Howlett*, but has a duty "to load the cargo so that an expert and experienced stevedore will be able to discharge the cargo with reasonable safety by exercising reasonable care." Couch v. Cro–Marine Transport, Inc., 44 F.3d 319, 1995 A.M.C. 1586 (5th Cir.1995). See also Young v. Armadores de Cabotaje, 645 So.2d 1266, 1995 A.M.C. 800 (La.App. 4th Cir.1994), in which the vessel owner and the onloading stevedore had been joined as defendants and the negligence charges 10% to the owner and 90% to the stevedore. After the decision was vacated and remanded for reconsideration in light of *Howlett*, the stevedore was assigned 100%.

CHAPTER 20

DEATH ACTIONS

Miles v. Apex Marine Corp.

Supreme Court of the United States, 1990.
498 U.S. 19, 111 S.Ct. 317, 112 L.Ed.2d 275.

■ JUSTICE O'CONNOR delivered the opinion of the Court.

We decide whether the parent of a seaman who died from injuries incurred aboard respondents' vessel may recover under general maritime law for loss of society, and whether a claim for the seaman's lost future earnings survives his death.

I

Ludwick Torregano was a seaman aboard the vessel *M/V Archon*. On the evening of July 18, 1984, Clifford Melrose, a fellow crew member, stabbed Torregano repeatedly, killing him. At the time, the ship was docked in the harbor of Vancouver, Washington.

Mercedel Miles, Torregano's mother and administratrix of his estate, sued Apex Marine Corporation and Westchester Marine Shipping Company, the vessel's operators, Archon Marine Company, the charterer, and Aeron Marine Company, the Archon's owner (collectively Apex), in United States District Court for the Eastern District of Louisiana. Miles alleged negligence under the Jones Act, 46 U.S.C. App. § 688, for failure to prevent the assault on her son, and breach of the warranty of seaworthiness under general maritime law for hiring a crew member unfit to serve. She sought compensation for loss of support and services and loss of society resulting from the death of her son, punitive damages, and compensation to the estate for Torregano's pain and suffering prior to his death and for his lost future income.

At trial, the District Court granted Apex's motion to strike the claim for punitive damages, ruled that the estate could not recover Torregano's lost future income, and denied Miles' motion for a directed verdict as to negligence and unseaworthiness. The court instructed the jury that Miles could not recover damages for loss of society if they found that she was not financially dependent on her son.

The jury found that Apex was negligent and that Torregano was 7% contributorily negligent in causing his death, but that the ship was seaworthy. After discounting for Torregano's contributory negligence, the jury awarded Miles $7,254 for the loss of support and services of her son and awarded the estate $130,200 for Torregano's pain and suffering. The jury also found that Miles was not financially dependent on her son and therefore not entitled to damages for loss of society. The District Court denied both parties' motions for judgment notwithstanding the verdict and entered judgment accordingly.

The United States Court of Appeals for the Fifth Circuit affirmed in part, reversed in part, and remanded. 882 F.2d 976 (1989). The court affirmed the judgment of negligence on the part of Apex, but held that there was insufficient evidence to support the contributory negligence finding. Id., at 983–985. Miles was therefore entitled to the full measure of $7,800 for loss of support and services, and the estate entitled to $140,000 for Torregano's pain and suffering. The court also found that Melrose's extraordinarily violent disposition demonstrated that he was unfit, and therefore that the Archon was unseaworthy as a matter of law. Id., at 983. Because this ruling revived Miles' general maritime claim, the court considered two questions concerning the scope of damages under general maritime law. The court reaffirmed its prior decision in Sistrunk v. Circle Bar Drilling Co., 770 F.2d 455 (C.A.5th.1985), holding that a nondependent parent may not recover for loss of society in a general maritime wrongful death action. 882 F.2d, at 989. It also held that general maritime law does not permit a survival action for decedent's lost future earnings. Id., at 987.

We granted Miles' petition for certiorari on these two issues, 494 U.S. 1003, 110 S.Ct. 1295, 108 L.Ed.2d 472 (1990), and now affirm the judgment of the Court of Appeals.

II

We rely primarily on Moragne v. States Marine Lines, Inc., 398 U.S. 375, 90 S.Ct. 1772, 26 L.Ed.2d 339 (1970). Edward Moragne was a longshoreman who had been killed aboard a vessel in United States and Florida territorial waters. His widow brought suit against the shipowner, seeking to recover damages for wrongful death due to the unseaworthiness of the ship. The District Court dismissed that portion of the complaint because neither federal nor Florida statutes allowed a wrongful death action sounding in unseaworthiness where death occurred in territorial waters. General maritime law was also no help; in *The Harrisburg*, 119 U.S. 199, 7 S.Ct. 140, 30 L.Ed. 358 (1886), this Court held that maritime law does not afford a cause of action for wrongful death. The Court of Appeals affirmed.

This Court overruled The Harrisburg. After questioning whether *The Harrisburg* was a proper statement of the law even in 1886, the Court set aside that issue because a "development of major significance ha[d] intervened." *Moragne*, supra, 398 U.S., at 388, 90 S.Ct., at 1781. Specifically, the state legislatures and Congress had rejected wholesale the rule against wrongful death. Every State in the Union had enacted a wrongful death statute. In 1920, Congress enacted two pieces of legislation creating a wrongful death action for most maritime deaths. The Jones Act, 46 U.S.C.App. § 688, through incorporation of the Federal Employers' Liability Act (FELA), 35 Stat. 65, as amended, 45 U.S.C. §§ 51–59, created a wrongful death action in favor of the personal representative of a seaman killed in the course of employment. The Death on the High Seas Act (DOHSA), 46 U.S.C.App. §§ 761 et seq., 762, created a similar action for the representative of anyone killed on the high seas.

These statutes established an unambiguous policy in abrogation of those principles that underlay *The Harrisburg*. Such a policy is "to be given its appropriate weight not only in matters of statutory construction but also in those of decisional law." *Moragne*, supra, at 391, 90 S.Ct., at 1782. Admiralty is not created in a vacuum; legislation has always served as an important source of both common law and admiralty principles. 398 U.S., at 391, 392, 90 S.Ct., at 1782, 1783, citing Landis, Statutes and the Sources of Law, in Harvard Legal Essays 213, 214, 226–227 (1934). The unanimous legislative judgment behind the Jones Act, DOHSA, and the many state statutes created a strong presumption in favor of a general maritime wrongful death action.

But legislation sends other signals to which an admiralty court must attend. "The legislature does not, of course, merely enact general policies. By the terms of a statute, it also indicates its conception of the sphere within which the policy is to have effect." *Moragne*, supra, at 392. 90 S.Ct., at 1783. Congress, in the exercise of its legislative powers, is free to say "this much and no more." An admiralty court is not free to go beyond those limits. The Jones Act and DOHSA established a policy in favor of maritime wrongful death recovery. The central issue in *Moragne* was whether the limits of those statutes proscribed a more general maritime cause of action. 398 U.S., at 393, 90 S.Ct., at 1783–1784.

The Court found no such proscription. Rather, the unfortunate situation of Moragne's widow had been created by a change in the maritime seascape that Congress could not have anticipated. At the time Congress passed the Jones Act and DOHSA, federal courts uniformly applied state wrongful death statutes for deaths occurring in state territorial waters. Except in those rare cases where state statutes were also intended to apply on the high seas, however, there was no recovery for wrongful death outside territorial waters. See *Moragne*, supra, at 393, and n. 10, 90 S.Ct., at 1784, and n. 10. DOHSA filled this void, creating a wrongful death action for all persons killed on the high seas, sounding in both negligence and unseaworthiness. Congress did not extend DOHSA to territorial waters because it believed state statutes sufficient in those areas. 398 U.S., at 397–398, 90 S.Ct., at 1786.

And so they were when DOHSA was passed. All state statutes allowed for wrongful death recovery in negligence, and virtually all DOHSA claims sounded in negligence. Unseaworthiness was "an obscure and relatively little used remedy," largely because a shipowner's duty at that time was only to use due diligence to provide a seaworthy ship. See G. Gilmore & C. Black, The Law of Admiralty 383, 375 (2d ed. 1975). Thus, although DOHSA permitted actions in both negligence and unseaworthiness, it worked essentially as did state wrongful death statutes. DOHSA created a near uniform system of wrongful death recovery.

"The revolution in the law began with Mahnich v. Southern S.S. Co., [321 U.S. 96, 64 S.Ct. 455, 88 L.Ed. 561 (1944)]", in which this Court transformed the warranty of seaworthiness into a strict liability obligation. Gilmore & Black, supra, at 384, 386. The shipowner became liable for failure to supply a safe ship irrespective of fault, and irrespective of the intervening negligence of crew members. *Mahnich*, supra, at 100, 64 S.Ct., at 458 ("[T]he exercise of due diligence does not relieve the owner of his obligation to the seaman to furnish adequate appliances * * * If the owner is liable for furnishing an unseaworthy appliance, even when he is not negligent, *a fortiori* his obligation is unaffected by the fact that the negligence of the officers of the vessel contributed to the unseaworthiness"). The Court reaffirmed the rule two years later in Seas Shipping Co. v. Sieracki, 328 U.S. 85, 94–95, 66 S.Ct. 872, 877–878, 90 L.Ed. 1099 (1946)("[Unseaworthiness] is essentially a species of liability without fault"). As a consequence of this radical change, unseaworthiness "[became] the principal vehicle for recovery by seamen for injury or death." *Moragne*, 398 U.S., at 399, 90 S.Ct., at 1787. DOHSA claims now sounded largely in unseaworthiness. "The resulting discrepancy between the remedies for deaths covered by [DOHSA] and for deaths that happen to fall within a state wrongful-death statute not encompassing unseaworthiness could not have been foreseen by Congress." Ibid.

The emergence of unseaworthiness as a widely used theory of liability made manifest certain anomalies in maritime law that had not previously caused great hardship. First, in territorial waters, general maritime law allowed a remedy for unseaworthiness resulting in injury, but not for death. Second, DOHSA allowed a remedy for death resulting from unseaworthiness on the high seas, but general maritime law did not allow such recovery for a similar death in territorial waters. Finally, in what *Moragne* called the "strangest" anomaly, in those States whose statutes allowed a claim for wrongful death resulting from unseaworthiness, recovery was available for the death of a longshoreman due to unseaworthiness, but not for the death of a Jones Act seaman. See *Moragne*, supra, at 395–396, 90 S.Ct., at 1785. This was because wrongful death actions under the Jones Act are limited to negligence, and the Jones Act pre-empts state law remedies for the death or injury of a seaman. See Gillespie v. United States Steel Corp., 379 U.S. 148, 154–156, 85 S.Ct. 308, 312–313, 13 L.Ed.2d 199 (1964).

The United States, as amicus curiae, urged the *Moragne* Court to eliminate these inconsistencies and render maritime wrongful death law uniform by creating a general maritime wrongful death action applicable in all waters. The territorial limitations placed on wrongful death actions by DOHSA did not bar such a solution. DOHSA was itself a manifestation of congressional intent "to achieve 'uniformity in the exercise of admiralty jurisdiction.'" *Moragne*, supra, 398 U.S., at 401, 90 S.Ct. at 1788, quoting *Gillespie*, supra, 379 U.S., at 155, 85 S.Ct., at 312. Nothing in that Act or in the Jones Act could be read to preclude this Court from exercising its admiralty power to remedy nonuniformities that could not have been anticipated when those statutes were passed. *Moragne*, supra, 398 U.S., at

399–400, 90 S.Ct., at 1787. The Court therefore overruled *The Harrisburg* and created a general maritime wrongful death cause of action. This result was not only consistent with the general policy of both 1920 Acts favoring wrongful death recovery, but also effectuated "the constitutionally based principle that federal admiralty law should be 'a system of law coextensive with, and operating uniformly in, the whole country.' " *Moragne*, supra, 398 U.S., at 402, 90 S.Ct., at 1788, quoting *The Lottawanna*, 88 U.S. 558, 22 L.Ed. 654, 21 Wall. 558, 575 (1875).

III

We have described Moragne at length because it exemplifies the fundamental principles that guide our decision in this case. We no longer live in an era when seamen and their loved ones must look primarily to the courts as a source of substantive legal protection from injury and death; Congress and the States have legislated extensively in these areas. In this era, an admiralty court should look primarily to these legislative enactments for policy guidance. We may supplement these statutory remedies where doing so would achieve the uniform vindication of such policies consistent with our constitutional mandate, but we must also keep strictly within the limits imposed by Congress. Congress retains superior authority in these matters, and an admiralty court must be vigilant not to overstep the well-considered boundaries imposed by federal legislation. These statutes both direct and delimit our actions.

Apex contends that *Moragne's* holding, creating a general maritime wrongful death action, does not apply in this case because Moragne was a longshoreman, whereas Torregano was a true seaman. Apex is correct that *Moragne* does not apply on its facts, but we decline to limit *Moragne* to its facts.

Historically, a shipowner's duty of seaworthiness under general maritime law ran to seamen in the ship's employ. See *Sieracki*, 328 U.S., at 90, 66 S.Ct., at 875. In *Sieracki*, we extended that duty to stevedores working aboard ship but employed by an independent contractor. Id., at 95, 66 S.Ct., at 877. As this was Moragne's situation, Moragne's widow was able to bring an action for unseaworthiness under general maritime law. In a narrow sense, *Moragne* extends only to suits upon the death of longshoremen like *Moragne*, so-called *Sieracki* seamen. Torregano was a true seaman, employed aboard the Archon. Were we to limit *Moragne* to its facts, Miles would have no general maritime wrongful death action. Indeed, were we to limit Moragne to its facts, that case would no longer have any applicability at all. In 1972, Congress amended the Longshore and Harbor Workers' Compensation Act (LHWCA), 86 Stat. 1251, as amended, 33 U.S.C. §§ 901–950, to bar any recovery from shipowners for the death or injury of a longshoreman or harbor worker resulting from breach of the duty of seaworthiness. See 33 U.S.C. § 905(b); American Export Lines, Inc. v. Alvez, 446 U.S. 274, 282, n. 9, 100 S.Ct. 1673, 1678, n. 9, 64 L.Ed.2d 284 (1980). If Moragne's widow brought her action today, it would be foreclosed by statute.

Apex asks us not to extend *Moragne* to suits for the death of true seamen. This limitation is warranted, they say, because true seamen, unlike longshoremen, are covered under the Jones Act. The Jones Act provides a cause of action against the seaman's employer for wrongful death resulting from negligence that Apex contends is preclusive of any recovery for death from unseaworthiness. See 46 U.S.C.App. § 688.

This Court first addressed the preclusive effect of the Jones Act wrongful death provision in Lindgren v. United States, 281 U.S. 38, 50 S.Ct. 207, 74 L.Ed. 686 (1930). Petitioner, who was not a wrongful death beneficiary under the Jones Act, attempted to recover for the negligence of the shipowner under a state wrongful death statute. The Court held that the Jones Act pre-empted the state statute: "[The Jones] Act is one of general application intended to bring about the uniformity in the exercise of admiralty jurisdiction required by the Constitution, and necessarily supersedes the application of the death statutes of the several States." Id., at 44, 50 S.Ct., at 210. The Court also concluded that the Jones Act, limited as it is to recovery for negligence, would preclude recovery for the wrongful death of a seaman resulting from the unseaworthiness of the vessel. Id., at 47–48, 50 S.Ct., at 211–212. In Gillespie v. United States Steel Corp., 379 U.S. 148, 85 S.Ct. 308, 13 L.Ed.2d 199 (1964), the Court reaffirmed *Lindgren*, and held that the Jones Act precludes recovery under a state statute for the wrongful death of a seaman due to unseaworthiness. Id., at 154–156, 85 S.Ct., at 312–313.

Neither *Lindgren* nor *Gillespie* considered the effect of the Jones Act on a general maritime wrongful death action. Indeed, no such action existed at the time those cases were decided. *Moragne* addressed the question explicitly. The Court explained there that the preclusive effect of the Jones Act established in *Lindgren* and *Gillespie* extends only to state remedies and not to a general maritime wrongful death action. See *Moragne*, 398 U.S., at 396, n. 12, 90 S.Ct., at 1785, n. 12.

The Jones Act provides an action in negligence for the death or injury of a seaman. It thereby overruled The Osceola, 189 U.S. 158, 23 S.Ct. 483, 47 L.Ed. 760 (1903), which established that seamen could recover under general maritime law for injuries resulting from unseaworthiness, but not negligence. The Jones Act evinces no general hostility to recovery under maritime law. It does not disturb seamen's general maritime claims for injuries resulting from unseaworthiness, Pacific Steamship Co. v. Peterson, 278 U.S. 130, 139, 49 S.Ct. 75, 78, 73 L.Ed. 220 (1928), and it does not preclude the recovery for wrongful death due to unseaworthiness created by its companion statute DOHSA. Kernan v. American Dredging Co., 355 U.S. 426, 430, n. 4, 78 S.Ct. 394, 397, n. 4, 2 L.Ed.2d 382 (1958). Rather, the Jones Act establishes a uniform system of seamen's tort law parallel to that available to employees of interstate railway carriers under FELA. As the Court concluded in *Moragne*, the extension of the DOHSA wrongful death action to territorial waters furthers rather than hinders uniformity in the exercise of admiralty jurisdiction. *Moragne*, supra, 398 U.S., at 396, n. 12, 90 S.Ct., at 1785, n. 12.

There is also little question that *Moragne* intended to create a general maritime wrongful death action applicable beyond the situation of longshoremen.   For one thing, *Moragne* explicitly overruled *The Harrisburg*. *Moragne*, supra, 398 U.S., at 409, 90 S.Ct., at 1792.   *The Harrisburg* involved a true seaman.   *The Harrisburg*, 119 U.S., at 200, 7 S.Ct., at 141. In addition, all three of the "anomalies" to which the *Moragne* cause of action was directed involved seamen.   The "strangest" anomaly—that recovery was available for the wrongful death in territorial waters of a longshoreman, but not a true seaman—could only be remedied if the *Moragne* wrongful death action extended to seamen.   It would be strange indeed were we to read *Moragne* as not addressing a problem that in large part motivated its result.   If there has been any doubt about the matter, we today make explicit that there is a general maritime cause of action for the wrongful death of a seaman, adopting the reasoning of the unanimous and carefully crafted opinion in *Moragne*.

IV

Moragne did not set forth the scope of the damages recoverable under the maritime wrongful death action.   The Court first considered that question in Sea–Land Services, Inc. v. Gaudet, 414 U.S. 573, 94 S.Ct. 806, 39 L.Ed.2d 9 (1974).   Respondent brought a general maritime action to recover for the wrongful death of her husband, a longshoreman.   The Court held that a dependent plaintiff in a maritime wrongful death action could recover for the pecuniary losses of support, services, and funeral expenses, as well as for the nonpecuniary loss of society suffered as the result of the death.   Id., at 691, 94 S.Ct., at 818.   Gaudet involved the death of a longshoreman in territorial waters.[1]   Consequently, the Court had no need to consider the preclusive effect of DOHSA for deaths on the high seas, or the Jones Act for deaths of true seamen.

We considered DOHSA in Mobil Oil Corp. v. Higginbotham, 436 U.S. 618, 98 S.Ct. 2010, 56 L.Ed.2d 581 (1978).   That case involved death on the high seas and, like *Gaudet*, presented the question of loss of society damages in a maritime wrongful death action.   The Court began by recognizing that *Gaudet*, although broadly written, applied only in territorial waters and therefore did not decide the precise question presented.   Id., at 622–623, 98 S.Ct., at 2013–2014.   Congress made the decision for us. DOHSA, by its terms, limits recoverable damages in wrongful death suits to "pecuniary loss sustained by the persons for whose benefit the suit is brought."   46 U.S.C.App. § 762 (emphasis added).   This explicit limitation forecloses recovery for non-pecuniary loss, such as loss of society, in a general maritime action.

Respondents argued that admiralty courts have traditionally undertaken to supplement maritime statutes.   The Court's answer in *Higginbotham* is fully consistent with those principles we have here derived from Mo-

---

1. As with *Moragne*, the 1972 amendments to LHWCA have rendered *Gaudet* inapplicable on its facts. See supra, at 323; 33 U.S.C. § 905(b).   Suit in *Gaudet* was filed before 1972.   Gaudet v. Sea–Land Services, Inc., 463 F.2d 1331, 1332 (C.A.5 1972).

ragne: Congress has spoken directly to the question of recoverable damages on the high seas, and "when it does speak directly to a question, the courts are not free to 'supplement' Congress' answer so thoroughly that the Act becomes meaningless." *Higginbotham*, supra, at 625, 98 S.Ct., at 2015. *Moragne* involved gap-filling in an area left open by statute; supplementation was entirely appropriate. But in an "area covered by the statute, it would be no more appropriate to prescribe a different measure of damages than to prescribe a different statute of limitations, or a different class of beneficiaries." *Higginbotham*, supra, at 625, 98 S.Ct., at 2015.

The logic of *Higginbotham* controls our decision here. The holding of *Gaudet* applies only in territorial waters, and it applies only to longshoremen. *Gaudet* did not consider the preclusive effect of the Jones Act for deaths of true seamen. We do so now.

Unlike DOHSA, the Jones Act does not explicitly limit damages to any particular form. Enacted in 1920, the Jones Act makes applicable to seamen the substantive recovery provisions of the older FELA. See 46 U.S.C.App. § 688. FELA recites only that employers shall be liable in "damages" for the injury or death of one protected under the Act. 45 U.S.C. § 51. In Michigan Central R. Co. v. Vreeland, 227 U.S. 59, 33 S.Ct. 192, 57 L.Ed. 417 (1913), however, the Court explained that the language of the FELA wrongful death provision is essentially identical to that of Lord Campbell's Act, 9 & 10 Vict. ch. 93 (1846), the first wrongful death statute. Lord Campbell's Act also did not limit explicitly the "damages" to be recovered, but that Act and the many state statutes that followed it consistently had been interpreted as providing recovery only for pecuniary loss. Vreeland, supra, at 69–71, 33 S.Ct., at 195–196. The Court so construed FELA. Ibid.

When Congress passed the Jones Act, the Vreeland gloss on FELA, and the hoary tradition behind it, were well established. Incorporating FELA unaltered into the Jones Act, Congress must have intended to incorporate the pecuniary limitation on damages as well. We assume that Congress is aware of existing law when it passes legislation. See Cannon v. University of Chicago, 441 U.S. 677, 696–697, 99 S.Ct. 1946, 1957, 60 L.Ed.2d 560 (1979). There is no recovery for loss of society in a Jones Act wrongful death action.

The Jones Act also precludes recovery for loss of society in this case. The Jones Act applies when a seaman has been killed as a result of negligence and it limits recovery to pecuniary loss. The general maritime claim here alleged that Torregano had been killed as a result of the unseaworthiness of the vessel. It would be inconsistent with our place in the constitutional scheme were we to sanction more expansive remedies in a judicially-created cause of action in which liability is without fault than Congress has allowed in cases of death resulting from negligence. We must conclude that there is no recovery for loss of society in a general maritime action for the wrongful death of a Jones Act seaman.

Our decision also remedies an anomaly we created in *Higginbotham*. Respondents in that case warned that the elimination of loss of society damages for wrongful deaths on the high seas would create an unwarranted inconsistency between deaths in territorial waters, where loss of society was available under *Gaudet*, and deaths on the high seas. We recognized the value of uniformity, but concluded that a concern for consistency could not override the statute. *Higginbotham*, 436 U.S., at 624, 98 S.Ct., at 2014. Today we restore a uniform rule applicable to all actions for the wrongful death of a seaman, whether under DOHSA, the Jones Act, or general maritime law.

V

We next must decide whether, in a general maritime action surviving the death of a seaman, the estate can recover decedent's lost future earnings. Under traditional maritime law, as under common law, there is no right of survival; a seaman's personal cause of action does not survive the seaman's death. Cortes v. Baltimore Insular Line, Inc., 287 U.S. 367, 371, 53 S.Ct. 173, 174, 77 L.Ed. 368 (1932); Romero v. International Terminal Operating Co., 358 U.S. 354, 373, 79 S.Ct. 468, 480, 3 L.Ed.2d 368 (1959); *Gillespie*, 379 U.S., at 157, 85 S.Ct., at 313–314.

 Congress and the States have changed the rule in many instances. The Jones Act, through its incorporation of FELA, provides that a seaman's right of action for injuries due to negligence survives to the seaman's personal representative. See 45 U.S.C. § 59; *Gillespie*, supra, at 157, 85 S.Ct., at 313. Most States have survival statutes applicable to tort actions generally, see 1 S. Speiser, Recovery for Wrongful Death 2d § 3.2, (1975 and Supp.1989), 2 id., §§ 14.1, 14.3, App.A., and admiralty courts have applied these state statutes in many instances to preserve suits for injury at sea. See, e.g., Just v. Chambers, 312 U.S. 383, 391, 61 S.Ct. 687, 693, 85 L.Ed. 903 (1941). See also Kernan v. American Dredging Co., 355 U.S. 426, 430, n. 4, 78 S.Ct. 394, 397, n. 4, 2 L.Ed.2d 382 (1958); Kossick v. United Fruit Co., 365 U.S. 731, 739, 81 S.Ct. 886, 892, 6 L.Ed.2d 56 (1961); *Gillespie*, supra, 379 U.S., at 157, 85 S.Ct., at 313–314; Comment, Application of State Survival Statutes in Maritime Causes, 60 Colum.L.Rev. 534, 535, n. 11 (1960); Nagy, The General Maritime Law Survival Action: What are the Elements of Recoverable Damages?, 9 U.Haw.L.Rev. 5, 27 (1987). Where these state statutes do not apply,[2] however, or where there is no state survival statute, there is no survival of unseaworthiness claims absent a change in the traditional maritime rule.

Several Courts of Appeals have relied on *Moragne* to hold that there is a general maritime right of survival. See Spiller v. Thomas M. Lowe, Jr., & Assocs., Inc., 466 F.2d 903, 909 (C.A.8 1972); Barbe v. Drummond, 507 F.2d 794, 799–800 (C.A.1 1974); Law v. Sea Drilling Corp., 523 F.2d 793, 795 (C.A.5 1975); Evich v. Connelly, 759 F.2d 1432, 1434 (C.A.9 1985). As we have noted, *Moragne* found that congressional and state abrogation of

---

2. In Offshore Logistics, Inc. v. Tallentire, 477 U.S. 207, 215, n. 1, 106 S.Ct. 2485, 2490, n. 1, 91 L.Ed.2d 174 (1986), we declined to approve or disapprove the practice of some courts of applying state survival statutes to cases involving death on the high seas.

the maritime rule against wrongful death actions demonstrated a strong policy judgment, to which the Court deferred. *Moragne*, 398 U.S., at 388–393, 90 S.Ct., at 1781–1784. Following this reasoning, the lower courts have looked to the Jones Act and the many state survival statutes and concluded that these enactments dictate a change in the general maritime rule against survival. See, e.g., Spiller, supra, at 909; Barbe, supra, at 799–800, and n. 6.

Miles argues that we should follow the Courts of Appeals and recognize a general maritime survival right. Apex urges us to reaffirm the traditional maritime rule and overrule these decisions. We decline to address the issue, because its resolution is unnecessary to our decision on the narrow question presented: whether the income decedent would have earned but for his death is recoverable. We hold that it is not.

Recovery of lost future income in a survival suit will, in many instances, be duplicative of recovery by dependents for loss of support in a wrongful death action; the support dependents lose as a result of a seaman's death would have come from the seaman's future earnings. Perhaps for this reason, there is little legislative support for such recovery in survival. In only a few States can an estate recover in a survival action for income decedent would have received but for death.[3] At the federal level, DOHSA contains no survival provision. The Jones Act incorporates FELA's survival provision, but, as in most States, recovery is limited to losses suffered during the decedent's lifetime. See 45 U.S.C. § 59; Van Beeck v. Sabine Towing Co., 300 U.S. 342, 347, 57 S.Ct. 452, 45s455, 81 L.Ed. 685 (1937); St. Louis, I.M. & S.R. Co. v. Craft, 237 U.S. 648, 658, 35 S.Ct. 704, 706, 59 L.Ed. 1160 (1915).

This state and federal legislation hardly constitutes the kind of "wholesale" and "unanimous" policy judgment that prompted the Court to create a new cause of action in *Moragne*. See *Moragne*, supra, 398 U.S., at 388, 389, 90 S.Ct., at 1781, 1782. To the contrary, the considered judgment of a large majority of American legislatures is that lost future income is not recoverable in a survival action. Were we to recognize a right to such recovery under maritime law, we would be adopting a distinctly minority view.

This fact alone would not necessarily deter us, if recovery of lost future income were more consistent with the general principles of maritime tort law. There are indeed strong policy arguments for allowing such recovery. See, e.g., R. Posner, Economic Analysis of Law 176–181 (3d ed. 1986)(recovery of lost future income provides efficient incentives to take care by

---

3. See Mich.Comp.Laws §§ 600.2921, 600.2922 (1986); Olivier v. Houghton County St. R. Co., 134 Mich. 367, 368–370, 96 N.W. 434, 435 (1903); 42 Pa.Cons.Stat. § 8302 (1988); Incollingo v. Ewing, 444 Pa. 263, 307–308, 282 A.2d 206, 229 (1971); Wash. Rev.Code § 4.20.060 (1989); Balmer v. Dilley, 81 Wash.2d 367, 370, 502 P.2d 456, 458 (1972). See generally 2 S. Speiser, Recovery for Wrongful Death 2d § 14.7, App. A (1975 and Supp.1989). Speiser explains that many states do not allow any recovery of lost earnings in survival, and that among those that do, recovery is generally limited to earnings lost from the time of injury to the time of death. Ibid.

insuring that the tortfeasor will have to bear the total cost of the victim's injury or death). Moreover, Miles reminds us that admiralty courts have always shown a special solicitude for the welfare of seamen and their families. "[C]ertainly it better becomes the humane and liberal character of proceedings in admiralty to give than to withhold the remedy." *Moragne,* supra, at 387, 90 S.Ct., at 1781, quoting Chief Justice Chase in The Sea Gull, 21 F.Cas. 909, 910 (No. 12,578)(CC Md.1865). See also Gaudet, 414 U.S., at 583, 94 S.Ct., at 814.

We are not unmindful of these principles, but they are insufficient in this case. We sail in occupied waters. Maritime tort law is now dominated by federal statute, and we are not free to expand remedies at will simply because it might work to the benefit of seaman and those dependent upon them. Congress has placed limits on recovery in survival actions that we cannot exceed. Because this case involves the death of a seaman, we must look to the Jones Act.

The Jones Act/FELA survival provision limits recovery to losses suffered during the decedent's lifetime. See 45 U.S.C. § 59. This was the established rule under FELA when Congress passed the Jones Act, incorporating FELA, see St. Louis, I.M. & S.R. Co., supra, 237 U.S., at 658, 35 S.Ct., at 706, and it is the rule under the Jones Act. See Van Beeck, supra, 300 U.S., at 347, 57 S.Ct., at 454–455. Congress has limited the survival right for seamen's injuries resulting from negligence. As with loss of society in wrongful death actions, this forecloses more expansive remedies in a general maritime action founded on strict liability. We will not create, under our admiralty powers, a remedy disfavored by a clear majority of the States and that goes well beyond the limits of Congress' ordered system of recovery for seamen's injury and death. Because Torregano's estate cannot recover for his lost future income under the Jones Act, it cannot do so under general maritime law

VI

Cognizant of the constitutional relationship between the courts and Congress, we today act in accordance with the uniform plan of maritime tort law Congress created in DOHSA and the Jones Act. We hold that there is a general maritime cause of action for the wrongful death of a seaman, but that damages recoverable in such an action do not include loss of society. We also hold that a general maritime survival action cannot include recovery for decedent's lost future earnings. Accordingly, the judgment of the Court of Appeals is

Affirmed.

■ JUSTICE SOUTER took no part in the consideration or decision of this case.

NOTE

When Carey v. Berkshire Railroad, 1 Cush. 475 (1848) was decided by the Massachusetts court, Baker v. Bolton, in which the English court had first indicated that the common law did not recognize a cause of action for wrongful death, was forty years old, and Lord Campbell's Act (1846) had been enacted. Although there were a few ripples in the pattern, the English model of rejecting common law development of death actions in favor of statutory treatment became universal in the States. Congress never adopted a generally applicable statute on the subject, perhaps because in diversity cases, which would account for the large bulk of such actions, the Rules of Decision Act required the application of state statutes, and while the state statutes varied in detail, they were generally patterned after Lord Campbell's Act and there seems to have been no groundswell in support of a change in substance. The issue did not reach the Supreme Court until 1878, In Mobile Life Ins. Co. v. Brame, 95 U.S. (5 Otto) 754, 24 L.Ed. 580 (1877), in which the insurer of the life of a murder victim sued the murderer for its alleged damage in having to pay the proceeds of the policy. In *Brame*, there was a State statute, but like the other state statutes, it created a cause of action only for the benefit of named relatives. The Court declined to create a common law cause of action that would permit recovery by others.

The question of wrongful death in the admiralty was somewhat different. The Rules of Decision Act did not require the application of state statutes in admiralty cases. In The Harrisburg, 119 U.S. 199, 7 S.Ct. 140, 30 L.Ed. 358 (1886), the death took place in Massachusetts, which had long had a wrongful death statute, but the plaintiff had let the statute of limitations run on his claim, and his lawyer was therefore obliged to sue in admiralty, which had no statute of limitation, and argue that the maritime law gave him a cause of action independent of the state statute. The Supreme Court, having rejected this argument at common law in *Brame* found no reason to depart from it in admiralty cases. It indicated that where applicable the state statutes would be applied in admiralty. Some adjustments remained. In The Corsair, 145 U.S. 335, 12 S.Ct. 949, 36 L.Ed. 727 (1892), it was held that an action under the state statute could not be prosecuted in the admiralty court in rem unless the statute created a lien, and indicated that by analogy to the home port lien for necessaries, such a lien would be enforced by the admiralty court. In The Hamilton, 207 U.S. 398, 28 S.Ct. 133, 52 L.Ed. 264 (1907), the dictum in The Harrisburg was made holding, and it was indicated that where applicable, the state statutes would ne enforced in actions involving death on the high seas.

The first of the federal Acts was the Employer's Liability Act (FELA) in 1908. The FELA, in principal part, made carriers by railroad liable for negligent injury to their employees in the course of their employment, free from the common law defense of fellow servant negligence, the bar of contributory negligence and assumption of risk. The wrongful death provision was typical of the state statutes. It appears to have been designed to guard against the possibility that the State statutes might be construed as not covering the broader liability created by the Act, e.g., fellow servant negligence. Although the FELA was not generally applicable, it imposed liability on carriers by railroad for injuries or death as a result of defect or insufficiency due to its negligence, in, inter alia, it "boats, wharves, or other equipment."

In 1915, Congress took the first step in the elimination of the fellow servant doctrine in maritime cases with the passage of § 20 of the Shipping Act, which narrowed the concept of a fellow servant doctrine to permit the seaman to sue for injuries caused by the negligence of his superiors. By this time the fashion of reform had passed from statutory abrogation of the fellow servant defense to workmen's compensation. In 1916 Congress enacted the Federal Employees Compensation Act, and in 1917, after it was held in *Jensen* that the state workmen's compensation acts could not be applied in maritime cases, it amended the Saving to Suitors Clause to include such in the remedies saved. 40 Stat. 395 (1917).

In 1918, the Supreme Court in effect nullified § 20, read The Osceola to hold that, independent of the fellow servant doctrine a seaman had no maritime cause of action, and held that a the maritime law governs all maritime causes whether in a common law court state or federal, or an admiralty court. Chelentis v. Luckenbach. See Chap. 11–B above.

As 1920 dawned, the decision in *Jensen* barred the application of state workmen's compensation remedies to maritime torts, and the decision upholding the Act of 1917 had been appealed and the appeal had been argued argued in the Supreme Court. *Chelentis* preserved the fellow servant doctrine in admiralty cases, albeit by another name. Meanwhile doubts had grown about the extent to which state statutes applied to deaths outside the boundaries of the state. This appears to have had no particular connection between the problem of death on the high seas and the problem of the limitations of The Osceola in maritime law of master-servant torts.

The DOHSA was general in its application, with no special reference to seamen, and was crafted to preserve the application of the state statutes in the case of wrongful death in domestic waters. It was carefully limited to deaths on the high seas, and the state remedies for death on domestic waters was carefully preserved, it gave no hint of dissatisfaction with the state law remedies apart from the fear that they did not reach the case of death on the high seas.

Also in March the Supreme Court handed down its decision in Knickerbocker Ice. Co. v. Stewart. See Chap.11–B above, striking down the statute of 1917 extending the state workmen's compensation remedy to maritime cases, and in June the Jones Act was enacted, extending the FELA to seamen. Does this history suggest that the Congress intended to apply a different rule in connection with the death of seamen on the high seas from the rule to be applied to the case of death on domestic waters? Or was it designed as a gap filler, permitting an employee action for negligence in the case of injury, with the death provision tacked on to make certain that the action for death would be coextensive with the newly created cause action for injury.

Is there another possibility? Is it possible that the Congress might have assumed that the Jones Act was coextensive with the employer's liability? Carlisle Packing Co. v. Sandanger, 259 U.S. 255, 42 S.Ct. 475, 66 L.Ed. 927 (1922), hinting at the absolute nature of the duty to provide a seaworthy vessel at the time the vessel leaves the pier, was two years off, and Mahnich v. Southern Steamship Co., 321 U.S. 96, 64 S.Ct. 455, 88 L.Ed. 561 (1944), extending the absolute duty post departure, was twenty-four years in the future. The FELA dealt with two separate categories of negligence. The carrier was made liable for injury to and death of an employee "resulting in whole or in part from the negligence of any of the officers, agents, or employees of such carrier, or by reason of any defect or insufficiency, due to its negligence, in its cars, engines, appliances, machinery, track, roadbed, works, boats, wharves, or other equipment." If seaworthiness is conceived of as negligence, doesn't this provision cover "the whole thing"?

In this connection it is to be noted that the Jones Act is not only limited to actions by seamen but to actions against the seaman's employer. In all other cases, presumably, seamen's actions respecting incidents on domestic waters were left to state law, and incidents on the high seas to the DOHSA. In short, the Jones Act reformed the law of master and servant torts within the maritime jurisdiction.

As applied in death cases, did the decision in *Mahnich*, turn The Osceola upside down? In The Osceola it was stated that the maritime law provided no general action for negligence of the master and crew, but there was an action for unseaworthiness. If an action under the Jones Act required negligence, and an action for unseaworthiness required no proof of negligence, then on domestic waters there was no action for unseaworthiness. And indeed this is what was held in Lindgren v. The United States, 281 U.S. 38, 50 S.Ct. 207, 74 L.Ed. 686 (1930), and reiterated in Gillespie v. United States Steel Corp., 379 U.S. 148, 85 S.Ct. 308, 13 L.Ed.2d 199 (1964). This is what was referred to in *Moragne* as "the strangest anomaly" at which the creation of a action for wrongful death under the general maritime law.

Are Justice O'Connor's "other signals" new ones, or echos of signals long unattended to? Does the decision in *Miles* solve the problem?

In the 1920 statutory scheme, there was no provision for an action for wrongful death of a longshoreman or harborworker. The reason for this appears to be straightforward. Congress read the decision in *Knickerbocker* to rest on the Saving to Suitors Clause and in 1922 it amended the statute to cover longshoremen under the state workmen's compensation schemes. When this scheme failed, it enacted the Longshoremen's and Harbor Workers' Compensation Act in 1926. Since the LHWCA also included a death benefit provision, the action for wrongful death against the employer was covered by federal law, but in actions against third persons, the state statutes were applied. In Seas Shipping Co. v. Sieracki, 328 U.S. 85, 66 S.Ct. 872, 90 L.Ed. 1099 (1946), the Court extended to longshoremen and other persons "doing the work of seamen" the benefit of the the *Mahnich* rule in actions against a vessel or its owner as a third-person tortfeasor. This created another hiatus in the actions for wrongful death, for some state statutes were construed to cover cases of absolute liability, while others, like the Jones Act, required negligence. Persons not seamen under the Jones Act and who did not die from an incident on the high seas, passengers and victims of accidents in pleasure boats, for example, were governed by the state statutes. Since such persons were not given the benefit of *Mahnich* unseaworthiness, generally had a remedy, but were subject to whatever limitations the state acts imposed, such as limitations on the type of damages or limit on the amount of damages.

In *Miles*, Justice O'Connor first stated that the decision in *Gaudet* applies "only to territorial waters, and it applies only to longshoremen," adding in a footnote, "As with *Moragne*, the 1972 amendments to LHWCA have rendered *Gaudet* inapplicable on its facts." Why is this so? Suppose the survivors of a longshore worker sues the vessel under 46 U.S.C. § 905(b) for wrongful death brought about by negligence. Why doesn't the same issue of damages arise?

Why does the Court suggest that *Gaudet* applied only to longshoremen? What would be the law applied to the death of a passenger on domestic waters? Is there any reason why a longshoreman, who is a resident of the state should be protected against possible deficiencies in the state wrongful death Act, and a foreign passenger on an ocean liner whose death took place within the three mile limit should be left to its mercy?

Does *Miles* govern the issue of eligibility as well as the issue of damages? For example, if a seaman's death takes place on domestic waters, leaving a spouse or child, may a *Moragne* action be brought on behalf of a dependent brother as well, or, following the Jones Act, only on behalf of the spouse or child? Does the fact that the Congressional signals in the Jones Act and the DOHSA differ leave the Court free to pick one? Must it grant relief to the brother in the event of a verdict of unseaworthiness, but not on a verdict of negligence?

The courts have had some trouble measuring the fallout from *Miles*. Consider the following possibilities:

(1) The survivors of a longshoreman, such as received the benefit of *Gaudet*, sue under § 905(b). See Randall v. Chevron U.S.A., 13 F.3d 888, 1994 A.M.C. 1217 (5th Cir.1994), modified 22 F.3d 568 (5th Cir.1994), holding that *Gaudet* and not *Miles* controls. Holding that *Miles* precludes non-pecuniary loss damages in an action by a covered employee under § 905(b), see Smallwood v. American Trading, 839 F.Supp. 1377, 1994 A.M.C. 1384 (N.D.Cal.1993)

(2) In an action against a third-party tortfeasor not a "vessel" the court in *Smallwood* supra held that *Miles* precludes non-pecuniary damages but that they can be awarded under state law.

(3) A longshoreman whose death takes place on the high seas. Holding that *Higginbotham* and *Miles* control and the damages are controlled by the DOHSA. Nichols v. Petroleum Helicopters, 17 F.3d 119, 1994 A.M.C. 1710 (5th Cir.1994).

(4) An action by a Jones Act seaman against a person not his employer (and therefore not within the Jones Act). Holding that *Miles* precludes damages for loss of consortium, see Davis v. Bender Shipbuilding and Repair Co., Inc., 27 F.3d 426, 1994 A.M.C. 2587 (9th Cir.1994). To the contrary, Cleveland Tankers Lim. Procs., 843 F.Supp. 1157, 1994 A.M.C. 2538 (E.D.Mich.1994).

(5) Although there have been no cases that raise the issue of whether a commercial passenger may recover non-pecuniary damages decided since *Miles*, it has been decided that such damages are not precluded in a personal injury case brought by a passenger. See Chan v. Society Expeditions, Inc., 39 F.3d 1398, 1994 A.M.C. 2642 (9th Cir.1994)(high seas); Emery v. Rock Island Boatworks, Inc., 847 F.Supp. 114, 1994 A.M.C. 2329 (C.D.Ill.1994)(territorial waters).

(6) The cases involving the survivors of accidents in pleasure boats cannot be reconciled. Holding that *Miles* applies and that plaintiff cannot recover for loss of society, at least where the person for whom the action is brought was not a dependent of the deceased, see Wahlstrom v. Kawasaki Heavy Industries, Ltd., 4 F.3d 1084, 1994 A.M.C. 13 (2d Cir.1993). To the contrary, see Earles v. United States, 26 F.3d 903, 1994 A.M.C. 2007 (9th Cir.1994).

(7) Does *Miles* apply to preclude damages for loss of consortium or loss of society in actions for personal injury as well as actions for wrongful death? Holding "yes," see Horsley v. Mobil Oil Corporation, 15 F.3d 200, 1994 A.M.C. 1372 (1st Cir.1994),

The question of whether *Miles* or *Gaudet* or *Alvis* applies assumes the application of the federal admiralty law, and does not reach the question of whether the state wrongful death and survival statutes can be applied as a supplementary remedy. In Offshore Logistics, Inc. v. Tallentire, 477 U.S. 207, 106 S.Ct. 2485, 91 L.Ed.2d 174, 1986 A.M.C. 2113 (1986), it was held that the state wrongful death statute could not be used to award nonpecuniary damages in an action under the DOHSA. The Court declined to address the question of whether the state survival statute could be applied to permit recovery of pain and suffering. The courts of appeals had differed on the issue. Cf. Barbe v. Drummond, 507 F.2d 794 (1st Cir.1974) with Dugas v. National Aircraft Corp., 438 F.2d 1386 (3d Cir.1971).

In Calhoun v. Yamaha Motor Corp., U.S.A., 40 F.3d 622, 1995 A.M.C. 1 (3d Cir.1994), it was held that state law provides the rule of decision in a case involving injuries incurred in recreational boating in domestic waters. *Calhoun* was affirmed in Yamaha Motor Corp., U.S.A. v. Calhoun, ___ U.S. ___, 116 S.Ct. 619, 133 L.Ed.2d 578 (1996), reproduced in Chap. 22, infra.

In *Miles*, the Court indicated that although the Jones Act does not govern actions for unseaworthiness, and although DOHSA does not govern actions for seamen's injuries or death on domestic waters, the limitations of these statutory remedies to pecuniary damages reveals the congressional resolution of the issue and therefore when the Court fills gaps in the legislation, it should not go beyond the congressional design. Is it thinkable that in 1920 the Congress deliberately chose to create a system in which the seaman had an action for negligence, wherever occurring, and an action for unseaworthiness if it occurred on the high seas, but not on domestic waters? Is it likely that it deliberately created a system in which an action for the death of a seaman killed on the high seas would be brought on behalf of one set of relatives and an action for death on domestic waters on behalf of another? Justice O'Connor recognized the fact in that in 1920 the Congress could be assumed to believe that unseaworthiness was a breed of negligence. Is there some verbal support for this supposition in the FELA itself? Until unseaworthiness became a basis for liability without fault nearly a quarter of a century after the enactment of the Jones Act, was there ever any need for the application of the DOHSA to the death of a seaman?

Was there any necessity for the application of the state wrongful death statutes in seamen's actions? Note that there does remain the question of whether an action for wrongful death can be brought in rem. Is there any discernible reason for permitting everyone whose death occurred on the high seas a lien but the seaman?

Can you put together a sensible construction of the doctrine of The Harrisburg and The Hamilton, and the Jones Act and the DOHSA?

CHAPTER 21

LIMITATION OF LIABILITY

A. VESSELS

The Yacht Julaine

(Petition of H.T. Porter)

United States District Court, Southern District of Texas, 1967.
272 F.Supp. 282, 1968 A.M.C. 2310.[1]

■ WOODROW B. SEALS, D.J. Claimants Katheryn Skinner Bell and Jack R. Fulton and wife, Mae Belle G. Fulton, have filed a motion to dismiss the above styled and numbered cause for want of jurisdiction. Claimants further request that in the event that the motion to dismiss is denied, this Court certify an interlocutory appeal to the Court of Appeals. The sole question presented for determination at this time is whether the Limitation of Liability Act may be properly applied to a twenty-nine foot pleasure craft such as the Julaine. The portions of the statute relevant to this discussion are found in 46 U.S.C.A. §§ 183 and 188.

The petition for exoneration from or limitation of liability was occasioned by the explosion of the Julaine on August 2, 1964. Claimants were guests on board the vessel at that time. They claim aggregate damages in the amount of $125,000 from petitioners Porter and Bell as a result of their injuries received in the explosion. If petitioners are able to limit their liability under the Act, claimants' recovery, if any, will probably be restricted to less than three thousand dollars.

The original Limitation of Liability Statute was enacted in 1851. 9 Stat. 635. The purpose of the Act was plainly to promote American commercial shipping by protecting private investment against financially staggering claims arising out of shipboard disasters. Cong.Globe, 31st Cong., 2nd Sess. 331, 332, 713–720 (1851). In one of the first cases that considered the application of the Act, the court concluded that the statute was restricted in its application to vessels of a commercial nature. Mamie, 5 F. 813 (E.D.Mich.1881). Accordingly limitation of liability was denied to the owners of a steam pleasure yacht involved in a collision on the Detroit River. In fact, Section 7 of the 1851 Act provided that it should not apply to "any canal boat, barge, or lighter, or to any vessel of any description whatsoever, used in rivers or inland navigation."

1. Footnotes omitted.

1026

But in 1886, Congress amended the Act to extend its application to "all sea-going vessels, and also to all vessels used on lakes or rivers or in inland navigation, including canal-boats, barges, and lighters." 24 Stat. 80 (now 46 U.S.C.A. § 188). Thereafter, judicial interpretation of the Act in relation to pleasure craft changed accordingly. By 1937, the Court of Appeals for the Sixth Circuit specifically held that the Act applied to any vessel; in this case a fifteen-foot Chris–Craft motorboat used for pleasure on the Ohio River. Feige v. Hurley, 89 F.2d 575, 1937 A.M.C. 913 (6 Cir.1937).

The reasoning of the courts in this respect is best illustrated by a district court decision of the same year:

"Since the amendment taking out the exception, it has uniformly been held by the courts that the question of the right to limitation of liability is not based upon the engagement of the vessel in maritime commerce, and further it is not based upon the question of the size of the craft." Francesca, 19 F.Supp. 829, 832, 1937 A.M.C. 1006, 1011 (W.D.N.Y.1937).

Case law since 1937 is also in accord. See, Petition of Reading, 169 F.Supp. 165, 1959 A.M.C. 1753 (N.D.N.Y.1958), aff'd 271 F.2d 959, 1960 A.M.C. 214 (2 Cir.1959); Petition of Colonial Trust, 124 F.Supp. 73, 1955 A.M.C. 1290 (D.Conn.1954); Trillora, 76 F.Supp. 50, 1948 A.M.C. 132 (E.D.S.C.1947). In addition, the leading textual authorities at least recognize this conclusion as the present status of the law. Gilmore & Black, *The Law of Admiralty,* sec. 10–12, at 674 (1957); Benedict on *Admiralty* (6th ed., Knauth, 1940), sec. 494, at 403–405.

On at least three occasions the Supreme Court has considered cases of the Act with the explosion of a motorboat of a well-to-do owner. Petition of Reading, supra, 169 F.Supp. at 167, 1959 A.M.C. at 1755. The same court in 1960 (on this occasion denying limitation because the injury did not occur on the navigable waters of the United States) elaborated on the situation in this manner:

"I am sure the ever-growing number of purchasers of these small pleasure craft do not check the limitation statutes before they purchase and never will. The financial protection and regulation necessary to alleviate the burden of society where the widow and orphan, maimed and crippled, are with us as a result of unfortunate highway accidents seem to me just as important in these boating accidents." Petition of Madsen, 187 F.Supp. 411, 413, 1963 A.M.C. 488, 489 (N.D.N.Y.1960).

More outspoken in their denunciation of the inequities that may arise when limitation is accorded to pleasure craft are the textual authors and other legal writers. This criticism is best summed up by the commentary of Gilmore & Black, sec. 10–23, at 700:

"Most of the recent individual ownership cases involve pleasure yachts and owners who are amateur yachtsmen. The Limitation Act, originally passed to afford a measure of relief to a hard pressed and highly competitive industry, has become a charter of irresponsibility for a few wealthy individuals. The individual owner of, say, a small fishing vessel which explodes in port may well find himself liable to respond in damages under circumstances where the absentee yacht-owner will go free. No theory can justify the results reached in Coryell v. Phipps or *Trillora,* under which the owner of the yacht or speedboat, who is provident enough to hire someone else to run the boat for him, is granted a general license to kill and destroy."

Recent law review articles have echoed this sentiment. These articles have pointed out that as small boat sales and traffic increase, so will the number of accidents and potential situations in which claimants may find themselves with pitifully inadequate recompense for serious injuries or death. It is urged that the result of this situation is to allow liability insurance companies to become the true beneficiaries by limiting their liability to the value of the vessel. See generally, Harolds, Limitation of Liability and Its Application to Pleasure Boats, 37 Temp.L.I. 423 (1964); Stolz, Pleasure Boating and Admiralty: Erie at Sea, 51 Calif.L.Rev. 661 (1963); Comment, Limitation of Liability in Admiralty: An Anachronism from the Days of Privity, 19 Vill.L.Rev. 721 (1965).

Appealing as these arguments may be, this Court does not consider itself justified in deviating from the settled case law in this matter. It is significant that no reported case in recent times has denied limitation of liability for the reason that the vessel was a pleasure craft and, therefore, not within the scope of the Limitation Act. It may be assumed that the more recent decisions holding the Act applicable to pleasure craft have been unable to find fault with the conclusion that "the evident purpose of the amendment (of 1886) was to make the statute applicable to all vessels, irrespective of the purpose to which they are put." Francesca, supra, 19 F.Supp. at 832, 1937 A.M.C. at 1011.

This conclusion is buttressed by the fact that in 1935, Congress amended the statute to provide for the "$60 per ton fund" to be used to compensate claimants for loss of life or bodily injury where the owner's liability was limited under the Act. 49 Stat. 960 (now 46 U.S.C.A. § 183(b)–(f)). At that time yachts along with towboats, lighters, barges and other craft were specifically excluded from the operation of this portion of the Act. 46 U.S.C.A. § 183(f). Prior to that time, however, the courts had held that yachts or pleasure boats were entitled to limitation under the Act. Warnken v. Moody, 22 F.2d 960 (5 Cir.1927); Alola, 228 F. 1006 (E.D.Va.1915); Mistral, 50 F.2d 957, 1931 A.M.C. 1973 (W.D.N.Y.1931). Likewise, lighters and towboats had also been held to be covered by the Act. See Wessel, Duval & Co. v. Charleston Lighterage & Transfer Co., 25 F.2d 126, 1928 A.M.C. 826 (E.D.S.C.1928), and M. Moran, 120 F. 556 (E.D.N.Y.1903). This leads to the conclusion that Congress realized that these types of craft were within the scope of the general limitation provisions of section 183(a), but were not to be included for purposes of the "$60 per ton fund."

It should also be recognized that the Limitation Act is not the only instance in which Congress has shown an inclination to legislate in regard to pleasure craft. The Rules of the Road are applicable to all vessels, including pleasure craft, and, except for the International Rules, make a violation thereof a criminal offense. 33 U.S.C.A. §§ 144–147d; 33 U.S.C.A.

§§ 151–232; 33 U.S.C.A. §§ 241–295; 33 U.S.C.A. §§ 302–356. The Motor Boat Act of 1940 specifies the equipment to be carried on engine powered vessels on the navigable waters of the United States. 46 U.S.C.A. §§ 526–526u.

It is the opinion of this Court that Congress intended the Limitation of Liability Act to apply to pleasure craft such as the Julaine as well as those vessels used for commercial purposes. Although it may reduce claimants' recovery drastically if it is later determined that petitioners are entitled to limit their liability, the remedy lies with congressional, not judicial action.

After careful consideration of all issues raised by claimants in this matter, it is the opinion of this Court that the motion to certify an interlocutory appeal under 28 U.S.C.A. § 1292(b) should be granted. If the Court of Appeals is of the opinion that the Julaine is not covered by the Limitation of Liability Act, this Court is without jurisdiction in this cause of action and proceedings herein would be ended. The sharp criticism of legal writers and some lower courts concerning applicability of the Act to pleasure craft indicates there is substantial ground for difference of opinion involving this controlling question of law. This is emphasized by the silence of the Supreme Court and the Court of Appeals for the Fifth Circuit on this issue.

For the reasons stated herein, the motion to dismiss for want of jurisdiction is denied. * * *

NOTE

What constitutes a vessel is discussed above in Chap. 4. In brief, a structure is a vessel if it is built with the intent that it be used in navigation as a means of transportation, is not permanently attached to the shore or the seabed, and is subject to the perils of the sea. See Grubart, Inc. v. Great Lakes Dredge & Dock Co., 513 U.S. ___, 115 S.Ct. 1043, 130 L.Ed.2d 1024, 1995 A.M.C. 913 (1995), in which the Supreme Court observed that it was not seriously contended that a barge on which a crane was brought to the worksite was not a vessel for the purposes of the Limitation Act despite the fact that at the time of the occurrence giving rise to the petition it was fixed to the bottom with spuds and used as a work platform.

The application of the Act to recreational vessels was reiterated by the Supreme Court in Sisson v. Ruby, discussed in chap. 3–B–3 above. The size of vessels held to be within the Act has worked its way down to a seven foot "jet ski." Keys Jet Ski, Inc. v. Kays, 893 F.2d 1225 (11th Cir.1990). In Davis v. Jacksonville Beach, p. 97, above, sustaining admiralty jurisdiction of an action arising out of a surfing accident, the court observed that there was no necessity to determine whether the surfboard was a vessel. Is that the limiting case?

Carolina Floral Import, Inc. v. M. v. Eurypylus

United States District Court, Southern District of New York, 1976.
416 F.Supp. 371, 1976 A.M.C. 1895.

MEMORANDUM

■ TENNEY, DISTRICT JUDGE. In accordance with the order entered herein on February 4, 1976, in Carolina Floral Import Inc., et al. v. M.V. *Eurypylus*, etc., 75 Civ. 5768, the attorneys for petitioner Ta Chi Navigation (Panama) Corp. S.A., as owner of the M.V. *Eurypylus,* for exoneration from or limitation of liability, and for cargo claimants, have agreed to submit the following question for determination in the above-captioned limitation proceeding (75 Civ. 5994):

> 1.   Whether the United States Limitation of Liability Act, Sections 4283, 4284, 4285 and 4289 of the Revised Statutes of the United States (46 U.S.C.A. §§ 183–185, 188) or the law of the Republic of Panama, applies to the limitation proceeding and governs the items comprising the limitation fund herein.

> (A) If the Court decides that United States law applies, irrespective of whether Panamanian law is substantive or procedural, then the Limitation Fund shall be fixed according to United States Limitation of Liability Act (46 U.S.C.A. § 183).

> (B) If the Court determines that Panamanian law could apply, if *substantive,* then counsel have agreed to obtain pertinent testimony in Panama for later submission to the Court regarding the nature of a shipowner's exoneration from or the limitation of liability provided for in the Commercial Code of the Republic of Panama.

A brief statement of assumed facts may prove helpful before embarking on what, until now, were believed to be charted waters.

On or about October 25, 1975, there was received on board M.V. *Eurypylus* at the port of Kobe, Japan, various shipments which together with other cargo received on board at Hong Kong and Taiwan were destined for discharge and delivery at Cristobal C.Z., San Juan, Puerto Rico, and at various ports on the Gulf and east coasts of the United States, including Charleston, Philadelphia, Baltimore and New York. Thereafter, the vessel departed from Kobe with some 7,767 tons of general cargo shipped under 322 bills of lading. M.V. *Eurypylus* was owned by Ta Chi Navigation (Panama) Corp. S.A. (hereinafter "Ta Chi Navigation").[1] The bills of lading were issued by Ta Peng Lines (or by Ta Peng Steamship Co., Ltd.). Both corporations conduct business in New York City through an agent, Transnational Maritime, Inc., 25 Broadway, New York City.

On November 10, 1975 the vessel sustained serious damage as the result of an explosion and fire in her engine room, the fire spreading rapidly to the after three cargo holds. After unsuccessfully attempting to control the fire, the crew abandoned the vessel then lying some 700 miles south of Los Angeles and on the high seas. Thereafter the vessel was delivered to Los Angeles, California, by salvors.

On November 17, 1975, the first claim for failure to deliver cargo was filed in this Court as an admiralty or maritime claim within the meaning of Rule 9(h) of the Federal Rules of Civil Procedure. An amended and supplemental complaint was filed in that action on January 22, 1976 adding

---

1. In an action by cargo claimants, not parties to the instant proceeding, the ownership of the vessel is alleged to be either Ta Peng Lines, Ta Chi Navigation Corp. S.A., or Compania Maritima San Basilio, S.A., I.T.A.D. Associates, Inc., et al. v. S.S. "*Eurypylus*", et al., 75 Civ. 6481.

more than 50 additional cargo claimants as party plaintiffs, consisting for the most part of United States corporations. Also added as party plaintiffs were numerous underwriters who "by virtue of policies of insurance issued by them to shippers or consignees or some of the cargo-plaintiffs hereinbefore identified, are obligated to pay plaintiffs the amount of their losses pursuant to the terms and conditions of said policies of insurance and the underwriter-plaintiffs have already issued salvage guarantees for the discharged cargoes insured under said policies." (Amended and Supplemental Complaint, 75 Civ. 5768, ¶ Sixth).

Following the filing, on November 17, 1975, of the initial claim against the shipowner Ta Chi Navigation, the shipowner commenced the subject limitation proceeding by filing a complaint seeking exoneration from or limitation of liability pursuant to the United States Limitation of Liability Act, 46 U.S.C. §§ 183–185, 188. A dispute having arisen as to the law to be applied in determining "the amount or value of the interest of [the] owner in the vessel", this Court, on February 4, 1976, ordered Ta Chi Navigation in 75 Civ. 5768, the pending suit by the cargo claimants, to post surety in the pending limitation proceeding, 75 Civ. 5994, in the sum of $268,246.30, that being the value of M.V. *Eurypylus* after the casualty, plus her pending freight on the voyage concerned, less salvage liens arising from the casualty, but without prejudice to plaintiffs' right to demand additional security in the limitation proceeding in the event: (1) that the Court determine that the salvage liens or any part thereof should be added to the present limitation funds, thereby increasing same to a sum not exceeding $624,246.30, pursuant to 46 U.S.C. § 183;[2] and/or (2) that the limitation fund is determined to be governed by some law other than as provided for by the said United States Limitation of Liability Act. In connection with the determination of the governing law as to the limitation fund, plaintiff cargo-claimants assert that the rights of the parties are governed and controlled by the law of the flag of M.V. *Eurypylus,* i.e., the laws of the Republic of Panama and, we assume, specifically by Sections 1078, 1079 and 1093 of the Commercial Code of the Republic of Panama. Petition of Chadade Steamship Co. (Yarmouth Castle), 266 F.Supp. 517 (S.D.Fla.1967)(hereinafter *"Chadade"*). Cargo claimants' attraction to *Chadade* is due to the holding therein that under similar circumstances Panamanian law was applicable in determining the "amount or interest of the owner in the vessel," and that under such law the court in *Chadade* determined that hull insurance, and protection and indemnity insurance, up to the amount necessary to cover the value of the claims pleaded or the face value of such insurance, whichever sum was smaller, was to be included in determining the owner's interest.

No claim is made by any of the parties hereto that hull or liability insurance is includable under 46 U.S.C. § 183, except insofar as the claim is made inferentially that in a proceeding under Section 183 the value of the *res* to be surrendered or for which surety may be given shall in the

---

2. No request for such determination has been made in the instant proceeding, and accordingly the Court refrains from any such determination at this time.

instant case be determined by the Panamanian definition of that *res,* which definition states that "[t]he indemnization of the insurance is part of the patrimony of the vessel." Article 1078 of the Commercial Code of the Republic of Panama, *quoted in Chadade,* supra, 266 F.Supp. at 521. Indeed, under our law such insurance must be excluded. The City of Norwich, 118 U.S. 468, 6 S.Ct. 1150, 30 L.Ed. 134 (1886); Pettus v. Jones & Laughlin Steel Corporation, 322 F.Supp. 1078, 1080–81 (W.D.Pa.1971); In re Pacific Inland Navigation Company, 263 F.Supp. 915, 919 (D.Hawai'i 1967); In re Sheridan's Petition, 226 F.Supp. 136, 140 (S.D.N.Y.1964); Gilmore and Black, *The Law of Admiralty,* 907–908 (2d ed. 1975). See also Maryland Casualty Co. v. Cushing, 347 U.S. 409, 419, 74 S.Ct. 608, 613, 98 L.Ed. 806, 816 (1954).

DISCUSSION

Section 183 is the very heart of the Limitation Act and subsection (a), containing the general provision, has been virtually unchanged since the Act was initially passed in 1851. It now reads as follows:

> "The liability of the owner of any vessel, *whether American or Foreign,*[3] for any embezzlement, loss, or destruction by any person of any property, goods or merchandise shipped or put on board of such vessel, or for any loss, damage, or injury by collision, or for any act, matter, or thing, loss, damage, or forfeiture, done, occasioned, or incurred, without the privity or knowledge of such owner or owners, shall not, *except in the cases provided for in subsection (b) of this section,*[4] exceed the amount or value of the interest of such owner in such vessel, and her freight then pending." (The italicized words were added by amendment in 1936).

The leading decision on the effect of foreign limitation statutes on actions brought by owners of foreign vessels in our courts under the United States Limitation of Liability Act is Oceanic Steam Navigation Company v. Mellor (The Titanic), 233 U.S. 718, 34 S.Ct. 754, 58 L.Ed. 1171 (1914)(hereinafter *"The Titanic"*). Before discussing *The Titanic,* reference should be made to two earlier cases decided by the Supreme Court, i.e., The Scotland, 105 U.S. 24, 26 L.Ed. 1001 (1881), and La Bourgogne, 210 U.S. 95, 28 S.Ct. 664, 52 L.Ed. 973 (1908), both of which involved collisions on the high seas between foreign flag vessels.

The Scotland, supra, 105 U.S. 24, 26 L.Ed. 1001, involved a collision in 1866 on the high seas between the British steamship, Scotland, and an American ship. The American ship sank immediately with all its cargo. The British vessel attempted to return to New York but also sank and became a total loss with the exception of some ship's material salvaged before she went down. Libels *in personam* were filed in the District Court for the Eastern District of New York against the British shipowner by the

---

3. The Limitation Act had been held applicable to foreign vessels as early as 1881. The Scotland, 105 U.S. 24, 31, 26 L.Ed. 1001, 1003 (1881).

4. The excepted cases provided for in subsection (b) are those involving loss of life or bodily injury, in which cases, where the limitation is insufficient to pay all losses in full, the portion applicable to the payment of claims for loss of life or bodily injury must be increased to an amount equal to $60 per ton of the vessel's tonnage.

owners of the American ship, cargo interests, and others. The District
Court rendered a decree in favor of libellants and denied the defense of the
limited liability law, a similar decision being reached on trial in the Circuit
Court. The principal question on the appeal to the Supreme Court was
whether the British shipowner was entitled to the benefit of limited
liability either under the general maritime law or under the United States
Limitation of Liability Act. The libellants contended that, in addition to
procedural deficiencies on the part of the owner, the general maritime law
on the subject (if there be any) was not in force in the United States and
the benefit of the United States statute could not be claimed by foreign
vessels. After declaring that limitation of liability is now part of United
States' maritime law, the Supreme Court noted that, nevertheless, it was
statute law and was to be interpreted and administered as such. The
question was, did the United States statute govern the case? In holding
that it did apply, Mr. Justice Bradley, in writing for the Court stated:

> "In administering justice between parties it is essential to know by
> what law or code or system of laws, their mutual rights are to be
> determined. When they arise in a particular country or State, they are
> generally to be determined by the laws of that State. Those laws pervade
> all transactions which take place where they prevail, and give them their
> color and legal effect. Hence, if a collision should occur in British waters,
> at least between British ships, and the injured party should seek relief in
> our courts, we would administer justice according to the British law, so far
> as the rights and liabilities of the parties were concerned, provided it were
> shown what that law was. If not shown, we would apply our own law to
> the case. In the French or Dutch tribunals they would do the same. *But,*
> *if a collision occurs on the high seas, where the law of no particular State*
> *has exclusive force, but all are equal, any forum called upon to settle the*
> *rights of the parties would, prima facie, determine them by its own law as*
> *presumptively expressing the rules of justice; but if the contesting vessels*
> *belonged to the same foreign nation, the court would assume that they were*
> *subject to the law of their Nation carried under their common flag, and*
> *would determine the controversy accordingly. If they belonged to different*
> *Nations, having different laws, since it would be unjust to apply the laws of*
> *either to the exclusion of the other, the law of the forum, that is, the*
> *maritime law as received and practiced therein, would properly furnish the*
> *rule of decision. In all other cases, each Nation will also administer justice*
> *according to its own laws."* Id. at 29–30, 26 L.Ed. at 1003 (emphasis
> added).

"Each Nation, however, may declare what it will accept and, by its courts,
enforce as the law of the sea, when parties choose to resort to its forum for
redress. And no persons subject to its jurisdiction, or seeking justice in its
courts, can complain of the determination of their rights by that law, unless
they can propound some other law by which they ought to be judged; and
this they cannot do except where both parties belong to the same foreign
Nation; in which case, it is true, they may well claim to have their
controversy settled by their own law. Perhaps a like claim might be made
where the parties belong to different Nations having the same system of
law. *But where they belong to the country in whose forum the litigation is*
instituted, or to different countries having different systems of law, the court

will administer the maritime law as accepted and used by its own sovereignty." Id. at 31–32, 26 L.Ed. at 1004 (emphasis added).

"[P]ublic policy, in our view, requires that the rules of the maritime law as accepted by the United States should apply to all alike, as far as it can properly be done. If there are any specific provisions of our law which cannot be applied to foreigners, or foreign ships, they are not such as interfere with the operation of the general rule of limited responsibility. That rule and the mode of enforcing it are equally applicable to all. They are not restricted by the terms of the statute to any nationality or domicile. We think they should not be restricted by construction. Our opinion, therefore, is that in this case the National Steamship Company was entitled to the benefit of the law of limited responsibility." Id. at 33, 26 L.Ed. at 1004.

La Bourgogne, supra, 210 U.S. 95, 28 S.Ct. 664, 52 L.Ed. 973, involved a collision on the high seas, in 1898, between a British ship and a French ship, the latter vessel sinking with heavy loss of life and property. Numerous suits in admiralty and actions at law were brought in various federal and state courts against the French vessel, or her owners, to recover damages for loss of life, baggage, and personal effects. Thereafter, the owner of the French vessel petitioned in this district for limitation liability. No question appears to have been raised in the lower courts as to the applicability of the United States limitation statute. The Supreme Court, in an opinion by Mr. Justice White, observed that it had been "settled in The Scotland, 105 U.S. 24, 26 L.Ed. 1001, that a foreign ship is entitled to obtain in the courts of the United States the benefit of the law for the limitation of liability of shipowners." Id. at 115, 28 S.Ct. at 670, 52 L.Ed. at 983. However, in the Supreme Court it was argued that the "fault" of the French vessel should be determined by French law rather than by the law of the forum. After quoting from Mr. Justice Bradley's opinion in The Scotland, supra, 105 U.S. at 29–30, 26 L.Ed. at 1003, relating to collisions on the high seas, as quoted above, Mr. Justice White concluded that

"we are of the opinion that we must decide the case before us by the international rule as interpreted in the courts of the United States, and not by the practice under that rule prevailing in the French courts, if there be a difference between the two countries. The petitioner is here seeking the benefits conferred by a statute of the United States, which it could not enjoy under the general maritime law. *Strictly speaking, the application for a limitation of liability is in effect a concession that liability exists, but, because of the absence of privity or knowledge, the benefits of the statute should be awarded.*" La Bourgogne, supra, 210 U.S. at 116, 28 S.Ct. at 671, 52 L.Ed. at 984 (emphasis added).

As has already been noted, *The Scotland* and *La Bourgogne* involved collisions between ships on the high seas. The Titanic, supra, 233 U.S. 718, 34 S.Ct. 754, 58 L.Ed. 1171, involved a British ship sunk in a collision with an iceberg on the high seas with total loss of the vessel and heavy loss of life, cargo, and other property. After a number of actions to recover for loss of life and personal injuries had been brought against the British shipowner in federal and state courts, the shipowner filed a petition for limitation of its liability under the United States Limitation of Liability

Act. Claimants, both English and American, argued that English limitation law, which provided a fund for recovery even though the ship was lost, should apply. The Second Circuit Court of Appeals certified three questions to the Supreme Court as follows:

"A. Whether, in the case of a disaster upon the high seas, where (1) only a single vessel of British nationality is concerned and there are claimants of many different nationalities; and where (2) there is nothing before the court to show what, if any, is the law of the foreign country to which the vessel belongs, touching the owner's liability for such disaster,— such owner can maintain a proceeding under §§ 4283–4285 U.S. Revised Statutes and the 54th and 56th Rules in Admiralty?

"B. Whether if, in such a case it appears that the law of the foreign country to which the vessel belongs makes provision for the limitation of the vessel owner's liability, *upon terms and conditions different from those prescribed in the statutes of this country,* the owner of such foreign vessel can maintain a proceeding in the courts of the United States, under said statutes and rules?

"In the event of the answer to question B being in the affirmative,

"C. Will the courts of the United States in such proceeding enforce the law of the United States or of the foreign country *in respect to the amount of such owner's liability?*" Id. at 731, 34 S.Ct. at 755, 58 L.Ed. at 1179 (emphasis added).

The Supreme Court, in an opinion by Mr. Justice Holmes, answered both questions A and B in the affirmative and with respect to question C declared that our courts would enforce the law of the United States and not that of the foreign country. The opinion of Mr. Justice Holmes is clear and to the point.

"It is true that the act of Congress does not control or profess to control the conduct of a British ship on the high seas. See American Banana Co. v. United Fruit Co., 213 U.S. 347, 356 [53 L.Ed. 826, 29 S.Ct. 511.] It is true that the foundation for a recovery upon a British tort is an obligation created by British law. But it also is true that the laws of the forum may decline altogether to enforce that obligation on the ground that it is contrary to the domestic policy, or may decline to enforce it except within such limits as it may impose. Cuba Railroad Co. v. Crosby, 222 U.S. 473, 478, 480 [56 L.Ed. 274, 32 S.Ct. 132.] Dicey, Conflict of Laws, 2d ed., 647. It is competent therefore for Congress to enact that in certain matters belonging to admiralty jurisdiction parties resorting to our courts shall recover only to such extent or in such way as it may mark out. Butler v. Boston & Savannah Steamship Co., 130 U.S. 527 [32 L.Ed. 1017, 9 S.Ct. 612.] *The question is not whether the owner of the Titanic by this proceeding can require all claimants to come in and can cut down rights vested under English law, as against, for instance, Englishman living in England who do not appear. It is only whether those who do see fit to sue in this country are limited in their recovery irrespective of the English law.* That they are so limited results in our opinion from the decisions of this court. For on what ground was the limitation of liability allowed in *The Scotland* or *La Bourgogne*? Not on their being subject to the act of Congress or any law of the United States in their conduct, but if not on that ground then it must have been because our statute permits a foreign vessel to limit its liability according to the act when sued in the United States. There may be some little uncertainty in the language of Mr. Justice Bradley in the earlier case. A slight suggestion that the statute is applied because of a vacuum,—the absence of any law properly governing the transaction. But it was no necessary part of his argument that people were to be made liable after the event by the mere choice of a forum; and if they were it would not be because of the act of Congress. That does not impose but only limits, the liability—a liability assumed already to exist on other grounds. *The essential point was that the limitation might be applied to foreign ships if sued in this country although they were not subject to our substantive law.*" Id. at 732–33, 34 S.Ct. at 755–56, 58 L.Ed. at 1180 (emphasis added).

The decision in *The Titanic* was accepted law until 1949 when the Supreme Court decided Black Diamond Steamship Corp. v. Robert Stewart & Sons, Ltd. (*The Norwalk–Victory*), 336 U.S. 386, 69 S.Ct. 622, 93 L.Ed. 754 (1949)(hereinafter "*The Norwalk Victory*"), and still is the controlling law in the instant case.

Briefly, *The Norwalk Victory* involved a collision between an American vessel and a British steamer in the Schelde River, within the territorial waters of Belgium, which resulted in the sinking of the British vessel with loss or damage to its cargo. The cargo owners sued the owners of the American vessel in federal court whereupon the owners petitioned for limitation under 46 U.S.C. § 185, but limited their tender of security to the amount of $325,000 under the alleged applicability of the Belgium statute, rather than $1,000,000, the value of the ship as determined by the provisions of Section 185. The owner's petition for limitation was dismissed by the district judge and his decree affirmed by the Court of Appeals for this Circuit because the amount of the security was not sufficient under the United States Limitation of Liability statute. In a 5–4 decision, the Supreme Court held that the shipowner should be given an opportunity to submit proof as to the nature of Belgian statute with particular reference to whether it was a procedural rule or a substantive law, and that if the latter was shown to be the case the shipowner should have the benefit of the Belgian law. The case was reversed and remanded with the suggestion that the shipowners be required to post a bond in the amount of $1,000,000 (the value of the vessel) to preserve the *status quo*. Unfortunately, Mr. Justice Frankfurter's citation to *The Titanic* in The Norwalk Victory, supra, 336 U.S. at 395, 69 S.Ct. at 627, 93 L.Ed. at 768, is somewhat ambiguous:

> "Having decided that the case must be remanded because the petition was improperly dismissed, we turn to the question whether there are any circumstances under which the Belgian limitation would be enforceable by our courts. On this point we agree with the Court of Appeals—and disagree with the District Court—that if, indeed, the Belgian limitation attaches to the right, then nothing in The Titanic, 233 U.S. 718 [34 S.Ct. 754, 58 L.Ed. 1171], stands in the way of observing that limitation. The Court in that case was dealing with 'a liability assumed already to exist on other grounds.' Id. at 733 [34 S.Ct. 754, 58 L.Ed. 1171]." Id.

The final sentence quoted above is perhaps misleading, and the quotation from Mr. Justice Holmes' opinion may have been taken out of context. In describing the United States Limitation of Liability Act, he noted that the Act itself does not impose, but only limits the liability—"a liability assumed [by the Act] already to exist on other grounds [other than by virtue of the Act]." Id. This is true in any case brought under the Limitation of Liability Act and does not distinguish *The Titanic* from any other such case. The following sentence in Mr. Justice Holmes' opinion makes it very clear that the limitation under the United States' statute might be applied to foreign ships if sued in the United States although they were not subject to United States' substantive law, i.e., they were subject to foreign substantive law. Even were it to have affected *The Titanic*, which it did not, *The Norwalk Victory* is clearly distinguishable from the instant case involving, as it does, a disaster on the high seas rather than in territorial waters and one with entirely different issues involved. Furthermore, in this Circuit it seems clear that *The Titanic* doctrine is still good law. Kloeckner Reederei und Kohlenhandel v. A/S Hakedal, 210 F.2d 754, 757 (2d Cir.1954).[5]

And so we finally reach *Chadade,* supra, 266 F.Supp. 517, upon which the claimants in effect rest their case. *Chadade* involved the Panamanian-flag cruise ship Yarmouth Castle, which on November 13, 1965, burned and sank on the high seas with resultant death, injury and property claims totalling more than 59 million dollars. The shipowners filed a petition for limitation of and exoneration from liability on December 8, 1965, claiming the benefit of the United States Limitation of Liability Act or "any applicable Convention or Foreign law" relating to limitation of liability. Id. at 519. The shipowner offered an interim stipulation for value in the sum of $33,000, and further offered to file such stipulation or other security as the court might fix, not to exceed $60.00 per ton, presumably to comply with Section 183(b) of the limitation statute relating to death or personal injury claims. By order of the court the shipowner amended the petition to claim the benefit of certain provisions of the Commercial Code of the Republic of Panama granting exoneration from or limitation of liability in the event it be determined that the rights of the parties were governed by

---

5. There would appear to be nothing inconsistent between the results reached in *The Titanic* and *The Norwalk Victory*. In *The Titanic* the amount recoverable under British law (The Merchants Shipping Act of 1894) was *much greater* than the limits set by § 183, whereas in *The Norwalk Victory* the amount recoverable under Belgian law was *far less* than the § 183 limitation. Accordingly, the question in *The Titanic* was whether, assuming the British law attached to the right, that right was subject to limitation as to those who sued to enforce it in our courts. The question in *The Norwalk Victory* related to the security to be given pursuant to § 185.

If the Belgian law attached to the right, the liability of the shipowner would be less than, rather than being limited by, the amount fixed by the provisions of § 183. The majority opinion clearly indicated that if the District Court determined that Belgian law controlled, § 185 would be read in the light of § 183, and the surety would be allowed in the lesser amount to reflect the liability established by the foreign law. In other words, the United States Limitation statute cannot be interpreted as *creating* a greater liability than is established by foreign law, but only as *limiting* the foreign liability in United States courts.

such foreign law. The court discussed *The Titanic* and *The Norwalk Victory,* and concluded, as had the Second Circuit Court of Appeals, that the latter case had not overruled the former. However, it determined that the Panamanian law was substantive rather than procedural, and applied that law to fix the surety bond to be filed by the shipowner. This would appear to run contrary to the holding by Mr. Justice Holmes that the limitation under the United States Limitation of Liability Act might be applied to foreign ships if they are sued in the United States even though they were subject to foreign substantive law. Indeed the opinion in *Chadade* suggests that the foreign law will be applied as substantive if it sets higher limits of liability than does the United States Limitation of Liability Act. However, it would appear that only when the foreign substantive law sets lower limits will it affect the surety to be posted under the United States' statute. Significantly, the provisions of Section 183 state that the liability thereunder *shall not exceed* the "amount or value of the interest of" the shipowner. In a proper case it can be less. The Norwalk Victory, supra, 336 U.S. 386, 69 S.Ct. 622, 93 L.Ed. 754. See also note 5, supra.

Chadade, like *The Titanic,* involved a foreign law which, it would appear, set higher limits of liability. It seems difficult to reconcile the different conclusions reached in the two cases, and since *Chadade* has apparently never been cited by any court, it certainly cannot be regarded as defining the law in this Circuit.

The learned Judge in *Chadade* suggested that if his analysis of *The Titanic* and *The Norwalk Victory* were not correct, *The Titanic* should be reexamined in the light of the conflict of laws "based upon a more realistic appraisal of world conditions and more responsive to the practicalities of modern maritime commerce." *Chadade,* supra, 266 F.Supp. at 523. This, however, is a legislative, rather than a judicial prerogative. There is nothing ambiguous about the statute.

Moreover, the instant controversy is not one which appeals to the conscience of the court. None of the claimants herein represent the interests of deceased seamen, and if Panamanian law grants a right of action for wrongful death on the high seas, they are free to sue in our courts outside the limitation proceeding. Death on the High Seas Act, 46 U.S.C. § 764; The Vestris, 53 F.2d 847, 853 (S.D.N.Y.1931).[6] The claimants, not the shipowner, selected the forum, and claimants may still have remedies available in the Republic of Panama, since any decree entered herein will have no extraterritorial effect. Petition of Bloomfield Steamship Company, 422 F.2d 728, 736 (2d Cir.1970). In the final analysis, and as is so often the case, the Court is dealing in great part herein with the conflicting interests of insurance underwriters. If the shipowner's hull and

---

6. It is possible that Panamanian law does not grant such a cause of action, since no mention of § 764 of the Death on the High Seas Act was made in *Chadade.* The bulk of the claims were death claims which must have been asserted under § 761 of that Act and therefore subject to limitation unlike claims under § 764.

liability insurance can be brought into the limitation fund, to that extent the insurers of the cargo claimants are relieved of their burden.

Accordingly, the Court holds that the United States Limitation of Liability Act, 46 U.S.C. §§ 183–185, 188, applies to the limitation proceeding and governs the items comprising the limitation fund herein in the absence of any proof that the substantive law of the Republic of Panama would fix the shipowner's liability in a lesser amount than fixed under 46 U.S.C. § 183(a).

So ordered.

B. OWNERS

In re Marine Recreational Opportunities, Inc.

United States Court of Appeals, Second Circuit, 1994.
15 F.3d 270, 1994 A.M.C. 1288.

■ WINTER, CIRCUIT JUDGE:

Marine Recreational Opportunities, Inc. ("MRO") appeals from Judge Keenan's order dismissing its complaint for lack of subject matter jurisdiction. MRO commenced this action under 46 U.S.C.App. § 183 (1988), seeking exoneration from, or limitation of, its liability for injuries to Gerald Berman. Berman's injuries were suffered aboard a vessel previously sold by MRO. We conclude that MRO was not an "owner" of the vessel within the meaning of Section 183. We therefore affirm the district court's dismissal.

In 1991, MRO purchased a pleasure craft, a 1987 Cruisers, Inc. 286 Rogue Sport ("p/c Rogue Sport") at a public auction. On May 31, 1991, MRO sold the vessel to Zachary Berman, Gerald Berman's son, for $41,000, and title and possession of the vessel transferred from MRO to Zachary Berman on that date. On June 2, 1991, Zachary Berman, accompanied by Gerald and Josephina Berman, took the p/c. Rogue Sport out on Long Island Sound. When the boat hit a large wave or wake, Gerald Berman was allegedly thrown around the boat and seriously injured.

Gerald and Josephina Berman filed suit against MRO in New York State Supreme Court, Bronx County, to recover damages for Gerald's injuries. In their complaint, the Bermans alleged, *inter alia* that MRO sold Zachary Berman a vessel with defective trim tabs, was negligent in failing to inspect the trim tabs before delivery, was negligent in failing to warn the purchaser of "a known dangerous, defective and hazardous condition," and was negligent in failing to train him in the proper operation of the vessel.

MRO then brought the instant action pursuant to Fed.R.Civ.P.Supp.F. seeking exoneration from, or limitation of, its liability for the alleged injuries. Pursuant to the Bermans' motion, the district court dismissed the action for lack of subject matter jurisdiction. This appeal followed.

Section 183(a) provides in pertinent part:

> The liability of the owner of any vessel, whether American or foreign, . . . for any loss, damage or injury by collision, or for any act, matter, or thing, loss, damage, or forfeiture, done, occasioned, or incurred, without the privity or knowledge of such owner or owners, shall not . . . exceed the amount or value of the interest of such owner in such vessel, and her freight then pending.

We conclude that this statute does not apply to MRO because it was not the owner of the p/c Rogue Sport at the time of the accident, and it is not being sued in that capacity.

Section 183 was enacted in 1851 "to encourage investments in ships and their employment in commerce," so that "the shipping interests of this country might not suffer in competition with foreign vessels." American Car & Foundry Co. v. Brassert, 289 U.S. 261, 263, 53 S.Ct. 618, 619; 77 L.Ed. 1162 (1933). To effectuate this purpose, the term "owner" as used in the statute has been interpreted in a "liberal way." Dick v. United States, 671 F.2d 724, 727 (2d Cir.1982)(quoting Flink v. Paladini, 279 U.S. 59, 63, 49 S.Ct. 255, 255, 73 L.Ed. 613 (1929)). In *Dick v. United States*, we stated that "[a]s a general rule, one who is subjected to a shipowner's liability because of his exercise of dominion over a vessel should be able to limit his liability to that of an owner." 671 F.2d at 727. MRO argues that under this liberal interpretation of the term "owner," it is entitled to limit its liability, because the Bermans seek to hold it liable for alleged negligence that occurred when the vessel was under its dominion and control. However, in most of the cases that purport to apply a broad interpretation of "owner," the party seeking to limit liability had actual title or was capable of exercising some measure of dominion or control over the vessel at the time of the accident. See id. at 726–28; In re Exoneration from or Limitation of Liability of Shell Oil Co., 780 F.Supp. 1086, 1087, 1089–90 (E.D.La.1991)(parent corporation that conveyed vessel to subsidiary but retained record title is "owner" because "the act is designed to cover one who is a 'likely target' for liability claims predicated on his status as the person perhaps ultimately responsible for the vessel's maintenance and operation"); In re Barracuda Tanker Corp., 281 F.Supp. 228, 231 (S.D.N.Y.1968)(plaintiff considered "owner" where it sold and leased back vessel prior to accident), remanded on other grounds, 409 F.2d 1013 (2d Cir.1969). MRO cites only one case that allowed limitation of liability by a prior owner who lacked any measure of control over the vessel at the time of the accident giving rise to liability. In re The Trojan, 167 F.Supp. 576, 578 (N.D.Cal.1958). aff'd sub nom. Todd Shipyards Corp. v. United States, 274 F.2d 402 (9th Cir.1960). We decline to follow *The Trojan*. Other courts have uniformly held that the time of the accident determines "ownership" under Section 183. Indeed, after *The Trojan*, the Ninth Circuit itself held that a plaintiff who acted as an agent in the sale of a fishing boat was not an owner within the meaning of the statute. See Calkins v. Graham, 667 F.2d 1292 (9th Cir.1982). In reaching its conclusion, the court stated, "When the accident occurred, Calkins no longer had possession or control of the vessel, nor was he responsible for its maintenance and operation...." Id. at 1294; see also Complaint of Sheen, 709 F.Supp. 1123, 1128 (S.D.Fla.1989)("... [T]he appropriate time of owner-ship for [Section 183] purposes must be the period encompassing the maritime accident"). One does not have to become a plain-meaning-of-the-statutory-language fanatic to conclude that a complete absence of legal title and of any practical control over a vessel at the time of the relevant accident precludes resort to Section 183. The use of the term "owner" in Section 183 is in the singular and does not suggest other persons in this chain of title. Extension of Section 183 to others in the chain of title is a rather extraordinary step, and any intent to afford prior owners the benefits of limitation or exoneration certainly would have found expression in the statutory language. Moreover, a contrary ruling would create a conflict among the circuits without our having any compelling reason to depart from the precedents of other circuits. International Soc'y for Krishna Consciousness, Inc. v. Lee, 925 F.2d 576, 580 (2d Cir.1991), affd. in part, 505 U.S. 672, 112 S.Ct. 2701, 120 L.Ed.2d 541 (1992); Feeney v. Port Authority Trans–Hudson Corp., 873 F.2d 628, 631–32 (2d Cir.1989), affd. 495 U.S. 299, 110 S.Ct. 1868, 109 L.Ed.2d 264 (1990). The district court therefore properly dismissed the complaint for lack of subject matter jurisdiction. We affirm.

Lady Jane, Inc., Lim. Procs.

United States District Court, Middle District of Florida, 1992.
818 F.Supp. 1470, 1993 A.M.C. 490.

■ JOHN H. MOORE, D.J.:

I. Background Facts

From 1986 until February 1989, petitioner Jane Steen was the owner of the F/V *Lady Jane*, a shrimping and fishing vessel engaged in commercial fishing. In February 1989, Steen formed the corporation Lady Jane, Inc., of which Steen is the sole shareholder. At that time, ownership of the *Lady Jane* was transferred from Steen to petitioner Lady Jane, Inc. On July 31, 1990, the *Lady Jane* was delivered to Xynides Boat Yard in St. Augustine, Florida, by her three crew members, Carl Frank Canova, Paul Groff, and Rob Hidenrick. Xynides and Steen entered into an oral contract whereby Xynides would make repairs to the *Lady Jane*. Specifically, Xynides was to reattach a water tank which had broken loose on a recent fishing voyage, striking the bottom of the vessel and dislodging several hull planks. During the course of the repairs an Xynides employee, Jerry Hamilton, performed some welding work in order to reattach the tank to the vessel. The welding was performed during the afternoon of August 2, 1990. Sometime during the late evening of August 2, or the early morning hours of August 3, a fire erupted on the *Lady Jane* which rendered the vessel a constructive total loss. On September 25, 1990, petitioner Steen filed a complaint for exoneration from or limitation of liability. Claimant Xynides Boat Yard, Inc. filed its claim against Steen on November 29, 1990, alleging Steen's failure to pay for services rendered and failure to remove the burned-out hulk from the shipyard. Petitioner Steen filed counter-claims against Xynides Boat Yard, Inc., Nicholas Xynides, and Harry Xynides for breach of contract, negligence, and breach of a bailment contract. On September 9, 1991, petitioner Steen, as owner *pro hac vice* of the *Lady Jane*, joined by petitioner Lady Jane, Inc., filed an amended complaint for exoneration from or limitation of liability, and an amended counterclaim. No written claim has been asserted against petitioner Lady Jane, Inc.

* * *

III. Ownership

The Limitation of Liability Act provides that "the owner of any vessel" may seek the protection of the Act. 46 U.S.C. App. § 183. Claimant contends that Steen is not an "owner" entitled to protection under the Limitation of Liability Act because Steen is merely the sole stockholder of the company, Lady Jane, Inc., which does own the vessel. The Court disagrees with claimant's conclusion. The Supreme Court has declared that the terms of the Limitation Act should be construed broadly so as to promote the Act's purposes of encouraging and inducing investment in shipping. See Flink v. Paladini, 279 U.S. 59, 1929 AMC 327 (1929); see also Admiral Towing Co. v. Woolen, 1961 AMC 2333, 2338, 290 F.2d 641, 645 (9 Cir.1961); In re Barracuda Tanker Corp., 1968 AMC 1711, 1717, 281 F.Supp. 228, 232 (S.D.N.Y.1968). In *Admiral Towing*, an "owner" was described as one whose

> "relationship to the vessel is such as might reasonably afford grounds upon which a claim of liability for damages might be asserted against him, a claim predicated on his status as the person perhaps ultimately responsible for the vessel's maintenance and operation and a claim against which the Limitation Act is designed to furnish protection." 1961 AMC at 2338, 290 F.2d at 645.

Steen was unquestionably the person ultimately responsible for the Lady Jane's maintenance and operation at the time of the fire even though the vessel was the property of Lady Jane, Inc., Steen was a person whose relationship to the vessel, as sole stockholder and president of Lady Jane, Inc., was such as might reasonably afford grounds for a claim of liability for damages to be asserted directly against her, possibly on a theory of piercing the corporate veil, or on a claim for acting as the agent for an undisclosed principal.[4] The Supreme Court in *Flink* held that the stockholders of a corporation which held title to a vessel were entitled to the protection of the Limitation Act. *Flink*, 279 U.S. at 63, 1929 AMC at 328 (stating that the term "owner" as used in the Act is an "untechnical word" that should be interpreted in a liberal way); see Dick v. United States, 1982 AMC 913, 917, 671 F.2d 724, 727 (2 Cir.1982). In addition to her status as stockholder, Steen had exclusive possession, management, and control of the Lady

---

4. The evidence at trial showed that Steen failed to inform the boatyard that Steen was acting on behalf of Lady Jane, Inc.

Jane. Cf. *Admiral Towing*, 1961 AMC at 2338, 290 F.2d at 645. For these reasons, the Court finds that Steen is an "owner" entitled to invoke the protection of the Act.

Claimant also disputes the right of Lady Jane, Inc. to seek protection under the Act, although for different reasons. Claimant contends that Lady Jane, Inc. should be time-barred from seeking protection under the Act, since Lady Jane, Inc. did not file a complaint for exoneration from or limitation of liability until after the Act's six-month statute of limitations for filing a complaint had passed. See 46 U.S.C.App. § 185 (requiring the vessel owner to file its limitation complaint "within six months after a claimant shall have given to or filed with such owner written notice of claim....."). The Court rejects this contention for two reasons. First, Lady Jane, Inc. has never been on notice of any claim against it, as to this date no claim has been asserted against Lady Jane, Inc. by Xynides Boat Yard, Inc. Second, to the extent there is a statute of limitations issue, the Court finds that the amended complaint which adds Lady Jane, Inc. as a second petitioner does not prejudice the claimant. See generally Wright, Miller & Kane, *Federal Practice and Procedure: Civil 2d* § 1501 (1990). The addition of Lady Jane, Inc. as a petitioner adds no new counterclaims against claimant, and adds no new transactions or occurrences to the case.

* * *

NOTE

In Dick v. United States, mentioned in both *Marine Recreation* and *Lady Jane* above, it was held that the United States was liable under the Public Vessels Act for damage done by an auxiliary Coast Guard vessel but as owner pro hac vice it could limit its liability. Judge Mansfield dissented, observing that "[t]he unavoidable fact here is that the Coast Guard did not exercise any dominion over the *Galaxy*, which was at all times operated and controlled by its owner."

A corporation contracting with the owner of vessels to man them, and described in the complaint as "manager" and as "employer of the crew," was not an owner under § 183. Chesapeake Shpg., Lim. Procs., 778 F.Supp. 153, 1992 A.M.C. 769 (S.D.N.Y.1991).

It has been held that to qualify as an owner it is necessary to show the required ownership existed at the time of the incident giving rise to the liability, and therefore the seller of a vessel cannot limit in an action by the buyer for products liability in respect of an accident taking place after the sale. Marine Recreational Opportunities, Lim. Procs., 15 F.3d 270, 1994 A.M.C. 1288 (2d Cir.1994), declining to follow The Trojan, 167 F.Supp. 576, 578, 1959 A.M.C. 201, 203–204 (N.D.Cal. 1958), aff'd sub nom. Todd Shipyards v. United States, 274 F.2d 402, 1960 A.M.C. 772 (9th Cir.1960).

A manufacturer participating with a radio station in a joint promotional scheme was not an "owner" of a vessel demise chartered by the radio station when it was not a party to the charter and did not participate in controlling the vessel. Anheuser–Busch, Lim. Procs., 742 F.Supp. 1143, 1994 A.M.C. 1518 (S.D.Fla.1990).

A liability insurer does not qualify as an owner, and therefore has no standing to petition for limitation or join the owner in doing so. Nobles Lim. Procs., 842

F.Supp. 1430, 1994 A.M.C. 51 (N.D.Fla.1993). See also Matter of Magnolia Marine Transport Co., Inc. v. Laplace Towing Corp., 964 F.2d 1571, 1994 A.M.C. 303 (5th Cir.1992).

Suppose that the record ownership and dominion are split. E.g., one entity is the owner of record and a former owner, but has transferred ownership to a wholly owned subsidiary of a wholly owned subsidiary, retaining the record title and Coast Guard registration in its name. May they both limit? See Shell Oil Co., Lim. Procs. M/V/ Eb II, 780 F.Supp. 1086, 1992 A.M.C. 2062 (E.D.La.1991), holding they may be able to. With *Shell Oil*, cf. Amoco Cadiz, Lim. Procs., 954 F.2d 1279, 1992 A.M.C. 913 (7th Cir.1992), holding that it was not error to deny subsidiaries of the vessel owner the right to limit and at the same time hold them liable because each of them was negligent in tanker's design, operation maintenance, repair, and crew training.

Under § 186 the charterer of a vessel "in case he shall man, victual, and navigate such vessel at his own expense," is "deemed to be the owner of such vessel within the meaning of the provisions of this chapter relating to the limitation of the liability of the owners of vessels," and the vessel remains liable, when so chartered, "in the same manner as if navigated by the owner thereof." It has been assumed that this is but a backhanded way of saying that a bare boat charterer may limit its liability. See Gilmore & Black, *Law of Admiralty*, § 10–10 (1975), suggesting that the chief significance of the provision is the negative implication that a time or voyage charterer cannot limit liability. See discussion of the Torre Canyon litigation in Gilmore and Black, loc.cit. raising the question whether a time charterer can ever be an "owner" under § 183, though not qualifying as a charterer deemed to be an owner under § 186. Cf. Dick v. United States, supra.

C.   LIMITABLE CLAIMS

1.   DEBTS AND LIABILITIES

Seven Resorts v. Cantlen

United States Court of Appeals, Ninth Circuit, 1995.
57 F.3d 771 , 1995 A.M.C. 2087.

■ FLOYD R. GIBSON, Senior Ct.J.:

Appellant Seven Resorts, Inc., a Nevada corporation, appeals the district court's dismissal for lack of subject matter jurisdiction of its petition in admiralty for indemnification pursuant to a rental contract and limitation of liability under 46 U.S.C. § 183 (1988). We have jurisdiction over this appeal pursuant to 28 U.S.C. § 1291 (1988), and we affirm.

I.   Facts

On May 7, 1992, Appellee James Cantlen, a member of the Delta Upsilon fraternity, rented a houseboat on Lake Shasta from Appellant Seven Resorts. Cantlen signed a rental contract whereby he agreed to be responsible for the safe operation of the houseboat and to hold Seven Resorts harmless from any liability arising out of his rental of the boat. Later that afternoon on Lake Shasta, Cantlen attempted to back the boat up while its engines were running. Unfortunately, Appellee Stacey Epping was swimming behind the boat. As the boat reversed, the propeller blades struck Epping, causing her serious injury.

On January 13, 1993, Epping filed suit in Shasta County Superior Court against Seven Resorts and James Cantlen, among others. On August 2,1993, Seven Resorts filed an amended complaint in admiralty in the United States District Court for the Eastern District of California, seeking indemnification under the rental contract or a limitation of liability under the Limitation of Liability Act, 46 U.S.C. App. § 183.[1] The district court dismissed the complaint for lack of subject matter jurisdiction. The district court explained that it lacked admiralty jurisdiction over the incident because it occurred on nonnavigable waters, and that it lacked jurisdiction under the Limitation of Liability Act because jurisdiction under that statute is coextensive with that of admiralty jurisdiction. Seven Resorts appeals, claiming jurisdiction under the Limitation of Liability Act, admiralty jurisdiction, or diversity of citizenship.

II. Discussion

A. *Jurisdiction under the Limited Liabilities Act.*

The Limitation of Liability Act, 46 U.S.C. app. § 183, ("the Act") provides a procedure in admiralty whereby vessel owners can limit their liability for maritime damages to the value of the vessel. Seven Resorts claims that the Act independently confers jurisdiction over its claim. The Supreme Court has expressly left this question unanswered. Sisson v. Ruby, 497 U.S. 358, 359, 1990 AMC 1801, 1802, n.1 (1990), but all five federal appellate courts that have addressed this issue have rejected Seven Resorts' argument. See David Wright Charter Service v. Wright, 1991 A.M.C. 2927, 2929, 925 F.2d 783, 785 (4 Cir.1991); Guillory v. Outboard Motor Corp., 956 F.2d 114, 115, 1993 AMC 605 [DRO] (5 Cir.1992); Complaint of Sisson, 1989 AMC 609, 624, 867 F.2d 341, 350 (7 Cir.1989), rev'd on other grounds, 497 U.S. 358, 1990 AMC 1801 (1990); Three Buoys Houseboat Vacations U.S.A. Ltd. v. Morts, 1991 AMC 1356, 1363, 921 F.2d 775, 780 (8 Cir.1990), cert. denied, 502 U.S. 898, 1992 AMC 2704 (1991); Lewis Charters, Inc. v. Huckins Yacht Corp., 1989 AMC 1521, 1530–33, 871 F.2d 1046, 1052–54 (11 Cir.1989). The Ninth Circuit has not yet addressed this question. We review the district court's dismissal for lack of subject matter Jurisdiction de novo. Kruso v. Int'l Tel. & Tel. Corp., 872 F.2d 1416, 1421 (9 Cir.1989), cert. denied, 496 U.S. 937 (1990).

Seven Resorts bases its claim on Richardson v. Harmon, 222 U.S. 96 (1911), in which the Supreme Court interpreted an amendment to the Act to confer jurisdiction beyond the reach of admiralty jurisdiction as it stood

---

1. 46 U.S.C. § 183:

The liability of the owner of any vessel, whether American or foreign, for any embezzlement. Loss or destruction by a person of any property, goods or merchandise shipped or put on board of such vessel, or for any loss, damage, or injury by collision ... done, occasioned, or incurred, without the privity or knowledge of such owner or owners, shall not ... exceed the amount or value of the interest of such owner in such vessel, and her freight then pending.

at that time. In that case, the Court allowed the owner of a commercial steam barge which had collided with a bridge to limit his liability under the Act. Id. at 106. The Court recognized that, prior to the enactment of § 18 of the Shipping Act of 1884 (now § 189 of the Act),[2] damage to a land-based object such as a bridge was "a nonmaritime tort and as such not within the cognizance of an admiralty court." *Richardson*, 222 U.S. at 101. Nevertheless, the Court expanded the jurisdictional reach of the Act beyond the then-existing parameters of admiralty jurisdiction in order to effect the amendment's goal of improving the competitive posture of American shipping. Id. at 101–102. Congress has since subsumed Richardson's expansion of the Act within the greater aegis of admiralty jurisdiction by passing the Extension of Admiralty Jurisdiction Act, 46 U.S.C. app. § 740, which extended admiralty jurisdiction to encompass "all cases of damage or injury, to person or property, caused by a vessel on navigable water, notwithstanding that such damage or injury be done or consummated on land." *Richardson* undeniably holds that the Act is capable of conferring independent jurisdiction beyond admiralty jurisdiction. Now that the reach of the Act and admiralty jurisdiction are once more coextensive, we must now determine whether jurisdiction of the Act should once again be expanded beyond admiralty jurisdiction.

We see no reason to extend the scope of the Act beyond the parameters of modern admiralty jurisdiction. Congress' passage of the Extension of Admiralty Jurisdiction Act has clearly obviated the rationale behind *Richardson's* expansion of the Act. Further extension of the Act to encompass torts occurring on non-navigable waterways with no relation to commercial shipping would do little to further the Act's purpose of making United States shipping more competitive worldwide through the limitation of shipping liability. See *Sisson,* 1989 AMC at 623–24, 867 F.2d at 350. In addition, further expansion of the Act would ill-serve the need for uniformity in maritime law. See e.g., Sisson v. Ruby, 497 U.S. 358, 367, 1990 AMC 1801, 1808 (1990).

We also believe that expansion of the Act's jurisdiction beyond the current scope of admiralty jurisdiction would unnecessarily undercut the Supreme Court's post-*Richardson* cases delineating the reach of maritime jurisdiction. Under this line of cases, "the party seeking to invoke maritime jurisdiction must show a substantial relationship between the activity giving rise to the incident and traditional maritime activity." *Sisson,* 497 U.S. at 364, 1990 AMC at 1806. See also Foremost Ins. Co. v. Richardson, 457 U.S. 668, 674, 1982 AMC 2253, 2258 (1982); Executive Jet Aviation, Inc. v. City of Cleveland, 409 U.S. 249, 268, 1973 AMC 1, 15–16 (1972). We can see little point in limiting maritime jurisdiction on the one hand to incidents substantially related to traditional maritime activities, while freely conferring such jurisdiction on the other hand to incidents utterly

---

2. 46 U.S.C. § 189:

The individual liability of a ship owner shall be limited to the proportion of any or all debts that his individual share of the vessel bears to the whole; and the aggregate liabilities of all the owners of a vessel on account of the same shall exceed the value of such vessels and freight pending.

unrelated to traditional maritime activities merely because a party wishes to limit his liability under the Act. As such, we view Richardson as a historical anomaly that cannot be fairly reconciled with modern admiralty jurisdiction, and conclude that the jurisdiction conferred by the Act remains coextensive with that of modern admiralty and maritime jurisdiction.

Seven Resorts alternatively argues that the Act creates federal question jurisdiction independent of admiralty jurisdiction as "arising under federal law." We disagree. An action arises under federal law for purposes of federal question jurisdiction if that law creates the cause of action, American Well Works Co. v. Layne & Bowler Co., 241 U.S. 257, 260 (1916), or if a substantial question of federal law is a necessary element of the plaintiff's cause of action, Smith v. Kansas City Title & Trust Co., 255 U.S. 180, 199–202 (1921). Under the "well-pleaded complaint" rule, however, the federal question must appear on the face of the plaintiff's well-pleaded complaint in order to create federal question jurisdiction. Franchise Tax Bd. v. Construction Laborers Vacation Trust, 463 U.S. 1, 9–10 (1983). "A defense that raises a federal question is inadequate to confer federal jurisdiction." Merrell Dow Pharmaceuticals Inc. v. Thompson, 478 U.S. 804, 808 (1986). In this case, Seven Resorts' assertion of the Act is clearly in the nature of a defense and, as such, cannot create federal question jurisdiction. *Three Buoys*, 1991 AMC at 1363, 921 F.2d at 779–80 (8 Cir.1990).

B. *Admiralty Jurisdiction*

Under 28 U.S.C. § 1333, the district courts have jurisdiction over "[a]ny civil case of admiralty or maritime jurisdiction." Seven Resorts does not challenge the district court's finding that Lake Shasta is not a navigable waterway for purposes of admiralty jurisdiction.[3] Instead it argues that the district court had jurisdiction over the charter contract regardless of whether Lake Shasta is a navigable waterway because charter contracts are by definition maritime contracts.

Admiralty jurisdiction over maritime contracts, however, is merely a subset of admiralty jurisdiction as a whole. The "primary focus of admiralty jurisdiction is unquestionably the protection of maritime commerce." *Foremost*, 457 U.S. at 674, 1982 AMC at 2258. "Commerce for the purpose of admiralty jurisdiction means activities related to the business of shipping." Adams v. Montana Power Co., 1978 AMC 680, 681, 528 F.2d 437, 439 (9 Cir.1975). As such, admiralty jurisdiction over both tort and contract issues requires a connection to navigable waters. Kossick v. United Fruit Co., 365 U.S. 731, 736, 1961 AMC 833, 838 (1961)("The only question is whether the transaction relates to ships and vessels, masters and mariners, as the agents of commerce. . . ." (quoting I Benedict, Admiralty, 131)); *People's Ferry Co. of Boston v. Beers*, 61 U.S. 393, 401 (1857)("The admiralty jurisdiction, in cases of contract, depends primarily upon the nature of the contract, and is limited to contracts, claims, and services, purely maritime, and touching rights and duties appertaining to commerce

---

3. In his reply brief, Seven Resorts concedes the nonnavigability of Lake Shasta.

and navigation."); *Adams*, 1978 AMC at 682, 528 F.2d at 439 ("admiralty jurisdiction need and should extend only to those waters traversed or susceptible of being traversed by commercial craft"). Consequently, the district court properly determined that it lacked admiralty jurisdiction over claims arising from incidents occurring on a nonnavigable waterway such as Lake Shasta.

C.   *Diversity Jurisdiction*

Seven Resorts claims that the district court had diversity jurisdiction over its claim.[4] We disagree. The federal diversity statute, 28 U.S.C. § 1332, requires both diversity of citizenship and an amount in controversy in excess of $50,000.00. Seven Resorts' complaint alleges neither. The complaint merely alleges that Seven Resorts is a Nevada corporation and that defendant James Cantlen is a resident of Oregon. It is black letter law that, for purposes of diversity, "[r]esidence and citizenship are not the same thing." Mantin v. Broadcast Music, Inc., 244 F.2d 204, 206 (9 Cir.1957). In addition, the complaint does not even attempt to allege an amount over $50,000.00 in controversy. Consequently, we conclude that Seven Resorts' complaint fails to plead diversity jurisdiction.

III.   Conclusion

For the above reasons, we affirm the order of the district court.[5]

N O T E

The statement in Richardson v. Harmon on which the petitioner relied in *Seven Resorts* was as follows: "Thus construed, the section harmonizes with the policy of limiting the owner's risk to his interest in the ship in respect of all claims arising out of the conduct of the master and crew, whether the liability be strictly maritime or from a tort nonmaritime, but leaves him liable for his own fault, neglect and contracts." Apart from the case of operation of a vessel on waters not part of the navigable waters of the United States, such as the *Seven Resorts* above, how many cases are there since the enactment of the Admiralty Extension Act of 1945 in which the owner of a vessel would be liable for nonmaritime torts? Cases have been rare. In Yacht Charlotte (Petition of Colonial Trust Co.), 124 F.Supp. 73, 1955 A.M.C. 1290 (D.Conn.1954), limitation was allowed in connection with the explosion of a boat while it was located in a boathouse on land.

4. The district court concluded that Seven Resorts failed to plead diversity in its complaint. Fed. R. Civ. Pro. Stat. requires "a short and plain statement of the grounds upon which the court's jurisdiction depends ..." Rule 204 of the Local Rules of the United States District Court of the Eastern District of California additionally requires that the complaint "shall state the claimed statutory or other basis of federal jurisdiction and shall also state the facts supporting such claim ..." Seven Resorts claims that it properly invoked diversity jurisdiction nonetheless by alleging facts giving rise to such jurisdiction in its complaint. Because we conclude that Seven Resorts' complaint failed to allege such necessary predicate facts, we need not reach this issue.

5. Because we do not find this appeal frivolous or dilatory, we deny the Appellee's request for attorneys' fees and double costs pursuant to Fed. R. App. P. 38 and 28 U.S.C. § 1912.

If *Seven Resorts* is correct and the only claims that are limitable are those within the admiralty jurisdiction, limitability requires maritime nexus as well as maritime location. See Delta Country Ventures v. Magana, 986 F.2d 1260, 1993 A.M.C. 855 (9th Cir.1993), denying limitation in connection with the injury of a fifteen year old boy, guest on a houseboat anchored in navigable water, who was injured when he dived into the water. The court believed that under the *Sisson* criteria recreational swimming lacks the requisite maritime nexus for admiralty jurisdiction. Judge Kozinski dissented.

Following *Magana* several cases in the District of Hawaii denied limitation in the case of injuries to scuba divers. But see McClenahan v. Paradise Cruises, 888 F.Supp. 120, 1995 A.M.C. 1899 (D.Haw.1995), in which the court reconsidered the issue in light of the decision in *Grubart*, and upheld the jurisdiction.

In Complaint of N.J. Theriot, Inc., 841 F.Supp. 209, 1994 A.M.C. 2700 (S.D.Tex.1994), limitation was denied in the case of a Jones Act claim for injury to a seaman in an automobile accident while he was being transported to the vessel to join the crew. The court held that assuming that there would be liability under the Jones Act, the incident did not have sufficient maritime nexus to support admiralty jurisdiction, and hence a limitation petition.

Contract claims as well as tort claims are limitable unless they come within the "personal contracts" doctrine, to be discussed, and the Act is specifically preserved as to cargo claims in both the Harter Act and the COGSA. Are there contracts on which the vessel owner may be liable as owner that are not maritime contracts? Claims for wages due to persons employed by shipowners are exempted in § 189. And it has been held that by analogy that claims for maintenance and cure are not limitable. Brister v. A.W.I., Inc., 946 F.2d 350, 1993 A.M.C. 1990 (5th Cir.1991).

Some statutory claims are not subject to limitation under the Limitation Act. In some cases the statutes or applicable international agreements provide their own limitation provisions. See, e.g., the Federal Water Pollution Control Act, 33 U.S.C.A. § 1321, and the Comprehensive Environmental Compensation and Liability Act (CERCLA) 42 U.S.C. § 9601. The relationship between these environmental protection Acts and the Limitation Act must be examined carefully. It is held, for example that while an action for cleanup costs under § 1321(f) is not limitable under the Limitation Act, an action for civil penalties under the FWPCA 1321(b)(6)(A) for civil penalties is. Korea Wonyang, Li. Procs., 1994 A.M.C. 804 (D.Alaska 1992). And liability for response costs under CERCLA are not limitable, once the hazardous material has been removed from a wreck located on a reef in nonnavigable water does not come within either CERCLA or the Wreck Act. To the contrary, see United States v. CF Industries, Inc., 542 F.Supp. 952, 1982 A.M.C. 2440 (D.Minn.1982).

In Wyandotte Transportation Co. v. United States, 389 U.S. 191, 88 S.Ct. 379, 19 L.Ed.2d 407 (1967), the Supreme Court avoided the question of whether liability to the United States for costs of removing a wreck is subject to limitation. The courts of appeals have held that it is not. See, e.g., University of Texas Medical Branch v. United States, 557 F.2d 438, 1977 A.M.C. 2607 (5th Cir.1977)(action against one who negligently caused the vessel to sink).

The Trans Alaska Pipeline Authorization Act (TAPAA), where applicable, has been held to effect an implicit repeal of the Limitation Act. In re The Glacier Bay, 944 F.2d 577, 1992 A.M.C. 448 (9th Cir.1991).

But the Submarine Cable Act, 47 U.S.C.A. §§ 21–33, has been held to create no private cause of action; since the cable-owner's action is under the general maritime law, the Limitation Act is applicable. American Telephone & Telegraph Co. v. M/V Cape Fear, 967 F.2d 864, 1992 A.M.C. 2492 (3d Cir.1992).

2.   PERSONAL CONTRACTS

Cullen Fuel Co. Inc. v. W.E. Hedger, Inc.

Supreme Court of the United States, 1933.
290 U.S. 82, 54 S.Ct. 10, 78 L.Ed. 189.

■ MR. JUSTICE ROBERTS delivered the opinion of the Court.

The petitioner owned a deck scow known as Cullen No. 32. The respondent wished to use her to lighter ore from ship-side in New York Harbor to the plant of the Grasselli Chemical Company, the consignee of the ore. A charter for an indefinite term, at a fixed daily rate of hire, was orally arranged by telephone with the petitioner's marine superintendent. The day following the demise, while being loaded from the ship, the scow capsized, dumped her cargo, and damaged an adjacent wharf and vessel. Suits ensued, one of them by the respondent as bailee of the cargo, against the petitioner as owner of the scow. Limitation of liability was sought by the petitioner, but the district court refused a decree for limitation, finding that the scow was unseaworthy at the time of the demise.

The Circuit Court of Appeals concurred in this finding and based its affirmance of the trial court's decision upon the ground that as the charter was the personal contract of the owner and included an implied warranty of seaworthiness the petitioner was precluded from the benefit of the limitation statutes.

The petitioner, conceding that where the owner personally expressly warrants seaworthiness he is not entitled to the benefit of the limited liability statutes (Pendleton v. Benner Line, 246 U.S. 353, 38 S.Ct. 330, 62 L.Ed. 770 (1918), Luckenbach v. McCahan Sugar Refining Co., 248 U.S. 139, 39 S.Ct. 53, 63 L.Ed. 170, 1 A.L.R. 1522 (1919)), correctly states that despite the decision of this court in Capitol Transportation Co. v. Cambria Steel Co., 249 U.S. 334, 39 S.Ct. 292, 63 L.Ed. 631 (1919), the contrariety of opinion which existed in the various circuits prior to that case, as to the effect of the implied warranty of the owner, still persists. We therefore granted certiorari.

We pass, without discussion, the contentions that the court below erred in its rulings that the owner's contract was personal and that the respondent as bailee of the cargo was entitled to recover from the charterer, as we are of opinion that both points were correctly decided (The Benjamin Noble, 232 F. 382 (D.C.Mich., 1916); Id., 244 F. 95 (6 Cir.1917); Capitol Transportation Co. v. Cambria Steel Co., supra; Pendleton v. Benner Line, supra, pages 355–356 of 246 U.S., 38 S.Ct. 330), and come to the question of petitioner's right of limitation notwithstanding the implied warranty of seaworthiness. The *Capitol Transportation* Case is an authority against the right. As appears by the opinion of the District Court (232 Fed. 382), the contract of the owner in that case was oral and no express warranty was given.

We see no reason to restrict or modify the rule there announced. The warranty of seaworthiness is implied from the circumstances of the parties and the subject-matter of the contract and may be negatived only by express covenant. It is as much a part of the contract as any express stipulation. Delaware & Hudson Canal Co. v. Penna. Coal Co., 8 Wall. 276, 288, 19 L.Ed. 349 (1868); Grossman v. Schenker, 100 N.E. 39, 206 N.Y. 466, 469 (1912); United States v. A. Bentley & Sons Co., 293 F. 229 (D.C.Ohio 1923).

The petitioner urges that the denial of limitation in cases like this will sweep away much of the protection afforded to ship owners by the acts of Congress. But this view disregards the nature of the warranty. The fitness of the ship at the moment of breaking ground is the matter warranted, and not her suitability under conditions thereafter arising which are beyond the owner's control. Compare Armour & Co. v. Fort Morgan S.S. Co., 270 U.S. 253, 46 S.Ct. 212, 70 L.Ed. 571 (1926); The Ice King, 261 F. 897 (2 Cir.1919); The Soerstad, 257 F. 130 (D.C.N.Y.1919).

The judgment is affirmed.

NOTE

The charter in the Cullen case was a demise charter. Would the result be the same if it had been a time charter? A voyage charter? See The Barge Ivernia, 1958 A.M.C. 2196 (S.D.N.Y.1958), in which a voyage charter of a barge was held to come within the doctrine. It is generally held that bills of lading are not personal contracts, however. See Gilmore and Black, Law of Admiralty 899 (1975). Their prediction in their first edition that this would be so even if the bills were signed by the president of the company himself has proved to be correct. See The Ionnasis P. Goulandris, 173 F.Supp. 140, 1959 A.M.C. 1462 (S.D.N.Y.1959), where the bills were signed by thirty per cent of ownership. The court held that the "personal contracts" doctrine is limited to charter parties. Gilmore and Black, supra, also take the position that "* * * it is probable that all repair and supply contracts are 'personal,' home port or foreign port, lien or no lien." Is this consistent with the reading of § 189 in Richardson v. Harmon? Is it consistent with any fair reading of § 189?

In The Soerstad, 257 Fed. 130 (S.D.N.Y.1919), Judge Learned Hand held that the breach as well as the undertaking would have to be "personal." Thus the owner who had entered into a towing contract assumed to be personal would not be liable without limitation for damage attributable to the negligent navigation of the vessel by its master. As far as implied warranties go, does the doctrine of *The Soerstad* make the "personal contracts" doctrine almost identical to the nondelegable duty doctrine? In this connection, see The Mormackite, 272 F.2d 873, 1960 A.M.C. 185 (2 Cir.1959). There a barge sank because it was overloaded. Judge Hand first found that there was no personal knowledge of the stowage on the part of the four persons who were sufficiently high in the corporate hierarchy to bind the corporate owners. Then, in answer to the argument that the vessel was unseaworthy because of the improper stowage, he stated, "The charter did indeed warrant that she was 'tight, staunch and strong and in every way fitted for the voyage,' but there was no warranty as to her stowage, especially on the return voyage. Moreover, the charter contained a provision that the bills of lading should be subject to the Carriage of Goods by Sea Act, and that provision would be ineffective unless there was a limitation of liability in the absence of privity or knowledge of the owner—sec. 1308, Title 46."

A claim under a contract to indemnify is not limitable. See S & E Shipping Corp. v. Chesapeake & O. Ry. Co., 678 F.2d 636, 1982 A.M.C. 2359 (6th Cir.1982). But to preclude limitation under the personal contracts doctrine the indemnity claim must be a claim under a personal contract. See, e.g., Signal Oil and Gas Co. v. Barge W–701, 654 F.2d 1164, 1982 A.M.C. 2603 (5th Cir.1981) cert. denied 455 U.S. 944, 102 S.Ct. 1440, 1441, 71 L.Ed.2d 656 (1982). There the owner of a pipeline granted permission to the owner of another pipeline to make a connection, and in their agreement owner two agreed to indemnify owner one for damage, independent of negligence. Pipeline Owner 2 hired a contractor under a contract by which contractor agreed to indemnify Pipeline Owner 2. Contractor did the work from a barge owned by Vessel Owner, who supplied the master. Through the negligence of the master in "dogging" the anchor the pipeline was ruptured. The court held that Vessel Owner was liable to Pipeline Owner 1 in tort, Pipeline Owner 2 was liable to Pipeline Owner 1 for contract indemnity. Contractor was liable to Pipeline Owner 2 for contract indemnity, and Vessel Owner was liable to Contractor and Pipeline Owner 2 under principles of indemnity in the maritime law of torts. Under these circumstances, the court held that Vessel Owner was not precluded from limitation, inasmuch as the action by Contractor against Vessel Owner and the vessel did not arise under a contract. "McDermott makes no claim that Williams should be denied limitation simply because it personally agreed to provide the vessel in aid of the construction operation. We leave, then, further consideration of the scope of the personal contracts doctrine to scholarly commentators and to judges directly confronting the issue." 654 F.2d at 1169.

There is an interesting discussion in Gilmore & Black, § 10–26 (1975), in which the authors express surprise that lawyers have been "uncharacteristically meek" in accepting as "holy writ" the rule in The Susan (Petition of Wood), 230 F.2d 197, 156 A.M.C. 547 (2d Cir.1956) to the effect that the warranty of seaworthiness is not a "personal contract," in light of the subsequent holdings that claims for maintenance and cure fall within the doctrine.

In Complaint of Great Lakes Dredge & Dock Co., 1993 A.M.C. 2046 (N.D.Ill. 1993), the district dismissed a petition for limitation filed by Great Lakes in connection with the great Chicago flood on the ground that the negligence asserted to have caused the flood was in the execution of a contract between the City and the petitioner. This decision was reversed at 3 F.3d 225, 1993 A.M.C.2409 (7th Cir.1993). The court of appeals took the contract for indemnity to be the only contract called to its attention that might be "personal," the claims of businesses injured by the flood being plainly tort claims. Since the record was insufficient to determine by whom the indemnity contract was signed, it was too early to decide its effect. The court added, "In no event, however, will the personal contracts doctrine affect Great Lakes' ability to obtain limitation of liability against anyone but the City, and, even with respect to the City, the doctrine does not affect the potential limitation of tort liability." On petition for rehearing, which was denied, the court revised this passage to read, "Nor is it clear whether the contract imposes liability on Great Lakes for injuries to third parties. These are all matters that can be addressed by the district court on remand. In no event, however, will the personal contracts doctrine affect the potential limitation of tort liability." The *Great Lakes* decision was affirmed in *Great Lakes Dredge & Dock Co. v. Grubart*, reproduced beginning on p. 104.

Remember the M/V Floridian, p. 475 above. There the breach of a contract of carriage was held to be a tort when it was also a violation of the statutory duties under COGSA, thus elevating the claim to tort priority. Can you design a good news—bad news situation where characterizing a claim as tort will permit the defendant to limit his liability, but characterizing it as contract will permit tort claimants to eat up all the assets?

D. PRIVITY OR KNOWLEDGE

1. CORPORATIONS

Petition of Kinsman Transit Co.

United States Court of Appeals, Second District, 1964.
338 F.2d 708, 1964 A.M.C. 2503.

■ HENRY M. FRIENDLY, CT. J. * * *

(3) *Limitation of Kinsman's liability.*

We find this issue more difficult; some further statement of the facts is required.

Kinsman's principal office is in Cleveland. It owned five vessels, four of which were in Buffalo in the winter of 1958–59. Kinsman is a family corporation; Henry Steinbrenner was its president and his son, George, then only twenty-eight years old and without maritime studies or experience, had become its vice president and treasurer in 1957.

The Shiras arrived in Buffalo with a cargo of grain for Continental late in November and was moored for the winter at the coal dock of the Lackawanna Railroad in the ship canal. Inspection of the grain revealed heating, which made it desirable to unload the Shiras and then reload her for further storage. George Steinbrenner went to Buffalo on December 8 to work out the plans; he returned to Cleveland on the 12th and, having gone to Florida on a vacation, was not in Buffalo again until after the accident. It is not shown that he had knowledge of the precise place where or the manner in which the Shiras would ultimately be moored.

When Kinsman had mooring or loading problems in Buffalo during the winter, it sometimes relied on its agents, Boland & Cornelius, and sometimes would dispatch one of its masters, grounded for the winter, who were paid for such work on a per diem basis. On this occasion it took the latter course. Henry Steinbrenner assigned the task to Captain Davies who had been master of the Shiras during the 1958 season. Davies came to Buffalo on three occasions. On the first he supervised the shifting of the Shiras to the unloading leg of the Concrete Elevator dock, on the second to the loading leg, and on the third, January 7, to the place east of the loading leg where she was expected to remain moored for the rest of the winter. The remooring was effected, without the aid of tugs, by a gang of Continental employees bossed by Kruptavich, which placed the lines on the shore. Kinsman had never made any effort to obtain information as to winter weather or harbor conditions in Buffalo but relied on inspection and approval by United States Salvage Association, which was employed to that end by the Great Lakes Protective Association, a mutual insurance association of steamship operators. Rozycki, a marine surveyor employed by United States Salvage, inspected the mooring on January 8 and made a favorable report; a formal certificate of approval was later sent to Henry Steinbrenner.

The case gives point to the comment that the statutory phrase, "without the privity or knowledge of such owner," is largely "devoid of meaning," Gilmore & Black, *Admiralty*, 695 (1957)—a statement supplemented with the admittedly unhelpful comment: "Where a vessel is held in corporate ownership, the imputation of 'privity or knowledge' to the corporate owner will be made if a corporate officer sufficiently high in the hierarchy of management is chargeable with the requisite knowledge or is himself responsible on a negligence rationale. How high is 'sufficiently high' will depend on the facts of particular cases * * *." Ibid. 701. Henry and George Steinbrenner were "sufficiently high," but George had no knowledge of the mooring, and Henry had none save for Davies' report on his return from Buffalo and the United States Salvage certificate, both of which were reassuring rather than the reverse. They were not negligent in assigning the task to Davies, whose competence was established. Davies was not "sufficiently high," under the authorities cited below. His knowledge is imputed to the corporation on the issue of exoneration, but that is precisely what the statute forbids on the issue of limitation. Still it seems likely that if Kinsman's headquarters had been in Buffalo, limitation would be denied under Spencer Kellogg & Sons v. Hicks, 285 U.S. 502, 52 S.Ct. 450, 76 L.Ed. 903 (1932), on the basis that it was negligent not to check the adequacy of the mooring of the Shiras when dangerous conditions threatened on January 21, or even that it was negligent to fail to make a cautionary inspection of the moorings of Kinsman's vessels in the harbor at an earlier date. If the latter view were taken, one might query the good sense of a distinction that would lead to a different result in this age of rapid transportation and communication because Kinsman's office was a few hundred miles away from the harbor where four of its five ships were berthed. The query seems especially pertinent when, as here, there is every indication that nothing different would have been done if George Steinbrenner had been on the scene during the final mooring as he had entrusted the operation to one admittedly more competent to oversee it than he was. Indeed, the whole rationale of the doctrine is of questionable application in a case like this where there was no need for the owner to rely on the skill of a master or other agents as he must when a vessel is at sea or in a distant port. All this, however, is not for us; shipowners and their insurers are entitled to rely on the statute and the decisions applying it, and we must take these as we find them until a higher authority intervenes. Although we doubt that the decisions can all be reconciled, this case is closer to Craig v. Continental Ins. Co., 141 U.S. 638, 12 S.Ct. 97, 35 L.Ed. 886 (1891); Quinlan v. Pew, 56 F. 111 (1 Cir.1893); The Annie Faxon, 75 F. 312 (9 Cir.1896), and The Erie Lighter 108, 250 F. 490 (D.N.J.1918), allowing limitation, than to McGill v. Michigan SS. Co., 144 F. 788 (9 Cir.), cert. denied 203 U.S. 593, 27 S.Ct. 782, 51 L.Ed. 332 (1906); The Marguerite, 140 F.2d 491 (7 Cir.1944); The Cleveco, 154 F.2d 605 (6 Cir.1946); The Edmund Fanning, 105 F.Supp. 353, 363–366, 371 (S.D.N.Y.1952), aff'd as to this point, 201 F.2d 281 (2 Cir.1953), and States SS. Co. v. United States, 259 F.2d 458 (9 Cir.1957), cert. denied 358 U.S. 933, 79 S.Ct. 316, 3 L.Ed.2d 305 (1959); Admiral Towing Co. v. Woolen, 290 F.2d 641 (9 Cir.1961), and The Derrick Trenton, 189 F.Supp. 400 (S.D.N.Y.1960), denying it. We are aware of the difference in the ages of the two sets of decisions, but we find nothing in the later cases reflecting on the authority of the earlier ones on fact situations within their sweep—a view which Coryell v. Phipps, 317 U.S. 406, 63 S.Ct. 291, 87 L.Ed. 363 (1943), tends to confirm.

Two other points must be considered. If the Shiras was not seaworthy in what has been termed the "primitive sense" of being "tight, staunch, strong and well and sufficiently tackled, appareled, furnished and equipped," a corporate owner who has failed in his duty to provide such a ship does not escape full liability, Gilmore & Black, supra, 702. It is argued that the Shiras was unseaworthy in this sense on the basis that although she put out all the mooring lines she had, their number was inadequate. The latter claim was the subject of conflicting testimony, and we take the judge's failure to fault the Shiras on this score as a finding, not clearly erroneous, that the claim was not established. Continental's claim that, under the "personal contract" exception, Gilmore & Black, *Admiralty*, §§ 10–26ff., Kinsman may not limit liability to it because of breach of the warranty of seaworthiness in the storage contract signed by Henry Steinbrenner, is defeated both by lack of proof of breach[3] and by the fact that the exception would apply only to damage to the stored cargo, which did not occur. See 3 Benedict, *Admiralty,* 373 (1940).

NOTE

In The Linseed King, cited by Judge Friendly in Petition of Kinsman, the Court found that the executive officers of the corporation were aware that the boat should not be run when there was ice on the river and had so instructed the works manager. It found further that the works manager was negligent in simply instructing the master not to operate when there was ice, the condition being apparent some days before. It found, therefore, that the negligence was within the

---

3. Although the shipkeeper's failure to ready the anchors may have rendered the Shiras unseaworthy in the expanded sense used in seamen's personal injury actions, the contractual warranty is for "The fitness of the ship at the moment of breaking ground * * *, and not her suitability under conditions thereafter arising which are beyond the owner's control." Cullen Fuel Co. v. W.E. Hedger, Inc., 290 U.S. 82, 89, 54 S.Ct. 10, 11, 78 L.Ed. 189 (1933); The Soerstad, 257 F. 130 (S.D.N.Y.1919).

privity and knowledge of the works manager, and that he was sufficiently high in the corporate hierarchy to make his privity and knowledge that of the corporation.

In cases in which responsible management personnel on shore are aware of dangerous practices in the operation of a vessel, privity has often been found, despite the fact that management has no knowledge of the particular negligence that gave rise to the accident. See, e.g., In re Adventure Bound Sports, Inc. 837 F.Supp. 1244, 1994 A.M.C. 1517 (S.D.Ga.1993). There the boat on a diving trip with customers was manned by a licensed captain and a divemaster and the captain dived with the customers, leaving the vessel with the divemaster. In an action by an injured customer, charging unsafe diving practices, it was held that the knowledge of the sole owner the corporate owner of the boat that the captain occasionally did this was held to make the corporation privy to the negligence.

In an action in which a pleasure craft struck a dredge pipe line, which had been partially opened to permit the crossing of traffic, and brought an action against the owner of the dredge, charging insufficiently lighting, it was held that the dredge owner could not limit because supervisory personnel had offices nearby and knew or should have known of the lighting practices. Complaint of American Dredging Co., 873 F.Supp. 1539, 1994 A.M.C. 2833 (S.D.Fla.1994).

And in PG & E Resources Offshore Co. v. Zapata Gulf Marine Corp., 1994 A.M.C. 2447 (S.D.Tex.1994), privity was found in the knowledge of the owner's shorebased operations manager that his captain moored off platforms with fully loaded tows and turned off the engine, waiting for bad weather to pass, and should have known that it would take as long as ten minutes to start the engine again.

Similarly, privity was found in the knowledge of the owner's managing officer that tug operated in the high wind, that she routinely did so, and occasionally became windbound. Brunet v. United Gas Pipeline Co., 15 F.3d 500, 1994 A.M.C. 1565 (5th Cir.1994); and in Pennzoil Producing Co. v. Offshore Express, Inc., 943 F.2d 1465, 1994 A.M.C. 1034 (5th Cir.1991), an action charging vessel that struck a natural gas pipeline failed to use a fathometer and spotlight and had no lookout on the bow, the the knowledge of executive personnel of the vessel's operating practices in the fog.

Of course where the boat is actually being operated by a corporate office or managing agent, there is privity. See Marine Sports, Lim. Procs., 840 F.Supp. 46, 1994 A.M.C. 1678 (D.Md.1993).

The question of who is a managing agent for the purpose of imputation of knowledge that will bar limitation has been troublesome. There are cases that hold that the the knowledge must be that of a policy-making office or employee. In Cupit v. McClanahan Contractors, 1 F.3d 346, 1994 A.M.C. 784 (5th Cir.1993), for example, it was held that knowledge of a tool pusher in charge of a movable drilling rig could not be imputed to the owner, since his authority was limited to his shift and did not extend to basic business decisions made by the drilling supervisors and the president of the company.

It has been held, however, that it must be a managing agent "with respect to the field of operation in which the negligence occurred." In Continental Oil Co. v. Bonanza Corp., 706 F.2d 1365, 1983 A.M.C. 2059 (5th Cir.1983)(en banc), the court indicated that the fact that the master of the vessel is an officer of the corporate owner does not automatically result in imputing his knowledge to the corporation. Nevertheless, limitation was denied on the ground of privity and knowledge of the corporation through the master, who was neither a stockholder nor an officer of the close corporation that owned the vessel, but had been given so much control over the vessel, its use, maintenance, etc., that the court could characterize him as a "managing agent" with respect to the operation of the vessel.

Similarly, in The Chickasaw (Petition of Waterman S.S. Corp.), 265 F.Supp. 595, 1966 A.M.C. 2219 (S.D.Cal.1966), the vessel was on a return trip from Japan, and departed the Orient with a defective fathometer. In holding the owners liable without limitation, the court observed, "Evidence failed to disclose anyone of higher rank in the managerial hierarchy or with greater authority in the Orient than Captain Patronis."

Cedarville—Topdalsfjord, 1967 A.M.C. 1965 (N.D.Ohio 1967). There the master of a vessel involved in a collision in the Straits of Mackinac and taking water at a rapid rate refused to order the ship abandoned and made an ill-fated run for the beach, resulting in the loss of ten of the crew. After the collision occurred, the master had reported it by telephone to the corporate office in Pittsburgh where the information had been relayed to the fleet superintendent who was in conference with the head of the whole shipping operation. These officials were made aware of the fact that the vessel had a hole in her, and that the master was trying to beach her. Further, they knew that with a hole in her, "she would sink like a brick." The fleet superintendent testified that he did not contact the vessel by telephone because in these situations the master is in full command and would "have no time for the telephone." In holding that the corporation was liable without limitation, and even for punitive damages, the court made two separate findings. The first was to the effect that the petitioner had placed such authority in the master as to make him the "alter ego" of the corporation. The second was that by their acquiescence in the master's decision to attempt to beach the vessel the corporate officials in effect ratified his conduct.

In Avera v. Florida Towing Corp., 322 F.2d 155, 1963 A.M.C. 2110 (5 Cir.1963), where the sole stockholder and corporate manager of a company operating tugs reserved to himself all management decisions, including the hiring of personnel, and required tug captains to report to him at designated intervals by radio telephone, it was held that the corporation was liable without limitation for injury to an inexperienced 17 year old deck hand that had been employed by the master, though the corporate manager had not been advised of his employment until after the accident. The court found that the manager could not operate everything himself by standing rule without undertaking to police compliance with such rules.

For an interesting variant on this theme, See Tug Ocean Prince v. United States, 584 F.2d 1151, 1978 A.M.C. 1786 (2 Cir.1978), cert. denied 440 U.S. 959, 99 S.Ct. 1499, 59 L.Ed.2d 772 (1979), in which limitation was denied on the ground that the vessel was unseaworthy, inter alia, because it was sent out to be operated by two pilots without appointing one of them captain.

Where do such cases leave us? If the corporation delegates full responsibility to the master, he becomes the alter ego of the corporation (*Cedarville* and *The Chickasaw*); if it reserves the decisions to management personnel, it is liable for failure to see that the master carries out the instructions (*Avera*).

Note that in *The Chickasaw* the duty that the court holds is delegated to the master is the duty to make the vessel seaworthy at the beginning of the return voyage. It has been held in some cases that the requirement of use of due diligence to make the vessel seaworthy at the beginning of the voyage is "nondelegable." See, e.g., Federazione Italiana v. Mandask Compania de Vapores, 388 F.2d 434, 1968 A.M.C. 315 (2 Cir.1968). If this is so, would it have mattered if there had been management personnel in the Orient in The Chickasaw, or if the corporate manager in *Avera* had not assumed the role of back seat driver? The *Cedarville* case is more difficult. If there is anything that can be delegated to the master of a vessel, it is its navigation. Putting aside the question of ratification, what happens to the doctrine of privity and knowledge if the master is characterized as the "alter ego" of the corporate owner because he is in complete command of the navigation of the vessel?

Most of the decisions appear to require either actual notice of the unseaworthy condition or negligence in not discovering it. See, e.g., Complaint of Bankers Trust Co., 651 F.2d 160, 1981 A.M.C. 1497 (3d Cir.1981), cert. denied 455 U.S. 942, 102 S.Ct. 1436, 71 L.Ed.2d 653 (1982), in which the court of appeals reversed the decision of the district court denying limitation on the finding of unseaworthiness in the form of a defective valve and turbine, on the ground of want of privity and knowledge. And see Empresa Lineas Maritimas Argentinas, S.A. v. United States, 730 F.2d 153, 1984 A.M.C. 1698 (4th Cir.1984), in which the court observed, "To preclude limitation under § 183(a), the shipowner's knowledge need not be actual. The shipowner is chargeable with knowledge of acts or events or conditions of unseaworthiness that could have been discovered through reasonable diligence." Id., at 155. And see Hercules Carriers, Inc. v. Claimant State of Florida 768 F.2d 1558 (11th Cir.1985) in which it was held that failure of the owner's operating agent to provide a competent crew and licensed officers precluded limitation.

It is suggested in Gilmore and Black, supra, that perhaps the duty to furnish a ship seaworthy in the "primitive sense" is absolute, and not discharged by a showing of due diligence. In most cases of "primitive" unseaworthiness, of course, it is possible to state that if due diligence had been exercised the condition would have been discovered. In Barge NL–5—Chesapeake Bay Bridge–Tunnel, 298 F.Supp. 881, 1968 A.M.C. 1427 (E.D.Va.1968), for example, the vessel's capstan was inoperable, her master and mate unlicensed, and her only deckhand had only three weeks experience when it started out to tow a barge with 1800 tons of cargo in the Chesapeake Bay in winter. Certainly due diligence would have discovered these defects. Indeed, the court observes that the owner knew of the inoperable capstan. In The Barcelona, 1968 A.M.C. 331 (S.D.Fla.1967), the presumption that a vessel that is seaworthy does not sink in calm seas and fair weather was relied upon to deny limitation. The relationship between such a presumption and the effort to prove due diligence is of interest. The court in *The Barcelona* held that the burden to show due diligence required that the owner establish by evidence the cause of the sinking. It found as a fact "That the cause of the loss of the S.S. Barcelona not having been established, it cannot be found that the loss of the S.S. Barcelona was from a cause without the actual fault and privity of the owner and/or charterer."

Farrell Lines, Inc. v. Jones

United States Court of Appeals, Fifth Circuit, 1976.
530 F.2d 7, 1976 A.M.C. 1639.

■ DYER, CIRCUIT JUDGE. Farrell Lines, Inc., owner of the Steamship *African Neptune,* appeals the judgment of the district court denying its petition for limitation of liability. We reverse.

On November 7, 1972, at 9:36 P.M., the *African Neptune,* left its berth at Brunswick, Georgia and proceeded down the East River on its way out of the harbor. The *African Neptune* was required to proceed down the river, turn 50 degrees to port to the Turtle River Lower Range course of 113 degrees true and thereafter pass through the 250 foot wide open draw of the Sidney Lanier Bridge on about 113 degrees true.

Two pilots directed the *African Neptune's* transit out of the port. At all times material, both pilots were on the bridge along with the master of the vessel, a watch officer and a helmsman. As the *African Neptune* approached the bridge, the pilot ordered the helmsman to put the rudder left 20 degrees. The helmsman repeated the order correctly when he received it, but executed the order incorrectly by putting the rudder 20 degrees right instead of left.

This error was tragic. A short time later, the watch officer detected the mistake and tried to indicate to the helmsman that the wheel should be put left. Both pilots also became aware of the mistake, as did the master. One of the pilots instinctively ordered hard left rudder followed by full astern. Other emergency measures were taken, but to no avail. At approximately 9:49 P.M., the *African Neptune* struck the bridge. Ten people were killed and ten others were injured.

Farrell filed a petition for exoneration from or limitation of liability. Farrell thereafter conceded that it was not entitled to exoneration. The district court was thus concerned solely with the issue of limitation. At the conclusion of trial, the district court ruled from the bench that Farrell was not entitled to limitation. It later made findings of fact and conclusions of law, 378 F.Supp. 1354. It is those findings and conclusions which Farrell complains of here.

Under 46 U.S.C.A. § 183, the liability of a shipowner for any loss, damage, or injury by collision may not exceed the amount or value of the interest of the owner in the vessel, if "done, occasioned or incurred" without the privity or knowledge of the owner. Subsection (e) provides that with respect to loss of life or bodily injury, the privity or knowledge of the master of the vessel at or prior to the commencement of each voyage is deemed conclusively the privity or knowledge of the owner.

The district court found that the procedures mandated by the shipowner and the procedures utilized by those in command of the *African Neptune*, on the night of the collision were inadequate and did not include "failsafe" precautions. The specific shortcomings in these procedures found by the district court were: (1) insufficient personnel on the bridge to insure proper helmsmanship; (2) delegation to the watch officer of the duty to keep the bell log book in addition to his duty to oversee execution of the pilot's orders to the helmsman; and (3) improper positioning of the rudder angle indicator on the pilot house bulkhead on the bridge which did not conveniently permit prompt detection of the helmsman's error.

Based on these findings, the district court concluded that Farrell had "failed to sustain its burden of proving that navigational errors which caused the collision were without its privity or knowledge." We reject this conclusion of the district court as being inconsistent with the standards required of a shipowner in order to avail himself of the benefits of the Limitation Act.

The determination of whether a shipowner is entitled to limitation employs a two-step process. First, the court must determine what acts of negligence or conditions of unseaworthiness caused the accident. Second, the court must determine whether the shipowner had knowledge or privity of those same acts of negligence or conditions of unseaworthiness. Knowledge or privity of any fact or act causing the accident is not enough for denial of limitation; it is only knowledge or privity of negligent acts or unseaworthy conditions which trigger a denial of limitation. Coleman v. Jahncke Service, Inc., 5 Cir.1965, 341 F.2d 956; Avera v. Florida Towing Corp., 5 Cir.1963, 322 F.2d 155.[1] And, although the petitioner in limitation bears the burden of proving lack of privity or knowledge, the initial burden of proving negligence or unseaworthiness rests with the libelants. Coleman v. Jahncke Service, Inc., supra.

In this case, all agree that the predominating cause of the accident was the navigational error of the helmsman in improperly executing his orders. There is also agreement that this navigational error was without privity or knowledge of Farrell. Thus, claimants have attempted to establish acts or conditions other than this navigational error which contributed to the accident and of which Farrell had knowledge. Specifically, the claimants argued below that Farrell utilized procedures, personnel, and equipment which were inadequate to prevent the human navigational error which directly caused the accident.

As outlined above, we are not concerned solely with the question of whether Farrell had knowledge of the allegedly inadequate procedures, personnel and equipment. Rather, we must first consider whether the procedures, personnel or equipment utilized involved negligence or rendered the *African Neptune,* unseaworthy.[2] Of course, we should not overturn the findings of the district court unless we conclude that they are clearly erroneous. Nuccio v. Royal Indemnity Co., 5 Cir.1969, 415 F.2d 228; Empire Seafoods, Inc. v. Anderson, 5 Cir.1968, 398 F.2d 204. But, by the same token we should not hesitate to overturn those findings if we are left with the definite and firm conviction that a mistake has been committed by the district court. Wade v. Mississippi Cooperative Extension Service, 5 Cir.1976, 528 F.2d 508. With these standards in mind, we consider seriatim the grounds relied on by the district court.

1. As stated in Avera v. Florida Towing Corp., supra, at 158:

> For the problem always exists, and certainly does here, of determining just what specific acts of negligence were committed against which the admiralty court subsequently applies the privity-knowledge yardstick.

See also 3 Benedict on *Admiralty,* § 41, p. 5–5:

> Without negligence there can be no privity or knowledge for there is nothing then to which the shipowner, however familiar with facts that establish his innocence, can be said to be privity (sic).

2. In making this analysis, we note that the determination of negligence overlaps the determination of unseaworthiness. Seaworthiness is defined as *reasonable* fitness to perform or do the work at hand. Walker v. Harris, 5 Cir.1964, 335 F.2d 185. The standard of reasonableness thus pervades both determinations.

PROCEDURES AND PERSONNEL

When the *African Neptune* left its berth there were five persons on the bridge: the master, the watch officer, the helmsman, and two pilots. According to Farrell's "Manual for Ship's Officers," the watch officer "must observe the steering, and see that all steering and engine orders are promptly and carefully carried out." He or she must "observe the steering closely" and is responsible for "seeing to it that the course set and steered is made good."

When a pilot is employed, the Manual provides that the Master "shall see that the officer of the deck renders the pilot all necessary assistance in the navigation of the ship and that there is no relaxation of vigilance on the part of the officer of the deck or lookouts."

In addition, the Manual contains repeated assertions that safety is the paramount concern of each ship's officer. Hence, there was no failure on Farrell's part in recognizing the importance of the watch officer's role of observing the execution of steering orders, and Farrell very clearly stressed the safety principle pervasively throughout the Manual.

Therefore, the only question is whether Farrell's Manual or the Master should have provided that additional persons be on the bridge during the transit of restricted waters such as existed at Brunswick. More specifically, we must ask whether the absence of such additional persons was negligent or rendered the vessel unseaworthy.

The only testimony in the record which suggests that there should have been extra persons on the bridge was that of Captain Kennedy, a former commander in the United States Navy, called as an expert witness by claimants.[3] He testified that in the Navy it was customary to place an extra person on the bridge to oversee the helmsman's execution of orders when a vessel was operating in confined or restricted waters. But Captain Kennedy also testified that two pilots, a master, a watch officer and a helmsman on the bridge was a sufficient complement if one of them was continually monitoring the helm and engine order telegraph.[4] Thus, even

---

3. All other experts for claimants and Farrell testified that the *African Neptune's* bridge complement was adequate, safe, and standard in the merchant marine.

4. The following colloquy took place during cross-examination of Captain Kennedy:

Q: [F]or a merchant ship, in going out of a harbor with a complement on the bridge of a docking pilot, river pilot, Captain, a watch officer, and a man at the wheel, do you consider that unreasonable or imprudent to go out with that complement on the bridge?

A: If one of them were continually monitoring the helm and your engine order telegraph, I would say that would be sufficient complement.

Q: Well, suppose one of them were available to continually do that, would that be sufficient?

A: Well, I tried to answer your question, sir, if one of those persons were continually available to monitor the helm and the telegraph operator, I would say yes, it was sufficient complement, to see that the helm did not go in the opposite direction from which it was ordered.

Q: * * * So actually, in addition to the navigating pilot, there were three people who could have picked up the helmsman's mistake, is that correct?

A: Right.

Captain Kennedy, the claimant's expert, testified that the bridge complement utilized by Farrell was reasonable and prudent, if one person out of that complement was "continually available" to monitor the helm.

The testimony established that the watch officer had the duty to keep the bell log book as well as to oversee execution of the pilot's orders to the helmsman. The evidence establishes without contradiction, however, that, in spite of this dual responsibility, the watch officer was nevertheless "continually available" to monitor the helm.

Captain Kennedy testified that it was common sense for a watch officer to verify a rudder angle rather than make a bell book entry; that it takes only a couple of seconds to make such an entry; and that the specific bell book entries made on the *African Neptune* shortly before the accident should not have significantly affected the watch officer's duty to verify the accuracy of the helmsman's actions. This latter testimony establishes that, *at the time of the accident*,[5] the watch officer was, or under the procedures mandated by Farrell should have been, continually available to monitor the helm.

Two other expert witnesses testified on behalf of claimants. One testified that a watch officer could check a helmsman for error even at night simply by turning his head which takes only a second; that maintaining a bell book does not interfere with checking the helmsman; and that it is more important to check the helmsman than to make bell book entries. The other expert testified that it was his standard practice as well as that in the merchant marine to have the watch officer handle the engine telegraph, keep the bell book and make sure that the helmsman carried out orders correctly.

In light of this evidence, we can only conclude that the watch officer was continually available to monitor the helm, notwithstanding his dual responsibility. Thus, in light of this determination, all testimony, even that of Captain Kennedy, supports the conclusion that the bridge complement, and the assignment of duties to those on the bridge, was reasonably safe under the circumstances. The finding of the district court that the *African Neptune* was unseaworthy, or Farrell negligent on those bases is therefore clearly erroneous.

EQUIPMENT

Claimants argue, and the district court agreed, that the rudder angle indicator was positioned so as to hinder prompt detection of the helmsman's error. They argue, and the district court agreed, that this rendered the vessel unseaworthy at the time of the accident.

The rudder angle indicator is a lighted dial which indicates the actual angle of the rudder to port or starboard. It was located high up on the

---

5. We do not question whether the duties might have interfered with each other at other times. Bound by the requirement of causation, we only consider negligent or un- seaworthy conditions which existed at the time of the accident and contributed to that accident.

forward bulkhead just to the left of the centerline of the wheelhouse. It is directly in front of the helmsman and is immediately visible to the watch officer. Both pilots testified that they had to step back a few paces to see it, but that they knew where it was located. There was also testimony that the indicator does not instantly reflect a change in the angle; there is a time lag between a rudder shift and the reaction of the indicator. Thus, those responsible on the bridge had ample time and opportunity to check the rudder angle indicator if they so desired. Their failure to do so was not caused by the position of the rudder angle indicator, but rather by their own inattention or inadvertence, acts not within the knowledge or privity of Farrell. On these facts, the positioning of the indicator was not a proper basis for a finding of unseaworthiness. The district court clearly erred in finding otherwise.

In sum, neither the absence of an additional watch officer nor the location of the rudder angle indicator involved negligence or rendered the vessel unseaworthy. Although the presence of an additional officer or the relocation of the indicator might have reduced the possibility of collision,[6] that is not the standard by which we are to determine whether Farrell is entitled to limitation. Rather, we must ask whether the procedures and equipment utilized rendered the vessel *reasonably* fit under the circumstances. Here, we conclude, as in United States v. Sandra & Dennis Fishing Corp., 1 Cir.1967, 372 F.2d 189, that the vessel as equipped was reasonably capable of performing the intended mission if properly operated. The accident resulted from lack of care and failure to exercise proper procedures by those on the bridge. For this Farrell is liable, but it is also entitled to limit.

Reversed.

■ CLARK, CIRCUIT JUDGE (dissenting).

Despite my great respect for the experience and expertise in this field of law of the majority and the deference which I do and should accord to their judgment, I hear a different drummer. I cannot bring myself to that critical point necessary to reverse the equally learned district judge—a definite and firm conviction that as trier of fact he made a mistake.

This was not a routine harbor departure, nor was it an ordinary passage through confined or restricted waters. One single maneuver which those in charge of the *African Neptune* planned for her to make on her course to the sea was so critical that a six-second error in its execution irrevocably consigned ten human beings to their death and injured ten others. Indeed, the majority does not contest the correctness of the district judge's determination that a high degree of care was demanded in the

---

6. As stated by Captain Kennedy:
"No system is infallible, sir, if people are running it, there's no infallible system. All you can hope for is to get one that is less infallible than another."

But just because one system is less perfect than another does not mean that the use of the former is negligent or renders the vessel unseaworthy.

ship's approach to and clearance of the bridge and that it was not a routine operation.

Additionally, on this disastrous evening almost every possible adverse factor was aligned against a safe transit of the bridge opening by the *African Neptune* and every one of them was known. *Before she left the dock* the master knew, and therefore Farrell knew, these things: the ship was in a light condition, which meant much more of her freeboard and her rudder was above the water line. Her propeller was barely under the surface. There was a westerly wind of some 10 to 15 knots. A full tide had begun to ebb. A fairly strong current in the river was flowing seaward. Thus, maneuverability at the crucial point was hampered in every conceivable fashion, so much so in fact that one expert testified he would not have put to sea under those conditions. The district judge determined in an unchallenged finding that the helmsman's error was detected by the third mate about six seconds after it occurred. Although correction was instantly begun, the ship was already irrevocably committed to its peril.

In reversing, the majority focuses upon two *general* faults—whether Farrell should have required additional persons to man the bridge during departures or whether the rudder angle indicator should have been differently positioned. Though I agreed with the majority's conclusions that neither of these findings formed a proper factual basis for denying limitation, I would come out differently. While the district judge listed them among the shortcomings, I do not feel that they formed the real basis for his determination that the ship and its master failed to *specifically* prepare for the delicate risks they were about to undertake on this departure.

The evidence is uncontradicted that on this fateful evening no safety procedures were discussed with either of the pilots aboard or with the bridge crew. No thought was taken for the safe navigation through the bridge span "because we didn't anticipate any danger."

The crucial finding of the district judge was that prior to the vessel's departure from the dock the master failed to coordinate procedures and understandings with all concerned with respect to approach to the bridge and its transit—a fault which contributed to the collision. It cannot be gainsaid that the accident happened because the helmsman erred. However, neither the errant helmsman nor the third mate assigned the duty of watching him were ever told that this particular turn, which the master and pilots know would have to be made to enter the bridge span, was so highly critical and dangerous that an error in its prompt, correct execution carried the portent of death and destruction and that mere seconds in its detection and correction would render its consequences inevitable.

Although the district judge may have chosen too harsh a term when he described the procedures that night as lacking in "fail safe" precautions, I cannot fault his ultimate determination that before the *African Neptune* got underway Farrell or its master should have taken a moment to tell those about to be charged with this ultra-hazardous undertaking what to expect and how they could minimize or prevent hazard to life and limb in the maneuver that lay ahead.

NOTE

The failure of the master to make specific plans for the safe execution of this unusually dangerous operation and discuss them with the pilots and officers responsible for its execution, adverted to by Judge Clark and found to be negligent by the district court, would suffice to establish privity or knowledge of the owner under § 183(e) as to claims for personal injury and death. What of a claim for damage to the bridge? See, e.g., The Mormackite, 272 F.2d 873, 1960 A.M.C. 185 (2 Cir.1959), in which the court of appeals affirmed a decree denying limitation as to personal injury claims but modified the decree to permit limitation of cargo claims upon a finding that the master must have known of improper stowage but no official high enough in the corporate hierarchy to have his privity or knowledge imputed to the owner was shown to be aware of it. In *The African Neptune*, however, the district court found that the "procedures" held to be inadequate were within the knowledge of the owner. See 378 F.Supp. 1354, 1976 A.M.C. 1649 (S.D.Ga.1974).

Cf. Hercules Carriers, Inc. v. Claimant State of Florida, 768 F.2d 1558 (11th Cir.1985), in which the failure of the owner's corporate operational agent to train the crew and assure that the vessel was not placed in the hands of unlicensed officers was held to constitute privity and knowledge.

2. INDIVIDUALS

Coryell Et Al. v. Phipps Et Al.

(The Seminole)

Supreme Court of the United States, 1943.
317 U.S. 406, 63 S.Ct. 291, 87 L.Ed. 363.

■ MR. JUSTICE DOUGLAS delivered the opinion of the Court.

Petitioners instituted a suit in Admiralty in the federal District Court to recover damages for the destruction of vessels owned by them as a result of a fire which occurred in June, 1935, while the vessels were afloat at Pilkington's storage basin at Fort Lauderdale, Florida. The fire was caused by an explosion of gasoline fumes in the engine room of the yacht Seminole, registered in the name of Seminole Boat Co. and owned by it. Prior to 1929 the Seminole was owned by respondent Phipps and his brother. At that time they transferred the yacht to the Seminole Boat Co., a Delaware corporation, all of the stock of which was issued to the two brothers. At the time of the fire respondent Phipps still owned half of the shares of stock, the other half having been acquired by his sister. Neither she nor Phipps was an officer or director of the company.

Respondent Phipps was sued on the theory that he was the owner of the yacht and operated and controlled her and that the Seminole Boat Co.

was a dummy corporation. In his answer Phipps set up, inter alia, the defense of limitation of liability contained in R.S. § 4283, 46 U.S.C. § 183, 46 U.S.C.A. § 183. The District Court found negligence on the part of the Seminole Boat Co. It held that the corporation was not a sham or a fraud but adequate to insulate Phipps as a stockholder from liability for this tort. It went on to hold that even if the corporation be disregarded Phipps was without "privity, or knowledge" of the events which caused the fire and hence could limit his liability to the value of his interest in the yacht. 39 F.Supp. 142. The Circuit Court of Appeals affirmed. 128 F.2d 702. The case is here on a petition for a writ of certiorari which we granted because of an asserted conflict on the point of limitation of liability under § 4283 between the decision below and In re New York Dock Co., 61 F.2d 777 (2 Cir.1933) and In re Great Lakes Transit Corp., 81 F.2d 441 (6 Cir.1936).

The sole questions raised by the petition relate to the liability of Phipps. Petitioners renew here their contention that the corporate existence of the Seminole Boat Co. should be disregarded and that it should be treated as a mere dummy or sham. We need not recite the facts on which that argument rests nor express an opinion on it. For even if we assume, without deciding, that the contention is a valid one and that Phipps should be treated as owner of the yacht for the purposes of this litigation, we nevertheless conclude that the courts below were correct in allowing the limitation of liability under § 4283.

That section, as it read at the time of the fire, provided as we have stated that the "liability of the owner" might be limited to the "amount or value of the interest of such owner" in the vessel, where the loss was occasioned or incurred without his "privity, or knowledge". The District Court found that the proximate cause of the fire was the presence of gasoline fumes in the engine room caused by a leak in some part of the machinery or equipment. That leak, it concluded, occurred not from faulty original installation of the gasoline tanks but with the passage of time. The Circuit Court of Appeals sustained those findings. It was not found by either of the courts below, nor is it claimed, that Phipps had knowledge of that condition. It is urged, however, that the agents of Phipps and the Seminole Boat Co. selected to manage and inspect the yacht were incompetent and negligent, that their negligence is attributable to Phipps, and that in any event he could not establish his claim for limitation of liability without showing that he had appointed competent persons to make the inspection. See McGill v. Michigan S.S. Co., 144 F. 788 (9 Cir.1906); In re Reichert Towing Line, 251 F. 214 (2 Cir.1918); The Silver Palm, 94 F.2d 776 (9 Cir.1938). The Circuit Court of Appeals found that the vessel had been examined and pronounced fit by an experienced ship surveyor in February, 1935, that she developed no faults in a cruise between February and April of that year when she was turned over to Pilkington for storage, that "the crew left her gasoline valves closed, her electric switches open, her gas tanks registering empty, and her bilges clean and free of gasoline or gasoline vapor," and that "she was repeatedly examined by competent men between April 15 and June 24, 1935, who discovered nothing wrong with her." [128 F.2d 703.] There is evidence to support those findings and we will not disturb them.   Thus respondent has satisfied the burden of proof, which is on those who seek the benefit of § 4283, of establishing the lack of privity or knowledge, McGill v. Michigan S.S. Co., supra; In re Reichert Towing Line, supra; *The Silver Palm,* supra, and is entitled to limit his liability, unless any neglect of those to whom duties were delegated may be attributed to him for purposes of § 4283.

Petitioners press several lines of cases on us.   We are not concerned here, however, with the question of limitation of liability where the loss was occasioned by the unseaworthiness of the vessel.   The limitations acts have long been held not to apply where the liability of the owner rests on his personal contract.   Pendleton v. Benner Line, 246 U.S. 353, 38 S.Ct. 330, 62 L.Ed. 770 (1918); Luckenbach v. McCahan Sugar Co., 248 U.S. 139, 39 S.Ct. 53, 63 L.Ed. 170, 1 A.L.R. 1522 (1919); Capitol Transportation Co. v. Cambria Steel Co., 249 U.S. 334, 39 S.Ct. 292, 63 L.Ed. 631 (1919).   As stated by Chief Justice Hughes in American Car & Foundry Co. v. Brassert, 289 U.S. 261, 264, 53 S.Ct. 618, 619, 77 L.Ed. 1162 (1933), "For his own fault, neglect, and contracts the owner remains liable."   And that exception extends to an implied as well as to an express warranty of seaworthiness. Cullen Fuel Co., Inc., v. Hedger, Inc., 290 U.S. 82, 54 S.Ct. 10, 78 L.Ed. 189 (1933).   But whatever limit there may be to that exception (290 U.S. page 89, 54 S.Ct. page 11; cf. Earle & Stoddart, Inc., v. Ellerman's Wilson Line, Ltd., 287 U.S. 420, 53 S.Ct. 200, 77 L.Ed. 403 (1933), arising under the fire statute), those cases are no authority for imputing to the individual owner the neglect of another so as to establish on his part privity within the meaning of the statute.

Petitioners also rely on cases involving corporate shipowners.   In those cases it is held that liability may not be limited under the statute where the negligence is that of an executive officer, manager or superintendent whose scope of authority includes supervision over the phase of the business out of which the loss or injury occurred.   Spencer Kellogg & Sons, Inc., v. Hicks, 285 U.S. 502, 52 S.Ct. 450, 76 L.Ed. 903 (1932), and cases cited; 3 Benedict, *Admiralty* (6th Ed.) § 490.   But those cases are no authority for holding that the negligence of a subordinate may be imputed to an individual owner so as to place him in privity within the meaning of the statute.   A corporation necessarily acts through human beings.   The privity of some of those persons must be the privity of the corporation else it could always limit its liability.   Hence the search in those cases to see where in the managerial hierarchy the fault lay.

In the case of individual owners it has been commonly held or declared that privity as used in the statute means some personal participation of the owner in the fault or negligence which caused or contributed to the loss or injury.   The 84-H, 296 F. 427 (2 Cir.1924); Warnken v. Moody, 22 F.2d 960 (5 Cir.1928); Flat–Top Fuel Co. v. Martin, 85 F.2d 39 (2 Cir.1936); and see La Bourgogne, 210 U.S. 95, 122, 28 S.Ct. 664, 673, 52 L.Ed. 973 (1908); Richardson v. Harmon, 222 U.S. 96, 103, 32 S.Ct. 27, 29, 56 L.Ed. 110 (1912); 3 Benedict, *Admiralty* (6th Ed.) § 489.   That construction stems from the well settled policy to administer the statute not "with a tight and grudging hand" (Mr. Justice Bradley in Providence & New York S.S. Co. v. Hill Mfg. Co., 109 U.S. 578, 589, 3 S.Ct. 379, 386, 27 L.Ed. 1038 (1883)) but "broadly and liberally" so as "to achieve its purpose to encourage investments in shipbuilding and to afford an opportunity for the determination of claims against the vessel and its owner." Just v. Chambers, 312 U.S. 383, 385, 61 S.Ct. 687, 690, 85 L.Ed. 903 (1941). And see Larsen v. Northland Transportation Co., 292 U.S. 20, 24, 54 S.Ct. 584, 585, 78 L.Ed. 1096 (1934); Flink v. Paladini, 279 U.S. 59, 62, 49 S.Ct. 255, 73 L.Ed. 613 (1929); Richardson v. Harmon, supra, 222 U.S. page 103, 32 S.Ct. page 29, 56 L.Ed. 110 (1912). Some cases, however, have barred the individual owner from the benefits of the statute even though the element of personal participation in the fault or negligence was not present. Thus it has been thought that the scope of authority delegated by an individual owner to a subordinate may be so broad as to justify imputing privity (In re New York Dock Co., supra, 61 F.2d page 779) as well as knowledge. In re Great Lakes Transit Corp., supra, 81 F.2d page 444. We need not reach those questions in this case. Privity like knowledge turns on the facts of particular cases. Here two courts have found the absence of both. We accept concurrent findings upon such matters. Just v. Chambers, supra, 312 U.S. page 385, 61 S.Ct. page 690, 85 L.Ed. 903. And even were we to assume without deciding that for the purposes of § 4283 privity as well as knowledge of an individual owner may be constructive rather than actual, it does not follow that Phipps should be barred from limiting his liability. One who selects competent men to store and inspect a vessel and who is not on notice as to the existence of any defect in it cannot be denied the benefit of the limitation as respects a loss incurred by an explosion during the period of storage, unless "privity" or "knowledge" are to become empty words. If § 4283 does not give protection to the individual owner in these circumstances, it is difficult to imagine when it would.

Affirmed.[14]

NOTE

See also The Frank L. III, 1964 A.M.C. 1543 (W.D.Wash.1964), aff'd 349 F.2d 660, 1965 A.M.C. 2492 (9th Cir.1965), where Judge Boldt observed:

"Under the law pertaining to limitation and exoneration, an owner is not required to know the stern from the bow of his ship. He has no obligation to undertake a course of study about navigation, the mysteries of the sea and the like. Within the law of limitation an owner may be a drygoods merchant in the Midwest and rely upon competent people to build his ship, to equip it and run it and do that which they request and suggest to him. Even if their suggestions turn out to be unwise, negligent, or result in unseaworthiness, the owner will not be precluded from limitation in or exoneration from liability for a casualty resulting from unseaworthiness or negligence outside the knowledge or privity of the owner."

14. Notes by the Court have been omitted.

In The Trillora II (Petition of Guggenheim), 76 F.Supp. 50, 1948 A.M.C. 132 (E.D.S.C.1947), it was stated that if an individual vessel owner turns over the vessel's upkeep, management, etc. to an "alter ego," the privity or knowledge of such a person will be imputed to the owner. Does it matter whether the "alter ego" is also the master? Doesn't the vessel owner always delegate broad authority to the master in the navigation and operation of the vessel? Why should it matter that he also is in charge of its upkeep? See The Tug Companion (Admiral Towing Co. v. Woolen), 290 F.2d 641, 1961 A.M.C. 2333 (9th Cir.1961), where privity was found in the failure of the owner to check on the identity of a crew member hired by the master when he was on notice that the new member might be inadequate, but the court indicated that if the unlimited agent of the owner is also the master and the cause of the accident is an error in seamanship the fact that the master is also vested with broad responsibilities for maintenance and repair should not be used to find privity. Why is the owner more culpable in hiring a competent general overseer than in retaining the management in his own incompetent hands?

Of course when a yachtsman operates his own vessel, he is liable without limitation. See, e.g., Follett, Lim. Procs., 172 F.Supp. 304, 1959 A.M.C. 258 (S.D.Tex.1958); Davis v. United States, 185 F.2d 938, 1951 A.M.C. 93 (9th Cir. 1950), cert. denied 340 U.S. 932, 71 S.Ct. 495, 95 L.Ed. 673 (1951). While it has been suggested that the same "rationale" applies when the vessel owner's wife is operating the vessel (Gilmore and Black, *Law of Admiralty* 882, n. 93 (1975)), the authority cited for that proposition, Schoremoyer v. Barnes, 190 F.2d 14, 1951 A.M.C. 1527 (5th Cir.1951), does not seem to go so far. There the wife was a co-owner. Further, the limitation issue was of no importance in the case as the stipulated value of the vessel came to within less than three hundred dollars of the judgment and the appeal was taken purely on the question of application of the state guest-host statute. It has been held that there is no privity or knowledge that will impute the negligence of a fifteen year old son to the father-owner when the son had been instructed in the operation of power boats and had been operating them since he was ten. Petition of Hocking, 158 F.Supp. 620, 1958 A.M.C. 1749 (D.N.J.1958). See also Complaint of Rowley, 425 F.Supp. 116 (D.Idaho 1977).

What if the owner is assisting in the operation of the vessel, but is not himself negligent. See Hanke Lim.Proc., F/V Atka, 1982 A.M.C. 140 (D.Or.1980), where it was held that the owner in such a situation must be given an opportunity to demonstrate the absence of privity and knowledge.

It is indicated in Gilmore and Black, supra, that the presence of the owner on board is enough to constitute privity under the limitation statute. The case they cite is Petition of H. & H. Wheel Service, Inc., 219 F.2d 904, 1955 A.M.C. 1017 (6th Cir.1955), a case in which the vessel was owned by a corporation and used for the personal pleasure of the corporation's president, manager, and almost sole stockholder, and for entertaining business guests. The vessel was found to be operated in a grossly negligent manner when it ran down a small boat. Two persons were killed in the accident. In finding privity, the court found that the president, who was aboard, "had knowledge of all happenings aboard * * * that night." See also Robertson Lim. Procs., 1958 A.M.C. 1697 (D.Mass.1958), where limitation was denied when the owner was aboard and probably conversing with the pilot from the galley at the time of the accident. The fault in the *Robertson* case was failure to maintain a proper lookout. Why should not the two necessary factors mentioned by Judge Friendly in The Petition of Kinsman Transit Corp., knowledge by someone high enough up to bind the corporation, *and* charged with the requisite knowledge, apply whether the negligence occurs on the water or on the land? In Petition of H. & H. Wheel Service, Inc., for example, suppose the negligence involved had been in the manner of operating the engines, something, we shall assume, the president knew nothing about, instead of grossly negligent navigation, something that might be charged to anyone who kept his eyes open. Would the result have been the same? Suppose an ocean liner is involved in a collision at night when the vice-president in charge of public relations is asleep in his cabin. See Blackler v. F. Jacobus Tr. Co., 243 F.2d 733, 1960 A.M.C. 581 (2d Cir.1957). There the court held that an allegation that the owner was on board is not incompatible with limitation of liability. Privity and knowledge, the court went on to state, "is a term of art meaning complicity in the fault that caused the accident, and if the petitioner is free from fault his actual knowledge of the facts of the accident does not prevent limitation." See also The Meridian, 224 F.Supp. 241, 1967 A.M.C. 645 (S.D.Fla. 1963), in which the owner of a yacht was permitted to limit though he was on the yacht but did not know, nor should have known, of the defect in a winch that produced the injury in question. And when the bodies of the owner and sole passenger were found in swimming trunks, with the empty boat floating nearby, the owner's estate should not be denied limitation on summary judgment, since at that stage the cause of death had not been determined. Polly v. Carlson, 859 F.Supp. 270, 1994 A.M.C. 2878 (E.D.Mich.1994).

E.   LIMITATION PROCEEDINGS

1.   AMOUNT OF THE FUND

In The City of Norwich, 118 U.S. 468, 6 S.Ct. 1150, 30 L.Ed. 134 (1885), the Supreme Court construed the language "shall not * * * exceed the amount or value of the interest of such owner in such vessel, and her freight then pending" to mean the interest of the owner at the time the voyage is terminated. In the particular case the vessel sank but was later salvaged. Subsequent events, such as salvage operations, whether carried on by the owner or others had nothing to do with the value, the Court observed, except as evidence of what the interest was worth at the breaking up of the voyage. In The City of Norwich, for example, the vessel was raised and brought to New York where it was appraised as worth $25,000. From this the district court had subtracted $22,500, which was the cost of raising her, leaving an appraised value of the interest of the owners at $2,500. The Court noted that if the vessel is a total loss, the interest is worth zero.

The fact that the bond is not sufficient to cover the claims is irrelevant if it is in an amount that equals the ship and freight then pending. Nobles Lim. Procs., 842 F.Supp. 1430, 1994 A.M.C. 51 (N.D.Fla.1993). And the bond is in respect of the personal liability of the petitioner. Thus when the petitioner is exonerated, the security must be released; it cannot be held to secure the liability of, in the particular instance his son. Churchill v. Fjord, 5 F.3d 374, 1994 A.M.C. 867 (9th Cir.1993).

The second matter taken up by the *Norwich* court was the question of whether the hull insurance must be deposited in the limitation fund. It held that it need not be. The owner is not required to insure, Justice Bradley reasoned; therefore he should not be denied the benefit of his insurance.

In The Great Western, 118 U.S. 520, 6 S.Ct. 1172, 30 L.Ed. 156 (1886), the following year, the Court, again through Mr. Justice Bradley, held that when a vessel was in a collision in which it was at fault and was worth $150,000 immediately after the collision but later in the same voyage was wrecked and abandoned to the underwriters who subsequently sold the materials saved for $1,796.14, this latter amount was the total of the limitation fund. Again it was held that hull insurance, in this case amounting to some £ 34,000, need not be surrendered.

The rule of The City of Norwich still obtains in the United States as to all claims save personal injury claims. It is a harsh rule, of course. See, e.g., In re Barracuda Tanker Corp., 281 F.Supp. 228, 1968 A.M.C. 1711 (S.D.N.Y.1968), rev'd and remanded 409 F.2d 1013, 1969 A.M.C. 1442 (2 Cir.1969), in which millions of dollars in claims were filed against the tanker Torrey Canyon, a vessel carrying a cargo of 119,328 tons when it was stranded ultimately causing a total loss of the ship and cargo. The court determined that the amount to be deposited was $50, reflecting the fact that the only thing found intact was a $48 lifeboat. The International Convention Relating to the Limitation of the Liability of Owners of Seagoing Ships—1957 (The Brussels Convention), as yet unratified by the United States or the number of states required to put it in effect, provides for a per ton limitation figure. In 1958, Great Britain adopted similar legislation. 6 & 7 Eliz. II, ch. 62 (1958).

The question as to whether the rule in The City of Norwich to the effect that insurance is independent of the limitation proceeding and need not be surrendered extends to liability insurance as well as hull insurance has caused some trouble. The question came before the Supreme Court in Maryland Casualty Co. v. Cushing, 347 U.S. 409, 74 S.Ct. 608, 98 L.Ed. 806 (1954). At issue in that case was whether claimants in a limitation proceeding and enjoined from prosecuting separate actions against the petitioner could nevertheless proceed against the petitioner's insurer under the Louisiana direct action statute. Four members of the Court, in an opinion by Mr. Justice Frankfurter, held that the application of the direct action statute in admiralty was unconstitutional in that it entered upon an area of admiralty jurisdiction withdrawn from the states. First, the federal law entitled the petitioner to a concursus of claims in the limitation proceedings; second, under the City of Norwich the petitioner was entitled to the protection of his insurance. Since the plaintiffs in the direct action might exhaust the limits of the policy the petitioner might later be called upon to pay claims of others at the limitation proceeding without the benefit of his insurance. Justice Black, the Chief Justice, and Justices Minton and Douglas dissented. They believed that the limitation act did not apply to the liability of insurance carriers and saw nothing in the state statute that interfered with the uniform administration of the admiralty law in the federal courts. Indeed, to them the state act was supplementary to the admiralty law as it provided for "relief not otherwise available for maritime wrongs." Mr. Justice Clark, speaking for himself alone, found no unconstitutionality in the state statute insofar as it imposed a liability on the insurer. He believed, however, that to permit the owner to be denied the full benefit of his insurance was inconsistent with the reasoning, though not the holding, of The City of Norwich. He proposed as a compromise, that the direct actions be enjoined until the limitation proceeding was completed and then be allowed to proceed. This way whatever part of the coverage necessary to cover the claims allowed at the limitation proceeding would be available for that purpose. If there were coverage in excess of this amount, however, the insurance company would be liable under the state law, and suable in a direct action as provided for by the state statute. The four justices who believed the direct action statute unconstitutional joined in this disposition of the case. What is the majority view? Five justices were of the opinion that the statute making the insurer liable is not invalid. Five justices were of the opinion that it could not be applied in a way that would increase the liability of the petitioner by depriving him of part of his insurance coverage.

Are there times when a *Cushing* type injunction would be unnecessary to protect the insured? Suppose that the claims exceed the limitation fund but not the policy limits. In such a case does the concern of the Frankfurter four in *Cushing* over providing the limitation petitioner with a concursus of claims dictate postponement of the direct action? See The Barge Murray Mac (Guillot v. Cenac Towing Co.), 366 F.2d 898, 1966 A.M.C. 2685 (5th Cir.1966), indicating that direct actions should be enjoined when permitting them to proceed would create an unmanageable problem of collateral estoppel on some issues and as to some parties but not on other issues and parties in the ultimate trial of the limitation action. Can this be avoided by consolidating the actions? See Olympic Towing Corp. v. Nebel Towing Co., 419 F.2d 230, 1969 A.M.C. 1571 (5th Cir.1969), cert. denied 397 U.S. 989, 90 S.Ct. 1120, 25 L.Ed.2d 396 (1970). Would there be jurisdiction under § 1333 if the action was on a marine policy? In *Nebel Towing* the direct action was brought under the diversity jurisdiction; but note 28 U.S.C.A. § 1332(c), governing the citizenship of insurers in direct actions, which had not been enacted at the time the case was filed and accordingly was not applied.

Nebel Towing held that under the Louisiana statute the insurer was liable for the full loss to the policy limits. See Judge Brown's dissenting opinion from denial of rehearing en banc. Is there any way in which the policy could be written to provide by contract what the court declined to read into the relevant statutes? See Crown Zellerbach Corp. v. Ingram Industries, Inc., 783 F.2d 1296 (5th Cir.1986)(en banc), holding that a policy clause limiting the insurance amount to the amount of the limitation fund in case the insured is held to have the right to limit, is enforceable. The panel that originally heard *Crown Zellerbach* held that such a clause was illegal under the Louisiana law, and hence unenforceable. See 745 F.2d 995, 1985 A.M.C. 305 (5th Cir.1984). No special language is required in a *Crown Zellerbach* clause, so long as it limits the liability on the policy to the amount for which the insured is liable. Rogers v. Texaco, 638 So.2d 347, 1994 A.M.C. 2148 (La.Ct.App.4th Cir.1994).

Third party indemnity claims raise problems similar to that posed by insurance. It is held that the limitation fund must include claims for hull damage against third parties, for these claims go to the value of the vessel surrendered. When the indemnity claims are independent of the value of the vessel, however, it has been held that the stipulation needn't include them. The Barge Murray Mac, supra.

The statute specifically provides that the owner must also surrender freight then pending. This does not mean the cargo on board, of course. The Main v. Williams, 152 U.S. 122, 14 S.Ct. 486, 38 L.Ed. 381 (1894). Freight has been given a broad construction and includes, e.g., charter hire. See In re Barracuda Tanker Corp., supra.

But "freight then pending" is construed to refer to the freight that has been fully earned on the voyage resulting in limitation. When freight has been paid in advance, is it "pending" despite the fact that the voyage is broken up by the limitable occurrence? Or does it depend upon whether the shipper would be entitled to return of the freight? See Complaint of Caribbean Sea Transport, Ltd., 753 F.2d 948, 1985 A.M.C. 1995 (11th Cir.1985), where it was held that freight on cargo shown by the cargo manifest to have been delivered prior to the incident resulting in the limitation petition had been fully earned and must be included, but that remand was necessary for findings as to freight on the cargo still aboard at the time of the incident.

The statute refers to the owner's interest "in such vessel." Suppose that the incident out of which the damage sought to be limited arose involved several vessels operating as a unit, e.g., a tug and her tow or a tug with a barge lashed to its side. Is the measure of the liability of the tug owner the value of the tug alone, or the value of the whole flotilla? It has already been noted that the passive barge is not liable in rem for the damage, and it may be assumed that if the barge is not owned by the tug owner the tug owner's interest is limited to the value of the tug. In Liverpool, Brazil & River Plate Steam Nav. Co. v. Brooklyn Eastern District Terminal, 251 U.S. 48, 40 S.Ct. 66, 64 L.Ed. 130 (1919), it was argued that when the tug and tow were both owned by the same person, the limitation statute should be read as limiting the liability to the amount the owner had invested in the "adventure." Therefore both tug and tow (in the particular case a car flat loaded with railroad cars and lashed to the side of the tug) should be surrendered. The Court, through Mr. Justice Holmes, read "such vessel" to mean literally what it said. Although Mr. Justice Holmes's statement is unequivocal, it has been held that the doctrine of the *Liverpool* case does not apply when the damage is done to a party to whom the offending flotilla is bound by contract. Thus when a corporation had undertaken to provide services to offshore gas well equipment and in the course of its work under the contract struck and damaged an off-shore rig with a barge that together with another barge was being pushed by a tug, it was held that the owner must surrender all three vessels. Brown & Root Marine v. Zapata Co., 377 F.2d 724, 1967 A.M.C.

2684 (5th Cir.1967). The same distinction was drawn in Rincon Hills—Long Branch, 258 F.2d 757, 1959 A.M.C. 28 (2d Cir.1958).

The *Liverpool* case was applied in a pure tort case, a collision between the tug and tow with a bridge, in South Carolina Hwy. Dept. v. Jacksonville Shipyards, 1976 A.M.C. 456 (S.D.Ga.1975), but reluctantly and with an invitation to the Supreme Court that it reconsider the question.

It is to be noticed that the limitation proceeding is not a proceeding *in rem* in which the vessel is seized. Supplemental Rule F provides two alternatives for the creation of the limitation fund. The first is to deposit the sum determined or security for it. The second is to transfer to a trustee the petitioners interest in the vessel and pending freight. If the petitioner elects to transfer his interest to a trustee, under the rule he must also deposit such sums, or security, "as the court may from time to time fix as necessary to carry out the provisions of the statutes." It is held that the "interest" spoken of in the statute means the petitioner's fractional interest in the full value of the vessel. Lien claims against the vessel are not subtracted in determining such interest. In Gilmore and Black, *Law of Admiralty* § 950 (1975), it is stated that before limitation will be granted, claims for prior voyages must be paid off or secured. They conceded that there was very little case support for this position, but noted statements in three previous treatises. Since that time the Fifth circuit has rejected the rule of the treatises, finding no support for it in the statute, the rule, or any decisional law. Rodco Marine Services, Inc. v. Migliaccio, 651 F.2d 1101, 1985 A.M.C. 605 [DRO] (5th Cir.1981). See also Petition of Zebroid Trawling Corp., 428 F.2d 226, 228–229, 1970 A.M.C. 113 (1st Cir.1970). In *Rodco Marine* the only preexisting encumbrances that existed were a preferred ship mortgage, which under the Ship Mortgage Act would be subordinated to the tort claims, and a salvage claim that appeared to have related to the disaster voyage. The court was able to note, therefore, that even if the act did require discharge of previous encumbrances, the particular claims considered by the court below would not come within the rule.

Ordinarily, claims that are not subject to limitation, or may not be subject to limitation, are not brought in the limitation proceeding, and Supplemental Rule F(3) provides for injunction of further prosecution "of any action or proceeding against the plaintiff or his property with respect to any claim *subject to limitation in the action*" [emphasis supplied]. Of course it may not be possible to tell in advance what claims may be limitable. Under § 183(e), for example, the privity or knowledge of the master may be imputed to the owners as to personal injury claims, and limitation denied, while limitation is granted as to cargo claims. In this situation it has been held that if the petitioner is solvent, the equitable doctrine of marshalling of assets will prevail and the personal injury and death claimants will be required to look to assets the limited claims cannot reach in the satisfaction of their judgments. The Moore–McCormack Lines v. Richardson, 295 F.2d 583, 1962 A.M.C. 804 (2d Cir.1961).

Under § 183(b), in the case of a seagoing vessel, if the amount allocable to death or personal injury claimants is less than $420 a ton, the petitioner must deposit enough to bring it up to that figure. Under (d) of that section it is provided that in the event death or personal injury claims arise out of distinct occasions, the owner is to be liable "to the same extent as if no other loss of life or bodily injury had arisen."

The language "amount applicable" that appears in § 183(b) has been interpreted to mean "amount [of the limitation fund] applicable." Thus the fact that the other party in a mutual fault collision is also liable on the personal injury claims does not excuse the limiting party from putting up the $60 a ton. See *Howard Olson—Marine Leopard,* supra, p. 984.

For an argument purely from the text that § 183(d) might require a limiting vessel to put up a new § 183(a) fund as well as a new § 183(b) fund for each separate occasion, see Gilmore and Black, supra, p. 723. What is a separate occasion? In M/T Alva Cape, 262 F.Supp. 328, 1967 A.M.C. 2362 (S.D.N.Y.1966), the vessel was in a collision and twelve days later it blew up. Judge Bonsal held that he could not rule on whether the explosion was a separate occasion without a full evidentiary hearing, but in the meanwhile ordered the petitioner to post two separate bonds.

As to what is a "seagoing vessel" under §§ 183(b), and 183(f), see Petition of Hocking, 158 F.Supp. 620, 1958 A.M.C. 1749 (D.N.J.1958), in which it was held that a 21' motor boat capable of a speed of 42 miles per hour was not "sea going" under the section. Note that in § 183(f), among the types of craft defined as not seagoing vessels is "tank vessels." What of the Torrey Canyon? See Petition of The Dodge—Michael, 282 F.2d 86, 1960 A.M.C. 233 (2d Cir.1960), in which the court held that it was not clearly erroneous to find that a coastwise tanker 250' long and 1,140 gross tons was a seagoing vessel, the term "tank vessels" in the statute being limited by judicial decision to "a tanker of the river or harbor type."

2. ISSUES TRIABLE IN A LIMITATION PROCEEDING

British Transport Commission v. United States

(The Haiti Victory)

Supreme Court of the United States, 1957.
354 U.S. 129, 77 S.Ct. 1103, 1 L.Ed.2d 1234.

■ MR. JUSTICE CLARK delivered the opinion of the Court.

The British Transport Commission, owner of the overnight ferry, Duke of York, questions the power of a District Court sitting in an admiralty limitation proceeding to permit the parties to cross-claim against each other for damages arising out of the same maritime collision. The United States, as owner of the U.S.N.S. Haiti Victory, had filed the original proceeding in which the Commission along with others filed claims. While the proceeding was pending some of the claimants against the Haiti filed cross-claims against the Duke and, in addition, the United States asserted a "set-off" and "cross-claim" against the Duke in answer to the latter's claim. The District Court dismissed all of the cross-claims on the ground that "a limitation proceeding does not provide a forum for the adjudication of liability of co-claimants to each other." The Court of Appeals reversed holding that "As a practical matter as well as an equitable one, the claimants herein should be allowed to implead the Commission." 230 F.2d 139, 144 (4 Cir.1956). Because the question is an important one of admiralty jurisdiction we granted certiorari, limited to the limitation proceeding question. 352 U.S. 821, 77 S.Ct. 59, 1 L.Ed.2d 46 (1956). We agree with the Court of Appeals.

On May 6, 1953, in the North Sea, the Naval Transport, Haiti Victory, owned by the United States, rammed the overnight channel ferry, Duke of York, owned by petitioner. The bow of the Duke broke away from the vessel and sank as a result of a deep cut on her port side just forward of the bridge inflicted by the Haiti. While the Haiti suffered only minor damage the Duke's loss was claimed to be $1,500,000. In addition several of the 437 persons aboard the Duke were killed, many were injured, and many of them lost their baggage. The Haiti returned to the United States and, thereafter, this proceeding was filed under §§ 183–186 of the Limited Liability Act, R.S. §§ 4281–4289, as amended, 46 U.S.C.A. §§ 181–196, for exoneration from, or limitation of, liability for loss or damage resulting from the collision. The United States as petitioner further alleged that the collision was "caused by the fault and neglect of the S.S. Duke of York and the persons in charge of her * * * and occurred without fault on the part of the petitioner * * *."

The Duke filed a claim in the proceeding for $1,500,000 and in addition an answer in which it claimed, inter alia, that the damages resulting from the collision were "not caused or contributed to by any fault or negligence on the part of this claimant * * * but were done, occasioned or incurred with the privity or knowledge of and were caused by the Petitioner and its managing officers and supervising agents and the master of the Haiti Victory * * * which will be shown on the trial." The United States answered that the collision "was occasioned by either the sole fault of the Duke of York or the joint fault of both the Duke of York and the Haiti Victory"; it alleged damage to the Haiti in the sum of $65,000, and that in addition it "has also been subjected to claims by passengers and members of the crews of both vessels filed herein, which presently approximate $809,714 for personal injury and death, and $45,975 for property damage other than that claimed by the Duke of York; all of which damage it prays to set off and recoup against the claimant, British Transport Commission, as owner of the Duke of York * * *." Various of the claimants against the Haiti in the meanwhile filed impleading petitions against the Duke alleging the collision was "caused or contributed to by the fault and negligence of the S.S. 'Duke of York' * * *" setting out, as did the United States, the particular acts upon which the claim of negligence was based. The District Court dismissed all of these cross-claims holding that the Act offers "a forum for the complete adjudication and recovery of all claims * * * against the petitioner only. * * * To permit one claimant to prosecute another claimant in the limitation litigation would be unfair. The latter has intervened under compulsion, the court enjoining his resort to any other tribunal. Therefore, his responsibility should not be enlarged beyond that incident to his claim. Obedience to the injunction should not expose him to an attack to which, in regular course, he would be subject only in the jurisdiction of his residence or other place of voluntary entrance."

On a hearing "restricted to the issues of the asserted liabilities of the two vessels, Duke of York and Haiti Victory, for the collision," the court exonerated the Haiti from all liability, holding the Duke solely to blame for the collision. 131 F.Supp. 712 (D.C.Va.1955). This finding was subsequently affirmed by the Court of Appeals and is not before us.[1] In reversing the dismissal of the cross-claims the Court of Appeals reasoned that "Modern codes of procedure have reflected two facets: (1) all rights, if this can fairly be done, should be decided in a single legal proceeding; (2) parties who submit themselves to the jurisdiction of a court in a legal proceeding should be bound by that court's decision on all questions, appropriate to and seasonably raised in, that proceeding. Those ideas, we think, can reasonably be deduced from the spirit, if not the letter, of the 56th Admiralty Rule." 230 F.2d, at 145.

* * *

The Congress by the provisions of the Act left the form and modes of procedure to the judiciary. Twenty years after passage of the Act this Court adopted some general rules with respect to admiralty practice. See 13 Wall. xii and xiii. Rule 56 first came into the General Admiralty Rules as Rule 59.[2] As will be noted, it was originally fashioned to accommodate cross-libels in marine collision cases, but acting upon the same inherent power to bring into the proceeding other parties whose presence would enable the court to do substantial justice in regard to the entire matter, the

---

1. The United States had not filed a cross-claim against the Duke for damage to its vessel because, as it alleges, its counsel felt that it had waived recovery of any claim against a vessel of the British Government by virtue of the "Knock for Knock" Agreement, 56 Stat. 1780, E.A.S. 282, Dec. 4, 1942. Subsequently, while the appeal was pending, the British Government advised that it did not consider the Duke as a government vessel. Consequently, following the Court of Appeals decision, the United States filed a cross-claim against the Duke in the proceedings before the District Court.

2. Rule 56 was adopted as Rule 59 in 1883 as a codification of the decision in The Hudson, 15 F. 162, (D.C.N.Y., 1883). The Rule then provided in part:

"In a suit for damage by collision, if the claimant of any vessel proceeded against, or any respondent proceeded against *in personam,* shall, by petition, on oath, presented before or at the time of answering the libel, or within such further time as the court may allow, and containing suitable allegations showing fault or negligence in any other vessel contributing to the same collision, and the particulars thereof, and that such other vessel or any other party ought to be proceeded against in the same suit for such damage, pray that process be issued against such vessel or party to that end, such process may be issued * * *." 112 U.S. 743.

The remainder of Rule 59 in its original form is substantially similar to the last two sentences of the present Rule 56.

courts soon began to extend the practice by analogy to cases other than collision. See, e.g., The Alert, 40 F. 836 (D.C.N.Y., 1889); 3 Moore, Federal Practice (2d ed. 1948), 450–456. As it is expressed in 2 Benedict, *Admiralty* (6th ed. 1940), § 349, at 534, "the 'equity of the rule' was given wide extension and the principle * * * was applied by analogy to require the appearance of any additional respondent who might be responsible for the claim or a part thereof." In the 1920 revision the 59th Rule became the 56th General Admiralty Rule and, as amended by this Court, authorized either a claimant or respondent to bring in any other vessel or person "partly or wholly liable * * * by way of remedy over, contribution or otherwise, growing out of the same matter." 254 U.S. 707.[3] The present-day limitation proceeding, therefore, springs from the 1851 Act and this Court's rules. Neither source indicates that admiralty limitation precluded other ordinary admiralty procedures. In fact, as Mr. Justice Bradley put it in The Scotland, 105 U.S. 24, 33, 26 L.Ed. 1001 (1881), "we may say, once for all, that [the rules] were not intended to restrict parties claiming the benefit of the law, but to aid them. * * * The rules referred to were adopted for the purpose of formulating a proceeding that would give full protection to the ship-owners in such a case. They were not intended to prevent them from availing themselves of any other remedy or process which the law itself might entitle them to adopt." Accord, Ex parte Slayton, 105 U.S. 451, 26 L.Ed. 1066 (1882).

It is the Commission's contention that Rule 56 is wholly inapplicable to the adjudication of a claim of one co-claimant against another in a limitation proceeding. The rule, it says, refers to libels and the use of the word "claimant" includes only the claimant of the vessel involved and not to those making claims against the vessel. But we have seen that Rule 56 has

---

3. The present Rule 56 provides:

"In any suit, whether *in rem* or *in personam,* the claimant or respondent (as the case may be) shall be entitled to bring in any other vessel or person (individual or corporation) who may be partly or wholly liable either to the libellant or to such claimant or respondent by way of remedy over, contribution or otherwise, growing out of the same matter. This shall be done by petition, on oath, presented before or at the time of answering the libel, or at any later time during the progress of the cause that the court may allow. Such petition shall contain suitable allegations showing such liability, and the particulars thereof, and that such other vessel or person ought to be proceeded against in the same suit for such damage, and shall pray that process be issued against such vessel or person to that end. Thereupon such process shall issue, and if duly served, such suit shall proceed as if such vessel or person had been originally proceeded against; the other parties in the suit shall answer the petition; the claimant of such vessel or such new party shall answer the libel; and such further proceedings shall be had and decree rendered by the court in the suit as to law and justice shall appertain. But every such petitioner shall, upon filing his petition, give a stipulation, with sufficient sureties, or an approved corporate surety, to pay the libellant and to any claimant or any new party brought in by virtue of such process, all such costs, damages, and expenses as shall be awarded against the petitioner by the court on the final decree, whether rendered in the original or appellate court; and any such claimant or new party shall give the same bonds or stipulations which are required in the like cases from parties brought in under process issued on the prayer of a libellant." 254 U.S. 707.

long been held to encompass cross-claims between parties in libel actions. This Court has held that limitation of liability petitions may also be determined by appropriate pleading in libel actions. See The North Star, 106 U.S. 17, 1 S.Ct. 41, 27 L.Ed. 91 (1882), and the discussion infra. It may therefore be said that a limitation proceeding not only provides concourse but serves the function of a cross-libel to determine the rights between petitioner and claimants as well; and equitable rights between the limitation petitioner and a claimant have long been recognized as encompassed in Rule 50.[4] Moore–McCormack Lines, Inc. v. McMahon, 235 F.2d 142 (2 Cir., 1956). It appears then that had this proceeding started out as a libel the Commission admittedly would have no complaint. And as we have pointed out, the Rules were not promulgated as technicalities restricting the parties as well as the admiralty court in the adjudication of relevant issues before it. There should therefore be no requirement that the facts of a case be tailored to fit the exact language of a rule. The initial petition filed in the limitation proceeding alleged that the Duke was wholly or partly at fault and asked for a "set-off" or "cross-claim" against it; the Commission entered the case not only to prove its claim but to contest this allegation of negligence against the Duke. The claimants are all present in the litigation. The United States has now filed a cross-claim or cross-libel against the Commission, it already being a party to the suit and before the court. The question is not what "tag" we put on the proceeding, or whether it is a "suit" under Rule 56 or a libel *in personam,* or whether the pleading is of an offensive or defensive nature, but rather whether the Court has jurisdiction of the subject matter and of the parties. It is sufficient to say as did Chief Justice Taft for a unanimous Court in Hartford Accident & Indemnity Co. v. Southern Pacific Co., 273 U.S. 207, 47 S.Ct. 357, 71 L.Ed. 612 (1927), "that all the ease with which rights can be adjusted in equity is intended to be given to the [limitation] proceeding. It is the administration of equity in an admiralty court. * * * It looks to a complete and just disposition of a many cornered controversy * * *." Id., at 216. See also the opinion of Chief Justice Hughes for a unanimous Court in Just v. Chambers, 312 U.S. 383, 386–387, 61 S.Ct. 687, 690, 85 L.Ed. 903 (1941). We do not believe that the analogy to equity is shadowy. The claimants in this proceeding have just claims arising out of the collision of the Haiti and the Duke. They have as much interest in the potential liability resulting from that marine disaster as has the equity receiver in perfecting the *res* of the estate. The scope of the proceeding is not limited to a determination of the petitioner's fault nor to its interest in the Haiti. In fact, here the fault of the disaster, a matter of legitimate interest to the claimants, has been adjudicated against the Commission and

---

4. Rule 50 provides:

"Whenever a cross-libel is filed upon any counterclaim arising out of the same contract or cause of action for which the original libel was filed, and the respondent or claimant in the original suit shall have given security to respond in damages, the respondent in the cross-libel shall give security in the usual amount and form to respond in damages to the claims set forth in said cross-libel, unless the court, for cause shown, shall otherwise direct; and all proceedings on the original libel shall be stayed until such security be given unless the court otherwise directs." 254 U.S. 702.

it admits this judgment is *res judicata* in all courts. Why does it not follow that the claimants, scattered as they are in eight countries of the world but all present in this proceeding, should recover judgment for their damages? Why should each be required to file a secondary action in the courts of another country merely to prove the amount of his due when the same evidence is already before the admiralty court here?

Logic and efficient judicial administration require that recovery against all parties at fault is as necessary to the claimants as is the fund which limited the liability of the initial petitioner. Otherwise this proceeding is but a "water haul" for the claimants, a result completely out of character in admiralty practice. Furthermore, the Commission entered this proceeding voluntarily without compulsion. It filed an answer asking that justice be done regarding the subject matter, the collision; it denied all fault on its part and affirmatively sought to place all blame on the Haiti; it claimed damage in the sum of $1,500,000; and it contested the Haiti's claim of limitation or exoneration. In all of these respects judgment went against the Commission—it lost. Now having lost, it claims that the court has wholly lost jurisdiction while had it won, jurisdiction to enter judgment on all claims would have continued. It asserts that neither the Haiti, which was damaged to the extent of some $65,000, nor any of the other 115 claimants may prove their losses against it. But reason compels the conclusion that if the court had power to administer justice in the event the Commission had won, it should have like power when it lost. Whether it is by analogy to Rule 56 or by virtue of Rule 44,[5] or by admiralty's general rules heretofore promulgated by this Court, we hold it a necessary concomitant of jurisdiction in a factual situation such as this one that the Court have power to adjudicate all of the demands made and arising out of the same disaster. This too reflects the basic policy of the Federal Rules of Civil Procedure. Admiralty practice, which has served as the origin of much of our modern federal procedure, should not be tied to the mast of legal technicalities it has been the forerunner in eliminating from other federal practices.

Petitioner points to the many dire consequences that may flow from exposing claimants to cross-claims. While these predictions are entirely speculative and not before us, we comment on those which petitioner believes to be the more serious. First it says foreign claimants will be frightened away and will not file claims in American limitation proceedings. This result is more, says petitioner, "than just robbing Peter to pay Paul." But if petitioner prevailed both Peter and Paul would be robbed. While it is true that no compulsion could be exerted on foreign claimants to file claims and some would not do so thus preventing the determination of fault from being *res judicata* as to them; and while an injunction against suits being filed in foreign jurisdictions would be ineffective unless comity

---

5. Rule 44 provides:

"In suits in admiralty in all cases not provided for by these rules or by statute, the district courts are to regulate their practice in such a manner as they deem most expedient for the due administration of justice, provided the same are not inconsistent with these rules." 254 U.S. 698.

required its recognition; and assuming all this would encourage the filing of foreign suits and the levying of attachments on any offending American vessel while in a foreign port, or for that matter against any vessel of the same American owner; still this would have little practical effect on the operation of our limitation law. Most foreign claimants are foreign shipowners whose vessels visit American ports and are subject to like action by claimants living here. Self-protection would balance things out. But even if it did not, of what good is a judgment as to fault, even if *res judicata*, if a claimant recovers nothing? The proceeding here would become entirely abortive. Petitioner's theory makes the claimants no more than pawns in a game between the offending shipowners in which all that the claimants win after the successful battle is the right to fight another day for their due and in another court. It appears to us, therefore, that fairness in litigation requires that those who seek affirmative recovery in a court should be subject therein to like exposure for the damage resulting from their acts connected with the identical incident. The claimants here ask no more. That no foreign country permits such impleading should not force litigants in United States courts to forego such procedures. Foreign limitation of liability procedures are for the most part different from ours where not only fault but claims are determined as part and parcel of the limitation action itself. We conclude that in the final analysis the manifest advantages of this cross-claim procedure serve the best interests of all of the parties before a court of the United States who find themselves the unfortunate victims of maritime disaster.

Other questions of procedural detail raised by the petitioner we leave to the trial courts. This has been the policy of this Court in the past in admiralty practice.

Affirmed.

■ * * * [JUSTICES BRENNAN, FRANKFURTER, and HARLAN dissented]

NOTE

For a review of the cases and discussion of third-party practice in admiralty under Rule 14(c), see Petition of Howard Klarman, owner of the Sloop Fling, 270 F.Supp. 1001, 1967 A.M.C. 2641 (D.Conn.1967). The fact that impleader may be freely resorted to in limitation proceedings does not, of course, answer questions about the extent of impleader in admiralty. See McCann v. Falgout Boat Co., 44 F.R.D. 34, 1968 A.M.C. 650 (S.D.Tex.1968), and Chapter 5(c)(3), p. 157 supra.

If a counterclaim such as that of the United States in The Haiti Victory may be brought, since the merger rules of 1966, is it not true that it *must* be brought? NOTE, supra, p. 163.

3. LIMITATION AND THE SAVINGS CLAUSE

Jefferson Barracks Marine Services, Inc. v. Casey

United States Court of Appeals, Eighth Circuit, 1985.
763 F.2d 1007, 1986 A.M.C. 374.

■ HENRY WOODS, DISTRICT JUDGE.

I. BACKGROUND

On October 2, 1983 the M/V WALTER E. BLESSEY, a towboat handling fifteen barges on the upper Mississippi River struck a pleasure craft with four aboard, including appellants' decedent, Richard D. Saal. Saal and one other passenger, Harold Byington, Jr., were drowned. Byington's father filed suit for wrongful death in the Circuit Court of Madison County, Illinois. Jean L. Saal, in her individual capacity as widow and as guardian of Richard F. Saal, the decedent's minor son, filed a wrongful death action in the Circuit Court of St. Louis County against the owners and Jefferson Barracks Marine Service, Inc., the charterer of the M/V WALTER E. BLESSEY. Thereafter, Patricia Groller, Doris Buchert and Rhonda Jo Saal, the adult children of Richard D. Saal, sought leave to intervene in the St. Louis County action to assert wrongful death claims.

On March 28, 1984, appellees Jefferson Barracks Marine Service, Inc., and the owners of the vessel filed a limitations of liability proceeding in the United States District Court for the Eastern District of Missouri, pursuant to 46 U.S.C. § 183. This Act provides that the liability of the owner of any vessel for damages occasioned or incurred without the privity or knowledge of the owner shall not exceed the value of his interest in the vessel and her freight then pending. Along with their complaint, appellees filed a stipulation of value in which they attested that the value of the vessel and freight was $1,001,970.84. At the same time they obtained an injunction prohibiting all claimants "from the prosecution of any action against plaintiffs on the M/V WALTER E. BLESSEY, arising out of the alleged accident * * * other than by filing claims in these proceedings." A June 15, 1984, deadline was fixed for the filing of claims. The three adult children, the minor child, and the widow of Richard Saal, named above, all filed claims along with the personal representative of the estate. The father of Harold Byington also filed a claim, subsequently settled for $87,500, leaving a balance in the limitation fund of ($914,470.84).

The appellants, who are the Saal claimants, on October 18, 1984 filed a motion to dissolve the injunction to permit them to proceed with the St. Louis County wrongful death action. At the same time the claimants stipulated that the amount of any recovery would be limited to the amount remaining in the limitation fund, and that the U.S. District Court would retain jurisdiction of all limitation issues. The district judge denied the motion to dissolve the injunction: "Due to the conflicting views as to the identities of Richard D. Saals' wives and children, and consequently, the obvious uncertainty that exists as to future claimants, dissolution of the injunction would be improper. It would make plaintiffs amenable to additional claims in state court, consequently prejudicing their right to limit liability." (Memorandum Opinion of District Judge, A–1). In their interlocutory appeal the Saal claimants challenge the district court's right to bar them from the Circuit Court of St. Louis County, which forum they have chosen under the "saving to suitors" clause of the Judiciary Act of 1789, 28 U.S.C. § 1333.

The injunction issued by the District Judge was predicated on decedent's rather tangled marital history. He was concerned because decedent had been married four times before contracting a common law marriage to Jean L. Saal. The record clearly shows that Saal first married Gladys Saal, nee Tinker, in 1950 and had two children by her, Patricia Groller and Doris Buchert, both of whom are adult claimants herein. The latter two testified that their mother divorced Saal in 1957. He then married Brenda Saal, divorced her and in 1960 married Jackie Dempsey, who is the mother of Rhonda Jo Saal, another claimant in these proceedings. The marriage to Jackie Dempsey ended in divorce in 1962, and Saal then married Bonnie Delaney, the sister of his first wife. Bonnie Delaney Saal has been dead for five years. There were no children born to either Brenda Saal or Bonnie Saal. After divorcing Bonnie Delaney Saal, Richard Saal entered into a common-law relationship with Jean L. Saal in Texas, a jurisdiction which recognizes common-law marriages. A minor child, Richard F. Saal, survives from that relationship, which existed at the time of the fatal collision. Both the minor and his mother are claimants herein.

The above marital history is established by one or more family members. There are disputes among the claimants themselves about certain aspects of the family history. For instance, the children of Gladys Saal question whether Rhonda Jo Saal and Richard F. Saal are actually the children of the decedent. Jean Saal, the last of decedent's five wives, is hazy about his early marital history, which is understandable. She questions whether Rhonda Jo Saal is his daughter but does not question that he was married to Jackie Saal, who is Rhonda Jo's mother. "Jean Saal claims that she is the common-law wife of decedent Richard D. Saal. Prior to this relationship, Richard D. Saal had been married four times. Jean Saal denies that Rhonda Jo Saal is the daughter of Richard D. Saal; however, Rhonda Jo Saal claims that she is the daughter of Richard D. Saal by one of his previous wives. Doris Buchert testified that she did not know whether Richard F. Saal was Richard D. Saal's son, and Patricia Groller testified that he was not." (Memorandum Opinion of District Judge, A–3). These disputes, however, are between parties who are before the state and federal courts. The state court can sort out these conflicting claims as well as a federal court. Appellees' argument is based on these interparty disputes. We fail to see how these conflicts would invite the appearance of some phantom claimant whose claim might exhaust the limitation fund. No such phantom claimant has been definitively identified in the testimony. We believe the possibility of some additional claimant appearing in these proceedings is extremely remote and that the district court erred in enjoining the state court action.

II. THE APPLICABLE SUPREME COURT DECISION

The conflict between the Limitation of Liability Act, 46 U.S.C. § 183, and the "saving to suitors" clause, 28 U.S.C. § 1333, has been troublesome for the courts. When the aggregate of all multiple claims will not exhaust the available limitation fund, the district court will not enjoin the prosecution of claims in other courts. If multiple claims exceed the amount of the fund, then other proceedings will be enjoined. What if the amount of the claims exceed the fund but the parties stipulate that they will not enter judgment in any court for more than the amount of the Limitation Fund? In Lake Tankers Corporation v. Henn, 354 U.S. 147, 77 S.Ct. 1269, 1 L.Ed.2d 1246 (1957) the Supreme Court held that such a stipulation must be accepted and the injunction dissolved since "the respondent must not be thwarted in her attempt to employ her common law remedy in the state court where she may obtain trial by jury." Id. at 153, 77 S.Ct. at 1273. Justice Clark, writing for the majority reasoned as follows:

> The state proceeding could have no possible effect on the petitioner's claim for limited liability in the admiralty court and the provisions of the Act, therefore, do not control. Langnes v. Green, 282 U.S. 531, 539–540 [51 S.Ct. 243, 246–247, 75 L.Ed. 520] (1931). It follows that there can be no reason why a shipowner, under such conditions, should be treated any more favorably than an airline, bus, or railroad company. None of them can force a damage claimant to trial without a jury. They, too, must suffer a multiplicity of suits. Likewise, the shipowner, so long as his claim of limited liability is not jeopardized, is subject to all common-law remedies available against other parties in damage actions.

354 U.S. at 153, 77 S.Ct. at 1273.

Langnes v. Green, 282 U.S. 531, 51 S.Ct. 243, 75 L.Ed. 520 (1931), cited by Justice Clark in the above quotation, involved a single claimant in contrast to multiple claimants. However, the Supreme Court had previously held that the Limitation Act applied in this situation, as well as in one involving multiple claims. White v. Island Transportation Co., 233 U.S. 346, 34 S.Ct. 589, 58 L.Ed. 993 (1914). The value of the vessel in Langnes v. Green, supra, was $5,000, and Green's claim was for $25,000. The district court enjoined the state court proceeding and proceeded to try Green's claim. The Supreme Court, overruling White v. Island Transportation Co., supra, held that the district court should have allowed the state court action to proceed, "retaining as a matter of precaution, the petition for a limitation of liability to be dealt with in the possible but * * * unlikely event that the right of petitioner to limited liability might be brought into question in the state court." 282 U.S. at 541, 51 S.Ct. at 247. Only in this way, said the Court, can the rights of both parties [i.e., under the Limitation Act and under the "saving to suitors" clause] be preserved.

The procedure that has been worked out for a single-claim plaintiff as a result of the decision in Langnes v. Green, supra, and a subsequent decision interpreting the mandate in Ex parte Green, 286 U.S. 437, 52 S.Ct. 602, 76 L.Ed. 1212 (1932) has been summarized in a leading admiralty text.[1] The state court plaintiff must comply with the following requirements:

   a) file his claim in the limitation proceeding;

---

1. See Gilmore and Black, *The Law of Admiralty* (2d Ed. 1975), p. 871 and particu-   larly cases cited in n. 84.

b) where a stipulation for value has been filed in lieu of the transfer of the ship to a trustee, concede the sufficiency in amount of the stipulation;

c) consent to waive any claim of *res judicata* relevant to the issue of limited liability based on any judgment obtained in the state court;

d) concede petitioner shipowner's right to litigate all issues relating to limitation in the limitation proceeding.

In their motion to dissolve the injunction, appellants stipulated as follows:

1. That if the District Court saw fit to dissolve its Order of Injunction, dated March 29, 1984, which prohibited Appellants from maintaining a direct action against Appellees in state court, Appellants would proceed as party-plaintiffs in the Circuit Court of St. Louis County, Missouri in Cause No. 897969 which had been filed prior to the issuance of the District Court's Order of Injunction.

2. That upon the dissolution of the Order of Injunction, the District Court sitting in admiralty would retain its exclusive jurisdiction over the issues of (1) Appellees' right to limit liability, (2) the proper value of the Limitation Fund, and (3) all matters affecting the right of Appellees to limit liability herein, and that any decision in the above described state court action would not be *res judicata* as to those issues should they in any manner be embraced by any such decision in state court.

3. That if Appellants obtained in the aggregate a verdict or judgment against Appellees, or any of them, in the Circuit Court of St. Louis County in excess of the difference of the amount of the Limitation Fund as was previously stipulated by Appellees less the amount agreed to be paid by Appellees to Harold Byington, Sr. as and for his claim, Appellants would consent to a remittitur so that judgment would be entered in the aggregate equal to the difference between the amount of the Limitation Fund as originally stipulated by Appellees less the amount agreed to be paid by Appellees to Harold Byington, Sr.—each of the Appellants remitting in proportion to his or her respective loss—and that an injunction would issue restraining Appellants from executing thereon to the extent that any such judgment exceeded the amount remaining in the Limitation Fund.

The stipulation in our opinion met the requirements of Lake Tankers Corporation v. Henn, supra, and Langnes v. Green, supra. The effect of these cases and a stipulation such as entered here was thoroughly discussed in Universal Towing Co. v. Barrale, 595 F.2d 414 (8th Cir.1979). "In the case of either a single claim or of multiple claims that do not exceed, the limitation fund, however, the court's discretion is narrowly circumscribed. *The District Court must dissolve the injunction unless the owner can demonstrate that his right to limit liability would be prejudiced.*" Id. at 420 (emphasis added). Here the owner has not made the required demonstration. His reliance on Helena Marine Service, Inc. v. Sioux City and New Orleans Barge Lines, Inc., 564 F.2d 15 (8th Cir.1977) is misplaced. The facts of that case bear little relationship to those of the case at bar. It involved not a "phantom claimant" but one readily identified and poised in a position to assert at any time a claim that would exceed the limitation fund. Lake Tankers Corp. v. Henn, supra, is factually and legally akin to the case under consideration.

III. APPELLEES' OTHER CONTENTIONS

We are not impressed by appellees' argument that the state court proceeding deprives it of the use of Rule 14(c) of the Federal Rules of Civil Procedure. If claimants have a substantive right to pursue their cause of action under the "saving to suitors clause," it can hardly be abrogated by a federal procedural rule.[2] Apparently, appellees are claiming that by impleading Paul Luster and Richard Stiles, the pleasure boat survivors, under 14(c), and assigning fault to them, the towboat owner would be absolved of that proportion of fault. Appellees misapprehend the law. Any judgment in favor of claimants in the limitation proceeding would be joint and several. As the Supreme Court recently pointed out, the maritime rule "is in accord with the common law, which allows an injured party to sue a tortfeasor for the full amount of damages for an indivisible injury that the tortfeasor's negligence was a substantial factor in causing, even if the concurrent negligence of others contributed to the incident." Edmonds v. Compagnie Generale Transatlantique, 443 U.S. 256, 260, 99 S.Ct. 2753, 2756, 61 L.Ed.2d 521 (1979). The towboat owner would only have the right of contribution from Stiles and Luster for any fault assigned to them. The towboat owner has the same rights under Missouri state law. It can implead Stiles and Luster and have the jury apportion fault for the purpose of contribution. Missouri P.R. Co. v. Whitehead & Kales Co., 566 S.W.2d 466 (Mo.1978). The liability, however, in both forums is joint and several. That Stiles was defaulted in the limitation proceeding on January 31, 1985, cannot affect this proceeding which is an appeal from an order entered on December 20, 1984, with the notice of appeal filed on January 9, 1985. At any rate, we fail to see how claimant could lose a valuable statutory substantive right through the default of a third-party defendant.

The case is remanded to the district court with directions to dissolve the injunction and permit claimants to proceed with their action in the St. Louis state court. Pursuant to the stipulation, which we hold is binding on all the claimants, the district court shall retain its exclusive jurisdiction over the issues of (1) appellees' right to limit liability, (2) the proper value of the limitation fund, and (3) all matters affecting the right of appellees to limit liability.

NOTE

In Lake Tankers Corp. v. Henn (The Eastern Cities—L.T.C. No. 38), 354 U.S. 147, 77 S.Ct. 1269, 1 L.Ed.2d 1246 (1957), thought closely analogous by the *Casey* court, personal injury claimants and a death claimant had filed claims in a limitation proceeding in which there was a contested issue of liability between two vessels that had been involved in a collision. The death claimant moved to be permitted to proceed with her action in the state court and stipulated that she would seek an amount that taken together with the personal injury claims, would not exhaust the limitation fund. The majority of the Supreme Court, in an opinion by Mr. Justice

---

2. See 28 U.S.C. § 2072 authorizing promulgation of the Federal Rules of Procedure. "Such rules shall not abridge, enlarge or modify any substantive right and shall preserve the right of trial by jury as at common law."

Clark, pointed out that in such a case permitting the claimant to pursue the common law remedy could in no way interfere with the right to limit liability, and that the right to limit liability is the only right conferred by the act. Mr. Justice Whittaker took no part, and Justices Harlan, Frankfurter, and Burton dissented. They believed that the jurisdiction of the court, having been properly invoked, could not be affected by the subsequent act of the claimant in reducing her claim and allocating her damages between the two vessels involved.

The "phantom claimants" sometimes show up. See Valley Line Co. v. Ryan, 771 F.2d 366 (8th Cir.1985), where the petition named only one claimant, though it had notice of several other claims. The one claimant moved to default other claims and dismiss the petition, and two persons moved for permission to file late claims. The court granted the permission to file late and determined that the fund totalled $900,000. Since the original claimant sought $800,000 and the two late claimants, between them, $75,000, the court found that the fund exceeded the claims and dissolved the injunction, whereupon the original claimant filed his action in the state court. Subsequently the petitioner sent notice to other claimants and the total amount claimed climbed to $950,000. The petitioner moved to reinstate the injunction; then original claimant stipulated that he would seek no more than $700,000. In these circumstances, the court of appeals held that the claimant should have been permitted to pursue his state court action to judgment, and bring the judgment into the limitation for satisfaction.

In *Casey* and in *Ryan* above, and in Langnes v. Green, the question is one of whether the federal court will permit the claims to be tried in one court and one defense in another. At best this is a somewhat inefficient way of handling the matter. In *Casey,* for example, how many times should the claimant be permitted to abandon a thin slice of the ad damnum and stay within the limitation fund in a case in which the court tolerates late claims? See, however, n. 3 to the *Ryan* opinion, 771 F.2d at 373, where the court questions any necessity for the stipulation to take less, pointing out that whatever the judgment in the state court, if the claims in the limitation proceeding should exceed the fund, the judgment would yield only the claimant's pro rata share of the fund.

Sometimes the substantive action and the limitation proceeding are both initiated in the federal court, but brought in different districts. See, e.g., Wheeler v. Marine Navigation Sulphur Carriers, Inc., 764 F.2d 1008 (4th Cir.1985), in which plaintiffs commenced actions under the Jones Act in the district court in the Eastern District of Pennsylvania, and defendant filed a limitation proceeding in the Eastern District of Virginia, which enjoined the actions in Pennsylvania. After the court in Virginia denied limitation, it lifted the injunction and the plaintiffs returned to Pennsylvania. The district court in Pennsylvania then transferred the actions back to Virginia on ground of forum non conveniens. Despite the fact that the action had previously been pending the Eastern District of Virginia in admiralty, the court of appeals held that upon return to the district after resumption of the proceedings in Pennsylvania the plaintiffs were entitled to a jury trial.

And the question of entitlement to a jury trial can arise without either a state court/federal court conflict, or the involvement of different districts. See, e.g., Famiano v. Enyeart, 398 F.2d 661, 1968 A.M.C. 2147 (7th Cir.1968). There plaintiff, injured in a water skiing accident sued the operator and the owner of a boat that was towing him. The action was brought at law under the diversity jurisdiction, with a demand for a jury trial. The defendants answered separately, denying negligence and raising affirmative defenses. The owner also raised the defense of limitation of liability. The plaintiff argued in his pretrial brief that he was entitled to a jury trial as to both defendants under the "saving" clause, and the case was set for jury trial. Subsequently, however, the plaintiff moved that all issues be tried to the court in admiralty. The motion was denied, and when the plaintiff refused to appear at the jury trial, the action was dismissed under Rule 41 for failure to prosecute. In affirming the court of appeals indicated that the plaintiff had a right to a jury trial under Langnes v. Green and Lake Tankers Corp. v. Henn, and that being so, once the jury demand was made, it could not be withdrawn without consent. See Chap. 6, supra.

4. Limitations in Limitation Proceedings

Section 185 of the act provides "The vessel owner, within six months after a claimant shall have given to or filed with such owner written notice of claim, may petition * * *." Does this provision relate to the right or only to the proceeding provided for in Supplemental Rule F? In their first edition Gilmore and Black noted some divergence of view on the matter in the lower courts. *Law of Admiralty* 685 (1957). The Third Circuit Rule in The Chickie, 141 F.2d 80, 1944 A.M.C. 635 (3d Cir.1944), to the effect that limitation can be pleaded by way of defense after the six months has passed was adopted by the Second Circuit. See Rincon Hills—Long Branch, 258 F.2d 757, 1959 A.M.C. 28 (2d Cir.1958); Murray v. N.Y. Central R.R., 287 F.2d 152, 1961 A.M.C. 1118 (2d Cir.1961). In their second edition they took the matter as settled. *Law of Admiralty* 855 (1975).

Cincinnati Gas & Elec. Co. v. Abel

United States Court of Appeals, Sixth Circuit, 1976.
533 F.2d 1001, 1976 A.M.C. 567.

■ Lively, Circuit Judge. This is an admiralty case. May a shipowner who has been sued in a state court for damages arising out of the operation of his vessel on navigable waters rely on a defense of limitation of liability under 46 U.S.C. § 183(a) pled in his answer in the state court proceedings or must he file a petition for limitation in a federal district court within six months after receiving notice of a claim as provided in 46 U.S.C. § 185? This is the only question presented by this appeal.

FACTS AND COURT PROCEEDINGS

The tugboat "Reddy Kilowatt," owned by Cincinnati Gas & Electric Company (CGE), collided with a marina on the Ohio River owned by Patricia Abel, d/b/a New Richmond Boating Center (Abel), on July 7, 1972. On January 30, 1974 Abel wrote CGE demanding payment for the damage to the marina and consequential damages alleged to have resulted from the negligent operation of CGE's vessel. On May 7, 1974 Abel filed an action in the Court of Common Pleas of Hamilton County, Ohio seeking $435,000 from CGE for injury to its marina, loss of profits and other damages. A jury trial was demanded. In its answer, filed on June 19, 1974, CGE pled, *inter alia*, that the value of its tugboat was $52,500 and "[i]n the event this answering defendant shall be held liable for all or any part of any loss and damage claimed by the plaintiff in her complaint, this answering defendant, as owner of the M/V Reddy Kilowatt, claims the benefit of limitation of liability as provided for in Sections 4281, 4282, 4283, 4284 and 4285 of the Revised Statutes of the United States (46 U.S.C. §§ 181–185), and the various statutes supplementary thereto and amendatory thereof."

CGE made a motion for partial summary judgment limiting its liability to $52,500, citing 46 U.S.C. § 183(a).[1] Abel opposed this motion on the ground that material issues of fact existed as to the privity or knowledge of the owner, the care exercised in choice of the master and crew and whether the limitation doctrine applies to consequential damages. By a supplemental memorandum Abel opposed the motion for summary judgment on the ground that CGE had failed to comply with the terms of 46 U.S.C. § 185[2] which provides that a shipowner may seek limitation of liability by filing a petition in the proper federal district court within six months after written notice of a claim. On November 5, 1974 CGE made a motion for stay of all proceedings in the state court "until such time as the movant shall have had an opportunity to have invoked the jurisdiction of the United States District Court for the Southern District of Ohio for a determination of such right and that Court shall have relinquished jurisdiction of these proceedings."

Though Abel agreed that the state court was without jurisdiction to decide the pure admiralty issue[3] of CGE's right to limited liability, she opposed the motion on the ground that a petition in the district court at that time was barred by the six months provision of Section 185. The Court of Common Pleas entered an order denying summary judgment and granting a stay for 30 days for CGE to file a proceeding in the district court. On December 3, 1974 CGE filed a complaint in the district court seeking exoneration from, or limitation of, liability together with a stipula-

---

1. 183.

(a) The liability of the owner of any vessel, whether American or foreign, for any embezzlement, loss, or destruction by any person of any property, goods, or merchandise shipped or put on board of such vessel, or for any loss, damage, or injury by collision, or for any act, matter, or thing, loss, damage, or forfeiture, done, occasioned, or incurred, without the privity or knowledge of such owner or owners, shall not, except in the cases provided for in subsection (b) of this section, exceed the amount or value of the interest of such owner in such vessel, and her freight then pending.

2. 185.

The vessel owner, within six months after a claimant shall have given to or filed with such owner written notice of claim, may petition a district court of the United States of competent jurisdiction for limitation of liability within the provisions of this chapter and the owner (a) shall deposit with the

court, for the benefit of claimants, a sum equal to the amount or value of the interest of such owner in the vessel and freight, or approved security therefor, and in addition such sums, or approved security therefor, as the court may from time to time fix as necessary to carry out the provisions of section 183 of this title, or (b) at his option shall transfer, for the benefit of claimants, to a trustee to be appointed by the court his interest in the vessel and freight, together with such sums, or approved security therefor, as the court may from time to time fix as necessary to carry out the provisions of section 183 of this title. Upon compliance with the requirements of this section all claims and proceedings against the owner with respect to the matter in question shall cease. R.S. § 4285; June 5, 1936, c. 521, § 3, 49 Stat. 1480.

3. See United States v. Peters, 9 U.S. (5 Cranch) 115 (1809).

tion (bond) for $52,500, interest and costs. Abel pled the six months requirement of 46 U.S.C. § 185 as a complete bar to CGE's action. Following briefing the district court granted summary judgment to Abel and dismissed CGE's complaint.

THE LEGAL ISSUE

Prior to 1936 a vessel owner could seek limitation of liability at any time, even by instituting an independent proceeding for this purpose after the issue of liability had been decided adversely to him. See Deep Sea Tankers v. The Long Branch, 258 F.2d 757, 772 (2d Cir.1958), cert. denied, 358 U.S. 933, 79 S.Ct. 316, 3 L.Ed.2d 305 (1959). Congress amended Section 185 in 1936 to provide, *inter alia,* that such a petition must be filed within six months after written notice of a claim. Though the statute uses the word "may," it has been held to mean "must" in the sense that an owner may file such proceedings within six months or not at all. Petition of American M.A.R.C., Inc., 224 F.Supp. 573, 574 (S.D.Calif.1963). After considering the legislative history of the 1936 amendment the court concluded in The Grasselli, 20 F.Supp. 394, 395 (S.D.N.Y.1937), that the purpose of the six months limitation in Section 185 was "to cut down the rights and privileges of the ship owner." In Petition of Goulandris, 50 F.Supp. 452 (S.D.N.Y.1943), aff'd, 140 F.2d 780 (2d Cir.), cert. denied, 322 U.S. 755, 64 S.Ct. 1268, 88 L.Ed. 1584 (1944), it was held that since a proceeding under Section 185 is purely statutory one who seeks to avail himself of its benefits must comply fully with its terms. The requirement that a petition under Section 185 be filed within six months of notice has been held to be a condition precedent which must be met in order for an admiralty court to have jurisdiction of a limitation proceeding. The Maine, 28 F.Supp. 578, 582 (D.Md.1939), aff'd. sub nom. Standard Wholesale P. & A. Works v. Travelers Insurance Co., 107 F.2d 373 (4th Cir.1939).

CGE does not quarrel with any of these propositions. It maintains, however, that by raising the defense of limitation of liability in its timely answer in the state court it relied on the grant of limitation in 46 U.S.C. § 183(a) which has no time limit. It only filed the complaint in the district court after Abel had contested its right to limitation and raised an issue outside the jurisdiction of the state court. It has long been recognized that limitation of liability may be invoked by a shipowner either as a defense in an action seeking damages or by an independent petition in admiralty. Deep Sea Tankers v. The Long Branch, supra, 258 F.2d at 772.

In Langnes v. Green, 282 U.S. 531, 51 S.Ct. 243, 75 L.Ed. 520 (1931), the Supreme Court held that a state court was competent to render relief by way of limitation of liability if the claimant, an injured seaman, did not contest the right of the shipowner to limit its liability. The shipowner had filed an independent federal court proceeding after the claimant had sued for damages in a state court. The Supreme Court directed that proceedings go forward in the state court, with the federal court retaining the petition for limitation as a matter of precaution, to be acted upon only if the claimant should bring into question the owner's right to limitation. The Court quoted from The Lotta, 150 F. 219 (D.S.C.1907), as follows:

> The owner of the vessel, therefore, can by answer in the state court set up as a defense that he is not liable beyond the value of the vessel * * *. 282 U.S. at 543, 51 S.Ct. at 247, 75 L.Ed. at 527.

Subsequently, the claimant in Langnes v. Green, supra, did contest the right of the owner to limit its liability and the Supreme Court held that the federal court was "authorized to resume jurisdiction and dispose of the whole case." Ex parte Green, 286 U.S. 437, 440, 52 S.Ct. 602, 603, 76 L.Ed. 1212, 1214 (1932).

The *Green* cases established that a shipowner may obtain the advantage of Section 183(a) by proper pleading in a state court, at least in situations such as the present one where there is only one claimant. See also Carlisle Packing Co. v. Sandanger, 259 U.S. 255, 260, 42 S.Ct. 475, 477, 66 L.Ed. 927, 930 (1922). However, these cases were not concerned with the six months requirement of Section 185 since they were decided prior to the 1936 amendments to the Limited Liability Act.

In The Chickie, 141 F.2d 80 (3d Cir.1944), the court considered the question of whether the six months limitation period of Section 185 governs a claim for limitation of liability asserted by way of an answer. Finding that two methods of obtaining limited liability had always been available, the court concluded that the time limitation of Section 185 should not be read into Section 183(a). The court stated—

> The 1936 Amendments did not abolish the right of a ship owner to plead limitation in his answer; both methods are still available thereunder. What may be termed the substantive section of the statute, § 3 of the 1851 Act, which gave the ship owner the defense of limitation of liability, is still in force, without any express time limitation in it. See § 183(a). The six months limitation was inserted only in what may be called the procedural section, § 185. 141 F.2d at 85. (footnote omitted).

The Second Circuit followed the ruling of *The Chickie* in its decision in Deep Sea Tankers v. The Long Branch, supra, noting that the abuses at which the 1936 amendments were directed "are not encountered when limitation is pleaded by way of answer, because the libellant, by filing its libel, controls the time within which the remedy must be invoked." 258 F.2d at 772–73.

Abel contends that both *The Chickie* and *Deep Sea Tankers* are distinguishable because in both cases the claimants brought admiralty actions in federal courts and the answers containing the pleas of limited liability were filed there, not in state courts. We have been cited to, and have found no case decided since the effective date of the 1936 amendments which holds that an answer containing a plea of limited liability which is filed in a state court satisfies the requirements of Section 185. CGE cites Murray v. New York Central R.R. Co., 287 F.2d 152 (2d Cir.), cert. denied, 366 U.S. 945, 81 S.Ct. 1674, 6 L.Ed.2d 856 (1961), in which a deckhand brought a civil suit in federal court, rather than an admiralty action, to recover for personal injuries suffered aboard a barge which was being maneuvered by the defendant's tug. In its answer, which was filed more than six months after notice of the claim, the owner of the tug claimed the right to limit its liability under Section 183(a). The court held that the six months provision of Section 185 did not apply since the issue of limitation of liability was raised by answer. The court found that it was immaterial whether the original claim was filed on the "admiralty side" or the "civil side" of the court. Holding that the owner was not required under these circumstances to file an independent action under Section 185 the court stated "[t]he rule for which appellant contends disregards the desirability of one trial only, where all rights can be fairly decided in a single legal proceeding." Id. at 153.

We find *Murray* to be persuasive, but not conclusive. The court noted that though the claimant's primary cause of action was a Jones Act claim, by including a claim for maintenance he had invoked the admiralty jurisdiction of the district court. Thus the case was already on the "admiralty side" with respect to one of its claims before the petition for limited liability was filed. Furthermore, the entire case was before the district court from its inception. It is apparent that there is a difference, in terms of jurisdictional considerations, between transferring an issue for separate trial from one division or "side" of a single court and transferring it for separate trial in an entirely different court system. This is the jurisdictional obstacle which the district court found impassable in this case, as did the court in Ohio River Co. v. City of Wheeling, 225 F.Supp. 733 (N.D.W.Va. 1964). We note also that the strongest argument in *Murray* related to the desirability of disposing of all issues in a single legal proceeding. This may be achieved in a case such as this one only in a federal court. When the right to limited liability is contested it becomes impossible to dispose of all the issues in a single proceeding in a state court.

While conceding that Abel's action could not have been removed to a federal court because of the "savings to suitors" clause of 28 U.S.C. § 1333[4] and that there is no procedure for transferring an issue from a state to a federal court, CGE argues that the state court "yielded jurisdiction" to the federal court on the issue of limitation of liability. Regardless of how the procedure is described, the fact remains that the state court lost jurisdiction of the limitation of liability issue when the claimant contested the owner's right to avail itself of limitation and only an admiralty court had jurisdiction to decide the issue. Furthermore, the only method available to CGE for invoking that jurisdiction was to follow the procedures prescribed by Section 185 and Supplemental Rule F for Admiralty and Maritime Claims which incorporates the six months requirement of Section 185.

The question presented here is a close one. See 3 Benedict on *Admiralty* § 73, at 8–11–14; Gilmore & Black, *The Law of Admiralty* 855

---

4. 1333.

The district courts shall have original jurisdiction, exclusive of the courts of the States, of:

(1) Any civil case of admiralty or maritime jurisdiction, saving to suitors in all cases all other remedies to which they are otherwise entitled.

* * *

(1975). When a shipowner is faced with a claim or claims in excess of the value of his vessel, the prudent thing for him to do is to file a protective petition in the proper federal court pursuant to Section 185. See The Bremen v. Zapata Off–Shore Co., 407 U.S. 1, 19–20 n. 20, 92 S.Ct. 1907, 1918, 32 L.Ed.2d 513, 525–526 (1972); Gilmore & Black, supra at 858–59. A petition for limitation of liability has been described as "an *anticipatory* protective measure to avoid full personal responsibility if liability shall later be imposed." Petition of United States, 367 F.2d 505, 508 (3d Cir.1966), cert. denied, 386 U.S. 932, 87 S.Ct. 953, 17 L.Ed.2d 805 (1967)(emphasis added). Prior to the adoption of the 1936 amendments it was not necessary to anticipate the possibility of claims exceeding the value of the vessel; it was sufficient to raise the issue after judgment. Now, however, an owner who receives a notice of a claim acts at his peril if he fails to file a petition for limitation in a federal court within six months. Having done this, if he is then sued in the district court, he can move for consolidation of the petition for limitation with the damage action. The procedure which the Supreme Court prescribed in Langnes v. Green, supra, modified to reflect the six months provision of Section 185, remains the preferred way of dealing with a contested issue of limitation of liability where the case has originated in a state court. At the time the owner files a petition under Section 185 he may make a motion to stay proceedings on his petition until it is determined whether it will be necessary to decide the limitation question. If the right to limitation is not contested in the state court and a final judgment is entered there without the necessity of litigating the limitation issue, the Section 185 proceedings in the district court can then be dismissed. See Rubenstein v. Bryant, 522 F.2d 1351 (5th Cir.1975); Great Lakes Dredge & Dock Co. v. Lynch, 173 F.2d 281 (6th Cir.1949).

Since the purpose of amending Section 185 was to cut down the right of a shipowner to limit his liability, the time limit imposed by the amendments should be strictly enforced. Cf. Donnelly v. Brown, 230 F.2d 169 (6th Cir.1956). Any ambiguity in the amended version of the Limited Liability Act should be resolved in favor of permitting full recoveries and requiring strict adherence to the statutory requisites for limiting liability. See Maryland Casualty Co. v. Cushing, 347 U.S. 409, 437, 74 S.Ct. 608, 622, 98 L.Ed. 806, 825 (1954)(Black, J., dissenting); Petition of Dodge, Inc., 282 F.2d 86, 89 (2d Cir.1960). Knowing of previous decisions permitting the right to limited liability to be raised by answer in state court proceedings, Congress could have provided for the continuance of this procedure with a reasonable time limit. However, both the amendment to Section 185 and Rule F, supra, require that a petition be filed in a district court of the United States. Failure to so file within six months of written notice of a claim deprives the vessel owner of the benefits of limitation of liability.

The judgment of the district court is affirmed.

NOTE

Abel was followed in substance in Vatican Shrimp Co., Inc. v. Solis, 820 F.2d 674, 1987 A.M.C. 2426 (5th Cir.1987), in which plaintiff sued in the state court, defendant raised limitation as a substantive defense, plaintiff contested it, defendant filed a petition in the district court, the court denied it as untimely and remanded to the state court, the defendant appealed from the order of remand, and the court of appeals affirmed. In both *Abel* and *Vatican Shrimp* the court read the *Green* cases as holding that the defendant in a state court case may plead a claim for limitation but if the claim is controverted, the court has no jurisdiction to try the issue. This principle has been spoken of as having been made clear by the decisions of the Supreme Court. See 7A Moore's Federal Practice, by Moore and Palaez, ¶ F.3 (1993).

In *Vatican Shrimp* it was stated by way of dictum that this jurisdictional objection would not arise if the issue were raised as a defense in an action in the federal court. The courts of appeals that have faced this question have sustained the jurisdiction to entertain a claim of limitation pleaded as a defense in an action in the federal court. See The Chickie, 141 F.2d 80, 1944 A.M.C. 635 (3d Cir.1944). The rule of The Chickie was followed in the Second Circuit in Deep Sea Tankers v. The Long Branch, 258 F.2d 757, 1959 A.M.C. 28 (2d Cir.1958), and reiterated in Murray v. New York Central Railroad Co., 287 F.2d 152, 1961 A.M.C. 1118 (2d Cir.1961). Gilmore & Black, writing in 1975, referred to the rule in The Chickie as "entirely satisfactory." The Law of Admiralty, § 10–15 (1975).

Assuming that the state court would not have the tools to achieve a concursus of claims because it could not stay litigation in other states, and its judgment could not bind absent persons, why does the *Abel* court reach the conclusion that the questions of the right to limit and the amount of the fund are "pure admiralty" questions and as such beyond the jurisdiction of the state court? For this proposition the court cites United States v. Peters, in 1808, in which the Supreme Court held that the a sentence given by the Court of Commissioners in Prize Cases, which during the time of the Articles of Confederation, had the power to revise the sentences of the state admiralty courts, must be enforced despite the instructions of the Pennsylvania legislature to the Governor to prevent its execution by military force. How much relevance does this have to the issue in *Abel*?

The Supreme Court of Tennessee has read *Vatican Shrimp* and *Abel* as limited to cases in which a petition is filed in the federal court, or in the alternative found that they misread Langnes v. Green and Ex Parte Green. Mapco Petroleum, Inc. v. Memphis Barge Lines, Inc., 849 S.W.2d 312, 1993 A.M.C. 2113 (Sup.Ct.Tenn.1993), a single claim case for damages to a dock when it was struck by a barge being towed by the defendant's vessel.

In such a case why should the Congress have chosen to provide that only the federal district court could appraise the value of the vessel?

With *Mapco*, compare Hellweg v. Baja Boats, Inc., 818 F.Supp. 1022, 1993 A.M.C. 2122 (E.D.Mich.1992), holding that even in the case of an action brought in the first instance in the federal court, the issue of limitation cannot be raised by answer if the complaint has not be designated as maritime. The court perceived this as a matter of jurisdiction. Quare if a contested limitation issue is within the exclusive maritime jurisdiction of the district court, how can failure to identify it as maritime remove it from the jurisdiction? See Rule 9(h).

The 6–months period runs from the date on which "a claimant shall have given to or filed with such owner written notice of claim." The court in L.W. Richardson, Lim. Procs., 850 F.Supp. 555, 1994 A.M.C. 313 (S.D.Tex.1993) give a run-down on what constitutes sufficient notice.

... Although the Fifth Circuit has not specifically addressed what constitutes "written notice of claim," it has stated that "[t]he purpose of the six-month prescription on the limitation of liability petition is to require the shipowner to act promptly to gain the benefit of the statutory right to limit liability." *Exxon Shipping Co.*, 869 F.2d at 486, 1989 AMC at 1425. Other courts that have considered whether a letter was sufficient to constitute written notice of a claim have examined such factors as whether the letter (*l*) informs the vessel owner of claimant's "demand of a right or supposed right," (2) blames the vessel owner "for any damage or loss," or (3) calls upon the vessel owner for something due Rodriguez Moreira v. Lemay, 659 F.Supp. 89, 91 (S.D.Fla.1987). See also In re Oceanic Fleet, Inc., 807 F.Supp. 1261, 1262 (E.D.La.1992)(examining factors such as notice of the alleged injury, the date and place on which it occurred, and "the adversary nature of the situation").

"[A] writing may constitute sufficient notice even if it is couched in tentative terms, referring only to the 'possibility' of legal action." In re Complaint of Bayview Charter Boats, Inc., 692 F.Supp. 1480, 1485, 1989 AMC 1289, 1297 (E.D.N.Y.1988)(paraphrasing holding of Petition of Allan N. Spooner & Sons, Inc., 1958 A. 1050, 1053, 253 F.2d 584, 586 (2d Cir.)), cert. dismissed 358 U.S. 30, 79 S.Ct. 9, 3 L.Ed.2d 48 (1958). In such a case the letter should be "read in its entirety," however, to determine if it constitutes a notice of claim sufficient to trigger § 185's time period. *Spooner*, 253 F.2d 584, 586, 1958 AMC 1050, 1053.

The statute has been construed as providing a single 6–months period running from the first notice with respect to a single event. A new notice does not trigger a new period. Esta Later Charters, Inc. v. Ignacio, 875 F.2d 234, 236, 1989 A.M.C. 1480 (9th Cir.1989).

The term "given to or filed with" has received fairly liberal construction. Notice from plaintiff's attorney to defendant's attorney defending plaintiff's compensation claim stating that he intended to file a state court negligence suit was held sufficient even though the attorney never told the vessel owner about it. Kiewit Pacific Co., Lim Procs., 1994 A.M.C. 1537 (N.D.Cal.1994). And a letter from seaman's counsel to the vessel owner's insurer's adjuster was hel to be enough in Doxee Sea Clam Co., Inc., 13 F.3d 550, 1994 A.M.C. 305 (2d Cir.1994).

The placement of the phrase "within six months ..." raises a question of whether the deposit or transfer of interest in the vessel to a trustee must occur within the same period. Rule F(1) is not wholly clear on the subject. See Guey v. Gulf Ins. Co., 46 F.3d 478, 1995 A.M.C. 1217, holding that the provision for security is not jurisdictional and is better enforced after filing and in the discretion of the court. Cf. Fed.R.App.Proc. 3, dealing with the notice of appeal.

In The M/S Bremen v. Zapata Off–Shore Co., 407 U.S. 1, 92 S.Ct. 1907, 32 L.Ed.2d 513, 1972 A.M.C. 1407 (1972), discussed in another connection on p. 628, supra, the defendant was executing a contract to tow an oil-drilling rig from a point in the United States to a point in Europe. The towage contract contained a clause providing that all disputes under the contract should be litigated in London, England. The tow was damaged in a storm and brought into Tampa. There plaintiff filed a libel in rem. Defendant moved to dismiss on the ground that plaintiff was bound by the forum selection clause, and at the same time commenced an action against plaintiff in London. The end of the six months allowed for the filing of a limitation proceeding approached and shortly before it expired, defendant filed the limitation petition. The Supreme Court rejected the argument that in thus filing a protective petition the defendant had subjected itself to the jurisdiction of the court and waived the issue of the forum selection clause, pointing out that the running of the six months period under the Limitation Act placed the defendant in a dilemma, since later raising his right to limit as a defense "was not without risk * * * that Unterweser's attempt to limit its liability by answer would be held invalid." In commenting on The M/S Bremen, Gilmore and Black, *Law of Admiralty*, 857 (1975), express the hope that "* * * the Chief Justice's language will not be used by over-zealous counsel to suggest that the entirely satisfactory rule of *The Chickie* is in any way open to doubt." And later district court authority in the Sixth Circuit treats it as undisturbed. Erie Sand S.S. Co. v. Peter Kiewit & Sons Co., 1978 A.M.C. 2241 (N.D.Ohio 1978).

If the result of the *Abel* decision is to permit the defendant to raise limitation of liability in the answer in an action in the federal court though six months has elapsed since the defendant was notified of the claims, but not in the state court, wouldn't counsel for the plaintiff in respect of such claims be well advised to file them in the state court. Is this sort of inducement to choose one forum or another useful?

If the six months has not run at the time of the filing of the action in the state court, and there are multiple claims in excess of the limitation fund, the pending actions will be enjoined and the plaintiffs forced to litigate their claims within the limitation proceeding. If there is a single claim, the *Abel* court suggests that the defendant may petition for limitation in the federal court and move to stay the proceeding until it becomes apparent whether it will be necessary to try the limitation issue. How efficient is this procedure? See, e.g., Ohio River Co. v. Carrillo, 754 F.2d 236, (7 Cir.1985). There, four years after the injunction was lifted and the limitation proceeding continued to permit the plaintiff to pursue his state court action, an order dismissing the limitation petition without prejudice for failure to prosecute was reversed on the ground of doubt about the ability to return to the federal court after such a dismissal, and the district court ordered to stay the proceedings.

The six months period runs from the date on which the defendant received written notice of the claim. To trigger the running of the six months, the claim of which the defendant receives written notice must be a claim that would be limitable. In Sook v. Great Pacific Shipping Co., 632 F.2d 100, 1981 A.M.C. 1232 (9th Cir.1980), for example, it was held that a crewmember's complaint in an action filed in a Korean court did not constitute "notice of claim" under the statute, inasmuch as a restraining order by a court in the United States would have no effect in Korea, where a shipowner is not permitted to limit his liability to a crewmember.

And since a shipowner is entitled to a limitation decree only when there are claims in excess of the value of the vessel and freight then pending, the six months does not commence to run until he has received written notice of a claim or claims in excess of the value of the vessel and freight then pending. See Complaint of Morania Barge No. 190, Inc., 690 F.2d 32, 1982 A.M.C. 2679 (2d Cir.1982), in which the court stressed that the petition should be filed within the six months following notification of the claim if there is any uncertainty, but held since plaintiff had made affirmative representation that the claim was not in excess of $366,563.94, and four and a half years later amended its complaint and bill of particulars to raise the claim to two and a half million, the six months period ran from the amendment.

Timeliness of claims

Supplemental Rule F provides that the court shall issue a notice to all persons asserting claims with respect to which the complaint seeks limitation, admonishing them to file their claims with the clerk and serve a copy on the attorney for the plaintiff before a date named in the notice, which may not be less than 30 days after issuance of the notice. This "monition period" may be extended for cause shown, and the grant or denial of permission to file late is reviewed on a standard of abuse of discretion. See American Commercial Lines, Inc. v. United States, 746 F.2d 1351, 1985 A.M.C. 1892 (8th Cir.1984), affirming the district in its denial of a motion to file a late claim when the result would be postponement of an already scheduled trial and the claimant who filed on time might be prejudiced, since the fund might be shared between them. The court noted that the latter might be eliminated by subordinating the claim of the late filer to those of claimants who filed on time, a method employed to avoid prejudice in Esso Brussels—C.V. Sea Witch, 1975 A.M.C. 1121 (S.D.N.Y.1975), but declined to reverse on this ground since the claimant had not requested below that this be done. With *American Commercial Lines,* cf. Sagastume v. Lampsis Navigation Ltd., 579 F.2d 222, 1978 A.M.C. 2130 (2d Cir.1978), in which denial of permission to file a late claim by Honduran seamen whose affidavit indicated that they had not had notice of the proceedings, when the only objection to permitting the filing of the claim rested on the fact that they had signed releases; the court of appeals found this objection wanting inasmuch as the burden of demonstrating that the releases were freely entered into rests on the vessel owner and the seamen, who were aboard when the vessel sank off Cape Hatteras, were under the control and supervision of the shipowner from the time they were rescued to the time they returned to Honduras, were without independent advice, and had executed releases for sums between $1,115 and $3,500.

F.   Note on Limitation of Liability in Water Pollution Cases

The Water Quality Improvement Act of 1970, reenacted in 1972 as an amendment to the Federal Water Pollution Control Act, 33 U.S.C.A. §§ 1251–1376, in addition to providing for a civil penalty of $5,000 per occurrence for discharging oil or a hazardous substance into or upon the navigable waters of the United States [§ 1321(b)(6)], requires that the person in charge of a vessel or of an onshore facility or offshore facility discharging oil or a hazardous substance into or upon navigable waters shall immediately notify the appropriate agency of the United States, on pain of fine or imprisonment [§ 1321(b)(5)]. Under § 1321(f)(1), the owner or operator is made liable for the cost of removal of the oil or hazardous substance unless he can show that it was caused by an act of God, an act of war, negligence on the part of the United States, an act or omission of a third party, without regard to whether the third party was negligent, or any combination of these. If the discharge was the result of "willful negligence or willful misconduct within the privity and knowledge of the owner," the owner or operator is made liable for the full cost of removal. Otherwise to an amount not to exceed $100 per gross ton of the vessel, or $14,000,000, whichever is lesser. The liability is made a lien on the vessel and collectable either in an action in rem or in an action against the owner or operator in any court of competent jurisdiction. Since the liability is imposed "notwithstanding any other provision of law," liability cannot be escaped by pleading the Limitation of Liability Act.

The definitions section of the Act defines "owner or operator" as meaning, in the case of a vessel, "any person owning, operating, or chartering by demise, such vessel."

Of the Act, Gilmore and Black, *Law of Admiralty* 827–828 (1975), observe, "Enough has been said to indicate that the Act is as soft and spineless in its drafting as it is muddle-headed in its policy. If it is destined to remain on the books, the courts will have their work cut out for them in making some sort of sense out of its vague, ambiguous, and contradictory terms." If it should happen that the limitation fund provided for by the Limitation of Liability Act would be in excess of that provided for in the WQIA, could the United States proceed in admiralty and ignore the WQIA? Gilmore and Black suggest that they might. They suggest further that if "willful negligence or willful misconduct within the privity and knowledge of the owner" is given a more restrictive interpretation than "privity and knowledge" or "design or neglect," the phrases used in the Limitation of Liability Act and the Fire Statute respectively, the United States might disregard the statute and sue in maritime tort.

There are other distressing ambiguities in the text of the statute. When the Act makes the owner or operator liable, does this mean that the United States may collect from either one? Notice that in the definition of "owner or operator" above, it is clear that a demise charterer is one or the other. Which? Limitation is denied when the willful negligence or willful misconduct is with the privity or knowledge of the *owner*. Suppose that it is with the privity or knowledge of the demise charterer. The owner could limit, but could the charterer? According to the text, he could. Does this make any sense? Even when the willful negligence or willful misconduct is that of the operator, the Act appears to provide that he can limit his liability if the owner is not privy to his acts?

The Congress has not dealt with the liability of vessels for private actions against vessels for damages from water pollution. Some states have statutes imposing liability upon water polluters, including the owners and operators of vessels, and the validity of such statutes was upheld in Askew v. American Waterways Operators, Inc., reproduced beginning on p. 403, supra. In the *Askew* case, Justice Douglas left open the question of the application of the Limitation of Liability Act to actions under such a statute.

CHAPTER 22

POSTSCRIPT ON FEDERAL PREEMPTION

Yamaha Motor Corp., U.S.A. v. Calhoun

Supreme Court of the United States, 1996.
___ U.S. ___, 116 S.Ct. 619, 133 L.Ed.2d 578.

■ JUSTICE GINSBERG delivered the opinion of the Court.

Twelve-year-old Natalie Calhoun was killed in a jet ski accident on July 6, 1989. At the time of her death, she was vacationing with family friends at a beach-front resort in Puerto Rico. Alleging that the jet ski was defectively designed or made, Natalie's parents sought to recover from the manufacturer pursuant to state survival and wrongful death statutes. The manufacturer contended that state remedies could not be applied because Natalie died on navigable waters; federal, judge-declared maritime law, the manufacturer urged, controlled to the exclusion of state law.

Traditionally, state remedies have been applied in accident cases of this order—maritime wrongful death cases in which no federal statute specifies the appropriate relief and the decedent was not a seaman, longshore worker, or person otherwise engaged in a maritime trade. We hold, in accord with the United States Court of Appeals for the Third Circuit, that state remedies remain applicable in such cases and have not been displaced by the federal maritime wrongful death action recognized in Moragne v. States Marine Lines, Inc., 398 U.S. 375, 90 S.Ct. 1772, 26 L.Ed.2d 339 (1970).

I

Natalie Calhoun, the twelve-year-old daughter of respondents Lucien and Robin Calhoun, died in a tragic accident on July 6, 1989. On vacation with family friends at a resort hotel in Puerto Rico, Natalie had rented a "WaveJammer" jet ski manufactured by Yamaha Motor Company, Ltd., and distributed by Yamaha Motor Corporation, U.S.A. (collectively, "Yamaha"), the petitioners in this case. While riding the WaveJammer, Natalie slammed into a vessel anchored in the waters off the hotel frontage, and was killed.

The Calhouns, individually and in their capacities as administrators of their daughter's estate, sued Yamaha in the United States District Court for the Eastern District of Pennsylvania. Invoking Pennsylvania's wrongful death and survival statutes, 42 Pa. Cons.Stat. §§ 8301–8309 (1982 and Supp. 1995), the Calhouns asserted several bases for recovery (including negligence, strict liability, and breach of implied warranties), and sought damages for lost future earnings, loss of society, loss of support and services, and funeral expenses, as well as punitive damages. They grounded federal jurisdiction on both diversity of citizenship, 28 U.S.C. § 1332,[1] and admiralty, 28 U.S.C. § 1333.

Yamaha moved for partial summary judgment, arguing that the federal maritime wrongful death action this Court recognized in Moragne v. States Marine Lines, Inc., 398 U.S. 375, 90 S.Ct. 1772, 26 L.Ed.2d 339 (1970), provided the exclusive basis for recovery, displacing all remedies afforded by state law. Under *Moragne*, Yamaha contended, the Calhouns could recover as damages only Natalie's funeral expenses. The District Court agreed with Yamaha that Moragne's maritime death action displaced state remedies; the court held, however, that loss of society and loss of support and services were compensable under *Moragne*.

Both sides asked the District Court to present questions for immediate interlocutory appeal pursuant to 28 U.S.C. § 1292(b). The District Court granted the parties' requests, and in its § 1292(b) certifying order stated:

> "Natalie Calhoun, the minor child of plaintiffs Lucien B. Calhoun and Robin L. Calhoun, who are Pennsylvania residents, was killed in an accident not far off shore in Puerto Rico, in the territorial waters of the United States. Plaintiffs have brought a diversity suit against, inter alia, defendants Yamaha Motor Corporation, U.S.A. and Yamaha Motor Co., Ltd. The counts of the complaint directed against the Yamaha defendants allege that the accident was caused by a defect or defects in a Yamaha jet ski which Natalie Calhoun had rented and was using at the time of the fatal accident. Those counts sound in negligence, in strict liability, and in implied warranties of merchantability and fitness. The district court has concluded that admiralty jurisdiction attaches to these several counts and that they constitute a federal maritime cause of action. The questions of law certified to the Court of Appeals are whether, pursuant to such a maritime cause of action, plaintiffs may seek to recover (1) damages for the loss of the society of their deceased minor child, (2) damages for the loss of their child's future earnings, and (3) punitive damages." App. to Pet. for Cert. A–78.

Although the Court of Appeals granted the interlocutory review petition, the panel to which the appeal was assigned did not reach the questions presented in the certified order, for it determined that an anterior issue was pivotal. The District Court, as just recounted, had concluded that any damages the Calhouns might recover from Yamaha would be governed exclusively by federal maritime law. But the Third Circuit panel questioned that conclusion and inquired whether state wrongful death and survival statutes supplied the remedial prescriptions for the Calhouns' complaint. The appellate panel asked whether the state remedies endured or were "displaced by a federal maritime rule of decision."

---

1. The Calhouns are citizens of Pennsylvania. Yamaha Motor Corporation, U.S.A. is incorporated and has its principal place of business in California; Yamaha Motor Company, Ltd. is incorporated and has its principal place of business in Japan.

40 F.3d 622, 624 (1994).   Ultimately, the Court of Appeals ruled that state law remedies apply in this case.   Id., at 644.

II

In our order granting certiorari, we asked the parties to brief a preliminary question: "Under 28 U.S.C. § 1292(b), can the courts of appeals exercise jurisdiction over any question that is included within the order that contains the controlling question of law identified by the district court?" 514 U.S. ___, 115 S.Ct. 1998, 131 L.Ed.2d 999 (1995).   The answer to that question, we are satisfied, is yes.

* * *

We therefore proceed to the issue on which certiorari was granted: Does the federal maritime claim for wrongful death recognized in *Moragne* supply the exclusive remedy in cases involving the deaths of nonseafarers[2] in territorial waters?

III

Because this case involves a watercraft collision on navigable waters, it falls within admiralty's domain.   See Sisson v. Ruby, 497 U.S. 358, 361–367, 110 S.Ct. 2892, 2896–2898, 111 L.Ed.2d 292 (1990); Foremost Ins. Co. v. Richardson, 457 U.S. 668, 677, 102 S.Ct. 2654, 2659, 73 L.Ed.2d 300 (1982). "With admiralty jurisdiction," we have often said, "comes the application of substantive admiralty law."   East River S.S. Corp. v. Transamerica Delaval Inc., 476 U.S. 858, 864, 106 S.Ct. 2295, 2298–2299, 90 L.Ed.2d 865 (1986).   The exercise of admiralty jurisdiction, however, "does not result in automatic displacement of state law."   Jerome B. Grubart, Inc. v. Great Lakes Dredge & Dock Co., 513 U.S. ___, 115 S.Ct. 1043, 1046, 130 L.Ed.2d 1024 (1995).   Indeed, prior to *Moragne*, federal admiralty courts routinely applied state wrongful death and survival statutes in maritime accident cases.[3]   The question before us is whether *Moragne* should be read to stop that practice.

Our review of maritime wrongful death law begins with The Harrisburg, 119 U.S. 199, 7 S.Ct. 140, 30 L.Ed. 358 (1886), where we held that the general maritime law (a species of judge-made federal common law) did not afford a cause of action for wrongful death.   The *Harrisburg* Court said that wrongful death actions are statutory and may not be created by judicial decree.   The Court did not question the soundness of this view, or examine the historical justifications that account for it.   Instead, the Court merely noted that common law in the United States, like the common law of England, did not allow recovery "for an injury which results in death," id., at 204, 7 S.Ct., at 142 (internal quotation marks omitted), and that no

---

2. By nonseafarers, we mean persons who are neither seamen covered by the Jones Act, 46 U.S.C. App. § 688, (1988 ed.), nor longshore workers covered by the Longshore and Harbor Workers Compensation Act. 33 U.S.C. § 901 et seq.

3. Throughout this opinion, for economy, we use the term wrongful death remedies or statutes to include survival statutes.

country had "adopted a different rule on this subject for the sea from that which it maintains on the land," id., at 213, 7 S.Ct., at 146. The Court did not consider itself free to chart a different course by crafting a judge-made wrongful death action under our maritime law.

Federal admiralty courts tempered the harshness of The Harrisburg's rule by allowing recovery under state wrongful death statutes. See, e.g., The Hamilton, 207 U.S. 398, 28 S.Ct. 133, 52 L.Ed. 264 (1907); The City of Norwalk, 55 F. 98 (S.D.N.Y.1893).[4] We reaffirmed this practice in Western Fuel Co. v. Garcia, 257 U.S. 233, 42 S.Ct. 89, 66 L.Ed. 210 (1921), by holding that California's wrongful death statute governed a suit brought by the widow of a maritime worker killed in that State's territorial waters. Though we had generally refused to give effect to state laws regarded as inconsonant with the substance of federal maritime law, we concluded that extending state wrongful death statutes to fatal accidents in territorial waters was compatible with substantive maritime policies: "The subject is maritime and local in character and the specified modification of or supplement to the rule applied in admiralty courts ... will not work material prejudice to the characteristic features of the general maritime law, nor interfere with the proper harmony and uniformity of that law in its international and interstate relations." Id., at 242, 42 S.Ct., at 90.[5] On similar reasoning, we also held that state survival statutes may be applied in cases arising out of accidents in territorial waters. See Just v. Chambers, 312 U.S. 383, 391–392, 61 S.Ct. 687, 692–693, 85 L.Ed. 903 (1941).

State wrongful death statutes proved an adequate supplement to federal maritime law, until a series of this Court's decisions transformed the maritime doctrine of unseaworthiness into a strict liability rule. Prior to 1944, unseaworthiness "was an obscure and relatively little used" liability standard, largely because "a shipowner's duty at that time was only to use due diligence to provide a seaworthy ship." Miles v. Apex Marine Corp., 498 U.S. 19, 25, 111 S.Ct. 317, 322, 112 L.Ed.2d 275 (1990)(internal quotation marks omitted). See also *Moragne* 398 U.S., at 398–399, 90 S.Ct., at 1786–1787. Mahnich v. Southern S.S. Co., 321 U.S. 96, 64 S.Ct. 465, 88 L.Ed. 561 (1944), however, notably expanded a shipowner's liability to injured seamen by imposing a nondelegable duty "to furnish a vessel and appurtenances reasonably fit for their intended

---

4. Congress also mitigated the impact of The Harrisburg by enacting two statutes affording recovery for wrongful death. In 1920, Congress passed the Death on the High Seas Act (DOHSA) 46 U.S.C.App. § 761 et seq. (1988 ed.), which provides a federal claim for wrongful death occurring more than three nautical miles from the shore of any State or Territory. In that same year, Congress also passed the Jones Act, 46 U.S.C.App. § 688 (1988 ed.), which provides a wrongful death claim to the survivors of seamen killed in the course of their employment, whether on the high seas or in territorial waters.

5. Indeed, years before The Harrisburg, this Court rendered a pathmarking decision, Steamboat Co. v. Chase, 83 U.S. 522, 21 L.Ed. 369, 16 Wall. 522 (1873). In *Steamboat*, the Court upheld, under the "saving-to-suitors" proviso of the Judiciary Act of 1789 (surviving currently in 28 U.S.C. § 1333(1)), a state court's application of the State's wrongful death statute to a fatality caused by a collision in territorial waters between defendants' steamboat and a sailboat in which plaintiff's decedent was passing.

use." Mitchell v. Trawler Racer, Inc., 362 U.S. 539, 550, 80 S.Ct. 926, 933, 4 L.Ed.2d 941 (1960). The duty imposed was absolute; failure to supply a safe ship resulted in liability "irrespective of fault and irrespective of the intervening negligence of crew members." *Miles*, 498 U.S., at 25, 111 S.Ct., at 322. The unseaworthiness doctrine thus became a "species of liability without fault," Seas Shipping Co. v. Sieracki, 328 U.S. 85, 94, 66 S.Ct. 872, 877, 90 L.Ed. 1099 (1946), and soon eclipsed ordinary negligence as the primary basis of recovery when a seafarer was injured or killed. *Miles*, 498 U.S., at 25–26, 111 S.Ct., at 321–322.[6]

The disparity between the unseaworthiness doctrine's strict liability standard and negligence-based state wrongful death statutes figured prominently in our landmark *Moragne* decision. Petsonella Moragne, the widow of a longshore worker killed in Florida's territorial waters, brought suit under Florida's wrongful death and survival statutes, alleging both negligence and unseaworthiness. The district court dismissed the claim for wrongful death based on unseaworthiness, citing this Court's decision in The Tungus v. Skovgaard, 358 U.S. 588, 79 S.Ct. 503, 3 L.Ed.2d 524 (1959). There, a sharply divided Court held that "when admiralty adopts a State's right of action for wrongful death, it must enforce the right as an integrated whole, with whatever conditions and limitations the creating State has attached." Id., at 592, 79 S.Ct., at 506. Thus, in wrongful death actions involving fatalities in territorial waters, state statutes provided the standard of liability as well as the remedial regime. Because the Florida Supreme Court had previously held that Florida's wrongful death statute did not encompass unseaworthiness as a basis of liability, the Court of Appeals affirmed the dismissal of Moragne's unseaworthiness claim. See *Moragne*, 398 U.S., at 377, 90 S.Ct., at 1775–1776.

The Court acknowledged in *Moragne* that The Tungus had led to considerable uncertainty over the role state law should play in remedying deaths in territorial waters, but concluded that "the primary source of the confusion is not to be found in The Tungus, but in The Harrisburg." 398 U.S., at 378, 90 S.Ct., at 1776. Upon reexamining the soundness of The Harrisburg, we decided that its holding, "somewhat dubious even when rendered, is such an unjustifiable anomaly in the present maritime law that it should no longer be followed." 398 U.S., at 378, 90 S.Ct., at 1776. Accordingly, the Court overruled The Harrisburg and held that an action "lie[s] under general maritime law for death caused by violation of maritime duties." 398 U.S., at 409, 90 S.Ct., at 1792.

---

6. The Court extended the duty to provide a seaworthy ship, once owed only to seamen, to longshore workers in Seas Shipping Co. v. Sieracki, 328 U.S. 85, 66 S.Ct. 872, 90 L.Ed. 1099 (1946). Congress effectively overruled this extension in its 1972 amendments to the Longshore and Harbor Workers Compensation Act, 33 U.S.C. § 901 et seq. See 33 U.S.C. § 905(b). We have thus far declined to extend the duty further. See Kermarec v. Compagnie Generale Transatlantique, 358 U.S. 625, 629, 79 S.Ct. 406, 409, 3 L.Ed.2d 550 (1959)(unseaworthiness doctrine inapplicable to invitee aboard vessel).

IV

Yamaha argues that *Moragne*—despite its focus on "maritime duties" owed to maritime workers—covers the waters, creating a uniform federal maritime remedy for all deaths occurring in state territorial waters, and ousting all previously available state remedies. In Yamaha's view, state remedies can no longer supplement general maritime law (as they routinely did before Moragne), because *Moragne* launched a solitary federal scheme.[7] Yamaha's reading of *Moragne* is not without force; in several contexts, we have recognized that vindication of maritime policies demanded uniform adherence to a federal rule of decision, with no leeway for variation or supplementation by state law. See, e.g., Kossick v. United Fruit Co., 365 U.S. 731, 742, 81 S.Ct. 886, 894, 6 L.Ed.2d 56 (1961)(federal maritime rule validating oral contracts precluded application of state Statute of Frauds); Pope & Talbot, Inc. v. Hawn, 346 U.S. 406, 409, 74 S.Ct. 202, 204–205, 98 L.Ed. 143 (1953)(admiralty's comparative negligence rule barred application of state contributory negligence rule); Garrett v. Moore–McCormack Co., 317 U.S. 239, 248–249, 63 S.Ct. 246, 252–253, 87 L.Ed. 239 (1942)(federal maritime rule allocating burden of proof displaced conflicting state rule).[8] In addition, Yamaha correctly points out that uniformity concerns informed our decision in *Moragne*.

The uniformity concerns that prompted us to overrule The Harrisburg, however, were of a different order than those invoked by Yamaha. Moragne did not reexamine the soundness of The Harrisburg out of concern that state damage awards in maritime wrongful death cases were excessive, or that variations in the remedies afforded by the States threatened to interfere with the harmonious operation of maritime law. Variations of this sort had long been deemed compatible with federal maritime interests. See *Western Fuel*, 257 U.S., at 242, 42 S.Ct., at 90–91. The uniformity

---

7. If *Moragne's* wrongful death action did not extend to nonseafarers like Natalie, one could hardly argue that *Moragne* displaced the state law remedies the Calhouns seek. Lower courts have held that *Moragne's* wrongful death action extends to nonseafarers. See, e.g., Sutton v. Earles, 26 F.3d 903 (C.A.9 1994)(recreational boater); Wahlstrom v. Kawasaki Heavy Industries. Ltd., 4 F.3d 1084 (C.A.2 1993)(jet skier), cert. denied, 510 U.S. ___, 114 S.Ct. 1060, 127 L.Ed.2d 380 (1994). We assume, for purposes of this decision, the correctness of that position. Similarly, as in prior encounters, we assume without deciding that *Moragne* also provides a survival action. See Miles v. Apex Marine Corp., 498 U.S. 19, 34, 111 S.Ct. 317, 326–327, 112 L.Ed.2d 275 (1990). The question we confront is not what *Moragne* added to the remedial arsenal in maritime cases, but what, if anything, it removed from admiralty's stock.

8. The federal cast of admiralty law, we have observed, means that "state law must yield to the needs of a uniform federal maritime law when this Court finds inroads on a harmonious system [,] [b]ut this limitation still leaves the States a wide scope." Romero v. International Terminal Operating Co., 358 U.S. 354, 373, 79 S.Ct. 468, 480, 3 L.Ed.2d 368 (1959). Our precedent does not precisely delineate that scope. As we recently acknowledged, "[i]t would be idle to pretend that the line separating permissible from impermissible state regulation is readily discernible in our admiralty jurisprudence." American Dredging Co. v. Miller, 510 U.S. ___, ___, 114 S.Ct. 981, 987, 127 L.Ed.2d 285 (1994). We attempt no grand synthesis or reconciliation of our precedent today, but confine our inquiry to the modest question whether it was *Moragne's* design to terminate recourse to state remedies when nonseafarers meet death in territorial waters.

concern that drove our decision in *Moragne* related, instead, to the availability of unseaworthiness as a basis of liability.

By 1970, when *Moragne* was decided, claims premised on unseaworthiness had become "the principal vehicle for recovery" by seamen and other maritime workers injured or killed in the course of their employment. *Moragne*, 398 U.S., at 399, 90 S.Ct., at 1786–1787. But with The Harrisburg in place, troubling anomalies had developed that many times precluded the survivors of maritime workers from recovering for deaths caused by an unseaworthy vessel. The *Moragne* Court identified three anomalies and concluded they could no longer be tolerated.

First, the Court noted that "within territorial waters, identical conduct violating federal law (here the furnishing of an unseaworthy vessel) produces liability if the victim is merely injured, but frequently not if he is killed." Id., at 395, 90 S.Ct., at 1785. This occurred because in nonfatal injury cases, state substantive liability standards were superseded by federal maritime law, see Kermarec v. Compagnie Generale Transatlantique, 358 U.S. 625, 628, 79 S.Ct. 406, 408–409, 3 L.Ed.2d 550 (1969); *Pope & Talbot*, 346 U.S., at 409, 74 S.Ct., at 204–206, which provided for maritime worker recovery based on unseaworthiness. But if the same worker met death in the territorial waters of a State whose wrongful death statute did not encompass unseaworthiness (as was the case in *Moragne* itself), the survivors could not proceed under that generous standard of liability. See The Tungus, 358 U.S., at 592–593, 79 S.Ct., at 506–507.

Second, we explained in *Moragne* that "identical breaches of the duty to provide a seaworthy ship, resulting in death, produce liability outside the three-mile limit . . . but not within the territorial waters of a State whose local statute excludes unseaworthiness claims." *Moragne*, 398 U.S., at 395, 90 S.Ct., at 1785. This occurred because survivors of a maritime worker killed on the high seas could sue for wrongful death under the Death on the High Seas Act (DOHSA), 46 U.S.C.App. § 761 et seq. (1988 ed.), which encompasses unseaworthiness as a basis of liability. *Moragne*, 398 U.S., at 395, 90 S.Ct., at 1784–1785 (citing Kernan v. American Dredging Co., 355 U.S. 426, 430, n. 4, 78 S.Ct. 394, 397 n. 4, 2 L.Ed.2d 382 (1958)).

Finally, we pointed out that "a true seaman [a member of a ship's company] . . . is provided no remedy for death caused by unseaworthiness within territorial waters, while a longshoreman, to whom the duty of seaworthiness was extended only because he performs work traditionally done by seamen, does have such a remedy when allowed by a state statute." 398 U.S., at 395–396, 90 S.Ct., at 1785. This anomaly stemmed from the Court's rulings in Lindgren v. United States, 281 U.S. 38, 50 S.Ct. 207, 74 L.Ed. 686 (1930), and Gillespie v. United States Steel Corp., 379 U.S. 148, 85 S.Ct. 308, 13 L.Ed.2d 199 (1964) that the Jones Act, 46 U.S.C.App. § 688 (1988 ed.), which provides only a negligence-based claim for the wrongful death of seamen, precludes any state remedy, even one accommodating unseaworthiness. As a result, at the time *Moragne* was decided, the survivors of a longshore worker killed in the territorial waters of a State whose wrongful death statute incorporated unseaworthiness could sue under that theory but the survivors of a similarly-situated seaman could not.[9]

The anomalies described in *Moragne* relate to ships and the workers who serve them, and to a distinctly maritime "substantive concept"—the unseaworthiness doctrine. The Court surely meant to "assure uniform vindication of federal policies," 398 U.S., at 401, 90 S.Ct., at 1788, with respect to the matters it examined. The law as it developed under The Harrisburg had forced on the States more than they could bear—the task of "provid[ing] the sole remedy" in cases that did not involve "traditional common-law concepts" but "concepts peculiar to maritime law." 398 U.S., at 401, n. 15, 90 S.Ct., at 1788, n. 15 (internal quotation marks omitted). Discarding The Harrisburg and declaring a wrongful death right of action under general maritime law, the Court concluded, would "remov[e] the tensions and discrepancies" occasioned by the need "to accommodate state remedial statutes to exclusively maritime substantive concepts." 398 U.S., at 401 90 S.Ct., at 1788.[10]

Moragne, in sum, centered on the extension of relief, not on the contraction of remedies. The decision recalled that " 'it better becomes the humane and liberal character of proceedings in admiralty to give than to withhold the remedy, when not required to withhold it by established and inflexible rules' " Id., at 387, 90 S.Ct., at 1781 (quoting The Sea Gull, 21 F.C. (C.C.Md.1865)(Chase, C. J.)). The Court tied Petsonella Moragne's plea based on unseaworthiness to a federal right-of-action anchor,[11] but notably left in place the negligence claim she had stated under Florida's law. See 398 U.S., at 376–377, 90 S.Ct. at 1775–1776.[12]

---

9. As noted earlier, unseaworthiness recovery by longshore workers was terminated by Congress in its 1972 amendments to the Longshore and Harbor Workers Compensation Act, 33 U.S.C. § 901 et seq. See 33 U.S.C. § 905(b).

10. The Court might have simply overruled The Tungus, see supra pp. 624–625, thus permitting plaintiffs to rely on federal liability standards to obtain state wrongful death remedies. The petitioner in *Moragne*, widow of a longshore worker, had urged that course when she sought certiorari. See Moragne v. States Marine Lines, Inc., 398 U.S. 375, 378 n. 90 S.Ct. 1772, 1776, n. 1, 26 L.Ed.2d 339 (1970). But training *Moragne* solely on The Tungus would have left untouched the survivors of seamen, who remain blocked by the Jones Act from pursuing state wrongful death claims—whether under a theory of negligence or unseaworthiness. See Gillespie v. United States Steel Corp., 379 U.S. 148, 154–155, 85 S.Ct. 308, 312–313, 13 L.Ed.2d 199 (1964). Thus, nothing short of a federal maritime right of action for wrongful

death could have achieved uniform access by seafarers to the unseaworthiness doctrine, the Court's driving concern in *Moragne*. See 398 U.S., at 396, n. 12, 90 S.Ct., at 1785, n. 12.

11. While unseaworthiness was the doctrine immediately at stake in *Moragne*, the right of action, as stated in the Court's opinion, is "for death caused by violation of maritime duties." *Moragne*, 398 U.S., at 409, 90 S.Ct., at 1792. See East River Steamship Corp. v. Transamerica Delaval, Inc., 476 U.S. 858, 865, 106 S.Ct. 2295, 2299, 90 L.Ed.2d 865 (1986)(maritime law incorporates strict product liability); *Kermarec*, 358 U.S., at 630, 79 S.Ct., at 409–410 (negligence). See also 2 G. Gilmore & C. Black, The Law of Admiralty 368 (2d ed.1975).

12. *Moragne* was entertained by the Court of Appeals pursuant to a 28 U.S.C. § 1292(b) certification directed to the District Court's order dismissing the unseaworthiness claim. See 398 U.S., at 376, 90 S.Ct., at 1775.

Our understanding of *Moragne* accords with that of the Third Circuit, which Judge Becker set out as follows:

> "*Moragne* . . . showed no hostility to concurrent application of state wrongful death statutes. Indeed, to read into Moragne the idea that it was placing a ceiling on recovery for wrongful death, rather than a floor, is somewhat ahistorical. The *Moragne* cause of action was in many respects a gap-filling measure to ensure that seamen (and their survivors) would all be treated alike. The 'humane and liberal' purpose underlying the general maritime remedy of Moragne was driven by the idea that survivors of seamen killed in state territorial waters should not have been barred from recovery simply because the tort system of the particular state in which a seaman died did not incorporate special maritime doctrines. It is difficult to see how this purpose can be taken as an intent to preclude the operation of state laws that do supply a remedy." 40 F.3d, at 641–442 (citation omitted).

We have reasoned similarly in Sun Ship, Inc. v. Pennsylvania, 447 U.S. 715, 100 S.Ct. 2432, 65 L.Ed.2d 458 (1980), where we held that a State may apply its workers' compensation scheme to land-based injuries that fall within the compass of the Longshore and Harbor Workers' Compensation Act, 33 U.S.C. § 901 et seq. See Sun Ship, 447 U.S., at 724, 100 S.Ct., at 2438–2439 (a State's remedial scheme might be "more generous than federal law" but nevertheless could apply because Congress indicated no concern "about a disparity between adequate federal benefits and superior state benefits")(emphasis in original).[13]

When Congress has prescribed a comprehensive tort recovery regime to be uniformly applied, there is, we have generally recognized, no cause for enlargement of the damages statutorily provided. See *Miles*, 498 U.S., at 30–36, 111 S.Ct., at 324–328 (Jones Act, rather than general maritime law, determines damages recoverable in action for wrongful death of seamen); Offshore Logistics, Inc. v. Tallentire, 477 U.S. 207, 232, 106 S.Ct. 2485, 2499, 91 L.Ed.2d 174 (1986)(DOHSA, which limits damages to pecuniary losses, may not be supplemented by nonpecuniary damages under a state wrongful death statute); Mobil Oil Corp. v. Higginbotham; 436 U.S. 618, 624–625, 98 S.Ct. 2010, 2014–2015, 56 L.Ed.2d 581 (1978)(DOHSA precludes damages for loss of society under general maritime law). But Congress has not prescribed remedies for the wrongful deaths of nonseafar-

---

13. Federal maritime law has long accommodated the States' interest in regulating maritime affairs within their territorial waters. See, e.g., Just v. Chambers, 312 U.S. 383, 390, 61 S.Ct. 687, 692, 85 L.Ed. 903 (1941)("maritime law [is] not a complete and perfect system"; "a considerable body of municipal law . . . underlies . . . its administration"). States have thus traditionally contributed to the provision of environmental and safety standards for maritime activities. See, e.g., Askew v. American Waterways Operators, Inc., 411 U.S. 325, 93 S.Ct. 1590, 36 L.Ed.2d 280 (1973)(oil pollution); Huron Portland Cement Co. v. Detroit, 362 U.S. 440, 80 S.Ct. 813, 4 L.Ed.2d 852 (1960)(air pollution); Kelly v. Washington ex rel. Foss Co., 302 U.S. 1, 58 S.Ct. 87, 82 L.Ed. 3 (1937)(safety inspection); Cooley v. Board of Wardens of Port of Philadelphia ex rel. Soc. for Relief of Distressed Pilots, 53 U.S. 299, 13 L.Ed. 996, 12 How. 299 (1852)(pilotage regulation). Permissible state regulation, we have recognized, must be consistent with federal maritime principles and policies. See *Romero*, 358 U.S., at 373–374, 79 S.Ct., at 480–481.

ers in territorial waters. See *Miles*, 498 U.S., at 31, 111 S.Ct., at 325. There is, however, a relevant congressional disposition. Section 7 of DOHSA states: "The provisions of any State statute giving or regulating rights of action or remedies for death shall not be affected by this chapter." 46 U.S.C.App. § 767. This statement, by its terms, simply stops DOHSA from displacing state law in territorial waters. See *Miles*, 498 U.S., at 25, 111 S.Ct., at 321–322; *Tallentire*, 477 U.S., at 224–225, 106 S.Ct., at 2495–2496; *Moragne*, 398 U.S., at 397–398, 90 S.Ct., at 1785–1786. Taking into account what Congress sought to achieve, we preserve the application of state statutes to deaths within territorial waters.

For the reasons stated, we hold that the damages available for the ski jet death of Natalie Calhoun are properly governed by state law.[14] The judgment of the Court of Appeals for the Third Circuit is accordingly Affirmed.

NOTE

Where does the *Calhoun* decision leave the *Moragne* remedy? Review the sample rulings following *Miles* that are given on p. 1024, supra. If a longshore worker sues a vessel owner for negligent injury under § 205 of the LHWCA, or a third party under § 933, may the estate of the worker in Pennsylvania sue for future lost income while the longshore worker in a neighboring state may not? What of the death of a blue water seaman in an action against a third-party for negligence or strict liability? Does the availability of non-pecuniary damages and future lost income turn on the law of the state in which the death took place? Was this just what the decision in *Moragne* was designed to eliminate? Or does the distinction lie between a difference in the standard of care and a difference in damages?

To what extent is wrongful death, like insurance in *Wilburn Boat*, a special case? In *Calhoun*, the Court could find specific provision in the DOHSA indicating a congressional preference for preserving the state remedies in the case of deaths on domestic waters. Was this intended merely to indicate that the kind of deference to congressional "policy" that was found to control in *Miles* was unnecessary?

---

14. The Third Circuit left for initial consideration by the District Court the question whether Pennsylvania's wrongful death remedies or Puerto Rico's apply. 40 F.3d 622, 644 (1994). The Court of Appeals also left open, as do we, the source—federal or state—of the standards governing liability, as distinguished from the rules on remedies. We thus reserve for another day reconciliation of the maritime personal injury decisions that rejected state substantive liability standards, and the maritime wrongful death cases in which state law has held sway. Compare *Kermarec*, 358 U.S. at 628, 79 S.Ct., at 408–

409 (personal injury); Pope & Talbot, Inc. v. Hawn, 346 U.S. 406, 409, 74 S.Ct. 202, 204–205, 98 L.Ed. 143 (1953)(same), with Hess v. United States, 361 U.S. 314, 319, 80 S.Ct. 341, 345–346, 4 L.Ed.2d 305 (1960)(wrongful death); The Tungus v. Skovgaard, 358 U.S. 588, 592–594, 79 S.Ct. 503, 506–508, 3 L.Ed.2d 524 (1959)(same).

Together with No. 94–1477, Korean Air Lines Co., Ltd. v. Zicherman, Individually and as Executrix of the Estate of Kole, et al., also on certiorari to the same court.

INDEX

References are to pages

ACT OF GOD
See Carriage of Goods; Collisions

ACTIONS
Common law forfeitures, see Jurisdiction
Foreclosure of liens, see Jurisdiction; Maritime Liens
Injunctions, see Jurisdiction
Municipal corporations, actions against, see Government, Actions Against
Replevin, see Jurisdiction
Specific Performance,
    Arbitration, see Jurisdiction
    Contract of sale, see Jurisdiction
State courts, actions in, see Jurisdiction
States, actions against, see Government, Actions Against
Unseaworthiness, see Seaworthiness, Warranty of

ADVANCES
See Maritime Liens

APPEALS
Interlocutory Appeals in admiralty cases, 308
Scope of review in admiralty appeals, 308

ATTACHMENT
See Jurisdiction

BAGGAGE
See Carriage of Goods

BILL OF LADING
See Carriage of Goods

BOTTOMRY BONDS
See Maritime Liens

CARRIAGE OF GOODS
Baggage, 603
Bill of Lading, 587
Charter parties, 559
    Bareboat charters, 574
    Demise charters, 574
    Oral charters, 573
    Time charters, 575
    Voyage charters, 575
COGSA,
    Carrier's responsibilities, 603
        Care and custody of cargo, 607

CARRIAGE OF GOODS—Cont'd
COGSA—Cont'd
    Carrier's responsibilities—Cont'd
        Seaworthy vessel, 603
    Coverage, 596
        Loading to discharge, 601
        To or from ports of the United States, 596
        Vessels, 596
    Deviation, 649
        Departure from basic terms of the contract as, 656
        Liberties clauses, 649
        Reasonableness of, 649
    Excepted perils, 610
        Act of God, 610
        Error in management, 631
        Error in navigation, 632
        Fire, 621
        Other causes without fault or neglect, 633
        Perils of the sea, 617
        Restraint of princes, 616
    Limitation of liability per package, 639
    Live animals, 602
    Stowage on deck, 603
Common Carriers, 558
Fire Statute, 621
    Neglect or design of owner, 621
    Preserved in COGSA, 621, 631
    Preserved in Harter Act, 621
Hague Convention, 596
Harter Act, 589
    Baggage, 603
    Charter parties, 596
    Coverage, 596
    Exculpatory clauses in bills of lading, 588
    Fire, see Fire Statute
    Latent defect, 589
    Seaworthiness, warranty of, 589
Ocean tramp, 558
Passengers, see Carriage of Passengers
Private carriers, 558
Public carriers, 558
Seaworthiness, warranty of,
    Commencement of voyage, 605
    Due diligence under Harter Act and COGSA, 606

CARRIAGE OF GOODS—Cont'd
Seaworthiness—Cont'd
　Presumption of seaworthiness when ship
　　sinks in calm seas, 606
Towage contracts, 576

CARRIAGE OF GOODS BY SEA ACT
See Carriage of Goods

CARRIAGE OF PASSENGERS
Breach of Duty as a Tort, 545
Standard of care, 552

CARRIER
See Carriage of Goods

CHARTER PARTIES
See Carriage of Goods; Maritime Liens

COLLISIONS
　In general, 759
Damages, 784
　Apportionment, 806
　　Innocent interests, 810
　　Moieties rule, 806
　　　Abrogation of moieties rule, 811
　　　Mechanics of divided damages, 810
　Detention, 802
　Duty to minimize, 801
　Economic loss, 801
　Interest and costs, 806
　Lost earnings, 801
　　Fishing catch, 804
　Punitive damages, 805
　Repairs, 800
　　Made by owner himself, 801
　　New for old allowance, 800
　　Temporary, 801
　Substitute ship, 802
　Valuation, 799
　Weak boat doctrine, 800
Fault, 759
　Act of God, 763
　Error in extremis, 780
　Inscrutable fault, 759
　Last clear chance, 779
　Major-minor fault rule, 774
Statutory fault, 763
　Customs, 764
　General precautionary rules, 765
　Local ordinances and regulations, 764
　Pilot rules, 763
　Rule of *The Pennsylvania*, 765
　Rules of navigation, 763

COMPULSORY PILOTS
See Maritime Liens

CUSTODIA LEGIS
See Maritime Liens

CUSTOMS
See Collisions

DAMAGES
See Carriage of Goods; Collisions; Torts

DEATH ACTIONS
See Wrongful Death

DEVIATION
See Carriage of Goods

DIVIDED DAMAGE RULE
See Collisions

ERRORS IN EXTREMIS
See Collisions

FEDERAL RULES OF CIVIL PROCEDURE
Effect of merger with admiralty rules, see
　Jurisdiction

FELLOW SERVANT DOCTRINE
See Torts

FIRE STATUTE
See Carriage of Goods; Limitation of Liability

FORUM NON CONVENIENS
See Venue

GENERAL AVERAGE
　In general, 720
Common adventure, 737
Damage by fire, heat, smoke, 732
Extraordinary expenses, 746
Jason Clause, 741,746
Laws of Oleron, 720
Peril, 733
　Mistake as to existence of, 736
　Must be imminent, 733
　Result of negligence, 741
Salvage expenses, 757
Voluntary sacrifice, 721
Voluntary stranding, 721
York–Antwerp Rules, 725, 731

GOVERNMENT, ACTIONS AGAINST
Foreign states, 340
Municipal governments, 340
States of the United States, 338
United States, 312

GOVERNMENT EMPLOYEES
See Torts

HAGUE CONVENTION
See Carriage of Goods

HARBOR WORKERS
　See also, Carriage of Goods; Longshore
　　and Harbor Workers

HARTER ACT
See Carriage of Goods

HOME PORT LIEN DOCTRINE
See Maritime Liens

INSCRUTABLE FAULT
See Collisions

INSOLVENCY
See Maritime Liens

INTEREST AND COSTS
See Collisions

JASON CLAUSE
See General Average

JONES ACT
See Torts

JURISDICTION
Admiralty Extension Act of 1948, p. 97
Amount in controversy, 131
Ancillary and pendent jurisdiction, 162
    Counterclaims, 163
    Joinder of non-maritime claims, 162
    Joinder of parties, 168
    Third-party claims, 165
Attachment and garnishment, 272
    Presence of defendant in district, 272
Body of the county as test, 2
Constitution, 1
Contracts, 56
    Affreightment contracts, see Carriage of
        Goods
    Agency contracts, 79
    Executory contracts, 72
    Joint venture and partnership contracts,
        91
    Lease-purchase contracts, 86
    Marine insurance, 56
        Contracts to procure insurance, 86
    Mixed maritime and nonmaritime con-
        tracts, 91
    Negligent breach, 475, 544, 837
    Passenger tickets, see Carriage of Passen-
        gers
    Pilotage contracts, 75
    Rental of boat slip, 75
    Repairs and necessaries, 67
    Sale of a vessel, 90
    Salvage contracts, see Salvage
    Separable contracts, 86
    Shipbuilding contracts, 76
        Breach of warranty, 839
    Stevedoring contracts, 74
    Storage of a vessel on land, 75
    Supply a crew, contract to, 85
    Wages, 75
    Wharfage, 74
Counterclaims, 163
Criminal jurisdiction, 126
Death on the High Seas Act, 161; see Wrong-
    ful Death
Federal claims, admiralty actions as, 205
Federal Rules of Civil Procedure, merger of
    admiralty rules with, 204
Historical development, 1
Joinder of non-maritime claims, 163
Joinder of parties, 168
Jurisdiction in personam, 281
    Service on an agent within the district,
        281
    Long-arm jurisdiction, 284
Jurisdiction in rem, 247
    Arrest, 247

JURISDICTION—Cont'd
Jurisdiction in rem—Cont'd
    Conflict between state and federal juris-
        diction over the res, 254
    Order to bring the res within the district,
        259
    Process in rem under F.R.C.P., 262
    Release of cargo, 256
    Service of process, traditional method, 247
    Security, release of the res, 264
    Seizure, necessity of, 261
Limitation of liability proceedings; see Limi-
    tation of liability
Location as test, 56, 92
Maritime connection, 104
Navigable waters, 8
    Artificial waterways, 40
    Determination of navigability in fact, 49
    Historical navigability, 40
    Inland lakes and rivers, 41
    Interstate and foreign commerce, 41
    Navigability in fact, 38
    Potential navigability, 40
    Present navigability, 41
    Regulation, 50
    Statutory definitions, 54
Outer Continental Shelf Act, 129
Petitory and possessory suits, 177
Prize jurisdiction, 128
Remedies in admiralty actions, 177
    Defenses of fraud, 194
    Equitable relief, 178
    Indebitatis assumpsit, 183
    Injunctions, 197
    Partition suits, 180
    Reformation of contracts, 178
    Specific performance, 189
        Arbitration agreements, 186
        Contract for the sale of a vessel, 90
Removal jurisdiction, 174
Saving to suitors clause, 144
    Attachment in state courts, 155
    Common law forfeiture proceedings, 147
    Foreclosure of maritime liens, 144
    Foreclosure of possessory liens, 159
    Quiet title proceedings, 159
    Replevin, 161
    Specific performance in state court, 161
Ship Mortgage Act of 1920, p. 162
Statutes of Richard II, p. 2
Third-party practice, 157
Tidewater as criterion, 29
Torts, 92
    Airplanes, 124, 143
    Extension Act of 1948, p. 97
    Gangplank, 92
    Hole in pier, 96
    Indemnity and contribution, 840
    Land, 97, 123
    Maritime nexus, 104
    On navigable water, 96
    Piers, 95
    Place of impact, 92
    Ship to shore collisions, 97

JURISDICTION—Cont'd
Torts—Cont'd
    Surfboard accident, 97
    Victim suspended from ship's equipment,
        96
Transfer of cases between admiralty and civil
    dockets, 205
Vessels and jurisdiction, 132
    Floating casino, 132
    Helicopter, 143
    Houseboat, 142
    Permanent connection with land, 139
    Wharfboat, 139

LAST CLEAR CHANCE
See Collisions

LATENT DEFECT
See Carriage of Goods

LIENS
See Maritime Liens

LIMITATION OF LIABILITY
    In general, 161, 1026
Foreign Vessel, see Vessels
Fund, amount, 1070
    Freight pending, 1073
    Insurance, 1071
        Hull, 1071
        Liability, 1071
        Personal injury and death, special
            fund, 1075
Limitable claims, 1044
    Debts and liabilities, 1044
    Personal contracts, 1050
Limitation proceedings, 1070
    In state courts under the saving to suitors
        clause, 1081
    Injunctions against prosecution of claims
        outside the proceeding, 1081
    Issues triable, 1075
        Counterclaims, 1081
        Crossclaims, 1075
        Exoneration, 1075
        Third-party claims, 1081
    Statute of limitations in limitation pro-
        ceeding, 1088
Persons entitled to limit, 1039
    Charterers, 1044
    Owners, 1039
Privity and knowledge, 1053
    Corporate owner, 1053
    Individual owner, 1065
Timeliness of claims, 1096
Vessels, 1026
    Foreign vessels, 1032
    Pleasure craft, 1026
    Seagoing, 1075
    Size, 1029
Water pollution cases, 1097

LONGSHORE AND HARBOR WORKERS
See Seaworthiness Warranty of; Torts

MAINTENANCE AND CURE
See Torts

MAJOR–MINOR FAULT RULE
See Collisions

MARITIME LIENS
    In general, 386
Advances, 480
Affreightment contracts, 417
    Baggage, 421
    Charter hire, 429
    Freight, overpayment of, 422
    Union of ship and cargo, 417
Arising while vessel owned by government,
    400
Bottomry bonds, 478
Cargo, liens on, 411, 428
Charter party, breach of, 478
Compulsory pilots, 399
Custodia legis, expenses when ship in, 401,
    410
Extinguishment of liens, 511
    Destruction of the res, 511
    Insolvency, 536
    Judicial sale, 513
    Laches, 531
    Reduction of claim to judgment in person-
        am, 520
    Release of vessel on bond, 516
    Waiver, 525
General agency contracts, 485
General average expenses, 478
Indelibility, 389
Lien Act of 1910, p. 430
Origin and nature, 386
Passenger tickets, 544
Personal jurisdiction, 281
    Long arm jurisdiction, 284
    Service on agent, 281
Personality of the ship, 400
Preferred ship mortgages, 465
    Foreign mortgages, 511
    Partial payment, effect of, 465
Priority of liens, 486
    By class of lien, 486
        Cargo claims, 475
        Contract liens, 492
        Collision damage, 492
        Maintenance and cure, 492
        Negligent towage, 587
        Preferred maritime liens, 504
        Preferred ship mortgages, 465
        Salvage liens, 490
        Tort liens, 497
        Wages of mariners, 416
    By time of accrual, 499
        Calendar year rule, 501
        New York harbor rule, 508
        Preferred ship mortgage, effect of, 508
        Season rule, 506
        Voyage rule, 501
Provision of services to a vessel, 433
Repairs, supplies, and necessaries, 430

MARITIME LIENS—Cont'd
Repairs—Cont'd
    Charter clauses prohibiting liens, 453
    Definition of "necessaries," 433
    Furnishing to the ship, 434
    Home port lien doctrine, 146, 430
    Master, authorization by, 446
    Owners, authorization by, 440
    Person authorized by owner, 447
    Reliance on credit of the vessel, 462
Respondentia bonds, 478
Ship Mortgage Act of 1920, pp. 162, 465
State law, liens under, 479
Subject of lien, 387
Subrogation, liens by, 480
Tort liens, 469
    Assault, actions for, 473
    Collision damage, 469
    Conversion of a vessel, 473
    Jones Act, under, 473
    Negligent damage to cargo, 475
    Personal injuries and death claims, 469
Transactions importing liens, 414
Union of ship and cargo, 426
Vessel in hands of state official pursuant to attachment, 410
Wages of crew after seizure of vessel, 410
Wages of mariners, 414
    Defined, 416
    Extra hazardous duty, 416
    Fish spotters, 416
    "Lay" arrangements, 414
    Master's wages, 416
    Repatriation expenses, 487
    Statutory penalties, 416
Withholding taxes, 417

NAVIGABLE WATERS
See Jurisdiction

PASSENGERS
See Carriage of Passengers; Salvage; Torts

PERSONALITY OF SHIP
See Maritime Liens

PIERS AND DOCKS
Piers and docks as an extension of land, see Jurisdiction

PRIORITY OF LIENS
See Maritime Liens

PRIZE CASES
See Jurisdiction.

PRIVITY AND KNOWLEDGE
See Maritime Liens

REMEDIES IN ADMIRALTY ACTIONS
See Jurisdiction

RESPONDENTIA BONDS
See Maritime Liens

RULES OF NAVIGATION
See Collisions

SALVAGE
    Generally, 664
Amount of award, 701
Conduct forfeiting award, 694
Contracts for salvage, 76, 713
Distribution of salvage award, 701
Duty of master to assist persons in danger, 713
Life salvage, 701, 708
Necessity for request, 693
Professional salvors, 673
Property subject to salvage, 664
Rival salvors, 696
Salvage acts, 683
Salvage situations, 677
    Peril, 677
Salvage statute, 710
Who may be a salvor, 668
    Crew of the salved vessel, 668
    Firemen, 673
    Passengers, 673
    Pilots, 673
    Professional salvors, 673

SAVING TO SUITORS CLAUSE
See Jurisdiction

SEAMEN
See Liens; Seaworthiness Warranty of; Torts

SEAWORTHINESS WARRANTY OF
Absoluteness of, 896
Affreightment contract, see Carriage of Goods
Crew, 909
Gear and appurtenances, 909
    Cargo containers, 976
    Stevedores' equipment, 968
Nondelegable duty, 909
Personal injuries, 909
    Impact on shore, 976
    Invitees, 821
    Longshoremen, 966
    Passengers, 545
    Seamen, 844
Seaman pro hac vice, 966
Seamen, 844
Vessels warranted seaworthy, 910
    Vessel withdrawn from navigation, 910

SHIP MORTGAGE ACT OF 1920
See Maritime Liens

SOURCES OF SUBSTANTIVE LAW
Common law, 357
Custom, 355
Sea codes and text writers, 343
Sovereign immunity, see Government, Actions Against
State law, 377
    Choice of law problems, 377
    Federal borrowing of state law, 377

SUBSTITUTE SHIP
See Collisions

THIRD PARTY PRACTICE
See Jurisdiction

TIDEWATER
See Jurisdiction

TORTS
In general, 820
Breach of affreightment contract, inducing, 824
Collisions; see Collisions
Fellow servant doctrine, 955
Government employees, 954, 990
Industrial accidents in general, 844
Jones Act, 911
    Action for wrongful death, 953
    Application of state wrongful death statutes, 1099
    Member of a crew of a vessel, 844, 911
    Negligence, 941
    Standard of care, 941
Longshore and Harbor Workers' Compensation Act, 980
    Accidents on the pier, 975
    Coverage, 980
    Exclusions, 989
    1972 Amendments, 982
    1984 Amendments, 989
    State law, 989
    Third person liability, 991
Longshoremen and harbor workers, 955
    Action for unseaworthiness, see Seaworthiness Warranty of
    Workmen's compensation, 374
Maintenance and cure, 866
    Abandonment of treatment, 895
    Amount, 893
    Attorney's fees, 885
    Earnings, subtraction of, 893
    Duration, 877
    Fights and affrays, 876
    Immorality, 875

TORTS—Cont'd
Maintenance and cure—Cont'd
    Service of the ship, 866, 871
    Shore leave, 866, 871
    Wages, 877, 885
    Wilful misconduct, 875
Products liability, 839
Seamen,
    Jones Act, action under, 911
    Maintenance and cure, action for, 866
    Traditional remedies, 859
    Unseaworthiness, action for, 896; see Seaworthiness Warranty of
Shipowner's action over against stevedore, 973
Warranty in the sale of a vessel, 839
Warranty of workmanlike service, 973

TOWAGE
See Carriage of Goods; Collisions; Torts

UNION OF SHIP AND CARGO
See Maritime Liens

VENUE
Forum non conveniens, 298
Jones Act, 296
Tradition rule in admiralty, 295
Transfer of actions under 28 U.S.C.A. §§ 1404(a), 1406(a), p. 297

VESSELS
See Jurisdiction; Limitation of Liability; Maritime Liens

WEAK BOAT DOCTRINE
See Collisions

WRONGFUL DEATH
Admiralty rule, 1020
Death on the High Seas Act, 161, 1013
Jones Act, 953
State law, 377, 1010, 1099
Survival of actions, 377, 1099

†

1–56662–337–5

90000

9 781566 623377